Interdisciplinary Contributions to Archaeology

Series Editor
Jelmer Eerkens, University of California, Davis, CA, USA

Editorial Board Members
Canan Çakırlar, University of Groningen, Groningen, The Netherlands
Fumie Iizuka, University of California, Merced, CA, USA
Krish Seetah, Stanford University, Stanford, CA, USA
Nuria Sugranes, Instituto de Evolución, Ecología Histórica y Ambiente
San Rafael, Mendoza, Argentina
Shannon Tushingham, Washington State University, Pullman, WA, USA
Chris Wilson, Flinders University, Bedford Park, Australia

Archaeology stands alone among the sciences in its attempt to enlighten us about the entire record of humankind. To cover such a broad range of time and space, archaeologists must ensure that their findings are integrated into broader spheres of scientific knowledge. The IDCA series aims to highlight the collaborative and interdisciplinary nature of contemporary archaeological research.

Topics the series has covered include:

- Paleoecology
- Archaeological Landscapes
- Statistical Approaches
- Laboratory Methods
- Human Biological and Cultural Evolution
- Human Nutrition
- Emergence of Agriculture and Pastoralism

For a copy of the proposal form, please contact Christi Lue (christi.lue@springer.com). Initial proposals can be sent to the Series Editor, Jelmer Eerkens (jweerkens@ucdavis.edu). Proposals should include:

- A short synopsis of the work or the introduction chapter
- The proposed Table of Contents
- The CV of the lead author(s)
- If available: one sample chapter

We aim to make a first decision within 1 month of submission. In case of a positive first decision the work will be provisionally contracted: the final decision about publication will depend upon the result of the anonymous peer review of the complete manuscript. We aim to have the complete work peer-reviewed within 3 months of submission.

This book series is indexed in SCOPUS.

For more information, please contact the Series Editor at (jweerkens@ucdavis.edu).

Erez Ben-Yosef • Ian W. N. Jones
Editors

"And in Length of Days Understanding" (Job 12:12)

Essays on Archaeology in the Eastern Mediterranean and Beyond in Honor of Thomas E. Levy

Volume 1

Editors
Erez Ben-Yosef
Department of Archaeology and Ancient
Near Eastern Cultures
Tel Aviv University
Tel Aviv, Israel

Ian W. N. Jones
Department of Anthropology
University of California, San Diego
La Jolla, CA, USA

ISSN 1568-2722   ISSN 2730-6984 (electronic)
Interdisciplinary Contributions to Archaeology
ISBN 978-3-031-27329-2   ISBN 978-3-031-27330-8 (eBook)
https://doi.org/10.1007/978-3-031-27330-8

© The Editor(s) (if applicable) and The Author(s), under exclusive license to Springer Nature Switzerland AG 2023, corrected publication 2023
This work is subject to copyright. All rights are solely and exclusively licensed by the Publisher, whether the whole or part of the material is concerned, specifically the rights of translation, reprinting, reuse of illustrations, recitation, broadcasting, reproduction on microfilms or in any other physical way, and transmission or information storage and retrieval, electronic adaptation, computer software, or by similar or dissimilar methodology now known or hereafter developed.
The use of general descriptive names, registered names, trademarks, service marks, etc. in this publication does not imply, even in the absence of a specific statement, that such names are exempt from the relevant protective laws and regulations and therefore free for general use.
The publisher, the authors, and the editors are safe to assume that the advice and information in this book are believed to be true and accurate at the date of publication. Neither the publisher nor the authors or the editors give a warranty, expressed or implied, with respect to the material contained herein or for any errors or omissions that may have been made. The publisher remains neutral with regard to jurisdictional claims in published maps and institutional affiliations.

Cover illustration: Thomas E. Levy exploring the region of al-Quseir, an Iron Age Edomite stronghold in southern Jordan (photo by Erez Ben-Yosef, March 2009)

This Springer imprint is published by the registered company Springer Nature Switzerland AG
The registered company address is: Gewerbestrasse 11, 6330 Cham, Switzerland

Introduction: Thomas E. Levy and Archaeology in the Twenty-First Century

No; the two kinds of people on earth I mean,
Are the people who lift, and the people who lean.

— Ella Wheeler Wilcox, *Custer and Other Poems* (1896)

Tom Levy's distinguished career in archaeology is a captivating story of perseverance and significance. He embodies the essence of what Wheeler Wilcox referred to as a "lifter", particularly in his contributions to his students, colleagues, and the scholarly community as a whole.[1] Since earning his PhD from the University of Sheffield in 1981, Tom has remained actively involved in archaeological research, embracing various aspects of the discipline. From leading challenging archaeological expeditions in Israel, Jordan, and Greece to utilizing archaeological sciences and cyber-archaeology for artifact analysis and archaeological information curation, Tom has displayed unwavering dedication. His work consistently demonstrates a deep appreciation for the research community and the responsibilities it entails.

Throughout his illustrious career, Tom has served as a mentor to numerous graduate students, including the editors of this book,[2] and postgraduate researchers. Additionally, he has selflessly assisted colleagues in advancing their own research

---

[1] According to a social network analysis by Steven Edwards of the University of Toronto, based on publications of the American Society of Overseas (previously Schools of Oriental) Research, Tom was found to be "the most connected scholar in the field" (https://socialsciences.ucsd.edu/news/newsletter/2018-tom-levy-most-connected-ASOR-scholar.html; the study was presented at the organization's 2018 Annual Meeting). This observation is yet another testimony to Tom's pivotal role within the research community, often serving as a catalyst to promote collaborations and research.

[2] One of us (EB-Y) commenced working with Tom while still a graduate student at the Hebrew University. This was part of a study focused on the magnetic properties of ancient copper slag, serving as an initial step in the ongoing endeavor to establish a comprehensive reference database for archaeomagnetic dating in the Levant. After a short meeting at the Hebrew Union College in Jerusalem, Tom invited me to join his upcoming expedition to Wadi Faynan, and that is how I found myself trekking through the Jordanian desert in the summer of 2004, looking for a tent camp somewhere on the outskirts of the Bedouin village of Quraiqira. Because of some difficulties descending the cliffs of the Edomite Plateau coming from the village of Shobak, I arrived at the

endeavors. Tom's contagious enthusiasm for archaeology, combined with his willingness to share research access, has had a profound and enduring impact on countless scholars in the field. This festschrift celebrating Tom's remarkable achievements serves as a testament to the magnitude of his influence.

Over 140 of Tom's friends and colleagues have contributed to this book, offering insights that align with his diverse research interests. These range from the late prehistory of the southern Levant to cyber-archaeology and the archaeological sciences. The resulting publication comprises two voluminous books (82 chapters) that make a significant contribution to the study of archaeology in the Eastern Mediterranean and beyond. These volumes also reflect the cutting-edge nature of archaeology in the early twenty-first century, incorporating advancements in methods and theory, many of which Tom has played a role in developing.

For instance, Tom's expedition to Wadi Faynan, conducted in collaboration with Mohammad Najjar, was among the first in the southern Levant to fully embrace digitized recording methods. This pioneering project employed geographic information systems (GIS) to generate daily top plans and final maps. Visitors to the expedition camp in the late 1990s witnessed the practical application of the project's visionary approach. While the team slept in electricity-free tents and showered with cold water, data processing occurred in a nearby Bedouin village. There, a collection of laptops, state-of-the-art photography and documentation instruments, and cutting-edge technology were deployed in a rented house. This expedition, spanning the transition into the third millennium, served as a testing ground for other methodologies that would become integral to twenty-first-century archaeology, including 3D LiDAR documentation, balloon photography, drone-based documentation, and more.

The book covers various themes, including the late prehistory of the southern Levant, biblical archaeology, Wadi Faynan, archaeometallurgy, marine archaeology, cyber-archaeology, archaeological sciences, and anthropological archaeology.

---

camp well past midnight, prompting the Bedouin guard to rouse Tom from his sleep to inquire about the unexpected late-night visitor. During this visit, Tom, his wife Alina, and I spent several days together, exploring various copper smelting sites in this wild and beautiful region. This, for me, was an important benchmark in the long journey of developing a career in research and academia. Tom's mentorship, which started then in the field, amidst millennia-old mounds of industrial waste, has in fact never ceased, and I am most grateful to him for his guidance and friendship. I am also thankful for our mutual love for the desert and archaeology, which brought us together, about 20 years ago. The other (IWNJ) began working with Tom at the beginning of my graduate studies at UC San Diego in 2008. On realizing that my prior excavation experience could be expressed in days, rather than weeks or months, Tom set me up to spend six months of 2009 on various archaeological projects in Israel and Jordan, including his excavations at Khirbat en-Nahas. Although there were occasional setbacks—including Tom having to send a rescue team for Kyle Knabb and myself when the old Land Rover we had been tasked with retrieving from the CBRL in Amman broke down at the Dead Sea, luckily within walking distance of the Mövenpick ice cream counter—this experience established my lasting love of archaeological fieldwork, and of the southern Levant, of course. It was around the same time that Tom encouraged me to consider writing my MA thesis on a small, Islamic period copper smelting site near KEN called Khirbat Nuqayb al-Asaymir, the excavation of which eventually formed the core of my doctoral research. These were pivotal moments in my career, and at this earliest stage of our collaboration, Tom set me down a path that I continue to explore, with his continued mentorship and encouragement, today.

Introduction: Thomas E. Levy and Archaeology in the Twenty-First Century   vii

These thematic sections trace the trajectory of Tom's extensive career, from its early days to his most recent endeavors. Although Tom retired from his longstanding academic home at the University of California San Diego in the summer of 2022 and will celebrate his 70th birthday with the publication of this book (late 2023), these milestones merely mark chapters in a continuous journey of exploration. The years ahead undoubtedly hold tremendous potential as Tom leverages his wealth of experience, echoing the sentiment expressed in the Book of Job (12:12, *NKJV*): "Wisdom is with aged men, and with length of days, understanding".

Tom Levy in Wadi Faynan, fall of 2006. (Photo courtesy of Erez Ben-Yosef)

Volume 1: The Southern Levant from Late Prehistory to Biblical Times

This volume is devoted to new research on the two main periods that have been the focus of Tom's archaeological research: late prehistory (from the Neolithic period to the Early Bronze Age) and the Biblical periods (primarily the Iron Age). Tom's research trajectory began in late prehistory with his work on the Late Chalcolithic period in Israel at Shiqmim, Gilat, Abu Hof, and other sites in the northern Negev desert, and he further developed this research when he began working in the Faynan region of Jordan in the late 1990s with excavations at the Pre-Pottery Neolithic site of Tall Tifdan, the Early Bronze Age I site of Wadi Fidan 4, and the EB III–IV site of Khirbat Hamra Ifdan, among others. In the 2000s, his work expanded into the Iron Age with his extensive excavations at the large copper smelting center of Khirbat en-Nahas and smaller smelting sites like Khirbat al-Jariya. While ongoing research on these sites in Jordan is the focus of Part III in Volume 2, Volume 1 instead demonstrates the scope of Tom's influence on research into these periods throughout the southern Levant.

Part I focuses on the late prehistoric archaeology of the southern Levant. It begins with a personal reflection by Simmons on his excavations at the Neolithic site of Ghwair I in the eastern part of the Faynan region at the same time Tom was leading excavations in the western part of the region. Several chapters present regional syntheses of recent research on late prehistory (Finlayson, who also conducted substantial research in Faynan, and Flohr on the Neolithic in the Jordanian *badia*, Rollefson on the Late Neolithic of the eastern *badia*, Shalem and Getzov on the Late Chalcolithic Galilee, and Garfinkel on the Late Chalcolithic Elah Valley), while several others present the results of in-depth research into specific sites (Shooval and colleagues on Tel 'Ein Jezreel, Davidovitch on 'En Gedi and Nahal Mishmar). Others take a more thematic approach, focusing on burials, cemeteries, and analysis of human remains (Milevski; Smith and colleagues; Najjar; Shafiq); botanical (Langgut) and faunal (Namdar and Sapir-Hen; Greenfield and Beller on Shiqmim) remains; specific aspects of material culture (Ilan and Rowan; Rosenberg and colleagues; Freikman and colleagues; Braun; Paz and Walzer); and overarching themes such as urbanism and increasing social complexity (Abadi-Reiss; Getzov and Milevski).

Part II follows Tom's shift in research focus, from late prehistory into the Iron Age and biblical archaeology. It commences with several methodological and theoretical reflections on the present state of biblical archaeology, particularly in light of the "architectural bias" (Ben-Yosef 2019, *Vetus Testamentum* 69(3)), a novel understanding of the significance of nomads during this transformative era, as emphasized by Levy's research in Edom. These reflections include Ben-Yosef and Thomas' extended critique of how social complexity has been deduced from the archaeological record in the Levant, presenting the case for a radical shift in methodology; Malena's examination of the challenges posed by the Iron Age as a historical period in regions with limited or absent written sources; and Thomas' investigation into the implications of the nomenclature employed for Iron Age archaeology in the Levant.

Several contributions take a wide view, focusing on specific themes in the Late Bronze and Iron Age archaeology of the Levant (Maeir; Wolff; Halpern) and Egypt (Bányai; Schneider), while others present thematic regional syntheses (Ben Dor Evian and Martin on Philistine burials; Hardin on social transformation in the Hesi region; Gadot and colleagues on interactions between Jerusalem and Samaria; Gibson and colleagues on the economy of the Buqei'a Plateau; Daviau on decorated Moabite ceramics). Many of the contributions explore themes central to Tom's research—such as chronology and dating methods (radiocarbon dating, archaeomagnetic dating), trade and the economy, religion, and the relationship between archaeology and historical texts—through new analyses of the material culture of specific sites (Ben-Shlomo; Maher and Nahshoni; Shai; Ortiz; Finkelstein; Vaknin and colleagues; Bruins; Roddy and colleagues; Younker; Bárta; and Fischer). Noteworthy is the wide range of scholars, spanning various—and at times opposing—approaches to biblical archaeology. This is a testimony to Tom's extensive impact, and his role in promoting a wider discussion and bridging gaps.

Volume 2: From Archaeological Sciences to Archaeological Theory

This volume celebrates Tom's substantial work in the Wadi Faynan region of southern Jordan, his contributions to the development of several important subdisciplines of archaeology, notably archaeometallurgy, marine archaeology, cyber-archaeology, and archaeological sciences, and the impacts these have had on anthropological archaeology as a field.

Part III is focused on the Faynan copper ore district of southern Jordan, where from 1997 to 2015 Tom conducted research on the role of copper mining and metallurgy in sociopolitical change as co-director of the UC San Diego Edom Lowlands Regional Archaeology Project (ELRAP). This section contains contributions from many of Tom's current and former students and collaborators at UCSD, as well as colleagues inspired by Tom's research to explore Faynan's connections to the southern Levant and other parts of West Asia. Gidding opens this section with an analysis of changes in the organization of copper production during the Early Bronze Age based on Levy's excavations at Khirbat Hamra Ifdan, which is followed by several contributions (Howland and Liss, Stroth and colleagues, and Beherec) using Levy's excavations at Khirbat en-Nahas and Khirbat al-Jariya to explore several aspects of Iron Age copper production. This is followed by several chapters (Yahalom-Mack and colleagues, Klassen and Danielson, and Ben-David) that consider the implications of Levy's work in Faynan for our understanding of the copper trade during the Iron Age and later periods. Finally, Jones explores the potential religious and socioeconomic implications of a surprising sherd found during Levy's excavations at Khirbat Faynan (Biblical Punon and Roman Phaino).

Part IV expands on Part III, recognizing the contributions of Tom's early work on Chalcolithic copper metallurgy in the Negev and later work with ELRAP in southern Jordan to wider discussions in archaeometallurgy. The contributions in this volume expand many of the conversations started by Tom, notably his focus on the social, economic, and political impacts of metallurgy, to other periods and regions of the world. Erel considers how lead concentrations in human remains can be used to understand fluctuations in the intensity of lead production, comparing individuals buried in Rome and the Levant. Eshel and colleagues address the question of the source of silver and lead circulating in the Levant during the Hellenistic period. Several contributions (Knapp, Kassianidou, and Papasavvas) consider questions related to the archaeometallurgy of Bronze Age Cyprus, at scales ranging from regional to microscopic. Lehner and colleagues engage Levy's work through a comparative study of Iron Age copper production in southeast Arabia. Schultze and Stanish, likewise, provide a comparative case study in copper production, which takes the form of a synthetic overview of the development of copper metallurgy in the Andes. Finally, Eliyahu-Behar explores the potential of experimental archaeometallurgy for understanding Levantine iron production.

In recent years, Tom's expansive scholarly interests have taken him from the desert to the Mediterranean coast. In **Part V**, Tom's recent work in marine archaeology is celebrated by scholars working in the eastern Mediterranean and beyond. Many of the contributions in this section approach marine archaeology from the perspective of theoretical and methodological approaches Tom developed over the course of his career, including craft production and spatial analysis. Tsiafaki bridges the gap between this section and Part IV by exploring the evidence for crafting activities at an Archaic period harbor site in northern Greece. Shtienberg and Cantu use coring to address the question of a possible inland anchorage at Tel Dor, Israel, the site of Levy's recent research. Demesticha and Polidorou consider the interpretation of "stray" finds in harbors through an analysis of a "stray" pottery assemblage found off the southeastern coast of Cyprus. Gambash considers the implications of changes in shipbuilding technologies in the southern Levant during the first millennium CE. Finally, Byrd and Brandy provide a thematic transition between this and the next section by using Geographic Information Systems (GIS) to explore the choices made by Indigenous groups living around what is today the San Francisco Bay between maritime and overland transport routes.

Part VI includes contributions on the topics of cyber-archaeology, an exciting field that Tom often defines as "the marriage of archaeology, computer science, engineering, and the natural sciences", and archaeological sciences. Throughout his career, Tom made many important contributions to these fields, beginning with his early adoption of digital recording technologies in the field for his excavations in Jordan in the late 1990s and continuing to today through experimentation with new developments in underwater photogrammetry and scanning. The contributions in this chapter celebrate this ongoing legacy and showcase the latest developments in these dynamic, diverse, and constantly evolving fields, with chapters exploring topics ranging from archaeogaming and virtual storytelling to erosion modeling and archaeomagnetism. Avni and colleagues address this at a large scale through a discussion of the system used by the Israel Antiquities Authority (IAA) to digitize and publish the data from the hundreds of excavations and surveys it conducts. Ridder and colleagues return to the theme of GIS modeling, in this case to analyze the erosion and deposition of sediments at a Bronze Age site in central Cyprus. Pavlidis bridges the gap between past, present, and future by exploring both present 3D-documentation technologies and possible future uses of Artificial Intelligence (AI) in archaeology. Smith considers the potential of video game technologies to allow archaeologists to visualize digitized versions of excavations in real time. Vincent considers the potential of digital documentation to help recover heritage post-conflict, using work conducted at the Mosul Cultural Museum as a case study, while Richard and Clark consider the potential of technology to aid in community archaeology during periods when travel is difficult, using their own work conducted early in the Covid-19 pandemic as a test case. Sobieralski engages Levy's work on both cyber-archaeology and copper production through the creation of a 3D game allowing users to simulate the experience of smelting copper firsthand. Tauxe and colleagues explore the same relationship with a very different technology, instead exploring archaeomagnetic research conducted on archaeological materials, including copper slag from Levy's excavations in Faynan.

The final part of the book, **Part VII**, expands the focus of the volume to anthropological archaeology as a whole. It begins with chapters exploring theoretical issues Tom addressed throughout his career, including archaeological interpretation, pragmatism (a body of theory that formed the basis of a volume Tom edited in 2010), state formation, ancient economies, and ethnic identity. It ends with several chapters exploring the recent historical archaeology and history of archaeology in the southern Levant. Greenberg commences by addressing theory directly, considering the questions of how archaeological interpretation happens and, at some level, what archaeology is. Dever builds on Levy's explorations of pragmatism in the last decade to consider the limitations and "ends" of archaeological theory. LaBianca returns to a theme that loomed large not only in Tom's work, but twentieth century anthropological archaeology more generally: the issue of state formation, in this case focusing on the southern Levant. Braswell expands this into the political-economic dimension by considering markets and the origins of money in early states. Ji addresses a related theme by considering the expansion of the Nabataean kingdom into central Jordan from the third century BCE to the first century CE. Arbel explores the question of religious imagery and religious identification, considering a surprising use of the hexagram symbol in Late Ottoman period Jaffa. Killebrew and Skinner use a combination of archival and archaeological research to investigate contradictory claims about Napoleon's presence (or not) at the site of Tel 'Akko. Finally, Cline uses archival research to investigate a mysterious potential conflict between William F. Albright and the University of Chicago excavations at Megiddo, providing a unique look into many key archaeological figures of the early twentieth century.

It would be difficult—indeed, perhaps impossible—for any book to fully encompass the breadth of Tom's contributions to archaeology over his long and distinguished career. Nonetheless, the wide scope of topics covered by these two volumes demonstrate the extensive impact Tom has had on the archaeology of the Eastern Mediterranean and beyond, in addition to providing a useful introduction to the current state-of-the-art in these subfields. We hope Tom will find it a fitting tribute.

Acknowledgments

This book represents the culmination of several years of hard work involving numerous individuals. We would like to express our gratitude to the authors for their dedication and patience, as well as the publisher's production team for their accommodating and efficient workflow. We extend our thanks to Myrna Polak for her English editing of several chapters in the book, which greatly improved its quality. Her contributions were invaluable. We are also grateful for the support received to produce this book. We acknowledge the partial funding provided by the Israel Science Foundation grant #408/22 (to E.B.-Y.) and the contributions from the Koret Foundation and the Murray Galinson San Diego-Israel Initiative (MGSDII). Furthermore, we would like to thank Susan and Bob Lapidus, Alina Levy, Paul and Maggie Meyer, and Stacy and Don Rosenberg for their generous contributions, which played a significant role in making this book possible.

Erez Ben-Yosef

Ian W.N. Jones

Levy in Paradise: From Israel to San Diego

A Tribute

Every now and then a scholar comes along who is more than just good. This magical scholar doesn't merely play the game well. He or she changes the very nature of the enterprise. I'm talking about Thomas Levy. With this *Festschrift* we honor him, true, but really he honors us, the contributors and readers of this collection. Tom had done significant work before he joined the faculty of the University of California in San Diego, but it seems fair to say that the symbiosis between Tom and UCSD produced a plethora of innovation. Two things in particular that that institution had to offer to Tom were capable of providing significant potential development, and in his willing hands they blossomed. The first was a group of colleagues with well-known records in biblical research. Not only the permanent UC faculty: Freedman, Friedman, Propp, and Goodblatt, but also a host of eminent guests who came as visiting faculty, guest lecturers, and participants in a long chain of international conferences: Frank Cross, Moshe Weinfeld, Baruch Halpern, Jo Ann Hackett, Alan Cooper, Moshe Greenberg, Jacob Milgrom, Menahem Haran, Arnaldo Momigliano, Moshe Goshen-Gottstein, Randy Garr, Ronald Hendel, Tomoo Ishida, Hugh Williamson, John Emerton, Shalom Paul, Carol Meyers – and that is just a sample. Levy interacted with all the guests, and he became a true friend to all of the permanent colleagues. When Tom first arrived in La Jolla, his interests were largely too early for exchange with most of us. As far as I could tell, for any period when people knew how to write, Tom lost interest. In a way, it served us right. For so long we had chuckled at classicists and others who were latecomers from our point of view as scholars of the Hebrew Bible and the ancient Near East. So now we got a much-needed lesson in relativity of time from a colleague to whom we were the Johnny-come-latelies in human development. So now Tom and we mutually profited from expansion of our horizons of time and civilization.

The second thing that UCSD had to offer Professor Levy was its special character as an advanced institution in the natural sciences. During Levy's years in the field, archaeology has gone from washing pots to radiocarbon dating to awesome three-dimensional virtual reality visualizations of sites within buildings on his campus to visualizing sites beneath the surface before excavating to sea-level change to the strength of the earth's magnetic field and its implications for dating Pre-Pottery to Pottery Neolithic sites. UCSD's advanced status in technology and engineering enabled him to do pretty much anything he wanted to do in this new state of the field. And its top-ranking Scripps School of Oceanography was in driving distance of his house—just as underwater archeology was offering a *tehom* of new discoveries. Fearless in the face of each new opportunity, Tom had to pass a swimming endurance test that was more suited to a young Olympic athlete than to a senior professor.

It's almost as if archaeology was waiting for this convergence: the arrival of new tools at a quantum leap higher than ever before and the right person who would know how to put all this to use. He not only mastered the new tech himself; he was a prime mover in the field, attracting others to the new archaeology as well.

It was there from the beginning. After years in Israel, Levy was interested in returning to the United States, preferably back to California, where he had grown up. And just then San Diego had moved to the forefront of research in the Hebrew Bible and was ready for an archaeologist. The job was advertised at a level that was below Levy's professional status at the time, but he applied anyway. When I asked a colleague what he thought about this, he answered: "If you can get Tom Levy at this level you'll be getting the bargain of the century." And we did. And Tom moved at warp speed through the ranks to full professor and eventually to an endowed chair. In his first year in La Jolla, he proposed an international conference that would bring together a tremendous who's who of archaeologists. He found the funding for it himself (another of his gifts) and published a substantial book of the fruits of that gathering. More conferences and more volumes followed.

He attracted students as well, both to his courses and to his excavations in Israel and Jordan. And several of his fine graduate students have gone on to careers in the field.

In all, I can't think of a scholar more deserving of a *Festschrift* than Professor Thomas Levy. From all of us: לחיים Tom. עד מאה ועשרים

Ann & Jay Davis Professor of Jewish Studies Emeritus University of Georgia Athens, GA, USA	Richard Elliott Friedman

Katzin Professor of Jewish Civilization Emeritus
University of California, San Diego
La Jolla, CA, USA

Contents of Volume 1

Volume 1: The Southern Levant from Late Prehistory to Biblical Times

Part I   The Later Prehistory of the Southern Levant

Tom Levy and "Deep Time": Forays into the Neolithic   3
Alan H. Simmons

The Neolithic of the Jordanian *Badia*   7
Bill Finlayson and Pascal Flohr

The Emergence of Fruit Tree Horticulture
in Chalcolithic Southern Levant 39
Dafna Langgut and Arik Sasi

Animal Economy in the Chalcolithic of the Southern Levant:
From Meat Source to Marketable Commodity 59
Linoy Namdar and Lidar Sapir-Hen

Butchering Patterns and Technology in a Chalcolithic Settlement:
Analysis of the Butchered Fauna from Shiqmim, Israel 83
Haskel J. Greenfield and Jeremy A. Beller

The Concept of Burial Modes as a Research Tool
in the Late Prehistory of the Southern Levant. 113
Ianir Milevski

Home on the Range: Late Neolithic Architecture
and Subsistence in Jordan's Black Desert 147
Gary Rollefson

Tel 'Ein Jezreel in the Neolithic and Chalcolithic Periods:
New Finds, New Insights 173
Tamar Shooval, Ian Cipin, Sonia Pinsky, Jennie Ebeling,
Norma Franklin, and Danny Rosenberg

Interpreting the Chalcolithic Steles of the Southern Levant 191
David Ilan and Yorke Rowan

The En Gedi Shrine and the Cave of the Treasure:
Disentangling the Entangled 205
Uri Davidovich

The Ghassulian Galilean Sub-Culture
in the Late Chalcolithic Period 219
Dina Shalem and Nimrod Getzov

The Late Chalcolithic in the Valley of Elah, Israel 245
Yosef Garfinkel

Cultural, Socio-economic and Environmental Influences
on Health Status of Chalcolithic Populations
in the Northern Negev.. 267
Patricia Smith, Marina Faerman, and Liora Kolska Horwitz

Socio-economic Complexity in Chalcolithic Villages:
A Re-evaluation in Light of New Excavations 295
Yael Abadi-Reiss

Perforated and Unperforated Flint Discs
from Late Chalcolithic Fazael: A Note on Their Characteristics
and Possible Implications..................................... 323
Danny Rosenberg, Sonia Pinsky, and Shay Bar

V-Shaped Bowls and Feasting Ceremonies
in the Late Chalcolithic Period in the Southern Levant:
The Case Study of Neve Ur 343
Michael Freikman, David Ben-Shlomo, Jacob Damm,
and Oren Gutfeld

Pottery Production in Late Phases of Early Bronze 1
in the Southern Levant.. 359
Eliot Braun

The Outline and Design of Fortified Cities
of the Early Bronze IB and II 389
Nimrod Getzov and Ianir Milevski

An-Naqʻ and Fifa in the Southern Ghor, Jordan:
A Tale of Two Cemeteries..................................... 411
Mohammad Najjar

A Note on the Earliest Appearance of the Hand-Made,
Straight-Sided Cooking Pot in the Southern Levant................ 443
Yitzhak Paz and Naama Walzer

Can DISH Be a Marker for Greater Social Stratification:
Jericho's Early Bronze IV and Tell Atchana, Alalakh   453
Rula Shafiq

Part II   New Directions in Biblical Archaeology

Theoretical and Methodological Comments on Social Complexity
and State Formation in Biblical Archaeology   471
Erez Ben-Yosef and Zachary Thomas

History Without Texts: Interdisciplinary Interpretive
Methods for Understanding the Early Iron Age   535
Sarah Malena

What Is the Name of Our Discipline? Or, the Onomastic Stew
That Is Archaeology in the Southern Levant   555
Zachary Thomas

"Their Voice Carries Throughout the Earth, Their Words
to the End of the World" (Ps 19, 5): Thoughts on Long-Range
Trade in Organics in the Bronze and Iron Age Levant   573
Aren M. Maeir

The Site of Khirbet 'Aujah el-Foqa:
Identifying Its Iron Age Architecture   601
David Ben-Shlomo

Die Like an Egyptian: Burial Customs in Iron Age I Philistia   625
Shirly Ben Dor Evian and Mario A. S. Martin

Philistine Rural Temple Economy: The Early Iron Age Fauna
from Nahal Patish   639
Edward F. Maher and Pirhiya Nahshoni

The Hesi Region: A Regional Perspective on Interaction
and Integration Processes During the Iron I/II Transition   681
James W. Hardin

Agricultural and Economic Change in the Iron
II Judean Shephelah as a Result of Geopolitical Shifts:
A View from Tel Burna   711
Itzhaq Shai

Gezer Destructions: A Case Study of a Border City   723
Steven M. Ortiz

Jerusalem's Settlement History: Rejoinders and Updates   753
Israel Finkelstein

The Interconnections Between Jerusalem and Samaria in the Ninth to Eighth Centuries BCE: Material Culture, Connectivity and Politics 771
Yuval Gadot, Assaf Kleiman, and Joe Uziel

Tel Beth-Shean in the Tenth–Ninth Centuries BCE: A Chronological Query and Its Possible Archaeomagnetic Resolution 787
Yoav Vaknin, Amihai Mazar, Ron Shaar, and Erez Ben-Yosef

Time and Paradigm at Tel Megiddo: David, Shoshenq I, Hazael and Radiocarbon Dating 811
Hendrik J. Bruins

The Buqei'a Plateau of the Judean Desert in the Southern Levant During the Seventh to Early Sixth Centuries BCE: Iron Age Run-off Farmland or a Pastoralist Rangeland? 839
Shimon Gibson, Rafael Y. Lewis, and Joan E. Taylor

Recognizing Ceramic Traditions: Moabite Painted and Decorated Wares 899
P. M. Michèle Daviau

The Qasr at Balu'a 923
Kent Bramlett, Monique Roddy, Craig Tyson, and Friedbert Ninow

The Case for Jalul as Biblical Bezer 943
Randall W. Younker

Remarks on the Typology and Chronology of Iron Age and Persian Period Winepresses 961
Samuel Richard Wolff

My Heart Is To …: Some Cruxes in Identity Formation in Iron I Israel? 977
Baruch Halpern

Merenptah and Amenmesse – Egyptian Rumors Concerning the Exodus 1013
Michael Bányai

Moses the Egyptian? A Reassessment of the Etymology of the Name "Moses" 1047
Thomas Schneider

Heraclitus' Law and the Late Period Shaft Tombs of Abusir 1057
Miroslav Bárta

Hala Sultan Tekke, Cyprus. Trade with Egypt in the Bronze Age 1069
Peter M. Fischer

Contents of Volume 2

Volume 2: From Archaeological Sciences to Archaeological Theory

Part III   New Research on the Archaeology of Faynan, Southern Jordan

Organizing Principles in Early Bronze Age Copper Manufacturing 1087
Aaron Gidding

Maps and Models: Applications of GIS and Image-Based
Modeling to Field Archaeology in Faynan, Jordan 1107
Matthew D. Howland and Brady Liss

Archaeological Evidence of Casual Snacking and Resource
Provisioning at Khirbat al-Jariya (ca. Eleventh to Tenth
Centuries BCE), an Iron-Age Copper Production Site 1133
Luke Stroth, Arianna Garvin Suero, Brady Liss, Matthew D. Howland,
and Jade D'Alpoim Guedes

City of Copper, Ruin of Copper: Rethinking Nelson Glueck's
Identifications of Ir Nahash and Ge Harashim 1155
Marc A. Beherec

Assessing the Circulation of Arabah Copper (Timna vs. Faynan)
from the End of the Late Bronze and Iron Age in the Southern
Levant by Combining Lead Isotopic Ratios
with Lead Concentrations 1181
Naama Yahalom-Mack, Daniel M. Finn, and Yigal Erel

Copper Trade Networks from the Arabah:
Re-assessing the Impact on Early Iron Age Moab 1201
Stanley Klassen and Andrew J. Danielson

The Negev Highlands — A Corridor for the Copper
and Incense Trade during Nonconsecutive Periods
between the Chalcolithic and Roman Periods 1227
Chaim Ben David

Fragments of an Archaeology of Late Roman Religion at Phaino
(Khirbat Faynān, Southern Jordan) 1255
Ian W. N. Jones

Part IV   Archaeometallurgy Beyond Faynan

Lead in Human Bones and Teeth Reflecting Historical
Changes in Lead Production: Rome and the Levant 1275
Yigal Erel

The Source of Southern Levantine Hellenistic Silver and Lead 1287
Tzilla Eshel, Gideon Hadas, Asaf Oron, Irina Segal, Ofir Tirosh,
and Yehiel Zelinger

A Social Archaeometallurgy of Bronze Age Cyprus 1303
A. Bernard Knapp

Early Types of Cypriot Bronze Age Metal Ingots 1323
Vasiliki Kassianidou

A Change in Attitude: X-Ray Images of the Ingot
God from Enkomi 1355
George Papasavvas

Iron Age Copper Metallurgy in Southeast Arabia: A Comparative
Perspective 1391
Joseph W. Lehner, Ioana A. Dumitru, Abigail Buffington, Eli Dollarhide,
Smiti Nathan, Paige Paulsen, Mary L. Young, Alexander J. Sivitskis,
Frances Wiig, and Michael J. Harrower

Copper Metallurgy in the Andes 1419
Carol Schultze and Charles Stanish

Experimental Bloomery Iron Smelting in the Study
of Iron Technology in the Southern Levant 1449
Adi Eliyahu Behar

Part V   Marine Archaeology and Maritime Trade
         in the Eastern Mediterranean and Beyond

Unearthing Craft Activities in the North Aegean:
The Karabournaki Settlement 1469
Despoina Tsiafaki

The Inland Late Bronze – Iron Age Anchorage of Dor: Ancient Reality or Fantasy? 1493
Gilad Shtienberg and Katrina Cantu

Stray Finds in the Periphery of Harbours: The Case of Paralimni-*Louma*, Famagusta Bay, Cyprus 1507
Stella Demesticha and Miltiadis Polidorou

The Shell and the Skeleton: The Circumstances for the Transition in Shipbuilding Technologies in the Late-Antique Southern Levant 1539
Gil Gambash

By Boat or by Land – GIS Least-Cost Modeling of Indigenous Native American Transportation Choices in the San Francisco Bay Area 1553
Brian F. Byrd and Paul Brandy

Part VI Cyber-Archaeology and Archaeological Science: The Future of the Past

From the Field to the Web: Towards an Integrative Approach in Data Processing from Excavations and Surveys into Quantitative Digital Archaeology – The Israeli Case Study 1581
Gideon Avni, Avraham S. Tendler, and Liat Weinblum

Photogrammetric and GIS-Based Modeling of Rapid Sediment Erosion and Deposition on the Taskscape of Bronze Age Politiko-*Troullia*, Cyprus 1603
Elizabeth Ridder, Patricia L. Fall, and Steven E. Falconer

From Digital Recording to Advanced AI Applications in Archaeology and Cultural Heritage 1627
George Pavlidis

New Approaches to Real-Time Rendering in Cyber-Archaeology 1657
Neil G. Smith

Preservation of the Memory of Lost Cultural Heritage in Post-conflict Communities 1683
Matthew Vincent

Local Voices, Storytelling, and Virtual Reality: Fostering Community Archaeology and Preserving Cultural Heritage in a COVID Lockdown 1701
Suzanne Richard and Douglas R. Clark

"Cult and Copper": A VR Game Exploring
the Intangible Heritage of Copper Smelting 1723
Casondra Sobieralski

Uncertainties in Archaeointensity Research:
Implications for the Levantine Archaeomagnetic Curve............. 1753
Lisa Tauxe, Ron Shaar, Brendan Cych, and Erez Ben-Yosef

Part VII Anthropological Archaeology in the Southern
Levant and Beyond

More than Antiquity: How Archaeologists See 1777
Raphael Greenberg

Pragmatism in Archaeology: The End of Theory? 1789
William G. Dever

Polycentrism and the Rise of Secondary States
in the Eastern Mediterranean: Aspects of a Southern
Levantine Cultural Paradigm 1801
Øystein S. LaBianca

Markets, Barter, and the Origins of Money: How Archaic States
and Empires Organized Their Economies 1823
Geoffrey E. Braswell

Making Peoples: The Nabatean Settlement
of the Dhiban Plateau and Beyond 1855
Chang-ho Ji

The Hexagram Graves: Symbols and Identity in Ottoman Jaffa....... 1889
Yoav Arbel

"Napoleon's Hill" and the 1799 Siege of Acre/Akko, Israel 1911
Ann E. Killebrew and Jane C. Skinner

The Curious Case of Albright at Megiddo
(aka "A Mysterious Affair at Armageddon")....................... 1933
Eric H. Cline

Correction to: "And in Length of Days Understanding" (Job 12:12) ... C1
Erez Ben-Yosef and Ian W. N. Jones

Index... 1953

Contributors

Yael Abadi-Reiss Israel Antiquities Authority, Jerusalem, Israel

Yoav Arbel Israel Antiquities Authority, Jerusalem, Israel

Gideon Avni Israel Antiquities Authority, Jerusalem, Israel

Michael Bányai Independent Scholar, Stuttgart, Germany

Shay Bar University of Haifa, Haifa, Israel

Miroslav Bárta Charles University, Prague, Czechia

Marc A. Beherec Independent Scholar, Los Angeles, CA, USA
Michael Baker International, Los Angeles, CA, USA

Jeremy A. Beller Simon Fraser University, Burnaby, BC, Canada

Chaim Ben-David Kinneret College on the Sea of Galilee, Zemach, Israel

Shirly Ben Dor Evian University of Haifa, Haifa, Israel

David Ben-Shlomo Ariel University, Ariel, Israel

Erez Ben-Yosef Tel Aviv University, Tel Aviv, Israel

Kent Bramlett La Sierra University, Riverside, CA, USA

Paul Brandy Far Western Anthropological Research Group, Davis, CA, USA

Geoffrey E. Braswell University of California, San Diego, La Jolla, CA, USA

Eliot Braun W.F. Albright Institute of Archaeological Research, Jerusalem, Israel

Hendrik J. Bruins Ben-Gurion University of the Negev, Beer-Sheva, Israel

Abigail Buffington College of William and Mary, Williamsburg, VA, USA

Brian Byrd Far Western Anthropological Research Group, Davis, CA, USA

Katrina Cantu University of California, San Diego, La Jolla, CA, USA

Ian Cipin University of Haifa, Haifa, Israel

Douglas R. Clark La Sierra University, Riverside, CA, USA

Eric H. Cline George Washington University, Washington, DC, USA

Brendan Cych Scripps Institution of Oceanography, La Jolla, CA, USA
University of Liverpool, Liverpool, UK

Jade D'Alpoim Guedes University of California, San Diego, La Jolla, CA, USA

Jacob Damm Cornell University, Ithaca, NY, USA

Andrew J. Danielson University of British Columbia, Vancouver, BC, Canada

P. M. Michèle Daviau Wilfrid Laurier University, Waterloo, ON, Canada

Uri Davidovich The Hebrew University of Jerusalem, Jerusalem, Israel

Stella Demesticha University of Cyprus, Nicosia, Cyprus

William G. Dever Lycoming College, Williamsport, PA, USA
University of Arizona, Tucson, AZ, USA

Eli N. Dollarhide New York University Abu Dhabi, Abu Dhabi, UAE

Ioana A. Dumitru Aarhus University, Aarhus, Denmark

Jennie Ebeling University of Evansville, Evansville, IN, USA

Adi Eliyahu-Behar Ariel University, Ariel, Israel

Yigal Erel The Hebrew University of Jerusalem, Jerusalem, Israel

Tzilla Eshel University of Haifa, Haifa, Israel

Marina Faerman The Hebrew University of Jerusalem, Jerusalem, Israel

Steven E. Falconer University of North Carolina at Charlotte, Charlotte, NC, USA

Patricia L. Fall University of North Carolina at Charlotte, Charlotte, NC, USA

Israel Finkelstein Tel Aviv University, Tel Aviv, Israel
University of Haifa, Haifa, Israel

Bill Finlayson University of Oxford, Oxford, UK

Daniel M. Finn The Hebrew University of Jerusalem, Jerusalem, Israel

Peter M. Fischer University of Gothenburg, Gothenburg, Sweden

Pascal Flohr University of Kiel, Kiel, Germany
University of Oxford, Oxford, UK

Norma Franklin University of Haifa, Haifa, Israel

Michael Freikman The Hebrew University of Jerusalem, Jerusalem, Israel

Contributors

Richard Elliott Friedman University of Georgia, Athens, GA, USA

Yuval Gadot Tel Aviv University, Tel Aviv, Israel

Gil Gambash University of Haifa, Haifa, Israel

Yosef Garfinkel The Hebrew University of Jerusalem, Jerusalem, Israel

Arianna Garvin Suero University of California, San Diego, La Jolla, CA, USA

Nimrod Getzov Israel Antiquities Authority, Jerusalem, Israel

Shimon Gibson University of North Carolina at Charlotte, Charlotte, NC, USA

Aaron D. Gidding University of California, Santa Barbara, Santa Barbara, CA, USA

Raphael Greenberg Tel Aviv University, Tel Aviv, Israel

Haskel J. Greenfield University of Manitoba, Winnipeg, MB, Canada

Oren Gutfeld The Hebrew University of Jerusalem, Jerusalem, Israel

Gideon Hadas Dead Sea and Arava Science Center, Jerusalem, Israel

Baruch Halpern University of Georgia, Athens, GA, USA

James W. Hardin Mississippi State University, Mississippi State, MS, USA

Michael J. Harrower Johns Hopkins University, Baltimore, MD, USA

Liora Kolska Horwitz The Hebrew University of Jerusalem, Jerusalem, Israel

Matthew D. Howland University of Georgia, Athens, GA, USA

David Ilan Hebrew Union College, Jerusalem, Israel

Chang-ho Ji La Sierra University, Riverside, CA, USA

Ian W. N. Jones University of California, San Diego, La Jolla, CA, USA

Vasiliki Kassianidou University of Cyprus, Nicosia, Cyprus

Ann E. Killebrew The Pennsylvania State University, University Park, PA, USA

Stanley Klassen University of Toronto, Toronto, ON, Canada

Assaf Kleiman Ben-Gurion University of the Negev, Beer-Sheva, Israel

A. Bernard Knapp University of Glasgow, Glasgow, Scotland, UK
Cyprus American Archaeological Research Institute, Nicosia, Cyprus

Øystein LaBianca Andrews University, MI, USA

Dafna Langgut Tel Aviv University, Tel Aviv, Israel

Joseph W. Lehner University of Sydney, Sydney, NSW, Australia

Rafael Y. Lewis Ashkelon Academic College, Ashkelon, Israel
University of Haifa, Haifa, Israel

Brady Liss University of California, San Diego, La Jolla, CA, USA

Aren M. Maeir Bar-Ilan University, Ramat Gan, Israel

Edward F. Maher Northeastern Illinois University, Chicago, IL, USA

Sarah Malena St. Mary's College of Maryland, MD, USA

Mario A. S. Martin University of Innsbruck, Innsbruck, Austria

Amihai Mazar The Hebrew University of Jerusalem, Jerusalem, Israel

Ianir Milevski Israel Antiquities Authority, Jerusalem, Israel
National Scientific and Technical Research Council, Buenos Aires, Argentina

Pirhiya Nahshoni Independent Scholar, Beer-Sheva, Israel

Mohammad Najjar Independent Scholar, Amman, Jordan

Linoy Namdar Tel Aviv University, Tel Aviv, Israel

Smiti Nathan Anthico LLC, Baltimore, MD, USA

Friedbert Ninow La Sierra University, Riverside, CA, USA
Theologische Hochschule Friedensau, Möckern, Germany

Asaf Oron Tel Aviv Museum of Art, Tel Aviv, Israel

Steven M. Ortiz Lipscomb University, Nashville, TN, USA

George Papasavvas University of Cyprus, Nicosia, Cyprus

Page E. Paulsen Johns Hopkins University, Baltimore, MD, USA

George Pavlidis Athena Research Center, Xanthi, Greece

Yitzhak Paz Israel Antiquities Authority, Jerusalem, Israel

Sonia Pinsky University of Haifa, Haifa, Israel

Miltiadis Polidorou National and Kapodistrian University of Athens, Athens, Greece

Suzanne Richard Gannon University, Erie, PA, USA

Elizabeth Ridder California State University, San Marcos, San Marcos, CA, USA

Monique Roddy La Sierra University, Riverside, CA, USA
Walla Walla University, WA, USA

Gary Rollefson Whitman College, Walla Walla, WA, USA

Danny Rosenberg University of Haifa, Haifa, Israel

Yorke Rowan University of Chicago, Chicago, IL, USA

Lidar Sapir-Hen Tel Aviv University, Tel Aviv, Israel

Arik Sasi Tel Aviv University, Tel Aviv, Israel

Thomas Schneider University of British Columbia, Vancouver, BC, Canada

Carol A. Schultze WestLand Engineering & Environmental Services, Seattle, WA, USA

Irina Segal Geological Survey of Israel, Jerusalem, Israel

Ron Shaar The Hebrew University of Jerusalem, Jerusalem, Israel

Rula Shafiq Yeditepe University, Istanbul, Turkey

Itzhaq Shai Ariel University, Ariel, Israel

Dina Shalem Israel Antiquities Authority, Jerusalem, Israel
Kinneret College on the Sea of Galilee, Zemach, Israel

Tamar Shooval University of Haifa, Haifa, Israel

Gilad Shtienberg University of California, San Diego, La Jolla, CA, USA

Alan H. Simmons University of Nevada, Las Vegas, Paradise, NV, USA
Desert Research Institute, Reno, NV, USA

Alexander J. Sivitskis Teton Science Schools, Jackson, WY, USA

Jane C. Skinner The Pennsylvania State University, University Park, PA, USA

Neil G. Smith University of California, San Diego, La Jolla, CA, USA

Patricia Smith The Hebrew University of Jerusalem, Jerusalem, Israel

Casondra Sobieralski University of California, Santa Cruz, Santa Cruz, CA, USA

Charles Stanish University of South Florida, Tampa, FL, USA

Luke Stroth University of California, San Diego, La Jolla, CA, USA

Lisa Tauxe Scripps Institution of Oceanography, La Jolla, CA, USA

Joan E. Taylor King's College London, London, UK

Avraham Tendler Israel Antiquities Authority, Jerusalem, Israel

Zachary Thomas Tel Aviv University, Tel Aviv, Israel

Ofir Tirosh The Hebrew University of Jerusalem, Jerusalem, Israel

Despoina Tsiafaki Athena Research Center, Xanthi, Greece

Craig Tyson D'Youville University, Buffalo, NY, USA

Joe Uziel Israel Antiquities Authority, Jerusalem, Israel

Yoav Vaknin Tel Aviv University, Tel Aviv, Israel
The Hebrew University of Jerusalem, Jerusalem, Israel

Matthew Vincent American Center of Research, Amman, Jordan

Naama Walzer Tel Aviv University, Tel Aviv, Israel

Liat Weinblum Israel Antiquities Authority, Jerusalem, Israel

Frances Wiig University of New South Wales, Sydney, NSW, Australia

Samuel R. Wolff W.F. Albright Institute of Archaeological Research, Jerusalem, Israel

Naama Yahalom-Mack The Hebrew University of Jerusalem, Jerusalem, Israel

Mary L. Young College of William and Mary, Williamsburg, VA, USA

Randall W. Younker Andrews University, MI, USA

Yehiel Zelinger Israel Antiquities Authority, Jerusalem, Israel

Part I
The Later Prehistory of the Southern Levant

Tom Levy in an excavated subterranean feature at the Chalcolithic village of Shiqmim, southern Israel, 1989. (Photo courtesy of T.E. Levy)

Tom Levy and "Deep Time": Forays into the Neolithic

Alan H. Simmons

Abstract Tom Levy usually is not associated with more "deep-time" archaeology, such as the Neolithic. He has, however, contributed to early time periods in more ways than one. In this short essay, I would like to share some personal observations and comments on how Tom has impacted Neolithic studies, especially in the Wadi Feinan of Jordan, where Mohammad Najjar and I conducted extensive excavations at a major Pre-Pottery Neolithic B (PPNB) site, Ghwair I. Tom was always supportive of our studies. Both in the field and back at our home bases, Tom always offered considerable insights into the cultural processes leading up to later cultural periods. And while he was not directly involved with such early studies, he certainly was aware of their importance. As just one example, his major work "The Archaeology of Society in the Holy Land" had several chapters devoted to prehistoric periods. And, Tom's use of state-of-the-art technology has led to technological improvements in earlier periods. This illustrates Tom's broad range of interest in archaeology as a discipline, rather than just one time period. Finally, Tom's many students continue to have an impact on the discipline.

Keywords Neolithic · Fieldwork · Jordan

I have never worked with Tom Levy but we have excavated in the same geographic area (Wadi Feinan, Jordan). While I do not know Tom all that well, I am appreciative of the opportunity to provide a few words about him in this volume. So, this is more of a personal essay, rather than a data-based one. And, certainly we all know of Tom's huge contributions to high tech and archaeology…a model to aspire to. But, I am sure that other contributions here address that more specifically.

A. H. Simmons (✉)
University of Nevada, Las Vegas, Las Vegas, NV, USA

Desert Research Institute, Reno, NV, USA
e-mail: simmonsa@unlv.nevada.edu

© The Author(s), under exclusive license to Springer Nature Switzerland AG 2023
E. Ben-Yosef, I. W. N. Jones (eds.), *"And in Length of Days Understanding" (Job 12:12): Essays on Archaeology in the Eastern Mediterranean and Beyond in Honor of Thomas E. Levy*, Interdisciplinary Contributions to Archaeology, https://doi.org/10.1007/978-3-031-27330-8_1

Tom and I work in different time periods, and he is not associated with more "deep-time" archaeology, such as the Neolithic. For me, though, anything after the Neolithic becomes fuzzy, while Tom specializes in later periods. But he has had a considerable impact on Neolithic research. In his long-term investigations into the Wadi Feinan (and elsewhere I'm sure), Tom has always been cognizant of earlier periods, and has contributed valuable insights into these. Indeed, his now dated and often difficult to find edited book "The Archaeology of Society in the Holy Land" (Levy, 1998) was one I used for years in teaching Near Eastern prehistory. Fourteen of the 32 chapters were devoted either to prehistory (here I include up to the Chalcolithic), anthropology, and the environment. There was (and really still is) little else available that addressed early prehistory in such detail, and Tom's inclusion of very important syntheses by prominent prehistorians in his volume was something that I am sure more than one of us was grateful for. It also is worth noting that, especially for the time, this volume had a very anthropological perspective to it, including an introduction by Kent Flannery. I mention this simply because anthropological approaches to much of Near Eastern archaeology at the time were limited.

In more personal terms, I think I first met Tom in the Wadi Feinan, when Mohammad Najjar and I were co-directing excavations at Neolithic Ghwair I (Figs. 1 and 2; Simmons & Najjar, 2006, 2007). And, of course, Mohammad has worked closely with Tom for years. During those field seasons, under very difficult conditions, Tom has always forthcoming in sharing resources and information.

Fig. 1 Overview of the Neolithic site of Ghwair I in the Wadi Feinan, Jordan

Tom Levy and "Deep Time": Forays into the Neolithic

Fig. 2 One of the architectural blocks at Ghwair I

While our teams did not interact too much (perhaps for the better?), Tom was always around to share questions and concerns with. These were wide-ranging, from specifics of life in the wadi, to more general research topics that crosscut our time differences. These usually related to issues of human adaptations to this very extreme environment.

Our seasons rarely overlapped, as we excavated during winter break to avoid much of the extreme heat of the wadi. Tom, on the other hand, often excavated, with quite large teams, during the heat of the summer. His team lived in a "tent city" and amenities were few. I have always marveled at this logistical achievement.

One of Tom's many accomplishments, of course, is his application of hi-tech methodologies to archaeology. These were readily apparent in the Wadi, and Tom was always willing to share thoughts on why or why not a particular technique might be of help to us. His field applications and data storage methods are ones that many projects could envy, and I am certain that many essays in this volume address those.

Another contribution is Tom's ability to navigate the always difficult terrain of doing archaeology in a political sensitive region. He seems to have accomplished this with great success, as attested to by his projects in both Israel and Jordan. And, his contributions are not restricted to archaeology alone. He has been a tireless advocate for heritage preservation in this volatile part of the world, to which we (Simmons & Najjar, 2013) have made an effort at Ghwair I.

Tom's other legacy, of course, relates to the numerous students he has mentored over the years, many of whom are now professional archaeologists in their own rights. And, it is not only students, but other young professionals, often starting out on their careers, to whom Tom has provided invaluable guidance.

During the field and at professional meetings, usually the annual meeting of the American Schools of Oriental Research, were really the only times I interacted with Tom, although we frequently shared information via email. Then one year I gave an Archaeological Institute of America lecture in San Diego that Tom hosted. Once again, I was impressed with his ease of organization of a very large AIA chapter. I'm sure his skills in organizing large field projects were of help here. The "potluck" dinner was something to be seen! All of this made that particular lecture something to remember.

So, I have only been able to make a few brief remarks about Tom here. I leave it to others to chronicle his considerable research achievements. But, Tom's broad range of interest in archaeology as a discipline, rather than just one time period, will be a lasting contribution. To me, Tom is what more of us need to be: a collegial scholar not afraid to share data and ideas.

References

Levy, T. (Ed.). (1998). *Archaeology of society in the Holy Land.* Leicester University Press.
Simmons, A., & Najjar, M. (2006). Ghwair I: A small but complex Neolithic community in Southern Jordan. *Journal of Field Archaeology, 31,* 77–95.
Simmons, A., & Najjar, M. (2007). Is big really better? Life in the Resort Corridor: Ghwair I, a small but elaborate Neolithic community in Southern Jordan. In T. Levy, P. Daviau, R. Younker, & M. Shaer (Eds.), *Crossing Jordan: North American contributions to the archaeology of Jordan* (pp. 233–241). Equinox Press.
Simmons, A., & Najjar, M. (2013). Joint custody: An archaeological park at Neolithic Ghwair I, Jordan. *Near Eastern Archaeology, 76,* 177–184.

The Neolithic of the Jordanian *Badia*

Bill Finlayson ⓘ and Pascal Flohr ⓘ

Abstract Much research has been conducted in the arid zone of Jordan, beyond the Mediterranean environments traditionally understood as the Neolithic core developmental area. The Neolithic of this arid zone has often been framed as marginal, as specially adapted to the dry environmental conditions, as maintaining hunting traditions, as providing protein to the settled communities of the core, and as made possible by new developments in pastoralism. As more evidence is discovered, an increasingly nuanced picture emerges. Not least, our understanding of the environment suggests that rather than adaptation to arid conditions much of this Neolithic expansion may relate to the exploitation of extensive areas that were better watered than today. Nonetheless, new ways of living did emerge, although typically Neolithic in their intensification of the exploitation of resources leading to the carving out of new cultural and environmental niches. The relationships between people living in these lands and those living in the core established the foundations of the economic networks that become visible in the Chalcolithic and into the Early Bronze Age.

Keywords Steppe · Desert · Neolithic · Pastoralism · Hunter-gatherer · Gazelle

---

B. Finlayson (✉)
School of Archaeology, University of Oxford, Oxford, UK
e-mail: bill.finlayson@arch.ox.ac.uk

P. Flohr
Institute for Pre- and Protohistory and Cluster of Excellence ROOTS, Christian Albrechts University of Kiel, Kiel, Germany

School of Archaeology, University of Oxford, Oxford, UK
e-mail: pflohr@roots.uni-kiel.de

© The Author(s), under exclusive license to Springer Nature Switzerland AG 2023
E. Ben-Yosef, I. W. N. Jones (eds.), *"And in Length of Days Understanding" (Job 12:12): Essays on Archaeology in the Eastern Mediterranean and Beyond in Honor of Thomas E. Levy*, Interdisciplinary Contributions to Archaeology, https://doi.org/10.1007/978-3-031-27330-8_2

1 Introduction

The Neolithic occupation of Jordan's (currently) arid zone, both steppe and desert, has a long history of research (Betts, 1982; Garrard et al., 1975). Not surprisingly, how this occupation is understood has undergone enormous change over time. This includes a more complex understanding of the nature of occupation, but also a considerable change in how we conceive of those arid margins in themselves. When one of the present authors (BF) first commenced work in Wadi Faynan in 1996, close to where Tom Levy's major Wadi Fidan project was to take place, the area was generally perceived of as marginal, both in terms of (early) Neolithic settlement and in environment (Goring-Morris & Belfer-Cohen, 2011). After many years of work, it is now clear that in the (early) Neolithic there was nothing marginal about either.

The arid zone of Jordan, and beyond, is generally referred to as the *badia*. This term is formally used for the area receiving less than 200 mm of precipitation per year, consisting of the semi-arid and arid steppe, desert, and hyper-arid desert, which together comprise about 80% of Jordan (Betts et al., 2013; The Hashemite Fund for the Development of Jordanian Badia) (Fig. 1). These areas are generally too arid for rain-fed (or 'dry') farming and are traditionally used as grazing grounds

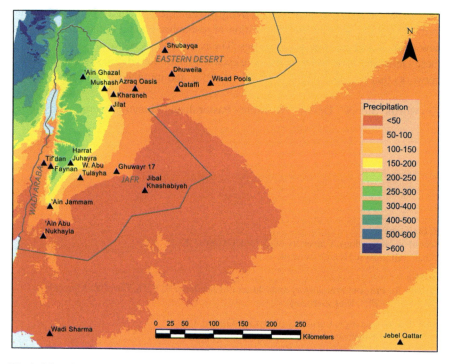

Fig. 1 Map of Jordan and surroundings with current mean annual precipitation gradients (in mm) and locations of main sites and areas mentioned in the text. The *badia* is the <200 mm red-yellow zone. Precipitation from WorldClim 2. (Fick and Hijmans 2017)

by Bedouin, although they incorporate a number of areas with additional waters from springs or run-off from more distant rain. This is probably why the area is conceived of as environmentally marginal, but when not overgrazed many parts of the area are richly vegetated (Fig. 2). Moreover, as explored further below, the

Fig. 2 Shauamari Nature Reserve, near Azraq, showing the contrast between vegetation present inside the fence (**a**) and land outside under grazing pressure (**b**), in June 2017

environment appears to have been wetter during the Neolithic (Jones et al., 2019). Due to the wealth of research in the Jordanian *badia* over the last decades, it is now clear that also in terms of Neolithic occupation the area was not marginal, certainly not during the Late Neolithic (c. 6500–5000 BCE[1]) for which period a wealth of evidence is now present, perhaps most remarkably from the Black Desert (e.g. Akkermans et al., 2014; Betts et al., 2013; Rowan et al., 2017).

Key research questions for the *badia* have been: In the mosaic of development paths that led to farming and pastoralism as we know them, how much was the Neolithic occupation of the *badia* the result of a more favourable environment than that which pertains today, how much may it have been based on resource needs from the more settled zones, or how much on the development of new practises in hunting and pastoralism? These traditional questions have recently been rephrased by Henton et al. (2018) as to whether the *badia* was only seasonally occupied by hunter-gatherers or hunter-herders during the Epipalaeolithic and Neolithic, or was occupied year-round by societies who had adapted to steppe conditions. It is becoming increasingly possible to move on from these questions, as we now know considerably more regarding the early stages of herd management and the movement of herd animals (Makarewicz, 2017; Makarewicz & Tuross, 2012), a process of domestication that appears to have been closely connected to the growth of Neolithic settlements, agriculture, and the development of a mixed farming economy (Bogaard et al., 2013). However, although the development of mixed farming is a well-known Neolithic development path, it is only one Neolithic trajectory, and in Jordan the emergence of untethered nomadic pastoralism has been a significant area of research, at least since Köhler-Rollefson used ethnoarchaeological analogy with contemporary Bedouin to argue for the development of transhumant pastoralism in PPNC 'Ain Ghazal (Köhler-Rollefson et al., 1988; Köhler-Rollefson, 1992). Recent field research has focussed on a possible major colonisation of the *badia* by Late Neolithic full-time pastoralists (e.g. Rollefson, 2011). An almost entirely separate strand of research has examined the technological improvements in water management during the PPNB that may have made agriculture possible beyond areas with sufficient rain, such as in the Jafr basin, and possibly even into Arabia (Fujii, 2007, 2011).

In this chapter we will consider which questions have been resolved, and what new, more nuanced questions our increasing knowledge permits. Much Neolithic research focuses on the development of a mixed farming system that led to the successful spread of the Neolithic into Europe and the establishment of economies and societies that enabled the development of urbanism. We wish to explore the potential of research into understanding the exploitation of the *badia* not just as an early trajectory to forms of pastoralism that became a significant way of life in the arid lands of Southwest Asia, but also as a route that enabled a more intensive exploitation of this vast landscape and made an important contribution to early civilizations. Perhaps surprisingly, although the diversity of the *badia* has been recognised, and different regional trends noted, relatively little focus has been given to the potential

---

[1] All dates in this chapter are calibrated, i.e. in calendar years BCE.

presence of simultaneous multiple ways of life adapted to local conditions within the *badia* (with the exception of Miller et al., 2018).

2 Present and Past Climate and Environment of Jordan's *Badia*

The Jordanian *badia* is currently reliant on precipitation generated over the Mediterranean and Atlantic, which falls almost exclusively during late autumn, winter and early spring. Currently, rainfall ranges from around 200 mm per year (on average, fluctuations can be large) in the north and northwest to less than 50 mm in the hyper-arid southeast (Fig. 1). Fluctuations between years are large, and importantly rain in the most arid regions often falls in one or two events only (Jones et al., 2021). Nonetheless, areas collecting runoff from wider catchments (wadis or seasonal streams, and *qe'an*[2] or seasonal lakes or mudflats) as well as those in the semi-arid (steppe) parts in the north and northwest show the potential for rich vegetation (Fig. 2) and even opportunistic growing of crops such as barley (Fig. 3). The Azraq Basin is of particular interest as water from an even larger catchment including the wetter Jebel Druze drains in this large depression towards the Azraq Oasis (Jones

Fig. 3 Barley growing in the Qa' Shubayqa, June 2017

---

[2] As plural of *qa'*, after Jones et al. 2021.

and Richter, 2011). In this oasis, as well as in some other areas of the *badia*, especially those on the western edge of the escarpment, perennial springs are present (MWI & BGR, 2019). The arid Wadi Araba also contains some locations with springs and streams, as in Wadis Faynan and Fidan. It is therefore important that the *badia* is not seen as one homogeneous area, but rather one containing a gradient from at least seasonally vegetated rainfed steppes to much less vegetated deserts, rainfed wadi courses and *qe'an*, as well as springfed, perennial wadis. Both the environmental impact and the changes in human behaviour need to be assessed in terms of these distinctions, which will in turn reveal more about what drove the decisions made.

While considerable uncertainty remains and no local high-resolution palaeoclimate records are available for the *badia*, the majority of Southwest Asian climate records indicate a wetter Early Holocene (c. 9700–6200 BCE, i.e. containing much of the Neolithic), wetter than after, including the present (Jones et al., 2019). Precipitation coming from the North Atlantic-Mediterranean system appears to have been higher: Soreq and Jeita speleothem records show more negative oxygen isotope values, which is for Southwest Asia frequently interpreted as indicating higher precipitation (Bar-Matthews et al., 1997; Cheng et al., 2015). It can be expected that this will also have affected especially the north-western edge of the *badia*, essentially moving the current rainfall zones further east- and southwards. However, it is not clear how much wetter it was exactly, and how far into the current *badia* >200 mm annual rainfall would have reached. No evidence for early Holocene standing (i.e. perennial) water has so far been found in Qa' Shubayqa, Wisad, or Qataffi in the Jordanian Black Desert (Jones et al., 2021). Nonetheless, the basins were still deeper than today and therefore had the capacity to hold more water, keeping seasonal rain available for longer periods (Jones et al., 2021). While records like Soreq, Jeita and others generally indicate an increase in precipitation from around the start of the Early Holocene, there are indications that during the Epipalaeolithic conditions in parts of the *badia*, like the Azraq basin, were at least at times also relatively wet, with soils and palaeolakes and/or wetlands, possibly because of lower evaporation rates (Cordova et al., 2013; Garrard et al., 1986). When this wetter period would have ended is unclear.

The Arabian Peninsula, bordering the Jordanian *badia* to its south, is also affected by other climate systems, which appear to have been more important in the region during the Early into the Mid Holocene. The Indian Monsoon has clearly been shown to have reached further north, but still stopping well south of the Jordanian *badia* (Fleitmann and Matter, 2009). In northern Saudi Arabia there is nonetheless good evidence for a wetter period between roughly 8000 and 4000 BCE (no high-precision well-dated records are available so the dating is approximate) (Petraglia et al., 2020). Modelling has shown that this was most likely driven by the African Monsoon, which, however, also did not reach as far north as Jordan (Guagnin et al., 2016). This might nonetheless be of relevance, since northern Saudi Arabia and Jordan share aquifers, with groundwater flowing northwards into southern Jordan.

Southern Jordan might also have been affected by Red Sea-generated moisture (Enzel et al., 2015). If these systems indeed caused wetter conditions in Early-Mid Holocene southern, but not northeastern, Jordan, this would have further reinforced the environmental variability between different areas of the Jordanian *badia*.

The current precipitation gradients are to a large extent influenced by the topography and can therefore be expected to have been the same relatively speaking, but more south- and eastwards, with the possible exception of Red Sea precipitation plumes causing increased rainfall in southern Jordan. Potential increased available groundwater as well as large-scale drainage patterns would have further influenced the availability of water.

In any case, it is clear that the environment of the *badia* was somehow 'wetter' during the Neolithic compared to the present. Without the present-day, and historical, intensive grazing, and with (some) increase in annual precipitation, areas that are now parts of Jordan's semi-arid steppe would have once been part of savannah lands that formerly likely extended further to the east and south than they do today, for example potentially placing the Wadi Jilat in the dry farming zone during the Neolithic (cereals were found at several Late PPNB Jilat sites (Colledge, 2001)). Until relatively recent intensive groundwater use, the Azraq Oasis was a place of wetlands, although the Early Holocene saw flood sediments rather than evidence for marshy conditions (Jones and Richter, 2011). For the Epipalaeolithic Azraq oasis the presence of palaeolakes and wetlands has been shown (Cordova et al., 2013), with evidence for soil formation in the Wadi Jilat (Garrard, 1998; Richter, 2020). At Shubayqa, lake or wetland environments have been attested for the Late Natufian period by the presence of ducks and rushes in the archaeological records (Yeomans & Richter, 2018). Work at Wisad Pools in the eastern *badia*, now a seasonal water resource located within the hyper-arid desert, shows this desert may have only developed in the last three or four millennia, and a lusher vegetation, including tabor oak, growing on an absorbent topsoil that was present around the transition from PPNC to Late Neolithic, while fig, a 'wet' species, has been found at Wadi Qataffi (Rollefson et al., 2015, 2018; Rowan et al., 2017). However, especially outside wetter locales, environments would have still been relatively arid, even if less so than today. Mostly steppe-adapted fauna has been uncovered from most studied Epipalaeolithic and Neolithic sites in the Azraq Basin and Black Desert (Martin et al., 2016), while arid-adapted plant species were found at Wadi Qataffi (Rowan et al., 2017). Farming in the Jafr basin, for example, would probably have required irrigation, as any eastwards increase in rainfall would not have occurred this far south (Wasse et al., 2020). The apparent discrepancy is perhaps also partly explained by a grazing effect on more recent landscapes: even today, protecting desert areas from grazing has a remarkable impact not only on vegetation, but on the development of moisture retaining soils that extend both the growing season and range of plants present (Hatough et al., 1986).

3 The *Badia* as Resource

The *badia* is often discussed from the perspective of the settled farming lands as a resource pool, whether that be in the form of additional protein for the growing population associated with increasingly large settled populations, or the production of commodities, such as beads (or the raw materials used to make them, such as malachite), tabular flint, or wool, all helping to later underpin the development of Bronze Age urban societies. In such scenarios, it is often assumed that the people obtaining these resources were, at least in the first instance, effectively conducting expeditions into the *badia*, whether these were to mine flint or move herds. The question whether people in the prehistoric *badia* were 'local' or not is one of the most-discussed in the archaeology of this region.

3.1 Hunting in the Badia

The debate relating to hunter-gatherer populations in the Jordanian *badia* has focused on seasonality and mobility: were 'independent' local populations present year-round in the *badia*, or did they visit the area seasonally between spending time in wetter locales? One problem we face is that we do not know where the boundaries between Mediterranean woodland and steppe zones were during any given period. Recently, Henton et al. (2018) argued, primarily from isotopic evidence, that in the better watered Eastern Desert of the Epipalaeolithic and Early Neolithic, gazelle populations did not undertake the long-distance migrations known from the recent past. This would have allowed human populations to hunt gazelle year-round in the *badia*. However, the authors also note that there were preferred hunting seasons (winter/spring in Epipalaeolithic, summer/autumn in the Neolithic), interpreted not as the result of resource availability, but, for the Neolithic, as a result of scheduling hunting to fit within the seasonal activities relating to farming (Rollefson & Köhler-Rollefson, 1993). This is important, as if correct would indicate that the people hunting gazelle in the *badia* were the same as the farmers to the west. It also still assumes that early Neolithic settlements were generally confined to our contemporary Mediterranean zone, or at least its ecotonal margins and that transhumance involved these settlements – in other words that the wetter parts of the *badia*, such as the Azraq basin, did not provide a tethering point.

A topic also relevant to the study of the people of the *badia* is whether observed changes in fauna from archaeological sites represent anthropogenic hunting pressure, selective hunting choices, or natural developments in the availability of wildlife (Martin et al., 2016), thus incorporating the key research theme of the role of climate/environment. Interestingly, throughout the Epipalaeolithic there is no sign of hunting pressure on gazelle herds, but in the PPNB there are indications for some human impact on gazelles, especially at Dhuweila during the LPPNB (Martin et al., 2016). This site, in a more arid part of the *badia*, contains no evidence for caprine herding and has therefore been interpreted as a specialised hunting site (Martin et al., 2016). This would accord with the association of the site with kites first recorded by Betts, suggesting that the use of kites for mass-hunting of gazelle commenced during this time (Betts 1998, 2014), perhaps by specialised hunters to gain meat and hides for exchange (Martin et al., 2016). The complete absence of caprines might suggest that these hunters were not pastoralists or farmers, but unfortunately not conclusively as the site could simply be the location for a highly specialised task. A LPPNB date for kites (and their function as hunting traps) has now been confirmed at least for a group of kites in southeast Jordan, which is of further interest as the use of these kites appears to have stopped at least by the Late Neolithic and probably before (Abu Azizeh et al., 2021).

Nonetheless, it seems hunting remained important in the *badia*, at least in the Azraq basin and the Eastern Desert, from which most of the data come, throughout the Neolithic. *Badia* sites continued to have wild animals represented in their fauna and it appears caprines are just added to the prey list, suggesting an adoption of caprines by existing populations, rather than the arrival of new herding people (Martin, 1999). However, Henton et al. (2018) note that in the Neolithic gazelle were pushed away from the immediate surroundings of the main settlements in the west, possibly due to local habitat changes caused by increased pastoralism still tethered to the settlements. The pattern observed may also have other causes such as keeping (domestic and wild) animals away from crops. As such, spatial patterns are also relevant. It has for example been argued that by the Late Neolithic a difference has developed between the western *badia*, where gazelle have become less numerous due to domesticate grazing pressure, and in the eastern *badia* where they remain abundant (Henton et al., 2018). In this scenario, hunting kites are a 'response' to increased pastoralism.

While important progress has been made over the last decades, the role of climate in the various developments remains unclear. After an apparently wetter Early Holocene, it has been suggested that increased aridification post-6600 BCE shifted gazelle into long-distance migration patterns, making the kites a more viable hunting mechanism (Henton et al., 2018). However, while aridification after c. 6600 BCE has been shown in palaeoclimate proxy records from the North Atlantic (Rohling & Pälike, 2005) and while more arid conditions than in the Early Holocene appear to have started at some point between 6000 and 4000 BCE, local timings and conditions are far from resolved. The above-mentioned work at Wisad Pools, for example, shows the presence of intact soil and 'wetter' vegetation during the Late Neolithic at this site.

3.2 *Pastoralism*

Pastoralism in Southwest Asia is usually understood as a sheep-goat, and/or cattle subsistence economy, generally divided into village-based and (semi-)nomadic, but in reality on a continuum between fully sedentary to fully mobile (Abdi, 2003;

Bar-Yosef & Khazanov, 1992; Levy, 1992; Makarewicz, 2013a, b). The separation of these forms of pastoralism has been generally understood as emerging in the Chalcolithic to Early Bronze Age, but perhaps going back into the Neolithic (Abdi, 2003; Cauvin, 2000; Hole, 1974, 1977; Levy, 1983; Makarewicz, 2013a, b; Rollefson, 2004). Neolithic origins have been sought through either a development arising from the Late PPNB agricultural settlements (Köhler-Rollefson, 1992; Rollefson & Köhler-Rollefson, 1992), or as indigenous developments with local hunter-gatherers in the arid lands adopting domesticates within their overall subsistence strategies (Baird et al., 1992; Garrard et al., 1996; Martin, 1999). Pastoralists in southwest Asia are understood, when not directly tethered to agricultural settlements, to be reliant on farmers (Bar-Yosef & Khazanov, 1992; Khazanov, 2009), however this conception is largely based in modern ethnography of environmentally and politically marginalised pastoralists (Makarewicz, 2013a). Makarewicz (2013a) notes that the focus of research on the origins of mobile pastoralism in the arid margins of Jordan maintains a marginalisation of nomadic pastoralism from the main trajectories of Neolithic development. The assumption that only farmers can create surplus and wealth limits the role of pastoralism in the subsequent developments of the Chalcolithic and Bronze Age, despite a clear potential for pastoralism to have created wealth (Makarewicz, 2013a, b; Rollefson, 2004). Similarly, the description of Late PPNB pastoralists as "paleobedouins" (Gebel, 2010) makes tacit assumptions about past ways of life that allows for over-interpretation without analysis.

The Late Neolithic colonisation of the *badia* is generally assumed to relate to this development of new forms of pastoralism, be it transhumant or (semi-)nomadic. The central argument that increased settlement of the *badia* was linked to pastoralism is clearly made by Rollefson et al. (2014: 285): "One likely territory was a region whose climatic conditions were inimical to agriculture: landscapes that could not support perennial farming because of a lack of reliably sufficient rainfall, but whose phytogeographic cover could be converted into energy and other requirements through the agency of the herding of caprines." Substantial research effort has been expended on the nature of early pastoralism, and how caprines are introduced to the *badia* – in particular whether they are adopted gradually by indigenous hunter-gatherer populations, or by herders coming from settlements to the west. A migration of herding people has two potential routes – a relatively gradual development of transhumant pastoralism, or a more dramatic migration. Rollefson et al. (2014) have argued that the population leaving shrinking Late PPNB 'mega-sites' may have provided the impetus for this, usefully making the *badia* a potential target for Late Neolithic populations dislocated and dispersing from PPNB agricultural settlements. This arrival of new populations would mean that 'nomadic pastoralism' is not a long slow development or "timid experimentation" (Rollefson et al., 2014: 287) amongst indigenous hunter-gatherer populations, but a rapid development at the start of the Late Neolithic (Rollefson, 2011; Rollefson et al., 2014). Martin (1999), however, saw more evidence for indigenous development, i.e. separate herding systems based, for example, on the percentage of caprines not being very low or very high, and when known derived from young/sub-adults. In reality, neither the faunal nor the isotopic evidence supports the idea that pre-pottery 'Ain

Ghazal was involved in the development of mobile pastoralism, neither in seasonal movement of flocks to the *badia*, nor in moving from an emphasis on meat production to secondary products (Makarewicz, 2014).

Increasingly the evidence appears to show that the reality was more complex, perhaps a combination of different strands. Caprine stable isotope evidence appears to show that herds both at the non-*badia* site of PPNB and PPNC 'Ain Ghazal and at the, at least currently *badia*, Early Late Neolithic (ELN; for an explanation see Sect. 4.4) site of Jilat 13 grazed locally or at least in areas environmentally similar to where the sites are located (Mediterranean and steppe, respectively), while those at current *badia* ELN site Jilat 25 roamed into higher rainfall area(s) (Makarewicz, 2014; Miller et al., 2018). The multiple strands can be seen in analyses that propose a tethered seasonal transhumant pastoralism in PPNC (and even Yarmoukian) 'Ain Ghazal, while by the start of the Late Neolithic, a fully separate, 'full-time' pastoralist population existed in the *badia* (Rollefson, 2011). Tethered pastoralism may well have long-continued as an aspect of major settlements, even as pastoralists in the *badia* became more mobile.

Other important issues relating to pastoralism in the *badia* are firstly the use of dairy products, about which virtually nothing is known yet for the Neolithic Jordanian *badia* (while in contemporary northern Mesopotamia dairy products have been attested (Evershed et al., 2008)). Secondly, in contrast to the Eastern Desert and Black Desert of Jordan where the focus appears to have been, as today, on sheep and goats, towards the south in Arabia cattle pastoralism was important (Makarewicz, 2020). Considering this is present as well in the Levant, potential routes for expansion could have gone through the Jafr Basin and/or the Wadi Araba (Makarewicz, 2020), which was perhaps better watered than the Eastern Desert at the time. This leads to the third related issue, the role of climate. It is tempting to relate the increase in settlement and pastoralism in the *badia* to either a general aridification starting around or after 6600 BCE (but see the comments above), or a more severe 'sudden' arid period between c. 6250 and 6000 BCE, the so-called 8.2 ka event (Alley et al., 1997; Rohling & Pälike, 2005). While pastoralism was clearly present in the *badia* prior to at least the latter (Fig. 4) (Flohr et al., 2016), the potential role of intensified pastoralism as a diversification strategy is certainly of interest (Martin et al., 2013).

4 The *Badia* Through Time

4.1 *Epipalaeolithic Backdrop*

Early work in the Jordanian Eastern Desert encountered numerous Epipalaeolithic sites, apparently more common than in the better watered areas of western Jordan (Betts, 1998). Some of this frequency is likely the result of better visibility and preservation, where flint scatter sites are more readily seen in a landscape today mostly bare of vegetation and relatively unaffected by modern development.

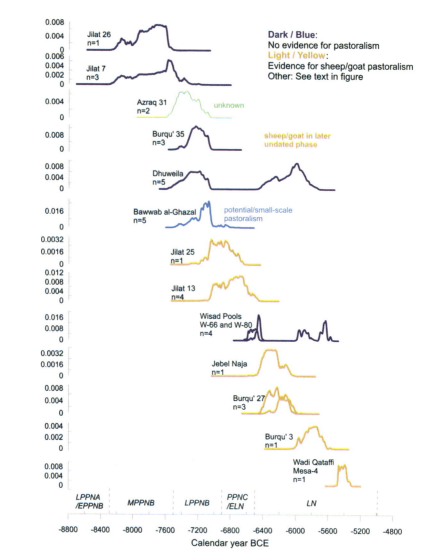

Fig. 4 Summed probability plots showing 14C-dated Neolithic sites in the Jordanian Eastern Desert and the presence or absence of sheep and goat (i.e. pastoralism) at these sites (after Flohr et al., 2016: Fig. 7; Martin in Garrard et al., 1994; Martin in Betts, 1998; Martin, 1999; Betts et al., 2013; Rollefson et al., 1999, 2014). Dark blue lines show sites without evidence of sheep/goat pastoralism, yellow lines indicate sites that do have evidence

However, the early and middle Epipalaeolithic of at least the (current) steppe zone of the *badia* were also characterised by large sites, areas of repeated occupation that appear to have drawn together different communities. Sites such as Jilat 6 and Kharaneh IV are widely understood as hunter-gatherer aggregation sites and nodes of interaction (Maher et al., 2015; Richter et al., 2011). These suggest that late

Pleistocene hunter-gatherer societies thrived, and that in certain favoured (and in these cases relatively wet) locations, they were able to gather in extended groups. Maher et al. (2015) have argued that given the plausible multi-season availability of resources at these locations, repeated occupation may have been long-term and multi-seasonal. Subsequently, Natufian occupation, especially in the Azraq oasis and around Qa' Shubayqa, shows that these hunter-gatherer societies were able to flourish beyond what was once understood as the Natufian core territory of the Mediterranean woodland zone (Richter et al., 2017). It appears that this was achieved through a combination of the presence of locally rich environments, and local fine tuning of Natufian economic strategies. However, one trait of this entire Epipalaeolithic period is that the history of occupation is patchy – in time and space. There are, for example, no early or middle Epipalaeolithic sites known at Shubayqa, and the Natufian is absent from a number of likely oasis settings. Wadi Faynan has no evidence for occupation between the Palaeolithic and the Neolithic (Finlayson & Mithen, 2007), although the adjacent Barqa area has clear evidence for Epipalaolithic, but no, or very limited, Neolithic occupation. With a palaeolake or palaeowetland present at the time, this locality might, as at Shubayqa, have been chosen for its wetland resources that helped provide the broad spectrum of subsistence that allowed Natufian communities to reduce their mobility. Nonetheless it is clear, while local environments clearly changed repeatedly over the time period under consideration, it appears implausible that the diversity of settlement patterns was driven by anything as simple as the availability of suitable locations.

There is no evidence of hunting pressure, although the number of sites examined remains small (Martin et al., 2016). Gazelle bones are dominant at all studied Epipalaeolithic *badia* sites, although in the Middle and Late Epipalaeolithic small game counts increase, like hare and birds and at Shubayqa 1 including waterfowl (Martin, 1999; Martin et al., 2016; Yeomans et al., 2017). Cattle are rare except at the wet localities of Azraq 18, 'Ain Qasiyya, and Shubayqa, and steppe adapted equids are more common (Martin, 1999; Martin et al., 2016; Yeomans et al., 2017). Plant evidence is limited, although Natufian Shubayqa shows an intensive use of wetland plants, with only limited use of cereals (Arranz-Otaegui et al., 2018), illustrating the ability of Natufian hunter-gatherers to tune their subsistence to local environments.

4.2 The PPNA and EPPNB

Known PPNA settlement is extremely rare in what today are the arid margins (Betts, 1998; see also Richter, 2020). Where present, sites were clearly in wetter environmental niches, such as in the Azraq oasis (Garrard et al., 1996), Shubayqa 6 near Qa' Shubayqa (Richter, 2020), or Wadi Faynan 16 on a wadi fed by perennial springs and downstream from a higher rainfall catchment area. Material culture at these sites is essentially typical of the range of PPNA material found elsewhere in Jordan. There is no sign of any PPNA 'arid' *badia* development – perhaps simply because PPNA people were only choosing to live in locales that were sufficiently wet to maintain the way of life within their normal range of activities. Both Natufian and PPNA occupation appears within a fairly classic cultural pattern, and the simplest explanation for this is that there was very limited fine-tuning to the environment, rather settlements only developed where little change was required to the lifeways that were developing. If there was continued settlement of the drier regions, it might not be readily detected from the background of earlier hunter-gatherer flint scatter sites.

Intriguingly, the identification of Early PPNB sites in Jordan is mostly restricted to marginal zones in both Jilat and the edge of the Jafr (Jilat 7 (Garrard et al., 1986, 1994); Harrat-Juhayra 202 (Fujii et al., 2019)) – possibly indicating the settlement of Early PPNB colonists in locations not exploited by indigenous PPNA communities and overlapping chronologically. Mushash 163 (8900/8800–8600/8500 BCE), located in the semi-arid steppe west of Azraq, is reported as having two phases, the first being PPNA, the later EPPNB, but both chronology and even the flint assemblage suggest it may be more EPPNB in character (Rokitta-Krumnow, 2019). These EPPNB arid steppe sites appear to date from very early in the EPPNB, at least Harrat Juhayra 202 appears to represent a fully developed EPPN from its start date c. 9000 BCE, although Mushash 163 appears to grow more EPPNB in character over time. The final phase of WF16, which contains evidence for an indigenous Late PPNA (Finlayson & Makarewicz, 2017), overlaps chronologically with this steppic EPPNB.

The site of Jebel Qattar 101 in Jubbah, Saudi Arabia (Crassard et al., 2013), is the first site in Arabia to show early PPN connections. It appears to have been a lakeside settlement, and in common with the Jordanian early PPN, suggests that colonisation was restricted to well-watered environments. Unfortunately, no structural evidence survives, and it is not clear if this is the result of erosion, or if the inhabitants of the site built no permanent structures. There are six el-Khiam and four Helwan points from the site, together with a flake-based assemblage that generally would accord with Jordanian PPNA and EPPNB dates. However, this flint scatter site also has 55 other points with tangs, mostly of Late Neolithic types. The argument that the PPN phase of the site represents a local adaptation is largely based on the absence of naviform technology, however, for the PPNA naviform technology would not be expected, and certainly in Jordan it is not always present even in the EPPNB. Continued connectivity with the Levant through the later projectile points suggests that the occupants of this site may have been migrants from the North, who maintained their connections.

In contrast to the continued importance of gazelle elsewhere in the PPNA, the fauna hunted at WF16 are massively dominated by caprines, although it is not certain what proportion are aegagrus (the wild ancestors of the domestic goat) and what are ibex (Carruthers & Dennis, 2007). Kill patterns indicate some sophistication in wild herd management. Other animals are hunted, including cattle and rare boar, illustrating the wetter environment around the site. There is a large assemblage of bird bones, many of them from birds of prey, with analysis suggesting that one purpose of the hunting was for feathers (White et al., 2021).

4.3 The Middle and Late PPNB

In the Middle PPNB an increasing difference appears to develop between sites in the *badia* and settlements to the west that become increasingly reliant on agriculture and domesticated herds. The evidence from 'Ain Ghazal indicates that gazelle ceased to be a significant resource by the MPPNB at this non-*badia* site. What gazelle are present appear not to come from its immediate environment, but the distances involved may be quite short (as little as 17 km) (Henton et al., 2018). The replacement of gazelle by managed caprine herds may simply indicate the end of hunting as a major subsistence activity, although if it is happening at increasing distance from the settlement, perhaps as gazelle were either deliberately kept away from fields or faced too much competition from the managed herds, then it would be reasonable to presume that greater processing of carcasses took place before meat was transported back to the site, explaining the lack of direct zooarchaeological evidence. An alternative is that transhumant pastoralism was developing, and that wherever hunting took place happened on the transhumant round.

One of the indications of how wet the region was in the Middle PPNB is the presence of domestic emmer, wild and domestic barley, and wild and domestic einkorn at Jilat 7 (Colledge, 2001). While harvested cereals could have been imported to the site from the west, the more parsimonious explanation is that they were grown here. Preservation, and a focus on the development of (semi-)nomadic pastoralism, may have led to an over-focus on the exploitation of animals in the Neolithic, even if we know from Shubayqa how important wetland plants were to local Natufian diets (Arranz-Otaegui et al., 2018), while Fujii's work in the Jafr at Wadi Abu Tulayha has stressed the value of cereal cropping in a more arid region (Fujii, 2009). Calculations on the potential meat input from mass gazelle slaughter at kite sites to Neolithic diets based on daily consumption of 0.5 kg per day per adult (Rollefson, 2021) do not fit our knowledge of the amount of meat eaten in traditional hunter-gatherer, farmer, or pastoralist diets, except in extreme latitudes.

Wasse et al. (2020) suggest that a discrete *badia* development only begins to emerge in the northern limestone *badia* by the end of the Middle PPNB. In any case settlement density increases during this period (Richter, 2020). Local lithic traditions began to develop separately from the Late PPNB into the Late Neolithic, suggesting to some that there was limited contact between the groups (Cropper, 2011). However, it is equally clear that in general Late PPNB lithic assemblages in the *badia* were similar to those on the plateau edge, and probably reflect a general PPNB expansion (Edwards, 2016). Within this general Late PPNB cultural milieu, the nature of settlement of the arid lands appears increasingly specialised, such as Fujii's 'outpost' at Wadi Abu Tulayha, which he argues is a seasonal site located to take advantage of seasonal rains and grow a quick cereal crop – very much as an outpost activity relating to the permanent settlements on the plateau edge (Fujii, 2009). Those permanent Late PPNB settlements on the plateau, often described as mega-sites, are generally understood as occupying a finger of well-watered landscapes that runs down the Jordanian plateau edge, reaching as far south as 'Ain

Jammam. At Wadi Abu Tulayha there is evidence for a precocious water management system including a cistern and barrage, a system that allowed cereal cultivation to expand far beyond the limits of dry farming (Fujii, 2007, 2008). A mixed economy is evident with carbonized seeds, some domestic sheep and goat bones, and numbers of hunted animals, dominated by gazelle. The material culture is typically PPNB, employing naviform technology and including Amuq and Byblos points. Further out into the Jafr the site of Ghuwayr 17 appears as a smaller version of the same, including the water-management features, illustrating the ability of PPNB people to move far into the desert. LPPNB Jilat 13 has a similar suite of cereals to Jilat 7, reinforcing the idea that dryland farming was possible in the Wadi Jilat at this time. However, it is notable that sickle elements are relatively rare in the chipped stone assemblage here (Baird, 1993).

PPNB settlements in the Wadi Araba are relatively rare, but where found, as at Ghwayr 1 and in Tom Levy's Wadi Fidan project at Tel Tif'dan, they don't show any major signs of adaptation to an arid environment, but appear to be typical PPNB settlements with densely built predominantly rectilinear stone architecture, with fauna dominated by caprines (Simmons & Najjar, 2006; Twiss, 2008). One distinctive feature is the absence of suids from southern PPNB sites, interesting as not only are wild suids relatively rare in these semi-arid environments (although wild boar were hunted at PPNA WF16), but there appears to be no introduction of any domesticated animals. Wild and domestic cattle are present in assemblages, but their numbers are low.

In contrast, Neolithic settlement around the Azraq oasis has generally been interpreted as continuing the nomadic lifeways of hunter-gatherer groups, although there is some (limited) evidence for plant cultivars and domestic sheep and goat from about 7000 BC (Garrard & Byrd, 2013). Occupation of the *badia* has been interpreted as simply providing additional protein to the large populations of these sites (Bar-Yosef, 2001). Interpretation of desert kites as mass-kill gazelle hunting traps that have their origins at the end of the Late PPNB provides further support to the idea of a relatively arid *badia* occupied, probably seasonally, by people pursuing specialist roles that helped support the large settlements on the plateau edge (Abu-Azizeh & Tarawneh, 2015; Helms & Betts, 1987). However, the lithic assemblage from settlements near the kites in Jibal Khashabiyeh is markedly different from both Late PPNB or PPNC assemblages elsewhere, suggesting this occupation may belong to a different technocomplex (Crassard & Hilbert, 2019).

One southern Jordanian site that may be critical to the transition to pastoralism is the site of 'Ayn Abu Nukhayla, located in the Wadi Rum world heritage site. This site, excavated in the 1990s by Henry, has produced some interesting but conflicting data (Henry & Beaver, 2014). Henry's current interpretation of the site is that it is largely Middle PPNB in date, and represents an early instance of sheep management, with herds being moved between 'Ayn Abu Nukhayla and the plateau edge on a transhumant seasonal basis. The Amuq points which dominate the diagnostic elements of the flint assemblage, however, suggest that the settlement might be later, dating to the Late PPNB/PPNC. This chronology would also fit better with the introduction of sheep this far south. 'Ayn Abu Nukhayla does provide evidence for developments in mobile pastoralism, still within the framework of a society employing the material culture of the settled communities to the west. (The retention of circular architecture appears typical of the most southern PPNB/C sites, such as Nahal Issaron (Carmi et al., 1994)). As such, 'Ayn Abu Nukhayla may be a critical site in the development of Late Neolithic nomadic pastoralism, critical for understanding both the settlement of the Jordanian *badia* and a new wave of settlement in Arabia. In fact, the recently excavated site of Wadi Sharma 1 in Saudi Arabia has many strong parallels with Ayn Abu Nukhayla, and is clearly dated to the LPPNB with a predominance of Amuq points (Fujii et al., 2021). The fauna and any plant remains have yet to be examined, but the presence of sickle elements and grinding stones suggests cereal cultivation. Doorways are sealed, suggesting the site was only seasonally occupied. With the exception of Jebel Qattar 101 this is the furthest south manifestation of the PPNB, and the site's Late PPNB date confirms that this is the start of expansion into this more arid zone, not yet representing fully nomadic pastoralists, but another form of seasonal migration.

Wadi Sharma 1 has a very limited lithic repertoire and no naviform cores, although some blades may have been produced by naviform technology and imported. To the East there is a small cluster of PPNB sites with naviform technology at Dumat al-Jandal in the al-Jawf province – at a similar latitude to 'Ayn Abu Nukhayla although far removed from the main concentration of Jordanian sites (Cressard & Hilbert, 2019). However, the naviform technology is not standard, but appears to have local adaptations, raising questions over its relationship with the Levantine PPNB.

4.4 PPNC and Early Late Neolithic (ELN)

In the arid margins/current steppes and deserts the PPNC (often called the Early Late Neolithic (ELN) in the eastern *badia*) is mostly known from Wadi Jilat 13 and 25 although the limited radiometric dating evidence that gives a broad range of 6900–6300 BCE includes both the PPNC as well as the start of Pottery or Late Neolithic (Garrard et al., 1994).

By the PPNC there is a shift in settlement patterns across Jordan. Unfortunately, many of the Late PPNB 'mega-sites' are poorly known and poorly published, but it appears from 'Ain Ghazal, that their permanent populations may decline after the LPPNB and there may be an increase in seasonal mobility (Rollefson & Köhler-Rollefson, 1989). This has been interpreted as the consequence of overexploitation of the land around the mega-sites, leading to developments in mobile pastoralism, and a decreased tethering of pastoralists from the major settlements (Rollefson, 2011; Rowan et al., 2020). This interpretation is not uniformly accepted, and it is notable that western sites such as Beisamoun and Motza may reach their peak in the PPNC (Khalaily et al., 2020; Bocquentin et al., 2020). It is also clear that occupation does continue into the Late Neolithic at both 'Ain Ghazal and Basta, although at a reduced scale (Gebel et al., 2006). The presence of massive anthropogenic rubble deposits at several sites implies considerable human activity. The PPNC appears to be a southern Levantine reflection of a wider set of changes to the Late Neolithic, in the northern Levant generally associated with the adoption of ceramics.

This period is when apparently herded sheep and goat herding in the *badia* first appear, as seen at Jilat 13 and 25 (Martin, 1999: 94–5; Miller et al., 2018) (Fig. 4). The change in settlement pattern to the west has been argued to be part of the same innovation, with a large part of the population at sites such as 'Ain Ghazal becoming transhumant herders (Rollefson, 2021). The possibility has been raised that these transhumant herders may have made it as far as the Eastern Desert. An alternative hypothesis is that herding was adopted by indigenous hunters, who rather than become transhumant, moved directly to fully mobile pastoralism (Miller et al., 2018). The evidence used, combining the animal remains, stable isotopes and chipped stone, suggests a complex pattern, where the inhabitants of Jilat 13 may be indigenous mobile pastoralists, while those at close-by Jilat 25 are more likely to be part of a tethered, transhumant pastoralist network (Miller et al., 2018).

Martin (1999: 94) also notes that the *badia* sites continue to have considerable numbers of wild animals represented in their fauna (Martin, 1999: Table 4, based on MNE counts 6–30% gazelle and 24–35% hare) – suggesting there is no grazing pressure from herded caprines, which would also suggest people simply did not have any/many caprines with them. Martin argues for continuity in faunal assemblages from the PPNB to the Late Neolithic with caprines just added to the mix, suggesting an adoption of caprines by existing populations, rather than the arrival of new herding people. She also notes that different kill patterns in the steppe suggest a distinct local herding system. Martin's analysis of *badia* faunal assemblages does not suggest the development of nomadic pastoralism in the PPNC/ELN, but she also argues for strong local continuity. Martin argues that given it is clear wild animals remained a good source of meat in the steppe, caprines were most likely adopted as part of a social process. In turn, they (especially sheep) have different requirements in terms of water and pasture, therefore may have in themselves created new mobility patterns.

In the Jafr, the abandonment of water management systems may reflect a drying environment, but may also illustrate a change in adaptation to the area, no longer based on agro-pastoralist economies of the PPNB, but on an increasingly nomadic pastoralism (Fujii, 2013).

Rollefson et al. (1992), and Martin and Edwards (2013), have argued that nomadic or transhumant pastoralism may have emerged in the *badia* in the ELN, contemporaneous with the PPNC, or perhaps the very end of the Late PPNB. Rollefson's initial argument was based on evidence from 'Ain Ghazal that part of the population became seasonally nomadic. The same evidence has been used to support the idea that the burin Neolithic was associated with pastoralism, with a suggestion that the burin spalls were used to make combs for collecting wool from moulting sheep within a single settlement system in the Late PPNB and PPNC/Early Late Neolithic. Mixed sheep and goat herds, as well as secondary products would have been essential for the development of pastoralism and a tethered pastoralist system connecting the steppe and desert with the western settlement (Quintero et al., 2004; Wasse et al., 2020). However, as noted by Makarewicz (2014) and Martin (1999), there is no faunal or isotopic evidence for pastoralism based on secondary products, nor for a mobile system linking the desert and the plateau edge. Furthermore, there is good evidence that whenever the burin spalls are found, they show signs of use as drills, both microscopically and macroscopically, and by association with bead manufacture waste (e.g. Finlayson & Betts, 1990; Baird in Garrard et al., 1994). The burins begin to appear in Middle PPNB contexts, suggesting that they are not a marker of sheep pastoralism (Baird, 1993).

As noted above, recent excavations in the south-eastern *badia* have confirmed a hunting function for the kites, and have produced dates from the very end of the PPNB and start of the ELN (Abu-Azizeh et al., 2021), indicating a highly specialised hunting economy.

4.5 Late Neolithic (c. 6500–5000 BCE)

The first Late Neolithic developments in the *badia* predate the so-called 8.2 ka event (Flohr et al., 2016, Rowan et al., 2020), suggesting that they are not a response to climate change, although these developments could have been reinforced by adaption to increased aridity. There are other changes in climate, but the data is not very clear, and at present connecting the uncertain impacts of climate change with our limited archaeological knowledge remains difficult.

A considerable amount of research has taken place on the Late Neolithic in the *badia*, especially in the Eastern Desert and around Azraq and Jilat (e.g., Betts et al., 2013; Rollefson, 2011, 2021; Rollefson et al., 2014; Rowan et al., 2017). Late Neolithic sites appear abundant in all types of *badia* regions: the (current) steppe, oases, (seasonal) lakes, and more clearly than before in areas with lower rainfall, although still with water resources such as at Wisad Pools, Wadi Araba and south-eastern Jordan (see also the map in Flohr, 2022). Not only do there appear to be more (or more visible) sites in more areas, they are also more diverse and include temporary camps such as Jebel Naja, and Jilat 13, longer-lived sites such as Wadi Qataffi and Wisad Pools, and funerary sites with cairns in SE Jordan (Rowan et al., 2020), and kites may continue into this period, although they have not yet been directly dated (Akkermans et al., 2014). Late Neolithic Dhuweila continues to be dominated by gazelle hunting (at 90% of the faunal remains) and still only a very low caprine presence (Martin, 1999). In other places, caprines form a more substantial part of the assemblage, like at Burqu 27 (38%) and Jebel Naja (50%); but with continued hunting (gazelle 10% and 25% respectively, hare 16% and 25%) (Martin, 1999: 94, Table 4). It is possible that hunting is now assisted by domestic dogs. Dogs as aids to hunting have been attested from the PPNA onwards in the *badia* (Yeomans et al., 2019) and domesticated dogs have been found at Late Neolithic Wisad pools (Rollefson et al., 2014).

It has been proposed that by the Late Neolithic a difference has developed between the western *badia*, where gazelle have become less numerous due to domesticate grazing pressure, than in the eastern *badia* where they remain abundant (Henton et al., 2018). This would provide further support for Rollefson et al.'s suggestion that pastoralism had become a major activity in the *badia* by the Late Neolithic (Rollefson et al., 2014). In this scenario, kites are therefore a 'response' to increased pastoralism, although Abu-Azizeh et al.'s (2021) new excavation results suggest that kites may emerge before this, at the end of the LPPNB/ELN.

A further argument to explain continued hunting of gazelle, is that this was a response to dairying, where caprine herds are increasingly kept 'live'. Meat is provided by hunting gazelle, who are separated from herding lands by the kite systems. Keeping caprine herds 'live' is used to explain why caprine bones are rare from faunal assemblages left by people who are assumed to have been at least semi-nomadic herders: the herds were not being culled (Henton et al., 2018; see also Martin, 1999). However, evidence for dairying in the Late PPNB and ELN remains limited, with no zooarchaeological evidence for dairying as kill patterns of caprines in the *badia* suggest they are kept for meat and not being culled to enhance dairy production (Martin, 1999). Martin argues that Late Neolithic assemblages suggest that caprines are just hunted in the same way as gazelle – no specialisation, nor different treatment between caprines and gazelle. She also notes that the kill-off of prime animals at *badia* sites does not support the idea that herds were fattened in the *badia* before return to the plateau edge for eating. Evidence from the *badia* is that very few caprines were being killed for any reason. Either all culling took place to the west, or in a possibility rarely mentioned, caprines were still rare in the *badia*, a difficulty for arguments that fully untethered pastoralism had developed by the Late Neolithic.

It has been suggested that cattle pastoralism may have been introduced to Arabia from the Jordanian *badia*, however, as described above, it appears that early pastoralism in the *badia* was based on caprine herding making the *badia* an unlikely source (Makarewicz, 2020). Cattle, including wild aurochsen, require open water to drink, and this might have been available in wetter early Holocene Arabia. However, there is no clear evidence for wild aurochsen, making local domestication unlikely (Makarewicz, 2020). The best examples of cattle on rock art appear to have horn shapes that suggest they are domesticated (Guagnin et al., 2015). Cattle may have been introduced along the Gulf from southern Mesopotamia. However, evidence appears to be mounting that domesticated cattle were present at Late PPNB settlements in the South of Jordan, including at Basta (Becker, 2002), and at Tel Tif'Dan in the Wadi Araba (Makarewicz, 2020; Twiss, 2008). It is possible that rather than via the northern *badia* and the Wadi Sirhan, cattle may have reached Arabia either through the Late PPNB in the Jafr Basin, or down the Wadi Araba (Makarewicz, 2020). This appears to match emerging evidence of PPNB connections.

The Jafr sequence has been interpreted to indicate that the isolated cemetery and ritual sites of the Late Neolithic may indicate early nomadic pastoralism, but fully nomadic pastoralism may not appear until the EBA when it is visible in the large-scale cairn fields that appear without associated settlements (Fujii, 2013).

5 Development in the Margins

After an initial phase of Neolithic exploitation of the savannah lands during the PPNA that appears to have been limited and restricted to locations where there was no need for any significant adaptation to a different environment, adaptation in the PPNB appears to commence. Where dryland farming could be achieved, as in Jilat, it was. Where some additional water-management allowed for farming at least of a seasonal nature, as in the Jafr margins, that was also implemented. More marked local adaptations appear in the later course of the Neolithic, and the changing nature of Neolithic settlement patterns and landscape occupation continues from the PPNC into subsequent Late Neolithic phases. Several dramatic developments appear to occur at around the same time.

The first is the establishment of so-called desert kites. These, most plausibly interpreted as hunting traps for mass killing of migrating gazelle, are known from an extensive system that runs predominately north-south down desert margins of the *badia*. Very few have received even exploratory excavation, but so far what is known suggests a date around the end of the PPN, and confirms their role in gazelle hunting (Abu-Azizeh et al., 2021). It appears that they continued to be used over time, and it is not clear if the appearance of a system of kites emerged rapidly, or consists of a long development of addition. It is conceivable that their construction follows a shift in gazelle migratory patterns, following increasing pressure on grazing lands to the west, but equally plausible that it represents a new exploitation of migratory gazelle once their less mobile western populations were reduced. Suggestions have been made that they were constructed to provide protein for settled communities to the west or to feed a herder population who kept their sheep and goats alive while in the east (Bar-Yosef, 2001; Henton et al., 2018). Both suggestions are problematic, partly as they both reflect an assumed relationship between pastoralist and farmer, where the *badia* serves to provide food to the settled population. The distances some kites are from the settled world also make provisioning implausible. Further, if the kites appear after the major settlements are abandoned or reduced in size, who would they provision? Equally, it appears unlikely that a population of nomadic pastoralists would have either required meat on this scale, nor been unable to obtain protein from their own herds through both dairy and culling practices.

The second development is the emergence of an entirely new form of Neolithic settlement. Known from locations such as Wisad Pools and the 'Mesas' these comprise Late Neolithic structures including enclosures and structures. Markedly different from the preceding LPPNB densely built settlements, these spread out over extensive areas of land. Although frequently discussed in the context of arid lands, a growing body of evidence suggests that when occupied their environment supported a fertile topsoil and woodland (Rowan et al., 2020). Settlement patterns hint that this environment may have been more extensive than what could be described as oasis settlement. However, interpretation still leans towards one of seasonal pastoralism, taking advantage of seasonal bounty. Notably the Late Neolithic here is still described as "The Black Desert Neolithic" (Rowan et al., 2020), perhaps unintentionally emphasising its relationship to arid margins. Faunal assemblages that are dominated by wild taxa, and flint assemblages characterised by arrowheads, have both been used to argue that these herders were depending substantially on wild resources, and reserving the domestic herds they are assumed to have kept, for exchange with western settled populations (again, problematically if the mega-sites are now abandoned). In contrast, if these sites can be related to processes where the tethers to western settlements are finally broken, it is interesting that such a marked change in architecture and settlement organisation appears. Does this reflect a major social change, triggered by new relationships to the landscape? If so, is this similar to other Late Neolithic landscape changes – where farmers appear to live closer to their fields – as argued in both Dhra' and the Wadi Ziqlab (Banning et al., 2013; Kuijt et al., 2007)? Without the ritual and social constraints holding the densely occupied mega-sites together, were people able to reduce social stress by reducing their demographic density, at the same time as living more closely to their subsistence resources? For the Late Neolithic pastoralists did this represent a pastoralist escape from settled constraints?

A third development is the apparent growth of specialist industrial sites on the *badia* edge. This so-called 'burin' Neolithic – associated with the presence of large numbers of burins, burin spalls, and sometimes bead manufacture, has been seen as another activity developed by mobile pastoralists to produce commodities for exchange with settled populations. Indeed, either of the main interpretations of the burin Neolithic – that the burins are used for combing wool, or that the spalls are used as drill bits, would have the same role in producing commodities. In that sense they possibly serve as a precursor of Chalcolithic flint mining activity and Bronze Age wool trade. If this is the beginning of extensive patterns of trade, perhaps it would become easier to accept the idea of quantities of dried meat being moved within a 'global' exchange system.

6 Conclusion – The Diverse Desert

It is perhaps important to note that amongst the reasons that researchers have been drawn to these areas is that the absence of substantial development in the last few thousand years has created landscapes of survival (cf Akkermans, 2020), as well as the romantic pull of the desert landscapes (e.g. Bell, 1907). Neither may be relevant to Neolithic occupation of course, as both relate to the contemporary environment.

The historical context of human occupation of the *badia* appears to start with societies who take advantage of periods of increased moisture, and who largely maintain the societies and subsistence systems of populations in areas of greater rainfall to the west. Such adaptations, such as the use of tubers at Natufian Shubyqa, are fine-tuning of contemporary Natufian lifeways (and in this case fine-tuning to a wetland environment, not a desert). PPNA lifeways seem to have followed a similar route, with locations such as WF16 taking advantage of local water availability. It may not be until the PPNB, and probably not until the Late PPNB, that adaptation of emerging Neolithic economies to an arid landscape can begin to be seen, most notably in the outposts identified by Fujii in the Jafr, with their barrages and cisterns. By the end of the LPPNB and into the Early Late Neolithic, this process appears to extend with the appearance of the extensive system of kites and mass hunting of gazelle. By the Late Neolithic this specialised hunting adaptation is joined, or perhaps replaced if the kites are no longer used, by a transhumant system seen in the extensive settlements of the Eastern Desert.

Work over the past decade/s, especially at Wisad Pools and Wadi Qataffi, has illustrated an expansion of population and settlement in the Late Neolithic. Rowan et al. (2020) outline possibilities for Late Neolithic settlement of the Eastern Desert as being a single community of *badia* adapted hunter-herders, or separate communities of migrant pastoralists coming from the west meeting indigenous 'hunter-forager-herders' coming from well-watered eastern niches. These possibilities encapsulate a wider range of issues that both go back in time and require an improved understanding of the wider geographical context.

All of this unprecedented activity suggests a complete re-adjustment of human-landscape interaction. There is at present no reason to assume a dramatic improvement in the environment that allowed this to happen at this time, indeed the Late Neolithic is more associated with a phase of drying and the 8.2 k event. Equally, if the environment was so productive, why did the nature of settlement construction change so much – to these new and relatively dispersed sites? Our knowledge of the precise effects and chronology of climate change makes correlation between human behaviour and environment difficult (Contreras & Makarewicz, 2016; Flohr et al., 2016; Makarewicz & Tuross, 2012; Stein, 2014; Torfstein et al., 2013; Richter et al., 2017). It is vital to understand the environment through time if we wish to understand when a new technology is required to exploit new landscapes, or when increased rainfall, or a raised water table, may permit an extension of existing technologies to new areas, and equally necessary to understand why reduced rainfall may not have the catastrophic impact that might be expected.

Even in the Late Neolithic, the evidence for the development of mobile pastoralism is still largely circumstantial – if the *badia* west of the Black Desert was greener, why develop pastoralism rather than extend the nascent PPNB mixed farming system at locales such as Wadi Qataffi? How good is our evidence that these people depended on pastoralism? In the absence of significant caprine domestic faunal remains, is the argument for pastoralism based largely on the presence of possible animal enclosures at the sites? The animal management systems that developed into pastoralism arose as part of the process of domestication occurring around increasingly settled sites – perhaps best illustrated by the transhumant practises of the PPNB (Makarewicz, 2017), which are presumably the foundation of more distant movements. It seems implausible that these management systems, built up over many generations and incorporating skills, the establishment of social territories, and ownership of domesticated species, could be easily picked up by desert hunter-gatherers and translated into a sophisticated mobile pastoralist system. Equally, the new systems of kites, possibly relating to new gazelle behaviours, and perhaps only relevant within a system of exchange that included large populations to create demand, appear unlikely to have appeared from nothing. The people who begin to experiment with new ways of exploiting the *badia* are those in the Jafr outposts, coincidentally the same people who start to build long low wall systems to create their barrages to guide water.

To understand these changes, our concern is not solely with the Eastern Desert, but with all of the *badia* lands. This includes the semi-arid areas most likely affected by climate change. The *badia* is not the same everywhere but a 'diverse desert', with different environments, different uses, and different communities. The human presence has not been dependent on favourable climate change, people have been present in the *badia* at least from the Epipalaeolithic during times of increasing aridity (Maher et al., 2011). Emergent evidence, perhaps best seen from the Jilat assemblages, suggests that different communities are present, some possibly still tethered to more settled communities to the west, others perhaps becoming less tethered – but still linked to sites with agricultural potential.

We still need to improve our understanding of the impacts of both climate change and increased grazing. We also need to improve our understanding of the relationship between these populations and those who inhabit lands suitable for dry farming. In particular, does the *badia* simply become a resource for settled communities – providing resources such as protein, flint, and increasingly importantly, wool, with much of its occupation restricted to seasonal expeditions and migrations? Alternatively, is this when increasingly mobile pastoralism first becomes an independent lifestyle, no longer tethered to the settled communities? These are vital issues for our understanding of the development of early urbanism, where control over wool appears to have played a major role in the development of trade and wealth. Finally, and often assumed to be part of the development of mobile pastoralism, it appears that there is a new wave of outward migration – in particular into the Arabian peninsula. Similar questions apply regarding how and why this jumps off, how much its early phase may relate to the increased water availability in this area.

Unfortunately, our contextual knowledge of this period in the 'core' region is relatively poor. Evidence from a number of the mega-sites suggests that occupation continued, although in an altered and probably reduced form. The substantial layers of rubble that appear in some cases appear to be largely anthropogenic, indicating continued activity. Other sites appear to become more diffuse than preceding PPN activity, such as the Late Neolithic occupation at Dhra'. There are, as again visible at Dhra', indications of an increasingly managed landscape (Kuijt et al., 2007) – and while there are lacunae in our knowledge, it does appear that while settlement patterns change, people don't vanish. The focus on large-scale settlement in the PPNB, and even the initial interest on whether this was an early expression of urbanism, has drawn attention away from indications that Late Neolithic settlement patterns may have been more scattered, but quite possibly more consistently present throughout the landscape than ever before, just harder to find (Banning et al., 2013). In some ways, the Late Neolithic settlement systems, more dispersed, more closely located adjacent to resources – be those fields or pastures, may be a social reaction to the controls required to maintain the densely populated intensive settlements of the Late

PPNB. People chose increasingly mobile pastoralist lives not because they had to, but as a choice.

One explanation for this is that the transition to the Late Neolithic involves many of the major changes in human-environment relations often assumed to occur earlier in the process. Locally appropriate methods for exploiting the environment start to come of age, with mixed farming, tethered pastoralism, and nomadic pastoralism (potentially including seasonal crop growing) all representing viable ways of life. Neolithic exploitation of the *badia* sets the ground for subsequent use, the presence of mobile pastoralists and people using water management techniques to live in fortified settlements farming and herding (Betts & Tarawneh, 2010; Müller-Neuhof, 2017). It is possible that the kites, at least in Jordan, go out of use as there is no evidence connecting them to Chalcolithic or Bronze Age use (Betts & Burke, 2022). Connections between these diverse systems doubtless helped promote regional networks, trade, and an increasingly intensive use of the landscape for other resources, such as tabular flint, or copper mining in Wadi Faynan.

References

Abdi, K. (2003). The early development of pastoralism in the central Zagros Mountains. *Journal of World Prehistory, 17*(4), 395–448. https://doi.org/10.1023/B:JOWO.0000020195.39133.4c

Abu-Azizeh, W., & Tarawneh, M. B. (2015). Out of the *harra*: Desert kites in southeastern Jordan. New results from the south eastern Badia archaeological project. *Arabian Archaeology and Epigraphy, 26*, 95–119.

Abu-Azizeh, W., Tarawneh, M., Crassard, R., & Sánchez Priego, J. A. (2021). Discovery and excavation of desert kites in the south-eastern Badia of Jordan. In A. Betts & P. van Pelt (Eds.), *The gazelle's dream: Game drives of the old and new worlds* (pp. 225–251). Sydney University Press.

Akkermans, P. (Ed) (2020). *Landscapes of Survival: International Conference on The Archaeology and Epigraphy of Jordan's North-Eastern Desert*. Sidestone Press Academics.

Akkermans, P. M. M. G., Huigens, H. O., & Brüning, M. L. (2014). A landscape of preservation: Late prehistoric settlement and sequence in the Jebel Qurma region, North-Eastern Jordan. *Levant, 46*(2), 186–205.

Alley, R. B., Mayewski, P. A., Sowers, T., Stuiver, M., Taylor, K. C., & Clark, P. U. (1997). Holocene climatic instability: A prominent, widespread event 8200 yr ago. *Geology, 25*(6), 483–486

Arranz-Otaegui, A., González Carretero, L., Roe, J., & Richter, T. (2018). "Founder crops" v. wild plants: Assessing the plant-based diet of the last hunter-gatherers in Southwest Asia. *Quaternary Science Reviews, 186*, 263–283.

Baird, D. (1993). *Neolithic chipped stone assemblages from the Azraq basin, Jordan and the significance of the Neolithic of the arid zones of the Levant*. University of Edinburgh (unpublished PhD thesis).

Baird, D., Garrard, A., Martin, L., & Wright, K. (1992). Prehistoric environment and settlement in the Azraq Basin: An interim report on the 1989 excavation season. *Levant, 24*, 1–31.

Banning, E. B., Hitchings, P., Abu Jayyab, K., Edwards, S., Elendari, R., Gibbs, K., Jablonkay, D., Al-Jarrah, H., Letham, B., Razzaz, S., Ullah, I., & Weston, R. (2013). 2013 archaeological survey in Wadi Qusayba and the Mandah plateau, Irbid region, Jordan. *Annual of the Department of Antiquities in Jordan, 57*, 463–475.

Bar-Matthews, M., Ayalon, A., & Kaufman, A. (1997). Late quaternary paleoclimate in the eastern Mediterranean region from stable isotope analysis of speleothems at Soreq cave, Israel. *Quaternary Research, 47*, 155–168.

Bar-Yosef, O. (2001). From sedentary foragers to village hierarchies: The emergence of social institutions. In G. Runciman (Ed.), *The origin of human social institutions* (pp. 1–38). Oxford University Press.

Bar-Yosef, O., & Khazanov, A. (Eds.). (1992). *Pastoralism in the Levant*. Prehistory Press.

Becker, C. (2002). Nothing to do with indigenous domestication? Cattle from late PPNB cattle. In A. M. Buitenhuis, M. Choyke, M. Mashkour, & A. H. Al-Shiyab (Eds.), Archaeozoology of the near east V: Proceedings of the fifth international symposium on the Archaeozoology of southwestern Asia and adjacent areas (pp. 112–137). ARC Publications.

Bell, G. L. (1907). *The desert and the sown*. W. Heinemann.

Betts, A. (1982). Prehistoric sites at Qa'a Mejalla, eastern Jordan. *Levant, 14*, 1–34.

Betts, A. V. G. (1998). *The Harra and the Hamad: Excavations and surveys in eastern Jordan* (Vol. 1). Sheffield Academic Press.

Betts, A. (2014). A response to Zeder, Bar-Oz, Rufolo and Hole (2013). *Quaternary International, 338*, 125–127. https://doi.org/10.1016/j.quaint.2014.01.006

Betts, A., & Burke, D. (2022). Game drives in the Black Desert, eastern Jordan. In A. Betts & P. van Pelt (Eds.), *The gazelle's dream: Game drives of the old and new worlds* (pp. 187–224). Sydney University Press.

Betts, A. V. G., & Tarawneh, M. (2010). Changing patterns of land use and subsistence in the Badiyat al-sham in the late Neolithic and chalcolithic periods: New data from Burqu' and Bayir. In M. al-Maqdissi, F. Braemer, & J.-M. Dentzer (Eds.), Bibliothèque Archéologique et Historique de l'IFPO. HAURAN V La Syrie du Sud du néolithique à l'antiquité tardive (pp. 69–80). Actes du colloque de Damas 2007.

Betts, A. V. G., Cropper, D., Martin, L., & McCartney, C. (2013). *The later prehistory of the Badia: Excavations and surveys in eastern Jordan* (Vol. 2). Oxbow Books.

Bocquentin, F., Khalaily, H., Boaretto, E., Dubreui, L., Schechter, H., Bar-Yosef, D., Greenberg, H., Berna, F., Anton, M., Borrell, F., Le Bourdonnec, F., Davin,, L., Noûs, C., Samuelian, N., Vieugué, J., & Horwitz, L. (2020). Between Two Worlds: The PPNB-PPNC Transition in the Central Levant as Seen Through Discoveries at Beisamoun. In H. Khalaily, A. Re'em, J. Vardi, I. Milevski (Eds) *The Mega Project at Motza (Moẓa): The Neolithic and Later Occupations up to the 20th Century*. New Studies in the Archaeology of Jerusalem and Its Region. (pp 163–200) Israel Antiquities Authority.

Bogaard, A., Fraser, R., Heaton, T. H. E., Wallace, M., Vaiglova, P., Charles, M., et al. (2013). Crop manuring and intensive land management by Europe's first farmers. *Proceedings of the National Academy of Sciences, 110*(31), 12589–12594. https://doi.org/10.1073/pnas.1305918110

Carmi, I., Segal, D., Goring-Morris, A. N., & Gopher, A. (1994). Dating the prehistoric site Nahal Issaron in the southern Negev, Israel. *Radiocarbon, 36*(3), 391–398.

Carruthers, D. B., & Dennis, S. (2007). The mammalian faunal remains. In B. Finlayson & S. Mithen (Eds.), *The early prehistory of Wadi Faynan, southern Jordan, archaeological survey of Wadis Faynan, Ghuwayr and al-Bustan and evaluation of the pre-pottery Neolithic a site of WF16* (pp. 372–386). Oxbow Books.

Cauvin, J. (2000). *The birth of the gods and the origins of agriculture*. Cambridge University Press.

Cheng, H., Sinha, A., Verheyden, S., Nader, F. H., Li, X. L., Zhang, P. Z., et al. (2015). The climate variability in northern Levant over the past 20,000 years. *Geophysical Research Letters, 42*(20), 8641–8650. https://doi.org/10.1002/2015GL065397

Colledge, S. (2001). *Plant exploitation on Epipalaeolithic and Early Neolithic sites in the Levant*. BAR International Series, p 986.

Contreras, D., & Makarewicz, C. (2016). Regional climate, local palaeoenvironment and early cultivation in the middle Wadi el-Hasa, Jordan. In D. Contreras (Ed.), *The archaeology of human-environment interactions* (pp. 96–120). Routledge.

Cordova, C. E., Nowell, A., Bisson, M., Ames, C. J. H., Pokines, J., Chang, M., & al-Nahar, M. (2013). Interglacial and glacial desert refugia and the middle Paleolithic of the Azraq oasis, Jordan. *Quaternary International, 300*, 94–110.

Crassard, R., & Hilbert, Y. H. (2019). Bidirectional blade technology on naviform cores from northern Arabia: New evidence of Arabian-Levantine interactions in the Neolithic. *Arabian Archaeology and Epigraphy, 31*, 93–101.

Crassard, R., Petraglia, M. D., Drake, N. A., Breeze, P., Gratuze, B., Alsharekh, A., et al. (2013). Middle Palaeolithic and Neolithic occupations around Mundafan Palaeolake, Saudi Arabia: Implications for climate change and human dispersals. *PLoS One, 8*(7), e69665. https://doi.org/10.1371/journal.pone.0069665

Cropper, D. (2011). *Lithic technology and regional variation in late Neolithic Jordan*. Archaeopress.

Edwards, P. C. (2016). The chronology and dispersal of the pre-pottery Neolithic B cultural complex in the Levant. *Paléorient, 42*(2), 53–72. https://doi.org/10.3406/paleo.2016.5720

Enzel, Y., Kushnir, Y., & Quade, J. (2015). The middle Holocene climatic records from Arabia: Reassessing lacustrine environments, shift of ITCZ in Arabian Sea, and impacts of the southwest Indian and African monsoons. *Global and Planetary Change, 129*, 69–91. https://doi.org/10.1016/j.gloplacha.2015.03.004

Evershed, R., Payne, S., Sherratt, A., et al. (2008). Earliest date for milk use in the near east and southeastern Europe linked to cattle herding. *Nature, 455*, 528–531. https://doi.org/10.1038/nature07180

Fick, S. E., & Hijmans, R. J. (2017). WorldClim 2: New 1km spatial resolution climate surfaces for global land areas. *International Journal of Climatology, 37*(12), 4302–4315.

Finlayson, B., & Betts, A. V. G. (1990). Functional analysis of chipped stone artefacts from the late Neolithic site of Gabal Na'ja, eastern Jordan. *Paléorient, 16*, 13–20.

Finlayson B., & Makarewicz C. (2017). The Neolithic of Southern Jordan. In O. Bar-Yosef and Y. Enzel (Eds) *Quaternary Environments, Climate Change, and Humans in the Levant*. Cambridge University Press.

Finlayson, B., & Mithen, S. (2007). *The early prehistory of Wadi Faynan, southern Jordan. Archaeological survey of Wadis Faynan, Ghuwayr and al-Bustan and evaluation of pre-pottery Neolithic a site of WF16*. Oxbow.

Fleitmann, D., & Matter, A. (2009). The speleothem record of climate variability in southern Arabia. *Comptes Rendus Geoscience, 341*(8–9), 633–642. https://doi.org/10.1016/j.crte.2009.01.006

Flohr, P. (2022). A new overview of late Neolithic sites in Jordan. *Studies of the History and Archaeology of Jordan, 14*, 97–121.

Flohr, P., Fleitmann, D., Matthews, R., Matthews, W., & Black, S. (2016). Evidence of resilience to past climate change in Southwest Asia: Early farming communities and the 9.2 and 8.2 ka events. *Quaternary Science Reviews, 136*, 23–39. https://doi.org/10.1016/j.quascirev.2015.06.022

Fuji, S., Al-Mansoor, A. A., Adachi, T., Al-Khalifa, K. K., & Nagaya, K. (2021). Excavations at Wadi Sharma 1: New insights into the Hijaz Neolithic, North-Western Arabia. In M. Luciani (Ed.), *The archaeology of the Arabian peninsula 2* (pp. 15–42). Austrian Academy of Sciences.

Fujii, S. (2007). PPNB barrage systems at Wadi Abu Tulayha and Wadi ar-Ruwayshid ash-Sharqi: A preliminary report of the 2006 spring field season of the Jafr Basin prehistoric project, phase 2. *Annual of the Department of Antiquities in Jordan, 51*, 403–427.

Fujii, S. (2008). Wadi Abu Tulayha: A preliminary report on the 2007 summer field season of the Jafr Basin prehistoric project, phase 2. *Annual of the Department of Antiquities in Jordan, 52*, 445–479.

Fujii, S. (2009). Wadi Abu Tulayha: A preliminary report of the 2008 summer final field season of the Jafr Basin prehistoric project, phase 2. *Annual of the Department of Antiquities in Jordan, 53*, 173–209.

Fujii, S. (2011). Domestication of runoff surface water: Current evidence and new perspectives from the Jafr pastoral Neolithic. *Neo-Lithics, 2*(10), 14–32.

Fujii, S. (2013). Chronology of the Jafr prehistory and protohistory: A key to the process of pastoral nomadization in the southern Levant. *Syria, 90*, 49–125. https://doi.org/10.4000/syria.1723

Fujii, S., Adachi, T., & Nagaya, K. (2019). Harrat-Juhayra 202, an early PPNB flint assemblage in the Jafr basin, southern Jordan. In L. Astruc, C. McCartney, F. Briois, & V. Kassianidou (Eds.), *Neolithic technologies on the move. Interactions and contexts in Neolithic traditions* (pp. 185–198). Astrom.

Garrard, A. N. (1998). Environment and cultural adaptations in the Azraq basin: 24,000 – 7,000 B.P. In D. O. Henry (Ed.), *The prehistoric archaeology of Jordan* (pp. 139–148). British Archaeological Reports. (International Series 705).

Garrard, A, & Byrd, B. (2013). Beyond the fertile crescent: Late palaeolithic and neolithic communities of the Jordanian Steppe. In *The azraq basin project* (Project background and the Late Palaeolithic) (Vol. 1), Oxbow Books.

Garrard, A. N., Stanley Price, N. P., & Copeland, L. (1975). A survey of prehistoric sites in the Azraq Basin, eastern Jordan. *Paléorient, 3*, 109–126.

Garrard, A. N., Byrd, B., & Betts, A. V. G. (1986). Prehistoric environment and settlement in the Azraq Basin: An interim report on the 1984 excavation season. *Levant, 18*, 5–24.

Garrard, A., Baird, D., & Byrd, B. F. (1994). The chronological basis and significance of the late Palaeolithic and Neolithic sequence in the Azraq Basin, Jordan. In O. Bar-Yosef & R. S. Kra (Eds.), *Late quaternary chronology and paleoclimates of the eastern Mediterranean* (pp. 177–199). Radiocarbon & American School of Prehistoric Research.

Garrard, A., Colledge, S., & Martin, L. (1996). The emergence of crop cultivation and caprine herding in the "marginal zone" of the southern Levant. In D. R. Harris (Ed.), *The origins and spread of agriculture and pastoralism in Eurasia* (pp. 204–226). University College London.

Gebel, H. G. K. (2010). Commodification and the formation of early Neolithic social identity. The issues as seen from the southern Jordanian highlands. In M. Benz (Ed.), *The principle of sharing. Segregation and construction of social identities at the transition from foraging to farming* (pp. 35–80). ex oriente.

Gebel, H. G. K., Nissen, H. J., & Zaid, Z. (2006). *Basta II: The architecture and stratigraphy*. ex oriente.

Goring-Morris, A. N., & Belfer-Cohen, A. (2011). Neolithization processes in the Levant: The outer envelope. *Current Anthropology, 52*, S195–S208. https://doi.org/10.1086/658860

Guagnin, M., Jennings, R. P., Clark-Balzan, L., Groucutt, H. W., Parton, A., & Petraglia, M. D. (2015). Hunters and herders: Exploring the Neolithic transition in the rock art of Shuwaymis, Saudi Arabia. *Archaeological Research in Asia, 4*, 3–16.

Guagnin, M., Jennings, R., Eager, H., Parton, A., Stimpson, C., Stepanek, C., et al. (2016). Rock art imagery as a proxy for Holocene environmental change: A view from Shuwaymis. *NW Saudi Arabia. The Holocene, 26*(11), 1822–1834. https://doi.org/10.1177/0959683616645949

Hatough, A. M. A., Al-Eisawi, D. M. H., & Disi, A. M. (1986). The effect of conservation on wildlife in Jordan. *Environmental Conservation, 13*(4), 331–335.

Helms, S., & Betts, A. (1987). The desert 'kites' of the Badiyat Esh-sham and North Arabia. *Paléorient, 13*(1), 41–67.

Henry, D. O., & Beaver, J. O. (Eds.). (2014). *The sands of time: The desert Neolithic settlement at Ayn Abū Nukhayla*. ex oriente.

Henton, E., Roe, J., Martin, L., Garrard, A., Boles, O., Lewis, J., et al. (2018). Epipalaeolithic and Neolithic gazelle hunting in the Badia of north-East Jordan. Reconstruction of seasonal movements of herds by stable isotope and dental microwear analyses. *Levant, 50*(2), 127–172. https://doi.org/10.1080/00758914.2019.1598764

Hole, F. (1974). Tepe Tula'i: An early campsite in Khuzistan, Iran. *Paléorient, 2*(2), 219–242.

Hole, F. (1977). *Studies in the archaeological history of the Deh Lureh plain: Excavations at Choga Sefid*. University of Michigan Museum of Anthropology.

Jones, M. D., & Richter, T. (2011). Paleoclimatic and archeological implications of Pleistocene and Holocene environments in Azraq, Jordan. *Quaternary Research, 76*(3), 363–372. https://doi.org/10.1016/j.yqres.2011.07.005

Jones, M. D., Abu-Jaber, N., AlShdaifat, A., Baird, D., Cook, B. I., Cuthbert, M. O., et al. (2019). 20,000 years of societal vulnerability and adaptation to climate change in Southwest Asia. *WIREs Water, 6*(2), e1330. https://doi.org/10.1002/wat2.1330

Jones, M. D., Richter, T., Rollefson, G., Rowan, Y., Roe, J., Toms, P., et al. (2021). The palaeoenvironmental potential of the eastern Jordanian desert basins (Qe'an). *Quaternary International, 635*(4). https://doi.org/10.1016/j.quaint.2021.06.023

Khalaily, H., Re'em, A., Vardi, J., & Milevski, I. (Eds) (2020). The Mega Project at Motza (Moẓa): The Neolithic and Later Occupations up to the 20th Century. New Studies in the Archaeology of Jerusalem and Its Region. Israel Antiquities Authority.

Khazanov, A. M. (2009). Specific characteristics of chalcolithic and bronze age pastoralism in the near east. In J. Szuchman (Ed.), *Nomads, tribes and the state in the ancient near east: Cross-disciplinary perspectives* (pp. 119–128). Oriental Institute Press.

Köhler-Rollefson, I. (1992). A model for the development of nomadic pastoralism on the Transjordanian plateau. In O. Bar-Yosef & A. Khazanov (Eds.), *Pastoralism in the Levant. Archaeological materials in anthropological perspectives* (pp. 11–18). Prehistory Press.

Köhler-Rollefson, I., Gillespie, W., & Metzger, M. (1988). The fauna from Neolithic 'Ain Ghazal. In A. N. Garrard & H. G. K. Gebel (Eds.), *The prehistory of Jordan. The state of research in 1986* (pp. 423–430). Archaeopress.

Kuijt, I., Finlayson, B., & MacKay, J. (2007). Pottery Neolithic landscape modification at Dhra. *Antiquity, 81*(311), 106–118.

Levy, T. E. (1983). The emergence of specialized pastoralism in the southern Levant. *World Archaeology, 15*, 15–36.

Levy, T. E. (1992). Transhumance, subsistence, and social evolution in the northern Negev Desert. In O. Bar-Yosef & A. Khazanov (Eds.), *Pastoralism in the Levant. Archaeological materials in anthropological perspectives* (pp. 65–82). Prehistory Press.

Maher, L. A., Banning, E., & Chazan, M. (2011). Oasis or mirage: The role of abrupt climate change in the prehistory of the southern Levant. *Cambridge Archaeological Journal, 21*(1), 1–29.

Maher, L., Macdonald, D., Allentuck, A., Martin, L., Spyrou, A., & Jones, M. (2015). Occupying wide open spaces? Late Pleistocene hunter–gatherer activities in the eastern Levant. *Quaternary International, 396*, 79–94. https://doi.org/10.1016/j.quaint.2015.07.054

Makarewicz, C. (2013a). A pastoralist manifesto: Breaking stereotypes and re-conceptualizing pastoralism in the near eastern Neolithic. *Levant, 45*(2), 159–174.

Makarewicz, C. A. (2013b). More than meat: Diversity in caprine harvesting strategies and the emergence of complex production systems during the late pre-pottery Neolithic B. *Levant, 45*(2), 236–261. https://doi.org/10.1179/0075891413Z.00000000027

Makarewicz, C. (2014). Bridgehead to the Badia: New biometrical and isotopic perspectives on early Neolithic caprine exploitation systems at 'Ain Ghazal. In B. Finlayson & C. Makarewicz (Eds.), *Settlement, survey, and stone: Essays on near eastern prehistory in honour of Gary Rollefson* (pp. 117–131). ex oriente.

Makarewicz, C. A. (2017). Sequential $\delta^{13}C$ and $\delta^{18}O$ analyses of early Holocene bovid tooth enamel: Resolving vertical transhumance in Neolithic domesticated sheep and goats. *Palaeogeography, Palaeoclimatology, Palaeoecology, 485*, 16–29. https://doi.org/10.1016/j.palaeo.2017.01.028

Makarewicz, C. A. (2020). The adoption of cattle pastoralism in the Arabian peninsula: A reappraisal. *Arabian Archaeology and Epigraphy, 31*(1), 168–177. https://doi.org/10.1111/aae.12156

Makarewicz, C., & Tuross, N. (2012). Finding fodder and tracking transhumance: Isotopic detection of goat domestication processes in the near east. *Current Anthropology, 53*(4), 495–505. https://doi.org/10.1086/665829

Martin, L. (1999). Mammal remains from the eastern Jordanian Neolithic, and the nature of caprine herding in the steppe. *Paléorient, 25*(2), 87–104.

Martin, L., & Edwards, Y. (2013). Diverse strategies: Evaluating the appearance and spread of domestic caprines in the southern Levant. In S. Colledge, J. Conolly, K. Dobney, S. Manning,

& S. Shennan (Eds.), *The origins and spread of domestic animals in Southwest Asia and Europe* (pp. 49–82). Left Coast Press.

Martin, L., Edwards, Y.H., & Garrard, A. (2013). Broad spectrum or specialized activity? Birds and tortoises at the Epipalaeolithic site of Wadi Jilat 22 in the eastern Jordan steppe. *Antiquity, 87*, 649–665.

Martin, L., Edwards, Y., Roe, J., & Garrard, A. (2016). Faunal turnover in the Azraq Basin, eastern Jordan 28,000 to 9,000 cal BP, signalling climate change and human impact. *Quaternary Research, 86*, 200–219. https://doi.org/10.1016/j.yqres.2016.07.001

Miller, H., Baird, D., Pearson, J., Lamb, A. L., Grove, M., Martin, L., & Garrard, A. (2018). The origins of nomadic pastoralism in the eastern Jordanian steppe: A combined stable isotope and chipped stone assessment. *Levant, 50*(3), 281–304. https://doi.org/10.1080/0075891 4.2019.1651560

Müller-Neuhof, B. (2017). The chalcolithic/early bronze age hillfort phenomenon in the northern Badia. *Near Eastern Archaeology, 80*(2), 124–131.

MWI & BGR (Ministry of Water and Irrigation; Bundesanstalt für Geowissenschaften und Rohstoffe). (2019). *Groundwater resource assessment of jordan 2017.*

Petraglia, M. D., Groucutt, H. S., Guagnin, M., Breeze, P. S., & Boivin, N. (2020). Human responses to climate and ecosystem change in ancient Arabia. *Proceedings of the National Academy of Sciences, 117*(15), 8263–8270. https://doi.org/10.1073/pnas.1920211117

Quintero, L., Wilke, P., & Rollefson, G. O. (2004). Highland towns and desert settlements: Origins of nomadic pastoralism in the Jordanian Neolithic. In H. Bienert, H. G. K. Gebel, & R. Neef (Eds.), *Central settlements in Neolithic Jordan* (pp. 201–213). ex oriente.

Richter, T. (2020). First inhabitants: The early prehistory of north- East Jordan. In P. Akkermans (Ed.), *Landscapes of survival: International conference on the archaeology and epigraphy of Jordan's north-Eastern Desert* (pp. 17–36). Sidestone Press Academics.

Richter, T., Garrard, A., Allock, S., & Maher, L. (2011). Interaction before agriculture: Exchanging material and sharing knowledge in the final Pleistocene Levant. *Cambridge Archaeological Journal, 21*(1), 95–114. https://doi.org/10.1017/S0959774311000060

Richter, T., Arranz-Otaegui, A., Yeomans, L., et al. (2017). High resolution AMS dates from Shubayqa 1, Northeast Jordan reveal complex origins of late Epipalaeolithic Natufian in the Levant. *Scientific Reports, 7*, 17025. https://doi.org/10.1038/s41598-017-17096-5

Rohling, E. J., & Pälike, H. (2005). Centennial-scale climate cooling with a sudden cold event around 8,200 years ago. *Nature, 434*(7036), 975–979. https://doi.org/10.1038/Nature03421

Rokkita-Krumnow, D. (2019). The chipped stone industry of Mushash 163, a PPNA/EPPNB site in the badia/northeastern Jordan. In L. Astruc, C. McCartney, F. Briois, & V. Kassianidou (Eds.), *Neolithic technologies on the move. Interactions and contexts in Neolithic traditions* (pp. 173–184). Astrom.

Rollefson, G. O. (2004). The character of LPPNB social organization. In H.-D. Bienert, H. G. K. Gebel, & R. Neef (Eds.), *Central settlements in Neolithic Jordan* (pp. 145–155). ex oriente.

Rollefson, G. O. (2011). The greening of the badlands: Pastoral nomads and the 'conclusion' of Neolithization in the southern Levant. *Paléorient, 37*(1), 101–109.

Rollefson, G. O. (2021). The Crowded Desert: Late Neolithic Megasites in the Black Desert of Jordan. In C. Bührig, M. van Ess, I. Gerlach, A. Hausleiter, & B. Müller-Neuhof (Eds.), *Klänge der Archäologie: Festschrift für Ricardo Eichmann* (pp. 343–350). Harrassowitz.

Rollefson, G. O., & Köhler-Rollefson, I. (1989). The collapse of early neolithic settlements in the southern Levant. In I. Hershkowitz (Ed.), *People and cultures in change* (pp. 73–89). British Archaeological Reports. (BAR International Series 308).

Rollefson, G. O., & Köhler-Rollefson, I. (1992). Early Neolithic exploitation patterns in the Levant: Cultural impact on the environment. *Population and Environment, 13*, 243–253.

Rollefson, G. O., & Köhler-Rollefson, I. (1993). PPNC adaptations in the first half of the 6th millennium B.C. *Paléorient, 19*(1), 33–41.

Rollefson, G. O., Simmons, A., & Kafafi, Z. (1992). Neolithic cultures at 'Ain Ghazal, Jordan. *Journal of Field Archaeology, 19*, 443–470.

Rollefson, G. O., Rowan, Y., & Wasse, A. (2014). The late Neolithic colonization of the eastern Badia of Jordan. *Levant, 46*(2), 285–301.

Rollefson, G., Quintero, L., & Wilke, P. (1999). Bawwab al-Ghazal: Preliminary report on the 1998 testing season. *Neo-Lithics, 1/99*, 2–4.

Rollefson, G. O., Rowan, Y., Wasse, A., Hill, A. C., Kersel, M., Lorentzen, B., et al. (2015). Investigations of a late Neolithic structure at Mesa 7, Wadi al-Qattafi, Black Desert, 2015. *Neo-Lithics, 1*(16), 3–12.

Rollefson, G. O., Rowan, Y., Wasse, A., Kersel, M., Hill, A. C., Lorentzen, B., et al. (2018). Excavations of structure W-80, a complex late Neolithic building at Wisad pools, Black Desert. *Annual of the Department of Antiquities in Jordan, 59*, 531–544.

Rowan, Y. M., Rollefson, G., Wasse, A., Hill, A. C., & Kersel, M. M. (2017). The late Neolithic presence in the Black Desert. *Near Eastern Archaeology, 80*(2), 102–113.

Rowan, Y., Rollefson, G., & Wasse, A. (2020). Populating the Black Desert: The late Neolithic presence. In P. Akkermans (Ed.), *Landscapes of survival: International conference on the archaeology and epigraphy of Jordan's north-Eastern Desert* (pp. 59–78). Sidestone Press.

Simmons, A. H., & Najjar, M. (2006). Ghwair I: A small, complex Neolithic community in southern Jordan. *Journal of Field Archaeology, 31*, 77–95.

Stein, M. (2014). The evolution of Neogene-quaternary water-bodies in the Dead Sea Rift Valley. In Z. Garfunkel, Z. Ben-Avraham, & E. Kagan (Eds.), *Dead Sea transform fault system: Reviews*. Springer.

The Hashemite Fund for Development of Jordan Badia. (n.d.). *The jordan badia*. Retrieved January 3, 2022, from http://www.badiafund.gov.jo/en/node/310

Torfstein, A., Goldstein, S. L., Stein, M., & Enzel, Y. (2013). Impacts of abrupt climate changes in the Levant from last glacial Dead Sea levels. *Quaternary Science Reviews, 69*, 1–7. https://doi.org/10.1016/j.quascirev.2013.02.015

Twiss, K. (2008). The zooarchaeology of Tel Tif-dan (Wadi Fidan 001), southern Jordan. *Paléorient, 33*, 127–145.

Wasse, A., Rollefson, G., & Rowan, Y. (2020). Flamingos in the desert: How a chance encounter shed light on 79 the 'burin Neolithic' of eastern Jordan. In P. Akkermans (Ed.), *Landscapes of survival: International conference on the archaeology and epigraphy of Jordan's north-Eastern Desert* (pp. 79–102). Sidestone Press.

White, J., Finlayson, B., Makarewicz, C., Khoury, F., Greet, B., & Mithen, S. (2021). The bird remains from WF16, an early Neolithic settlement in southern Jordan: Assemblage composition, chronology and spatial distribution. *International Journal of Osteoarchaeology, 31*(6), 1030–1045. https://doi.org/10.1002/oa.3016

Yeomans, L., & Richter, T. (2018). Exploitation of a seasonal resource: Bird hunting during the late Natufian at Shubayqa 1. *International Journal of Osteoarchaeology, 28*(2), 95–108. https://doi.org/10.1002/oa.2533

Yeomans, L., Richter, T., & Martin, L. (2017). Environment, seasonality and hunting strategies as influences on Natufian food procurement: The faunal remains from Shubayqa 1. *Levant, 49*(2), 85–104. https://doi.org/10.1080/00758914.2017.1368820

Yeomans, L., Martin, L., & Richter, T. (2019). Close companions: Early evidence for dogs in Northeast Jordan and the potential impact of new hunting methods. *Journal of Anthropological Archaeology, 53*, 161–173.

The Emergence of Fruit Tree Horticulture in Chalcolithic Southern Levant

Dafna Langgut and Arik Sasi

Abstract This paper reviews our current knowledge of fruit tree cultivation in the Levantine region. Plant remains recovered from archaeological excavations indicate that the olive, grapevine, fig, date palm, and pomegranate were the first fruit trees to be domesticated in southwest Asia and Europe. Compared to the evidence for the origin of cultivated cereals and pulses in the Old World, the information on the beginning of horticulture is fragmentary. This paper gathers all recent archaeological and archaeobotanical information regarding early fruit tree cultivation and argues that the central Jordan Valley may have been the primary area of their domestication. The onset of this development, which can be considered part of the Secondary Product Revolution, is dated to ca. 7000 years BP.

Keywords Fruit tree cultivation · Fruit tree domestication · Olive (*Olea*) · Fig (*Ficus carica*) · Grape (*Vitis vinifera*) · Date palm (*Phoenix dactylifera*) · Chalcolithic period

This paper[1] addresses four crucial questions about fruit tree cultivation: what, where, when, and why.

---

[1] We are delighted to dedicate this article to Prof. Tomas E. Levy, an inspiring, encouraging, and forward-thinking colleague and peer on the occasion of his 70th birthday.

D. Langgut (✉)
The Laboratory of Archaeobotany and Ancient Environments, Institute of Archaeology, and the Steinhardt Museum of Natural History, Tel Aviv University, Tel Aviv, Israel
e-mail: langgut@tauex.tau.ac.il

A. Sasi
The Department of Archaeology and Ancient Near Eastern Cultures, Tel Aviv University, Tel Aviv, Israel
e-mail: ariksasi@mail.tau.ac.il

© The Author(s), under exclusive license to Springer Nature Switzerland AG 2023
E. Ben-Yosef, I. W. N. Jones (eds.), *"And in Length of Days Understanding" (Job 12:12): Essays on Archaeology in the Eastern Mediterranean and Beyond in Honor of Thomas E. Levy*, Interdisciplinary Contributions to Archaeology,
https://doi.org/10.1007/978-3-031-27330-8_3

1 What?

Five founder fruit trees established horticulture in the late prehistoric Levant (Fig. 1; Zohary & Spiegel-Roy, 1975; Zohary et al., 2012; Weiss, 2015): olive (*Olea europea*), common fig (*Ficus carica*), grapevine (*Vitis vinifera*), date palm (*Phoenix dactylifera*), and pomegranate (*Punica granatum*). Let us discuss them one at a time.

1.1 Olive (Olea europea)

The earliest archaeological and archaeobotanical evidence for olive oil production derives from the southern Levant and is dated to the Late Pottery Neolithic/Early Chalcolithic period (~7500–7000 BP; Galili et al., 1997, 2018). In the submerged site of Kfar Samir on the northern Israeli coast (Fig. 1), thousands of crushed olive pits (Fig. 2a) were found in association with stone basins and woven baskets, probably strainers, and interpreted as remnants of large-scale olive oil extraction facilities (Galili et al., 1997). In the contemporaneous site of 'Ain Zippori in the Lower Galilee, olive oil residues were discovered in a pottery vessel (Namdar et al., 2015), indicating that olive oil was being produced and consumed in the northern parts of the country at this time. The earliest evidence for the processing of table olives, however, is a little later. It consists of small elliptical installations at the submerged site Hishuley Carmel dated to ca. 6600 years cal. BP. These installations contained thousands of olive pits (Fig. 2b) and were presumably used for large-scale processing of table olives. Perhaps, olive oil production evolved first, whereas the processing of table olives followed later (Galili et al., 2021).

Crucially, given their location in the natural distribution area of wild olives, it is impossible to say whether these industries relied on an infrastructure of domesticated or cultivated trees. Conversely, solid indications for purposeful olive tree cultivation were recently identified at Middle Chalcolithic Tel Tsaf in the central Jordan Valley (ca. 7200–6700 cal. BP Fig. 1; Langgut and Garfinkel, 2022). They consist of a substantial amount of charred olive wood (Fig. 3) in a region located outside the wild olive's natural habitat (Fig. 4). Unlike seeds and fruits that can be traded over considerable distances, it is widely accepted that wood and charcoal derive from a site's immediate vicinity (Lev-Yadun, 2007; Liphschitz, 2007:103–104, 108), which, in turn, strongly suggests systematic human intervention when sizeable assemblages of a fruit tree's wood are found in a site located outside this tree's natural habitat.[2] Thus, Middle Chalcolithic Tel Tsaf provides the earliest charred olive wood remains in the central and Lower Jordan Valley, followed by Late Chalcolithic sites like Abu Hamid (Neef, 1990), Teleilat Ghassul (Meadows, 2001), and Pella which also produced large amounts of olive-pressing waste (Dighton et al., 2017).

---

[2] A few charcoal remains of olive as well as some olive stones were also reported in previous studies from the site (Gophna & Kislev, 1979; Liphschitz, 1988; Graham, 2014; Rosenberg et al., 2014).

The Emergence of Fruit Tree Horticulture in Chalcolithic Southern Levant

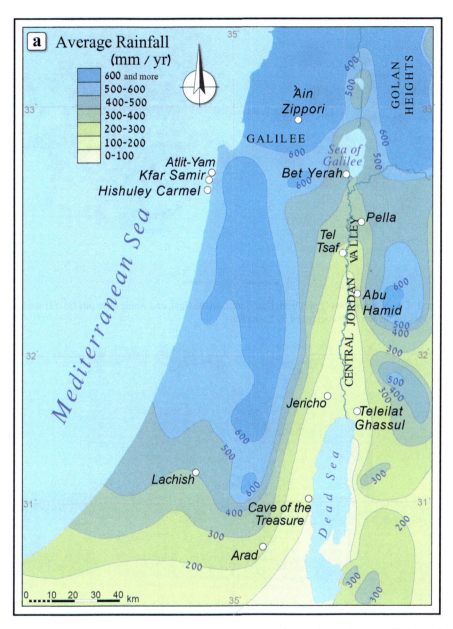

Fig. 1 Map of the southern Levant indicating mean annual precipitation in mm. (Srebro and Soffer, 2011)

Numerous olive stones, olive wood remains, and crushing basins found at Late Chalcolithic sites in the Golan Heights (Epstein, 1993) and Samaria (Eitam, 1993) strongly suggest that, by ca. 6000 cal. BP, olive horticulture was well established in

Fig. 2 Crushed olive pits (*gefet*) from Kfar Samir, on the right, and whole olive pits from Hishuley Carmel, on the left. (Photographed by Sasha Flit)

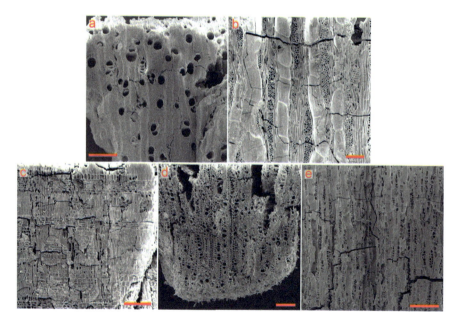

Fig. 3 SEM images of charred-wood sections of taxa indicating early fruit tree horticulture at Tel Tsaf: (**a**) *Olea europaea*, radial section, scale 200 μm; (**b**) *Olea europaea*, transverse longitudinal section, scale 200 μm; (**c**) *Olea europaea*, tangential longitudinal section, scale 200 μm; (**d**) *Ficus carica*, transverse longitudinal section, scale 500 μm; (**e**) *Ficus carica*, tangential longitudinal section, scale 100 μm. (Photographed by Mark Cavanagh, using a Tescan VEGA3 LMH scanning electron microscope)

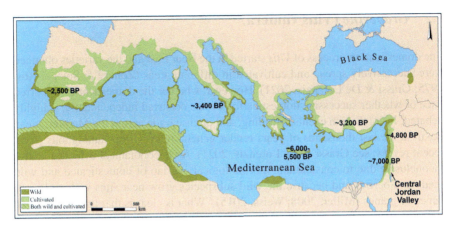

Fig. 4 Geographical distribution of wild olive (*Olea europaea* subsp. *oleaster*) and cultivated olive in the Mediterranean Basin. (Modified after Carrión et al. 2010, Lavee and Zohary 2011) together with suggested dates for the beginning of olive horticulture in the Mediterranean regions. (Langgut et al. 2019)

these regions and the southern Levant as a whole. This estimate accords well with Zohary and Spiegel-Roy's (1975) suggestion of almost five decades ago that olive horticulture was already practiced at Tuleilat Ghassul.

On a broader scope, a comprehensive palynological investigation, covering the entire Mediterranean Basin, observed a sudden increase in olive pollen during the first half of the seventh millennium BP in the southern Levant while the frequencies of other Mediterranean broadleaved trees (e.g., oaks and pistachios) remained more-or-less the same, thus rejecting a climate-related change (Langgut et al., 2019). The earliest of these anthropogenic olive pollen increases was registered at the Sea of Galilee, ca. 7000 cal. BP (Schiebel, 2013), followed by other locations along the Jordan Valley rift—the Dead Sea (Litt et al., 2012), the Hula Valley (Van-Zeist et al., 2009), and Birkat Ram (Neumann et al., 2007; Schiebel, 2013)—at ca. 6500 cal. BP.

Thus, archaeological and botanical evidence suggests that olive cultivation began in northern Israel (Carmel coast and the Galilee) towards the end of the eighth millennium BP, probably drawing on naturally occurring wild olive species [*Olea europaea* L. subsp. *Europaea* var. *sylvestris* (Mill.) Lehr.]. A few centuries later, at ca. 7000 cal. BP, the settlers of Tel Tsaf engaged in full-fledged olive cultivation, indicated by their location outside *Olea europaea*'s natural distribution (Fig. 4).[3]

---

[3] To accomplish this geographical shift, a transfer of both knowledge and seedlings from northern Israel to the central Jordan Valley must have occurred.

1.2 Grapevine (Vitis vinifera)

The domestication process of *Vitis* started in the Near East and the varieties obtained were successively spread and cultivated in different areas (Zohary & Spiegel-Roy, 1975; Grassi & De Lorenzis, 2021). However, whether the domestication occurred once or whether successive domestication events occurred independently, is highly debated. Introgression events, breeding, and intense trade across the Mediterranean Basin in the last thousands of years render genetic relationships ambiguous (for a recent review, see Grassi & De Lorenzis, 2021). Archaeobotanical evidence is also inconclusive due to considerable morphological overlap of domesticated and wild seeds and berries and because the wild subspecies grow near sites with early evidence of grapes (Miller, 2008; Weiss, 2015).[4] What is clear is that the period when grapevines spread beyond their natural wild distribution, can be taken as indicative of cultivation, if not domestication (Miller, 2008; Fuller & Stevens, 2019).

Many scholars consider the area of the southern Caucasus the most likely origin of grape cultivation. The region is notable for the wide diversity of wild populations and cultivars (Bouby et al., 2021), and it provides the earliest evidence of wine production, manifested in chemical residues in early eighth-millennium BP pottery vessels from Georgia (McGovern et al., 1996, 2017; but see critique by Fuller & Stevens, 2019:270). However, like in the case of early production of olive oil (Galili et al., 1997; Namdar et al., 2015), it is unclear whether this Georgian wine was produced from wild or domesticated grapes (Bouby et al., 2021; Miller, 2008). Moreover, further solid archaeological evidence of grapes (pollen, fruit remains, and wood) does not turn up in this area until 3000 years later, in the mid-fifth millennium BP (Miller, 2008).

In the southern Levant, the wild grapevine occurs in wet habitats such as the upper Jordan River and the Hula Valley, but not as a common component of the vegetation. Two pips of *Vitis* were recovered from Ohalo II[5] on the south-eastern shore of the Sea of Galilee (Kislev et al., 1992) and several fossil pollen grains were extracted from an Epipaleolithic site on the southern shore of paleolake Hula (Langgut et al., 2021a) and from Early Holocene Sea of Galilee (Schiebel, 2013). The wild grapevine is much more widespread in wetter habitats such as in river valley of the Zagros and Pontus ridges in Turkey in comparison to the Levant wet environments. Indeed, most wild grapevine habitats have annual precipitation levels exceeding 600 mm, and the southern Levant is on the cusp and below this figure. Nevertheless, ecological studies have shown that the wild populations are remarkably adaptable, capable of growing in a broad range of habitats and various soils,

---

[4] Two subspecies are recognized: the wild form, *V. vinifera* subsp. *sylvestris*, and the domesticated one, *V. vinifera* subsp. *Vinifera* (or *sativa*).

[5] The site of Ohalo II is adjacent to Bet Yerah (Fig. 1). The two sites can be found along the Jordan River estuary at the southernmost part of the Sea of Galilee, which is considered to be the beginning of the central Jordan Valley. The Ohalo II Epipaleolithic fishercamp was dated to 23,000 cal. Years BP (Nadel et al., 2012).

including along seasonal rivers in closed forests, forested wetlands, and sand dune shrublands (Zohary, 1973; Naqinezhad et al., 2018).

Domesticated grapevines capitalized on this adaptability; they were carried over into drier regions—as far as the Negev Desert—and supported the southern Levant's establishment as a center of ancient winemaking that lasted until the collapse of the Byzantine Empire (Fuks et al., 2020; Langgut et al., 2021b). When this began is unclear. But, the discovery of pips, charred berries, and wood in Early Bronze I Jericho (Hopf, 1983), a site too dry and too warm to support wild *V. sylvestris* (Fig. 1), offers a *terminus ante quem* for this event.[6] Other Early Bronze Age sites from the region that include grapevine remains, are: Bet Yerah (Berger, 2013), Numeira and Bab edh-Dhra on the eastern side of the Dead Sea (McCreery, 1979), Arad (Hopf, 1978), and Lachish (Helbaek, 1958). Grape remains also appear in Egypt at this time, apparently as an import (Weiss, 2015, and references therein).

Perhaps the northern part of the Jordan Valley served as an independent domestication center, and from there it spread during the Chalcolithic period southwards,[7] reaching Jericho by the mid-sixth millennium BP. This hypothesis receives some support from Sivan et al.'s (2020) observation that the Levantine grapevine varieties have a distinct genomic background. However, they also stress that it remains unclear whether ancient Levantine varieties stemmed from extensive gene-flows across the Near East or directly domesticated Levantine wild grapevines.

1.3 Common Fig (Ficus carica)

The literature on the timing of fig domestication is mired in inconclusive and sometimes contradictory results. To date, several hypotheses have been put forth. The most widely accepted theory suggests that the common fig was domesticated, with other founder fruit trees, during the Chalcolithic period, some 6000 years ago (Zohary & Spiegel-Roy, 1975; Weiss, 2015). Another hypothesis offered by Kislev et al. (2006) suggested that the common fig was domesticated in the lower Jordan Valley 11,400–11,200 years ago (Pre-Pottery Neolithic A), even before the beginning of grain crop agriculture at about 10,500 years ago. However, this hypothesis was subsequently rejected since the parthenocarpic female figs discussed by Kislev et al. (2006) occur naturally due to a genetic mutation (Lev-Yadun et al., 2006; Denham, 2007; Zohary et al., 2012; Abbo et al., 2015; Weiss, 2015; Lev-Yadun, 2022).

It is also unclear whether common fig domestication was a single innovation that occurred at a specific time and place, gradually spreading throughout the Mediterranean Basin, or multiple culturally unrelated events. This indeterminacy is

---

[6] The presence of fruit remains as well as wood from the grape plant in a site where wild grapevine could not grow, provides solid proof for horticulture-type domestication (Miller, 2008; Weiss, 2015).
[7] To accomplish this geographical shift, a transfer of both knowledge and seedlings from the northern Jordan Valley to the central and southern segments of the Valley must have occurred.

rooted in the female common fig's clonality and the lack of anatomical differences between wild and domesticated types, rendering the distinction between primary and secondary locations difficult to trace (Lev-Yadun, 2022).[8]

Most recently, Langgut and Garfinkel (2022) reported a sizeable assemblage of *Ficus carica* charred wood from Middle Chalcolithic Tel Tsaf, suggesting it constitutes one of the earliest instances of cultivated figure. This argument is based on the observation that a substantial portion of the charcoals originated from young branches that may have derived from pruning. Pruning is standard practice in fruit tree horticulture: it allows sunlight to reach all of a tree's branches, maintains a desired size and shape, and facilitates fruit harvest (Flaishman et al., 2008). After pruning, the trimmed branches are removed to prevent the spreading of fungi and pests onto healthy trees, subsequently serving as a readily available fuel source at the site (Langgut et al., 2014; Benzaquen et al., 2019), a practice still common among traditional Levantine societies (Hobbs, 1989:53; Andersen et al., 2014). Two additional points are noteworthy: A charred fig wood specimen was ^{14}C dated and yielded an age of ca. 7000 cal. BP (Langgut & Garfinkel, 2022), and the evidence of fig pruning reinforce and align with earlier reports about the presence of the species' seeds (pips) at Tel Tsaf (Gophna & Kislev, 1979:113).

One should bear in mind that unlike the tree's seeds and fruit, common fig wood is a rare find in archaeological sites, comprising, at most, a small fraction of the wood assemblage. This scarcity of fig wood is attributed to its limited usefulness: it does not provide long and sturdy beams, and it is unknown to have been traded for other purposes. Therefore, when fig wood remains are found in an archaeological context, it may be deduced that fig trees grew nearby (Lev-Yadun, 2022). Early Bronze Age Tel Bet Yerah is a case in point (Fig. 1): A substantial number of young fig branches were found in the charcoal assemblage, suggesting fig cultivation was practiced (Mor, 2022).

*1.4 Date Palm (*Phoenix dactylifera*)*

The date palm is native and economically significant in arid and semi-arid regions of the southern Mediterranean Basin and southwest Asia (Fig. 5; Zohary et al., 2012). Present-day populations of *P. dactylifera* are comprised of wild forms, segregating escapees, and domesticated clones, which are all genetically interconnected by occasional hybridization (Fig. 5; Zohary et al., 2012:132).[9] Since it is also

---

[8] Similar to the grapevine and pomegranate, fig trees can be easily propagated from branch/stem cuttings (Flaishman et al., 2008; Abbo et al., 2015). However, it is impossible to distinguish wild from domesticated fig on the grounds of wood anatomy and seed morphology (Zohary et al., 2012; Lev-Yadun, 2022).

[9] Yet, Zohary et al. (2012:132) suggest that at the southern base of the Zagros Range facing the Persian Gulf —and at the southern parts of the Dead Sea Basin, wild-type *dactylifera* palms are present. The wild forms are characterized by small and mostly inedible fruits.

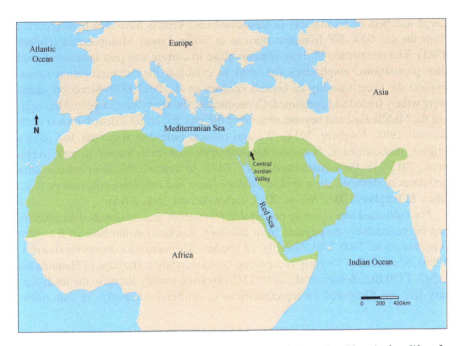

Fig. 5 Geographical distribution of wild and feral forms of date palm, *Phoenix dactylifera*. In south Arabia, Sudan, Eritrea, Somalia, and Senegal they sometimes cross with the Native *P. reclinata*; and in the Indus Basin with *P. sylvestris*. The figure is modified after Zohary et al. (2012, Map 18)

difficult to distinguish wild from domesticated date palms in the archaeobotanical record (e.g., Weiss, 2015), scholars have been relying on marked increases in the frequency of date kernels to trace domestication.[10] In the southern Levant,[11] such increased frequencies have been reported from Tuleilat Ghassul (Zohary & Spiegel-Roy, 1975) and the "Cave of the Treasure" (Zaitschek, 1961) in the Dead Sea region.

---

[10] Date palm thrived in at the hot and dry parts of southern Mediterranean and southwest Asia (Fig. 5) long before the initiation of agriculture, as attested by date palm remains from the Late Middle Palaeolithic (Solecki & Leroi-Gourhan, 1961; Miller-Rosen, 1995; Madella et al., 2002; Henry et al., 2011). Later on, 23,000 years old Ohalo II produced charred pieces of *P. dactylifera* wood (Liphschitz & Nadel, 1997). Date palm remains of the Pre-Pottery Neolithic period were found off the Israeli coast at Atlit-Yam (Liphschitz, 2007:39) and in the Jordanian Desert at Ghuwayr 1 (Simmons & Najjar, 2003) and Tell Wadi Feinan (Jenkins et al., 2011).

[11] A strange episode in the long history of south Levantine date palm horticultural deserves special mention. At some point after the Byzantine period, *P. dactylifera* trees began to slowly disappear, and, by the eighteenth century AD, travelers reported that "not even a single palm tree was found in Jericho" (Amar, 1996; Bernstein, 2004). The causes of this are unknown, although a natural enemy, such as the red palm weevil (*Rhynchophorus ferrugineus Olivier*; Faleiro, 2006), may have been responsible. In the first half of the twentieth century, date palm trees of the same native species (*P. dactylifera*), were intentionally brought back to the region from Egypt and Iraq (Bernstein, 2004).

Large numbers of presumably domesticated date kernels have also been reported from the ca. 6000 BP Ubaidian horizon at Eridu, Lower Mesopotamia (Gillett, 1981). The occurrence of these remains close to current and past habitats of wild date populations, emphasizes the need to establish their domestication status, beyond the sheer quantity of kernels (Zohary et al., 2012:134). Moreover, dates were widely traded and consumed. Consequently, the seeds were dispersed throughout the Middle East and beyond, obscuring the species' original distribution (Fig. 5; Barrow, 1998; Tengberg, 2012). We thus possess little data about the date palm's origins, domestication, historical biogeography, and evolutionary history (Abbo et al., 2015:338; Gros-Balthazard et al., 2017). As a result, efforts to indicate sites and dates of domestication tend to produce loose and indefinite conclusions (e.g., Méry & Tengberg, 2009; Weiss, 2015; Zehdi-Azouzi et al., 2015).

The cultivated tree is easily propagated from seeds and, unlike its wild relative, can be vegetatively propagated from offshoots (suckers) at the base of the plant (Fig. 6; Janick, 2005:276). Notably, all species of *Phoenix* are dioecious (Barrow, 1998), which called for early recognition of sex, already at the days of Hammurabi (1792–1750 BC; Zohary et al., 2012:131). Assyrian murals dating to the tenth century BC, are illustrated by representations of artificial pollination of date palms

Fig. 6 An offshoot (a sucker) of a juvenile date palm's axillary bud groomed for vegetative propagation. When at ground level or when surrounded boxed (in the past) or wrapped by plastic sheets (today), by soil or potting mixture, these offshoots may develop an adventitious root system and following 3–5 years can be removed from the mother tree and replanted. The photo was taken by Dafna Langgut in a date palm plantation in the central Jordan Valley, Israel

(Paley, 1976; Bryant, 1990). They also attest to the ancient understanding of the importance of the pollination process and its sophisticated culture in ancient Mesopotamia.

1.5 *Pomegranate* (**Punica granatum**)

Wild forms of *P. granatum* grow in masses in the south Caspian belt, northeastern Turkey, and in Albania and Montenegro (Zohary et al., 2012: 134),[12] and it is assumed that the tree was cultivated there (Abbo et al., 2015: 340). Though the earliest archaeobotanical findings of Pomegranate were found in the Early Bronze Age southern Levant, the region was ruled out as a possible center of domestication as the tree does not occur in a wild state in this region[13] (Zohary et al., 2012: 135). However, the recent discovery of waterlogged pomegranate wood and charcoals in the south Levantine Epipaleolithic site of Jordan River Durijat (Gonen Sharon, personal communication) calls this assumption into doubt and demands further examination. The pomegranate is an appreciated minor crop in traditional Mediterranean horticulture (Zohary et al., 2012: 134). Its fruits are not amenable to simple preservation, which is probably responsible for their relatively low status. In the traditional Near Eastern fruit culture, the pomegranate is a common component of home gardens or mixed orchards (*bustan*), but it never attains a dominant economic role and is never cultivated at a wide-scale comparable with olive, date palm, or grapevine (Bonfil & Hadas, 2011; Abbo et al., 2015: 365). For these reasons, the pomegranate will not be discussed further in this article.

2 Where?

Since, as of the Pottery Neolithic, the Near East should be regarded a mono-cultural unit (Gopher et al., 2021), it is unlikely that fruit tree horticulture could have been introduced several times and independently in this restricted area (Abbo et al., 2015). Instead, we propose the central Jordan Valley (Fig. 1) as the primary origin of fruit tree cultivation.

This suggestion is based on the geographical overlap distribution of the founder fruit trees which established horticulture. The common fig is native to the central Jordan Valley and seems to have been cultivated there as early as ca. 7000 cal. BP (Langgut & Garfinkel, 2022). Similarly, the central Jordan Valley also presents the

---

[12] The wild types of pomegranate occupy a wide range of elevations from below sea level to ca. 2000 m above sea level, indicating that while certain genotypes tolerate high temperatures, others withstand low ones (Browicz, 1996).

[13] At Early Bronze Age Jericho (Hopf, 1983), Arad (Hopf, 1978) and Bet Yerah (Mor, 2022) *Punica* remains were found, suggesting well-established cultivation in the Early Bronze southern Levant.

earliest robust evidence for olive domestication based on the occurrence of *Olea* remains outside its present natural habitat (Langgut & Garfinkel, 2022). Concerning grapevine and date palm, it is telling that they have both been observed in the Epipaleolithic site of Ohalo II, on the Lake of Galilee (Kislev et al., 1992; Liphschitz & Nadel, 1997). Given these species' distinct northern and southern distributions, their concurrence here constitutes the central Jordan Valley as their only point of convergence.

While olive, common fig, and grapevine are native to the Levantine Mediterranean climatic zones, the date palm is best adjusted to arid conditions. To yield high-quality fruits, the palm tree requires high temperatures and low humidity; trees that grow in areas with mild summers (e.g., the Mediterranean coast of Israel and Lebanon) are likely to bear low-grade fruits. Thus, the central Jordan Valley is the only place in the world where these four horticulture founder species can all thrive and gain economic clout.

3 When?

The process of fruit tree domestication can be divided into three principal phases: (1) management of wild material (manipulations such as pruning), (2) selection of desirable basic domestication traits, and (3) dispersal of the domesticated material. While presently available archaeological and archaeobotanical evidence supports the reconstruction of all three phases of olive domestication (Langgut et al., 2019), it is too fragmentary to do the same for the other three founder species. It seems that the settlers of the Carmel Coast and the Galilee were manipulating olives already at ca. 7500 cal. BP (phase 1). By ca. 7000 cal. BP, olive trees spread beyond their natural distribution area (phase 3), and the common fig was being pruned (phase 1). Thus, during the late-eighth/early-seventh millennium BP, both trees were undergoing the early stages of domestication. Concerning the date palm, evidence suggests it was domesticated sometime during the Chalcolithic period, while definite indications of grapevine horticulture emerged slightly later, during the beginning of the Early Bronze Age.

4 Why?

4.1 What Is the Motivation?

It remains unclear what triggered the Neolithic process of plant and animal domestication, causing large groups of people to live close to one another and wrestle with the many problems inherent in such an arrangement. Undoubtedly, the decision to domesticate fruit trees somewhere during the late-eighth/early-seventh millennium BP made the situation considerably more complex.

When integrating fruit trees into an agro-economic system that relies mainly on grain crops, it is important to consider several key themes. Unlike annually renewed crops, fruit tree cultivation is a long-term investment that offers relatively delayed returns and requires years of investment in research and development. A fruit tree plantation might not attain its full yield potential within the planter's lifetime due to fruit trees' long juvenility (even if clonally propagated; Abbo et al., 2015). Furthermore, unlike annual plants, fruit trees cannot be rotated between plots, necessitating, therefore, careful premeditation and planning when land is being allocated for a fruit tree plantation (Abbo et al., 2015). Lastly, orchards' longevity has considerable implications for land ownership and its passing down to future generations. All these features call for more elaborate social contracts and institutions (Langgut & Garfinkel, 2022).

Middle Chalcolithic Tel Tsaf is a case in point. The site provides not only one of the earliest examples of fruit tree cultivation worldwide but also the earliest stamp seal in the southern Levant (Freikman et al., 2021) and an unprecedented concentration of large storage facilities (Garfinkel et al., 2009; Rosenberg et al., 2017). The occurrence of rare exotic objects at Tel Tsaf suggests wealth accumulation, probably driven by grain and fruit products' surplus. Ultimately, it seems Tel Tsaf's inhabitants knowingly and purposefully chose to cultivate fruit trees and were not forced into it by external pressures. The climatic conditions, for instance, were favorable and did not seem to have acted as direct catalysts of large-scale transformations as they sometimes do (e.g., Langgut et al., 2018; Grove, 2021). Indeed, climate reconstructions for the Chalcolithic Levantine Mediterranean region point to higher humidity levels than today, with precipitation originating from both the North Atlantic/Mediterranean climate system (Bar-Matthews & Ayalon, 2011) and the low-latitude monsoonal system (Langgut, 2018). There were, therefore, no climate-related deterioration or stress factors that would have driven the settlers to change their subsistence strategy. Moreover, in the central Jordan Valley, proposed here to have been the site of primary fruit horticulture, the proximity to the Jordan River implies that water shortage was not an issue or limiting factor either. Suggested changes in social organization, shifts in settlement patterns and population growth were also proposed to explain the dramatic changes in the economic subsistence (Levy, 1983, 1986).

Two major benefits are likely to have been at the front of early cultivators' minds. The first benefit is better nutrition, as the traditional cereals and legumes diet was augmented by complementary ingredients like olive oil and sugar. Moreover, olive oil's and fruits' suitability for prolonged storage via curing or drying went a long way to guarantee a long-term and stable supply of these products. The second benefit is social. It pertains to the conceptualization of fruits as exotic foods and their dovetailed capacity to act as status symbols. In the same way that rare exotic objects (such as copper awls, obsidian, Ubaid pottery, foreign beads, and Nilotic shells; Garfinkel et al., 2007, 2014) served as social markers at Tel Tsaf, so did the fruits and their products (Langgut & Garfinkel, 2022).

4.2 The Creation of Surplus

Five decades ago, Renfrew (1972) underscored the importance of fruit tree cultivation, in general, and the olive, in particular. He proposed that the emergence of the Mycenaean and Minoan civilizations was linked to the development of a polycultural triad comprised of wheat, vine, and olive. In his view, olive was cultivated on marginal agricultural lands, making way for surplus production, population growth, socio-economic change, expanded exchange networks, and technological advances. Though this suggestion was heavily criticized (e.g., Hamilakis, 1996; Runnels & Hansen, 1986), it demonstrates the importance ascribed to olive cultivation and industries.

The crystallization of fruit tree horticulture explored in this study is intertwined with the establishment of the Mediterranean village economy and the Secondary Products Revolution (Sherratt, 1983), not with urbanization or state formation (Langgut et al., 2019). It was primarily a rural staple economic strategy that was only much later co-opted by Early Bronze Age elites as an instrument of economic leverage (Canellas-Bolta et al., 2018; Langgut et al., 2019). Since fruit tree cultivation is a long-term investment with delayed returns (Abbo et al., 2015) and since we ruled out climate change or water scarcity as an explanation for its emergence, we must ask what pushed human societies towards such a shift.

Recently, Mayshar et al. (2022) made an interesting suggestion regarding the Near East Neolithic Revolution. They argued that societies occupying areas more suited for growing cereals are more likely to develop some sort of governance over time. The reason is the long shelf life of cereals that support the possibility of taxation, contrary to roots and tubers (like cassava and potatoes), whose short shelf life renders taxation implausible. Mayshar et al. (2022) used statistical analysis to test the appearance of a complex society, mainly, against two variables: (i) cereal grain cultivation and (ii) soil productivity. They found that when cereal grains are cultivated in a specific location, the productivity of the soil is rendered statistically insignificant, and they suggested that social elites drive the accumulation of surplus, not driven by it. Thus, inequality and elites did not emerge from societies with preexisting surpluses. Instead, elites and inequality were the force that pushed surplus production because they made way for taxation: "We challenge the conventional productivity theory, contending that it was not an increase in food production that led to complex hierarchies and states, but rather the transition to reliance on appropriable cereal grains that facilitate taxation by the emerging elite" (Mayshar et al., 2022: 2). Insofar as this theory is correct, its conclusions must hold equally well for fruit tree horticulture. As indicated above, fruit trees produce products with long shelf lives, such as table olives, olive oil, raisins, wine, and dried figs and dates, and, therefore, are highly suitable for long-distance trade and taxation .

A ruler's incentive to provide its territories with long-term prospects was introduced by Olsen (1993) in his theory of roving and stationary bandits. In a world where wheat is domesticated, there are two types of players: (i) the sedentary type that grows crops and (ii) the nomadic bandits. Since they are roving and occasionally plunder the farmers, they are called "roving bandits," and their strategy aims to maximize immediate yields (of plunder) with little concern for long-term effects. At some point, the roving bandits might decide to settle, which, according to Olsen (1993, 2000), could be suggested by the farmers as they prefer fixed and low taxation over uncertainty. Now, the bandits may "plunder"—i.e., levy taxes— the same village more than once. Under these circumstances, the pay-off matrix is different, and the ruler will not strive to maximize short-term yields but invest in long-term prospects. Olsen (1993, 2000) argues that this mechanism encourages stationary bandits (i.e., long-term rulers) to invest in the village, not for the farmers' sake but their own. Undoubtedly, the introduction of fruit trees and their industries opened new avenues of profitable conduct, but they also necessitated the establishment of a much more complex economic and political system.

References

Abbo, S., Gopher, A., & Lev-Yadun, S. (2015). Fruit domestication in the near east. *Plant Breeding Reviews, 39*, 325–377.

Amar, Z. (1996). Agricultural products in the Jordan valley in the middle ages. In S. Dar & Z. Safrai (Eds.), *The village in ancient Israel* (pp. 297–326). Ereztz.

Andersen, G. L., Krzywinski, K., Talib, M., Saadallah, A. E. M., Hobbs, J. J., & Pierce, R. H. (2014). Traditional nomadic tending of trees in the Red Sea Hills. *Journal of Arid Environments, 106*, 36–44.

Bar-Matthews, M., & Ayalon, A. (2011). Mid-Holocene climate variations revealed by high-resolution speleothem records from Soreq Cave, Israel and their correlation with cultural changes. *The Holocene, 21*, 163–171.

Barrow, S. C. (1998). A monograph of *Phoenix* L. (Palmae: Coryphoideae). *Kew Bulletin, 53*, 513–575.

Benzaquen, M., Finkelstein, I., & Langgut, D. (2019). Vegetation history and human impact on the environs of Tel Megiddo in the bronze and iron ages: A dendroarchaeological analysis. *Tel Aviv, 49*, 1–23.

Berger, A. (2013). *Plant economy and ecology in Early Bronze Age Tel Bet Yerah*. Master thesis, Tel Aviv University. https://primage.tau.ac.il/libraries/theses/arc/002870666.pdf

Bernstein, Z. (2004). *The date palm*. The Israeli Council for Production and Distribution of Fruits LTD.

Bonfil, D. J., & Hadas, A. (2011). Ancient field-crop yields and land-carrying capacity. In Y. Dagan (Ed.), *The Ramat Beit Shemesh regional project: Landscapes of settlement: From the Palaeolithic to the Ottoman periods* (pp. 199–210). Israel Antiquities Authority.

Bouby, L., Wales, N., Jalabadze, M., Rusishvili, N., Bonhomme, V., Ramos-Madrigal, J., Evin, A., Ivorra, S., Lacombe, T., Pagnoux, C., & Boaretto, E. (2021). Tracking the history of grapevine cultivation in Georgia by combining geometric morphometrics and ancient DNA. *Vegetation History and Archaeobotany, 30*, 63–76. https://doi.org/10.1007/s00334-020-00803-0

Browicz, K. (1996). *Chorology of trees and shrubs in south-west Asia and adjacent regions*. Institute of Dendrology.

Bryant, V. M. (1990). Pollen: Nature's fingerprints of plants. In D. Calhoun (Ed.), *Yearbook of science and the future* (pp. 92–111). Encyclopedia Britannica.

Cañellas-Boltà, N., Riera-Mora, S., Orengo, H. A., Livarda, A., & Knappett, C. (2018). Human management and landscape changes at Palaikastro (Eastern Crete) from the Late Neolithic to the Early Minoan period. *Quaternary Science Reviews, 183*, 59–75. https://doi.org/10.1016/j.quascirev.2018.01.010

Carrión, Y., Ntinou, M., & Bada, E. (2010). *Olea europaea* L. in the north Mediterranean Basin during the Pleniglacial and the Early–Middle Holocene. *Quaternary Science Reviews, 29*, 952–968. https://doi.org/10.1016/j.quascirev.2009.12.015

Denham, T. P. (2007). Early fig domestication, or gathering of wild parthenocarpic figs? *Antiquity, 81*, 457–461.

Dighton, A., Fairbairn, A., Bourke, S., Faith, J. T., & Habgood, P. (2017). Bronze Age olive domestication in the North Jordan valley: New morphological evidence for regional complexity in early arboricultural practice from Pella in Jordan. *Vegetation History and Archaeobotany, 26*, 403–413. https://doi.org/10.1007/s00334-016-0601-z

Eitam, D. (1993). Between the [olive] rows, oil will be produced, presses will be trod. (Job 24, 11). In M. C. Amouretti & J. P. Brun (Eds.), *La Production du Vin et l'Huile en Mediterranée* (pp. 65–90). Ecole Francaise d'Athènes.

Epstein, C. (1993). Oil production in the golan heights during the chalcolithic period. *Tel Aviv, 20*, 133–146. https://doi.org/10.1179/tav.1993.1993.2.133

Faleiro, J. R. (2006). A review of the issues and management of the red palm weevil Rhynchophorus ferrugineus (Coleoptera: Rhynchophoridae) in coconut and date palm during the last one hundred years. *International Journal of Tropical Insect Science, 26*, 135–154. https://doi.org/10.1079/IJT2006113

Flaishman, M., Rodov, V., & Stover, E. (2008). The fig: Botany, horticulture and breeding. In J. Janick (Ed.), *Horticultural Reviews* (Vol. 34, pp. 113–196). Wiley. https://doi.org/10.1002/9780470380147.ch2

Freikman, M., Ben-Shlomo, D., & Garfinkel, Y. A. (2021). A stamped sealing from Middle Chalcolithic Tel Tsaf: Implications for the rise of administrative practices in the Levant. *The Journal of the Council for British Research in the Levant, 53*, 1–12. https://doi.org/10.1080/00758914.2021.1923906

Fuks, D., Bar-Oz, G., Tepper, Y., Erickson-Gini, T., Langgut, D., Weissbrod, L., & Weiss, E. (2020). The rise and fall of viticulture in the Late Antique Negev Highlands reconstructed from archaeobotanical and ceramic data. *PNAS: Proceedings of the American National Academy of Sciences, 117*, 19780–19791. https://doi.org/10.1073/pnas.1922200117

Fuller, D. Q., & Stevens, C. J. (2019). Between domestication and civilization: The role of agriculture and arboriculture in the emergence of the first urban societies. *Vegetation History and Archaeobotany, 28*, 263–282. https://doi.org/10.1007/s00334-019-00727-4

Galili, E., Stanley, D. J., Sharvit, J., & Weinstein-Evron, M. (1997). Evidence for earliest olive-oil production in submerged settlements off the Carmel Coast, Israel. *Journal of Archaeological Science, 24*, 1141–1150. https://doi.org/10.1006/jasc.1997.0193

Galili, E., Weinstein-Evron, M., Chaim, S., Cvikel, D., Benjamin, J., McCarthy, J., Langgut, D., Cavanagh, M., Sapir, S., Rosen, B., & Kolska Horwitz, L. (2018). The archaeology and paleoenvironment of the submerged Pottery Neolithic settlement of Kfar Samir (Israel). *Paléorient, 44*, 113–132.

Galili, E., Langgut, D., Terral, J. F., Barazani, O., Dag, A., Kolska Horwitz, L., Ogloblin Ramirez, I., Rosen, B., Weinstein-Evron, M., Chaim, S., Kremer, E., Lev-Yadun, S., Boaretto, E., Ben-Barak-Zelas, Z., & Fishman, A. (2021). Early production of Table Olives at a mid-7th millennium BP submerged site off the Carmel Coast (Israel). *Scientific Reports, 11*, 1–15. https://doi.org/10.1038/s41598-020-80772-6

Garfinkel, Y., Ben-Shlomo, D., Freikman, M., & Vered, A. (2007). Tel Tsaf: The 2004–2006 excavation seasons. *Israel Exploration Journal, 57*, 1–33. http://www.jstor.org/stable/27927153

Garfinkel, Y., Ben-Shlomo, D., & Kuperman, T. (2009). Large-scale storage of grain surplus in the sixth millennium BC: The silos of Tel Tsaf. *Antiquity, 83*, 309–325.

Garfinkel, Y., Klimscha, F., Shalev, S., & Rosenberg, D. (2014). The beginning of metallurgy in the southern Levant: A late 6th millennium Cal BC copper Awl from Tel Tsaf, Israel. *PLoS One, 9*, 1–6.

Gillett, J. B. (1981). Botanical samples. In F. Safar, M. A. Mustafa, & S. Lloyd (Eds.), *State organization of antiquities and heritage* (pp. 317–318). Eridu.
Gopher, A., Lev-Yadun, S., & Abbo, S. (2021). Breaking ground: Plant domestication in the Neolithic Levant: The "Core-area one-event" model. Tel Aviv University.
Gophna, R., & Kislev, M. (1979). Finds at Tel-Saf (1977–1978). *Revue Biblique, 86,* 112–114.
Graham, P. (2014). Archaeobotanical remains from late 6th/early 5th millennium BC Tel Tsaf, Israel. *Journal of Archaeological Science, 43,* 105–110. https://doi.org/10.1016/j.jas.2013.12.018
Grassi, F., & De Lorenzis, G. (2021). Back to the origins: Background and perspectives of grapevine domestication. *International Journal of Molecular Sciences, 22,* 4518. https://doi.org/10.3390/ijms22094518
Gros-Balthazard, M., Galimberti, M., Kousathanas, A., Newton, C., Ivorra, S., Paradis, L., Vigouroux, Y., Carter, R., Tengberg, M., Battesti, V., Santoni, S., Falquet, L., Pintaud, J. C., Terral, J. F., & Wegmann, D. (2017). The discovery of wild date palms in Oman reveals a complex domestication history involving centers in the Middle East and Africa. *Current Biology, 27,* 2211–2218. https://doi.org/10.1016/j.cub.2017.06.045
Grove, M. (2021). Climatic change and climatic variability: An objective decomposition. *Quaternary Science Reviews, 271,* 107196.
Hamilakis, Y. (1996). Wine, oil and the dialectics of power in Bronze Age Crete: A review of the evidence. *Oxford Journal of Archaeology, 15,* 1–32.
Helbaek, H. (1958). Plant remains in ancient Lachish. *Lachish IV (Tell ed-Duweir).* In *The Bronze Age.* Oxford University Press.
Henry, A., Alison, G., Brooks, S., & Piperno, D. R. (2011). Microfossils in calculus demonstrate consumption of plants and cooked foods in Neanderthal diets (Shanidar III, Iraq; Spy I and II, Belgium). *Proceedings of the National Academy of Sciences of the United States of America, 108,* 486–491. https://doi.org/10.1073/pnas.1016868108
Hobbs, J. J. (1989). *Bedouin life in the Egyptian wilderness.* University of Texas Press.
Hopf, M. (1978). Plant remains, strata V-I. In R. Amiran & O. Ilan (Eds.), *Early Arad* (pp. 64–82). Jerusalem.
Hopf, M. (1983). Jericho plant remains. In K. M. Kenyon & T. A. Holland (Eds.), *Excavations at Jericho* (pp. 576–621). London.
Janick, J. (2005). The origins of fruits, fruit growing, and fruit breeding. In J. Janick (Ed.), *Plant breeding reviews* (Vol. 25, pp. 255–320). Wiley & Sons. https://doi.org/10.1002/9780470650301.ch8
Jenkins, E., Baker, A., & Elliott, S. (2011). Past plant use in Jordan as revealed by archaeological and ethnoarchaeological phytolith signatures. In S. Mithen (Ed.), *Water, life and civilization: Climate, environment and society in the Jordan Valley* (pp. 381–400). Cambridge University Press.
Kislev, M. E., Nadel, D., & Carmi, I. (1992). Epipalaeolithic (19,000 BP) cereal and fruit diet at Ohalo II, Sea of Galilee, Israel. *Review of Palaeobotany and Palynology, 73,* 161–166. https://doi.org/10.1016/0034-6667(92)90054-K
Kislev, M. E., Hartman, A., & Bar-Yosef, O. (2006). Early domesticated fig in the Jordan Valley. *Science, 312,* 1372–1374. https://doi.org/10.1126/science.1125910
Langgut, D. (2018). Late Quaternary Nile flows as recorded in the Levantine Basin: The palynological evidence. *Quaternary International, 464,* 273–284. https://doi.org/10.1016/j.quaint.2017.07.006
Langgut, D., & Garfinkel, Y. (2022). 7000-year-old evidence of fruit tree cultivation in the Jordan Valley, Israel. *Scientific Reports, 12*(1), 1–12. https://doi.org/10.1038/s41598-022-10743-6
Langgut, D., Lev-Yadun, S., & Finkelstein, I. (2014). The impact of olive orchard abandonment and rehabilitation on pollen signature: An experimental approach to evaluating fossil pollen data. *Ethnoarchaeology, 6,* 121–135. https://doi.org/10.1179/1944289014Z.00000000016
Langgut, D., Almogi-Labin, A., Bar-Matthews, M., Pickarski, N., & Weinstein-Evron, M. (2018). Evidence for a humid interval at ~56–44 ka in the Levant and its potential link to mod-

ern humans dispersal out of Africa. *Journal of Human Evolution, 124*, 75–90. https://doi.org/10.1016/j.jhevol.2018.08.002

Langgut, D., Cheddadi, R., Carrión, J. S., Cavanagh, M., Colombaroli, D., Eastwood, W. J., Greenberg, R., Litt, T., Mercuri, A. M., Miebach, A., & Roberts, C. N. (2019). The origin and spread of olive cultivation in the Mediterranean Basin: The fossil pollen evidence. *The Holocene, 29*, 902–922. https://doi.org/10.1177/0959683619826654

Langgut, D., Cheddadi, R., & Sharon, G. (2021a). Climate and environmental reconstruction of the Epipaleolithic Mediterranean Levant (22.0–11.9 ka cal. BP). *Quaternary Science Reviews, 270*, 107170. https://doi.org/10.1016/j.quascirev.2021.107170

Langgut, D., Tepper, Y., Benzaquen, M., Erickson-Gini, T., & Bar-Oz, G. (2021b). Environment and horticulture in the byzantine Negev Desert, Israel: Sustainability, prosperity and enigmatic decline. *Quaternary International, 593*, 160–177.

Lavee, S., & Zohary, D. (2011). The potential of genetic diversity and the effect of geographically isolated resources in olive breeding. *Israel Journal of Plant Sciences, 59*, 3–13. https://doi.org/10.1560/IJPS.59.1.3

Levy, T. E. (1983). The emergence of specialized pastoralism in the southern Levant. *World Archaeology, 15*, 15–36. https://doi.org/10.1080/00438243.1983.9979882

Levy, T. E. (1986). Archaeological sources for the study of Palestine: The chalcolithic period. *Biblical Archaeology, 49*, 82–108. https://doi.org/10.2307/3210005

Lev-Yadun, S. (2007). Wood remains from archaeological excavations: A review with a near Eastern perspective. *Israel Journal of Earth Sciences, 56*, 139–162. https://doi.org/10.1560/IJES.56.2-4.139

Lev-Yadun, S. (2022). The common fig (*Ficus carica*) remains in the archaeological record and its domestication processes. In M. A. Flaishman & U. Aksoy (Eds.), *The fig: Advances in research and sustainable production* (pp. 11–25). CABI.

Lev-Yadun, S., Ne'eman, G., Abbo, S., & Flaishman, M. A. (2006). Comment on "early domesticated Fig in the Jordan Valley." *Science, 314*, 1683.

Liphschitz, N. (2007). *Timber in ancient Israel dendroarchaeology and dendrochronology.* Monograph series, 26, of the Institute of Archaeology of Tel Aviv University.

Liphschitz, N., & Nadel, D. (1997). Charred wood remains from Ohalo II (19,000 BP), Sea of Galilee, Israel. *Journal of the Israel Prehistoric Society, 27*, 5–18.

Lipshchitz, N. (1988). Analysis of the botanical remains from Tel Tsaf. *Journal of the Institute of Archaeology of Tel Aviv University, 15*, 52–54.

Litt, T., Ohlwein, C., Neumann, F. H., Hense, A., & Stein, M. (2012). Holocene climate variability in the Levant from the Dead Sea pollen record. *Quaternary Science Reviews, 49*, 95–105.

Madella, M., Jones, M. K., Goldberg, P., Goren, Y., & Hovers, E. (2002). The exploitation of plant resources by Neanderthals in Amud Cave (Israel): The evidence from phytolith studies. *Journal of Archaeological Science, 29*, 703–719.

Mayshar, J., Moav, M., & Pascali, L. (2022). The origin of the state: Productivity or appropriability? *Journal of Political Economy., 130*, 1091–1144. https://doi.org/10.1086/718372

McCreery, D. W. (1979). Flotation of the Bab edh-Dhra and Numeira plant remains. *Annual of the American Schools of Oriental Research, 46*, 165.

McGovern, P., Glusker, D. L., Exner, L. J., Voigt, M. M., McGovern, P., Glusker, D. L., Exner, L. J., & Voigt, M. M. (1996). Neolithic resinated wine. *Nature, 381*(6582), 480–481.

McGovern, P., Jalabadze, M., Batiuk, S., Callahan, M. P., Smith, K. E., Hall, G. R., Kvavadze, E., Maghradze, D., Rusishvili, N., Bouby, L., & Failla, O. (2017). Early Neolithic wine of Georgia in the South Caucasus. *Proceedings of the National Academy of Sciences, 114*, E10309–E10318. https://doi.org/10.1073/pnas.1714728114

Meadows, J. (2001). Olive domestication at Teleilat Ghassul. In L. Hopkins & A. Parker (Eds.), *Archaeology of the Near East: An Australian perspective* (pp. 13–18). University of Sydney.

Méry, S., & Tengberg, M. (2009). Food for eternity? The analysis of a date offering from a 3rd millennium BC grave at Hili N, Abu Dhabi (United Arab Emirates). *Journal of Archaeological Science, 36*, 2012–2017. https://doi.org/10.1016/j.jas.2009.05.017

Miller, N. F. (2008). Sweeter than wine? The use of the grape in early western Asia. *Antiquity, 82*, 937–946.

Miller-Rosen, A. (1995). Preliminary analysis of phytoliths from prehistoric sites in southern Jordan. In D. O. Henry (Ed.), *Prehistoric cultural ecology and evolution insights from southern Jordan* (pp. 399–403). Springer.

Mor, E. (2022). *Reconstructing Tel bet Yerah's natural and anthropogenic environment during the early bronze age through wood remains* MA thesis, Tel Aviv University. MA Thesis (in Hebrew with English abstract).

Nadel, D., Piperno, D. R., Holst, I., Snir, A., & Weiss, E. (2012). New evidence for the processing of wild cereal grains at Ohalo II, a 23 000-year-old campsite on the shore of the sea of Galilee, Israel. *Antiquity, 86*, 990–1003.

Namdar, D., Amrani, A., Getzov, N., & Milevski, I. (2015). Olive oil storage during the fifth and sixth millennia BC at Ein Zippori, Northern Israel. *Israel Journal of Plant Sciences, 62*, 65–74. https://doi.org/10.1080/07929978.2014.960733

Naqinezhad, A., Ramezani, E., Djamali, M., Schnitzler, A., & Arnold, C. (2018). Wild grapevine (*Vitis vinifera* subsp. *sylvestris*) in the Hyrcanian relict forests of northern Iran: An overview of current taxonomy, ecology and palaeorecords. *Journal of Forestry Research, 29*, 1757–1768. https://doi.org/10.1007/s11676-017-0549-6

Neef, R. (1990). Introduction, development and environmental implications of olive culture: The evidence from Jordan. In S. Bottema, G. Entjes-Nieborg, & W. Van Zeist (Eds.), *Man's role in the shaping of the eastern Mediterranean landscape* (pp. 295–306). A. A. Balkema Rotterdam.

Neumann, F., Schölzel, C., Litt, T., Hense, A., & Stein, M. (2007). Holocene vegetation and climate history of the northern Golan heights (Near East). *Vegetation History and Archaeobotany, 16*, 329–347.

Olsen, M. (1993). Dictatorship, democracy, and development. *American Political Science Review, 87*, 567–576.

Olsen, M. (2000). *Power and prosperity: Outgrowing communist and capitalist dictatorships*. Basic books.

Paley, S. M. (1976). *King of the world: Ashur-nasir-pal II of Assyria 883–859 BC*. Brooklyn Museum.

Renfrew, C. (1972). *The emergence of civilization: The Cyclades and the Aegean in the third millennium BC*.

Rosenberg, D., Klimscha, F., Graham, P. J., Hill, A., Weissbrod, L., Ktalav, I., Love, S., Pinsky, S., Hubbard, E., & Boaretto, E. (2014). Back to Tel Tsaf: A preliminary report on the 2013 season of the renewed project. *Journal of the Israel Prehistoric Society, 44*, 148–179. http://www.jstor.org/stable/24312158

Rosenberg, D., Garfinkel, Y., & Klimscha, F. (2017). Large-scale storage and storage symbolism in the ancient Near East: A clay silo model from Tel Tsaf. *Antiquity, 91*, 885–900. https://doi.org/10.15184/AQY.2017.75

Runnels, C. N., & Hansen, J. (1986). The olive in the prehistoric Aegean: The evidence for domestication in the early bronze age. *Oxford Journal of Archaeology, 5*, 299–308.

Schiebel, V. (2013). *Vegetation and climate history of the southern Levant during the last 30,000 years based on palynological investigation*. PhD dissertation, University of Bonn. Bonn.

Sherratt, A. G. (1983). The secondary products revolution of animals in the Old World. *World Archaeology, 15*, 90–104. http://www.jstor.org/stable/124640

Simmons, A. H., & Najjar, M. (2003). Ghuwayr I, a pre-pottery Neolithic B settlement in Southern Jordan. Report of the 1996–2000 campaigns. *Annual of the Department of Antiquities of Jordan, 47*, 407–430.

Sivan, A., Rahimi, O., Weiss, E., Drori, E., & Hübner, S. (2020). Genomic evidence support an independent history of grapevine domestication in the Levant. *bioRxiv*. https://doi.org/10.1101/2020.07.11.198358

Solecki, R. S., & Leroi-Gourhan, A. (1961). Palaeoclimatology and archaeology in the near East. *Annals of the New York Academy of Sciences, 95*, 729–739. https://doi.org/10.1111/j.1749-6632.1961.tb50073.x

Srebro, H., & Soffer, T. (2011). *The new Atlas of Israel: The national Atlas*. The Hebrew University of Jerusalem.

Tengberg, M. (2012). Beginnings and early history of date palm garden cultivation in the Middle East. *Journal of Arid Environments, 86*, 139–147.

Van Zeist, W., Baruch, U., & Bottema, S. (2009). Holocene palaeoecology of the hula area, northeastern Israel. In K. Kaptijn & L. P. Petit (Eds.), *A timeless Vale, archaeological and related essays on the Jordan Valley* (pp. 29–64). Leiden University Press.

Weiss, E. (2015). Beginnings of fruit growing in the old world two generations later. *Israel Journal of Plant Sciences, 62*, 75–85. https://doi.org/10.1080/07929978.2015.1007718

Zaitschek, D. V. (1961). Remains of cultivated plants from the cave of Nahal Mishmar: Preliminary note. *Israel Exploration Journal, 11*, 70–72.

Zehdi-Azouzi, S., Cherif, E., Moussouni, S., Gros-Balthazard, M., Abbas Naqvi, S., Ludena, B., Castillo, K., Chabrillange, N., Bouguedoura, N., Bennaceur, M., & Si-Dehbi, F. (2015). Genetic structure of the date palm (*Phoenix dactylifera*) in the Old World reveals a strong differentiation between eastern and western populations. *Annals of Botany, 116*, 101–112. https://doi.org/10.1093/aob/mcv132

Zohary, M. (1973). *Geobotanical foundations of the Middle East*. Gustav Gischer Verlag.

Zohary, D., & Spiegel-Roy, P. (1975). Beginnings of fruit growing in the Old World. *Science, 187*, 319–327. https://doi.org/10.1126/science.187.4174.319

Zohary, D., Hopf, M., & Weiss, E. (2012). *Domestication of plants in the old world* (4th ed.). Oxford University Press. https://doi.org/10.1093/acprof:osobl/9780199549061.001.0001

Animal Economy in the Chalcolithic of the Southern Levant: From Meat Source to Marketable Commodity

Linoy Namdar and Lidar Sapir-Hen

Abstract Economic development resulting from the exploitation of animals in the Chalcolithic period is considered one of the major factors that promoted early urbanism in the period that followed. In the current paper, we examine the animal economy in two phases of the Chalcolithic period, and track changes in exploitation of animals over time. We examine when and where exploitation of secondary products became intense. To do this, we reviewed published faunal assemblages from the southern Levant, and, based on models, estimated the exploitation of animals. Our results suggest that evidence for the exploitation of cattle for work and caprines for milk is present only beginning in the Late Chalcolithic-Ghassulian, and not from the earlier Wadi Raba and Pre-Ghassulian cultures. This significant economic advance, which transformed animal roles from a source of meat into a marketable commodity, occurred gradually across the studied period.

Keywords Livestock management · Southern Levant · Chalcolithic · Secondary products · Zooarchaeology

1 Introduction

In contrast to early fifth millennium BCE southern Mesopotamia, where urbanism had already developed, creating intensification of agriculture, centralization of urban settlements, and cultural consistency, in the southern Levant autonomous villages were just emerging with their own new culture and technology (Greenberg, 2019: 15). This new urbanism spread to the northwest Negev and the lower Jordan Valley (Levy, 1995: 230), where the settlements no longer based their economic strategies on hunting activities alone, but on mixed farming and pastoralism, alongside the cultivation of cereals and legumes (Grigson, 1995: 249). The expansion of extensive livestock husbandry and crop field management became possible as a result of sophisticated water systems, and the development of ceramic storage pithoi (Greenberg, 2019: 17).

Studies of faunal remains of the earlier period, Late Pottery Neolithic,[1] show that the economy was based on livestock animals, mostly sheep and goats, as well as cattle, and pigs (e.g., Wasse, 2002; Marom & Bar-Oz, 2013; Horwitz, 2002, 2017; Horwitz et al., 2002; Haber & Dayan, 2004; Getzov et al., 2009; Davis, 2012; Nativ et al., 2014; Namdar et al., 2021). Similar to that of the Late Pottery Neolithic, the Chalcolithic economy was also based on domesticated sheep, goats, cattle, and pigs. One of the influencing factors in the decision of which species to raise in this period was the local climate. While sheep and goats were relatively "easy" to raise in different environments, pigs and cattle required a nearby water source, and specific humid and colder environments (Grigson, 1987, 1995; Hesse 1990). Therefore, it is not surprising that caprines were common at most sites, while pigs and cattle were absent in the southern areas (Grigson, 1995: 251). For example, the drying of the natural springs made the northern Negev unsuitable for raising pigs, which had been an important part of some of the more northern settlements' economies (Levy, 1995).

The prosperity during the Chalcolithic period is characterized by the intensive growth of agricultural fields and farming (Levy et al., 1991), as well as wide market trade relations between Palestine, Egypt, Syria, and Mesopotamia (Grigson, 1995: 245). It is known that livestock animals were exploited for their meat; the question is, when did their exploitation for secondary products (milk, wool, and work) begin, and when did this exploitation become intense (see below Sect. 1.1)? This question is especially intriguing as the exploitation of cattle for its main secondary product, the plow, and the exploitation of caprines for milk are considered to be primary factors in promoting early urbanism in the Chalcolithic period (Greenfield & Arnold, 2015).

Although different aspects of the Chalcolithic period are widely discussed, and it is acknowledged that the provisioning of food is what drives human society (Grigson, 1995: 245), an updated comprehensive study to review the changes in animal economy throughout the Chalcolithic period is still lacking. Therefore, in this paper, we review the evidence for the animal economy in two phases of the Late Pottery Neolithic/Early Chalcolithic and Late Chalcolithic periods (see below Sect. 1.2 on the terminology). The review explores published data on species exploitation, herd management strategies, and paleo-pathologies, with the aim to understand the advent in the exploitation of animals, in relation to social processes of these periods.

---

[1] 4900–4500 BCE, dates according to Levy 1995: 226.

1.1 Exploitation for Secondary Products

Several millennia after the Neolithic revolution, animals were no longer used only for primary products (e.g., meat, leather, bones), but also for their secondary products (e.g., milk, wool, and work, and later for riding). The exploitation of animals for their secondary products soon became an important element of the animal economy, and played a major role in the construction of early complex societies and empires of the Bronze Age (Sherratt, 1981, 1983; Greenfield & Arnold, 2015).

When and where in the southern Levant the "secondary products revolution" began is still an unresolved question. Often, researchers follow Sherratt's suggestion that it began in the Near East during the late fifth millennium BCE (Sherratt, 1981: 280–282, 287). As for milk exploitation, Sherratt claimed that in order to produce milk, sheep, goats, and cattle would already have had to be fully domesticated. Otherwise, they would not have been capable of producing enough milk for their offspring as well as for human consumption. A special enzyme is required to digest milk (Silanikove et al., 2006), which prehistoric humans did not have (Sherratt, 1981: 276–277). Thus, secondary products, beginning with milk exploitation, required longer adaptation (Sherratt, 1981: 276–7; Levy, 1983), and could not develop soon after the Neolithic revolution (but see Bar-Yosef & Khazanov, 1992: 11–18).

Smith and Horwiz's (1984) study, which was based on measuring the cortical bone thickness in caprines' long bones from the Pre-Pottery Neolithic B (PPNB) to the Early Bronze Age, suggested that reduction of bone thickness that is related to milking caprines, started later than the Chalcolithic-Ghassulian period. Later studies argue that dairying exploitation began before cattle were used for traction and sheep for wool (Vigne & Helmer, 2007; Evershed et al., 2008; Allentuck, 2015), while these inventions occurred at different times at various locations (Greenfield, 2010; Marciniak, 2011). Cattle were found to be used for milk later than caprines, in 6500 BCE (Evershed et al., 2008), based on residue analysis of ceramic vessels from Shiqmim, Tell Sabi Abyad, and Sha'ar Hagolan.

As for wool exploitation, the first appearance of loom weights, and the decrease in flax (*Linum usitatissimum*) (Orrelle et al., 2012: 632) as a main component of the textile production, was dated to the Early Chalcolithic period (Shamir 2002, 2014), but studies that examine the advent of this exploitation through the faunal remains are lacking.

As for exploitation of work, cattle are the main candidate in these periods, as other work animals (donkeys) were domesticated later (Grigson, 2012). Cattle frequencies increase between the Pottery Neolithic and Iron Age, with the expansion of agriculture (Grigson, 1995: 252, 259–262). Their use for draft and traction is known from the mid-fourth millennium BCE in Mesopotamia (Sherratt, 1981: 267) and Europe (Greenfield, 2005), but lately it has been suggested that it should date earlier to 6000 BCE (Gaastra et al., 2018). A bull figurine carrying a churn from Ein Gedi implies that cattle were used to transport loads in the Chalcolithic period (Grigson, 1995: 267–268), while the churn might also indicate the production of butter, as was found at other sites from this period (e.g., Kaplan, 1954; Gopher, 2012: 1488–1489).

Apart from demographic differences, pathological conditions in livestock bones are used to understand the way they were treated and used (Bartosiewicz, 2013: 43; Bartosiewicz, 2021). Identification of the pathological types, the area in the skeleton where they appear, and the relative frequency in relation to the total number of individuals, can offer information about their lives. These conditions can result from different management strategies, environmental conditions, nutrition, healed bone fractures, and old age (Baker & Brothwell, 1980).

1.2 A Note on the Chalcolithic Period Terminology

The transition from the Pottery Neolithic to the Chalcolithic period is represented by the Wadi Raba culture, which, to date, has not been conventionally ascribed to either period. Garstang, in 1935 at his Jericho excavation, identified "Layer VIII" as Chalcolithic, and then in 1936 as Neolithic (Garstang, 1935; Garstang et al., 1936). When Kenyon excavated Jericho in the 1950s, this chronological term changed again. The Pottery Neolithic (PN) period was divided into two phases: PNA (equals Garstang's Layer IX) and PNB (equals Garstang's Layer VIII). Kenyon included the Ghassulian culture as part of the following Chalcolithic period, which was first identified at Tuleilat el-Ghassul (Kenyon, 1960). Later, when Kaplan discovered the Wadi Raba culture (Kaplan, 1958), its dating was parallel to Garstang's Layer VIII, and Kenyon's PNB. Today, while some scholars refer to Wadi Raba as Early Chalcolithic (Garfinkel, 2009), others still classify it as Pottery Neolithic, such as Gopher (2012) who attributes this phase to the "Second Neolithic Revolution" (Gopher, 2012: 1577). At the final stages of the Wadi Raba culture, it extended into central and northern Israel, as the new Post-Wadi Raba/Pre-Ghassulian culture (4700–4500 BCE). This entity had a rather short occurrence of only 200 years (Gopher, 2012: 1533). Thus, in this paper, when we use the term "Late Pottery Neolithic/Early Chalcolithic," we refer to assemblages attributed to the Wadi Raba and Pre-Ghassulian cultures (4900–4500 BCE).

Following this phase, the Chalcolithic-Ghassulian period emerged (4500–3500 BCE), which is also referred to as "Late Chalcolithic" (Garfinkel, 2009: 326). We refer to these phases when we use the term Late Chalcolithic-Ghassulian.

2 Models for Herd Management Strategies

To review the animal economy and compare various published faunal databases, we employed models of herd management strategies. These models are based on age and sex profiles, and they are used to identify exploitation for primary and secondary products (e.g., Payne, 1973; Helmer et al., 2007). The most prominent model is Payne's (1973) "kill-off patterns in sheep and goats," which is based on anthropological observation of the villages in Asvan in Eastern Anatolia. It describes three herd management models:

Model A: meat production – males are culled between the ages of two and three, when they reach their optimum weight gain (once they have finished growing and the resources required to raise them are no longer counterbalanced by their meat value). Young lambs are kept for future reproduction, and to preserve the herd's size in case of unpredicted losses. Young females are usually kept alive for future reproduction, but if not needed then they are culled at the age of two. Female caprines can deliver between 5 and 7 lambs, of which the fourth lamb is considered to be the best, while the younger lambs are of lower quality. Caprines can live for eight to ten years, but when a female fails to give birth after two years from the first birth, it is slaughtered for meat.

Model B: milk production – lambs are culled shortly after birth; their mothers' milk in its entirety is then collected for human use.

Model C: wool production – when both domesticated male and female sheep reach early adulthood, their wool is sheered. This process is repeated every summer. Thus, sheep are culled at a late age.

Helmer et al. (2007) created a broader model for herd exploitation, differentiating between sheep and goat meat, milk, and wool production. This new model was inferred from conversations with herders in southern France:

Meat type A – lambs are culled between six months to one year of age. This fits domestic household consumption.

Meat type B – Young adults are culled between one to two years of age. They are kept to this stage and fattened, in order to exploit their tender meat but still at the maximum weight. Culling also takes place in this model, in the case of barren females.

Milk type A – lambs are culled before weaning, between birth and three months. This model suggests high production of dairy for trade or commerce.

Milk type B – The unweaned lambs are kept separately from the rest of the flock, to preserve their mothers' milk. While the females have passed their production peak, usually between two to four years of age, and at times four to six years of age, they are culled for meat.

Fleece – Female sheep managed for wool are kept later than four years of age, but culled when their milk production, or their fleece quality, decrease, usually between four to six years of age. Nevertheless, it is noted that fine fleece results from human selection, which only began in the Bronze Age, while evidence for wool (as we know it today) appears even later (Ryder, 1992, 1993). Moreover, they argue that wool management will eventually look the same as for dairy, and thus they suggest it is the subjective interpretation of the researcher. Helmer et al. (2007) further refer to cattle herds managed for milk. In this case, the herd is composed of young calves and adult females, because in contrast to caprines, the female cow requires her offspring near her to produce milk. Calves are culled only after they reach their post-lactation stage, which is usually between six and twelve months.

Nevertheless, it should be noted that even though Payne's (1973) "kill-off patterns" model, and Helmer et al. (2007) model are generally used by zooarchaeologists, they are critiqued (e.g., Greenfield, 2005). The main issue regards the lack of statistical ability to distinguish between meat and milk models, or meat and wool models (Marom & Bar-Oz, 2009, but see Brochier, 2013), which often result from small bone sample sizes (Price et al., 2016).

3 Review of the Faunal Evidence

3.1 Fauna of the Late Pottery Neolithic/Early Chalcolithic Period

Data from 17 published faunal assemblages (Table 1) dated the Wadi Raba and Post-Wadi Raba/Pre-Ghassulian cultures (4900–4500 BCE), are reviewed here, revealing the economy of the Late Pottery Neolithic/Early Chalcolithic period. Most of the assemblages have a small sample size (<200 NISP), which in most cases made age and sex profiles impossible to analyze.

Caprines (combined sheep and goat category) are the most common species in all Wadi Raba and Post-Wadi Raba/Pre-Ghassulian assemblages (Table 2), except in Yiftahel, where gazelles are the most common species, representing 43% of all identified specimens.

Mortality profiles of caprines are similar in all Wadi Raba assemblages, as young adults were culled between 1.5 to two or three years (Table 3). Caprines gain their optimum weight during those years and this pattern testifies that they were slaughtered for their meat (Payne, 1973: Model A, meat production; Helmer et al., 2007: Meat type B). In Hagoshrim, the caprine age profile is similar in all Neolithic phases, which suggested continuity in exploitation of meat until Wadi Raba. This is true also for Yiftahel, as caprines were raised for meat during Jericho IX and Wadi Raba cultures (Namdar et al., 2021). In Wadi Raba Abu Zureiq, and Post-Wadi-Raba/Pre-Ghassulian Abu-Ghosh, researchers suggest that caprines were, possibly, exploited for milk in addition to meat (Horwitz, 2002; Milevski et al., 2015). These assumptions rely on very few elements that could be estimated for their age, of caprines older than two years, thus, they cannot be conclusive. For other assemblages, the sample size was too small and thus, no conclusions were made regarding the demographic profiles, such as in Kfar Samir (NISP:8), Magadim (NISP:1), Hanaton (NISP:78,92), Nahal Betzet II (NISP:25), and Arad el-Samra (NISP:133).

In addition to caprines, pigs and cattle dominated the economy, and their presence suggests mixed farming and pastoralism. The preference for raising either more pigs or cattle probably depended in this period on the environment and local climate. All Wadi Raba sites presented here are in the Mediterranean zone, with wet winters and ample vegetation, and thus, suitable for raising both pigs and cattle (Harris, 1987: 73). The differences between cattle and pig frequencies in the Carmel

Table 1 Chalcolithic sites, their total mammal's assemblage size (NISP), and most common species

Period	Culture	Geographical area	Site	Total NISP	Common species	References
Late Neolithic/ early chalcolithic	Wadi Raba (4900–4700 BCE)	Carmel	Neve yam	491	Cattle	Horwitz et al. (2006)
			Kfar Galim	31	Pig	Horwitz et al. (2002)
			Tel Hariz	106	Cattle	Davis (2012)
		Menashe hills	Nahal Zehora II		Caprines	
		Galilee	Hanaton	78	Caprines	Nativ et al. (2014)
			Ahihud	1259	Pig	Namdar et al. (2021)
			Yiftahel	858	Gazelles	
			Abu Zureiq	146	Cattle	Horwitz (2002)
			Tel Dan	63	Cattle	Horwitz (1987)
			Tel Eli	64	Pig	Jarman (1974)
		Hula valley	Nahal Betzet II	25	Caprines	Getzov et al. (2009)
			Arad El- Samra	59	Caprines	
			Hagoshrim	3850	Caprines	Haber et al. (2004)
	Post Wadi Raba/ Pre-Ghassulian (4700–4500 BCE)	Galilee	Hanaton	92	Cattle	Nativ et al. (2014)
		Judean Hills	Abu gosh	138	Caprines and pig	Milevski et al. (2015)
			Motza	168	Caprines	Namdar (2019)

(continued)

Table 1 (continued)

Period	Culture	Geographical area	Site	Total NISP	Common species	References
Late chalcolithic	Ghassulian (4500–3500 BCE)	Lod Valley	Shoham (north) cave 4	698	Caprines	Horwitz (2007)
		Galilee	Marj Rabba	2410	Caprines	Price et al. (2013)
			Marj Rabba (pit 559C)	3720	Caprines	Hil et al. (2016)
			Marj Rabba (Bulding I)	485	Gazelles	Price et al. (2016)
		Negev	Shiqmim	416	Caprines	Grigson (1987); Levy et al. (1991)
			Gilat	6706	Caprines	Grigson (2006)
			Horvat hor	93	Caprines	Horwitz (1990)
		Jordan Valley	Teleilat Ghassul	1108	Caprines	Bourke et al. (2000)
			Tell el-Mafjer	1026	Caprines	Al-Zawahra (2008)
			Tel Tsaf	14,380	Caprines	Hill (2011)
		Judean Hills	Yesodot (Khirbet umm el-Kalkha)	161	Cattle	Sapir-Hen (2022)
			Beqo'a	33	Caprines	Maher (2018)

Table 2 The main species (NISP%) in Late Neolithic/Early Chalcolithic sites. (Reference in Table 1)

Culture	Site	Caprines	Cattle	Pigs	Gazelle/Deer
Wadi Raba	Neve yam	34%	36%	26%	4%
	Kfar Galim	4%	28%	68%	0%
	Tel Hariz	18%	61%	16%	4%
	Hanaton	40%	25%	27%	8%
	Ahihud	25%	21%	39%	15%
	Yiftahel	44%	6%	9%	41%
	Abu Zureiq	27%	49%	22%	3%
	Tel Dan	24%	60%	16%	0%
	Tel Eli	30%	17%	43%	10%
	Nahal Betzet II	44%	20%	36%	0%
	Arad El- Samra	37%	36%	20%	7%
	Hagoshrim	50%	22%	12%	10%
	Nahal Zehora II (stratum I)	43%	13%	26%	17%
	Nahal Zehora II (stratum II)	48%	14%	27%	8%
Post Wadi Raba/ pre-Ghassulian	Hanaton	20%	40%	37%	3%
	Abu gosh	43%	11%	43%	2%
	Motza	37%	11%	31%	22%

($\chi2 = 21.50$, $p < 0.0001$, $dF = 2$, Cramer's $V = 0.23$), and in the Galilee ($\chi2 = 67.30$, $p < 0.0001$, $dF = 5$, Cramer's $V = 0.28$) are significant, in contrast to their differences in the Hula Valley ($\chi2 = 2.10$, $p = 0.3521$, $dF = 2$, Cramer's $V = 0.51$). When pigs are more common than cattle, it can imply lower intensity of agriculture, which can be related to the local landscape, the site's function, and cultural preferences (Harris, 1987: 73; Hesse, 1990; Grigson, 1995: 255).

In most Wadi Raba sites, cattle exploitation was less intense in comparison to caprines but more common in comparison to pig exploitation, such as in Tel Hariz, Abu Zureiq, Tel Dan, and Arad El- Samra. In older excavations, high representation of cattle can result from a bias toward collecting larger and easily identifiable fragments, but in recent excavations, the protocol for collecting faunal remains is more adequate. The high frequency of cattle is often correlated to an agricultural motivation of the population (Grigson, 1995: 252, 259–262). However, this frequency should be considered in combination with other evidence such as the herds' demography and notification of any pathological lesions. In case cattle were used for labor, there is a preference to keep both females and males to adulthood (Lyman, 1994; Greenfield, 2010).

In Neve Yam, Kfar Galim, Yiftahel, Abu Zureiq, Tel Eli, and Abu Gosh, cattle were kept to adulthood, but it was suggested that they were only used for meat. In Kfar Galim and Yiftahel, it has been suggested that cattle were used to some degree for labor, and possibly even milk. These sites presented large numbers of adult

Table 3 Economic exploitation of Late Neolithic/Early Chalcolithic sites (**Demography** = aging and sexing, m = months, y = years; **Exploitation:** original publication, as was interpreted by the authors of publications referred here. **Current paper,** as suggested by us; **Hunting intensity:** Low <2%, Medium 2%–4%, High >5%, Very high >20%). (Site references are in Table 1)

Culture	Site	Caprines Demography	Exploitation (original publication)	Exploitation (Current paper)	Cattle Demography	Exploitation (origin)	Exploitation (Current)	Pigs	Hunting intensity
Wadi Raba	Neve yam	Culled young under 21 m, four adults 3-4 year	No conclusion	Meat and possible milk	Culled adults older than 40 m	Meat	Meat and possible labor	Domesticated and wild. Young under 20 m	Medium
	Kfar Galim	One young 6-12 m	Meat	Meat	Adults	Meat and possible milk	Meat and possible labor	One young less than 24 m	None
	Kfar Samir	No data							None
	Magadim	No data							None
	Tel Hariz	One young less than 1 year, two young adults 1-2 year, one adult 3-4 year	Meat	Meat	Two young less than 1 year, and one 1–1.5 year, one 2 year	Meat	Meat	Domesticated and wild. All young less than 1 year, one adult 3.5 year.	Medium
	Hanaton	No data							High
	Ahihud	Culled mostly young adults 18-30 m	Meat	Meat	Culled young adults 1.5–2.5 year. None survived to adulthood	Meat	Meat	Culled mostly young-adults 2–3 year. Some survived to 4-5 year. All domesticated	High
	Yiftahel	Survived young adults 18-30 m, culled old 30-48 m	Meat	Meat	Culled between 1.5–3 year. Some survived to 3.5–4 year	Meat, some maybe for labor	Meat and possible labor	Culled mostly old 4-5 year. All domesticated	Very high
	Abu Zurik	Mostly adults over 2 year	Meat and possible milk	Meat and possible milk	Some kept to adulthood	Meat and possible labor and milk	Meat and possible labor	Mostly young, one 6 m, one 12–16 m, and one 17–22 m	Medium
	Tel Dan	Young	No conclusion	Meat	Young	No conclusion	Meat	Only wild boar	None

		Culled young adults over 2 year	Meat	Meat	Culled young adults over 2 year	Meat	Meat	Culled young 6–12 m and 2 year	High
	Tel Eli								
	Nahal Betzet II	No data							None
	Arad El-Samra	No data							High
	Hagoshrim	No data	Meat	No data	No data	Meat	No data	Culling young, fully domesticated	High
	Nahal Zehora II	Culled young adults 2–3 year	Meat	Meat and possible milk	No data	Meat	No data	No data	High
Post Wadi Raba/ pre-Ghassulian	Hanaton	No data							Low
	Abu gosh	One young 10 m, one 13–16 m, one young adult 2.5–3 year	Young for meat, adults milk or reproduction		One young adult and one adult	No conclusion	No conclusion	Mostly young less than 10 m, three young adults 2–2.5 year	Low
	Motza	Culled young adults 12–30 m	Meat		Survived until 2.5 year	Meat	Meat	Culled young 7–8 m and young adults 2–3 year	High

cattle. In Abu Zureiq, exploitation for labor has also been suggested, but this assumption was based on only one fused bone of an adult individual. In Motza, cattle were probably not used for work, as there are no fused elements older than 2.5 years. If we consider that training cattle for draft or traction requires knowledge and skills, as well as land to cultivate and produce enough crops for cattle and humans (Halstead & Isaakidou, 2011: 62), during the PN cattle could not be tamed for labor so close to their domestication (Namdar et al., 2021).

In Post-Wadi Raba/Pre-Ghassulian Abu Gosh caprines and pigs were equally represented (29%), which express the growing importance of pigs in the economy. In contrast to cattle and caprines, pigs cannot be used for secondary products. Nevertheless, they are an important source of protein, due to their high caloric meat and fat, which no other livestock can supply (Marom & Bar-Oz, 2013). Moreover, their numbers can increase fast, as a female pig can deliver several offspring in one birth, a couple of times a year (Nelson, 1998: 68). When human populations turned sedentary, pigs were easy to raise (Nelson, 1998: 67). Pigs probably also maintained an important part of daily life, consuming human waste (Dursteler, 2020: 223) and thus preventing the spread of disease (Grigson, 2007).

Pigs were usually culled after their second year, when they had reached their optimum weight, as can be seen in Ahihud, Yiftahel, Tel Eli, and Motza. Still, at most sites, age profiles suggest that the majority of pigs were culled young, at less than a year old, while in some cases a few were kept to adulthood, probably for reproduction. Culling young and young-adult pigs was suitable for domestic populations, which needed to restrain pig population growth while sustaining their meat to keep other livestock for herding and secondary products. If the herd was small, population growth was under control, and as pork was not the main meat supply, then pigs could be raised to adulthood (Nelson, 1998: 67).

The only site that showed high frequencies of wild animals was Yiftahel, with 43% of the assemblage. Gazelles were also highly frequent during the Middle Pre-Pottery Neolithic period (MPPNB), representing 69% of all identified specimens. During the later period in the Late Pre-Pottery Neolithic (LPPNB) and the beginning of the Pre-Pottery Neolithic C (PPNC), their frequency decreased to 5.6% (Sapir-Hen et al., 2016). During the Pottery Neolithic period (Jericho IX culture), gazelle hunting was resumed, and their frequency increased to 12% (Namdar et al., 2021). Hunting intensified during Wadi Raba, just to decline again in the EB I to only 4% (Horwitz & Lernau, 2003). The unique case of Yiftahel could be linked to the natural cold habitat of the site, with rich vegetation and a flowing river (Horwitz & Lernau, 2003). And yet, no other sites in northern Israel show similar patterns. On the contrary, the frequency of hunted species is much lower, and in some assemblages, there is no evidence of hunting at all (e.g., Kfar Galim, Kfar Samir, Magadim, Tel Dan, and Nahal Betzet II).

3.2 Fauna of the Late Chalcolithic-Ghassulian Period

Data from 12 published faunal assemblages (Table 1) dated the Late Chalcolithic-Ghassulian (4500–3500 BCE), are reviewed here, focusing on species abundance and livestock exploitation strategies. Although the number of assemblages is smaller in comparison to the Late Pottery Neolithic/Early Chalcolithic assemblages, the total sample size of the identified specimens is much larger.

Livestock animals assembled most of the Late Chalcolithic-Ghassulian economy, with caprines as the most common species in all assemblages (Table 4). Cattle and pigs are the second most common species, followed by donkeys and in some cases also dogs. Wild species, mainly gazelles, are scarce and represent between 1% and 2% of all identified specimens. The decrease in hunting range is linked to the growing intensity of mixed farming and pastoralist economy (Rowan & Golden, 2009).

Based on age estimation, and in rare cases also available sex profiles, the possibility that caprines and cattle were exploited for secondary products seems more probable and more conclusive than in the earlier period as described in Sect. 3.1. At most sites, such as Shoham (Noth), Marj Rabba, Tel Tsaf, and Beqo'a, caprines were kept to adulthood (older than 3 years), and at some sites, such as Marj Rabba, Gilat, and Teleilat Ghassoul, mostly young caprines were culled for meat (Payne, 1973: Model A, meat production; Helmer et al., 2007: meat type A). In Gilat, most goats were also identified as females. The combination of culling juveniles, keeping other animals to older ages, and a preference for females, suggest that these herds might have been exploited for their milk (Payne, 1973: Model B, milk production; Helmer et al., 2007: Milk type A and B). The results are inconclusive only in Shiqmim, as only two young individuals were identified (Table 5).

Table 4 The main species (NISP%) in Late Chalcolithic period sites (Ghassulian culture). (References in Table 1)

Site	Caprines (%)	Cattle (%)	Pigs (%)	Gazelle/Deer (%)
Shoham (North) Cave 4	63	20	15	3
Marj Rabba	54	11	33	2
Marj Rabba (Pit 559C)	55	14	29	2
Marj Rabba (Building I)	29	4	13	53
Shiqmim	85	14	0	1
Gilat	69	15	14	2
Horvat Hor	98	2	0	0
Teleilat Ghassul	76	11	11	2
Tell el-Mafjer	51	16	31	1
Tel Tsaf	46	16	36	3
Yesodot (Khirbet Umm el-Kalkha)	31	66	1	2
Beqo'a	69	25	6	0

Table 5 Economic exploitation of Late Chalcolithic sites (**Demography** = aging and sexing, m = months, y = years; **Exploitation: original publication**, as was interpreted by the authors of publications referred here. **Current paper, Exploitation**, as suggested by us; **Hunting intensity**: Low <2%, Medium 2%–4%, High >5%, Very high >20%). Site references are in Table 1

Culture	Site	Caprines Demography	Exploitation (original publication)	Exploitation (Current paper)	Cattle Demography	Exploitation (origin)	Exploitation (Current)	Pigs	Hunting intensity
Ghassulian (4500–3500 BCE)	Shoham (north) cave 4	Mostly adults	Meat	Meat	Mostly adults	Meat	Meat and possible labor	Mostly young	Low
	Marj Rabba	Culling young and keeping some to adulthood	Primary and secondary	Meat and possible milk	Culling young before 3 year	Meat	Meat	Most culled before 2 year, some kept after 2 year	High
	Shiqmim	Two young	No conclusion		One young	No conclusion		Absent	Low
	Gilat	Culling young adults under 2 year. Mostly female goats	Meat and wool. Maybe milk		Culling old at 5 year	Meat and milk. No labor (no pathologies)	Possible labor	Culling at 1 year and 2 year	Medium
	Horvat hor	Two young under 1 year, and three over 2.5 year	No data	Meat and possible milk	No data			None	None
	Teleilat Ghassul	Culling young	Primary and secondary	Meat	Mostly adults	Meat, milk, reproduction	Possible labor	Younger	Low
	Tel el-Mafjer	Culled between 1–3 year	Meat and wool	Meat	Mostly older than 3 year	Meat and labor	Possible labor	Culled between 1–2 year, some adults 3.5 year	Low

Site							
Tel Tsaf	Adults	Meat, milk, and wool	Meat and possible milk	Adults	Labor	Possible labor	Culling young adults 2.5 year. Some kept to adulthood 3.5 year	Low
Yesodot (Khirbet Umm el-Kalkha)	Young adult 1.5–2 year and adults 3–3.5 year	No conclusion	Meat	Adults 3-4y	Labor	Possible labor	No data	Low
Beqo'a	Young adults 2–3 year	Primary and secondary	Meat and possible milk	No data	Labor	No conclusion	No data	Low

Wool is another secondary product discussed in relation to adult sheep. Still, the assumption that sheep were exploited for this product should be tested based on ageing sheep elements. However, in most studies, reliance is on the ageing profile for the total caprine herd (goats and sheep). In Tel Tsaf, although both sheep and goats were slaughtered for meat when they reached optimum weight at two years of age, sheep were kept to an older age (Payne, 1973: Model A, meat production; Helmer et al., 2007: Meat type B). These differences in ages suggest that sheep were not only exploited for milk but also for wool (Hill, 2011: 164) (Payne, 1973: Model C: wool production; Helmer et al., 2007: fleece). In Marj Rabba, the researchers suggested that the textile industry could still be based on flax rather than wool of sheep, which were exploited, but not in a specialized way (Price et al., 2013).

While paleo-pathologies are often scarce in relation to the total assemblage (Namdar et al., forthcoming), paleo-pathologies are more common in Late Chalcolithic sites than in previous periods and are found especially in livestock and not in wild species. Most published pathological cases were recorded in cattle (Grigson, 1987; Hill, 2011; Price et al., 2013; Price et al., 2020), and attributed to degenerative joint diseases, in relation to draught, traction and carrying heavy loads. Pathological cases driven by these activities are usually located on the feet and vertebrae of cattle, horses, and donkeys (e.g., Mariani-Costantini et al., 1996, Johannsen, 2005, Fabis, 2005, Telldahl, 2002, Markovic' et al., 2014).

In Shiqmim, one pathology on a metapodial of an ox was related to draft (Grigson, 1987). In Marj Rabba, cattle's distal metapodial, phalanges, and pelvis were identified with different pathological outgrowths, suggested as resulting from traction (Price et al., 2013). In later studies, based on stable isotopes, these pathologies were identified as the result of long walks, as cattle were exchanged between different regions (Price et al., 2020). In Tel Tsaf, cattle were raised to adulthood, and some individuals developed exostoses and osteoarthritis on the lower limb bones, suggesting they had been used for plowing fields. In addition, this site reveals an increase in cattle's relative abundance and degree of pathologies during the Chalcolithic period, in comparison to earlier phases (Hill, 2011: 164–166).

In addition to cattle, a new "beast of burden" was domesticated during the Chalcolithic period, the donkey (*Equids asinus*), which was descended from the African wild ass (*Equus africanus*) (Milevski & Horwitz, 2019: 97). It originated in Egypt during the pre-Dynastic/Dynastic period (4600–4400 BC) and spread from there to the Sudan and southern Levant (Stine et al., 2008). Recently, donkey domestication was identified through genetic analyses in three main areas: the Near East, northeast Africa, and the Arabian Peninsula (Rosenbom et al., 2015).

In the Chalcolithic southern Levant, Equid remains (either domesticated or wild) were identified in many sites, such as Gilat (Grigson, 2006), Shiqmim (Grigson, 1987), Abu Matar (Josien, 1955), Horvat Beter (Angress, 1959), and Wadi Gaza (Ducos, 1968). It was proposed that during the Late Chalcolithic period, donkeys were used to transport copper ores from mines in Faynan to the Beersheva Valley, which can suggest that donkeys were already exploited in an extensive and progressive way (Levy, 2007). And yet, donkey remains frequencies were rather low (between 1%–2%), and they became an important part of the economy only in the later Early Bronze Age (with an average of 10%) (Milevski & Horwitz, 2019: 101). A decrease in donkey body size is observed between the Chalcolithic and the Early Bronze Age (Grigson, 2012), suggesting they were fully domesticated by that time.

When domesticated, donkeys were used in Mesopotamia for draft and plowing (Jans & Bretschneider, 1998), while in the southern Levant it was mainly done by cattle. Donkeys were presumed to be used as pack animals, and to transport commodities, based on foot pathologies, texts (Partridge, 1996: 95–99), and ceramic figurines from the Early Bronze Age (e.g., Milevski, 2011). And yet, it is still unknown whether donkeys were ridden in the Chalcolithic, or just walked in "donkey trains" (Grigson, 2012).

Pigs, either domesticated or wild, were highly important sources of meat for ancient humans, while in the Chalcolithic period they were either highly consumed or not at all (see Rowan & Golden, 2009, Table 1; Fig. 3; and Grigson, 1987; Gilead, 1989; Hesse, 1990; Josien, 1955; Horwitz, 1990). In our data, it seems that pigs were slaughtered at the peak of their weight, mostly between one and two years, while some were kept to adulthood (Table 5) probably for reproduction, such as at Marj Rabba, Tel el-Mafjer, and Tel Tsaf.

The need for water sources and moist environments made it difficult to raise pigs in drier areas (Grigson, 1995; Levy et al., 1991). Pig remains were indeed absent at Chalcolithic sites with only 200 mm of rainfall yearly, such as Shiqmim (Grigson, 1987), Tel Abu Matar (Josien, 1955), Bir es-Safadi (Josien, 1955), and Horvat Hor (Horwitz, 1990). In contrast, pigs were highly common at sites located in the northern Negev with over 250 mm of rainfall yearly, such as Gilat (Levy, 1981), and Wadi Gaza D (Ducos, 1971) (see Levy et al., 1991, Table 5: 408; Rowan & Golden, 2009, Table 3). In Teleilat Ghassul, pigs were culled young, perhaps to replace caprines and cattle as main meat producers, while these were held to adulthood for secondary products (Bourke et al., 2000).

Finally, although wild animals constitute only 1–2% of most assemblages, in Building I in Marj Rabba gazelles are the majority with 55% of all the assemblage (Table 4). Most of the gazelle bones in this assemblage are half-burned articulated phalanges, leading the authors to reconstruct the building as part of a ritualistic place (Price et al., 2016).

4 Conclusions

We presented here, for the first time, a detailed review of the Chalcolithic economy, based on previous zooarchaeological publications. We included Wadi Raba and post Wadi Raba assemblages, to examine the transition between the Neolithic to the Chalcolithic periods. Based on species abundance, demographic profiles, and site distribution, we found great economic differences between the earlier phases and the later Chalcolithic period.

The Late Pottery Neolithic/Early Chalcolithic subsistence economy relied on caprines, cattle and pigs, exploited only for their meat. In this period livestock animals were the base of the human diet, while game hunting, mostly gazelles, decreased with time. At large, as the local climate and their surroundings are different between the sites, the variation in livestock and wild animals frequencies also differ. But, considering the age profiles as well, it seems that the animal economy of the Wadi Raba cultures corresponds more to the earlier Pottery Neolithic economy (Jericho and Lodian phases; Namdar et al., 2021) and differs more from the later Chalcolithic-Ghassulian.

In the Chalcolithic-Ghassulian period, as caprine frequencies increased in comparison to other species, pastoralism became more common. Among the different types of pastoralism (such as 'mobile pastoralism', and 'nomadic pastoralism') the most common type is the transhumant pastoralism, which is based on permanent settlements, with seasonal movement of the herd. This type of pastoralism can also be called "village-based herding", which set the ground for the emergence of early farming communities in the later periods (Abdi, 2003). As a possible result, evidence for secondary products only presented itself from the Late Chalcolithic-Ghassulian. The first exploitation for secondary products was done with sheep and goats for dairy, perhaps only butter in this stage. These assumptions rely mostly on demographic profiles but are supported by the appearance of the churn in ceramic assemblages (Gopher, 2012: 1488–1489)Sheep may also have been used, to some degree, for wool, according to the high number of adults at some sites, and the appearance of loom weights in the Early Chalcolithic period (Orrelle et al., 2012: 632; Shamir, 2014). Still, the selective selection of sheep for fleece was suggested to only have begun at that time, which enabled the development of wool for textile in later periods. Evolutionary developments based on human selection are part of a long process, which almost always presented their outcome much later in time. Finally, it should be noted that when interpretating wool exploitation, sheep demographic models cannot be the sole evidence, as it resembles the milk exploitation model.

It is still not clear whether cattle were used for dairy, as sex profiles were almost always impossible to provide. Nevertheless, cattle kept to adulthood are often assumed to be maintained for labor and plowing fields. These activities can be the reason for pathological outgrowth developed in cattle feet bones. And yet, pathologies, especially those caused by degenerative joint diseases, are scarce. Additionally, the domestication of donkeys in the Late Chalcolithic period, can imply the growing need for beasts of burden, in addition to cattle. Donkeys were used mainly for long-distance trade, while in the following Early Bronze Age they played a greater role in the economy.

In conclusion, this study shows that the changes in animal economy of the Chalcolithic period were gradual. While the early phase of the Chalcolithic period was a continuation of the earlier Neolithic economy, the later phase of the Chalcolithic-Ghassulian period saw an important development in livestock economy and agriculture, reflected in the establishment of the exploitation of secondary products, specifically cattle for work and caprines for milk. The advent of the exploitation of these products had far-reaching impact on the economy and on human society (reviewed in Allentuck, 2015). Exploitation of livestock for work enabled the exploitation of vaster fields in a more efficient way. It intensified the agricultural products, while freeing humans for other activities. Exploiting caprines for milk enabled an additional food source. At the same time, it created social complexity, as owning cattle necessitated water and food, investment in training, and large fields (Greenfield & Arnold, 2015). Owning caprines for milk necessitated keeping them near the settlements in pens for daily contact (Hubbard, 2010). Owning donkeys enabled long-distance trade of wool and other products (Milevski & Horwitz, 2019: 101). These changes transformed animal roles, from meat suppliers to economic investments. Thus, exploiting animals for their secondary products promoted the ownership of lands, property, and animals. These economic changes enabled the growth and expansion of settlements, trade relations with Syria (Grigson, 1995: 245), and thus promoted social changes and the rise of urbanism and empires in the following Early Bronze Age.

References

Abdi, K. (2003). The early development of pastoralism in the central Zagros Mountains. *Journal of World Prehistory, 17*(4), 395–448. https://doi.org/10.1023/B:JOWO.0000020195.39133.4c

Allentuck, A. (2015). Temporalities of human-livestock relationships in the late prehistory of the Southern Levant. *Journal of Social Archaeology, 15*(1), 94–115.

Al-Zawahra, M. (2008). The faunal remains from Tell el-Mafjer, a Chalcolithic site in the lower Jordan valley, Palestine. *Archaeozoology of the Near East, VIII*, 431–449.

Angress, S. (1959). Mammal remains from Horvat Beter (Beersheva). *Atiqot, 11*, 53–71.

Baker, J., & Brothwell, D. (1980). *Animal diseases in archaeology*. Academic.

Bartosiewicz, L. (2013). *Shuffling nags, lame ducks*. Oxbow Books.

Bartosiewicz, L. (2021). What is a rare disease in animal paleopathology? *International Journal of Paleopathology, 33*, 13–24.

Bar-Yosef, O., & Khazanov, A. M. (1992). *Pastoralism in the Levant: Archaeological materials in anthropological perspective*. Prehistory Pr.

Bourke, S., Lovell, J., Sparks, R., Seaton, P., Mairs, L., & Meadows, J. (2000). Preliminary report on a second and third season of renewed excavations at Teleilat Ghassul by the university of Sydney, 1995/1997. *Annual of the Department of Antiquities of Jordan, 44*, 37–89.

Brochier, J. É. (2013). The use and abuse of culling profiles in recent zooarchaeological studies: Some methodological comments on "frequency correction" and its consequences. *Journal of Archaeological Science, 40*(2), 1416–1420.

Davis, S. J. M. (2012). Animal bones at the Nahal Zehora sites. In A. Gopher (Ed.), *Village communities of the Pottery Neolithic period in the Menashe Hills, Israel. Archaeological investigations at the sites of Nahal Zehora* (Vol. III, pp. 1258–1320). Emery and Claire Yass Publications in Archaeology.

Ducos, P. (1968). *L'Origine des Animaux Domestiques en Palestine*. Publications de l'Institut de Préhistoire de l'Université de Bordeaux, Mémoire 6), Delmas Mémoire 6). Delmas.

Dursteler, E. R. (2020). The 'abominable pig' and the 'mother of all vices': Pork, wine, and the culinary clash of civilizations in the early modern Mediterranean. In K. Dmitriev, J. Hauser, & B. Orfali (Eds.), *Insatiable appetite food as cultural signifier in the Middle East and beyond* (pp. 214–241). Brill.

Evershed, R. P., Payne, S., Sherratt, A. G., Copley, M. S., Coolidge, J., Urem-Kotsu, D., Kotsakis, K., Özdoğan, M., Özdoğan, A. E., Nieuwenhuyse, O., Akkermans, P. M. M. G., Bailey, D., Andeescu, R. R., Campbell, S., Farid, S., Hodder, I., Yalman, N., Özbasaran, M., Bcakc, E.,

Garfinkel, Y., Levy, T., & Burton, M. M. (2008). Earliest date for milk use in the near East and Southeastern Europe linked to cattle herding. *Nature, 455*, 528–531.

Fabis, M. (2005). Pathological alteration of cattle skeletons- evidence for the draught exploitation of animals? In J. Davies, M. Fabis, I. Mainland, M. Richards, & R. Thomas (Eds.), *Diet and health in past animal populations* (Proceedings of the 9th conference of the International Council of Archaeozoology, Durham, August 2002) (pp. 58–62). Oxbow Books.

Garfinkel, Y. (2009). The transition from Neolithic to Chalcolithic in the Southern Levant: The material culture sequence. In J. J. Shea & D. E. Lieberman (Eds.), *Transitions in prehistory* (Essays in Honor of Ofer Bar-Yosef). Oxbow Books.

Garstang, J. (1935). Jericho: City and necropolis (fifth report). *Annals of Archaeology and Anthropology, 22*, 143–168.

Garstang, J., Ben-Dor, I., & Fitzgerald, G. M. (1936). Jericho: City and necropolis (report for sixth and concluding season). *Annals of Archaeology and Anthropology, 23*, 67–90.

Getzov, N., Barzilai, O., Le Dosseur, G., Eirikh-Rose, A., Ktalav, I., Marder, O., Marom, N., & Milevski, I. (2009). Nahal Betzet II and Ard el Samra: Two late prehistoric sites and settlement patterns in the Akko plain. *Journal of the Israel Prehistoric Society, 39*, 81–158.

Ducos, P. (1971). Le cheval de Soleb. In M. S. Giorgini (Ed.), *Soleb 11-Les Nécropoles* (pp. 471–479). Florence.

Gopher, A. (2012). Village communities of the Pottery Neolithic period in the Menashe Hills, Israel. In *Archaeological investigations at the sites of Nahal Zehora* (Vol. III, pp. 1258–1320). Emery and Claire Yass Publications in Archaeology.

Greenberg, R. (2019). *The archaeology of the bronze age levant*. Cambridge University Press.

Greenfield, H. J. (2005). A reconsideration of the secondary products revolution: 20 years of research in the Central Balkans. In J. Mulville & A. Outram (Eds.), *The zooarachaeology of milk and fats. Proceedings of the 9th ICAZ conference, Durham 2002* (pp. 14–31). Oxbow Books.

Greenfield, H. J. (2010). The secondary products revolution: The past, the present and the future. *World Archaeology, 42*(1), 29–54.

Greenfield, H. J., & Arnold, E. R. (2015). 'Go(a)t milk?' New perspectives on the zooarchaeological evidence for the earliest intensification of dairying in South Eastern Europe. *World Archaeology, 47*(5), 792–818.

Grigson, C. (1987). Shiqmim: Pastoralism and other aspects of animal management in the Chalcolithic of the Northern Negev. In T. E. Levy (Ed.), *Shiqmim I, studies concerning chalcolithic societies in the Northern Negev Desert, Israel* (pp. 219–241). Oxbow Books.

Grigson, C. (1995). Plough and pasture in the early economy of the southern Levant. In T. E. Levy (Ed.), *The archaeology of society in the holy land* (pp. 245–263). Leicester University Press.

Grigson, C. (2006). Farming? Feasting? Herding? Large mammals from the Chalcolithic of Gilat. In T. E. Levy (Ed.), *Archaeology, anthropology, and cult: The sanctuary at Gilat, Israel* (pp. 215–319). Equinox Publishing.

Grigson, C. (2007). Culture, ecology, and pigs from the 5th to the 3rd millennium be around the Fertile Crescent. In U. Albarella, K. Dobney, A. Ervynck, & P. Rowley- Conwy (Eds.), *Pigs and humans: 10,000 years of interaction* (pp. 83–108). Oxford University Press.

Grigson, C. (2012). Size matters-donkeys and horses in the prehistory of the Southernmost Levant. *Paléorient, 38*(1/2), 185–201.

Haber, A., & Dayan, T. (2004). Analyzing the process of domestication: Hagoshrim as a case study. *Journal of Archaeological Science, 31*(11), 1587–1601.

Halstead, P., & Isaakidou, V. (2011). Revolutionary secondary products: The development and significance of milking, animal-traction and wool-gathering in later prehistoric Europe and the near East. In T. C. Wilkinson, S. Sherrat, & J. Bennet (Eds.), *Interweaving worlds: Systemic interactions in Eurasia,7th to 1st Millennia BC* (pp. 61–76). Oxbow Books.

Harris, M. (1987). *The sacred cow and the abominable pig: Riddles of food and culture*. Touchstone Books.

Helmer, D., Gourichon, L., & Vila, E. (2007). The development of the exploitation of products from Capra and Ovis (meat, milk and fleece) from the PPNB to the early bronze in the northern near East (8700 to 2000 BC cal.). *Anthropozoologica, 42*(2), 41–69.

Hesse, B. (1990). Pig lovers and pig haters: Patterns of Palestinian pork production. *Journal of Ethnobiology, 10*, 195–225.

Hill, A. C. (2011). *Specialized pastoralism and Social stratification-analysis of the Fauna from Chalcolithic Tel Tsaf, Israel.* PhD dissertation. University of Connecticut.

Horwitz, K. L. (1987). Animal remains from the Pottery Neolithic levels at Tel Dan. *Mitekufat Haeven- Journal of the Israel Prehistoric Society, 20*, 114–118.

Horwitz, L. K. (1990). Animal bones from the site of Horvat Hor. *Mitekufat Ha'even: Journal of the Israel Prehistoric Society, 23*, 153–159.

Horwitz, L. K. (2002). Fauna from the Wadi Raba site of Abu Zureiq. *Israel Exploration Journal, 52*(2), 167–178.

Horwitz, L. K. (2007). Faunal remains from late Chalcolithic–bronze age Dwelling and Burial Caves at Shoham (North), Lod valley. *Atiqot, 55*, 1–15.

Horwitz, L. K. (2017). Pottery Neolithic (Yarmukian) faunal remains from Hamadiya. In A. Gopher, R. Gophna, R. Eyal, & Y. Paz (Eds.), *Jacob Kaplan's excavations of protohistoric sites 1950s–1980s* (Vol. I–II, pp. 503–515). Eisenbrauns.

Horwitz, L. K., & Lernau, O. (2003). Temporal and spatial variation in Neolithic caprine exploitation strategies: A case study of fauna from the site of Yiftah'el (Israel). *Paléorient, 29*(1), 19–58.

Horwitz, L. K., Galili, E., Sharvit, J., & Lernau, O. (2002). Fauna from five submerged Pottery Neolithic sites off the Carmel coast. *Journal of the Israel Prehistory Society, 32*, 147–174.

Horwitz, L., Galili, E., & Lernau, O. (2006). Fauna from the submerged Pottery Neolithic site of Newe Yam, Northern Israel. *Journal of Israel Prehistoric Society, 36*, 139–171.

Hubbard, E. M. (2010). Livestock and people in a middle Chalcolithic settlement: A micromorphological investigation from Tel Tsaf, Israel. *Antiquity, 84*, 1123–1134.

Jans, G., & Joachim, B. (1998). Wagon and chariot representations in the early dynastic Glyptic: 'Tey came to tell Beydar with wagon and equid'. In M. Lebeau (Ed.), *About Subartu: Studies devoted to upper Mesopotamia: II. culture, society, image* (pp. 155–194). Brepols.

Jarman, M. (1974). The fauna and economy of Tel Eli. *Mitekufat Haeven, 12*, 50–70.

Johannsen, N. N. (2005). Paleopathology and Neolithic cattle traction: Methodological issues and archaeological perspectives. In J. Davies, M. Fabis, I. Mainland, M. Richards, & R. Thomas (Eds.), *Diet and health in past animal populations* (Proceedings of the 9th conference of the international council of Archaeozoology, Durham, August 2002) (pp. 39–51). Oxbow Books.

Josien, T. (1955). La faune chalcolithique des gisements Palestiniens de Bir es-Safudi et Abou Matar. *Israel Exploration Journal, 5*, 246–258.

Kaplan, J. (1958). Excavations at Wadi Rabah. *Israel Exploration Journal, 8*(3), 149–160.

Kaplan, L. (1954). Two chalcolithic vessels from Palestine. *Palestine Exploration Journal, 86*, 97–101.

Kenyon, K. H. (1960). *Archaeology in the Holy Land.* E. Benn.

Levy, T. E. (1981). *Chalcolithic settlement and subsistence in the Northern Negev Désert.* University Microfilms.

Levy, T. E. (1983). The emergence of specialized pastoralism in the Southern Levant. *World Archaeology, 15*, 15–36.

Levy, T. E. (1995). Cult, metallurgy and rank societies-chalcolithic period (CA.4500-3500 BCE). In T. E. Levy (Ed.), *The archaeology of society in the holy land* (pp. 226–244). Leicester University Press.

Levy, T. E. (2007). Journey to the copper age. archaeology in the Holy Land. .

Levy, T. E., Grigson, C., Holl, A., Goldberg, P., Rowan, Y., & Smith, P. (1991). Subterranean settlement and adaptation in the Negev Desert, c. 4500–3700 BC. *National Geographic Research and Exploration, 7*(4), 394–413.

Lyman, R. L. (1994). *Vertebrate Taphonomy.* Cambridge University Press.

Maher, E. F. (2018). Chalcolithic and early bronze age IB Fauna from Beqo'a. *Atiqot, 90*, 67–74.

Marciniak, A. (2011). The secondary products revolution: Empirical evidence and its current zooarchaeological critique. *Journal of World Prehistory, 24*, 117–130.

Mariani-Costantini, R. M., Ottini, L., & Capasso, L. (1996). On Paleopathological fossil bovid phalanx from the late middle Pleistocene Aurelia Fromation, near Rome. *Journal of Paleopathology, 8*(3), 169–176.

Marković, N., Stevanović, O., Nešić, V., Marinković, D., Krstić, N., Nedeljković, D., Radmanović, D., & Janeczek, M. (2014). Paleopathological study of cattle and horse bone remains of the ancient Roman city of Sirmium (Pannonia/Serbia). *Revue de Médecine Vétérinaire, 165*(3–4), 77–88.

Marom, N., & Bar-Oz, G. (2009). Culling profiles: The indeterminacy of archeozoological data to survivorship curve modelling of sheep and goat herd maintenance strategies. *Journal of Archaeological Science, 36*, 1184–1187.

Marom, N., & Bar-Oz, G. (2013). The prey pathway: A regional history of cattle (*Bos taurus*) and pig (*sus scrofa*) domestication in the Northern Jordan valley, Israel. *PLoS One, 8*(2), 1–13.

Milevski, I. (2011). *Early bronze goods exchange in the Southern Levant: A marxist perspective*. Equinox Publishing.

Milevski, I., & Horwitz, L. K. (2019). Domestication of the donkey (*Equus asinus*) in the southern Levant: Archaeozoology, iconography and economy. In R. Kowner, G. Bar-Oz, M. Biran, M. Shahar, & G. Shelach-Lavi (Eds.), *Animals and human Society in Asia* (pp. 93–148). Springer International Publishing. https://doi.org/10.1007/978-3-030-24363-0_4

Milevski, I., Marder, O., Mienis, H. K., & Horwitz, L. K. (2015). Abu Ghosh, jasmine street: A Pre-Ghassulian site in the Judean Hills. *Atiqot, 82*, 85–130.

Namdar, L. (2019). *Human-animal relationships through the remains of animal bones, during the late Pottery Neolithic period in the Southern Levant*. M.A thesis, Tel Aviv University (in Hebrew).

Namdar, L., Vardi, J., Paz, Y., & Sapir- Hen, L. (2021). Variation in economic specialization is revealed through the study of Pottery Neolithic faunal assemblages from the Southern Levant. *Archaeological and Anthropological science, 13*(207), 1–19.

Namdar, L., Bartosiewicz, L., May, H., & Sapir- Hen, L. (forthcoming). Human – Livestock interaction: Examining paleopathology evidence from the Neolithic to early modern period in the southern levant. *Journal of Social Archaeology. 15*(1).

Nativ, A., Shimelmitz, R., Agha, N., Ktalav, I., & Rosenberg, D. (2014). Hanaton: Interim report on a Neolithic- Chalcolithic settlement in the lower galilee. *Journal of the Israel Prehistoric Society, Mitekufat Haeven, 44*, 117–147.

Nelson, S. M. (1998). *Ancestors for the pigs: Pigs in prehistory*. University of Pennsylvania Museum of Archaeology and Anthropology.

Orrelle, E., Eyal, R., & Gopher, A. (2012). Spindle whorls and their blanks. In A. Gopher (Ed.), *Village communities of the Pottery Neolithic period in the Menashe Hills, Israel. Archaeological investigations at the sites of Nahal Zehora* (Vol. III, pp. 632–656). Emery and Claire Yass Publications in Archaeology.

Partridge, R. (1996). *Transport in ancient Egypt*. Stacey International.

Payne, S. (1973). Kill-off patterns in sheep and goats: The mandibles from Asvan Kale. *Anatolian Studies, 23*, 281–303.

Price, M. D., Buckley, M., Rowan, Y. M., & Kersel, M. (2013). Animal management strategies during the Chalcolithic in the lower galilee: New data from Marj Rabba. *Paléorient, 39*, 183–200.

Price, M. D., Hill, A. C., Rowan, Y. M., & Kersel, M. M. (2016). Gazelles, liminality, and Chalcolithic ritual: A case study from Marj Rabba, Israel. *BASOR, 376*, 7–27.

Price, M. D., Rowan, Y. M., Kersel, M. M., & Makarewicz, C. A. (2020). Fodder, pasture, and the development of complex society in the Chalcolithic: Isotopic perspectives on animal husbandry at Marj Rabba. *Archaeological and Anthropological Science, 12*(95), 1–14.

Rosenbom, S., Costa, V., Chen, S., Khalatbari, L., Yusefi, G. H., Abdukadir, A., Yangzom, C., Kebede, F., Teclai, R., Yohannes, H., Hagos, F., Moehlman, P. D., & Beja-Pereira, A. (2015). Reassessing the evolutionary history of Ass-like equids: Insights from patterns of genetic variation in contemporary extant populations. *Molecular Phylogenetics and Evolution, 85*, 88–96. https://doi.org/10.1016/j.ympev.2015.01.005

Rowan, Y. M., & Golden, J. (2009). The Chalcolithic period of the Southern Levant: A synthetic review. *Journal of World Prehistory, 22*, 1–92.

Ryder, M. L. (1992). The interaction between biological and technological change during the development of different fleece types in sheep. *Anthropozoologica, 16*, 131–140.

Ryder, M. L. (1993). The use of goat hair. An introductory historical review. *Anthropozoologica, 17*, 37–46.

Sapir-Hen, L. (2022). The post-ghassulian and middle bronze age faunal assemblages. *Salvage Excavation Reports, 11*, 241–249.

Sapir-Hen, L., Dayan, T., Khalaily, H., & Munro, N. (2016). Human hunting and nascent animal management at middle pre-pottery Neolithic Yiftah'el, Israel. *PLoS One, 11*(7), 1–18.

Shamir, O. (2002). Textile production in Eretz-Israel. *Michmanim, 16*, 19–32.

Shamir, O. (2014). Textiles, basketry and other organic artifacts of the Chalcolithic period in the southern Levant. In M. Sebbane, O. Misch-Brandel, & D. M. Master (Eds.), *Masters of fire: Copper age art from Israel* (pp. 138–152). Princeton University Art Museum.

Sherratt, A. (1981). Plough and pastoralism: Aspects of the secondary products revolution. In I. Hodder, G. Isaac, & N. Hammond (Eds.), *Pattern of the past: Studies in honour of David Clarke* (pp. 261–306). Cambridge University Press.

Sherratt, A. (1983). The secondary exploitation of animals in the old world. *World Archaeology, 15*(1), 90–104.

Silanikove, N., Merin, U., & Leitner, G. (2006). Physiological role of indigenous milk enzymes: An overview of an evolving picture. *International Dairy Journal, 16*(6), 533–545.

Smith, P., & Horwitz, L. K. (1984). Radiographic evidence for changing patterns of animal exploitation in the Southern Levant. *Journal of Archaeological Science, 11*, 467–475.

Stine, R., Marshall, F., Peters, J., Pilgram, T., Adams, M. D., & O'Connor, D. (2008). Domestication of the donkey: Timing, processes, and indicators. *Proceedings of the National Academy of Sciences, 105*(10), 3715–3720.

Telldahl, Y. (2002). Can palaeopathology be used as evidence for draught animals? In J. Davies, M. Fabis, I. Mainland, M. Richards, & R. Thomas (Eds.), *Diet and health in past animal populations. Current research and future directions* (Proceedings of the 9th ICAZ conference, Durham) (pp. 63–67). Oxbow Books.

Vigne, J. D., & Helmer, D. (2007). Was milk a "secondary product" in the old world neolithisation process? Its role in the domestication of cattle, sheep and goats. *Anthropozoologica, 42*(2), 9–40.

Wasse, A. (2002). Final results of an analysis of the sheep and goat bones from Ain Ghazal, Jordan. *Levant, 34*, 59–82.

Butchering Patterns and Technology in a Chalcolithic Settlement: Analysis of the Butchered Fauna from Shiqmim, Israel

Haskel J. Greenfield 🄳 and Jeremy A. Beller

Abstract This paper presents the analysis of the butchered animal bones recovered from the Chalcolithic site of Shiqmim, excavated by Thomas E. Levy in [1993]. Despite the fact that the bones are fragmented, it is possible to document the types of tools used in the process as well as the stages of butchering. The butchered taxa are primarily domestic taxa and exhibit a wide range of butchering related activities (skinning to toolmaking). The results of light optical and scanning electron microscope (SEM) readings indicate that all butchering slice marks were made by unretouched chipped stone tool implements (flakes/blades). It is possible to deduce that the occupants of Shiqmim relied on both young and old livestock for consumption and had not integrated metal technology into such quotidian activities as animal carcass processing. This is the first time that Chalcolithic butchering processes have been systematically investigated. The results lay the foundation for comparison to later periods, when metal technologies were introduced.

Keywords Shiqmim · Chalcolithic · Negev · Zooarchaeology · Fauna · Animal butchering · Chipped stone tools · Lithics · Scanning electron microscopy

Foreword HJG met Tom many years ago on one of his many trips to Israel. HJG had just published his article on the Secondary Products Revolution (Greenfield, 1988). Tom made several cogent comments about how the model related to the Chalcolithic of the Levant, the time period and region in which Tom was interested (Levy, 1988). Tom, Steve Rosen, and HJG subsequently gathered at a coffee shop on Ben Yehuda Street to talk about archaeological issues and discovered the wealth

H. J. Greenfield (✉)
University of Manitoba and St. Paul's College, Winnipeg, MB, Canada
e-mail: haskel.greenfield@umanitoba.ca

J. A. Beller
Simon Fraser University, Burnaby, BC, Canada
e-mail: beller.jeremy.a@gmail.com

© The Author(s), under exclusive license to Springer Nature Switzerland AG 2023
E. Ben-Yosef, I. W. N. Jones (eds.), *"And in Length of Days Understanding" (Job 12:12): Essays on Archaeology in the Eastern Mediterranean and Beyond in Honor of Thomas E. Levy*, Interdisciplinary Contributions to Archaeology, https://doi.org/10.1007/978-3-031-27330-8_5

of common interests. Unfortunately, HJG was deeply involved in his Balkan research at the time and was not able to follow up on Tom's suggestions. Many years later, HJG had the opportunity to begin to work in Israel and reached out to Tom for permission to analyze the Shiqmim and other faunal assemblages that he had excavated. Since then, they regularly keep in touch at meetings and through correspondence. HJG invited Beller, his former student, to join him in this publication. Together with Tom, HJG and Beller have previously published data on the faunal assemblage from Nahal Tillah, an EB I site that Tom excavated.

1 Introduction

In recent years, it has become possible to determine the type of technology employed in the butchering of animals based upon the microscopic analysis of butchering marks (e.g., chop, slice, scrape) on the bones. The butchering patterns and style are reconstructed from the location and frequency of the type and distribution of marks on each osteological element. The specific frequencies and distribution of marks can vary over time and cross-culturally and are typically influenced by the available technology (Burke, 2001). These provide insight into the nature of carcass processing, diet, specialization, and technology of past communities (Binford, 1981; Cope, 2004; Lyman, 1987, 1994).

The Chalcolithic is a period of dramatic change in the Near East (ca. 4500–3600 BCE Cal ^{14}C). It is when new technologies develop, namely copper metallurgy, and an expansion of regional populations and the beginnings of specialized production, including pastoralism. These are all evident at Shiqmim, Israel, a Chalcolithic settlement excavated by Thomas E. Levy (Golden et al., 2001; Grigson, 1995; Levy et al., 2006, 2007; Whitcher et al., 1998).

In this contribution to Tom's festschrift volume, the faunal remains from Shiqmim are reanalyzed from the perspective of butchering process and technology. The questions investigated in this study are: which raw material (stone or metal) and tool types (e.g., flake, blade, scraper) were utilized, the state of the implements (e.g., sharp, dull, retouched), and the nature of the butchering process? This contribution is another component in the study of the transition from a stone- to a metal-based butchering technology in the Levant (Greenfield, 2004, 2005, 2008, 2013, 2017, 2021; Greenfield et al., 2018, 2021; Greenfield & Brown, 2016; Greenfield & Horwitz, 2012; Saidel et al., 2006).

2 The Site of Shiqmim

Shiqmim is a single period site that dates to the fifth millennium BCE. It is situated on the banks of a seasonal watercourse (the *Nahal Be'er Sheva*) in the northern Negev Desert of Israel (Fig. 1). Excavations of the site began in 1979 and continued until 1993. They were co-directed by Thomas Levy (University of California,

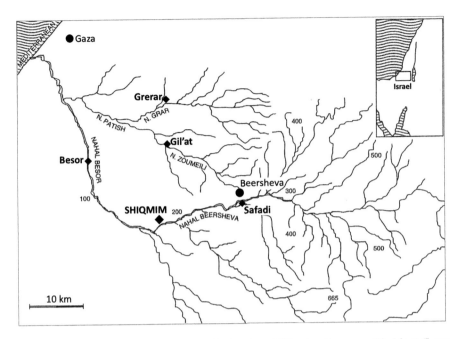

Fig. 1 Map of Nahal Be'er Sheva depicting the location of Shiqmim. (Image modified from (Levy et al., 2006, p. 42))

San Diego) and David Alon (Hebrew Union College, Jerusalem). The aim was to identify the processes that led to the rise of early social complexity in the southern Levant during the late fifth and early fourth millennium BCE (Levy, 1995). The site is about 10 ha in size with a number of domestic residences and middens.

The lithic assemblage includes a wide variety of axes, adzes, blades, borers, chisels, cores, denticulates, flakes, scrapers, and debitage. Most of the chipped stone tools were likely produced from local chert and other raw materials (Levy & Rosen, 1987). There is evidence for metal (copper) use and/or production at the site in the form of awls, axes, chisel, mace head, crucibles, and slag (Levy et al., 1991; Levy & Shalev, 1989). While the chipped stone (Levy et al., 1991; Levy & Rosen, 1987; Rowan & Levy, 1991) and metal assemblages (Golden et al., 2001; Hansen, 2021; Oakberg et al., 2000) from the site have yielded insights into the nature of stone tool use and the evolution of early copper metallurgy, neither sets of studies addressed whether the stone and/or metal tools were used as part of the butchering toolkit.

3 Methods and Materials

All identifiable and unidentifiable bones and bone splinters were sorted and examined with a hand-held magnifying glass for evidence of butchering marks. Potential butchering marks were further examined with a medium-power light optical microscope to ensure that they were not taphonomic in origin (e.g., modern or ancient scratches, root marks) or anatomical features (e.g., grooves made by blood vessels). Each bone identified with slicing marks was subsequently subjected to a full taxonomic, taphonomic, and cultural-modification analysis (e.g., including identification of taxon, domestic or wild status, symmetry, part of the element). The type of butchery damage was also noted through the identification of the location, type, and number of marks. All interpretations related to the butchering process (e.g., slaughtering, skinning, filleting) were based on these data.

The data were quantified using two measures: Number of Individual Specimens (NISP) and Number of Butchering Incidences (NBI). NISP quantifies a single specimen once even though there may be many different incidents of butchering on it. In contrast, the NBI quantifies the number of butchering episodes on the same specimen. A butchering incidence is when there is an isolated mark or a cluster of marks that are part of the same action. Marks found on different faces of the same bone and/or at different locations on the same face of the bone would correspond to separate incidences, as would different types of butchering marks (e.g., bashes, chops, slices). Thus, when two separate butchering grooves were found at either end of a bone, the NISP was 1 and NBI was 2. NISP is useful when quantifying by taxon in order not to inflate species counts. It is very susceptible to the influence of differential fragmentation and may overrepresent what was there. For butchering analyses, the NBI is a more suitable measure of butchering patterns (Beller et al., 2022b; Greenfield et al., 2016, 2018; Greenfield & Brown, 2016).

After the initial stage of analysis, each specimen with a slice mark was examined in greater detail under a light optical microscope. Based on this level of analysis, the raw material of the implement used in the butchering process (stone or metal) could be determined. Interpretations of butchering technology were based on experimental research conducted by HJG and the method is described in detail elsewhere (Greenfield, 1999, 2000, 2002, 2006). All identifications and conclusions made about specimens during the analysis was conducted by both the primary analyst (HJG) and at least one assistant. All conclusions as to the type of tool and its raw material had to be agreed upon by both analysts to ensure that a firm identification was made for the data to be included in the analysis, thus ensuring a level of accuracy not normally reached in such studies.

To ensure a high level of accuracy in the identification of the raw material and the type of butchering technology, the morphologies of the slice marks were analyzed with a scanning electron microscope (SEM). Silicone molds were made of slice marks and transported back to the University of Manitoba. In the SEM, the molds of the slice marks appear as reverse images – rather than being troughs in a medium (bone), they appear as raised peaks.

4 The General Faunal Assemblage

The faunal assemblage was analyzed many years ago by Caroline Grigson (Grigson, 1987, 1989, 1995; Levy et al., 1991) and Sarah Whitcher Kansa (Whitcher et al., 1998). However, neither analyses dealt with the butchered remains nor with butchering technology, the subject at hand. For example, Whitcher et al. (1998, p. 112) note the following about the butchering of cattle at the site:

> The most convincing evidence for cattle being used for meat at Shiqmim is seen in cut marks on an articulating group of limb bones (calcaneum, astragalus, centroquatial and metatarsal) found in a pit. The calcaneum and astragalus have heavy cut marks on the lateral side, indicating an attempt to sever the extremity from the meat-bearing upper limb. The unfused calcaneum reveals that the animal was less than three years old when it died, suggesting that it was intentionally killed at a young age.

The current study investigates aspects of the butchering from only the 1993 faunal assemblage (Whitcher et al., 1998). Therefore, only the zooarchaeological data from this part of the larger assemblage are summarized next. Most of these faunal remains derive from pits, namely secondary rubbish/midden deposits (Whitcher et al., 1998, p. 111). They are curated as part of the National Natural History Collections, Institute of Earth Sciences of The Hebrew University of Jerusalem, and available for future analyses.

A total of 1558 bones was recovered during the 1993 excavations, of which 1504 were identified to a specific taxon (Whitcher et al., 1998, pp. 104, table 101). Most of the identifiable assemblage is composed of domestic animals (96.9%), with the rest composed of wild taxa (3.1%). Wild animals include gazelle (0.8%), hare (0.4%), cat (0.3%), fox (<0.1%), rodents (0.7%), birds (0.6%), amphibians (frog), and fish (0.1%) in very small quantities (Whitcher et al., 1998, table 1). The domestic assemblage is dominated by sheep and goats (85%, with a sheep:goat ratio of 1.2:1). There are much lower frequencies of cattle (11.5%) and equids (0.13%). Dogs (0.3%) are the only other domestic fauna found at the site (Whitcher et al., 1998, Table 1).

As noted above, each of the bones described in the following sections was originally identified by Sarah Whitcher Kansa, who gave each a unique identification (ID) number. This sequence of numbers was written on the tag for each bone bag in the curatorial facility (Jerusalem). For the butchering analysis, each bone with slice marks was separated and assigned a sequence of identification numbers beginning with #200 for each specimen. Each analyzed butchered specimen was placed in its own plastic bag and stored in a box in the Jerusalem curatorial facility. The silicone molds are stored at the University of Manitoba. Both numbering systems are synchronized in Appendix 1.

5 The Butchered Assemblage

Of the more general taxonomic level of identification, only 63 specimens with clear butchering marks were identified on them (representing 5.1% of the assemblage) (Table 1). Those with impact fractures were not recorded, as the means by which they shattered could not always be determined at the time of original lab analysis (2003). This is a similar frequency to what is seen in other prehistoric assemblages from terrestrial sites in the region (Greenfield, 2013; Greenfield et al., 2016).

Table 1 Taxa of the butchered assemblage by phase by NISP

Taxon		Phase						Phase				
		Unknown	I	II	I/II	Total		Unknown	I	II	I/II	Total
Unknown	Unknown (total)		1	4		5			4.8%	12.9%		7.9%
	Large mammal		1	4		5			4.8%	12.9%		7.9%
Domestic	Domestic (total)	5	19	27	6	57		100.0%	90.5%	87.1%	100.0%	90.5%
	Bos taurus			4	2	6				12.9%	33.3%	9.5%
	Capra hircus	2	8	9	1	20		40.0%	38.1%	29.0%	16.7%	31.7%
	Ovis aries	1	4	7	3	15		20.0%	19.0%	22.6%	50.0%	23.8%
	Ovis/Capra	2	7	7		16		40.0%	33.3%	22.6%		25.4%
Wild	Wild (total)		1			1			4.8%			1.6%
	Lepus sp.		1			1			4.8%			1.6%
Grand total		5	21	31	6	63		100.0%	100.0%	100.0%	100.0%	100.0%

The most common taxon identified in the butchered assemblage are similar to those in the general assemblage: goat, sheep, and cattle. Ovicaprines combined (sheep and goat) form the largest component (81%). These are broken down as *Capra hircus* (31.7%) + *Ovis aries* (23.8%) + *Ovis/Capra* (25.4%). This is followed by cattle (*Bos taurus*) at 9.5%. A similar percentage (7.9%) could only be identified as indeterminate large mammal. Only one specimen in the butchered assemblage was identified as a wild animal: hare (1.6%). No other wild or domestic animals were found (e.g., equids, dog, gazelle, fox, rodent, cat, fish, bird, and frog).

While the majority of remains (96.9%) are domesticated taxa in the general assemblage (Whitcher et al., 1998), they are less dominant in the butchered assemblage (90.5%). This is partly because we include the taxonomically indeterminate large mammal remains. If these are domestic cattle (as we suspect), then the frequencies of taxa are the same for the general and the butchered assemblage.

Unfortunately, the small overall number of butchered remains and frequencies of taxa do not permit the secure identification of temporal variation. These small sample sizes are subject to such random variations that it is of little use to consider their temporal variability except in the most general terms. Both butchered domestic livestock and wild taxa decrease from Phase I (90.5%, 4.8% respectively) to Phase II (87.1%, 0% respectively). Part of this change is attributable to the variability in large mammals which triples in frequency over time from Phase I (4.8%) to Phase II (12.9%). If the large mammal remains are attributed to cattle, then the frequency of domestic taxa increases from Phase I (95.3%) to Phase II (100%).

The majority of the specimens are of adult (46%) and subadult (29%) age (Table 2). The collective Ovicaprines exhibit age profiles slightly skewed toward older categories. The indeterminate *Ovis/Capra* are largely subadult (50%) and juvenile (25%). Sheep have a greater distribution with subadult (33%) followed by subadult/adult (27%) and adult (27%). Goats are predominantly represented by older specimens with adults (75%) in a high frequency followed by subadult and subadult/adult (both 17%). The profiles are slightly different for cattle where specimens of an older age are identified (adult 67%). Similarly, indeterminate large mammals are also represented by older profiles (subadult/adult 60%, adult 40%). The lone *Lepus* sp. specimen is an adult specimen.

6 Taphonomy of the Assemblage

Two types of natural causes of bone attrition were recorded on the butchered assemblage from Shiqmim: weathering and gnawing (Tables 3 and 4). The bones are for the most part lightly weathered (77.8%). Far fewer exhibit a medium level of weathering (20.6%) where the compact surface (periosteum) is slightly cracked and/or damaged (slightly removed or pitted). Very few (1.6%) were heavily weathered. Many sources can account for such weathering, including carbonate intrusion into bone cavities, soil acidity, water activity in the soil, root action, and exposure to the elements. None of the bones were abraded or water-worn as if they were being

Table 2 Age profiles of the butchered assemblage by NISP

Taxon		Age categories					
		Infant	Juvenile	Subadult	Subadult/adult	Adult	Total
Unknown	Unknown (total)				3	2	5
	Large mammal				3	2	5
Domestic	Domestic (total)	2	6	18	5	26	57
	Bos taurus			1	1	4	6
	Capra hircus	1		4		15	20
	Ovis aries		2	5	4	4	15
	Ovis/Capra	1	4	8		3	16
Wild	Wild (total)					1	1
	Lepus sp.					1	1
Grand total		2	6	18	8	29	63
		Infant	Juvenile	Subadult	Subadult/adult	Adult	Total
Unknown	Unknown (total)				60%	40%	100%
	Large mammal				60%	40%	100%
Domestic	Domestic (total)	4%	11%	32%	9%	46%	100%
	Bos taurus			17%	17%	67%	100%
	Capra hircus	5%		20%		75%	100%
	Ovis aries		13%	33%	27%	27%	100%
	Ovis/Capra	6%	25%	50%		19%	100%
Wild	Wild (total)					100%	100%
	Lepus sp.					100%	100%
Total		3%	10%	29%	13%	46%	100%

Table 3 Weathering patterns of the butchered assemblage by NISP

Taxon	Weathering							
	Light	Medium	Heavy	Total	Light	Medium	Heavy	Total
Bos taurus	3	3		6	50.0%	50.0%	0.0%	100.0%
Capra hircus	16	4		20	80.0%	20.0%	0.0%	100.0%
Large mammal	3	2		5	60.0%	40.0%	0.0%	100.0%
Lepus sp.	1			1	100.0%	0.0%	0.0%	100.0%
Ovis aries	14		1	15	93.3%	0.0%	6.7%	100.0%
Ovis/Capra	12	4		16	75.0%	25.0%	0.0%	100.0%
Total	49	13	1	63	77.8%	20.6%	1.6%	100.0%
Ovicaprines combined	42			51				82.4%

actively rolled around and then redeposited. The frequencies of weathered bone vary wildly, largely because of the small numbers in the butchered assemblage. But if we consider only the larger sample sizes (sheep, goat, and sheep/goat), they are similar to the overall pattern of weathering (82.4% light).

Only a single butchered bones exhibited any evidence of canid gnawing (Table 4). The absence of natural causes of attrition on most of the bones indicates that the major sources of damage and attrition in the assemblage are likely to be cultural in origin.

Table 4 Gnawing patterns of the butchered assemblage by NISP

Taxon	Canid	None	Total	Canid	None	Total
Bos taurus		6	6	0.0%	100.0%	100.0%
Capra hircus	1	19	20	5.0%	95.0%	100.0%
Large mammal		5	5	0.0%	100.0%	100.0%
Lepus sp.		1	1	0.0%	100.0%	100.0%
Ovis aries		15	15	0.0%	100.0%	100.0%
Ovis/Capra		16	16	0.0%	100.0%	100.0%
Total	1	62	63	1.6%	98.4%	100.0%

Table 5 Occurrence of calcium carbonate on the butchered assemblage by NISP

Taxon	Yes	No	Total	Yes	No	Total
Bos taurus	1	5	6	16.7%	83.3%	100.0%
Capra hircus	1	19	20	5.0%	95.0%	100.0%
Large mammal		5	5	0.0%	100.0%	100.0%
Lepus sp.		1	1	0.0%	100.0%	100.0%
Ovis aries		15	15	0.0%	100.0%	100.0%
Ovis/Capra	1	15	16	6.2%	93.8%	100.0%
Total	3	60	63	4.8%	95.2%	100.0%

At some sites in the region, there is substantial calcium carbonate concretions that have developed on the surface of the bones. Its development is indicative of changing climatic and water conditions at the site after deposition. Such concretions hinder the search for microscopic butchering marks on the bone surface. At Shiqmim, there is little evidence of this problem where 93.7% of the bones do not exhibit it at all (Table 5).

Two types of cultural causes of bone modification beyond butchering were identified in the assemblage: heat treatment and tool/ornament manufacture (Tables 6 and 7). Basically, 95.2% of the assemblage showed no evidence of heat treatment. Only three butchered bones exhibited some evidence of having been cooked (burned and/or boiled). Cooking was evidenced in both medium (Ovicaprines) and large taxa (indeterminate). Thus, it is important to recognize that unbutchered bones do not necessarily show evidence of having been cooked. Butchering is a process which may or may not include cooking.

At other sites (e.g., Halif, Nahal Tillah, Tall Zirā'a, Tell eṣ-Ṣâfi/Gath), many of the bones with butchering marks exhibit evidence that they were culturally modified to be used as tools, game pieces, and/or ornaments. This should not be surprising since all the soft tissue must be removed from bones to enable them to be modified and/or used for a secondary function (Albaz et al., 2017; Beller et al., 2022b; Greenfield et al., 2018; Greenfield & Brown, 2016). At Shiqmim, we observed a similar pattern with a substantial relative frequency (23.8%) exhibiting evidence of both butchering and cultural modification (Table 7). All taxa in the butchered assemblage, except for Lepus sp. (hare), showed such evidence. This does not include the formal bone tools that were not available for this phase of the analysis.

Table 6 Heat treatment patterns of the butchered assemblage by NISP

	Heat treatment pattern								
Taxon	Burn-black	Burn-brown	Boiled	None	Total	Burn-black	Burn-brown	Boiled	None	Total
Bos taurus				6	6	0.0%	0.0%	0.0%	100.0%	100.0%
Capra hircus				20	20	0.0%	0.0%	0.0%	100.0%	100.0%
Large mammal			1	4	5	0.0%	0.0%	20.0%	80.0%	100.0%
Lepus sp.				1	1	0.0%	0.0%	0.0%	100.0%	100.0%
Ovis aries				15	15	0.0%	0.0%	0.0%	100.0%	100.0%
Ovis/Capra	1	1		14	16	6.3%	6.3%	0.0%	87.5%	100.0%
Total	1	1	1	60	63	1.6%	1.6%	1.6%	95.2%	100.0%

Table 7 Bone tools within the butchered assemblage by NISP

Taxon	Unknown tool	Game piece	None	Total	Unknown tool	Game piece	None	Total
Bos taurus	3		3	6	50.0%	0.0%	50.0%	100.0%
Capra hircus	2		18	20	10.0%	0.0%	90.0%	100.0%
Large mammal	4		1	5	80.0%	0.0%	20.0%	100.0%
Lepus sp.			1	1	0.0%	0.0%	100.0%	100.0%
Ovis aries	4	1	10	15	26.7%	6.7%	66.7%	100.0%
Ovis/Capra	1		15	16	6.3%	0.0%	93.8%	100.0%
Total	14	1	48	63	22.2%	1.6%	76.2%	100.0%

7 Butchering Patterns

A number of previous studies, including Binford (1978, 1981) and Lyman (1994), and the authors' personal observations of modern butchers and slaughterers were drawn upon for conclusions regarding the types of butchering activities in relation to the location of butchering marks. Several common activities and their indicative marks are listed in Table 8 and examples from the Shiqmim assemblage are found in Fig. 2. It is impossible to identify actual slaughter since animals can be killed in ways that do not leave evidence on the bones. However, some marks on neck vertebrae may indicate decapitation, possibily associated with slaughter. Fortunately, many stages of the butchering process are still evident in the assemblage.

A total of 89 butchering incidences are distributed among four taxa: sheep, goats, cattle, and hare (Table 9, Appendices 1 and 2). As is typical of prehistoric sites, most of the butchered specimens exhibit filleting activities (91%). Two specimens with saw marks were observed. In both cases, there were many slice marks in the same place to create a deep groove that mimics a saw (Fig. 2 - Specimen 262). Both were

Table 8 Diagnostic features of butchering activities

Activity	Mark	Location on skeleton	Purpose
Brain extraction	Chop	Cranium	Open cranium to access and remove brain
Disarticulation	Slice, chop	Typically around articular joints or facets	Calculated division of one bone from another, typically division of limb into smaller units
Dismemberment	Chop, bash, heavy slice	Typically a separation of a limb from the trunk regardless of articular joints	Forceful division of body regardless of anatomical joint location
Filleting	Slice, scrape	Typically shaft portions	Removal of meat around and along bones
Marrow extraction	Bash, chop	Shaft of long bones	Retrieval of marrow within interior shaft
Skinning	Slice	Mainly exterior processing, typically around the head and lower limb	Removal of hide and skin
Slaughter	Slice, chop	Typically around the neck or head	Intended to kill animal
Toolmaking	Slice	Anywhere, but mostly shafts of long bones	Removal of residual flesh to completely expose bone

Adapted from Beller et al. (2022b)

from domestic cattle and large mammal (probably *Bos taurus*) specimens. There were five scraping incidences to fillet meat off the bone – all limited to Ovicaprine specimens (sheep and goat). The relative frequency of slicing marks on both medium and large taxa was very similar (ca. 89–94%) which suggests that meat was similarly valued from sized animals and that despite the difference in size, it was filleted close to the bone. The lone chop mark occurs on the ventral face of the centrum of a goat atlas (Specimen 254). Such a strong blow in this location is indicative of decapitation or dismemberment, but possibly slaughter as well. The following sections discuss the distribution of butchering marks and their associated activities and refers to Appendix 2.

7.1 Goats

Twenty-two specimens of domestic goat (*Capra hircus*) displayed butchering marks (Fig. 3). These are found on a variety of elements including the trunk (vertebra), proximal front limb (humerus, scapula, radius, ulna), proximal hindlimb (innominate, femur, tibia), and distal limb (astragalus, metacarpus). Interestingly, no cranial fragments with butchering marks were found. Even so, this suggests that entire carcasses were processed at the site.

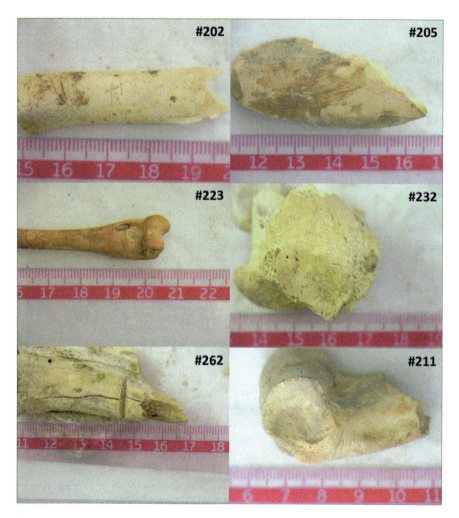

Fig. 2 Examples of butchering marks on the Shiqmim faunal assemblage. All grooves are slices made by unifacial unretouched chipped stone tools (flakes/blades), except on specimen #262, where the groove is made by sawing back and forth

Table 9 Occurrence of types of butchering marks within the butchered assemblage by NBI

Taxon	Mark type					Mark type %				
Row labels	Chop	Saw	Scrape	Slice	Total	Chop	Saw	Scrape	Slice	Total
Bos taurus		1		11	12		8.3%		91.7%	100.0%
Capra hircus	1		2	25	28	3.6%		7.1%	89.3%	100.0%
Large mammal		1		5	6		16.7%		83.3%	100.0%
Lepus sp.				1	1				100.0%	100.0%
Ovis aries			2	23	25			8.0%	92.0%	100.0%
Ovis/Capra			1	16	17			5.9%	94.1%	100.0%
Total	1	2	5	81	89	1.1%	2.2%	5.6%	91.0%	100.0%

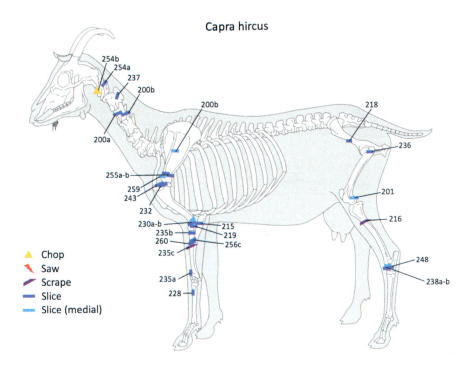

Fig. 3 Distribution of butchering marks on goats

Several stages of the butchering process were also present, including evidence for decapitation (around the epistropheus/2nd neck vertebra – Specimen #254), disarticulation between the joints of various vertebral (Specimens #200 and #237) and limb bones, filleting of the meat off bones, and skinning around the metapodia. One specimen also exhibited both slice and chop marks on the element (Specimen #254).

7.2 Sheep

Eighteen domestic sheep (*Ovis aries*) specimens displayed butchering marks (Fig. 4). These were found on a variety of elements including the trunk (vertebra), proximal front limb (humerus, scapula, radius, ulna), proximal hindlimb (innominate), and distal limb (metacarpus, astragalus, and phalange 1). There are more distal limb and fewer proximal hindlimb than in goats. This suggests that entire carcasses were processed at the site.

Several stages of the butchering process were present – i.e., decapitation (around the atlas/first neck vertebra – Specimens #246 and #222), disarticulation between the joints of various vertebral (Specimen #222) and limb bones (Specimens #204, #211, #220, #229, #239, #240, #242, #250, #256, and #257), filleting of meat (Specimens #204, #226, #229, #241, #256), and skinning around a posterior

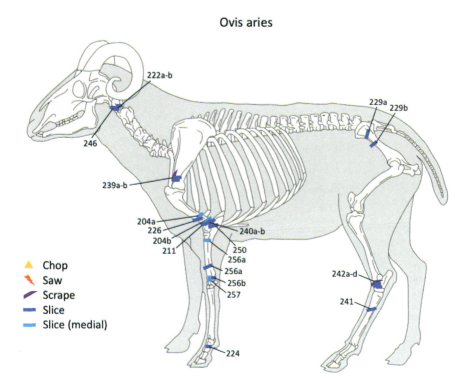

Fig. 4 Distribution of butchering marks on sheep

phalange 1 (Specimen #224). One specimen also exhibited both slice and chop marks on the element (Specimen #254). Similar to goats, no cranial fragments with butchering marks were found.

7.3 Sheep/Goat

The rib specimens with evidence of butchering (n = 3) are present among the indeterminate domestic sheep/goat specimens simply because of the difficulty of taxonomically distinguishing ribs between them. Hence, they are lumped together here. Their presence fills out the missing part of the carcass and again reinforces the evidence for household level of butchering of animals.

A smaller quantity and range of sheep/goat element types were identified. Only 16 indeterminate sheep/goat specimens displayed butchering marks. These were found on a variety of elements including the trunk (rib and vertebra – both cervical and sacrum), proximal front limb (humerus), proximal hindlimb (innominate and femur), and distal limb (metatarsus). For the first time, there were cranial elements present (mandible). This distribution helped to support our assertation that entire carcasses were processed at the site (Fig. 5).

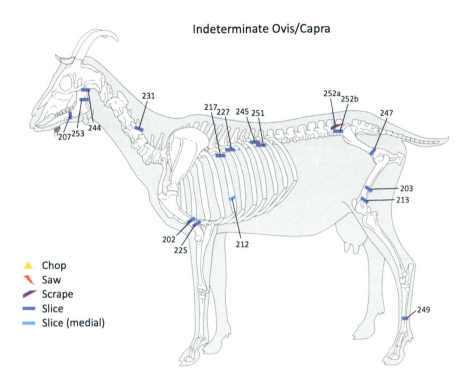

Fig. 5 Distribution of butchering marks on indeterminate Ovis/Capra

Only two stages of the butchering process were present: disarticulation of the mandible from the cranium (Specimens #207, #244, and #253), disarticulation between the joints of various vertebral (Specimens #231 and #252), ribs from vertebrae (Specimens #217, #245, and #251) and limb bones (Specimens #202, #213, #225, #247, and #249). There is no evidence of decapitation, filleting, or skinning. Similar to sheep and goats, no cranial fragments with butchering marks were found.

7.4 Cattle

A smaller quantity and range of domestic cattle specimens (*Bos taurus*) were identified. This number doubles if the large mammals are included. For analytical purposes, the two taxa are discussed separately even though the large mammals are likely the remains of cattle.

Only four types of elements were found representing the trunk (rib), proximal front limb (scapula), proximal hindlimb (innominate), and distal limb (metacarpus). This is a much smaller range of elements than seen in sheep and goats. Once again, no cranial elements were present (either cranium or mandible).

Only two stages of the butchering process were present: filleting (of meat off bones) and disarticulation (Fig. 6). The specimens with filleting activity (Specimens

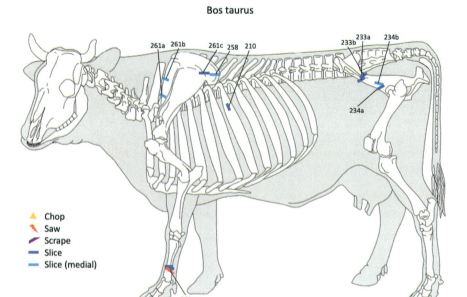

Fig. 6 Distribution of butchering marks on cattle

#210, #261 and #262) seem to be part of the toolmaking process. Also, Specimen #262 had marks that sawed back and forth to shape the bone into a tool of some sort. Disarticulation between limb bones was evident from the other three specimens (sacrum from innominate, innominate from femur, and scapula from humerus – Specimen #233, #234, #258, and #261).

7.5 Indeterminate Large Mammal

Among the six large mammal remains, five were long bones and one was a rib. All butchering marks represented filleting activity associated with bone tool production. Hence, it is less clear if entire carcasses of cattle were processed at the site based on the butchered remains. There was no evidence for decapitation or skinning. Similar to sheep and goats, no cranial fragments with butchering marks were found.

7.6 Hare

One specimen of an adult hare (*Lepus* sp.) was found, a distal humerus (Specimen #223). It had slice marks near the epiphyseal line, indicative of disarticulation and separation of the distal joint.

8 Butchering Technology

The technology, both raw material and tool types, can be determined through the evaluation of butchering marks and their groove morphology. The data in this section are quantified by Number of Butchering Incidence (NBI).

8.1 Types of Chipped Stone Tool Marks

For the most part, certain marks (i.e., bashes) could not be recorded systematically. They were numerous as evidenced by the number of fractured bones (nearly the entire assemblage) and those with conchoidal fractures and spalls from impact. This suggests that ground stone axes were used primarily to break open bones.

Based on the light optical microscopic level of analysis, all the slice marks were made by chipped stone tools (Table 10). There is no evidence of metal marks in the assemblage. While flakes and blades are listed separately in Table 10, it is nearly impossible to distinguish between the two since their overall morphology is similar unless they were retouched. Flakes and blades are distinguished based on a putative stage of production. When there is no evidence of retouch, they are classified as unmodified flakes. When there is evidence of retouch, they are classified as blades – either unifacially or bifacially. This has been confirmed by selecting several specimens for analysis in a SEM.

Almost all the slice marks are made by unifacially produced, but unretouched flakes (Table 10). Taxa of all sizes (from small to large) were butchered using this type of tool. Flakes are ubiquitous at the site and are examples of an ad hoc technology (Levy & Rosen, 1987). Only a few slicing incidences could be associated with unifacially retouched chipped stone tools. In general, the butchering marks mirror what we see in the lithic industry, where most chipped stone tools are ad hoc and used for household or domestic activities.

Several specimens (#234, #240, #258, and #260) were subjected to SEM analysis to confirm or negate the light optical readings (Fig. 7). In general, each of the specimens confirms the light optical readings. They exhibit an asymmetrical profile with one side rising at a steeper angle than the other. This is most apparent on Specimens #234 and #240 where the steeper (unifacial) slide is crisper and smoother (even better illuminated) than the shallower (cortex) side. The grooves on the other two specimens (#258 and 260) are less well defined, but follow the same pattern as noted above.

Table 10 Slice mark distribution by tool type by NBI

Material	Blade	Flake	Saw	Total	Blade	Flake	Saw	Total
Stone	3	83	1	87	3.4%	95.4%	1.1%	100.0%
Unclear, stone?		2		2		100.0%		100.0%
Total	3	85	1	89	3.4%	95.5%	1.1%	100.0%

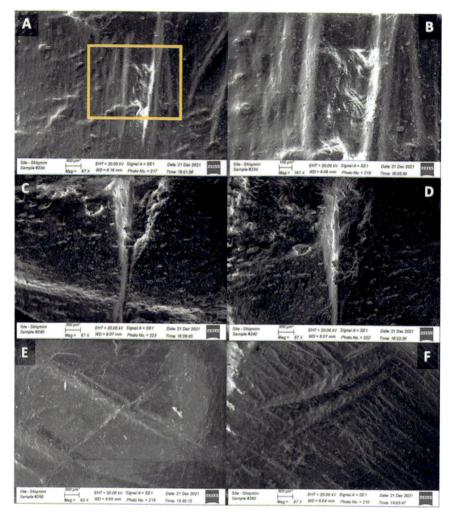

Fig. 7 SEM images of silicone moulds from various butchering marks. (**a–b**) Unifacial unretouched chipped stone tool slice mark on bone specimen #234 – innominate (ilium) of a Bos taurus (**b** is yellow square in **a**). (**c–d**) Unifacial unretouched chipped stone tool slice mark on bone specimen #240 – distal end and shaft of a humerus of an Ovis aries. (**e**) Unifacial unretouched chipped stone tool slice mark on bone specimen #258 – distal end of a scapula of a Bos taurus. (**f**) Unifacial unretouched chipped stone tool slice mark on bone specimen #260 – proximal shaft of a radius of a Capra hircus

The width of the slice marks, as measured by the SEM, fell into a relatively narrow range (150–200 µm), indicating the use of relatively narrow, sharp slicing tools. This width accords well with the use of unmodified flakes or blades as the primary butchering tool. The width is also within the range of grooves made with chert or similar geological materials since they are wider and more coarse than materials found at sites where obsidian is pervasive (Greenfield & Marciniak, 2019). Hence, the light optical readings that all the butchering marks were made by stone tools are confirmed by the SEM readings. At Shiqmim, the slice marks on butchered animal bones were made by sharp, relatively thin, unmodified stone flakes or blades. This is very similar to other Early Bronze Age assemblages (e.g., Tel Halif), but very different from earlier sites, such as Neolithic Neve Yam, where unifacially retouched tools were involved in the butchering process. There is no evidence for bifacially retouched tools being used in the butchering process. Furthermore, spectrographic analysis of the area on and around the butchering grooves on each of the samples did not display any evidence of metals of any kind.

8.2 Butchering Efficiency

The Butchering Efficiency Index (BEI) is calculated by dividing the total number of slice marks by the NBI – for example, if there are 10 slices in a single incidence, the BEI would be 10. If there is only 1 slice per incidence, then the BEI would be 1. The higher the BEI value, the lower the efficiency. The lower the BEI value, the higher the efficiency.

Butchering efficiency has been successfully monitored elsewhere by examining the average frequency of slices with respect to slicing incidences (Greenfield, 2013; Greenfield & Brown, 2016). The number of slices per slicing incidence for each taxon observed under light optical microscope are summed and then divided by the number of incidences (Table 11).

It is clear that the overall relative efficiency of the butchering assemblage is low. The average BEI is 8.7. However, the BEI varies quite widely between taxa – from 5.4 to 10. It does not appear to be affected by the size of the animal since both small, medium and large animals have overlapping ranges. As well, the range does not appear to vary with the assemblage size for each taxon – the larger sample sizes are found at either end of the range. Cattle have intermediate butchery efficiency (BEI 7.2) when compared to goat (BEI 5.4) and sheep (BEI 10). The average BEI is very similar to other later prehistoric assemblages (Beller et al., 2022a; Greenfield et al., 2016, 2018). All of this suggests that butchering efficiency is not very high at Shiqmim and there is little evidence of productive specialization in meat processing.

Table 11 Butchering efficiency associated with slice incidences

Taxon	Sum of slice marks	Sum of slice incidence	BEI
Bos taurus	87	12	7.2
Capra hircus	152	28	5.4
Large mammal	73	6	12.2
Lepus sp.	10	1	20
Ovis aries	252	25	10.1
Ovis/Capra	122	17	7.2
Total	696	89	8.7

9 Conclusions

Even though the sample of butchered remains from Chalcolithic Shiqmim is relatively small (n = 63), significant conclusions can be drawn from the present study.

1. All except one specimen of the butchered assemblage are from domestic animals. On the face, this is very different than in the overall assemblage. However, wild animals are not common in the larger assemblage in general. The absence of butchered gazelle bones in the assemblage is significant as they are a source for bone tools. Their long bones tend to be straighter and more gracile than those of domestic animals of a comparable size and therefore more appropriately shaped for bone tools (Horwitz, 1997).
2. The entire skeleton for medium-sized mammals (i.e., sheep and goat) are butchered and consumed on site. It is not clear if this is true also of large mammals (i.e., cattle).
3. There is little evidence of butchered bone attrition, suggesting that the assemblage is relatively intact.
4. Despite the small sample size, several phases of the butchering process could be identified — skinning, dismemberment, disarticulation, filleting, and toolmaking. There is one possible case of slaughter, but it is not possible to demonstrate that slaughter took place on or off the site for all animals.
5. All the butchering marks are made by stone tools, either chipped or ground stone. Almost all slice marks were made by unmodified unifacially produced flakes, while only a few were possibly made by blades with unifacial retouch.

When compared with other Chalcolithic assemblages, it becomes possible to make some tentative conclusions with regard to butchery practices and technology during this critical period in the evolution of early metallurgical societies.

First, animals were butchered with a very limited set of stone tools, in almost all cases, chert flakes (or blades), which were unifacially produced, without any evidence of retouch. These unworked flakes are part of the relatively abundant debitage that is scattered across sites.

Second, the Chalcolithic appears to fill the gap in the chronological continuity in stone tool butchering technology that extends from the Neolithic into the Early Bronze Age. Regardless of whether they are metal-using societies or not, butchering is conducted for the most part with the same types of tools – i.e., unmodified flakes or simple blades.

Third, the common assumption that Chalcolithic societies were developing metallurgy and that this must have affect all domains of life is not necessarily true. Metals during this period were for the most part for prestige and display. Animal butchering is a quotidian activity that continued to be dominated by a stone tool technology. The extremely high frequency of chipped stone tools at such sites is testimony that they continued to be of importance in a variety of functions (Levy et al., 1991; Levy & Rosen, 1987; Rosen, 1996, 1997). Hence, this study reaffirms the continued importance of ad hoc tools in animal butchering. Unfortunately, until recently, most lithic studies focused on the formal tools (e.g., Canaanean blades, tabular scrapers). These are clearly not intensively used in the butchering process. The greater quantity of flakes often ignored and/or not even recovered need to be the focus instead. Ultimately, if archaeologists are interested in identifying meaningful activity areas, such as butchering locales, they need to not only collect and analyze the bones, but also the ad hoc chipped stone tools. Animal remains are often collected and disposed of elsewhere away from the locus of domestic activities since their size and the smell of decay make their presence unpleasant. However, the small, chipped stone tools used in food processing might be found closer to where they were used. It is then apparent that archaeologists need to collect and map out the distributions of not only the formal tools, but also the seemingly innocuous waste that is generated by tool making. Otherwise, the location of butchering and a variety of other activities will continue to remain invisible.

Acknowledgments We gratefully acknowledge and thank all of the following for their hospitality, collegiality, assistance, and the opportunities that made this analysis possible — Tom Levy, Sarah Whitcher Kansa, and Caroline Grigson granted for permission to analyze the material; Yorke Rowan helped to sort out the stratigraphy and context; Rivka Rabinovich provided us with continued access to the zooarchaeology depot and her laboratory (part of the National Natural History Collections, Institute of Earth Sciences) of The Hebrew University of Jerusalem; Elizabeth Arnold, Tina Jongsma Greenfield, and Matthew Singer helped to collect the data in Israel. The research was funded by grants and infrastructure funding to HJG from the Social Science and Humanities Research Council of Canada and the University of Manitoba (UM/SSHRC) and St. Paul's College.

Appendices

Appendix 1: List of Butchered Bones and Their Contexts

Butchering bone #	1993 assemblage bone ID #	Area	Square #	Locus #	Basket #	Area of site	Context
200	598–599	D	N13/N13	4146	A364	Main village	Bell shaped pit (w/ fills L. 4140, L. 4143)
201	306–324	D	P13	4041	A146	Main village	Pit fill, in L. 4056
202	1168–1176	X	P17	4517	B48	East edge of main village	Topsoil
203	69–78	D	O12/O13	4087	A200	Main village	Cleaning pit, L. 4103
204	702	Mizrah	O4	34	H3	Satellite site	Occupation horizon on pebbles
205	691	E	A14	5035	C105	Main village	Division of probe #1

(continued)

Butchering bone #	1993 assemblage bone ID #	Area	Square #	Locus #	Basket #	Area of site	Context
206	459–461	D	O13	4005	A40	Main village	Pit fill, in L. 4265
207	1483–1496	D	Q13	4195	A438	Main village	Fill in pit L. 4194
208	1483–1496	D	Q13	4195	A438	Main village	Fill in pit L. 4194
209	1483–1496	D	Q13	4195	A438	Main village	Fill in pit L. 4194
210	1003–1011	X	P17-P18	4522	B81	East edge of main village	Pit
211	816–824	D	V16	4561	S257	Main village	Pit
212	816–824	D	V16	4561	S257	Main village	Pit
213	769–791	X	P20-Q20	4527	B136	East edge of main village	Pit
214	1382–1394	X		4507	B19	East edge of main village	Fill
215	380–381	D	O12/O13	4219	A534	Main village	Cleaning
216	1095–1099	D	O12/O13	4087	A219	Main village	Cleaning pit, L. 4103
217	1095–1099	D	O12/O13	4087	A219	Main village	Cleaning pit, L. 4103
218	1516–1517	D	H14	4036	A101	Main village	Pit fill, in L. 4037, under L. 4033
219	1033–1053	D	Q14	0	A1	Main village	Cleaning
220	1033–1053	D	Q14	0	A1	Main village	Cleaning
221	1426–1437	Z	T2	5004	C33	East edge of main village	Ash pit
222	483–502	D	P14	4084	A277	Main village	FILL, SR 16, SAME AS L. 3507 (1989)
223	483–502	D	P14	4084	A277	Main village	FILL, SR 16, SAME AS L. 3507 (1989)
224	984–1002	X	P1/P2	4521	B93	East edge of main village	Pit
225	1477–1478	D	N14	2020	A74	Main village	Locus not in db

(continued)

Butchering Patterns and Technology in a Chalcolithic Settlement...

Butchering bone #	1993 assemblage bone ID #	Area	Square #	Locus #	Basket #	Area of site	Context
226	343–348	D	o11/12	4158	A397	Main village	Fill, silts
227	1614–1615	X	O17	4511	B35	East edge of main village	Topsoil
228	1537–1539	D	Q14	4149	A387	Main village	Fill/collapse in SR 16 and SR 17
229	363–367	D	R13	4235	A523	Main village	Fill in pit L. 4236 in SR 15
230	363–367	D	R13	4235	A523	Main village	Fill in pit L. 4236 in SR 15
231	657–669	D	O12	4178	A414	Main village	Fill of pit L. 4190
232	657–669	D	O12	4178	A414	Main village	Fill of pit L. 4190
233		X	O18/P18	4529	B19	East edge of main village	Tunnel
234		X	O18/P18	4529	B19	East edge of main village	Tunnel
235	1177–1187	X	O17	4514	B47	East edge of main village	Rubbish dump
236	1177–1187	X	O17	4514	B47	East edge of main village	Rubbish dump
237	522–556	D	P14	4084	A301	Main village	FILL, SR 16, SAME AS L. 3507 (1989)
238		D	Q13	4217	A568	Main village	Fill in pit L. 4214
239	1127–1129	D	D13	4113	A288	Main village	Fill in pit, L. 4116
240	843–844	X	O17	4514	B47	East edge of main village	Rubbish dump
241	150–166	D	O12/O11	4158	A391	Main village	Fill, silts
242	199	D	O12	4107	A265	Main village	Fill
243	64–68	D	O13	4077	A214	Main village	Fill
244	794–797	X	P20/Q20	4537	B140	East edge of main village	No information

(continued)

Butchering bone #	1993 assemblage bone ID #	Area	Square #	Locus #	Basket #	Area of site	Context
245	200–234	D	P14	4198	A564	Main village	Fill in pit L. 4197
246	123–149	D	P13/O13	4147	A374	Main village	Ashy fill in pit L. 4160
247	1321–1327	D	H17	4544	B161	Main village	Fill, ash
248	521	D	Q13	4118	A303	Main village	Fill in pit, L. 4226
249	272–276	X	P17	4518	B52	East edge of main village	Rubbish dump
250	885–917	X	P20-Q20	4527	B117	East edge of main village	Pit
251	885–917	X	P20-Q20	4527	B117	East edge of main village	Pit
252	1354–1362	Z	T1	5003	C8	East edge of main village	Circular pit
253	1354–1362	Z	T1	5003	C8	East edge of main village	Circular pit
254	557–575	D	P13	4041	A146	Main village	Pit fill, in L. 4056
255		D	P13/O13	4147	A374	Main village	Ashy fill in pit L. 4160
256		D	P13/O13	4147	A374	Main village	Ashy fill in pit L. 4160
257		D	P13/O13	4147	A374	Main village	Ashy fill in pit L. 4160
258	1444–1451	D	R13	4245	A559	Main village	Fill in SR 15
259	1444–1451	D	R13	4245	A559	Main village	Fill in SR 15
260	1512	X	P17-P18	4531	B113	East edge of main village	Sub-room, fill
261	79–93	D	N13/N12	4143	A362	Main village	Ashy fill in L. 4146 (bell shaped pit)
262	79–93	D	N13/N12	4143	A362	Main village	Ashy fill in L. 4146 (bell shaped pit)

Appendix 2: Distribution of Butchering Marks and Related Activities by Taxon by NBI

Taxon	Element	Location	Mark	Decapitation	Disarticulation	Filleting	Modern	Skinning	Toolmaking	Grand Total
Bos taurus	Total				6	5			1	12
	Innominate	Ilium shaft	Slice		4					4
	Metacarpus	Proximal shaft	Saw						1	1
			Slice			2				2
	Rib	Distal shaft	Slice			1				1
	Scapula	Distal end	Slice		1					1
		Distal shaft	Slice		1	2				3
Capra hircus	Total			2	19	4		3		28
	Astragalus	Proximal and distal shaft	Slice					2		2
		Proximal shaft	Slice					1		1
	Femur	Distal epiphysis	Slice		1					1
		Proximal epiphysis	Slice		1					1
	Humerus	Distal epiphysis	Slice		1					1
		Distal shaft	Slice		2					2
		Tuberculum major	Slice		2					2
	Innominate	Ilium shaft	Slice		1					1
	Metacarpus	Proximal shaft	Slice			1				1
	Radius	Distal epiphysis	Slice		1					1
		Proximal end	Slice		1					1
		Proximal epiphysis	Slice		1					1
		Proximal shaft	Scrape		1					1
			Slice		1					1

(continued)

Taxon	Element	Location	Mark	Decapitation	Disarticulation	Filleting	Modern	Skinning	Toolmaking	Grand Total
	Scapula	Distal end	Slice		2					2
		Midshaft	Slice			1				1
		Distal shaft	Slice			1				1
	Tibia	Proximal shaft	Scrape			1				1
	Ulna	Proximal end	Slice		1					1
	Vertebra	Body	Slice		1					1
		Centrum	Chop	1						1
			Slice	1						1
		Cranial end	Slice		1					1
		Lateral process	Slice		1					1
Indeterminate large mammal	Total					5			1	6
	Long bone	Shaft	Saw						1	1
			Slice			3				3
		Distal shaft	Slice			1				1
	Rib	Proximal shaft	Slice			1				1
Lepus sp.	Total				1					1
	Humerus	Distal shaft	Slice		1					1
Ovis aries	Total			3	15	5	1	1		25
	Humerus	Distal epiphysis	Slice		1					1
		Distal shaft	Slice		3	2				5
	Innominate	Ilium	Slice		1	1				2
	Metacarpus	Proximal and midshaft	Slice			1				1
	Phalange 1	Distal shaft	Slice					1		1
	Radius	Distal epiphysis	Slice		1					1
		Proximal end	Slice		1					1
		Proximal shaft	Slice		1	1				2

	Scapula	Distal end	Scrape					1
			Slice	1				1
		Distal shaft	Slice	1				1
	Tarsal	Distal condyle	Scrape					1
		Midshaft	Slice	3		1		3
	Ulna	Olecranon	Slice	1				1
	Vertebra	Body	Slice		1			1
		Cranial body	Slice		1			1
		Lateral process	Slice		1			1
Ovis/Capra	Total			14	3			17
	Femur	Midshaft	Slice		1			1
		Distal shaft	Slice	1				1
	Humerus	Distal shaft	Slice	2				2
	Innominate	Ilium shaft	Slice	1				1
	Mandible	Horizontal ramus	Slice	1				1
		Vertical ramus	Slice	2				2
	Metatarsus	Distal shaft	Slice	1				1
	Rib	Proximal neck	Slice	1				1
		Proximal shaft	Slice	1				1
		Proximal shaft	Slice	1				1
		Distal shaft	Slice		1			1
		Proximal shaft	Slice		1			1
	Vertebra	Centrum	Scrape	1				1
		Spinous process	Slice	1				1
Total				55	22	1	4	2	89

References

Albaz, S., Shai, I., Greenfield, H. J., & Maeir, A. M. (2017). Board games in Biblical Gath. *Biblical Archaeology Review, 43*(5), 22, 68.

Beller, J. A., Greenfield, H. J., & Gaastra, J. (2022a). Changes in butchering technology and efficiency patterns between the Early and Middle Bronze Ages from Tell Zirā'a, Jordan. In D. Vieweger & J. Häser (Eds.), *Tall Zirā'a, The Gadara Region Project (2001–2011) Final Report Volume 3: Early and Middle Bronze Age (Strata 25–17)* (Vol. 3, pp. 649–727). Deutsches Evangelisches Institut.

Beller, J. A., Greenfield, H. J., & Levy, T. E. (2022b). The butchered faunal remains from Nahal Tillah, an EB I Egypto-Levantine settlement in the southern Levant. In J. Daujat, A. Hadjikoumis, & R. Berthon (Eds.), *Archaeozoology of Southwest Asia and Adjacent Areas XIII: Proceedings of the 10th ICAZ-ASWA conference, Nicosia, Cyprus, June 4–10, 2017* (pp. 61–80). Lockwood Press.

Binford, L. R. (1978). *Nunamiut ethnoarchaeology*. Academic.

Binford, L. R. (1981). *Bones: Ancient men and modern myths*. Academic.

Burke, A. M. (2001). Butchery of a sheep in rural Tunisia (North Africa): Repercussions for the archaeological study of patterns of bone disposal. *Anthropozoologica, 32*, 3–9.

Cope, C. R. (2004). The butchering patterns of Gamla and Yodefat: Beginning the search for kosher practicies. In S. Jones O'Day, W. van Neer, & A. Ervynck (Eds.), *Behaviour beyond bones: The zooarchaeology of ritual, religion, status and identity* (pp. 25–34). Oxbow Books. (Reprinted from: IN FILE)

Golden, J., Levy, T. E., & Hauptmann, A. (2001). Recent discoveries concerning Chalcolithic metallurgy at Shiqmim, Israel. *Journal of Archaeological Science, 28*, 951–963.

Greenfield, H. J. (1988). The origins of milk and wool production in the Old World: A zooarchaeological perspective from the central Balkans. *Current Anthropology, 29*(4), 573–593.

Greenfield, H. J. (1999). The origins of metallurgy: Distinguishing stone from metal cut marks on bones from archaeological sites. *Journal of Archaeological Science, 26*(7), 797–808.

Greenfield, H. J. (2000). Monitoring the origins of metallurgy: An application of cut mark analysis on animals bones from the Central Balkans. *Environmental Archaeology, 5*, 119–132.

Greenfield, H. J. (2002). Origins of metallurgy: A zooarchaeological perspective. In R. Harrison, M. Gillespie, & M. Peuramaki-Brown (Eds.), *Eureka: The Archaeology of Innovation and Science: Proceedings of the 27th annual conference of the Archaeological Association of the University of Calgary* (pp. 430–448). The Archaeological Association of the University of Calgary.

Greenfield, H. J. (2004). The butchered animal bone remains from Ashqelon, Afridar-Area G. *'Atiqot, 45*, 243–261.

Greenfield, H. J. (2005). The origins of metallurgy at Jericho (Tel es-Sultan): A preliminary report on distinguishing stone from metal cut marks on mammalian remains. In H. Buitenhuis, A. Choyke, L. Martin, L. Bartosiewicz, & M. Mashkour (Eds.), *Archaeozoology of the Near East VI: Proceedings of the 6th Sixth International Symposium on the Archaeozoology of Southwestern Asia and Adjacent Areas* (pp. 178–186). Archeological Research and Consultancy.

Greenfield, H. J. (2006). Slicing cut marks on animal bones: Diagnostics for identifying stone tool type and raw material. *Journal of Field Archaeology, 31*, 147–163.

Greenfield, H. J. (2008). Metallurgy in the Near East. A zooarchaeological perspective on the origins of metallurgy in the Near East: Analysis of stone and metal cut marks on bone from Israel. In H. Selin (Ed.), *Encyclopedia of the History of Science, Technology, and Medicine in Non-Western Cultures* (2nd ed., pp. 1639–1647). Springer Academic Publishers.

Greenfield, H. J. (2013). "The Fall of the House of Flint": A zooarchaeological perspective on the decline of chipped stone tools for butchering animals in the Bronze and Iron Ages of the southern Levant. *Lithic Technology, 38*(3), 161–178.

Greenfield, H. J. (2017). The spread of productive and technological innovations in Europe and Near East: An integrated zooarchaeological perspective on secondary animal products and bronze utilitarian metallurgy. In P. W. Stockhammer & J. Moran (Eds.), *Appropriating Innovations (Proceedings of the Entangled Knowledge in Late Neolithic and Early Bronze Age Eurasia Conference, Heidelberg, 15th–17th January 2015)* (pp. 50–68). Oxbow Books.

Greenfield, H. J. (2021). Insufficient evidence for metal butchering marks at Tell el-Hesi during the Early Bronze Age: Critique of the analysis of microscopic grooves in 'Cultural modification analyses on faunal remains in relation to space use and direct provisioning from Field VI EBIIIA Tell el-Hesi' by Kara Larson, James W. Hardin, and Sara Cody. *Palestine Exploration Quarterly, 160*(2), 144–155. https://doi.org/10.1080/00310328.2021.1921436

Greenfield, H. J., & Brown, A. (2016). 'Making the cut': Changes in butchering technology and efficiency patterns from the Chalcolithic to modern Arab occupations at Tell Halif, Israel. In N. Marom, R. Yeshurun, L. Weissbrod, & G. Bar-Oz (Eds.), *Bones and identity: Zooarchaeological approaches to reconstructing social and cultural landscapes in Southwest Asia (Proceedings of the ICAZ-SW Asia conference, Haifa, June 23–28, 2013)* (pp. 273–291). Oxbow Press.

Greenfield, H. J., & Horwitz, L. K. (2012). Reconstructing animal butchering technology: Slicing cut marks from the submerged Pottery Neolithic site of Neve Yam Israel. In K. Seetah & B. Gravina (Eds.), *Bones for Tools – Tools for Bones: The Interplay between Objects and Objectives (Proceedings of a Conference organized at the McDonald Institute of Archaeological Research)* (pp. 77–87). MacDonald Institute for Archaeological Research, University of Cambridge.

Greenfield, H. J., & Marciniak, A. (2019). Retention of old technologies following the end of the Neolithic: Microscopic analysis of the butchering marks on animal bones from Çatalhöyük East. *World Archaeology, 51*(1), 76–103. https://doi.org/10.1080/00438243.2018.1525310

Greenfield, H. J., Cheney, T., & Galili, E. (2016). A taphonomic and technological analysis of the butchered animal bone remains from Atlit Yam, a submerged PPNC site off the coast of Israel. In N. Marom, R. Yeshurun, L. Weissbrod, & G. Bar-Oz (Eds.), *Bones and Identity: Zooarchaeological Approaches to Reconstructing Social and Cultural Landscapes in southwest Asia (Proceedings of the ICAZ-SW Asia Conference, Haifa, June 23–28, 2013)* (pp. 89–112). Oxbow Press.

Greenfield, H. J., Beller, J. A., & Levy, T. E. (2018). Butchering technology during the Early Bronze Age I: An examination of microscopic cut marks on animal bones from Nahal Tillah, Israel. In I. Shai, J. R. Chadwick, L. Hitchcock, A. Dagam, C. McKinny, & J. Uziel (Eds.), *Tell it in Gath: Studies in the History and Archaeology of Israel. Essays in Honor of A. M. Maeir on the Occasion of his Sixtieth Birthday, Ägypten und Altes Testament – Studien zu Geschichte, Kultur und religion Ägyptens und des Alten Testaments, Band 90* (pp. 20–40). Zaphon.

Greenfield, H. J., Brown, A., & De Miroschedji, P. (2021). Origins of metallurgy in the southern Levant: Microscopic examination of butchering marks on animal bones at Tel Yarmuth, Israel. In U. Albarella, C. Detry, S. Gabriel, C. Ginja, A. E. Pires, & J. P. Tereso (Eds.), *Themes in old world zooarchaeology: From the Mediterranean to the Atlantic* (pp. 95–107). Oxbow Books.

Grigson, C. (1987). Shiqmim: Pastoralism and other aspects of animal management in the Chalcolithic in the northern Negev. In T. E. Levy & D. Alon (Eds.), *Shiqmim I: Studies concerning Chalcolithic Societies in the Northern Negev Desert, Israel (1982–1984)* (British Archaeological Reports, International Series 356) (pp. 219–241). BAR.

Grigson, C. (1989). Shiqmim I- archaeozoological aspects. *Mitekufat Haeven, 22*, 111–114.

Grigson, C. (1995). Plough and pasture in the early economy of the southern Levant. In T. E. Levy (Ed.), *The archaeology of society in the Holy Land* (pp. 245–268). Facts on File.

Hansen, S. (2021). Arsenic bronze: An archaeological introduction into a key innovation. *Eurasia Antiqua, 23*(2017), 139–162.

Horwitz, L. K. (1997). Faunal remains. In E. Braun (Ed.), *Yiftaḥ'el: Salvage and rescue excavations at a Prehistoric Village in the Lower Galilee, Israel* (Israel Archaeological Antiquity Reports, No. 2) (pp. 155–172). Israel Antiquities Authority.

Levy, T. E. (1988). On the origins of milk and wool production in the Old World: Reply to comments. *Current Anthropology, 29*(5), 744–745.

Levy, T. E. (1995). Cult, metallurgy and rank societies – Chalcolithic period (ca. 4500–3500 BCE). In T. E. Levy (Ed.), *The archaeology of society in the Holy Land* (pp. 227–244). Leicester University Press.

Levy, T. E., & Rosen, S. A. (1987). The chipped stone industry at Shiqmim: Typological considerations. In T. E. Levy & D. Alon (Eds.), *Shiqmim I: Studies concerning Chalcolithic Societies in the Northern Negev Desert, Israel (1982–1984)* (pp. 281–294). British Archaeological Reports.

Levy, T. E., & Shalev, S. (1989). Prehistoric metalworking in the southern Levant: Archaeometallurgical and social perspectives. *World Archaeology, 20*(3), 353–372.

Levy, T. E., Grigson, C., Buikstra, J. E., Alon, D., Smith, P., Shatev, S., & Ben Yosef, A. (1991). Protohistoric investigations at the Shiqmim Chalcolithic village and cemetery: Interim report on the 1987 season. *Bulletin of the American Schools of Oriental Research, 27*, 29–46.

Levy, T. E., Burton, M. M., & Rowan, Y. M. (2006). Chalcolithic hamlet excavations near Shiqmim, Negev Desert, Israel. *Journal of Field Archaelogy, 31*, 41–60.

Levy, T. E., Yorke, M. R., & Burton, M. M. (2007). *Desert Chiefdom: Dimensions of subterranean settlement and society in Israel's Negev Desert (c. 4500–3600 BC) based on new data from Shiqmim*. Equinox.

Lyman, R. L. (1987). Archaeofaunas and butchery studies: A taphonomic perspective. *Advances in Archaeological Method and Theory, 10*, 249–337.

Lyman, R. L. (1994). *Vertebrate taphonomy*. Cambridge University Press.

Oakberg, K., Levy, T., & Smith, P. (2000). A method for skeletal arsenic analysis, applied to the Chalcolithic copper smelting site of Shiqmim, Israel. *Journal of Archaeological Science, 27*(10), 895–901.

Rosen, S. A. (1996). The decline and fall of flint. In G. H. Odell (Ed.), *Stone tools, theoretical insights into human prehistory* (pp. 129–158). Plenum Press. (Reprinted from: IN FILE)

Rosen, S. A. (1997). *Lithics after the Stone Age: A handbook of stone tools from the Levant*. Altamira Press.

Rowan, Y., & Levy, T. E. (1991). Use wear analysis of Chalcolithic scraper assemblage from Shiqmim. *Journal of the Israel Prehistoric Society, 24*, 112–134.

Saidel, B., Erickson-Gini, T., Vardi, J., Rosen, S. A., Maher, E. F., & Greenfield, H. J. (2006). Egypt, copper, and microlithic drills: The test excavations at Rogem Be'erotayim in western Negev. *Mitkufat Haeven (Journal of the Israel Prehistoric Society), 36*, 201–229.

Whitcher, S. E., Grigson, C., & Levy, T. E. (1998). Recent faunal analyses at Shiqmim, Israel: A preliminary analysis on the 1993 assemblage. In H. Buitenhuis, L. Bartosiewicz, & A. M. Choyke (Eds.), *Archaeozoology of the Near East III: Proceedings of the third international symposium on the archaeozoology of southwestern Asia and adjacent areas* (pp. 103–116). ARC.

The Concept of Burial Modes as a Research Tool in the Late Prehistory of the Southern Levant

Ianir Milevski

Abstract As the Neolithic Revolution made its entrance on the stage of the southern Levant, it brought with it major changes in human society. As man progressed from primitive modes of production in the Pre-Pottery Neolithic, Pottery Neolithic and Early Chalcolithic periods, into the Early Bronze Age, as he moved on to agriculture and the domestication of animals, as he developed socially and his knowledge of metals and trade and economy grew, so, too, he changed his ways of burying his dead.

Throughout these periods, the spiritual world and burial customs of early man developed from in-house burials in the Pre-Pottery Neolithic period to cemeteries in the Ghassulian Chalcolithic and to socially separated cemeteries in the Early Bronze Age. In this paper, we will attempt to define the burial customs of late prehistory in the southern Levant and its relationship to economy and society. In this sense, we will present the concept of burial modes as a research tool for archaeology as a scientific discipline.

Keywords Burial modes · Funerary customs · Modes of production · Late prehistory · Southern Levant

1 Mortuary Practices and the Concept of Burial Modes

In this paper we will first present the main characteristics of burial practices in terms of the socio-economic aspects of the late prehistoric societies of the southern Levant (Fig. 1). Subsequently, we will describe the main aspects of the mortuary practices of the local Neolithic, Chalcolithic and Early Bronze periods by introducing a new

I. Milevski (✉)
Israel Antiquities Authority, Jerusalem, Israel

National Scientific and Technical Research Council, Buenos Aires, Argentina
e-mail: ianirmilevski@gmail.com

© The Author(s), under exclusive license to Springer Nature Switzerland AG 2023
E. Ben-Yosef, I. W. N. Jones (eds.), *"And in Length of Days Understanding" (Job 12:12): Essays on Archaeology in the Eastern Mediterranean and Beyond in Honor of Thomas E. Levy*, Interdisciplinary Contributions to Archaeology, https://doi.org/10.1007/978-3-031-27330-8_6

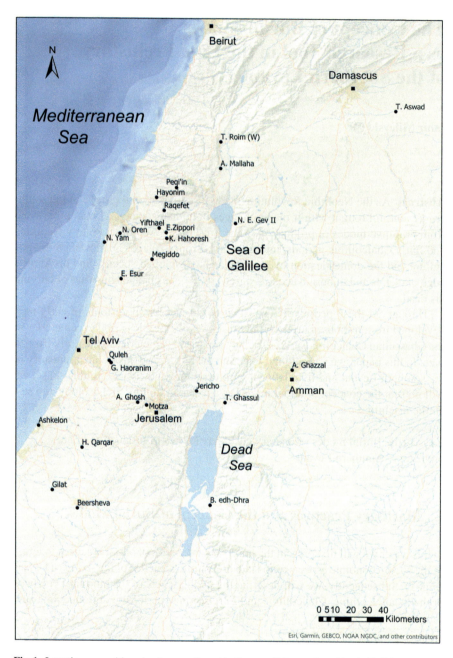

Fig. 1 Location map with main sites mentioned in the text. (Map produced by A. Fadida with Esri, ARC-GIS)

concept based also in Materialistic Dialectical archaeology. This concept encompasses both burial practices and social formations, setting a model of these burial modes for late Prehistory in the southern Levant.

1.1 Introduction

Approaches to investigating mortuary practices in archaeology have focused on different aspects of burial assemblages, treatment of the dead, location of graves and social dimensions of ritual practices. These mortuary practices relate to the society of the living, and not to the buried individual (see Parker Pearson, 2001).

Funerary rituals belong to the category of rites by means of which society sanctions the passage of a person from one qualitative state to another, among them rituals connected with childbirth, initiation and marriage. Burial customs indicate the transfer of the deceased member of the community to another state, another realm. Different communities conceived of that realm in various ways, hence the great variety of burial customs recorded by archaeologists in excavations of ancient burial grounds (Alekshin, 1983: 137).

In this sense, the anthropological work of Bloch and Parry (1999) has shown that in several places of the world, fertility and death are related through ceremonial practices and burial customs. These authors suggest that death is then related to the idea of regeneration of life through the enacting of funeral rites. It is suggested here that burial customs reflected the relationship between the dead with the community to which they belonged, i.e., organization of the dead in terms of production and reproduction of these communities.

Flexed (or semiflexed) burial position can be interpreted as the re-birth of the dead after burial (Gimbutas, 1999). A common interpretation is that the burial of the deceased in this position is a metaphor for the fetus in the womb (Naumov, 2007: 258) independent of tomb location within the settlement or in caves.

Scholars based on archaeothanatology (e.g., Bocquentin, 2003; Lengyel et al., 2013) have suggested the utilization of funerary bags during the Epi-palaeolilthic and Neolithic periods into which the bodies of the deceased were placed. This is confirmed by the fact that skeletons show constrictions which are not the result of the narrow pit effect. These bags were then interred in pits within houses or under floors. For Naumov (2007: 260, and bibliography therein) the bag represents the womb or alternatively, the bag could represent the neonate's placenta. In sum, the flexed position and the utilization of funerary bags reinforce the concept that the dead were considered as departing from the present with the idea of regeneration.

When pottery was utilized as a burial container, one of the symbolic features of the ceramic vessels, either in form or applied decoration, were human bodies, or more precisely the body of women (Naumov, 2008). From the Late Pottery Neolithic/Early Chalcolithic period to the Early Bronze Age (e.g., Lepetit, 2017), infants (and very rarely adults) were found mostly interred in pottery jars or under large sherds of broken jars, signifying they were being returned to their mothers (see below).

For the Palaeolithic and Epi-Palaeolithic periods, caves were the natural places for shelter and habitation; however, after the Neolithic Revolution and the increase in agriculture, both caves and the subterranean dimension in general were probably viewed as locales of mysteries. Most probably from the Neolithic period onward, caves (e.g., Bar-Yosef & Alon, 1988) were understood as a contact with "other-worldliness" (Rowan & Ilan, 2012). Furthermore, caves were compared with the womb of women, the entrance to the earth (Couto-Ferreira & Verderame, 2018; and especially Lupo, 2018, and the relation with the Mother Godess suggested by Gimbutas, 1999).

While biological aspects, pathologies and aDNA studies (e.g., Lazaridis et al., 2016; Harney et al., 2018), are not presented in this paper, we include some elements of the archaeothanatological approach (Duday, 2009). The objective of this approach is to reconstruct the attitudes of ancient populations towards death by focusing on the study of the human skeleton and analyzing the acts linked to the management and treatment of the body and funerary structures and their environment and the individuals.

One of the important aspects of mortuary practices is the potential to show kinship networks and gender and age differentiation among the burials. Taking into consideration that aDNA studies could address these aspects, there is significant potential aDNA research as well as palaeopathology which can shed light on those networks in the southern Levant (e.g., Alt et al., 2015; Nagar, 2013). Unfortunately, until a greater number of anthropological reports has been published, it is difficult to apply this mode of investigation in late prehistory (see Sheridan, 2017, Table 2), as already pointed out by Hodder (2011).

1.2 Archaeological Approaches to Death and to the Dead

The approaches to death and society in archaeology have been divided into four major viewpoints. First, the traditional approach, principally influenced by cultural-historic archaeologies, in which burial remains are the expression of the world of religious beliefs with assemblages usually interpreted by ideological metaphors, and extensive corpora of objects utilized for defining cultures and ethnic groups as in biblical archaeology (e.g., Bloch-Smith, 1992). The second approach is based on the processualist archaeological school which stresses the social reality behind mortuary practices and the complexity of burial customs related to ranked or complex societies (Binford, 1971; see Levy & Alon, 1982). One of the innovations in this approach is the demand for quantitative methods.

The third approach is related to the post-processual school or as Lull (2000) described it, the return of symbolic historicism in archaeological interpretation. In this case, post-processual approaches do not see a direct reflection of social systems nor a reflection of individual status in the funerary remains, but the negotiation of conflicts as stressed by Giddens (1979) within the living societies by other means, utilizing social symbols (Shanks & Tilley, 1982; see Nativ, 2014).

Both processual and post-processual studies (e.g., Saxe, 1970; Tainter, 1975; Parker Pearson, 1982) have included important quantitative elements in the research of mortuary practices (see Milevski et al., in press). In other studies (e.g., Binford, 1971) available ethnographic information on differentiation between individuals in death does seem to confirm the relationship between dimensions of disposal and the form of social organization.

The fourth approach in world archaeology, the Dialectical Materialist (Marxist) method, has also been applied to the interpretation of funeral customs (Lull & Picazo, 1989; Lull, 2000). According to these scholars, burials are deposits of social work produced by the society of the living with a social value. Just as the value of goods in the production of the living is calculated on the basis of the labor socially necessary to produce these products (Marx, 1977 [1867], 1993a [1859]), the value of mortuary products must be calculated on the basis of the socially necessary work related to the funeral customs, including the work invested in the graves and the goods included in the burials. In this article we will utilize Materialistic Dialectic methods, basing our premises on the understanding of social formations in late prehistory (see below), although we will analyze the development of these funeral customs over various periods.

Production, exchange and consumption are part of a single process (Marx, 1993b [1939]: 88–100). For this approach, human social relations have as a target the production and reproduction of society and its social relations, including life and death. The death and burial-related objects are like commodities for the living, whereas the dead are the consumers (see Parker Pearson, 1982). For this approach, as well, the individual is responsible for his life and for his own sustenance, i.e., his own reproduction as a member of the community (see Marx, 1993b [1939]: 471). His reproduction, as a member of the community, independent of the type of society, brings us to the idea of continuation of life after death present in most of the burial practices and mortuary beliefs.

However, as Gordon Childe (1945: 17), on a Materialistic Dialectic background, suggested, there is a kind of social advertisement in mortuary practices that can express changing relations of domination and re-structuring and consolidation of new social positions (see Parker Pearson, 1982).

1.3 Introducing the *Burial Mode* Concept

In this paper we introduce the concept of *burial mode* as a synthesis of the concept of mode of production and social formation which characterizes the ways societies (in this case late prehistoric communities) organize their production and reproduction, and the ways they treat the dead (burial customs) while keeping them within their communities.

Our concept is a simplified and ideal representation of mechanisms that related the mortuary practices and social formations, i.e., a model related to the nature of its components and its evolution in time (see Godelier, 1964: 9). Pre-Capitalistic formations were analyzed by Marx (e.g., 1993b [1939]); his methods are still valid for us. However, as Hobsbawn (1965: 65) pointed out, the acceptance of the method does not mean the automatic acceptance of all Marx's suggestions since they were constructed before anthropology and archaeology developed in the twentieth and twenty-first centuries (see Palerm, 2008: 45–58).

2 The Socio-Economic Framework of Late Prehistory in the Southern Levant

The Neolithic Revolution, as most scholars agree, replaced the hunter-gatherer's mode of production and style of life, beginning with the domestication of plants and agriculture, and following with the domestication of animals and herding as shown in Table 1 and Fig. 2. We would suggest, following Childe (1936: 142), that labor division was the result of the Neolithic/Agricultural Revolution, producing a social division that probably influenced the different ways of people's access to land, tools and animals (but see Abbo & Gopher, 2022).

Subsistence strategies during the non-sedentary Epi-Paleolithic period were based on family and tribal community, which jointly appropriated resources such as

Table 1 The evolution of economic activities from the Neolithic period to the Early Bronze Age in late prehistoric in the southern Levant

Years Cal BCE	Period/ culture	Hunter-Gathering fishing	Agriculture	Husbandry secondary products	Metallurgy	Inter-site exchange
3100–2400	Early Bronze Age II-III					
3700–3100	Early Bronze Age I					
4500–3700	Ghassulian Chalcolithic					
5800–4500	Late PN /Early Chalcolithic					
6400–5800	Early PN					
7000–6400	PPNC					
8500–7000	PPNB					
9500–8500	PPNA					
12000–9500	Khiamian Natufian					

The darker the color, the greater the relative intensity of the activity during the period

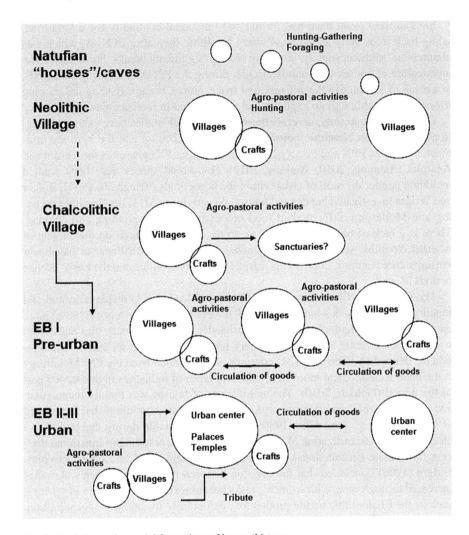

Fig. 2 South Levantine social formations of late prehistory

soil and water, vegetation and animals throughout most of this period, yet changing towards its end, i.e., in the Natufian period (see Goring-Morris, 1995).

Rollefson (2000) and Gebel (2010) both suggested that the establishment of the social order of the Neolithic period relied on establishing claims on certain commodities for the exclusive exploitation by certain segments of the society: the establishment of corporate kinship groups based on descent. They further suggested that unilinear descent groups were the most effective means of maintaining social order in the threat of warfare and intense competition for resources. A notable outcome of the emergence of unilinear corporate groups would have manifested in equality in terms of what has been described as "inalienable possessions"; these include both physical assets as well as social entities such as names, myths, ceremonies and other intangible goods.

Sites in the Levant have had formal and functional continuity for a long time, going back to as early as the Pre-Pottery Neolithic (hereafter PPN) A, which was a hunter- and gatherer society. Yet, there are also significant breaks. For instance, the architecture of houses was mainly circular during the PPNA, but during the PPNB, as a result of a change in the utilization of space, houses became rectangular (Goring Morris, 2005), although no explicit changes are noted in food acquisition.

Concerning continuity, several ethnoarchaeological studies have examined relationships between Neolithic household social organization and the built environment, both in its PPN and Pottery Neolithic (hereafter PN) phases in the Levant and Anatolia (Banning, 2010; Watkins, 2012). Household spaces have been studied including gender division of tasks within the households (Tringham, 1994). Bolger and Wright investigated gender and household activities (2013) for Neolithic societies, and Molleson (2007) studied food processing through grinding and cooking. There is a lack of biological as well as archaeological research on the subject of whether Neolithic societies were organized according to matrilinear or patrilinear kinships, (see Naumov, 2008). This is true for the Chalcolithic and the Early Bronze periods as well.

The Ghassulian Chalcolithic (as defined by Gilead, 2011) displays formal and functional continuity in some aspects with the PN but the subsistence is based more on agriculture, horticulture and animal husbandry (sheep and goats, pigs and cattle) with only small-scale hunting. Secondary products derived from animal exploitation (as defined by Sherratt, 1981) continue and expanded from the PN. Metallurgy is the main technological innovation with two types of industries in the second part of the period (Golden, 2010). The architecture of houses was mainly rectangular, and the settlements were densely settled, with designated buildings that functioned as sanctuaries (e.g., Ussishkin, 1980; Levy, 2006). Notable during this period is a clear change in the utilization of space within the house resulting in functional division for storage (installations), flint knapping, metallurgical and other activities. Wright (1996) concluded that the division between men's and women's activities increased through time, with women's tasks becoming related to household settings, such as the Chalcolithic textile production, particularly for domestic consumption, which is a highly gendered craft (e.g., Levy & Gilead, 2012).

In the Ghassulian Chalcolithic, these domestic spaces became more complex with many multi-storied structures, agglutinated cellular plans with contiguous rooms and certainly village-related elites emerged (e.g., Mallon et al., 1934; Levy, 1987). The "spatial syntax" at these sites documents an increasing control (Banning, 2010).

The Early Bronze Age (hereafter EB) I initially exhibits a kind of recession in village complexity displayed by oval separated structures (households?) (Braun, 1989). Several elements change in the economy of this period, although they show some continuity with the previous Ghassulian Chalcolithic (Milevski, 2013). While there is a continuation in agriculture and animal husbandry strategies and some technologies, there is a notable increase in the production of diverse pottery types, flint blades and networks of metallurgical production. The latter produced a growth of exchanged products in the southern Levant. These arrived at the end of the EB I/ beginning of the EB II and led to the creation of urban sites with defensive walls and public buildings, both palaces and temples (e.g., Greenberg, 2011, 2019), the Urban Revolution of Gordon Childe (1950). The EB II–III sites provide testimony to the growing aspects of a network of production, exchange and consumption (Milevski, 2011).

3 The Mortuary Practices of Late Prehistory in the Southern Levant

Detailed archaeological documentation of mortuary practices and the spatial and conceptual relationships between the dead and the living are now available in larger numbers for south Levantine prehistory. The following sections describe late Prehistoric burial patterns by periods (see Table 2).

3.1 Natufian

It seems probable that the burial customs of the PPN began during the Epi-Palaeolithic Natufian culture. We base this synthesis on the Natufian burial patterns primarily on the work of Belfer-Cohen (1988), Bar-Yosef (1998) and Bocquentin et al. (2016). Natufians buried their dead in graves at base camps and caves, in the Natufian heartland as well as in smaller sites.

Hayonim Cave, Ain Mallaha (Eynan) and el-Wad demonstrate that graves were dug in deserted dwellings and outside of houses, but not under the floors of active

Table 2 Burial patterns according to periods in southern Levantine late prehistory.

Periods Burial patterns	Natufian	Pre-Pottery Neolithic	Early PN	Late PN/Early Chalcolithic	Ghassulian Chalcolithic	Early Bronze Age
Primary	X	X	X	X	X	X
Secondary	X	X	X	X	X	?
Removing and decorating skulls	X	X			?	
Infant burials in ottery vessels				X	X	X
Ossuaries					X	
Cemeteries				?	X	X
Social differentiated cemeteries						X

houses. Burials were in pits, rarely paved with stones or plaster (Bocquentin, 2003; Wenstein-Evron et al., 2018: 52–55). Lime plaster covered burials at Natufian burials in Nahal Ein Gev II (Friesem et al., 2019). The pattern of body disposition in primary burials is supine, semiflexed or flexed, with various orientations of the head. A special type of mortuary practice is indicated by human and dog burials in two graves, one in Ain Mallaha and the other at Hayonim Terrace. According to Bar-Yosef (1998), these burials mark a departure from the Paleolithic dichotomous division of the natural world between humans and wildlife (see below). The fauna (small mammals, birds and reptiles) of various caves as Raqefet probably reflect a somewhat different type of communal meal (Yeshurun et al., 2013).

In several cases human skull removals were observed in the late Natufian, for instance at Hayonim Cave, Nahal Oren and Ain Mallaha (Eynan) (Fig. 3: 1) (Bocquentin et al., 2016). Other burials show complete skeletons and animals. At el-Wad terrace the skull was decorated (see Fig. 3: 2).

The suggestion pointed to in the past that differences within these mortuary practices reflect a social hierarchy seems to us unsubstantiated (Belfer-Cohen, 1991). Most burials are single with no grave goods, in primary or secondary deposition. Skull removal, a practice begun during the late Natufian, was performed only on adults; child burials were left intact.

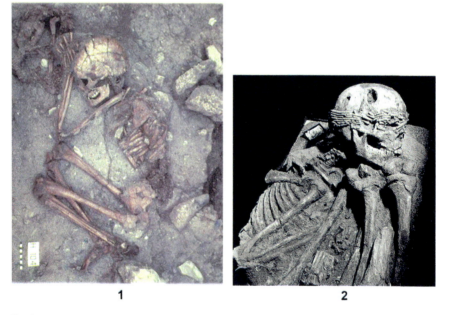

Fig. 3 Natufian burials. (1) Ain Mallaha (Eynan). (Courtesy of H. Khalaily). (2) El-Wad Terrace, Nahal Hamearot. (Courtesy of the IAA)

3.2 Neolithic Period

The variability in the mortuary practices of the Pre-Potttery Neolithic has been treated by Bocquentin (2003), Goring Morris (2005), Benz (2010), and Al-Shorman and Khwaileh (2011: 92–93) for Transjordan. The Neolithic population buried the dead in permanent sites. Stratigraphic indications from Beisamoun, Kfar Hahoresh, Jericho, Ain Ghazal, Abu Ghosh, Motza, as well as Yiftahel (e.g., Fig. 4: 1) and others, demonstrate that graves were dug in the dwellings under and close to the houses, *id est*, under the floors of active households (Kuijt, 2008). Graves were in pits, several of them covered by new plaster layers, some stone-lined. In some instances limestone slabs were put over the graves; all graves generally were filled with sediment. The pattern of body disposition in primary burials was supine, semiflexed or flexed, with various orientations of the head. The number of inhumations per grave varies from single to multiple. Some burials probably designate family groups, with children (Goring Morris, 2005; Anton, 2020). Secondary burials appear together with primary burials.

Skull removal was also practiced during the PPNA, both in the northern (Kanjou et al., 2013) as well as the southern Levant (Bocquentin et al., 2016). However, skull removal and decoration was one of the main characteristics of the PPNB mortuary practices (e.g., Fig. 4: 2). A current interpretation views skull removal as evidence of the veneration of ancestors; a long-term social value was attributed to adults, as shown by the conservation of their skulls (Bonogofsky, 2003, 2006; Milevski et al., 2008). In the Final PPNB or even before, evidence of cremation was found at Beisamoun and other sites (Bocquentin et al., 2020).

Sometimes primary burials also appear with caches of skulls, as at Tel Aswad (Stordeur & Khawam, 2007). Here, scattered human bones occurred above the occupational deposits, indicating that in Neolithic times burials also took place after the sites were abandoned, as in Yiftahel (Hershkovitz et al., 1986; Garfinkel et al.,

Fig. 4 (1) Yiftahel. Middle PPNB burial under the floor of Building 501, Area I. Two individuals in Locus 5528, looking northwest. (Courtesy of the IAA, photograph: I. Milevski). (2) Cache of three Middle PPNB plastered skulls from Yiftahel, Area I. Locus 4187, looking east. (Courtesy of the IAA, photograph: I. Milevski)

2012: 13–35). Babies and children comprise a part of the dead, for instance 17% in Yiftahel, probably indicating a relatively high mortality among fetuses, infants and small children (Abramov, 2018).

There is a tendency to introduce objects into burials during the PPNB, with pendants, beads and bracelets made of shells and stones, mainly in the Late and Final PPNB (or PPNC) (Bentz et al., 2019; Anton, 2020; Milevski et al., 2022) (e.g., Fig. 5). At Yiftahel some green stone axes were found near Middle PPNB burials, probably of serpentine, an exotic material found in the southern Levant (Khalaily et al., 2008).

In a few cases, anatomical research, based on the study of teeth, was able to point to the existence of biological relationships between some of the analyzed individuals, for example at Kfar Hahoresh (Alt et al., 2015). The researchers suggested that matrilocal biological relationships may have played a role in the burial practice. However, other individuals buried in the same location did not show biological relationships, and therefore a final conclusion on group homogeneities and residence patterns can only be made when the final analyses of the whole skeletal corpus is made available. Yet, the study shows that biological relationships in some cases correlated with architecture and this suggests in the view of this author household organization.

Burial customs of the early and late PN (Early Chalcolithic) periods are still less known in spite of several recent studies (e.g., Kuperman, 2010; Lepetit, 2017). In this regard, some sites such as Tel Roim West, Ein Zippori and Ein Assawir can clarify the mortuary practices and possibly alter the present observations, yet the publication of these and other sites is preliminary. Burial customs of the late PN include graves containing one individual in primary burial with the skull, in flexed or semi-flexed position, communal burials with two or three individuals and pits containing one or more individuals in secondary burial (Eshed & Nadel, 2005: 126). In some cases (Tel Roim West, Ein Zippori, e.g., Fig. 6: 1); Ein Assawir), individuals were interred in rectangular-built stone structures within the settlements (i.e., Eshed & Nadel, 2005, Fig. 11; Yaroshevich, 2016; Lepetit, 2017; D. Shalem and Y. Paz, pers. comm.) During the PN, skull removal was documented only in Anatolia (e.g., Özbek, 2009) but not in the southern Levant. Infants were buried in jars or under large potsherds that were laid within or between houses, or in offering depostis; they are a ubiquitous phenomenon of the PN (Lepetit, 2017) (e.g., Fig. 6: 2).

Animals were in general not buried with humans. A special type of mortuary practice during the aceramic PPN is indicated by the burial of anatomical parts of animals, mainly *Bos primigenius* (aurochs) but also fox, wild capra and others (Horwitz & Goring-Morris, 2004; Khalaily et al., 2008; Reshef et al., 2019). This could be understood as marking the transition of the departure of humans from the wild species, still present in the Neolithic world, and the beginning of animal domestication. Furthermore, in the late PN (Early Chalcolithic) a complete *bos taurus* was found at Ein Zippori (Milevski & Getzov, 2014).

The departure from the natural world and wildlife began with the Neolithic expression of the fact that domestication of plants and animals was the arsenal that

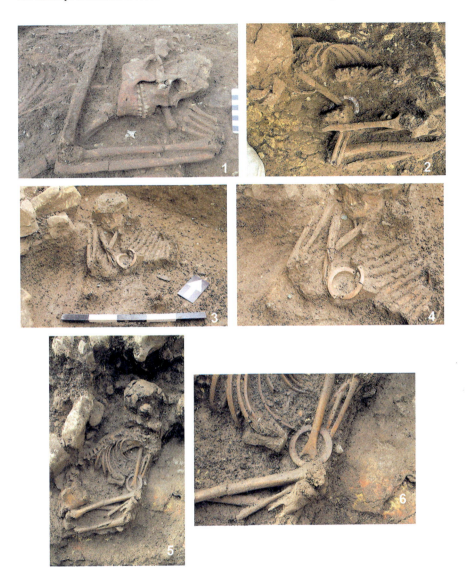

Fig. 5 Motza, Late PPNB burials of individuals with bracelets, pendants and other luxury objects. (1) and (2) Burial of Subarea C7. (3) and (4) Burial of Subarea C4. (5) and (6) Burial of Subarea C8 (Courtesy of H. Khalaily and J. Vardi, IAA, photographs: H. Khalaily and J. Vardi)

provided both the means and the materials of labor, and also the location, i.e., sedentary villages (see Marx, 1993b [1939]: 472). Still, in some semi-desertic areas, late PN burials and shrines bear animal offerings from a range of species, including several wild animals (Avner & Horwitz, 2017).

It has been claimed that at the late PN site of Newe Yam was a cemetery, i.e., a burial ground separated from the houses (Galili et al., 2009). This could be the

Fig. 6 Late Pottery Neolithic/Early Chalcolithic burials at Ein Zippori. (1) Area N5, Locus 345, looking. (Courtesy of Alla Yaroshevich, IAA; photograph: A. Yaroshevich). (2) Burial of an infant within pieces of jars, Area B, Locus 3552, looking north. (Courtesy of the IAA, photograph: N. Getzov)

prolegomena to the Ghassulian Chalcolthic which was to occur some centuries later. Yet the fact that this is a unique case (at least for the moment) indicated that prior to 4500 BCE there were no institutionalized cemeteries related to villages (see Kuperman, 2010).

3.3 Chalcolithic (Ghassulian) Period

Important changes occurred in the middle of the fifth millennium BCE. When it comes to the Ghassulian Chalcolithic, we find primary burials within the site (e.g., Perrot, 1955; Levy, 1987, 2006; Gilead, 1995), but then the bones were removed, placed in ossuaries, and re-buried in cemeteries in the caves, i.e., there were community burials. It could be suggested that ossuaries were "funeral homes" since several of the ossuaries were domiforms, however Bar-Yosef and Ayalon (2001) suggested that the ossuaries "copied" granaries or storage buildings.

Indeed, the late Chalcolithic period had a bimodal burial practice with primary burials in the settlement (e.g., Fig. 7: 1) and collective secondary burials with ossuaries placed in caves or structures outside the settlements (e.g., Fig. 7: 2, 3) (Nativ, 2014; Scheftelowitz, 2016; Milevski et al., in press). Primary burials within the villages are certainly a continuation of the Pottery Neolithic burial practices, with flexed position skeletons within the houses or in underground facilities such as those excavated in Teleilat Ghassul (Mallon et al., 1934 25: 3; Koepel, 1940: 19), the Beer-sheba sites (Perrot, 1955) and their surroundings (Gilead, 1995: 59–61; Smith et al., 2006). Infants are also buried within jars inside the settlements (e.g., Mallon et al. 25: 4; Eshed & Bar, 2012), but also in flexed positions without jars (e.g., Koepel, 1940: 29). A special case is Shiqmim (e.g., Levy & Alon, 1982, 1985) where primary and secondary burials are within and close to the settlement.

Furthermore, massive secondary burials suggest that death did not demand the immediate preservation of the individual but he or she continued to be part of the community outside the perimeter of the settlement.

It has been suggested by Ilan and Rowan (2012, Table 7.1), in their idea of death and regeneration, that the Chalcolithic period ossuaries were the receptacles in which the deceased would not only have been contained but also resurrected. If burial customs were related to the idea that human life is like agriculture, in which people live, die and are resurrected, as in the natural cycle of plants, for instance (Milevski, 2002), then there is a clear relationship between fertility and death (see Bloch & Parry, 1999).

Moreover, the interpretation that ossuaries were houses or buildings where the human remains were deposited seemed to express the idea that households or other forms of social organization within the villages continued to exist in a certain way in the cemeteries of the Chalcolithic period.

Evidence for age differentiation in burial practices during the Chalcolithic period is noted in the cemeteries where primarily adults (and scarcely any infants) were interred. The absence of new-borns and infants in the caves may be attributed to

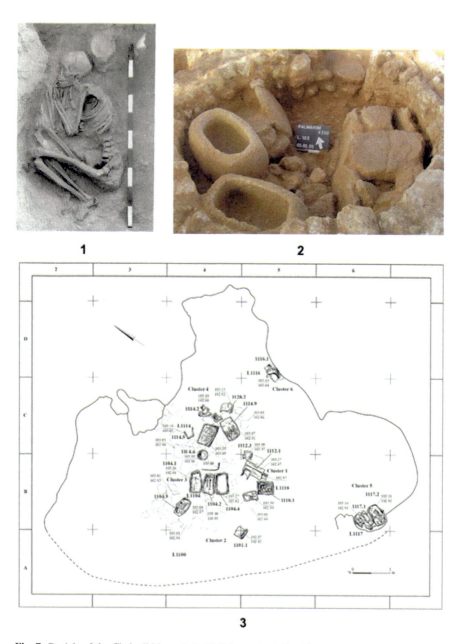

Fig. 7 Burials of the Chalcolithic period. (1) Primary burial in Gilat, Locus 806, looking north. (Courtesy of Thomas E. Levy, University of California San Diego). (2) Stone ossuaries in a burial at Palmahim (North). (Courtesy of the IAA, photo: A: Gorzalczany). (3) Plan of Cave K-1 at Quleh with ossuaries *in situ*, Chalcolithic Phase III. (Courtesy of the IAA, drawing: O. Dubowsky)

ritual practices, probably related to agriculture and fertility as well (Orrelle, 2008), or to the idea proposed by Hertz (1960: 95) that people who suffer violent deaths, death by accident, suicide, or death in childbirth, received different mortuary treatment.

Children were probably considered too young to be members of the community, or as several ethnographic examples indicate, children did not, in the words of Binford (1971: 7; see Faerman & Smith, 2008), become members of the "visible society".

While gender divisions are difficult to assess (see Fadida & Milevski, in press) differential burials have been recovered, some with elaborate finds, many with few finds, but in general the variability in burials during the Chalcolithic shows several common elements which can also be quantified (Nativ, 2014; Scheftelowitz, 2016; Fadida & Milevski, in press). Rowan (2014, following Levy, 1995) hints at a non-egalitarian social structure, but he also suggests that because the exotic finds are found with secondary burials, it leaves open the question of whether or not inherited status may be inferred based on this mortuary information. We believe that it is not that social ranking did not exist but that mortuary practices do not necessarily directly reflect individual status but mainly the relationship of the dead with the living village communities of the time.

Animal bones were found in burial caves but their interpreting their presence is still under debate. Did they represent faunal remains of community feasts (Yeshurun et al., 2013)? Were they animal burials related to the humans (Horwitz, 2007)? Were the residues a result of different activities (Agha, in press; Horwitz, in press)?

The retrieval of bones, inclusion of mortuary finds and production of ossuaries for the dead was an extended ceremonial process, probably with aspects of a social event (Rowan, 2014). Ossuaries were probably prepared at the settlements since fragments were found at several habitation sites (Fadida & Milevski, in press, Table 21.2), and recently at Ashkelon-Agamim (Y. Abadi-Reiss and D. Varga, pers. comm.). The fact that probably more than one settlement buried its dead in one cemetery (Boness et al., 2016; Cohen-Weinberger, in press) and several cemeteries served a single site (Milevski et al., in press) suggests that Chalcolithic mortuary practices involved numerous inter-site activities that included, by other means, the settling of regional conflicts and probably inter-tribal negotiations.

3.4 Early Bronze Age

For the Early Bronze Age, there are some examples of cemeteries attached to their settlements, including Jericho (Kenyon, 1965), Bab edh-Dhra (Schaub & Rast, 1989) and Assawir (Yannai, 2016). In these cases, the tombs contained a large number of interments. The EB I is a period of transition to urbanism, also from the point of view of the burial modes.

Bab edh-Dhra, located in the southeastern plain of the Dead Sea, is one of the most researched sites in the southern Levant It has been suggested that the cemetery functioned as a regional burial center where thousands of bodies were interred from the mid-fourth millennium to the late third millennium BCE, spanning the entire Early Bronze Age (Sheridan et al., 2014).

Studies in recent decades (e.g. Harrison, 2001; Ilan, 2002; Ben-Ari, 2010) demonstrate that burial patterns and mortuary practices from the EB I are more complex than the previous ones of the Chalcolithic period, showing a ranked society. However as, in general, data regarding the EB IA is still incomplete, the EB IB seems to be the prologue to the urban society of the EB II.

At the same time, some sites are an extension of previous periods. For instance, the EB IA cemetery of Bab edh-Dhra (Schaub & Rast, 1989: Figs. 15, 61; Sheridan et al., 2014) shows a continuation in the secondary arrangement of bones as in the Chalcoltihic period. Chesson (2001: 110) suggested that these customs were directed to mark a continuity with the previous generations.

The EB IB population continued to utilize burial caves in the vicinity of the settlements with mostly primary, but also secondary burials. Contrary to the Chalcolithic period, there are more interments per burial cave, there is no evidence for burial "containers" and there is an increase in burial offerings (Ben-Ari, 2010; Yannai, 2016) (e.g., Fig. 8: 1). Moreover, spatial and quantitative analysis of these burial goods help to determine the basic EB IB burial kit according to regions, contrary to the Chalcolithic period. The interregional comparison of the EB IB burial kits discern differences in the composition of each of their components, for instance, imports (Ben-Ari, 2010). Megiddo Tombs 903 and 910 (Guy, 1938: Figs. 11, 14), huge and finely-masoned tombs, are the largest and richest found in the EB, probably contemporaneous with the the EB IB complex of temples (Adams et al., 2014). Unfortunately, all the human remains and most of the finds were removed in antiquity, which makes it difficult to learn about these cases (see Ilan, 2002: 94–95), though there are clear signs of social stratification at the site.

During the EB II-III, marked social differentiation emerged, with burials containing vessels of local origin, and the larger tombs, grave goods including gold, faience, mother-of-pearl, jewelry, stone blades and other luxury items, plus imported ceramic vessels (Chesson, 1999; Chesson & Philip, 2003). The increase in social differentiation at each site over time from the EB I to the EB III, is evident although the scale of differentiation is limited to what Chesson (2015: 59–60) calls groups with greater and lesser degrees of access to local and non-local goods. Osteological evidence and mortuary contexts from Bab edh-Dhra (Sheridan et al., 2014) indicate that funerary rituals shifted over time to reflect altered settlement patterns and changing social dynamics.

At this site during the EB II-III a charnel house contemporary with the planned, fortified settlement—housed the remains of a smaller number of multigenerational families (Chesson, 1999, 2015) (Fig. 8: 2). Such tombs also contained metal weapons and mace-heads, probable signs of political and military powers. Other cemeteries, such as the one at Jericho, showed a social division reflective of the urban, hitherto not seen (Kenyon, 1981). Infants are still found buried in jars on site as in the Chalcolithic period at EB IA sites (Yekutieli & Gophna, 1994; Braun & Gophna, 2004) but also at EB IB or II sites (Golani, 2019, 110–112; Milevski & Getzov,

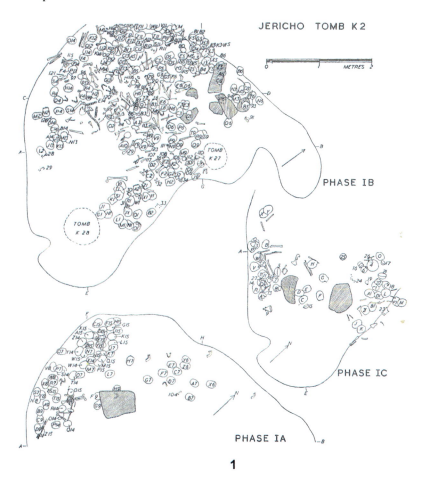

Fig. 8 Burials of the Early Bronze Age in the southern Levant. (1) Plan of Jericho Tomb K2, Phase I, EB IB. (Adapted from Kenyon, 1965, Fig. 1). (2) Charnel house A41, Bab edh-Dhra, EB II-III. (Reconstruction by Eric Carlson, courtesy of Meredith Chesson, the Expedition to the Dead Sea Plain)

2014). Ilan (2002: 95) has pointed out that gender does not seem to be a factor for selection, yet, similar to the practices noted during the Chalcolithic period, there are multiple burials with poor state of preservation which preclude conclusions regarding gender and age differentiation.

One interesting aspect of burial practices in the EB is the presence in several burial caves as well as in some settlements of donkey figurines Because these figurines are related to a large presence of domesticated donkeys (*Equus asinus*) for the first time in the southern Levant we suggested they represent the cult of traders utilizing this animal as a mean of transportation. In the EB settlements donkey skeletons were found as well, probably buried or part of some ceremonial ritual (Milevski, 2011: 177–197; Milevski & Horwitz, 2019). The presence of animal bones in mortuary contexts is still under debate. The fact that several burials from the EB I-III contain faunal remains from both wild and domestic species (including donkeys) was interpreted as burial offerings (e.g., Hesse & Wapnish, 1979) or as domestic activities in the caves (e.g., Horwitz, 2007).

4 The *Burial Modes* of Late Prehistory in the Southern Levant

As stressed above. this concept was born as a synthesis of the concept of mode of production and social formation, which characterizes the ways societies organize their production and re-production. Our concept is a simplified representation of mechanisms which connect the mortuary practices and social formations.

We begin the study of mortuary practices as a means of social inference from archaeological data (e.g., Milevski, 2013; Jaruf et al., 2014), moving beyond the use of this data for studying these practices per se or the ideological meaning of them, but to see what the burials can tell us about the wider time sequence of grave goods and the statistics of past populations (see Chapman, 2003).

Quantitative variables (Saxe, 1970), which could measure the notion of energy expenditure on deceased individuals for determining the grade of ranking and social differences (e.g., Tainter, 1975; Lull, 2000), are necessary. Furthermore, the burial evidence should be integrated with other archaeological parameters such as settlement hierarchy and location, craft specialization and gender division when possible.

In prehistoric societies, the relationship of the individual to the objective conditions of labor is one of ownership. In this system of production, labor has a tribal and communal character (see Marx, 1977 [1939]: 471–447, 1993a [1859]).

The communal system on which this mode of production is based prevents the labor of an individual from becoming private labor, and his product the private product of a separate individual; it causes individual labor to appear rather as the direct function of a member of the social organization. The common property which formerly absorbed everything and embraced them all, then subsists as a special common land. Neolithic and Chalcolithic societies have modes of production, generally termed "primitive" social formations, which have their specificities depending on geographical, historical and technological characteristics (Fig. 2).

For the Early Bronze Age, mainly the EB II-III urban entities, it seems that surplus labor exists, although labor is not creation of value in modern terms; it belongs to the higher community, which ultimately appears as a person, king, governor or high priest. This surplus labor is rendered both as tribute and as common labor for the ruler or the elite (Marx, 1977 [1939]: 472–474). For the Early Bronze defensive walls and public buildings of the urban centers, taxes should have been collected from residents of nearby settlements as well. The social reality of these centers seems to be that of a ranked and stratified society: probably *corvée* laborers, working under the guidance of professionals or bureaucrats (Shalev, 2018) (Fig. 2).

While kingship relationships continue to exist, the suggestion that the construction of urban centers and the whole EB society was a collaborative enterprise, the result of a corporate village or a house society (Chesson & Philip, 2003) is more a remnant of the past.

By taking into consideration all the elements of mortuary practices, the *burial mode* concept does not separate these practices from the mode of production of the communities that gave birth to them. These practices are immersed in the ideology of these communities, not as a conscious desire of these peoples but as a concept dictated by their social experience. Mortuary practices as part of the ideology of these prehistoric communities can never be anything else than their conscious existence, i.e., their actual life-process (Marx & Engels, 1977 [1932]), echoing this life-process.

Furthermore, the *burial mode* concept contains and takes in mind Binford's (1971) suggestion that *social personae* were commonly recognized in mortuary rituals varying significantly with the organizational complexity of the society as measured by different forms of subsistence practice. However we do not take in mind sole individuals; there are social groups, communally related in their life and modes of production. Then mortuary practices do not reflect the status of the individuals but the social formations in which they lived and were buried.

Following are the main *burial modes* for late prehistory in the southern Levant (Fig. 9). Since the Natufian culture is a sort of prolegomena of the PPNA, but without the fully developed villages and households, we will start with the Neolithic period. The Natufian burial mode should be a transition between tribe organization and the Neolithic household mode.

4.1 Neolithic Household Burial Mode

The mode of Neolithic production could be a variant of what Marx (1993b [1939]; Hobsbawm, 1965) defined as the primitive or communal mode of production, and other anthropologists, such as Sahlins (1972) called the domestic mode of production, albeit in a neo-evolutionary understanding. This mode of production, which could be understood as a household social formation as previously described in the

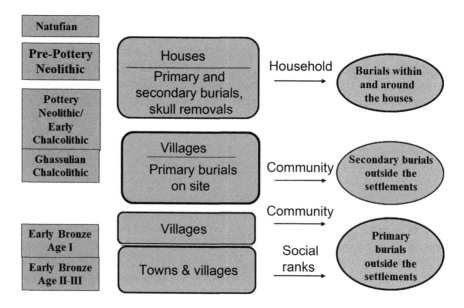

Fig. 9 Late prehistoric *burial modes* in the southern Levant

first sections of this paper, represents a formation in which the productive unit is mainly household-based in the extended family within the village. While the burial mode of the Natufian prescribes graves to be placed in abandoned houses, this changes in the Neolithic, and from the PPNA onwards the burials are below the houses or attached to them. The Neolithic burial mode is based on households; this includes not only the graves within the houses but also the plastering and decoration of the skulls and all the ceremonies and the cycle which includes re-burying them.

Kuijt (2001, 2008) argued that mortuary rituals were organized by a series of ordering principles. These were based on the age, and possibly status, of the deceased. We do not know if gender affected these principles but suggest that gender as well as age took an important volume of social differentiation in these Neolithic communities. Peterson (2002), however, suggested that during the Neolithic, male activities changed and began to resemble female activities while the activity patterns themselves became more intense for both sexes. Several dimensions of regional mortuary practices were pointed out on the social impact of secondary mortuary practices and skull caching on community integration and cohesion. At the same time, and continuing the tradition starting in the Natufian, the body is treated and the skulls applied with various materials, mainly plaster (Bonogofsky, 2003; Fletcher et al., 2008; Milevski et al., 2008; Slon et al., 2014) but also bitumen (Bar-Yosef & Alon, 1988). The transformative aspect of the work invested in this treatment is undeniable, and all this was done at a cost, therefore the labor on the body was also a commodity (see Parker Pearson, 1982; Lull, 2000).

It is suggested that the development of specific ritual practices was linked to the need to maintain existing household political, economic and social ties during times of social, resource and environmental stress as a result of the changes undergone within the Neolithic communities (Kuijt, 2008). Watkins (2012: 154) even concluded that the consciousness of the community should be kept alive through manipulation of symbols for the individual and the community. Ceremonies and performance were embedded in the manipulation of symbols and the way that ceremonies and rituals were repeatedly performed. For Watkins (2012), based on Assmann (1995), this was the key to understanding the nature of collective memory and sense of identity in the Neolithic communities. In any case, this indicates the clues of ceremonial burial practices and the communal building as resulting from social contradictions in these societies.

Totemic elements, as explained by Frazer (2014 [1887]: 118) could be related perhaps to the interment of animals as suggested further above, but also to the identification of households and extended families. Goring-Morris and Belfer-Cohen (2002) suggested that totemism was a part of the Natufian and early Neolithic communities and functioned as a traditional system that had been in use among hunter-gatherer societies since the Natufian (Goring-Morris & Belfer-Cohen, 2002). Totemism however could also reflect the organization of sedentary tribes and *gentes* as shown by Morgan (1877), but totemism in ancient societies does not have sharp divisions, and it represents stages in continuous transition (Lévi-Strauss, 1991), which may have made it difficult for us to follow the influence of this phenomenon in burial practices. At any rate, cultic practices in the PPN expressed the emergence of differential wealth and the development of differential inherited status from the middle PPNB onwards. Some studies show that biological relationships in a number of cases (Alt et al., 2015) correlated with architecture and this suggests in the view of this author household organization. The power of ritual, as well as the Neolithic burial mode, was household-based.

4.2 The Chalcolithic (Ghassulian) Communal Burial Mode

We can define the Chalcolithic burial customs compared to previous and later burials as a communal form of burial, where the community would be the unit that prevailed over households, but where social differentiation was not yet obvious. Still, totemic elements should also be present, which can explain some of the differences in the iconography of Chalcolithic cultures in general and that of the ossuaries in particular (Milevski et al., in press).

A visible change during the Chalcolithic period, when a bi-modal burial practice with primary burials in the settlement and collective secondary burials in caves or other places outside the settlements becomes the norm. During the Ghassulian Chalcolithic, the pre-condition to everyone to accede to possession was still the community, with the family organization still existing but in a second range. Property actually was the realm of the whole village; however tribal and individual possession, for instance of houses, storage installations, tools, etc., actually could have existed (Milevski, 2013). A major division of labor was created regarding the previous PN communities, since pottery, flint, basalt and metal products enlarged the economy of the Chalcolithic villages, not to speak of the agriculture, horticulture and products derived from animal husbandry.

The transformative aspect in mortuary practices of building specific containers is undeniable, and all this was done at a cost. Therefore, treatment of the body was a commodity, as was secondary burial of bones in ossuaries. Energy was also invested in cave burials; although the caves existed naturally, they had to be hewn and modified (Rowan, 2014: 111–112). And when caves were not available construction of burial rooms had to be constructed on the coastal plain (e.g., Goren & Fabian, 2002; Gorzalczany, 2018). The conjuncture of fertility and death motifs in Chalcolithic art is very clear as suggested by us earlier (Milevski, 2002), and by other colleagues (Ilan & Rowan, 2012). The Chalcolithic burial mode is a communal one in which all the iconographical motifs seem to to be related to ensuring fertility, rebirth and continuity. If the interpretation of different populations re-burying their relatives in the same cemetery is correct, this may indicate that groups negotiated and resolved (or not) confrontations with regard to burial practices (Milevski et al., in press).

4.3 The Early Bronze Social Ranks Burial Mode

If the Chalcolithic burial mode represents the separated communities, the EB shows the passage from that burial mode to one in which social differentiation is clearly observed in the burials during the urban EB II-III. The mode of production which resulted from the urban revolution has been defined in general as the Asiatic mode of production or tributary mode of production in a general way (Hobsbawm, 1965). Yet there are several expressions of this mode of production. One of them occurs during the Levantine urban Early Bronze Age (see Milevski, 2013).

The transformative aspect in the mortuary practices continued in caves, some of them as in Megiddo or charnel houses as in Bab edh-Dhra with considerable invested energy.

If the Chalcolithic burial mode is a communal one utilizing several cemeteries where regional or tribal groups negotiated confrontations, the Early Bronze Age seemed to express the new relations of domination, including consolidation of new social positions as suggested by Gordon Childe (1956). One of the new elements is the possible existence of a group of traders, as suggested by the cultic activities of donkey figurines in several burials.

The burial mode of the urban Early Bronze Age is an extension of social ranks in mortuary practices. The division of labor that began in the EB I with a major circulation of goods crystalizes in the EB II-III with a burial mode that expresses the division of the society in those practices.

5 Discussion

By discussing the late Prehistoric ritual and mortuary practices in the southern Levant (Table 2) we suggest that the organization of the burial practices is related to the socio-economic formations present among the living (Figs. 2 and 9). Numerous scholars agree that these practices were intentionally employed as a means of consolidating community membership at least until the Ghassulian Chalcolithic. During the Early Bronze Age it seems that these practices were intended to have an effect on conflicts within and among these communities. However, the *burial mode* concept makes a link within societies and mortuary practices because the ideological factors involved in burial customs are the result of the living societies that produce, exchange and consume goods. These burial customs are part of this process. In this sense, the concept of *burial mode* seems to put an end to the discussion of weather mortuary practices reflect more the living or the dead, since the dead are part of the communities and a continuation of life in different ways.

As was suggested above, mortuary practices are a form of public action rather than a direct reflection of personal status. From this, we should conclude that the mortuary practices are not related to the individual but rather to the individual as part of the household and community in late prehistoric villages of the southern Levant. This, however, means that it is difficult to identify personal status in burial practices, even in specific cases such as those of the plastered skulls of the PPNB. After the Pottery Neolithic, households were not the unit for secondary burials. Cemeteries existed outside the villages and these cemeteries represented the whole community or village Still, primary burials within the villages could attest to the existence of households in the Chalcolithic. Since there seemed to be much interaction between different sites at different cemeteries, this should indicate a continuation of the living inter-site relationships with death at these communities.

During the Early Bronze Age, a transition from villages to urban states occurred and the *de facto* existence of social groups differentiated one to another by social statuses, craft specialization, geographical location (town or village), as well as their belonging to bureaucratic classes. However, there is also probable continuation of households dedicated to some traditional works. The burial mode of the urban Early Bronze Age is related to the fact that the superior unity (represented by the rulers of the towns) is the real owner of the numerous communities. The cemeteries are the continuation of these communities, showing their internal social differences in their assemblages.

The Early Bronze Age is probably the first period in which social differences and surpluses were directed in favor of elites in an "organized" way. *Burial modes* during this period albeit continue certain elements of the Chalcolithic burial practices, among them the utilization of caves outside the settlement, but now the cemeteries are located in the immediate vicinity of the settlement sites of the living. The *burial mode* of the urban Early Bronze is the first expression of a social differentiaton within the settlements since the first Neolithic farmers institutionalized the household burials in their villages.

Burial modes as a research tool should be proven in later periods of the Levant and other places of the world in order to be admitted as a framework to analyze past societies. Certainly, local and regional differences will be observed not only in our southern Levantine laboratory but in archaeological studies worldwide. A careful study of ancient social formations and mortuary practices is still indispensable in order to build a scheme of *burial modes* in antiquity.

Acknowledgments This paper, warmly dedicated to Thomas E. Levy, is based on lectures given in Hebrew at the conference organized by the Southern District of the Israel Antiquities Authority and Ben-Gurion University of the Negev in 2019 in Beersheva, and in a seminar for advanced students at the same university. I would like to thank Karen Covallo-Paran (IAA), and the editors of this volume for their comments and the editing of the English text. I also want to thank Thomas, Meredith Chesson and my colleagues at the IAA, Hamoudi Khalaily, Jacob Vardi, Nimrod Getzov, and Alla Yaroshevich, for allowing me to reproduce figures from their and our common excavations (Figs. 3: 1, 4–8). Last but not least, I am indebted to Atalya Fadida and Olga Dubowsky (also from the IAA) for the drawings and production of the general map (Fig. 1) and the the plan of Cave K-1 from Quleh (Fig. 7: 3).

References

Abbo, S., & Gopher, A. (2022). *Plant domestication and the origins of agriculture in the Ancient Near East*. Cambridge University Press.

Abramov, J. (2018). *The inhabitants of the Middle and Late Pre-Pottery Neolithic B (ca. 10,000-9,000 Cal BP) site of Yiftahel: An anthropological, bio-archaeological, and cultural analysis*. MA dissertation, Tel Aviv University. (Hebrew with English summary)

Adams, M. J., Finkelstein, I., & Ussishkin, D. (2014). The great temple of Early Bronze I Megiddo. *American Journal of Archaeology, 118*(2), 285–305.

Agha, N. (in press). Faunal remains from Quleh. In I. Milevski, R. Lupu, & A. Cohen-Weinberger (Eds.), *Excavations at Quleh and Mazor (West). Iconography and burial practices in southern Levantine Chalcolithic cemeteries*. Austrian Academy of Sciences.

Alekshin, V. A. (1983). Burial customs as an archaeological source. *Current Anthropology, 24*(2), 137–150.

Al-Shorman, A., & Khwaileh, A. (2011). Burial practices in Jordan from the Natufians to the Persians. *Estonian Journal of Archaeology, 15*(2), 88–108. https://doi.org/10.3176/arch.2011.2.02

Alt, K. W., Benz, M., Vach, W., Simmons, T. L., & Goring-Morris, A. N. (2015). Insights into the social structure of the PPNB site of Kfar HaHoresh, Israel, based on dental remains. *PLoS ONE, 10*(9), Article e0134528. https://doi.org/10.1371/journal.pone.0134528

Anton, M. (2020). Death at Motza: Variability in the treatment of human remains. In H. Khalaily, A. Re'em, J. Vardi, & I. Milevski (Eds.), *The mega project at Motza (Moza): The Neolithic and later occupations up to the 20th century* (pp. 201–222). Israel Antiquities Authority.

Assmann, J. (1995). Collective memory and cultural identity. *New German Critique, 65*, 125–133.

Avner, U., & Horwitz, L. K. (2017). Sacrifices and offerings from cult and mortuary sites in the Negev and Sinai, 6th–3rd millennia BC. *Aram, 29*(1-2), 35–70.

Banning, E. (2010). Houses, households, and changing society in the Late Neolithic and Chalcolithic of the southern Levant. *Paléorient, 36*(1), 45–83.

Bar-Yosef, O. (1998). The Natufian culture in the Levant, threshold to the origins of agriculture. *Evolutionary Anthropology, 6*, 159–177.

Bar-Yosef, O., & Alon, D. (1988). *Nahal Hemar cave* ('Atiqot 18). Israel Department of Antiquities.

Bar-Yosef, O., & Ayalon, E. (2001). Chalcolithic ossuaries – What do they imitate and why? *Qadmoniot, 121*, 34–43. (Hebrew)

Belfer-Cohen, A. (1988). *The Natufian settlement at Hayonim Cave: A hunter-gatherer band on the threshold of agriculture*. Ph.D. thesis, The Hebrew University of Jerusalem.

Belfer-Cohen, A. (1991). The Natufian in the Levant. *Annual Review of Anthropology, 20*, 167–186.

Ben-Ari, N. (2010). *Mortuary practices in Israel's costal plain during the Early Bronze Age IB and their social implications*. MA thesis, Tel Aviv University. (Hebrew with English summary)

Bentz, M., Gresky, J., Štefanisko, D., Alarashi, H., Knipper, C., Purschwitz, C., Bauer, J., & Gebel, H. G. K. (2019). Burying power: New insights into incipient leadership in the Late Pre-Pottery Neolithic from an outstanding burial at Ba'ja, southern Jordan. *PLoS ONE, 14*(8), Article e0221171. https://doi.org/10.1371/journal.pone.0221171

Benz, M. (2010). Beyond death – The construction of social identities at the transition from foraging to farming. In M. Benz (Ed.), *The principle of sharing. Segregation and construction of social identities at the transition from foraging to farming* (pp. 249–276). ex oriente.

Binford, L. R. (1971). Mortuary practices: Their study and their potential. *Memoirs of the Society for American Archaeology, 25*, 6–29.

Bloch, M., & Parry, J. (Eds.). (1999). *Death and the regeneration of life*. Cambridge University Press.

Bloch-Smith, E. (1992). *Judahite burial practices and beliefs about the dead*. Journal for the Study of the Old Testament/ASOR Monograph Series.

Bocquentin, F. (2003). *Pratiques funéraires, paramètres biologiques et identités culturelles au Natoufien: une analyse archéo-anthropologique*. PhD thesis, Université Bordeaux 1.

Bocquentin, F., Kodas, E., & Ortiz, A. (2016). Headless but still eloquent! Acephalous skeletons as witnesses of Pre-Pottery Neolithic North-South Levant connections and disconnections. *Paléorient, 42*(2), 35–55.

Bocquentin, F., Anton, M., Berna, F., Rosen, A., Khalaily, H., Greenberg, H., Hart, T. C., Lernau, O., & Horwitz, L. K. (2020). Emergence of corpse cremation during the Pre-Pottery Neolithic of the Southern Levant: A multidisciplinary study of a pyre-pit burial. *PLoS ONE, 16*(1), Article e0246488. https://doi.org/10.1371/journal.pone.0246488

Bolger, D., & Wright, R. (2013). Gender in southwest Asian prehistory. In D. Bolger (Ed.), *Companion to gender prehistory* (pp. 372–394). Wiley.

Boness, D., Scheftelowitz, N., Fabian, P., Gilead, I., & Goren, Y. (2016). Petrographic study of the pottery assemblages from Ḥorvat Qarqar South, a Ghassulian Chalcolithic cemetery in the southern Levant. *Bulletin of the American Schools of Oriental Research, 375*, 185–213.

Bonogofsky, M. (2003). Neolithic plastered skulls and railroading epistemologies. *Bulletin of the American Schools of Oriental Research, 331*, 1–10.

Bonogofsky, M. (2006). *Skull collection, modification and decoration*. British Archaeological Reports.

Braun, E. (1989). The problem of the apsidal house: New aspects of Early Bronze I domestic architecture in Israel, Jordan, and Lebanon. *Palestine Exploration Quarterly, 121*, 1–43.

Braun, E., & Gophna, R. (2004). Salvage excavations at Afridar (Ashqelon, Israel) in Area G. *'Atiqot, 45*, 185–242.

Chapman, R. (2003). Death, society and archaeology: The social dimensions of mortuary practices. *Mortality, 8*(3), 305–312.

Chesson, M. (1999). Libraries of the dead: Early Bronze Age charnel houses and social identity at urban Bab edh-Dhra', Jordan. *Journal of Anthropological Archaeology, 18*, 137–164.

Chesson, M. (2001). *Social memory, identity and death: Ethnographic and archaeological perspectives on mortuary rituals*. American Anthropological Association.

Chesson, M. A. (2015). Reconceptualizing the Early Bronze Age Southern Levant without cities: Local histories and walled communities of EB II-III society. *Journal of Mediterranean Archaeology, 28*(1), 51–79.

Chesson, M. A., & Philip, G. (2003). Tales of the city? Urbanism in the Early Bronze Age Levant from Mediterranean and Levantine perspectives. *Journal of Mediterranean Archaeology, 16*, 3–16.

Childe, V. G. (1936). *Man makes himself*. Watts & Company.
Childe, V. G. (1945). Directional changes in funerary practices during 50,000 years. *Man, 4*, 13–19.
Childe, V. G. (1950). The urban revolution. *Town Planning Review, 21*, 3–171.
Childe, V.G. (1956). *Society and knowledge: The growth of human traditions*.
Cohen-Weinberger, A. (in press). Petrographic analyses of ceramic vessels and ossuaries from Quleh and Mazor (West). In I. Milevski, R. Lupu, & A. Cohen-Weinberger (Eds.), *Excavations at Quleh and Mazor (West). Iconography and burial practices in southern Levantine Chalcolithic cemeteries*. Austrian Academy of Sciences.
Couto-Ferreira, M. E., & Verderame, L. (2018). *Uterus in pre-modern societies, past and present*. Cambridge Scholars Publishing.
Duday, H. (2009). *The archaeology of the dead. Lectures in archaeothanatology*. Oxford University Press.
Eshed, V., & Bar, S. (2012). An innovative analysis of infant burials from the Chalcolithic site of Fazael 2, Israel. *Israel Exploration Journal, 62*(2), 129–140.
Eshed, V., & Nadel, D. (2005). Changes in burial customs from the Pre-Pottery to the Pottery Neolithic periods in the Levant: The case-study of Tel Roim West, Northern Israel. *Paléorient, 41*(2), 115–131.
Fadida, A., & Milevski, I. (in press). Quleh and Mazor (West): A comparison with other Chalcolithic cemeteries. In I. Milevski, R. Lupu, & A. Cohen-Weinberger (Eds.), *Excavations at Quleh and Mazor (West). Iconography and burial practices in southern Levantine Chalcolithic cemeteries*. Austrian Academy of Sciences.
Faerman, M., & Smith, P. (2008). Has society changed its attitude to infants and children? Evidence from archaeological sites in the southern Levant. In F. Gusi, S. Muriel, & C. Olària (Eds.), *"Nasciturus: Infans, puerulus. Vobis mater terra". La muerte en la infancia* (pp. 211–229) Servei d'Investigacions Arqueològiques i Prehistòriques
Fletcher, A., Pearson, J., & Ambers, J. (2008). The manipulation for social and physical identity in the Pre-Pottery Neolithic. Radiographic evidence for cranial modification at Jericho and its implications for the plastering of skulls. *Cambridge Archaeological Journal, 18*, 302–325.
Frazer, J. G. (2014). *Totemism*. Kindle. (Original work published 1887)
Friesem, D. E., Abadi, I., Shaham, D., & Grosman, L. (2019). Lime plaster cover of the dead 12,000 years ago – New evidence for the origins of lime plaster technology. *Evolutionary Human Sciences, 1*. https://doi.org/10.1017/ehs.2019.9
Galili, E., Eshed, V., Rosen, B., Kislev, M. E., Simchoni, O., Hershkovitz, I., & Gopher, A. (2009). Evidence for a separate burial ground at the submerged Pottery Neolithic site of Neve-Yam, Israel. *Paléorient, 35*(1), 31–46.
Garfinkel, Y., Dag, D., Khalaily, H., Marder, O., Milevski, I., & Ronen, A. (2012). *The Pre-Pottery Neolithic B village of Yiftahel: The 1980s–1990s excavations*. ex oriente.
Gebel, H. G. K. (2010). Commodification and the formation of Early Neolithic social identity. The issues as seen from the southern Jordanian highlands. In M. Benz (Ed.), *The principle of sharing. Segregation and construction of social identities at the transition from foraging to farming* (pp. 35–80). ex oriente.
Giddens, A. (1979). *Central problems in social theory. Action, structure, and contradiction in social analysis*. University of California Press.
Gilead, I. (1995). *Grar. A Chalcolithic site in the northern Negev*. Ben-Gurion University of the Negev.
Gilead, I. (2011). Fifth millennium culture history Ghassulian and other Chalcolithic entities in the southern Levant. In J. L. Lovell & Y. M. Rowan (Eds.), *Culture, chronology, and the Chalcolithic: Theory and transition* (pp. 12–24). Oxbow Books.
Gimbutas, M. (1999). *The living goddess* (M. R. Dexter, Ed.). University of California Press.
Godelier, M. (1964). *La notion de "mode de production asiatique" et les schémas marxistes d'évolution des sociétés*. Centre de recherches marxistes.
Golani, A. (2019). *Ashqelon Barne'a: The Early Bronze Age site. Volume I: The excavations*. Israel Antiquities Authority.

Golden, J. (2010). *Dawn of the metal age. Technology and society during the Levantine Chalcolithic*. Equinox Publishing.

Goren, Y., & Fabian, P. (2002). *Kissufim Road: A Chalcolithic mortuary site*. Israel Antiquities Authority.

Goring Morris, A. N. (2005). Life, death and the emergence of differential status in the Near Eastern Neolithic. Evidence from Kfar Hahoresh, Lower Galilee, Israel. In J. Clarke (Ed.), *Archaeological perspectives on the transmission and transformation of culture in the eastern Mediterranean* (pp. 89–105). Oxbow Books.

Goring-Morris, A. N. (1995). Complex hunter/gatherers at the end of the Paleolithic (20,000–10,000 BP). In T. E. Levy (Ed.), *The archaeology of society in the Holy Land* (pp. 141–167). Leicester University Press.

Goring-Morris, A. N., & Belfer-Cohen, A. (2002). Symbolic behaviour from the Epipalaeolithic and Early Neolithic of the Near East: Preliminary observations on continuity and change. In H. G. K. Gebel, B. D. Hermansen, & C. H. Jensen (Eds.), *Magic practices and ritual in the Near Eastern Neolithic* (pp. 67–79). ex oriente.

Gorzalczany, A. (2018). The Chalcolithic cemetery at Palmahim (North): New evidence of burial patterns from the central coastal plain. *'Atiqot, 91*, 1–94.

Greenberg, R. (2011). Travelling in (world) time. Transformation, commoditization and the beginnings of urbanization. In T. C. Wilkinson, S. Sherrat, & J. Benet (Eds.), *Intervieawing worlds. Systematic interactions in Eurasia, 7th–1st millennia BC*. Papers from a conference in Memory of Professor Andrew Sherratt (pp. 231–240). Oxbow Books.

Greenberg, R. (2019). *The archaeology of the Bronze Age Levant. From urban ortgins to the demise of city-states, 3700–1000 BCE*. Cambridge University Press.

Guy, P. L. O. (1938). *Megiddo tombs*. University of Chicago Press.

Harney, É., May, H., Shalem, D., Rohland, N., Mallick, S., Lazaridis, I., Sarig, R., Stewardson, K., Nordenfelt, S., Patterson, S., Hershkovitz, I., & Reich, D. (2018). Ancient DNA from Chalcolithic Israel reveals the role of population mixture in cultural transformation. *Nature Communications, 9*, 3336. https://doi.org/10.1038/s41467-018-05649-9

Harrison, T. (2001). Early Bronze organization as reflected burial patterns from the southern Levant. In S. Wolff (Ed.), *Studies in the archaeology of Israel and neighbouring countries in memory of Douglas L. Esse* (pp. 215–236). University of Chicago Press.

Hershkovitz, I., Garfinkel, Y., & Arensburg, B. (1986). Neolithic skeletal remains at Yiftahel, Area C (Israel). *Paléorient, 12*(1), 73–81.

Hertz, R. (1960). *Death and the right hand*. Free Press.

Hesse, B., & Wapnish, P. (1979). Animal remains from the Bab edh-Dhra cemetery. *The Annual of the American Schools of Oriental Research, 246*, 133–136.

Hobsbawm, E. (1965). Introduction. In K. Marx, *Pre-capitalist economic formations* (pp. 1-67). International Publishers

Hodder, I. (2011). Human-thing entanglement: Towards an integrated archaeological perspective. *Journal of the Royal Anthropological Institute (N.S.), 17*, 154–177.

Horwitz, L. K. (2007). Faunal remains from Late Chalcolithic–Bronze Age dwelling and burial caves at Shoham (North), Lod valley. *'Atiqot, 55*, 1*–15*.

Horwitz, L. K. (in press). In I. Milevski, R. Lupu, & A. Cohen-Weinberger (Eds.), *Excavations at Quleh and Mazor (West). Iconography and burial practices in southern Levantine Chalcolithic cemeteries*. Austrian Academy of Sciences.

Horwitz, L. K., & Goring-Morris, A. N. (2004). Animals and ritual during the Levantine PPNB: A case study from the site of Kfar Hahoresh, Israel. *Anthropozoologica, 39*(1), 165–178.

Ilan, D. (2002). Mortuary practices in Early Bronze Age Canaan. *Near Eastern Archaeology, 65*(2), 92–104.

Ilan, D., & Rowan, Y. M. (2012). Deconstructing and recomposing the narrative of spiritual life in the Chalcolithic of the southern Levant (4500–3600 B.C.E.). *Archeological Papers of the American Anthropological Association, 21*(1), 89–113.

Jaruf, P., Milevski, I., & Gandulla, B. (2014). La estructura social del calcolítico palestinense: una propuesta de interpretación desde el materialismo histórico. *Antiguo Oriente, 12*, 149–184.

Kanjou, Y., Kuijt, I., Erdal, Y. S., & Kondo, O. (2013). Early human decapitation, 11,700–10,700 cal bp, within the Pre-Pottery Neolithic village of Tell Qaramel, north Syria. *Internationl Journal of Osteoarchaeology, 25*(5), 743–752.

Kenyon, K. (1965). *Excavations at Jericho. Volume 2. The tombs excavated in 1955-58.* British School of Achaeology in Jerusalem.

Kenyon, K. (1981). *Excavations at Jericho. Volume 3. The architecture and stratigraphy at the tell. Plates.* British School of Achaeology in Jerusalem.

Khalaily, H., Milevski, I., Getzov, N., Hershkovitz, I., Barzilai, O., Yarosevich, A., Shlomi, V., Najjar, A., Zidan, O., Smithline, H., & Liran, R. (2008). Recent excavations at the Neolithic site of Yiftahel (Khalet Khalladyiah), Lower Galilee. *Neo-Lithics, 2*(08), 3–11.

Koepel, R. (1940). *Teleilat Ghassul II. Compte rendu des fouilles de l'Institut Biblique Pointificial 1932-1936.* Institut Biblique Pointificial.

Kuijt, I. (2001). Meaningful masks: Place, death, and the transmission of social memory in early agricultural communities of the Near Eastern Pre-Pottery Neolithic. In M. Chesson (Ed.), *Social memory, identity and death: Intradisciplinary perspectives on mortuary rituals* (pp. 80–99). American Anthropolgial Association.

Kuijt, I. (2008). The regeneration of life. Neolithic structures of symbolic remembering and forgetting. *Current Anthropology, 49*, 171–197.

Kuperman, T. (2010). *Anthropological aspects and burial customs in the Pottery Neolithic period (8350–6800 B.P.).* MA thesis, University of Tel Aviv. (Hebrew with English summary)

Lazaridis, I., Nadel, D., Rollefson, G., Merrett, D. C., Rohland, N., Mallick, S., Fernandes, D., Novak, M., Gamarra, B., Sirak, K., Connell, S., Stewardson, K., Harney, E., Fu, Q., Gonzalez-Fortes, G., Jones, E. P., Alpaslan Roodenberg, S., Lengyel, G., Bocquentin, F., Gasparian, B., Monge, J. M., Gregg, M., Eshed, V., Mizrahi, A. S., Meiklejohn, C., Gerritsen, F., Bejenaru, L., Blüher, M., Campbell, A., Cavalleri, G., Comas, D., Froguel, P., Gilbert, E., Kerr, S. M., Kovacs, P., Krause, J., McGettigan, D., Merrigan, M., Merriwether, D. A., O'Reilly, S., Richards, M. B., Semino, O., Shamoon-Pour, M., Stefanescu, G., Stumvoll, M., Tönjes, A., Torroni, A., Wilson, J. F., Yengo, L., Hovhannisyan, N. A., Patterson, N., Pinhasi, R., & Reich, D. (2016). Genomic insight into the origin of farming in the Ancient Near East. *Nature, 536*(7617), 419–424. https://doi.org/10.1038/nature19310

Lengyel, G., Nadel, D., & Bocquentin, F. (2013). The Natufian at Raqefet Cave. In O. Bar-Yosef & F. Valla (Eds.), *Natufian foragers in the Levant: Terminal Pleistocene social changes in western Asia in prehistory* (pp. 478–504). International Monographs in Prehistory.

Lepetit, A. (2017). *La transition VIe-V^e millénaire au Levant sud à travers les tombes de la fin du Néolithique/Chalcolithique Ancien du site d'Ein Zippori (Israël).* MA thesis, Université d`Aix-Marseille.

Lévi-Strauss, C. (1991). *Totemism.* Merlin Press.

Levy, J., & Gilead, I. (2012). Spinning in the 5th millennium in the southern Levant: Aspects of textile Economy. *Paléorient, 38*, 127–139.

Levy, T. E. (Ed.). (1987). *Shiqmim I: Studies concerning Chalcolithic societies in the northern Negev desert, Israel.* BAR.

Levy, T. E. (1995). Cult, metallurgy and rank societies – Chalcolithic period (ca. 4500–3500 BCE). In T. E. Levy (Ed.), *The archaeology of society in the Holy Land* (pp. 226–244). Leicester University Press.

Levy, T. E. (Ed.). (2006). *Archaeology, anthropology and cult. The Sanctuary at Gilat, Israel.* Equinox Publishing.

Levy, T. E., & Alon, D. (1982). The Chalcolithic mortuary site near Mezad Aluf, northern Negev desert: A preliminary study. *Bulletin of the American Schools of Oriental Research, 248*, 37–59.

Levy, T. E., & Alon, D. (1985). Shiqmim: A Chalcolithic village and mortuary centre in the Northern Negev. *Paléorient, 11*(1), 71–83. https://doi.org/10.3406/paleo.1985.4362

Lull, V. (2000). Death and society: A Marxist approach. *Antiquity, 74*, 576–580.

Lull, V., & Picazo, M. (1989). Arqueología de la muerte y estructura social. *Archivo español de arqueología, 62*, 5–20.

Lupo, A. (2018). Dalle sette caverne alla parto: un excursus su concezione e pratiche intorno all'utero nel Messico antico e modern. In E. Couto-Ferrerira & L. Verderame (Eds.), *Cultural constructions of the uterus in pre-modern societies, past and present* (pp. 57–86). Cambridge Scholars Publishing.

Mallon, A., Koepel, R., & Neuville, R. (1934). *Teleilat Ghassul I. Compte Rendu des Fouilles de l'Insitut Biblique Pontificial 1929–1932*. Pontificial Biblical Institute.

Marx, K. (1977). *Capital. A critique of political economy, vol. I* (E. Mandel, Intr.; B. Fowkes, Trans.). Vintage Books. (Original work published 1867)

Marx, K. (1993a [1859]). *Contribution to the critique of the political economy* (S. W. Ryazanskaya, Trans.). Progress Publishers. (Original work published 1859)

Marx, K. (1993b [1939]). *Grundisse. Foundations of political economy (Rough draft)* (M. Nicolaus, Trans.). Penguin Books. (Original work published 1939)

Marx, K., & Engels, F. (1977). *The German ideology* (Edited and introduced by C. J. Arthur). Lawrence & Wishart. (Original work published 1932)

Milevski, I. (2002). A new fertility figurine and new animal motifs from the Chalcolithic of the southern Levant: Finds from Cave K-1 at Quleh, Israel. *Paléorient, 34*(2), 37–46.

Milevski, I. (2011). *Early Bronze Age goods exchange in the southern Levant: A Marxist perspective*. Equinox Publishing.

Milevski, I. (2013). The transition from the Chalcolithic to the Early Bronze Age of the southern Levant in socioeconomic context. *Paléorient, 39*(1), 193–208.

Milevski, I., & Getzov, N. (2014). 'En Zippori. *Hadashot Arkheologiyot-Excavations and Surveys in Israel, 126*. http://www.hadashot-esi.org.il/Report_Detail_Eng.aspx?id=13675&mag_id=121

Milevski, I., & Horwitz, L. K. (2019). Domestication of the donkey (*Equus asinus*) in the Southern Levant: Archaeozoology, iconography and economy. In R. Kowner, G. Bar-Oz, M. Biran, M. Shahar, & G. Shelach-Lavi (Eds.), *Animals and human society in Asia. Historical, cultural and ethical perspectives* (pp. 93–148). Palgrave Macmillan.

Milevski, I., Khalaily, H., Getzov, N., & Hershkovitz, I. (2008). The plastered skulls and other PPNB finds from Yiftahel, lower Galilee (Israel). *Paléorient, 34*(2), 37–46.

Milevski, I., Vardi, J., & Khalaily, H. (2022). Typology, material and cultural role of stone bracelets (bangles) from the Neolithic megasite of Motza – Preliminary report. In Y. Nishiaki, O. Maeda, & M. Arimura (Eds.), *Tracks of the Near Eastern Neolithic – Lithic perspectives on its origins, development and dispersals* (pp. 141–152). Sidestone Press.

Milevski, I., Lupu, R., & Cohen-Weinberger, A. (Eds.). (in press). *Excavations at Quleh and Mazor (West). Iconography and burial practices in southern Levantine Chalcolithic cemeteries*. Austrian Academy of Sciences.

Molleson, T. I. (2007). Bones of work at the origins of labour. In S. Hamilton, R. D. Whitehouse, & K. I. Wright (Eds.), *Archaeology and women: Ancient and modern issues* (pp. 185–198). Altamira Press.

Morgan, L. H. (1877). *Ancient society or researches in the lines of human progress from savagery through barbarism to civilization*. Bharti Library.

Nagar, Y. (2013). The physical anthropology of the Peqi'in population. In D. Shalem, Z. Gal, & Smithline (Eds.), *The Peqiin Cave: A Late Chalcolithic Cemetery. Upper Galilee, Israel* (Land og Galilee 2) (pp. 391–406). Ostracon & Israel Antiquities Authority.

Nativ, A. (2014). *Priorizing death and society. The archaeology of Chalcolithic and contemporary cemeteries in the southern Levant*. Equinox Publishing.

Naumov, A. (2007). Housing the dead: Burials inside houses and vessels in the Neolithic Balkans. In J. K. Kozłowsky & M. Nowak (Eds.), *Mesolithic/Neolithic interactions in the Balkans and in the middle Danube basin* (BAR international series 1726) (pp. 255–266). BAR.

Naumov, G. (2008). The vessel as a human body: Neolithic anthropomorphic vessels and their reflection in later periods. In I. Berg (Ed.), *Breaking the mould: Challenging the past through pottery* (BAR international series 1864) (pp. 93–101). BAR.

Orrelle, E. (2008). Infant jar burials: A ritual associated with early agriculture? In K. Buchvarov (Ed.), *Babies reborn: Infant/child burials in pre- and protohistory* (pp. 71–78). Archaeopress.

Özbek, M. (2009). Remodeled human skulls in Köşk Höyük (Neolithic Age, Anatolia): A new appraisal in view of recent discoveries. *Journal of Archaeological Science, 36*, 379–386.

Palerm, A. (2008). *Antropología y marxismo* (E. R. Wolf, Ed.). Universidad Autónoma Metropolitana.

Parker Pearson, M. (1982). Mortuary practices, society and ideology: An ethnoarchaeological study. In I. Hodder (Ed.), *Symbolic and structural archaeology* (pp. 99–113). Cambridge University Press.

Parker Pearson, M. (2001). *The archaeology of death and burial*. Cambridge University Press.

Perrot, J. (1955). The excavations at Tell Abu Matar, near Beersheba. *Israel Exploration Journal, 5*, 17–41.

Peterson, J. (2002). *Sexual revolutions: Gender and labor at the dawn of agriculture*. Altamira Press.

Reshef, H., Anton, M., Bocquentin, F., Vardi, J., Khalaily, H., Davis, L., Bar-Oz, G., & Marom, N. (2019). Tails of animism: A joint burial of humans and foxes in Pre-Pottery Neolithic Motza, Israel. *Antiquity Project Gallery, 93*(371), Article e28. https://doi.org/10.15184/aqy.2019.165

Rollefson, G. O. (2000). Ritual and social structure at Neolithic 'Ain Ghazal. In I. Kuijt (Ed.), *Life in Neolithic farming communities: Social organization, identity, and differentiation* (pp. 165–180). Kluwer Academic Publications.

Rowan, Y. M. (2014). The mortuary process in the Chalcolithic period. In M. Sebbane, O. Mischbrandl, & D. Master (Eds.), *Masters of fire* (pp. 100–113). Institute for the Study of the Ancient World, New York University.

Rowan, Y. M., & Ilan, D. (2012). The subterranean landscape in the southern Levant during the Chalcolithic period. In H. Moyes (Ed.), *Sacred darkness. A global perspective on the ritual use of caves* (pp. 87–107). University Press of Colorado.

Sahlins, M. (1972). *Stone age economics*. University of Chicago Press.

Saxe, A. (1970). *Social dimensions of mortuary practices*. PhD thesis, University of Michigan.

Schaub, R. T., & Rast, W. E. (1989). *Bâb edh–Dhrâc excavations in the cemetery directed by Paul W. Lapp (1965–1967)*. Eisenbrauns.

Scheftelowitz, N. (2016). *Chalcolithic burial customs in the southern Levant – The case study of Horvat Qarqar South and Palmahim*. PhD thesis, Ben-Gurion University in the Negev. (Hebrew with English summary)

Shalev, O. (2018). The fortification wall of Tel Erani: A labour perspective. *Tel Aviv, 45*, 193–215.

Shanks, M., & Tilley, M. (1982). Ideology, symbolic power and ritual communication: A reinterpretation of Neolithic mortuary practices. In I. Hodder (Ed.), *Symbolic and structural archaeology* (pp. 129–154). Cambridge University Press.

Sheridan, S. G. (2017). Bioarchaeology in the ancient Near East: Challenges and future directions for the southern Levant. *American Journal of Physical Anthropology, 165*, 110–152.

Sheridan, S. G., Ullinger, J., Gregoricka, L., & Chesson, M. (2014). Bioarchaeological reconstruction of group identity at Early Bronze Age Bab edh-Dhra'. In B. W. Porter & A. T. Boutin (Eds.), *Remembering the death in the Ancient Near East. Recent contributions from bioarchaeology and mortuary archaeology* (pp. 133–184). University Press of Colorado.

Sherratt, A. (1981). Plough and pastoralism: Aspects of the secondary products revolution. In I. Hodder, G. Isaac, & M. Hammond (Eds.), *Patterns of the past: Studies in honor of David Clarke* (pp. 261–305). Cambridge University Press.

Slon, V., Sarig, R., Hershkovitz, H., Khalaily, H., & Milevski, I. (2014). The plastered skulls from the Pre-Pottery Neolithic B site of Yiftahel (Israel) – A computed tomography-based analysis. *PLoS ONE, 9*(2), Article e89242. https://doi.org/10.1371/journal.pone.0089242

Smith, P., Zagerrons, T., Sabari, P., Golden, J., Levy, T. E., & Dawson, L. (2006). Death and the sanctuary. The human remains from Gilat. In T. E. Levy (Ed.), *Archaeology, anthropology and cult. The Sanctuary at Gilat, Israel* (pp. 327–366). Equinox Publishing.

Stordeur, D., & Khawam, R. (2007). Les crânes surmodelés de Tell Aswad (PPNB, Syrie). Premier regard sur l'ensemble, premières réflexions. *Syria, 84*, 5–32.

Tainter, J. A. (1975). Social inference and mortuary practices: An experiment in numerical classification. *World Archaeology, 7*(1), 1–15.

Tringham, R. (1994). Engendered places in prehistory. *Gender Place and Culture. A Journal of Feminist Geography, 1*(2), 169–203.

Ussishkin, D. (1980). The Ghassulian shrine. *Tel Aviv, 7*, 1–44.

Watkins, T. (2012). Household, community and social landscape: Mainting social memory in the Early Neolithic of southwest Asia. In M. Furtholt, M. Hinz, & D. Mischka (Eds.), *"As times goes by"? Monumentality, landscapes and temporal perspective* (pp. 23–44). Verlag Dr. Rudolf Habelt.

Wenstein-Evron, M., Yeshurun, R., Ashkenazi, H., Chasan, R., Rosenberg, D., Bachrach, N., Boaretto, E., Caracuta, V., & Kaufman, D. (2018). After 80 years – Deeper in the Natufian layers of el-Wad Terrace, Mount Carmel, Israel. *Mitekufat Haeven – Journal of the Israel Prehistoric Society, 48*, 5–61.

Wright, R. P. (1996). *Gender and archaeology*. University of Pensylvannia Press.

Yannai, E. (2016). *En Esur ('Ein Asawir) II. Excavations at the Cemeteries*. Ostracon & Israel Antiquities Authority.

Yaroshevich, A. (2016). Giv'at Rabbi. *Hadashot Arkheologiyot- Excavations and Surveys in Israel, 128*. http://www.hadashot-esi.org.il/Report_Detail_Eng.aspx?id=24973&mag_id=124

Yekutieli, Y., & Gophna, R. (1994). Excavation at an Early Bronze Age site near Nizzanim. *Tel Aviv, 21*, 162–185.

Yeshurun, R., Bar-Oz, G., & Nadel, D. (2013). The social role of food in the Natufian cemetery of Raqefet Cave, Mount Carmel, Israel. *Journal of Anthropological Archaeology, 32*, 511–526.

Home on the Range: Late Neolithic Architecture and Subsistence in Jordan's Black Desert

Gary Rollefson

Abstract Architecture during the seventh and sixth millennia BCE reflects some distinctive differences between buildings on the slopes of mesas in the Wadi al-Qattafi and along the Wisad Pools in Jordan's Black Desert, but the buildings share basic aspects as well: all are generally circular, built of flood basalt slabs, and have no preserved superstructure. Pollen from one structure at Wisad Pools indicates marshy habitats around the *qe'an* (dry lake beds), and the location of the structures near *qe'an* suggest roofing may have used aquatic plants to create roofing. Large numbers of structures in dense association at both sites as well as faunal remains indicate large groups of hunter-herders associated with mass slaughter of gazelles using "kites" to trap entire herds. The problems associated with moving hundreds of killed animals as whole carcasses or as skinned and butchered masses of meat and hides are discussed.

Keywords Late Neolithic · Neighborhoods · Architecture · Phragmites · Gazelle meat and hides · Transport

1 Introduction

Beginning at ca. 9500 cal BCE the climate in the eastern Mediterranean area began a dramatic change (Rollefson, 2021a: Fig. 1), becoming increasingly wetter until ca. 5000 BCE, when severe oscillations of rainfall began, leading to the onset of arid and hyperarid desertification in the Harrat ash-Sham (Black Desert) of eastern Jordan (Fig. 1). Populations of hunter-gatherer groups in this region can't be estimated with any accuracy, but it is probable that pre-seventh millennium BCE groups were clearly small and very mobile. But after 7000 BCE, the number of people in

G. Rollefson (✉)
Whitman College, Walla Walla, WA, USA
e-mail: rollefgo@whitman.edu

Fig. 1 Location of Wisad Pools and Wadi al-Qattafi in the Black Desert

the Black Desert mushroomed in size (Rollefson, 2021a), not due to increased precipitation, but to a radical new tactic of hunting gazelle: stampeding entire herds into special hunting traps called "kites."

The Eastern Badia Archaeological Project (EBAP) has undertaken surveys and excavations at Wisad Pools and Wadi al-Qattafi, two "megasites" in the volcanic flood basalt field popularly known as the Black Desert since 2008. Wisad Pools has an estimated 400 structures that are not animal enclosures spread through approximately 1.8 km^2, and the mesas at Qattafi host about 800 structures along 7 km on both sides of the wadi. A total of five Late Neolithic (LN) structures have been excavated: one at M7 and one at M4 in the Wadi al-Qattafi, and three from Wisad Pools.

2 Wisad Pools

Wisad Pools are natural depressions and built dry-stone dikes in the short (ca. 1.5 km long) Wadi Wisad that drains a broad plateau (ca. 2 km² catchment area) during the rainy season and empties into the Qa al-Wisad ca. 0.5 km² in area to the SE of the site. There is some scant evidence of Lower Paleolithic presence, and looting in the past destroyed a Late PPNB camp (second half of the eighth millennium BCE), but late in the first half of the seventh millennium (ca. 6600 BCE) LN structures appear at the site in clusters of ca. 8–25 buildings each in "neighborhoods" (Rollefson et al., n.d.). Post-Neolithic architecture, perhaps spanning parts of the Chalcolithic and Early Bronze Age, is much less dense, and except for a few tens of pastoral complexes of huts and animal enclosures, most of the buildings from the fifth and fourth millennia BCE appear to be funereal in purpose. There are late Iron Age tower tombs, but little evidence of any intensive building during the second millennium BCE. Safaitic people evidently made use of the water in the pools, but the only buildings they left behind are three modified and re-used late Iron Age burial towers.

2.1 Wisad Pools Excavations

Two seasons of survey (2008–2009) and six campaigns of excavations (2011, 2013–2014, 2018–2019, 2022) have been undertaken at Wisad Pools.

2.1.1 W-400

W-400 is located near the northern edge of the site. It is a relatively small hut of irregular subcircular shape with a ca. 4 m interior diameter (and 6 m exterior); it appears to have some association with an elliptical animal enclosure (Fig. 2a; cf. Wasse et al., n.d., 2018), although it has not yet been verified if the two were physically attached. The walls of both the hut and the corral, built with pyroclastic basalt boulders rather than flood basalt slabs, are low, preserved to a height of 60–70 cm, although there has been considerable collapse, especially the hut; the instability of using boulders has probably contributed to the damage. It has not yet been possible to detect a doorway, although it is possible it is in the northern wall. There are several "bays" inside the hut, spaces that are delineated by short stub walls (Fig. 2b). Two radiocarbon dates indicate occupation intermittently from the beginning of the seventh millennium until its end.

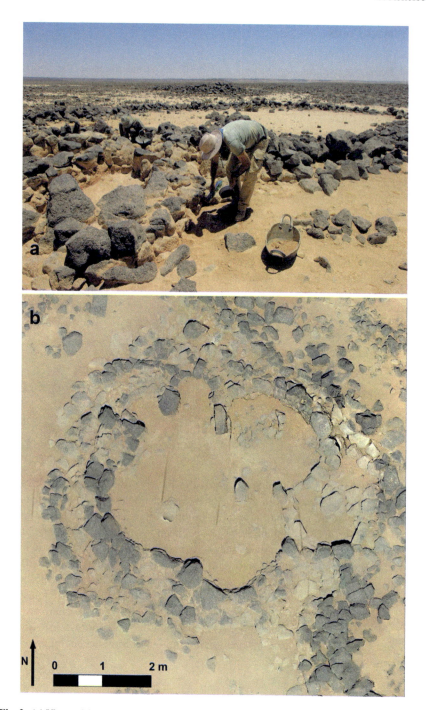

Fig. 2 (a) View to NE of the excavation of W-400; in the background is a large oval animal enclosure. (b) Aerial view of W-400 (photos: Y. Rowan)

2.1.2 W-66

W-66 is about the same size as W-400, and it also has an irregular wall contour, but the similarities end there. The southern and eastern wall were constructed with flat slabs set as deeply corbelled stretchers in a bonded pattern. The northern wall appears to have been breached, then rapidly and sloppily rebuilt using slabs set on end (Fig. 3). A vertical stone (marked P in Fig. 3b) measuring 102 x 44 x 30 cm stood near the center of the structure, and a thin flat slab (93 × 90 × 10 cm) was erected at the eastern wall (Rollefson et al., 2012: Fig. 16). At the western side of the structure, an apsidal alcove was constructed measuring 1.5 × 0.85 m. Gypsum plaster was used to surface the floor of the alcove at least four times with accumulated dirt up to 10 cm between the plaster laminae; the last plastering episode is 28-35 cm higher than the floor level in the main room (Rollefson et al., 2012: Fig. 15). The original floor of the entire structure was coated with a ca. 1–2 cm layer of gypsum plaster, and just to the east of the alcove an elliptical basin 58 x 44 cm was excavated 5 cm below the floor and coated with 1 cm of gypsum plaster. A single radiocarbon date from the charcoal in the plaster yielded a date of 6600 to 6460 cal BCE for the founding of the building (Table 1).

2.1.3 W-80

W-80 is a large and very complex structure. Six radiocarbon dates range from the middle of the seventh millennium to the middle of the sixth (Table 1). The main room is just over 6 m in interior diameter (ca. 8.5 m exterior diameter). There is a central pillar about a meter high, 60 cm wide and 20 cm thick that probably had some ritual importance in view of specific faunal remains at its base (Wasse et al., 2018) (Fig. 4). A similar upright stood against the western wall; an allied companion was not found on the eastern wall, but the major renovations of W-80 over its use-life (as much as a millennium or more) may have removed it. In places the room's walls were preserved to a height of ca. 90 cm. Two narrow (35 cm wide) benches were aligned along the northwestern wall and along the southeastern wall. A large thin (ca. 30 × 20 × 1 cm) patch of gypsum plaster was found along the western wall (Rollefson et al., 2018), evoking the situation in W-66.

There was a window in the south wall in the earliest phase of occupation, framed by two thin slabs standing on edge on the flat slab that formed the base of the window (f, above a in Fig. 4b); the window was later blocked. There are two doorways in W-80, marked as red circles in Fig. 4; The earliest NE doorway was 2.3 m wide (Fig. 4b), which in a later phase was narrowed to only 60 cm (Fig. 4a). Figure 5a was taken at about 7:00 a.m. five days after the summer solstice, and the alignment of the shadow, the doorway (a), and the window (above b, blocked in this later phase of the building) suggests some importance of this orientation. The other door is in the southwestern part of the room and measures ca. 55 cm wide but only 40 cm high; the large rock that imitates a lintel may be a tumble from the wall (Rollefson et al., 2013: 12–13 and Fig. 9a).

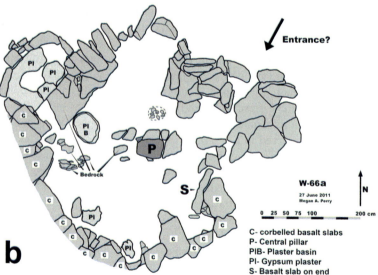

Fig. 3 (**a**) View to the west of the interior of W-66 (Photo: G. Rollefson). (**b**) Final top plan of W-66 (Drawing: Y. Rowan)

Outside the SW door is a roughly circular addition to the main room we've named the "porch" (P in Fig. 5b). In later phases this appears to have been an outdoor work area (a large dimpled grinding slab was found in the latest phase, but

Home on the Range: Late Neolithic Architecture and Subsistence in Jordan's Black Desert   153

Table 1 Radiocarbon dates from Wisad Pools and Wadi al-Qattafi

Site	Structure	Sample	Locus	Cal BCE
Wisad	W-66	Beta 46621	6	6600-6460
Wisad	W-80	Beta 395440	073	5765-5670
Wisad	W-80	Beta 366675	011	5710-5610/6570-6440
Wisad	W-80	Beta 395441	078	5890-5740
Wisad	W-80	Beta 366677	033	6000-5840
Wisad	W-80	Beta 524015	108	6068-5986
Wisad	W-80	Beta 366676	022	6590-6580/6570-6440
Wisad	W-400	UGAMS 53254	070	5920-5800
Wisad	W-400	UGAMS 53256	053	7040-6680
Mesa 4	SS-11	Beta 346614	015	5480-5320
Mesa 7	SS-1	Beta 431871	026	6455-6390
Mesa 7	SS-1	Beta 431872	029	6490-6430
Mesa 7	SS-1	Beta 464324	063	6383-6236
Mesa 7	SS-1	Beta 364325	073	6432-6336/6315-6255

earlier there was a ring of thin stones set on edge into the soil that defined a circular pit with a diameter of one meter. Adjacent to the NW was an elliptical area about 12 m in diameter bounded by slabs set on edge with no clear indication of use; it appears to have been another work area.

2.2 *Excavations at the Wadi al-Qattafi Mesas*

Three branches of the Wadi al-Qattafi (North, Central and South) converge at the Qa al-Qattafi. The qa is 6 km² in area, and the catchment area of the three branches is approximately 175 km². The high number of structures around and on the mesas in the Wadi al-Qattafi is matched by the density of architecture (Fig. 6). There are at least 278 structures that are not animal enclosures at the base of M7, more than 50 on the northern and northeastern slopes of M5, and more than 40 just across the wadi at M8 (Rowan et al., 2017). Two seasons of survey were conducted at the Wadi al-Qattafi plus two excavation campaigns on the south slope of M7 and one more at the base of M4.

2.2.1 Mesa 7, SS-1

Drone photography rapidly recorded the locations of the dense numbers of structures in Fig. 7, and examination of the photos revealed that there was a pattern of clustering of the buildings (Fig. 6b). Figure 7a shows one cluster that included the large building that was excavated (SS-1, labeled with a "1" in a white circle). Structure SS-2 was sampled, but perhaps 75% or more was destroyed in antiquity;

Fig. 4 (**a**) View to the SE of the early half of the first half of the seventh millennium LN interior of W-80 (red circle); note the narrow NE doorway at left center (photo: Y. Rowan). (**b**) the same view, but of the last half of the seventh millennium phase of W-80; note the wide door at left center (red circles indicate doorways). (Photo: Y. Rowan). (**a**) alcove; (**b**) "porch"; (**c**) central pillar; (**d**) hearth; (**e**): western forecourt; (**f**) window through the wall blocked in the later phase

Fig. 5 (a) Photo to SW with the later doorway and b the blocked window (photo: G. Rollefson). (b) View towards the west across a large forecourt of W-80. P is the "Porch"; W is the western forecourt; S is a probable shrine; and "?" is a post-Neolithic addition of unknown age (photo: Y. Rowan)

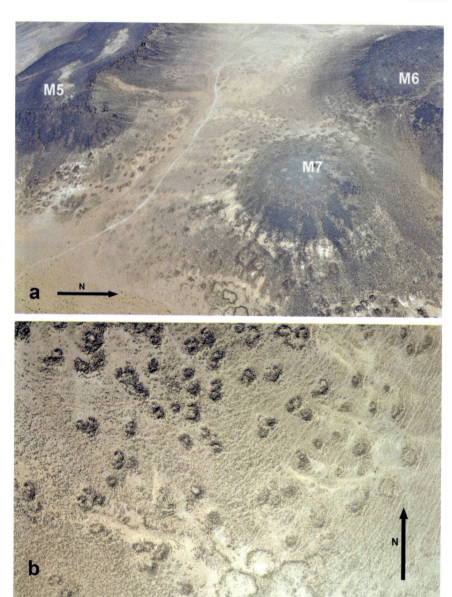

Fig. 6 (**a**) Mesa 7 between Mesas 5 and 6 (photo APAAME_20080909_DLK-285 by David Kennedy, by permission). (**b**) Drone photograph showing clustering of structures on the southern slope of Mesa 7 (photo: A.C. Hill)

the other structures (SS-3 through SS-7) were not sampled during our two seasons at this mesa.

Two configurations of structures were evident: one was a simple circular wall of stacked slabs around the interior, and the other a circular wall made of rectangular

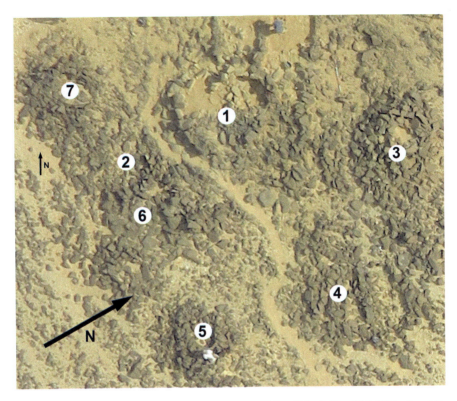

Fig. 7 Drone view of one cluster on the south slope of Mesa 7, including SS-1 (#1 in the white circle at an early stage of excavation) and SS-2 through SS-7 (photo: A.C. Hill)

slabs set on edge. SS-1 added a slight variant, with a simple wall that was modified once (the dotted line in Fig. 8b), probably changing an original circular shape to the structure to an oval one, and once again when a layer of slabs set on end were added to the interior face of the simple wall (Fig. 8a, b).

Five radiocarbonn samples place SS-1 throughout the last half of the seventh millennium BCE (Table 1). It had an oval shape whose dimensions were 8 m E-W by 6 m N-S on the exterior and 5 m E-W by 4 m N-S. The interior of SS-1 incorporated three standing stones (marked with a red "s" in Fig. 8a), one in the northern wall and another in the southern one; a third standing stone was slightly off the center of the north-south axis. The 60 cm wide entrance to the building is marked with a red circle in Fig. 8a, and because the structure was constructed on a slope, a flight of 4 steps led into the interior (the shaded area in Fig. 8b) to a threshold about 15 cm above the floor. Note that the sun can be seen lighting the steps as it rises in this photo taken around the time of the summer solstice (Rollefson et al., 2017: Fig. 5), paralleling the situation at W-80. A large and deep hearth against a huge basalt slab set on edge in the southeastern part of the room appears to have been hot enough to crack the block.

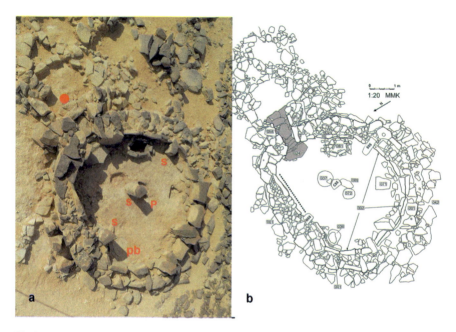

Fig. 8 (**a**) Drone shot of a structure cluster at M7 SS-1 (photo: A.C. Hill). (**b**) Top plan of M7 SS-1 (drawing: M. Kersel)

Substantial plaster features were associated with the floor of the building. A cylindrical pit 38 cm in diameter had been cut 34 cm into the bedrock and coated with brilliant white plaster; the volume of this feature was 38.5 liters (Rollefson et al., 2017: 20, Fig. 6). Plaster was also used to make a shallow oval-shaped basin (65 × 50 × 10 cm) on the floor against the northwestern corner of SS-1. A period of non-use or abandonment resulted in a 3 cm accumulation of silt in the basin on which a slightly smaller plaster basin was made; long finger marks were still in place after the fashioning of the second basin (Rollefson et al., 2016: Figs. 4–6). The basin plaster is gypsum based, but the pit plaster is lime plaster (K. al-Bashaireh, personal communication: cf. Rollefson et al., 2016).

A study of patination on flint tools and debitage indicates that only the eastern half of SS-1 was roofed. To the east of the N-S axis defined by the standing stones and central pillar, 96.5 of the artifacts bore no patina, while to the west of the axis, 64% of the tools and debitage were lightly to heavily patinated.

2.2.2 Mesa 4, SS-11

A survey of the slopes of M4 tallied 60 structures excluding animal enclosures that probably dated to the seventh through the end of the sixth millennia. Among these were two clusters of buildings likely representing small communities of LN hunter-herders, although one of the clusters was less involved in hunting than the other.

Figure 9a shows the SW edge of M4, and the clusters are distinctly separate entities. The 11 black circles (three are just off the photo to the left) are circular structures similar to the rest of the mesas along the wadi, probably late seventh to mid-sixth millennia in age. The second group includes nine white circles in a configuration that is very different: each of the shelters is attached to a large circular corral. Included in this group is SS-11 (Fig. 9b), attached to a large (ca. 15 m in diameter) animal enclosure.

SS-11 was a small oval hut measuring ca. 3 m (N-S) by 2 m (E-W) (Fig. 10a); the original height of the walls can't be determined because of the collapsed corbelling into the interior. An especially curious design was the incorporation of two doors. The trapezoidal western door led to the western side of the mesa slope. It was small, only 85 cm high and 78 cm wide at the threshold; a person would have had crawl into the room. The eastern door was more rectangular (89 x 61 cm) and it led into the corral. The building was occupied in two main phases. The earlier had a dirt floor, succeeded by a major alteration that included the blocking of the doorway leading to the corral and the intricate paving of the room with basalt slabs 35 x 50 cm in size. A radiocarbon sample taken from a hearth just to the east of the eastern door dated the structure to the last half of the sixth millennium (Table 1), but it is not certain to which phase of the building it might pertain (Wasse et al., 2012).

3 Shutting Out the Sky

With walls standing as much as one meter high, the LN residents at Wisad and Wadi al-Qattafi built what amounted to a labor-draining wind break with improved yet still meager protection against rain/snow, intense heat, and high winds, depending on the seasons of habitation. The roofing of structures goes back as far as the Upper Paleolithic in eastern Europe (Iakovleva, 2015), and protection was necessary enough that structures in the Levant at Epipaleolithic Kharaneh IV were built huts of brush, probably incorporating a roof of brush as well (Maher et al., 2021); the same was also the case at Ohalo II in the Jordan Valley (Nadel & Werker, 1999).

3.1 The Late Neolithic Vegetational Landscape in the Southern Black Desert

In view of the current conditions in the Black Desert it would be difficult to build shelters of brush. In Wadi al-Qattafi *Atriplex* sp. (called *kataf* by bedouins [Musil, 1927: 608; 1928: 338] and thus from which the wadi's name is derived) is prominent, but it is a low-lying subshrub of little use beyond fuel. *Atriplex* is rare at Wisad Pools.

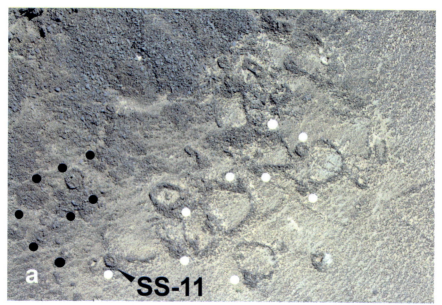

Fig. 9 (**a**) Location of SS-11 on the SW slope of Mesa 4; black circles are late seventh millennium or early sixth millennium, white circles are late sixth millennium (photo: APAAME_20080909_DLK-272 by D. Kennedy). (**b**) View to the west of the eastern façade of SS-11 (Photo: G. Rollefson)

The excavation of structure W-80 at Wisad also included sampling of sediments at a local qa (dry lake bed) where a gritty red soil was visible in a section left by a bulldozer excavating a deep reservoir to catch water for bedouin herders. The soil

Fig. 10 (**a**) Aerial view of the interior of SS-11; red circles show two doors. The one at the top is the largest door in Fig. 9b (photo: Y. Rowan). (**b**) View towards the east through both doors (photo: Y. Rowan)

was identical to the dirt on which W-80 and W-66 were built, and which prevented the dirt from being eroded away.

A palynological analysis of sediment samples from the bulldozer section revealed that non-arboreal pollen (NAP) dominated over arboreal pollen (AP) by 93.7% to 6.3%, with *Poaceae* (formerly called *Graminae*) ranging between 60–80% of the NAP. Included in the NAP was *Lemna* sp. (duckweed), indicating that "the site was once occupied by still water, especially with the presence of algae material", supported as well by the presence of *Typha latifolia* (bulrush) (Ikram, 2016: 28).

AP included *Quercus ithaburensis* (oak), *Pinus* sp. (pine), and *Juniperus* sp. (juniper) (Ikram, 2016: Fig. 5). The presence of oak pollen (which isn't transported through the atmosphere over more than several hundred meters) mirrors the presence of oak charcoal from hearths at W-80 and W-66; *Q. ithaburensis* requires ca. 300–350 mm of rainfall, and while it is unlikely that precipitation was that high during the seventh and sixth millennia, refugia probably existed within a short distance from the site. Another indicator of a more humid setting is the presence of Salix sp. (willow) charcoal (Wasse et al., 2018), which usually requires moving water to transport pollen.

The dominance of Poaceae pollen obscures what the actual phytoscape was; the family has more than 10,000 species world-wide, and the pollen of the different genera and species is difficult to distinguish. One of the genera in this family is *Phragmites*, the reeds that until the early twenty-first century grew in such luxuriance around the pools in Azraq. That it is likely that *Phragmites* was another member of the wetland plant community around and in the *qe'an* (plural of *qa*) is the recovery of two basalt shaft-scrapers from W-80, which would have smoothed the joint ridges or nodes of the reeds, as well as to remove the papery outer layers of the stalk, to manufacture arrow shafts, important commodities that made up around half of the tools for the hunters who used W-80 (Rowan et al., 2015: Table 1).

Soil samples from Qadi al-Qattafi have not undergone pollen analysis. Charcoal is identified as local seeds and brush that still occur in the area today, but the recovery of a burned fig achene from M7 SS-1 reflects increased moisture in the area of the mesas, for figs generally "seem to be flourishing by water courses" (J. Andrews, pers. com 17.02.2022).

3.2 *Organic Material Useful for Roofing*

Phragmites is ideal construction material, as the cathedral-like structures of the Marsh Arabs demonstrate (Thesiger, 2008: Figs. 94–99). Reeds are light-weight but strong and durable. Phragmites is a versatile resource that can be used in a number of ways (Erini, 2021), even for medicinal and psychotropic purposes (Cleversley, 2002). Beating individual stalks with a flat hammerstone on a flat rock shatters the stalk into splints that can be plaited to make mats and baskets (Thesiger, 2008: 30). Bundling numbers of whole stalks together produces thick shafts for use as parts of frames (Thesiger, 2008: Figs. 88,90), against which mats can be placed to act as shades or as elements of a conical roof, appropriate for circular buildings (cf. Juwono & Susanto, 2018: Figs. 6, 7, & 8). Because of the light weight of reeds, superstructures can be dismantled and transported to other sites during the annual round (Thesiger, 2008: Fig. 89).

Bulrushes are also versatile in their potentials. Uses for *Typha latifolia* include as thatch in roofing and can be woven into mats, bags, baskets, furniture, and hats, and it can also be used as insulation and as wound dressing (Global Invasive Species Database [2022]). Mats placed across reed frames would provide shade, and if structures were used in the rainy season, gazelle hides could be used over the matting to provide waterproof roofing and to reduce heat loss from hearths; as seasons change, the hides would be removed.

Holding all the architectural elements together would require cordage and rope. *Typha latifolia* is one source: the leaves of the plant are shredded, soaked, and twisted. *Juncus* sp. (rushes) can be used in basketry, thatching, and ropemaking as well; the stalks are dried and used whole (Keith, n.d.). Although *Juncus* was not specifically identified in the Wisad Pools pollen, it occurs around the pools at South Azraq in dense patches of the drier parts of the edges of the pools (Katbeh-Bader, 1997: 56), and it is likely that *Juncus* was also present at Wisad *qe'an*, too. Another resource for making rope is bast, a fibrous material from the inner bark of a tree such as oak, used for making cordage and textiles; bast close to the bark is relatively coarse, but "tree bast fibers farthest from the bark can be very fine and their morphology can resemble that of flax fibers (Rast-Eicher et al., 2021: 1129). Other plants also provide fibers for cordage, including *Cyperus* sp., *Scirpus* sp., *Sparganium erectum*, and *Phoenix dactylifers* (Nadel et al., 1994: 455).

4 Subsistence Economy

In the Black Desert throughout the Early Holocene until the last century of the eighth millennium BCE, hunting of both small and large mammals, as well as birds, appears to have been undertaken by small bands of people stalking their prey, based on the small area and reduced artifact counts and the absence of architecture at most find spots (e.g., Betts et al., 2013; Wasse & Rollefson, 2005). By the beginning of the seventh millennium a major change in hunting strategy emerged relatively rapidly coincident with the collapse of the LPPNB megasites in the Mediterranean zone, accompanied by the addition of a new and important source of nutrition: maintaining herds of caprines for dairy exploitation.

4.1 Caprine Herding

The following section on hunting points out that hunting was the fundamental source of nutrition for the population of the Black Desert at the very end of the eighth millennium and throughout the seventh and sixth millennia as well. But one aspect of faunal analysis of faunal analysis of the excavated sites from this time reveal a persistent, albeit generally small, proportion of caprine bones across the Black Desert. Since the caprine contribution to the diet of the hunting groups was virtually superfluous, it is appropriate to investigate what may have been the motivation for the hunters to bring into a landscape that was not their natural habitat.

Drinking fresh caprine milk by current pastoralist populations in the deserts of Jordan is not a common phenomenon after early childhood, but "culturing" milk (Rosenstock et al., 2021: 256) for consumption as different derivatives of milk is a customary practice that provides diversity in the diet, including butter, clarified butter (*samn*), defatted yoghurt (*laban*) and dry yoghurt (*jamid*); the last form can be stored for months (Palmer 2002: 182–186; Figs. 9–13). It is probably the storable nature of *jamid* that induced gazelle hunters to adopt caprines.

Vigne and Helmer analyzed archaeosteological collections from the Levant and Mediterranean Europe, and based on "slaughtering age profiles", they concluded that fresh and/or processed dairy exploitation of caprines and cattle began as early as the mid-eighth millennium BCE (2007: 18; Helmer et al., 2007: 49). Intensive analyses using a similar approach of herd demographic implications (Namdar et al., 2021) did not reflect dairy exploitation, on the other hand, and the authors argued that osteological evidence showed that caprines were raised for meat.

Based on lipid residues extracted from Late Neolithic potsherds from two sites in Jordan, Gregg et al. (2009: 939, Table 1) determined that caprine dairy residues were present and that dairy exploitation began at least as early as the seventh millennium (Kadowaki et al., 2008), a conclusion that was reinforced by examination of fatty acid residues from seventh millennium Tell Sabi Abyad in Syria (Nieuwenhuyse et al., 2015: Table 1). Stable isotope analysis of widely distributed caprine populations now shows that caprine dairying was a strategy that emerged in the Levant perhaps as early as the ninth millennium BCE (Rosenstock et al., 2021: 256) and certainly by the end of the eighth millennium (Makarewicz, 2013, 2022).

Caprine bones are found routinely in Black Desert LN sites (e.g., Martin, 1998), usually at low percentages. From W-66 and W-80 at Wisad Pools and Mesa 7 SS-1, caprines make up to 20-30% at all three structures (Martin and Saritas 2022). They do not appear at LPPNB sites in the limestone steppe at Wadi Jilat, although they account for 20% of the fauna remains at PPNC Jilat J13 and 59% at PPNC J25. (Gazelle bones make up only 18% and 5%, respectively (Garrard et al., 1994: Tables 7–8 and 10; notably, there are no known kites in the vicinity). In contrast, however, at six excavated LN sites at Burqu' at the eastern edge of the Black Desert, only two of them had relatively well-preserved bones; at B03500 caprines accounted for 43% of the material (Betts et al., 2013: Table 15b), and at B11000 they reached 42% (Betts et al., 2013: Table 3.44). The relatively high numbers suggest these sites may have functioned differently than other LN habitations, or that they were occupied at seasons different from other sites.

How caprine pastoralism developed in the steppes and deserts of eastern Jordan was addressed by Köhler-Rollefson (1992), who developed of model that was based on a growing population of Pre-Pottery Neolithic sedentary farmers and the requirements for sufficient pasturage for their herds of sheep and goats, a model that was enhanced by the calculations of Rollefson (2011, 2014). Other models were advanced that did not involve portions of sedentary farmers bringing sheep and goats into the arid regions, eventually settling permanently in those areas, especially after the collapse of the 11 LPPNB megasites in highland Jordan (Rollefson, 2021b); instead, indigenous communities in the steppe and desert adopted caprine pastoralism simply saw its benefits and adopted the practice.

Results of the investigation of stable isotopes ($\delta^{13}C$) and nitrogen ($\delta^{15}N$) in caprine samples of bone collagen from Wadi Jilat's PPNC sites of J13 and J25 were compared with samples from 'Ain Ghazal (Miller et al., 2019). "… the model of Kohler-Rollefson (1992), which states that animals in the steppe must have been present as part of herds from sedentary villages, cannot be supported as an exclusive phenomenon on the grounds of the Wadi Jilat 13 isotope evidence" (Miller et al., 2019: 295–296), and "the Wadi Jilat 25 evidence, which indicates that, in addition, animals who spent a significant proportion of their time in the better watered areas of the Mediterranean zone, were introduced to the steppe of the southern Levant at a similar time as the emergence of steppe pastoralism" (Miller et al., 2019) can be interpreted to show that the W25 animals arrived at Wadi Jilat some (considerable?) time ahead of the caprines from J13, which may have adapted to steppe conditions long after the W25 herds had moved on.

4.2 Mass Slaughter of Gazelles

There has been an extensive array of publications that have reported on research concerning the construction and function of "mega-traps" (Crassard et al., 2022) as structures into which entire herds of gazelle were stampeded by hunters and their dogs for mass slaughter (Helms & Betts, 1987; Legge & Rowley-Conwy, 1987; but see Kirkbride, 1946; Svizzero & Tisdell, 2018). The contrast in productivity between kite trapping and stalking is difficult to exaggerate, particularly considering the impact this source of meat and other material had on local and regional population sizes, density of substantial archaeological sites across the Black Desert, and the intensity and frequency of occupational episodes on a seasonal basis.

This is shown in part by examining the animal bone from sites in the Black Desert. Dhuweila is a very small site repeatedly occupied intensively during the LPPNB and LN periods; the proportion of gazelle remains among the large faunal inventory is overwhelming: 93% in the LPPNB layer and 94% in the LN strata (Betts, 1998; Martin, 1998: Tables 8-2a & 8-2b). The small excavated LPPNB structure was built over a kite guiding wall, which not only dates the kite to the last century or two of the eighth millennium, but also shows the efficacy of kites for hunting success.

The same dominance of gazelle presence in the animal bones of LN sites is the situation for the excavation at two mid- to late seventh millennium structures (W-66 and W-80) at Wisad Pools (cf. Wasse et al., 2018) and at the Late seventh millennium building SS-1 at Mesa 7 in the Wadi al-Qattafi (Rollefson et al., 2017). In all three cases, gazelle contributed more than 50% of the remains, with caprines at 20-30%, and small mammals (fox and hare) making up an estimated 10% each). As with Dhuweila, there are kites near Wisad and within the Wadi al-Qattafi. The wealth of available meat from such "harvests" was enormous (see next section, "Coping"), perhaps indicating that the hunting of smaller mammals may have been simply to provide some diversity to the local diet.

5 Coping with Abundance: Transport

The development of the mass slaughter of gazelles using kites has been well studied over the past several decades (Betts & Burke, 2015; Betts & van Pelt, 2021). Kempe and al-Malabeh (2010) produced an account of the cost in labor to build kites, calculating that a moderate-sized kite would take ten people about 56 days to finish. The most efficient time to use kites in the hunt for gazelle would be during two migration seasons, when herds would reach hundreds – perhaps even thousands – of animals (Martin, 2000: 23); Martin notes that there is an autumn/spring season and a summer one in some areas (Martin, 2000: 25), although Blank and colleagues claim a migration in March/April and another in October in Kazakhstan (Blank et al., 2012a, 2012b: 153). For the rest of the year herd sizes are small, and the period from early November through early March would probably be the best time to extend the distribution of kites in view of summer temperatures and the heavy labor involved; the rainy season would also provide more drinking water on a reliable basis as well.

The rewards in terms of meat and hide yield from kite-based mass slaughter would have been enormous. However, this wealth of meat introduces another aspect of cost beyond constructing and maintenance of the kites and kite walls: transporting the gazelle meat and hides from the kite to the home base.

5.1 Contrasting Problems of Transport

5.1.1 Jibal al-Khashabiyeh

In 2018 Abu-Azizeh and his team continued the excavation of a final LPPNB/early PPNC camp near a kite in the in the Jibal al-Khashabiyeh area on the southern edge of the Jafr Basin of southern Jordan (Crassard et al., 2022). One pit was filled with gazelle bones, and after analysis it was concluded that the minimum number of gazelles was 148, a sizeable herd caught in a kite with a diameter of ca. 150 m. The average amount of meat available in *Gazella subgutturosa* is 15 kg (Cichon et al., 2011; cf. Kingswood & Blank, 1996: 518)., and that calculates to 2220 kg; additionally, there would be the weight of gazelle hides, which might be estimated at 4 kg each, in view of their probable economic value (Bar-Yosef, 2016), adding another ca. 600 kg.

The weight of meat could be diminished between 20–70% depending on the literature consulted (Spyroua et al., 2019; FAO, n.d.), so the weight of the meat alone might be reduced to between 666–1772 kg, but with the hides added, there would still be at least a ton to move. There is no information where a home base may have been for the Jibal al-Khashabiyeh hunters, but transporting nearly a ton or two of material would have posed a major challenge. The number of hunters at the camp is not known, nor can it be estimated how many people may have been accessible at the home base to summon for assistance using backpacks or other containers. Pack animals might have provided some help (e.g. Sutliff, 2019; Upreti et al., 2005), but how large a herd of caprines would have been available? Using a travois made of bundled reeds hauled by people or dogs (e.g. Henderson, 1994; Welker, 2021) may have been productive, but like backpacks, etc., there is no evidence preserved in the archaeological record.

5.1.2 Wadi al-Qattafi and Wisad Pools

The problems of transporting meat and hides from the kites in Jibal al-Khashabiyeh to a home base are much less severe in the Wadi al-Qattafi and Wisad Pools. At Wisad Pools 50% or more of the faunal remains are gazelle bones; caprines account for a substantial amount of the bones, and hare and fox bones c. 10% each. (Rowan et al., 2015), and a similar faunal array holds for M7 SS-1 (Rollefson et al., 2017: 28). But the gazelle bones indicate that the animals were butchered at these two sites, not at some remote camp site.

At Qattafi there are at least 34 kites in the immediate vicinity of the wadi (there is one kite at the base of M9, one and perhaps two at the base of M10, a kite between M11 and M12, and even a massive kite on top of M2 (https://www.flickr.com/search/?text=Qattafi%20kites). In this case, there was probably a large enough population along the immediate banks of the wadi to lug the harvest back to individual building clusters for butchering and hide cleaning, but the hunters would have been lugging whole gazelles, not just the meat and hides. The situation at Wisad Pools was somewhat more problematic. There are at least 50 kites in the vicinity of Wisad Pools, but none closer than ca. 5 km (https://www.flickr.com/search/?q=wisad%20kites). Transporting entire carcasses would have been laborious, but the use of travois would have alleviated the labor.

6 Discussion

Despite the grim vistas of today's Black Desert, the view of the landscape of the seventh and eighth millennia BCE dreadful; one might say it was of a different color altogether, including a variety of green hues from horizon to horizon. Increased precipitation had increased the quantity and quality of the vegetation which in turn augmented the numbers and density of wildlife, including the *Gazella subgutturosa* population. The construction of kites resulted in a major increase in the population of hunter-herders that resulted in more and more kites in an expanding positive feedback loop.

Today's *qe'an* store the occasional rainfall in the winter, but the depth of depressions today is very shallow as a consequence of the deposition of eroded silt from higher elevations in the region, and the captured water evaporates relatively rapidly. That was not the case during the Late Neolithic period: wadis were deeper as were the basins that were filled by the wadis (Jones et al., 2021), permitting longer stays in one locality by hunters and herders both.

Construction material for buildings is readily available at both Qattafi and Wisad, particularly slabs of flood basalt. Vegetation, especially *Phragmites*, *Typha*, and *Juncus*, was probably dense in and around the Qa al-Qattafi and Qa al-Wisad; for anyone who visited the wetlands in North and South Azraq in the 1980s and 1990s will recall the presence of imported water buffalo to keep the vegetation manageable. Qa al-Wisad is small, only about half a square kilometer, but Jawrat al-Wisad is another qa adjacent to the eastern edge of the site, measuring 5 km^2. The area of this qa and of Qa al-Qattafi fall within the size range of the North Azraq wetlands (3.25 km^2) and the wetlands of South Azraq (14.5 km^2), suggesting abundant aquatic resources for the hunter-herders.

The management of the processing of the rewards of kite hunting remain somewhat obscure. Skinning and butchering 148 gazelles at Jibal al-Khashabiyeh required a lot of labor: if the team consisted of four people, that would mean each was responsible for 37 gazelles; for ten people, 15 gazelles. For transport of the meat and hides, four people would each have to move 703 kg; for 10 people, 190 kg per person. At Wisad and Qattafi, where complete carcasses were brought to the site and skinned and butchered, open spaces (especially the courtyards) were probably scenes of intensive activity during the day and probably tempted foxes at night to scavenge offal.

Research at Qattafi and Wisad will continue, and one of the many objectives will be to seek evidence that will determine seasonality of habitation at each site. The dates for Wisad and Qattafi indicate contemporaneity in the last half of the seventh millennium BCE, abut it can't be determined if the occupations represent seasonal movement of one population from one site to the other, or that there were two populations separated by ca. 50 km.

References

Bar-Yosef, O. (2016). Changes in 'demand and supply' for mass killings of gazelles during the Holocene. In N. Marom, R. Yeshuran, L. Weissbrod, & G. Bar-Oz (Eds.), *Bones and identity: Zooarchaeological approaches to reconstructing social and cultural landscapes in Southwest Asia* (pp. 113–124). Oxbow Books.

Betts, A. (1998). Dhuweila: Stratigraphy and construction. In A. Betts (Ed.), *The Harra and the Hamad* (Excavations and surveys in Eastern Jordan) (Vol. 1, pp. 27–58). Sheffield Academic Press.

Betts, A., & Burke, D. (2015). Desert kites in Jordan – A new appraisal. *Arabian Archaeology and Epigraphy, 26*, 74–94.

Betts, A., & van Pelt, W. (2021). *The Gazelle's dream: Game drives of the old and new worlds.* University of Sydney Press. https://doi.org/10.2307/j.ctv24q4zh6

Betts, A., Martin, L., Matsaert, F., & McCartney, C. (2013). Prehistoric sites at Burqu. In A. Betts (Ed.), *The later prehistory of the Badia* (Excavations and surveys in Eastern Jordan) (pp. 52–142). Oxbow Books.

Blank, D., Ruckstuhl, K., & Yang, W. (2012a). Influence of population density on group sizes in goitered gazelle (Gazella subgutturosa Guld., 1780). *European Journal of Wildlife Research, 58*, 981–989. https://doi.org/10.1007/s10344-012-0641-3

Blank, D., Yang, C., Xia, C., & Xu, W. (2012b). Grouping pattern of the goitered gazelle, Gazella subgutturosa (Cetartiodactyla: Bovidae) in Kazakhstan. *Mammalia, 76*, 149–155.

Cichon, C., Woo, Y. & Woo, K. (2011). *"Gazella subgutturosa" (On-line), Animal Diversity Web.* https://animaldiversity.org/accounts/Gazella_subgutturosa/

Cleversley, K. (2002). *Phragmites australis – Common reed.* http://entheology.com/plants/phragmites-australis-common-reed/

Crassard, R., Abu-Azizeh, W., Barge, O., Brochier, J., Chahoud, J., & Régagnon, E. (2022). The use of desert kites as hunting mega-traps: Functional evidence and potential impacts on socio-economic and ecological spheres. *Journal of World Archaeology, 35*, 1–44.

Eirini, M. (2021). *"Phragmites": A network of producing and processing reed at the island of Kimolos.* https://www.archisearch.gr/student-works/phragmites-a-network-of-producing-and-processing-reed-at-the-island-of-kimolos/

FAO. Food and Agricultural Organization of the UN. (n.d.). *2. Simple techniques for production of dried meat.* https://www.fao.org/3/x6932e/X6932E02.htm

Garrard, A., Douglas Baird, D., Susan Colledge, S., Martin, L., & Wright, K. (1994). Prehistoric environment and settlement in the Azraq Basin: An interim report on the 1987and 1988 excavation seasons. *Levant, 26*, 73–109.

Global Invasive Species Database. (2022). *Species profile: Typha latifolia.* http://www.iucngisd.org/gisd/species.php?sc=895 on 19-01-2022.

Gregg, M., Banning, E., Gibbs, K., & Slater, G. (2009). Subsistence practices and pottery use in Neolithic Jordan: Molecular and isotopic evidence. *Journal of Archaeological Science, 36*, 937–946.

Helmer, D., Gourichon, L., & Vila, E. (2007). The development of the exploitation of productsfrom Capra and Ovis (meat, milk and fleece) from the PPNB to the Early Bronze in the northern near East (8700 to 2000 BC cal.). *Anthropozoologica, 42*(2), 41–69.

Helms, S., & Betts, A. (1987). The desert "kites" of the Badiyat Esh-Sham and North Arabia. *Paléorient, 13*(1), 41–67.

Henderson, N. (1994). Replicating dog travois travel on the Northern Plains. *Plains Anthropologist, 39*(148), 145–159.

Iakovleva, L. (2015). The architecture of mammoth bone circular dwellings of the Upper Palaeolithic settlements in central and Eastern Europe and their sociosymbolic meanings. *Quaternary International, 359–360*, 324–324.

Ikram, H. (2016). The paleoenvironments of Wisad, south-east Jordan. Honors BSc dissertation, University of Nottingham.

Jones, M., Richter, T., Rollefson, G., Rowan, Y., Wasse, A., & Alshdaifa, A. (2021). The palaeoenvironmental potential of the eastern Jordanian desert basins (Qe'an). *Quaternary International, 635*, 73–82. https://doi.org/10.1016/j.quaint.2021.06.023

Juwono, J., & Susanto, D. (2018). The reeds performance study on traditional architecture as building material in Wae Rebo Village. *E3S Web of Conferences, 67*, 04015. https://doi.org/10.1051/e3sconf/20186704015

Kadowaki, S., Gibbs, K., Allentuck, A., & Banning, E. (2008). Late Neolithic settlement in Wadi Ziqlab, Jordan: al-Basatîn. *Paléorient, 34*(1), 105–129.

Katbeh-Bader, A. (1997). On the common Insecta of Al Azraq. *Entomologist's Gazette, 48*, 55–66.

Keith, B. (n.d.). *Ropemaker, Chapter 9*. http://bkeithropemaker.com/Rope_Chapt_9.html

Kempe, S. & Malabeh, A. (2010). Kites and other archaeological structures along the Eastern Rim of the Harrat (Lava plain) of Jordan, signs of intensive usage in prehistoric time, a google earth images study. Proceedings of the 14th international symposium on Vulcanospeleology (pp. 199-215).

Kingswood, S., & Blank, D. (1996). Gazella subgutturosa. *Mammalian Species, 518*, 1–10.

Kirkbride, A. (1946). Desert kites. *Journal of the Palestine Oriental Society, 20*, 1–5.

Köhler-Rollefson, I. (1992). A model for the development of nomadic pastoralism on the Transjordanian Plateau. In O. Bar-Yosef & A. Khazanov (Eds.), *Pastoralism in the Levant; archaeological materials in anthropological perspectives* (pp. 11–18). Prehistory Press.

Legge, A., & Rowley-Conwy, P. (1987). Gazelle killing in Stone Age Syria. *Scientific American, 257*, 88–95.

Maher, L., Macdonald, D., Pomeroy, E., & Stock, J. (2021). Life, death, and the destruction of architecture: Hunter-gatherer mortuary behaviors in prehistoric Jordan. *Journal of Anthropological Archaeology, 61*. https://doi.org/10.1016/j.jaa.2020.101262

Makarewicz, C. (2013). More than meat: Diversity in caprine harvesting strategies and the emergence of complex production systems during the late pre-pottery Neolithic B. *Levant, 45*(2), 236–261.

Makarewicz, C., Kendall, I., Palmer, K., Winter-Schuh, C., Mike Buckley, M., Evershed R. & Rollefson, G. (2022). Human dietary dynamics and early caprine husbandry: isotopic and proteomic analyses of skeletal tissues and Dental Calculus from 'Ain Ghazal. Paper presented to the 28th EAA Annual Meeting in Budapest, Hungary, 31 August – 3 September 2022.

Martin, L. (1998). The animal bones. In A. Betts (Ed.), *The Harra and Hamad* (Excavations and surveys in Eastern Jordan) (Vol. 1, pp. 159–189). Sheffield Academic Press.

Martin, L. (2000). Gazelle (Gazella spp.) behavioural ecology: Predicting animal behaviour for prehistoric environments in south-West Asia. *Journal of Zoology, 250*, 13–30.

Martin, L. & Saritas, O. (2022). New insights into Late Neolithic herding in the Jordanian harra: zooarchaeological results from Wisad Pools and Wadi al-Qattafi. Paper presented to the 15th International ICAZ/AWS Meeting, Tokyo, 1 December 2022.

Miller, H., Baird, D., Pearson, J., Lamb, A., Grove, M., Martin, L., & Garrard, A. (2019). The origins of nomadic pastoralism in the eastern Jordanian steppe: A combined stable isotope and chipped stone assessment. *Levant, 50*(3), 281–304.

Musil, A. (1927). *Arabia Deserta, a topographical itinerary*. American Geographical Society.

Musil, A. (1928). *The manners and customs of the Rwala bedouins*. American Geographical Society.

Nadel, D., & Werker, E. (1999). The oldest ever brush hut plant remains from Ohalo II, Jordan Valley, Israel (19,000 BP). *Antiquity, 73*, 755–764.

Nadel, D., Danin, A., Werker, E., Schick, T., Kislev, E., & Stewart, K. (1994). I9,000-year-old twisted fibers from Ohalo II. *Current Anthropology, 35*(4), 451–457.

Namdar, L., Vardi, J., Paz, Y., & Sapir-Hen, L. (2021). Variation in economic specialization as revealed through the study of pottery Neolithic faunal assemblages from the southern Levant. *Archaeological and Anthropological Sciences, 13*, 206–225.

Nieuwenhuyse, O., Roffet-Salque, M., Evershed, R., Akkermans, P., & Russell, A. (2015). Tracing pottery use and the emergence of secondary product exploitation through lipid residue analysis at late Neolithic tell Sabi Abyad (Syria). *Journal of Archaeological Science, 64*, 54–66.

Palmer, C. (2002). Milk and cereals: Identifying food and food identity among fallahin and bedouin in Jordan. *Levant, 34*, 173–195.

Rast-Eicher, A., Karg, S., & S. & Jørgensen, L. (2021). The use of local fibres for textiles at Neolithic Çatalhöyük. *Antiquity, 95*(383), 1129–1144.

Rollefson, G. (2011). The greening of the Badlands: Pastoral nomads and the "conclusion" of neolithization in the Southern Levant. *Paléorient, 37*(1), 101–109.

Rollefson, G. (2014). The Fat of the Land: Neolithic Origins of "Wealth" in the Southern Levant. In *Akkadica Supplementum XII* (pp. 19–26).

Rollefson, G. (2021a). The Crowded Desert: Late Neolithic megasites in the Black Desert of Jordan. In C. Bührig, I. Gerlach, A. Hausleiter, & B. Müller-Neuhof (Eds.), *Klänge der Archäologie. Festschrift für Ricardo Eichmann* (pp. 343–350). Harrassowitz.

Rollefson, G. (2021b). The great eastward migration into the late Neolithic Black Desert, Jordan. *Jordan Journal for History and Archaeology, 51*(2), 87–111.

Rollefson, G., Rowan, Y., Perry, M., & Abu-Azizeh, W. (2012). The 2022 season at wisad pools, Black Desert: Preliminary report. *Annual of the Department of Antiquities of Jordan, 56,* 29–44.

Rollefson, G., Rowan, Y., & Wasse, A. (2013). Neolithic settlement at wisad pools, Black Desert, Jordan. *Neo-Lithics, 1*(13), 11–23.

Rollefson, G., Rowan, Y., Wasse, A., Hill, A. C., Kersel, M., Lorentzen, B., & al-Bashaireh K. and Ramsay J. (2016). Investigations of a late neolithic structure at mesa 7, Wadi al-Qattafi, Black Desert, 2015. *Neo-Lithics, 1*(16), 3–12.

Rollefson, G., Wasse, A., Rowan, Y., Kersel, M., Jones, M., Lorentzen, B., Hill, A. C., & Ramsay, J. (2017). The 2016 excavation season at the late Neolithic structure SS-1 on Mesa 7, Black Desert. *Neo-Lithics, 2*(17), 19–29.

Rollefson, G., Rowan, Y., Wasse, A., Kersel, M., Hill, A. C., Lorentzen, B., Ramsay, J., & Jones, M. (2018). Excavation of structure W-80, a complex late neolithic building at wisad pools, Black Desert. *Annual of the Department of Antiquities of Jordan, 59,* 531–544.

Rollefson, G., Wasse, A., Rowan, Y., Abu-Azizeh, W. & Hill, A.C. (n.d.). The multifaceted site of wisad pools, Black Desert. In R. Repper, M.C. Bishop and R. Bewley (Eds.), *Reframing the 'Desert Frontier': Studies in the Ancient Near East and Northern Arabia in Honour of David Kennedy (in review).*

Rosenstock, E., Ebert, J., & Scheibner, A. (2021). Cultured Milk: Fermented dairy foods along the Southwest Asian–European neolithic trajectory. *Current Anthropology, S-24,* 254–275.

Rowan, Y., Wasse, A., Rollefson, G., Kersel, M., Jones, M., & Lorentzen, B. (2015). Late Neolithic architectural complexity at wisad pools. *Black Desert. Neo-Lithics, 1*(15), 3–10.

Rowan, Y., Rollefson, G., Wasse, A., Hill, A. C., & Kersel, M. (2017). The late neolithic presence in the Black Desert. *Near Eastern Archaeology, 80*(2), 102–113.

Spyroua, A., Maher, L., Martin, L. D., Macdonald, A., & D. & Garrard, A. (2019). Meat outside the freezer: Drying, smoking, salting and sealing meat in fat at an Epipalaeolithic megasite in eastern Jordan. *Journal of Anthropological Anthropology, 54,* 84–101.

Sutliff, D. (2019). Pack goats in the Neolithic Middle East. *Anthropozoologica, 54*(5), 45–53.

Svizzero, S., & Tisdell, C. (2018). Desert kites: Were they used for hunting or for herding? A review of the recent academic literature. *Journal of Zoological Research, 24,* 7–28.

Thesiger, W. (2008). *The marsh Arabs*. Penguin.

Upreti, C., Bahadur, S., Kuwar, B., & Panday., S. (2005). Development and evaluation of improved feeders for goats suitable to stall-fed management system. *Nepal Agricultural Research Journal, 6,* 78–83.

Vigne, J.-D., & Helmer, D. (2007). Was milk a "secondary product" in the Old World Neolithisation process? Its role in the domestication of cattle, sheep and goats. *Archaeozoologica, 42*(2), 9–40.

Wasse, A., & Rollefson, G. (2005). The Wadi Sirhan project: Report on the 2002 archaeological reconnaissance of Wadi Hudruj and Jabal Thawra, Jordan. *Levant, 37,* 1–20.

Wasse, A., Rowan, Y., & Rollefson, G. (2012). A seventh millennium BC late Neolithic village at Mesa 4 in Wadi -Qattafi, eastern Jordan. *Neo-Lithics, 1*(12), 15–24.

Wasse, W., Rollefson, G., Rowan, Y., Braun, G., Heidkamp, B., Hill, A., Kersel, M., Lorentzen, B., & Ramsay, J. (2018). Eastern Badiyah archaeological project: Preliminary report on the 2018 excavation season at late neolithic structure W-80, wisad pools. *Annual of the Department of Antiquities of Jordan, 60,* 249–269.

Wasse, A., Rowan, Y. & Rollefson, G. (n.d.). *Wisad Pools: Report on the 2019 season of excavation. Annual of the Department of Antiquities of Jordan (in review).*

Welker, M. (2021). Travois transport and field processing: The role of dogs in intermountain and plains food transport. *Human Ecology, 2021*(49), 721–733.

Tel 'Ein Jezreel in the Neolithic and Chalcolithic Periods: New Finds, New Insights

Tamar Shooval, Ian Cipin, Sonia Pinsky, Jennie Ebeling, Norma Franklin, and Danny Rosenberg

Abstract Recent survey and excavation at Tel 'Ein Jezreel, located in the Jezreel Valley directly above the spring of 'Ein Jezreel, revealed evidence for settlement from the Neolithic Period through the modern era. (The Jezreel Expedition was sponsored by The Zinman Institute of Archaeology, University of Haifa, Israel and the University of Evansville, Indiana, USA. One survey season (2012) and six seasons of excavation (2013–2018) were co-directed by Norma Franklin (University of Haifa) and Jennie Ebeling (University of Evansville). While most of the finds date to the Early Bronze Age, there is also substantial evidence for settlement in the Late Neolithic and Chalcolithic periods. This essay presents some of the pottery, flint, and ground stone artifacts from the Yarmukian culture of the Pottery Neolithic period, the Wadi Rabah culture of the Late Pottery Neolithic/Early Chalcolithic, and the Ghassulian culture of the Late Chalcolithic period. The significance of these finds is discussed within the broader context of Neolithic and Chalcolithic settlement in the Jezreel Valley and adjacent areas.

Keywords Yarmukian · Wadi Rabah · Chalcolithic · Jezreel Valley · Pottery · Flint · Ground stone artifacts

---

T. Shooval (✉) · I. Cipin · D. Rosenberg
Laboratory for Ancient Food Processing Technologies (LAFPT), The Zinman Institute of Archaeology, University of Haifa, Haifa, Israel
e-mail: tamartour@gmail.com; iancipin@gmail.com; drosen@research.haifa.ac.il

S. Pinsky · N. Franklin
The Zinman Institute of Archaeology, University of Haifa, Haifa, Israel
e-mail: spinsky@univ.haifa.ac.il; norma_f@netvision.net.il

J. Ebeling
University of Evansville, Evansville, IN, USA
e-mail: je55@evansville.edu

© The Author(s), under exclusive license to Springer Nature Switzerland AG 2023
E. Ben-Yosef, I. W. N. Jones (eds.), *"And in Length of Days Understanding" (Job 12:12): Essays on Archaeology in the Eastern Mediterranean and Beyond in Honor of Thomas E. Levy*, Interdisciplinary Contributions to Archaeology,
https://doi.org/10.1007/978-3-031-27330-8_8

1 Introduction

Tel 'Ein Jezreel is a relatively unknown site in contrast to its sister site Tel Jezreel, which is famous for its Iron Age settlement and biblical connections. However, recent survey and excavation at Tel 'Ein Jezreel have revealed a rich history dating from the Neolithic to the Byzantine period (Ebeling et al., 2012; Ebeling, 2020). The site is strategically located at the midpoint of the Jezreel Valley nearly equidistant from Megiddo to the west and Beth Shean to the east. The Jezreel Valley served as a natural corridor connecting the Jordan Valley with the Lower Galilee and the coastal plain that provided passage for different cultures whose presence can be traced in the rich archaeological assemblages they left behind. This paper will focus on the late prehistory of the Jezreel Valley with a focus on the material culture recently excavated from the central site of Tel 'Ein Jezreel.

Archaeological sites with material dating to the Pottery Neolithic and Early Chalcolithic periods are well-known across the northern part of Israel (Garfinkel, 1993, 1999; Gopher, 2012; Gopher & Gophna, 1993: Figs. 6, 10, 15). However, sites where the Yarmukian and Wadi Rabah cultures were dominant are located mainly in central and southern Israel, stretching from Israel's northern coastal plain south to the Shephelah and from the central Jordan Valley east to the Jordanian plateau (Garfinkel, 2019, p. 11). These cultures are less well-known in the Jezreel and Beth Shean valleys of northern Israel. Late Chalcolithic sites belonging mainly to the Ghassulian culture are also absent from the map of early settlements in the region (Fig. 1). The material from Tel 'Ein Jezreel thus provides new insights about the distribution of Yarmukian, Wadi Rabah, and Ghassulian settlements in the northern valleys and sheds light on the inter-regional connections between these sites during the proto-historic period.

2 Tel 'Ein Jezreel in the Late Neolithic and Chalcolithic Periods

Tel 'Ein Jezreel is located on a basaltic terrace ca 10 m above sea level, directly above the spring of 'Ein Jezreel, with elevation of ca 5 m below sea level, and overlooking the narrowest point of the Jezreel Valley (Fig. 1). It is ca 800 m northeast of Tel Jezreel which is ca 100 m above sea level. Earlier surveys of Tel 'Ein Jezreel (Gophna & Shlomi, 1997; Zori, 1977) revealed evidence for settlement during the Late Neolithic and Early Chalcolithic periods in the form of characteristic pottery, flint tools, and ground stone artifacts[1] (Gophna & Shlomi, 1997). The site was

---

[1] This material came from a very brief survey conducted in the mid-1990s by a few team members of the Tel Jezreel excavation team of Tel Aviv University and the British School of Archaeology in Jerusalem (BSAJ).

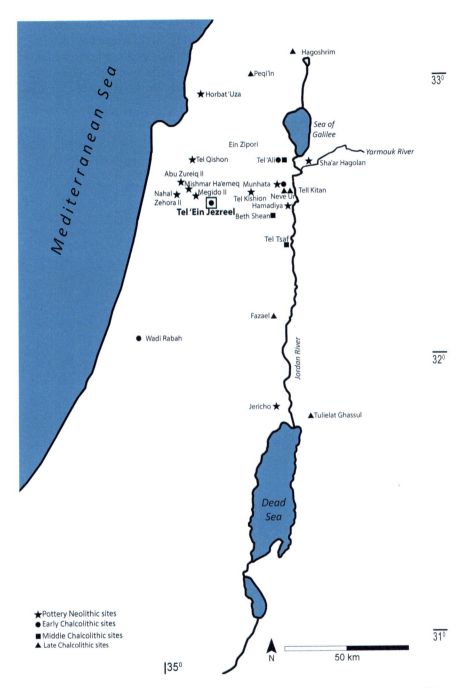

Fig. 1 Map showing the location of Tel 'Ein Jezreel and other Pottery Neolithic and Chalcolithic sites mentioned in the text

surveyed again by members of the Jezreel Expedition team in 2012 and areas were chosen for excavation in the 2013–2018 seasons (Fig. 2) (Ebeling et al., 2012).

A series of Early Bronze Age occupation levels was exposed in Area S along with material culture dating to the Pottery Neolithic and Early and Late Chalcolithic periods. Since the material culture pre-dating the Early Bronze Age I was not found

Fig. 2 Tel 'Ein Jezreel: View Looking East (upper photo) and LIDAR scan of the site (lower photo). Area S is Tel 'Ein Jezreel. Photos courtesy of the Jezreel Expedition

in clear stratigraphic context, only the indicative finds were selected for inclusion in this study. This was achieved by separating them from the mixed loci that also contained material dating from the Early Bronze Age through to the modern era. The artifact assemblages (pottery, flint, and ground stone artifacts) unearthed during six seasons of excavation at the site are currently being studied by specialists and their reports will appear in the final excavation report (Ebeling, Cipin, and Stehney forthcoming; Pinsky forthcoming). It should be noted that no quantitative or qualitative analyses were conducted as part of this study since many of the finds are derived from unclear contexts; still, this material has provided significant insights about the nature of the Pottery Neolithic and Chalcolithic presence in the Jezreel Valley that will be presented and discussed below.

2.1 Yarmukian Material Culture

The Yarmukian culture of the Pottery Neolithic period (ca. 6400–5800 cal. BC) is mainly located in the Mediterranean zone of the southern Levant with Sha'ar Hagolan being the hallmark site (Garfinkel, 1999:16–67, 2019:7–12; Gopher & Gophna, 1993). The Yarmukian culture is the first pottery bearing culture in the region and produced distinctive pottery that was often decorated with an incised herringbone pattern. The flint assemblages consist of arrowheads and denticulate sickle blades. Unique clay and pebbles figurines are another key feature of this culture (Garfinkel, 2019:12) as well as notable ground stone tools assemblages (Rosenberg, 2011; Rosenberg & Garfinkel, 2014).

The Yarmukian finds from Tel 'Ein Jezreel (Fig. 3) include dozens of sickle blades and a few pottery sherds. The Yarmukian sherds include a jar neck fragment (Fig. 3:1), possibly of a typical 'Sha'ar Hagolan' jar (Garfinkel, 1999, pp. 43–48), and three decorated body fragments (Fig. 3:2–4), one of which probably belongs to another jar (Fig. 3:2). Three of the body sherds have the typical incised herringbone Yarmukian decoration, and one (Fig. 3:4) has only painted decoration (for parallels see Garfinkel, 1992: Fig. 39:11,12; see also Garfinkel, 1999:59–67 for a detailed description of decoration styles). Other less clear Yarmukian sherds were not included in this report.

The typical sickle blades with deep denticulations (Fig. 3:5–8) that are characteristic of this period (e.g. Gopher, 1995; Gopher & Gophna, 1993; Vardi, 2011) are also common here. These deeply serrated sickle blades are usually found intact, and many of them show a long period of use noticeable by their worn-down denticulations. Although it was not possible to securely identify any Yarmukian ground stone artifacts in the assemblage, some of the stone vessels show correspondences with the known Yarmukian repertoire (see e.g. Rosenberg, 2011; Rosenberg & Garfinkel, 2014).

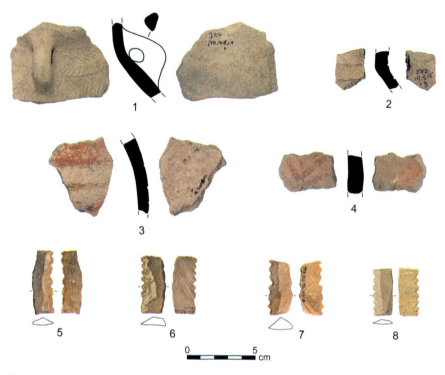

Fig. 3 Yarmukian finds: 1–4. Yarmukian sherds; 5–8. Yarmukian sickle blades

2.2 Early Chalcolithic Material Culture

The Early Chalcolithic period (ca. 5800–5300 cal. BC, sometimes termed the Late Neolithic or Pottery Neolithic period) has been subject to a lively debate regarding its chronological placement and its division into sub-periods (Banning, 2007; Garfinkel, 1999, 2009; Gilead, 2009; Gopher, 2012, 2019; Gopher & Gophna, 1993; Rosenberg, 2011). Some scholars consider the Wadi Rabah culture to be a late Pottery Neolithic phenomenon (Gopher, 2012:1525, 2019; Khalaily et al., 2016), while others believe it to be Early Chalcolithic (e.g. Garfinkel, 1999, 2009; Getzov, 2015; Getzov et al., 2009; Gopher & Gophna, 1993; Gophna & Sadeh, 1988–89; Kaplan, 1958; Sadeh & Gophna, 1991). Here, we use the general term Early Chalcolithic as defined by Kaplan (1958) and has large equivalent with the Wadi Rabah culture.

The Wadi Rabah culture spread over a wide geographic area, from northern Israel south to the Shephelah and from the coastal plain east to the Jordanian highlands (Banning, 2007). The Wadi Rabah culture is characterized by new pottery types, such as carinated bowls and bow-rim jars, that display a considerable investment in treatment and decoration. Flint tools also exhibit major changes, including the absence of small arrowheads and the appearance of new types of sickle blades. Biconical slingstones are a characteristic feature of the Wadi Rabah culture as well (Rosenberg, 2009). These and other distinctive artifact types provide evidence for close connections between the southern Levantine and northern cultures like the Halafian (Garfinkel, 2009).

The majority of the late prehistoric finds from Tel 'Ein Jezreel can be attributed to the Early Chalcolithic period. The typical Early Chalcolithic pottery assemblage includes many decorated body sherds (Figs. 4, 5 and 6) as well as a few bow-rim jars (Fig. 7), one of the most distinctive vessel types for this period (Garfinkel, 1999: Fig. 8:4–11). The decorated sherds include combed decoration (4:1–13), incised decoration (Figs. 4:14–26, 5:23–27, 29–32), and different types of impressed decoration, including a rouletted impression (Fig. 5:2–3, 5), punctured decoration (Fig. 5:1, 4, 6–22), and lunar impressions (Fig. 6). A number of slipped and highly burnished sherds characteristic of Early Chalcolithic pottery traditions were also identified in this assemblage and a few sherds with plastic decoration were also noted (Fig. 5:28). These decorative styles are well-known from other Early Chalcolithic sites (Garfinkel, 1999; Gopher & Eyal, 2012; Rosenberg et al., 2017). Other Wadi Rabah sherds which are less characteristics were not included in this report.

The Early Chalcolithic lithic assemblage includes examples of the wide, rectangular sickle blades typical of this period (Fig 8:1–10) with truncations on both extremities, a retouched back, and a retouched active side (e.g. Gopher, 1989: Fig 41: type C; Rosenberg et al., 2017: Fig 48; Vardi, 2011). Some of the bifacial tools in the assemblage might also be attributed to the Early Chalcolithic period (Pinsky forthcoming).

Among the ground stone artifacts are large fragments of nine full-based basalt pedestals (Fig. 8:11–17) typical of the Early Chalcolithic period (Rosenberg, 2011). All nine were carved from dense, fine-grained, basalt. The possibility that they were intentionally broken should be considered. In addition, over 100 slingstones that exhibit the typical attributes of slingstones from this period (Rosenberg, 2009:102) were collected from different contexts across the site (Fig. 9). Slingstones have long been recognized as one of the primary *fossiles directeurs* of the "normative" Wadi Rabah culture in the southern Levant (Gopher & Gophna, 1993; Kaplan, 1972; Rosenberg, 2009). Most are made of limestone and were pecked and abraded to achieve the desired elongated or biconical form with an elliptical shape, wider central part, and narrower ends.

2.3 Late Chalcolithic Material Culture

The Late Chalcolithic period (ca. 4500–3800 cal. BC) is often defined by the 'Ghassulian' culture first recognized at the site of Teleilat al-Ghassul. This period is known for its pronounced regionalism with major differences between the Golan, Hula Valley, Jordan Valley, and Beer-Sheva Valley areas (Rowan & Golden, 2009).

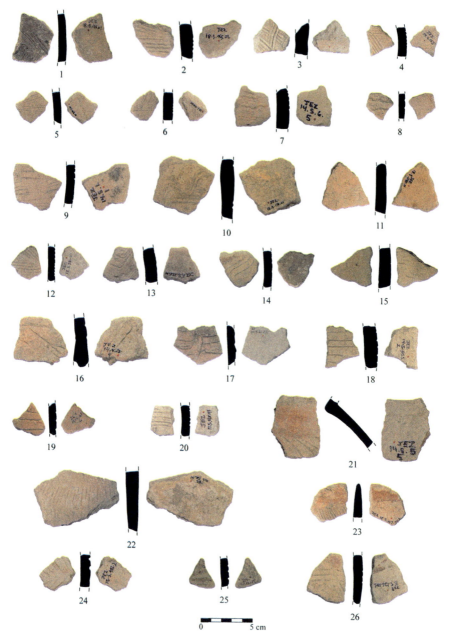

Fig. 4 Early Chalcolithic: Decorated sherds

Fundamental changes took place in all aspects of life, including settlement size, craft specialization, mortuary practices, architecture, and material culture. The most prominent innovation is the appearance of copper artifacts (Shalev, 1991; Shuger &

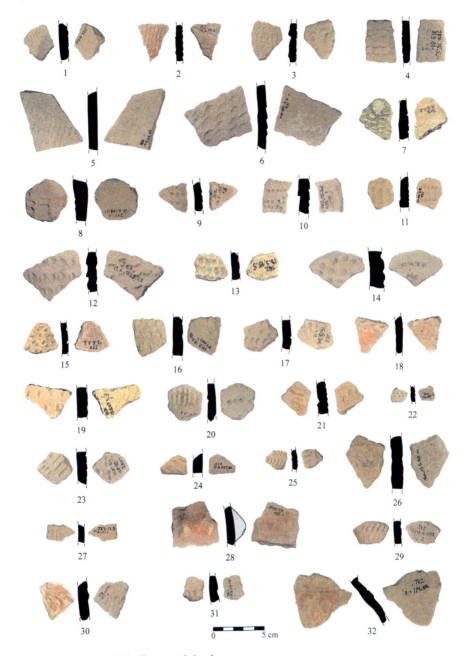

Fig. 5 Early Chalcolithic: Decorated sherds

Gohm, 2011; Rosenberg et al., 2020; Rowan & Golden, 2009). All this provides evidence for rise in socio-political organization and technological know-how during this period (Klimscha et al., 2021; Rowan, 2014).

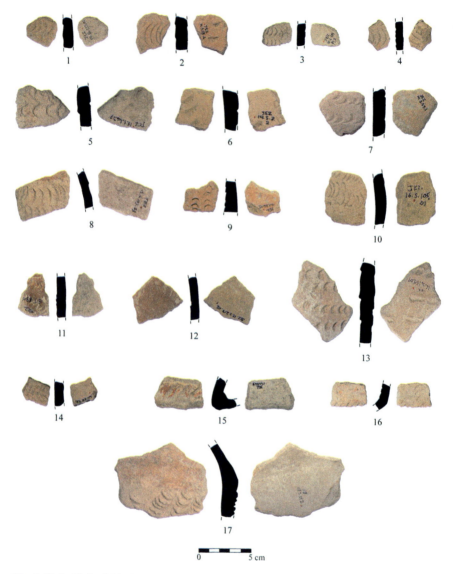

Fig. 6 Early Chalcolithic: Decorated sherds

While a large number of possible Late Chalcolithic pottery sherds were noted in the Tel 'Ein Jezreel assemblage, none can be securely attributed to this period. In addition, the flint assemblage is meagre, although there are a few typical sickle blades with truncations on both extremities, a retouched back, and retouched active side that are narrower and more elongated than the Wadi Rabah forms (Fig. 10:1–4). A single perforated flint disc was also noted (Fig. 10:5) that is comparable to those found mainly in the north of Israel (Rosenberg & Shimelmitz, 2017; Rosenberg

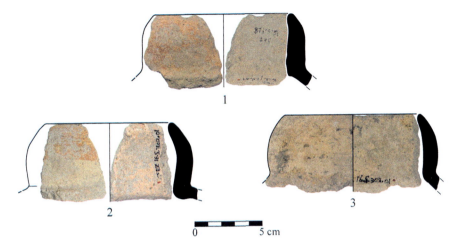

Fig. 7 Early Chalcolithic: Bow-Rim jars

et al. this volume). It is also probable that the bifacial tools, specifically the adzes, should be attributed to this period.

Although the ground stone artifacts from Tel 'Ein Jezreel included a large number of basalt vessels of different types, only a few could be securely attributed to the Late Chalcolithic period. Among them are seven fenestrated pedestals (Fig. 10:6–8) that are the *fossiles directeurs* for this period and have been found in large numbers in the southern Levant (Rowan, 1998; Chasan & Rosenberg, 2018; Rosenberg et al., 2016). Other stone artifacts typical for this period include maceheads (Rosenberg, 2010; Sebbane, 2016) and large perforated stones (frequently referred to as 'digging stick weights', Gopher & Orrelle, 1996; Ilan, 2016).

3 Discussion

The results of the recent survey and excavation of Tel 'Ein Jezreel suggest that the site was occupied almost continuously from late prehistory through the modern era. Despite the damage wrought by later inhabitants who robbed out the earlier architecture and obscured the evidence of the earliest phases of occupation, the finds presented here clearly testify to continuous settlement at the site from the Late Neolithic through the Late Chalcolithic period (see also Gophna & Shlomi, 1997).

A number of sites in the Jezreel Valley and the surrounding areas have yielded evidence for the Yarmukian culture, e.g., Tel Kishion in Nahal Tavor (Arnon & Amiran, 1981, 1993), Nahal Zehora II in the Menashe Hills (Gopher, 2012), Megiddo (Shipton, 1939), Hazorea (Anati, 1973), Abu Zureiq (Anati, 1973), and Mishmar Ha'emek (Barzilai & Getzov, 2008) within the valley fringes (Garfinkel, 2019:10; Gopher & Gophna, 1993). New evidence from Tel 'Ein Jezreel has

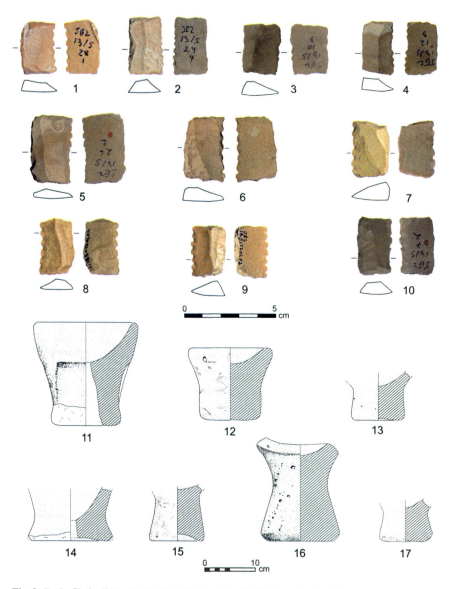

Fig. 8 Early Chalcolithic: 1–10. Sickle blades; 11–17. Full-based pedestals

enabled a connection to be made with the well- known Yarmukian sites in the Jordan Valley, e.g., Sha'ar Hagolan (Garfinkel, 2019), Hamadiyah (Garfinkel et al., 2017), and Munhata (Garfinkel, 1992). Thus, the Yarmukian material from Tel 'Ein Jezreel provides a link between the Jezreel Valley sites and sites to the east and north (Fig. 1) that can be seen in the pottery, flint, and ground stone artifact assemblages.

Tel 'Ein Jezreel in the Neolithic and Chalcolithic Periods: New Finds, New Insights 185

Fig. 9 Early Chalcolithic: Slingstones

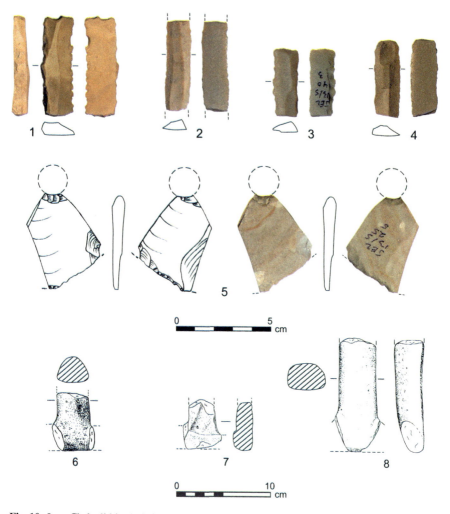

Fig. 10 Late Chalcolithic: 1–4. Sickle blades; 5. Perforated disc; 6–8. Fenestrated pedestals

The Early Chalcolithic period is represented by the typical Wadi Rabah pottery assemblage as defined by Kaplan (1958, 1969) and previously noted at the site by Gophna and Shlomi (Gophna & Shlomi, 1997: Fig. 1). The recently-excavated material presented here accords with their findings: the abundance of decorated sherds clearly demonstrates a Wadi Rabah presence and the pottery is consistent with other Wadi Rabah assemblages (e.g. Garfinkel, 1992: Fig. 140:5, 6, 1999: Fig. 90; Kaplan, 1969). The Early Chalcolithic period is also clearly reflected in the flint and ground stone artifact assemblages (Gopher, 1989; Rosenberg, 2011; Rosenberg et al., 2017; Vardi, 2011).

The Wadi Rabah presence at Tel 'Ein Jezreel may constitute the eastern limit of the so-called 'normative' Wadi Rabah culture (Gopher & Gophna, 1993) within the Jezreel Valley, located as it is to the east of other known Wadi Rabah sites, e.g., 'Ein el Jarba (Kaplan, 1969; Streit, 2015) and Hazorea (Anati, 1973). In the Beth Shean Valley, which lies to the east of Tel 'Ein Jezreel, no normative Wadi Rabah sites were found. Instead, other variants of the early and Middle Chalcolithic cultures of the 5th millennium BC are known in this region (Gophna & Sadeh, 1988; Rosenberg et al., 2014, 2021; Sadeh & Gophna, 1991).

Gophna and Shlomi (1997) recognized the Ghassulian occupation at the site, and this is reinforced by the new finds. These suggest connections between Tel 'Ein Jezreel and sites such as Neve Ur (Perrot et al., 1967) and Tell Kitan (Sadeh & Gophna, 1991) in the central Jordan Valley (see Fig. 1).

Summing up, the recent excavations at Tel 'Ein Jezreel have revealed evidence for a succession of Late Neolithic, Early Chalcolithic, and Late Chalcolithic communities that relied on cereal agriculture. The site's location next to a perennial spring, the abundant agricultural land surrounding it, the large assemblage of sickle blades, the exceptionally large and diverse assemblage of basalt grinding stones and other ground stone artifacts, and the site's position directly on top of a basalt outcrop suggests that the early settlers were attracted to this spot for its great agricultural potential. These new finds from Tel 'Ein Jezreel shed new light on the earliest permanent settlements in the Jezreel Valley, possible interregional connections between sites in the vicinity of the valley, and connections between the inhabitants of these sites and those in the central Jordan Valley and Lower Galilee.

Acknowledgments The Jezreel Expedition was co-sponsored by The Zinman Institute of Archaeology of the University of Haifa and the University of Evansville; consortium partners include Campbell University, Chapman University, Moravian Theological Seminary, San Francisco Theological Seminary/Graduate Theological Union, University of Arizona, Vanderbilt University, Villanova University, and Wesley Theological Seminary. We thank the Foundation for Biblical Archaeology, the American Society of Overseas Research (ASOR), members of Kibbutz Yizrael, and many others for their support. Thanks are also due to S. Haad for preparing the plates.

References

Anati, E. (1973). *Hazorea* (Vol. 5). Edizioni del Centro.
Arnon, C., & Amiran, R. (1981). Excavations at Tel Qishon – Preliminary report on the 1977–1978 seasons. *Eretz Israel, 15*, 205–212. (in Hebrew with English summary).
Arnon, C., & Amiran, R. (1993). Kishion. *The new encyclopedia of archaeological excavations in the Holy Land, 3*, 873–874.
Banning, E. B. (2007). Time and tradition in the transition from Late Neolithic to Chalcolithic: Summary and conclusions. *Paléorient, 33*(1), 137–142. https://doi.org/10.3406/paleo.2007.5210
Barzilai, O., & Getzov, N. (2008). Mishmar Ha'emeq: A Neolithic Site in the Jezreel Valley. *Neo-Lithics, 2*(08), 12–17.

Chasan, R., & Rosenberg, D. (2018). Basalt vessels in Chalcolithic burial caves: Variations in prestige burial offerings during the Chalcolithic period of the southern Levant and their social significance. *Quaternary International, 464*, 226–240.

Ebeling, J. (2020). Gone to the dogs: Zerʻin through western eyes. In J. Ebeling & P. Guillaume (Eds.), *The woman in the pith helmet: A tribute to archaeologist Norma Franklin* (pp. 35–56). Lockwood Press.

Ebeling, J., Franklin, N., & Cipin, I. (2012). Jezreel revealed in laser scans: A preliminary report of the 2012 survey season. *Near Eastern Archaeology, 75*(4), 232–239.

Garfinkel, Y. (1992). *The pottery assemblages of the Shaʼar Hagolan and Rabah stages of Munhata (Israel)*. Association Paléorient.

Garfinkel, Y. (1993). The Yarmukian culture in Israel. *Paléorient, 19*(1), 115–134.

Garfinkel, Y. (1999). *Neolithic and Chalcolithic Pottery of the southern Levant (Qedem 39)*. Institute of Archaeology, The Hebrew University of Jerusalem.

Garfinkel, Y. (2009). The transition from Neolithic to Chalcolithic in the southern Levant: The material culture sequence. In J. J. Shea & D. E. Lieberman (Eds.), *Transitions in prehistory: Essays in honor of Ofer Bar-Yosef* (pp. 325–333). Oxbow Books.

Garfinkel, Y. (2019). *Shaʻar Hagolan volume 5*. Institute of Archaeology, Hebrew University of Jerusalem.

Garfinkel, Y., Goldman, T., Rosenberg, D., Eirikh-Rose, A., & Matskevich, Z. (2017). Hamadiya in the Central Jordan Valley: A Yarmukian Pottery Neolithic site (1964). In A. Gopher, R. Gophna, R. Eyal, & Y. Paz (Eds.), *Jacob Kaplan's excavations of protohistoric sites 1950s–1980s, Vol. 2 (Monograph series of the Institute Of Archaeology 36)* (pp. 455–502). Tel Aviv University.

Getzov, N. (2015). Relative chronology of the proto-historic remains at Nahal Saflul 71 in the Galʻed Hills. *ʼAtiqot, 82*, 1*–20*. (Hebrew with English summary, pp. 221–223).

Getzov, N., Lieberman-Wander, R., Smithline, H., & Syon, D. (2009). *Horbat ʻUza: The 1991 excavations, volume I: The early periods (IAA reports 41)*. Israel Antiquities Authority.

Gilead, I. (2009). The Neolithic–Chalcolithic transition in the southern Levant: Late sixth–fifth millennium culture history. In J. J. Shea & D. E. Lieberman (Eds.), *Transitions in prehistory: Essays in honor of Ofer Bar-Yosef* (pp. 335–355). Oxbow Books.

Gopher, A. (1989). *The flint assemblages of Munhata (Israel): Final report*. In *Les Cahiers du Centre de Recherche Français de Jérusalem* (Vol. 4). Paris.

Gopher, A. (1995). Early pottery-bearing groups in Israel – The pottery Neolithic period. In T. E. Levy (Ed.), *The archaeology of society in the Holy Land* (pp. 205–225). Leicester University Press.

Gopher, A. (2012). The Pottery Neolithic in the southern Levant – A second Neolithic revolution. In A. Gopher (Ed.), *Village communities of the Pottery Neolithic period in the Menasheh Hills, Israel: Archaeological Investigations at the sites of Nahal Zehora* (pp. 1525–1581). Institute of Archaeology, Tel-Aviv University.

Gopher, A. (2019). Unresolved Pottery Neolithic chrono-stratigraphic and chrono-cultural issues: Comments on the beginning and the end of the Pottery Neolithic period. In H. Goldfus, M. I. Gruber, S. Yona, & P. Fabian (Eds.), *Studies in archaeology and ancient cultures in Honor of Isaac Gilead* (pp. 96–108). Archaeopress Archaeology.

Gopher, A., & Eyal, R. (2012). Nahal Zehora pottery assemblages: Typology. In A. Gopher (Ed.), *Village communities of the Pottery Neolithic period in the Menasheh Hills, Israel: Archaeological investigations at the sites of Nahal Zehora* (pp. 359–523). Institution of Archaeology, Tel Aviv University.

Gopher, A., & Gophna, R. (1993). Cultures of the eighth and seventh millennia BP in the southern Levant: A review for the 1990s. *Journal of World Prehistory, 7*(3), 297–353. https://doi.org/10.1007/BF00974722

Gopher, A., & Orrelle, E. (1996). The ground stone assemblages of Munhata, a Neolithic site in the Jordan valley, Israel: A report. *Les cahiers des missions archéologiques Françaises en Israel.*

Gophna, R., & Sadeh, S. (1988–89). Excavations at Tel Tsaf: An early Chalcolithic site in the Jordan Valley. *Tel Aviv, 15–16*(1), 3–36

Gophna, R., & Shlomi, V. (1997). Some notes on Early Chalcolithic and Early Bronze Age material from the sites of 'En Jezreel and Tel Jezreel. *Tel Aviv, 24*, 73–82.

Ilan, D. (2016). The ground stone components of drills in the ancient Near East: Sockets, flywheels, cobble weights, and drill bits. *Journal of Lithic Studies, 3*(3), 261–277.

Kaplan, J. (1958). Excavations at Wadi Rabah. *Israel Exploration Journal, 8*, 149–160.

Kaplan, J. (1969). 'Ein el Jarba: Chalcolithic remains in the Plain of Esdraelon. *Bulletin of the American Schools of Oriental Research, 194*, 2–39. https://www.jstor.org/stable/1356425

Kaplan, J. (1972). Twenty years to the discovery of the Chalcolithic culture of Wadi Rabah. *Annual of the Ha'aretz Museum, 14*, 9–13. (Hebrew).

Khalaily, H., Milevski, I., Kolska Horwitz, L., & Marder, O. (2016). Early Wadi Rabah and Chalcolithic occupations at Tel Dover: Environmental and chronological insights. In S. Ganor, I. Kreimerman, K. Streit, & M. Mumcuoglu (Eds.), *From Sha'ar Hagolan to Shaaraim. Essays in honor of Prof. Yosef Garfinkel* (pp. 109–154). Israel Exploration Society.

Klimscha, F., Hansen, S., & Renn, J. (2021). *Contextualising ancient technology: From archaeological case studies towards a social theory of ancient innovation processes. Berlin Studies of the Ancient World, 73*. https://doi.org/10.17171/3-73

Perrot, J., Zori, N., & Reich, Y. (1967). Neve Ur, un nouvel aspect du Ghassoulien. *Israel Exploration Journal, 17*(4), 201–232.

Rosenberg, D. (2009). Flying stones – The slingstones of the Wadi Rabah culture of the southern Levant. *Paléorient, 35*(2), 99–112.

Rosenberg, D. (2010). Early Maceheads in the southern Levant: A "Chalcolithic" hallmark in Neolithic context. *Journal of Field Archaeology, 35*(2), 204–216.

Rosenberg, D. (2011). *Development, continuity and change: The stone industries of the early ceramic bearing cultures of the southern Levant*. Unpublished Ph.D. Dissertation. Haifa: The University of Haifa (Hebrew with English summary)

Rosenberg, D., & Garfinkel, Y. (2014). *Sha'ar Hagolan Volume 4: The ground-stone industry: Stone working at the Dawn of Pottery production in the southern Levant*. Israel Exploration Society and Institute of Archaeology, Hebrew University.

Rosenberg, D., & Shimelmitz, R. (2017). Perforated stars: Networks of prestige item exchange and the role of perforated flint objects in the Late Chalcolithic of the southern Levant. *Current Anthropology, 58*(2), 295–306.

Rosenberg, D., Klimscha, F., Graham, P. J., Hill, A. C., Weissbrod, L., Ktalav, I., Love, S., Pinsky, S., Hubbard, E., & Boaretto, E. (2014). Back to Tel Tsaf: A preliminary report on the 2013 season of the renewed project. *Journal of the Israel Prehistoric Society, 44*, 148–179.

Rosenberg, D., Chasan, R., & van den Brink, E. C. (2016). Craft specialization, production and exchange in the Chalcolithic of the southern Levant: Insights from the study of the basalt bowl assemblage from Namir Road, Tel Aviv, Israel. *Euroasian Prehistory, 13*(1–2), 105–128.

Rosenberg, D., van den Brink, E. C. M., Shimelmitz, R., Nativ, A., Mienis, H. K., Shamir, O., Chasan, R., & Shooval, T. (2017). Pits and their contents: The Wadi Rabah site of Qidron in the Shephela, Israel. *Journal of the Israel Prehistoric Society, 47*, 33–147.

Rosenberg, D., Pinsky, S., Shooval, T., Tzin, B., Reshef, H., Liu, C., Ktalav, I., & Chasan, R. (2020). Lost and found: 66B, a Late Chalcolithic site in the northern Negev, Israel and its material culture. *Journal of the Israel Prehistoric Society, 50*, 104–137.

Rosenberg, D., Pinsky, S., & Klimscha, F. (2021). Tel Ẓaf. *Hadashot*, 133. Retrieved from www.hadashot-esi.org.il/Report_Detail_Eng.aspx?print=all&id=25891

Rowan, Y. (1998). *Ancient distribution and deposition of prestige objects: Basalt vessels during late prehistory in the southern Levant*. Unpublished Ph.D. dissertation, University of Texas at Austin.

Rowan, Y. M. (2014). The southern Levant (Cisjordan) during the Chalcolithic period. In M. L. Steiner & A. Killebrew (Eds.), *The Oxford handbook of the archaeology of the Levant (ca. 8000 – 332 BCE)*. Oxford University Press.

Rowan, Y. M., & Golden, J. (2009). The Chalcolithic period of the southern Levant: A synthetic review. *Journal of World Prehistory, 22*(1), 1–92.

Sadeh, S., & Gophna, R. (1991). Observations on the Chalcolithic ceramic sequence in the Middle Jordan Valley. *Journal of The Israel Prehistoric Society, 24*, 135–148.

Sebbane, M. (2016). Ceremonial and ritual maces in the temples of the ancient Near East, and the nature of the hoard from Nahal Mishmar. In I. Finkelstein, C. Robin, & T. Römer (Eds.), *Alphabets, texts and artifacts in the ancient Near East: Studies presented to Benjamin Sass* (pp. 421–473). Van Dieren.

Shalev, S. (1991). Two different copper industries in the Chalcolithic culture of Israel. In C. Eluere & J. P. Mohen (Eds.), *Découverte du méta* (pp. 413–424). Picard.

Shipton, G. M. (1939). *Notes on the Megiddo pottery of Strata VI-XX. Oriental Institute of the University of Chicago, Studies in Ancient Oriental Civilizations 17.* University of Chicago Press.

Shuger, A. N., & Gohm, C. J. (2011). Developmental trends in Chalcolithic copper metallurgy: a radiometric perspective. In J. L. Lovell & Y. M. Rowan (Eds.), *Culture, chronology and the Chalcolithic: Theory and transition* (pp. 133–148). Oxbow Books.

Streit, K. (2015). Exploring the Wadi Rabah Culture from the 6th millennium cal BCE: Renewed Excavations at Ein el-Jarba in the Jezreel Valley, Israel (2013–2015). *Strata: Bulletin of the Anglo-Israel Archaeological Society, 33*, 11–35.

Vardi, J. (2011). *Sickle Blades and Sickles of the Sixth and Fifth Millennia BCE in light of the finds from the Chalcolithic Sickle Blade Workshop Site of Beit Eshel.* Unpublished Ph.D. Dissertation. The Ben-Gurion University of the Negev

Zori, N. (1977). *The land of Issachar: Archaeological survey* [Hebrew]. Israel Exploration Society

Interpreting the Chalcolithic Steles of the Southern Levant

David Ilan and Yorke Rowan

Abstract Upright stones (steles/monoliths/mazzeboth/menhirs) are a widespread occurrence in the archaeology of the Levant, beginning in the Natufian. The Chalcolithic Period (c. 4500–3700 BCE) is no exception. In this paper, we examine Chalcolithic upright stones in their contexts. Lacking inscriptions or figurative representation, archaeological context and associated material culture is the key to interpretation. We find that upright stones in the Chalcolithic correlate strongly to mortuary contexts, more so than in earlier or later periods, though this correlation may be weaker in the desert regions.

Keywords Steles · Standing stones · Upright stones · Mazzeboth · Menhirs · Chalcolithic ritual · Chalcolithic religion · Netherworld · Mortuary temple · Gilat · Marj Rabba · Shiqmim · Palmahim · Kissufim · Nevatim · Ramot Nof · Tulaylat Ghassul · Quleh · Horvat Qarqar

1 Introduction

Found on different continents, in different periods, and in diverse contexts, upright stones (steles/monoliths/mazzeboth/menhirs) have long been the subject of scholarly inquiry (e.g., Fitzhugh 2017; Gebel 2013; Keall 1998; Khalidi 2008; Schmidt 2006, 2010). Defining a stele is not necessarily straightforward. Upright stones can have various functions; they can be structural elements—orthostats as ceiling supports or as wall components, for example (Fig. 1; Betts et al., 2013: 54, 87; Fig. 3.4).

D. Ilan (✉)
Hebrew Union College, Jerusalem, Israel
e-mail: dilan@huc.edu

Y. Rowan
University of Chicago, Chicago, IL, USA
e-mail: ymrowan@uchicago.edu

© The Author(s), under exclusive license to Springer Nature Switzerland AG 2023
E. Ben-Yosef, I. W. N. Jones (eds.), *"And in Length of Days Understanding" (Job 12:12): Essays on Archaeology in the Eastern Mediterranean and Beyond in Honor of Thomas E. Levy*, Interdisciplinary Contributions to Archaeology, https://doi.org/10.1007/978-3-031-27330-8_9

Fig. 1 An upright stone incorporated within a Late Neolithic structure (W400) in the Black Desert, Jordan, possibly blocking an earlier entrance. (Photo: Y. Rowan, courtesy of the Eastern Badia Archaeological Project)

We define a stele/mazzebah/menhir as *a stone, usually taller than it is wide, placed upright, without a support function and imbued with symbolic meaning*. Steles range in size from the diminutive to the megalithic.

In the Levant, steles found in prehistoric contexts typically lack figurative representation, the hallmark exception being the pillars in the Neolithic temple at Göbekli Tepe and its surrounding region (Moetz & Celik, 2012; Schmidt 2006, 2010), which can also be viewed as steles. In the case of aniconic steles, interpretation is contingent upon context and associated material culture. Lacking iconographical evidence, archaeological context may suggest symbolic meaning. An example of this might be the late PPNB megalithic semicircle at the submerged site of Atlit Yam. Seven megaliths, ranging from one to two meters high, were set upright around a freshwater spring, possibly as part of a shrine (Galili et al. 2020: 452–454, Fig. 23.7).

Steles of a ritual-symbolic nature are a widespread occurrence in the archaeology of the Levant (e.g., Avner 1984, 1993, 2002; Graesser 1972; La Rocca-Pitts, 2001: 205–228; Mettinger 1995), a tradition that apparently begins in the Natufian (Avner 2002: 70–76). In no period, however, are they ubiquitous, at least not in the Mediterranean climate zone (steles are more visible and perhaps more common in the deserts). They do not seem to have been a quotidian feature of daily life.

In this paper, we catalog and discuss the steles of the Levantine Chalcolithic period (c. 4500–3700 BCE), offering interpretations based on their archaeological contexts.

2 Chalcolithic Steles in Context

Chalcolithic steles can be made of limestone, chalk, kurkar (calcareous sandstone), or even terra cotta (see Tables 1, 2 and 3). They tend to be between 25 and 125 cm. high and between 20 and 45 cm. across, and rectangular, oval, trapezoidal, pyramidal, or "cigar-shaped". Some are worked and some are not, which may indicate that there existed a conceptual template of what a proper standing stone should look like. Some show signs of ochre paint and it is possible that some, many, or all were originally decorated. Most are rather simple, rough forms with no preserved iconography. Therefore, it is likely that the stone itself was the operative symbol.

At least 20 steles from Chalcolithic contexts have been documented; we have mapped their distribution in Fig. 2. Table 1 is a compilation of most of the known Chalcolithic examples from settlement sites. The paucity of settlement sites with steles is somewhat striking. In such contexts, they often seem to co-occur with symbolically charged artifacts and features. One possible stele was reported at the village of Shiqmim, in Subterranean Room 18 (L4244), lying on its side just to the right of the entrance. In Subterranean Room 16/17 at Shiqmim another limestone slab (stele?) was reported (L4201). This area was associated with numerous disarticulated human remains (Levy et al., forthcoming), and as an underground space it is very likely this stone was originally upright. At the cemetery of Shiqmim, on the ridge above the site, steles formed part of a grave circle (Table 2).

At Marj Rabba, a standing stone forms the center of a circular stone feature (Fig. 3) blocking an entrance to an interior room inside of Building #1, a well-built structure containing human skeletal remains (foot bones), not far from the stele. At Tulaylat al-Ghassul, one standing stone discovered in the Area E Sanctuary is mentioned, but with little detail (Seaton 2008: Table 2.1).

Table 1 An inventory of standing stones in Chalcolithic architectural contexts

Site	N=	Remarks	References
Gilat various contexts (see Table 3)	8	5 single stones, one group of 3; 1 painted blue; one in pit	Levy et al. (2006a); see Table 3
Nevatim	+3	In pits and at surface; limestone, worked, rectangular, ca. 50 cm. High; at least one associated with burial	Gilead and Fabian (2002): 73, 75, Fig. 8
Ramot Nof	3	2 in one pit, 1 in another; worked limestone, 1 rectangular, 1 oval-shaped, 1 hybrid rectilinear	Nachshoni et al. (2002): 16*, Fig. 9
Ghassul	3	Area E sanctuary, areas A, Q	Seaton (2008): Table 2.1
Marj Rabba	1	Area B, interior of building 1; limestone	Rowan (personal observation), see Fig. 3
Shiqmim - east	1	Fallen, chalk	Levy et al. (2006b): Fig. 9, 47

Table 2 An inventory of steles in Chalcolithic tomb contexts

Site	N=	Remarks	References
Azor	1	Kurkar fragment	Perrot and Ladiray (1980): Fig. 77.5
Ben Shemen, Tomb 502	1	Limestone, fragment	Perrot and Ladiray (1980): 76, Figs. 117, 134:3
Ben Shemen, Tomb 506	1	Limestone, shaped	Perrot and Ladiray (1980): 76, Figs. 117, 134:3
Ben Shemen, Tomb 510	1	Limestone, shaped, fragment,	Perrot and Ladiray (1980): 76, Figs. 117, 134:3
Bene Beraq, Tomb B	1	Limestone	Kaplan (1993)
Giv'atayim, Cave 2	x	Kurkar, shaped	Sussman and Ben-Arieh (1966): Fig. 7
Giv'atayim cave 7	4	Kurkar, shaped, 4 painted red	Sussman and Ben-Arieh (1966): Fig. 7
Givat Ha'Oranim, Cave 1185	c. 23	Flat, dressed fieldstone, c. 14 singles, 5 in group of 2 or more, 2 single at the centers of pits; 1 perforated	Scheftelowitz (2004): 60
Kissufim Rd. L99	9	Chalk, shaped	Fabian and Goren (2002): 44–46
Kissufim Rd. L99	9	Chalk, shaped	Fabian and Goren (2002): 44–46
Kissufim Rd. L501	1	Chalk, shaped	Fabian and Goren (2002): 44–46
Kissufim Rd. L500–502	1	Chalk, shaped	Fabian and Goren (2002): 44–46
Mazor, Cave B-2, phase III	1	Limestone, said to be shaped	I. Milevski, pers. comm.
Quleh, Cave E-1	1	Limestone, shaped	I. Milevski, pers. comm.
Shoham (N) Cave 4	2	Limestone, shaped	Rowan (2005): Figs. 9.19–9.20
Palmahim	58 (in more than 20 tombs)	Kurkar, rectangular, trapezoidal and oval	Gorzalczany, A. (2018: 58–63)
Horvat Qarqar, south Caves 2, 3, 5, 7, 8, 10, 14, 15	8 (one in each cave)	7 limestone, flat or cigar-shaped; 1 terra cotta, "cigar-shaped" 125 × 37 cm.; in general 54–131 cm high	Fabian et al. (2015)
Shiqmim SR 18	1	Chalk, large, flat	Levy et al. (in prep)

(continued)

Table 2 (continued)

Site	N=	Remarks	References
Shiqmim cemetery?	?	? Stele are mentioned in Alon and Levy 1989: 183. However, there is no mention of steles in the more comprehensive reports on the Shiqmim cemeteries Levy and Alon (1985: 78–81), Levy and Alon (1987: 333–356), Levy et al. (1991: 409–411)	

Table 3 Standing stone contexts at Gilat

Stratum	Area/ Square	Loci	Description/associated features	Illustration in Levy et al. (2006)	Gilat Ref.
2B	D	Room A = room 1	One standing stone[a]	n/a	Alon and Levy (1989): 183–184; Levy et al. (2006a): Table 5.2
2C	D	Room A = room 1	One standing stone	n/a	Alon and Levy (1989): 183–184; Levy et al. (2006a): Table 5.2
2C	J/K2	1154, 1083	One large standing stone in a line of 12 smaller standing stones in an open plaza. The large stone bore faint signs of blue paint. Many pits and symbolic artifacts in plaza.	Pls. 5.28, 5.29	Levy et al. (2006a): 110
2C	Y/J5	589	Three small standing stones above 3B pit 586 (which contained a torpedo vessel). The stones faced a small wall 591 with mudbrick protrusions extending from each end.	Pl. 5.64	Levy et al. (2006a): 129
2C	T/S0	1510	In a burial pit, a standing stone was found 20 cm from the cranium of a flexed adult mail burial	n/a	Levy et al. (2006a): 124
?	D	?	Incised standing stone of chalk	Pl. 5.12	From Alon excavations – unprovenienced

[a]One of the steles noted by Alon and Levy (1989: 183) is perforated (cf. the perforated steles in the Negev, Avner 2002: 68). It is not clear which of these it is.

In the Mediterranean zone, in contrast to the desert regions, standing stones appear to be mainly a feature of mortuary contexts. Steles are documented, for example, at Ben Shemen, Bene Berak, Giv'atayim, Kissufim, Peqi'in, Horvat Qarqar South, Quleh (Fig. 4), and Shoham. The four steles found in Tomb 7 at Giv'atayim may be indicative of the original configuration and treatment of steles in other tombs where steles were present but collapsed. The two *in situ* limestone

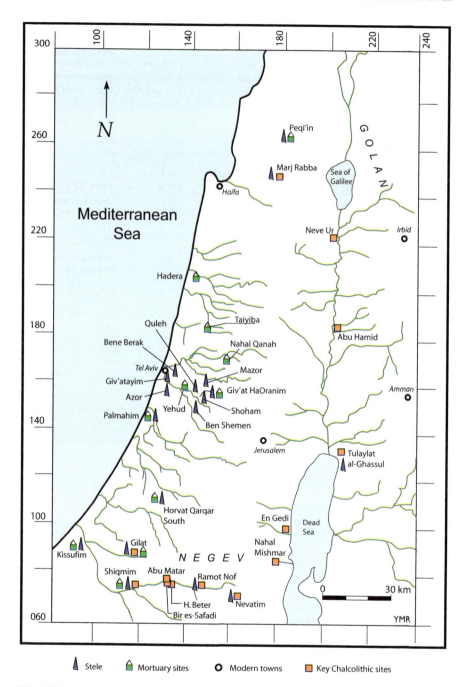

Fig. 2 Distribution map of steles found at Chalcolithic settlements and burial sites

Interpreting the Chalcolithic Steles of the Southern Levant

Fig. 3 Standing stone feature at Marj Rabba, side view, looking south (top) and overhead view (bottom). (Photo courtesy of the Galilee Prehistory Project)

steles, in particular, flanking an ossuary, demonstrate succinctly the relationship between the remains of the dead and the standing stones. Moreover, the red painted stele suggests that others may have been similarly treated. The Palmahim cemetery contains the largest assemblage of steles. These were incorporated into the eastern

Fig. 4 A stele from Cave 10 at Horvat Qarqar South (top, courtesy P. Fabian) and a drawing of a stele found in a Chalcolithic tomb at Quleh (bottom, courtesy I. Milevski)

wall of each tomb, typically within a niche. Between one and four steles were found in each, with no correlation to the number of interments (Gorzalczany 2018: 58–63). Traces of burning were evident in places, such as on the pavement next to a stele, or in a ceramic vessel within the niche of a tomb wall. Many burial contexts contain just one standing stone, regardless of how many individuals were present in the tomb.

Interpreting the Chalcolithic Steles of the Southern Levant

Fig. 5 Stele at the mortuary temple at Gilat, Locus 589, Stratum 2C (courtesy T. Levy)

The stele configurations at Gilat (Fig. 5) appear to be anomalous within the broader Chalcolithic context. The context summary in the Gilat volume (Levy et al. 2006a: 152, Table 5.4) shows four standing stone contexts, one in Stratum 2B and three in Stratum 2C, the two main strata of the site. A search in the locus table (Levy et al. 2006a: Table 5.1) results in a count of seven such contexts; five from Stratum 2C, one from 2B, and one unknown. Beyond this, an earlier publication lists seven standing stones, without context, from the Phase 1 excavations of Alon in Area D, apparently pulled up by plowing (Alon and Levy 1989: 182–184). Table 3 is our own compendium, which results in a total of eight steles at Gilat, five as single stones and three in a group. We have suggested that the Gilat sanctuary is a mortuary complex in light of the large number of primary burials and skeletal fragments (N = 90+) and in light of the iconographic associations (Rowan and Ilan 2007: 251–252; Ilan and Rowan 2012: 102). The plethora of standing stone configurations at Gilat seems to provide further support for the site being a mortuary complex and for the deathly association of steles.

We have also suggested that the Ghassulian Chalcolithic temple at Ein Gedi is a mortuary temple related to the Judean Desert necropolis (Ilan & Rowan, 2015). If this interpretation is correct, and given our interpretation of the Gilat sanctuary as a mortuary temple, the question arises: where is/are the Ein Gedi temple stele/s? Given how close the Chalcolithic remains were to the surface and given the recurring settlement at the Ein Gedi oasis in the Iron Age through the Byzantine period it would not be surprising for upright monoliths to be uprooted. Amihai Mazar (2000) proposed that the circular stone installation in the center of the Ein Gedi temple courtyard enclosed a sacred tree. This is doubtful because the bedrock is quite close to the surface. A better proposal, albeit also speculative, is that the installation enclosed a large stele, similar to some of the installations in the Negev and Sinai (see below).

3 Chalcolithic Steles in the Arid Margins of the Levant

Identifying Chalcolithic sites in the arid margins of the southern and eastern Levant—the Negev, Sinai, Jordan and Arabia—is still difficult. The material culture of the sixth-third millennia BCE is usually meager and displays long-term continuity. Several scholars now identify a separate cultural sphere called the "Timnian", with three phases (e.g., Rosen 2013): early (late fifth to early fourth millennium BCE), middle (mid-fourth millennium BCE), and late (late fourth millennium BCE), where the Chalcolithic of the north is coeval with the middle phase. In his survey of the cultic installations in the desert regions Avner (2002: 70–76, Table 13) has documented eight or nine sites with steles attributable to the middle Timnian phase (Table 4).

Only a few steles found at arid zone sites are clearly associated with burial remains, Wadi Zalaqa being the most prominent of these (Avner 1984: 117). However, many of the Negev and Sinai tumuli contain upright stones, and some of these tumuli contain human remains (Avner 1984: 117; 1993: 166; 2002: 69–70). Only a few of these can be dated to the Chalcolithic period proper (ca. 4500–3700 BCE) but others probably belong to this time frame as well. In any case, the specific dates are perhaps not so important for what is a more general, long-term cultural phenomenon.

Table 4 An inventory of standing stones in the Negev, Sinai, and Arabah attributable to the Chalcolithic / Middle Timnian culture, ca. 4500–3500 BCE

Site	Steles	Reference
Eilat tomb IV	2 steles	Avner (2002): 69
Eilat tomb V	Two cells with 3 and 4 steles, respectively	Avner (2002): 69
Uvda Valley 124/IV	1 stele adjacent to habitation site; 400 m to the south another single stele with shrine	Avner (2002): 72
Maaleh Shaharut	69 steles in concentric circles; open air shrine	Avner (2002): 73
Samar	1 stele; habitation site	Avner (2002): 73
Wadi Watir	3 steles; habitation site	Avner (2002): 74
Wadi Zalaqa 307, tomb 2	1 broad stele; nearby six other steles in open-air shrines, associated with tumuli	Avner (2002): 75
Wadi Sa'al	Two sites with groups of 7 and 9 steles, respectively; open air shrines	Avner (2002): 75–76
Wadi Daba'iya	5 steles; next to large habitation site	Avner (2002): 76
W. Aheimar	Two locations with 7 and 3 steles, respectively; open-air shrines	Smith and Neimi (1994): 481
Wadi Saminiya	Single steles at either end of one of the stone ovals dated to the Chalcolithic and interpreted as burial rings.	Smith et al. (1997): 52

The steles of the southern Levant's arid margins show some of the characteristics of those of the Mediterranean zone to the north. Many seem to have mortuary associations (Avner 2002: 69–70). While single steles seem to be more the rule in Mediterranean zone burial contexts, multiple stele groups are more frequent in the arid zone, though single stones are still the majority (Avner 2002: 67). Arid zone steles are rarely worked; they are selected for their particular shape, which implies that morphology is significant (Avner 2002: 79–80). Tabular scrapers are frequently found in ritual sites and often next to steles (Avner 2002: 76–78). The steles in the arid regions typically occur with offering tables, basins, or altars (Avner 1984: 118); steles in the agrarian regions are not associated with these features.

4 Interpreting Chalcolithic Steles

Steles were a feature of the religious and ritual lives of most, if not all, the peoples of the ancient Levant. They have been interpreted in various ways, usually depending on their find contexts, and in the Bronze and Iron Age, at least, against the background of textual references, especially the Hebrew Bible (Avner 2002: 84–98 and references there). The options can be narrowed somewhat in the Levantine Chalcolithic, by archaeological context.

Chalcolithic steles are most often associated with burial contexts—cave tombs in the Mediterranean zone and tumuli tombs in the arid zone (see Tables 2 and 4). Steles found in tombs of the Mediterranean zone are almost always singles (see Table 3; the exception being a couple of possible groups at Givat HaOranim). In the Negev and Sinai, on the other hand, the numbers of those found in tumuli vary; the majority contain single stones, but two stones and more have been documented (Avner 2002: 90–91). Therefore, their role may have been perceived somewhat differently than that of the singletons of the north.

At Gilat, Nevatim, and Ramot Nof (see Tables 1 and 3), steles are found in pits, often with evocative ritual objects. One of the pits at Nevatim contained human remains as well, as did some of those at Givat HaOranim. Pit interment suggests intentionality—once again, accessing the subterranean. The fact that steles are most often placed in tombs or pits suggests that they are not grave markers *per se* (cf. Avner 2002: 85) because they were not visible to the living.

Steles are inserted into the earth. This is a purposeful ritual act with religious motivations. Being partly above ground and partly below, steles may have served as vehicles for communication between the dead and the living, between the newly dead and the ancestor dead, and/or between the chthonic deity and the newly dead and/or the living (cf. Avner 2002: 86–92).[1] One of us has recently proposed that the famous Gilat Lady figurine is an embodiment of this concept (Ilan 2022).

---

[1] Avner infers that steles were held to embody or "house" deities. This may have been so, at least when the deity was summoned. However, from our perspective, they are more conduits for communication than an actual materialization of the divine.

The steles that occur outside of underground burial contexts occur most often in, or near, the loci of ritual performance. These *were* visible to the living and seem to have had a more public, collective function. Their uprightness served as a focusing device. One infers that these steles may have been the focus of communal, commemorative rituals, communicating with the ancestors and/or with the chthonic deity. At Gilat, in particular, we would argue that all the steles are associated with that site's function as a mortuary temple. Farther to the north, in the Galilee, the Marj Rabba stele is also part of an installation with human bones nearby.[2] At Gilat the remains of feasting are ample; we would interpret this as funerary feasting.[3] At Marj Rabba, too, feasting remains have been documented (Hill et al. 2016), though they were not proximate to the stele or the human remains.

As to the matter of orientation, this seems to be one of the criteria where the steles of the sown differ from the steles of the desert. While the desert steles most often show an orientation to the east, and less frequently to the west (Avner 2002: 83), those in the sown regions to the north, whether underground or in the open, do not seem to have any consistent orientation. This may have something to do with the fact that desert burial and ritual contexts are not usually underground; they are located on the surface, and open to the sky. Avner's proposal that the west is the direction of death (the setting sun) and the east the direction of rebirth (the rising sun) may be more natural to the desert. In contrast, the religious precepts of the sown regions were more oriented towards what came out of the ground—water, pasture and cultivated crops.

In essence then, Chalcolithic steles are associated with the dead and with the netherworld. We propose that they were media of communication between the netherworld and those in the world above, perhaps in phases of liminality achieved through the process of primary burial, secondary burial and above-ground ritual action, in the presence of steles. Steles were an integral component of the Chalcolithic life cycle religion and ritual action.

References

Alon, D., & Levy, T. E. (1989). The archaeology of cult and the chalcolithic sanctuary at Gilat. *Journal of Mediterranean Archaeology, 2*, 163–221.

Avner, U. (1984). Ancient cult sites in the Negev and Sinai deserts. *Tel Aviv, 11*(2), 115–131.

Avner, U. (1993). Masseboth sites in the Negev and Sinai and their significance. In A. Biran & J. Aviram (Eds.), *Proceedings of the second international congress on biblical archaeology today 1990* (pp. 166–181). Jerusalem.

Avner, U. (2002). Studies in the material and spiritual culture of the Negev and Sinai populations, during the 6th—3rd Millennia B.C.

---

[2] The Marj Rabba installation is highly reminiscent of some stele installations in the Negev and Sinai (cf. Avner 2002: Fig. 5:93, and more generally, Figs. 4.56–4.63).

[3] Grigson 2006 does not interpret the Gilat faunal assemblage this way, but we make the case that feasting is clearly implicated (Rowan and Ilan, forthcoming).

Betts, A. V., Cropper, D., Martin, L., McCartney, C., Cooke, L., Garrard, A., & Willcox, G. (2013). *The later prehistory of the Badia*. Oxbow Books.

Fabian, Peter & Goren, Yuval. (2002). The Stone Artifacts. In *Kissufim Road: A Chalcolithic Mortuary site* (pp. 44–48).

Fabian, P., Scheftelowitz, N., & Gilead, I. (2015). Horvat Qarqar South: Report on a Chalcolithic cemetery near Qiryat Gat, Israel. *Israel Exploration Journal, 65*(1), 1–30.

Fitzhugh, W. W. (2017). Mongolian deer stones, European Menhirs, and Canadian Arctic Inuksuit: Collective memory and the function of northern monument traditions. *Journal of Archaeological Method and Theory, 24*(1), 149–187. https://doi.org/10.1007/s10816-017-9328-0

Galili, E., Rosen, B., Weinstein Evron, M., Hershokovitz, I., Eshed, V., & Kolska Horwitz, L. (2020). Israel: Submerged prehistoric sites and settlements on the Mediterranean coastline— The current state of the art. In B. Bailey, N. Galanidou, H. Peeters, H. Jons, & M. Mennenga (Eds.), *The archaeology of Europe's drowned landscapes* (pp. 443–481). Springer.

Gebel, H. G. (2013). Arabia's fifth millennium BCE pastoral well cultures: Hypotheses on the origins of oasis life. In *Proceedings of the Seminar for Arabian Studies* (Vol. 43, pp. 111–126). Archaeopress.

Gilead, I. & Fabian, P. (2002). Nevatim: A site of the Chalcolithic period in the Northern Negev [in Hebrew]. In *Settlement, civilization and culture: Proceedings of the conference in memory of David Alon* (pp. 67–86). Ramat-Gan: Bar-Ilan University, The Faculty of Jewish Studies. The Martin (Szuz) Department of Land of Israel Studies, The Institute of Archaeology.

Gorzalczany, A. (2018). Final report of the 2005 salvage excavations of the Chalcolithic cemetery at Palmahim (North). New evidence of chalcolithic burial patterns from the central coast plain of Israel. *Atiqot, 91*, 1–94.

Graesser, C. (1972). Standing stones in ancient Palestine. *Biblical Archaeologist, 35*, 34–63.

Grigson, C. (2006). Farming? Feasting? Herding? Large mammals from the Chalcolithic of Gilat. In Levy, T.E. (Ed.), *Archaeology, anthropology and cult: The sanctuary at Gilat, Israel* (pp. 215–319). London: Equinox.

Hill, A. C., Price, M. D., & Rowan, Y. M. (2016). Feasting at Marj Rabba, an early Chalcolithic site in the Galilee. *Oxford Journal of Archaeology, 35*(2), 127–140.

Ilan, D. (2022). The weeping lady of Gilat. In K. Garroway, C. Palmer, & A. Erisman (Eds.), *The body lived, cultured, adorned: A Festschrift in honor of Nili S. Fox* (pp. 301–315). Hebrew Union College Press.

Ilan, D., & Rowan, Y. M. (2012). Deconstructing and recomposing the narrative of spiritual life in the chalcolithic of the Southern Levant (4500–3600 B.C.E.). In Y. M. Rowan (Ed.), *Beyond belief: The archaeology of religion and ritual* (pp. 89–113). American Anthropology Association and University of California Press.

Ilan, D., & Rowan, Y. M. (2015). The Judean Desert as a Chalcolithic Necropolis. *Journal of Mediterranean Archaeology, 28*(2), 171–194.

Kaplan, J. (1993). Bene Barak. In *New Encyclopedia of Archaeological Excavations in the Holy Land* (Vol. 1, pp. 186–187).

Keall, E. J. (1998). Encountering megaliths on the Tihamah coastal plain of Yemen. *Proceedings of the Seminar for Arabian Studies, 28*, 139–147.

Khalidi, L. (2008). The late prehistoric standing stones of the Tihâma (Yemen): The domestication of space and the construction of human-landscape identity. *Revue des mondes musulmans et de la Méditerranée, 121-122*, 17–33.

LaRocca-Pitts, E. (2001). *"Of wood and stone" the significance of Israelite cultic items in the bible and its early interpreters*. Eisenbrauns.

Levy, T. E., & Alon, D. (1985). Shiqmim: a Chalcolithic village and mortuary centre in the northern Negev. *Paléorient, 11*, 71–83.

Levy, T. E., & Alon, D. (1987). Excavations in Shiqmim Cemetery 3: Final report on the 1982 excavations. In T. E. Levy, (Ed.), *Shiqmim I*, BAR International Series 356 (pp. 333–355).

Levy, T. E., Alon, D., Anderson, J., Rowan, Y. M., & Kersel, M. (2006a). The Sanctuary Sequence: Excavations at Gilat: 1975–77, 1989, 1990–1992. In *Archaeology, Anthropology and Cult: The Sanctuary at Gilat* (pp. 95–212).

Levy, T. E., Burton, M., & Rowan, Y. M. (2006b). Chalcolithic hamlet excavations near Shiqmim, Negev Desert, Israel. *Journal of Field Archaeology, 31*(1), 41–60.

Levy, T. E., Alon, D., Grigson, C., Holl, A. Goldberg. P., Rowan, Y. & Smith P. (1991). Subterranean Negev Settlement. *National Geographic Research and Exploration, 7*, 394–413.

Levy, T. E., Rowan, Y. M., & Burton, M. (in prep). *Excavations, subsistence and human population at a Chalcolithic settlement center in the Northern Negev Desert, Israel (1987–1989, 1993)*.

Mazar, A. (2000). A sacred tree in the Chalcolithic shrine at En-Gedi: A suggestion. *Bulletin of the Anglo Israel Society, 18*, 31–36.

Mettinger, T. (1995). *No graven image? Israelite aniconism in its ancient Near Eastern context*. Almquist & Wiksell.

Moetz, F. K., & Celik, B. (2012). T-shaped pillar sites in the landscape around Urfa. In R. Matthews & J. Curtis (Eds.), *Proceedings of the 7th international congress on the archaeology of the ancient near east* (pp. 695–703). Harrossowitz Verlag.

Nahshoni, P., Goren, Y., Marder, O., & Goring Morris, N. (2002). A Chalcolithic site at Ramot Nof, Be'er Sheva. *Atiqot, 48*, 1–24.

Perrot, J., & Ladiray, D. (1980). *Tombes a ossuaires de la region cotiere Palestinienne au IVe millennaire avant l'ere Chretienne, Memoires et Travaux du Centre de Recherches Prehistoriques Francais de Jerusalem* (Vol. 1). Association Paléorient.

Rosen, S. A. (2013). Evolution in the desert: Scale and discontinuity in the Central Negev (Israel) in the fourth millennium BCE. *Paléorient, 39*(1), 39–148.

Rowan, Y. M. (2005). Basalt bowls and ground stone assemblage. In E. C. M. Van den Brink & R. Gophna (Eds.), *Shoham (North), Lod Valley, Israel: Excavations of three Chalcolithic burial caves* (pp. 113–139). Israel Antiquities Authority.

Rowan, Y. M., & Ilan, D. (2007). The meaning of ritual diversity in the chalcolithic of the Southern Levant. In D. Barrowclough & C. Malone (Eds.), *Cult in context: Reconsidering ritual in archaeology* (pp. 249–256). Oxbow.

Scheftelowitz, N. (2004). Stone Artefacts. In *Giv'at Ha-Oranim: A Chalcolithic Site*. (pp. 59–67). Tel Aviv University.

Schmidt, K. (2006). *Sie bauten die ersten Tempel. Das rätselhafte Heiligtum der Steinzeitjäger*. C. H. Beck.

Schmidt, K. (2010). Göbekli Tepe – The stone age sanctuaries: New results of ongoing excavations with a special focus on sculptures and high reliefs. *Documenta Praehistorica, 37*, 239–256. https://doi.org/10.4312/dp.37.21

Seaton, P. (2008). *Chalcolithic cult and risk management at Teleilat Ghassul*. Archaeopress.

Smith, A. M., & Neimi, T. (1994). Results of the southeast Arabian reconnaissance. *Annual of the Department of Antiquities of Jordan, 38*(38), 469–483.

Smith, A. M., Stevens, M., & Neimi, T. (1997). The Southeast Araba archaeological survey: A preliminary report of the 1994 season. *BASOR, 305*, 45–71.

Sussman, V., & Ben-Arieh, S. (1966). Ancient burials in Giv'atayim. *Atiqot, 3*, 27–39.

The En Gedi Shrine and the Cave of the Treasure: Disentangling the Entangled

Uri Davidovich

Abstract Two Judean Desert sites excavated in the early 1960s—the En Gedi Shrine and the Cave of the Treasure in Nahal Mishmar—assumed a prominent role in the scholarly discourse of Late Chalcolithic southern Levant. In 1971, David Ussishkin formulated what became a prevailing convention that linked the two sites, suggesting that the Nahal Mishmar hoard was an ephemeral cache of objects that originally served as the cultic paraphernalia of the En Gedi Shrine, hidden in the remote cave by the shrine's caretakers at a time of distress. While reservations and alternative interpretations were raised over the years, this suggested connection was widely accepted in Late Chalcolithic scholarship and has been reconceptualized several times over the years. The present contribution maintains that the long-standing ties between En Gedi and Nahal Mishmar should be disentangled, and that the material dichotomy between En Gedi and the Judean Desert cliff caves (Nahal Mishmar included) implies that the two phenomena represent different chronological *facies* within the Late Chalcolithic Ghassulian culture.

Keywords Late chalcolithic · Southern Levant · Ghassulian culture · Ritual behavior · Refuge · Judean Desert

1 Introduction

The early 1960s witnessed two major discoveries that forever changed the study of the Chalcolithic era in the southern Levant, and, in a broader sense, the study of the advent of metallurgy in Old-World late prehistory. In the spring of 1961, a cache of over 400 ingeniously-crafted copper-alloyed objects was uncovered by P. Bar-Adon in a remote, difficult-to-access cave on a cliff in Wadi Mahras (Heb. Nahal Mishmar)

U. Davidovich (✉)
The Hebrew University of Jerusalem, Jerusalem, Israel
e-mail: uri.davidovich@mail.huji.ac.il

during the second season of a concerted operation of the Israeli archaeological institutions at that time to unearth hidden Roman period scrolls in the Judean Desert (Aviram, 1961; Bar-Adon, 1980). The cave yielded evidence of a Chalcolithic occupation that included large assemblages of material and ecofactual remains recovered from mixed accumulations of geogenic, biogenic and anthropogenic deposits. The hoard was found wrapped in a reed mat concealed below a rock ledge on the northern side of the main hall of the cave. A year later, the Hebrew University expedition to the En Gedi Oasis, led by B. Mazar, I. Dunayevsky and T. Dothan, exposed an isolated edifice above the En Gedi Spring, ca. 10 km northeast of the Nahal Mishmar cave. The edifice, comprised of two broadroom structures, a main gatehouse and a secondary gate connected by a polygonal fence, immediately evoked a cultic interpretation owing to its unique spatial organization, architectural features and cultural remains (Mazar, 1963: 107). Although a 1956 sounding had already disclosed the structure's date and significance (Naveh, 1958), it was only during the 1962 excavations (supervised by D. Ussishkin, who was also entrusted with the final publication) that the most elaborate Chalcolithic ritual compound known to date came to light.

The two sites—the En Gedi Shrine (or temple) and the Cave of the Treasure, as they came to be known—quickly assumed a prominent role in the scholarly discourse of the south Levantine Late Chalcolithic (LC) Ghassulian culture (ca. 4500–3800 BCE). The vast literature concerning these two sites encompasses almost all aspects of research, including metallurgy (e.g., Key, 1964; Levy & Shalev, 1989; Shalev & Northover, 1993; Tadmor et al., 1995; Goren, 2008; Golden, 2009a), art, iconography and symbolism (e.g., Epstein, 1978; Bar-Adon, 1980; Amiran, 1985; Merhav, 1993; Ziffer, 2007; Shalem, 2015; Amzallag, 2018), ritual, cult and society (e.g., Ussishkin, 1980; Levy, 1995; Gilead, 2002; Ilan & Rowan, 2012; Gošić & Gilead, 2015; Gošić, 2016), architecture and material culture (e.g., Porath, 1985; Roux & Courty, 2007; Shamir, 2014; Levy, 2020), as well as the circumstances that led to the deposition of the hoard and the abandonment of the shrine and their possible relation to the demise of the Ghassulian and the end of the Chalcolithic era (e.g., Bar-Adon, 1980; Ussishkin, 1980; Moorey, 1988; Tadmor, 1989; Gates, 1992; Garfinkel, 1994; Joffe & Dessel, 1995; Davidovich, 2013; Sebbane, 2016). A common thread underlying many of these studies is that the two sites are intrinsically connected, as postulated by Ussishkin (1971) some 50 years ago. According to his suggestion, the hoard from Nahal Mishmar initially comprised the cultic paraphernalia of the En Gedi Shrine, and these, following the hasty abandonment of the latter (possibly in times of turmoil), were cached in a desolate, hardly-accessible cliff cave by the shrine's caretakers. Although this reconstruction was questioned as early as the late 1980s, the very connection between the two sites is still widely accepted and has been reconceptualized several times over the years.

The time has come to untangle this long-standing tie between En Gedi and Nahal Mishmar. This paper is divided into three sections, devoted to the three major manifestations of the "connection hypothesis" (Ussishkin, 1971; Goren, 2008; Ilan & Rowan, 2015, respectively). The concluding section will address several implications that arise from the disentangling of the two sites within the broader research of the LC Ghassulian Culture. I wish to devote this inquiry to Tom, a prominent scholar of the south Levantine Chalcolithic and a true supporter of the renewed work in the Judean Desert cliff caves.

2 A Play in Three Acts

2.1 Act One

In 1971, nearly a decade after the initial discoveries, the first detailed publications of the hoard from Nahal Mishmar (Bar-Adon, 1971 [Hebrew], with the English version following in 1980) and the En Gedi Shrine (Ussishkin, 1971, a semi-popular version of the final report that followed in 1980) appeared. The main thesis of Ussishkin's 1971 article was disclosed in the title, *The "Ghassulian" Temple in Ein Gedi and the Origin of the Hoard from Nahal Mishmar*, and was further developed in the second part of the article, following the presentation of the excavation results in the shrine (Ussishkin, 1971: 34–35):

> ...the temple was found empty with all its cultic equipment missing. Hardly any objects, with the exception of the alabaster fragment, were found in the enclosure. The absence of such equipment becomes even more conspicuous when we remember the relative richness of the finds in the Ghassulian sites. One has to conclude that when the temple was abandoned its equipment was carried away by the priests. Unfortunately, they were rather thorough, and nothing was left behind. What happened to the temple's equipment and whence was it taken?

Subsequently, he described the basic data concerning the Cave of the Treasure and its remains, and concluded with an answer to the above question (Ussishkin, 1971: 37–39):

> The hoard contains an unusually rich series of articles, together forming a unique collection of equipment for use in the Ghassulian ritual. The articles of the hoard must have been in use in a central Ghassulian sanctuary; and it seems that the Ein Gedi temple, being a central shrine and a place for a pilgrimage, is the only candidate to which the articles of the hoard can be attributed. All data fit this conclusion and we can attempt the following reconstruction. The articles of the hoard formed the cultic equipment of the temple... When the decision to abandon the temple had been reached, the "priests" methodically assembled all the ritual equipment without leaving even one article behind, and left for good. They traveled only a few miles until they reached the Nahal Mishmar cave, where they stayed for a while. There they decided to continue their journey, and, considering their future return to be certain, chose to leave the ritual equipment in the cave. They carefully wrapped the articles in a straw mat and hid them in a niche never to see them again.

Ussishkin's hypothesis thus connected the En Gedi Shrine and the hoard from Nahal Mishmar based on two complementing arguments: the relative geographic proximity, and the fact that the shrine contained (according to his view) no cultic paraphernalia. Ussishkin was of course aware of other data that may have complicated this immaculate account of the events. For example, the fact that cliff caves with Ghassulian deposits were found much closer to En Gedi (e.g., the Cave of the Pool in Nahal David; Aharoni, 1958; Avigad, 1962), and thus there was no necessity to drag the hoard as far as Nahal Mishmar. In fact, Ussishkin himself was a staff member in Yadin's expedition to Nahal Hever as part of the "Judean Desert Operation" in the early 1960s, and participated in the excavation of a LC occupation in the Cave of Letters, approximately halfway between Nahal Mishmar and En Gedi (Yadin, 1962, 1963). In addition, Ussishkin's claim that no cultic paraphernalia were found in En Gedi underscores his reductive approach to the multiple remains associated with rituals in the shrine, including cultic-related installations (the rounded installation in the courtyard, the altar in the center of the" sanctuary"), activities (e.g., the deposition of ceramic "offerings" in refuse pits or "favissae" on both sides of the sanctuary) and artifacts (i.e., the ceramic figurine of a horned animal laden with churns found in the altar, and the base of a rare alabaster vase found in the courtyard). Evidently, he did not consider these arguments as hampering the suggested narrative. Ussishkin reiterated his view in more detail in the final publication of the excavations (1980: 38–41; reprinted in 2007), and again in a retrospect celebrating 50 years of the excavations of the shrine (Ussishkin, 2014: 22–26), where he already countered some of the critiques that were offered by that time (see below).

The narrative formulated by Ussishkin was warmly adopted, both by scholars specializing in the study of the Ghassulian Culture (e.g., Epstein, 1978: 26; Levy, 1986: 89) and in more general accounts on the archaeology of the southern Levant (e.g., Kenyon, 1979: 62–63; Aharoni, 1982: 43–45; Coogan, 1987: 3–4; Mazar, 1990: 68). In tandem, during the 1980s and 1990s a floruit of suggestions concerning the nature of the hoard and the circumstances that led to its concealment surfaced in the scholarly literature, some adhering to its origin in a ritual or public precinct, though not necessarily En Gedi (Bar-Adon, 1980: 12–13, 202; Moorey, 1988: 182; Garfinkel, 1994: 174–176), while others advocated different approaches altogether (Tadmor, 1989; Gates, 1992). More recent commentators were inclined to associate the original systemic context of the hoard with a public domain related to ritual activities within the Ghassulian settled zone, whereas its connection specifically to En Gedi is disputed (Joffe et al., 2001: 18, n. 8; Goren, 2008: 391–393; Goren, 2014: 263–265; Ussishkin, 2014: 22–26; Gilead & Gošić, 2014: 234–235; Sebbane, 2014: 132–134; Gošić & Gilead, 2015: 171–172; Ilan & Rowan, 2015: 177; Sebbane, 2016: 464).

The petrographic examination of Ghassulian pottery carried out by Y. Goren in the late 1980s and early 1990s was the first study to question the connection between En Gedi and the Cave of the Treasure on empirical grounds. While the results of his MA study (Goren, 1987; Gilead & Goren, 1989) were later amended based on larger sample collections and improved optical identifications (Goren, 1991, 1995), the notion that the petrographic profile of the two sites was markedly different was already suggested following the first stage of analysis (Gilead & Goren, 1989: 7), and solidified in the second stage (Goren, 1995). According to the latter version, the petrographic profile of En Gedi is rather homogenous and comprises two closely-related groups originating in the Cenomanian segment of the Judea Group, and considered to represent a local or "Judean" (regional) origin of the pottery assemblage. Conversely, the pottery from the Cave of the Treasure is composed of various petrographic groups of distant geological sources (Northern Negev, Coastal Plain, Lower Jordan Valley) in addition to the "Judean" groups. Thus, Goren (1995: 296–297) concluded that (1) En Gedi should be viewed as a ritual center serving a local population or more distant communities which made use of locally-produced vessels in their ritual activities; (2) the Cave of the Treasure assemblage reflects a different model of interregional ritual center, which was located either in the cave itself or (more likely) in an unknown site somewhere within the settled zone of the Ghassulian, and its contents were later transported for a final deposition in the cave; and (3) the two sites should be disconnected due to the substantial differences in the petrographic composition of the ceramic assemblages. Although Ussishkin (2014: 24–25) recently attempted to discredit Goren's changing petrographic readings in order to throw the baby out with the bathwater, it seems that even if challenges may be raised with respect to certain empirical identifications, the general picture of conspicuous petrographic disparity between the two sites stands out.

The petrographic disparity, however, is only one facet of a much broader incongruity between the two sites, whose clearer manifestation can be traced in the typological diversity of the pottery assemblages (Fig. 1). In my MA thesis (2008) I conducted a detailed study of the Nahal Mishmar cave complex and its material-cultural remains as part of a regional investigation of cave exploitation patterns in the Judean Desert. A comparative analysis of the typological composition of the Cave of the Treasure (n = 175 vessels; Davidovich, 2008: 236–259) and the En Gedi shrine (Ussishkin, 1980: 18–34) reveals a clear dichotomy: three of the four most common vessel types in the shrine—the cornet, the fenestrated chalice and the basin (for definitions, see Davidovich, 2008: 91–101, based on Gilead & Goren, 1995)—are entirely absent from the Cave of the Treasure, and, in effect, from all cliff cave assemblages in the Judean Desert, with a single exception for each type (Davidovich, 2008: 109–111). On the other hand, vessel types commonly found in the cliff caves, e.g., the churn, the medium-sized bowl with a soft S profile below the rim, the holemouth pithos and the large jar (Davidovich, 2008, types CN, BL2-a, HL2, JR4, respectively), are nonexistent at En Gedi. While quantitative variations in the frequency of certain types in the assemblages may account for functional differences, the typological dichotomy cannot but be interpreted as a cultural and/or chronological distinction between the two sites, and, more generally, between En Gedi and the cliff cave occupations (Davidovich, 2008: 109–112). This dichotomy is evinced in other material realms as well (e.g., the presence of metal, shell and ivory objects in the cliff caves vs. their absence at En Gedi).

In the concluding section of my thesis, I suggested that En Gedi and the Cave of the Treasure belong to two different *facies* of the Ghassulian Culture (Davidovich, 2008: 160–162): Whereas En Gedi finds its closest equivalent at Ghassul, the material assemblages from the cliff caves, including Nahal Mishmar, resemble those of the Beer Sheva Valley sites (as noted already by some of the early excavators of the caves: e.g., Aharoni, 1961: 14). At that time, I was hesitant to determine with certainty that this divergent cultural affiliation expresses a chronological distinction. Given the results of the systematic work of I. Gilead on Ghassulian inner chronology and sub cultures (e.g., Gilead, 1994, 2007, 2011; Gilead & Gošić, 2014:

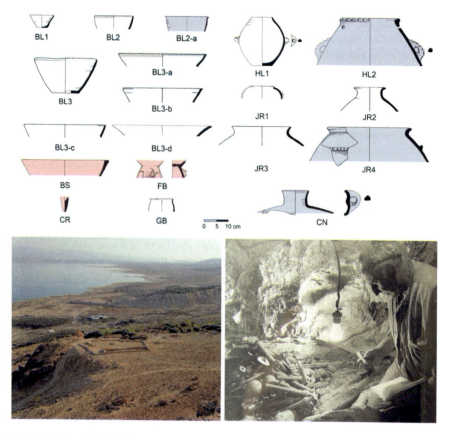

Fig. 1 The Late Chalcolithic ceramic typology of the Judean Desert (following Davidovich 2008, figs. 22–23), emphasizing vessel categories typical to the En Gedi shrine (in red) and the cliff caves (in blue). The shrine is seen on the lower left, looking southeast towards the En Gedi Oasis and the Dead Sea. The hoard from Nahal Mishmar is shown in the lower right, inspected by Bar-Adon inside the Cave of the Treasure

231–235), a chronological separation between Nahal Mishmar and En Gedi seems the most plausible solution. According to Gilead's model, En Gedi fits well within the Early Ghassulian represented at sites such as Ghassul, Grar and Gilat, while the Cave of the Treasure belongs to the Late Ghassulian phase of the Beer Sheva Valley sites. Apart from ceramic distinctions denoted by changes in vessel frequencies, the two Ghassulian phases differ in other cultural spheres, metallurgy being the most notable difference (see further below).

2.2 Act Two

In 2008, Goren published his extensive work on the provenance of ceramic residues of the molds used in the production of the Ghassulian copper-alloyed objects made in the lost wax technique. This research included dozens of objects from the Nahal Mishmar hoard and similar objects found in other Ghassulian sites. In this publication, in which he revised his conclusions from an earlier work that were based on a much smaller sample (Goren, 1995: 295–296, appendix II), Goren suggested that the molds were made of different compositions originating in multiple geological settings located on both sides of the Dead Sea Rift. Since in several cases more than one composition was associated with the same object, indicating the creation of layered molds made of different source materials, it was convincingly suggested that (at least one of) the production center(s) of the copper-alloyed objects is to be located along the Rift Valley (Goren, 2008: 391–392; 2014: 263–265). From this point, Goren went on to speculate that this production center should be sought in the En Gedi Shrine, while reviving the connection between the shrine and the Nahal Mishmar hoard. In order to allow this interpretation, he had to tackle (or bypass) two main hurdles: his own assertion of the petrographic disparity between En Gedi and the Cave of the Treasure, discussed in detail above, and the absence of metallurgic remains at En Gedi.

Regarding the first issue, Goren used several statements made by Bar-Adon in the final report of the excavations at the Cave of the Treasure (1980: 7), implying that the hoard was inserted into the "niche" where it was found through a pit dug from the upper level of the so-called Chalcolithic layer, in an attempt to disconnect the hoard from the Chalcolithic occupation in the cave (Goren, 2008: 392). While this assertion contradicts his own earlier assessment of the same statements (Goren, 1995: 297), it is important to briefly remark on the problems involved in using Bar-Adon's portrayal of the stratigraphy of the cave. By and large, Bar-Adon attempted to apply a standard version of archaeological stratigraphy, based on his own experience in excavating multi-strata mound sites (e.g., Bet Yerah), in interpreting the excavation results in the cave. By doing so, he failed to recognize the entirely different nature of formation processes in the Judean Desert caves, which typically contain mixed accumulations that were deposited, turbated and transported by multiple geological, biological and anthropological agents that operated in the caves throughout the Holocene (Davidovich, 2008: 76–83; Lazagabaster et al., 2021). This fundamental lapse, coupled with major oversights related to the chronostratigraphy of the cave (e.g., the existence of an unrecognized Early Bronze IB occupation: Davidovich, 2012) and the numerous errors found in the final report (Davidovich, 2008: 239–244; Gilead & Gošić, 2014: 227–232), make it impossible, in my view, to accept Bar-Adon's aforementioned stratigraphic reconstruction. As such, there is no basis for disconnecting the hoard from the Chalcolithic occupation in the cave, and this connection should be viewed as a parsimonious explanation for the cultural context of the hoard (see also Gilead & Gošić, 2014).

As for En Gedi, Goren (2008: 392) suggested that the methods applied in the 1960s excavations of the shrine were inadequate to identify residues related to the production of metal objects in the lost wax technique. Ussishkin and others criticized this view (Ussishkin, 2014: 25; Gilead & Gošić, 2014: 234) for its lack of factual basis. In addition, the attribution of En Gedi to an Early Ghassulian phase discussed above, chronologically distinct from the Late Ghassulian affiliation of the Cave of the Treasure, coincides with the notion of the Early Ghassulian as a "premetallic" phase (Golden, 2009b: 47; Gilead & Gošić, 2014: 235). While a detailed inspection of the advent of metallurgy in the Ghassulian is beyond the scope of this paper, suffice it to state that En Gedi and Nahal Mishmar cannot be connected on metallurgic grounds.

2.3 Act Three

The final attempt to link the shrine at En Gedi to the Nahal Mishmar Hoard was made by D. Ilan and Y. Rowan (2015; also 2012: 103–104) as part of their reconstruction of the Judean Desert as a Ghassulian necropolis. According to this theory, the cliff caves of the Judean Desert were used primarily for mortuary purposes, and the hoard from Nahal Mishmar should be viewed as a group of burial offerings (found in either primary or secondary deposition) associated with the skeletal remains excavated by Bar-Adon in the cave (Rowan & Ilan, 2012: 94–95; Ilan & Rowan, 2015: 174–177). En Gedi, according to their suggestion, functioned as a mortuary shrine directly related to the burial activities in the caves hanging in the cliffs of the nearby canyons (Ilan & Rowan, 2015: 182–187).

Offering a detailed critique of Ilan and Rowan's theoretical, methodological and interpretative frameworks would require a separate essay; therefore, I will only state the obvious problems. First, only three LC cave sites in the entire area that stretches between Qumran and Masada (the Nahal Mishmar Cave Complex, the Cave of Horror in Nahal Hever, and the Cave of Skulls of the Large Cave Complex in Nahal Ze'elim) yielded human skeletal remains, rendering the characterization of the Judean Desert as a Chalcolithic necropolis unviable (Davidovich, 2008: 130–131). Second, nothing in the material culture of the cliff caves invokes mortuary-related interpretations, even if Ghassulian burial caves elsewhere in the southern Levant share some of their material traits with contemporary settlement sites and with the Judean Desert caves. Third, the En Gedi shrine produced no evidence whatsoever that would imply the practice of mortuary rituals. And, finally, the disparity between the material assemblages of En Gedi and the cliff caves, detailed above, places them in separate cultural contexts altogether.

3 Conclusions

Ussishkin's half-century-old postulation connecting the En Gedi Shrine and the Nahal Mishmar Hoard, two of the most important late prehistoric discoveries ever made in the southern Levant, proved to be a compelling premise in the scholarship of the Late Chalcolithic period. Over the years, this premise has been formulated as behavioral (the flight of the shrine's caretakers with its ritual paraphernalia to a remote cliff cave; Ussishkin, 1971), technological (production of the hoard's copper-alloyed objects in En Gedi; Goren, 2008), and ritual (En Gedi as a mortuary shrine associated with burials in the cliff caves, with the hoard interpreted as burial offerings; Ilan & Rowan, 2015). These incarnations enabled the underlying premise to endure growing criticism and competing interpretations. They also testify to the powerful impact of (relative) geographic proximity on archaeological inference, even though the sites are located 10 km apart and in greatly divergent landscapes. Nonetheless, it is time for this long-standing construction to fall apart once and for all.

The ritual complex at En Gedi is part and parcel of the Early Ghassulian phase of the Late Chalcolithic (Fig. 2). The high frequency of cornets in the ceramic

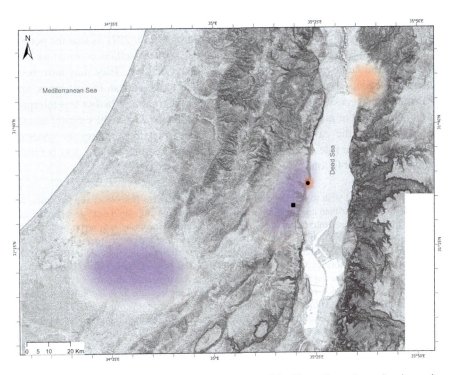

Fig. 2 Terrain (hillshade) map of the southern provinces of the Ghassulian culture, showing major nodes in the distribution of the Early Ghassulian (red) and the Late Ghassulian (blue), as well as the location of En Gedi (black circle) and the Cave of the Treasure (black square)

assemblage and the lack of metallurgic remains and other traits of the "late" phase (e.g., ivories) not only indicate its chronological position within the LC even in the absence of radiometric data, but also associate En Gedi with the other two Ghassulian ritual complexes known to-date—Ghassul Area E and Gilat (Gošić, 2016). This observation may lend further support to the hypothesis that the transition between the Early and Late Ghassulian involved marked changes in the realm of the ritual, including (but not limited to) the emergence of metallurgy as a new axis of ritual praxis (Gošić & Gilead, 2015). En Gedi was most probably a ritual edifice serving primarily a local community (Davidovich, 2008: 53–57), as indicated by the rather homogenous petrographic profile of the ceramic assemblage of the shrine, that is based on geological formations outcropping in the oasis.

The Cave of the Treasure, on the other hand, is but one (albeit unique) example of a regional phenomenon of ephemeral occupations in hardly-accessible cliff caves in the Judean Desert, interpreted by the author in the context of temporary refuge episode/s associated with times of societal strife (Davidovich, 2008, 2013; compare Levy, 1995: 239–243). The material assemblages from these caves, on the whole, set them apart from En Gedi and place the entire phenomenon within the Late Ghassulian. The Cave of the Treasure is exceptional in comparison with other cliff caves in the quantity and diversity of material remains, in the petrographic variation of the ceramic assemblage, and, obviously, in producing the largest collection of metal objects found in a single Ghassulian context. In my opinion, the best explanation for the uniqueness of the cave, following Goren (1995: 297), is that the people who took refuge there came from an unknown, affluent settled community that housed a ritual center, possibly of interregional significance. They may have been among the leaders of the societal fraction that fled to the Judean Desert caves, and as a result, had access to the communal ritual paraphernalia. Whether this interpretation is accepted or not, the association between the hoard and the cultural assemblages found in the cave should form the basis for reconstructing its systemic context and unique role in the latter phase of the Ghassulian culture, just before it disappeared into oblivion.

Acknowledgments I wish to thank the editors of this volume, Erez Ben-Yosef and Ian Jones, for their invitation to contribute an essay in honor of Prof. Tom Levy, to whom I am deeply indebted. Mika Sarig from the Institute of Archaeology of the Hebrew University was responsible for the pottery drawings, and Eran Shefi assisted in the graphic design of the pottery plate. Processing the finds from the Cave of the Treasure and other cliff caves stored in the national treasures of the Israel Antiquities Authorities was made possible with the help of Galit Litani, curator of the Chalcolithic and Bronze Age periods, and Michael Sebanne, chief director of the National Treasures. Doron Bar-Adon contributed the photograph of the treasure included in Fig. 1, and Ido Wachtel (GIS) and Micka Ullman (graphic design) assisted in the production of Fig. 2. Assaf Nativ and Micka Ullman read an early version of this article and offered important insights. I offer my thanks and great appreciation to all of them.

References

Aharoni, Y. (1958). Archaeological survey of 'Ein Gedi. *Bulletin of the Israel Exploration Society, 22*, 27–45. (Hebrew).

Aharoni, Y. (1961). Expedition B. *Israel Exploration Journal, 11*(1–2), 11–24.

Aharoni, Y. (1982). *The archaeology of the land of Israel, from the prehistoric beginnings to the end of the first temple period*. Westminster Press.

Amiran, R. (1985). A suggestion to see the copper 'crowns' of the Judean desert treasure as drums or stand-like altars. In J. Tubb (Ed.), *Palestine in the Bronze and Iron Ages, papers in honour of Olga Tufnell* (pp. 10–14). Institute of Archaeology.

Amzallag, N. (2018). Visual code in the Nahal Mishmar Hoard: The earliest case of protowriting? *Antiguo Oriente, 16*, 45–92.

Avigad, N. (1962). Expedition A – Nahal David. *Israel Exploration Journal, 12*(3–4), 169–183.

Aviram, J. (1961). Introduction. *Israel Exploration Journal, 11*(1–2), 2–5.

Bar-Adon, P. (1971). *The Cave of the Treasure: The finds from the caves in Nahal Mishmar*. Mosad Bialik and Israel Exploration Society (Hebrew).

Bar-Adon, P. (1980). *The Cave of the Treasure: The finds from the caves in Nahal Mishmar*. Israel Exploration Society.

Coogan, M. D. (1987). Of cults and cultures: Reflections on the interpretation of archaeological evidence. *Palestine Exploration Quarterly, 119*, 1–8.

Davidovich, U. (2008). *The Late chalcolithic period in the Judean desert: Identification, settlement pattern and material culture as a basis for social and environmental reconstruction*. Unpublished MA dissertation, The Hebrew University (Hebrew), Jerusalem.

Davidovich, U. (2012). The early Bronze IB in the Judean desert caves. *Tel Aviv, 39*(1), 3–19.

Davidovich, U. (2013). The chalcolithic-early Bronze transition: A view from the Judean desert caves. *Paléorient, 39*(1), 125–138.

Epstein, C. (1978). Aspects of symbolism in chalcolithic Palestine. In P. R. S. Moorey & P. Parr (Eds.), *Archaeology in the Levant: Essays for Kathleen Kenyon* (pp. 23–35). Aris & Phillips.

Garfinkel, Y. (1994). Ritual burial of cultic objects: The earliest evidence. *Cambridge Archaeological Journal, 4*(2), 159–188.

Gates, M. H. (1992). Nomadic pastoralists and the chalcolithic hoard from Nahal Mishmar. *Levant, 24*, 131–139.

Gilead, I. (1994). The history of the chalcolithic settlement in the Nahal Beer Sheva area: The radiocarbon aspect. *Bulletin of the American Schools of Oriental Research, 296*, 1–13.

Gilead, I. (2002). Religio-magic behavior in the chalcolithic period of Palestine. In S. Ahituv & E. D. Oren (Eds.), *Studies in archaeology and related disciplines, Aaron Kempinski memorial volume* (pp. 103–128). Ben-Gurion University of the Negev Press.

Gilead, I. (2007). The Besorian: A pre-Ghassulian cultural entity. *Paléorient, 33*(1), 33–49.

Gilead, I. (2011). Chalcolithic culture history: The Ghassulian and other entities in the southern Levant. In J. L. Lovell & Y. M. Rowan (Eds.), *Culture, chronology and the chalcolithic: Theory and transition* (pp. 12–24). The Council for British Research in the Levant and Oxbow Books.

Gilead, I., & Goren, Y. (1989). Petrographic analyses of fourth millennium B.C. pottery and stone vessels from the Northern Negev, Israel. *Bulletin of the American Schools of Oriental Research, 275*, 5–14.

Gilead, I., & Goren, Y. (1995). The pottery assemblages from Grar. In I. Gilead (Ed.), *Grar: A chalcolithic site in the Northern Negev* (Beer-Sheva VII) (pp. 137–221). Ben-Gurion University of the Negev Press.

Gilead, I., & Gošić, M. (2014). Fifty years later: A critical review of the stratigraphy, chronology and context of the Nahal Mishmar Hoard. *Mitekufat Haeven – Journal of the Israel Prehistoric Society, 44*, 226–239.

Golden, J. M. (2009a). New light on the development of chalcolithic metal technology in the southern Levant. *Journal of World Prehistory, 22*(3), 283–300.

Golden, J. M. (2009b). *Dawn of the Metal Age. Technology and society during the Levantine chalcolithic*. Equinox.

Goren, Y. (1987). *Petrography of chalcolithic period pottery assemblages from southern Israel*. Unpublished M.A. dissertation. The Hebrew University (Hebrew), Jerusalem.

Goren, Y. (1991). *The beginnings of pottery production in Israel: Technology and typology of proto-historic ceramic assemblages in Eretz-Israel (6th–4th millennia B.C.E.)*. Unpublished PhD. dissertation. The Hebrew University (Hebrew), Jerusalem.

Goren, Y. (1995). Shrines and ceramics in chalcolithic Israel: The view through the petrographic microscope. *Archaeometry, 37*, 287–305.

Goren, Y. (2008). The location of specialized copper production by the lost wax technique in the chalcolithic Southern Levant. *Geoarchaeology, 23*, 374–397.

Goren, Y. (2014). Gods, caves, and scholars: Chalcolithic cult and metallurgy in the Judean Desert. *Near Eastern Archaeology, 77*(4), 260–266.

Gošić, M. (2016). Temples in the Ghassulian culture: Terminology and social implications. *Issues in Ethnology and Anthropology, 11*(3), 869–893.

Gošić, M., & Gilead, I. (2015). Casting the sacred: Chalcolithic metallurgy and ritual in the southern Levant. In N. Laneri (Ed.), *Defining the sacred: Approaches to the archaeology of religion in the near East* (pp. 161–175). Oxbow.

Ilan, D., & Rowan, Y. M. (2012). Deconstructing and recomposing the narrative of spiritual life in the chalcolithic of the southern Levant (4500–3700 BC). In Y. M. Rowan (Ed.), *Beyond belief: The archaeology of religion and ritual* (Archaeological papers of the American anthropology association 21) (pp. 89–113). Wiley-Blackwell.

Ilan, D., & Rowan, Y. M. (2015). The Judean desert as a chalcolithic necropolis. *Journal of Mediterranean Archaeology, 28*(2), 171–194.

Joffe, A. H., & Dessel, J. P. (1995). Redefining chronology and terminology for the chalcolithic of the Southern Levant. *Current Anthropology, 36*, 507–518.

Joffe, A. H., Dessel, J. P., & Hallote, R. S. (2001). The "Gilat Woman": Female iconography, chalcolithic cult, and the end of Southern Levantine prehistory. *Near Eastern Archaeology, 64*(1–2), 8–23.

Kenyon, K. M. (1979). *Archaeology in the Holy Land* (4th ed.). E. Benn.

Key, C. A. (1964). Ancient copper and copper-arsenic alloy artefacts: Composition and metallurgical implications. *Science, 146*, 1578–1580.

Lazagabaster, I. L., Ullman, M., Porat, R., Halevi, R., Porat, N., Davidovich, U., & Marom, N. (2021). Changes in the large carnivore community structure of the Judean Desert in connection to Holocene human settlement dynamics. *Scientific Reports, 11*, 3458. https://doi.org/10.1038/s41598-021-82996-6

Levy, T. E. (1986). Archaeological sources for the study of Palestine: The Chalcolithic period. *Biblical Archaeologist, 49*, 82–108.

Levy, T. E. (1995). Cult, metallurgy and rank societies – Chalcolithic period (ca. 4500–3500 BCE). In T. E. Levy (Ed.), *The archaeology of society in the holy land* (pp. 226–244). Leicester University Press.

Levy, J. (2020). *The genesis of the textile industry from adorned nudity to ritual regalia: The changing role of fibre craft and their evolving techniques of manufacture in the ancient near east from the Natufian to the Ghassulian*. Archaeopress.

Levy, T. E., & Shalev, S. (1989). Prehistoric metalworking in the Southern Levant: Archaeometallurgical and social perspectives. *World Archaeology, 20*, 352–372.

Mazar, B. (1963). Excavations at the oasis of Engedi. *Archaeology, 16*, 99–107.

Mazar, A. (1990). *Archaeology of the land of the bible: 10,000–586 B.C.E.* Douhleday.

Merhav, R. (1993). Scepters of the divine from the cave of the treasure at Nahal Mishmar. In M. Heltzer, A. Segal, & D. Kaufman (Eds.), *Studies in the archaeology and history of ancient Israel in honour of Moshe Dothan* (pp. 21–42). Haifa University Press. (Hebrew).

Moorey, P. R. S. (1988). The chalcolithic hoard from Nahal Mishmar, Israel, in context. *World Archaeology, 20*, 171–189.

Naveh, J. (1958). Chalcolithic remains at 'Ein Gedi. *Bulletin of the Israel Exploration Society, 22,* 46–48. (Hebrew).
Porath, Y. (1985). A chalcolithic building at Fasa'el. *Atiqot, 17,* 1–19.
Roux, V., & Courty, M. A. (2007). Analyse techno-pétrographique céramique et interpretation fonctionnelle des sites: un exemple d'application dans le Levant Sud chalcolithique. In A. Bain, J. Chabot, & M. Moussette (Eds.), *La mesure du passé: contributions à la recherche en archéométrie (2000–2006)* (BAR international series 1700) (pp. 153–167). BAR.
Rowan, Y. M., & Ilan, D. (2012). The subterranean landscape of the southern Levant during the chalcolithic period. In H. Moyes (Ed.), *Sacred darkness: A global perspective on the ritual use of caves* (pp. 87–108). University of Colorado Press.
Sebbane, M. (2014). The hoard from Nahal Mishmar, and the metalworking industry in Israel in the chalcolithic period. In M. Sebbane, O. Misch-Brandl, & D. M. Master (Eds.), *Masters of fire: Copper Age art from Israel* (pp. 114–136). Princeton University Press.
Sebbane, M. (2016). Ceremonial and ritual maces in the temples of the ancient near East, and the nature of the hoard from Nahal Mishmar. In I. Finkelstein, C. Robin, & T. Römer (Eds.), *Alphabets, texts and Artifacts in the ancient near East: Studies presented to Benjamin Sass* (pp. 421–473). Van Dieren.
Shalem, D. (2015). Motifs on the Nahal Mishmar hoard and the ossuaries: Comparative observations and interpretations. *Mitekufat Haeven – Journal of the Israel Prehistoric Society, 45,* 217–237.
Shalev, S., & Northover, P. J. (1993). The metallurgy of the Nahal Mishmar hoard reconsidered. *Archaeometry, 35*(1), 35–47.
Shamir, O. (2014). Textiles, basketry, and other organic artifacts of the chalcolithic period in the Southern Levant. In M. Sebbane, O. Misch-Brandl, & D. M. Master (Eds.), *Masters of fire: Copper Age art from Israel* (pp. 138–152). Princeton University Press.
Tadmor, M. (1989). The Judean Desert treasure from Nahal Mishmar: A chalcolithic traders' hoard? In A. J. Leonard & B. B. Williams (Eds.), *Essays in ancient civilization presented to Helen J. Kantor* (pp. 249–261). The Oriental Institute of the University of Chicago.
Tadmor, M., Kedem, D., Begemann, F., Hauptmann, A., Pernicka, E., & Schmitt-Strecker, S. (1995). The Nahal Mishmar hoard from the Judean Desert: Technology, composition, and provenance. *Atiqot, 27,* 95–148.
Ussishkin, D. (1971). The "Ghassulian" temple in Ein Gedi and the origin of the hoard from Nahal Mishmar. *Biblical Archaeologist, 34,* 23–39.
Ussishkin, D. (1980). The Ghassulian shrine at En-Gedi. *Tel Aviv, 7,* 1–44.
Ussishkin, D. (2007). The Ghassulian shrine at En-Gedi. In E. Stern (Ed.), *En Gedi excavations I, final report (1961–1965)* (pp. 29–68). Israel Exploration Society.
Ussishkin, D. (2014). The chalcolithic temple in En Gedi: Fifty years after its discovery. *Near Eastern Archaeology, 77*(1), 15–26.
Yadin, Y. (1962). Expedition D – The Cave of Letters. *Israel Exploration Journal, 12*(3–4), 227–257.
Yadin, Y. (1963). *The finds from the Bar Kokhba period in the Cave of Letters*. Israel Exploration Society.
Ziffer, I. (2007). A note on the Nahal Mishmar "crowns". In J. Cheng & M. H. Feldman (Eds.), *Ancient near eastern art in context: Studies in honor of Irene J. winter by her students* (pp. 47–67). Brill.

The Ghassulian Galilean Sub-Culture in the Late Chalcolithic Period

Dina Shalem and **Nimrod Getzov**

Abstract In 1986, when Tom Levy indicated that distinct regional cultures emerged in the Late Chalcolithic period, he did not refer to the Galilee, as available information on that region was sparse. In the same year, Frankel and Gophna defined Galilean painted "Abu-Sinan" pottery, but additional information regarding the Late Chalcolithic material culture in the mountainous Galilee was still scarce and mainly based on a few survey collections. The discovery of the Peqi'in secondary-burial cave in 1995 changed the hitherto general impression that the Galilee during the second half of the fifth millennium BCE was a barely populated periphery. Since then, interest in the mountainous Galilee during this period has increased, engendering additional surveys and some excavations. The updated information shows that this area housed more than 30 settlements, and that its material culture was in general typical of the period and the Ghassulian culture. However, variations in pottery types, decoration, and motifs as well as flint, differentiates this area. We suggest that these distinctive Galilean characteristics should be considered a Ghassulian Galilean sub-culture.

Keywords Late Chalcolithic · Galilee · Ghassulian Galilean culture · Sub-culture · Material culture · Burial cave

---

D. Shalem (✉)
Israel Antiquities Authority, Jerusalem, Israel

Kinneret College on the Sea of Galilee, Zemach, Israel
e-mail: shalemdina@gmail.com

N. Getzov
Israel Antiquities Authority, Jerusalem, Israel
e-mail: getzovarch@gmail.com

© The Author(s), under exclusive license to Springer Nature Switzerland AG 2023
E. Ben-Yosef, I. W. N. Jones (eds.), *"And in Length of Days Understanding" (Job 12:12): Essays on Archaeology in the Eastern Mediterranean and Beyond in Honor of Thomas E. Levy*, Interdisciplinary Contributions to Archaeology, https://doi.org/10.1007/978-3-031-27330-8_11

1 Introduction

Many years of surveys and excavations have extended our knowledge of settlement during the Late Chalcolithic period (ca. 4500–3900 BCE; henceforth LC) in the southern Levant, from the Galilee (e.g., Shalem, 2003) and the Golan Heights (Epstein, 1998), through the central parts of Israel (e.g., Dothan, 1959; Finkelstein & Gophna, 1993; Gibson et al., 1991; Perrot et al., 1967; Yannai, 2006) and Jordan (e.g., Bourke, 2002; Lovell, 2000), to the Negev (e.g., Alon & Levy, 1980; Baumgarten & Eldar, 1984; Gilead, 1995; Gilead et al., 1991; Perrot, 1955, 1959). The small, medium-sized, and sometimes large villages are located in open areas close to water sources. The remains and finds of the main culture associated with the period—the Ghassulian—are well documented and discussed in some comprehensive studies, and the social structure of its communities has been debated by several scholars (e.g., Bourke, 2002; Gilead, 1988; Levy, 1986; Rowan & Golden, 2009). As these studies are mainly concerned with the northern Negev, central Israel, Jordan and the Golan Heights, this paper gives an updated presentation of the Galilean Late Chalcolithic finds and discusses its main cultural characteristics.

1.1 Geographic and Chronological Context

The various finds which are considered in this paper and represent a homogeneous material culture were obtained in surveys and excavations of sites located in the mountainous Galilee. The boundaries of this region are the Mediterranean Sea in the west, the border with Lebanon in the north, the Jordan Valley in the east and Mount Atzmon in the south. While the eastern and western boundaries are natural, the northern one is arbitrary, and the southern one was defined by us according to distinguishing features of the material culture. Further studies of this area and adjacent regions will allow a more accurate definition of the boundaries of the material culture presented here as characterizing the Galilee. Except for the coastal plain, the discussed area comprises mountainous landscape of mainly limestone and dolomite, with its highest peak being Mount Meron (1208 m asl) and lowest being Mount Atzmon (545 m asl). There are a few small valleys, such as 'Aqrav, Bet Ha-Kerem and Sahnin.

The term used here for the discussed period—the LC—is equivalent to Levy's "Chalcolithic" period (Levy, 1986) and to Garfinkel's "Late Chalcolithic" (Garfinkel, 1999). By definition LC is a relative term, and is thus used by scholars who consider material cultures from the sixth and first half of the fifth millennia within the Chalcolithic (Garfinkel, 1999; Getzov, 2015; Kaplan, 1958), but not by those who see the Neolithic period as continuing up to the middle of the fifth millennium BCE (Gilead, 2009; Gopher, 2012: Fig. 41.1; for a summary of the various terms used by scholars, see Garfinkel, 1999: Table 1), and therefore do not sub-divide it.

Table 1 Late Chalcolithic settlements in mountainous Galilee

No.	Site	Map ref		Estimated size	References
1	ʿEn Eder	2173	7763	0.4 ha	Frankel et al. (2001): Site 117 and Shalem (2003): Site 2
2	Yiron	2429	7756	?	Frankel et al. (2001): Site 350 and Shalem 2003: Site 9
3	Har Ukhman 1	2213	7755	0.5 ha	Frankel et al. (2001): Site 194, Aviam and Shalem (2020): Site 38
4	Bereikhat Kaskas	2246	7744	0.7	Aviam and Shalem (2020): Site 62
5	Mitzpe Yiron	2440	7751	0.3 ha	Shalem (2003): Site 10
6	Shelomi (south)	2138	7749	1 ha	Frankel et al. (2001): Site 80
7	Beʾer Zonam	2291	7743	4.5 ha	Shalem (2003): Site 6, Shalem (2006) and Aviam and Shalem (2020): Site 68
8	Kh. Muʿaddemiya	2411	7728	2 ha	Frankel et al. (2001): Site 343 and Shalem (2003): Site 11
9	Rihaniya	2458	7728	?	Shalem (2003): Site 12
10	Bereikhat Fassuta	2282	7724	1 ha	Shalem (2003): Site 5 and Aviam and Shalem (2020): Site 96
11	Nahariyya (north)	2095	7708	1 ha	Frankel et al. (2001): Site 10
12	Bereikhat Teitaba	2453	7690	0.5 ha	Frankel et al. (2001): Site 317 and Shalem (2003): Site 15
13	Agam Dalton site	2427	7689	1 ha	Frankel et al. (2001): Site 309 and Shalem (2003): Site 13
14	Ḥurfeish, el-Khirbe	2331	7686	1.2 ha	Frankel et al. (2001): Site 252 and Shalem (2003): Site 7
15	Tel Kabri	2143	7680	Very small	Getzov (2013b)
16	Ḥ. Raviz	2432	7678	0.4 ha	Frankel et al. (2001): Site 312
17	Meron	2414	7653	2 ha	Frankel et al. (2001): Site 305 and Shalem (2003): Site 16
18	Naḥal Sekhvi	2454	7648	Large?	Wachtel and Davidovich (2021)
19	Peqiʿin	2316	7645	9 ha	Getzov (2007) and Shalem and Bekker-Shamir (in press)
20	Asherat	2153	7643	Cave	Smithline (2001)
21	Bet haʿEmeq site	2157	7639	Cluster	Getzov and Gur (in press)
22	Naḥal Kishor cave	2235	7630	?	Info. from Z. Rosen
23	Abu Sinan	2164	7627	Cave	Frankel and Getzov (2012): Site. 187
24	Meʿarat Tefen	2241	7625	Cave	Frankel et al. (2001): Site 159
25	Ha-Yonim terrace	2206	7587	Very small	Khalaily et al. (1993)
26	Ḥ. ʿUza	2145	7576	?	Getzov et al. (2009)
27	ʿEn Aqar	2517	7575	?	Shalem (2003): Site 17

(continued)

Table 1 (continued)

No.	Site	Map ref		Estimated size	References
28	Ard el-Samra	2167	7559	Cluster	Getzov et al. (in press)
29	Ya'ad (east)	2239	7531	0.2 ha	Shalem (2003): Site 18
30	Marj Rabba	2266	7499	4.5 ha	Urban et al. (2014)
31	Kaukab Springs	2244	7484	7 ha	Getzov (2016a)
32	'Ibillin (east)	2201	7482	0.4 ha	Shalem (2003): Ste. 19
33	Kh. Wadi Ḥamam	2460	7479	?	Davidovich et al. (2013)

Only two Galilean sites were dated by ^{14}C. One is Peqi'in Cave (4450–3960 calBC; Shalem et al., 2013) and the other is Marj Rabba (4600–4200 calBC; Price et al., 2020). Both dates fall within the undisputed range of the period (4500–3900 calBC, e.g., Gilead, 2011).

1.2 History of Research

In 1966 de Vaux presumed that the Chalcolithic period "…scarcely reached as far as the mountains and the north of the country" (de Vaux, 1966: 530–531), and only in the 1980s the Chalcolithic of the Galilee was defined by Frankel and Gophna according to ceramic finds from Abu Sinan and some previously reported finds from Kabri, Ḥ. Uẓa and Bet Ha-'Emeq (Frankel & Gophna, 2008 and see references there; Frankel & Getzov, 2012: Figs. 187.7–187.8). Nevertheless, the information about this region remained very limited and when Levy (1986) defined the various cultural entities of the Chalcolithic period he could not refer to the Galilee due to lack of information.

The extraordinary artifacts from Peqi'in Cave in the Upper Galilee (Shalem et al., 2013), which was found and excavated in 1995, changed the attitude of researchers to this hitherto neglected region. A study of the LC Galilean sites and their ceramic assemblages was conducted (Shalem, 2003; 2008), and the Galilee was included in studies concerning burial caves (e.g., van den Brink & Gophna, 2005) and other presentations and discussions (e.g., Rowan & Golden, 2009).

In his comprehensive study of Neolithic and Chalcolithic pottery, Garfinkel mentioned the main known finds from the "Galilean Hills" (Garfinkel, 1999:206), and the Ghassulian "Ware"—in which he included finds from the Galilean Peqi'in Cave—as distinct from the Golan Ware and the Hula Ware. Gilead also defined the settlements in the Galilee as Ghassulian, but he did not consider the Galilee as one of the main areas of the culture and stated that in this area "… there are more cultural entities, probably of a lower order, that still await recognition and definition in time and space" (Gilead, 2011:13, 16, 22).

Excavations of some of the Galilean settlements—Asherat (Smithline, 2001), Be'er Zonam (Shalem, 2006), Peqi'in settlement (Getzov, 2007; Shalem & Bekker-Shamir, in press), Kaukab Springs (Getzov, 2016a), Ard el-Samra (Getzov et al., in press) and Marj Rabba (Rowan & Kersel, 2014)—have enriched our knowledge. When considered with survey finds (Frankel et al., 2001, Frankel & Getzov, 2012; Aviam & Shalem, 2020), it is now possible to update the previous summary of the LC Galilean sites and ceramic finds (Shalem, 2003, 2008) and give a wider presentation of the cultural characteristics of the LC period in the Galilee.

1.3 Method of Presentation

A presentation of the types of settlements and their locations within the geographic frame of this paper will be followed by a description of the characteristics of the relatively few architectural remains that were found in excavations. The bulk of the information that will be presented derives from ceramic finds collected in surveys and excavated, iconography and motifs, as well as flint tools and stone vessels, and some data from faunal remains. In most cases we will not refer to all the known subtypes of vessels, and only examples of relevant finds will be illustrated. Our intention is to compare the Galilean finds as a whole to those from other regions, highlighting the characteristics that distinguish the Galilean assemblages. Therefore, when relating to finds that are considered as typically LC of the southern Levant (such as V-shaped bowls and churns) we will use Garfinkel's, 1999 as a general reference for ceramics from sites in other regions. The material culture of the Golan Heights, which is often considered to be a different culture than the Ghassulian, will receive special consideration (e.g., Gilead, 2011).

1.4 "Material" and "Culture"

A variety of finds that share common characteristics, and are found within specific geographic and chronological boundaries, form what is often named "material culture", which characterizes and differentiates community/ies. Obviously, the only information available from prehistoric periods includes remains of architecture and objects created by humans, or of food consumed by them, which survived *and* was retrieved in modern times—hence the term "material." Not only are these finds only partial remains of the man-made items, but man-made items are only part of a larger picture—often referred to as "culture," other elements of which, like language and music, remain unknown to us.

Innumerable papers and books discuss the definition and the usage of the term "culture" from various points of view: anthropological, historical, psychological, political and more (e.g., Brumann, 1999 and references there). We have no intention of joining this valuable discussion, but wish to clarify our meaning when we use the term "material culture," sometimes referred to as just "culture." We believe that although man-made archaeological finds are only a small part of a large and complex reality, it is a part that can and should be described, defined and compared, as we usually do in archaeology, following Clarke (1978). In his presentation of Ghassulian and other entities Gilead rightly wrote in favor of using the terms "culture" and "material culture" (Gilead, 2011), as Brumann (1999) did when discussing archaeological cultures in general.

Nevertheless, although when collecting and arranging the data one may try to be as unbiased as possible, there is a tendency by some to see the common characteristics, and by others to emphasize the diversity. There is no single right way to understand the information, but various interpretations, which enrich science. We tend to see the common characteristics when comparing LC finds from the various areas of the southern Levant. At the same time, we believe that types of artifacts, decoration or motifs, as well as technology, that are typical only to a certain area were chosen, at least to a certain degree, deliberately to identify and differentiate one group of people from another. The way in which one defines these groups and the degree of differentiation between them that can be determined by the finds, is also subject to personal views that extend beyond being archaeologists. It is also obvious that a community that belongs to a certain culture may share some traditions with one or more other cultural group/s. When different cultural groups share cultural customs, they can be defined as sub-cultures of a larger mutual culture (Brumann, 1999; Clarke, 1978).

1.5 "Culture" and "Chronology"

The division of the periods and cultures, and the names used, differ among scholars (for a summary of the use from the PN to the LC, see Garfinkel, 1999: Table 1). There are chrono-terms, which follow the classification of ancient finds by Thomsen (1836) and define time periods and their subdivisions according to raw materials (e.g., the Stone Age, the Iron Age). Other terms relate to cultural affiliation, and these often use the names of the sites where the cultures were first defined according to a particular assemblage of finds (e.g., the Wadi Rabah culture, the Ghassulian culture). Researchers of prehistoric and protohistoric sites in Israel use terms that relate to cultural affiliation also as alternative chrono-terms.

While Garfinkel divided the Chalcolithic period into three sub-periods and chose to describe wares (and not cultural entities) (Garfinkel, 1999: 104), Getzov (2015) divided the same time span into two, and further sub-divided the first part into three phases (thus four phases altogether), and assigned cultures to each phase. Gopher also divided the same period into four phases, but related the first three to the second half of the Pottery Neolithic, and although they are shown as chronological phases, he used cultural terms to name them (Gopher, 2012: Fig. 41.1). Some cultures are often used as chrono-terms, as for example the Wadi Rabah culture (e.g., Yannai,

2006: Table 1.3), while some periods, like the PPN, are not associated with any specific culture.

2 Settlements

2.1 Site Distribution

Thirty-three LC settlements are known in the mountainous Galilee (Fig. 1; Table 1), and seven of them were excavated (HaYonim Terrace, Asherat, Be'er Zonam, Kaukab Springs, Peqi'in, Marj Rabba, Bet Ha-'Emeq Site and Ard el-Samra). Detailed information from surveys shows that in the Early Chalcolithic most settlements, especially the large ones like Tel Kabri and H. Uza, were located in the coastal plain, while in the LC the distribution changed, and more settlements were located in the mountainous area (Getzov et al., in press).

2.2 The Settlements

Settlements in the Galilee, like elsewhere, were located in open areas and in proximity to water sources, such as small rivers (Be'er Zonam), springs (Kaukab Springs) or seasonal pools (*birke*; Bereikhat Fassuta) that were often enlarged by man. The settlements can be divided into four groups:

Isolated Caves Caves of various sizes were used for habitation. Some, like Tefen Cave (Frankel et al., 2001) are large, others are small, like the cave at Asherat (Smithline, 2001). Inhabited caves could also be associated with settlements, as at Ard el-Samra and perhaps other sites, but these are not mentioned here, since they are not isolated.

Small Settlements These sites, which constitute most of the settlements, span areas up to 1 ha.

Clusters of Small Settlements At Ard el-Samra and Bet Ha-'Emeq Site remains of LC finds were defined in isolated spots separated by areas empty of ancient remains. In Bet Ha-'Emeq Site the finds were found in three areas (A, D and F) (Getzov & Gur, in press), and close to this cluster were two isolated caves, Asherat and Abu Sinan. The site in Nahal Sekhvi may also be a cluster of small habitations (Wachtel & Davidovich, 2021: Figs. 4 and 5).

Large Settlements Four or five sites are approximately 4.5 ha or more, the largest being Kaukab Springs (ca. 7 ha) and Peqi'in, which is estimated to be ca. 9 ha.

Fig. 1 Map showing areas and sites mentioned in the paper

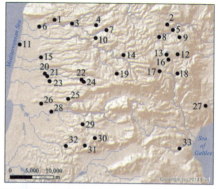
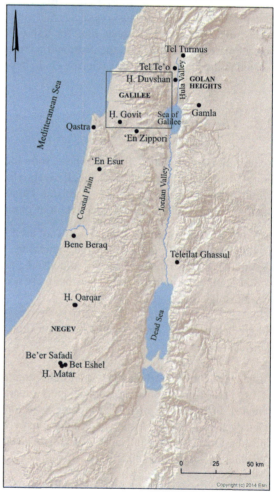

Another site that may be large is the one in Naḥal Sekhvi, unless it is a cluster of sites, as mentioned above.

3 Architecture

Excavated architectural remains from the mountainous Galilee are rather scarce and partial and none provide a plan of a settlement, hardly even a full plan of a building. Nevertheless, the characteristics of the architecture are similar to buildings excavated in other regions—broad rooms, earth- or stone-floors, silos and various installations. The main difference when compared to other regions is the building technique. In the Galilee, the Golan Heights (Epstein, 1998) and Tel Teo (Eisenberg, 2001) the houses were built from stones, whereas bricks, often on stone foundations, were the main building material in other regions (e.g., Yannai, 2006: 25).

Be'er Ẓonam A small excavation at this large site revealed a straight wall (at least 12 m long) and the remains of another building with straight corners (Shalem, 2006).

Peqi'in Two excavations were conducted at Peqi'in, the large site located 300 m east of Peqi'in Cave (Fig. 2; Getzov, 2007; Shalem & Bekker Shamir, in press). In the more recent excavation, conducted in 2019, architectural remains were exposed, including a wall extending over a length of at least 20 m (Shalem & Bekker Shamir, in press), which may have functioned as a circumference wall, similar to the one that was found at 'En Esur (Yannai, 2006:19–20). The excavated area on the southeastern side of the wall included a curvilinear building, floors and circular structures (Shalem & Bekker Shamir, in press).

Bet Ha-'Emeq Site Excavations revealed a segment of a wall built on the rock that functioned as the floor of the building. A later floor made of earth and small stones was defined above it (Getzov & Gur, in press).

Fig. 2 (**a**) Peqi'in, general view to the east seen from the cave (photo D. Shalem); (**b**) Kaukab Springs, general view to southeast (photo N. Getzov)

Fig. 3 Kaukab Springs, corner of a stone building (photo N. Getzov, courtesy of the Israel Antiquities Authority)

Marj Rabba Excavations conducted at the site by the Oriental Institute exposed phases of rectilinear buildings and pavements constructed of stones, and circular features (the largest 5 m in diameter)—possibly silos—paved with smaller stones (Rowan & Kersel, 2013: 2014). A geophysical investigation of the site showed that this settlement was intensely built (Urban et al., 2014).

Kaukab Springs Two strata were defined, in which parts of a rectangular stone building were exposed (Figs. 2 and 3). Earth and stone floors, as well as installations and pits whose walls were carefully constructed with small stones were found (Getzov, 2016a).

4 Pottery Vessels

Definitions of cultures from the Pottery Neolithic onwards are often based on comparisons of ceramic vessel types and decoration. A large number of LC ceramic vessel types are common to all regions, including the Golan Heights, although the ware in this area differs due to the local raw material. The common types include pithoi, jars with high necks, holemouth jars, open bowls and jugs with high necks, as well as handles with triangular sections. As mentioned above, vessel types that are common in all or most regions will be given a general reference from Garfinkel, 1999.

4.1 Selected Vessel Types (Fig. 4)

V-Shaped Bowls Simple open bowls with straight walls and flat base—so called V-shaped bowls—are widely common in the southern Levant (Garfinkel, 1999: Figs. 127, 128), as well as in the Galilee (Kaukab Springs: Getzov, 2016a: Fig. 6:1–10; Peqi'in Cave: Shalem et al., 2013: Fig. 9; Asherat: Smithline, 2001: Fig. 6) but not in the Golan Heights where only a small number are known (Epstein, 1998:164). However, one technological difference is striking. V-shaped bowls from the Galilean sites and the Golan Heights bear no indications of turning marks, except for few examples from Peqi'in Cave (Fig. 4:1; Kamaisky & Ben-Gal, 2013: Fig. 2.30), while small V-shaped bowls produced on a slow potter's wheel (tournette) are common in other regions (Garfinkel, 1999:206). To the best of our knowledge the northernmost site where V-shaped bowls were made on the slow wheel is H. Govit, located southeast of Qiryat Ata (van den Brink & Commenge, 2008: Fig. 6: 1–6).

Spouted Kraters Kraters are defined here as large vessels, open or slightly closing towards the top, which can be easily moved (as opposed to holemouth jars or pithoi that are often defined as kraters). They usually have a pair of handles and sometimes a spout (Garfinkel, 1999: Figs. 136, 137, 139). Spouted kraters are very common in the Golan Heights (Epstein, 1998: Pls. XII–XIV), but seemingly much less so in the Galilee, where only about 10 examples in total are known from all sites (Fig. 4:2; Peqi'in Cave: Shalem et al., 2013: Fig. 6.4:3, 4; Abu Sinan: Frankel & Getzov, 2012: Fig. 187.7:18; Marj Rabba: Shalem pers. knowledge; Kaukab Springs: Getzov, 2016a: Fig. 22:4).

Jars with Outturned Rim While jars with high necks are widely spread in all regions, jars with outturned rims are not found in the Golan Heights, although they are known from all other regions (Garfinkel, 1999, Fig. 148), including the Galilee (Fig. 4:6; Kaukab Springs: Getzov, 2016a: Fig. 19:1–4; Peqi'in Cave: Shalem et al., 2013: Figs. 4.102, 4.107:1, 3; Marj Rabba: Shalem pers. knowledge).

Jars with Multiple Handles Typical to the LC, although less common, are jars with multiple handles (Fig. 4:8; Garfinkel, 1999: Fig. 142), which appear in the Galilee as well (Kaukab Springs: Getzov, 2016a: Fig. 19:1–4; Peqi'in Cave: Shalem et al., 2013: Figs. 4.115, 4.116, 4.121) but are rare in the Golan Heights (Epstein, 1998: Pl. V:8).

Chalices Chalices, or bowls with high-footed base that is typically fenestrated, are one of the characteristics of the period in all regions, although less so in the Golan Heights (Epstein, 1998: Pl. XXII; Garfinkel, 1999: Fig. 134). Many of the chalices in the Galilee and the Golan Heights have applied rope decoration surrounding the junction between the bowl and base (Fig. 4:3), but this addition is less common in other regions.

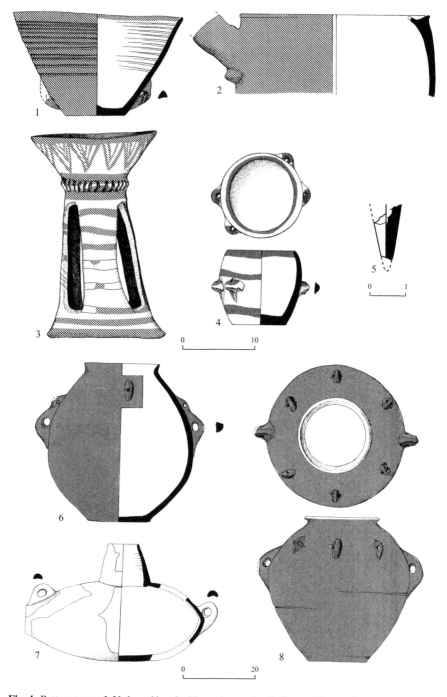

Fig. 4 Pottery types: 1. V-shaped bowl with turning marks; 2. Spouted krater; 3. Fenestrated chalice; 4. Bowl with two pairs of double-handles; 5. Cornet; 6. Jars with outturned rim; 7. Churn; 8. Jar with multiple handles. Nos. 2 and 5 from Marj Rabba (drawings H. Tahan, courtesy of the Oriental Institute). Nos 1, 3, 4, 6–8 (drawings N. Zeevi and L. Kirifov, courtesy of the Israel Antiquities Authority)

Churns Churns of various sizes are very common in all regions (Garfinkel, 1999: Figs. 158–160), including the Galilee (Fig. 4:7; Kaukab Springs: Getzov, 2016a: Fig. 22:1–3; HaYonim Terrace: Khalaily et al., 1993: Fig. 4:9, 10; Marj Rabba: Shalem pers. knowledge; Yiron: Shalem, 2003: Fig. 12.3; Peqi'in Cave: Shalem et al., 2013: Figs. 6.8, 6.9), but not in the Golan Heights (Epstein, 1998:164).

Cornets Cornets characterize the period in all regions from the Negev up to the lower Galilee where they are found in small numbers (Fig. 4:5; Marj Rabba: Shalem pers. knowledge; Kaukab Springs: Getzov, 2016a: Fig. 16:14–15). None have been found in other parts of the Galilee, nor in the Golan.

Vessels with Two Pairs of Double-Handles Vessels with two pairs of double-handles are known from all regions (Garfinkel, 1999: Figs. 130:5, 7; 133:4, 6, 8; 141:3), including the Galilee (Fig. 4:4; Peqi'in Cave: Shalem et al., 2013: Fig. 6.2:7–9,11) and the Golan Heights (Epstein, 1998: Pl. XIX).

4.2 Decoration

Slip and Painted Decoration Fully painted vessels are very common in the Galilee (Fig. 5; Shalem, 2003, 2008), the color being red or red-brown. In other regions the red slip is usually absent, and Garfinkel points to it as being rare and "typical for this period" (1999: 273, 275). The slip is also absent from the Golan Heights, although one should keep in mind that the ware itself is red due to the basalt inclusions. While open bowls and especially V-shaped bowls in most regions have a red band painted along the rim (Garfinkel, 1999:272), in the Galilee it is less common and more often the bowls are red-slipped. While painted geometric patterns sometimes occur on small vessels (Garfinkel ,1999:272), including light-colored-ware vessels from the southern Golan Heights (Epstein, 1998:160), in the Galilee red-painted patterns are

Fig. 5 (**a**) Peqi'in Cave, a red-slipped jar (photo M. Saltzberger, courtesy of Israel Antiquities Authority); (**b**) Bet Ha-'Emeq Site, Ḥula Ware (photo N. Getzov, courtesy of Israel Antiquities Authority); (**c**) Bet Ha-'Emeq Site, Abu Sinan Ware (photo N. Getzov, courtesy of Israel Antiquities Authority)

Fig. 6 (**a**) Kaukab Springs, interwoven rope impression (photo N. Getzov, courtesy of the Israel Antiquities Authority); (**b**) Marj Rabba, applied rope decoration (photo A. Hill, courtesy of the Oriental Institute; (**c**) Kaukab Springs, bowl with thumb -impressed rim (drawing H. Tahan, courtesy of the Israel Antiquities Authority)

common. The decoration is sometimes painted on light wash (so called Abu Sinan ware; Fig. 5) and usually appear on bowls and chalices (Frankel & Getzov, 2012: Figs. 187.7–187.8).

Rope Decoration Rope decoration made by applied bands that were thumb-impressed or impressed by tools is typical of vessels from the Galilee (Fig. 6; e.g., Shalem, 2003: Fig. 26; Getzov, 2016a: Fig. 21) and the Jordan Valley (Garfinkel, 1999: 272), and is even more common in the Golan Heights where jars and pithoi are sometimes completely covered by the rope pattern (Epstein, 1998: Pls. III–VIII). In other regions, the applied rope design seems to be infrequent (Garfinkel, 1999:272).

Thumb-Impressions on Rims Thumb-impressions along the rims, mainly of kraters and pithoi, are well known in all regions (Garfinkel, 1999: 171), except for the Galilee where they are rare (Fig. 6; Getzov, 2016a: Fig. 16:1, 11), and the Golan Heights, where they are absent.

Hula Decoration The so called Ḥula Ware (Fig. 5), which was first described in the excavation of Tel Turmus (Dayan, 1969), is often considered to belong exclusively to sites in the Hula Valley, but sherds bearing this decoration were found at Asherat (Smithline, 2001: Fig. 8), Be'er Zonam (Shalem, 2008: Fig. 4), Marj Rabba (Shalem pers. observ.) and Kaukab Springs (Getzov, 2016a). It seems that this group may be divided into two: thin-walled fine ware with black or red slip, burnish, with geometric incised decoration, the incisions filled with white chalk (Eisenberg, 2001: 105–106), and coarser ware with thicker walls, reddish slip with incised decoration, possibly burnished and probably missing the white chalk filling (Shalem pers. observ.). Petrographic analyses suggest that these vessels were made of at least two different raw materials, one of them from the Hula Valley (Shalem et al., 2019: 274).

4.3 Impressions of Interwoven Ropes

Very common in the Galilee are impressions on large vessels made by thin, often interwoven ropes (Fig. 6; e.g., Shalem et al., 2013: Figs. 4.117–4.119; Getzov, 2016a: Fig. 23). The ropes were wrapped around the vessels during its preparation, perhaps as support.

4.4 Imported Ware

Golan Vessels Golan ceramic vessels are found in several western Galilean sites (Shalem et al., 2013: 4.126–4.131). According to petrographic analysis they were most probably imported from the Golan Heights and not from the eastern basaltic Galilee (Shalem, 2008: 102*–105*; Shalem et al., 2019: 269–272).

5 Flint Tools

Detailed information about flint tools is known only from two Galilean settlements—Kaukab Springs and Ard el-Samra—and from the Peqi'in Cave. In general, the flint from the Galilee is comparable to that of other regions (Hermon, 2008).

Sickle Blades Typical to the LC are steeply backed sickle blades with straight truncated ends and fine denticulation on the working edge. At Peqi'in Cave (Getzov, 2013a: 293–294, Table 7.3) and Tel Turmus (Hermon, 2008: 73, Table 15) the sickle blades are rather wide (15.3 mm and 16.6 mm on average respectively), as are the blades from the Golan Heights (17–18 mm wide; Noy, 1998: 287). At Kaukab Springs and Ard el-Samra, the sickle blades are highly standardized, and they are narrower (13.6 mm and 12.7 mm on average respectively), as they are in sites in the northern Negev (11.3 mm average width at Abu Matar and Bir Es-Safadi: Hermon, 2008: 28).

Remains of a workshop that was found at Ard el-Samra, indicate that sickle blades and adzes were produced at the site (Getzov et al. forthcoming). The production technology is identical to the one known from sites in the Negev, such as Bet Eshel (Vardi & Gilead, 2013).

Perforated Disks Perforated flint disks were found at Bet Ha-'Emeq Site, in the fields of Kibbutz Hanita in the Shefa'Valley (Ronen, 1968: Fig. 13:2) and at Marj Rabba (Rowan & Kersel, 2014: Fig. 9). The perforation is in the center of these objects, and the retouch is bifacial. Such tools are well known from the Golan Heights (Noy, 1998: Pls. LIV–LVI), Tel Turmus and the northern Jordan Valley

Fig. 7 Perforated flint disks from Peqi'in Cave (photo H. Smithline, courtesy of the Israel Antiquities Authority)

(Rosenberg et al., 2019 and see references there). A large homogeneous group of perforated disks was also found in Peqi'in Cave (Fig. 7). This is an assemblage of a different type, as the perforation is not at the center, and the retouch is only along the edge of the dorsal face (Getzov, 2013a: 302–303).

6 Stone Artifacts

Stone tools and vessels were found in all the surveys and excavations in the Galilee, but more information is needed for a comprehensive comparison with other regions. Nevertheless, one noticeable detail concerns the fenestrated chalices, which are found in all regions, although rarely in the Golan Heights (Epstein, 1998: 235). These vessels are often decorated with a row of incised triangles along the rim (Chasan & Rosenberg, 2019). In the Galilee (Fig. 8; and the Golan Heights) however, this decoration is only known from Bet Ha-'Emeq Site (Getzov & Gur, in press).

7 Burials

One of the characteristics of the LC is a dramatic change in burial customs, which is manifest in public secondary-burial cemeteries located outside the settlements (e.g., van den Brink & Gophna, 2005). In the Galilee only one such cemetery,

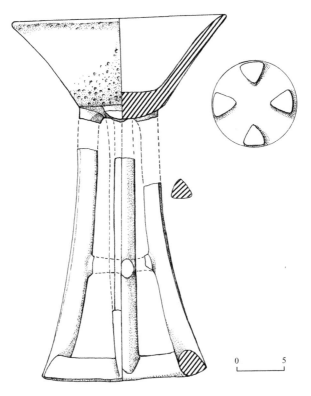

Fig. 8 Peqi'in Cave, fenestrated basalt chalice (drawing N. Ze'evi, courtesy of the Israel Antiquities Authority)

although a very large one, is known, at Peqi'in (Fig. 9) Shalem et al., 2013). In the Golan Heights no secondary-burial cemeteries have been found, but it should be emphasized that in common with most of the sites in all other regions, no burials at all were found in the Golan settlements, and therefore it is plausible to conclude that burials were located outside the settlements in this region as well.

Ossuaries and other large vessels that were either intentionally -made for secondary-burials, or fulfilled this function in secondary use, are found in all secondary-burial cemeteries. Ossuaries that comprise a box and a lid were found only at Peqi'in Cave and at Qastra. The more common single-unit ossuaries have openings at their front, apart from Peqi'in where the opening may be either at the front or the back. Bene Beraq is the southernmost burial site with ossuaries that have feet, a feature known as far north as Peqi'in, and the northernmost site with stone ossuaries and burial jars with a knob at the top, two features that are missing at Peqi'in (Shalem, 2015:221).

Fig. 9 (a) Peqi'in Cave, general view (photo H. Smithline, courtesy of the Israel Antiquities Authority); (b) ossuary of in the shape of a male figure from Peqi'in Cave (photo M. Saltzberger, courtesy of Israel Antiquities Authority)

8 Ritual Objects, Imagery and Motifs

The LC period is known for its extraordinary burst of iconographic motifs that were applied and painted on various finds, such as ossuaries, ceramic vessels, copper objects, basalt chalices and ivory artifacts. The main motifs were a large nose, large open eyes, horns or horned animals and geometric designs. Peqi'in Cave is the only Galilean site in which a few copper scepters and ivory items, one of them the head of a figurine, were found. No metal or ivory artifacts are known in the Golan Heights.

The ossuaries from Peqi'in Cave have the most ornate anthropomorphic features and designs, including male images with beards, ears, mouths with teeth, and arms with hands and fingers—none of which are shown on ossuaries from other caves (Shalem, 2015: 221). Other motifs that are common on ossuaries, such as big noses and female breasts, are shared by Peqi'in Cave and other sites, and one particular type of female ossuary, with fan-shaped front, large nose, small button-like eyes and often molded breasts, is distributed from Peqi'in Cave in the north to cemeteries on the coastal plain (Shalem, 2017:162).

One motif which is common in other regions—the horns—is missing from Peqi'in Cave and from the Galilee in general, although the cave contains ossuaries with molded tails and typical zoomorphic facial features (Shalem, 2015:227–228). Horns and horned animals are also common in the Golan Heights, where they are depicted on the basalt "pillar figures" and on ceramic vessels (Epstein, 1998: Pls. XXIII–XXIV, XXX–XXXIII), as well as on ossuaries from some of the coastal plain caves, on kraters from Ḥ. Qarqar and on several of the copper objects (Shalem, 2015: 227–228 and see references there).

Violin figurines are known from various sites in the southern Levant, usually in small numbers. The exception is Gilat, where more than 50 figurines were found (Commenge et al., 2006). In the Galilee ten figurines were found in Peqi'in Cave

Fig. 10 Violin-shaped figurines from Peqi'in Cave, (**a**) made of bone, (**b**) made of stone, scale 2:4 (photo M. Saltzberger, courtesy of Israel Antiquities Authority)

(Fig. 10) and one in Kaukab Springs (Getzov, 2016a). A single violin-figurine was found in the Golan Heights, at Gamla (Getzov, 2016b: Fig. 18.1:7).

9 Fauna (Table 2)

Detailed information about fauna is available for three sites in the Galilee—Kaukab Springs (Getzov, 2016a), Ard el-Samra (Getzov et al. forthcoming) and Marj Rabba (Price et al., 2020).The first two have Early Chalcolithic remains as well, and these show an increase in sheep and goat towards the LC, and a decrease in domesticated pig. At Marj Rabba too, sheep and goat dominate the LC assemblage—a change in animal husbandry that occurred in the whole southern Levant (Price et al., 2020).

Table 2 Identified specimens from three Galilean sites

Site/Specimens	Cattle	Sheep and goAT	Pigs	Wild animals and dogs	NISP
Kaukab Springs LC	**13%**	**48%**	**26%**	**13%**	**95**
Kaukab Springs EC	18%	27%	47%	8%	60
Ard el-Samra LC	**13%**	**47%**	**25%**	**16%**	**103**
Ard el-Samra EC	13%	43%	41%	4%	56
Marj Rabba	**13%**	**50%**	**30%**	**7%**	**5663**

10 Summary and Discussion

10.1 Main Characteristics of the Galilean Material Culture

Stone building is a primary characteristic that distinguishes the Galilee from other regions, except for the Golan Heights. Although stone-building may be expected in this area, architecture before the LC comprised brick-walls over stone foundations (Getzov, 2016a: 34*–35*). Another distinction concerns the local pottery production and is one of technology—the rare usage of the potter's wheel.

The ceramic vessels from Galilean sites include the typical LC repertoire, but are differentiated by the general exclusion of cornets, kraters with thumb-impressed rims and spouted kraters, all of which appear to be found only in sites in the southern part of the mountainous Galilee. They are also distinguished by red slip that often occurs on all types of vessels, applied rope-decoration and impressions of thin interwoven ropes. Moreover, in addition to the typical LC repertoire, vessels bearing Hula Decoration were found in the Galilee, and were probably produced there. Vessels from the Golan Heights were imported to Galilean sites but not beyond. Vessels with light wash and red-painted decoration seem, with some variations, to be common in the coastal area from the Galilee to 'En Esur (Yannai, 2006:75, 275). In the mountainous Galilean sites, the painted vessels have no light wash, as in the case of the chalices, bowls and other vessels from Peqi'in Cave (Shalem et al., 2013: Figs. 5.3–5.20, 6.2, 6.5).

The lithics also show some distinguishing features. A striking local variation is found in the perforated flint disks that are almost absent outside the Galilean sites. Moreover, Galilean sickle blades are wider than the ones in the southern regions, except for blades from two sites located in the southern part of the Galilee. Another typical LC characteristic—the incised decoration of triangles along the rims of fenestrated chalices—is absent in the Galilee, with a single exception.

When it comes to iconography, the most remarkable difference is the absence of depictions of horns and the choice of tails and zoomorphic facial features, plausibly representing sheep or goats, to represent animals on ossuaries instead.

10.2 Connections and Influence

The import of ceramic vessels from the Golan Heights testifies to strong connections between the two regions. Also common to both regions are stone-building and the absence/rare usage of tournettes. The flint disks, which can plausibly be considered as ritual objects, were perhaps the northern—Galilean and Golan Heights—local scepters (Shalem, 2015: Fig. 4a). Also common to the Galilee and the Golan Heights, are the width of sickle blades, and the applied rope decorations, as well as the absence of cornets, thumb-impressed rims and decoration on the basalt chalices.

Some influence from the south did reach the southern parts of the Galilee (Shalem, 2008: 106*). To this can be attributed the cornets, spouted kraters and vessels with thumb-impressed rims, possibly red-painted rims, together with narrow sickle blades and the decorated rims of basalt chalices. Petrographic analysis of cornets from the Galilee shows that they were most probably produced of local material (Shalem et al., 2019) and should therefore be explained as an influence of the Ghassulian from the south. This conclusion may also apply to the other southern influence.

The red-painted decoration on light wash is a coastal characteristic of the LC, extending from Ras Shamra in the north to 'En Esur in the south. Although there are slight differences between the vessels from Abu Sinan and 'En Esur this is an interesting example of a pottery group that is shared by parts of two distinct regions.

10.3 The Ghassulian Galilean Sub-Culture

In our opinion, the Galilean LC material culture includes more similarities with the Ghassulian culture than dissimilarities. However, the existing distinctions suggest that the Galilean population chose to keep some old traditions. Most of the LC ceramic types in the Galilee (as in other regions) continue from the Early Chalcolithic period. These include churns, as well as particular features such as handles with triangular section, and red slip, all of which appear in the Early Chalcolithic 3 (Getzov, 2016a) and become main characteristics of the LC. Violin figurines are also known in the Galilee in strata that predate the LC (Getzov et al., 2009: 101–102). The Galilean population usually chose not to use the tournettes in pottery manufacture, and differentiated itself to a certain degree when it came to the new LC customs, such as the production and use of flint disks and the preference to exclude cornets. Since the traditions that are shared with the Ghassulian culture are obvious and encompass all parts of the material culture—architecture, pottery, flint, basalt and fauna, as well as secondary burial and motifs—the Galilee should be considered as belonging to the Ghassulian sphere. Nevertheless, the Galilean population did choose to differentiate itself to a certain extent and therefore it should be defined as Ghassulian Galilean sub-culture of the main Ghassulian culture. Future studies of other regions may suggest additional sub-cultures.

The large variety of ossuaries and the rich imagery from Peqi'in, which is unique when compared to other caves, considered together with the high variety of decorations on chalices and other vessels from the same cave, as well as the painted Abu Sinan decorations on the coastal vessels and the Hula Decoration, present a rich variety far more expressive than any that can be found in other regions. It may be suggested that the high variety of artistic expression in the Galilean material culture influenced regions to its south.

10.4 A Note Concerning the Golan Heights

The LC material culture in the Golan is usually considered to be related to a discrete culture (e.g., Isaac Gilead, 2011:14–16). We suggest a different opinion, which considers the finds from the Golan as a sub-culture of the main Ghassulian culture. One of the prominent features of this sub-culture are the ceramic vessels that have a dark-red color due to the local basaltic material. While Epstein attributed the typical Golan ware only to the local available material (Epstein, 1998:160), Hartal pointed to the southern Golan, where ceramic vessels were produced from a different material although the settlements are also located in a basaltic area (Hartal, n.d.). An example to the contrary is Ḥ. Duvshan, located in a basaltic area but in proximity to chalky soils. The population of this settlement chose to belong to the Golan sub-culture by producing typical Golan Ware vessels (Smithline, 2013). It seems therefore that the basaltic reddish ware was not merely an expression of available local resources, but also a cultural preference.

The Golan sub-culture comprises first and foremost general Ghassulian characteristics: broad houses and absence of burials in the settlements, as well as several of the pottery types, motifs such as the large nose and horns and the violin figurines. It also shares characteristics with the Galilean sub-culture: stone-building, perforated disks, wider sickle blades and rich usage of rope-decoration, as well as the absence/rare usage of tournettes and cornets, and of decorated rims on basalt chalices. Altogether, we see more common characteristics than differences between the Ghassulian culture and the Golan sub-culture, while the Golan sub-culture is more distinct than its Galilean neighbor.

Acknowledgments We are grateful to Y. Rowan of the Oriental Institute, for approving the use unpublished information from Marj Rabba, to A. Shapiro for the preparation of the GIS map and to S. Gabrieli for the English editing.

References

Alon, D., & Levy, T. E. (1980). Preliminary note on the distribution of chalcolithic sites on the Wadi Beer-Sheba—Lower Wadi Besor drainage system. *Israel Exploration Journal, 30*(3/4), 140–147.

Aviam, M., & Shalem, D. (2020). *The land of lost villages: Shomera map survey (3). Land of Galilee 6*. Ostracon.
Baumgarten, Y., & Eldar, I. (1984). Neveh Noy—A Chalcolithic site near Beer-Sheba. *Qadmoniot, 66–67*, 51–56.
Bourke, S. J. (2002). The origins of social complexity in the southern Levant: New evidence from Teleilat Ghassul, Jordan. *Palestine Exploration Quarterly, 134*(1), 2–27.
Brumann, C. (1999). Writing for culture: Why a successful concept should not be discarded. *Current Anthropology, 40*(S1), S1–S27.
Chasan, R., & Rosenberg, D. (2019). Getting into shape: The characteristics and significance of late Chalcolithic basalt vessel decoration in the southern Levant. *Paléorient, 45*(1), 53–68.
Clarke, D. L. (1978). *Analytical archaeology*. Roultledge.
Commenge, C., Levy, T. E., Alon, D., & Kansa, E. (2006). Gilat's figurines: Exploring the social and symbolic dimensions of representation. In T. E. Levy (Ed.), *Archaeology, anthropology and cult. The sanctuary at Gilat, Israel* (pp. 739–830). Equinox.
Davidovich, U., Ullamn, M., & Leibner, U. (2013). Late prehistoric occurrences in Har Nitai and Khirbat Wadi Hamam, northeastern lower Galilee. *Journal of the Israel Prehistoric Society, 43*, 186–204.
Dayan, Y. (1969). Tel Turmus in the Huleh Valley. *Israel Exploration Journal, 19*, 65–78.
Dothan, M. (1959). Excavations at Meṣer, 1957: Preliminary report on the second season. *Israel Exploration Journal, 9*(1), 13–29.
Eisenberg, E. (2001). Pottery of Strata VII-VI, the chalcolithic period. In E. Eisenberg, A. Gopher, & R. Greenberg (Eds.), *Tell Te'o a Neolithic, Chalcolithic and Early Bronze Age site in the Hula Valley* (pp. 105–116). Israel Antiquities Authority.
Epstein, C. (1998). *The Chalcolithic culture of the Golan*. Israel Antiquities Authority.
Finkelstein, I., & Gophna, R. (1993). Settlement, demographic, and economic patterns in the highlands of Palestine in the Chalcolithic and Early Bronze periods and the beginning of urbanism. *Bulletin of the American Schools of Oriental Research, 289*(1), 1–22.
Frankel, R., & Getzov, N. (2012). The archaeological survey of Israel. In *Map of 'Amqa* (p. 5). http://survey.antiquities.org.il/index_Eng.html#/MapSurvey/4/site/979
Frankel, R., & Gophna, R. (2008). Chalcolithic pottery from a burial cave in western Galilee. In M. Yedaya (Ed.), *The western Galilee antiquities* (pp. 37–43). Israel's Ministry of Defense.
Frankel, R., Getzov, N., Aviam, M., & Dagan, A. (2001). *Settlement dynamics and regional diversity in ancient Upper Galilee: Archaeological survey of Upper Galilee*. (IAA Reports 14).
Garfinkel, Y. (1999). *Neolithic and Chalcolithic pottery of the Southern Levant*. Institute of Archaeology, Hebrew University of Jerusalem. https://www.jstor.org/stable/43588816. Accessed 23 November 2021
Getzov, N. (2007). A late chalcolithic and early bronze age settlement at Peqi'in, in upper Galilee. *Atiqot, 56*, 1–12.
Getzov, N. (2013a). Flint assemblage. In D. Shalem, Z. Gal, & H. Smithline (Eds.), *Peqi'in: A late Chalcolithic burial site Upper Galilee, Israel* (pp. 293–318). Ostracon.
Getzov, N. (2013b). Tel Kabri. *Excavations and Surveys in Israel, 125*. http://www.hadashot-esi.org.il/report_detail_eng.aspx?id=2256&mag_id=120. Accessed 30 December 2021.
Getzov, N. (2015). Relative chronology of the proto-historic remains at Nahal Saflul 71 in the Gal'ed Hills. *Atiqot, 82*, 1–20.
Getzov, N. (2016a). Remains from the end of the early Chalcolithic and the Late Chalcolithic periods at Kaukab Springs in the Western Galilee. *Atiqot, 87*, 1–41.
Getzov, N. (2016b). Seals, seal impressions and a violin figurine. In I. D. Syon (Ed.), *Gamla III, The Shmarya Gutmann excavations 1976–1989, finds and studies, Part 2* (pp. 283–286) (IAA Reports 59).
Getzov, N., & Gur, Y. (in press). Excavations at Bet Ha-'Emeq Site: A Late Chalcolithic rural settlement and an Early Bronze City on a Slope. *'Atiqot*. (Hebrew).
Getzov, N., Lieberman-Wander, R., Smithline, H., & Syon, D. (2009). *Horbat "Uza, the 1991 excavations (Vol. I): The early periods* (IAA Reports 14).

Getzov, N., Vardi, J., & Marom, N. (in press). The Ard el-Samra 2010 excavations: A protohistoric settlement on the fringe of the 'Akko plain. *'Atiqot*. (Hebrew).

Gibson, S., Ibbs, B., & Kloner, A. (1991). The Sataf project of landscape archaeology in the Judaean Hills: A preliminary report on four seasons of survey and excavation (1987–89). *Levant, 23*(1), 29–54.

Gilead, I. (1988). The chalcolithic period in the Levant. *Journal of World Prehistory, 2*(4), 397–443. https://doi.org/10.1007/BF00976197

Gilead, I. (1995). *Grar: A chalcolithic site in the Northern Negev*. Ben-Gurion University of the Negev Press.

Gilead, I. (2009). The Neolithic-Chalcolithic transition in the southern Levant: Late sixth–fifth millennium culture history. In J. J. Shea & D. E. Lieberman (Eds.), *Transitions in prehistory: Essays in honor of Ofer Bar-Yosef* (pp. 339–359). Oxbow Books.

Gilead, I. (2011). Chalcolithic culture history: Ghassulian and other entities in the southern Levant. In J. L. Lovell & Y. M. Rowan (Eds.), *Culture, chronology and the Chalcolithic. Theory and transition* (pp. 12–24). Oxbow Books.

Gilead, I., Rosen, S., & Fabian, P. (1991). Excavations at tell Abu-Matar (the Hatzerim Neighborhood), Beer Sheva. *Journal of the Israel Prehistoric Society, 24*, 173–179.

Gopher, A. (2012). *Village communities of the pottery Neolithic period in the Menashe Hills, Israel: Archaeological investigations at the sites of Naḥal Zehora* (Vol. 1). Institute of Archaeology, Tel Aviv University.

Hartal M. (n.d.). *The archaeological survey of Israel. Golan survey — introduction*. (Hebrew). http://survey.antiquities.org.il/index.html#/Golan

Hermon, S. (2008). *Socio-economic aspects of chalcolithic (4500–3500 BC) societies in the southern Levant: A lithic perspective*. Archaeopress.

Kamaisky, E., & Ben-Gal, M. (2013). Appendix 2: The manufacturing techniques of the pottery vessels. In D. Shalem, Z. Gal, & H. Smithline (Eds.), *Peqi'in: A late chalcolithic burial site, upper Galilee, Israel*. Ostracon.

Kaplan, J. (1958). Excavations at Wadi Rabah. *Israel Exploration Journal, 8*(3), 149–160.

Khalaily, H., Goren, Y., & Valla, F. R. (1993). A late pottery Neolithic assemblage from Hayonim terrace, Western Galilee. *Journal of the Israel Prehistoric Society, 25*, 132–144.

Levy, T. E. (1986). Archaeological sources for the study of Palestine: The Chalcolithic period. *The Biblical Archaeologist, 49*(2), 82–108. https://doi.org/10.2307/3210005

Lovell, J. L. (2000). Pella in Jordan in the chalcolithic period. In G. Philip & D. Baird (Eds.), *Breaking with the past: Ceramics and change in the early bronze age of the southern Levant* (pp. 59–71). Sheffield Academic Press.

Noy, T. (1998). The flint artifacts. In C. Epstein (Ed.), *The Chalcolithic culture of the Golan* (pp. 269–332). Israel Antiquities Authority.

Perrot, J. (1955). The excavations at tell Abu Matar, near Beersheba. *Israel Exploration Journal, 5*(3), 167–189.

Perrot, J. (1959). *Bir es-Safadi. Israel Exploration Journal, 9*(9), 141–142.

Perrot, J., Zori, N., & Reich, Y. (1967). Neve Ur, un nouvel aspect du Ghassoulien. *Israel Exploration Journal, 17*(4), 201–232.

Price, M., Rowan, Y. M., Kersel, M. M., & Makarewicz, C. A. (2020). Fodder, pasture, and the development of complex society in the Chalcolithic: Isotopic perspectives on animal husbandry at Marj Rabba. *Archaeological and Anthropological Sciences, 12*(4), 95. https://doi.org/10.1007/s12520-020-01043-z

Ronen, A. (1968). *The flint implements in the Hanita Museum*. Hanita Museum. (Hebrew).

Rosenberg, D., Groman-Yaroslavski, I., Chasan, R., & Shimelmitz, R. (2019). Additional thoughts on the production of chalcolithic perforated flint tools: A test case from Tel Turmus, Hula Valley, Israel. In L. Astruc, C. McCartney, F. Briois, & V. Kassianidou (Eds.), *Near Eastern lithic technologies on the move. Interactions and contexts in Neolithic traditions. 8th international confrence on PPN chipped and ground stone industries of the near East, Nicosia, Novmber 23rd-27th 2016* (pp. 415–426). Astrom.

Rowan, Y. M., & Golden, J. (2009). The Chalcolithic period of the southern Levant: A synthetic review. *Journal of World Prehistory, 22*, 1–92. https://doi.org/10.1007/s10963-009-9016-4

Rowan, Y. M., & Kersel, M. M. (2013). Marj Rabba. *The Oriental Institue Annual Report, 91*–98.

Rowan, Y. M., & Kersel, M. M. (2014). New perspectives on the Chalcolithic period in the Galilee: Investigations at the site of Marj Rabba. In J. R. Spencer, R. A. Mullins, & A. J. Brody (Eds.), *Material culture matters: Essays on the archaeology of the southern Levant in honor of Seymour Gitin* (pp. 221–238). Eisenbrauns.

Shalem, D. (2003). *The Chalcolithic period sites in the mountains of the Galilee–settlement distribution and ceramic characteristics.* . Thesis, The University of Haifa, Haifa.

Shalem, D. (2006). Be'er Zonam. In *Excavations and Surveys in Israel*, (pp. 118). https://www.jstor.org/stable/26583825. Accessed 25 Nov 2021.

Shalem, D. (2008). The upper and lower Galilee in the late Chalcolithic period. In S. Bar (Ed.), *In the hill-country, and in the shephelah, and in the arabah (Joshua 12, 8): Studies and researches presented to Adam Zertal in the thirtieth anniversary of the Manasseh Hill-country survey* (pp. 99–110). Ariel publishing house.

Shalem, D. (2015). Motifs on the Nahal Mishmar hoard and the ossuaries: Comparative observations and interpretations. *Journal of the Israel Prehistoric Society, 45*, 217–237.

Shalem, D. (2017). Cultural continuity and changes in south Levantine late Chalcolithic burial customs and iconographic imagery: An interpretation of the finds from Peqi'in Cave. *Journal of the Israel Prehistoric Society, 47*, 148–170.

Shalem, D. & Bekker Shamir, M. (in press). Peqi'in. In *Excavations and Surveys in Israel*.

Shalem, D., Gal, Z., & Smithline, H. (2013). *Peqi'in: A late Chalcolithic burial site, upper Galilee, Israel*. Ostracon.

Shalem, D., Cohen-Weinberger, A., Gandulla, B., & Milevski, I. (2019). Ceramic connections and regional entities: The petrography of late Chalcolithic pottery from sites in the Galilee (Israel). In H. Goldfus, M. I. Gruber, S. Yonah, & P. Fabian (Eds.), *Studies in archaeology and ancient cultures in honor of Isaac Gilead* (pp. 262–277). Archaeopress Archaeology.

Smithline, H. (2001). Chalcolithic and Early Bronze Age caves at Asherat, Western Galilee. *Atiqot, 42*, 35–78.

Smithline, H. (2013). Horbat Duvshan: A 'Golan' Chalcolithic site in eastern Galilee. *Atiqot, 73*, 19–35.

Thomsen, C. J. (1836). Ledetrad til Nordiske Oldkindigbed. .

Urban, T. M., Rowan, Y. M., & Kersel, M. M. (2014). Ground-penetrating radar investigations at Marj Rabba, a Chalcolithic site in the lower Galilee of Israel. *Journal of Archaeological Science, 46*, 96–106.

van den Brink, E. C. M., & Commenge, C. (2008). A Chalcolithic burial near Ḥorbat Govit in lower Galilee. *Atiqot, 60*, 1–18.

van den Brink, E. C. M., & Gophna, R. (2005). *Shoham (North): Late Chalcolithic burial caves in the Lod Valley Israel*. Israel Antiquities Authority.

Vardi, J., & Gilead, I. (2013). Keeping the razor sharp: Hafting and maintenance of sickles in the southern Levant during the 6th and 5th millennia BC. In F. Borrell, J.-J. Ibáñez, & M. Molist (Eds.), *Stone tools in transition: From hunter-gatherers to farming societies in the near East: Papers presented to the 7th conference on PPN chipped and ground stone industries of the fertile crescent* (pp. 377–395). Universitat Autònoma de Barcelona.

Vaux, R., de (1966). Palestine during the Neolithic and Chacolithic periods. . : Cambridge University Press.

Wachtel, I., & Davidovich, U. (2021). Qedesh in the Galilee: The emergence of an early bronze age Levantine Megasite. *Journal of Field Archaeology, 46*(4), 260–274. https://doi.org/10.1080/00934690.2021.1901025

Yannai, E. (2006). *ʿEn Esur (ʿEin Asawir) I: Excavations at a protohistoric site in the coastal plain of Israel*. Israel Antiquities Authority.

The Late Chalcolithic in the Valley of Elah, Israel

Yosef Garfinkel

Abstract Late Chalcolithic finds were unearthed at Khirbet Qeiyafa, a site overlooking the Valley of Elah in Israel's Judean Shephelah. The small assemblage includes pottery, flint, a fenestrated basalt chalice, a hematite mace head, and a limestone seal. These discoveries, as well as fresh data from various neighboring sites, permit us to add this region to the map of Late Chalcolithic activities.

Keywords Late Chalcolithic · Valley of Elah · Khirbet Qeiyafa · Fenestrated basalt chalice · Hematite mace-head · Seal · Cornets

1 Introduction

Khirbet Qeiyafa is a 2.3-hectare site surrounded by massive fortifications, built from megalithic stones, that still stand to a height of 2–3 m. It is located in the western part of the upper Shephelah (Israel map grid 14603–12267), on the summit of a hill that borders the Valley of Elah on the north (Fig. 1). The site has attracted much attention due to the excavation of the heavily fortified Iron IIA city dated to the early tenth century BCE (Garfinkel & Ganor, 2009; Garfinkel et al., 2014, 2016; Garfinkel, 2017). The site was occupied in two earlier periods, the remains of which were badly damaged by the construction of the Iron Age city. The structures of the city (two gates, a city wall, public structures, and dwellings) were built directly on bedrock. All remnants of earlier habitation were cleared away and the only indications of these earlier periods were artifacts uncovered in secondary deposition or in shallow sediments in bedrock cavities.

Y. Garfinkel (✉)
Institute of Archaeology, The Hebrew University of Jerusalem, Jerusalem, Israel
e-mail: Garfinkel@mail.huji.ac.il

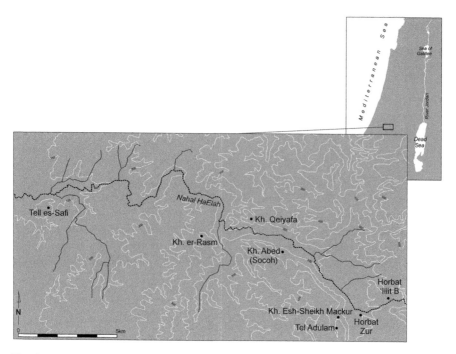

Fig. 1 Map of the Judean Shephelah and the location of the main Late Chalcolithic sites mentioned in the article

The earliest occupation on the site is dated to the Late Chalcolithic period. It was discerned only in later excavation seasons, and is published here for the first time. The second occupation, that of the Middle Bronze Age, was already identified in the first excavation season and was reported in the first excavation report (Garfinkel & Ganor, 2009: 43–46).

The Late Chalcolithic remains include no architecture but comprise a small assemblage of artifacts: pottery sherds, flint objects, a fenestrated basalt chalice, a hematite mace head, and a seal. These artifacts, together with the accumulation of data from some ten different sites in the Valley of Elah and other sites in the vicinity, shed light on a previously neglected region of Late Chalcolithic activity.

2 The Distribution of Late Chalcolithic Finds at Khirbet Qeiyafa

During the excavations two loci were identified as dating from the Late Chalcolithic period: Fill C6484 and Fill C6500 (Fig. 2). Both are located in the same square, DD11 in the northern part of Area C, and were described as "dark compact sediments" (Sang-Yeup, 2014). The finds in this spot included about 60 small, crudely handmade pottery sherds, which seem to signify a primary depositional context.

The Late Chalcolithic in the Valley of Elah, Israel   247

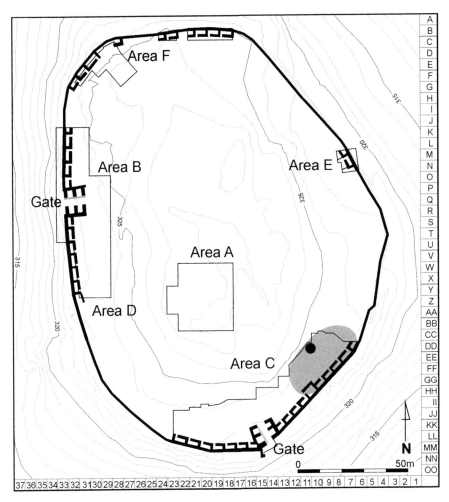

Fig. 2 Map of the Khirbet Qeiyafa excavations showing the location of the Late Chalcolithic remains on the eastern side of Area C. The black dot indicates the remains in situ, and the gray area indicates the distribution of finds in later contexts

This humble find spot contributes little information on the Late Chalcolithic settlement. The site's significance in the period can be understood, however, from other Late Chalcolithic artifacts found out of context in Area C: a fragment of a fenestrated basalt chalice, a fragment of a hematite mace head, and a stone seal. Hematite mace heads and seals are rarely found in Late Chalcolithic sites, and hence their appearance together at Khirbet Qeiyafa points to the importance of the site during that period.

Table 1 presents the relevant data on the Late Chalcolithic remains at Khirbet Qeiyafa. The data is organized by location, from the core area of Square DD11 through nearby squares and then further away. Most of the items were found on the eastern side of Area CC. Four sherds were found in Area E, also located on the

Table 1 The distribution of Late Chalcolithic finds at Khirbet Qeiyafa

Square	Bucket	Locus	Context	Object
CC9	C10531	C6659	Late Persian	1 sherd (cornet)
CC9	C10581	C6666	Iron IIa	1 sherd
CC9	C10828	C6696	Iron IIa	1 sherd
DD9	C10315	C6566	Iron Age	1 sherd
DD10	C10013	C6472	Topsoil	1 sherd (cornet)
DD10	C10038	C6481	Iron IIa	1 sherd
DD10	C10075	C6500	Late Chalc.	2 sherds (cornet)
DD10	C10102	C6515	Iron IIa	2 sherds
DD10	C10158	C6528	Iron Age	1 sherd (bowl rim)
DD10	C10166	C6508	Iron Age	1 sherd (churn handle)
DD10	C10225	C6526	Iron IIa	6 sherds
DD10	C10393	C6561	Iron IIa	1 sherd
DD11	C10039	C6484	Late Chalc.	17 sherds
DD11	C10072	C6492	Iron IIa	3 sherds
DD11	C10073	C6484	Late Chalc.	18 sherds
DD11	C10074	C6500	Late Chalc.	25 sherds
DD7	C7887	C6123	Topsoil	Flint
DD7	C8209	C6072	Topsoil	1 sherd
DD7	C8447	C6106	Iron IIa	2 sherds
DD7-8	C9065	C6211	Iron IIa	Flint
DD7-8	C9066	C6211	Iron IIa	Fenestrated basalt chalice, fragment
DD10	C10013	C6472	Topsoil	1 sherd (cornet)
EE9	C9082	C6179	Late Persian	1 sherd
EE10	C8459	C6084	Late Persian	1 sherd (cornet)
EE11	C10043	C6476	Topsoil	1 sherd (cornet)
EE11	C10322	C6576	Iron IIa	1 sherd
EE12	C10511	C6657	Iron IIa	3 sherd
FF8-9	C8930	C6192	Iron Age	1 sherd (cornet)
FF8-9	C8476	C6091	Late Persian	2 sherds (cornet & handle)
FF10	C8807	C6140	Late Persian	Hematite mace head, fragment
FF11	C8817	C6174	Late Persian	1 sherd
FF12	C10168	C6543	Iron Age IIa	2 sherd
FF12	C10246	C6543	Iron IIa	1 sherd
FF12	C10302	C6577	Iron Age	2 sherd (2 kraters)
GG10	C11037	C6807	Iron Age	2 sherds (one painted red line)
GG11	C8723	C6161	Late Persian	Flint adze
GG11	C8723	C6161	Late Persian	1 sherd (krater rim)
GG13	C10104	C6517	Iron Age	3 sherds
GG13	C10173	C6493	Iron Age	1 sherd
HH10-11	C7502	C5205	Topsoil	Flint axe
HH14	C10114	C6513	Topsoil	Stone seal, broken handle
II18	C6818	C6818	Bedrock	Basin cut in bedrock

(continued)

The Late Chalcolithic in the Valley of Elah, Israel   249

Table 1 (continued)

Square	Bucket	Locus	Context	Object
JJ14	C7334	C5099	Persian	1 sherd
JJ14	C7365	C5112	Iron Age	1 sherd (strainer)
JJ17	C10612	C6684	Iron Age	1 sherd
JJ19, KK20	C11212	C6854	Topsoil	1 sherd
LL18	C10370	C6599	Topsoil	1 sherd (cornet)
LL22	C11390	C6902	Late Persian	1 sherd (cornet)
MM20	C11088	C6739	Late Persian	1 sherd (krater rim)
Area C	C10360	C6591	Dump	1 sherd
N5 (Area E)	E55	E29	Late Persian	4 sherds (cornet & handle)
Area A	A202	A100	Topsoil	Flint chisel

eastern side of the site. Two sherds were found in Area A at the center of the site, close to Area C. Late Chalcolithic finds were not observed in Areas B, D, or F. This distribution indicates that the settlement was rather small, occupying only part of the eastern side of the site.

To the various finds we add a rock-hewn installation. This is an elongated cup-mark or vat found in Square II18 of Area C. The cup-mark was observed in Stone C6818, which was quarried away from the exposed bedrock (Ovadia, 2014; Keimer, 2014: Figs. 11:10, 11:13). Quarries like this, found in various parts of the site, supplied stones for the construction of the Iron Age fortifications (Keimer, 2014; Keimer et al., 2015). Since the cup-mark was damaged by quarrying, it attests to earlier activity. Such cup marks, sometimes in groups of hundreds, are characteristic of Late Chalcolithic sites in this region (Van den Brink, 2008; Dagan, 2010: 173–174 and photograph on book cover; Dagan et al., 2011: 219, Figs. 15.3–15.4). In the survey of Khirbet Beit 'Awwa in the Judean Shephelah, where a large number of Late Chalcolithic pottery sherds was collected, seven basins and 20 cup marks were observed on a nearby rock exposure (Dagan, 2006, Site 556). Consequently, it seems likely that the installation cut into Stone C6818 at Khirbet Qeiyafa also dates from the Late Chalcolithic period.

3 The Finds

The Late Chalcolithic remains include artifacts of various types:

3.1 Pottery

The entire pottery assemblage is composed of small sherds, most of them undiagnostic fragments. As the pottery is crude and handmade, it is easily differentiated from the wheel-made pottery of the Middle Bronze Age or Iron Age. Some of the sherds, especially many of the cornets, are characterized by their white clay. Decades ago it was suggested that these vessels were made from kaolin clay (Amiran, 1955, 1969). Petrographic analysis of such sherds, however, indicates that they were made from Eocene chalk, which is common in many sections of the Beer-sheba Basin and the southern Shephelah (Gilead & Goren, 1989: 7–10).

The pottery of the Late Chalcolithic period is well known and has been published from a large number of sites (Mallon et al., 1934; Koeppel et al,. 1940; Dothan, 1959; Amiran, 1969; Levy & Alon, 1987; Garfinkel, 1999; Gilead, 2005; Levy, 2006). The diagnostic Late Chalcolithic sherds from Khirbet Qeiyafa include the following typical shapes:

1. Basin (Fig. 3: 1).
2. Cornet (Fig. 4). This is the most common vessel in the assemblage (ca. ten sherds). Most are base fragments, probably a result of the thick and massive shape of the base, which resists erosion. Indeed, this part of the vessel is reported from later fills at tell sites such as Megiddo or Ashkelon (Loud, 1948, Pl. 92: 18–24; L. Stager, personal communication). Cornets have been collected from site surfaces during surveys, for instance at Harei Yattir (Govrin, 1991, Site 10, Fig. 5: 8–11) and Khirbet Beit 'Awwa (Dagan, 2006, Site 556, Fig. 566.2: 12–13).
3. Large holemouth krater with thumb-impressed rim (Fig. 3: 2–4). Thanks to its thick rim, this vessel type resists erosion and is consequently reported from various surveys, such as those of Nahal Beer-sheba (Govrin, 1991: Site 249, Figs. 5: 14–17, 6: 1–8) and Khirbet Beit 'Awwa (Dagan, 2006: Site 556, Fig. 566.1: 4–6). A few complete examples of such vessels are reported from the Kissufim Road burial site (Goren & Fabian, 2002: Fig. 4.3: 2–3).
4. Strainer (Fig. 3: 5). One rounded sherd has five holes pointing to its function as a strainer. From its rounded shape, it seems that it was originally located at the base of the neck of a vessel, like the strainers located in small churns, tall-necked jars, and spouted holemouth jars (Perrot & Ladiray, 1980: Fig. 71: 1, 3–6, 8; Garfinkel, 1999: Fig. 145:3; Van den Brink & Lazar, 2019: Fig. 54: 7).
5. Typical Late Chalcolithic handle (Fig. 5). These include handles with a triangular shape, a large rounded hole, and a triangular cross-section. Two of the handles may have come from churns.

Although most of the sherds were undecorated, in a few cases traces of paint, including red or white lines, were observed. A few sherds bear rope decoration, created either by adding strips of clay (plastic decoration) or by incisions made directly into the surface of the clay (Fig. 3: 6–7).

While the pottery assemblage is indeed small, its dating to the Late Chalcolithic period is indisputable due to the large number of cornets, a pottery type typical of the Late Chalcolithic period. The large holemouth krater with thumb-impressed rim is another pottery type that is characteristic of the Late Chalcolithic period.

The Late Chalcolithic in the Valley of Elah, Israel

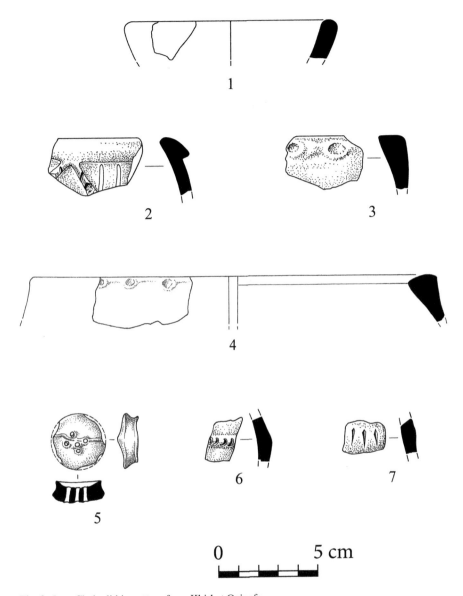

Fig. 3 Late Chalcolithic pottery from Khirbet Qeiyafa

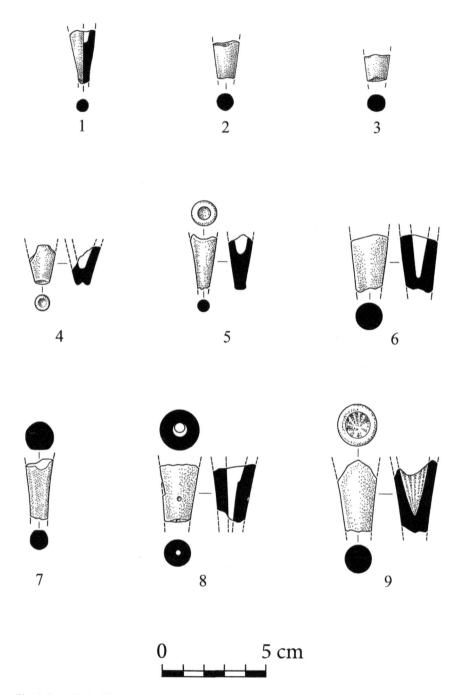

Fig. 4 Late Chalcolithic pottery from Khirbet Qeiyafa: Cornets

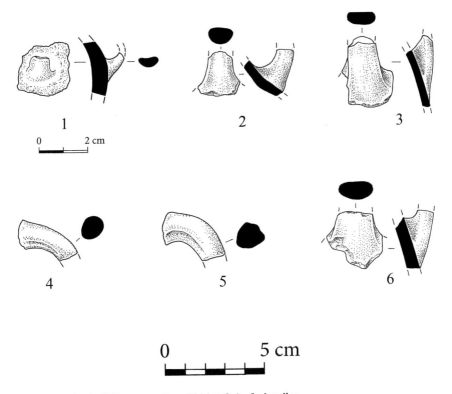

Fig. 5 Late Chalcolithic pottery from Khirbet Qeiyafa: handles

3.2 Flint

Three bifacial flint tools, two axes and one chisel, were found (Fig. 6).

3.3 Fenestrated Basalt Chalice

A fragment of a stone vessel made of fine basalt was found in Squares DD7–8 (Fig. 7: 1). This is the lower part of a fenestrated chalice, a fragment of the ring base. The item is well made and smoothed, displaying a high level of craftsmanship. The fenestrated chalice is a common vessel in Late Chalcolithic sites (Van den Brink et al., 1999). Such vessels are reported, for example, from the nearby site of Horbat 'Illit B (Milevski et al., 2013: Fig. 57: 4–6) and from sites farther away, such as burial caves at Shoham (Rowan, 2005: Fig. 9.12).

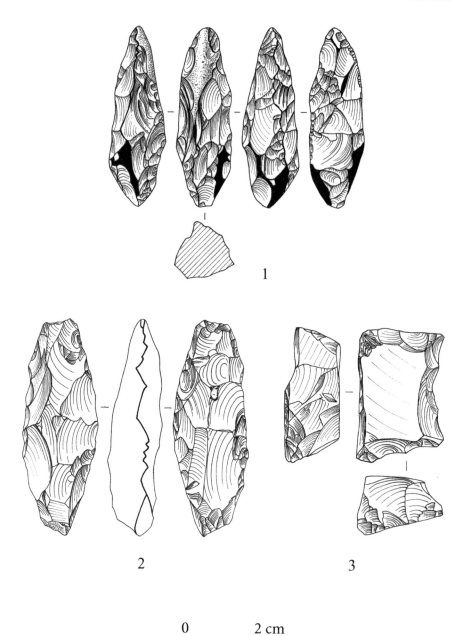

Fig. 6 Late Chalcolithic flint artifacts from Khirbet Qeiyafa

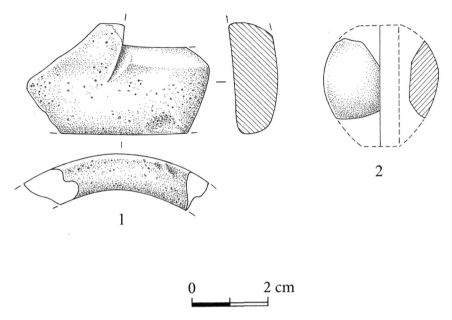

Fig. 7 Late Chalcolithic stone artifacts from Khirbet Qeiyafa: **1**. fenestrated basalt chalice; **2**. Hematite mace head

3.4 Hematite Mace Head

One fragment of a well-polished rounded mace head, made from black hematite, was found (Fig. 7: 2). The complete object was probably piriform in shape. Maceheads, which are characteristic of the Late Chalcolithic period, were made from limestone, basalt, hematite, and copper (Sebbane, 1998). Hematite mace heads, however, are quite rare. Six of them are reported from the Nahal Mishmar hoard (Bar-Adon, 1980, Nos. 185–190) and three from Gilat (Rowan et al., 2006: 591, Fig. 12.25: 3). Usually, however, only one or two were uncovered at a particular site: Tuleilat Ghassul (Mallon et al., 1934: Pl. 35: 3; Bourke et al., 2000: Fig. 23: 2), Horvat Beter (Dothan, 1959: 27, Fig. 18:5 5), Benei Braq (Kaplan, 1963: Fig. 9: 14), Azor (Perrot & Ladiray, 1980: Fig. 77: 4), Shoham (Nadelman, 1995), Nahal Qana Cave (Gopher & Tsuk, 1996: Figs. 4.17, 4.18), Giv'at ha-Oranim (Scheftelowitz, 2004: 67, Fig. 4.8), and Peqi'in (Shalem et al., 2013: Fig. 9.3: 3–4). Two hematite mace heads were found in Early Bronze Age I contexts at Nesher-Ramla Quarry, but probably originated from the Late Chalcolithic occupation of the site (Avrutis, 2012: 187–188).

3.5 Seal

An outstanding discovery at Khirbet Qeiyafa is a limestone seal. It measures 3.3 × 4.6 cm. The seal, in the common button shape, is rectangular in outline and has a raised handle, now broken, on its back. The pattern engraved on the seal is composed of parallel wavy lines (Figs. 8 and 9).

Chalcolithic seals and seal impressions are quite rare. From the Early Chalcolithic period (ca. 5800–5200 BCE) almost all the known seals were found at one site, Hagoshrim in the upper Jordan Valley, where about 40 seals were found on the surface or in excavations (Bar-Yosef & Garfinkel, 2008: 296–297; Getzov, 2011). Another example comes from Cave 53 near Qumran (Freikman et al., 2020). From the Middle Chalcolithic period (ca. 5200–4500 BCE) two seals are reported from Herzliya and Tel Tsaf (Garfinkel et al., 1992; Freikman & Garfinkel, 2017: Fig. 22; Freikman et al., 2021). At Tel Tsaf nearly 140 unstamped clay sealings were found as well, and a sealing from the site bearing two seal impressions was identified only recently (Freikman & Garfinkel, 2017: 2021).

Although Late Chalcolithic seals and sealings have been found in a few sites, they are very rare. A few seals are reported from Teleilat Ghassul (Mallon et al.,

Fig. 8 Photograph of the Late Chalcolithic limestone seal from Khirbet Qeiyafa

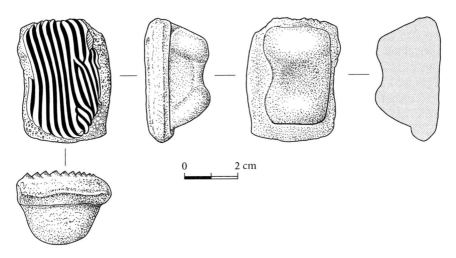

Fig. 9 Drawing of the Late Chalcolithic limestone seal from Khirbet Qeiyafa

1934: Fig. 28: 1; Bourke et al., 2000: Fig. 23: 1), and a seal and a clay sealing are reported from Grar (Ben-Tor, 2005). The seal from Khirbet Qeiyafa thus makes an important contribution to this very rare-find category.

4 Late Chalcolithic Sites in the Valley of Elah and Its Vicinity

The Valley of Elah (Wadi es-Sunt) is a shallow valley running from east to west, draining the hill country of Jerusalem and the Judean Shephelah into the Mediterranean Sea. Here I will present the data known from a particular part of the valley, in the area of the Judean Shephelah. The relevant sites are presented from east to west (Fig. 1):

Horbat 'Illit B This site is located on the border between the Shephelah and the Judean Hills. It was first published as Nahal Ha-Elah after a survey carried out in 2004, when Late Chalcolithic artifacts were observed in two locations, Site 14 and Site 20 (Stark, 2006). *Later, a large-scale excavation uncovered the remains of* a substantial village with stone-walled houses, 1 hectare in area (Eirikh-Rose & Milevski, 2008: 111–114; Milevski et al., 2013). The excavation unearthed a rich assemblage of pottery, remains of intensive flint knapping, and stone objects. A few basalt bowls and a pedestaled chalice made of fine basalt were found as well (Milevski et al., 2013: Fig. 57: 4–6). A number of cup-marks cut in a bedrock exposure were observed some 50 m from the site.

Horbat Zur Small-scale salvage excavations were conducted at this site after it was damaged by construction. Four excavation areas were opened. In Area A a Late Chalcolithic burial cave was unearthed, with typical secondary burials in pottery containers. Another cave, used for various daily tasks and probably for flint quarrying as well, was excavated in Area B. In Areas C and D the Late Chalcolithic remains were disturbed by later activities (Eirikh-Rose, 2009; Eirikh-Rose & Milevski, 2008: *108–111*). *Eirikh-Rose and Milevski* suggest that this location was used for activities that took place outside the nearby village sites of Horbat 'Illit B and Khirbat esh-Sheikh Madkur.

Khirbat esh-Sheikh Madkur This site is located at the foot of Tel Adulam. No excavations have taken place in this location, but Late Chalcolithic pottery has been collected during surveys *(*Eirikh-Rose & Milevski, 2008*)*.

Tel Adulam (Khirbat esh-Sheikh Madkur West) Late Chalcolithic pottery has been collected from the site surface (Dagan, 1992: 149–150, 272; Radashkovsky & Liraz, 2017), but no excavations have taken place.

Khirbet Abed (Socoh) Late Chalcolithic pottery has been collected from the site surface (Hasel et al., 2017: 54–55), but no excavations have taken place.

Khirbet Qeiyafa Late Chalcolithic remains were scattered over the site, with remains *in situ* uncovered in one small area, as presented above in this article.

Khirbet er-Rasm This site is located south of Tel Azeka, near the local gasoline station (Faust & Erlich, 2011: 3). The excavations concentrated on the Hellenistic level, but Late Chalcolithic remains of pottery and flint without clear context were observed in later fills.

Tell es-Safi/Gath This site is located in the lower Shephelah, near the modern village of Kefar Menahem. Intensive site survey revealed typical pottery of the Late Chalcolithic period (Uziel & Maeir, 2005). No settlement level of this period was reached in the excavations.

In addition, in the district north of Khirbet Qeiyafa known as Ramat Bet Shemesh, an area of some 3000 hectares was allotted for the construction of new neighborhoods. Consequently, an extensive survey and excavations took place in this region in 1994–2000 (Dagan, 2010; Dagan et al., 2011). The material relating to the Late Chalcolithic period has been described in detail (Dagan et al., 2011: 234–240) and, as described in the report, "opens a new chapter in the history of settlement in the Judean Shephelah." The survey defined 14 sites as settlements, one site as an isolated structure, and 35 places as "findspots." In addition to the surveys, excavations were conducted in three sites (222, 226, and 228). To date, only preliminary results from these sites have been presented. In Site 222, which spreads across 7000 sq. m, three phases of occupation were discerned. The excavation uncovered rectangular structures, one circular structure, courtyards, and a silo lined with stone slabs. On exposed bedrock south of the site, 46 oval vats and 19 cup-marks were observed, while in another nearby spot 19 vats and four cup-marks were counted. The finds from the excavated area include pottery sherds and flint implements (Dagan, 2010: 173–174, Fig. 222.1). In Site 226, spreading over 2000 sq. m, the remains of structures and vats were observed. Three structures were excavated and 12 oval vats were counted on a nearby bedrock exposure of nearly 10 sq. m. The finds include pottery sherds and flint implements (Dagan, 2010: 176). In Site 228 the excavations unearthed a few Late Chalcolithic structures inside and outside a collapsed cave. The finds include pottery sherds and flint implements (Dagan, 2010: 177). It should be noted that although Khirbet Qeiyafa was also examined in this survey, remains of Late Chalcolithic occupation were not identified (Dagan, 2010: 279–283).

The extensive survey that preceded construction in Ramat Bet Shemesh hence revealed numerous Late Chalcolithic sites, all of them quite small. All of the sites located along the Valley of Elah are fairly small as well.

5 Discussion

There are numerous implications to the identification of Late Chalcolithic activity at Khirbet Qeiyafa.

5.1 Site Formation Processes

The site of Khirbet Qeiyafa is located on a hilltop where bedrock is exposed in significant parts of the area. In two periods, the Iron Age and the Byzantine era, massive construction took place at the site. The Iron Age city was built on bedrock over the entire hilltop. Before construction, the entire area was cleared to bedrock and any architectural remains of the two earlier periods (the Late Chalcolithic and the Middle Bronze Age) were erased. In the Late Persian–Early Hellenistic era (Sandhaus & Kreimerman, 2015; Garfinkel, 2021) the site was reoccupied, but in this period the construction was less massive and generally reused the remains of the Iron Age city without erasing the earlier level. In the Byzantine era, small-scale activity took place at the site and a farmhouse was built at the summit of the site. This structure was built on bedrock and before its construction the entire area was cleared, an activity that erased most of the earlier remains in this location.

In sites built on a hilltop with exposed bedrock, the builders of each successive level aim to found their structures on solid rock and hence erase all, or large parts, of the earlier occupation. At sites located in valleys or in areas with a thick cover of soil it is difficult if not impossible to reach bedrock, and consequently, new occupation levels do not erase earlier phases but build on top of them. As a result, we do not see large tell sites in hilly areas of the southern Levant.

At Khirbet Qeiyafa the Iron Age building program indeed destroyed large parts of the Late Chalcolithic level. The stones of walls, if there were any, were reused for the construction of the city. Basins cut into bedrock were damaged by quarrying, as we see in Installation C6818. The various finds (pottery, flint, and stone vessels) were scattered and deposited in levels of the Iron Age or later periods. It is likely that the vast majority of the Late Chalcolithic finds disappeared over time. Nevertheless, a small percentage has survived and testifies to the activity that took place at the site in the Late Chalcolithic period.

5.2 The Character of the Site in the Late Chalcolithic Era

In this section I will attempt to evaluate the size and character of the Late Chalcolithic settlement at Khirbet Qeiyafa. As the remains of this period are distributed over a rather small area on the eastern side of the site and no signs of them were found in Area A, B, D, or F, it seems that the Late Chalcolithic activity was not widespread but occupied a small area in the eastern part of the site. This occupation may have spread over some 1000 sq. m. If the Late Chalcolithic settlement continued to the east, beyond the line of the Iron Age fortifications, it may have been a little larger.

The character of the site in the Late Chalcolithic period can be evaluated by the objects uncovered at the site. Although the excavations yielded very few artifacts of this period, these include somewhat rare prestige objects: a fenestrated basalt chalice, a hematite mace head, and a stone seal. Such items are rarely reported even from large-scale excavations at Late Chalcolithic sites. The small pottery assemblage is untypical as well, as it contains a very high proportion of cornets. Granted, this high proportion may be partly due to the thick and massive shape of the cornet base, which resists erosion. There are, however, other vessels with thick body parts, such as large holemouth kraters, jars, pithoi, and churns, that are not present in the assemblage.

The discovery of the hematite mace head and the seal at Khirbet Qeiyafa is reminiscent of the situation at Tuleilat Ghassul, where a hematite mace head and a seal were found together in the same spot (Bourke et al., 2000). The high concentration of prestige objects in the very small assemblage indicates that Khirbet Qeiyafa was of regional importance, beyond the local population that lived there.

5.3 The Limitations of Surveys

The Shephelah area was intensively surveyed by Dagan over several decades. In the area of Ramat Bet Shemesh, four Late Chalcolithic sites were initially identified (Dagan et al., 2011: 47–48). Later, when the entire area was earmarked for the construction of new neighborhoods, an intensive survey took place in this region and four additional Late Chalcolithic sites were located. Later, when the entire area was condemned to destruction by development, mechanical trenches were dug over large areas (Dagan et al., 2011: 329, Fig. 15: 12) and seven additional sites were discovered (Dagan et al., 2011: 48, Table 4.1). With the intensification of archaeological investigation, altogether 15 Late Chalcolithic sites were identified in three phases.

Although Khirbet Qeiyafa was also surveyed during these years, the Late Chalcolithic settlement was not recognized, and even the heavily fortified city of the Iron IIA was incorrectly dated by the survey (Garfinkel & Ganor, 2010). These examples highlight the limitations of surveys, in which a significant part of the archaeological data remains unknown.

Nevertheless, surveys are an important tool in archaeological research, as they are the only way to achieve a regional picture over and above the excavated sites in a region. All in all, one needs to be aware of the limitations of this method when drawing conclusions based on the sites and periods represented in a survey: basing theories on a lack of data is unsound methodology.

5.4 The Late Chalcolithic Settlement Pattern on the Regional Scale

The concentration of Late Chalcolithic sites along the Valley of Elah fits the pattern observed in the Ramat Bet Shemesh survey. As summarized by Dagan et al. (2011: 235), "It is evident that the Late Chalcolithic settlers preferred to locate their villages on elevated alluvial terraces near the wadis (local valleys), in proximity to both water sources and fertile soil." Similar locations of Late Chalcolithic sites near river beds were observed in the survey of Late Chalcolithic sites in the northern Negev (Gophna, 1979; Levy & Alon, 1983).

There is, however, a notable difference between the Ramat Bet Shemesh sites and those along the Valley of Elah: prestige objects have been found only in the latter. This difference is a function of the geographical conditions. Unlike the local small-scale valleys of Ramat Bet Shemesh, the Valley of Elah is a major drainage system, extending from the Jerusalem Hills to the Mediterranean Sea. Besides the advantages of fertile alluvial soil and water, it was a major transportation route from east to west. In accordance, the Late Chalcolithic sites along the Valley of Elah seem to be larger and richer in finds.

5.5 The Late Chalcolithic Settlement Pattern in the Southern Levant

It was marginal areas of the southern Levant that saw the discovery of the first Late Chalcolithic sites, like the large village of Tuleilat Ghassul in the arid climatic zone of the Dead Sea environs (Mallon et al., 1934; Koeppel et al., 1940) and Abu Matar,

Bir es-Safadi, and Horvat Beter around the city of Beer Sheba in the Negev (Perrot, 1955, 1956, 1959a, 1960; Dothan, 1959). Later on, additional sites of large-scale Late Chalcolithic activity were identified in the northern Negev, at Shiqmim, Gilat, and Grar (Levy & Alon, 1987; Gilead, 2005; Levy, 2006). Similarly, the Ein Gedi temple was discovered in the marginal area of the Judean Desert (Ussishkin, 1980), as well as activities of various kinds in many caves in the region (Bar-Adon, 1980; Davidovich et al., 2015). Sites in these marginal areas yielded many of the most spectacular Late Chalcolithic discoveries, such as rich metal objects, wall paintings, ivories, and violin-shaped figurines (Bar-Adon, 1980; Mallon et al., 1934: frontispiece; Perrot, 1959b; Levy & Golden, 1996; Scham & Garfinkel, 2000; Commenge, 2006).

It seems that in the Mediterranean zones of the southern Levant, which enjoy more favorable climatic conditions, Late Chalcolithic activities were less dominant. Large village sites and spectacular Late Chalcolithic artifacts are not reported from central and northern Israel, where the sites appear to be smaller. The only aspect that is more dominant in the Mediterranean zones is that of burial customs, such as the abundant and impressive burial caves with secondary burial in ossuaries (see, for example, Perrot & Ladiray, 1980; Van den Brink, 2005; Shalem et al., 2013).

How can we relate to the fact that among the Late Chalcolithic settlements of the southern Levant the sites in the Mediterranean zones do not display the same scale of size, architecture, and richness of finds as the southern sites? Basically, there are two possible approaches. The first is that this is a distorted picture: due to site formation processes, Late Chalcolithic sites in the northern area have simply vanished over time, as they were buried under natural erosion, covered by many later levels of occupation in tell sites, or simply destroyed, as in the case of Khirbet Qeiyafa.

The second approach is that this is indeed the real picture. Even if the destruction of Late Chalcolithic sites was more intensive in the north than in the south, the difference between the two regions still reflects an authentic situation. The finds from the Valley of Elah and its vicinity seem to point to rather small-scale activities in all of the sites mentioned above. Thus, it seems to me that in the Late Chalcolithic period the marginal areas of the southern Levant were indeed more dominant.

References

Amiran, R. B. (1955). The 'cream ware' of Gezer and the Beersheba late Chalcolithic. *Israel Exploration Journal, 5*, 240–245.

Amiran, R. (1969). *Ancient pottery of the Holy Land: From its beginnings in the Neolithic period to the end of the Iron Age*. Massada Press.

Avrutis, V. W. (2012). *Late Chalcolithic and Early Bronze Age I remains at Nesher-Ramla Quarry*. Institute of Archaeology, University of Haifa.

Bar-Adon, P. (1980). *The cave of the treasure: The finds from the caves in Nahal Mishmar*. Israel Exploration Society.

Bar-Yosef, O., & Garfinkel, Y. (2008). *The prehistory of Israel*. Ariel. (Hebrew).

Ben-Tor, A. (2005). A stamp seal and a seal impression of the Chalcolithic period from Grar. In I. Gilead (Ed.), *Grar. A Chalcolithic site in the northern Negev* (pp. 361–375). Ben-Gurion University of the Negev.

Bourke, S., Lovell, J., Sparks, R., et al. (2000). A second and third season of renewed excavation by the University of Sydney at Tulaylat al-Ghassul (1995–1997). *Annual of the Department of Antiquities of Jordan, 44*, 37–89.

Commenge, C. (2006). Gilat's figurines: Exploring the social and symbolic dimensions of representation. In T. E. Levy (Ed.), *Archaeology, anthropology and cult: The sanctuary at Gilat, Israel* (pp. 739–830). Equinox.

Dagan, Y. (1992). *The Shephelah during the period of the monarchy in light of archaeological excavations and surveys*. Unpublished MA thesis, Tel Aviv University (Hebrew).

Dagan, Y. (2006). *Map of Amazya (109), Vol. 2: The southern sector*. Israel Antiquities Authority.

Dagan, Y. (2010). *The Ramat bet Shemesh regional project: The gazetteer (IAA Reports 46)*. Israel Antiquities Authority.

Dagan, Y., Bonfil, R., & Sharon, I. (2011). *The Ramat Bet Shemesh regional project: Landscapes of settlement from the Paleolithic to the Ottoman periods (IAA Reports 47)*. Israel Antiquities Authority.

Davidovich, U., Porat, R., & Ullman, M. (2015). Judean Desert caves: Archaeology and history. In A. Frumkin (Ed.), *Holy Land Atlas. Judean Desert caves* (pp. 23–37). Magness Press.

Dothan, M. (1959). Excavations at Horvat Beter (Beersheba). *Atiqot, 2*, 1–42.

Eirikh-Rose, A. (2009). *Nahal Ha-Ela. Preliminary report. Hadashot Arkheologyiot– Excavations and Surveys 121*. http://www.hadashot-esi.org.il/report_detail_eng.asp?id=1011&mag_id=115.

Eirikh-Rose, A., & Milevski, I. (2008). Chalcolithic sites in the Elah Valley. *New Studies in the Archaeology of Jerusalem and its Region, 2*, 105–115.

Faust, A., & Erlich, A. (2011). *The excavations of Khirbet er-Rasm, Israel* (BAR international series 2187). BAR.

Freikman, M., & Garfinkel, Y. (2017). Sealings before cities: New evidence on the beginnings of administration in the ancient near East. *Levant, 49*, 1–22. https://doi.org/10.1080/00758914.2017.1323290

Freikman, M., Gutfeld, O., & Ovadia, A. (2020). A stamp seal from Cave 53 near Qumran. *Mitekufat Haeven: Journal of the Israel Prehistoric Society, 50*, 93–103.

Freikman, M., Ben-Shlomo, D., & Garfinkel, Y. (2021). A stamped sealing from Middle Chalcolithic Tel Tsaf: Implications for the rise of administrative practices in the Levant. *Levant, 53*, 1–12. https://doi.org/10.1080/00758914.2021.1923906

Garfinkel, Y. (1999). *Neolithic and Chalcolithic pottery of the Southern Levant* (Qedem 39). Institute of Archaeology, Hebrew University of Jerusalem.

Garfinkel, Y. (2017). Khirbet Qeiyafa in the Shephelah: Data and interpretations. In S. Schroer & S. Münger (Eds.), *Khirbet Qeiyafa in the Shephelah. Papers presented at a colloquium of the Swiss society for ancient near Eastern studies held at the University of Bern, September 6, 2014* (Orbis Biblicus et Orientalis 282) (pp. 5–59). Academic.

Garfinkel, Y. (2021). Khirbet Qeiyafa in the late Persian and early Hellenistic periods. In S. Honigman, C. Nihan, & O. Lipschits (Eds.), *Times of transition: Judea in the early Hellenistic period* (Studies on ancient Israel 1) (pp. 81–101). Institute of Archaeology, Tel Aviv University.

Garfinkel, Y., & Ganor, S. (2009). *Khirbet Qeiyafa Vol. 1. The 2007–2008 excavation seasons*. Israel Exploration Society.

Garfinkel, Y., & Ganor, S. (2010). Khirbet Qeiyafa in survey and in excavations: A response to Y. Dagan. *Tel Aviv, 37*, 67–78. https://doi.org/10.1179/033443510x12632070179702

Garfinkel, Y., Burian, F., & Friedman, E. (1992). A late Neolithic seal from Herzliya. *Bulletin of the American Schools of Oriental Research, 286*, 7–13.

Garfinkel, Y., Ganor, S., & Hasel, M. G. (2014). *Khirbet Qeiyafa Vol. 2. The 2009–2013 excavation seasons: Stratigraphy and architecture (Areas B, C, D, E)*. Israel Exploration Society.

Garfinkel, Y., Kreimerman, I., & Zilberg, P. (2016). *Debating Khirbet Qeiyafa: A fortified city in Judah from the time of King David*. Israel Exploration Society.

Getzov, N. (2011). Seals and figurines from the beginning of the early Chalcolithic period at Ha-Gosherim. *Atiqot, 61*, 1–26. (Hebrew).

Gilead, I. (2005). *Grar. A Chalcolithic site in the Northern Negev* (Beer-Sheva 7). Ben-Gurion University of the Negev.

Gilead, I., & Goren, Y. (1989). Petrographic analyses of fourth millennium BC pottery and stone vessels from the northern Negev, Israel. *Bulletin of the American Schools of Oriental Research, 275*, 5–14. https://doi.org/10.2307/1356874

Gopher, A., & Tsuk, T. (1996). *The Nahal Qanah cave. earliest gold in the Southern Levant* (Monograph series 12). Institute of Archaeology, Tel Aviv University.

Gophna, R. (1979). The settlement of the North-Western Negev during the Chalcolithic period (the fourth millennium B.C.). In A. Shmueli, Y. Gardos, & F. Mor (Eds.), *The land of the Negev, men and desert (Part 1)* (pp. 203–208). Ministry of Defence (Hebrew).

Goren, Y., & Fabian, F. (2002). *Kissufim road. A Chalcolithic mortuary site* (IAA reports 16). Israel Antiquities Authority.

Govrin, Y. (1991). *Map of Nahal Yattir (139)*. Israel Antiquities Authority.

Hasel, M. G., Garfinkel, Y., & Weiss, S. (2017). *Socoh of the Judean Shephelah: The 2010 survey*. Eisenbrauns.

Kaplan, J. (1963). Excavations at Benei Braq 1951. *Israel Exploration Journal, 13*, 300–312.

Keimer, K. H. (2014). The Iron Age quarries. In Y. Garfinkel, S. Ganor, & M. G. Hasel (Eds.), *Khirbet Qeiyafa Vol. 2. The 2009–2013 excavation seasons: Stratigraphy and architecture (Areas B, C, D, E)* (pp. 333–345). Israel Exploration Society.

Keimer, K. H., Kreimerman, I., & Garfinkel, Y. (2015). From quarry to completion: *Hirbet Qeiyafa* as a case study in the building of ancient near eastern settlements. *Zeitschrift des Deutschen Palästina-Vereins, 131*, 109–128.

Koeppel, R., Senes, H., Murphy, J. W., et al. (1940). *Teleilat Ghassul II (1932–1936)*. Pontifical Biblical Institute.

Levy, T. E. (2006). *Archaeology, anthropology and cult: The sanctuary at Gilat, Israel*. Equinox.

Levy, T. E., & Alon, D. (1983). Chalcolithic settlement patterns in the northern Negev desert. *Current Anthropology, 24*(1), 105–107.

Levy, T. E., & Alon, D. (1987). *Shiqmim 1: Studies concerning Chalcolithic societies in the northern Negev Desert, Israel (1982–1984)* (BAR international series 356). BAR.

Levy, T. E., & Golden, J. (1996). Syncretistic and mnemonic dimensions of Chalcolithic art: A new human figurine from Shiqmim. *Biblical Archaeologist, 59*, 150–159.

Loud, G. (1948). *Megiddo II: Seasons of 1935–39* (Oriental institute publications 62). Oriental Institute of the University of Chicago.

Mallon, A. S. J., Koeppel, R. S. J., & Neuville, R. (1934). *Teleilat Ghassul I*. Institut Biblique Pontifical.

Milevski, I., Vardi, J., Gilead, I., et al. (2013). Excavations at Horbat 'Illit B: A Chalcolithic (Ghassulian) site in the Haelah valley. *Journal of the Israel Prehistoric Society, 43*, 73–147.

Nadelman, Y. (1995). Shoham. *Excavations and Surveys in Israel, 14*, 80–81.

Ovadia, A. (2014). The stratigraphy of square II18. In Y. Garfinkel, S. Ganor, & M. G. Hasel (Eds.), *Khirbet Qeiyafa Vol. 2. The 2009–2013 excavation seasons: Stratigraphy and architecture (Areas B, C, D, E)* (pp. 475–476). Israel Exploration Society.

Perrot, J. (1955). The excavations at Tell Abu Matar, near Beersheba. *Israel Exploration Journal, 5*, 167–189.

Perrot, J. (1956). Beersheba: Bir es Safadi. *Israel Exploration Journal, 6*, 126–127.

Perrot, J. (1959a). Bir es Safadi. *Israel Exploration Journal, 9*, 141–142.

Perrot, J. (1959b). Statuettes en ivoire et autres objets en ivoire et en os provenant des gisements préhistoriques de la région de Beersheba. *Syria, 36*, 8–19.

Perrot, J. (1960). Beersheba: Bir es Safadi. *Israel Exploration Journal, 10*, 121–122.

Perrot, J., & Ladiray, D. (1980). *Tombes à ossuaries de la region côtière palestinienne au IVe millénaire avant l'ère chrétienne*. Association Paléorient.

Radashkovsky, I., & Liraz, E. (2017). Khirbat esh-Sheikh Madkur (west). In *Hadashot Arkheologiyot: Excavations and Surveys in Israel* (p. 129). https://www.hadashot-esi.org.il/report_detail.aspx?id=25234&mag_id=125

Rowan, Y. M. (2005). The groundstone assemblages. In E. Van den Brink & R. Gophna (Eds.), *Late Chalcolithic burial caves in the Lod Valley, Israel* (IAA reports 27) (pp. 113–139). Israel Antiquities Authority.

Rowan, Y. M., Levy, T. E., Alon, D., et al. (2006). Gilat's ground stone assemblage: Stone fenestrated stands, bowls, platters and related artifacts. In T. E. Levy (Ed.), *Archaeology, anthropology and cult: The sanctuary at Gilat, Israel* (pp. 575–684). Equinox.

Sandhaus, D., & Kreimerman, I. (2015). The late 4th/3rd century BCE transition in the Judean hinterland in light of the pottery of Khirbet Qeiyafa. *Tel Aviv, 42*, 251–271. https://doi.org/10.1179/0334435515Z.00000000051

Sang-Yeup, C. (2014). The stratigraphy of square DD11. In Y. Garfinkel, S. Ganor, & M. G. Hasel (Eds.), *Khirbet Qeiyafa Vol. 2. The 2009–2013 excavation seasons: Stratigraphy and architecture (Areas B, C, D, E)* (pp. 453–454). Israel Exploration Society.

Scham, S., & Garfinkel, Y. (2000). Perforated rods: A new Chalcolithic ivory type. *Bulletin of the American Schools of Oriental Research, 319*, 1–5. https://doi.org/10.2307/1357557

Scheftelowitz, N. (2004). Stone artifacts, Giv'at Ha-Oranim – A Chalcolithic site. *Salvage Excavation Reports, 1*, 59–67.

Sebbane, M. (1998). *The mace-head in Canaan in the fifth millennium and the beginning of the fourth millennium B.C.E.: Typology, technology, use and foreign relations*. Unpublished M.A. thesis, Hebrew University of Jerusalem (Hebrew).

Shalem, D., Gal, Z., & Smithline, H. (2013). *Peqi'in: A late Chalcolithic burial site, upper Galilee, Israel*. Kinneret Academic College.

Stark, H. (2006). Nahal Ha-Ela, final report. In *Hadashot Arkheologiyot* (p. 118). http://www.hadashot-esi.org.il/report_detail_eng.aspx?id=308&mag_id=111

Ussishkin, D. (1980). The Ghassulian shrine at En-gedi. *Tel Aviv, 7*, 1–44. https://doi.org/10.1179/033443580788441071

Uziel, J., & Maeir, A. M. (2005). Scratching the surface at Gath: Implications of the Tell es-Safi/Gath surface survey. *Tel Aviv, 32*, 50–75. https://doi.org/10.1179/033443505791198459

Van den Brink, E. C. M. (2005). Chalcolithic burial caves in coastal and inland Israel. In E. Van den Brink & R. Gophna (Eds.), *Late Chalcolithic burial caves in the Lod Valley, Israel* (IAA reports 27) (pp. 176–189). Israel Antiquities Authority.

Van den Brink, E. C. M. (2008). A new fossil director of the Chalcolithic landscape in the Shephelah and the Samarian and Judean Hill countries: Stationary grinding facilities in bedrock. *Israel Exploration Journal, 58*, 1–23.

Van den Brink, E. C. M., & Lazar, D. (2019). Horbat Nevallat. A Chalcolithic habitation site and agricultural installations in the Shephelah Foothills. *Atiqot, 94*, 1–88.

Van den Brink, E. C. M., Rowan, Y. M., & Braun, E. (1999). Pedestalled basalt bowls of the Chalcolithic: New variations. *Israel Exploration Journal, 49*, 161–183.

Cultural, Socio-economic and Environmental Influences on Health Status of Chalcolithic Populations in the Northern Negev

Patricia Smith, Marina Faerman, and Liora Kolska Horwitz

Abstract Reconstructions of material culture, subsistence base and lifestyle, show marked dissimilarities between two Late Chalcolithic site clusters from the Northern Negev; one cluster along the Beersheva stream and the second cluster along the Besor-Grar drainage. In this paper we have examined the extent to which these factors affected the health status of human populations from both clusters, as expressed in their age at death and skeletal and dental pathology.

We found marked differences in health status between the clusters that may relate to a combination of dietary and lifestyle differences between them, with the Besor-Grar cluster (e.g. the site of Gilat) exhibiting more deleterious health status than the Beersheva cluster (e.g. the site of Shiqmim). However, for Chalcolithic communities in the Southern Levant as a whole, life expectancy was short and preceded by chronic ill-health typical of populations with poor nutrition and a high prevalence of infectious diseases, many that were probably zoonotic in origin.

Keywords Human remains · Life history · Paleopathology · Zoonoses · Ghassulian · Secondary burial · Pastoralism

1 Introduction

Late prehistoric communities of the sixth–fifth millennia BC that inhabited the Southern Levant, experienced far-reaching transformations in all aspects of their lifestyle, economy and culture, a process that culminated in the Late Chalcolithic

P. Smith (✉)
Faculties of Dental Medicine and Medicine, The Hebrew University, Jerusalem, Israel

National Natural History Collections, The Hebrew University, Jerusalem, Israel
e-mail: pat.smith@mail.huji.ac.il

M. Faerman · L. K. Horwitz
National Natural History Collections, The Hebrew University, Jerusalem, Israel
e-mail: marinaf@cc.huji.ac.il; lix1000@gmail.com

© The Author(s), under exclusive license to Springer Nature Switzerland AG 2023
E. Ben-Yosef, I. W. N. Jones (eds.), *"And in Length of Days Understanding" (Job 12:12): Essays on Archaeology in the Eastern Mediterranean and Beyond in Honor of Thomas E. Levy*, Interdisciplinary Contributions to Archaeology,
https://doi.org/10.1007/978-3-031-27330-8_13

Ghassulian culture (~4500–3700 BC).[1] This "Chalcolithization Process" was defined by Holl (2019: 44) as the "adoption of the production and use of copper artifacts, polychrome pottery, and V-shape bowls." We extend this definition to include several other crucial socio-economic changes; aside from new technologies such as copper smelting we observe the establishment of craft specialization and workshops for ivory and stone carving, lithic artefact and textile manufacture (e.g. Gilead, 1988; Golden, 2014; Hermon, 2008; Levy, 1998; Levy, 2019; Levy & Alon, 1992; Levy & Gilead, 2012; Levy & Shalev, 1989; Perrot, 1959). Furthermore, the production of regional and distinctive traditions of ceramics is documented, as well as centralized production of objects such as ground stone and lithic artefacts (e.g. Garfinkel, 1999; Gilead, 1984; Gilead et al., 2004; Kerner, 2010; Manclossi & Rosen, 2022; Rowan & Golden, 2009). The use of broad-room architecture, subterranean structures and off-site cemeteries was also innovated and/or refined during this period, with both primary and secondary burial practiced, and with infants excluded from cemeteries where secondary burial was the norm (Gilead, 1988; Levy, 1982, 1987, 1998; Levy et al., 1991; Nagar & Eshed, 2001; Nativ, 2013; Perrot, 1959, 1984). It has been argued that at least in settlements in arid regions, a new system of social organization was established in the form of chiefdoms, denoting an addition stage in the development of non-egalitarian social structures (Levy, 1998, 2014; Levy et al., 2006).

In terms of the economy, there is evidence for intensification of agriculture including horticulture, particularly of olives (Langgut et al., 2019; Langgut & Garfinkel, 2022; Lovell et al., 2010), and the creation and storage of agricultural surplus (Garfinkel et al., 2009; Rosenberg et al., 2017). This was coupled with intensified animal husbandry, probably incorporating specialized pastoralism and transhumance in arid zones, as well as the exploitation of herd animals for their secondary products, especially milk (Levy, 1983, 1998; Grigson, 1995, 1998, 2006; Whitcher, 1999; Hill, 2011; but see Smith & Horwitz, 1984). Finally, a regional-scale trade system, probably based on barter, was established that was possibly associated with the use of donkeys as beasts of burden by the end of this period (Grigson, 2012; Rosen, 2019; but see Milevski, 2013; Milevski & Horwitz, 2019).

Another important development in the Chalcolithic was the expansion of village settlement into the arid margins, areas that had been previously unoccupied or only sparsely inhabited. Wetter climatic conditions ~4500 BC, facilitated movement of populations into these arid zones, including the Northern Negev and Judean Desert (Bar-Matthews & Ayalon, 2004; Litt et al., 2012; Miller Rosen, 2007). This environmental amelioration was associated with the establishment of large sedentary agro-pastoral communities in the Northern Negev, with smaller, satellite hamlets located along the same wadi systems, leading to an unprecedented aggregation of settlements in this region (Levy et al., 2006; Winter-Livneh et al., 2010). The improved

---

[1] Chronology followed here: Early Chalcolithic/Late Pottery Neolithic period, Wadi Rabah culture ~5800–4800 BC; Early Chalcolithic/Late Pottery Neolithic period, Qatifian/Besorian/Jericho VIII cultures ~4800–4500 BC; Late Chalcolithic period, Early Ghassulian culture ~4500–4300 BC; Late Chalcolithic period, Late Ghassulian culture ~4300–3700 BC.

climatic conditions proved advantageous for floodwater farming in marginal zones. Thus, it is not accidental that Chalcolithic settlements in the Northern Negev were located along the major river drainage systems—Nahal Beersheva, Nahal HaBesor and Nahal Grar-with their fields probably located in the seasonal floodplains (Winter-Livneh et al., 2010). As noted by Miller Rosen (2007: 100), floodwater farming "added a beneficial buffer to farming economies, reducing risk and allowing the higher cereal yields needed to support growing populations." As discussed by Grigson (2007), in marginal areas even slight shifts in the quantity of rainfall can result in sufficient latitudinal shifts in isohyets to facilitate dry farming. Indeed, research on grass phytoliths from Grar (Katz et al., 2007), has demonstrated that dry farming of crops was probably also practiced in these Northern Negev sites. Changing climate, leading to the onset of severe drought conditions towards the end of the third millennium, resulted in the unsustainability of both dry and floodwater farming in the Northern Negev sites, a factor that has been implicated as a major factor contributing to the collapse of Chalcolithic societies (Miller Rosen, 2007; see summary in Hermon, 2008: Chap. 1; Burton & Levy, 2011).

In this paper, we examine the effect of the extensive social, economic and cultural transformations that took place during the "Chalcolithization Process" on the health status and longevity of Late Chalcolithic human populations from two site clusters in the Northern Negev desert. The underlying assumption, based on modern clinical studies, is that human health is dependent both on *social context* i.e. socioeconomic and political constraints, as well as on the *living environment* i.e. the physical conditions experienced by people (e.g., Marmot et al., 2012; WHO, 2017). When changes take place in one or more of these factors, it is expected that health status and concomitantly mortality rates of a population, will be affected. The direction of change can be deleterious or beneficial, the outcome depending upon the type and severity of the change. As noted by Waldron (2008: 10), with reference to the study of skeletal remains, "what determines their actual state of health depends not only upon the diseases that affected their internal organs, but their mental state, their diet and many other environmental and social factors". For the Late Chalcolithic populations of the Northern Negev many of the latter factors are known, facilitating the contextualization of their health status. The latter is defined here as 'poor' or 'good' based upon inter-population comparison of the frequency and severity of skeletal and dental pathologies evident in two, roughly contemporaneous Late Chalcolithic regional site clusters.

1.1 Regional Clusters

Gilead (2011) highlighted significant differences between Ghassulian sites located along the Beersheva stream (Shiqmim, Bir es-Safadi, Horvat Beter, Abu Matar) and those situated along the Besor-Grar drainages (Grar, Gilat, Wadi Gazze D) (Fig. 1). He concluded that these two site clusters may represent geographic sub-cultures with inter-site differences expressed in terms of material culture– with copper

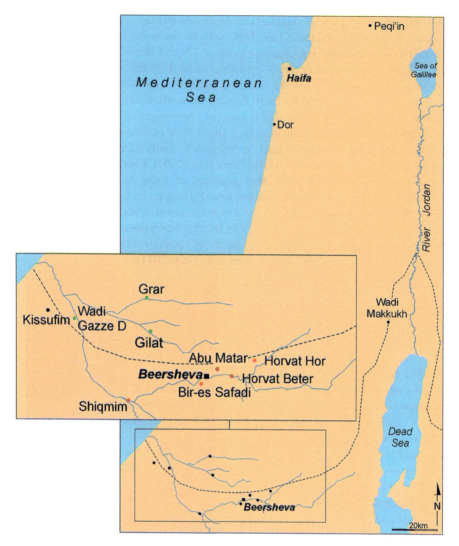

Fig. 1 Map showing location of Northern Negev and other Chalcolithic sites mentioned in the text. The dotted line represents the 200 mm isohyet. Red dots indicate sites without pigs, green dots those with pigs (drawing J. Rosenberg)

smelting and ivory carving absent in the Besor-Grar sites but present in the Beersheva settlements, while sickle blades, tabular scrapers and bifacial tools (adzes, axes, chisels) are found in significantly higher numbers in the Besor-Grar cluster than in the former sites. Frequencies of ceramic vessel types and technologies also differ between the clusters with, for example, pointed base cornets occurring in far higher numbers in the Besor-Grar sites, as do vessels with string-cut bases (Burton & Levy, 2011; Levy et al., 2006). Gilead also suggested that there were architectural differences in the use of stone versus mudbricks for building wall foundations, but these claims are apparently not upheld (Burton & Levy, 2012). In terms of economy, domestic pigs are absent in the Beersheva cluster sites while present in those from the Besor-Grar drainage (Grigson, 1987a, 1989, 2007; Horwitz, 1990). Notably, the sites lacking pigs are situated in more arid areas that lie below the 200 mm isohyet, which Grigson (2007) set as a limit for dry farming. This suggests that there may be differences between site clusters not only in the composition of animals kept and their association with rainfall quantity, but also in the types and/or extent of crops cultivated, with less cereal production in sites of the more arid Beersheva cluster. Gilead (2011: 20) concluded that "the fact that one group raised pigs and the other did not, in addition to the other differences listed above, is to be regarded as reflecting behavioral, cultural and socio-economic differences between the members of these two sub-cultures." Finally, there has been a discussion about the synchronicity of sites within and between the clusters, with Gilead (1994, 1995) suggesting that sites are not contemporaneous. However, based on analyses of radiocarbon dates and material culture, Levy and colleagues (Burton & Levy, 2011, 2012; Levy et al., 2006) have argued that they are at least partly synchronous and so comparable. Burton and Levy (2012) emphasized that it is possible for contemporaneous assemblages that comprise variable material culture, to co-exist and so represent distinct but inter-relating socio-cultural groups. Given the far-reaching variation evident between the clusters in many facets, we have examined the possible impact this may have had on the health status and longevity of the Ghassulian Chalcolithic communities inhabiting the Northern Negev.

In an insightful paper on social violence, Paul Farmer wrote, *"An anthropology that tallies the body count must of course look at the dead and those left for dead. Such inquiry seeks to understand how suffering is muted or elided altogether. It explores the complicity necessary to erase history and cover up the clear links between the dead and near-dead and those who are the winners in the struggle for survival"* (Farmer, 2004: 304). We have tried to rectify the objectification inherent in "body counts" in bioanthropology, by reconstructing the broader life history of Chalcolithic populations from these two specific site clusters. Pathologies (as evidenced in their bones and teeth) and age at death, together serve as invaluable sources of evidence on the success of different cultural and technological adaptations in past societies, and so contribute towards our understanding of the severity of socio-economic and environmental constraints as well as scalar stress experienced by them.

2 Materials

This study examines longevity and disease load as evident in the age profiles of deceased individuals and prevalence of pathological lesions in their bones and teeth. We have examined these parameters in human skeletal remains deriving from secondary and primary burials from the two identified Chalcolithic site clusters, for which primary bio-anthropological data have been collected by the two senior authors.

(a) The Beersheva cluster comprises aggregated households from Shiqmim village (Faerman et al., in press; Faerman & Smith, 2008; Levy et al., 1991, 1993), a site that has yielded primary and secondary burials, as well as partial remains in disturbed contexts. In addition, we included data from the tumulus cemeteries (grave circles 51 and 101) from Mezad Aluf (n = 76) that contained secondary burials and were probably associated with the Shiqmim village and adjoining hamlets (Levy et al., 1991, 1993; Levy & Alon, 1982). A total of 65 burials were identified at Shiqmim village, with the vast majority (n = 45) found in Stratum IIb. The remainder were isolated remains from Strata I and III.

(b) The Besor-Grar cluster comprises the village-sanctuary site of Gilat (Smith et al., 2006) and the aggregated household clusters at Grar (Gilead, 1995: 59–60, 76, 94). Primary, flexed burials were found at both sites as well as isolated bones in fill. Unfortunately, no detailed bio-anthropological data is available for Grar. At Gilat, remains from a total of 91 individuals were recovered. The uppermost Stratum I, yielded very fragmentary remains of 6 individuals including a possible secondary burial – the only one identified at the site. The majority of the remains from the site date to Stratum II, which yielded a total of 45 individuals. The breakdown by phase is: Stratum IIa with 17 primary flexed burials, Stratum IIb with 21 burials (including the collective burial with 9 individuals from a silo), and Stratum IIc with 7 burials. Stratum IIIa contained 11 burials. For a further 29 individuals, stratum attribution was uncertain.

Both Gilat and Shiqmim have yielded relatively large collections of human skeletal remains, as expressed in high minimum of individual counts (MNI). However, our analyses have been hampered by poor preservation so that most of the skeletal remains were incomplete and further affected by adverse environmental conditions that were exacerbated by burial type (e.g. secondary burial), post-depositional disturbances from grave robbers and/or accidental damage by later building activities in antiquity. Moreover, it should be borne in mind that the sites appear to have been in use for many generations, so that the number of individuals recovered represents a time-averaged series. To obtain large enough samples with which to obtain a broad temporal overview of the Late Chalcolithic, we have pooled all available data by site and in some instances, when no statistically significant inter-site differences were found, we combined data from sites. This approach has enabled us to explore the skeletal and dental evidence for differences in health status between the two site clusters, and between them and other Chalcolithic sites from the region.

As a reference population for evaluation of the age distribution and pathologies identified, we have referred to a skeletal series from the late eighteenth-early nineteenth century site of Dor, located on the Carmel coast just south of Haifa (Smith & Horwitz, 2009). The paleopathological findings from this site are reflected in historical records that describe this as a poverty-stricken hamlet inhabited by subsistence peasant-farmers and fisherfolk who were characterized by poor health and chronic disease.

3 Palaeodemography

Life expectancy is highly correlated with infant mortality rates and these are commonly used as a reliable measure of health status in the living. But several factors need to be considered when applying them to the analysis of skeletal remains, including age or sex related differences in burial practices, poor preservation of fragile infant bones (Guy et al., 1997), changes in population size over the period a cemetery was in use and so the relative number of births and deaths in a community. A number of methods have been developed to minimize the effect of the biases inherent in such studies (Larsen, 2015). Here, as a reference for comparison, we have chosen to use the age distribution from the relatively well preserved remains excavated in the Ottoman cemetery of Dor as representative of the expected frequency of deaths at different ages, before the advent of modern medicine or sanitation. We have further calculated the percentage of older adults within the adult sample, on the premise that this will provide a measure of relative of longevity while avoiding biases resulting from differential diagenesis or exclusion of infants.

In general, in Chalcolithic sites where primary burial was practiced, individuals of all ages—including infants and young children, are present. This is true for Shiqmim, Gilat, Tel Te'o and Horvat Qarqar South (Kahila Bar-Gal & Smith, 2001; Smith et al., 2006; Faerman & Smith, 2008; Faerman et al., in press; Fabian et al., 2015). However, infants are absent in secondary burial sites from this period, such as the Mezad Aluf cemeteries, Kissufim, Wadi Makkukh, Peqi'in and Ben Shemen, interpreted as due to differential burial practices exacerbated by biases in the preservation of their remains (Nagar, 2013; Nagar & Eshed, 2001; Smith et al., 2006; Zagerson & Smith, 2002).

Infants (aged less than 1 year) comprise 29% of all those identified from the intramural primary burials at Shiqmim, 28% of those at Gilat, and 19% of those from the Ottoman site of Dor (Faerman et al., in press; Smith et al., 2006; Smith & Horwitz, 2009). These findings are in keeping with the expected frequency of infant mortality during most of the past i.e., prior to the introduction of modern medical care and sanitation (Volk & Atkinson, 2013). In Israel, infant deaths only began to fall following the institution of public health measures in the 1920s during the British Mandate of Palestine (Kligler, 1924, 1932). Thus, the high frequency of infant mortality found at Gilat and Shiqmim suggests that the poor health status that characterized much of the Southern Levant in the late eighteenth-early nineteenth centuries i.e., at Dor, actually dates back to much earlier periods.

Figure 2a shows the percentage of adults in Chalcolithic sites with primary and secondary burials alongside Ottoman Dor (with primary burials). Using Fishers Exact Test, we found no significant difference in the proportion of adult to immature deaths (i.e., individuals aged 0–18 years) between Gilat and Shiqmim, but did find significantly more immature individuals when the combined data for Gilat/Shiqmim were compared to Dor (P = 0.009) or the secondary burial sites Mezad Aluf, Peqi'in and Wadi Makkukh. These results were expected given the absence of infants from secondary burial complexes, that are best explained as due to their disposal

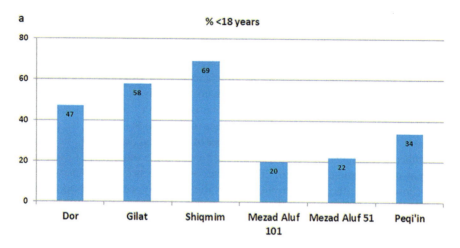

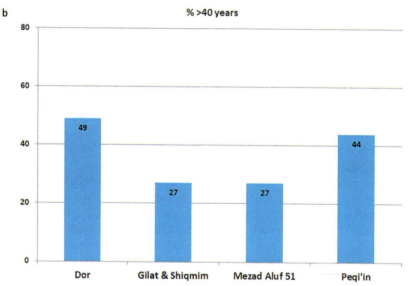

Fig. 2 (a) Frequency of immature individuals (<18 years) relative to adults (18+ years) in Chalcolithic sites and Ottoman Dor. (b) Frequency of mature adults (40+) out of all adults in Chalcolithic sites and Ottoman Dor. The data used here does not include the adults that could not be placed in a specific age category

elsewhere. This may relate to the fact that infants were not considered important enough for full burial rites which were both expensive and time consuming, or simply that it was not practical given (i) the high rates of infant mortality, and (ii) the problems of preserving fragile infant bones during the rites associated with secondary burial, that sometime included exposure and defleshing of the corpse (Le Mort & Rabinovich, 1994).

Figure 2b shows that the percentage of those surviving to age 40+ in the combined Gilat/Shiqmim sample and Mezad Aluf was less than at any of the other sites suggesting that these Northern Negev populations had a similar short life expectancy. This was markedly shorter than that found at Chalcolithic Peqi'in or even Ottoman period Dor (Fishers Exact Test P < 0.01).

4 Skeletal Pathology

The pathological lesions that were identified on the bones of Chalcolithic populations fall into several categories. They include conditions resulting from malnutrition or malabsorption, expressed in localized areas of surface pitting and porosity of the bone, especially on the cranium; evidence of stress in the form of periostitis resulting in shallow patches of new bone formation often in the form of parallel striations on the surface of the long bones; reduction in bone mass as measured by combined cortical thickness (CCT); function-related degenerative changes on joint surfaces; infectious lesions, tumors and genetic conditions affecting bones and or teeth. These conditions were scored after Ribot and Roberts (1996), Roberts and Manchester (2005), Ortner (2003) and Ortner and Frohlich (2008). Dental lesions studied included enamel hypoplasia in the form of linear enamel defects (LEH) reflecting episodes of ill-health during tooth formation, caries and periodontal disease (Hillson, 2012). In addition, tooth wear and ante-mortem tooth loss were scored (Hillson, 2012). Together, these skeletal and dental conditions provide an indication of the type and severity of dietary stress and/or disease load experienced by a human population.

The majority of Chalcolithic specimens in both clusters showed evidence of ill-health prior to death expressed in cribra orbitalia (pitting in the orbits), pitting of the parietal bones of the skull, and periostitis. All four individuals from Gilat with the orbital region of the cranium preserved exhibited cribra orbitalia (Fig. 3a), while parietal pitting was seen in the cranial bones of all children from the site (Fig. 3b). At Shiqmim, 75% out of a sample of 12 individuals (that had the relevant bones preserved), were affected by cribra orbitalia. At Peqi'in, with a much larger sample, Nagar (2013) reported that 83% of 101 individuals suffered from this condition, which is similar to the frequency seen at Ottoman Dor (84% of those studied). Both cribra orbitalia and parietal pitting have been associated with anaemia. This may result from dietary deficiencies, chronic loss of blood resulting from diseases such as malaria or intestinal parasites, or genetic mutations affecting the integrity of red blood corpuscles such as thalassemia, a disease known to have been present in the region at least since the Neolithic (Hershkovitz et al., 1991). Periostitis was most prevalent at Gilat affecting 85% of the femora of children that were examined, compared to 52% at Shiqmim and 51% at Ottoman Dor (Fig. 4). This finding is indicative of the poor health status of all populations, especially Gilat.

No CCT measurements were available for Shiqmim, but at Gilat CCT was measured in 4 individuals and values for the humerus ranged from 9.8 mm in a male and 7.5 to 7.3 mm for the three females (Smith et al., 2006). At Horvat Hor values for four individuals ranged from 10.5 mm to 7.5 mm (Smith & Sabari, 1995). At Ottoman Dor, mean values for the right humerus were even lower (7.3 mm in

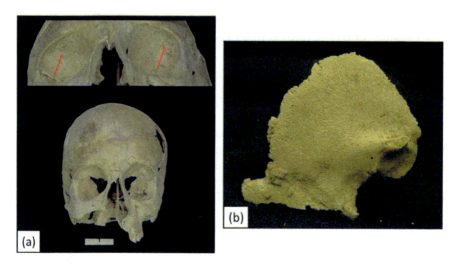

Fig. 3 (a) Cribra orbitalia (shown by arrows) in an adolescent from Shiqmim. (b) Pitting on the temporal bone of a child from Gilat

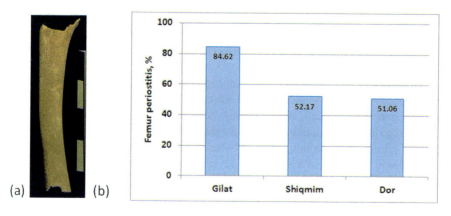

Fig. 4 (a) Photo of child's tibia from Gilat showing periostitis and bowing, probably from rickets. (b) Histogram showing frequency of periostitis in childrens' femora from Gilat (13 bones examined), Shiqmim (23 bones examined) versus Ottoman Dor (47 bones examined)

females and 9.4.mm in males (Smith & Horwitz, 2009). Notably, in all groups, mean values for females are much lower than for males, and show a significant reduction compared to Natufian (Epipaleolithic) hunter-gatherer populations that had mean values of 12.1 mm and 8.9 mm for males and females respectively (Smith & Horwitz, 1984). Cortical thickness in the humerus of less than 7.5 mm is considered evidence of osteoporosis, which is rare before the age of 40 years in healthy women (Bloom & Laws, 1970). Since the females from the Chalcolithic sites were all younger than 40, the low CCT values probably denote bone loss related to poor nutrition or poor health, compounded by frequent pregnancies.

Pathologies associated with specific diseases were seen in a number of individuals at Gilat; in a young child in the form of tibial bowing which is typical of rickets (Fig. 4a), in an adolescent in the form of inflammatory changes on the internal surface of the frontal bone possibly due to meningitis, in a young female with abscesses at the elbow joint of the ulna and collapsed cervical and thoracic vertebrae, and in a second young female in whom abscesses were present in the thoracic vertebrae (Smith et al., 2006). In both young women, the pathology identified is similar to, but not pathognomic of tuberculosis.

In sum, most of the individuals from Gilat and Shiqmim had one or more skeletal lesions, indicating they had been ill for some time before death, but all conditions were more common at Gilat than Shiqmim, indicating differences in the severity of environmental stress between these sites. Compared to Ottoman Dor, infants and children from Shiqmim showed less evidence of chronic disease, while disease rates at Gilat were even more severe than at Ottoman Dor. For adults too, the quantity and type of bony pathologies observed in all sites is indicative of a high disease load and poor nutrition, resulting in early death. Additional evidence for poor health status in Chalcolithic populations from the region has been reported by Hershkovitz et al. (2021), who found a significantly higher frequency of ear infections in them, relative to a diachronic series of skeletal remains from the region.

5 Dental Pathology

Lev-Tov Chattah (2005), carried out a detailed study of teeth and jaws of individuals aged 16+ years, in Chalcolithic samples from Israeli sites including those in the Northern Negev. She found (Fig. 5) that Peqi'in had the highest frequency of carious teeth (7.45%) while Gilat had the lowest frequency (2.1%), but that ante-mortem tooth loss (AMTL) showed a reverse trend with the highest frequency at Gilat (9.5%) followed by Wadi Makkukh with 8.9% (Fig. 6) and Peqi'in the lowest (6.8%). No ante-mortem tooth loss (AMTL) was observed at Shiqmim. Periapical lesions were similarly slightly more frequent at Wadi Makkukh and Gilat than Peqi'in (Fig. 5).

Many of the teeth had fallen out of the jaws post-mortem, especially the anterior single-rooted teeth, with Peqi'in and Wadi Makkukh most severely affected and this may have biased the results given above because of different susceptibility of anterior and posterior teeth to disease. In order to check this, Lev-Tov Chattah (2005) also examined the frequency of conditions by tooth type and found that the results for the first and second molars were similar in order of the ranking of the conditions studied: caries frequencies were highest at Peqi'in and lowest at Gilat with none at Shiqmim, while ante-mortem tooth loss was highest at Gilat followed by Wadi Makkukh and with Peqi'in lowest. Periapical lesions were similarly, slightly more frequent at Wadi Makkukh and Gilat than Peqi'in. Neither of the latter conditions were noted at Shiqmim. In view of the younger age of individuals with teeth and jaws from Gilat and Shiqmim, as well as the low frequency of carious lesions, we

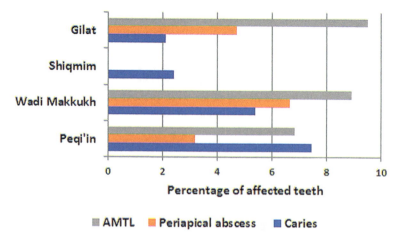

Fig. 5 Histogram showing frequencies of caries, and ante-mortem tooth loss (AMTL) and periapical lesions in teeth and tooth sockets from Gilat, Shiqmim, Wadi Makkukh and Peqi'in

Fig. 6 Photograph showing extensive ante-mortem tooth loss in an adult mandible from Wadi Makkukh

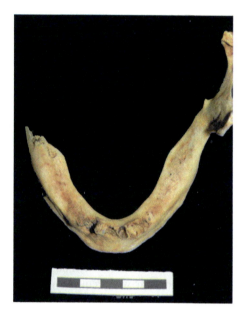

suggest that these data support the hypothesis that a combination of severe tooth wear and poor health contributing to periodontal disease were the probable causes of AMTL at Gilat, and reflects a more abrasive diet and impaired dental health relative to that of Peqi'in or Shiqmim.

Lev-Tov Chattah and Smith (2006) reported more severe rates of tooth wear in the Judean Desert site of Wadi Makkukh compared to Peqi'in in the Mediterranean region. Tooth wear at Wadi Makkukh appeared to be similar to that at Shiqmim, while Smith et al. (2006) commented on the extremely severe tooth wear in adolescents at Gilat. The data presented here also show that there was even less caries and more AMTL and periodontal abscesses at Gilat than at Wadi Makkukh. In their study of health status in Neolithic populations from the Southern Levant, Bocquentin et al. (2021) reported a significantly lower frequency of caries in sites from the steppe/desert regions compared to those in the Mediterranean zone, a finding that is echoed in the Chalcolithic data presented here. This they attributed to differences in the extent of carbohydrate intake, either due to dietary differences or regional variation in methods of food preparation. The latter factors also influence the rate of dental wear which has been shown to reduce the impact of caries by removing pits and fissures on the tooth crown where the majority of carious lesions originate (Hopcraft & Morgan, 2006), and may explain the low caries rates in the Northern Negev sites.

In contrast to the skeletal and dental conditions described above, that reflect the severity and type of disease experience throughout life, hypoplastic lesions of enamel (LEH; Fig. 7) constitute a record of developmental disturbances during infancy and childhood (Goodman et al., 1980). However, many of the anterior teeth in the Chalcolithic dentitions examined here had been lost post-mortem e.g., at Wadi Makkukh only two canines were present in the jaw, so that the findings for these teeth may be unreliable. Accordingly, the frequency of LEH was also calculated for the first molar where sample sizes were larger (Fig. 8).

The frequency of LEH in the canines (C) was similar at Peqi'in, Gilat and Dor (~90%) and markedly higher at these sites than at Shiqmim (76%). In the first molar (M1), the frequency of LEH at Gilat (90%) and Dor (67%) remained higher than that at Peqi'in (44.1%) and Wadi Makkukh (29.1%), while at Shiqmim it was 7.7%. The difference in the frequency of this condition seen between the canine and first molar is associated with differences in age and duration of formation of the

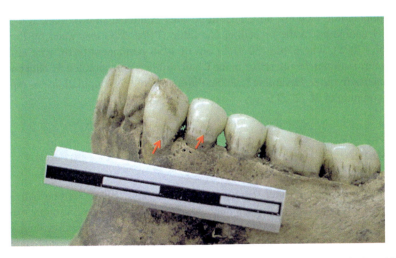

Fig. 7 Photograph showing hypoplastic lesions in a canine and first pre-molar (red arrows) in an adolescent from Shiqmim

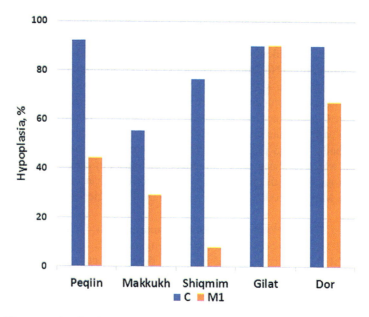

Fig. 8 Histogram showing frequencies of hypoplastic lesions (LEH) in canines (C) and first molars (M1)

permanent tooth crown. This begins *in utero* and is completed by 3.5–4 years in the first molar, but begins at 5–6 months and is completed only at 6 years in the canine (AlQahtani et al., 2010). Moreover, the location of most of the LEH lesions in Gilat covered more than half the canine, indicative of ill-health during the entire period of tooth formation. In contrast, in the other sites, the lesions were usually limited to less than 1/3 of the tooth crown, again emphasizing the poorer health status of the Gilat population. Notably, all Chalcolithic sites examined show a marked increase in LEH compared to the preceding Neolithic (PPNC/PN) examined by Lev-Tov Chattah (2005), where 463 (30.91%) out of 1498 permanent teeth were affected. The deterioration in health status in the Chalcolithic is corroborated by data on LEH frequencies in other, Levantine Late Neolithic (PPNC/PN) populations, as reported by Bocquentin et al. (2021).

6 Stature

Stature was calculated (after regressions given in Bass, 1995), for two individuals from the Northern Negev sites; a female humerus from Gilat gave a stature estimate of 155.4 ± 4.45 cm and for a male femur from Shiqmim, stature was calculated as 169.4 ± 3.94 cm. In Horvat Hor, a female humerus gave an estimated stature of 150–160 cm (Smith & Sabari, 1995). Stature estimates based on femur measurements of 10 females and 9 males from Wadi Makkukh were 148–160 cm in females and 162–172 cm in males (Smith unpublished data), and in Peqi'in stature for the left femur was 164 ± 5.8 cm for males and 149 ± 7.3 cm for females (Nagar, 2013). These estimates tally well with those published based on femur length for Nahal Mishmar (recalculated using the same regression from data given in Haas & Nathan, 1973) which averaged 165 ± 8 cm for 7 males and 155 ± 10 cm for 5 females, mean ± 2SD). All these estimates are similar to that seen at Ottoman Dor which ranged from 151.9–176.6 cm for males (mean 164.7 cm) and 148–170 cm for females (mean 157.3 cm) (Smith et al. 1984a, b). The frequent episodes of growth insults identified in the teeth, and pathologies identified in the bones, suggests that growth in the Chalcolithic populations was probably stunted and fell far short of their genetic potential for height.

7 Discussion

The Chalcolithic socio-economic and cultural innovations initiated in the Northern Negev were accompanied by large aggregations of people (Winter-Livneh et al., 2010). As noted by Michael E. Smith (2019) in his "energized crowding" model, although larger population aggregations[2] are more innovative and productive per capita than smaller groupings, they are also negatively characterized by high levels of scalar stress, increased levels of poverty and disease (see also Pimentel et al., 2007). Indeed, the synthesis of bioarchaeological data undertaken here (Fig. 9), demonstrates that for the Northern Negev Late Chalcolithic populations, life expectancy was low and associated with high levels of skeletal pathology and developmental defects of the teeth indicative of chronic ill-health. While poor health status was common in all Chalcolithic populations in the region, such as at Wadi Makkukh in the Judean Desert and Peqi'in in the Mediterranean zone, the prevalence and severity of health insults in Northern Negev sites—especially at Gilat, appear most severe. Health status at Gilat, as shown by the range and severity of skeletal pathology (cribra orbitalia, periostitis, osteoporosis in young females, possibly tuberculosis, rickets) and dental developmental defects (hypoplasia), was markedly poorer than at Shiqmim. We propose that these differences are related to manifold, intertwined factors in which environment played a major role. Moreover, the disease load in the Northern Negev sites was more severe than that observed at Ottoman Dor. This is also reflected in the earlier age at death of all Chalcolithic individuals examined compared to Dor.

Although all Northern Negev Late Chalcolithic sites engaged in a mixed economy founded on the cultivation of crops (grains and legumes) and products from domestic herds—primarily caprines (meat, milk and its products), some critical differences are evident that may have influenced lifestyle, diet and so health status in

---

[2] In his model M. E. Smith related to complex urban settlements, but we consider this as applicable to the Chalcolithic in the Northern Negev since this period saw an unprecedented rise in the number of settlements in this region.

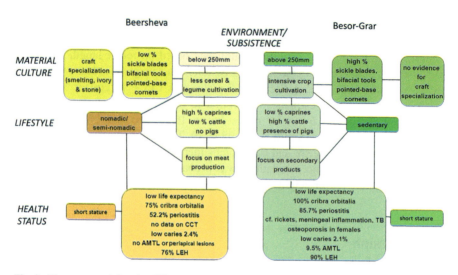

Fig. 9 Chart summarizing the differences between the Beersheva and Besor-Grar clusters

the two clusters. In Shiqmim and Abu Matar, carbonized crops were identified and comprised two-row barley (*Hordeum vulgare* or *distichon*), wheat (*Triticum turgidum*, subsp. *diccocum*), emmer wheat (*Triticum parvicoccum*), lentil (*Lens culinaris*), in addition to ca. 40 different species of wild plants and fruits, including fig, almond, pistachio, a weed (*Galium tricorne*) commonly found in lentil fields, and *Trigonella arabica* that is related to the herb fenugreek (Kislev, 1987; Negbi, 1955). In contrast to the Beersheva sites, burnt macro-botanical remains were not preserved at the Besor-Grar sites, but phytoliths of wheat and/or barley were identified at Grar (Katz et al., 2007). Exceptionally high frequencies of sickle blades (24% at Grar) and grinding stones in both Gilat and Grar may be taken to indicate intensive cereal cultivation at these sites. Sickle blades were relatively rare in the Beersheva sites, perhaps attesting to lower investment in cereal agriculture or, as suggested by Levy et al. (2006) it may be attributed to the application of different harvesting techniques. As reported by Winter-Livneh et al. (2010), inter-cluster differences in agricultural strategies may also relate to variance in the topography and volume of the wadi systems associated with each cluster. Based on the low frequencies of lentils at Shiqmim, Kislev (1987) suggested that this may indicate a greater reliance on animal protein at this site, a much richer source of essential amino acids (protein) than plants. Although providing a ready source of high energy food (carbohydrates), cereals lack essential amino acids, vitamins and minerals, while phytates in the husks of cereals retard absorption of iron contributing to anemia (Hallberg et al., 1987; Sommer, 2008; Yamamah et al., 2007).

Caprine (sheep and goat) frequencies are especially high in the Nahal Beersheva sites (≥85% of identified remains) but constitute only ≤60% of the remains in the Besor-Grar sites (Gilat, Grar, Wadi Gazze D), where significant quantities of cattle and pig remains are found (Ducos, 1968; Grigson, 1993, 1995, 1998, 2006; Horwitz,

1990). The caprine mortality data reflects some interesting inter-cluster differences in herding management (Fig. 9), despite the small and/or uneven sample sizes as well as differential survivorship of the more fragile bones and teeth of immature caprines that may have biased the survivorship curves. At the Besor-Grar cluster sites (Gilat and Grar), the caprine survivorship curves strongly suggest herding strategies geared towards secondary products i.e. milk and wool production, with relatively low numbers of animals culled when immature and high numbers of animals surviving into adulthood (Grigson, 1995, 2006). Age data for cattle is limited due to small samples, but at Grar remains of cattle suggest "a generalized policy allowing for meat and breeding, probably with some milk production" (Grigson, 1995: 412). The ruminant mortality profiles at Gilat and Grar can be coupled with the presence of churns- vessels said to have been used to produce butter or yoghurt (Grigson, 1998), an idea supported by residue analysis of ceramics from Gilat (Burton, 2004; Chasan et al., 2022). Based on examination of cortical bone thickness in caprines, Smith and Horwitz (1984) have suggested that although milking was practiced in Late Chalcolithic sites in the Southern Levant, it was probably on a small-scale, subsistence level.

In contrast, caprine kill-off profiles in the Beersheva cluster sites – Horvat Hor and Shiqmim (Grigson, 1987a; Horwitz, 1990; Whitcher, 1999; Whitcher et al., 1998) do not indicate intensive secondary product exploitation but rather herds primarily raised for meat. At the site of Bir es-Safadi, a more nuanced result was obtained through separation of sheep and goats by sex (Grigson, 1987b). Results indicate, that at this site, most male caprines were slaughtered young (for meat) while higher frequencies of females survived into adulthood, particularly female sheep (57%) which Grigson (1987b) interpreted as possibly reflecting that a sector of the herd was managed for wool production. The cull profile represents a mixed meat-secondary products strategy, with reproduction the main driving force behind female survivorship.

Another inter-cluster distinction is the absence of pigs in the Nahal Beersheva sites and their presence in the Besor-Grar cluster (Fig. 9; Horwitz, 1990; Grigson, 2007). This reflects differences in environment and water availability as expressed in rainfall and site location, with pigs absent in sites in the more arid region below the 200 mm isohyet (Grigson, 1989, 1998, 2007). Pigs require daily access to standing water for wallowing in to control body temperature (Ranjhan, 1997) and so are ill-adapted to arid regions. In addition, pigs have a poor capacity to digest structural carbohydrates (cellulose and hemicellulose) found in wild-growing bushes and grasses, which provides nutrition for ruminants such as caprines and cattle in arid zones. Thus, the natural vegetation cover in arid regions offers limited quantities of foods for pigs (Ditchkoff & Mayer, 2009). Pigs also serve as an indirect indicator of sedentism at a site, since in addition to their water dependency, their short legs and temperament make them unsuited to travel very long distances.

As implied by the presence of pigs, the presence of standing water at, or near to, Gilat may have had negative consequences for the human population in providing a breeding ground for malarial-carrying mosquitoes. Thalassemia, a genetic mutation that arose in response to malaria, was already present in the Southern Levant in the Neolithic (Hershkovitz et al., 1991). Even during the British Mandate in Palestine, malaria was still a major cause of death throughout the region, including the Northern Negev (Kligler, 1924; Abu-Rabia, 2005; Alexander & Dunkel, 2017), and was even cited by Flinders Petrie (1934) as the reason for the abandonment of Bronze Age Tel Ajjul (Gaza) and its re-establishment on higher ground. In areas where it is endemic, malaria is still the major cause of death in infants (Institute for Health Metrics and Evaluation [IHME], Malaria Atlas Project, 2020). Even those who survive suffer from recurrent attacks in later life that cause anaemia. As noted above, this condition may be linked to the high prevalence of cribra orbitalia observed in Chalcolithic populations from the Northern Negev.

Extensive animal husbandry associated with the Chalcolithic may also have provided new opportunities for zoonotic pathogens (viruses, bacterial, parasitic and fungal infections) to spread to humans. For example, the benefit gained at the Besor-Grar complex sites via access to a more varied spectrum of animal protein (given the higher numbers of cattle and presence of pigs), may have been offset by the potential of these domesticates to contribute to the spread of a broad spectrum of diseases, such as cysticercosis from intestinal helminths *Taenia solium*, anthrax and tuberculosis (Horwitz & Smith, 2000; Maudlin et al., 2009). In addition, the incorporation of the donkey into the Late Chalcolithic economy as suggested by Grigson (1993, 2006, 2012), but see Milevski & Horwitz, 2019), although offering an economic advantage for transport and trade over greater distances than before, may have served as a source of viral infections in humans, such as equine influenza (Thiemann, 2012). Indeed, close contact between people and domestic animals would have greatly increased opportunities for the passive transfer of pathogens (via insect vectors, parasites in contaminated foods, liquids, hides and wool). The greater mobility of people having beasts of burden would have exposed Chalcolithic societies (and their animals) to novel environments where they would have encountered diseases previously unknown to them, and for which they had no immunity. In the Besor-Grar cluster, zoonotic diseases would have been further fostered by the sedentary lifestyle of these communities, while in the Nahal Beersheva sites, the spread and maintenance of zoonoses may have been more constrained given their more nomadic lifestyle that best suits caprine herders in semi-arid regions (e.g. Krader, 1959; Meir, 2019). The absence of pigs and large numbers of caprines (coupled with the caprine survivorship data) support the idea that the Beersheva complex population were nomadic or at least semi-nomadic on a seasonal basis (Levy, 1983).

Transhumance to a new locality would have offered some relief from the insanitary and crowded conditions of village life, and greatly reduced infectious disease (including zoonoses) thereby contributing to better health status as observed in these populations. In contrast, although the Besor-Grar sites had access to a broader spectrum of resources (animal protein included pork, milk and its products) and had a greater investment in cultivation of crops, they appear to have suffered from poorer health. The data points to year-round sedentism in this cluster, which in itself would have promoted infectious diseases including the transmission of zoonoses. In addition, the Chalcolithic populations probably suffered high rates of disease and even mortality when exposed to new pathogens, such as through activities related to trade, for which they had not acquired immunity. However, infection rates in both sites would have been exacerbated by poor sanitation as attested to by refuse pits in and around living areas, that point to a cavalier attitude to hygiene.

Alongside the differences in agriculture and animal husbandry, the site clusters also differ in the presence and range of craft specialization (Fig. 9), as expressed by metal and ivory working in the Beersheva sites (Shiqmim, Neve Noy, Bir es-Safadi), activities that are absent in the Besor-Grar cluster sites (Eldar & Baumgarten, 1985; Levy & Alon, 1992; Levy & Shalev, 1989; Oakberg et al., 2000). Craft specialization in the Beersheva sites is also attested in the proficiency demonstrated in production of uniform small V-shaped bowls at Shiqmim (Burton et al., 2018). Notably, the presence of craftsmen in the Beersheva cluster points to access to food surpluses that could sustain them (e.g., Garfinkel et al., 2009), and so perhaps a more affluent economy than the Besor-Grar cluster. However, specialized crafts such as pottery, bone/ivory, metal working and tanning animal hides, add to the contamination of land and water supplies, as well as to depletion and degradation of the natural environment already disturbed by farming activities, all factors that are deleterious to human health. Specifically, the manipulation and use of metals has been associated with environmental pollution and even poisoning (e.g. Erel et al., 2021; Eshel et al., 2020). While the scale of such industries in the Chalcolithic may have been relatively small, they already had an impact on human health as attested by the presence of arsenic in human remains from Shiqmim (Oakberg et al., 2000). There is also evidence for pollution of sediments resulting from pre-modern metallurgical activities, although the extent varies spatiotemporally within settlements and does not appear to have deleteriously affected areas outside sites e.g. field systems (Knabb et al., 2016).

In conclusion, there are a multiplicity of factors that may have contributed to the observed disparity in health status between the Beersheva and Besor-Grar site clusters, although there are also marked similarities between them. Diet in all Northern Negev sites was based on cultivated crops (cereals and legumes), with consumption of milk and milk products alongside meat. Specifically, the economy and diet in the Besor-Grar sites appears to have been more focused on cultivated crops and secondary products such as milk, while the Beersheva sites focused more on meat. While milk is a rich source of protein, like cereals it lacks some essential minerals and vitamins that are present in meat, fresh fruit and vegetables. Indeed, even at the present time, Bedouin children in the Near East with a restricted diet based primarily on cereals (bread), have been shown to suffer severely from deficiencies in essential minerals and vitamins due to malabsorption resulting from chronic intestinal infections—bacterial and parasitic (Abu-Saad et al., 2009; Coles et al., 2004; Yamamah et al., 2007).

The absence of craft specialists in the Besor-Grar sites implies a poorer economic base than sites in the Beersheva cluster. By themselves or together, these factors may have contributed to the more deleterious health status of the Besor-Grar population compared to the Beersheva complex communities. It should be emphasized though, that both Chalcolithic communities suffered a heavy disease load resulting in mortality at an early age preceded by ill-health, such that the difference between them was primarily one of scale.

In large parts of the world, malaria is a major cause of infant mortality, and there is extensive evidence that this disease was endemic in the Northern Negev settlements. However, even in the absence of "killer diseases" the effect of chronic infections on health and morbidity can be severe. A high disease load contributes to malnutrition through impaired absorption. One result is reduced resistance, which increases the likelihood of death from otherwise minor infections especially in infants (e.g. Scott & Duncan, 2000), while affecting those who survive with pain, disability and chronic fatigue and so impacting day to day functioning.

Following the "Neolithic Revolution," past human societies in the Southern Levant experienced an ever-increasing infectious disease load, with longevity and human health status in antiquity showing a significant decline over time (e.g. Bocquentin et al., 2021; Eshed et al., 2006, 2010; Hershkovitz & Gopher, 2008; Smith & Horwitz, 1984, 1989, 2007; Stutz et al., 2021). Thus, the Chalcolithic period in the Southern Levant, represents just one point along a diachronic trajectory of declining health that continued into the first years of the British Mandate of Palestine, as evident in the deleterious health status of the inhabitants of Ottoman Dor, corroborated by early twentieth century medical census records for the region (Kligler et al., 1924; Cantor, 1927; Abu-Rabia, 2005; Davidovitch & Greenberg, 2007).

Probably, no single factor was responsible for the high levels of disease present in the Chalcolithic, and more specifically for communities inhabiting the Northern Negev. Most likely it was a constellation of the factors discussed above-diet, poor sanitation, crowding and zoonotic infections-that contributed to this shared life experience. Thus, in the light of our results, it is tempting to add ill-health to the list of factors that contributed to the demise of Chalcolithic societies in the arid regions of the Southern Levant.

The methodological approach applied here, one which integrates data from bioanthropology and human paleopathology with information on archaeozoology and archaeobotany, has been extremely rewarding, providing greater insights into the Late Chalcolithic of the Northern Negev. Additional data on these populations may be obtained in the future through the application of comprehensive scientific methods such as ancient DNA/paleoproteomic analyses of dental calculus for diet, molecular diagnosis of specific diseases by tracing pathogenic DNA, residue analysis of ceramic or lithic artefacts and paleodietary analysis using stable isotopes (Richards & Britton, 2020). What is assured is that the basic bioanthropological analysis of the human skeletal remains will continue to serve as the starting point for such research which highlights the significant, but often overlooked, role played by health status in the history of the human populations of the Southern Levant.

Acknowledgments We thank the editors for the opportunity to participate in this Festschrift honoring Tom Levy. This study is based on material from Tom's excavations in the Negev, which stand as milestones in Chalcolithic research in the Levant.

References

Abu-Rabia, A. (2005). Bedouin health services in mandated Palestine. *Middle Eastern Studies, 41*(3), 421–429. https://doi.org/10.1080/00263200500106081

Abu-Saad, K., Shai, I., Kaufman-Shriqui, V., German, L., Vardi, H., & Fraser, D. (2009). Bread type intake is associated with lifestyle and diet quality transition among Bedouin Arab adults. *The British Journal of Nutrition, 102*(10), 1513–1522. https://doi.org/10.1017/S0007114509990675

Alexander, A., & Dunkel, F. V. (2017). Local malaria elimination: A historical perspective from Palestine 100 years ago informs the current way forward in Sub-Saharan Africa. *American Entomologist, 63*(4), E1–E14. https://doi.org/10.1093/ae/tmx060

AlQahtani, S. J., Hector, M. P., & Liversidge, H. M. (2010). Brief communication: The London atlas of human tooth development and eruption. *American Journal of Physical Anthropology, 142*, 481–490.

Bar-Matthews, M. A., & Ayalon, A. (2004). Speleothems as paleoclimatic indicators: A case study from Soreq Cave located in the Eastern Mediterranean region, Israel. In R. Battarbee, F. Gasse, & C. E. Stickley (Eds.), *Past climate variability through Europe and Africa* (pp. 363–391). Springer.

Bass, W. (1995). *Human osteology. A laboratory and field manual* (4th ed.). Missouri Archaeological Society.

Bloom, R. A., & Laws, J. W. (1970). Humeral cortical thickness as an index of osteoporosis in women. *The British Journal of Radiology, 43*(512), 522–527. https://doi.org/10.1259/0007-1285-43-512-522

Bocquentin, F., Chamel, B., Anton, M., & Nous, C. (2021). The subsistence and foodways transition during the Neolithisation process. Glimpses from a contextualized dental perspective. *Food & History, 19*(1–2), 23–52. hal-03381426.

Burton, M. M. (2004). Collapse, continuity, and transformation: Tracking protohistoric social change through ceramic analysis. *Case studies of late 5th–early 4th millennium societies in the southern Levant*. PhD Dissertation, University of California, San Diego.

Burton, M. M., & Levy, T. E. (2011). The end of the Chalcolithic period (4500–3600 BC) in the northern Negev Desert, Israel. In J. L. Lovell & Y. M. Rowan (Eds.), *Culture, chronology and the Chalcolithic theory and transition* (pp. 178–191). Oxbow Books.

Burton, M. M., & Levy, T. E. (2012). Chalcolithic social organization reconsidered: Excavations at the Abu Hof village, northern Negev, Israel. *Mitekufat Haeven: Journal of the Israel Prehistoric Society, 42*, 92–137.

Burton, M. M., Quinn, P. S., Tamberino, A., & Levy, T. E. (2018). Ceramic composition at Chalcolithic Shiqmim, Northern Negev desert, Israel: Investigating technology and provenance using thin section petrography, instrumental geochemistry and calcareous nannofossils. *Levant, 50*(2), 237–257. https://doi.org/10.1080/00758914.2019.1625656

Cantor, L. (1927). Public health engineering progress in Palestine. *American Journal of Public Health, 17*(4), 341–348.

Chasan, R., Spiteri, C., & Rosenberg, D. (2022). Dietary continuation in the Southern Levant: A Neolithic-Chalcolithic perspective through organic residue analysis. *Archaeological and Anthropological Sciences, 14*, 49. https://doi.org/10.1007/s12520-022-01519-0

Coles, C. L., Levy, A., Gorodischer, R., Dagan, R., Deckelbaum, R. J., Blaner, W. S., & Fraser, D. (2004). Subclinical vitamin A deficiency in Israeli-Bedouin toddlers. *European Journal of Clinical Nutrition, 58*(5), 796–802. https://doi.org/10.1038/sj.ejcn.1601879

Davidovitch, N., & Greenberg, Z. (2007). Public health, culture, and colonial medicine: Smallpox and variolation in Palestine during the British mandate. *Public Health Reports, 122*(3), 398–406. https://doi.org/10.1177/003335490712200314

Ditchkoff, S. S., & Mayer, J. J. (2009). Wild pig food habits. In J. J. Mayer & I. L. Brisbin, Jr. (Eds.), *Wild pigs: Biology, damage, control techniques and management* (pp. 105–143). Savannah River National Laboratory.

Ducos, P. (1968). *L'Origine des animaux domestiques en Palestine* (p. 6). Publications de l'Institut de préhistoire de l'Université de Bordeaux.

Eldar, I., & Baumgarten, Y. (1985). Neve Noy: A Chalcolithic site of the Beer-Sheba culture. *Biblical Archaeologist, 48*(3), 134–139.

Erel, Y., Pinhasi, R., Coppa, A., Ticher, A., Tirosh, O., & Carmel, L. (2021). Lead in archeological human bones reflecting historical changes in lead production. *Environmental Science & Technology, 55*(21), 14407–14413. https://doi.org/10.1021/acs.est.1c00614

Eshed, V., Gopher, A., & Hershkovitz, I. (2006). Tooth wear and dental pathology at the advent of agriculture: New evidence from the Levant. *American Journal of Physical Anthropology, 130*(2), 145–159. https://doi.org/10.1002/ajpa.20362

Eshed, V., Gopher, A., Pinhasi, R., & Hershkovitz, I. (2010). Paleopathology and the origin of agriculture in the Levant. *American Journal of Physical Anthropology, 143*(1), 121–133. https://doi.org/10.1002/ajpa.21301

Eshel, T., Yahalom-Mack, N., Tirosh, O., Maeir, A. M., Harlavan, Y., Gilboa, A., & Erel, Y. (2020). Pollution and human mobility in the Southern Levant during the Iron Age using chemical and isotopic analysis of human tooth enamel. *Journal of Archaeological Science, 124*, 105262. https://doi.org/10.1016/j.jas.2020.105262

Fabian, P., Sheftolovitz, N., & Gilead, I. (2015). Horvat Qarqar South: Report on a Chalcolithic cemetery near Qiryat Gat, Israel. *Israel Exploration Journal, 65*, 1–30.

Faerman, M., & Smith, P. (2008). Has society changed its attitude to infants and children? Evidence from archaeological sites in the Southern Levant. In F. Gusi, S. Muriel, & C. Olària (Eds.), *Nasciturus: Infans, Puerulus. Vobis MaterTerra. La Muerte en la Infancia* (pp. 211–229). Servei d'Investigacions Arqueològiques I Prehistòriques (SIAP): Diputació de Castelló.

Faerman, M., Zagerson, T., Dawson, L., & Smith, P. (in press). Burial customs and human remains from the Shiqmim cemetery and village. In T.E. Levy, Y.M. Rowan, & M.M. Burton (Eds.), *Desert chiefdom: Dimensions of subterranean settlement and society in Israel's Negev Desert (ca. 4500-3600 BC) based on new data from Shiqmim*. London: Equinox.

Farmer, P. (2004). An anthropology of structural violence. *Current Anthropology, 45*(3), 305–325.

Garfinkel, Y. (1999). *Neolithic and Chalcolithic pottery of the Southern Levant* (*Qedem 39*). The Hebrew University of Jerusalem.

Garfinkel, Y., Ben-Shlomo, D., & Kuperman, T. (2009). Large-scale storage of grain surplus in the sixth millennium BC: The silos of Tel Tsaf. *Antiquity, 83*, 309–325.

Gilead, I. (1984). The micro-endscraper: A new tool type of the Chalcolithic period. *Tel-Aviv, 11*, 3–10.

Gilead, I. (1988). The Chalcolithic period in the Levant. *Journal of World Prehistory, 2*, 397–443.

Gilead, I. (1994). The history of the Chalcolithic settlement in the Nahal Beer Sheva area: The radiocarbon aspect. *Bulletin of the American Schools of Oriental Research, 296*, 1–13.

Gilead, I. (Ed.). (1995). *Grar. A Chalcolithic site in the Northern Negev*. Ben-Gurion University of the Negev Press.

Gilead, I. (2011). Chalcolithic culture history: Ghassulian and other entities in the Southern Levant. In J. L. Lovell & Y. M. Rowan (Eds.), *Culture, chronology and the Chalcolithic theory and transition* (pp. 12–24). Oxbow Books.

Gilead, I., Marder, O., Khalaily, H., Fabian, P., Abadi, Y., & Yisrael, Y. (2004). The Beit Eshel Chalcolithic flint workshop in Beer Sheva: A preliminary report. *Mitekufat Ha'even: Journal of the Israel Prehistoric Society, 34*, 245–263.

Golden, J. M. (2014). *Dawn of the Metal Age. Technology and society during the Levantine Chalcolithic*. Routledge.

Goodman, A. H., Armelagos, G. J., & Rose, J. C. (1980). Enamel hypoplasias as indicators of stress in three prehistoric populations from Illinois. *Human Biology, 52*(3), 515–528.

Grigson, C. (1987a). Shiqmim: Pastoralism and other aspects of animal management in the Chalcolithic of the Northern Negev. In T. E. Levy (Ed.), *Shiqmim I. Studies concerning Chalcolithic societies in the Northern Negev Desert, Israel (1982–1984)* (BAR International Series 356) (pp. 219–241). Archaeopress.

Grigson, C. (1987b). Different herding strategies for sheep and goats in the Chalcolithic of Beersheva. *Archaeozoologia, 12*, 115–126.

Grigson, C. (1989). Shiqmim I – Archaeozoological aspects. *Mitekufat Haeven: Journal of the Israel Prehistoric Society, 22*, 111*–114*.

Grigson, C. (1993). The mammalian remains from the Chalcolithic site of Horvat Beter, excavation of 1982. *Atiqot, 22*, 28–31.

Grigson, C. (1995). Cattle keepers of the northern Negev: Animal remains from the Chalcolithic site of Grar. In I. Gilead (Ed.), *Grar. A Chalcolithic site in the Northern Negev* (pp. 377–416). Ben-Gurion University of the Negev Press.

Grigson, C. (1998). Plough and pasture in the early economy of the Southern Levant. In T. E. Levy (Ed.), *The archaeology of society in the Holy Land* (pp. 245–268). Leicester University Press.

Grigson, C. (2006). Farming? Feasting? Herding? Large mammals from the Chalcolithic of Gilat. In T. E. Levy (Ed.), *Archaeology, anthropology and cult: The Sanctuary at Gilat, Israel* (pp. 215–319). Equinox.

Grigson, C. (2007). Culture, ecology, and pigs from the 5th to the 3rd millennium BC around the Fertile Crescent. In U. Albarella, K. Dobney, A. Ervynck, & P. Rowley-Conwy (Eds.), *Pigs and humans. 10,000 years of interaction* (pp. 83–108). Oxford University Press.

Grigson, C. (2012). Size matters – Donkeys and horses in the prehistory of the southernmost Levant. *Paléorient, 38*(1/2), 185–201. https://doi.org/10.3406/paleo.2012.5468

Guy, H., Masset, C., & Baud, C. (1997). Infant taphonomy. *International Journal of Osteoarchaeology, 7*(3), 221–229. https://doi.org/10.1002/(SICI)1099-1212(199705)7:3<221::AID-OA338>3.0.CO;2-Z

Haas, N., & Nathan, H. (1973). An attempt at a social interpretation of the Chalcolithic burials in the Nahal Mishmar caves. In Y. Aharoni (Ed.), *Excavations and studies: Essays in honour of Professor Shemuel Yeivin* (pp. 143–153). Tel-Aviv University. (Hebrew).

Hallberg, L., Rossander, L., & Skånberg, A. B. (1987). Phytates and the inhibitory effect of bran on iron absorption in man. *The American Journal of Clinical Nutrition, 45*(5), 988–996. https://doi.org/10.1093/ajcn/45.5.988

Hermon, S. (2008). *Socio-economic aspects of Chalcolithic (4500-3500 BC) societies in the Southern Levant – A lithic perspective* (BAR International Series 1744). Archaeopress.

Hershkovitz, I., & Gopher, A. (2008). Demographic, biological and cultural aspects of the Neolithic revolution: A view from the Southern Levant. In J.-P. Bocquet-Appel & O. Bar-Yosef (Eds.), *The Neolithic demographic transition and its consequences* (pp. 441–479). Springer Science+Business Media B.V.

Hershkovitz, I., Ring, B., Speirs, M., Galili, E., Kislev, M., Edelson, G., & Hershkovitz, A. (1991). Possible congenital hemolytic anemia in prehistoric coastal inhabitants of Israel. *American Journal of Physical Anthropology, 85*(1), 7–13. https://doi.org/10.1002/ajpa.1330850103

Hershkovitz, I., Sarig, R., & May, H. (2021). Trends in ancient populations' osteobiography during the Holocene: The Levantine perspective. *Paléorient, 47*(1), 71–82. https://journals.openedition.org/paleorient/907#quotation

Hill, A. C. (2011). *Specialized pastoralism and social stratification – Analysis of the fauna from Chalcolithic Tel Tsaf, Israel*. PhD Dissertation, University of Connecticut.

Hillson, S. (2012). *Teeth*. Cambridge University Press.

Holl, A. F. C. (2019). The Chalcolithization process: Dynamics of Shiqmim site-cluster (northern Negev, Israel). *International Journal of Archaeology, 7*(2), 30–46. https://doi.org/10.11648/j.ija.20190702.12

Hopcraft, M. S., & Morgan, M. V. (2006). Pattern of dental caries experience on tooth surfaces in an adult population. *Community Dental Oral Epidemiology, 34*(3), 174–183. https://doi.org/10.1111/j.1600-0528.2006.00270.x

Horwitz, L. K. (1990). Animal bones from the site of Horvat Hor: A Chalcolithic cave-dwelling. *Mitekufat Haeven: Journal of the Israel Prehistoric Society, 23*, 153–161.

Horwitz, L. K., & Smith, P. (2000). The contribution of animal domestication to the spread of zoonoses: A case study from the Southern Levant. *Anthropozoologica, 31*, 77–84.

Institute for Health Metrics and Evaluation (IHME), Malaria Atlas Project. Global Malaria Incidence, Prevalence, and Mortality Geospatial Estimates 2000–2019. Seattle, United States of America: Institute for Health Metrics and Evaluation (IHME), 2020. https://doi.org/10.6069/CG0J-2R97.

Kahila Bar-Gal, G., & Smith, P. (2001). The human remains. In E. Eisenberg, A. Gopher, & R. Greenberg (Eds.), *Tel Te'o: A Neolithic, Chalcolithic and Early Bronze Age settlement in the Hula Valley* (pp. 163–169). Israel Antiquities Authority Reports No. 13.

Katz, O., Gilead, I., Bar (Kutiel), P, & Shahack-Gross, R. (2007). Chalcolithic agricultural life at Grar, Northern Negev, Israel: Dry farmed cereals and dung-fueled hearths. *Paléorient, 33*(2), 101–116.

Kerner, S. (2010). Craft specialisation and its relation with social organisation in the late 6th to early 4th millennium BCE of the southern Levant. *Paléorient, 36*(1), 179–198.

Kislev, M. (1987). Chalcolithic plant husbandry and ancient vegetation at Shiqmim. In T. E. Levy (Ed.), *Shiqmim I: Studies concerning Chalcolithic societies in the Northern Negev Desert, Israel (1982–1984)* (BAR International Series 356) (pp. 251–279). Archaeopress.

Kligler, I. J. (1924). Malaria in rural settlements in Palestine: 1. Incidence and etiology of malaria. *The Journal of Hygiene, 23*(3), 280–316.7. https://doi.org/10.1017/s0022172400034215

Kligler, I. J. (1932). Public health in Palestine. *The Annals of the American Academy of Political and Social Science, 164*(1), 167–177. https://doi.org/10.1177/000271623216400119

Knabb, K. A., Erel, Y., Tirosh, O., Rittenour, T., Laparidou, S., Najjar, M., & Levy, T. E. (2016). Environmental impacts of ancient copper mining and metallurgy: Multi-proxy investigation of human-landscape dynamics in the Faynan Valley, Southern Jordan. *Journal of Archaeological Science, 74*, 85–101. https://doi.org/10.1016/j.jas.2016.09.003

Kock, R., Michel, A. L., Yeboah-Manu, D., Azhar, E. I., Torrelles, J. B., Cadmus, S. I., Brunton, L., et al. (2021). Zoonotic tuberculosis – The changing landscape. *International Journal of Infectious Diseases, 113*(Suppl 1), S68–S72. https://doi.org/10.1016/j.ijid.2021.02.091

Kontulainen, S., Sievänen, H., Kannus, P., Pasanen, M., & Vuori, I. (2002). Effect of long-term impact-loading on mass, size, and estimated strength of humerus and radius of female racquet-sports players: A peripheral quantitative computed tomography study between young and old starters and controls. *Journal of Bone and Mineral Research, 17*(12), 2281–2289. https://doi.org/10.1359/jbmr.2002.17.12.2281

Krader, L. (1959). The ecology of nomadic pastoralism. *International Social Science Journal, XI*(4), 499–510.

Langgut, D., & Garfinkel, Y. (2022). 7000-year-old evidence of fruit tree cultivation in the Jordan Valley, Israel. *Scientific Reports, 12*, 7463. https://doi.org/10.1038/s41598-022-10743-6

Langgut, D., Cheddadi, R., Carrión, J. S., Cavanagh, M., Colombaroli, D., Eastwood, W. J., Greenberg, R., Litt, T., Mercuri, A. M., Miebach, A., Roberts, C. N., Woldring, H., & Woodbridge, J. (2019). The origin and spread of olive cultivation in the Mediterranean Basin: The fossil pollen evidence. *Holocene, 29*(5), 902–922. https://doi.org/10.1177/0959683619826654

Larsen, C. S. (2015). *Interpreting behavior from the human skeleton* (2nd ed.). Cambridge University Press.

Le Mort, F., & Rabinovich, R. (1994). L'Apport de l'étude taphonomique des restes humains à la connaissance des pratiques funéraires: Exemple du site chalcolithique de Ben Shemen (Israël). *Paléorient, 20*(1), 69–98.

Lev-Tov Chattah, N. (2005). *Health patterns and dental disease during the Chalcolithic period in the Southern Levant: Inferences for regional variation in lifestyle*. Unpublished PhD thesis, The Hebrew University of Jerusalem.

Lev-Tov Chattah, N., & Smith, P. (2006). Variation in occlusal dental wear of two Chalcolithic populations in the Southern Levant. *American Journal of Physical Anthropology, 130*(4), 71–479. https://doi.org/10.1002/ajpa.20388

Lev-Tov, N., Gopher, A., & Smith, P. (2003). Dental evidence for dietary practices in the Chalcolithic period: The findings from a burial cave in Peqi'in (northern Israel). *Paléorient, 29*(1), 121–134.

Levy, T. E. (1982). The Chalcolithic mortuary site near Mezad Aluf, Northern Negev Desert. A preliminary study. *Bulletin of the American Schools of Oriental Research, 248*, 37–59.

Levy, T. E. (1983). The emergence of specialized pastoralism in the southern Levant. *World Archaeology, 15*(1), 15–36. https://doi.org/10.1080/00438243.1983.9979882

Levy, T. E. (1987). *Shiqmim I: Studies concerning Chalcolithic societies in the Northern Negev Desert, Israel (1982–1984)* (BAR International Series 356). Archaeopress.

Levy, T. E. (1998). Cult, metallurgy and rank societies: Chalcolithic period (ca. 4500-3500). In T. E. Levy (Ed.), *The archaeology of society in the Holy Land*. Leicester University Press.

Levy, T. E. (2014). Introduction to the Levant during the Chalcolithic period. Regional perspectives. In M. Steiner & A. E. Killebrew (Eds.), *The Oxford handbook of the archaeology of the Levant 8000–332 BC* (pp. 203–211). Oxford University Press.

Levy, J. (2019). Clothes Maketh (Hu)Man: Textile production in the Southern Levant in the Chalcolithic period. In H. Goldfus, M. I. Gruber, S. Yona, & P. Fabian (Eds.), *'Isaac went out to the field': Studies in archaeology and ancient cultures in honor of Isaac Gilead* (pp. 172–202). Archaeopress. https://doi.org/10.2307/j.ctvndv7gk.17

Levy, T. E., & Alon, D. (1982). The Chalcolithic mortuary site near Mezad Aluf, Northern Negev Desert: A preliminary study. *Bulletin of the American Schools of Oriental Research, 248*, 37–59.

Levy, T. E., & Alon, D. (1985a). The Chalcolithic mortuary site near Mezad Aluf, Northern Negev Desert: Third preliminary report, 1982 season. *Bulletin of the American Schools of Oriental Research, Supplement, 23*, 121–135.

Levy, T. E., & Alon, D. (1985b). Shiqmim: A Chalcolithic village and mortuary center in the Northern Negev. *Paleorient, 11*, 71–83.

Levy, T. E., & Alon, D. (1992). A corpus of ivories from Shiqmim. In E. Stern & T. E. Levy (Eds.), *Eretz-Israel: Archaeological, historical and geographical studies* (Vol. 23, pp. 65–71). Israel Exploration Society. (in Hebrew).

Levy, J., & Gilead, I. (2012). Spinning in the 5th millennium in the Southern Levant: Aspects of the textile economy. *Paléorient, 38*(1–2), 127–139.

Levy, T. E., & Shalev, S. (1989). Prehistoric metalworking in the Southern Levant: Archaeometallurgical and social perspectives. *World Archaeology, 20*(3), 352–372. https://doi.org/10.1080/00438243.1989.9980078

Levy, T. E., Alon, D., Goldberg, P., Grigson, C., Smith, P., Buikstra, J., Holl, A., Shalev, S., Ben Itzchak, S., & Ben Yosef, A. (1990). Protohistoric investigations at the Shiqmim Chalcolithic village and cemetery: An interim report on the 1987 season. *Bulletin of the American Schools of Oriental Research, 27*, 29–46.

Levy, T. E., Grigson, C., Buikstra, J. E., Alon, D., Smith, P., Shalev, S., Goldberg, P., et al. (1991). Protohistoric investigations at the Shiqmim Chalcolithic village and cemetery: Interim report on the 1987 season. *Bulletin of the American Schools of Oriental Research, Supplementary Studies, 27*, 29–46.

Levy, T. E., Alon, D., Goldberg, P., Grigson, C., Smith, P., Buikstra, J., Holl, A., & Sabari, P. (1993). Protohistoric investigations at the Shiqmim Chalcolithic village and cemetery: An interim report on the 1988 season. *The Annual of the American Schools of Oriental Research, 51*, 87–106.

Levy, T. E., Burton, M. M., & Rowan, Y. M. (2006). Chalcolithic hamlet excavations near Shiqmim, Negev Desert, Israel. *Journal of Field Archaeology, 31*(1), 41–60.

Litt, T., Ohlwein, C., Neumann, F. H., Hense, A., & Stein, M. (2012). Holocene climate variability in the Levant from the Dead Sea pollen record. *Quaternary Science Reviews, 49*, 95–105. https://doi.org/10.1016/j.quascirev.2012.06.012

Lovell, J., Meadows, J., & Jacobsen, G. E. (2010). Upland olive domestication in the Chalcolithic period: New 14C determinations from el-Khawarij (Ajlun), Jordan. *Radiocarbon, 52*(2), 364–371. https://doi.org/10.1017/S0033822200045410

Manclossi, F., & Rosen, S. A. (2022). *Flint trade in the protohistoric Levant*. Routledge.

Marmot, M., Allen, J., Bell, R., Bloomer, E., Goldblatt, P., & Consortium for the European Review of Social Determinants of Health and the Health Divide. (2012). WHO European review of social determinants of health and the health divide. *Lancet, 380*(9846), 1011–1029. https://doi.org/10.1016/S0140-6736(12)61228-8

Maudlin, I., Eisler, M. C., & Welburn, S. C. (2009). Neglected and endemic zoonoses. *Philosophical Transactions of the Royal Society of London. Series B, Biological Sciences, 364*(1530), 2777–2787. https://doi.org/10.1098/rstb.2009.0067

Meir, A. (2019). *As nomadism ends. The Israeli Bedouin of the Negev*. Routledge.

Milevski, I. (2013). The transition from the Chalcolithic to the Early Bronze Age of the Southern Levant in socio-economic context. *Paléorient, 39*(1), 193–208.

Milevski, I., & Horwitz, L. K. (2019). Domestication of the donkey (*Equus asinus*) in the Southern Levant: Archaeozoology, iconography and economy. In R. Kowner, G. Shelach, G. Bar-Oz, M. Shahar, & M. Biran (Eds.), *Animals and human Society in Asia: Historical, cultural and ethical perspectives* (pp. 93–148). Palgrave Macmillan.

Miller Rosen, A. M. (2007). *Civilizing climate: Social responses to climate change in the ancient near east*. Rowman Altamira.

Nagar, Y. (2013). Physical anthropology of the Peqi'in population. In Z. Gal, D. Shalem, & H. Smithline (Eds.), *Peqi'in – A Late Chalcolithic burial site, upper Galilee, Israel* (pp. 391–406). Ostracon Press.

Nagar, Y., & Eshed, V. (2001). Where are the children? Age-dependent burial practices in Peqi'in. *Israel Exploration Journal, 51*, 27–35.

Nativ, A. (2013). *Prioritizing death and society. The archaeology of Chalcolithic and contemporary cemeteries in the Southern Levant*. Routledge.

Negbi, M. (1955). The botanical finds at Tell Abu Matar, near Beersheba. *Israel Exploration Journal, 5*(4), 257–258.

Oakberg, K., Levy, T. E., & Smith, P. (2000). A method for skeletal arsenic analysis, applied to the Chalcolithic copper smelting site of Shiqmim, Israel. *Journal of Archaeological Science, 27*, 895–901. https://doi.org/10.1006/jasc.1999.0505

Ortner, D. J. (2003). *Identification of pathological conditions in human skeletal remains*. Academic.

Ortner, D. J., & Frohlich, B. (2008). *The Early Bronze Age I tombs and burials of Bâb edh-Dhrâ, Jordan*. AltaMira Press.

Perrot, J. (1959). Statuettes en ivoire et autres objets en ivoire et en os provenant des gisements prehistoriques de la region de Beersheba. *Syria, 36*, 8–19.

Perrot, J. (1984). Structures d'habitat, mode de vie et environment. Les villages souterrains des pasteurs de Beersheva dans le sud dTsrael, au IVe millénaire avant le l'ère chrétienne. *Paleorient, 10*, 75–96.

Petrie, W. F. (1934). *Ancient Gaza IV*. British School of Archaeology in Egypt, University College.

Pimentel, D., Cooperstein, S., Randell, H., Filiberto, D., Sorrentino, S., Kaye, B., Nicklin, C., Yagi, J., Brian, J., O'Hern, J., Habas, A., & Weinstein, C. (2007). Ecology of increasing diseases: Population growth and environmental degradation. *Human Ecology: An Interdisciplinary Journal, 35*(6), 653–668. https://doi.org/10.1007/s10745-007-9128-3

Ranjhan, S. K. (1997). *Animal nutrition and feeding practices* (5th ed.). Vishal Printers.

Ribot, I., & Roberts, C. (1996). A study of non-specific stress indicators and skeletal growth in two Mediaeval subadult populations. *Journal of Archaeological Science, 23*, 67–79. https://doi.org/10.1006/jasc.1996.0006

Richards, M. P., & Britton, K. (2020). *Archaeological science. An introduction*. Cambridge University Press.

Roberts, C. A., & Manchester, K. (2005). *Archaeology of disease*. Sutton Publishing.

Rosen, S. A. (2019). Trade through the desert: A long-term perspective on goods, animals, and polities in the Negev. *Chungara Revista de Antropología Chilena, 51*(1), 71–84.

Rosenberg, D., Garfinkel, Y., & Klimscha, F. (2017). Large-scale storage and storage symbolism in the ancient Near East: A clay silo model from Tel Tsaf. *Antiquity, 91*(358), 885–900. https://doi.org/10.15184/aqy.2017.75

Rowan, Y. M., & Golden, J. (2009). The Chalcolithic period of the Southern Levant: A synthetic review. *Journal of World Prehistory, 22*(1), 1–92. https://doi.org/10.1007/s10963-009-9016-4

Scott, S., & Duncan, C. J. (2000). Interacting effects of nutrition and social class differentials on fertility and infant mortality in the pre-industrial population. *Population Studies, 54*(1), 71–87. https://doi.org/10.1080/713779065

Smith, M. E. (2019). Energized crowding and the generative role of settlement aggregation and urbanization. In A. Gyucha (Ed.), *Coming together: Comparative approaches to population aggregation and early urbanization* (pp. 37–58). State University of New York Press.

Smith, P., & Horwitz, L. K. (1984). Radiographic evidence for changing patterns of animal exploitation in the Southern Levant. *Journal of Archaeological Science, 11*, 467–475. https://doi.org/10.1016/0305-4403(84)90025-6

Smith, P., & Horwitz, L. K. (1989). Culture, environment and disease: Paleo-anthropological findings for the Southern Levant. In C. L. Greenblatt (Ed.), *Digging for pathogens. Ancient emerging diseases – Their evolutionary, anthropological and archaeological context* (pp. 201–239). Balaban Publishers.

Smith, P., & Horwitz, L. K. (2007). Ancestors and inheritors: A bio-cultural perspective of the transition to agro-pastoralism in the Southern Levant. In M. N. Cohen & G. M. M. Crane-Kramer (Eds.), *Ancient health. Skeletal indicators of agricultural and economic intensification* (pp. 207–222). University Press of Florida.

Smith, P., & Horwitz, L. K. (2009). A synthetic approach to the study of diet, health and disease in an Ottoman period population from Palestine. *Al-Rafidian, 30*, 78–106.

Smith, P., & Sabari, P. (1995). The Chalcolithic skeletal remains from Ḥorvat Ḥor. *Israel Exploration Journal, 45*(2–3), 128–135.

Smith, P., Bar-Yosef, O., & Sillen, A. (1984a). Archaeological and skeletal evidence for dietary change during the late Pleistocene/Early Holocene in the Levant. In M. Cohen & G. Armelagos (Eds.), *Paleopathology at the origins of agriculture* (pp. 101–136). Academic Press.

Smith, P., Bloom, R. A., & Berkowitz, J. (1984b). Diachronic trends in humeral cortical thickness of Near Eastern populations. *Journal of Human Evolution, 13*(8), 603–611. https://doi.org/10.1016/S0047-2484(84)80017-2

Smith, P., Zagersen, T., Sabari, P., Golden, J., Levy, T. E., & Dawson, L. (2006). Death and the sanctuary: The human remains from Gilat. In D. Alon & T. E. Levy (Eds.), *Archaeology, anthropology and cult – The sanctuary at Gilat (Israel)* (pp. 327–366). Leicester University Press.

Sommer, A. (2008). Vitamin A deficiency and clinical disease: An historical overview. *Journal of Nutrition, 138*(10), 1835–1839. https://doi.org/10.1093/jn/138.10.1835

Stutz, A. J., Bocquentin, F., Chamel, B., & Anton, M. (2021). The effects of early childhood stress on mortality under Neolithization in the Levant: New perspectives on health disparities in the transition to agriculture. *Paléorient, 47*(1), 45–70.

Thiemann, A. K. (2012). Respiratory disease in the donkey. *Equine Veterinary Education, 24*(9), 469–478. https://doi.org/10.1111/j.2042-3292.2011.00292.x

Volk, A. A., & Atkinson, J. A. (2013). Infant and child death in the human environment of evolutionary adaptation. *Evolution and Human Behavior, 34*, 182–192.

Waldron, T. (2008). *Paleopathology*. Cambridge University Press.

Whitcher (Kansa), S. E. (1999). *Animals, environment and society: A zooarchaeological approach to the Late Chalcolithic–Early Bronze I Transition in the Southern Levant*. PhD dissertation, University of Edinburgh.

Whitcher (Kansa), S. E, Grigson, C., & Levy, T. E. (1998). Recent faunal analysis at Shiqmim, Israel: A preliminary analysis on the 1993 assemblage. In H. Buitenhuis, L. Bartosiewicz, & A. M. Choyke (Eds.), *Archaeozoology of the Near East III* (pp. 103–116). ARC – Publicatie 18.

WHO. (2017, February 2). *Determinants of health*. https://www.who.int/news-room/questions-and-answers/item/determinants-of-health

Winter-Livneh, R., Svoray, T., & Gilead, I. (2010). Settlement patterns, social complexity and agricultural strategies during the Chalcolithic period in the Northern Negev, Israel. *Journal of Archaeological Science, 37*(2), 284–294. https://doi.org/10.1016/j.jas.2009.09.039

Yamamah, G. A. N., Hassan, H. M. S., Salama, E. E. E., Ghanem, K. Z., Hassan, M. A., & Hussein, M. A. (2007). Health profile of Bedouin children living at South Sinai. *Journal of Medical Sciences, 7*(6), 1009–1014. https://scialert.net/abstract/?doi=jms.2007.1009.1014

Zagerson, T., & Smith, P. (2002). Human remains from Kissufim road. In Y. Goren & P. Fabian (Eds.), *Kissufim road. A Chalcolithic mortuary site* (Israel Antiquities Authority Reports No.16) (pp. 57–65). Israel Antiquities Authority.

Socio-economic Complexity in Chalcolithic Villages: A Re-evaluation in Light of New Excavations

Yael Abadi-Reiss

Abstract To a large extent, our understanding of the socio-economic system of the Chalcolithic period in the southern Levant is based on excavations of sites in Israel's northern Negev. While hundreds of sites are known, discoveries from excavations of less than ten large villages are those that have outlined the socio-economic conclusions currently drawn regarding Chalcolithic cultural entities.

Discussions in the 1980s regarding the level of complexity in Chalcolithic society ranged from seeing it as a broad egalitarian society to perceiving it as a localized chiefdom. Small excavations in the following decades did not change these perceptions. Recent excavations of several large Chalcolithic villages, however, have now provided much-needed quality data that has changed the status of research and analysis. Information from excavations conducted during the last decade at the Chalcolithic sites of Tel Sheva, Agamim and Kuseife enable a better reassessment of the socio-economic complexity in this period.

Keywords Chalcolithic · Levant · Society · Economy · Ghassulian · Chiefdom

1 Introduction

The Chalcolithic period in the southern Levant existed between the late fifth and the mid-fourth millennia (Bourke et al., 2007; Braun et al., 2013; Rowan & Golden, 2009). This period, and the cultures and phases within it, have been studied over the last one hundred years (Rowan & Golden, 2009; Lovell, 2001: 1–10; Gilead, 2011). Significant and noticeable developments occurred during the Chalcolithic period: A change in the settlement pattern models and a marked increase in the size of the settlements (Rowan & Golden, 2009: 27–29; Winter-Livneh et al., 2013; Levy &

Y. Abadi-Reiss (✉)
Israel Antiquities Authority, Jerusalem, Israel
e-mail: yaelab@israntique.org.il

© The Author(s), under exclusive license to Springer Nature Switzerland AG 2023
E. Ben-Yosef, I. W. N. Jones (eds.), *"And in Length of Days Understanding" (Job 12:12): Essays on Archaeology in the Eastern Mediterranean and Beyond in Honor of Thomas E. Levy*, Interdisciplinary Contributions to Archaeology, https://doi.org/10.1007/978-3-031-27330-8_14

Alon, 1987); development of craft production on the household level and above (Lovell, 2011; Roux, 2003; Bourke, 2001), including the emergence of metallurgy (Shalev, 1994; Gandulla & Jeruf, 2017; Shugar, 2000; Gošić, 2015); the beginnings and growth of the use of secondary products (Greenfield, 2010; Price et al., 2013; Sherratt, 1981); new mortuary practices (Gorzalczany, 2018; Shalem, 2017; Rowan, 2014; Rowan & Ilan, 2013); unique symbolic and ritual expression (Harney et al., 2018; Commenge et al., 2006; Drabsh & Bourke, 2019) and a general advance in social complexity (Kerner, 2010; Levy, 1986, 2006; Rowan & Golden, 2009). The depth of this complexity is debatable. Less dramatic, but no less significant developments were perceived in subsistence economy (Rowan & Golden, 2009: 23–26), which advanced the trajectories of development from the Neolithic periods.

Although surveys and small-scale excavations in northern Israel indicate widespread distribution of Chalcolithic sites (Gibson & Rowan, 2006; Rowan et al., 2021; Getzov, 2016: 35*), much of the knowledge of Chalcolithic societies derives from the few regions where extensive excavation took place. The northern Negev sites particularly dominate our understanding of this period.

In the Chalcolithic period, the Ghassulian culture was the most prominent and significant cultural entity (Gilead, 2011; Bourke, 2001; Seaton, 2008; Lovell, 2011; Gilead, 1988; Levy, 1995), and through it one can trace social development. This article will focus on the Ghassulian cultural entity in its core area–the northern Negev (Fig. 1).

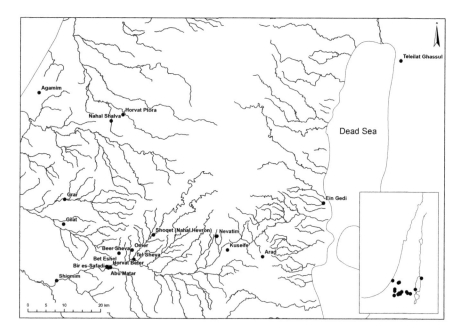

Fig. 1 Major Chalcolithic sites in the northern Negev. (E. Aladjem, IAA)

2 Identification of Social Complexity

The nature and the developmental paths of large-scale human social structures have long been of interest to archaeologists and anthropologists (see Carballo et al., 2014: 100–106). Interest in the Ghassulian entity is in the extent of its socio-economic complexity, that is in the socio-economic complexity during which transformation in a qualitatively and quantitatively different form of economic and social complex occurs, reflecting a new societal structure (Flannery, 1972: 409; Rothman, 2004; Parkinson & Galaty, 2007: 113;). The level of centralization of materials, methods and products and the difference in access to these resources within a society, are at the base of a complex society (Flannery, 1972: 409; Rothman, 2004: 76; Levy, 2006: 831). The more the signs of centralization occur, the higher the level of social complexity. Does everyone have the ability to get quality sickles? Can everyone learn how to work on a potter's wheel? Does everyone have access to ivory for sculpture? Can everyone use a loom? The 1980s saw an active discussion about the level of complexity in Chalcolithic society, ranging from viewing it as a broad egalitarian society to perceiving it as a localized chiefdom.

Levy (1986) suggested that the increase in social complexity and in ranked societies is the rise of chiefdom (Levy, 2006: 831), an idea that was accepted and strengthened in further studies (Gopher & Tsuk, 1996; Schick, 1998). The new trajectory of hierarchical and complex societies, Levy argued (2006: 835–842), was the consequence of maturing of several processes: the "secondary product revolution" (Greenfield, 2010; Levy, 1983, 1992; Price et al., 2013; Sherratt, 1981, 1983), the beginning of metallurgy (Shugar, 2003), the "fiber revolution" (McCorriston, 1997), the significant increase in population (Levy, 2006: 831) and the emergence of a regional cult center (Levy, 2006: 831). Some of these developments are widely accepted (and see Rowan & Golden, 2009), while others are less so.

Contrary to the complex society model, other studies enhanced the perception that the Ghassulian society was a simple, egalitarian one (Gilead, 1986; Gophna & Zuk, 1990). This perception undermined the settlement character of the northern Negev, suggesting that even in the Beer-sheba area, other than a separate group of farmers in villages, the people of the area were semi-nomads (Kenyon, 1979; Perrot, 1984: 79). According to this concept, the chiefdom model was more suitable, if only for a few sites in a small area in the south of the Ghassulian sphere (Gilead, 1986; Winter-Livneh et al., 2010). Some of the northern Negev sites that were interpreted as large villages, were actually a cluster of sub-sites, households that did not necessarily exist in parallel (Gilead & Fabian, 2001: 76). Gilead (1995a: 470; 1986) further suggested that the character of the Chalcolithic village was mixed farming—simple farmers and sheepherders, making them "the earliest *fellahin*[1] villagers in the Near East" (Gilead, 1995a: 470).

---

[1] 'Fallah' is the Arabic word for peasant, usually farmer.

3 Excavations at Ghassulian Sites in the Twenty-First Century

There have been many excavations at Ghassulian sites in the Mediterranean area over the past 20 years. Some have been extensive (van den Brink & Lazar, 2019; Elad et al., 2020 and see further references there; van den Brink et al., 2016; Eirikh-Rose et al., 2017; Barzilai et al., 2013; Kaplan et al., 2017; Milevski & Baumgarten, 2008; Gorzalczany, 2018), others on a medium and small scale (van den Brink et al., 2016; Jakoel & Be'eri, 2016; Agmon et al., 2019; Milevski et al., 2013; Govrin, 2015; Davidovich et al., 2013).

There are still entire areas where almost no large-scale excavations have been conducted at Chalcolithic village sites, although it is known that there are sites from the period. And as the results of Rowan and others (2021) research in the Lower Galilee shows the potential of sites not yet discovered is high (and see Getzov, 2016: 35*, of the Western Galilee).

The northern Negev is still the essential area of this culture, hence the core of the discussion is Ghassulian, with the understanding that the information added in the twenty-first century from excavations in the Mediterranean zone did not significantly alter the information on the Ghassulian culture.

Excavations at the large sites of the Chalcolithic period in the Beer-sheba Valley in the 1950s (Dothan, 1959; Perrot, 1984, 1955) formed the basis for the definition of the cultural entity. Additional excavations in the last third of the twentieth century, at new sites and returning to already excavated sites (Gilead et al., 1991; Levy, 1987, 2006; Levy et al., 1991; Levy & Alon, 1985; Baumgarten, 1986) were the basis for a reassessment of the cultural setting of the period (and see Rowan & Golden, 2009).

The most comprehensive analysis—353 sites in an area of 1252 sq. km in the northern Negev (Winter-Livneh et al., 2010)—collected data accumulated until 2008, but new sites are constantly being discovered. Even the large site of Agamim (below) was not known at all until it was excavated in 2018.

Several excavations were carried out in the current century. Some were studies carried out at already excavated sites (Abadi-Reiss, 2017; Abulafia, 2020), while new sites were constantly being discovered (Bischoff A8711/2021; Dobrinin A9126/2021). Alongside limited scale excavations a number of substantially large-scale excavations of Ghassulian sites took place in the northern Negev. In the Beer-sheba basin the Ghassulian village of Tel Sheva (Abadi-Reiss, 2016; Gilead, Talis and Aladjem A5631/2009;[2] Paz et al., 2014; Pasternak, 2020), the Shoqet site situated about nine kilometers to the northeast of Tel Sheva (Be'eri et al., 2017) and Kuseife village were excavated (Abadi-Reiss & Fraiberg, 2014) and on the southern Mediterranean coast, the large scale Agamim site was excavated (Abadi-Reiss & Varga, 2019, 2022; Varga et al., 2021). Smaller-scale excavations indicate other large and permanent settlements: Nahal Shalva (Israel et al., 2014), Nevatim (Gilead

---

[2] When referencing an unpublished excavation, the excavation license number and year appear.

& Fabian, 2001), Beer-sheba Compound C (Eisenberg-Degen & Talis, 2020; Vardi et al., 2020), Omer (Fraiberg A8916/2021), Beer-sheba Rakafot St. (Tchekhanovets et al., 2021) and Horbat Rakiq (Levi-Hevroni A8725/2020). Other types of sites were also excavated, such as the important sickle blade knapping industry site at Beit Eshel (Gilead et al., 2004) and the metallurgy industry in Horbat Beter (Ackerfeld et al., 2020). The existence of new data is extremely valuable and enables re-evaluating the social complexity of this culture.

Most of the data from the recent large-scale excavations are still being processed, but a review of the results that already exist allows the information to be incorporated into the discussion. The nature and the artifactual assemblages are clearly within the range of typical Ghassulian culture of the southern Levant: In all of them, the ceramic assemblage includes a wide diversity of open and closed forms. V-shaped bowls are common, and are considered hallmarks of the Chalcolithic pottery assemblages, alongside ceramic churns. The cornets—the *fossil director* of Ghassulian culture—complement the culture's identification according to the ceramic assemblage. Most vessels were hand-made, and bowls were finished on slow wheels. Clay was orange with gravel grits and burning was low. The flint industry basically used flake from local rock, producing typical tools such as backed sickle blades, bifacial celts and tabular scrapers.

Despite the significant differences in the methods of excavation, documentation, processing and analysis, the results confirm the description of the basic characteristics of this culture as concluded from the twentieth century excavations. The body of knowledge gathered in one hundred years of research is an empirical database and can be used.

3.1 Tel Sheva

The Ghassulian village of Tel Sheva is located on a small hill between Nahal Hevron and Nahal Beer-sheba. It was excavated by five different excavation expeditions (Baumgarten's excavation - A2062/1993; Abadi-Reiss, 2016; Gilead, Talis and Aladjem's excavation - A5631/2009; Pasternak, 2020; Paz et al., 2014), only one of which was fully published (Abadi-Reiss, 2016). The findings from all excavations reflect the intensity of the settlement array. In each excavation, subterranean complexes were discovered, as well as some remains of structures constructed on the surface.

Most of the excavated area seems to have been domestic, with hundreds of underground or semi-underground cavities that were discovered in Loess. The final stage for most of them was as a garbage dump (Abadi-Reiss, 2016). In the northern part of the site, however, it appears that the final use of several pits was for activities of a different sort altogether. Several of the pits, it seems, were used for the burial of objects and for human burials accompanied by offerings (Paz et al., 2014; Pasternak, 2020). Nearby, two pieces of a deliberately broken stone bowl were dumped separately (Paz et al., 2014). The burial in pits demonstrates the bowl's transition from storage vessel to another use that does not allow for continued activity in its previous state.

The pottery assemblage from two excavation areas (Abadi-Reiss, 2016; Abadi-Reiss & Pasternak, n.d.) presents a wide variety of tool types typical of the Ghassulian. These include V-shaped bowls, cornets and churns. The set of tools indicate storage, cooking, serving and ceremonies. The distribution of the tools does not indicate differences between the parts of the site, in accordance with the architecture, that is mostly residential. The same patterns are seen in the ceramic assemblages from Ghassulian sites in the vicinity of the nearby Beer-sheba sites: Abu Matar, Horbat Beter and Bir a-Safadi.

The dominance of bowls in the Ghassulian assemblies is striking when compared to ceramic assemblages from other, earlier, protohistoric cultures in the region (Fig. 2). V-shaped bowls are an important tool type for the identification of Ghassulian pottery. They are so prevalent in the ceramic complexes that they are the most common type in many pottery assemblages from large settlement sites, and are the only tool whose manufacturing process involves a potter's wheel. Their scattering pattern at sites, their high frequency and shape characteristics led to many suggestions that these were used for personal serving and eating—and very frequently (Commenge, 2006: 442), for pouring liquids or measuring volume (Commenge-Pellerin, 1987: 49). They were also used as candles (de Contenson, 1956: 173), for ceremonial purposes (Dollfus & Kafafi, 1993) and as receptacles serving the elite (Roux, 2010). Commenge (Commenge, 2006: 443) settled the apparent

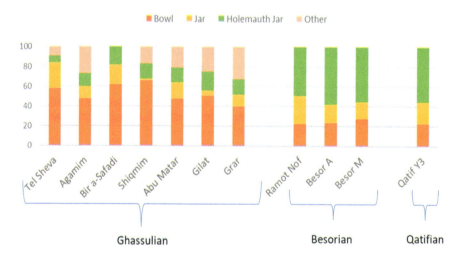

Fig. 2 Relative rate of pottery tool type in protohistoric assemblages. (Tel Sheva: Abadi-Reiss & Pasternk, n.d.; Bir a-Safadi: Commenge-Pellerin, 1990: Fig. 12; Shiqmim: Levy & Menachem, 1987: 315–7; Abu Matar: Commenge-Pellerin, 1987: Fig. 8; Gilat: Commenge, 2006: table 10.1; Grar: Gilead & Goren, 1995: Fig. 4.21; Ramot Nof: Nahshoni et al., 2002: Table 1; Besor A: Roshwalb, 1981: 74–80; Besor M: Roshwalb, 1981: 178–179; Qatif Y3: Abadi-Reiss, 2013: Table 3.4)

contradiction between daily and ceremonial use, defining them as multi-use tools utilized at different levels of the daily routine and social behavior of the individual.

In the Tel Sheva assemblage, half of the bowls are V-shaped, uniform in shape and in size, while the other half come in a wide variety of shapes and sizes. The scattering patterns of all the bowl types point in the direction of daily home use more than any other use. Examining their distribution in different areas of the site, types of spaces on the site and in relation to other tools, does not show a clear association between them and another variable.

Research at the Tel Sheva site confirms the conclusions about the nature of the large settlement sites that were previously excavated within the city of Beer-sheba. The intensive research of the site allows for a more accurate identification of the scattering of finds in the settlement area and of various stages that took place during the site's existence—including periods of different use of the quarried underground spaces, some of which moved from everyday domestic use to such one-time ceremonial uses as burial. This research enables us to distinguish between different areas of activity on the site. As for identifying the use of bowls, their spatial distribution at the Tel Sheva site is extremely wide; they are not limited to a particular location type and appear at all stages and sorts of activities.

3.2 Kuseife

Excavation in the eastern part of the Beer-sheba Valley unearthed the new multi-layer Chalcolithic site of **Kuseife** (Abadi-Reiss & Fraiberg, 2014; Abadi-Reiss & Fraiberg, n.d.). The Ghassulian settlement layers were discovered across the eastern and southern slopes of a hill, inside a natural cave (in Area D: Abadi-Reiss & Fraiberg, 2014: Plan 2, Fig. 7), above it (in Area D and Area B) and down the hill near other caves (Area A).

In Area A, there was an activity area: rooms built of narrow stone walls with a compacted earth floor and a stone floor covered with bitumen. Facilities were built in the rooms, including tabuns, and pits were hewn in the rock. The many floors, one above the other, indicate at least three phases of construction during the period. Up the hill (Area B), there was a domestic and cottage industry area, with rooms whose rounded walls were built of stone and mud bricks; pits fashioned in the rock, excavated in loess and hewn at the bottom; floors made of compacted soil and remnants of bonfires. In Area D, rectangular stone architecture was discovered inside and above a cave.

Intra-site differences can be identified in the artifacts. Focusing on Area A, most of the processed flint items (85%), most of the flint tools (94%), and most of the hammer stones (70%) were discovered there. It was a center of food storage and production, and craft manufacturing. The flint processing activity on the site was carried out near the northern cave, where there is also a natural source of flint. Half of the stone mortars and almost all the ground stone tools were discovered there, as well. Two large tabuns were also discovered there, surrounded by large amounts of ash, and a grain storage area was demarcated. Ninety-one percent of the animal bone finds were from sheep, which at that time were a food source. Up the hill, a larger area was devoted to residential buildings.

The Kuseife artifacts merge well with the technological and typological characteristics of Ghassulian culture. The most common pottery tool type is the V-shaped bowls, manufactured first by hand, and then on a potter's wheel. Also in the pottery assemblage were a variety of jars and holemouth jars, bowls and a few churns. The flint assemblage includes locally made ad-hoc tools, and a few scrapers, sickle blades and borers, made of a better-quality flint that originated far from the site.

The scarcity of sickles and ground stone tools suggests that the subsistence economy relied less on growing grain, compared to other sites in the Beer-sheba Valley. The material culture shows a clear cultural connection to the sites of the Ghassulian sphere, and the differences in the type of structures and the distribution of artifacts between the different areas demonstrate a clear regional division within the site. The various activity areas at the site are all at the household level, and no public activity was identified.

3.3 Agamim

Agamim is a Chalcolithic period site located in Ashkelon, on the southern coastal plain of Israel (Abadi-Reiss & Varga, 2019, 2022; Varga et al., 2021). It is a large, rural settlement that was buried under a cover of 2–3 m of alluvial soil; seven areas were excavated. Several Chalcolithic period strata were identified in each of these areas. The detailed analysis of the data is still in progress, but preliminary publications and some data can already be addressed.

The intensive and wide-ranging excavation, and the information from more than one thousand test trenches at a site that was covered and almost undamaged, allow an in-depth look at the question of social complexity.

All phases of life from the Chalcolithic period in Agamim belong to the Ghassulian culture, with the presence of the *fossile directeur* of the culture—the cornets, and assemblages of vessels typical of Ghassulian culture such as V-shaped bowls, churns, rectangular backed sickle blades, basalt bowls and copper artifacts.

The architecture at Agamim shows a separation of architectural spaces on the site according to different uses (Fig. 3). First, residential and domestic industry areas, constructed of narrow stone walls and mud bricks, where the general plan of each building varies from one layer to the next (Fig. 3: Area A, I, K, F. and see Abadi-Reiss & Varga, 2019: Fig. 4). Second, an industrial area that is separated from the village, next to which there is no domestic construction, but rather signs of copper processing (Fig. 3: Area E. Abadi-Reiss & Varga, 2019: Fig. 5).

Third, at the approximate center of the settlement, stand three remarkably large, rectangular buildings constructed of solid stone walls, about a meter wide (Fig. 3: Area C, J. Abadi-Reiss & Varga, 2019: Figs. 2, 3). They have been preserved up to a height of about one meter. These "broad room" buildings are also exceptional on the site with regard to the content of the artifacts on their floors. Dozens of large

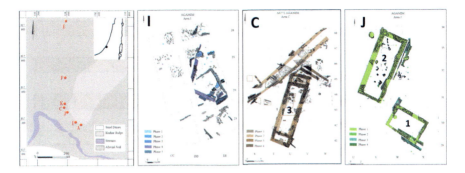

Fig. 3 Agamim: General plan of the Chalcolithic excavated areas; Layers plans of Areas I, C, J. (I. Azuolay, IAA)

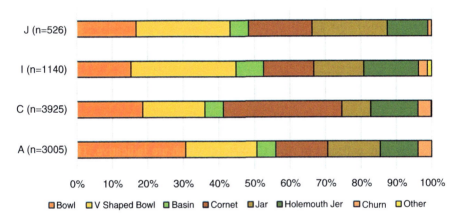

Fig. 4 Pottery types from four areas in Agamim

storage vessels in the middle of the hall, an ossuary, Canaanite blades, stone tablets and more, were discovered on the floor of Building 2, and copper axes were buried in two of its walls. Building 1 was almost completely empty, except for a jar buried under its floor. A large number of pottery vessels, half of which were cornets, were discovered in Building 3—an unusual rate relative to anything known in this culture (and see below).

While in the domestic areas there is no architectural continuity between the layers (Fig. 3: Area I), the continuity is evident in the plan of the large buildings: the plan of the building was maintained over a long period, and the changes and additions to it preserved its general plan.

The ceramic assemblage from Agamim shows a general resemblance between the various parts of the site (Fig. 4). On closer examination, mild differences between areas and layers can be discerned. Building 3 in Area C have a main hall in which two floors were identified: an early one made of crushed kurkar (Layer C3) and about 40 cm above it, a compacted earth floor (Layer C2). About 30,000

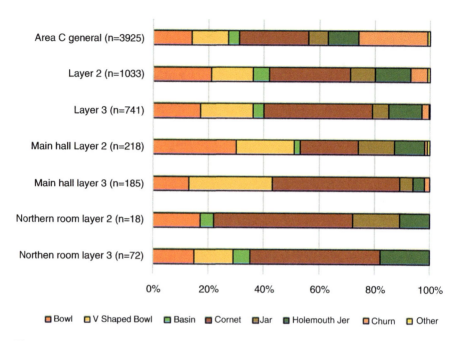

Fig. 5 Pottery types relative rate: different layers and parts in Area C, Agamim

potsherds were collected in Area C, 3925 of which are indicative. The complete cataloging of pottery by the four different layers in Area C makes it possible to identify models of space use through the types of pottery (Fig. 5). We focus here on Layers 2 and 3, in which the large structure was used. From a comparison of the typological distribution of the pottery tool types from Area C's different parts (Fig. 5), a very similar trend is observed in the relative rate of the types in general and in both layers. In all parts of Area C, and especially inside Structure 3, the relatively high proportion of cornets is notable. It is unusually high relative to ceramic assemblies from other sites (Table 1), and also high within the site of Agamim (Fig. 4). The highest relative rate is found within the floor of the main hall in Stratum 3, and the northern room in Strata 2 and 3. The unusual amount of this special tool, synchronized with the special structure, points to an unusual use for this structure, which should be linked to ceremonial activity. The use of cornets is intriguing. Since they could not stand on the pointed base, it is widely accepted that they were used for cultic purposes (Gilead & Goren, 1995; Ussishkin, 2014).

Upon examination of the distribution of tool types in the hall, there is a clear discrepancy between the number of cornet bases and their possible rims. Even assuming that all the bowl rims from this floor are cornet rims, a significant gap still remains. Hence, at least some of the cornets did not break inside the hall, and the negligible pattern of the fragments separated the base and rim of these tools systematically. The question about the use of this unusual tool, which despite many

Table 1 Relative rate (out of the total indicative sherds), and absolute number of cornets in Ghassulian sites

Site	% from indicative sherds	Absolute no.	
Ein-Gedi	40	200	Ussishkin (2014: 21; 1980: Table 1.18)
Agamim (area C)	25	969	
Agamim (general)	18	1512	
Horbat Zur	15.6	52	Eirikh-Rose et al. (2017: Table 1)
Namir road	14.3	43	van den Brink et al. (2016: 70)
Grar	11	138	Gilead & Goren (1995: Fig. 4.21)
Horvat Beter		65	Dothan (1959: 27), Rosen and Eldar (1993)
Tel Sheva north	1	20	Abadi-Reiss & Pasternak (n.d.)
Tel Sheva 36		7	Abadi-Reiss (2016: 52*)
Gilat	1	112	Commenge (2006: Table 10.1)
Omer	0.4	1	Fraiberg & Abadi-Reiss (n.d.)
Hatzerim	3	1	p.c. Bischoff
Abu-Matar	0.1–0.4		Commenge-Pellerin (1987: Tableau 2)
Bir es-Safadi	0.03		Commenge-Pellerin (1990: Tableau 1)
Shiqmim	0	0	Levy & Menachem (1987:319)
Nevatim	0	0	Gilead & Fabian (2001)
Kuseife	0	0	

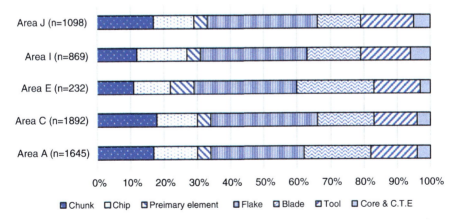

Fig. 6 Flint artifact types from five areas in Agamim

suggestions, is still open, and receives here for the first-time information about a special negligible model.

The uniformity in the relative proportion of flint artifacts of different types, between the areas (Fig. 6), indicates a similar function of flint use throughout the site. It is evident that most of the flint production did not take place in the excavated parts of the site. An unusual phenomenon is the presence of Canaanite blades as an integral part of the assemblage, both of tools and of debris and cores.

External relations of Agamim are expressed in two main ways: material connection and cultural connection. A wide variety of raw materials were discovered at the site, many of which did not originate locally: obsidian, hematite, pure copper and arsenic copper, shells from the Nile, basalt, tabular flint and metamorphic sandstone. Some of the prominent production specialties of the period, such as metallurgy, the use of a potter's wheel and basalt vessel production, all of which are represented at Agamim, clearly require the use of distant resources.

A clear separation of architectural spaces was identified according to different uses at Agamim village. This was found in different construction style, with different material culture characteristics and opposing trends of continuity throughout the stages of settlement of the site between the types of built spaces. The site reflects a complex social system, one that enables and requires public construction and separates uses between parts of the locality.

Agamim is part of the Ghassulian sphere in every aspect examined. Its resemblance to sites in the desert areas (Teleilat Ghassul, Shiqmim, Tel Sheva and others) stands out against the background of being located in the Mediterranean climate zone. In other words, its cultural affiliation is stronger than the characteristics of the environment. Moreover, it is characterized more as Ghassulian—as defined at the key site in a distance of one hundred kilometers away, Teleilat Ghassul—than one of the regional variants in the northern Negev.

4 Identifying Socio-economic Complexity

There are many aspects through which to test the degree of socio-economic complexity. The material indicator revealed in this century's excavations for the level of complexity—the asymmetrical social, economic and political relations within a society—can make the understanding of the degree of social complexity clearer. Following, I will review resource control, complex trade, Inter-and Intra-Site complexity and community cooperation.

4.1 Resource Control

The control over aspects of resources and production is an expression of social complexity (Schortman & Urban, 2004: 193; Costin, 1991; Carballo et al., 2014: 105). Identifying the distribution of resources accessible to everyone, or those that only a part of the population has access to, is a way of examining social and economic complexity. The means of production can be reflected in the control of the raw material, the appropriate tools required for production, and the required knowledge, as well as in product distribution mechanisms.

Some of the materials and manufacturing techniques were available to everyone and can be seen in household-level production systems ("cottage industry"): handmade pottery manufactured from local clay; production of ad hoc tools from local flint; ground stone tools from beach rock at Agamim and from limestone in the Beer-sheba basin; Mediterranean shells in Agamim. Alongside these systems, there were production systems that required the acquisition of remote raw materials, and sometimes also specific knowledge and production tools.

In the stone tool and vessel assemblages, the portion of raw materials originating far away from the sites stands out, to a greater (Abadi-Reiss & Varga, 2022; Lee, 1973; Perrot, 1955) or lesser degree (Abadi-Reiss, 2016: 59*–60*; Gilead, 1995b: Table 7.3; Rowan et al., 2006; Scheftelowitz, 2004). The distribution of stone tools is widespread, at every site and is noticeable in every household: 750 stone artifacts at Agamim, 123 in Grar (Gilead, 1995b: Table 7.3), 1922 in Gilat (Rowan et al., 2006 and Rowan, 2006: Table 12.34). It indicates regular manufacturing activity that partly relied on available sources and partly needed a regular supply system and hence a required consistent arrangement of foreign relations.

In the Ghassulian culture, there are two fields of production in which there is a great deal of centralization, both in terms of access to tools and technology, and in terms of access to knowledge itself: metalworking (Gošić, 2008; Golden, 1998; Ackerfeld et al., 2020), and the use of a potter's wheel (Roux, 2010, 2019; Roux & Miroshedji, 2009). Researchers in the field define this knowledge and use of tools as exclusive, but the products are found at many sites. Looking at Agamim, the two copper axes found hidden in two opposite walls of a building had to come from a highly professional metal workshop. The 1400 V-shaped bowls, many of which come with wheel marks, indicate the presence of a potter's wheel and an expert potter. Possibly, other products follow a similar pattern of specialized production centers. The sickle blade workshop in Beit Eshel (Gilead et al., 2004), and the tabular scrapers' workshops in the Negev (Manclossi & Rosen, 2021: 139) are an example. Possibly so are basalt quarries, production workshops (365 basalt artifacts at Agamim, no knapping waste), and Canaanean blade specialization (a few dozen blades, core and core trimming elements in Agamim).

The production systems above the household level indicate a high level of complexity. The differences between household-level production, cottage industry, and industrial and specialty industry centers, ensure a clear asymmetry within the society.

Another aspect reflecting limited access to resources is in obtaining rare or distant materials. The effort involved in obtaining these raw materials is also related to access to distant territories, through cooperative relations (with the possibility of access to the source), exchange or trade, or achieved by violence (raiding) (Abadi, 2003: 4–5).

Most of the large villages contain complex underground systems dug in the loess (Abadi-Reiss, 2021: 134) that reach hundreds of subterranean spaces (Abadi-Reiss,

2016; Baumgarten, 1999; Paz et al., 2014; Perrot, 1984). The importance of underground spaces as a reflection of socio-economic systems is great, in the context of the storage potential inherent in them. Storage itself reflects the ability to accumulate property, which is part of the growth of economic complexity. Storage is just one of a variety of potential uses for these spaces (Abadi-Reiss, 2021) but even in partial use for storage, there is plenty of room. Large and numerous storage spaces reflect storage capacity above the household level, which supports risk management and the economy of redistribution (Flannery, 1972; Levy, 1993). Storage at such a level is also evidence of the possibility of violent conflicts, whether as preparation for scarcity or as relief of power by large-scale construction (Clare, 2010: 21; Konrad & Leininger, 2011; Zhang et al., 2007).

4.2 Complex Trade

In the Chalcolithic artifact production system, there are raw materials that are available near the sites—for example, flint pebbles, limestone and herbal materials—and others that are located a few days' walk from most sites—basalt from the Golan and Arava, metamorphic sandstones from the Ramon Crater, tabular flint from the Negev, Mediterranean seashells, ochre and more. A few materials come from long distances away: obsidian, hematite, Nile shells and Red Sea shells, copper and arsenic copper, Ivory, hippopotamus teeth. This wide range of materials is found in many of the large Ghassulian sites (Perrot, 1955; Abadi-Reiss, 2016; Scheftelowitz, 2004; Wright, 1992; Gilead & Fabian, 2001; Bourk et al., 2000) and the three sites described above: obsidian, hematite, pure copper and arsenic copper, shells from the Nile, basalt, tabular flint, metamorphic sandstone. Long-distance intra-regional exchange networks required a degree of complexity (Baum, 2004: 72–3; Rupp, 1993: 3). The variety of artifacts whose source of raw material is far away from the areas of the Ghassulian culture, shows that there were connections with a distant population that did not belong to the Ghassulian cultural entity.

There were several supply chains, different from each other in character: in the range of attainment, in the nature of the ties with others—whether within or outside the Ghassulian cultural areas, in the rarity of the product, in the cost of transportation and in its overall value. In a society that produces surplus, it is likely that there was also trade in agricultural products and by-products. A parallel system of exports is likely. However, at this stage of the study it is difficult to validate this assumption.

4.3 Inter- and Intra-site Complexity

The characteristics of the socio-economic interactions inside the site and between sites, are a manifestation of the socio-economic attributes. As such, they are an indicator of the level of complexity. The built environment in the settlement is an indicator of the relationship between the household and the community (Banning, 2010). The settlement distribution patterns of a site within a landscape provide information about social and economic organization (Clarke, 1977; Conard, 2001). The settlement hierarchy is an indication of complexity (Wright, 1984: 43–4). Likewise, Mortuary segregation is a manifestation of complexity (Wright, 1984: 43–4). On a smaller scale, the architecture in the sites is a visible manifestation of the community organization (Byrd, 1994; Flannery, 1972; Wilson, 1988).

4.3.1 Inside the Site

The architecture and the spatial distribution of artifacts in it are a visible manifestation of community organization. In the three excavations of large settlement sites presented above, there is a certain degree of division into areas within the site. Any area in the village involving activities that are not at the level of the household is communal. At these sites, it is evident that such areas are permanent. In the Agamim site, it is also evident that a central location, investment in construction and maintenance, and unique artifacts have been devoted to the communal space. Unlike the large-scale sites, differences between households that indicate a social hierarchy have not been identified in Chalcolithic villages. Some degree of ranked society was identified at Palmahim cemetery (Gorzalczany, 2018: 73, 75).

Architectural differentiation is another sign of a complex society (Bourke, 2001: 151; Joffe, 2003: 53). Such differences become apparent in large-scale excavations at village sites, and especially in the three surveyed above. Public structure is harder to identify and it seems that Agamim is the only recent contribution to the subject. The three public buildings in Agamim, consistent in their plan and construction characteristics, and different from each other in their content, reflect the fulfillment of several different needs of the community. It is a manifestation of what is important for continuity (and what is not), reflecting a long-standing public investment and representing the ongoing needs of the community.

4.3.2 Site Hierarchy

The analysis of survey data (Winter-Livneh et al., 2010; 2013) shows the extent of the Chalcolithic presence in the northern Negev and strengthens the fact that the Ghassulian villages are base sites—site-centers—for hundreds of small ephemeral sites (Winter-Livneh et al., 2010: 286; Abadi-Reiss, 2021).

In the Chalcolithic northern Negev, sites were clustered, especially along riverbeds (Winter-Livneh et al., 2010). Out of hundreds of sites in this area (Winter-Livneh et al., 2010: 286), less than 20 have been defined as large sites (Abadi-Reiss, 2021: 134). The structure is of a few large rural settlements (Abadi-Reiss, 2021: 135–137), and many small settlements or other types of sites: mortuary sites (Fabian et al., 2015; Gal et al., 1997; Gorzalczany, 2018), an intentionally separated production area (Abadi-Reiss & Varga, 2022), worship sites, farmsteads and seasonal shepherds' camps (Gilead, 1988).

In such a system, the model of territories proposed by Levy (1986: Fig. 8) makes great sense, but it is necessary to re-examine and assimilate the current information.

The presence of large-scale underground formations in the large settlement sites is another difference between sites: the architecture of the big ones is more complex, and might serve the safe storage needs for the communities from the smaller settlements.

4.3.3 The Ghassulian Sphere

The resemblance between the characteristics of the material culture at Ghassulian sites that are distant from each other is significant. Teleilat Ghassul and Agamim are 100 km away from each other. The repeated appearance of characteristics of the Ghassulian cultural entity in hundreds of sites spread over hundreds of square kilometers (see Rowan & Golden, 2009: Fig. 1), allows the identification of a significant cultural sphere. It shows that there was a continuous connection, which was expressed both in daily life—in the great similarity in the tool kits—and in the socio-economic-religious system. A constant flow of ideas and information reassured and strengthened cultural identity in the Ghassulian sphere. This reflected in the long-term trading relationships presented above; in the basic package of V-shaped bowls, cornets and churns that appear again and again at the sites; in the uniformity of the two main ceramic technologies—hand-made and wheel-shaped (Roux, 2019)—and the distinctive artistic expressions (Harney et al., 2018). There are strong cultural ties within the Ghassulian sphere, within which the various levels of the settlements are located, in addition to the set of economic ties reviewed above.

4.4 Community Cooperation

During the Chalcolithic period, there was clear cooperation above the household level (Lovel, 2011), and large community structures in Agamim are a good example of such cooperation. The question is, to what extent the collaboration was reached, and how it was arranged. The issue can be explored through the signs of resource concentration, public construction and worship.

Dynamic relations exist among processes of production, consumption, distribution and the organization of power. These are signs of concentration of resources (Schortman & Urban, 2004: 187) and they need to be regulated and organized. Medium- and long-term trading systems, which provide raw materials for significant manufacturing activity, cannot rely on randomness but need to be managed.

The different levels of production systems, from the household level to specialized production centers (sickle blades, wheel-made pottery, metallurgy), are possible when there is a suitable economic and social organization. To these must be added the wide-range distribution arrays, thanks to which sickle blades travel from the workshop in Beit Eshel throughout the Negev, basalt bowls are brought to all the large villages and tabular flint is carried to sites far from its source. The arrangement of exchange arrays requires contact with neighboring cultures. For example, in the south, the source of many raw materials (metamorphic sandstones, granite, tabular flint, bitumen) is in the spreading areas of the Timnian culture (Rosen, 2013, 2017; Rosen & Goring-Morris, 2018; Manclossi & Rosen, 2021: 139).

The construction of storage spaces that are beyond the household level (Abadi-Reiss, 2021; Clare, 2010; Levy, 1993) reflects the need for storage at such a level, both for excess production and for a common community goal. It expresses the community's long-term need, and indirectly, the community's intention to deal collectively with scarcity.

The existence of central buildings, which are not used as a household, requires both concentrated work in cooperation, the joint agreement to place them in the settlement and conceptual support with regard to their meaning embedded within the society. At sites where there are differences between the parts of the village, above the level of the household, the community must give its consent, i.e., there are mechanisms involved in the agreement and a need for the right person to coordinate.

Several significant sites have been added to the existing knowledge regarding ceremonies and worship in Ghassulian culture. These include the cemetery in Palmachim (Gorzalczany, 2018); the ritual activities reflected in several artifacts buried at Tel Sheva (Pasternak, 2020; Paz et al., 2014); the unusual distribution models of finds in public buildings at Agamim—including the atypical number of cornets in one building, the dominance of storage vessels and ossuaries in the second building and the emptiness in the third building. Even if a particular definition of the manner of worship and rituals has not yet been formulated, their complex existence, public nature and place in the social fabric are clear and imply ritual activity.

The sub-systems of economic, social and religious structures of the Ghassulian culture required cooperation; these systems cannot be stable without it. Cooperation requires coordination. The coordinators are the key people in the community. The question of who regulated the activity in these areas is the question of associating this culture with defined social arrays.

5 Level of Complexity, Level of Leadership

In order to live as part of a complex community, people provide a portion of their production and autonomy for the economic and political arrangements of the society (Clark & Parry, 1990; Schortman & Urban, 2004: 187). The basic arrangement of production and distribution of a nuclear family or household is simpler than that of a bigger group. When a community is organized for cooperation, it needs someone to lead and arrange its members (Carballo et al., 2014: 100; Baum, 2004). The need also exists in organizing public construction, leading traditions of joint burial, forming a cultural identity and more. In the definition of who leads and organizes the collaborations of the community, its level of complexity will also be defined.

5.1 Big Man

A" big man" ("center man") is a natural leader in a small-scale hierarchical society (Baum, 2004; Sahlins, 1963). It is not as much a role as it is the functioning of a member of the community due to his personal abilities to initiate and motivate others (Baum, 2004; Sahlins, 1963). In this system the big man status is conditional, based on his ability to benefit the individuals—his followers—in a clear and immediate manner (Carballo et al., 2014: 100; Baum, 2004, Sahlins, 1963).

The level of economic, social and religious complexity of Ghassulian culture clearly requires an organizing leader. The big man political system is generally unstable and lasts for short terms. But in this culture, there is a constant need for regulation. Metallurgy, for instance, requires a group that holds the knowledge and materials from different and remote sources outside the Ghassulian sphere. In order for this to be an ongoing activity, coordination needs to be regular and long-lasting. The construction of a large, centralized structure can be the result of short-term, hard work investment, but its maintenance, while carefully preserving its original building plan changes, indicates continuity in decision-making and leadership. Also, the class asymmetry that is part of the Ghassulian system is not a temporary matter. Likewise, it seems that the authority could not have been temporary and therefore the "big man" model does not apply.

5.2 Chiefdom

A chiefdom society is a ranked socio-political entity with a stable redistribution system in which general social control activities are subsystem-based (Service, 1962: 144; Wright, 1977, 1984: 42; Bondarenko, 2014: 222; Abrutyn & Lawrence, 2010). The chiefdom authority position is more stable than that of the "big man." Chiefdom as a social system often includes not only the ability to collect sufficient labor to build large buildings, but also the ideology to justify the need for these efforts (Stanish, 2001: 44; DeMarrais et al., 1996).

The production, distribution, community organizing and ceremonial activities of the Ghassulian culture can take place in a society led by a chief. The array of Ghassulian sites where there are few large and complex settlements and many small and simple settlements is also suitable for a social structure that has a certain degree of centralization.

No signs of a definite class hierarchy were identified in domestic areas, but there are signs of some degree of a ranked society in cemeteries.

The ruling class in a chiefdom is stable and inherited, and the preservation of society's power structures can be seen reflected in the continuity of style and cultural characteristics.

5.3 Pre-State

The degree of hierarchy and status differentiation in a pre-state society is significantly higher than that of a tribal society (Feinman & Neitzel, 1984: 77; Baum, 2004: 77; Wright, 1977). Even if it does not necessarily reach the next level of complexity—urbanity—it is a very complex system, with considerable class differences.

Some regard the Pre-State as a "complex chiefdom" (Alizadeh, 1998: 31; Bondarenko, 2014: 219) in which there is a clear ranked group in a highly developed entity. However, increasing complexity for itself does not indicate a pre-state formation, and the emergence of a higher level of complexity is not a simple trajectory (Abrutyn & Lawrence, 2010; Rosen, 2021). According to the current data, it is difficult to support the idea of strong social differences, a non-productive status and an administrative system in the Ghassulian culture.

6 Conclusions

The definition of the socio-economic alignment of the Ghassulian cultural entity was placed in the range between a hierarchical tribal society (chiefdom) and a society that is mostly egalitarian.

The discussion of socio-economic complexity relied on information that was available to researchers at the time. Now that new information has been accumulated from sites excavated on a large scale in the core area of this culture, its level of complexity can be re-evaluated.

In the Ghassulian society of the Chalcolithic period there were complex systems of production, surplus, storage and trade economies, arranged over great distances as well as within the communities themselves. These separate levels and purposes of production differentiate between individuals within the group. Part of the communities lived in large villages, where there were collaborations at the community level that enabled the social regulation of tensions between the basic units that make up the community. Within the large settlement sites, the community separated areas according to the activities performed there and the meaning allocated to these areas. Outside the settlement, in growing circles, the communities maintained complex relationships with other communities that were part of the Ghassulian cultural sphere, as well as with distant communities belonging to other cultures.

The regulation and organization of these economic and social systems involved ideological, ceremonial, and religious development that confirmed to the group the existing array and strengthened it. These developments are evident in the large cemeteries, in the stylistic uniformity, in the fixed standard for V-shaped bowls and in the construction of public buildings.

The characteristics of the rule and authority are too complex and long-term to fit the pattern of a "big-man" model, and yet they do not reach the governmental and class level of the systems of pre-state and urbanity. The governmental system was composed of chiefdom arrays centered on large and complex permanent settlements, to which clusters of small settlements, temporary settlements, production centers, cemeteries and more belonged. All these are part of the array managed from the center. It is conceivable that in the periphery the array of a big-man, which suited the smaller and less complex communities, was preserved. This is similar to the manner in which the avoidant socio-economic array was preserved in the south.

1. Another thought

Did urbanity develop immediately in the wake of Chalcolithic society? The possibility that this culture was pre-urban must be ruled out as it did not continue to develop in that direction. The emergence of socio-economic complexity is not a single event, single threshold, or innovation (Abrutyn & Lawrence, 2010), as in the development of pastoral nomadism in the proto-historic Negev (Rosen, 2021). In the Chalcolithic period, the development towards increasing complexity (socio-economic-religious-governmental complexity) was interrupted and did not mature into urbanity and a state. It is possible that the sharp neglect of the Chalcolithic traditions—the all-too-distinctive ceramic tradition of V-shaped lipstick-covered bowls, churns and cornets; the ritual practice (copper items from Nahal Mishmar, in the purifiers); the settlement patterns—is related to renouncing the ruling religious elite. It can happen, as Flannery (1972: 410–421) shows, if the elite developed strategies that are more "self-serving" than "system-serving."

Acknowledgments I thank my colleagues Alexander Fraiberg and Daniel Varga of the Israel Antiquities Authority who worked with me in the field in our Chalcolithic excavations. Emil Aladjem made the map and Ilanit Azoulay, the Agamim plan. I thank Davida Degen-Eisenberg for stimulating discussions and useful insight on the first draft of this paper, and Ido Reiss for support in the statistical analysis.

References

Abadi, Y. (2003). *Early Bronze Age grinding stone production in the Negev highlands.* M. A. Thesis, Ben Gurion University of the Negev.
Abadi-Reiss, Y. (2013). *The site of Qatif Y3 and the Neolithic-Chalcolithic transition in the southern Lavant.* Ph.D. dissertation submitted to Ben-Gurion University of the Negev.
Abadi-Reiss, Y. (2016). Chalcolithic settlement in Tel Sheva. *'Atiqot, 87,* 43–69.
Abadi-Reiss, Y. (2017). *Be'er Sheva', Be'er Sheva', Yasmin Street (Horbat Beter).* Hadashot Arkheologiot – Excavations and Surveys in Israel, 129. https://www.hadashot-esi.org.il/report_detail.aspx?id=25375&mag_id=125

Abadi-Reiss, Y. (2021). Dug in the loess: A new look at the understanding of underground spaces during the Chalcolithic period in the Northern Negev. In A. Golani, D. Varga, G. Lehmann, & Y. Tchekanovets (Eds.), *The Annual 17th Southern Conference* (pp. 134–151). Beer-Sheva.

Abadi-Reiss, Y., & Fraiberg, A. (2014). Horbat Kasif (northwest). In *Hadashot Arkheologiot – Excavations and surveys in Israel* (Vol. 126). Israel Antiquities Authority. https://www.hadashot-esi.org.il/report_detail.aspx?id=14711&mag_id=121

Abadi-Reiss, Y., & Fraiberg, A. (n.d.). A site from the Chalcolithic period onwards in Kuseife. *'Atiqot*.

Abadi-Reiss, Y., & Pasternak, M. (n.d.). Aspects of V-shape: The pottery assemblage from Tal Sheva. *'Atiqot*.

Abadi-Reiss, Y., & Varga, D. (2019). Inter-site complexity in the Ghassulian Chalcolithic site of Agamim, Ashkelon. In D. Varga, Y. Abadi-Reiss, G. Lehmann, & D. Vainstub (Eds.), *Worship and burial in the Shfela and Negev regions throughout the ages* (pp. 67–78). The Annual 15th Southern Conference.

Abadi-Reiss, Y., & Varga, D. (2022). "Agamim" Neighborhood: in the Chalcolithic Period, in light of recent excavations and studies. In R. Y. Lewis, D. Varga, & A. Sason (Eds.), *Ashkelon: Landscape of peace and conflicts* (pp. 14–44). Studies of the Southern Coastal Plain and Judean Foothills. Ashkelon Studies Series.

Abrutyn, S., & Lawrence, K. (2010). From chiefdom to state: Toward an integrative theory of the evolution of polity. *Sociological Perspectives, 53*(3), 419–442.

Abulafia, T. (2020). Be'er Sheva', Horbat Beter. *Hadashot Arkheologiot – Excavations and Surveys in Israel, 132*. https://www.hadashot-esi.org.il/report_detail.aspx?id=25837&mag_id=128

Ackerfeld, D., Abadi-Reiss, Y., Yagel, O., Harlavan, Y., Abulafia, T., Yegorov, D., & Ben-Yosef, E. (2020). Firing up the furnace: New insights on metallurgical practices in the Chalcolithic Southern Levant from a recently discovered copper-smelting workshop at Horvat Beter (Israel). *Journal of Archaeological Science: Reports, 33*.

Agmon, Y., Elisha, Y., Jakoel, E., & Be'eri, R. (2019). Yehud, Ha-'Azma'ut Street. *Hadashot Arkheologiot – Excavations and Surveys in Israel, 131*. https://www.hadashot-esi.org.il/report_detail.aspx?id=25645&mag_id=127

Alizadeh, A. (1998). Socio-economic complexity in Southwestern Iran during the fifth and fourth millennia B.C.: The evidence from Tall-i Bakun A. *Iran, 26*, 17–34.

Banning, E. B. (2010). Houses, households, and changing society in the Late Neolithic and Chalcolithic of the Southern Levant. *Paléorient, 36*(1), 49–87.

Barzilai, O., Getzov, N., Gubenko, N., Marom, N., Milevsky, I., Vered, A., & Zheng, J. (2013). Proto-historic Ein Zippory: The 2007 excavation season. *Mitekufat Haeven. Journal of the Israel Prehistoric Society, 43*, 22–72.

Baum, R. (2004). The origin of polities: A preliminary inquiry into the evolution of command and control in human collectivities. *Social Evolution and History, 3*(2), 55–92.

Baumgarten, Y. Y. (1986). New aspects of the Chalcolithic site at Be'er Tspad (Neve Noi) following 1982 excavations. *Michmanim, 3*, 33–36.

Baumgarten, Y. Y. (1999). Subterranean Systems in the Chalcolithic period in Southern Israel: Were they used as dwellings? In *Centenary of Mediterranean Archaeology 1897–1997* (pp. 29–39). University Press.

Be'eri, R., Lifshits, V., Fraiberg, A., Balila, M., & Azoulay, I. (2017). Nahal Hevron. *Hadashot Arkheologiot – Excavations and Surveys in Israel, 129*. https://www.hadashot-esi.org.il/report_detail.aspx?id=25368&mag_id=125

Bondarenko, D. M. (2014). On the nature and features of the (early) state: An anthropological reanalysis. *Zeitschrift für Ethnologie, 139*(2), 215–232.

Bourke, S. J. (2001). The chalcolithic period. In B. MacDonald, R. Adams, & P. Bienkowski (Eds.), *The archaeology of Jordan* (pp. 107–162). Sheffield Academic Press.

Bourke, S. J., Lovell, J., Sparks, R., Seaton, P., Mairs, L., & Meadows, J. (2000). A second and third season of renewed excavation by the University of Sydney at Tulaylāt al-Ghassūl (1995–1997). *ADAJ, 44*, 37–89.

Bourke, S. J., Zoppi, U., Meadoes, J., Hua, Q., & Gibbins, S. (2007). The end of the chalcolithic period in the South Jordan Valley: New 14C determinations from Teleulat Ghassul, Jordan. *Radiocarbon, 46.*

Braun, E., van den Brink, E. C. M., Regev, J., Boaretto, E., & Bar, S. (2013). Aspects of radiocarbon determinations and the dating of the transition from the Chalcolithic period to Early Bronze Age I in the Southern Levant. *Paléorient, 39*(1), 23–46.

Byrd, F. B. (1994). Public and private, domestic and corporate: The emergence of the southwest Asian village. *American Antiquity, 59,* 639–666.

Carballo, D. M., Roscooe, P., & Feinman, G. M. (2014). Cooperation and collective action in the cultural evolution of complex societies. *Journal of Archaeological Method and Theory, 21*(1), 98–133.

Clare, L. (2010). Pastoral clashes: Conflict risk and mitigation at the pottery Neolithic transition in the Southern Levant. *Neo-Lithic, 1*(10), 13–23.

Clark, J. E., & Parry, W. J. (1990). Craft specialization and cultural complexity. *Research in Economic Anthropology, 12,* 289–346.

Clarke, D. L. (1977). *Spatial archaeology.* Academic Press INC.

Commenge, C. (2006). Gilat's ceramics: Cognitive dimensions of pottery production. In T. E. Levy (Ed.), *Archaeology, anthropology and cult; the sanctuary at Gilat, Israel. Approaches to anthropological archaeology* (pp. 394–506). Equinox Publishing Ltd.

Commenge, C., Levy, T. E., Alon, D., & Kansa, E. (2006). Gilat's figurines: Exploring the social and symbolic dimensions of representation. In T. E. Levy (Ed.), *Archaeology, anthropology and cult; the sanctuary at Gilat, Israel. Approaches to anthropological archaeology* (pp. 739–830). Equinox Publishing Ltd.

Commenge-Pellerin, C. (1987). *La Poterie D'Abou Matar et de L'ouadi Zoumeili (Beershéva) au IVe Millénaire avant L'ère Chrétienne.* Association Paléorient.

Commenge-Pellerin, C. (1990). *La Poterie de Safadi (Beershéva) au IVe Millénaire avant L'ère Chrétienne.* Association Paléorient.

Conard, N. J. (2001). Advances and problems in the study of Paleolithic settlement systems. In N. J. Conard (Ed.), *Settlement dynamics of the middle Paleolithic and Middle Stone Age, Kerns Verlag* (pp. 7–20).

Costin, C. L. (1991). Craft specialization: Issues in defining, documenting, and explaining the organization of production. *Archaeological Method and Theory, 3,* 1–56.

Davidovich, U., Ulman, M., & Leibner, U. (2013). Late prehistoric occurrences in Har Nitai and Khirbat Wadi Hamam, northeastern lower Galilee. *Mitekufat Haeven. Journal of the Israel Prehistoric Society, 43,* 186–204.

de Contenson, H. (1956). Tel Turmus in the Huleh Valley. *Israel Exploration Journal, 13,* 115–119.

DeMarrais, E., Castillo, L. J., & Earle, T. (1996). Ideology, materialization, and power strategies. *Current Anthropology, 37*(1), 15–31.

Dollfus, G., & Kafafi, Z. (1993). Recent researches at Abu Hamid. *Annual of the Department of Antiquities of Jordan, 37,* 241–262.

Dothan, M. (1959). Excavations at Horvat Beter (Beersheva). *Atiqot, 2,* 1–42.

Drabsch, B., & Bourke, S. (2019). Early visual communication: Introducing the 6000-year-old Buon Frescoes from Teleilat Ghassul, Jordan. *Arts, 8*(79), 1–14.

Eirikh-Rose, A., Milevsky, I., Barzilai, O., Matzkevich, Z., Nagar, Y., & Sklar, D. (2017). Horbat Zur: Burial and non-burial caves in the Ghassulian Chalcolithic and Early Bronze Age at the Haelah Vally. *Mitekufat Haeven. Journal of the Israel Prehistoric Society, 47,* 171–207.

Eisenberg-Degen, D., & Talis, S. (2020). Be'er Shevaʽ, Compound C. *Hadashot Arkhaeologiyot: Excavations and Surveys in Israel, 132.* https://www.hadashot-esi.org.il/report_detail.aspx?id=25706&mag_id=128

Elad, I., Paz, Y., & Shalem, D. (2020). *En Esur (Asawir), area N* (p. 132). Hadashot Arkhaeologiyot: Excavations and Surveys in Israel. https://www.hadashot-esi.org.il/report_detail.aspx?id=25833&mag_id=128

Fabian, P., Scheftelowitz, N., & Gilead, I. (2015). Ḥorvat Qarqar South: Report on a Chalcolithic Cemetery near Qiryat Gat, Israel. *Israel Exploration Journal, 65*(1), 1–30.
Feinman, G., & Neitzel, J. (1984). Too many types: An overview of sedentary Prestate societies in the Americas. *Advances in Archaeological Method and Theory, 7*, 39–102.
Flannery, K. V. (1972). The cultural evolution of civilizations. *Annual Review of Ecology and Systematics, 3*, 399–426.
Gal, Z., Smithline, H., & Shalem, D. (1997). A chalcolithic burial cave in Peqi'in, Upper Galilee. *Israel Exploration Journal, 47*(3/4), 145–154.
Gandulla, B., & Jaruf, P. (2017). Título: Otherness and interaction in copper metallurgy in the Chalcolithic of the Southern Levant: The Transcaucasian connection. *Claroscuro, 16*, 1–22.
Getzov, N. (2016). Remains from the end of the early Chalcolithic and the late Chalcolithic periods at Kaukab Springs in the Western Galilee. *Atiqot, 87*, 1–4.
Gibson, S., & Rowan, Y. M. (2006). The Chalcolithic in the central highlands of Palestine: A reassessment based on a new examination of Khirbet es-Sauma'a. *Levant, 38*, 85–108.
Gilead, I. (1986). Did they live in the underground buildings at the Be'er Sheba sites during the Chalcolithic period? A non-stratigraphic paradigm. *Archaeology: Israel Archaeologists Association, 1*, 40–48.
Gilead, I. (1988). The chalcolithic period in the Levant. *JWP, 2*, 397–443.
Gilead, I. (1995a). Summary and conclusions: Grar and the chalcolithic period in the Northern Negev. In I. Gilead (Ed.), *Grar: A Chalcolithic site in the Northern Negev (Beer-Sheva VII)* (pp. 463–480). Ben-Gurion University Press.
Gilead, I. (1995b). The stone industry. In I. Gilead (Ed.), *Grar: A Chalcolithic site in the Northern Negev (Beer-Sheva VII)* (pp. 309–333). Ben-Gurion University Press.
Gilead, I. (2011). Chalcolithic culture history: Ghassulian and other entities in the Southern Levant. In J. L. Lovell & Y. M. Rowan (Eds.), *Culture, chronology and the chalcolithic: Theory and transition* (pp. 12–24). Levant Suppl. S. 9.
Gilead, I., & Fabian, P. (2001). Nevatim: A site of the Chalcolithic period in the Northern Negev. In A. M. Maeir & E. Baruch (Eds.), *Settlement, civilization and culture. Proceedings of the Conference in Memory of David Alon* (pp. 67–86). Ramat Gan.
Gilead, I., & Goren, Y. (1995). The pottery assemblages from Grar. In I. Gilead (Ed.), *Grar: A Chalcolithic site in the Northern Negev (Beer-Sheva VII)* (pp. 137–221). Ben-Gurion University Press.
Gilead, I., Rosen, S. A., & Fabian, P. (1991). Excavations at Tell Abu-Matar (the Hatzerim neighborhood), Beer Sheva. *Mitekufat Haeven: Journal of the Israel Prehistoric Society, 24*, 173–179.
Gilead, I., Marder, O., Khalaily, O., Fabian, P., Abadi, Y., & Yisrael, Y. (2004). The Beit Eshel Chalcolithic flint workshop in Beer Sheva: A preliminary report. *Mitekufat Haeven. Journal of the Israel Prehistoric Society, 34*, 245–263.
Golden, J. M. (1998). *The Dawn of the Metal Age: Social complexity and the rise of copper metallurgy during the Chalcolithic of the Southern Levant, circa 4000–3500 BC*. Ph.D Dissertation, University of Pennsylvania.
Gopher, A., & Tsuk, T. (1996). The chalcolithic assemblages. In A. Gopher (Ed.), *The Nahal Qanah cave: Earliest gold in the southern Levant* (pp. 91–138). Monograph Series of the Institute of Archaeology Tel Aviv.
Gophna, R., & Zuk, Z. (1990). Chalcolithic settlements in Western Samaria. In *Eretz-Israel: Archaeological, historical and geographical studies 21* (pp. 111–118). Roth Amiran.
Gorzalczany, A. (2018). The Chalcolithic cemetery at Palmahim (North): New evidence of Chalcolithic burial patterns from the Central Coastal Plain of Israel. *Atiqot, 91*, 1–93.
Govrin, Y. (2015). Excavations at Yehud: The 2008–2009 seasons. *NGSBA Archaeology, 3*, 7–160. http://ngsba.org/wp-content/uploads/2018/05/NGSBA3.pdf
Gošić, M. (2008). Chalcolithic metallurgy of the Southern Levant: Production centers and social context. *Journal of Serbian Archaeological Society, 24*, 67–80.

Gošić, M. (2015). Casting the sacred: Chalcolithic metallurgy and ritual in the southern Levant. In N. Laneri (Ed.), *Defining the sacred: Approaches to the archaeology of religion in the near east* (pp. 161–175). Oxbow Books.

Greenfield, H. J. (2010). The secondary products revolution: The past, the present and the future. *World Archaeology, 42*(1), 29–54.

Harney, É., May, H., Shalem, D., et al. (2018). Ancient DNA from Chalcolithic Israel reveals the role of population mixture in cultural transformation. *Nature Communications, 9*, 3336. https://doi.org/10.1038/s41467-018-05649-9

Israel, Y., Aladjem, E., & Milevski, I. (2014). Nahal Shalva. *Hadashot Arkheologiot – Excavations and Surveys in Israel, 126.* https://www.hadashot-esi.org.il/report_detail.aspx?id=12656&mag_id=121

Jakoel, E., & Be'eri, R. (2016). Yehud, Ha-'Azma'ut Street. *Hadashot Arkheologiot– Excavations and Surveys in Israel, 128.* https://www.hadashot-esi.org.il/report_detail.aspx?id=24997&mag_id=124

Joffe, A. H. (2003). On the language of complex societies: Reply to Michael Heltzer. *Journal of the Economic and Social History of the Orient, 46*(4), 529–532.

Kaplan, J., Gophna, R., & Paz, Y. (2017). Jabotinsky street (Jamassin) excavations, Tel Aviv (1950–1951). In A. Gopher, R. Gophna, R. Eyal, & Y. Paz (Eds.), *Jacob Kaplan's excavations of Protohistoruc sites 1950s–1980s, 2* (pp. 558–621). Tel Aviv University.

Kenyon, K. M. (1979). *Archaeology of the Holy Land.*

Kerner, S. (2010). Craft specialization and its relation with social organisation in the late 6th to early 4th millennium BCE of the Southern Levant. *Paléorient, 36*(1), 179–198.

Konrad, K. A., & Leininger, W. (2011). Self-enforcing norms and efficient non-cooperative collective action in the provision of public goods. *Public Choice, 146*(3), 501–520.

Lee, J. R. (1973). *Chalcolithic Ghassul: New aspects and master typology.* Ph.D dissertation. The Hebrew University.

Levy, T. E. (1983). The emergence of specialized pastoralism in the southern Levant. *World Archaeology, 15*(1), 15–36.

Levy, T. E. (1986). Social archaeology and the chalcolithic period: Explaining social organizational change during the 4th millennium in Israel. *Michmanim, 3*, 5–20.

Levy, T. E. (Ed.). (1987). *Shiqmim I—Studies concerning chalcolithic societies in the Northern Negev Desert, Israel (1982–1984).* British Archaeological Reports, International Series 356.

Levy, T. E. (1992). Transhumance, subsistence, and social evolution in the northern Negev desert. In O. Bar-Yosef & A. Hazanov (Eds.), *Pastoralism in the Levant; archaeological materials in anthropological perspectives* (pp. 65–82). Monographs on World Archaeology, 10. Prehistory Press.

Levy, T. E. (1993). Production, space, and social change in protohistoric Palestine. In A. Holl & T. E. Levy (Eds.), *Spatial boundaries and social dynamics* (pp. 63–81). Ethnoarchaeological Series.

Levy, T. E. (1995). Cult, metallurgy and rank societies – Chalcolithic period (ca. 4500–3500 BCE). In T. E. Levy (Ed.), *The archaeology of Society in the Holy Land* (pp. 226–244). Leicester University Press.

Levy, T.E. (Ed.) (2006). *Archaeology, anthropology and cult: The sanctuary at Gilat, Israel.* .

Levy, T. E., & Alon, D. (1985). Shiqmim: A Chalcolithic Village and Mortuary Centre in the Northern Negev. *Paléorient, 11*(1), 71–83.

Levy, T. E., & Alon, D. (1987). Settlement patterns along the Nahal Beersheva–lower Nahal Besor: Models of subsistence in the Northern Negev. In T. E. Levy (Ed.), *Shiqmim I: Studies concerning Chalcolithic societies in the Northern Negev Desert, Israel (1982–1984)* (pp. 45–138). BAR Int. S. 356.

Levy, T. E., & Menachem, N. (1987). The pottery from the Shiqmim village: Typological and spatial considerations. In T. E. Levy (Ed.), *Shiqmim I: Studies concerning chalcolithic societies in the northern Negev Desert, Israel (1982–1984)* (pp. 313–331). BAR Int. S. 356.

Levy, T. E., Grigson, C., Holl, A., Goldberg, P., Rowan, Y., & Smith, P. (1991). Protohistoric investigations at the Shiqmim Chalcolithic village and cemetery: Interim report on the 1987 season. *Bulletin of the American Schools of Oriental Research, Supplement, 27*, 29–45.

Lovell, J. L. (2001). *The late Neolithic and Chalcolithic periods in the Southern Levant: New data from the site of Teleilat Ghassul, Jordan*. BAR Int. S. 974; Monographs of the Sydney University Teleilat Ghassul Project I.

Lovell, J. L. (2011). Community is cult, cult is community: Weaving the wen of meanings for the chalcolithic. *Paléorient, 36*, 103–122.

Manclossi, F., & Rosen, S. A. (2021). *Flint trade in the protohistoric levant*. Routledge: Taylor & Francis.

McCorriston, J. (1997). The fiber revolution: Textile extensification, alienation, and social stratification in ancient Mesopotamia. *Current Anthropology, 38*(4), 517–459.

Milevski, I., & Baumgarten, Y. (2008). Between Lachish and Tel 'Erani: Horvat Ptora, a new late prehistoric site in the Southern Levant. In J. M. Córdoba, M. Molist, C. Pérez, I. Rubio, & S. Martínez (Eds.), *Proceedings of the 5th International Congress on the Archaeology of the Ancient Near East: Madrid, April 3–8, 2006* (pp. 609–626).

Milevski, I., Vardi, J., Gilead, I., Eirikh-Rose, A., Birkenfeld, M., Mienis, H. K., & Kolska, H. L. (2013). Excavations at Horbat 'Illit B: A Chalcolithic (Ghassulian) site in the Haelah Valley. *Mitekufat Haeven. Journal of the Israel Prehistoric Society, 43*, 73–147.

Nahshoni, P., Goren, Y., Marder, O., & Goring-Morris, N. (2002). A Chalcolithic site at Ramot Nof, Be'er Sheva'. *'Atiqot, 43*, 253–254.

Parkinson, W. A., & Galaty, M. L. (2007). Secondary states in perspective: An integrated approach to state formation in the prehistoric Aegean. *American Anthropologist, 109*(1), 113–129.

Pasternak, M. D. (2020). Tel Sheva' in the chalcolithic period: Underground and aboveground in the Ghassulian culture. In Y. Abadi-Reiss, D. Varga, & G. Lehmann (Eds.), *Desert archaeology. The Annual 16th Southern Conference* (pp. 127–140).

Paz, Y., Aladjem, E., Abadi-Reiss, Y., Kahalani, N., & Timmer, N. (2014). Tel Sheva. *Hadashot Arkheologiot – Excavations and Surveys in Israel, 126*. https://www.hadashot-esi.org.il/report_detail.aspx?id=9566&mag_id=121

Perrot, J. (1955). The excavations at Tell Abu Matar near Beersheba. *IEJ, 5*, 17–40, 73–84, 167–189.

Perrot, J. (1984). Structures d'Habitat, Mode de Vie et Environnement. Les Villages Souterrains des Pasteurs de Beersheva, Dans le Sud d'Israel, au IVe Millénaire Avant l'Ere Chrétienne. *Paléorient, 10*(1), 75–96.

Price, M. D., Buckley, M., Kersel, M. M., & Rowan, Y. M. (2013). During the Chalcolithic in the lower Galilee: New data from Marj Rabba (Israel). *Paleorient, 39*(2), 183–200.

Rosen, S. A. (2013). Evolution in the desert: Scale and discontinuity in the Central Negev (Israel) in the fourth millennium BCE. *Paléorient, 39*(1), 139–148.

Rosen, S. A. (2017). *Revolutions in the desert*. Routledge: Taylor and Francis.

Rosen, S. A. (2021). The herding revolution in the desert: Adoption, adaptation, and social evolution in the Negev and Levantine deserts. In J. M. Rowland, G. Lucarin, & G. J. Tassie (Eds.), *Revolutions. The Neolithisation of the Mediterranean Basin: The transition to food producing economies in North Africa, Southern Europe and the Levant* (pp. 233–246). Berlin Studies of the Ancient World.

Rosen, S. A., & Eldar, I. (1993). Ḥorvat Beter revisited: The 1982 salvage excavations. *'Atiqot, 22*, 13–27.

Rosen, S. A., & Goring-Morris, N. A. (2018). Tabular scraper quarries: A view from Har Qeren in the Western Negev. *Mitekufat Haeven: Journal of the Israel Prehistoric Society, 48*, 82–96.

Roshwalb, A. F. (1981). *Protohistory in the Wadi Ghazzeh: A typological and technological study based on the Macdonald excavations*. Ph.D. diss. London: University of London.

Rothman, M. S. (2004). Studying the development of complex society: Mesopotamia in the late fifth and fourth millennia BC. *Journal of Archaeological Research, 12*(1), 75–119.

Roux, V. (2003). A dynamic systems framework for studying technological change: Application to the emergence of the Potter's wheel in the southern Levant. *Journal of Archaeological Method and Theory, 10*, 1–30.

Roux, V. (2010). Technological innovations and developmental trajectories: Social factors as evolutionary forces. In M. J. O'Brien & S. J. Shennan (Eds.), *Innovation in cultural systems. Contributions from evolutionary anthropology* (pp. 217–234). The MIT Press.

Roux, V. (2019). The Ghassulian Ceramic Tradition: A Single Chaîne Opératoire Prevalent throughout the Southern Levant. *Journal of Eastern Mediterranean Archaeology & Heritage Studies, 7*(1), 23–43.

Roux, V., & Miroshedji, P. (2009). Revisiting the history of the potter's wheel in the Southern Levant. *Levant, 41*(2), 155–173.

Rowan, Y. M. (2006). The chipped stone assemblage at Gilat. In T. E. Levy (Ed.), *Archaeology, anthropology and cult: The sanctuary at Gilat, Israel* (pp. 507–574).

Rowan, Y. M. (2014). The mortuary process in the chalcolithic period. In M. Sebbanne, O. Misch-Brandl, & D. M. Master (Eds.), *Masters of fire: Copper age art from Israel* (pp. 100–113). Princeton.

Rowan, Y. M., & Golden, J. (2009). The chalcolithic period of the Southern Levant: A synthetic review. *JWP, 22*, 1–92.

Rowan, Y. M., & Ilan, D. (2013). The subterranean landscape of the Southern Levant during the Chalcolithic period. In H. Moyes (Ed.), *Sacred darkness: A global perspective on the ritual use of caves* (pp. 87–107). University Press of Colorado.

Rowan, Y. M., Levy, T. E., Alon, D., & Goren, Y. (2006). Gilat's ground stone assemblage: Stone fenestrated stands, bowls, palettes, and related artifacts. In T. E. Levy (Ed.), *Archaeology, anthropology and cult: The sanctuary at Gilat, Israel* (pp. 575–684). Routledge.

Rowan, Y. M., Kersel, M. M., Hill, A. C., & Urban, T. M. (2021). Late prehistory of the lower Galilee: Multi-faceted investigations of the Wadi el-Ashert. *BASOR, 385*.

Rupp, D. W. (1993). Aspects of social complexity in Cyprus: Socioeconomic interaction and integration in the fourth through second millennia B. C. E. *Bulletin of the American Schools of Oriental Research, 292*, 1–8.

Sahlins, M. (1963). Poor man, rich man, big man, chief: Political types in Melanesia and Polynesia. *Comparative Studies in Society and History, 5*, 285–303.

Scheftelowitz, N. (2004). Stone artifacts. In N. Scheftelowitz & R. Oren (Eds.), *Giv'at Ha-oranim; A Chalcolithic site* (pp. 59–67). Salvage Excavation Report. Tel Aviv University.

Schick, T. (1998). *The cave of the warrior: A fourth millennium burial in the Judean Desert* (IAA reports 5). Jerusalem.

Schortman, E. M., & Urban, P. A. (2004). Modeling the roles of craft production in ancient political economies. *Journal of Archaeological Research, 12*(2), 185–226.

Seaton, P. (2008). *Chalcolithic cult and risk management at Teleilat Ghassul: The Area E Sanctuary*. Bar International Series.

Service, E. (1962). *Primitive social organization*. Random House.

Shalem, D. (2017). Cultural continuity and changes in south Levantine late chalcolithic burial customs and iconographic imagery: An interpretation of the finds from Peqi'in cave. *Mitekufat Haeven. Journal of the Israel Prehistoric Society, 47*, 148–170.

Shalev, S. (1994). The change in metal production from the Chalcolithic period to the Early Bronze Age in Israel and Jordan. *Antiquity, 68*, 630–637.

Sherratt, A. G. (1981). Plough and pastoralism: Aspects of the secondary products revolution. In I. Hodder, G. Isaac, & N. Hammond (Eds.), *Pattern of the past* (pp. 261–306). Cambridge University Press.

Sherratt, A. G. (1983). The secondary products revolution of animals in the Old World. *World Archaeology, 15*, 90–104.

Shugar, A. N. (2000). *Archaeometallurgical investigation of the chalcolithic site of Abu Matar, Israel: A re-assessment of technology and its implications for the Ghassulian culture*. PhD thesis. University College London.

Shugar, A. N. (2003). *Reconstructing the Chalcolithic metallurgical process at Abu Matar, Israel, international conference Archaeometallurgy in Europe.*, September 2003 (pp. 449–458). Milan.

Stanish, C. (2001). The origin of state societies in South America. *Annual Review of Anthropology, 30*, 41–64.

Tchekhanovets, Y., Lehavi, A., & Shaked, S. (2021). Be'er Sheva', Nahal 'Ashan. *Hadashot Arkheologiot – Excavations and Surveys in Israel, 133*. https://www.hadashot-esi.org.il/report_detail.aspx?id=26067&mag_id=133

Ussishkin, D. (2014). The Chalcolithic Temple in Ein Gedi: Fifty years after its discovery. *Near Eastern Archaeology, 77*(1), 15–26.

van den Brink, E. C. M., & Lazar, D. (2019). Horbat Nevallat: A Chalcolithic habitation site and agricultural installations in the Shephelah Foothills. *'Atiqot, 94*, 1–88.

van den Brink, E. C. M., Barzilay, O., Vardi, J., Cohen-Weiniberger, A., Lernau, O., Liphschitz, N., Bonani, G., Mienis, H. K., Rosenberg, D., Yzin, B., Katina, A., Shalev, S., Shilstein, S., & Horowitz, L. K. (2016). Late Chalcolithic settlement remains East of Namir road, Tel Aviv. *Mitekufat Haeven. Journal of the Israel Prehistoric Society, 46*, 20–121.

Vardi, J., Fabian, P., & Gilead, I. (2020). Ghassulian sickle blade workshops: The case of Mitḥam C, Beer Sheva, Israel. *Mitekufat Haeven. Journal of the Israel Prehistoric Society, 50*, 166–191.

Varga, D., Abadi-Reiss, Y., Pasternak, M. D., Kobrin, F., & Silberklang, H. (2021). Ashqelon, Agamim neighborhood (east). *Hadashot Arkheologiot – Excavations and Surveys in Israel, 133*. https://www.hadashot-esi.org.il/report_detail.aspx?id=25893&mag_id=133

Wilson, P. J. (1988). *The domestication of the human species.* Yale University Press.

Winter-Livneh, R., Svoray, T., & Gilead, I. (2010). Settlement patterns, social complexity and agricultural strategies during the Chalcolithic period in the Northern Negev, Israel. *Journal of Archaeological Science, 37*(2), 284–294.

Winter-Livneh, R., Svoray, T., & Gilead, I. (2013). Shape reproducibility and architectural symmetry during the chalcolithic period in the Southern Levant. *Journal of Archaeological Science, 40*(2), 1340–1353.

Wright, H. (1977). Recent research on the origin of the state. *Annual Review Anthropology, 6*, 379–397.

Wright, H. (1984). Prestate political formation. In T. Earle (Ed.), *On the evolution of complex societies: Essays in honor of Harry Hoijer 1982* (pp. 41–78). Malibu.

Wright, K. I. (1992). *Ground stone assemblage variations and subsistent strategies in the Levant, 22,000 to 5,500 b.p.* Ph.D dissertation submitted to the Yale University.

Zhang, D. D., Brecke, P., Lee, H. F., He, Y. Q., & Zhang, J. (2007). Global climate change, war, and population decline in recent human history. *PNAS, 104*(49), 19214–19219.

Perforated and Unperforated Flint Discs from Late Chalcolithic Fazael: A Note on Their Characteristics and Possible Implications

Danny Rosenberg, Sonia Pinsky, and Shay Bar

Abstract The Late Chalcolithic period of the southern Levant is frequently regarded as a tipping point, with a notable increase in social and technological complexity. This time span also features many examples of 'special' classes of artefacts that first appeared during this period and changed or disappeared during the transition to the Early Bronze Age. One of the oddest Late Chalcolithic tool types, which has no parallels in earlier or later periods, is the perforated flint disc. This paper presents a group of perforated objects and related items found at the Late Chalcolithic site of Fazael in the Jordan Valley. This assemblage attributes the site, recently acknowledged as a significant metallurgical center, additional importance. In the current paper we discuss the significance of the new finds in the context of the site and of the Chalcolithic period of the southern Levant.

Keywords Perforated flint objects · Jordan Valley · Chalcolithic period · Southern Levant · Craft specialization · Exchange networks

1 Introduction and Background

The Late Chalcolithic period of the southern Levant (about 4500–3900 BCE) is regarded by most scholars dealing with the later prehistory of the region as a tipping point, with a notable increase in social and technological complexity. This period marks significant changes from its predecessors, specifically in various aspects of

D. Rosenberg (✉)
Laboratory for Ancient Food Processing Technologies (LAFPT), Zinman Institute of Archaeology, University of Haifa, Haifa, Israel
e-mail: drosen@research.haifa.ac.il

S. Pinsky · S. Bar
Zinman Institute of Archaeology, University of Haifa, Haifa, Israel
e-mail: spinsky@univ.haifa.ac.il; bar.inbal.shay@gmail.com

© The Author(s), under exclusive license to Springer Nature Switzerland AG 2023
E. Ben-Yosef, I. W. N. Jones (eds.), *"And in Length of Days Understanding" (Job 12:12): Essays on Archaeology in the Eastern Mediterranean and Beyond in Honor of Thomas E. Levy*, Interdisciplinary Contributions to Archaeology, https://doi.org/10.1007/978-3-031-27330-8_15

social organization, subsistence economy, cult, and religion (e.g. Gilead, 1988; Joffe & Dessel, 1995; Levy, 1986, 2014; Rowan & Ilan, 2007; Shalem, 2015; van den Brink, 1998). Some suggest that the Late Chalcolithic demonstrates significant socio-political changes, although debate regarding the exact nature of the Chalcolithic socio-political structure continues (e.g. Bourke, 2001: 151; Gilead, 1988; Joffe, 2003: 53; Joffe & Dessel, 1995; Levy, 1986, 1998; Perrot & Ladiray, 1980: 131; Rowan & Golden, 2009).

Advances in various technologies have also been widely discussed (e.g. Albright, 1932; Bourke, 2001; Gilead, 1992; Rosenberg et al., 2016; Rowan & Golden, 2009). In this regard, the Late Chalcolithic period featured increased evidence for the development of craft specialization, apparent primarily in the appearance of metallurgy (e.g. Golden, 2009, 2010; Goren, 2008, 2014; Gošić, 2015; Levy & Shalev, 1989; Shalev, 1991, 2008; Shugar & Gohm, 2001), standardized production of certain ceramic vessel types (Kerner, 2010; Roux, 2003) and advanced production techniques, for example in basalt vessel production (e.g. Chasan et al., 2019; Chasan & Rosenberg, 2018, 2019; Rosenberg et al., 2016).

Specific components in the Late Chalcolithic lithic industry have also been claimed to reflect specialization (e.g. Gilead et al., 2004; Pinsky, 2019; Rosen, 1983, 1997; Rosenberg & Shimelmitz, 2017; Vardi, 2011). Regional variation occurred in lithic craft specialization and the use of its products (e.g. Gilead, 1984; Hermon, 2008; Pinsky, 2019; Rosen, 1997; Shimelmitz & Mendel, 2008). In this regard, the Late Chalcolithic lithic industry was composed of several chaînes opératoires (Hermon, 2008 and see Rosenberg et al., 2019). These included primarily expedient or ad hoc flake production (e.g. Rosen, 1997) and blade production, chiefly for the manufacture of sickle blades (e.g. Gilead et al., 2004; Pinsky, 2019; Roshwalb, 1981; Shimelmitz & Mendel, 2008; Vardi & Gilead, 2013). Other chaînes opératoires included bladelet production for microlith manufacture (Gilead, 1984; Shimelmitz, 2007), bifacial production primarily for adze manufacture (Barkai, 2005: 362), large cortical flake production for tabular scraper manufacture (e.g. Rosen, 1983) and large flake production for perforated tool manufacture (Rosenberg & Shimelmitz, 2017 and references therein).

Perforated flint objects are known from several Late Chalcolithic sites in the southern Levant, and are considered one of the hallmarks of the Late Chalcolithic material culture (Rosen, 1997: 84–85; Rosenberg & Shimelmitz, 2017; Rosenberg et al., 2019). Since they were first noted in the 1930s (Mallon et al., 1934: pl. 31, no. 4), perforated flint objects have been discovered at more than 40 sites, mainly clustered in northern Israel (the Galilee, Golan Heights and northern Jordan Valley), and also in Jordan, Lebanon and Syria (Rosenberg & Shimelmitz, 2017 and see references therein). So far, about 250 perforated flint objects have been documented in the region, although the number of objects per site is usually low.

It has recently been claimed that these, together with other aspects of the Late Chalcolithic material culture, should be regarded as indicators for regional variation, and that they reflect a specific technological trajectory (Rosenberg & Shimelmitz, 2017). In the current paper, we present a group of perforated objects and other items related to this industry found at the Late Chalcolithic site of

Fazael in the Jordan Valley. We will discuss these objects and their characteristics and significance in the context of the Late Chalcolithic period of the southern Levant.

2 Fazael and the Chalcolithic Settlements

The Chalcolithic site of Fazael is located in the Fazael Basin, in the central Jordan Valley, about 20 km north of Jericho (Fig. 1). The site was described by Glueck (1951), and salvage excavations were later conducted in the eastern part of the area by Porath (1985) and Peleg (2000). This area was surveyed in the framework of the Manasseh Hill Country Survey (Zertal & Bar, 2019), and further explored in the Fazael Valley Regional Project during the last 15 years (Bar, 2013, 2014).

Chalcolithic Fazael 'sites' (2, 5 and 7) are in fact a cluster of several segments of possibly one large site (Fig. 2) located along the northern terrace of Wadi Fazael, initially excavated as three separate areas. Another site located nearby, Fazael 1, was ascribed to an earlier phase of the Late Chalcolithic (Bar et al., 2014). Fazael 2, 5, and 7 were attributed to a late phase of the Late Chalcolithic period based on the pottery, lithics, and ^{14}C dates (Bar, 2013, 2014; Bar et al., 2013, 2014, 2015, 2017). These sites, specifically Fazael 2 that was the most intensively excavated, also yielded many copper items (Buchman, 2018; Rosenberg et al., 2020). Fazael 2 and 7 also yielded Canaanean blades (in Fazael 5, only one possible such blade has been found so far), a characteristic of the Early Bronze Age (Pinsky, 2019). Fazael 2 and 7, which were excavated more intensively than Fazael 5, also yielded the perforated and other atypical items that are the focus of this paper.

Fazael 2 is located in the northern area of the greater Late Chalcolithic Fazael site (Bar et al., 2013). Stratum II of this three-stratum site was dated to a late stage in the Late Chalcolithic continuum, with radiometric dates falling within the first century of the fourth millennium BCE (Bar, 2014: 319–320). The main feature discovered is a large courtyard house (Fig. 3), covering an area of about 620 m^2. The courtyard itself is about 500 m^2 in area, bounded by 80–100 cm-thick stone walls. Most of the courtyard has not yet been excavated. One broad room was found abutting the southeastern section of the courtyard, divided into two large cells, with its entrance facing east. At least five successive beaten-earth floors were detected, implying a long period of habitation. Another room, 40 m^2 in area, was excavated in the western part of the courtyard. An entrance flanked by two standing monoliths was set at the southern part of the room and another entrance faced the courtyard. The pottery, flint, and ground stone tool assemblages by and large match other contemporary sites, except for the Canaanean blade industry (Bar & Winter, 2010; Pinsky, 2019).

At Fazael 7 (Fig. 4), southeast of Fazael 2, one of the largest architectural complexes ever uncovered in the Late Chalcolithic was exposed (Bar et al., 2017). Two probes below the foundation level revealed additional Late Chalcolithic remains, which predate the large architectural complex (Bar et al., 2017). The architectural

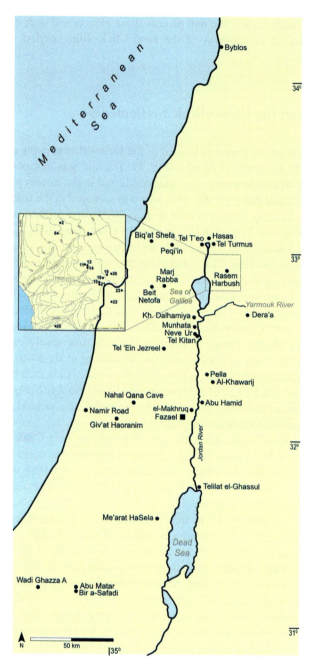

Fig. 1 A map showing the location of Fazael and other sites where perforated objects were found. (Modified from Rosenberg et al., 2017)

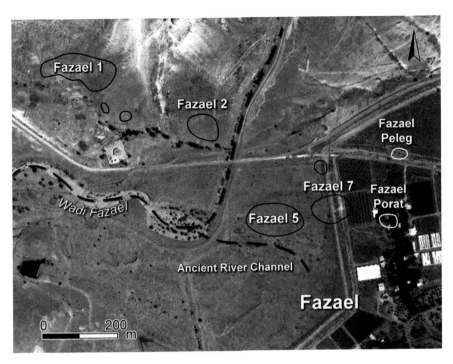

Fig. 2 General view of the location of the Chalcolithic site

complex is unique, and unlike typical Late Chalcolithic broad room structures found at Fazael 2 and Fazael 5. The architectural complex was probably roofed (120 m^2), and consists of four almost identical rectangular rooms created by the division of two roughly square units. This structure is surrounded by three large courtyards, which contain a subsidiary structure, altogether covering an area of about 1300 m^2. The pottery, flint, and ground stone tool assemblages parallel other contemporary sites (however, they lack some of the common types, such as churns and cornets), with significant evidence of the presence of the Canaanean blade industry (Pinsky, 2019).

3 The Fazael Perforated and Unperforated Flint Discs

The Fazael assemblage includes perforated ($n = 11$) and related unperforated ($n = 4$) flint discs (Tables 1 and 2, Figs. 5, 6, 7, 8 and 9). This is one of the largest assemblages of such items from a single site. The objects included here were found at Fazael 2 ($n = 9$) and Fazael 7 ($n = 6$). Discard patterns of the items show that they were abandoned mainly in rooms ($n = 12$), courtyards ($n = 1$), and the surface and topsoil ($n = 2$). They were found in loci defined as floors ($n = 3$), accumulation, fills and collapses above floors ($n = 9$) and one was found in a pit ($n = 1$).

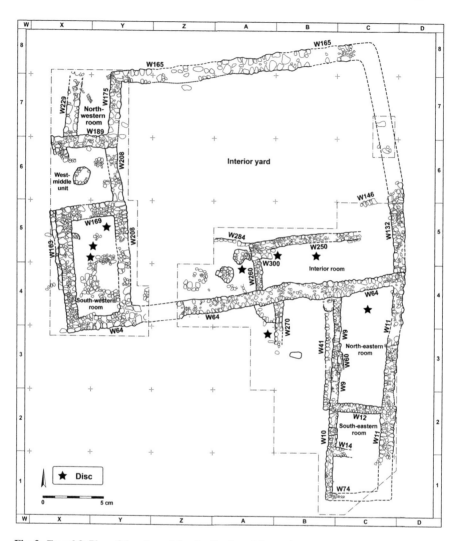

Fig. 3 Fazael 2: Plan of the site and the distribution of the perforated and unperforated flint discs

The perforated flint items were made of high-quality flint; its origin is still unknown (high quality flint was found a short distance from the site). The original blank production required large nodules, and the production of the large thin flakes used as blanks in most examples demanded the calculated and skilled effort of highly qualified knappers (Rosenberg & Shimelmitz, 2017). The items range from 39 to 144 mm across, and are 7 to 14 mm thick (Table 1).

Except for one complete item (damaged during the excavation), all the perforated flint objects are fragments (Figs. 5, 6 and 7). Most of these belong to Type A (Rosenberg & Shimelmitz, 2017), and a few could not be securely classified to a type. Most of these are oval flakes shaped by irregular circumferential retouch. The

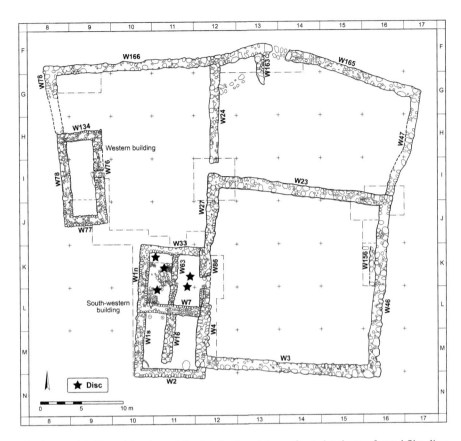

Fig. 4 Fazael 7: Plan of the site and the distribution of the perforated and unperforated flint discs

retouch is mainly fine to semi-abrupt direct. Bifacial retouch was noted in some cases (Fig. 7: 5), usually at the area of the bulb of percussion. This was probably applied to reduce the thickness of this area of the disc by flat, intrusive removals, creating a concave base (Fig. 7: 6–7). Two of the fragments were recycled, bearing post-fragmentation retouch (Fig. 6: 3; 6).

The perforations (Fig. 7: 1–4) are the most distinctive features assigned to this type of tool. The holes are mainly formed off-center. In most of the perforated items, the hole is biconical in section, except for one tool that has a conical hole. The holes were made by pecking, using a very sharp object (probably a flint tool with pointed tip), to create the apertures, similar to perforated discs found at other sites (Rosenberg & Shimelmitz, 2017), and in a few cases, the edges of the pecking scars are slightly abraded. One fragment has pecking marks covering the entire hole, and three fragments have retouch scars still exposed under the pecking marks. Two fragments have pecking only on one side of the hole, leaving exposed retouch on the other side. Two fragments do not show pecking at all. The hole diameters range from 8 to 15 mm.

Table 1 Breakdown of the Fazael perforated discs

Items	Site/Locus	Context	Preservation	Type	Radius (mm)	Maximum diameter (mm)	Fragment portion	Max thickness (mm)	Bifacial removal in some places	Retouched circumference	Hole profile	Hole diameter (mm)	Pecking of hole	Base diameter (mm)	Figure
1	F2/L348	Pit	Broken	A	52	–	1/5	11		Direct and semi-abrupt	A	–	5	40	5:4
2	F2/L354	Fill above floor	Broken	A	39	–	1/4	14	+	Irregular	B	12	1	–	6:3
3	F2/L379	Floor	Broken	A	41–67	111	1/2	11		Direct and semi-abrupt		13	4	–	6:1
4	F2/L311	Accumulations above floor	Broken	A	–	–	1/3	8	+	Bifacial	B	–	–	–	5:1
5	F2/L273	Accumulation above floor	Whole	A	–	96	1/2	7	+	Bifacial and direct		–	–	–	5:2
6	F2/L100	Top soil	Broken	A?	56	115	1/2	8		Direct and irregular inverse	B	15	3	–	6:2
7	F2/L106	Accumulation above floor	Broken	?	51	–	1/8	5		Direct and fine	B	8	5	–	6:4
8	F7/L112	Accumulation above floor	Broken	A	54–70	144	4/4	10	+	Bifacial and direct	B	15	2, 4	40	5:5
9	F7/L300	Fill	Broken	?	–	–	1/8	7	+	Bifacial and semi-abrupt		–	–	–	6:5
10	F7/L128	Fill below floor	Broken	A	46	–	1/8	7	+	Bifacial and direct	B	–	3	40	5:3
11	F7/L143	Fill above floor	Broken	A	59	101	1/2	7		Direct and fine		–	–	–	6:6

[a]Types are according to Rosenberg & Shimelmitz (2017). Hole profile: A. Cone on one face, B. Two opposed symmetrical cones, C. Two opposed unsymmetrical cones; Pecking: 1. Pecking covers entire hole, 2. Scar still visible to a minor extent, 3. Scars well visible below pecking, 4. Pecking on one side only, 5. No pecking

Table 2 Breakdown of the Fazael unperforated discs

Item	Site/Locus	Context	Preservation	Diameter (mm)	Thickness (mm)	Diameter of cavity (mm)	Depth of cavity (mm)	Cortex	Retouch on circumference	Ventral face	blank	Figure
12	F2/L299	Collapse above floor	Whole	–	13	12	<1		Direct, fine	Flat	Flake	8:3
13	F2/L298	Floor	Whole	57	13	16	1	+	Direct, irregular	Flat	Primary flake	8:4
14	F7	Site's surface	Broken	81	47	22	<1	+	Inverse	Intensive retouch	Flake core	8:2
15	F7/L149	Dismantling stratum II floor	Broken	94	30	27 (dorsal face)/22 (ventral face)	15 (dorsal face)/1 (ventral face)	+	Direct, abrupt	Flat	Flake	8:1

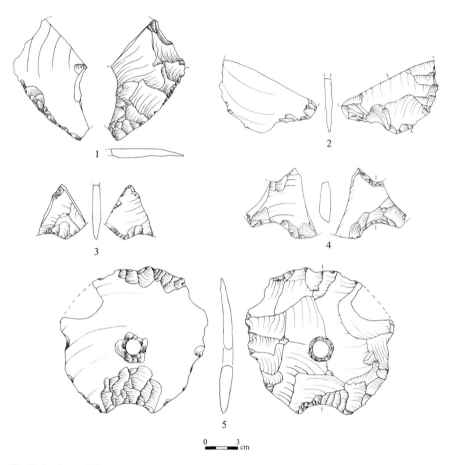

Fig. 5 Perforated flint discs

Four of the items included in the study are unperforated (Figs. 8 and 9, Table 2); however, their general shape is paired with one or two opposite round depressions made by pecking, allowing their inclusion in this group. The raw materials vary, but they are all of high quality. The blanks vary. Two are flakes with similar metrics (diameter 81 and 94 mm and thickness 47 and 30 mm, respectively), one of which is a cortical flake. Two of these are whole and thick (a core and a scraper, Fig. 8: 1–2), while the others are fragments of thinner objects that more closely resemble the perforated discs described above (Fig. 8: 3–4). While the latter may represent perforated discs discarded during perforation, probably because they were broken in preparation, the thicker examples are clearly not directly related to the perforated discs.

The unperforated discs have a flat ventral face, apart from one made on a core with an intensive centripetal retouch. The circumference retouch is usually direct, but its intensity varies, ranging from fine to abrupt and intensive. Cavities (Fig. 9) are not more than 1 mm deep, and are made by pecking, except for the deep dorsal one of a large scraper (Fig. 8: 1) 15 mm deep. The pecking, also probably made by a flint tool with a very thin pointed tip, mostly appears inside the cavity (Fig. 9:

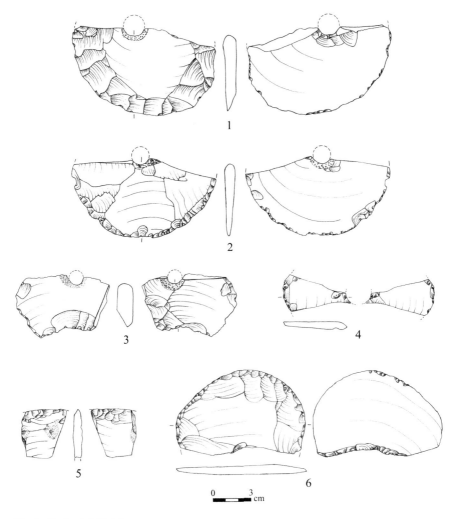

Fig. 6 Perforated flint discs

1–3), except in one case where it is spread loosely around it (Fig. 9: 4). The two thick items have cavities of diameter 22 and 27 mm, and those of the thinner examples range from 12 to 16 mm.

4 Discussion

The assemblage of the 11 perforated and the four unperforated discs with cavities produced by fine pecking include mainly Type A items (Rosenberg & Shimelmitz, 2017) and several unidentified fragments. Two of the unperforated specimens are considerably thicker, and should probably be regarded as a new type – Type

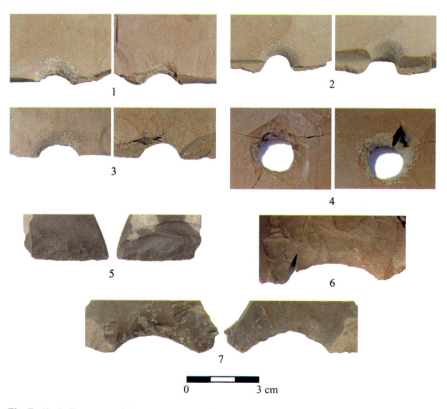

Fig. 7 (1–4) Close-ups of the perforations, (5) Bifacial retouch on one of the discs, (6, 7) Two of the concave bases

E. Discard patterns suggest that most of these were found broken and in accumulations on floors in rooms, rather in courtyards. Some had been recycled after being broken.

While preliminary observations did not establish the function or functions of these objects, results of different studies conducted on perforated discs from other sites in the region have so far also not been very helpful. Two perforated discs from Bir es-Safadi did not show use-wear traces, but one did bear a possible ochre residue (Yamada et al., 2020: 204–205. table 1). Twenty-one perforated discs from Tel Turmus were subjected to detailed use-wear analysis, and some of these showed indistinct use-wear (Rosenberg et al., 2019: table 3). On one of the Tel Turmus examples, a black substance was identified adhering to the smoothing traces, which might indicate contact with a basaltic smoothing surface. Further traces related to use were observed on the edges of two artefacts: this use-wear was associated with plant working. Four of the items show polish at the aperture, related to wood, stone, or sand polish (Rosenberg et al., 2019).

Putting aside the exact function of the Late Chalcolithic perforated discs, it is clear that they were formed using several production techniques, and their

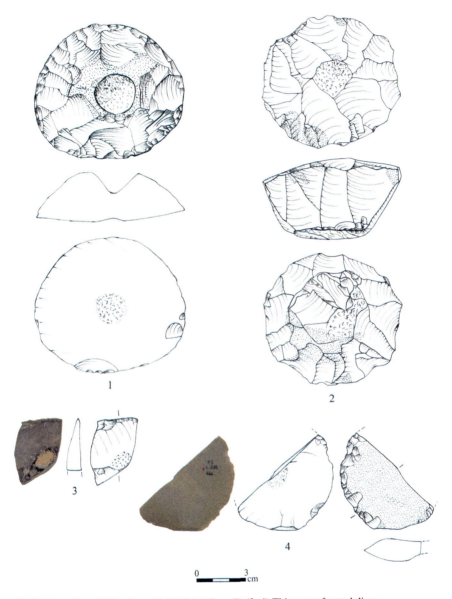

Fig. 8 Unperforated flint discs: (1, 2) Thick Type E, (3, 4) Thin unperforated discs

distribution reflects regional variability (Rosenberg & Shimelmitz, 2017). The number of types in the Fazael perforated disc assemblage is limited, and the technology of production suggests mainly unifacial shaping, although there are sporadic bifacial flakes on the periphery or base.

The aperture and the cavities were clearly formed by pecking applied from one or two faces of the large flake. This technology is the basic common denominator of

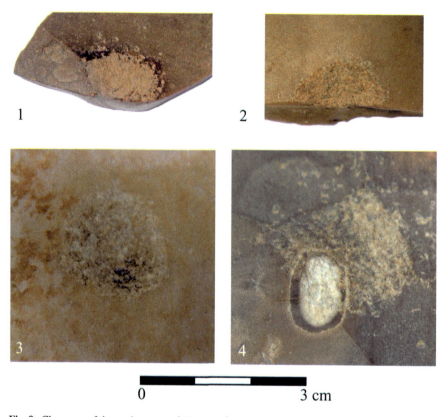

Fig. 9 Close-ups of the cavity areas of the unperforated objects

these items, and has not been identified in flint industries pre- or post-dating the Late Chalcolithic period. This technology reflects high-risk production (referring to the possibility of breakage during the perforation process) that was most probably conducted by specialist knappers (Rosenberg & Shimelmitz, 2017).

During the Late Chalcolithic period, craft production conducted by specialists increased in tandem with the advent and rise in social complexity and the consolidation of regional entities (e.g. Kerner, 2010; Rosenberg et al., 2016; Rosenberg & Shimelmitz, 2017; Roux & Courty, 2005; Rowan & Golden, 2009). These specialized crafts were adopted by numerous industries, including several flint tool types (e.g. Hermon, 2008; Pinsky, 2019; Rosen, 1983, 1997; Rosenberg & Shimelmitz, 2017), ceramics (e.g. Kerner, 1997, 2010; Roux, 2003; Roux & Courty, 2005), basalt vessels and other ground stone tools (e.g. Chasan et al., 2019; Rosenberg et al., 2016; Rosenberg & Golani, 2012) and metallurgy (e.g. Golden, 2009; Shalev, 1991; Shuger & Gohm, 2001).

While evidence of the production site (or sites) of the perforated flint disc is still not in hand (although at least two of the unperforated discs could imply production at Fazael 2), it is clear that the majority of the perforated discs currently known were found in the northern parts of the southern Levant, in the Dera'a area ($n = 27$, Nasrallah, 1948: 92; 1950: 28–30), the Golan Heights ($n = 70$, Freikman, 2014: Fig. 2.172; Noy, 1998: table 8a), Tel Turmus ($n = 48$, Rosenberg et al., 2019) and Tel Te'o ($n = 14$, Gopher & Rosen, 2001: 54, 58, table 42, Fig. 4.17: 1) in the Hula Valley, and at Peqi'in Cave ($n = 34$, Getzov, 2013: 298–300, figs. 7.8–7.12, pl. VII:1) in the upper Galilee. Neve Ur was probably also rich in perforated discs; however, the exact number is not clear, and only a few have been published ($n = 8$, Perrot et al., 1967). These numbers, forming the majority of the Late Chalcolithic perforated disc assemblage, suggest that production was centered around these regions.

Sites in Jordan and central and southern Israel, even if intensively excavated, e.g. Teleilat el-Ghassul (Hennessy, 1969: Fig. 10:10; Mallon et al., 1934: pl. 31:4), Abu Matar (Perrot et al., 1967), Bir es-Safadi (Hermon, 2008: 30; Perrot et al., 1967) and Namir Road in Tel Aviv (van den Brink et al., 2016), yielded only a few perforated items. Bearing these examples in mind, the assemblage of Fazael, located south of the main concentration of perforated flint discs, is outstanding, even compared to most sites south of the northern Jordan Valley. This raises the question of why these finds were relatively frequent at Fazael, and whether this relates to other characteristics of the site and its material culture.

While the answer to this question is not simple and straightforward, the Late Chalcolithic site of Fazael marks several significant characteristics unknown in most other Late Chalcolithic sites. These includes the site's size and its architectural features, especially at Fazael 7 with its large building and related open courtyards (Bar et al., 2017). Other remarkable aspects were noted in the material culture of Fazael: the relative rarity of cornets and churns, the proliferation of copper items and copper production (Rosenberg et al., 2020), and evidence of the Canaanean blade industry (Bar & Winter, 2010; Pinsky, 2019). Bearing all these in mind, and although its location is outside the main center of the perforated disc distribution area, it is not surprising that the site is also rich in perforated flint objects that may have been traded as part of an inter-site/inter-regional exchange network.

The new finds presented here reflect yet another aspect that adds to the significance of the Fazael Basin during the Late Chalcolithic period. It is possible that Fazael fulfilled a central role in copper production and recycling during this time (Rosenberg et al., 2020), and this, paired with its location close to possible routes leading from south to north and east to west, lent the site its economic significance. While the lack of clear evidence regarding the exact role of the flint discs militates against incorporating them into the wider site interpretation, it is clear that the value of these objects stemmed from their specialized high-risk production, and possibly their function. Whether these were involved in copper production centered at Fazael is unclear; however, we can cautiously postulate that the perforated flint disc and related objects form a link between the intensive copper industry at Fazael and the other unusual characteristics of the site.

Acknowledgments We would like to thank S. Haad for her assistance with the graphics, R. Chasan and J. Tresman for perusing and editing the text and H. Cohen-Klonymus for the Fazael 2 data.

References

Albright, W. F. (1932). The chalcolithic age in Palestine. *Bulletin of the American Schools of Oriental Research, 48*, 10–17. https://doi.org/10.2307/1354831

Bar, S. (2013). *Yogvim Venokdim I* (p. 325). Seker. (in Hebrew).

Bar, S. (2014). *The dawn of the Bronze Age* (Culture and history of the ancient near east 72) (607 pp). Brill.

Bar, S., & Winter, H. (2010). Canaanean flint blades in Chalcolithic context and the possible onset of the transition to the Early Bronze Age: A case study from Fazael 2. *Tel Aviv, 37*, 33–47. https://doi.org/10.1179/033443510x12632070179423

Bar, S., Bar-Oz, G., Ben Yosef, D., Boaretto, E., Raban-Gerstel, N., & Winter, H. (2013). Fazael 2, one of the latest chalcolithic sites in the Jordan Valley? Report of the 2007–2008 excavation seasons. *Journal of the Israel Prehistoric Society, 43*, 5–23. https://www.jstor.org/stable/23784049

Bar, S., Bar-Oz, G., Cohen-Klonymus, H., & Pinsky, S. (2014). Fazael 1, a Chalcolithic site in the Jordan valley: Report of the 2013–2014 excavation seasons. *Journal of the Israel Prehistoric Society, 44*, 180–201. https://www.jstor.org/stable/24312159

Bar, S., Cohen-Klonymus, H., Pinsky, S., Bar-Oz, G., & Shalvi, G. (2015). Fazael 5, soundings in a Chalcolithic site in the Jordan Valley. *Journal of the Israel Prehistoric Society, 45*, 193–216. https://www.jstor.org/stable/26572637

Bar, S., Cohen-Klonymus, H., Pinsky, S., Bar-Oz, G., Zukerman, R., Shalvi, G., & Davidovich, U. (2017). Fazael 7: A large Chalcolithic architectural complex in the Jordan Valley, the 2009-2016 excavations. *Journal of the Israel Prehistoric Society, 47*, 208–247. https://www.jstor.org/stable/26572673

Barkai, R. (2005). *Flint and stone axes as cultural markers: Socio-economic changes as reflected in Holocene Flint tool industries of the southern Levant: Studies in early near eastern production, subsistence and environment* (410 p). Ex-Oriente.

Bourke, S. J. (2001). The Chalcolithic period. In B. MacDonald, R. Adams, & P. Bienkowski (Eds.), *The archaeology of Jordan* (pp. 107–163). Sheffield Academic Press.

Buchman, E. (2018). *Copper finds in the Fazael sites and their meaning in understanding the copper industry in the Chalcolithic period in the south of the Levant* (p. 123). Unpublished MA thesis. University of Haifa. (in Hebrew).

Chasan, R., & Rosenberg, D. (2018). Basalt vessels in Chalcolithic burial caves: Variations in prestige burial offerings during the Chalcolithic period of the southern Levant and their social significance. *Quaternary International, 464*, 226–240. https://doi.org/10.1016/j.quaint.2017.02.026

Chasan, R., & Rosenberg, D. (2019). Getting into shape: The significance of decorated basalt vessels during the Chalcolithic period of the southern Levant. *Paléorient, 45*(1), 53–68.

Chasan, R., van den Brink, E. C. M., & Rosenberg, D. (2019). Crossing the lines – Elaborately decorated Chalcolithic basalt bowls in the southern Levant. *Bulletin of the American Schools of Oriental Research, 381*, 145–162. https://doi.org/10.1086/703077

Freikman, M. (2014). *Megalithic structures in the southern Levant: The Golan Heights as a Test Case* (312 p). Unpublished Ph.D. dissertation, Hebrew University of Jerusalem.

Getzov, N. (2013). Flint assemblage. In D. Shalem, Z. Gal, & H. Smithline (Eds.), *Peqi'in: A late Chalcolithic burial site, upper Galilee, Israel* (pp. 293–318). Land of the Galilee 2. Institute for Galilean Archaeology and Kinneret College, Kinneret.

Gilead, I. (1984). The micro-endscraper: A new tool type of the Chalcolithic period. *Tel Aviv, 11*, 3–10. https://doi.org/10.1179/tav.1984.1984.1.3

Gilead, I. (1988). The Chalcolithic period in the southern Levant. *Journal of World Prehistory*, 2(4), 397–443. https://www.jstor.org/stable/25800549

Gilead, I. (1992). Farmers and herders in southern Israel during the Chalcolithic period. In O. Bar-Yosef & A. Khazanof (Eds.), *Pastoralism in the Levant* (pp. 29–42). Prehistory Press.

Gilead, I., Marder, O., Khalaily, H., Fabian, P., Abadi, Y., & Yisrael, Y. (2004). The Beit Eshel Chalcolithic flint workshop in Beer Sheva: A preliminary report. *Journal of the Israel Prehistoric Society, 34*, 245–263. https://www.jstor.org/stable/23380638

Glueck, N. (1951). *Exploration in eastern Palestine IV (part I: Text)* (438 p). American Association of Oriental Research.

Golden, J. (2009). New light on the development of Chalcolithic metal technology in the southern Levant. *Journal of World Prehistory, 22*, 283–300. https://doi.org/10.1007/s10963-009-9022-6

Golden, J. (2010). *Dawn of the Metal age: Technology and society during the Levantine Chalcolithic* (256 p). Equinox.

Gopher, A., & Rosen, S. A. (2001). Lithics of Strata XIII-III, the pre-pottery Neolithic-Early Bronze Age. In E. Eisenberg, A. Gopher, & R. Greenberg (Eds.), *Tel Te'o: A Neolithic, Chalcolithic and Early Bronze Age site in the Hula Valley* (pp. 49–82). IAA Reports 13, Israel Antiquities Authority.

Goren, Y. (2008). The location of specialized copper production by the lost wax technique in the Chalcolithic southern Levant. *Geoarchaeology, 23*(3), 374–397. https://doi.org/10.1002/gea.20221

Goren, Y. (2014). Gods, caves, and scholars: Chalcolithic cult and metallurgy in the Judean Desert. *Near Eastern Archaeology, 77*(4), 260–266. https://doi.org/10.5615/neareastarch.77.4.0260

Gošić, M. (2015). Skeuomorphism, boundary objects and socialization of the Chalcolithic metallurgy in the southern Levant. *Issues in Ethnology Anthropology, 10*, 717–740. https://doi.org/10.21301/eap.v10i3.8

Hennessy, J. B. (1969). Preliminary report on a first season of excavations at Teleilat Ghassul. *Levant, 1*, 1–24. https://doi.org/10.1179/lev.1969.1.1.1

Hermon, S. (2008). *Socio-economic aspects of Chalcolithic (4500–3500 BC) societies in the southern Levant: A lithic perspective* (BAR International Series 1744) (212 p). Archaeopress.

Joffe, A. H. (2003). Slouching toward Beersheva: Chalcolithic mortuary practices in local and regional context. In B. A. Nakhai (Ed.), *The near East in the Southwest: Essays in Honor of William G. Dever* (pp. 45–67). Annual of the American Schools of Oriental Research 58, American Schools of Oriental Research.

Joffe, A., & Dessel, J. (1995). Redefining chronology and terminology for the Chalcolithic of the southern Levant. *Current Anthropology, 36*(3), 507–518. https://doi.org/10.1086/204388

Kerner, S. (1997). Specialization in the Chalcolithic in the southern Levant. In G. G. Hans, K. Zaydan, & G. O. Rollefson (Eds.), *The prehistory of Jordan, II: Perspectives from 1997* (pp. 419–427). Studies in Early Near Eastern Production, Subsistence, and Environment 4, Ex Oriente.

Kerner, S. (2010). Craft specialization and its relation with social organization in the late 6th to early 4th millennium BCE of the southern Levant. *Paléorient, 36*(1), 179–198.

Levy, T. E. (1986). Social archaeology and the Chalcolithic period: Explaining social organizational change during the 4th millennium in Israel. *Michmanim, 3*, 5–20.

Levy, T. E. (1998). Cult, metallurgy and rank societies—Chalcolithic period (ca. 4500–3500 BCE). In T. E. Levy (Ed.), *The archaeology of society in the holy land* (pp. 226–244). Leicester University Press.

Levy, T. E. (2014). Cultural transformations – The Chalcolithic southern Levant. In J. Chi (Ed.), *Faces of the Chalcolithic* (pp. 40–60). Princeton University Press.

Levy, T. E., & Shalev, S. (1989). Prehistoric metalworking in the southern Levant: Archaeometallurgical and social perspectives. *World Archaeology, 20*(3), 352–372. https://www.jstor.org/stable/124559

Mallon, A., Koeppel, R., & Neuville, R. (1934). *Teleilat Ghassul I, 1929–1932* (112 p). Pontifical Biblical Institute.

Nasrallah, J. (1948). Une station ghassulienne du Hauran. *Revue Biblique, 55*, 81–103.
Nasrallah, J. (1950). A carding comb from the Chalcolithic of Syria. *Man, 50*, 28–30. https://doi.org/10.2307/2793298
Noy, T. (1998). The flint artifacts. In C. Epstein (Ed.), *The Chalcolithic culture of the Golan* (pp. 269–299). IAA Reports 4, Israel Antiquities Authority.
Peleg, Y. (2000). Fasa'el (North). *Hadashot Arkheologiyot, 112*, 67–68. (in Hebrew).
Perrot, J., & Ladiray, D. (1980). *Tombes à Ossuaires de la Région Côtière Palestinienne au IVe Millénaire Avant l'ère Chrétienne* (400 p). Association Paléorient.
Perrot, J., Reich, I., & Tzori, N. (1967). Neve Ur: Un nouvel aspect du Ghassoulien. *Israel Exploration Journal, 17*, 201–232. https://www.jstor.org/stable/27925105
Pinsky, S. (2019). *The late Chalcolithic lithic industries of the Fazael sites and their relations to other late Chalcolithic lithic industries* (163 p). Unpublished MA thesis, University of Haifa.
Porath, Y. (1985). A Chalcolithic building in Fasa'el. *'Atiqot, 17*, 1–19.
Rosen, S. (1983). Tabular scraper trade: A model for material culture dispersion. *Bulletin of the American Schools of Oriental Research, 249*, 79–86. https://doi.org/10.2307/1356563
Rosen, S. (1997). *Lithics after the Stone Age: A handbook of stone tools from the Levant* (184 p). Altamira Press.
Rosenberg, D., & Golani, A. (2012). Groundstone tools of a 'coppersmiths' community: Understanding stone-related aspects of the Early Bronze Age site of Ashqelon Barnea. *Journal of Mediterranean Archaeology, 25*(1), 27–51. https://doi.org/10.1558/jma.v25i1.27
Rosenberg, D., & Shimelmitz, R. (2017). Perforated stars: Networks of prestige item exchange and the role of perforated flint objects in the late Chalcolithic of the southern Levant. *Current Anthropology, 58*(2), 295–306. https://doi.org/10.1086/690646
Rosenberg, D., Chasan, R., & van den Brink, E. C. M. (2016). Craft specialization, production and exchange in the Chalcolithic of the southern Levant: Insights from the study of the basalt vessel assemblage from Namir road (Tel Aviv, Israel). *Eurasian Prehistory, 13*(1/2), 105–128.
Rosenberg, D., Groman-Yaroslavski, I., Chasan, R., & Shimelmitz, R. (2019). Additional thoughts on the production of Chalcolithic perforated flint tools: A test case from Tel Turmus, Hula Valley, Israel. In L. Astruc, C. McCartney, F. Briois, & V. Kassiandaou (Eds.), *Near eastern lithic technologies on the move. Interactions and contexts in Neolithic traditions (studies in Mediterranean archaeology)* (pp. 415–426). Proceedings of the 8th International Conference on PPN Chipped and Ground Stone Industries of the Near East. Nicosia, November 23rd–27th 2016. Uppsala: Astrom Editions.
Rosenberg, D., Buchman, E., Shalev, S., & Bar, S. (2020). Evidence for Late Chalcolithic copper recycling in the southern Levant: New discoveries from the Fazael Basin. *Documenta Praehistorica, 47*, 246–261. https://doi.org/10.4312/dp.47.14
Roshwalb, A. F. (1981). *Protohistory in the Wadi Ghazzeh: A typological and technological study based on the Macdonald excavations* (506 p). Unpublished PhD, University College of London.
Roux, V. (2003). A dynamic systems framework for studying technological change: Application to the emergence of the potter's wheel in the southern Levant. *Journal of Archaeological Method and Theory, 10*(1), 1–30. https://doi.org/10.1023/A:1022869912427
Roux, V., & Courty, M.-A. (2005). Identifying social entities at a macro-regional level: Chalcolithic ceramics of south Levant as a case study. In A. L. Smith, D. Bosquet, & R. Martineau (Eds.), *Pottery manufacturing processes: Reconstruction and interpretation* (pp. 53–57). BAR International Series, Archaeopress.
Rowan, Y. M., & Golden, J. (2009). The Chalcolithic period of the southern Levant: A synthetic review. *Journal of World Prehistory, 22*(1), 1–92. https://doi.org/10.1007/s10963-009-9016-4
Rowan, Y. M., & Ilan, D. (2007). The meaning of ritual diversity in the Chalcolithic of the southern Levant. In C. Malone & B. Barrowclough (Eds.), *Cult in context: Reconsidering ritual in archaeology* (pp. 249–254). Oxbow Books.
Shalem, D. (2015). Motifs on the Nahal Mishmar Hoard and the ossuaries: Comparative observations and interpretations. *Journal of the Israel Prehistoric Society, 45*, 217–237. https://www.jstor.org/stable/26572638

Shalev, S. (1991). Two different copper industries in the Chalcolithic culture of Israel. In C. Eluère & J. P. Mohen (Eds.), *Découverte du Metal* (pp. 413–424). Picard.

Shalev, S. (2008). A brief outline summary of nonferrous archaeometallurgy in Israel. *Israel Journal of Earth Sciences, 56*, 133–138. https://doi.org/10.1560/IJES.56.2-4.133

Shimelmitz, R. (2007). The Chalcolithic lithic assemblage. In R. Gophna, I. Taxel, & A. Feldstein (Eds.), *Kafr Ana: A rural settlement in the Lod Valley* (pp. 77–87). Salvage Excavation Reports No. 4, Emery and Claire Yass Publications in Archaeology.

Shimelmitz, R., & Mendel, S. (2008). A Chalcolithic workshop for the production of blades and bi-facial tools at Khirbet Yoah, the Manasseh Hills. *Journal of the Israel Prehistoric Society, 38*, 229–256. https://www.jstor.org/stable/23386444

Shugar, A., & Gohm, C. J. (2001). Developmental trends in Chalcolithic metallurgy: A radiometric perspective. In J. L. Lovell & Y. M. Rowan (Eds.), *Culture, chronology and the Chalcolithic: Theory and transition* (pp. 133–149). Levant Supplementary Series 9, Oxbow Books.

van den Brink, E. C. M. (1998). An index to Chalcolithic mortuary caves in Israel. *Israel Exploration Journal, 48*(3/4), 165–173. https://www.jstor.org/stable/27926516

van den Brink, E. C. M., Barzilai, O., Vardi, J., Cohen-Weinberger, A., Larnau, O., Liphschitz, N., Bonani, G., Minies, H., Nagar, K., Rosenberg, Y. D., Tzin, B., Katina, A., Shalev, S., Shilstein, S., & Kolska-Horwitz, L. (2016). Late Chalcolithic settlement remains east of Namir road, Tel Aviv. *Journal of the Israel Prehistoric Society, 46*, 20–121. https://www.jstor.org/stable/26572646

Vardi, J. (2011). *Sickle blades and sickles of the sixth and fifth millennia BCE in light of the finds from the Chalcolithic sickle blade workshop site of Beit Eshel* (p. 426). Unpublished PhD dissertation, The Ben-Gurion University of the Negev. (in Hebrew).

Vardi, J., & Gilead, I. (2013). Keeping the razor sharp: Hafting and maintenance of sickles in the southern Levant during the 6th and 5th millennia BCE. In F. Borrell, J. J. Ibáñez, & M. Molist (Eds.), *Stone tools in transition: From hunter-gatherers to farming societies in the near east* (pp. 377–394). Proceedings of the 7th International Conference on the Chipped and Ground Stone Industries of the Pre-Pottery Neolithic, Universtat Autònoma de Barcelona.

Yamada, S., Birkenfeld, M., & Lili-Tafber, C. (2020). Use-wear analysis of cortical and tabular scrapers and discs from the Chalcolithic sites of Bir es-Safadi and Abu Matar. *Journal of the Israel Prehistoric Society, 50*, 192–208.

Zertal, A., & Bar, S. (2019). *Manasseh Hill Country Survey* (Vol. 5, 593 p). Brill.

V-Shaped Bowls and Feasting Ceremonies in the Late Chalcolithic Period in the Southern Levant: The Case Study of Neve Ur

Michael Freikman, David Ben-Shlomo, Jacob Damm, and Oren Gutfeld

Abstract The paper deals with a ceramic assemblage excavated at the Late Chalcolithic site of Neve Ur, specifically with Pit B116, where large numbers of V-shaped bowls, as well as other vessel types, were found. The high percentage of V-shaped bowls, compared to the percentage found in the surrounding excavated area, as well as their condition, suggests that the pit was used for a single event rather than for the disposal of random waste over a long time-span. We propose that the assemblage found in Pit B116 and the surrounding area implies that special feasting events related to burial practices were held here during the Late Chalcolithic period.

Keywords Late chalcolithic · Southern Levant · V-shaped bowls · Feasting · Neve Ur

1 Introduction

The Late Chalcolithic period in the southern Levant is characterized by remarkable changes in social and religious life, expressed in archaeological record by new cult practices and rich funerary traditions. The emergence of complex social structures brought with it religious buildings, such as the sanctuaries of Gilat and 'En Gedi, that were foci for intra- (and possibly inter-) regional interactions. Even the relations between the

---

M. Freikman (✉) · O. Gutfeld
Hebrew University of Jerusalem, Jerusalem, Israel
e-mail: indy424@gmail.com; gutfeldo@gmail.com

D. Ben-Shlomo
Ariel University, Ariel, Israel
e-mail: davben187@yahoo.com

J. Damm
Cornell University, Ithaca, NY, USA
e-mail: j.c.damm@gmail.com

© The Author(s), under exclusive license to Springer Nature Switzerland AG 2023
E. Ben-Yosef, I. W. N. Jones (eds.), *"And in Length of Days Understanding" (Job 12:12): Essays on Archaeology in the Eastern Mediterranean and Beyond in Honor of Thomas E. Levy*, Interdisciplinary Contributions to Archaeology,
https://doi.org/10.1007/978-3-031-27330-8_16

living and the dead increased in complexity: in contrast to the preceding periods, burials were now separated from dwellings and were usually located beyond the border of the settlement. The burials themselves were secondary and were much richer in funerary gifts, including large amounts of pottery used in funerary rites or to provide the dead with food in the netherworld. However, while we usually search for evidence for religious practices and their meaning in so-called "cultic contexts," such a strict division between the sacred and the profane (Eliade, 1961) seems to be a modern construct that makes the study of Chalcolithic society easier for scholars rather than being an authentic part of prehistoric reality. In a society in which the house and settlement are only one part of a greater physical and metaphysical reality, these two elements of life are frequently intertwined and are hard to separate. It would be not at all surprising to find evidence for ritual practices in contexts that we usually interpret as clearly mundane. In this paper we will present an analysis of a ceramic assemblage found during a salvage excavation near Kibbutz Neve Ur. The analysis is attempts to identify evidence for activities of possible ritualistic nature in a seemingly mundane context.

The settlement of Neve Ur (Fig. 1) rests on a thin layer of ca. 40–50 cm thick *Hawwar ha-Lashon* (Lisan marl), which in turn covers a colluvial wedge probably brought here from the west by the Tabor stream. The site of Neve Ur was discovered by the members of the kibbutz and was surveyed by N. Tzory in the 1950s (Tzory, 1958). The material collected during that survey, including ceramic and other evidence dated to the Late Chalcolithic period, was published (Perrot et al., 1967), and some of it is currently on display in the museum of the Gan Hashelosha National Park. However, no archaeological excavation was carried out at Neve Ur until recently, when prior to the installation of a gas pipeline a salvage excavation was conducted there in two stages. First, three test pits (Area A) were excavated by Tsur on behalf of the Israel Antiquities Authority. Next, in May–June 2018, a larger salvage excavation was conducted by Freikman and Gutfeld on behalf of the Hebrew University of Jerusalem. The entire area of 400 m², designated Area B, was e excavated down to virgin soil. The main part of this area is characterized by a number of shallow and deeper pits dug into the ground. The site was securely dated to the later part of the Late Chalcolithic period by analysis of the pottery typology and by two radiometric samples.

2 Description of the Assemblage

No architectural remains were uncovered in this area during the excavation, with the exception of a small circular structure built of a single course of stones and a number of mudbrick fragments that suggested the existence of buildings in the immediate vicinity. Five large pits were found in the western part of Area B (Fig. 2). These pits can be ascribed to two general types: Pits B116 and B137 are shallow pits 30–40 cm deep, while Pits B124, B142 and B150 are much deeper, reaching almost one m in depth. The shallower group of pits contained relatively large amounts of pottery and other objects, while the deeper group contained black and ashy sediments yielding fewer potsherds and other objects as well as considerable numbers

V-Shaped Bowls and Feasting Ceremonies in the Late Chalcolithic Period in...

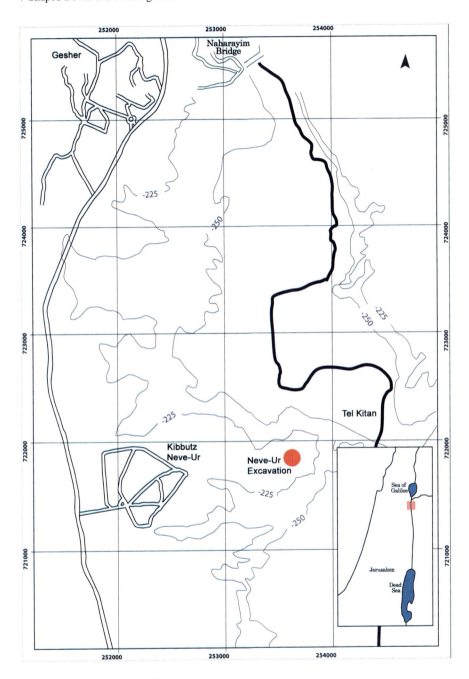

Fig. 1 The location of Neve Ur

Fig. 2 Aerial photograph of the pits and installations

of bones bearing signs of burning, mostly sheep and goats but also other species such as pigs. In general, we may assume that the shallower pits were used for disposal of disused vessels, while the deeper ones were related to cooking activities. The assemblage of pottery and other artifacts found inside Pit B116 was especially rich in both size and variety in comparison to those of the other pits. A small circular installation (B103), made of natural pebbles and possibly used as a hearth, was found in the same area. As we were restricted by the limits of the salvage excavation, we believe that the total number of pits and cooking installations may have been much larger, extending to the west and/or south.

The pottery assemblage is represented by various vessel types, such as miniature and larger V-shaped bowls as well as other bowl types, pedestalled bowls/chalices, basins and kraters, holemouth and necked jars, and pithoi.

1. V-shaped bowls comprise more than half of the assemblage. The great majority are miniature bowls less than 10 cm in diameter and with an average volume of only 130 cu cm (Fig. 3: 1–6). They are crudely made, and none is decorated with

V-Shaped Bowls and Feasting Ceremonies in the Late Chalcolithic Period in... 347

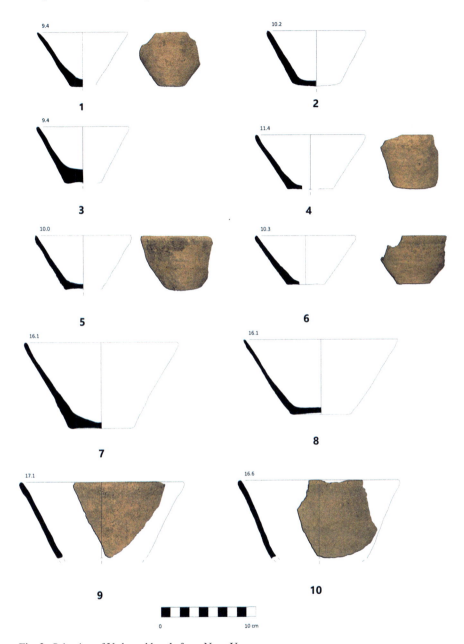

Fig. 3 Selection of V-shaped bowls from Neve Ur

red paint or plastic decoration of any kind. In contrast, the large V-shaped bowls measure 16–19 cm or more in diameter and have an average volume of 470 cu cm (Fig. 3: 7–10). These bowls generally have a better finish than the miniature vessels, and many of them bear "lipstick" decoration. Most of the rims of both miniature and large V-shaped bowls were finished on a slow wheel, and in a few cases wheel marks are discernible on the whole profile, including the base (Fig. 4). Notably, unlike other pottery types, many of the V-shaped bowls of both kinds were partially or fully restorable, sometimes preserving complete profiles. Semi-globular and deep bowls are also attested, although in significantly smaller numbers. These bowl types are usually much more richly decorated, bearing red painted decoration, incised decoration of various kinds, or both.

2. The holemouth jars frequently bear soot marks on their outer surface, suggesting that they were used in food preparation. At least four lids fashioned from clay or prepared from bases of pottery vessels in secondary use may have been intended for these vessels.
3. A number of necked jars and large pithoi were found inside the pits and around them. Additionally, several swollen-neck rims found in the area may be parts of churns. No restorable profiles of these vessels were found.
4. A large fragment belongs to a unique holemouth jar or krater with a basket handle and a strainer (Fig. 5). Spouted kraters (Garfinkel, 1999: 226–230, 237–240), rarely with basket handles (Goren & Fabian, 1993), are attested at various Late Chalcolithic funerary sites. However, with the single exception of one unpublished example found at Fazael (S. Bar, pers. comm.), this specific vessel type with a basket handle and strainer spout is to date unique at south Levantine sites,
5. Remains of at least 24 high stands and fenestrated vessels (21 *in situ*) were found in this area as well (Fig. 6).

Fig. 4 The interior of the base of a V-shaped bowl, showing marks of a slow wheel

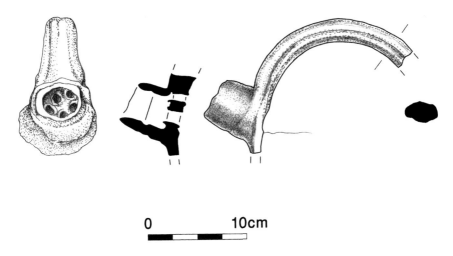

Fig. 5 A unique spouted vessel with a basket handle

3 Spatial Analysis

The distribution of the pottery in the excavated area seems to be fairly distinctive (Fig. 7, Table 1). The pottery in general, and the V-shaped bowls in particular, seem to be distributed unevenly. The great majority of bowls and pedestalled bowls (chalices) were found in or around Pits B116 and B142/150, amounting to almost 75% in each location. The absolute count of the pottery is even more telling: over 120 (minimum number) bowls were found in Pit B116 or in its immediate vicinity, while only 77 were found in the rest of the area, including all other pits and the living surface around them. Moreover, of these bowls, almost all (more than 95%) of the crudely made miniature bowls were found piled inside the pit and even above it (Fig. 8). We should add here that most of the V-shaped bowls found inside Pit B116 (90 of 95) are undecorated, and the percentage of decorated bowls found in the rest of the area (34%) is significantly higher than in Pit B116. It is noteworthy that none of the miniature V-shaped bowls was decorated. The distribution of closed vessels is also noteworthy: while Pit B116 yielded only 23 fragments of holemouth jars and 21 fragments of storage vessels such as jars and pithoi (27% of the assemblage found within the pit), in the other parts of the area their percentage of the assemblage is 50–70%. One may add that although no complete or even partially restorable profiles of holemouth jars, necked jars or other pottery types came from the pits (as well as the rest of the area), many of the V-shaped bowls were at least partially restorable with complete profiles (one is even whole). While fragments of no less than 24 pedestalled/fenestrated bowls were retrieved in this limited area (21 in situ), almost all of them were found within Pits B142/150 and especially Pit B116, which yielded 14 of them.

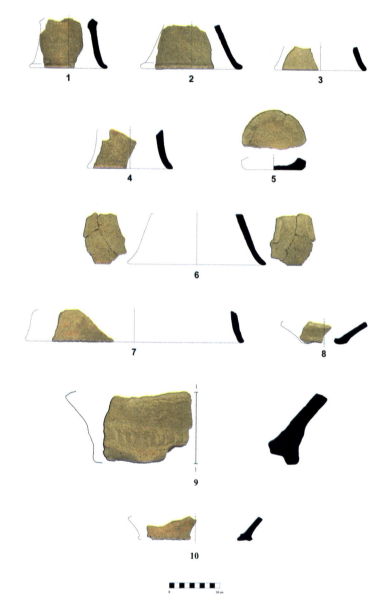

Fig. 6 Fenestrated and pedestalled bowls

4 Petrography

Petrographic analysis was carried out on seven of the V-shaped bowls as well as three additional vessels from Neve Ur. The petrographic groups are similar to those of Tel Tsaf, a large Middle Chalcolithic site 20 km to the south (see, e.g., Freikman

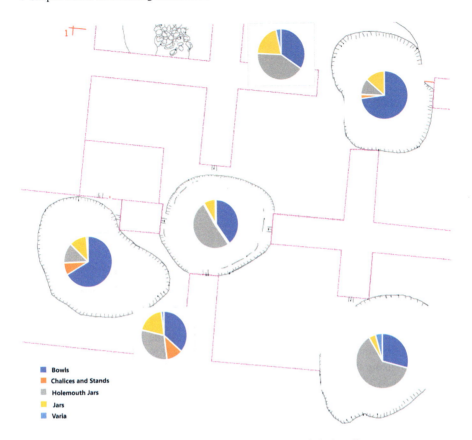

Fig. 7 Pie charts of the distribution of the main clusters of vessels in Area B

Table 1 Spatial distribution of the finds within and around the pits

Context	Bowls	Pedestalled bowls	Holemouth jars	Jars	Misc. pottery
Pit B116	120	14	23	21	2
Pit B137	7	0	15	1	0
Pit B124	14	0	18	3	0
Pit B142/150	27	1	4	5	0
Loc. B105	19	6	16	10	1
Loc. B111	10	0	12	6	1

et al., 2021: 80). All seven V-shaped bowls (and one open bowl) are made of the same fabric: a calcareous marl (denoted Group 2), silty, rich in microfossils, calcite and large-grained basalt. Some samples (Group 2a) have sand-sized chert, while others (Group 2b) do not. This group appears at Tel Tsaf too, but in view of the location of exposures of basalt (Hatzor, 2000), the source is more likely near Neve Ur. The two closed vessels are made of Lisan marl-type clay, rich in microfossils and chalk. This is the most common group at the site of Tel Tsaf (denoted Group 1a).

Fig. 8 The upper part of Pit B116; several V-shaped bowls are visible on top of the pit

5 Residue Analysis of the V-Shaped Bowls

Gas chromatography/mass spectrometry (GC/MS) residue analysis was conducted by Jacob C. Damm on five of the V-shaped bowls from Neve Ur (IAA Export Permit no. 14425) using the facilities of the Pasarow Mass Spectrometry Laboratory at the University of California, Los Angeles (UCLA). The bowls came from a single context (Pit B116), and for each vessel it was possible to take a sample from the soil that had been retained within the vessels since their excavation. Extraction, derivatization and instrumentation procedures followed methods developed by Kym Faull and Hans Barnard of UCLA. The soil samples yielded near-identical qualitative and quantitative results, indicating a homogenous post-depositional environment for the vessels. More importantly, however, the samples taken from the ceramic vessels yielded substantially different quantitative and qualitative fatty acid profiles in comparison to the soil samples, indicating the preservation of ancient organic residues within the vessel walls.

Traditionally, there are two methods for interpreting the significance of organic residues within ancient vessels. The first centers on the identification of diagnostic biomarkers that could only be derived from a narrow range of precursor substances (see Evershed, 2008). In the case of the bowls from Neve Ur, the vessels, unfortunately, yielded no such biomarkers. Instead, each sample almost exclusively presented evidence for common medium- and long-chain saturated fatty acids that are not inherently diagnostic, being present in a wide variety of plant- and animal-based products. Because of this, these results were cautiously analyzed using an alternative method that employs the ratios between several key saturated fatty acids (Eerkens, 2005, 2007; Malainey, 2007). This method remains controversial as its primary application has been to New World foodstuffs, meaning that the published parameters for various foodstuffs cannot be immediately projected onto samples from Old World contexts (McGovern & Hall, 2016). Because of this caution, these ratios were not used to identify the original function of the bowls, but rather the ratios were used as proxy evidence to determine whether the bowls were used in a similar fashion. In the case of the bowls from Neve Ur, close correspondence across separate ratios for three main saturated fatty acid groups—C16:0/C18:0, C12:0/C14:0 and (C15:0 + C17:0)/C18:0—suggests that each vessel was subject to similar use patterns prior to deposition. While it remains impossible to demonstrate exactly what that use was or what substances were originally in the bowls, the data from residue analysis in tandem with the single-event deposition of the bowls points towards a fixed sequence of practice, perhaps ritualized behaviors.

6 Discussion and Parallels

V-shaped bowls appear in the southern Levant in small numbers as early as the Middle Chalcolithic period and are still present during the initial phases of the Early Bronze Age. Their peak appearance, however, is in the Late Chalcolithic period, when they comprise a considerable part of ceramic assemblages all over the southern Levant, sometimes amounting to more than half of the vessels (Roux & Courty, 1997: 25). They frequently appear in domestic contexts associated with mundane activities (Commenge-Pelerin, 1987; Levy & Menahem, 1987). However, they also frequently appear in funerary assemblages (Epstein, 2001), where they acquire "another meaning" (Ilan & Rowan, 2011: 106). Large numbers of V-shaped bowls (and in particular small V-shaped bowls) have been found along with other vessels at various funerary sites, such as Hadera (Sukenik, 1937), Benei Brak (Ory, 1946), Azur (Perrot & Ladiray, 1980), Givʻataim, Palmahim (Gophna & Lifshitz, 1980), Ben Shemen (Perrot & Ladiray, 1980), Maʻabarot (Porath, 2006), Shaʻar Efraim (Oren & Scheftelowitz, 1998), Peqiʻin, Shiqmim (Levy & Alon, 1982), and many others.

Organic residues, which may still be intact, are sometimes found inside the bowls (Goren, 2002: 21), although it is not clear whether this food was left for the dead, was consumed by the living at ceremonial feasts of some kind during and/or after burial, or possibly both. A further link of the V-shaped bowls with the Chalcolithic funerary tradition is seen in the V-shaped or similar open receptacles that appear on top of the anthropomorphic stands found in the Peqiʻin cave (Shalem et al., 2013: 239–266) and the basalt anthropomorphic stands found in the Golan (Freikman, 2018). Direct evidence of an association between the V-shaped vessels and deceased persons is provided by the fact that bones of the dead, particularly their skulls or mandibles, were sometimes placed inside them (Levy et al., 1991: 409). V-shaped bowls are also attested at Chalcolithic sites of ritual significance in general, namely the sanctuaries of ʻEn Gedi (Ussishkin, 1980), Gilat (Levy, 2006), Shiqmim (Levy et al., 1991: 400) and Teleilat Ghassul (Seaton, 2008), as well as deep natural caves presumably used for ritual purposes (Freikman, 2017).

The relationship of some of the V-shaped bowls with Late Chalcolithic ritual in general, and with burial traditions in particular, is hence based on numerous finds from all over the region. However, the question of the particular way in which these bowls were used remains open. Were they merely a symbolic gesture, were they used as votive vessels, or were they used for the distribution and consumption of food or drink during funerary or memorial ceremonies?

Here we may propose a possible answer based on the assemblage excavated at Neve Ur. A number of features of the assemblage of this site may point to a special use of the bowls, perhaps related to feasting rather than everyday consumption of food or drink.

1. An exceptionally large concentration of V-shaped bowls was found here in a limited area. While large numbers of such vessels are not unusual in the Chalcolithic southern Levant, their intra-site distribution is noteworthy. Although only a few fragments were uncovered in Area A in contexts of domestic architecture, they were found in large numbers outside the settled space within the pits of Area B, and the great majority were literally piled into a single pit (B116) or around it. They constitute not only the majority of bowls but also the majority of the assemblage found there. It seems that placing most of them together in the same pit was a deliberate action.
2. Some of them, mostly those at the top of this pile, were found in restorable or even complete condition. Consequently, we may assume that they were placed in the pit or thrown into it as whole vessels. This observation stands in clear contradiction to the pottery vessels of other types, particularly closed forms, none of which was in restorable state and which were usually represented by isolated fragments.
3. The miniature bowls that make up the majority of the assemblage could contain only a very small amount of liquid or solid food (less than 150 cc), suggesting that the meal was symbolic or short-term in nature. Most of them apparently contained the same substance (although it is impossible at this stage to establish exactly what this was), indicating a certain degree of ritualization of the meal.
4. While most of the large hemispherical and deep bowls are decorated with red painted or incised designs, and among the general assemblage red painted decoration reaches almost 20%, none of the miniature V-shaped bowls is decorated in any way and only a few of the large V-shaped bowls bear red painted designs. On the other hand, with few exceptions, the V-shaped bowls were finished or entirely prepared on the slow wheel. Taking into consideration these two facts, we may speculate that the V-shaped bowls, particularly the miniature versions, had some symbolic meaning in the eyes of the inhabitants of Neve Ur but were intended for only a few events or even single use.
5. A large number of fenestrated stands, which in practice are V-shaped bowls installed on top of a high stand, were found within Pit B116 or nearby. Like the V-shaped bowls, they were not found in association with architecture in Area A. It is plausible that some of the fragments of the bowls or platters found here in fact belong to these vessels. Frequently associated with ritual or funerary

activity (Amiran, 1992; Seaton, 2008: 45), these vessels too may point to the ritual nature of the activity conducted here.
6. The two types of pits found in this area are also noteworthy. We may cautiously propose, based on the nature of these pits and the material found within them, that there was a functional difference between the shallow Pits B116 and B137 and the deeper Pits B124, B142 and B150: while the former were mainly used for disposal of broken pottery and other artifacts, the latter were mainly related to the cooking process. It is not clear, however, whether the cooking was actually conducted in the deeper pits or they were used for dumping the ashes and remains of other material related to this process. There may be another reason for the functional difference between the two types of pits: while the shallow pits were used for cooking bread and vegetables, the deeper pits were used to cook meat together with stones to increase heat transfer (Molist, 1985; Ben-Shlomo et al., 2009; Garfinkel et al., 2020: 229–236), and only after that were the shallow pits used for the disposal of vessels.

Overall, these observations indicate that the assemblage found in the area of the pits, and particularly within Pit B116, may be interpreted as the result of a planned series of actions in this area. We may hypothesize the order of these actions. Food was prepared within the deep pits, or alternatively was prepared in the immediate vicinity and the remains were dumped in these pits. Afterward, small equal portions of the same kind of food were dispensed into the miniature (and possibly the larger) bowls and consumed by a group of people numbering at least several dozen participants. After the food was eaten, all the receptacles used for this purpose, although still whole, were buried together inside one of the shallow pits, totally filling it. While it is possible that the consumption of the food and disposal of the vessels was a single event, a series of such feasting events may have been conducted in this open location. The latter possibility may be reinforced by the discovery of several pits dug in the same place, in one case even cutting into one another. Similar uses of pits as cooking pits/ovens or pits for the disposal of refuse from feasts, as well as the digging of new pits into existing ones, have already been interpreted as evidence of ceremonial feasts at Middle Chalcolithic Tel Tsaf (Ben-Shlomo et al., 2009; Garfinkel et al., 2020: 229). In both cases, an open area could have been designated for well-organized communal meals over a certain span of time. Moreover, the data presented above includes many of the characteristics viewed as evidence of feasting of a religious nature (Twiss, 2008). The assemblage of the pits can be interpreted as the remains of a collective meal with a large number of participants.

Although evidence of communal feasting is not always easy to identify in the field, new evidence that has accumulated during recent decades and reexamination of the material collected earlier suggest that such feasting events of communal food consumption already appear in the Early Neolithic period all over the ancient Near East (Twiss, 2008) and eventually develop into the complex ceremonies of the Chalcolithic period (Peltenburg, 1991; Helwing, 2003; Ben-Shlomo et al., 2009: 143–146; Garfinkel et al., 2020: 229–236). Moreover, the distinctive shape of the V-shaped bowls can be compared to similar ceramic shapes used in roughly contemporary periods in other parts of the ancient Near East. For instance, we may compare the phenomenon of Neve Ur with the roughly contemporary Late and Post-Ubaid "Coba" bowls. These bowls are very similar in shape to the V-shaped bowls from the southern Levant and may be found discarded in considerable numbers near firepits in communal spaces (Baldi, 2012), hence also reflecting practices of communal preparation and consumption of food and consequent discarding of the vessels participating in this act. Moreover, this role of the V-shaped bowls in the social interaction in the ritual/funerary context may be illustrated through comparison to a similar phenomenon well attested in the roughly contemporary fourth-millennium BCE Uruk period in Syria and Mesopotamia. This period is characterized by BRB vessels (beveled rim bowls), found in large numbers and often associated with public institutions. They have been interpreted in different ways as being used for food distribution and/or preparation, tax collection, or votive purposes (Beale, 1978: 304–305). While any of these options is possible, it is clear that BRB vessels, of essentially the same shape as V-shaped bowls from the southern Levant, were involved in the fairly complex social interaction mechanisms of Uruk society. While they are frequently found in contexts of mundane nature in which they were probably related to everyday activities, they can also be found in clearly cultic or funerary contexts. One such example is the site of Carchemish, where large numbers of BRB were found together with cultic stands in burials, whether as votive offerings or testifying to ritual consumption of burial meals performed on the graves (Hogarth et al., 1952: 215–218, Pl. 52).

7 Conclusions

In conclusion, the assemblage of V-shaped bowls, cooking and disposal pits, and other related material excavated at Neve Ur can be regarded as evidence of a previously unnoticed aspect of the social and religious life of Late Chalcolithic society, related to their ideology of death. At a lower level of interpretation, we may stress the importance of the V-shaped bowl not only as the most frequent vessel in Late Chalcolithic assemblages but also as a vessel bearing special meaning in the Chalcolithic world of symbols. Although they are also found in contexts that are usually regarded as mundane, the totality of the data collected at Neve Ur indicates that these bowls were an important element in activities that transcended the everyday preparation and consumption of food. We may interpret it as an integral part of the feasting ceremony, probably related to the interaction of the local population with their deceased relatives through communal consumption of small, almost symbolic amounts of food. We may also speculate that the V-shaped bowls, as well as the other vessels used in the pits during the feast, were discarded in perfect condition due to the fact that they were especially made for this ceremony, somewhat similar to the V-shaped bowls left as offerings in burials. The feasting events themselves took place around the residential areas rather than at the burial sites, and could have been conclusions to burial ceremonies conducted immediately after them or annual memorial ceremonies honoring the deceased. They could have been related to other communal events as well. In any case, we must stress the preliminary nature of these conclusions, based on a very small excavated portion of the site. It is our hope that future excavation of Chalcolithic settlements will yield additional data reinforcing our proposal and help to establish the link between the rituals performed at the funerary sites themselves and ceremonies related to the dead in the settlements.

References

Amiran, R. (1992). Development of the cultic stands in the Chalcolithic and Early Bronze periods. *Eretz-Israel, 23*, 72–75. (Hebrew).

Baldi, J. (2012). Coba bowls, mass-production and social change in post-Ubaid times. *Paléorient, 27*, 393–416.

Beale, T. (1978). Bevelled rim bowls and their implications for change and economic organization in the later fourth millennium B.C. *Journal of Near Eastern Studies, 37*, 289–313.

Ben-Shlomo, D., Hill, A., & Garfinkel, Y. (2009). Feasting between the revolutions: Evidence from Chalcolithic Tel Tsaf, Israel. *Journal of Mediterranean Archaeology, 22*, 129–150.

Commenge-Pelerin, C. (1987). *Le poterie d'Abou Matar et de l'ouadi Zoumeili (Beershéva) au IVe millénaire avant l'ère chrétienne (Cahiers du Centre de Recherche Français de Jérusalem 5)*. Association Paléorient.

Eerkens, J. W. (2005). GC–MS analysis and fatty acid ratios of archaeological potsherds from the Western Great Basin of North America. *Archaeometry, 47*(1), 83–102. https://doi.org/10.1111/j.1475-4754.2005.00189.x

Eerkens, J. W. (2007). Organic residue analysis and the decomposition of fatty acids in ancient potsherds. In H. Barnard & J. W. Eerkens (Eds.), *Theory and practice of archaeological residue analysis* (pp. 90–98). BAR International Series 1650. Archaeopress.

Eliade, M. (1961). *The sacred and profane: The nature of religion*. Harper.

Epstein, C. (2001). The significance of ceramic assemblages in chalcolithic burial contexts in Israel and neighbouring regions in the Southern Levant. *Levant, 33*, 81–94.

Evershed, R. P. (2008). Organic residue analysis in archaeology: The archaeological biomarker revolution. *Archaeometry, 50*(6), 895–924. https://doi.org/10.1111/j.1475-4754.2008.00446.x

Freikman, M. (2017). Into the darkness: Deep caves in the ancient Near East. *Journal of Landscape Ecology, 10*, 81–99.

Freikman, M. (2018). Chalcolithic pillar figures from the Golan: A new interpretation. *Eretz-Israel, 34*, 211–220. (Hebrew).

Freikman, M., Ben-Shlomo, D., & Garfinkel, Y. (2021). Architectural models from Tel Tsaf, Central Jordan Valley, Israel. A glimpse of the superstructure and roof of late prehistoric buildings. *Paléorient, 47*(2), 69–82.

Garfinkel, Y. (1999). *Neolithic and Chalcolithic pottery of the southern Levant. Qedem 39*. Hebrew University of Jerusalem.

Garfinkel, Y., Ben-Shlomo, D., & Freikman, M. (2020). *Excavations at Tel Tsaf 2004–2007: Final report, volume 1* (Ariel University Institute of Archaeology Monograph Series 3). Ariel University Press.

Gophna, R., & Lifshitz, S. (1980). A Chalcolithic burial cave at Palmahim. *'Atiqot, 14*(English Series), 1–8.

Goren, Y. (2002). The pottery assemblage. In Y. Goren & P. Fabian (Eds.), *Kissufim road. A Chalcolithic mortuary site* (pp. 28–41). Israel Antiquities Authority.

Goren, Y., & Fabian, P. (1993). Kissufim road. *Excavations and Surveys in Israel, 12*, 90–91.

Hatzor, Y. (2000). *Beth She'an map. Sheet 6-I, II. Geological maps of Israel 1:50,000*. Geological Survey.

Helwing, B. (2003). Feasts as a social dynamic in prehistoric Western Asia—Three case studies from Syria and Anatolia. *Paléorient, 29*, 63–85.

Hogarth, D., Campbell Thompson, R., & Woolley, L. (1952). *Carchemish. Report of the excavations at Jerablus on behalf of the British museum, part III*. Trustees of the British Museum.

Ilan, D., & Rowan, Y. (2011). Deconstructing and recomposing the narrative of spiritual life in the Chalcolithic of the Southern Levant (4500–3600 B.C.E.). *Archaeological Papers of the American Anthropological Association, 21*, 89–113.

Levy, T. (2006). *Archaeology, anthropology and cult: The sanctuary at Gilat*. Equinox.

Levy, T., & Alon, D. (1982). The Chalcolithic mortuary site near Mezad Aluf, northern Negev Desert: A preliminary study. *Bulletin of the American Schools of Oriental Research, 248*, 37–59.

Levy, T., & Menahem, N. (1987). The ceramic industry at Shiqmim: Typological and spatial considerations. In T. Levy (Ed.), *Shiqmim I, studies concerning Chalcolithic societies in the Northern Negev Desert, Israel (1982–1984)* (pp. 313–331). Archaeopress.

Levy, T., Grigson, C., Holl, A., & Goldberg, P. (1991). Subterranean settlement in the Negev Desert, ca. 4500–3700 B.C. *National Geographic Research and Exploration, 7*, 394–413.

Malainey, M. E. (2007). Fatty acid analysis of archaeological residues: Procedures and possibilities. In H. Barnard & J. W. Eerkens (Eds.), *Theory and practice of archaeological residue analysis* (pp. 77–89). BAR International Series 1650. Archaeopress.

McGovern, P. E., & Hall, G. R. (2016). Charting a future course for organic residue analysis in archaeology. *Journal of Archaeological Method and Theory, 23*(2), 592–622. https://doi.org/10.1007/s10816-015-9253-z

Molist, M. (1985). Les structures de combustion de Cafer Höyük (Malatya, Turquie). Étude préliminaire après trois campagnes. *Cahiers de l'Euphrate, 4*, 35–52.

Oren, R., & Scheftelowitz, N. (1998). The Tel Te'enim and Sha'ar Efraim Project. *Tel Aviv, 25*, 52–93.

Ory, J. (1946). A Chalcolithic Necropolis at Benei Beraq. *Quarterly of the Department of Antiquities in Palestine, 12*, 43–57.

Peltenburg, E. (1991). *Lemba Archaeological Project, Volume II.2. A ceremonial area at Kissonerga*. Paul Åströms.

Perrot, J., & Ladiray, D. (1980). *Tombes à ossuaires de la région côtière au IVe millénaire avant l'ére chrétienne. Mémoires et Travaux du Centre de Recherches Préhistoriques Français de Jérusalem 1*. Association Paléorient.

Perrot, J., Zori, N., & Reich, I. (1967). Neve Ur, un nouvel aspect du Ghassoulien. *IEJ, 17*, 201–232.

Porath, Y. (2006). Chalcolithic burial sites at Ma'abarot and Tel Ifshar. *'Atiqot, 53*, 45–63.

Roux, V., & Courty, M. (1997). Les bols élaborés au tour d'Abu Hamid: rupture technique au 4e millénaire avant J.-C. dans le Levant-Sud. *Paléorient, 23*, 25–43.

Seaton, P. (2008). *Chalcolithic cult and risk management at Teleilat Ghassul*. Archaeopress.

Shalem, D., Gal, Z., & Smithline, H. (2013). *Peqi'in. A late chalcolithic burial site, upper Galilee, Israel*. Kinneret Academic College.

Sukenik, E. (1937). A Chalcolithic necropolis at Haderah. *Journal of the Palestine Oriental Society, 17*, 15–30.

Tsory, N. (1958). Neolithic and Chalcolithic sites in the valley of Beth Shan. *Palestine Exploration Quarterly, 90*, 44–51.

Twiss, K. (2008). Transformations in an early agricultural society: Feasting in the Southern Levantine pre-pottery Neolithic. *Journal of Anthropological Archaeology, 27*, 418–442.

Ussishkin, D. (1980). The Ghassulian shrine at En-Gedi. *Tel Aviv, 7*, 1–44.

Pottery Production in Late Phases of Early Bronze 1 in the Southern Levant

Eliot Braun

Abstract Pottery in the Early Bronze 1 (EB1) (For numerous reasons I eschew the use of the terms EB IA and EB IB and their sub-periods purportedly representing the lengthy time span of ca 3700–3000 BCE (Braun E, Forging a link: evidence for a 'Lost Horizon' In: H Goldfus, MI Gruber, S Yona, P Fabian (eds) The Late Chalcolithic to EB 1 Transition in the Southern Levant. 'Isaac went out to the field': studies in Archaeology & Ancient Cultures in Honor of Isaac Gilead. Archeopress, Oxford, pp 66–95, 2019). That is because of the extreme regionality of EB 1 material culture and the revealed archaeological record that has failed to yield a single sequence for the entire southern Levant, thus making chronological correlations between ceramic groups entirely dependent on the degree of validity of archaeological deposits' associations with radiocarbon determinations (Regev et al., Radiocarbon 54(3–4):525–566, 2012: 528; Braun E, Early Megiddo on the East Slope (The "Megiddo Stages"). A Report on the Early Occupation of the East Slope of Megiddo–Results of the Oriental Institute's Excavations, 1925 – 1933 (Oriental Institute Publications 139). The Oriental Institute of the University of Chicago, 2013: 30–31). Our knowledge is too incomplete and regional differences too pronounced for such simplistic periodizations) was produced in two basic "modes," in limited quantities by semi-skilled individuals or small groups, or on larger scales by numerous skilled potters. The former type of activity, known as Domestic Mode of Production or DMP indicates part-time potters plying their craft for local consumption, possibly on a household level. Although there is some limited evidence for DMP in early phases of EB 1, most pottery during this lengthy period appears to have been made by potters of greater skills and was disseminated through trade or in some instances by itinerant practitioners of the craft. This latter activity accounts for very significant degrees of standardization of ceramic types found at numerous sites. Those levels of standardization argue for regional centers of production from which wares were dispersed. This paper discusses some of the outstanding evidence for those modes of pottery production in the archaeological record,

E. Braun (✉)
W.F. Albright Institute of Archaeological Research, Jerusalem, Israel
e-mail: eliotbraun@yahoo.com

© The Author(s), under exclusive license to Springer Nature Switzerland AG 2023
E. Ben-Yosef, I. W. N. Jones (eds.), *"And in Length of Days Understanding" (Job 12:12): Essays on Archaeology in the Eastern Mediterranean and Beyond in Honor of Thomas E. Levy*, Interdisciplinary Contributions to Archaeology, https://doi.org/10.1007/978-3-031-27330-8_17

and their implications for trade and other types of social intercourse in diverse regions of the southern Levant. The time span is the late to very early third millennia (ca 3700–3000).

Keywords Early Bronze Age Southern Levant · Pottery · Trade · Craft specialization · Standardization

1 Pre-EB 1 Pottery Production in the Southern Levant

Production of pottery in the southern Levant was already underway for millennia by the advent of EB 1 (Amiran, 1969; Goren, 1991). However, until recently the sole direct information on pre-EB 2 pottery production in the southern Levant was to be found only in vast quantities of potsherds and more complete vessels. Some of the earliest of these items were relatively crude, not very symmetrical, and often with lumpy walls and carelessly smeared finishes—products of potters of relatively limited skills. However, not long thereafter some potters were more capable practitioners of the art, producing vessels of considerable skill and evincing a degree of standardization. Often their products are of relatively hard (apparently well-fired) fabrics with smoothed walls of well-proportioned thicknesses. Many were decorated in finely stylized modes that included coloring, incising, burnishing and raised applications (Wright, 1937; Amiran, 1969:13–40; Garfinkel, 1999).

Two exemplary types of pottery that emphasize relatively early potters' skills are found at many sites, including vessels in the Sha'ar Hagolan style with incised herringbone and painted decorations (e.g., Garfinkel, 1992: Fig. 47.1; Gopher & Tsuk, 1996: Fig. 3.5:1,2,5; Kafafi, 2001: Pls. 13B, 13C,14A,14B). Another is in a group of bow-rim sherds of thin-walled, highly burnished black fabrics from Late Neolithic Munhatta[1] (e.g., Garfinkel, 1992: Figs. 99: 1–9, 12–14, 17, 19, 21, 22; 115: 2, 3). These last are some of the very finest examples of the art of sixth millennium BCE potters. In addition, there are also many finely fashioned red burnished vessels (e.g., Garfinkel, 1992: Figs. 99, 100: 1–6, 116). Similar skills may also be witnessed in much of the production of potters of the fifth and fourth millennia, with pronounced regional and chronological variations. Thus, there is copious evidence early in the southern Levant of skilled potters producing fine wares evincing relatively high degrees of standardization.

Despite considerable excavation of late prehistoric sites in the southern Levant resulting in massive quantities of unearthed pottery, until recently, nowhere was there any evidence of actual production locales where raw materials were converted into pottery. Now, however, after more than a century of archaeological excavation, a fortuitous and truly astounding discovery was made at Tall Abu Habil in the Jordan Valley. A large ceramic workshop dated to the Late Chalcolithic (LC) and LC-EB 1

---

[1] When I first saw them, they reminded me of black Attic Ware.

transitional horizons (late fifth to early fourth millennia), which offers an extraordinary view of a locale associated primarily with pottery production; presently unique for the southern Levant prior to EB 2.[2] The finds at this Jordan Valley site include more than a score of kilns (Baldi, 2020; Baldi et al., 2019) clearly representing a centralized and highly organized mode of production using very sophisticated firing techniques. Stratigraphic evidence indicates two types of kilns, and a development in production from the earlier to the later period. Future publications will, no doubt, greatly inform on the details of that site and enhance our understanding of early pottery production. A recent study on Chalcolithic pottery has suggested the likelihood of similar centers of production with regional implications (Shalem et al., 2019).

While Tall Abu Habil remains a unique, serendipitous find for early pottery production in the southern Levant, based on more than a century of ceramic investigation in the region at EB 1 sites, it is possible to extrapolate from that knowledge to suggest the existence of similar centers of production for this later period. Such a paucity of evidence in the presently revealed archaeological record may be explained by the Tall Abu Habil workshop, which appears to have been primarily devoted to production. Indeed early stages of exploration suggest that it may not even have been the locale of the potters' habitations. I postulate that other similar centers of the EB 1 period are to be found outside of settlements. Hopefully, future discoveries, which to date have been primarily limited to settlements, mortuary-related activities, and occasionally cultic-associated installations, will add to information on ceramic production in EB 1. The Tall Abu Habil workshop vindicates, in a very specific manner, N. Porat's (1989: 48) statement that: "Pottery during EB was usually manufactured in workshops by specialized potters, and not at home."

2 Early EB 1 Pottery Production

As the LC-EB 1 transition comes into greater view there is increasing evidence for continuity in material culture between these periods, particularly in the central and southern regions. Potting traditions are an exceptional expression of this (Braun, 1996, 2000a, 2011, 2019, in press; Braun & Gophna, 2004; Hourani, 2010; Roux et al., 2013). Unfortunately, however, the situation is less clear in the north as little is understood of what constitutes LC there, while the earliest definitively EB 1 sites in that region appear to evince diverse ceramic traditions, as suggested by the pottery of Tel Te'o VI compared with that of Tel Te'o V (Eisenberg et al., 2001) (Fig. 1: map).

The Yiftahel Stratum II ceramic assemblage (Braun, 1997, 2009) evinces a major dichotomy in modes of ceramic production with the bulk of large and medium-sized storage vessels showing a relatively low level of standardization, interpreted as

---

[2] Prior to this, the earliest-known kiln in the southern Levant, found at Tell Far'ah North, dates to the EB 2 (de Vaux, 1955: 558–563).

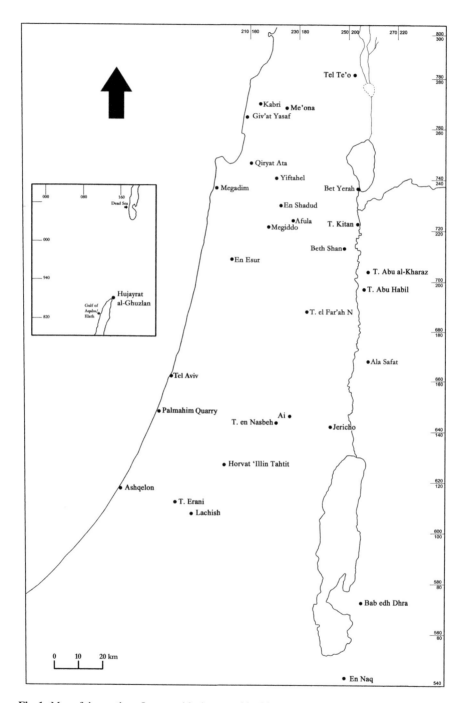

Fig. 1 Map of the southern Levant with sites noted in this paper

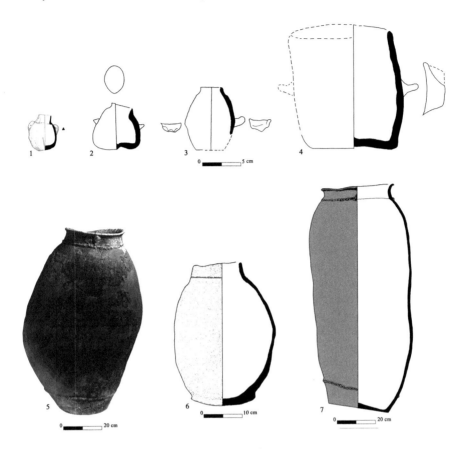

Fig. 2 Select Examples of Domestic Mode of Production

No	Site	References
1	Horvat 'Illin T	Unpublished (late EB 1)
2	Tell en Nasbeh	After Wampler, 1947: Pl. 9:142
3	Tell en Nasbeh	After Wampler, 1947: Pl. 9:143
4	Tell en Nasbeh	After Wampler, 1947:144
5	Yiftahel II	Courtesy Israel Department of Antiquities and Museums
6	Hujayrat al Ghuzlan, 'Aqaba	After Kerner, 2009: Fig. 39:1
7	Yiftahel II	After Braun, 1997: Fig. 9.15:1

evidence of DMP. I suggest that potters of very modest skills were active there and that they imbibed vaguely familiar morphological templates, which more or less conformed to accepted ceramic styles of that era (Fig. 2). Some examples of exceptionally crude vessels from that and other sites indicate just how unskilled some potters were (e.g., Fig. 2:1, 2, 4, 6). At Yiftahel many vessels conformed only slightly to accepted styles (e.g., Fig. 2:5, 7) as the assemblage of storage vessels evinces large variations in morphology and decorations and is remarkable for the relatively poor quality of the fabrics of which they were fashioned. The Yiftahel potters were likely locals unskilled in the craft, who fashioned most of their vessels using somewhat vague, generic templates. The result is an assemblage of storage vessels lacking uniformity and standardization.

A singular exception in the ceramic assemblage of Yiftahel is found in a finely fashioned holemouth vessel (Braun, 1997: Figs. 9. 10: 6) with a very close parallel at Tel Te'o (Eisenberg et al., 2001: Fig. 7.5: 11). Presumably those two holemouths derive from the same center of production, definitely not located at Yiftahel.

Another probably contemporary, albeit rather intriguing example of DMP is found in the pottery assemblages of Hujayrat al Ghuzlan (Kerner, 2009) and its sister community, Tall Magass (Khalil, 2009), two sites apparently primarily devoted to copper production. Despite an obvious degree of knowledge in pyrotechnology, the potters who produced those assemblages showed little skill and apparently had little taste for standardization. One extraordinary feature in vessels from those sites is the use of matts on which pots were fashioned. Their impressions on bottoms of bases are otherwise unknown in EB 1 pottery, although analogous features are found in Late Neolithic and early Chalcolithic ceramic assemblages (e.g., Stekelis, 1935: Pl. V: 2, 13).

A similar claim, for DMP by potters of limited skills, albeit for late phases of EB, is found in a corpus of cooking pots from Bet Yerah. Those vessels, somewhat rudely fashioned and which are often asymmetrical, are claimed to be of local materials and made at the site. Direct evidence is found there in kilns and unfired vessels of post EB 1 periods (Greenberg & Iserlis, 2014: 57). However, even in early EB 1, not all pottery was the production of unskilled potters.

2.1 Gray Burnished Ware (GBW)

This ware is a very distinctive group of bowls fashioned by highly skilled potters. Different morphological types (Braun, 2012a, b) within this category are associated with chronological phases with the most elaborate, understood as early examples, adorned with knobs and other raised decorations. Fabrics tend to be in different hues of gray, but occasional examples are ivory-colored, mustard yellow and brown. Almost every example of early types was burnished. Morphological cognates of the early and late types are of light-colored fabrics with earthen red slips, or sometimes in mottled hues of gray, red and brown. Vessels in these classes were invariably symmetrical; the earlier types were finely finished, with some of the most exceptional exemplars of GBW so well-burnished as to be shiny (Fig. 3:11, 13).

This specialized class of pottery was apparently the product of what is understood as a tradition of some duration associated with five different morphological types presumably originating in one or more workshops (Braun, 2012a, b; Cohen-Weinberger, 2022; Goren & Zuckerman, 2000). Vessels of early types of GBW (Type 1 and its sub-types and Type 5) and their cognates were widely dispersed and

Pottery Production in Late Phases of Early Bronze 1 in the Southern Levant

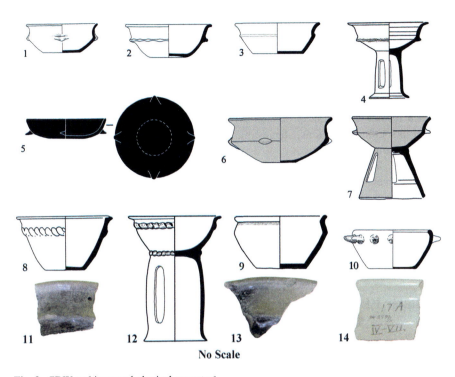

Fig. 3 GBW and its morphological cognates[a]

No.	Type	Description
1	GBW type 1a	Gray and burnished with pronounced flat protuberances
2	GBW type 1b	Gray and burnished with less pronounced protuberances
3	GBW type 1c	Gray and burnished with barely pronounced protuberances
4	GBW type 1a	Gray and burnished with pronounced protuberances, fenestrated pedestal
5	GBW type 5	Black and burnished with no carination and flat protuberances
6	Cognate type 1a	Buff, red painted and not burnished
7	Cognate type 1a	Buff, red painted and not burnished, fenestrated pedestal
8	GBW type 2	Gray
9	GBW type 3	Gray, not burnished
10	GBW type 4	Variations red or mottled red and gray or brown slipped
11	GBW type 1b	Fragment from Beth Shan, shiny, very highly burnished
12	GBW type 2	Gray or brown
13	GBW type 1	Fragment from Beth Shan, shiny, very highly burnished
14	GBW type 1 or 3	Fragment from Megiddo, east slope, light gray, shiny, continuous burnishing

[a]Numbers 3:1–10,12 (from Braun, 2013); numbers 3:11,13,14 are photos by the author of sherds from G.M. FitzGerald's excavation of Beth Shan (Braun, 2004) and Megiddo (Braun, 2013), now in a Student Gallery, Rockefeller Museum, Jerusalem, administered by the Israel Antiquities Authority

have been found in significant quantities at numerous sites in Galilee, in the Zebulon, Jezreel and Jordan Valleys as far south as Wad Qelt, just south of Jericho. There are also appreciable quantities from sites in the Samaria Incline and on the Mediterranean Littoral from Kabri in the north to as far south as Ashqelon (Fig. 1). Those assemblages indicate very copious production and extensive trade of this ware. Several examples of GBW from Palmahim Quarry (Braun, 2000a, b) and the Afridar and Barnea locales at Ashqelon (Cohen-Weinberger, 2022:97), were apparently produced in southern locations, suggesting the likelihood of itinerant potters working in that region.

Notably, later production of what are generally assumed to be associated types (3 and 4), however, seems to have been much more limited and the types less widely diffused primarily in the northern region. There is considerably less evidence of standardization and skill in these later exponents of so-called GBW, with many vessels unburnished, while morphological imitations are of quite different, often buff-colored fabrics and slipped in earthen reds or mottled in different hues.

3 Later EB 1 Pottery Production

In more advanced phases of EB 1 the evidence indicates a great deal of regional-related diversity that suggests the likelihood of numerous centers of production and their associated networks (Braun, 1996: 171–245). Following are a few outstanding examples. Many others may be observed in the archaeological record for this long period of ca eight centuries (Braun et al., 2013; Regev et al., 2012).

3.1 The Basket Style of Decoration

Lawrence Stager's (1990) astute recognition, based on Marque-Krause's (1949: 41, 90) observations, of the significance of a class of EB 1 pottery decorated in a very distinctive style of painting imitative of basketry, has led to its becoming known as the "basket style" (Braun, 2012a, b). The finest examples (e.g., Fig. 4:1–5, 8, 10) were painted with precise, thinly painted lines of red over light-colored fabrics. Such vessels are known from numerous sites in the southern and central-eastern regions and clearly originated in one or perhaps more centers of production. Their presence in tombs is indicative of the regard in which these vessels were held. Potters not only produced the style in morphological variations but were able to paint them with a significant degree of skill.

The finest examples are from advanced, but not very late EB 1 contexts as indicated by one example found in a royal Egyptian tomb (U-j at Abydos), dated earlier than the end of EB 1, together with additional south Levantine vessels of the Erani

Pottery Production in Late Phases of Early Bronze 1 in the Southern Levant 367

Fig. 4 Select examples of basket ware

No	Site	References
1	Tell en Nasbeh?	Rockefeller museum study collection; photo by author
2	Jericho, Tomb K2	After Kenyon, 1965: Fig. 7:3
3	Jericho, Tomb K2	After Kenyon, 1965: Fig. 7:7
4	Tell en Nasbeh?	Rockefeller museum study collection; photo by author
5	Ai (Et Tell)	After Marqet-Krause, 1949, Pl. LXVII, 7.587
6	Jericho, Tomb K2	Kenyon, 1965: Fig. 7:2
7	Tell en Nasbeh	After Wampler, 1947: Pl. 9:130
8	Ghor es Safi ?	Safi Museum, Jordan, photo by author
9	Jericho Tomb K2	After Kenyon, 1965: Fig. 7:1
10	Tell en Nasbeh	After Wampler, 1947: Pl. 9:130

C horizon[3] (Braun 2012–2013). It is possible this style of painting deteriorated over time as indicated by some less skilled examples (e.g., Fig. 4: 6,7) or alternately, some of the better ones were reasonably good imitations at least in regard to morphology (e.g., Fig. 4: 6). Other exemplars seem to evidence deterioration of the style, which was likely copied by potters of lesser skills (e.g., Fig. 4:7). This particular vessel is a miniature imitation of a vessel with false spout or rest for a dipper juglet. It is a rare example of the blending of two contemporary traditions of decoration; the second one is a feature common to vessels of the Erani C horizon (Braun, 2012a, b), a tiny band surrounding the base of the spout. Eventually, the basket style became completely debased, losing its original inspiration.

3.2 Grain-Wash and Its Relation to Pot Types: Evidence for Multiple Centers of Production

This rather distinctive style or mode of painting, sometimes known as "band slip," is a kind of painting in which broad stripes of wash (thin, watery applications of clay for creating color) are generally applied vertically or nearly so, presumably with a brush, over lighter-colored fabrics such that patches of the underlying surface remain uncovered. Darker slips are shades of gray and black, but most examples seem to be varying hues of earthen reds, browns and occasionally orange to yellow.[4] On some vessels, colors vary within the same stripes (e.g., Eisenberg & Rotem, 2016: Fig. 4), presumably due to firing conditions. I suggest there are several variations of this style(s) of painting that are generally recognized as grain-wash. Grain-wash is primarily associated with late EB 1 sites in the northern region.[5]

---

[3] This series of distinctive decorative styles is named after an advanced, but not very late phase of EB 1 first recognized at the site of Tel Erani (modern Qiryat Gat, Israel) (Fig. 1).

[4] Although shading in black and white drawings is generally used to indicate various hues of red, in the instance of grain-wash, shading also designates more somber colors.

[5] The style is also associated with EB 2 and/or EB 3 at the site of Khirbet ez Zeraqon (Genz, 2000).

1. One variation is of broad vertical or nearly vertical stripes applied unevenly such that only parts of the stripes are completely opaque, while others only sparsely cover or do not cover what is below (Figs. 4: 11, 5: 3–5, 8). Often stripes overlap producing an effect that sometimes resembles wood grain. This variant of the style is generally found on large vessels.
2. A second variation is the use of stripes in loose criss-cross patterns (Figs. 5: 6, 7, 9, 6: 10). This type of decoration should not be equated with some vessels decorated in broad, well-defined bands of paint also in similar patterns, although the latter may be inspired by the former. This style is also found on large vessels (e.g., Fig. 5: 1, 2, 6, 7, 9).
3. A third variation is the use of narrower stripes, generally painted in a slanting or even swirling pattern. Often, they emerge from a broad horizontal band above (e.g., Figs. 5: 10, 12, 6: 10). This variation appears to be mostly in earthen red tones and is found on medium to small vessels, but also on some pithoi (e.g., Fig. 6:10). Strictly speaking, this style is less similar to actual grain-wash because the stripes tend to be opaque. Nevertheless, this style of decoration is often recognized as such in the literature.
4. Although often these three basic variations are mutually exclusive, some examples have elements of two of them. The upper portion of the vessel illustrated in Fig. 6: 10 is decorated primarily in variation 3, but its lower wall has a modified criss-cross pattern similar to variation 2.

Differences in vessel morphology, associated with some non-contiguous regional patterns of distribution, suggest that grain-wash was a popular style of decoration adopted by potters in several centers of production over a span of time. That appears to be evident from the diffusion of two major types of pithoi with such decoration found in advanced and late EB 1 phases. In certain instances, the two morphological types are found at the same sites, but at other locales, either one or the other is known (see below).

The grain-wash painting technique, popular in the northern region, was one that required skill. As noted by Eisenberg and Rotem (2016: 5) concerning the pottery of late EB 1 Tel Kitan, including vessels decorated in grain-wash: "These characteristics indicate expertise in the various creative processes of ceramics manufacture—from the preparation of the raw material to the firing, which was conducted at high temperatures." Similar vessels are also found at Tall Abu-al Kharaz, across the Jordan (Fischer, 2008: Figs. 111–112) but were only red slipped or unslipped, suggesting they derived from some other center of production. Notably, those, as well as other pithoi are generally well made with smooth walls of even thicknesses and are symmetrical (Figs. 6 and 7, cf. Fig. 2:5–7).

3.2.1 Rail Rim Pithoi

Pithoi with thickened rims and incisions or striations, called "rail rims," are found at a number of advanced and late EB 1 sites in the Jezreel Valley and at settlements to the east in the area of the Kinneret (Sea of Galilee) and both sides of the Jordan

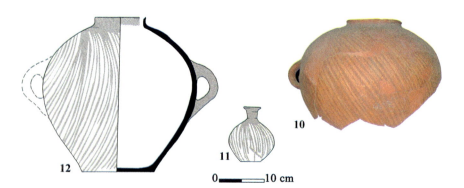

Fig. 5 Grain-wash (Band Slip)[a]

No	Site	References
1	Megiddo East of tell	With kind permission of Matthew Adams
2	Me'ona	Courtesy Israel Department of Antiquities and Museums
3	Megiddo	East slope
4	Megiddo	East slope
5	Giv'at Yasaf	With kind permission of E.C.M. van den Brink
6	Giv'at Yasaf	With kind permission of E.C.M. van den Brink
7	Giv'at Yasaf	With kind permission of E.C.M. van den Brink
8	Giv'at Yasaf	With kind permission of E.C.M. van den Brink
9	Giv'at Yasaf	With kind permission of E.C.M. van den Brink
10	Tel Kitan	Courtesy of Israel antiquities authority
11	Qiryat Ata	Golani, 2003: Fig. 2.41:4
12	Qiryat Ata	Golani, 2003: Fig. 2.41:7

[a]Photos by author, courtesy of Israel Antiquities Authority

Valley at Tel Kitan, Tel Yaqush (Rotem et al. 2019) and Tall Abu al-Kharaz (Fischer, 2008). Variations of the type sometimes have no necks (Fig. 6: 7, 8, 12), but others have low and more pronounced necks (Fig. 6: 1–6, 9–11). On some examples, the decoration is simple (e.g., Fig. 6: 1–9, 11), but on others, potters took great care in this decorative effect (e.g., Fig. 6:10). The type of decoration on the rims of these vessels suggest they derive from one tradition, and possibly even a single workshop. The differences in necks may indicate disparate functions. Some associated types have similar rims but are not striated. Many examples are decorated in the grain-wash style (e.g., Figs. 5: 1–9, 6: 10–12).

3.2.2 Bow Rim Pithoi

These vessels, with distinct, high rims (Fig. 7) are found at a number of sites in the Jezreel and Zebulon Valleys, Nahal 'Iron (En Esur/Assawir) and on the coast at Tel Megadim. There is some variation in the rims, with some higher and more curved than others, but the somewhat limited range suggests a single type, possibly associated with a specific function. While some are devoid of colored exteriors, many are red painted, and others are decorated in variation styles 1 and 3 of grain-wash (e.g., Fig. 7: 11). This morphological type of pithos appears to be absent at sites east of the Jezreel Valley, suggesting its limited distribution is related to trade between the western Jezreel Valley and the coast via Nahal 'Iron (the Megiddo Pass) at least as far as Tel Megadim, where several examples are known. Several of these vessels bear cylinder seal impressions, which suggest a possible accounting system, perhaps related to cultic activity associated with the Megiddo EB 1 temple(s) (Braun, 2013: 103–104; Braun, 2021a, b).

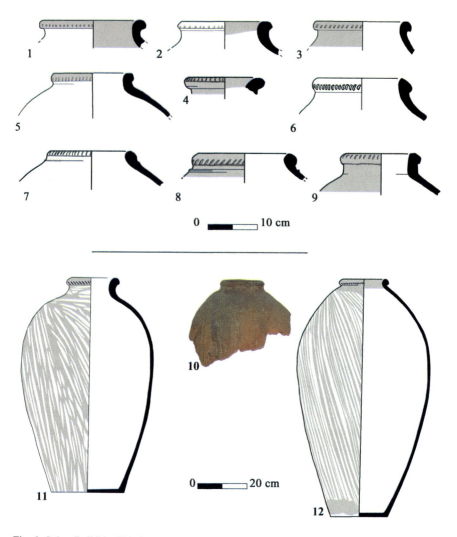

Fig. 6 Select Rail Rim Pithoi

No	Site	References
1	Bet Yerah	After Getzov, 2006: Fig. 2.16:5
2	Bet Yerah	After Getzov, 2006: Fig. 2.16:2
3	Bet Yerah	After Getzov, 2006: Fig. 2.16:3
4	En Shadud	After Braun, 1985: Fig. 23:5
5	Bet Yerah	After Getzov, 2006: Fig. 2.16:4
6	Bet Shan	After FitzGerald, 1935: Pl. 4:17
7	En Shadud	After Braun, 1985: Fig. 23:4
8	En Shadud	After Braun, 1985: Fig. 23:6
9	En Shadud	After Braun, 1985: Fig. 23:7
10	Tel Kitan	Large fragment of Fig. 6:11b; photo by author 10/2021
11	Tel Kitan	After Eisenberg & Rotem, 2016: Fig. 11:2
12	Tel Kitan	After Eisenberg & Rotem, 2016: Fig. 12:1

Pottery Production in Late Phases of Early Bronze 1 in the Southern Levant

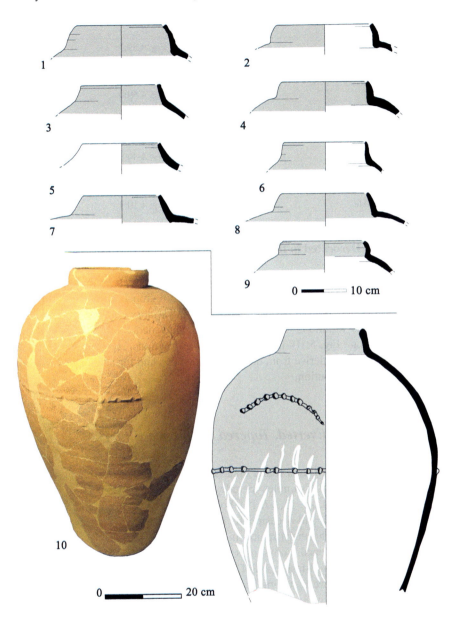

Fig. 7 Bow Rim Pithoi

No	Site	References
1	En Esur	After Yannai, 2006: Fig. 4.59:5
2	En Esur	After Yannai, 2006: Fig. 4.59:2
3	En Esur	After Yannai, 2006: Fig. 4.59:9
4	En Esur	After Yannai, 2006: Fig. 4.59:4
5	En Esur	After Yannai, 2006: Fig. 4.59:11
6	En Esur	After Yannai, 2006: Fig. 4.59:6
7	En Esur	After Yannai, 2006: Fig. 4.59:10
8	En Esur	After Yannai, 2006: Fig. 4.59:8
9	En Esur	After Yannai, 2006: Fig. 4.59:12
10	Megiddo, east slope	Photo by author (See Braun, 2013: Pl. 58)
11	Qiryat Ata	After Golani, 2003: Fig. 4.10:3

3.2.3 Vessels Decorated in the Grain-Wash (Band-Slip) Mode

Examples of vessels decorated in this mode of painting suggest that while the overall style was widely employed by potters, there are regional differences. Notably, some bow-rim pithoi, but not all, were decorated in variations in this painting style. Grain-wash in its variations was also often applied to medium and occasionally to small vessels (e.g., Fig. 5:10–12). These stylistic variations, represented by widely dispersed finds, likely derive from different workshops and further suggest overlapping systems of distribution.

3.3 Vessels with Everted, Tapered (S-Shaped Rims)

This distinctive type of rim is found on a large morphological variety of pots with large apertures (Fig. 8). Examples include medium sized bowls (Fig. 8: 3, 4, 15), kraters (Fig. 8: 1, 2, 10, 12, 13, 17, 19), holemouths (Fig. 8: 9, 18) and large bowls (Fig. 8: 11, 16, 20, 21), and occasionally small jars (Fig. 8: 14). They are found at numerous sites in the northern region in developed and late EB 1 contexts. Most examples were red slipped, sometimes only externally but also internally. These vessels are generally well-fashioned of hard-fired fabrics. Occasional examples are polished, but many have matt finishes. Some of these vessels are decorated with incised wavy lines (Fig. 8: 15, 17–21). Based on the popularity of this singular defining feature, the specialized rim, it seems likely vessels in this group derive from one or more related workshops of skilled potters. Those with the wavy-line decorations probably were made in a single workshop, as that style of decoration is unknown on other types of vessels of the period.

Pottery Production in Late Phases of Early Bronze 1 in the Southern Levant 375

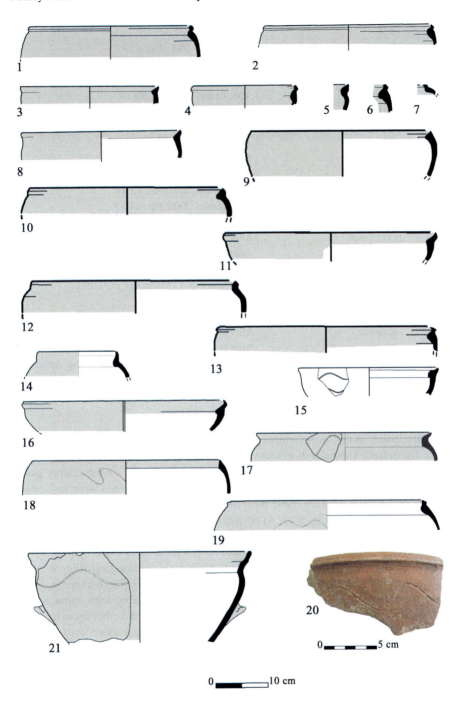

Fig. 8 Select vessels with s-profile rim/tapering rims

No	Site	References
1	En Esur	After Yannai, 2006: Fig. 4.53:2
2	En Esur	After Yannai, 2006: Fig. 4.53:6
3	En Shadud	After Braun, 1985: Fig. 19:11
4	En Shadud	After Braun, 1985: Fig. 19:14
5	En Esur	After Yannai, 2006: Fig. 4.53:9
6	En Esur	After Yannai, 2006: Fig. 4.53:1
7	En Esur	After Yannai, 2006: Fig. 4.53:7
8	En Shadud	After Braun, 1985: Fig.19:12
9	Qiryat Ata	After Golani, 2003: Fig. 4.1:15
10	Qiryat Ata	After Golani, 2003: Fig. 4.1:16
11	Qiryat Ata	After Golani, 2003: Fig. 4.1:17
12	Qiryat Ata	After Golani, 2003: Fig. 4.1:18
13	Qiryat Ata	After Golani, 2003: Fig. 4.1:19
14	Megiddo	After Braun, 2013: Pl 51:j
15	Beth Shan	After Mazar (Ed.) Mazar, 2012: Pl. 19:13
16	Beth Shan	After Mazar (Ed.) Mazar, 2012: Pl. 19:12
17	Megiddo	After Braun, 2013: Pl 51:k
18	Megiddo	After Braun, 2013: Pl 51:l
19	Megiddo	After Braun, 2013: Pl 51:m
20	Afula	After Gal & Covello-Paran, 1996: Fig. 4:6
21	Megiddo	East slope, photo by author courtesy of M. Adams

3.4 Tell Far'ahNorth Ware (TFN)

In a discussion of this large family of ceramics, I named it after the site where it was first discovered, although its center of production remains obscure (Braun, 2012a, b; Braun & van den Brink, 2022: 62–68). The ware is based on fabrication using simple rounded bowls from which different morphological types were fashioned. The bowls were apparently made on forms with central humps, which left distinctive slightly rounded (Fig. 9: 2, 4) or conical (Fig. 9:5,6), internal protuberances, sometimes referred to as "omphaloi". Some exemplars are bowls (e.g., Fig. 9: 5), but many others are closed vessels of small and medium sizes made by joining two bowls of slightly different diameters, with their rims overlapping (Fig. 9: 1–3). Often these joins are visible on the exteriors of such vessels. The manner in which they were fashioned may suggest divisions of labor, possibly with some potters fashioning basic bowls, others adorning them with handles and other appurtenances and perhaps still others slipping and polishing them to very smooth finishes. Final hard-fired products include both simple open and more elaborate closed forms. Creation of TFN ware was clearly labor intensive and its exponents were likely considered a kind of luxury ware, explaining, perhaps why they are known from many tomb assemblages.

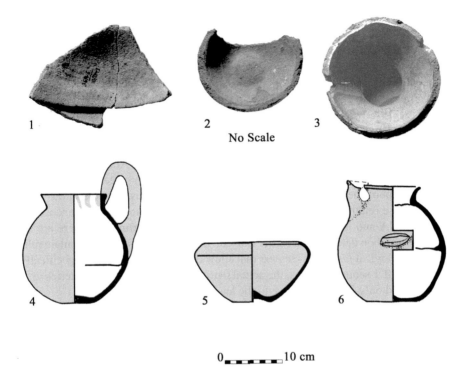

Fig. 9 Tell Far'ah North Ware (TFN Ware)

No	Site	References
1	Ha Qirya, Tel Aviv[a]	Braun & van den Brink, 2022: Fig. 5.7:7
2	Ha Qirya, Tel Aviv	Braun & van den Brink, 2022: Fig. 5.7:8
3	Ha Qirya, Tel Aviv	Braun & van den Brink, 2022: Fig. 5.7:9
4	Ha Qirya, Tel Aviv	Braun & van den Brink, 2022: Fig. 5.10:6
5	Ha Qirya, Tel Aviv	Braun & van den Brink, 2022: Fig. 5.8:5
6	Ha Qirya, Tel Aviv	Braun & van den Brink, 2022: Fig. 5.12:3

[a]The site is a cemetery of the EB 1 and EB 4-MB 1 horizons partially unearthed in salvage excavations in the Qirya Quarter of Tel Aviv

From the copious quantities known of this ware, it seems likely it was made in one or more centers from which it was traded. It is known in the hill country of Samaria and northern Judea, and to the west along the Coastal Plain as far south as Palmahim. The direction of that trade was likely to the south and west (if produced in the region of Tell el-Far'ah North, but apparently not farther north, as to the best of my knowledge this ware has not been found in the nearby Jezreel Valley nor in the adjacent Zebulon and Beth Shan valleys.

3.5 Site Specific Styles

3.5.1 Early Pottery from the EB 1 Cemetery at Bab edh Dhra

Systematic excavation of some previously untouched tombs in the badly looted cemeteries of Bab edh Dhra by Paul Lapp and later published by Tom Schaub and Walt Rast (1989) yielded a large assemblage of intact ceramic vessels evincing several features that are found almost exclusively at that site. Some of those vessels came from burials found below tombs containing quantities of definitively late EB 1 pot types, indicating the lower burials to be relatively earlier. Although the excavators identified the earlier tombs as EB IA, it is unclear just how early those burials are. When published, that EB IA labeling seemed likely, as the period was then deemed to be relatively short and therefore easily divided into an earlier and a later phase, EB IA and EB IB respectively (Mazar, 1990). Unfortunately, there are no good radiocarbon dates for the earlier Bab edh Dhra tombs, nor do they contain reliable chronological *fossiles directeurs* that allow them to be placed more specifically within an EB 1 sequence. Thus, the actual date of that phase of the cemeteries may be expressed only in terms relative to the later burials.

The pottery from the putative EB IA tombs, mostly looted, represents a very sizable assemblage of unknown proportions. Of the vessels I have seen in museums and other collections, it is quite clear that the potters responsible for that output were skilled. While most of the vessels were unpainted or unslipped,[6] they are of hard-fired fabrics and have symmetrical morphologies, most of which are typically EB 1. However, these early Bab edh Dhra types differ in the application of three kinds of decorative elements, which, with rare exceptions, are not found in other EB 1 assemblages. Those features make the early Bab edh Dhra pottery distinctive and easily recognizable. They are:

1. The most prevalent stylistic treatment is punctuate decoration generally in horizontal bands, although occasionally in simple patterns. The equidistant punctures seem to have been made by very thin, needle-like styli (Fig. 10: 2, 4, 5, 7, 8, 10). Examples of this type of decoration were generally fashioned with care.
2. Less prevalent are narrow raised bands of rope-like decoration or small, evenly spaced protuberances creating a similar effect (Fig. 10: 1, 6, 9). They differ from more usual types of rope-like embellishments on EB 1 pots and are, apparently, a virtually site-specific style peculiar to the early Bab edh Dhra tomb assemblage.
3. The application of knobs on many pots is another aspect of this special assemblage. While not unknown in other EB 1 assemblages, flat knobs or protuberances seem to be particularly favored by the potters who created many of the ceramic grave goods in the early EB 1 cemeteries of Bab edh Dhra (e.g., Fig. 10: 4, 6, 10).
4. A type of juglet (Fig. 10:3) of a rare morphology found at Bab edh Dhra, may also be uniquely associated with this site.

---

[6] I know of several apparently rare, red slipped and burnished vessels in this stylistic grouping.

Pottery Production in Late Phases of Early Bronze 1 in the Southern Levant

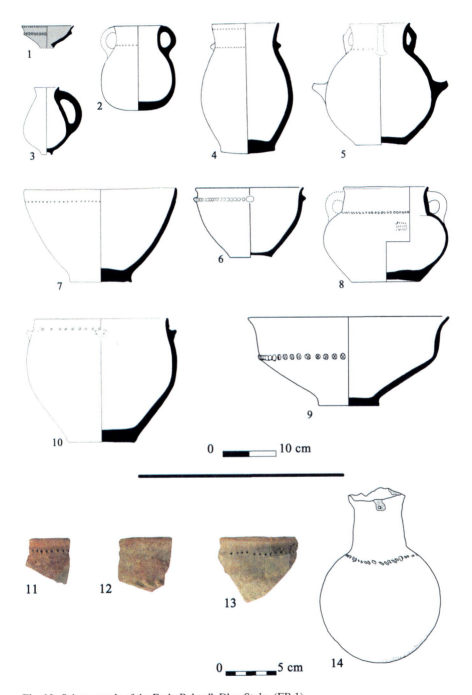

Fig. 10 Select vessels of the Early Bab edh Dhra Styles (EB 1)

No	Site	References
1	Lachish	After Tufnell et al., 1958: Pl. 56:13
2	Bab edh Dhra	After Schaub & Rast, 1989: Fig. 44:4
3	Bab edh Dhra	After Schaub & Rast, 1989: Fig. 30:2
4	Bab edh Dhra	After Schaub & Rast, 1989: Fig. 29:2
5	Bab edh Dhra	After Schaub & Rast, 1989: Fig. 29:4
6	Bab edh Dhra	After Schaub & Rast, 1989: Fig. 45:2
7	Bab edh Dhra	After Schaub & Rast, 1989: Fig. 30:11
8	Ala Safat	After Stekelis, 1961: Fig. 19:189
9	Bab edh Dhra	After Schaub & Rast, 1989: Fig. 122:7
10	Bab edh Dhra	After Schaub & Rast, 1989: Fig. 30:9
11	En Naq	Surface find; private collection
12	En Naq	Surface find; private collection
13	En Naq	Surface find; private collection
14	En Naq	After surface find; private collection; drawn from a photograph

My experience of over four decades of viewing south Levantine EB 1 pottery has yielded knowledge of only two published vessels with the distinctive punctuate decorations at sites other than Bab edh Dhra. One is from a cemetery at Ala Safat, farther north in the same rift valley (Fig. 10: 8); the other is from a site just adjacent to Tel Lachish (the so-called "Northwest Settlement") (Fig. 10: 1). Several additional finds of vessels in this group which I was able to photograph (Fig. 10: 11–14) are in a private collection. They are from the surface of the En Naq EB 1 Cemetery in the same rift valley, south of Bab edh Dhra (Braun, 2021a with references; see also below). Such types in that cemetery are rare, and thus, they may come from the same source as the Bab edh Dhra's ceramics. However, their fabrics are somewhat cruder, while the execution of their decorations seems to be less skillful than those of their corollaries from Bab edh Dhra, perhaps suggesting that those from En Naq are imitations.

The virtual singularity of the earlier EB 1 pottery from the Bab edh Dhra tombs, as well as the vast quantities of them known to have been looted from the cemetery (Saller, 1964–65),[7] clearly indicates that those vessels derive from at least one or more related major centers of production where skilled potters plied their craft. Quantitatively and qualitatively, the assemblage from these tombs far outweighs any possibility of it having been produced by a nomadic or even a semi-nomadic population.

---

[7] I know of scores of vessels of the Bab edh Dhra styles held in collections of the Jordan Department of Antiquities and in Israel; these last confiscated from illegal dealers. One such collection, once deposited in the W.F. Albright Institute of Archaeology, Jerusalem, was repatriated to the Jordan Department of Antiquites.

3.5.2 The "Safi Cup"

A single find of an unusual, and "unique" cup-like vessel at my excavation of an EB 1 site at Palmahim Quarry remained a mystery to me until a visit by a colleague, Russel Adams, revealed that it was one of perhaps hundreds known from the site of En Naq (Ghor es-Safi), which he called the "Safi Cup." A later visit to the EB cemetery of En Naq, and a subsequent study of some of the pottery from there (Braun, 2005a, b) indicated a distinction that made these differ from the high loop handled juglets typical of EB 1. The Safi examples, with small cups of varying morphologies, have one of two distinctive features: protuberances or very high, pronounced ridges at the tops of their handles above where they are attached to vessel rims (Fig. 11).

Perhaps hundreds or even more of this vessel type are known from the site. I have seen countless fragments of them strewn across the looted cemetery of En Naq, while colleagues have informed me of many others in private collections. Some have been confiscated from illegal sellers in Israel, while others were (are?) for sale from "authorized" antiquities dealers in Israel (e.g., Fig. 11: 3). These and many other vessels from the En Naq Cemetery are, as the pottery from the Bab edh Dhra cemeteries, clearly products of skilled potters. Enormous quantities of complete vessels and potsherds from the Bab edh Dhra and En Naq, as well as a cemetery at Fifa (Kersel & Chesson, 2013) in northeastern Arabah Valley attest to regional pottery production on a truly vast scale over a lengthy span of time within the EB 1 period.

Fig. 11 Select examples of Safi Cups

No	Site	References
1	En Naq	Courtesy of Konstantine Politis
2	En Naq	Courtesy of Konstantine Politis
3	En Naq	A Safi Cup (amidst many other looted vessels) in an antiquities store, via Dolorosa, Jerusalem; photo taken surreptitiously by author ca 1995
4	En Naq	Courtesy of Konstantine Politis
5	En Naq	Courtesy of Konstantine Politis
6	En Naq	Rendering of a Safi Cup

3.6 Summary

Early Bronze pottery production in the southern Levant is indicative of a long-range trend towards communal efforts in pottery production, which accounts for much of the long-understood standardization of types that allowed Petrie (1891) and others following him to use this important artifact type as an indicator of chronology. That trend, which began in the Late Neolithic period, and which continued throughout Chalcolithic times, seems to have been disrupted during the Late Chalcolithic transition to Early EB 1, when continuity in the cultural burden was greatly interrupted (Braun, 2011, 2019, 2021b), particularly in the northern region.

The assemblage of storage vessels associated with Yiftahel II and DMP, seems to illustrate one aspect of that discontinuity. It may have been born of necessity, possibly because aside from the case of GBW, there were no major producers of pottery extant in that time span. That, however, may be a confined view as to date that site has yielded the only large-scale assemblage of nearly complete pots in the region and thus, it is difficult to compare and contrast it with contemporaneous ceramic assemblages. The Tel Te'o assemblage suggests that the site may have had access to the production of more skilled potters other than the producers of GBW.

By contrast, information from the southern region suggests significant continuity with LC potting traditions (Braun, 2000a, b) in an LC-EB 1 transition period, although there is evidence of major discontinuity in settlement patterns and mortuary behavior at the end of the LC. That, however, is only part of the picture as the end of the Late Chalcolithic communities in the Beer-sheba region is an indication of a major break in settlement patterns. The picture of Chalcolithic communities on the Ashqelon Littoral (Braun, 2019), however, seems to be evidence of shifting patterns of settlement, perhaps associated with climatic desiccation.

In more advanced phases of EB 1 it is possible to see that pottery production was primarily on a massive scale with numerous centers active in different regions. That is not totally unexpected as the production of ceramics of the quality and types known in this period was no simple affair. Involved are technical knowledge of clays, their sources, their characteristics for working and after firing, types of materials used for coloring and pyrotechnology. No less important are the manual skills of potters and their aesthetic sensibilities. The assumption is that, as even in earlier times, there was a skilled class of potters working in different centers producing their wares for consumers throughout the southern Levant. That allows for the chronological classifications that have been basic to the study of this and many other periods. Of course, now more modern, scientific methods enhance our understanding, but pottery chronology still remains an essential method of understanding (Cohen-Weinberger, 2022; Roux, 2019; Roux et al., 2018).

Only a chosen few of many possible examples are discussed above to illustrate the kind of ceramic production and associated patterns of trade that appeared as early as the sixth millennium in the southern Levant. Although by no means unique, I have chosen the EB 1 period for my study as it is the most familiar to me and offers an excellent opportunity to understand pottery production in late prehistoric periods in the southern Levant. By studying those cited above and other groups (e.g., Egyptianized pottery; Braun, 2005b), it is possible to discern much about advanced and late EB 1 society through its pottery, even without direct knowledge of actual centers of production such as that recently excavated at Tall Abu Habil.

Centers of production may have been large-scale workshops in concentrations apparently similar to that of the Tall Abul Habil site. However, those centers may have been more diverse, similar to villages or regions where numerous potters engaged in their craft. Ethnographic evidence for that is replete in the literature, with vestiges of such activity still found in some traditional societies (e.g., London, 2000; Roux et al., 2018).

Understanding details of production and diffusion of ceramic artifacts such as the examples cited above, emphasizes the importance of studies of this kind. From this type of inquiry and the information it provides, it is possible to extrapolate and better understand late prehistoric, ceramic-producing societies in the region, especially in the way it details aspects of intercourse between sites and likely means by which those associations were accomplished. In short, understanding pottery production and dispersal of its exponents offers many insights into the warp and woof of those early societies (Roux, 2019).[8]

Acknowledgments Thanks are due to Galit Litani, curator and the crew of the Israel Antiquities Authority's storerooms at Beth Shemesh for help in accessing objects from different sites.

References

Amiran, R. (1969). *Ancient pottery of the holy land*. Massada.
Baldi, J. S. (2020). Broadening perspectives through the chaine operatoire approach: Scattered epistemological notes on the case study of Tell Abu Habil, Jordan. *Archaeological Review from Cambridge, 35*(1), 126–148. https://doi.org/10.17863/CAM.65448
Baldi, J. S., Hourani, F. & Pichon, F. (2019). *The LaP Job project team's first time in the field at Tell Abu Habil (Jordan)*. https://archeorient.hypotheses.org/12353

---

[8] A study of the myriad possibilities of the kinds of intercourse that pottery production and its dispersal suggest is beyond the scope of this paper. Roux's treatment offers an excellent summary on this subject.

Braun, E. (1985) *En Shadud: Salvage excavations at a farming community in the Jezreel Valley, Israel* (British archaeological reports international series 249).

Braun, E. (1996). *Cultural diversity and change in the early bronze I of Israel and Jordan: Towards an understanding of the chronological progression and patterns of regionalism in early bronze society*. Ph. D. Thesis: Tel Aviv University. https://independent.academia.edu/EliotBraun

Braun, E. (1997). *Yiftahel: Salvage & rescue excavations at a prehistoric village in lower Galilee, Israel* (IAA reports 2). Israel Antiquities Authority.

Braun, E. (2000a). Area G at Afridar, Palmahim Quarry 3 and the earliest pottery of Early Bronze I: Part of the missing link. In G. Philip & D. Baird (Eds.), *Breaking with the past: Ceramics and change in the Early Bronze Age of the Southern Levant* (pp. 113–128). Sheffield Academic Press.

Braun, E. (2000b). Post mortem: A late prehistoric site at Palmahim quarry. *Bulletin of the Anglo-Israel Archaeological Society, 17*, 17–28.

Braun, E. (2004). *Early Beth Shan (strata XIX-XIII): G. M. FitzGerald's deep cut on the tell* (University museum monograph 121). University of Pennsylvania Museum of archaeology and anthropology.

Braun, E. (2005a). Parochialism in EB I ceramic traditions: The case of a "Safi Cup" from the EB I site at Palmahim Quarry, Israel. In A. Maier & P. de Miroschedji (Eds.), *I will speak the riddle of ancient times: Festschrift in honor of Prof. Amihai Mazar* (pp. 3–7). Eisenbrauns.

Braun, E. (2005b). Identifying ethnicity from prehistoric pottery in ancient Egypt and the southern Levant. In J. Clarke (Ed.), *Archaeological perspectives on the transmission & transformation of culture in the eastern Mediterranean* (Levant supplementary series) (Vol. 2, pp. 140–154). Oxbow.

Braun, E. (2009). Social development and continuity in Early Bronze Age I of the southern Levant: Reflections on evidence for different modes of ceramic production. In S. A. Rosen & V. Roux (Eds.), *Techniques & people: Anthropological perspectives on technology in the archaeology of the proto-historic & early historic periods in the southern Levant* (Mémoires et travaux du Centre de Recherche Français à Jérusalem: Archéologie et sciences de l'antiquité et du Moyen Âge 9) (pp. 233–252). De Brocard.

Braun, E. (2011). Chapter 12: The transition from Chalcolithic to EB I in the southern Levant: A 'Lost Horizon' slowly revealed. In J. L. Lovell & Y. M. Rowan (Eds.), *Culture, chronology & the chalcolithic: Theory and transition* (CBRL Levant supplementary monograph series) (Vol. 9, pp. 160–177). Oxbow Books.

Braun, E. (2012a). On some Levantine Early Bronze Age ceramic "wares" and styles. *Palestine Exploration Quarterly, 144*(1), 5–32.

Braun, E. (2012b–2013). A note on relations between the southern Levant and Egypt during early Dynasty 0. *Egypt & the Levant XXII-XXIII*, 339–348.

Braun, E. (2013). *Early Megiddo on the East Slope (The "Megiddo Stages"). A Report on the Early Occupation of the East Slope of Megiddo—Results of the Oriental Institute's Excavations, 1925–1933* (Oriental Institute Publications 139). The Oriental Institute of the University of Chicago.

Braun, E. (2019). Forging a link: Evidence for a 'Lost Horizon'. In H. Goldfus, M. I. Gruber, S. Yona, & P. Fabian (Eds.), *The Late Chalcolithic to EB 1 Transition in the Southern Levant. 'Isaac went out to the field': Studies in Archaeology & Ancient Cultures in Honor of Isaac Gilead* (pp. 66–95). Archeopress.

Braun, E. (2021a). Chapter 10: Observations on the Early Bronze Age Cemetery at An-Naq'. In K. Politis (Ed). *Zoara I:Ancient Landscapes & Excavations at the Ghor as-Safi in Jordan, 1997–2018* (PEF annual XVII 2020) (pp. 127–140). Palestine Exploration Fund.

Braun, E. (2021b). They seek It here they seek it there, "That Demned Elusive" Late Chalcolithic to Early Bronze I transition. In M. J. Adams & V. Roux (Eds.), *Transitions during the Early Bronze Age in the Levant: Methodological problems & unterpretative perspectives* (Ägypten und Altes Testament 109) (pp. 7–35). Zaphon.

Braun, E., & Gophna, R. (2004). Excavations at Afridar--Area G. *Atiqot, 45*, 185–242.

Braun, E. & van den Brink, E. C. M. (2022). *Two Ancient Cemeteries in the Qirya Quarter of Tel Aviv* (Ägypten und Altes Testament 113). Zaphon.

Braun, E., van den Brink, E. C. M., Regev, J., Boaretto, E., & Bar, S. (2013). Aspects of radiocarbon determinations and the dating of the transition from the Chalcolithic period to Early Bronze Age I in the southern Levant. *Paléorient, 39*(1), 23–46.

Cohen-Weinberger, A. (2022). Chapter 2: Petrographic analysis of selected vessels. In A. Golani (Ed.), *Ashqelon Barne'a: The site, volume I* (IAA reports 170) (pp. 91–99). Israel Antiquities Authority.

Eisenberg, E., & , Y. (2016). The Early Bronze Age IB pottery assemblage from Tel Kitan, Central Jordan Valley. *Israel Excavation Journal, 66*(1), 1–34.

Eisenberg, E., Gopher, A. & Greenberg, R. (2001). *Tel Te'o: A Neolithic, Chalcolithic, and Early Bronze Age Site in the Hula Valley* (IAA reports 13). Israel Antiquities Authority.

Fischer, P. M. (2008). *Tell Abu Al-Kharaz in the Jordan Valley, Vol. I: The Early Bronze Age* (Österreichische Akademie der Wissenschaften Denkschriften der Gesamtakademie, Band 48). Österreichische Akademie der Wissenschaften.

FitzGerald, G. M. (1935). Beth Shan: Earliest pottery. *The Museum Journal* (The University Museum, University of Pennsylvania, Philadelphia), *XXIV*, 5–22.

Gal, Z., & Covello-Paran, C. (1996). Excavations at 'Afula, 1989. *Atiqot, XXX*, 25–67.

Garfinkel, Y. (1992). *The Pottery Assemblages of the Sha'ar Hagolan and Rabah Stages of Munhata (Israel) (Les Cahiers du Centre de Recherche Français de Jerusalem 6)*. Association Paléorient.

Garfinkel, Y. (1999). *Neolithic & Chalcolithic Pottery of the Southern Levant (Qedem 39)*. The Hebrew University of Jerusalem.

Genz, H. (2000). Chapter 15: Grain-wash ware in Early Bronze Age III? The evidence from Khirbet ez-Zeraqon. In G. Philip & D. Baird (Eds.), *Ceramics and change in the Early Bronze Age of the Southern Levant* (Levantine archaeology 2) (pp. 279–286). Sheffield Academic Press.

Getzov, N. (2006) *The Tel Bet Yerah Excavations, 1994–1995* (IAA reports 28). Israel Antiquities Authority.

Golani, A. (2003), *Salvage excavations at the Early Bronze Age site of Qiryat Ata* (IAA Reports 18). Israel Antiquities Authority.

Gopher, A. & Tsuk, TS. (1996). *The Nahal Qanah Cave: Earliest gold in the southern Levant* (Monograph series of the Institute of Archaeology, Tel Aviv University, no. 12). Tel Aviv University.

Goren, Y. (1991). *The beginnings of pottery production in Israel: Technology & typology of protohistoric ceramic assemblages in Eretz-Israel (6th-4th millennia B.C.E)*. Ph.D. thesis: The Hebrew University of Jerusalem (Hebrew with English Summary).

Goren, Y., & Zuckerman, S. (2000). An overview of the typology, provenance and technology of the Early Bronze Age I 'Gray Burnished Ware'. In G. Philip & D. Baird (Eds.), *Ceramics and change in the Early Bronze Age of the Southern Levant* (Levantine archaeology 2) (pp. 165–183). Sheffield Academic Press.

Greenberg, R., & Iserlis, M. (2014). Chapter 3: The early bronze pottery industries. In *Bet Yerah: The early bronze age mound. Volume II: Urban structure & material culture. 1933–1986 excavations* (IAA reports 54) (pp. 53–149). Israel Antiquities Authority.

Hourani, F. (2010). Late Chalcolithic/Early Bronze I transition settlements in the middle Jordan Valley: Investigating alluvial sequences as a chronostratigraphical framework, and cycles as a social organising component. *Paléorient, 26*(1), 123–139.

Kafafi, Z. (2001). *Jebel Abu Thawwab (er Rumman), Central Jordan: The Late Neolithic & Early Bronze Age I occupations* (Bibliotheca neolithica asiae meridionalis et occidentalis & Yarmouk University, Monograph of the Institute of Archaeology & anthropology 3). ex Oriente.

Kenyon, K. M. (1965). *Excavations at Jericho 2*. The British School of Archaeology of Jerusalem.

Kerner, S. (2009). The Pottery of Tall Gujarat al-Ghuzlan 2000-2004. In L. Khalil & K. Schmidt (Eds.), *Prehistoric 'Aqaba I* (Orient-Archäologie Band 23) (pp. 127–232). Verlag Marie Leidorf GmbH.

Kersel, M. M., & Chesson, M. S. (2013). Looting matters: Early Bronze Age cemeteries of Jordan's Southeast Dead Sea plain in the past and present. In S. Tarlow & L. Nilsson Stutz (Eds.), *The Oxford handbook of the archaeology of death and burial* (pp. 677–694). Oxford University Press.

Khalil, L. A. (2009). The Excavations at Tall al-Magass: Stratigraphy and architecture. In L. Khalil & K. Schmidt (Eds.), *Prehistoric ᶜAqaba I* (Orient-Archäologie Band 23) (pp. 1–15). Verlag Marie Leidorf GmbH.

London, G. (2000). Continuity and change in Cypriot pottery production. *Near Eastern Archaeology, 63*(2), 102–110.

Marqet-Krause, J. (1949). *Les Fouilles de 'Ay (et Tell) 1933–1935 : La Résurrection d'une grande cité biblique (texte)* (Bibliothèque archéologique et historique XLV). Librairie Orientaliste Paul Geuthner.

Mazar, A. (1990). *Archaeology of the Land of the Bible: 10,000–586*. Doubleday.

Mazar, A. (Ed.). (2012). *Excavations at Tel Beth Shean IV 1989–1996: The fourth & third millennia B C E*. The Israel Exploration Society & Hebrew University of Jerusalem.

Petrie, W. M. F. (1891). Chronology of pottery. *Palestine exploration fund quarterly statement* 23 *(for 1891)*, 68.

Porat, N. (1989). *Composition of pottery: Application to the study of the interrelations between Canaan and Egypt during the 3rd millennium B.C.* Ph. D. Thesis. The Hebrew University of Jerusalem.

Regev, J., de Miroschedji, P., Greenberg, R., Braun, E., Greenhut, Z., & Boaretto, E. (2012). Chronology of the Early Bronze Age in the southern Levant: New analysis for a high chronology. *Radiocarbon, 54*(3–4), 525–566.

Rotem, Y., Iserlis, M., Höflmayer, F., & Rowan, Y. M. (2019). Tel Yaqush: An Early Bronze Age village in the central Jordan Valley, Israel. *Bulletin of the American Schools of Oriental Research, 381,* 107–184.

Roux, V. (2019). Modeling the relational structure of ancient societies through the *chaîne opératoire*: The Late Chalcolithic societies of the southern Levant as a case study. In M. Saqalli & L. M. Vander (Eds.), *Integrating qualitative & social science factors in archaeological modelling* (pp. 163–184). Springer.

Roux, V., Van Den Brink, E. C. M., & Shalev, S. (2013). Continuity and discontinuity in the Shephela (Israel) between the Late Chalcolithc and the Early Bronze I: The Modi'in "deep deposits" ceramic assemblages as a case-study. *Paléorient, 39*(1), 63–81.

Roux, V., Bril, B., & Karasik, A. (2018). Weak ties and expertise. *Journal of archaeological method & theory, 25*, 1024–1050.

Saller, S. (1964–5). Bab edh-Dhra'. *Liber Annuus,* 1964–5, 137–219.

Schaub, R. T., & Rast, W. E. (1989). *Bâb edh-Dhrâᶜ: Excavations in the cemetery directed by Paul W. Lapp (1965-67)*. Eisenbrauns.

Shalem, D., Cohen-Weinberger, A., Gandulla, B., & Milevski, I. (2019). Ceramic connections and regional entities: The petrography of Late Chalcolithic pottery from sites in the Galilee. (Israel). In H. Goldfus, M. I. Gruber, S. Yona, & P. Fabian (Eds.), *The Late Chalcolithic to EB I transition in the southern Levant, 'Isaac went out to the field': Studies in archaeology & ancient cultures in honor of Isaac Gilead* (pp. 262–277). Archeopress.

Stager, L. E. (1990). Painted pottery and its relationship to the weaving crafts in Canaan during the Early Bronze Age I. *Eretz Israel, XXI,* 83–87.

Stekelis, M. (1935). *Les monuments mégalithiques de Palestine* (Archives de l'Institut de Paléontologie Humaine: Mémoire 15). Masson.

Stekelis, M. (1961). *La necropolis megalitica de Ala-Safat, Transjordania (Monografias, I, del Instituto de Prehistoria y Arqueologia)*. Diputacion Provincial de Barcelona.

Tufnell, O., et al. (1958). *Lachish IV (Tell ed-Duweir): The Bronze Age*. Oxford University Press.

de Vaux, R. (1955). Les fouilles de Tell el-Far'ah, près Naplouse: cinquième campagne. *Revue Biblique, 62,* 541–589.

Wampler, J. C. (1947). *Tell En-Nasbeh II: The pottery (excavated under the direction of the late William Frederic Badé)*. The Palestine Institute of Pacific School of Religion & the American Schools of Oriental Research.

Wright, G. E. (1937). *The Pottery of Palestine from the Earliest Times to the End of the Early Bronze Age*. American Schools of Oriental Research.

Yannai, E. (2006). *`En Esur ('Ein Asawir) I. Excavations at a protohistoric site in the coastal plain of Israel* (IAA Reports 31). The Israel Antiquities Authority.

The Outline and Design of Fortified Cities of the Early Bronze IB and II

Nimrod Getzov and Ianir Milevski

Abstract To date scholarship has maintained that urban centers emerged in the southern Levant during the Early Bronze IB in a process in which fortified cities were the skeletal formation of settlements of the region and were perceived as part of the archaeological landscape. A survey of the early urban topographical centers in the southern Levant shows that these early centers were built on summits, ridges or slopes, or a combination of these.

In this paper we will argue for a different perspective: while topographical elements could to some extent determine the location of the urban centers of the Early Bronze Age, human activity could have changed the landscape. Our argument is not based on objective conditions, but rather on the social organization within these centers.

The emergence of Early Bronze Age cities introduces the question of how much the configuration of the fortified cities was influenced by a known architectural design model or whether it reflects an existing topography whereby walls were erected on it. Similarly, we can study how much the construction of such fortified cities was inspired by common sources or whether these cities underwent particular processes for each community with little reciprocal influence.

Keywords Early Bronze Ib · Early Bronze II · Urbanization · Fortifications · Oil lamps · Southern Levant

N. Getzov (✉) · I. Milevski
Israel Antiquities Authority, Jerusalem, Israel
e-mail: nimrod@getzov.com; ianirmilevski@gmail.com

1 Introduction

Fortified urban centers or cities began to exist in the southern Levant during the Early Bronze (henceforth EB) IB (Paz, 2002; Milevski et al., 2021),[1] Large and planned settlements of earlier periods have been found. These include the Pre-Pottery Neolithic C settlement in Moza (Khalaily & Vardi, 2020), the Pottery Neolithic settlement in Sha'ar Ha-Golan (Ben-Shlomo & Garfinkel, 2009), and the Early Chalcolithic site of `En Zippori (Milevski & Getzov, 2014; Yaroshevich, 2016; Getzov & Milevski, 2017). In this site and others, dated earlier than the EB IB, wide walls can be identified as massive buildings or fortifications.[2] But these phenomena are sporadic and cannot be seen as truely urban; their presence merely underscores the fact that the cities of the EB did not appear unexpectedly.

Without going deeply into a discussion about the cause and effect of human activity on the landscape, we can say that different archaeological schools have drawn different interpretations from these relationships. Whereas the Processual perspectives largely gave importance to the study of demography and landscape relations within regional perspectives (e.g., Gophna, 1995; Getzov et al., 2001), the post-processual (interpretative) viewpoints emphasized the effects produced on the social and individual perception of the archaeological landscape (e.g., Ucko & Layton, 1999; Tilley, 2010; Greenberg, 2019: 207–209).

Gophna (1984), while seeking to draw the long-term development of the archaeological landscape and the demography of settlements and regions from at least the Chalcolithic period onwards (ca. 6500 years ago), explained how man can shape the landscape by building fortified cities in the southern Levant. Gophna suggested that the majority of the fortified EB II-III sites were located at the tops of hilly landscapes and that the larger settlements (e.g., `Ai, Tel Yarmouth) began to spill over onto the slopes of the hills. The opposite is true, however. The typical Middle Bronze urban cities, ubiquitous in the plains and valley landscape, were designed as fortified soil ramparts so. Furthermore, according to Herzog (1976: 77, 266).The visible architectural element in the cities of the EB II is their fortifications. He claimed that this period presents the first urban acropolis.

---

[1] For other opinions, see: Paz, 2010: 25–26, 229; de Miroschedji, 1989, 2012–13; Greenberg, 2019: 70–135.

[2] E.g.: the findings from the Early Chalcolithic at Wadi Rabah (Kaplan 1958, Building C), the Late Chalcolithic period at Ein Esur (Yannai, 2006: 24, Fig. 2.19) and the massive wall from the EB IA at Kafer Qana (H. Smithline, pers. comm.).

2 The Outline of Southern Levantine Cities

2.1 Research Questions

In this paper we argue for a different perspective. While topographical elements could to some degree determine the location of the urban centers of the Early Bronze Age, human activity could change the landscape, not because of objective conditions but because of the ways of social organization within these centers.

For that, the emergence of EB cities introduces a first question: what a city during this period is. Although, the state of archaeological research on cities in the Near East and the Levant from the times of Gordon Childe (1950) has been discussed some venerable questions are renewed, including how the cities of the southern Levant are characterized by, including interpretative explanations which sometimes denies the urban character of this period (Chesson, 2003, 2019).

From our point of view (Milevski et al., 2021, 128; Milevski & Yegorov, 2022, 115–116; with bibliography) a city is a permanent settlement, large enough, inhabited by a relatively small population, residing in close proximity and socially diversity, separated from its countryside, generally by defensive or enclosure walls. It contains public buildings, some of them for the political and religious elites, with different activity areas that could be distinguished, including domestic, production and exchange areas (Childe, 1950, Smith, 2009, Yoffe, 2015).

For us one of the main archaeological elements in the case of the EB centers, are fortifications which serve to define those who are inside and those who are outside the city, providing also a sense of identity to the people who live in the center and in the surrounding areas, and public buildings. Then the question is how much the outline of the fortified cities is influenced by a known architectural design model or whether it reflects an existing outline whereby walls are erected around it. Similarly, we can study how much the construction of such fortified cities is influenced by common sources or particular processes in each community with little mutual influence. Furthermore, a quick survey of the topographical "scenes" in which the early urban centers were located in the southern Levant shows that these are summits, ridges or slopes, or a combination of these.

To answer these questions, we will summarize and discuss the remains of 13 sites where EB IB and EB II fortifications were discovered and where enough information is available to provide the outline of the city (Fig. 1, Table 1). In some cases, it is unclear whether the fortification was built during the EB II or EB III and therefore they will be noted together.

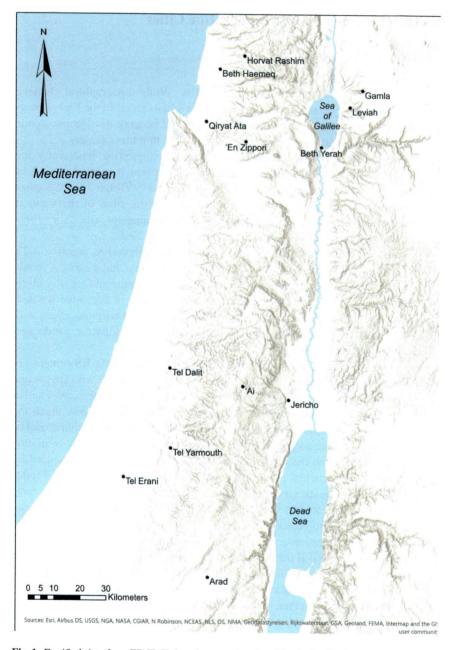

Fig. 1 Fortified sites from EB IB-II, location map (produced by Atalya Fadida in ESRI ArcGIS)

Table 1 EB IB and II urban fortified centers from the southern Levant according to topographical modes and fortification characteristics

	Site	Fortification date	Model	Estimated area (dunams)	Bastion	Gate
1	H. Rashim	EB II	Dome and Slope	40	Semi-circular	
2	Beth Haemeq Site	EB II	Slope	100		Postern gate
3	Gamla	EB II	Crest and slope	<100		
4	Qiryat Ata	EB II	Slope	30		
5	Leviah	EB II-III	Spur	50–90		Wide gate
6	'En Zippori	EB IB	Dome and slope	500	Square with rounded corners	Postern gate
7	Beth Yerah	EB IB	Spur	<300		Wide Gate
8	Tel Dalit	EB II	Dome and slope	40		Postern Gate
9	'Ai	EB II-III	Dome and slope	110	Semi- circular	Postern Gate
10	Jericho	EB II-III	Crest and slope	30	Semi- circular and square	Postern Gate?
11	Tel Yarmouth	EB II-III	Dome and slope	160		Wide gate
12	Tel Erani	EB IB	Dome and slope	160		
13	Arad	EB II	Crest and slope	90	Semi- circular and square	Wide gates and postern gates

2.2 Case Studies

2.2.1 Horbat Rashim (Fig. 2)

The site occupies two neighboring hills The northwestern hill bears the remains of a ca. 40 dunam EB city. Limited excavations were conducted in different areas of this site. In Area A, on a wide plateau southwest of the slope, an EB I fortification wall and an EB II semi-circular bastion were found (Braun, 1996: 3–8). In Area D, on the eastern slope, a portion of a massive structure was discovered from EB II and it is likely a portion of a fortified wall or a gate (Braun, 2010: 2–3). In Area B, at the top of the northern slope, remains were found of structures dated to the EB IB (Braun, 1999, 2010: 5–6). In Area G, at the top of the hill, remains of structures dated to the EB II were discovered (Getzov, 2017).[3] It became clear that during the EB IB the entire hillside had been occupied and during the EB II when the city was

---
[3] The naming of the sites on Fig. 1 in the diary of the excavation were faulty and instead of Area G it was noted as Area E.

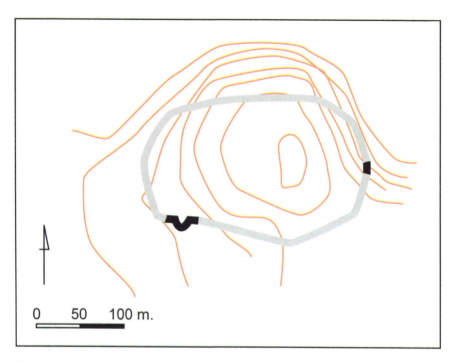

Fig. 2 Horbat Rashim plan with 5 m interval contours. (Drawing: N. Getzov)

fortified the city planners had decided to give up the northern slope and constructed their city in the "dome and slope" model at the top of the hill and on the remaining slopes.

2.2.2 Bet Haemeq (Fig. 3)

The remains of a city dated to the EB II were discovered on the western slope of a wide chalk hill north of Nahal Zach. At this site, early settlements were discovered from the late Chalcolithic period, EB I and EB II. During the EB II, a wall was built that surrounded a city that spans an area of ca. 100 dunams (Getzov & Gur, in press),

Area D on the lower part of the slope exposed foundations of a 3.5 m wide wall containing a postern gate. Area B near the top of the slope, but not quite at the top, revealed a rampart and it is assumed that a fortification wall existed at its base. According to limited excavations in four separate areas (Givon, 2002; Gur & Getzov, 2011; Spivak, pers. comm.), and based on the scattering of pottery sherds, it is assumed that a dense city was built on an area of ca. 100 dunam and was encased by a wall. According to reconstruction of the extent of the wall, it became apparent that the city occupied a slope of an extension, the top part on the shoulder of the extension and the lower part of a small valley of the Zach Stream. It is evident that the city was constructed according to the "Slope" model.

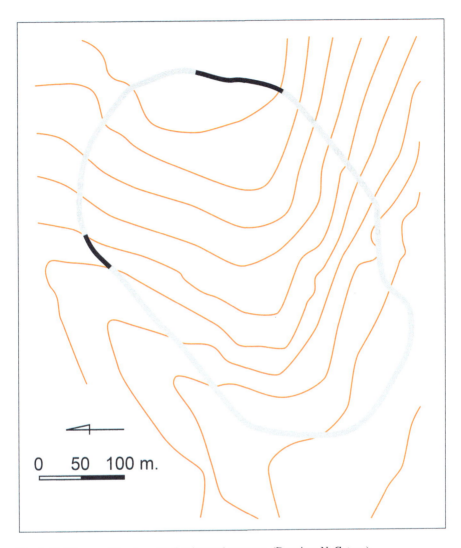

Fig. 3 Bet Haemeq Site plan with 5 m interval contours. (Drawing: N. Getzov)

2.2.3 Gamla

The site is mainly known as a city dating from the Second Temple period. It reached its peak in the first century BCE and spans ca. 140 dunams. The city occupied the southern slope of a narrow basalt ridge. Most of the excavated fields reveal pottery remains dating from the EB II (Paz, 2018: Figs. 6.4–6.5) and despite the fact that there is not enough information to state with certainty the extent of the city from that period, it is safe to assume that it was not less than 100 dunam. The eastern city wall dates from the Second Temple period. Excavators believe that it was partially built on the outline of a wall dating from the EB (Yavor, 2010: 25). Although, as noted, there is insufficient information available to allow for the reconstruction of the extent of the wall, the scattered remains of pottery reveals that the city was built according to the "crest and slope" city model.

2.2.4 Qiryat Ata (Fig. 4)

The remains of a small, fortified city dated to the EB II, spanning an area of 30 dunam. were found on a moderate slope of a wide-based hill (Golani, 2003, 2013: Fig. 1). The remains of a wall were found only in the south end of the city, at the bottom of the slope, but the extent of the remains shows that the settlement was not at the top of the hill and therefore it is apparent that it was constructed based on the "Slope" model.

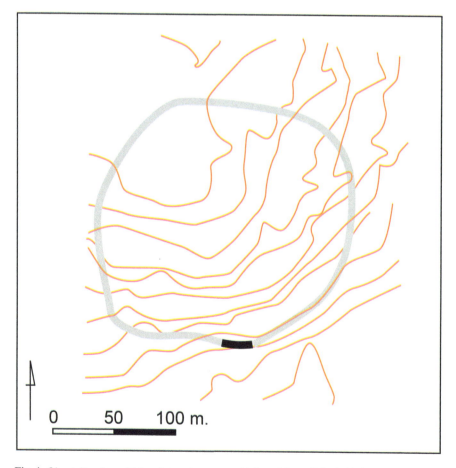

Fig. 4 Qiryat Ata plan with 1 m interval contours. (Adapted from Golani, 2013, Fig. 1, drawing: N. Getzov)

2.2.5 Leviah and Other Cities in the Golan (Fig. 5)

Leviah is a city built on a narrow planar spur, spanning an area of approximately 90 dunams. It was fortified during the EB II and its area was thereafter reduced to less than 50 dunams (Paz, 2018:161, Fig. 2.3). To the north and south, the extension had

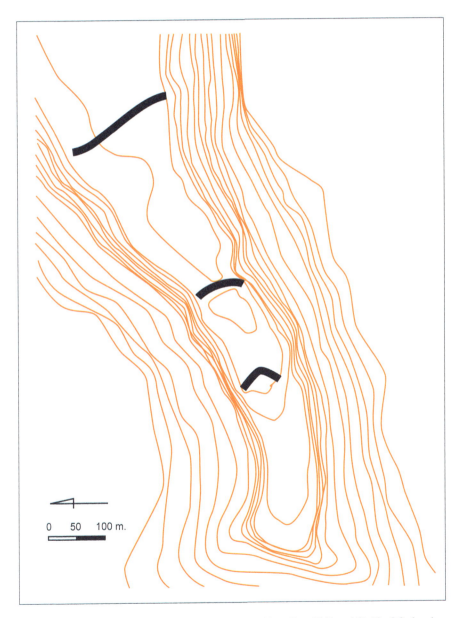

Fig. 5 Leviah plan with 5 m interval contours. (Adapted from Paz, 2018, p. 161, Fig. 2.3, drawing: N. Getzov)

very steep slopes, walls protected the EB II city to the east and the city followed a "spur" model. Paz illustrates that at the same time the Golan was home to other cities employing a similar layout (Paz, 2018:145–160). Most of them are known only from archaeological surveys and at this point of the research, no graphic illustration is available.

2.2.6 'En Zippori (Giva'at Rabi) (Fig. 6)

This is an extensive site built on a gentle slope, located at the foot of Giv'at Rabi and south of Nahal Zippori. Remains of a settlement dated to the EB IB were discovered (Milevski et al., 2014). These settlements contained double-apse structures, rectangular structures with rounded corners and circular structures. It is our opinion that the circular structures acted as foundations for towers that guarded the family complex and allowed for the storage of food and essential goods required during hard times. Other researchers claim that these structures were silos (Golani & Yannai, 2016). At the southeastern edge of the settlement, a 2 m-wide wall was discovered. A 70 m-long portion of the wall was revealed (Milevski et al., 2014, Yaroshevich, 2016). The portion that was revealed contained a postern gate and rectangular

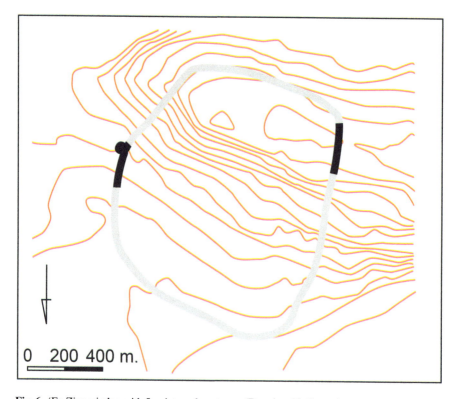

Fig. 6 'En Zippori plan with 5 m interval contours. (Drawing: N. Getzov)

bastion with rounded corners, like the structure discovered in many of the area's excavation fides. During the II the overall size of the settlement decreased, and it did not reach the line of the wall.

At the top of Giva'at Rabi, far above the settlement, there were multiple accumulations dating to the EB IB and EB II. The western area of the hilltop bordering the settlement housed a wide rampart and it is very likely that it contained the remains of a wall. It is also likely that the two portions are part of the same wall that surrounded the area at the bottom of the slope adjacent to Ein Zippori, a rocky area at the center of the slope, and an upper settlement at the top of the hill. The overall size of the city surrounded by a wall is believed to have been 500 dunam and it follows the "dome and slope" model.

2.2.7 Beth Yerah

Beth Yerah (Fig. 7) is a ca. 300 dunam EB city that sits on a narrow strip of dry land between the Sea of Galilee and the Jordan River(Greenberg, 2014: 8–9: Fig. 1.10). During the EB IB a tall and wide wall was erected that blocked access to the dry land strip from the southeast (Getzov, 2006: 7–39). Greenberg and Paz date the wall to the EB II. They explain the prominence of the EB IB pottery by the fact that the denizens of EB II had mined the building materials from earlier strata (Greenberg & Paz, 2014, plan 2.3). Their thesis, however, is faulty: Locus 179, located in the area Greenberg and Paz claim was the source of the building materials, strata containing remains of EB IB settlements, is evident. Additionally, the walls contain four distinct stages of extended building activity as well as additions and rebuilding after destruction. It is not possible that throughout the entire extended building period the EB II builders had made a concerted effort to use only material from one early source and did not use even one sherd from the current period. At this stage of research, it is not clear what the quality of EB II fortifications is at Bet Yerah, but it is possible to surmise that the later portion of the EB IB fortification was utilized and the city was planned according to the "spur" city model. The wall contained a wide gate. Note that the Bet Yerah excavations also revealed fortifications dating to the EB III, but these will not be discussed here.

2.2.8 Tel Dalit (Fig. 8)

The site is found at the top of a high hill. Excavations reveal remains from an EB I town as well as a small (ca. 49 dunam) urban settlement that dates to the EB II (Gophna, 1996). Area B at the top of the hill reveals foundations of a wide wall. Area A on the slope also contained similar foundations. Review of the entire outline of Tel Dalit (Gophna, 1996, Fig. 3) reveals that it was an urban settlement built according to the "dome and slope" model. A postern gate was incorporated into the wall.

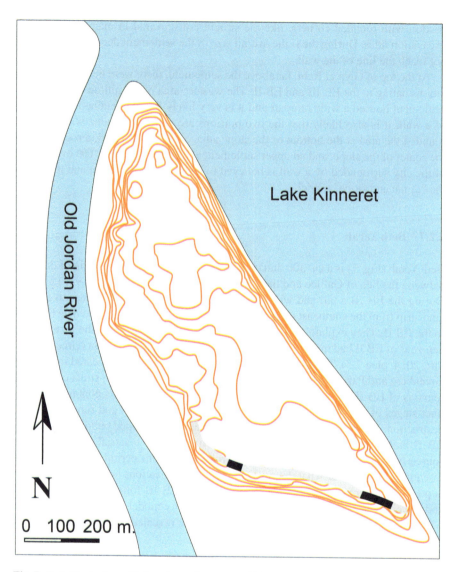

Fig. 7 Beth Yerah plan with 1 m interval contours. (Adapted from Greenberg, 2014, Fig. 1.10, drawing: N. Getzov)

2.2.9 'Ai (et-Tel) (Fig. 9)

The remains here are of a ca. 110 dunam city on top of a wide hill (Callaway, 1980, Fig. 2), surrounded by an EB II and EB III wall. To the west, adjacent to the top, were remains of fortifications and a fort or temple. Most of the remains were discovered along the eastern slope. It is apparent that the city was built according to the "dome and slope" model. The wall contains a postern gate and semi-circular towers.

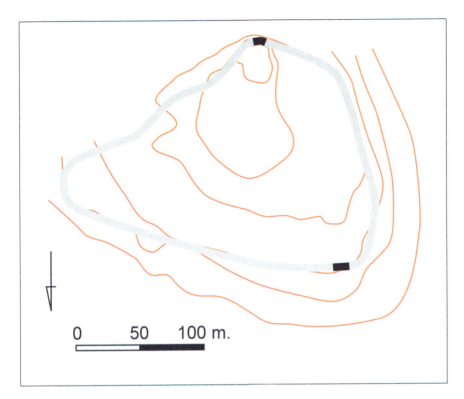

Fig. 8 Tel Dalit plan with 5 m interval contours. (Adapted from Gophna, 1996, Fig. 3, drawing: N. Getzov)

2.2.10 Jericho (Tell es-Sultan) (Fig. 10)

The remains of a small urban settlement dating to the EB II, spanning ca. 30 dunam, were discovered at the top of an ancient tell and its slope (Nigro, 2017, Fig. 8.7). The wall was constructed on a narrow western ridge at the edge of the battery and at the eastern edge the wall followed a spring at the plain just at the foot of the hill. The outline of the wall follows the "crest and slope" model. The wall contained semi-circular towers, a square tower and possibly postern gates.

2.2.11 Tel Yarmouth (Fig. 11)

The remains of a large fortified urban settlement dating to the EB II and EB III, spanning ca. 160 dunam were discovered along the top and slope of a small, wide but high tell (battery) (de Miroschedji, 2012–13, Fig. 1, 2013). Extensive excavations were conducted at different areas on the tell. The foundations of walls encompassing the remains on the slope were discovered in a number of the areas in addition to a large gate. The remains of the wall have not yet been excavated in the areas of

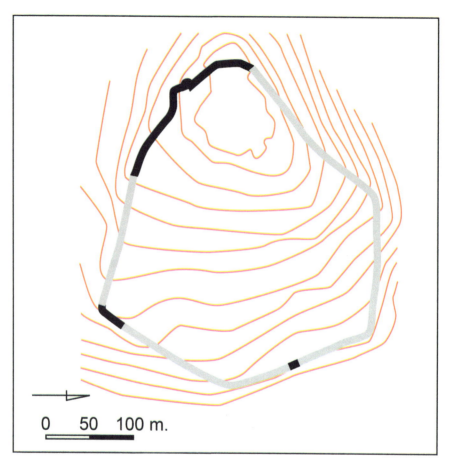

Fig. 9 'Ai plan with 5 m interval contours. (Adapted from Callaway, 1980, Fig. 2; drawing: N. Getzov)

the small tell but de Miroschedji assumes that the wall surrounded it. When comparing it to different sites mentioned above, such as `Ai and Tel Dalit, it is possible to assume that the wall was built adjacent to the top of the battery and that the city follows the "crest and slope" model.

2.2.12 Tel Erani (Fig. 12)

The site is located to the southwest of Nahal Lachish, has a hilltop ("acropolis") and two terraces, with a steep slope facing the stream and a moderate slope to the southwest. The remains of a wide brick wall were discovered at the bottom of the southwest and northwest slopes (Yeivin, 1961; Milevski et al., 2016, 2019; Yekutieli, 2016). The remains show that the wall was built over a long period of time, kept up

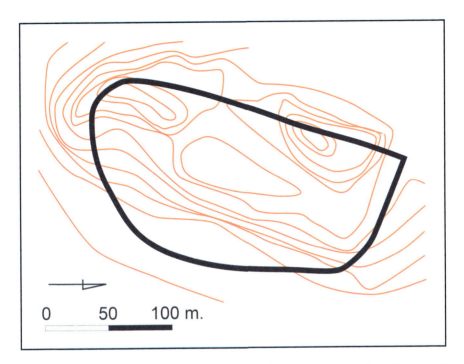

Fig. 10 Jericho (Tell es-Sultan) plan with 1 m interval contours. (Adapted from Nigro, 2017, drawing: N. Getzov)

and renewed and it is evident that it was maintained over at least two stages, all of which can be dated to the early part of EB IB ("Erani C" horizon; and see Kempinski & Gilead, 1991; Yekutieli, 2002). The top of the tell and the northern slope excavations did not extend to EB strata and did not reach virgin soil and therefore it is difficult to estimate the outline of the wall. We propose, however, that in comparison with the sites discussed above the city was built according to the "crest and slope" model and that the wall encompasses an area spanning ca. 160 dunams.

2.2.13 Arad (Fig. 13)

These are the remains of a medium sized, ca. 90 dunam city that was walled during the EB II (Amiran & Ilan, 1996: Pl.68). The city was built along the slopes of a small gorge on a wide hill that rose over the Arad Valley. The lion's share of the wall is found along the ridge, while part of it dissects the bottom of the ravine, adjacent to the mouth that exits the floor of the valley. The ridge where the wall was constructed extends over three domes. The wall surrounds the head of the highest peak towering above the other two. The outline of the wall along the ridge delineates it as a "crest and slope" model. The wall consists of semi-circular towers, square towers as well as two wide gates.

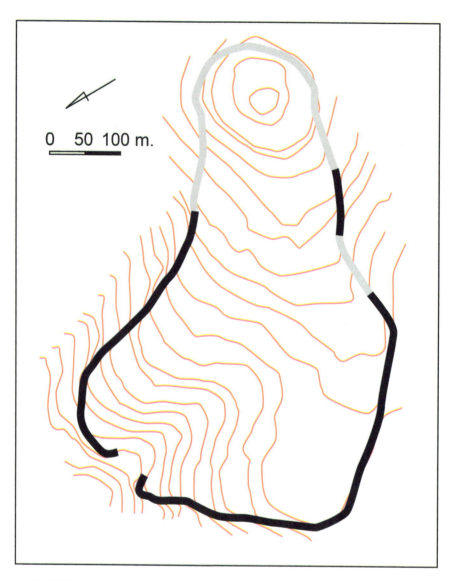

Fig. 11 Tel Yarmouth plan with 5 m interval contours. (Adapted from de Miroschedji, 2012–13, Fig. 1; drawing: N. Getzov)

3 Discussion

It is apparent that the slope constitutes a central element in the layout of many of the EB II cities. The selection of the EB II city at Horbat Rashim to build the city between the peak and bottom of its southern slope, by giving up the settlement on the northern slope, exemplifies that the Slope Type Model was an intended choice

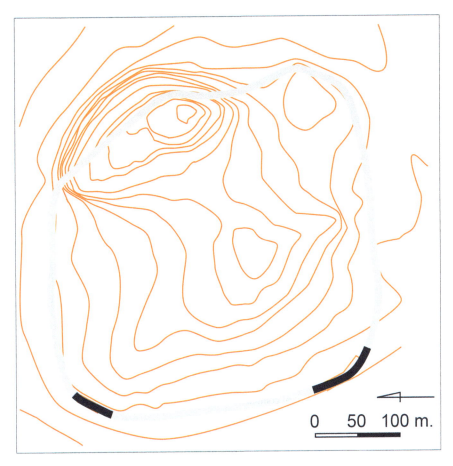

Fig. 12 Tel Erani plan with 1 m interval contours. (Adapted from Milevski et al., 2016, Fig. 1; drawing: N. Getzov)

and not the continuation of the earlier city planning from the time before fortification. At Beit Yerah in the Golan, there are known cities where the model may be different; the valley areas may possibly also have had some urban settlements that stray from this model (Gophna, 1984: 28), but those were far and few between. To date, there is no example of a fortified city dating from the EB whose walls circumvented the summit in a steady height, as was typical in many of the cities starting from Middle Bronze.

There is no explanation based on evidence as to the cause of the aforementioned period constructing their cities specifically on slopes, but we can offer two possible options that may be used as possible explanations. The first option is the primacy of urban settlements during the EB. It is at the very end of the EB I that cities began fortifying in the southern Levant; the large mass of fortified cities is a novelty of the EB II. It is possible that during that time the architects did not comprehend the

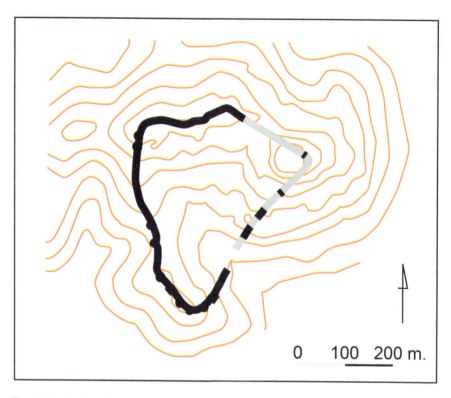

Fig. 13 Arad plan with 5 m interval contours. (Adapted from Amiran & Ilan, 1996, pl.68; drawing: N. Getzov)

military value of locating a city at the top of a hill and surrounding it with a wall. It is also possible that at that time, enemy threats were insufficient to justify such lines of defense. The second option is tied to the location of the urban elite who had not, at that stage, developed differentiation based on building large palaces (Herzog, 1997: 73–74). The Slope type city may have provided the elite the opportunity to stake their topographical claim to the top, thus differentiating themselves from the other residents. It is interesting to note that at Tel Yarmouth the first palace was constructed only during EB III. The enormous palace necessitated its being located atop the wide middle plateau of the slope rather than on top of the narrow peak. The design elements such as the postern gates, wide portals and colonnades were constructed in a similar manner in other urban settlements, but due to the minimal extent of the excavation they were only revealed in a small number of the excavation sites.

Following our survey, synthetized in Table 1, we can observe the characteristics of the outline, gates and bastions that were unveiled at the sites. There are great differences among the size/span of the cities we surveyed, however, there seem to be great similarities in their outline. There appears to be a common source and mutual influence among the different communities that founded the fortified cities in the region. Additionally, the same characteristics of the outline and elements of fortification are present in the early cities that were fortified, such as `En Zippori, Beit Yerah and most likely Tel Erani. This provides a clear clue to the source, continuity and the urbanization process that started as early as EB IB. Only later, during EB II, did the urbanization affect the different building elements within the cities, starting at the dwelling units (Milevski et al., 2021), the disappearance of the circular towers (Golani & Yannai, 2016: 33) and finally the construction of palaces during the EB III (de Miroschedji, 2012–13).

Acknowledgments We are indebted to Ayelet Gezow (Getzov) for the translation of a Hebrew version of this paper and to Atalya Fadida who produced the map in Fig. 1 based on an ArcGIS Esri program. We also are indebted to an anonymous reviewer and the editors of this volume, Erez Ben-Yosef and Ian Jones for critical observations and the editing of the text.

References

Amiran, R., & Ilan, O. (1996). *Early Arad II*. The Israel Museum and the Israel Exploration Society.
Ben-Shlomo, D., & Garfinkel, Y. (2009). Sha'ar Hagolan and new insights on Near Eastern protohistoric urban concepts. *Oxford Journal of Archaeology, 28*, 189–209.
Braun, E. (1996). Salvage excavations at the Early Bronze Age site of Me'ona: final report. *Atiqot, 28*, 1–39.
Braun, E. (1999). Me'ona. *Excavations and Surveys in Israel, 19*, 5*–6*.
Braun, E. (2010). The Early Bronze Age Site of Me'ona in the Western Galilee. *'Atiqot, 62*, 1–15.
Callaway, J. A. (1980). *The Early Bronze Age citadel and lower city at 'Ai (et-Tell)*. Harvard University Press.
Chesson, M. S. (2003). Households, houses, neighborhoods and corporate villages: Modeling the Early Bronze Age as a house society. *Journal of Mediterranean Archaeology, 16*(1), 79–102.
Chesson, M. S. (2019). The southern Levant during the early Bronze Age I–III. In A. Yassur, E. H. C. Landau, & Y. M. Rowan (Eds.), *The Social Archaeology of the Levant* (pp. 163–182). Cambridge University Press.
Childe, V. G. (1950). The Urban Revolution. *Town planning review, 21*(1), 3–17.
de Miroschedji, P. (1989). Le processus d'urbanisation de la Palestine au Bronce ancien: Chronologie et rythmes. In P. de Miroschedji (Ed.), *L 'urbanisation de la Palestine à l'âge du Bronze ancien* (Vol. I, pp. 357–388). British Archaeological Reports.
de Miroschedji, P. (2012–13). L'apparition des palais au Levant ancient au Bronze ancient et sa signication. In C. Michel (Ed.), *De la maison à la ville dans l'orient ancient : Bâtiments publics et lieux de pouvoir* (pp. 95–101). Centre National de la Recherche Scientifique.
de Miroschedji, P. (2013). Fouilles de Tel Yarmouth: Résultats des travaux de 2003 à 2009 (14e-18e campagnes). *Comptes rendus de l'Académie des inscriptions et Belles-Lettres, 157*(2), 759–796.
Getzov, N. (2006). The Tel Beth Yerah Excavations 1994–1995 (IAA Reports 28). Israel Antiquities Authority.
Getzov, N. (2017). Horbat Rashim, Final report, *Hadashot Arkheologiyot – Excavations and Surveys in Israel*, 129. https://www.hadashot-esi.org.il/Report_Detail_Eng.aspx?id=25274&mag_id=125
Getzov, N., & Gur, Y. (in press). Excavations at the Beth Ha-'Emeq site: A rural settlement from the Late Chalcolithic period and a slop city from the Early Bronze Age. *'Atiqot*.
Getzov, N., & Milevski, I. (2017). En Zippori. Preliminary report. *Hadashot Arkheologiyot-Excavations and Surveys in Israel*, 129. https://www.hadashot-esi.org.il/Report_Detail_Eng.aspx?id=25239&mag_id=125

Getzov, N., Paz, Y., & Gophna, R. (2001). *Shifting urban landscapes during the Early Bronze Age in the Land of Israel*. Ramot Publishing.

Givon, S. (2002). Beth Ha'emeq – Village of shepherds and farmers from the Chalcolithic Period and the Early Bronze Age. In E. C. M. van den Brink & E. Yannai (Eds.), *In quest of ancient settlements and landscapes. Archaeological studies in honour of Ram Gophna* (pp. 87–106). Ramot Publishing.

Golani, A. (2003). *Salvage excavations at the Early Bronze Age site of Qiryat Ata*. Israel Antiquities Authority.

Golani, A. (2013). Rescue excavations at the Early Bronze Age site of Qiryat Ata—Area O. *'Atiqot, 75*, 27–60.

Golani, A., & Yannai, E. (2016). Storage structures of the Late Early Bronze I in the southern Levant and the urbanization process. *Palestine Exploration Quarterly, 148*(1), 8–41.

Gophna, R. (1984). The settlement landscape of Palestine in the Early Bronze Age II-III and Middle Bronze Age II. *Israel Exploration Journal, 34*, 24–31.

Gophna, R. (1995). Early Bronze Age Canaan: Some spatial and demographic observation. In T. E. Levy (Ed.), *The Archaeology of society in the Holy Land* (pp. 269–280). Leicester University Press.

Gophna, R. (1996). *Excavations at Tel Dalit*. Ramot Publishing.

Greenberg, R. (2014). The formation of the mound of Beth Yerah. In R. Greenberg (Ed.), *Beth Yerah. The Early Bronze Age mound. Vol. II: Urban structure and material culture, 1933–1986 excavations* (pp. 1–14). Israel Antiquities Authority.

Greenberg, R. (2019). *The Archaeology of the Bronze Age Levant. From urban origins to the demise of the city-states, 3700–1000 BCE*. Cambridge University Press.

Greenberg, R., & Paz, S. (2014). Early Bronze Age architecture, function, and planning. In R. Greenberg & B. Yerah (Eds.), *The Early Bronze Age mound. Vol. II: Urban structure, and material culture, 1933–1986 excavations* (pp. 15–52). Israel Antiquities Authority.

Gur, Y., & Getzov, N. (2011). Bet Ha-'Emeq. Preliminary report, *Hadashot Arkheologiyot – Excavations and surveys in Israel*, 123, https://www.hadashot-esi.org.il/Report_Detail_Eng.aspx?id=1803&mag_id=118

Herzog, Z. (1976). *The city-gate in Eretz-Israel and its neighboring countries*. Tel Aviv University.

Herzog, Z. (1997). *Archaeology of the city. Urban planning in ancient Israel and its social implications*. Tel Aviv University.

Kaplan, J. (1958). Excavations at Wadi Rabah. *Israel Exploration Journal 8*, 149–160.

Kempinski, A., & Gilead, I. (1991). New excavations at Tel Erani: A preliminary report of the 1985–1988 season. *Tel Aviv, 18*, 164–191.

Khalaily, H., & Vardi, J. (2020). In H. Khalaily, A. Re'em, J. Vardi, & I. Milevski (Eds.), *The Mega Project at Motza (Moẓa): The Neolithic and Later Occupations up to the 20th Century*. Israel Antiquities Authority.

Milevsk, I., & Getzov, N. (2014). 'En Zippori. Preliminary report. *Hadashot Arkheologiyot, 126*. http://www.hadashot-esi.org.il/Report_Detail_Eng.aspx?id=13675

Milevski, I., & Yegorov, D. (2022). El origen de las primeras ciudades en el levante meridional. Una visión desde Tel Erani. In M. Campagno, B. Gandulla, & I. Milevski (Eds.), *Relaciones entre Egipto y Palestina en el IV milenio a.c. Modelos e interpretaciones* (Estudios del Mediterráneo Antiguo, PEFSCEA, 27). Miño y Dávila.

Milevski, I., Liran, R., & Getzov, N. (2014). The Early Bronze Age town of 'En Zippori in the Galilee (Israel). *Antiquity Project Gallery, 339*. http://antiquity.ac.uk/projgall/milevski339

Milevski, I., Yegorov, D., Aladjem, E., & Pasternak, M. D. (2016). Salvage excavation at Tel Erani, areas P to U. Preliminary report. In K. M. Ciałowicz, Y. Yekutieli, & M. Czarnowicz (Eds.), *Tel Erani I. Preliminary report of the 2013–2015 excavations* (pp. 45–57). Wydawnictwo Alter.

Milevski, I., Campagno, M., Gandulla, B., Jaruf, P., Daizo, M. B., Czarnowicz, M., Ochał-Czarnowicz, A., Karmowski, J., Yegorov, D., Cohen-Sasson, E., & Yekutieli, Y. (2019). Tel Erani, Israel: Reporte de la campaña arqueológica de 2018 y sus antecedentes. *Revista del Instituto de Historia Antigua Oriental, 20*, 5–22.

Milevski, I., Getzov, N., & Paz, Y. (2021). Uneven and combined: The Synchronization of the Early Bronze Age I and the first urbanization of the southern Levant. In M. J. Adams & V. Roux (Eds.), *Transitions during the Early Bronze Age in the Levant. Methodological problems and interpretative perspectives* (pp. 127–142). Zaphon.

Nigro, L. (2017). The end of the Early Bronze Age in the southern Levant. In T. Cunningham & J. Driessen (Eds.), *Crisis to collapse. The archaeology of social breakdown* (pp. 149–172). Presses Universitaires du Louvain.

Paz, S. (2010). *Life in the city: The birth of urban habitus in the Early Bronze Age of Israel*. Ph D dissertation, Tel Aviv University.

Paz, Y. (2002). Fortified settlements of the EB IB and the emergence of the first urban system. *Tel Aviv, 29*, 238–261.

Paz, Y. (2018). *Leviah, an Early Bronze Age fortified town in the megalithic landscape of the Golan*. Ostracon.

Smith, M. E. (2009). Centenary paper: V. Gordon Childe and the urban revolution: A historical perspective on a revolution in urban studies. *Town Planning Review, 80*(1), 3–29.

Tilley, C. (2010). *Interpreting landscapes. Geologies, topographies, identities. Explorations in landscape phenomenology*. Routledge.

Ucko, P. J., & Layton, R. (Eds.). (1999). *The archaeology and anthropology of landscape*. Routledge.

Yannai, E. (2006). *'En Esur ('Ein Asawir) I. Excavations at a protohistoric site in the coastal plain of Israel*. Israel Antiquities Authority.

Yaroshevich, A. (2016). 'En Zippori. Preliminary report. *Hadashot Arkheologyiot- Excavations and Surveys in Israel, 126*. http://www.hadashot-esi.org.il/Report_Detail_Eng.aspx?id=24979&mag_id=124

Yavor, Z. (2010). The srchitecture and stratigraphy of the eastern and western quarters. In I. D. Syon, Z. Yavor, & I. I. Gamla (Eds.), *The architecture, the Shmarya Gutmann excavations 1976–1988* (pp. 13–112). Israel Antiquities Authority.

Yeivin, S. (1961). *First preliminary report on the excavations at Tel "Gat" (Tell Sheykh Ahmed el-`Areyny): Seasons 1956–1958*. Israel Department of Antiquities.

Yekutieli, Y. (2002). The pottery assemblage of phase C from the Early Bronze IB1 in Area DII at Tel Erani. *Beer–Sheva, 15*, 59*–79*. (Hebrew).

Yekutieli, Y. (2016). Analysis of previous excavations at Area D. In K. Ciałowicz, Y. Yekutieli, & M. Czarnowicz (Eds.), *Tel Erani I: A preliminary report of the 2013–2015 excavations* (pp. 15–26). Wydawnictwo Alter.

Yoffe, N. (Ed.). (2015). *Early cities in comparative perspective, 4000 BCE – 1200 BCE* (Cambridge World History, 3). Cambridge University Press.

An-Naq' and Fifa in the Southern Ghor, Jordan: A Tale of Two Cemeteries

Mohammad Najjar

Abstract This report presents the long-awaited findings of salvage excavations conducted in 2001 at the Early Bronze IB cemeteries of Fifa and an-Naq' in the Southern Ghor, Jordan. While technological and statistical analyses of the ceramics and analysis of the human osteological remains are still incomplete, this report, which focuses on the ceramics, further facilitates its integration into the overall picture of Early Bronze Age pottery. By providing a descriptive analytic overview of the complete ceramic assemblages found in the tombs at an-Naq' and Fifa, the report enables comparative study and provides a window into understanding the character of urbanism in the region during the EBA.

Keywords An-Naq' · Fifa · Southern Ghor · Burials · Early Bronze Age · Pottery

1 Introduction

This report presents the long-awaited findings of salvage excavations conducted in 2001 at the archaeological sites of Fifa and an-Naq' in the Southern Ghor, Jordan (Figs. 1, 2, 3, 4 and Tables 1, 2, 3, 4).[1] Although the architectural drawings, pottery figures and other major material for this report were completed in 2001, directly after the termination of the excavation, unfortunately, the technological and statistical analyses of the ceramics and analysis of the human osteological remains were, and still are, incomplete.

---

[1] The project was directed by the author. The participants, in various capacities, were: Lotos Abu Karaki, Ghandi Abbadi, Qutaibah Dasouqi, Sabal Zaben, Samar Habahbeh, Tawfeeq Hnaiti, Usamah Gaber, Adnan Rafai'eh, and Ahmad Shami.

M. Najjar (✉)
Independent scholar, Amman, Jordan
e-mail: m.najjar@joscapes.com

© The Author(s), under exclusive license to Springer Nature Switzerland AG 2023
E. Ben-Yosef, I. W. N. Jones (eds.), *"And in Length of Days Understanding" (Job 12:12): Essays on Archaeology in the Eastern Mediterranean and Beyond in Honor of Thomas E. Levy*, Interdisciplinary Contributions to Archaeology, https://doi.org/10.1007/978-3-031-27330-8_19

Fig. 1 The Dead Sea area

We now publish our report with the understanding that it is only partially complete, in the hope that some day soon the full analyses will become available for publication, and in the knowledge that the data presented here will facilitate integration of the material from these excavations into the overall picture of Early Bronze Age (EBA) pottery.

Fig. 2 Naq' and Fifa site location

Current archaeological knowledge of stratified sites of the Early Bronze I (EB I) in Jordan is sketchy at best. Published whole or reconstructed whole forms (partial forms from which whole forms can be reasonably postulated) from domestic contexts are rare, and many of the published whole forms are from tombs in the Southern Ghor (Schaub & Rast, 1984, 1989, 2000). Thus, they may not accurately reflect domestic forms or geographical variation. Although this may not be an issue for

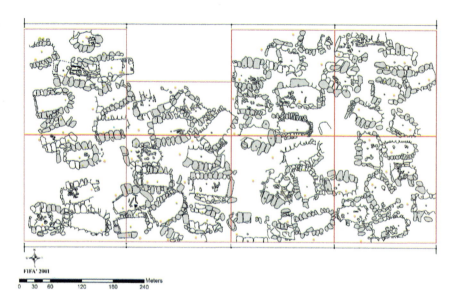

Fig. 3 Fifa tombs

determining pottery periodization, it may impact other cultural studies. While the material presented in this report is also from tombs, it is, nevertheless, useful for comparative study and for understanding the character of urbanism in the region. The publication of this material has been delayed, but it remains important, and honoring my good friend and colleague Tom is a good occasion for its publication.

1.1 Geological Setting

The Southern Ghor is part of the continental transform which runs from the southern mouth of the Red Sea to Anatolia. The Jordan Rift Valley separates the Arabian plate, where modern Jordan is located, from the African plate (Najjar, 2019: 25). The Arabian plate shifted north ca. 105 km relative to the African plate, and this transform remains active today. As the boundary between two plates (both moving to the north at different speeds and submerging under the Eurasian plate), the region is subject to moderate earthquakes that contribute to the destruction of archaeological sites and, most significantly, to alterations in the level of groundwater (Bandel & Salameh, 2013: 255–256). Changes in the level and locations where groundwater comes to the surface can greatly impact not only agriculture, communication, and trade routes, but also settlement patterns. These environmental changes may be the cause of the urban collapse at the end of the Early Bronze Age.

Due to the geological characteristics of the landscape, the nature of sediments in the Rift Valley can vary greatly over very short distances. While the main sediments

An-Naqʻ and Fifa in the Southern Ghor, Jordan: A Tale of Two Cemeteries

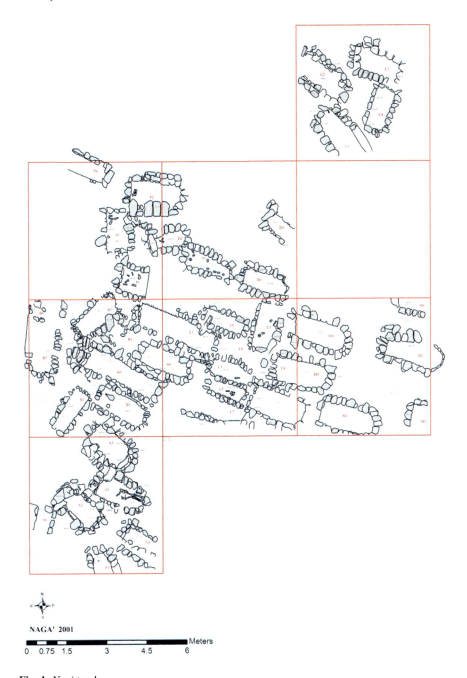

Fig. 4 Naqʻ tombs

Table 1 Ceramics from the 2001 excavations at Fifa

R. Number	Ex. number	Vessel	Height	Diameter	Rim/diameter	Base/Diameter	Handle	Decoration	Condition	Remarks
123	Area1,K7,124	Jar	370	260	Everted 130	Flat 160		None	Mended	Incomplete
124	A2,G6,123	Jar	260	220	Straight 100	Disk 108		None	Mended	Incomplete
125	A2,?1, 129	Jar	295	230	Everted	Flat 130		None		Chipped rim
126	A2,D3,113	Jar	280	200	Everted 85	Disk 105	Handleless	None	Mended	Some parts are missing
127	A2,?1125	Jar	200	195	Everted145	Flat 95		None	Mended	Chipped rim
130	A2,C1	Jar	146	111	Flaring 50	Ring 59		Incision band at base of neck	Broken rim	Incomplete
131	A2,?3115	Vase	203	165	Everted 100	Disk 75	Handleless	Incision band at base of neck	Intact	Chipped rim [ ]
132	A2,G7,112	Jar	195	150	Everted 95	Ring 70	Handleless	None	Intact	Chipped rim
133	A2,??,?	Jar	205	140	Everted 105	Ring 66	Handleless	None	Cracked	Some parts are missing
134	A2,C6,101	Jar	150	155	Everted	68	Handleless	Incision band at base of neck	Intact	Chipped rim
135	A2,K3,116	Vase	195	150	Everted 90	Disk 60	Handleless	Incision band at base of neck	Intact	Chipped rim
136	A2,?8,91	Jar	170	130	Everted 100	Ring 53	Handleless	None	Intact	Some parts are missing
137	A2,C1,119	Vase	185	140	Everted 90	Disk 68	Handleless	None	Intact	Chipped rim
138	A2,??118	Jar	160	145	Everted	Disk 60	Handleless	Six clay vertical lumps at the base of the neck	Intact	Chipped rim
139	A2,H6,104	Jar	165	145	Everted	Disk 73	Handleless	Incision band at base of neck	Cracked	Chipped rim
141	A2,K7,181	Vase	140	110	Everted 60	Flat 57	Handleless	None	Intact	Chipped rim
142	A?,??,?	Vase	112	85	Everted 73	Disk 41	Handleless	None	Intact	Complete

An-Naq' and Fifa in the Southern Ghor, Jordan: A Tale of Two Cemeteries

143	A2,F2	Vase	124	88	Everted	Ring 43	Handleless	None	Intact	Complete
144	A2,?,?,?	Vase	108	81	Everted 71	Disk 45	Handleless	None	Intact	Complete
145	A2,?3,50	Vase	100	76	Everted 65	Disk 36	Handleless	None	Intact	Chipped rim
146	A2,?,?,?	Vase	109	84	Everted 72	Concave 44	Handleless	None	Intact	Chipped rim
147	A2,?,?,?	Vase	91	62	Everted 44	Disk 31	Handleless	None	Intact	Complete
148	A2,A5,85	Vase	105	75	Everted rim	Flat 52	Handleless	None	Intact	Chipped rim
149	A2,B2,65	Vase	120	90	Cylindrical 75	Flat 50	Handleless	None	Intact	Some parts are missing
150	A2,G8,62	Vase	107	80	Everted 68	Disk 40	Handleless	None	Intact	Chipped rim
151	A2,G1,79	Vase	115	78	Everted 67	Disk 40	Handleless	None	Intact	Chipped rim
154	A2,K15,83	Vase	105	77	Everted 64	Ring 70	Handleless	None	Intact	Chipped rim
155	A1,A7,71	Vase	110	81	Everted 69	Disk 42	Handleless	None	Intact	Chipped rim
156	A1,?2,78	Vase	110	79	Everted 63	Disk 38	Handleless	None	Intact	Chipped rim
157	A2,A4,137	Vase	100	74	Everted 35	Ring 38	Handleless	Incision band at base of neck	Intact	Chipped rim
158	A2,?3,56	Vase	97	77	Flaring 59	Ring 38	Handleless	None	Intact	Chipped rim
159	A2,D1,86	Vase	113	87	Flaring 64	Disk 44	Handleless	None	Intact	Chipped rim
160	A2,?,?,?	Vase	104	73	Everted 37	Ring 37	Handleless	Incision band at base of neck	Intact	Chipped rim
160	A2,C8,84	Vase	107	83	Flaring 67	Ring 44	Handleless	None	Intact	Chipped rim
161	A2,A6,67	Vase	102	70	Flaring 64	Disk 37	Handleless	None	Cracked	Chipped rim
162	A2,H6,187	Vase	101	81	Flaring 53	Disk 46	Handleless	None	Intact	Chipped rim
163	?2,?,?	Vase	108	74	Flaring 55	Disk 47	Handleless	None	Intact	Complete
164	?2,?,?	Vase	110	77	Flaring 65	Disk 43	Handleless	None	Intact	Complete
165	A2,G1,80	Vase	103	74	Flaring 69	Disk 35	Handleless	None	Intact	Complete
166	A2,?4,72	Vase	105	86	Everted 61	Disk 45	Handleless	None	Intact	Complete
167	?2,?3139	Vase	107	79	Flaring 61	Ring 34	Handleless	None	Intact	Complete
168	A2,?2,70	Vase	99	75	Everted 56	Flat 50	Handleless	None	Intact	Chipped rim

(continued)

Table 1 (continued)

R. Number	Ex. number	Vessel	Height	Diameter	Rim/diameter	Base/Diameter	Handle	Decoration	Condition	Remarks
170	A?,??,?	Vase	99	74	Everted 64	Disk 43	Handleless	None	Intact	Chipped rim
172	A2,D1,168	Vase	115	92	Flaring 57	Disk 57	Handleless	None	Intact	Chipped rim
173	A2,C6,69	Vase	103	79	Flaring	Disk 39	Handleless	None	Cracked	Chipped rim
174	A?,??,?	Vase	108	77	Everted 67	Disk 42	Handleless	None	Intact	Chipped rim
175	A2,D1,178	Vase	105	85	Everted 62	Ring 53	Handleless	Incision band	Intact	Chipped
176	A?,?4,89	Vase	92	72	Everted 64	Disk 39	Handleless	None	Intact	Chipped
177	A1,F2,33	Vase	109	82	Everted 63	Disk 38	Handleless	None	Intact	Complete
178	A2,??,59	Vase	86	68	Everted 50	Disk 29	Handleless	None	Intact	Chipped
179	A2,A7,?	Vase	105	77	Everted	Disk 40	Handleless	None	Intact	Some parts are missing
180	A2,D5,81	Vase	82	62	Everted 54	Disk 33	Handleless	None	Cracked	Chipped
181	A1,?8,74	Vase	105	81	Everted 68	Disk 42	Handleless	None	Mended	Some parts missing
182	A2,B1,73	Vase	105	88	Everted 62	Disk 53	Handleless	None	Cracked	Holes in body
183	A?,??,?	Vase	110	80	Everted 70	Disk 43	Handleless	None	Intact	Chipped
184	A2,??,?	Vase	100	74	Everted	Disk 38	Handleless	None	Mended	Some parts missing
185	A?,??,?	Vase	102	80	Everted 67	Disk 41	Handleless	None	Intact	Chipped rim
186	A?,?8,93	Vase	94	73	Everted 50	Flat 43	Handleless	None	Intact	Complete
187	A?,??,?	Vase	100	75	Everted 62	Disk 39	Handleless	None	Intact	Some parts missing
189	A?,?1110	Jar	245	180	Straiht 85	Disk 97	Two loop handles	None	Intact	Rim missing
190	A2,F2,110	Jar	220	195	Everted 105	Flat 118	Two vertical loop handles at shoulder	Four clay knobs at each side	Intact	Chipped rim

An-Naq' and Fifa in the Southern Ghor, Jordan: A Tale of Two Cemeteries 419

191	A2,K7,130	Jar	200	195	Everted 113	Flat 115	Two lug handles, 2 horizontal loob handles	Four clay knobs at each side, the loop handles are decorated with 3 rows of holes	Intact	Chipped rim and missing handles
192	A2,A7,117	Jar	210	180	Everted 92	Disk 92	Two vertical loop handles neck to shoulder	None	Cracked	Rim missing
196	A?,?6103	Jar	170	130	Straight 53	Ring 50	One loop handle rim to shoulder	None	Intact	Rim missing
198	A2,D6,41	Jar	130	155	Everted 115	Disk 65	One loop handle rim to shoulder	Two clay lumps at the shoulder	Mended	Handle missing
199	A?,?3172	Jug	170	125	Cylindrical 41	Disk 60	Two lug handles	None	Mended	Incomplete
201	A?,?1102	Jar	170	135	Conical 40	Disk 53	Two lug handles horizontal	None	Intact	Complete
202	A2,A6,174	Jar	170	13	Conical 30	Disk 55	Two lug handles horizontal	None	Intact	Complete
204	A2,A4,106	Jar	140	115	Conical 30	Disk 51	Two lug handles horizontal	None	Intact	Complete
205	A?,D4,173	Jug	130	100	Cylindrical 45	Disk 45	Two lug handles	None	Intact	Complete
207	A2,?1126	Jar	140	115	Cylindrical 44	Ring 52	Two lug handles horizontal	None	Mended	Holes in body
208	A2,B5,169	Jug	140	105	Conical 25	Disk 42	Two lug handles	None	Intact	Hole in body
211	A?,K5,132	Jug	120	95	Conical 25	Ring 45	Two lug handles	None	Mended	Complete
212	A2,C6,183	Jug	110	85	Conical 35	Ring 35	Two lug handles	None	Intact	Complete
216	A2,?7182	Jar	93	67	Conical 29	Conical 33	Two lug handles horizontal	None	Intact	One handle missing
220	A?,C6,191	Jug	70	55	Everted 35	Disk 27	Two lug handles vertical	None	Intact	Complete
224	A?,?1,35	Jug	96	106	Everted 74	Flat 60	Loop, rim to body	None		Handle missing
225	A??1, 34	Jug	90	80	Everted	Flat 45	Loop, rim to shoulder	Two clay lumps at the shoulder	Intact	Complete

(continued)

Table 1 (continued)

R. Number	Ex. number	Vessel	Height	Diameter	Rim/diameter	Base/Diameter	Handle	Decoration	Condition	Remarks
227	A?,?1, 29	Mug	73	95	Inverted	Rounded	Loop, rim to body	None		Incomplete
228	A2,H1,37	Bowl	71	120	Inverted	Disk 49	Loop, rim to body with small knob	Six elongated clay lumps under rim	Intact	Complete
228	A?,?1,37	Mug	63	82	Everted	Flat 54	Loop, rim to body with clay knob	None	Chipped	Complete
230	A2,H1,28	Bowl	71	105	Inverted	Flattened	Loop, rim to shoulder with three vertical grooves	Five groups of red paint vertical lines $ lines in each group	Mended	Incomplete
231	A?,??,?	Bowl	57	95	Everted	Flattened	Loop, rim to base with small clay knob	None		Incomplete
232	?	Jug	80	80	Everted	Flat 55	Loop, rim to shoulder	Two clay lumps at shoulder	Intact	Complete
234	A2,H1,33	Mug	66	85	Everted 86	Flattened 49	Loop handle rim to shoulder	Two lumps of clay at shoulder	Intact	Chipped rim
235	A2,D6,40	Jug	76	86	Everted 75	Flat 56	Loop, rim to body with small knob	Two clay lumps at shoulder	Intact	Complete
236	A2,H1,39	Mug	65	87	Everted 84	Disk 45	Loop, rim to body	None	Intact	Complete
237	A?,?1,20	Jug	65	87	Everted 79	Disk 47	Loop, rim to body with clay knob	None	Intact	Complete
239	??,??,?	Jug	78	71	Flaring 46	Rounded	Loop handle rim to shoulder	Four vertical group lines of red paint (4 line each)	Intact	Complete

An-Naq' and Fifa in the Southern Ghor, Jordan: A Tale of Two Cemeteries

240	A2,H1,32	Bowl	66	91	Inverted rim 65	Flattened	Loop handle rim to shoulder	Four vertical group lines of red paint (5–10 line each)	Intact	Chipped rim
242	A?,??,?	Mug	62	78	Everted	Rounded	Loop, rim to base with small clay knob	None	Intact	Chipped
244	A2,H1,38	Bowl	59	81	Inverted	Flattened	Loop, rim to shoulder	Five groups of red paint vertical lines $ lines in each group	Intact	Handle missing
246	A1,?6,27	Mug	58	63	Everted	Rounded	Loop, rim to body with small knob	None	Intact	Handle missing
253	A?,??,?	Mug	50	80	Everted	Rounded	Loop, rim to base with small clay knob	None	Mended	Incomplete
255	A?,??,?	Bowl	44	90	Everted	Rounded	Loop, rim to base with small clay knob	None	Mended	Incomplete
256	A?,??,?	Bowl	44	108	Everted	Rounded	Loop, rim to base with small clay knob	None	Mended	Incomplete
263	?	Bowl	64	86	Inverted	Ring 38		None	Intact	Complete
265	A2,??,?	Bowl	51	81	Inverted	Omphalos		None	Intact	Complete
266	A2,C8,144	Lid	53	58	Inverted rim 48		Twin pierced lug handles	None	Intact	Complete
267	A2,C8,145	Lid	48	64	Inverted rim 60		Twin pierced lug handles	None	Intact	Chipped rim
268	A2,A8,142	Lid	44	56	Inverted 50		Twin pierced lug handles	None	Mended	Chipped rim
273	A2,K5,150	Lid	34	38	Inverted 34		Twin pierced lug handles	None	Intact	Chipped rim

Table 2 Ceramics from the 2001 excavations at an-Naq'

R. number	Ex. number	Vessel	Height	Diameter	Rim/ diameter	Base/ Diameter	Handles	Decoration	Condition	Remarks
128	A1,B3	Jar	275	210	Flaring 120	Flat 120	Handleless	None	Cracked	Some parts missing
129	A?,?2,19	Jar	180	170	Everted 135	Concave 75	Handleless	Five clay knobs at shoulder	Cracked and mended	Some parts missing
171	A?,?2,65	Jar	106	93	Everted 66	Ring 49	Handleless	None	Intact	Chipped rim
188	A1,??,44	Jar	66	95	Everted 79	Flattened	Handleless	Five clay knobs at shoulders	Mended	Incomplete
209	A1,?3194	Jar	140	90	Conical 35	Omphalos 40	Two lug handles horizontal	None	Intact	Complete
210	A1,M4,133	Jug	116	95	Conical 27	Ring 335	Two lug handles		Cracked	Some parts missing
213	A1,?2175	Jar	100	81	Everted 44	Flattened	Two vertical loop handles		Intact	Complete
215	A1,? 5135	Jug	110	81	Conical 37	Ring 40	Two lug handles	None	Intact	Chipped and one handle missing
217	A1,?2193	Jug	62	68	Everted 32	Flattened	Two lug handles vertical	5 clay knobs at shoulder	Intact	Complete
218	A1,D8,112	Jug	75	68	Everted 33	Flattened	Knob Handles (2)	None	Intact	One handle missing
219	A1,D2,190	Jug	55	65	Everted 38	Flattened	Two lug handles vertical	Four clay knobs at shoulder	Intact	Complete
226	A1,?1,25	Jug	81	83	Everted	Flat 46	Loop, rim to shoulder with clay knob	None	Cracked and mended	Some parts missing
233	A1,D1,179	Jug	104	80	Everted 59	Flat 48	Loop, rim to body with clay knob	None	Intact	Chipped rim

An-Naq' and Fifa in the Southern Ghor, Jordan: A Tale of Two Cemeteries

241	A?,?3,24	Mug	57	85	Everted 81	Rounded	Loop, rim to body with clay knob		Mended	
243	A?,?2,30	Mug	66	75	Everted 71	Rounded	Loop, rim to body with clay knob			
245	?	Mug	49	75	Everted 74	Rounded	Loop, rim to body with clay knob	None	Intact	Complete
249	A?,?3,10	Mug	49	100	Everted 98	Rounded	Loop, rim to body with small knob	None	Intact	Complete
250	A?,?2,12	Mug	48	100	Everted 96	Rounded	Loop, rim to body with small knob	None	Mended	Some parts missing
251	A?,?2,13	Mug	48	100	Everted 94	Rounded	Loop, rim to body with small knob	None	Intact	Complete
252	A?,??,16	Bowl	55	90	Everted	Flattened	Loop, rim to base with small clay knob	None	Intact	Complete
254	A?,?2,17	Bowl	39	80	Straight 100	Rounded	Loop, rim to base with small clay knob	None	Intact	Complete
257	A1,N4,11	Mug	32	91	Inverted	Flat	Loop, rim to body with clay knob	None	Intact	Complete
258	A1,D2,4	Platter	43	167	Inverted	Flattened	Loop, rim to base with clay knob	None	Mended	Some parts messing
259	A1,M4,5	Platter	39	135	Inverted	Flattened	Loop, rim to base with clay knob	None	Mended	Incomplete
260	A1,M4,3	Platter	24	152	Inverted	Flattened	Loop, rim to base with clay knob	None	Mended	Some parts missing
261	A1,D2,6	Platter	48	130	Inverted	Flattened	Loop, rim to base with clay knob	None	Mended	Some parts missing

(continued)

Table 2 (continued)

R. number	Ex. number	Vessel	Height	Diameter	Rim/ diameter	Base/ Diameter	Handles	Decoration	Condition	Remarks
262	A1,M4,2	Platter	18	135	Straight	Flattened	Loop, rim to base with clay knob	None	Mended	Complete
276	A1,M1,153	Mace head	56	62	Squat				Chipped	Hole in center 15 mm, limestone
277	A!,L8,155	Mace head	59	55	Conical upright				Chipped	Hole in center 16 mm, limestone
278	A1,??,157	Mace head	32	63	Discoid				Chipped	Hole in center 16 mm, limestone
152	A1,B3,131	Vase	110	94	Everted 56	Flattened 58	Handleless	None	Intact	Chipped rim
140	A1,??,60	Jar	126	150	Everted 103	Flat 73	Handleless	None	Intact	Complete
264	A1,H4,48	Bowl	47	110	Inverted 110	Omphalos 16		Red paint group lines from interior	Intact	Complete
282	A1,D2,2	Mortar	95	115	Everted 125	Flat 114	Handleless	None	Intact	Chipped rim, basalt
283	A1,D2,163	Mortar	80	95	Everted 100	Flat 90	Handleless	None	Intact	Chipped rim basalt
285	A1,D3,165	Mortar	49	71	Straight 71	Rounded 62	Handleless	None	Intact	Complete, basalt
153	A1,D1,180	Vase	115	85	Flaring 53	Flat 58	Handleless	None	Intact	Chipped rim
271	A1,M5,147	Lid	46	54	Inverted 47			None	Intact	Chipped rim
206	A1,M3,107	Jar	152	110	Conical 51	Disk 58	Two pierces horizontal lug handleless	None	Intact	Complete

Table 3 Tombs at Fifa

Number	Orientation	Capstones	Depth (cm)
Area 1,A03	40°	6 capstones	NA
Area 1,A02	46°	2 capstones	NA
Area 1,B07	139°	2 capstones	NA
Area 2,A01	99°	3 capstones	85
Area 2,A02	105°	2 capstones	78
Area 2,A03	110°	5 capstones	85
Area 2,A04	52°	None	77
Area 2,A05	95°	3 capstones	100
Area 2,A06	103°	2 capstones	84
Area 2,A07	55°	2 capstones	80
Area 2,A08	120°		NA
Area 2,A09	93°	None	118
Area 2,A10	130°	None	NA
Area 2,B01	60°	4 capstones	66
Area 2,B02	115°	3 capstones	100
Area 2,B03	90°	3 capstones	66
Area 2,B04	97°	2 capstones	NA
Area 2,B05	72°	None	84
Area 2,B06	340°	None	86
Area 2,C01	135	3 capstones	88
Area 2,C02	96°	2 capstones	72
Area 2,C03	84	4 capstones	92
Area 2,C04	93°	1 capstone	10
Area 2,C05	72°	2 capstones	86
Area 2,C06	85°	1 capstone	66
Area 2,C07	90°	2 capstones	79
Area 2,C08	5°	2 capstones	80
Area 2,D01	104°	2 capstones	100
Area 2,D02	120°	4 capstones	97
Area 2,D03	121°	4 capstones	85
Area 2,D04	113°	3 capstones	77
Area 2,D05	67°	2 capstones	126
Area 2,D06	117°	2 capstones	115
Area 2,D07	104°	5 capstones	81
Area 2,D08	NA	2 capstones	NA
Area 2,F01	62°	3 capstones	20
Area 2,F02	73°	3 capstones	70
Area 2,F03	130°	2 capstones	84
Area 2,G01	106°	3 capstones	120
Area 2,G02	78°	3 capstones	88
Area 2,G03	73°	2 capstones	109
Area 2,G05	260°	2 capstones	54

(continued)

Table 3 (continued)

Number	Orientation	Capstones	Depth (cm)
Area 2,G06	87°	3 capstones	102
Area 2,G07	60°	5 capstones	NA
Area 2,G08	90°	3 capstones	74
Area 2,H01	105°	3 capstones	93
Area 2,H02	118°	3 capstones	78
Area 2,H03	72°	3 capstones	100
Area 2,H04	67°	4 capstones	135
Area 2,H05	82°	3 capstones	64
Area 2,H06	60°	3 capstones	70
Area 2,K01	85°	4 capstones	93
Area 2,K02	88°	2 capstones	36
Area 2,K03	98°	2 capstones	82
Area 2,K04	88°	3 capstones	83
Area 2,K05	96°	3 capstones	96
Area 2,K06	106°	2 capstones	93
Area 2,K07	186°	None	55

in the largest Early Bronze Age site, Bab adh-Dhra' (Donahue, 1981: 137–154), are marl, shale, gypsum, and clastic intercalations (the Lisan Formation), only 10 km to the south the sediments change to terrestrial, fluviatile, and lacustrine unconsolidated sediments. This greatly impacted the types of burials in these otherwise closely—geographically and culturally—related areas.

1.2 Geographical Setting

The research area is located ca. 160 km south of Amman on the eastern side of the southern Jordan Valley (Fig. 1). The alluvial fans at the mouths of Wadi al-Hasa in Ghor as-Safi and Wadi Fifa are referred to by the local inhabitants as the Southern Ghor (Ar. *al-ghawr*, valley or lowland). Until recently, Wadi Araba was the most accessible approach to the southern Dead Sea plains. This isolation historically impacted the inhabitants' cultural interactions with the neighboring regions. The broad expanse of the plain between the mountains to the east and the Dead Sea shore to the west varies between 1.5 and 5 km. It is noteworthy that Early Bronze settlements were located on elevated areas away from the Dead Sea shoreline (Fig. 2). The occupational history of the region is reflected in abundant remains from the Early Bronze and Iron Ages and the Roman, Byzantine, and Medieval periods (Khouri, 1988).

Table 4 Tombs at an-Naq'

Number	Orientation
Area 1,A1	120°
Area 1,A2	140°
Area 1,A3	135°
Area 1,A4	116°
Area 1,A5	160°
Area 1,A6	194°
Area 1,B1	107°
Area 1,B2	205°
Area 1,B3	117°
Area 1,B4	110°
Area 1,B5	186°
Area 1,B6	145°
Area 1,B7	220°
Area 1,B8	112°
Area 1,C1	104°
Area 1,C2	125°
Area 1,C3	137°
Area 1,C4	200°
Area 1,D1	114°
Area 1,D2	111°
Area 1,D3	87°
Area 1,D4	130°
Area 1,L1	107°
Area 1,L2	109°
Area 1,L3	107°
Area 1,L4	108°
Area 1,L5	196°
Area 1,L6	109°
Area 1,L7	105°
Area 1,L8	110°
Area 1,M1	192°
Area 1,M2	107°
Area 1,M3	103°
Area 1,M4	102°
Area 1,M5	93°
Area 1,M6	97°
Area 1,P1	97°
Area 1,P2	92°
Area 1,P3	182°
Area 1,P4	120°

An-Naq' Cemetery is located in the alluvial fan of Wadi al-Hasa. The burial ground covers the area between Wadi al-Hasa in the north and agricultural fields in the south, and rugged hills to the east and the Dead Sea Highway to the west. Judging from looted tombs, the size of the burial ground is estimated to be 20 hectares (Schaub, 1992: 895). Fifa Cemetery, less than 10 km away (Fig. 2), is located to the east of the Dead Sea Highway within the alluvial fan of Wadi Fifa. It covers an area of ca. 17 hectares and is separated from the modern town of Fifa by the Dead Sea Highway.

Since both burial grounds were subjected to major looting activities related to the illicit trade of antiquities at the turn of the current millennium, it was decided to salvage and document as much as possible of the remaining burials at both sites. Because of the extensive damage to the cemeteries, excavations at both sites were conducted where the spoil heaps of the looting activities were dumped, in the hope that the burials covered by spoil heaps would be intact. After removing the spoil heaps, ca. 50 intact burials in cist tombs were exposed and excavated at each site.

2 Research at the Sites

2.1 Early Explorations

In 1818, Irby and Mangles identified the ruins of Bab edh-Dhra' with biblical Zoar. The American naval researcher Willian Lynch, during his survey of the Dead Sea in 1850, also identified Bab edh-Dhra' with Zoar. The last of these early researchers was Hoskins, who in 1905 visited the area in search of biblical Sodom and Gomorrah.

A turning point in the research was the expedition of W. Albright, M. Kyle, and A. Mallon to the Dead Sea region in 1924 (Albright, 1924: 1–12). The aim of this expedition was to locate the five biblical Cities of the Plain mentioned in Genesis. Ruins from different historical periods were documented, but the site of Bab edh-Dhra' was the only site that could in theory have had any connection with the biblical story. The discovery of Bab edh-Dhra', and its subsequent excavation by P. Lapp in 1964–1967 (Lapp, 1966: 104–111), was a significant achievement in studying the settlement patterns of the area during the Bronze Age.

2.1.1 Recent Fieldwork at an-Naq' and Fifa

Archaeological investigations in the Southern Ghor in recent decades have revealed a wealth of details. With the exception of Bab edh-Dhra' and Numayra, all of the information concerning the Early Bronze Age has come from cemeteries. Three vast necropolises with tens of thousands of tombs have been exposed, making an abundance of information on funeral practices of the Early Bronze Age available.

In 1973, a survey of Early Bronze Age sites in the Southern Ghor (Bab edh-Dhra', Numayra, an-Naq', Fifa, and Khunayzireh) was conducted in response to illicit digging at these sites (Rast and Schaub 1974: 5–53). The main aim was to evaluate the situation and to identify the research potential (Rast & Schaub, 1981). In 1985 these sites were revisited by B. Frohlich and W. Lancaster (Frohlich & Lancaster, 2000). In 1985–1986, the Southern Ghor and Northeast 'Arabah Archaeological Survey reported devastating illicit digging at the sites and recommended carrying out salvage excavations at an-Naq' and Fifa (MacDonald, 1992). In 1989–1990 a limited rescue project at Fifa was initiated by the Expedition to the Dead Sea Project. The number of the tombs was estimated at 5000 (Rast and Schaub 1974; Schaub and Rast 1990); all were cist tombs. In 1992, a survey was conducted by Mohammad Waheeb in preparation for the road connecting the Dead Sea Highway with Tafila (Waheeb 1993), and in 1995, ca. 100 tombs at an-Naq' were excavated by the Department of Antiquites and Mu'tah University in three excavation areas (Waheeb, 1995). In 1996, 14 additional cist tombs (Papadopoulos et al., 2001) at Naq' were excavated by the Department of Antiquities and Ionnina University (Greece). In 2001, the Department of Antiquities of Jordan conducted the rescue excavation project reported here (Najjar, 2001).

2.1.2 Methodology and Approach

This report presents a catalog of the ceramics from Naq' and Fifa, with analysis limited primarily to formal and decorative typology. It takes an essentially descriptive or classificatory approach, with discussion restricted to the identification of parallels. Although more concerned with the presentation of new material than with exploring the implications of this evidence, it raises numerous issues relevant to wider interpretation and discussion. Admittedly, this approach suffers from the methodological and interpretive limitations discussed above and lacks the analyses necessary to illuminate the technological, socio-economic, political, and cognitive systems which made up the Early Bronze landscape. That said, the use of pottery for relative dating has, almost by default, retained its importance despite doubts expressed regarding its reliability and the clear need for chronological revision in light of new radiocarbon evidence.

At the beginning of the excavations at Naq' and Fifa, grids were established at both sites and alphabetical letters assigned to each excavation trench. The burials were numbered sequentially in the order in which they were excavated. Elevations were taken based on a benchmark by the Department of Land and Surveys of Jordan. Tombs were drafted by Qutaiba Dasouqi of the Department of Antiquities of Jordan (DOAJ) and pottery was drawn by Tawfiq Hanaity of the DOAJ.

The pottery vessels were given an excavation number according to their findspots in tombs. Unfortunately, some of the original excavation numbers on the vessels are now missing, and these missing numbers are reflected as question marks in Tables 1 and 2. At a later stage, registration numbers in numerical series were added. The assemblages from both sites share a single sequence of registration numbers, but the findspots were indicated whenever possible (Tables 1 and 2).

The vessels were sorted into classes of closed and open forms. Within these classes, vessels were grouped into specific formal categories, e.g., jars, juglets, bowls, and miscellanea. No attempt was made to classify the ceramic wares, and this aspect of the assemblage requires further study.

2.1.3 Regional Assemblages of EB I

Bab edh-Dhra'

The EB IA tombs excavated at Bab edh-Dhra' were found to be divided into eight subgroups. The nature of burial was thought to reflect social organization, with the extended family the basic societal unit. According to Harrison (2001), the introduction of charnel houses in the EB IB indicates intensification of sedentarism. While demonstrating some continuity with the EB IA, the shift to charnel houses might imply participation of a greater number of individuals in burial services and greater empowerment of family and lineage as basic societal institutions. Familial ties may have broadened to integrate people not necessarily connected by blood ties. This alteration in social organization would have coincided with (or would have been triggered by) sedentarization and a shift to agriculture.

As for domestic contexts, the earliest Stratum V occupation is characterized by a local ceramic assemblage, in terms both of raw materials and specific stylistic attributes. It appears far more isolated than the assemblages from southern Palestine. Stratum IV, the first period of permanent occupation, witnessed the appearance of better fabrics and new morphological features (amphoriskoi, spouted bowls, and Safi cups) and two styles of painted decoration: red bands applied directly to the clay surface of small bowls and the Line Group Painted tradition (LGP), straight or wavy lines, arranged in groups, with patterns formed by their intersections, also directly painted on the vessel surface. These are the diagnostics of the later phases of the EB I (Schaub & Rast, 2000).

The pottery is all handmade, with the greater part consisting of a coarse cooking pot fabric. Red slipping and burnishing are relatively rare (14%) and are primarily restricted to small vessels such as cups, bowls, and little jars. The assemblage is mainly of local origin and appears to comprise a fairly limited range of forms and fabrics. LGP constitutes only a fraction of the painted pottery.

Changes in ceramic assemblages may reflect specific shifts in social organization or subsistence activities. Given the range of factors that can result in ceramic change, settlement evidence may provide a more effective indicator of the degree of overall continuity of human activity. Nonetheless, the existence of an east-west connection during the EB III that links the two sides of the Rift Valley contrasts with the very different assemblages which characterize these two regions during the EB I. This may well indicate a significant reorientation of economic and/or political connections during the third millennium BCE. Interactions with Egypt are attested during the EB IB by the presence of small quantities of imported Levantine wares in Egypt (Tell el-Farkha) and the export of Egyptian items to the Levant (Levy & van den Brink, 2002).

3 Discussion

3.1 Tombs

The tombs at both Fifa (Fig. 3) and Naq' (Fig. 4) differ from those at Bab edh-Dhra' in many ways. With the exception of two chamber burials found in 1995 at an-Naq', all the excavated tombs at both sites are cist burials. The shaft tombs, dominant at Bab edh-Dhra', are absent; so are the charnel houses. This difference is due to the geological settings of the sites; while the tombs at Bab edh-Dhra' were dug into the Lisan marl, the individual cist tombs at both Fifa and Naq' were dug into the alluvial fans and constructed using rock slabs and boulders. Despite these differences, the ceramic typologies are the same, which might indicate culturally-united inhabitants adapting burial practices to different geological formations and landscapes. Articulation is another distinction between funeral practices at Fifa and an-Naq' and those at Bab edh-Dhra'. According to some researchers (e.g., Chesson, 1999), a shift toward articulated burials might reflect the beginning of the settled life at Bab edh-Dhra'. The presence of articulated burials at Naq' and Fifa suggests that occupation at both sites began later than at Bab edh-Dhra' and ceased with the end of EB I.

At this stage of research, establishing the relationship between funerary gifts and the gender or age of buried individuals is impossible. Comparisons must be restricted to architectural variables. While no variation was noticed in the internal patterning of tomb contents (mainly due to displacement of these contents as a result of siltation and seepage of rainwater, as well as looting, both ancient and recent), slight variations in tomb structure exist. Various types of tomb architecture are attested at Naq' and Fifa, as they are at Bab edh-Dhra'. These include chamber-type, courted-cist tombs and regular cist tombs. All the tombs excavated during the 2001 season were of the regular cist tomb type with roughly shaped slabs or boulders with earthen floors.

3.2 Funerary Goods

Funerary goods consisted of ceramic and non-ceramic gifts. The offerings were presumably of food, drink, scents, and oils, but all that remained of these were the containers, in this case, pottery vessels. It is also possible that at least some of the vessels themselves were funerary gifts. Contrary to vessels from occupational levels, these vessels are mostly intact and can contribute greatly to our knowledge of the ceramic traditions of the period. It is assumed that a variation of funerary gifts might mirror the social position of the deceased in the community. Energy expenditure (in both funerary goods and architectural design) is taken as an indicator of social status.

3.2.1 Ceramics

In both technological and morphological properties, ceramics from the EB IB demonstrate strong affinities to those from the EB IA. Most of these vessels are shallow bowls with gently curved sides and small bag-shaped juglets with relatively large handles, sometimes rising well above the rim. Some of the bowls and jugs have a crude decoration of red or brown lines. The assemblage also includes some jars with ledge handles and high, projecting spouts. The sample size is small, limited to ca. 300 vessels from 90 tombs.

Basic Forms

The basic forms at both sites are bowls, jars, and juglets.

Bowls (Figs. 5, 6, 7 and 8)

Specific bowl forms include biconical bowls, mugs, Safi cups, hemispherical bowls, platters, spouted bowls, twin-cups, and V-shaped bowls. Bowls can be divided into bowls without handles and bowls with loop handles. The first group is hemispherical in shape, sometimes carinated, and usually decorated with Line Group Painting on the interior and exterior. The bowls with handles are subdivided into Safi cups, Safi platters, and mugs.

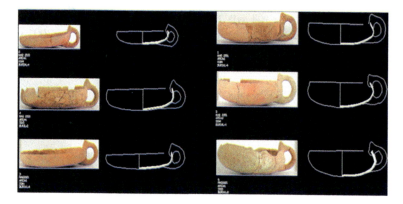

Fig. 5 Safi platters

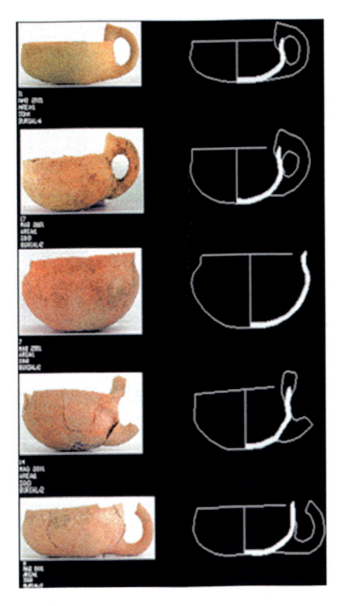

Fig. 6 Safi bowls and cup

- Safi cups (a key indicator of the EB IB in the Southern Ghor) are relatively shallow bowls with a clay horn at the upper ridge. The ratio of height to rim diameter and base diameter to rim diameter is 1:2. The rim of the bowl is either everted or slightly inverted.
- Safi platters are a related form, but with a height to rim diameter ratio of 1:5.5. Some of these platters have slightly inverted rims.

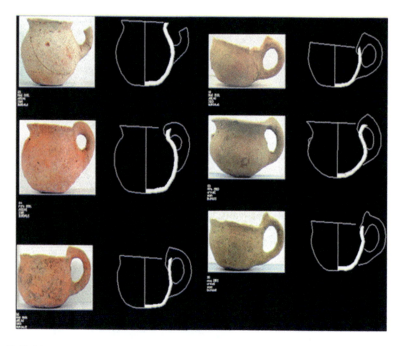

Fig. 7 Safi jugs

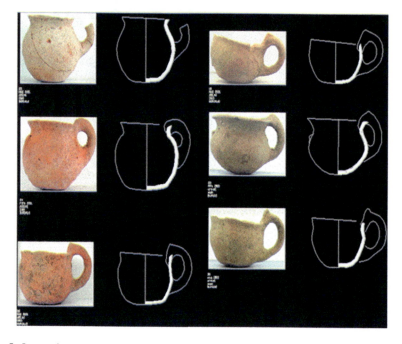

Fig. 8 Jugs and mugs

- Safi mugs are the same size as Safi cups but deeper and with everted rims. The ratio between the height and rim diameter is 1:1.35. Some of these mugs come with a loop handle, with or without a clay horn, and their exteriors are decorated with groups of red paint. One mug had three vertical incised lines along the handle and a second mug had plastic decoration in the form of clay lumps. The larger vessels were used as serving platters, while the smaller ones were probably used for individual dining.

Jars (Fig. 9)

Specific jar forms include amphoriskoi, column jars, and holemouth jars. Amphoriskoi with LGP and bag-shaped jars were characteristic of EB IB ceramics. Jars were sorted into jars without handles and jars with handles. The jars with handles were grouped into jars with tall, wide necks, flaring rims, and inflected points at the base of the neck; jars with short necks and flaring rims; and jars with tall, narrow necks. The jars with two or more handles were grouped into jars with tall, narrow necks and very small, pierced lug handles on the shoulder (amphoriskoi); and jars with loop handles. The handles can be vertical or horizontal and some of these jars were provided with additional duck-bill ledge handles. These jars usually have plastic decoration in the form of clay knobs. Most probably, jars of different sizes were used for serving food and drinks or eating and drinking. Towards the end

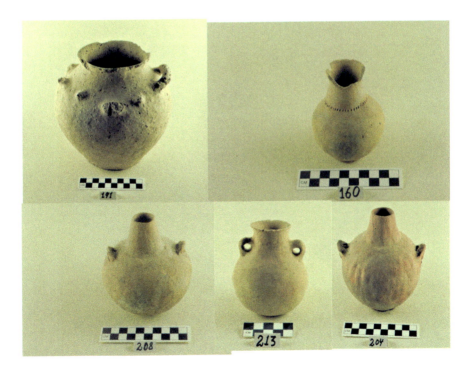

Fig. 9 Jars and Amphoriskoi

of the period, the small jars were replaced by the spouted jars attested in the EB IB at Bab edh-Dhra'. The absence of these spouted jars in Naq' and Fifa may simply be a result of the limited sample at hand but might also indicate that the assemblage should be considered transitional between the EB IA and EB IB. This might be the case in light of typical EB IB ceramic types, or at least their prototypes, at both sites.

Jugs (Fig. 10)

Specific jug forms include juglets, globular jugs, and piriform jugs. Juglets are deep vessels with one handle, short necks, and flaring rims. Some of them are decorated with clay knobs and have flat or rounded bases. These vessels might have been used as containers for wine, milk, or ointments.

Miscellaneous Forms and Vessel Parts

This category includes spoons, column handles, and ear-handled cups.

Surface Treatment (Fig. 11)

A variety of slips are found on ceramics from both sites, including pink slip, red slip, white slip, band slip, and grain wash. Slipping was sometimes combined with burnishing. Some vessels were wet-smoothed. Burnishing was observed on vessels

Fig. 10 Jugs

Fig. 11 Jugs

fired to red and gray. Line painting and Line Group Painting, characteristic of the EB IB, were present. Plastic decoration consists primarily of raised bands and clay knobs or dots applied to the exterior of many vessels. Finally, slashed bands and punctate lines were found incised on some vessels.

Ware and Manufacture

Plain ware, red burnished ware, and Line-Group Ware (LGW) commonly have calcite, chert, and sand inclusions. All vessels were handmade, with bowls being coiled-formed. Some vessels were tournette finished. Joined necks were attached to jars and jugs. The ceramics from both sites were generally well-fired.

3.2.2 Non-ceramic Goods (Fig. 12)

The presence of some "prestigious" artifacts and their rarity in the tombs might suggest social stratification. It is possible that variation in the proportion and type of the funerary gifts might indicate social status. The other possible explanation is that this variation reflects access to and use of these materials as a means to express societal and maybe professional identities, as suggested by Chesson (1999).

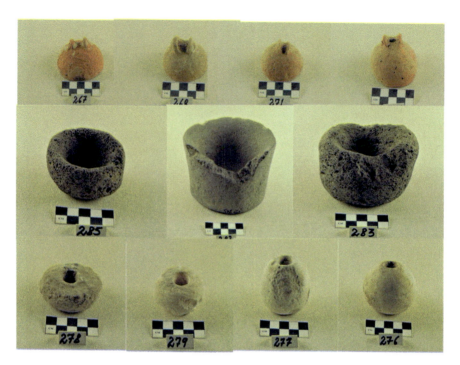

Fig. 12 Stone vessels

Basalt

Seven complete basalt vessels and more than 30 fragments were found during this project. These vessels along with mace heads were common during the EB I but less common in the later Early Bronze Age. These vessels, which were shaped like mortars, mostly with flat bases and flaring rims, were probably more ceremonial than utilitarian. Some of them were very simple with rounded bases. The raw material for manufacturing these vessels is available locally in the form of basalt boulders in Wadi al-Kerak and other adjacent wadis.

Mace Heads

Another class of artifacts, mace heads that might symbolize power and authority, were attested at both Fifa and Naq' (35 complete forms and fragments). These artifacts were made of limestone and, in one instance, alabaster. Their shapes vary from spheroidal to piriform. The fact that most of them were chipped or broken might indicate that they were more functional than votive, unless the breakage was post-depositional.

Lids

Small pottery lids were also attested. They were shaped as small cups with pierced knob handles attached to the base. Judging by their size and shape, these lids were used to cover amphoriskoi. Most probably they were affixed to their necks with a string attaching the knob handles on the lid to the knob handles on the shoulder of the vessel.

Metals

A dagger, probably of unalloyed copper, was found in one of the tombs at Naq'. Daggers were also reported in funerary contexts from the 1995 excavations. It is believed that their presence in the tombs might symbolize social status and gender. These daggers are rhomboid in section with wooden hafts. A golden ring was found in one of the chamber tombs during the 1995 excavation at Naq'.

Shell and Beads

Fragments of shell, shell bracelets, ostrich eggshell, and a few carnelian beads were attested at both sites.

3.3 Chronology

The chronological framework of both sites was based solely on the ceramic and tomb typologies. The fact that there is little change in cist tomb typology might indicate that the burial ground was used during one period, the EB I, regardless of the large size of the cemeteries, especially if we reconsider the duration of this period, which lasted at least 600–700 years. The ceramic typology can be compared to the ceramics from Bab adh-Dhra', which have been more intensively studied. The publication by Schaub and Rast of stratified EB I material from Bab edh-Dhra' Area H allows comparison with the better-known tomb deposits. The authors concluded that the two assemblages at Bab edh-Dhra' contain many of the same forms (bowls, jars, and juglets), but with the addition in domestic contexts of vessels associated with storage and cooking activities. A considerable degree of overlap between the pottery occurring in settlement and burial contexts is documented at many other sites. Similar forms were found in Jericho Tomb A 94, indicating the same date.

The EB I date of Naq' and Fifa was confirmed by the excavations of 1995, 2000, and 2001. In the absence of radiocarbon evidence, these tombs must be dated with reference to stratified material from tombs or occupational contexts at other sites, hence the reliance on pottery typologies. At present, we cannot say whether differences between the ceramic repertoires at these sites are a reflection of chronological and/or regional character, or the fact that they represent different categories of site. Various factors such as site size, function, location, and relationships to other sites might influence the range of ceramics present in individual sequences and thus the degree of chronological resolution obtainable in any single case. Taking into consideration the long duration of the EB I, delineation of sub-periods is potentially valuable, especially as it may be of regional rather than site-specific applicability.

Both Naq' and Fifa were abandoned at the transition to the EB II (in the case of Fifa, the site was reoccupied in the Iron II), while Bab edh-Dhra' developed at the same time into an urban center with impressive fortification walls. The nucleation of Bab edh-Dhra' as a regional center, therefore, likely caused the abandonment of Naq' and Fifa.

4 Conclusions

Use of both the Naq' and Fifa cemeteries commenced sometime during the transition between the EB IA and EB IB. Nucleation of regional settlement at Bab edh-Dhra' likely caused the abandonment of both Naq' and Fifa by the end of the EB IB. This nucleation coincided with (or was, perhaps, caused by) the shift to a sedentary agricultural lifestyle.

With the increasingly anthropological orientation of Levantine archaeology, it is obvious that deeper research on Naq' and Fifa should be conducted. Pottery analysis is an avenue for studying broader aspects of culture, such as shifts in settlement type and distribution, continuity and change in local cultures, connectivity, technological advancement, social stratification, and, most importantly, adaptation to environmental changes. To achieve these goals, however, research must shift towards the construction of ceramic typologies which draw upon a far broader range of ceramic information than presented here. This must go hand in hand with intensive use of AMS radiocarbon dating to create temporal anchors for these ceramic typologies.

One final factor must be mentioned in regard to the character of urbanism in Early Bronze Age Jordan. Urbanism should not be (mis)measured by the size of cities and towns, nor by the numbers of their inhabitants. It should rather be measured according to deeply-rooted political and socio-economic changes in society. Of course, compared to Mesopotamian urban centers, south Levantine city-states and urban centers look minuscule (Philip, 2008:163). Despite their small scale, however, their transition to urban society was bona fide, authentic, and very real.

References

Albright, W. F. (1924). The archaeological results of an expedition to Moab and the Dead Sea. *Bulletin of the American Schools of Oriental Research, 14*, 2–12.

Bandel, K., & Salameh, E. (2013). *Geologic development of Jordan: Evolution of its rocks and life*. self-Published.

Chesson, M. S. (1999). Libraries of the dead: Early bronze age charnel houses and social identity at urban Bab edh-Dhra', Jordan. *Journal of Anthropological Archaeology, 18*, 137–164.

Donahue, J. (1981). Geological investigations at early bronze sites. In W. E. Rast & R. T. Schaub (Eds.), *The Southeastern Dead Sea plain expedition: An interim report of the 1977 season* (pp. 137–154). American Schools of Oriental Research.

Frohlich, B., & Lancaster, D. (2000). Social and demographic implication of subadult inhumations in the ancient near east. In L. E. Stager, J. A. Greene, & M. D. Coogan (Eds.), *The archaeology of Jordan and beyond: Essays in honor of James A. Sauer* (pp. 122–132). Eisenbrauns.

Harrison, T. (2001). Early bronze social organization as reflected in burial patterns from the southern Levant. In S. R. Wolff (Ed.), *Studies in the archaeology of Israel and neighboring lands in memory of Douglas L. Esse* (pp. 215–236). Oriental Institute of the University of Chicago.

Khouri, R. (1988). *The antiquities of the Jordan Rift Valley*. Al Kutba.

Lapp, P. (1966). The cemetery at Bab edh-Dhra', Jordan. *Archaeology, 19*, 104–111.

Levy, T. E., & van den Brink, E. C. M. (2002). Interaction in context. In E. C. M. van den Brink & T. E. Levy (Eds.), *Egypt and the Levant: Interrelations from the 4th through the early 3rd millennium B.C.E* (pp. 3–38). Leicester University Press.

MacDonald, B. (1992). *The southern Ghors and northeast 'Arabah archaeological survey*. Dorset Press.

Najjar, M. (2001). *The Results of the Archaeological Excavations At Naq' and Fifa, 2001*. Report deposited at the Documentation Center of the Department of Antiquities of Jordan.

Najjar, M. (2019). Geology of the Levant. In M. Peilstöcker & S. Wolfram (Eds.), *Leben am Toten Meer: Archäologie aus dem Heiligen Land* (pp. 25–30). Landesamt für Archäologie Sachsen.

Papadopoulos, T., Kantorli-Papadopoulos, L., & Politis, K. (2001). Rescue excavations at An-Naqe' and Tulaylat Qasr Musa Al-Hamad 2000. *Annual of the Department of Antiquities of Jordan, 45*, 189–193.

Philip, G. (2008). The Early Bronze Age I–III. In R. B. Adams (Ed.), *Jordan: An archaeological reader*. Equinox.

Rast, W., & Schaub, R. T. (1981). The 1977 expedition to the southern Dead Sea plain, Jordan. In W. E. Rast & R. T. Schaub (Eds.), *The Southeastern Dead Sea plain expedition: An interim report of the 1977 season* (pp. 1–5). American Schools of Oriental Research.

Schaub, R. T. (1992). Safi. In D. N. Freedman (Ed.), *The anchor Bible dictionary* (Vol. 6). Yale University Press.

Schaub, R. T., & Rast, W. (1984). Preliminary report of the 1981 expedition to the Dead Sea plain, Jordan. *Bulletin of the American Schools of Oriental Research, 254*, 35–60.

Schaub, R. T., & Rast, W. (1989). *Bâb edh-Dhrâ' I: Excavations in the cemetery directed by Paul W. Lapp (1965–67)*. Scholars Press.

Schaub, R. T., & Rast, W. (2000). The Early Bronze Age I stratified ceramic sequences from Bab edh-Dhra'. In P. Graham & D. Baird (Eds.), *Ceramics and change in the Early Bronze Age of the Southern Levant* (pp. 73–90). Sheffield Academic Press.

Waheeb, M. (1995). The first season of the an-Naqe' project, Ghawr As-Safi. *Annual of the Department of Antiquities of Jordan, 39*, 553–555.

A Note on the Earliest Appearance of the Hand-Made, Straight-Sided Cooking Pot in the Southern Levant

Yitzhak Paz and Naama Walzer

Abstract The straight-sided, flat-based, hand-made cooking pot has long been considered one of the hallmark vessels of the early south Levantine Middle Bronze Age(MB), dated to the beginning of the second millennium BCE.

A growing body of evidence, however, now points to an earlier appearance of this vessel type in the Intermediate Bronze Age (IB) (mid-late third millennium BCE).

This article outlines the phenomenon, places its geographic origin along the eastern side of the Jordan Valley and portrays, in general terms, its cultural implications.

Keywords Straight-sided cooking pot · Jordan Valley · Intermediate Bronze Age · Middle Bronze Age · Ceramic typology · Spatial distribution · Cooking ware

1 The Straight-Sided Cooking Pot – Morphology, Technology and Traditional Dating

The hand-made, poorly fired (as indicated by its gray-black core) straight-sided cooking pot (SSCP), with its rectangular profile and flat base, is one of the most recognized ceramic types of the second millennium BCE.

Amiran (1971) distinguished between two successive sub-types of the vessel. She dated the earlier type, which had a straight or slightly everted rim, to the early

Y. Paz (✉)
Israel Antiquities Authority, Jerusalem, Israel
e-mail: yitzhakp@israntique.org.il

N. Walzer
Tel Aviv University, Tel Aviv, Israel
e-mail: naamawal@mail.tau.ac.il

© The Author(s), under exclusive license to Springer Nature Switzerland AG 2023
E. Ben-Yosef, I. W. N. Jones (eds.), *"And in Length of Days Understanding" (Job 12:12): Essays on Archaeology in the Eastern Mediterranean and Beyond in Honor of Thomas E. Levy*, Interdisciplinary Contributions to Archaeology, https://doi.org/10.1007/978-3-031-27330-8_20

second millennium BCE (MB IIA),[1] and the later type, which had a straight or slightly in-turned wall and was much less popular to the MB IIB–C (ca. 1,800–1550 BCE).[2] While both sub-types were decorated with plastic "rope" application, only the earlier sub-type was also lugged around its perimeter with small holes (termed "steam holes," also used here for convenience, regardless of their exact purpose). Alongside both sub-types, wheel-made cooking pots were also in use, and had gradually become the dominant and almost exclusive cooking ware type from the MB IIB onwards; (Amiran, 1971: 126–127).

Throughout the MB IIA the SSCP was common across the southern Levant, and parallels can be found from north to south (see Fig. 1): the Upper Galilee (e.g., Tel Hazor, Yadin et al., 1958: Pl. 93: 23), Lower Galilee (e.g., Tel Gat: Hefer, Alexandre et al., 2003: Fig. 6:7–9), the Jezreel Valley (e.g., Tel Qashsish: Ben-Tor & Bonfil, 2003: Fig. 81:16; Afula: Gal & Covello-Paran, 1996: Fig. 21: 14, 16–18), the Sharon region (e.g., Phase B at Tel Ifshar: Marcus et al., 2008: Fig. 4, 8: 6), the central coastal plain (e.g., pre-palace phase at Tel Aphek: Beck, 2000: Fig. 10.1:24; Tel Gerisah: Geva, 1982: Fig. 29:16), in the Judean Shephelah (e.g., Ramlah: Yasur-Landau & Samet, 2008: Fig. 2.6: 1–3; Tel Gezer: Dever, 1986: Pl. 4: 15, 22), and along the Jordan Valley (e.g., Beth Shean: see Maeir, 2007: 258–260).

Though much less common, as previously stated, the SSCP continues well into the MB IIB, with examples found within the Judean Shephelah (e.g., Khirbet Qeiyafa: Garfinkel, 2009: Fig. 3.38: 6–9; Tel Lachish: Singer-Avitz, 2004: Fig. 16.9:15; Nahal Ha-Elah Site: Paz, 2016) and in the Central Hill Region (e.g., Shiloh: Bunimovitz & Finkelstein, 1993: Fig. 6.8: 17–20).

2 The Early Appearance of Straight-Sided Cooking Pots in the Late Third Millennium BCE

The SSCP appears, along with Levantine Painted Ware, in what are considered the earliest MB IIA contexts of the southern Levant—the pre-palace phase at Tel Aphek (Kochavi & Yadin, 2002: Pl. 2), and in Phase B at Tel Ifshar (Marcus et al., 2008: Fig. 4; Fig. 8: 6). Thus, there is no doubt that this ceramic type was part of the local repertoire of the second millennium BCE.

Maeir suggested that SSCPs were manufactured in several production centers from which they were distributed already at the very beginning of the second millennium BCE (Maeir, 2007: 258–260). However, ample new data suggest that SSCPs were not a novelty of the MB. Rather, they had most likely already made their first appearance during the IBA along the Jordan Valley and in southern Syria, as already noted by Gophna (1989: 113) and by Cole (1984: 62).

---

[1] Note that an EB III-IBA-MB IIA-MB IIB nomenclature will be used here.
[2] Chronology is based on the *NEAEHL* chronological table.

A Note on the Earliest Appearance of the Hand-Made, Straight-Sided Cooking Pot...

Fig. 1 Sites in the southern Levant mentioned in the text – SSCP spatial distribution during the IBA-MBA

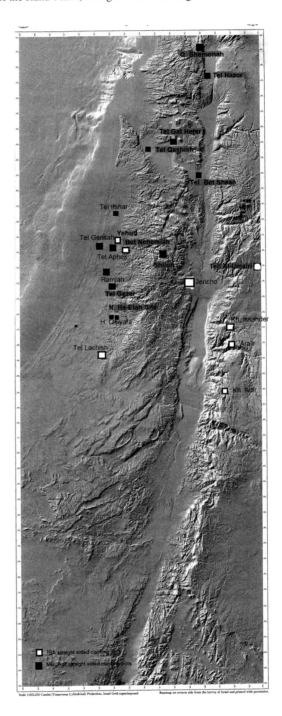

The following are SSCPs that were found in secure IBA contexts[3] and can safely be assigned to this period (see Fig. 1):

- D'Andrea (2012) attempted to discern earlier and later IBA assemblages. In her study of IBA pottery from south-central Transjordan,, the earlier ceramic horizon can be identified by its many shared traits with the former EB III's traditions. The later horizon is marked by the introduction of new ceramic types and decoration techniques (D'Andrea, 2012: 21–26). Of these new types the straight-sided cooking pot is found in the stratified IBA sites in Transjordan (e.g., Phase 3 at Khirbet Iskandar, Stratum VIa at Arôᶜer, and Kh. 'Adir, D'Andrea, 2012: 26–29, Fig. 11: 4). However, it must be noted that their appearance is relatively scarce, and was most likely used alongside the more common hole-mouthed cooking pots.
- Kh. Iskandar (Richard et al., 2010: Fig. 4.1: 15). The sole specimen published in the final report of the excavations in Area C may demonstrate its uniqueness, yet it had come from a clear and clean context, thus, cannot be overlooked.
- Tell el-Umeiri (Herr, 1997: Fig. 5.24: 30). Located at the Madaba Plain, out of the Jordan Valley proper but in direct contact with it. It is highly probable that the specimen presented from this site originated in the Jordan Valley.
- Arôᶜer (Olavárri, 1969: Fig. 5: 12). The restricted excavation at this site, conducted some 46 years ago. Yielded straight-sided cooking pots, as identified by the excavator.
- Jericho, located west of the Jordan River, but still within the boundaries of the Jordan Valley. The straight-sided cooking pot sherds were reported from trenches I and II from what was defined as "EB-MB" contexts (Kenyon & Holland, 1981: Fig. 21: 23; Fig. 70).

At sites outside of the Jordan Valley, sherds of straight-sided cooking pots were, until recently, considered intrusive from adjacent or juxtaposed MB strata, such as the sherd from Cemetery 2000 at Tel Lachish, found among IBA complete vessels that were placed as grave goods (Tufnell, 1958: Pl. 66: 415).

However, recently a sherd with rounded holes on its wall was found at Bet Nehemiah (Yekutieli et al., 2015: Fig. 5:10). Since no post-IBA occupation was detected at the site, dating this vessel to the IBA is secure.

Also, a sherd of a brown clayed cooking pot, very poorly fired, also with a lugged rounded hole, was found near Yehud (ca. 10 km northwest of Beit Nehemiah), in an IBA settlement where no MBA remains were found (observation of the pottery found in the excavation directed by G. Yitah. The authors wish to thank G. Yitah for allowing them to quote this information). Therefore, it can now safely be stated that straight-sided cooking pots made their appearance west of the Jordan Valley as early as the second half of the third millennium BCE.

---

[3] Though SSCP have previously been found at IBA sites, these were reported to have come from unsecure contexts and/or mixed with later MB material.

The southern cutoff of the straight-sided cooking pot's distribution in the Shephelah during the IBA can be explained with the use of Goren's (2010) petrographic examination of the pottery from Kh. Iskandar. This study indicates the site's inhabitants sought cultural ties northward, along the Jordan Valley. Thus, a lack of connections to those living to their south, in Wadi Feinan and the Negev, could provide some initial insight to the complete absence of the straight-sided cooking pot from Negebite sites (and see discussion below).

Considering the lack of reported SSCPs prior to the MBA from the Negev, Central Hill Region, Jezreel Valley, or the Galilee suggests within these regions hole-mouth forms were the sole cooking form used throughout the IBA. Returning to Goren's petrographic work, this distribution does indeed comply with the Jordan Valley connectivity testified by the pottery from Kh. Iskandar (Richard et al., 2010). However, it stands in contrast to what was expected following his work on the many vessels from the Negev sites, such as ᶜEin Ziq and Mashabe Sade, from which a Jordan Valley provenience was indicated for a prominent portion of their assemblages (Goren, 1996: 56). In this light, the complete absence of the SSCP from the regions west of the Jordan Valley, especially the Negev, is indeed intriguing.

The northern distribution border for the SSCP can be placed around the site of Kh. Al-Umbashi. During excavation, six specimens (one intact) were found within Tomb 49, dated by the excavators to the Late IBA/Early MBA (Braemer et al., 2004: 298; Fig. 551). The location of Kh. Al-Umbashi more than 100 km east of the Jordan Valley within the great basaltic Ledja of southern Syria may point to interregional trading links with the Jordan Valley. It should be noted that this cooking pot does not have the characteristic "steam holes" or plastic application that encircled the entire diameter of the vessel; instead it appears with two vestigial ledge handles. Oddly enough, an identical vessel type was found in clear MB IIA context at Qiryat Shemona, Israel (Yasur-Landau, 2012: Fig. 3.3: 8).

Also intriguing are the SSCPs reported from Kh. Ez-Zeraqon, located in the Gilead region, more than 100 km distant from the Jordan Valley. Unlike the sole small body sherds collected from IBA, the sites described above, at the EB III Kh. Ez-Zeraqon, large sherds (with plastic application and "steam-holes") and even one complete vessel (without holes) were found (Genz, 2002: Tafel 13:6; 54:4–6; 61:3; 123:2, 3). The vessels presented by Genz all belong to the latest settlement phase, which should be dated to the EB III. That said, a word of caution is needed here: the on-going strict examination of each and every context from which the SSCP sherds were unearthed, has resulted in the notion that most of them came from disturbed contexts in which IBA pottery was found along with EBA pottery (Genz: pers. Comm.). Still, one wonders why these cooking pots were the only "representatives" of post-EB III occupation levels, and why they were found along with pure EB III assemblages without a single IBA or MBA sherd.

During the survey that was conducted in the immediate region of Kh. Ez-Zeraqon between 1989–1994 (Kamlah, 2000), several sherds of straight-sided cooking pots were found at Hirbet Yariha esh-Shemaliye (Kamlah, 2000: Tafel 70: 5–11); most had plastic decoration but no "steam holes." While MBA remains were also found at the site, Kamlah (2000: 59) clearly assigns the sherds to the EBA and points to the vessels found at Zeraqon for parallels. Thus, one can speculate that at least within the Gilead region, and especially at Kh. Ez-Zeraqon, the straight-sided cooking pot was known already during the late EB III, towards the mid-third millennium BCE.

Further indications of an EB III precedent of the straight-sided cooking pot were sought in all available excavation reports. Not a single sherd of the type that can be securely dated to the EB III was found. The one exception, the sherds found at Beth Shean Strata XI–XII, mistakably published by Fitzgerald along with EBA pottery, were correctly dated to the MB IIB (Fitzgerald, 1935: Pl. IX: 4–6; Maeir, 2007: 258–261).

Moreover, sites where extensive EB III mound settlements flourished, such as Megiddo, ͨAi, Jericho, Tel Yarmouth, Tell eṣ-Ṣāfi/Gath, Tel Lachish, and Tell Halif bare no sign of the existence of the SSCP in pre-MBA contexts and again, one should postulate an eastern Jordan Valley origin for the type. The SSCP was not known from EB III contexts in any of the major excavated sites in the eastern Jordan Valley and further east, such as Tell esh-Shunah North, Tell Hammam, Khirbet el-Batrawi and Khirbet Iskander.

In addition, as previously noted, appearance of the SSCP in the IBA west of the Jordan Valley is extremely rare and in most cases is connected with later MBA contexts. In other words, sherds from MBA strata could have found their way into IBA strata. It is therefore important to stress that at IBA sites where no MBA strata were found, the SSCP was very rare, and thus we can hardly assign the type to a pre-MBA context.

It can be thus concluded that the earliest appearance of the SSCP was seen in northern Jordan and southern Syria, with two variants—one with a whole diameter "rope application" and "steam holes" and the other, with only a redundant ledge handle decoration. It seems that the two sub-types co-existed (both were found) at EB III/IV Kh. Ez-Zeraqon, and moreover, the "ledge handle" sub-type was the only specimen of SSCP found at MB IIA Qiryat Shemona (Yasur-Landau, 2012: Fig. 3.3: 8).

3 Discussion

As noted by Yasur-Landau (2012: 50), the appearance of the SSCP as early as the EB III/IV was observed by various scholars already in the 1980s and seems to reflect a continuity of tradition well into the MBA between northern Jordan, northern Israel and southern Syria. It is important to stress that the SSCP was completely absent and was virtually unknown in northern Syria, from the Jazira, the Amuq Plain and along the Euphrates Valley. The spatial distribution of the type can therefore be placed around the Jordan Valley towards the Gilead, Hauran and Bashan towards Damascus.

The data available to date is insufficient to pin-point the exact geographic origin of the SSCP. While it is plausible that it was well known at Khirbet ez-Zeraqon and in its immediate vicinity as early as the late EB III (mid-third millennium BCE), the curious absence of the type from other EBA sites may point tos a very restricted production and distribution mechanism that has resulted in the adoption of the type at Kh. Ez-Zeraqon.

The SSCP gained a bit more popularity during the IBA (mid-late third millennium BCE). It is curious that the type is said to belong to the later stages of the IBA as claimed by d'Andrea (2012: 26), since it may have appeared in its "classic" form with plastic rope application and "steam-holes" already in the late EB III/early IBA at Kh. Ez-Zeraqon, as shown above. This situation, along with the rather small number of sherds that belong to the type found in the Jordan Valley on the one hand and its remote appearance at Kh. El-Umbashi on the other hand, may hint at a lacuna in the available archaeological data, such that could have bridged the gap between the EB III and the late IBA. The almost complete absence of SSCPs at sites located west of the Jordan River may accord with the petrographic analysis that traced the origin of many IBA pottery types in the Jordan Valley. On the other hand, the SSCPs that were found at Kh. El-Umbashi point towards a wider distribution of this type.

Another word about the socio-economic implications of the early appearance of the straight-sided cooking pot should be added here. As was well-known in the research of the MBA in the southern Levant, the new wave of urbanization that took place at the beginning of the second millennium BCE was inspired and plausibly initiated by north-Syrian urbanization that was characterized, among other things, by ramparts, glacis, direct access gates, wheel-made pottery, advanced Bronze weapons processes (see, e.g., Bunimovitz, 1992).

It can thus be suggested that the hand-made crude and very poorly fired SSCP was the last gasp of an older tradition that was very much "low tech" and stands in sharp contrast to the well levigated, wheel-made and highly fired new type of cooking pot that predominated north Syrian assemblages and finally also became the predominant pot in the southern Levant. As expressed by London (2016: 107), cooking vessels characterized by steam holes were generally used to cook food slowly, which was probably suitable for rural habitation and less suitable for urban life where time was much more precious and cooking activities needed to be rapid (see, e.g., Iserlis & Paz, 2011: 43). For that reason, rounded based cooking pots became preferable over flat based vessels. Furthermore, cleaning round-based cooking vessels seems much easier than those with flat bases in which food remains can stick to the angular interior (London, 2016: 150).

It can be seen that at least in some south Levantine sites, the SSCP appeared in stages that pre-dated the fully urban phases (see, e.g., "pre-Palace" Aphek; Kochavi & Yadin, 2002) and thus it can be suggested that the vessel reflects a cooking tradition that prevailed in the late third millennium BCE in rural settlements and survived at least in the early stage of the renewed urbanization of the MBA, albeit on a modest scale. The decrease of the SSCP and its final disappearance during the mid-second millennium BCE may go hand in hand with the fully urban lifestyle that dictated more rapid cooking activities, such as could best be conducted with the round-based, wheel-made cooking pot.

The mortuary context in which the Kh. El-Umbashi SSCPs were found (and possibly also the Lachish and Ramat Bet Shemesh specimens; see above) may hint at a possible role in mortuary rites, that are beyond the scope of the current paper.

References

Alexandre, Y., Covello-Paran, K., & Gal, Z. (2003). Excavations at Tel Gat-Ḥefer in the Lower Galilee, Areas A and B. *'Atiqot, 44*, 143–170.

Amiran, R. (1971). *The ancient pottery of Eretz Yisrael*. The Bialik Institute and the Israel Exploration Society.

Beck, P. (2000). Area B: Pottery. In M. Kochavi, P. Beck, and E. Yadin, (eds), Aphek-Antipatris I – Excavations of Areas A and B – The 1972–1976 seasons, pp. 93–111. The Institute of Archaeology, Tel Aviv University.

Ben-Tor, A., & Bonfil, R. (2003). The stratigraphy and pottery assemblages of the Middle and Late Bronze Ages in Area A. In A. Ben-Tor, R. Bonfil, & S. Zuckerman (Eds.), *Tel Qashish, a village in the Jezreel Valley, final report of the archaeological excavations (1978–1987)* (pp. 185–276). Institute of Archaeology Hebrew University of Jerusalem.

Braemer, F., Échallier, J.-C., & Taraqji, A. (2004). *Khirbet el Umbashi: Villages et campements de pasteurs dans le «désert noir» (Syrie) à l'âge du Bronze*. Institut français du Proche-Orient.

Bunimovitz, S. (1992). The Middle Bronze Age fortifications in Palestine as a social phenomenon. *Tel Aviv, 19*(2), 221–234.

Bunimovitz, S., & Finkelstein, I. (1993). Chapter 6: The pottery. In I. Finkelstein (Ed.), *Shiloh, the archaeology of a Biblical Site* (pp. 81–196). The Institute of Archaeology, Tel Aviv University.

Cole, D. P. (1984). *Shechem I, Tel Balatah Shechem, the Middle Bronze IIB Pottery*. American School of Oriental Research.

D'Andrea, M. (2012). The Early Bronze IV Period in South-Central Transjordan: Reconsidering chronology through ceramic technology. *Levant, 44*, 17–50.

Dever, W. G. (1986). *Gezer IV: The 1969–71 seasons in Field VI, the "Acropolis"*. Israel Exploration Society.

Fitzgerald, G. M. (1935). The earliest pottery of Beth-Shan. *The Museum Journal, 24*, 5–22.

Gal, Z., & Covello-Paran, K. (1996). Excavations at Afula, 1989. *Atiqot, 30*, 25–67.

Garfinkel, Y. (2009). Pottery of the Middle Bronze Age II. In Y. Garfinkel & S. Ganor (Eds.), *Khirbet Qeiyafa vol. 1. Excavation report 2007–2008* (pp. 43–46). Israel Exploration Society and Institute of Archaeology, Hebrew University of Jerusalem.

Genz, H. (2002). *Die Frühbronzezeitliche Keramik von Hirbet ez-Zeraqon, Nordjordanien, und ihre Bedeutung für die Frühbronzezeitchronologie der Levante* (Arbeit, zur Erlangung des Grades eines Doctor der Philosophie). Harrassowitz Verlag.

Geva, S. (1982). *Tell Jerisha: The Sukenik excavations of the Middle Bronze Age fortifications* (Qedem 15). The Institute of Archaeology, Hebrew University of Jerusalem.

Gophna, R. (1989). The Intermediate Bronze Age. In A. Ben-Tor (Ed.), *The Archaeology of Ancient Israel*. Yale University Press and the Open University of Israel.

Goren, Y. (1996). The Southern Levant in the Early Bronze Age IV: The petrographic perspective. *Bulletin of the American School of Orient Research, 303*, 33–72.

Goren, Y. (2010). Chapter 6: Ceramic technology and provenance at Khirbat Iskandar. In S. Richard, J. C. Long Jr., P. Holdorf, & G. Peterman (Eds.), *Khirbat Iskandar: Final report on the Early Bronze IV Area C "Gateway" and cemeteries* (pp. 133–140). American Schools of Oriental Research.

Herr, L. G. (1997). *Madaba Plains project: The 1989 season at Tell el-'Umeiri and vicinity and subsequent studies*. Andrews University Press.

Iserlis, M., & Paz, Y. (2011). Urban cooking in the Early Bronze Age II—III: A comparative technological perspective. *Eretz Israel, 31*, 38–45. (Hebrew)

Kamlah, J. (2000). *Der Zeraqon-Survey: 1989–1994; mit Beiträgen zur Methodik und geschichtlichen Auswertung archäologischer Oberflächenuntersuchungen in Palästina.* Harrassowitz Verlag.

Kenyon, K. M., & Holland, T. A. (1981). *Excavation at Jericho (Vol. 3): The architecture and stratigraphy of the Tel.* British School of Archaeology at Jerusalem.

Kochavi, M., & Yadin, E. (2002). Typological analysis of the MB IIA pottery from Aphek according to its stratigraphic provenance. In M. Bietak (Ed.), *The Middle Bronze Age in the Levant* (pp. 189–225).

London, G. (2016). *Ancient cookware from the Levant, an Ethnoarchaeological perspective.* Equinox Publishing.

Maeir, A. M. (2002). Perspectives on the Early MBII Period in the Jordan Valley in the Middle Bronze Age culture in the Levant. In M. Bietak (Ed.), *Proceedings of an international conference on MB IIA ceramics, Vienna, 24th–28th of January 2001* (pp. 261–267). Austrian Academy of Sciences.

Maeir, A. (2007). Chapter 4: The Middle II pottery. In A. Mazar & R. Mullins (Eds.), *Excavations at Tel Beth Shean 1989–1996 vol II* (pp. 342–390). Israel Exploration Society and Institute of Archaeology, Hebrew University of Jerusalem.

Marcus, E., Porath, Y., & Paley, S. (2008). The Early Middle Bronze Age IIa Phases at Tel Ifshar and their external relations. *Egypt and the Levant, 18*, 221–244.

Olavárri, E. (1969). Fouilles aI l'Arôʿer sur l'Arnon, Les niveaux du Bronze Intermediare. *Revue biblique, 76*, 230–259.

Paz, Y. (2016). Nahal Ha-Elah Site. *Hadahot Arkheologiyot, 128.* https://www.hadashot-esi.org.il/Report_Detail_Eng.aspx?id=25011&mag_id=124

Richard, S., Long, J. C., Holdorf, P. S., & Peterman, G. (Eds.). (2010). *Archaeological expedition to Khirbat Iskander and its environs, Jordan: Khirbat Iskander: Final report on the Early Bronze IV Area C 'Gateway' and cemeteries* (pp. 133–140). The American School of Oriental Research.

Singer-Avitz, L. (2004). The Middle Bronze Age pottery from Areas D and P. In D. Ussishkin (Ed.), *The renewed archaeological excavations at Lachish (1973–1994)* (pp. 900–965). The Institute of Archaeology, Tel Aviv University.

Tufnell, O. (1958). *Lachish IV.* Oxford University Press.

Yadin, Y., Aharoni, Y., Dunayevski, E., Dothan, T., Amiran, R., & Perrot, J. (1958). *Hazor I: An account of the first season of excavations, 1955.* Israel Exploration Society.

Yasur-Landau, A. (2012). Chapter 3: The Middle Bronze Age Pottery of Strata VII-V: Typology and chronology. In Y. Gadot & A. Yasur-Landau (Eds.), *Qiryat Shemona (S), fort and village in the Hula Valley* (pp. 39–75). The Institute of Archaeology, Tel Aviv University.

Yasur-Landau, A., & Samet, I. (2008). The Middle Bronze Age: Stratigraphy and pottery. In O. Tal & I. Taxel (Eds.), *Ramla (South): An industrial site of the early Islamic period and remains of previous periods* (pp. 16–26). The Institute of Archaeology, Tel Aviv University.

Yekutieli, Y., Paran, N. S., & Ben-Yishai, Y. (2015). Bet Nehemya. *Hadashot Arkheologiyot, 127.* http://www.hadashot-esi.org.il/Report_Detail_Eng.aspx?id=24855&mag_id=122

Can DISH Be a Marker for Greater Social Stratification: Jericho's Early Bronze IV and Tell Atchana, Alalakh

Rula Shafiq

Abstract This study utilizes bioarchaeological analysis to investigate social stratification in past populations. The presence of diffuse idiopathic skeletal hyperostosis (DISH), a joint disease that is believed to be the outcome of obesity and type II diabetes, was found in the skeletal remains of six adult males: four from Jericho (Early Bronze IV) and two from Tell Atchana, Alalakh (Late Bronze I). The current study finds a correlation between burials of males of higher social status and the presence of DISH at both sites. At Jericho, Kenyon reported the presence of seven types of Early Bronze IV tombs that were suggested to represent different ethnic distinctions and social stratification within the population. Four males with DISH were found in Tombs O1, P12, P20 and P22, which belong to the outsize tomb type and were considered to represent a different social class of the society, in this case, the higher, elite class. This evidence is attributed to the successful rural/village social-complexity and prosperous times of the Early Bronze IV that provided accessibility to rich diets. The archaeological evidence from Tell Atchana, Alalakh, indicates a higher social status for the two adult males with DISH who were buried in two distinct ways: one in the Plastered Tomb (individual S4–09), a unique elite tomb located in the extramural cemetery, and one within an intramural cemetery, the so-called craftsmen area (Grave 100).

Keywords DISH · Late Bronze I · Joint disease · Outsize tomb · Elite class · Plastered Tomb

R. Shafiq (✉)
Anthropology Department, Yeditepe University, Istanbul, Turkey
e-mail: rula.shafiq@gmail.com

1 Introduction

Bioarchaeology, the study of human skeletal remains from archaeological contexts, implements a "contextual approach" in analyses and interpretations, integrated within socio-cultural contexts. This approach takes into account all the available lines of evidence, which include age and sex of the interment, burial position in relation to the grave goods, grave structure and location within the cemetery (Knüsel, 2010), along with osteobiographies of the remains (Hosek & Robb, 2019). In this study, the implementation of the contextual approach plays a pivotal role in understanding the socio-cultural contexts of past populations at two archaeological sites in the Levant (Fig. 1): Jericho (Palestinian Territories) and Tell Atchana, Alalakh (southeastern Turkey—Hatay region). Of particular interest are the remains of six individuals dating to the Early Bronze IV and Late Bronze I, respectively. At Jericho, the remains of four males were buried in the associated cemetery of Tell Es-Sultan in single tombs classified as the outsize type. At Tell Atchana, Alalakh, two males were buried in two separate locations within the settlement structure: one in the Plastered Tomb, located in the extramural cemetery, and one in an intramural

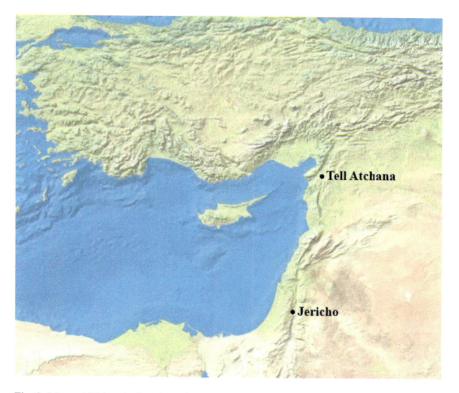

Fig. 1 Map exhibiting the location of the two sites: Jericho and Tell Atchana, Alalakh. (Map source: Natural Earth)

cemetery, in the so-called craftsmen area. All six individuals are characterized with the paleopathological condition of diffuse idiopathic skeletal hyperostosis (DISH).

2 Archaeological Context and Grave Description

2.1 Jericho/Tell Es-Sultan

The site of Jericho represents one of the earliest settlements in the Jordan Valley, with a long-standing occupation of several millennia. Its strategic location, in addition to its water resources, the permanent springs of `Ain Es-Sultan, made it a favorable node in trading networks, leading to the rise of urbanism in the Early Bronze Age. Of particular interest to this research is the Early Bronze IV (2300–2000 BCE), a period characterized as being a rural/village settlement. Recent excavations by the Italian-Palestine expedition have divided the Early Bronze IV into two phases based on architectural evidence from the tell. The earlier phase has the appearance of a rural village, with the later phase showing enlargement of the settlement with distinguishing ceramic and metal technologies (Nigro, 2019). The tombs dating to this period were excavated by Kathleen Kenyon's expedition in the 1950s, in which a total of 177 tombs were excavated. An additional 167 tombs were located, but not excavated, as they were damaged or looted, giving a total of 344 tombs. The material culture and burial customs of the Early Bronze IV tombs were different from those of the earlier Early Bronze III and later Middle Bronze Age, that being the only period characterized by single interment burials at Jericho. There were a few cases of double burials, but the majority were single, with much smaller burial chambers than in other periods (Kenyon, 1965). Kenyon (1960, 1965) divided the tombs into seven different types according to the composition of burial goods and the tomb's structural shape. She named them: square-shaft type, dagger type, pottery type, bead type, outsize type, composite type and multiple-burial type. Kenyon interpreted these seven tomb types as representative of different ethnic or tribal groups among the people of the Early Bronze IV (Kenyon, 1965). Palumbo's (1987) comprehensive research into Jericho's Early Bronze IV seven tomb types suggested that the differences found in burial practices were representative of social stratification and ethnic distinctions within the population. Nigro (2019) has interpreted this as indicating the arrival of a new population that settled Tell Es-Sultan during the Early Bronze IV.

The outsize tomb type (such as Tombs O1, P12, P20 and P22) was described by Kenyon (1965) as being very large in size (the shaft and the chamber), despite having a single interment, and situated at a distance from the tell. In general, the burial goods consisted of a rich assemblage of pots, beads, lamps, metal objects (which might have been attached to wooden artifacts) and animal remains. Tomb O1, published in Kenyon's volume two (1965), shows the remains of one intact individual in a flexed burial position with an assemblage of pots and animal bones at the center of the

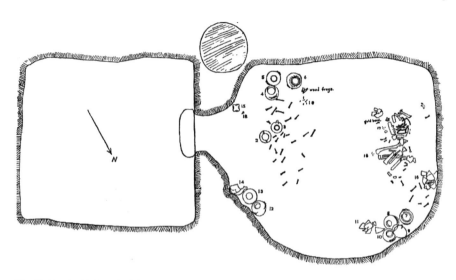

Fig. 2 Tomb O1 from Jericho, Early Bronze IV. (Kenyon, 1965:122)

chamber and a lamp at the entrance (Fig. 2). The interment had a string of beads placed in the neck region, two of which were made of gold. Tomb P12 had the remains of one individual that appears to have been partly disturbed as a result of water seeping into the chamber, but still showing a similar burial position: flexed at the knees. Placed towards the lower limbs were several pottery vessels, and on the opposite side were scattered animal bones. Other grave goods included several fragments of bronze objects, beads and a metallic knife (Kenyon, 1965). P20 is one of the tombs that has not been published; thus, very little information is found in Kenyon's Volumes I and II (1960, 1965). The few phases indicate a rich burial with the customary metallic objects (Kenyon, 1965). Tomb P22 had the remains of one individual, whose skeletal remains were scattered, making it difficult to observe the burial position. Adjacent to the disarticulated skeleton were several pots mixed with scattered animal bones that seemed like they belonged to a young animal. Other burial objects were a spindle whorl, fragments of metallic objects and beads (Kenyon, 1965).

2.2 Tell Atchana, Alalakh

The site of Tell Atchana, Alalakh, is located on the major crossroads between the Levant and Anatolia in the Amuq Valley (Hatay region of Turkey) and dates to the Middle and Late Bronze Ages (2000–1300 BCE). During the Middle Bronze Age, Alalakh was a small regional kingdom, which was a vassal of the Amorite kingdom centered in Aleppo. Following the destruction of Alalakh at the end of the Middle Bronze Age, purportedly by the Hittite king Hattusili I, the city became a vassal of the Mitannian empire. During the latter part of the Late Bronze Age, Alalakh fell under the control of the Hittite empire (Yener, 2010, 2013). The city's architectural features show evidence of rich palace and temple structures, known as the "Royal Precinct," within which several palace archives were recovered (Wooley, 1955; Wiseman, 1953; Von Dassow, 2008). Tell Atchana has one of the largest and richest cemeteries in the eastern Mediterranean region dating from the Middle Bronze II to the Late Bronze I. The majority of the graves are located in the extramural cemetery outside the city fortification walls and are represented by shallow pit-graves (Ingman, 2020), most probably where the majority of the population (commoners) were buried. Recent excavations have revealed the presence of an intramural cemetery located within the city, and it has been classified as a so-called craftsmen burial place (Shafiq, 2018).

Of particular interest to this study are two graves, whose occupants were buried in two distinct ways. The first one is called the Plastered Tomb, an elite tomb located in the extramural cemetery, and the second is Grave 100, located in the craftsmen cemetery. The Plastered Tomb is a unique grave that was constructed of plaster and contained the remains of four adults. The base of the grave was composed of cobblestones within a mixture of white plaster, where the body of the first individual, named S4–09, was placed. This individual, an adult male, was buried on his back with the head resting on a large pottery jar and the legs flexed at the knees. Individual S4–09 had several burial items associated with him: a gold ring, a possible earring made of gold, a piece of plaster placed in his mouth

Fig. 3 Individual S4–09 of the Plastered Tomb from Tell Atchana, Alalakh. (Photo courtesy of Tell Atchana archives, Hatay, Turkey)

(Fig. 3) and several metallic pins (silver and copper), as well as gold appliques with a rosette shape (Yener, 2013). S4–09 shared the Plastered Tomb with three other individuals, a female buried on the same level and a male and another female buried on a second level made of plaster (Boutin, 2010; Yener, 2013). The whole tomb was sealed, and a covering structure composed of mudbricks enclosed the tomb, but little of this superstructure was preserved. However, the tomb's structural evidence indicates that when built, the tomb was visible from afar (Yener, 2013). It is worth mentioning here that three of the four individuals have had their aDNA tested for genetic analyses, and the results indicated a biologically related kin group (Skourtanioti et al., 2020). Moreover, the recent study conducted by Ingman et al. (2021) reconstructed the genetic pedigree of the three individuals. The results indicated that two of the individuals ((S4–09) were father and daughter (first-degree relatives), while the other male was the grandson of S4–09 (second-degree relatives). The results of these genetic studies have confirmed that the Plastered Tomb is a unique and rich family burial reflecting the elite status of the individuals within (Ingman et al., 2021).

The second grave from Tell Atchana is Grave 100, found in the intramural cemetery, craftsmen area, dating to Late Bronze I. The grave is considered a pit inhumation with one interment buried in a supine position with the legs flexed at the raised knees (Fig. 4). Compared to the extramural cemetery, in which burial items are uncommon (Ingman, 2017), all the adult burials in the craftsmen area had associated grave items. Grave 100 had two pottery vessels, one held in the right hand and the second near the head. One of the characteristics of the craftsmen cemetery is the presence of a mudbrick platform placed on the right side of many interments that might have been used in the burial preparation.

3 Osteological Methods

All six individuals' skeletal remains have been fully studied and analyzed by this author, as well as the excavation of Grave 100 at Tell Atchana in 2016. Osteological analyses included age estimation, sex determination and identification of paleopathological conditions. The application of the different methodologies was affected by the degrees of preservation of the different bone elements. Age was estimated by the morphological changes of the auricular surface of the ilium (after Meindl & Lovejoy, 1989, cited in Buikstra & Ubelaker, 1994) and the pubic symphysis (after Brooks & Suchey, 1990, cited in Buikstra & Ubelaker, 1994). Determination of biological sex was based on the features present in the pelvis and the cranium following the standardized criteria listed in Buikstra and Ubelaker (1994), with the addition of pelvic arc compose (Sjovold, 1988). Sex was also determined using metrical analyses of the femoral head diameter, based on the work of this author for the skeletal assemblages of Jericho (Shafiq, 2010) and Tell Atchana. Diagnoses of the paleopathological conditions were conducted macroscopically and based

Fig. 4 Grave 100 of the craftsmen cemetery from Tell Atchana, Alalakh. The mudbrick platform is located under the black and white scale (Photo courtesy of Tell Atchana archives, Hatay, Turkey)

primarily on the visual appearance of the bones with the aid of a 10x and 30x magnification hand-held loupe.

Osteological analyses have identified the paleopathological condition of diffuse idiopathic skeletal hyperostosis (DISH), which is an asymptomatic joint disease. Modern studies have indicated that obesity and type II diabetes contribute to the development of DISH, and it occurs more frequently in men above the age of 40 than in women. Thus, it is considered an age-related condition that develops with the progression of age (Julkunen et al., 1971), leading to more advanced stages of the disease (Verlaan et al., 2007). The operational definition for DISH is characterized by the formation of new bone in the shape of flowing melted wax located along the right side of the vertebrae column. It develops in the thoracic region, causing vertebrae fusion. Early onset of DISH can be diagnosed when less than four bones are found fused with the "melted wax" on the right side. In archaeological cases affected by preservation, the presence of fewer than four fused bones can still be considered to represent DISH, since this feature is pathognomonic to DISH (Waldron, 2001, 2009). Additional diagnosis also depends on the evidence of ossified enthuses that can occur on different bone elements, along with preserved disc space between vertebral bodies (Burt et al., 2013). Rogers and Waldron's (2001) study has indicated that the high prevalence of DISH was connected with a "monastic way of life" or high status in a society. This kind of life provides and maintains the rich diets, which ultimately is a contributing factor in the development of DISH amongst monks or other high status individuals (Rogers & Waldron, 2001; Waldron, 2001, 2009).

4 Results

The results of the skeletal analyses for the six individuals, four from Jericho and two from Tell Atchana, reveal similar diagnoses. All six are mature adult males with auricular surface age estimations of phases 5 and 7, corresponding roughly to 40–45 and 50–60 years old, and pubic symphysis phase 6. The majority of the six individuals have good preservation of their skeletal elements, with the exception of Tomb P20, having around 40% preserved.

All six individuals exhibited similar pathological changes to their skeletal elements that match the operational definition for DISH. Diagnosis of DISH was based on the presence of (1) fused thoracic vertebrae, (2) marginal osteophytes in the form of melting wax located on the right side of the thoracic region, (3) preserved disc space between the vertebrae bodies, and (4) ossified enthesophytes (Burt et al., 2013; Rogers & Waldron, 2001; Waldron, 2001, 2009). The following is a brief description of each individual, outlining the pathological changes observed that indicate the diagnosis of DISH. At Jericho, the skeletal remains of O1 (Fig. 5) exhibited fusion and a candle-wax formation on the right side covering the thoracic (T), lumbar (L) and sacrum regions (T7, T8, T9, T10, T11, T12, L1, L2, skipping L3 and L4, to continue with L5 and sacrum). Similarly, the P12 (Fig. 6) and P20 (Fig. 7)

Fig. 5 Individual O1 from Jericho, exhibiting marginal osteophytes in the form of "melting wax" located on the right side of the thoracic region

Fig. 6 Individual P12 from Jericho, exhibiting fused lower thoracic vertebrae (T10 and T11) with "melting wax" formation and preserved disc space at the red arrow

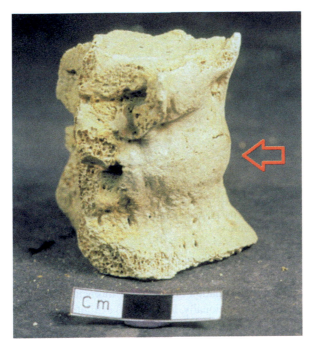

Fig. 7 Individual P20 from Jericho, exhibiting fully fused thoracic vertebrae with "melting wax" formation at the red arrow

Fig. 8 Individual P22 from Jericho, with fusion of the thoracic region in the form of "melting wax" along with ossification of the posterior longitudinal ligaments (OPLL) at the red arrows

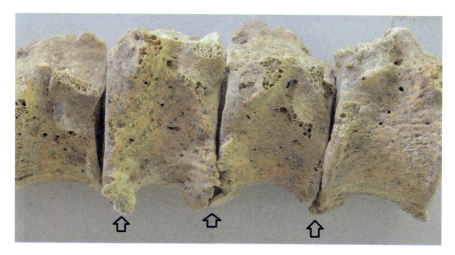

Fig. 9 Individual S4–09 from the Plastered Tomb, exhibiting the typical "melting wax" of DISH on the right side at the black arrows

individuals exhibited fully fused thoracic vertebrae with candle-wax formation. The vertebrae of individual P22 showed fusion of the thoracic region (T7, T8, T9 and T10), with a candle-wax formation on the lower thoracic and lumbar bones (T12, L1, L2, L3, L4 and L5). Additionally, P22 (Fig. 8) exhibited the pathological condition of ossification of the posterior longitudinal ligaments (OPLL) found in the lower thoracic vertebrae (T8, T9 and T10). This condition has a similar aetiology to DISH, as it occurs more in males than females; at the same time it is connected to obesity and type II diabetes (Waldron, 2009).

Fig. 10 Grave 100, exhibiting the typical "melting wax" of DISH on the right side at the black arrows

At Tell Atchana, individual S4–09 from the Plastered Tomb exhibited the typical "melting wax" of DISH on the thoracic vertebrae's right side (Fig. 9) (T4, T5, T6, T7, T8, T9 and T11, with the exception of T10 and T12). This is followed by the lumbar bones, which exhibited marginal osteophytes on the right side. Being a bone former, ossified enthesophytes were found on several of S4–09 bone elements. Similarly, the adult male in Grave 100 showed "melting wax" on the thoracic vertebrae (T7, T8, T9, T10, T11 and T12) (Fig. 10). Interestingly enough, this individual does not exhibit other joint pathological changes, in particular in the weight-bearing regions of the knee and pelvis. Moreover, the long bones are characterized by thin cortical bone and gracile morphology, especially attested at the muscular insertion area of the deltoideus.

5 Discussion

In this study, six individuals exhibited the skeletal changes that match the operational definition for DISH (Burt et al., 2013; Rogers & Waldron, 2001; Waldron, 2001, 2009): four individuals dating to the Early Bronze IV at Jericho (O1, P12, P20 and P22) and two dating to Late Bronze I from Tell Atchana (Plastered Tomb S4–09 and Grave 100). Examination of these pathological changes has indicated that there are variations between the degrees of the disease expression. The skeletal features observed on individual S4–09 can be considered to represent an early developmental stage of DISH. The two individuals, Grave 100 and P12, display further stages of DISH development. Advanced stages of DISH were observed in individuals P20, followed by O1 and P22. The former exhibited full fusion of the thoracic and lumbar vertebrae, while P22, in addition to his vertebrae fusion, showed the additional pathological condition of OPLL, which is known to have similar aetiology and association with DISH (Rogers & Waldron, 2001; Verlaan et al., 2007; Waldron, 2009).

The six adult males were aged between 40 to 50 and 50 to 60 years, mainly according to their pelvic auricular surface and other age estimation indicators. Previous studies have attributed the high prevalence rate of DISH to be associated with high status individuals in a society that provides and maintains the acquisition of rich diets (Rogers & Waldron, 2001). Based on the evidence of DISH found in the skeletal remains of the six males aged above 40, this study proposes that these individuals represent the higher elites of their societies during the Early Bronze IV and Late Bronze I.

At Jericho, four individuals out of 17 recovered from 16 outsize type tombs (Shafiq, 2010), have been diagnosed with DISH. It is worth noting that Kenyon (1965), in her description of Tombs O1 and P22, noted that the skeletal remains exhibited fused vertebrae. She also reported that the outsize type tomb was located the farthest distance away from the rest of the six tomb types distinguishing the Early Bronze IV. She further noted that the outsize type contained only one individual accompanied with rich burial items, including beads, pots, copper and metal objects, knives and animal remains (Kenyon, 1965). Cornwall (1965) reported that the animal bones found in the outsize tombs belonged to sheep and goat and were represented by ulna-radius and tibia portions. Cornwall interpreted this as representing "symbolic offerings" for the dead, since these bones were from the parts of the animals' bodies that had the least amount of meat. Palumbo (1987) also interpreted the outsize tomb type contents (such as Tomb O1) as being "very rich," especially for this period. He further indicated that the differences found in burial practices were representative of different ethnic distinctions and social stratification within the population.

The implementation of the contextual approach takes into account all the above information, along with osteobiographies of the skeletal remains. This study proposes the presence of different social class, specifically emphasized in the outsize tomb type. In particular, the adult males buried in this type of tomb are distinguished by having rich burial items, as well as being buried at a greater distance from the cluster of other types of Early Bronze IV tombs. Moreover, the presence of four individuals with the same diagnosis of DISH is rather high, thus lending further support to the association between rich tombs and the skeletal remains within, all of which indicate the elites of their society. This study further proposes that all the tombs classified as the outsize type are a representation of a different social class of the society, in this case, the higher elite class. This is also based on the analyses of the corpus of Jericho skeletal assemblage, which revealed that only the Early Bronze IV exhibited individuals with DISH (Shafiq, 2010).

Similarly, at Tell Atchana, is it possible to observe the differences in mortuary treatment of the dead between the higher classes and the commoners. Ingman (2017) and Akar (2017) reported that the lower percentage of goods and luxury items in the pit graves of the extramural cemetery indicate that the people who were buried there represent the commoners of the society of Alalakh. The higher classes were buried in specially designated tombs, such as the Plastered Tomb, as well as buried within the city limits in a private intramural cemetery, such as that of the craftsmen area. The rich gold burial objects found in association with individual

S4–09 indicate much higher class than Grave 100. The results of the osteobiographical analyses have shown that the individual in Grave 100 has very little pathological conditions at his joints, and the skeletal remains showed gracile bones with cortical thinning of the long bones. The evidence of DISH, along with the majority of his teeth being lost ante-mortem, further supports the notion of a high status sedentary life (Shafiq, 2018).

The ongoing study by this author of the skeletal remains recovered from the craftsmen cemetery area at Tell Atchana has shown the near absence of joint disease for the adults within this cemetery, such as at the major joint surfaces and the knee, which is rather notable, especially among older individuals. Based on these results, this study proposes that the craftsmen cemetery, including Grave 100, should be considered as representing an elevated portion of the society at Tell Atchana during the Late Bronze I. This study draws on further evidence collected from the written material found in the Late Bronze I Level IV archives indicating that Alalakh had a four-class society during the Late Bronze Age, as has been reported by Wiseman (1953) and later elaborated on by Von Dassow (2008). The highest was the elites, named *maryanni*, who owned horses and chariots, followed by the *ehelle*, who were classified as a class of craftsmen, and then the poor of the society and the foreigners, named ḫupše and ḫabirū, respectively. The texts also indicate that the *ehelle* owned land and were employed by either the palace or the *maryanni* class (Von Dassow, 2008). Of particular interest here is the *ehelle* social class, which, as indicated in the texts, was exempt from physical labor, as opposed to the majority of the population, especially the commoners (Von Dassow, 2008; Wiseman, 1953), who were involved in the type of harsh work that caused joint diseases and hand and feet crush fractures.

6 Conclusions

There is enough compelling evidence to demonstrate the association between DISH and males of high social status in both societies. This evidence reflects several aspects of the lifestyles once practiced by these males, having continuous access to rich diets. One could elaborate on the composition of these diets based on the reports of Rogers and Waldron (2001) who gave account of the monastic rich diet as a contributing factor for the development of DISH. Their diet was composed of bird and animal fats, meat, fish, dairy products, carbohydrates and more. Thus, it can be assumed that the six individuals presented here might have had a similar composition of rich diet leading to obesity and type II diabetes, predisposing later into DISH. Based on the association between the archaeological evidence presented above and the pathological findings of DISH, the current study proposes that the four males (O1, P12, P20 and P22) dating to Early Bronze IV at Jericho and the two males (S4–09 and Grave 100) dating to Late Bronze I at Tell Atchana, Alalakh, were individuals of high social status.

One might ask why only males during the Early Bronze IV at Jericho? The answer to this is related to the aetiology of DISH, having a higher incidence in males above the age of 40. The majority of the outsize tomb types belong to males, with four tombs (P27, P3 [with graffiti on the tomb walls; Kenyon, 1965], P30 and P9) of females with age-at-death of 45 and above. However, the bone preservation is rather poor in these, and the majority of the bone elements are fragmented and incomplete. In spite of the low preservation, the tombs showed rich burial items that are similar to the males' (Shafiq, 2010). However, there is no osteobiographical evidence to support the proposed high status of the four females in the outsize type. Thus, it is difficult to state that females might also have had a higher status, equal to males, with no supporting evidence based on skeletal markers, such as DISH. Regardless, this study takes the leap and proposes that, based on similarities in the archaeological contents, including the tomb type and the burial items within, all the tombs classified as outsize type can be considered to represent the elite of the society during the Early Bronze IV at Jericho. This is attributed to the successful rural/village setting and prosperous times of the Early Bronze IV. This proposition correlates well with others (Richard, 2020; D'Andrea D"Andrea, 2012) who analyzed the multiple lines of evidence from several archaeological sites in the Jordan Valley to indicate "social complexity" in these advanced rural-cities characterizing the Early Bronze IV.

Similar evidence points to a higher status at Tell Atchana for the two males, S4–09 and Grave 100. The former belongs to the elite, the *maryanni*, and the latter belongs to the craftsmen's class, the *ehelle*. This study proposes that this intramural cemetery might be an *ehelle* cemetery for the craftsmen and their extended families (Shafiq, 2018). This notion is further supported by an identical genetic marker found on the permanent upper incisor teeth of three individuals, thus supporting the idea of family burials. The near absence of joint disease, along with DISH, indicates a lack of hard physical labor for the males and females in the intramural craftsmen cemetery, as supported by the Level IV archival texts.

In general, these findings propose a correlation between grave structures, rich burial items, grave location and osteobiographies, in particular, the presence of DISH, all of which indicate social differentiation for the buried individuals and thus, putting forth an association between the level of nutrition, sedentary life and elevated social status. However, it should be noted that not every individual found with DISH should be assumed to represent high status (Waldron, 2019), other types of evidence should be evaluated within the contextual approach.

This study identifies certain males as having higher social status in their respective societies. Moreover, this elite status would have given them certain privileges that guaranteed continuous access and acquisition to rich diets, contributing to obesity and diabetes, thus leading to DISH. At Tell Atchana, higher social status provided the two males during their lifetime with access to rich diets and being elevated from the rest of the commoner class by not being involved in hard physical labor, as observed on their skeletal elements. The social structure of these societies guaranteed that elite individuals were distinguished during their lifetime and after their death. This study demonstrates that it is possible to observe social stratification based on the funerary treatment of the dead, along with osteobiographies of the skeletal remains.

Acknowledgments The author is thankful to Professor Dr. Aslıhan Yener for providing the opportunity to access and study the human skeletal remains of Tell Atchana, Alalakh. Thanks also goes to the Director of the site, Associate Professor Dr. Murat Akar (Mustafa Kemal University, Turkey) for his appreciated help. The author also thanks the Duckworth Laboratory, University of Cambridge, for permission to study Jericho's skeletal material within its collections. Thanks also goes to Dr. Tara Ingman for her supportive editorial comments.

References

Akar, M. (2017). Late Middle Bronze Age international connections: An egyptian style kohl pot from Alalakh. In E. Kozal, M. Akar, Y. Heffron, Ç. Çilingiroğlu, T. E. Şerifoğlu, C. Çakırlar, S. Ünlüsoy, & E. Jean (Eds.), *Questions, approaches, and dialogues in the eastern mediterranean archaeology. Studies in honor of Marie-Henriette and Charles Gates* (pp. 219–232). Ugarit Verlag.

Boutin, A. T. (2010). The burials. In K. A. Yener (Ed.), *The Amuq Valley Regional Projects: Excavations in the Plain of Antioch: Tell Atchana, Ancient Alalakh, Vol. 1: The 2003–2004 excavation seasons* (pp. 111–121). Koç University Press.

Brooks, S., & Suchey, J. (1990). Skeletal age determination based on the os pubis: A comparison of the Acsadi-Nemeskeri and Suchey-Brooks methods. *Human Evolution, 5*, 227–238. (Cited in Buikstra and Ubelaker 1994).

Buikstra, J., & Ubelaker, D. (1994). *Standards for data collection from human skeletal remains* (Arkansas archaeological survey research series no. 44). Arkansas Archaeological Survey.

Burt, N., Semple, D., Waterhouse, K., & Lovell, N. (2013). *Identification and interpretation of joint disease in paleopathology and forensic anthropology*. Charles C Thomas, Publisher, Ltd.

Cornwall, I. (1965). Collections of animal bones from tombs of E.B.-M.B. outsize type. In K. Kenyon (Ed.), *Excavations at Jericho. Volume two: The tombs excavated in 1955–1958* (pp. 702–703). British School of Archaeology in Jerusalem.

D"Andrea, M. (2012). The Early Bronze IV period in south-central Transjordan: Reconsidering chronology through ceramic technology. *Levant, 44*(1), 17–50. https://doi.org/10.1179/175638012X13285409187838

Hosek, L., & Robb, J. (2019). Osteobiography: A platform for bioarchaeological research. *Bioarchaeology International, 3*(1), 1–15. https://doi.org/10.5744/bi.2019.1005

Ingman, T. (2017). The extramural cemetery at Tell Atchana, ancient Alalakh and GIS modeling. In C. Maner, M. Horowitz, & A. Gilbert (Eds.), *Overturning certainties in near eastern archaeology: A festschrift in honor of K Aslıhan Yener* (pp. 245–258). Brill.

Ingman, T. (2020). *Identity and changing funerary rituals at Tell Atchana, Alalakh: Mortuary and isotopic analyses*. Ph.D. Thesis unpublished, Koç University.

Ingman, T., Eisenmann, S., Skourtanioti, E., Akar, M., Ilgner, J., Ruscone, G. A. G., le Roux, P., Shafiq, R., Neumann, G. U., Keller, M., Freund, C., Marzo, S., Lucas, M., Krause, J., Roberts, P., Yener, K. A., & Stockhammer, P. W. (2021). Human mobility at Tell Atchana (Alalakh), Hatay, Turkey during the 2nd millennium BC: Integration of isotopic and genomic evidence. *PLoS One, 16*(6), e0241883. https://doi.org/10.1371/journal.pone.0241883

Julkunen, H., Heinonen, O. P., & Pyörälä, K. (1971). Hyperostosis of the spine in an adult population. Its relation to hyperglycaemia and obesity. *Annals of the Rheumatic Diseases, 30*, 605–612. https://doi.org/10.1136/ard.30.6.605

Kenyon, K. (1960). *Excavation at Jericho. Volume one: The tombs excavated in 1952–4*. British School of Archaeology in Jerusalem.

Kenyon, K. (1965). *Excavations at Jericho. Volume two: The tombs excavated in 1955–1958*. British School of Archaeology in Jerusalem.

Knüsel, C. J. (2010). Bioarchaeology: A synthetic approach. *Bulletins et Mémoires de la Société d anthropologie de Paris, 22*(1), 62–73. https://doi.org/10.1007/s13219-010-0003-1

Meindl, R., & Lovejoy, C. (1989). Age changes in the pelvis: Implications for paleodemography. In M. Işcan (Ed.), *Age markers in the human skeleton*. Charles C. Thomas. (Cited in Buikstra and Ubelaker 1994).

Nigro, L. (2019). The Italian-Palestinian expedition to Tell es-Sultan, ancient Jericho (1997–2015): Archaeology and valorisation of material and immaterial heritage. In R. T. Sparks, B. Finlayson, B. Wagemakers, & J. M. Briffa (Eds.), *Digging up Jericho: Past, present and future* (pp. 175–214). Archaeopress Archaeology.

Palumbo, G. (1987). "Egalitarian" or "stratified" society? Some notes on mortuary practices and social structure at Jericho in EBIV. *BASOR, 267*, 43–59.

Richard, S. (2020). New vistas on the Early Bronze Age IV of the southern Levant: A case for "rural complexity" in the permanent sedentary sites. In S. Richard (Ed.), *New horizons in the study of the Early Bronze III and Early Bronze IV of the Levant* (pp. 417–453). University Park, Pennsylvania.

Rogers, J., & Waldron, T. (2001). DISH and the monastic way of life. *International Journal of Osteoarchaeology, 11*, 357–365.

Shafiq, R. N. (2010). *Diet and health in relation to changes of urban and rural living during the Bronze and Iron Ages, in the southern Levant*. Ph.D. Thesis unpublished, University College London.

Shafiq, R. (2018). Evidence of a possible elite cemetery at Alalakh/Tell Atchana. In *Vol 33 Arkeometri Sonuçları Toplantası* (pp. 193–203). Ankara.

Sjovold, T. (1988). Geschlechtsdisgnose am skelett. In R. Knussmann (Ed.), *Anthropologie. Handbuck der vergleichenden biologie des menschen* (pp. 444–480). Gustav Fischer Verlage.

Skourtanioti, E., Erdal, Y. S., Frangipane, M., Restelli, F. B., Yener, K. A., Pinnock, F., Matthiae, P., Özbal, R., Schoop, U. D., Guliyev, F., Akhundov, T., Lyonnet, B., Hammer, E. L., Nugent, S. E., Burri, M., Neumann, G., Penske, S., Ingman, T., Akar, M., Shafiq, R., Palumbi, G., Eisenmann, S., D'Andrea, M., Warinner, C., Jeong, C., Stockhammer, P. W., Haak, W., & Krause, J. (2020). Genomic history of Neolithic to Bronze Age Anatolia, Northern Levant and South Caucasus. *Cell, 181*, 1158–1175. https://doi.org/10.1016/j.cell.2020.04.044

Verlaan, J. J., Oner, F. C., & Maat, G. J. R. (2007). Diffuse idiopathic skeletal hyperostosis in ancient clergymen. *European Spine Journal, 16*, 1129–1135. https://doi.org/10.1007/s00586-007-0342-x

Von Dassow, E. (2008). State and society in the Late Bronze Age: Alalakh under the Mittani empire. In D. Owen & G. Wilhelm (Eds.), *Studies on the civilization and culture of Nuzi and the Hurrians* (Vol. 17). CDL Press.

Waldron, T. (2001). *Shadows in the soil: Human bones and archaeology*. Tempus Publishing Ltd.

Waldron, T. (2009). *Palaeopathology*. Cambridge University Press.

Waldron, T. (2019). Joint disease. In J. E. Buikstra (Ed.), *Ortner's identification of pathological conditions in human skeletal remains* (3rd ed., pp. 719–748). Academic Press, Elsevier Inc.

Wiseman, D. J. (1953). *The Alalakh tablets* (Occasional publications of the British Institute of Archaeology at Ankara) (Vol. 2). British Institute of Archaeology at Ankara.

Woolley, C. L. (1955). Alalakh: An account of the excavations at Tell Atchana in the Hatay, 1937-1949. In *Reports of the Research Committee of the Society of Antiquaries of London, Vol. 18*. Oxford University Press.

Yener, K. A. (2010). Introduction. In K. A. Yener (Ed.), *The Amuq Valley regional projects: Excavations in the plain of Antioch: Tell Atchana, ancient Alalakh, Vol. 1: The 2003–2004 excavation seasons* (pp. 1–6). Koç University Press.

Yener, K. A. (2013). A plaster encased multiple burial at Alalakh: Cist tomb 3017. In R. B. Koehl (Ed.), *Amilla: The quest for excellence. Studies in honor of Günter Kopcke on the occasion of his 75 birthday* (pp. 263–279). INSTAP Academic Press.

Part II
New Directions in Biblical Archaeology

Tom Levy at Tel Gezer, 1971. (Photo courtesy of William G. Dever)

Theoretical and Methodological Comments on Social Complexity and State Formation in Biblical Archaeology

Erez Ben-Yosef and Zachary Thomas

Abstract Archaeology has done nothing if not expose the amazing degree of cultural variation among both ancient and more recent pre-modern societies throughout the world, while archaeological theory has likewise broadened our ways of appreciation of this variability and the scope of interests and perspectives that the archaeological record invites. One such area worthy of attention is social complexity, the variations of which throughout world archaeology have received much attention, and it is well appreciated that older evolutionary theory cannot adequately make sense of such variation. Yet, biblical archaeology remains stuck with many outdated notions about social complexity and its archaeological manifestations. The assumption that complexity is necessarily attached to urbanism and monumentality is especially prevalent, and accordingly "state formation" of the biblical kingdoms is recognized only on the basis of architectural remains and simplistic evaluations of their substantiality. This paper seeks to untie this necessary association by demonstrating that complexity can occur in the absence of monumentality. Of particular importance to the early Iron Age, we demonstrate that societies that have a dominant or significant nomadic component can be complex in the absence of monumentality, while there are also cases in predominantly settled societies where monumentality is not demonstrably central to local ideologies of power and authority. The United Monarchy in ancient Israel, a mixed settled-nomadic society with both archaeological and textual sources, is presented as a case study for reorienting evaluations of complexity away from simple equations with monumentality and more towards contextually-imbedded, emic understandings of society and polity.

Keywords Social complexity · Archaeological theory · Nomadism · Polymorphic societies · Ancient Israel · Monumentality · Social evolution · Architectural bias

E. Ben-Yosef (✉) · Z. Thomas
Tel Aviv University, Tel Aviv, Israel
e-mail: ebenyose@tauex.tau.ac.il; thomasz1@mail.tau.ac.il

1 Introduction[1]

Social complexity is a primary preoccupation of archaeologists the world over. Strictly speaking, social complexity is an anthropological subject. When archaeologists deal with it, they are concerned with discovering and figuring out its nature and materialization in extinct social systems. The crucial questions that region-specific disciplines like biblical archaeology must ask, therefore, is what is the nature of complexity in the historical cultural context under study, and to what degree is that complexity actually *discoverable*? It should be noted that in biblical archaeology, the answers to these questions have fundamental implications for the study of the Hebrew Bible/Old Testament, in particular to issues related to the use of archaeology as the ground truth for the historicity of biblical accounts.

With limited (and often overlooked) exceptions, biblical archaeology has long been content to sidestep these questions, and to stick to a traditional set of assumptions about what social complexity is and is not, and to rest in the assurance that if it was present, it will be found. This belies the complexity, so to speak, of social complexity that is well understood within the theoretical and methodological richness of world archaeology; it is time for biblical archaeology to become exposed to this. Indeed, biblical archaeology's assumptions and assurances have recently received a serious challenge through arguments that complexity can be seen among nomadic groups in the early Iron Age southern Levant, and that nomads present an unavoidable problem for the detection of complexity. Why is this so? Consider first this observation:

> Scattered, opportunistic, and shifting, the nomads of popular imagination are the dark matter of history. Historians tend to look straight through them into entities that appear more substantial and seem to move history: settler empires, nation-states, agro-capitalist regimes. (Hämäläinen, 2013: 85)

Dark matter is indeed an excellent metaphor for nomads as historical actors, something not readily observable by standard means of observation but capable of exerting profound influence upon the system in which it exists. For pre-modern nomadic societies, a combination of the severe problems that archaeology has in detecting them and ingrained biases against them within theories of social progress and "complexity" has seen them frequently overlooked as historical actors on equal footing with sedentary societies. Being so much more easily visible to archaeological investigation, it is sedentary populations (or the sedentary components of social groups) that are upheld as the real historical actors, even when they may have shared their environment with mobile populations. As a result, archaeologists and historians privilege aspects of the archaeological record that are particular to sedentary life as material markers and proxies for a society's characteristics, namely its complexity.

---

[1] This is a longer and more elaborated version of a paper in the *Journal of Archaeological Research* entitled "Complexity Without Monumentality in Biblical Times" (Ben-Yosef & Thomas, 2023). Our thanks to the editors of JARE and to Springer Nature for their permission to reproduce material here.

This "sedentarocentrist" predisposition can be particularly associated with positivistic processual archaeology, but even post-processual approaches can fall afoul of it (Bernbeck, 2008). As stated by Honeychurch and Makarewicz (2016: 342): "Pastoral nomads, simultaneously admired and disparaged for their apparent separateness from the civilized world, have long been defined according to the perceptions of settled peoples."

We begin with nomads not because this is simply another paper on nomads, of which there are already many excellent examples, including the two just cited. Rather, pre-modern societies that were fully or largely nomadic and yet also socially complex present the starkest contradiction to what McIntosh calls the "conceptual tyranny of the monumental" (1999: 20). Monumentality remains deeply ingrained in the archaeology of social complexity to the point that monumentality is not just taken to be a material aspect of culture that can be associated with complexity, but one that *must* be associated with complexity (Kradin, 2006, 2013). Ergo, it is assumed that if monumentality is absent in the archaeological record of a society, that society cannot be said to be fully complex. It has thus been possible to downplay the possibility of complexity of pre-modern societies in regions with little to no monumentality, for example sub-Saharan Africa (McIntosh, 1999: 20). A reverse situation in which societies deemed "simple" could not have been responsible for ancient monuments pervaded much early archaeological scholarship in North America (Trigger, 1980). It is this necessary link that this paper seeks to question and ultimately to unravel, not because we deny that complexity and monumentality co-occur (they certainly do) or that any pre-modern society lacking monumentality was complex (obviously not all were). Archaeologists have to come to appreciate that social simplicity can develop in sedentary societies and that monumentality can occur without unambiguous complexity (Fowles, 2018; Miller, 2021). Rather, by holding fast to a fixed, generalizing idea of what complexity must be and thus ignoring the possibility of complexity without monumentality, we contend that world archaeology runs the serious risk of overlooking situations where this is the case, even if such cases are relatively uncommon. We intend for this study to inform other cases in world archaeology where a necessary association between complexity and monumentality is suspect, and where severing that association can help to advance understanding complexity at a locally contextualized level.

While consideration of complexity without monumentality in predominantly nomadic societies does serve to prompt the question, it is important to note that our critique and its implications are not limited to any one particular social form or subsistence base. We are hardly the first to suggest that nomads can form complex societies. If anything, however, the implications would seem to be greater for the study of complexity in sedentary societies, the usual locus for monumentality in the archaeological record. To speak of "sedentary" versus "nomadic" societies in the first place is very much a modern distinction that assumes societies do not take different forms simultaneously (Alizadeh, 2010; Barth, 1967; Fowles, 2002), a distinction reified in the early history of anthropology, which Eurocentrically equated sedentism with the evolution of "civilization." Ongoing discoveries and scholarship since the early days of anthropology though have shown that often Old World societies especially were comprised of a mix of settled and nomadic groups, though views have differed over the manner in which they were integrated. Rowton's older notion of a "dimorphic" society (1976), which sees a sharp distinction between nomadic and settled communities even when they participate in the same polity, is often cited for the Near East, one of the world's primary regions for the study of historical nomadism and pastoralism. It is now evident however that at least through to the Late Bronze Age in the Near East, pastoralism and farming were not two separate economies of distinct communities but rather strategies practiced simultaneously by the same community, which was neither only sedentary nor purely nomadic (Arbuckle & Hammer, 2019). This is better described as a "polymorphic" society (Lemche, 1985), which incorporated an organic, flexible mix of different lifestyles and economic strategies. Nomadism (including pastoralism) and sedentism should not themselves be imagined as polar opposites but rather as two ends of a continuum upon which individual social groups were located and along which they moved. Multiple sorts of combinations occur: nomads sometimes remain stationary for periods and practice agriculture, sedentary groups can revert to nomadism if they need to, while individual social groups (not just whole societies) can be simultaneously comprised of both nomadic and settled subsets (Cribb, 1991; Khazanov, 1994; Schloen, 2017; Silvia Castillo, 2005). The mobility or sedentariness of a society will have differential influences of the manner of social complexity, but it should not be assumed that the potential for complexity depends on the adoption of one particular form of subsistence (or anything in between). Where a society is truly polymorphic, as in the case study we present in this paper, there is a need for much more nuance in how complexity is evaluated, more than simply affiliating complexity with material markers like monumentality.

The context for the prevailing enchainment of complexity to monumentality, as well as our critique here, is to be found in the general trends in the history of archaeological theory, more specifically its utilization of the social sciences and ethnographic work (see Trigger, 2006; Johnson, 2020). The earliest primary phase in the history of archaeology, in the nineteenth century up until roughly World War II, was a period of romantic exploration, of competition among colonializing European nations to claim ownership of the past through the excavation and acquisition of museum-worthy pieces, in the biblical and classical Mediterranean world especially, and eventually the culture-historical approach with its links to nationalism. At the level above the direct study of artifacts, the dominant theoretical framework was social evolution (cultural evolution to some) as associated with early anthropologists such as Spencer and Morgan, by which archaeologists sought to trace how simple and primitive societies had evolved into the idealized, complex European civilization. Confidence in being able to discover historical developments and character of ancient societies ran high, while for societies that left little behind, ethnography was used to fill in the gap. Following World War II archaeology underwent its "loss of innocence" (Clarke, 1973), becoming both much more theoretically self-aware and more informed by both scientific methods and a scientific orientation in its philosophy of epistemology and explanation. Within the "New" or processual archaeology and its nomothetic designs, social evolutionism flourished once again, with its discreet typological stages serving as seemingly natural, even objective categories for ordering the cultural world studied. With the recognition that the archaeologist still needed to infer the behavioral and social context in which their data were produced, ethnography could provide an empirical source for such inference (as per Renfrew & Bahn, 2019: 175). Post-processualism (Hodder, 1985) has tended to challenge at a philosophical level the objectivity and positivism of processualism and its more uniform conclusions, instead emphasizing the instability of interpretations and multiple dimensions of both being in the past and for studying those ways of being from the vantage of the present. The uniqueness and idiosyncrasies of individual cultures with their particular histories of development and the role of the agency of actors within them have been emphasized against attempts to flatten them under universalizing interpretative structures like social evolution (Geertz, 1973; Martin, 2005). This has been accompanied by more awareness of the distinction between the etic views of the Western analyst and the emic or native understanding of society and culture within an embedded system of symbols and language (Hodder, 1992).

Post-processualism has opened up a wide vista of different interpretative dimensions, and for the study of social complexity it has stimulated a freedom to move beyond the constraints of Eurocentric definitions and their criteria such as monumentality. We can now formulate "alternative complexities" (Honeychurch, 2014), complexities which do not start from ethnocentric assumptions about what sorts of societies can or cannot be complex, and which take seriously the emic understanding of socio-political structures of power within the context studied. Here we recognize a problem however, in how the differential quality of the archaeological records can stimulate differential applications of theory. We observe that post-processual interpretations, in all their various nuances, tend to be applied to societies that have a rich archaeological record and often textual evidence as well, providing fodder for investigations of context-specific cultural phenomena such as ideology, as well as the unique history of the subject society. Conversely, we observe that in cases where the archaeological record of a society is poor (and texts unavailable), there tends to be a default to processualist and social evolutionary interpretation. In such cases archaeology does not provide an artefactual baseline from which to launch investigation of cultural phenomena in their context-specific form. As such, the pre-defined and even predictive concepts of explanatory framework of processualism-evolutionism would seem an attractive recourse, a ready-made way to fill in the gaps. Setting aside the general validity of social evolutionism, the difficulty with such a recourse is that it substantially narrows the range of possibilities that archaeologists would consider for the characteristics of said society, including its complexity. Ethnography becomes a tyrannical rather than a liberating source of analogy and comparison, constraining the possibilities that are considered (Belfer-Cohen & Goring-Morris, 2009; Wobst, 1978). Empirically-accessible markers like fellow tyrant monumentality become the deciding criteria for judging complexity, even if the possibility remains that monumentality did not play a critical role in the formation and maintenance of socio-political relationships in the cultural context at hand.

We would situate our critique as another step in post-processualism's history of broadening the horizons of social archaeology and exposing just how complex social complexity really is. Though the proposition of complexity without monumentality appears rather more radical within the methodological confines of our own field (Levantine archaeology), as we shall explain, within world archaeology and the specialization of archaeological theory, this is hardly a revolutionary new proposal so much as a natural extension of existing developments in the study of social complexity. To demonstrate the application of our critique and to show its implications, we present a case study from the southern Levant, the case of the United Monarchy, the earliest phase of monarchic political organization in ancient Israel during the early Iron Age, a polymorphous society with a primarily nomadic background. The study of the United Monarchy, like that of many other polities in the Bronze and Iron Age Levant, has taken place insulated from many advances in archaeological theory of complex societies, being mostly conducted within a simplified positivist and evolutionist framework. Archaeological evaluations of complexity and "state formation" in early Iron Age Israel have concentrated on the presence or absence of material markers of which monumentality is one prominent example. This has recently been challenged in two ways, in the (chance) discovery of a complex nomadic society in the neighboring region of Edom that was contemporary with the United Monarchy, and the application of an emic model of social organization deriving from the wider ancient Near Eastern studies. Before laying out this case study, we first discuss the problem of the archaeological visibility of ancient nomadic and polymorphous societies, leading into a more in-depth discussion of social evolution, complexity and monumentality. Here we present our reasons for rejecting a stadial evolutionist model while retaining the concept of complexity, albeit in a form that can be adapted to be sensitive to the context of societies like ancient Israel where, we argue, monumentality was not a central cog within the workings of complexity or an inevitable outcome of it.

2 Defining and Discerning Complexity: The Archaeological and Anthropological Dimensions

2.1 The Visibility Problem

Regarding how the physical status of an ancient polity relates to its actual power, Thucydides made the following prescient observation:

> For just suppose the city of Sparta were wiped out and all that was left were its shrines and the foundations of its buildings, I think that years later future generations would find it hard to believe that its power matched up to its reputation...[B]ecause they are not united in one city and have no lavish shrines or public buildings but instead live in village settlements in the traditional Greek manner, they would be underestimated. On the other hand, if the Athenians were to suffer the same fate they would be thought twice as powerful as they actually are *just on the evidence of what one can see*. (2013: I.10, emphasis added)

Here the father of "scientific" history recognizes that there is in fact no simple, directly-perceptible equation between the material qualities of a society (including the monumentality familiar from his native Athens) and its complexity, in rather archaeological terms, no less. We can ask, how much more might Thucydides have insisted upon this if he had known of the great nomadic empires to come of later centuries, like that of Genghis Khan?

There are two interrelated sides to the issue of archaeological detectability: First, there is the extent to which the social institutions and characteristics of a particular culture should or should not have a proportionate material correlate. This is exactly the overall issue that this paper addresses, in the spirit of Thucydides' skepticism that archaeological remains directly bespeak social complexity. Second, and currently in focus, is the very availability of archaeological remains. Contrary to any notion that the archaeological record of even a highly urbanized society is an exact fossilization of said society, it is in fact shaped by cultural and post-depositional factors that can obscure the sorts of things that we would wish to investigate (Schiffer, 1996). But for nomadic societies or the nomadic segments of polymorphic societies this is much more so. Dwelling in tents, mobility without residency in any one location for an extended period, and lifeways that made use of primarily perishable organic materials mean that pastoral and nomadic life leave little if any archaeological imprint. So much has been evident at least since Childe (1936: 91).

Near Eastern archaeology, and more specifically the archaeology of the southern Levant, offers an instructive exemplar for how this plays out in research endeavors (as well as providing some relevant background to our case study below). Nomadic groups have largely been overlooked as part of the region's cultural landscape and especially as part of social complexity there as a result of being largely invisible to archaeology, a situation which persists even despite the fact that they are mentioned in written sources including in the Hebrew Bible, cuneiform and Egyptian texts, where they do appear in some cases as much more than fringe players. In just the small area of the southern Levant and Sinai, nomadic peoples, for whom there is little to no archaeological evidence are attested in textual sources during several periods, from the Iron Age Arabs who appear in Assyrian sources all the way to the Bedouin of the Islamic and Ottoman periods (Finkelstein, 1992b; Finkelstein & Perevolotsky, 1990; Frendo, 1996; Riehl, 2006; Wilkinson, 2000: 250). Even in places where environmental conditions could be conducive to the preservation of minimal remains of nomadic life, other environmental factors often have a detrimental effect on preservation. For instance, a systematic study of paleo-floods in the deserts of southern Israel have demonstrated the infrequent occurrences of unexpected "mega-floods" that would have washed away much of the remains of nomadic activity deposited on the surface (Ben-Yosef, 2019: 366; Ginat et al., 2018). Research specifically designed to detect the remains of nomads, with targeted surveys and sampling (Knabb et al., 2014; Rosen, 2017: 53–70), is viable in certain landscapes (and particular kinds of nomadism), but still unlikely to produce the kind of data that can lead to insights beyond the level of basic subsistence and lifeways (Ben-Yosef, 2019: 362, 366).

In non-desert areas, we have the additional problem of changes to the historical environment introduced by settled communities and their land-use practices that have obscured its place in the historical nomadic landscape. Based on their archaeological excavations and surveys along with a study of historical environment and settlement patterns in the region around Tell el-Hesi in southwestern Israel, Blakeley and Hardin argue that the region was likely to have been a pasturage going back at least to the early Iron Age and continuing as late as the end of Ottoman rule. The nature of the region's soil meant that permanent settlement and rain-fed agriculture was unviable except in limited circumstances, becoming viable only much more recently with the technological introduction of drilled wells and mechanical pumps (Blakeley, 2021; Hardin & Blakeley, 2019). This serves to remind us that as we assess the place of nomadic communities within a wider social landscape, we should be wary of doing so purely on the basis of the present environment.

In his influential volume *Nomads in archaeology,* Cribb (1991), while taking a more positive approach to the possibilities of locating nomads archaeologically, acknowledges the problem of visibility and also points out that it is often not possible to actually distinguish the material culture used by nomads from their settled counterpart. The two do not necessarily represent distinct *archaeological* cultures or preferences for different types of materials. Cribb offers some examples of fixed features that could indicate the use of a site as a nomadic camp, such as leveled floors, but setting aside the issue of preservation for the moment, it is difficult to know to what extent the practices Cribb documented among the nomads in modern Turkey and Iran, are representative of nomadic practices in other contexts, misleading ethnographic comparison always being a risk (see below).

This raises the question of whether there are any other types of remains that can be associated with nomads with any degree of confidence, and that would not so easily be lost to the vagaries of the environment? Honeychurch and Makarewicz (2016: 347) suggest types of features and sites that can be related to nomads, including "seasonal camps, rock art panels, burials and cemeteries, and ritual areas," and indeed such features and sites do seem promising sources of evidence if, again, they are preserved, if they can be dated and if a possible association with sedentary communities can be excluded with a degree of confidence. The burials and cemeteries of nomadic communities clearly do hold much potential for providing data and insights, though their visibility in the landscape varies depending on the regional and cultural context. Burials of the ancient nomadic Xiongnu found in Siberia and Mongolia had prominent, labor-intensive surface structures and were used to inter a small number of related individuals, perhaps presenting an elite, while the majority of the population appears to have been buried in ways less likely to survive into the archaeological record (Honeychurch, 2014: 303–304). Compare this with the early Iron Age cemetery of Wadi Fidan 40 in the Wadi Aravah, Jordan, which contains more than one thousand stone cist graves. The construction and prominence of these graves were not prominent in the landscape, but the cemetery offers a much larger number of individuals as a dataset and a much larger cross-section of society (Beherec, 2011; Beherec et al., 2014). Cultural domains like burial practices are of course as much a matter of cultural values and ideology as they are of lifestyle and subsistence base, so it would be improper to look for a single "nomadic" burial practice or to assume that all nomadic (or sedentary) burials will be of a type likely to be archaeologically visible.

We would note briefly here that even where archaeological evidence produced by mobile groups is available, this does not mean its historical significance will be readily apparent. Bioarcheological evidence related to the passage of Hannibal's Carthaginian army across the Alps in 281 BCE has been found through a specialized environmental study (Mahaney et al., 2017a, b), but the significance of such evidence would be entirely unrealized if we did not have Roman historical sources to indicate that it was produced by a large army on a single march from Iberia to Italy.

We offer these points to establish that at a basic level one cannot simply assume that the archaeological record provides direct, uncomplicated access to a society's complexity, which holds true even in the archaeologically rich contexts of settled and highly urbanized societies. The correlation is much more problematic for societies that have some form of polymorphism or that are properly nomadic, owing to the substantial difficulties in the archaeological detection of mobile groups of their activities. Nomads in particular only become visible in rather specific and uncommon circumstances, and this visibility is dependent in part on cultural practices that leave more than a fleeting material trace. Though we agree with Arbuckle and Hammer (2019) that polymorphism is the more accurate characterization for the social context in which much mobility occurred in the ancient Near East and we share their skepticism in retrojecting ethnographic accounts of modern pastoralists and nomads back into antiquity, still their overall evaluation does rely on a positivistic methodology: the only kinds of mobile communities are those that are archaeologically visible, in this instance pastoralists tied to settled communities. This leads them to reject the likelihood that there were properly nomadic groups sharing the same environment in the periods they survey, from the Neolithic to the end of the Late Bronze Age (Arbuckle & Hammer, 2019: 404, 419, 432–433). Though they do admit that the late second and first millennia BCE saw the emergence of proper nomads in the Near East, they understand this as a development made possible by the increased use of camels as beasts of burden (2019: 420–421, 427). As we will discuss in our case study below, however, the early Iron Age southern Levant may be exceptional, as evidence for the activities of complex nomadic polities pre-dates good evidence for the use of domesticated camels there (Sapir-Hen & Ben-Yosef, 2013).

In a more methodologically-neutral world, scholars might be more willing to admit to the limitations of evaluating social complexity on purely archaeological grounds, especially in societies with significant mobile components. Rather than admit that in such cases the question of complexity is an open one without a clearly demonstrable answer, there is a tendency to resort to interpretative schemas like evolutionism that come preloaded with answers about what sorts of societies had what manner of complexity, and what sorts of archaeological correlates are indicative of it, such as monumentality. We turn next to examine these subjects.

2.2 Social Evolution and the Primitive-Civilized Dichotomy

To reconstruct ancient societies, archaeologists move from their evidence and what it indicates about basic technological, economic and subsistence practices to inferences at higher orders, inferences about social, political, and religious institutions that permeate and structure societies. Because such institutions are first and foremost products of human relationships, agency and practice, discerning them requires a certain intellectual leap, and a degree of interpretative creativity (Gallay, 1989; Hawkes, 1954; MacWhite, 1956). It is notable that the turn towards the physical and natural sciences within processual archaeology did much to increase evidence relating lifeways and exchange of goods, while no equivalent revolution has taken place for the archaeology of societal phenomena. Such a revolution would not really be possible, as such phenomena are by virtue of their social nature incorporeal and thus unmeasurable. In the archaeology of historical periods, the natural inclination is to draw direct information regarding society, polity and religion from texts. Archaeology has a complicated history with the use of texts however, especially in the post-romantic phase of the discipline's history. Archaeologists have often been suspicious that texts are too biased, subjective, products of an elite or otherwise limited in their historical veracity (Moreland, 2001). The case study presented below is a good example of where disagreement over historical texts as a source relatable to archaeology (in this case the Hebrew Bible) has added another dimension to the study of an ancient society. Ideally then, archaeological theory serves as a scaffolding for drawing inferences about social institutions, their internal nature and relationship to other institutions out of the archaeological record.

But theory, broadly conceived, has also served to guide evaluations of ancient societies according to definable cross-cultural characteristics, of which complexity is perhaps the most prominent. Such evaluation serves to satisfy our desire to discover how ancient societies were or came to be "like us" (Chapman, 2003; Alt, 2010), for we of course are complex and know in what way we are complex. How one defines and characterizes "us" and where we stand in relation to the historical development of human society therefore will shape (if not dictate) how our theory evaluates societies that are not really "like us," especially if we see our society as in some way superior, ideal or more advanced, rather than simply different. This was very much the case with practitioners in the early history of anthropology during the nineteenth century, who dichotomized their subjects, the evolutionarily stagnant and backwards "primitives" from ascendant "civilization" of their own world. Rather than make a clean break from this outdated and problematic thinking, social evolution as utilized by archaeologists is still rooted in this intellectual history (Alt, 2010: 2–3; Chapman, 2003: 7; Fowles, 2018: 19; Kuper, 2005; Pluciennik, 2005: 102–103). So perhaps it is more honest to say that these nineteenth century origins are really "shackles" (Shanks & Tilley, 1987: 144), by which evolutionary theory weights archaeological and anthropological theory with a certain valorization of modern-day Eurocentric categories, values, and experience of history, to the point that what constitutes European complexity and its realization in the state becomes the benchmarks for evolutionary assessments anywhere (a "temporal ethnocentrism" [Rowlands, 1984: 108]). This continues to be held even when modern practitioners are aware of the variation they encounter across the myriad human cultures and time periods they study (Alt, 2010: 2; Pluciennik, 2005: 95–97; Rowlands, 1989). It would hardly be controversial to say that urbanism, for instance, can appear in many different forms in the different contexts where it is used as a criterion for social complexity or state-formation, but the basic idea of urbanism itself is still borne directly from Eurocentric underpinnings of such theory, not to mention the reliable archaeological preservation of urban contexts.

Indeed, the cultural context for the molding of anthropological and ethnographic theory that archaeologists would take up, as the product of a small set of Anglo-American gentlemen, must be confronted when considering the applicability of social evolution and the notion of progress from simple to complex. The early history of the disciplines of anthropology and ethnography with their fundamental notions of primitive vs civilized, European vs the "other" is inseparable from Euro-American colonialism and the need for justifications thereto, individuals sometimes being engaged quite directly in the colonial program (Diaz-Andreu, 2007; Hingley, 2013; Kuper, 2005; Pluciennik, 2005). In the course of colonial encounters and ethnographic work, early practitioners encountered societies with stark enough differences from the European familiar to allow them to create and confirm sharp dichotomies between the civilized world and the primitive, the latter visible in living fossils that had survived into the modern day, but without having evolved (for the southern Levant, see the case of the Bedouins below). Mobility, subsistence through foraging and pastoralism, and kinship-based social structure were on the primitive side, while the achievement of civilization was equated with sedentarization, agriculture, and super-kinship political structures, that is to say government (Kuper, 2005; Pluciennik, 2005). There was no room for a notion that complexity was within the faculties of the forager or pastoral nomad, as their potential had been completely exhausted by the need to adapt to their environment, and in this primitive state they remained frozen on the evolutionary ladder (Sneath, 2007a, b: 120–122):

> The Nomads and the Eskimos have fallen into an arrest through an excessive concentration of all their faculties on their shepherding and hunting techniques. Their single-track lives have condemned them to a retrogression towards an animalism which is the negation of human versatility. (Toynbee, 1946: 327)

Nomads in particular were seen as saddled with characteristics seen as inevitably limiting their evolutionary potential and trapping them in simplicity. Being by definition tribal, egalitarian and unable to accumulate wealth, nomads were thus deemed unable to achieve the hierarchic form of evolved societies like state familiar from the settled world (Sneath, 2007b). Even when it was later suggested that nomads could form states (that is, be complex) it was only after they became socially divided between the ruling/non-producing class and a subordinate/producing class, and adopted writing, characteristics based on settled societies (Krader, 1978).

2.3 Monumentality (or the Monument Mentality)

Childe (1950) put the outbreak of urbanism, his "urban revolution," squarely at the center of society's progress towards civilization. The beginnings of urbanism involved and was enabled by the exploitation of a non-productive elite that took control of agricultural and craft surpluses, through the administrative technology of writing, concentrating their surplus in monumental construction. This reified the evolutionist position of the nineteenth and much of the twentieth centuries that posits not only an artificial distinction between mobility/nomadism and sedentism/urbanism, but also a dichotomy between their evolutionary status, equating the latter with humankind's progress towards civilization. Processual archaeology would continue to view sedentarization as an inevitable, irreversible outcome of improving adaptation and urbanism as bound up with the evolution of the state (Bernbeck, 2008: 45–50; Jennings & Earle, 2016: 475). As such, it comes as no surprise that monumentality, as a phenomenon treated as inseparable from urbanism, would come to have the status of a necessary element within complexity and higher evolutionary forms. Yet this raises several difficult methodological questions concerning the concept of "monumentality" itself: why and on what grounds do we designate something in archaeology, usually architecture, as monumental? Does monumentality (as we designate it) have an agentive role in socio-political relations, or is it just an epiphenomenon of complexity? How is this role shaped by the cultural context in which any instances of monumentality occur? The most important question for our purposes here is whether or not the dynamics and structure of socio-political authority somehow depend on monumentality? A functionalist approach that enchains complexity to monumentality, McIntosh's "conceptual tyranny of the monumental" (1999: 20), must assume that they are, one way or another. Childe himself did not really engage these problems, stating only that "monumental public buildings...symbolize the concentration of the social surplus" (Childe, 1950: 12). Theorizing about the archaeology of complexity in the neo-evolutionary school has continued in this same vein, treating monumental or "public" buildings (palaces, temples, tombs) more as outcomes of a society becoming complex than as active participants in that process (Smith, 2003: 42–43).

To begin answering these questions, it is clear that "monumentality" is an etic analytic type, which groups certain constructions or kinds of constructions into one simplified class according to a certain trait, not much different from the stadial types of neo-evolutionism (see below). Trigger (1990) provided the classic and most influential definition of monumental architecture: working from the assumption that people seek to conserve energy (physical output and resources), the construction of monumental architecture deploys more energy than is necessary, such that it can be said to be deliberately overbuilt. This sets up a false dichotomy between what is monumental and what is not monumental. But where does one draw the line? What do we do with structures that fall somewhere in the middle, or those that have a non-domestic or non-prosaic use but that are not monumental as defined by Trigger? The relative scale of non-monumental to monumental will also vary depending on cultural context; what is monumental in one place will not look so impressive in another (Hildebrand, 2013). Additionally, the assumption that the builders of "monumental" architecture were deliberately applying more energy than was necessary is highly subjective and in most cases it would be difficult if not impossible to prove that they were working in accordance with such logic. For instance, could "monumental" defenses (walls, ramparts, etc.) ever be unnecessarily strong (Thomas, 2019a, b)?

Yet more problematic is Trigger's (1974, 1990, 2004) functionalist and materialist view of the actual socio-political role of monumentality as a form of conspicuous consumption on the part of the ruling authority that commissioned it, which serves the dual function of visibly projecting the ruling authority's high status and command of both human and physical resources, as well as reminding the subordinate population responsible for the actual construction work of its subordinate social position. As such, monumentality could serve as a direct archaeological indicator of the presence of a state and the kind of government that characterizes it. Such functionalist and materialist perspectives are inevitably circular in positing that the construction of monumental architecture was productive of a social hierarchy that already had to exist to enable the ruling authority to command the labor of its subordinate population (Hildebrand, 2013; Thomas, 2019a, b). As Marcus (2003: 115) notes, such an approach to monumentality relies on the dubious, simplistic logic that "(1) monumentality equals power; (2) early states had less power than later states; (3) the bigger the monument, the more powerful the ruler or government that commissioned it." Typical of the positivistic approach in processual archaeology discussed below, monumentality under the influence particularly of Trigger and Childe has been used as an index of the scale of a society's complexity (Osborne, 2014a, b). What exactly is imagined to happen in the absence of monumentality within such functionalist and materialistic perspectives is quite clear even if never stated outright: a lack of monumentality effectively disables complexity, so if it is not found by the archaeologist, it was not present.

It is certainly true that the functionalism of Trigger and others is not the only way to approach monumentality; there are also phenomenological approaches that seek to understand how a monument's original audience interacted with it and the effects that it had upon them, and the agentive social role that monuments had, affected by and affecting its embedded socio-cultural world (Delitz & Levenson, 2019; Hildebrand, 2013: 158–159; Osborne, 2014b). Though these approaches are eminently preferable to functionalism, they still have the problem that there is often no basis upon which to choose between different viable interpretations, as well as the risk of the archaeologist importing modern, ethnocentric concepts and models (Hildebrand, 2013: 158–159). This would appear to be what Delitz and Levenson do when they state that:

> Societies–like the nomadic–that exhibit no monumental architecture must rather be described as ones that defend themselves against monumental buildings and artifacts. Collective strategies are associated with this: the accumulations of power that accompany monumental and impressive architecture are to be avoided. The intention is to moderate social inequalities and hierarchies in the mode of architecture. (2019: 114)

This view manages to centralize monumentality even when it is absent, and assumes that a lack of monumentality must be a statement against what it represented socially, rather than to related to completely different cultural relationship with architecture. It is difficult to counteract such subjectivity or ethnocentrism when there is no available native, emic conceptualization of what we would call "monumentality" and its socio-political role available, primarily from texts, upon which to base interpretations. But the problem goes beyond this, because with such a native and emic conceptualization available, on what basis can we assume that monumentality was in fact critical to the dynamics and structure of socio-political authority in the first place? To explore the workings of complexity without monumentality, we must disabuse ourselves of the idea that monumentality is an absolutely necessary and universal component of complexity. Again, we do not claim that monumentality (as we designate it) does not play an active role in complexity in some cultural contexts; certainly it does, but archaeologists are under no obligation to assume this is the case in the absence of positive evidence to that effect for the society they are studying. This should apply in any case, but particularly when the textual and archaeological evidence for the native structuration of socio-political relations is rich. For an archaeologist to assume that monumentality (or the lack thereof) was critical to the complexity of a pre-modern society in such a situation would effectively be to claim that the structuration of socio-political authority in its native linguistic expression is either naïve about how power actually worked there or a deliberate ideological mask hiding the "real" nature of relationships of authority and social hierarchy, which worked by rules familiar to the modern Western interpreter (Schloen, 2001). Below, we point to cases from world archaeology and history where complexity existed *sans* monumentality, while much scholarship concerning our case study, the United Monarchy in early Iron Age Israel, has assumed an importance for monumentality that no native text (ancient Israelite or Near Eastern) clearly supports.

2.4 Neo-evolutionism in Archaeology

Social evolution's second flourishing in what is commonly known as "neo-evolutionism" continued the effort to categorize societies into different types of social organization that could be placed on an evolutionary ladder, as a series of steps ascending teleologically to the highest step, that of civilization in the Western mold. Again, the cultural context cannot be ignored; neo-evolutionism truly crystalized in the post-World War II United States, where economic prosperity encouraged a focus on the material and a belief in the upward march of progress and improvement (Trigger, 2006: 386–387). Service's (1971 [1962]) influential model of progression of types from band to tribe, to chiefdom, to state, provided a schema by which anthropologists and archaeologists could classify societies in an even more specific way according to certain characteristics. Here a basic dichotomy is again fundamental, that between the kinship-based organization of lower order social types like the tribe, and the supersession of kinship by a specialized elite hierarchy that held a centralized administrative authority, as in the state. Service called this division between kinship and civil society "The Great Divide" (Service, 1975). It seems appropriate to emphasize the universalizing ambitions of neo-evolutionism, unattenuated from earlier social evolutionary thought. In making his distinction between specific and general evolution, Sahlins recognized cultural variation and evolutionary differences that went with it, but still held that there were overall trends in evolutionary progress that could be seen transculturally (Sahlins, 1960). Though ethnographic and archaeological information had increased since the pioneering days of anthropology, neo-evolutionist models were still derived from a limited number of cases, which were taken to be representative of broadly-applicable types, somewhat blurring the specific-general boundary (Whallon, 1982). As Sahlin's and Service's theories were based on their study of Melanesian and Polynesian societies, this led to what McIntosh (1999: 4) called "the Oceanic hegemony in complex society archaeology."

Neo-evolutionism was embraced by Anglophone archaeology with the rise of the "New" or processual archaeology, as a field in which archaeology was capable of making serious contribution to anthropology (Binford, 1962). The positivism inherent in the evolutionary program of classifying societies into types according to their characteristics along a primitive-civilized or simple-complex progression sat comfortably within processualism's scientifically-oriented approach to adducing and explaining the archaeological record. Culture was now to be treated as a natural phenomenon, and so like other natural phenomena, its regularities and rules, the objective things that comprise it could be discovered by proper testing. On the social level it was Service's very specific types that would come to be the regularities that could be demonstrated empirically (Wenke, 1981; White, 1959). As a result, past social reality becomes fully accessible by way of the functionalist assumption that "when distortions of archaeological post-depositional formation processes have been subtracted, there exists a rather direct relationship between the archaeological record and past cultural systems" (Kristiansen, 1984: 76). In his paper, "Archaeology as Anthropology" a foundational processualist text, Binford offers a highly positivistic assessment of how culture can and does allow access to social systems. Though conceding that "we cannot excavate a kinship terminology or a philosophy,"

[W]e can and do excavate the material items which functioned together with these more behavioral elements within the appropriate cultural sub-systems. The formal structure of artifact assemblages together with the between element contextual relationships should and do present a systematic and understandable picture of the *total extinct* cultural system. (Binford, 1962: 218–219, emphasis original)

Neo-evolutionist types, especially those of Service, can be seen within broader processualist aim to grasp the breadth and change of culture within categories and covering laws. Observable and measurable factors like population growth were understood as drivers of change, problems for societies that forced them to change and improve their adaptation (Dan-Cohen, 2020: 736; Patterson, 2003; Sanders & Price, 1968; Wenke, 1981: 82). Comparing societies and using similarities or differences to categorize them into these different types had been part of evolutionism for a long time, but neo-evolutionism's emphasis on comparison has been said to have contributed significantly to world archaeology. Likewise, the use of ethnography had long been central to evolutionism, the study of supposed "survivals" of humanity's primitive beginnings, but neo-evolutionism now stimulated the more nuanced field of ethnoarchaeology (e.g. Kramer, 1979), to study modern societies at the same typological level (tribe, chiefdom etc.) that one wished to understand in the archaeological record (Kohl, 2007: 4).

But how viable does evolutionism remain today? Marcus (2008) has recently defended social evolution in quite a direct manner, in a paper simply entitled "The Archaeological Evidence for Social Evolution." While not stating outright that culture is a natural phenomenon, she does view nature as the appropriate analogy:

> The relationship between ethnology and archaeology is analogous to that between zoology and vertebrate paleontology. Zoologists are able to study both muscle tissue and behavior at a level of detail unavailable to paleontologists. Paleontologists, however, can find the muscle attachments on fossil bones that provide evidence for specific muscles; they can then draw on the zoological literature both on those muscles and on the behavior they reflect. (2008: 253)

She extends this analogy to societal typology: "Imagine the problems that would result if zoologists were forbidden to create categories such as 'amphibian,' 'reptile,' and 'mammal'" (2008: 253). This position hangs precariously on the appropriateness of the analogy, but even if one accepts that discrete categorizations in the natural world (taxonomy) are ontologically absolute, which is doubtful, it is hardly clear that this applies to human society in all its variations across time and space. Likewise, it is hardly clear that ethnography can or even should inform archaeology in the straightforward, uncomplicated way that Marcus seems to hold. The search for "evidence" for social evolution as per the paper's title only works on the positivistic basis that social evolutionism is a phenomenon *out there* to be discovered, rather than an etic analytic structure of concepts and values taken and applied to data by the scholar. But social evolution is not an objective reality but "above all a particular narrative which says much about the holder's or opposer's world view and incorporates deeply held convictions about the nature and meaning of human history" (Pluciennik, 2005: 13). Formulating an archaeological analysis determined by evolutionism but then claiming to produce "evidence" for social evolution runs into circular reasoning (Kristiansen, 1984: 72). We do not mean to imply that Marcus or other contemporary proponents of social evolutionism hold to the ethnocentric, teleological or colonialist convictions of those founding figures of the theory. But we cannot avoid the reality that such convictions are essential to the original formulation of social evolutionism. As Kuper points out, the very idea of primitive society, without which there could not be evolution to civilization, is an "illusion….a myth that was constructed by speculative lawyers in the late nineteenth century" (2005: 10). One cannot therefore argue for social evolution on purely ontological grounds. It does not simply exist as part of the natural world in the same way that Darwinian biological evolution does, but is a very particular way of ordering societies on the basis of very particular preconceptions and values.

Aside from the question of its ontology, social evolutionist theory has been critiqued both from within processualism and more forcefully from without by post-processualists, on quite a number of grounds, one of which, its underlying ethnocentricity, we have already discussed. Though the literature here is quite vast and opinions most various, certain criticisms do stand out. Its use in archaeology has been criticized on the grounds that the theory was not developed in response to archaeological evidence, of which there was little available to early anthropologists who ultimately relied on ethnography to build their typology, a reliance that remained important even into the neo-evolutionist school. Notwithstanding the acceptance of neo-evolutionists like Sahlins (1960) that evolution did not happen in the same way in every culture, many have criticized as universalizing and essentializing social evolutionism's pretense to apply to any culture. Much criticism of the theory has centered on this issue, that evolutionism overlooks or bypasses both synchronic differences between cultures that it would group together in the same stage and in the particular contingencies of history that play out across the history of any culture and society. The very idea of stage-based progression like Service's (1971) has been criticized as an illogical and simplistic framing of socio-cultural development, as societies do not simply jump between substantially different forms of organization (Bawden, 1989; Giddens, 1984; Kuper, 2005; Pauketat, 2007; Pluciennik, 2005; Routledge, 2004; Shanks & Tilley, 1987; Stein, 1998; Wenke, 1981; Yoffee, 1979, 1993, 2005).

Stages such as tribe, chiefdom and state are simply ways to classify and group societies according to arbitrary criteria imposed from the outside, and it is not clear that they really possess more explanatory potential than typologies of various sorts of archaeological finds like ceramics. Nor do these types have much explanatory potential for understanding how and why societies change in significant ways, including how they become noticeably more complex (Dunnell, 1980; Kohl, 2007: 11; McGuire, 1983). Processual and neo-evolutionist theory has tended to explain change through various combinations of "prime movers" that provide some external stimulant to a society to evolve rather than change through purely internal stimulants like the agency of a charismatic individual (Flannery, 1972; Sanders & Price, 1968; Shanks & Tilley, 1987: 140). We have already referred above to one prominent example, that of population pressure, which brings us back for a moment to the problem of visibility, especially for polymorphous or nomadic societies; if a significant portion of the population is difficult to detect archaeologically, how effectively can a metric like population size be used to explain change? Even where sedentary polities are concerned, it is not at all clear that population size is either something that can be clearly discerned or directly linked to substantive structural transformations due to a number of issues, including differences in scales of organization between polities and difficulties in actually finding their boundaries archaeologically, or the problem of simple demographic fluctuations over time (Feinman, 1998).

The specific neo-evolutionist stages and their forms, namely Service's (1971, 1975) tribes, chiefdoms and states, have themselves been individually subject to serious criticism as well, not least in Pauketat calling the chiefdom an "archaeological delusion" (2007) that collapses variability and local historical contingencies into a single, monolithic and ultimately quite artificial type. Nor have attempts to divide up the chiefdom type into a multitude of subtypes proved convincing (Feinman & Neitzel, 1984). The state, on the other hand, has more ontological security owing to the fact that unlike chiefdoms, the state is something that is natively recognized as really existing by those within it. But is a state, even if one adds modifiers like "archaic" (Feinman & Marcus, 1998), the right way to characterize many complex pre-modern polities, even those that look superficially like a modern state? This once again raises the dual problem of ethnocentrism and etic versus emic; the state looks like the apogee of social evolution because that is what its benchmark is in the modern West. But if it is projected back onto ancient societies that did not conceptualize themselves as state or organize themselves as a state does, then for the archaeologist this type can only ever be an etic one (Smith, 2003). Weber's definition of the state has been highly influential in anthropological and archaeological work on the state. It emphasizes the monopoly on the legitimate use of violence on a given territory. Though Weber defined different ways in which authority could be seen as legitimate, there has been less awareness that Weber also defined the state as a legal and administrative order established in legislation and managed by a professional staff, that is to say, a specifically rational and bureaucratic order (Weber, 1978).

The Near East (including Pharaonic Egypt) provides another good exemplar, in this case for regional scholarship retrojecting the state type back onto ancient complex polities, even when aware of their differences from the modern state and the complex difficulties that exist in mapping structures of authority and administration in ancient polities onto the characteristics of the modern state (Joffe, 2018; Scheidel, 2013). Some Near Eastern scholars have, however, presented alternatives either maintaining the term "state" while arguing effectively that it was not bureaucratic (Garfinkle, 2008) or rejecting the term as applicable altogether (Schloen, 2001; Thomas, 2021; Younker, 1997). Research in the latter vein has made light of the importance that kinship-based tribal structures have on the structure of ancient Near Eastern kingdoms (Master, 2001; Porter, 2012), of which our case study is a good example. Even in the modern Middle East, tribes remain integral to the social and political fabric rather than the marginal, the Hashemite Kingdom of Jordan being a good example (Alon, 2005). This directly contradicts the sharp evolutionist distinction between kinship and "higher" form of political organization such as (but not limited to) states (as per Ribeiro, 1968; Service, 1975), as well as the notion that the tribe is not a potentially complex social form, that while "some segmentary societies have officials and even a capital or seat of government, such officials lack the economic base necessary for effective use of power" (Renfrew & Bahn, 2019: 176). In fact, the ancient Israelite tribe, described in the Hebrew Bible as a kinship unit composed of clans composed of households (Stager, 1985) is the original ethnographic tribe, the *ur*-tribe. But as an anthropological and evolutionary concept, the tribe has become a much more problematic term, not only because of its pejorative connotations and colonialist uses but also because its wide application in different places tends to submerge a wide degree of socio-cultural variation, and often relies on the use of ethnographic analogy (Fowles, 2002; Fried, 1975). It seems that one can hardly find a reliable, uncontroversial rung on the evolutionist ladder.

This brings us to the fundamental question: To what extent can culturally, geographically, and temporally unrelated societies be compared to each other and assessed against a set of universalized, culturally non-specific criteria? The social evolutionist program rather depends on a positive response: doing so must be seen as basically legitimate, even though, as we have discussed, its criteria are far from universal or non-specific to any culture, in that they were derived from certain norms, ideals and values that are very much specific to the Western experience, and were initially the experience of the West's colonial domination during the nineteenth century. This is in fact a point on which evolutionism was criticized quite early in the work of Boas (1896, 1920) and his students, who held that societies had to be understood as distinctive, individual systems on their own terms and within their own historical and environmental contingencies, as opposed to grand narratives like social evolution. Though influential for a time, the Boasian school was eventually quashed by the fluorescence of the neo-evolutionist school (Kuper, 2005; Pluciennik, 2005). In the early twenty-first century, post-processual archaeology, under the influence of more recent cultural anthropology, as well as the availability of a much greater amount of data, has returned to a somewhat Boasian position in rejecting evolutionism in favor of particularism (Trigger, 2006: 8–9, 521). This does not mean that advances in understanding brought by processualism, particularly as regards the importance of the environment and adaptation, should be discarded (*pace* Mithen, 1989), but moving from evolutionism back to taking any particular society on its own terms without assumptions of pre-defined rules about what types of societies must behave in what ways is a first step towards considering situations such as social complexity accruing *sans* monumentality that evolutionism struggles to comprehend.

2.5 *Revisiting Social Complexity in Archaeology*

Having established the reasons for a deep methodological suspicion of social evolutionist theory and its stadial types, we can now return to the subject of social complexity more specifically and ask if this concept, used on its own, holds up any better? Is this a more neutral or less ethnocentric way to discuss the nature of a society and how it compares to others? We would argue that social complexity as a concept does hold such potential, but only if used in a certain way that takes this processualist concept and transforms it through post-processual considerations; this necessitates some discussion of its place in theory so far. Though we see no *a priori* reason why social complexity cannot be applied independently from social evolution, as we have already noted the two have been very much intertwined in the history of anthropological and archaeological theory (Chapman, 2007: 13–15; Kuper, 2005; Pluciennik, 2005). The basic term "complex society" has effectively been a metonym for the state, but one that has sometimes been adopted by those who do not hold to the assumption that the developmentally-advanced societies must always be states *per se*. The concept of complexity is, or at least has been, as "ideologically loaded" as social evolution, but a simple-complex continuum does at least have the advantage of being less binary than primitive/civilized or tribe/state dichotomies (Fowles, 2018; Shanks & Tilley, 1987: 163–164). Much would then depend on how one defines social complexity and what, if anything, one assumes to be significant about being complex. Often the definition of social complexity in theory and as correlated in archaeology is left less than precisely defined, probably on the assumption that the term will be implicitly understood. Flannery's definition, however, seems to get at what most understand complexity implicitly to be (Honeychurch, 2014: 281; Chapman, 2007):

> [C]omplexity can be measured in terms of its segregation (the amount of internal differentiation and specialization of subsystems) and centralization (the degree of linkage between the various subsystems and the highest-order controls in society. (Flannery, 1972: 409)

This focus on the number of moving parts, their interconnections and connections to a center of control in Flannery's definition appears more neutral, and on its own avoids any direct dependence on any one particular or culturally-dependent preconception of what complex societies are and what they should look like. But it is important to acknowledge that this definition is informed by Flannery's view of "human society as one class of living system" (1972: 409), a direct application of the processualist view of culture as a natural phenomenon whose characteristics, in this case social complexity, can be scientifically measured and quantified. In spite of his wording of the definition, Flannery was clear in what he understood full social complexity to look like when he posited the state, with its internal specialization, administrative elite and super-kinship organization, as the highest form of complexity (1972: 403–404). As such, this definition can still be applied to produce an evaluation of a society's complexity that assesses how much it is or is not "like us," with ourselves as the benchmark (Alt, 2010; Chapman, 2003). It also takes complexity to be a rather unified and undifferentiated quality that a society has, tying together different characteristics that a society might have such as degrees of social differentiation and hierarchization, characteristics that are better understood as independent variables that can take on different forms and appear in different ways depending on the cultural context being examined (McGuire, 1983). It is not hard to see how societies in which kinship structures and/or mobility play important roles could be denied their complexity, since these characteristics tend to mitigate against the particular kinds of differentiation and centralization found in the rather narrow set of societies that have set the agenda for what is complex (Honeychurch, 2014: 281–282; Smith, 2003: 90–94). Broadly speaking, social complexity has been treated in scholarship as something associated with sedentism and urbanism practically by default, monumentality being a primary material indicator of complexity's presence (Adams, 2001; Chapman, 2003; Cowgill, 2004; Flannery, 1972, 1998; Kradin, 2006, 2013; Renfrew & Bahn, 2019; Ross & Steadman, 2017; Scheidel, 2013; Tainter, 1988; Trigger, 2003; Yoffee, 2005). Unsurprisingly, this repeats the same patterns we have seen with social evolutionism; if societies that are complex are "like us," they must be completely sedentary because we in the modern Western state are so.

More recent theoretical scholarship has been able to "complexify" social complexity, breaking it down into different variables and exposing its myriad ways of manifesting, no less than when it comes to the crucial question of centralization and hierarchy. While a "fundamental equation incorporating complexity with hierarchy, social stratification, centralized power and authority is often taken for granted within archaeological modelling" (Souvatzi, 2007: 37), buttressed by the use of material markers such as monumentality as outward signs of complexity, scholars have offered much more diverse, less dichotomized and more graded dimensions of organization such at heterarchy, corporate and network governance, and more focus on the historical and culturally-embedded contingencies through which sociopolitical relations are negotiated and maintained (Feinman, 2017; Feinman & Carballo, 2019; Honeychurch, 2014). Hierarchy and centralization even within complex societies are now understood as organizational dimension articulated in much more nuanced ways that are influenced by both cultural and environmental context. Building on older work, LaBianca has recently highlighted the continuum between polycentric and unicentric political organization in the history of the Middle/Near East. The degree to which a polity tends towards one or the other is influenced by cultural factors including that nature of social relations or the degree of sedentism versus mobility, and geographical factors that constrain or allow communication (Hartshorne, 1950; LaBianca, 2009, 2021; Meir, 1988). Centralization can thus be understood as a dynamic, and negotiated variable within complex societies, rather than as something that is simply present to this or that degree. Hierarchy meanwhile, while a characteristic certainly found often in complex society, should not be assumed to be coterminous with complexity (Souvatzi, 2007).

Looking at some real-world cases only emphasizes on a practical level what was becoming increasingly clear to many on a theoretical level: (a) there is "an increasingly poor fit between the 'facts' as we know them and traditional evolutionary constructs" (Possehl, 1998: 279; see also Graeber & Wengrow 2021). The social evolutionary model and its constitutive ideas of discrete social types cannot fully comprehend the dynamic, multivariate, contextually-dependent forms that societies can take, especially complex societies, and; (b) the complexity of such societies needs to be understood as a function of each particular cultural context rather than of a limiting, transcultural definition that is actually derived from the modern Western experience. Complicating this further is the factor of what complexity a society had as opposed to what degree it is manifested in the archaeological record, and then the degree to which that manifestation is actually preserved (Chapman, 2007: 18–19). The expanding ethnographic record, the ultimate basis of evolutionist models, has itself produced examples that contradict the neat predictions of evolutionist types. Chapman points to the case of the Iroquoian Native Americans, who maintained an egalitarian social structure yet also had hereditary chiefs, a contradiction in terms from the evolutionist viewpoint, as well as to work in the Pacific since the formulation of Sahlins and Service's "Oceanic hegemony" (McIntosh, 1999: 4), which has broken down a sharp trait-based distinction between chiefdom and tribal societies in Melanesia and Polynesia (Chapman, 2003: 42).

World archaeology has arguably dealt even more serious blows, even with cases of settled societies. While forms of evolutionism have long been dominant in the archaeology of the Bronze Age Minoans and Myceneans, Hamilakis (2002) has described how the ongoing accumulation of data has confounded a simple progression from simple to complex socio-political organization with its apogee in the formation of palatial institutions, and has failed to show an association between complexity and archaeological indications of social heterogeneity. It has also become more evident that the history of change at different places around the Mycenean and Minoan world were local and would have involved local historical contingencies. While palatial Mycenaean and Minoan societies are widely accepted as complex and their rulers are attested in written texts, monumental inscriptions and artistic depictions relating to rulers are absent and seemingly not part of the communicative program of ruling individuals or dynasties—a stark material contrast to what was found in the contemporary Near East (Blakolmer, 2019). This somewhat recalls the situation in the Mature phase of the Indus Valley or "Harappan" civilization, where there is a complete absence of representations of any ruler, and while there are texts, they are short and undeciphered. Otherwise, the Indus Valley civilization shows several traditional archaeological signs of social complexity including urbanism, technological development, trade (including contemporary third millennium BCE Mesopotamia) and some monumentality, yet no structures that can be identified as temples and palaces, and no material culture or urban-planning patterns that clearly indicate a distinction between elite and non-elite segments of the population. It should be pointed out that pastoralism was clearly part of the economic base and pastoralist camp sites are known archaeologically, and while Possehl for one has considered the possibility that some were engaged in pastoral nomadism, he acknowledges that this relies on the more recent ethnohistoric record of India and Pakistan and the dangers involved with ethnographic analogy. In any event, the Indus Valley is a good example of an idiosyncratic form of social complexity, to whatever extent a segment of the population was non-sedentary (Possehl, 1979, 1998, 1999, 2002; Shaffer, 1982; Swayam, 2006).

The emergence of the Mesoamerican Olmec culture provides an example of a settled society whose accepted social complexity is not associated with the adoption of agriculture, which only later succeeded in developing a mixed subsistence base directed at wild resources (Killion, 2013). O'shea (1980) argues that even at their height the Omec were not complex and populous enough to be considered a state in the evolutionist sense, despite that fact that they practiced regional trade and had the organizational capacity to mobilize the labor needed for elaborate ceremonial centers and monumental construction. Kristiansen (2007) points to southern Scandinavia during the Bronze Age as an example of what he terms "decentralized complexity," in which all "the traditional diagnostic features of ranking and complexity" appear but without urbanism, monumentality and overt materializations of centralized authority. Instead, built features in the landscape appear to have substituted for such materialization. He also notes the social complexity of Bronze Age society has been downplayed even though its archaeological record is fundamentally similar to that of the Viking period, whose social complexity is directly recorded in texts, concluding that "we have generally been too unwilling to admit ranking and complex social organization to societies without written records, by downplaying indications of social and institutional complexity" (Kristiansen, 2007: 66–68). It is also interesting to note that in the Near East the use of seals that marked clay sealings, a core administrative practice in the Bronze and Iron Ages, is already attested as far back as the Neolithic period (Freikman et al., 2021), another concrete indication that sociopolitical practices associated with complexity are not tightly bound to only certain types or levels of complex society.

The cases that provide both the starkest contradiction to the dictates of evolution and the clearest evidence for unbounded variation in which social complexity can appear are societies where mobility played an important role. An example is the simple case of the Mughal emperor's use of both a fixed, monumental capital and mobile tent capital that carried his entire court and its functions, including the royal mint, as he traveled around the country (Sinopoli, 1994). At the other end of the continuum, the complexity of properly nomadic polities has sometimes been denied even when they exercised significant power *vis a vis* settled neighbors. Barfield (2001) has argued that historically nomads only formed "shadow empires" that copied their sedentary neighbors, upon whom they relied, parasitically, for resources, without duplicating the latter's internal complexity. Drompp (2005), however, has shown this to be inaccurate through the case of early nomadic Turkic empires that interacted with China, pointing out that the former not only flourished when they were able to extract from the latter, and that the Turkic empires did in fact have their own important internal dynamics, as well as trade contacts that went well beyond just China. The Turkic nomadic empire of the later half of the first millennium CE stands amidst a long tradition of such empires in Central and East Asia, going back to the Xiongnu of the late first millennium BCE, their successors the Huns who established a short-lived empire in Europe in the late fourth–fifth centuries CE, and culminating with the rapid expansion of Mongols, first under Genghis Khan, in the thirteenth–fourteenth centuries CE. The complexity of these empires is undeniable; they were certainly not an unsophisticated rabble that swamped settled civilization before disintegrating. The Mongols in particular adapted administrative practices from conquered peoples as needed but kept their own tribal socio-political structure which Genghis Khan subtly manipulated to his own ends. Along the way he and his successors directly and indirectly stimulated trade, technology and craft production throughout their vast, multicultural realm. Asian nomadic empires were able to maintain, if only for a time, political cohesion and economic connections over a scale that is simply not comprehensible within the limited view of evolutionary types. They did at times make use of architecture, often for apparently defensive purposes, but their complexity was never associated with or dependent upon a conversion to widespread settlement and urbanism. Otherwise, the archaeological record of these empires is at best partial, and without historical sources, Thucydides' dictum applies: what is visible does not necessarily equate with what is present

(Biran, 2015; Fitzhugh et al., 2009; Frachetti, 2012; Honeychurch, 2013; Kim, 2016; Kradin et al., 2016).

Though not discussed in terms of nomadism in the same manner as one finds in scholarship concerning the Old World, the social complexity of societies with a tribal structure and movement along a mobile-settled continuum also appears as a theme in the archaeology of Native Americans, particularly for the Southwest and Great Plains (Brooks, 2016; Herr & Clark, 2002). Between the mid-eighteenth and mid-nineteenth centuries CE the region was dominated by a decentralized but powerful empire of the Comanche people, which remained a serious, even feared obstacle to both American and Spanish-Mexican expansion. The power of the Comanches was based on their nomadic horsemanship abilities, and they used it to extract tribute from both fellow Native American and colonial European communities. Politically, the Comanches did not have a single supreme ruler but rather made decisions in periodic assemblies of chiefs. Most of the time, however, affairs were handled at much more local levels, with the different segments of Comanche society living quite independently of each other. Despite the wealth they accrued, much of it from the European communities they dominated, this decentralized empire never felt the need to express itself in those ways thought typical of complex polities and especially empires, such as monumental art and architecture (Hämäläinen, 2008, 2013).

The eastern Mediterranean sphere provides some of the best historical examples of complex societies in which mobility was important. In North Africa, while sedentary and highly monumental Pharaonic Egypt is widely considered a classic case of what an ancient complex polity looks like, the region also played host to complex polities in which mobility was important. Egypt's problematic southern neighbor Kush incorporated both settled urban and mobile pastoralist populations (Emberling, 2014). Evidence for writing in early Kushite sites including the capital Kerma is absent, yet inscriptions in other places indicate that writing was used at the royal level, through co-opting Egyptian writing and Egyptian scribes (Cooper, 2018). In the Late Antique and Early Islamic periods, a pastoral-nomadic kingdom of the Blemmyean people dominated the Eastern Desert and southern reaches of the Nile. In common with other mobile polities, the Blemmyean kingdom had a confederated tribal structure with positions of authority taken by members of the ruling dynasty, as opposed to a more rationalized bureaucratic elite (Cooper, 2020). Importantly, this kingdom is known primarily through inscriptional evidence rather than any direct indication from archaeology. This provides a useful corollary to Kristiansen's warning against downplaying the complexity of societies that cannot speak for themselves due to an absence of written records (2007: 66–68), as written records can also demonstrate social complexity that would not otherwise be evident on purely archaeological grounds.

In the Near East, the most notable case is the Middle Bronze Age kingdom of Mari in the region of the Euphrates and Ḫabur Rivers, which again is known primarily through its extensive textual record. The scholarship on Mari is extensive, but for our purposes it is sufficient to summarize the relevant characteristics of the kingdom. Though centered at the urban site of Mari itself, this extensive kingdom integrated both settled and mobile groups, to the point that a strict separation between the two does not seem to have characterized the kingdom's internal social relations or political structure. In addition to vassals and landed communities on the banks of the Euphrates, King Zimri-Lim of Mari ruled over two tribal confederations, the Yaminites and Simalites. Both included towns as well as mobile groups referred to in the Akkadian language by the rather complicated term ḫana, which may mean "those who dwell in tents." Zimri-Lim was himself a member of the Simalites and these tribal confederations exercised significant influence within the kingdom's internal affairs, as well as providing the basis of the king's military forces (Charpin & Durand, 1986; Fleming, 2004, 2009; Miglio, 2014). Exactly how their mobile components should be understood, as proper nomads or as pastoralists associated with settled communities, is debatable (Arbuckle & Hammer, 2019; Rosen & Lehmann, 2010), and complicated by the apparent use in the texts from Mari of terms that can be translated as "town" or "city" but which refer in some cases to tent encampments (Kupper, 1957: 13–14; van Driel, 2001: 109). Either way, the centrality of both tribal structures even in the case of the king's affiliation and the influence wielded by mobile populations within the kingdom of Mari cast doubt on tribe/state or settled/mobile dichotomies as operational within social complexity in the ancient near Eastern world. The idea of kings themselves dwelling in tents was certainly not foreign to this world; the Assyrian kings list begins with "kings who dwelt in tents" (Glassner, 2004). Alizadeh (2010) has argued that "mobile highland pastoralists" in Iran dominated lowland sedentary communities and formed the Elamite kingdom, a major player in political-military history of Mesopotamia, during the third millennium BCE. Arbuckle and Hammer (2019) have criticized Alizadeh for his uncritical reliance on the ethnographic record, in this case his analogy with socially-complex, independent Irian tribes who have occupied the same environment in the modern day, and we agree with them on this methodological point. But still, setting aside ethnographic support does not itself disprove Alizadeh's reconstruction. Arbuckle and Hammer cite Potts' (2014) criticism that Alizadeh has too little concrete evidence for the existence and importance of nomads in the creation of the Elamite kingdom, as compared to what is known of its settled communities. However, Potts' volume on the history of nomadism in Iran has itself been criticized for adopting a positivist and trait-list approach to nomadism that ignores the possibility of their importance at any time when they are not directly attested textually (Alden, 2015).

In the later history of the ancient Near East, mobility is no less coincident with complexity. In the late second and first millennia BCE Assyrian kings fought constantly against Aramean tribal polities in Syria-Mesopotamia, and from Assyrian texts it is evident that these tribes could be settled, mobile or both at the same time. This seems to have been the case even as late as the eighth century BCE when Assyrian kings were dealing with longstanding Aramean kingdoms to the west (Younger, 2016). We would also point to the later case of the Nabateans, the famed masters of the Arabian trade in the Hellenistic-Roman periods. Historical references clearly indicate that the Nabateans had already formed into a kingdom which was a potent military and geopolitical influence already in the fourth–third centuries BCE, some time before any archaeological evidence of their sedentarization in the first century BCE (Pearson, 2011). *Contra* Graf (2007, 2013), there is no need to search for an early Nabatean sedentarization process to account for this, and we note that his invocation of early Hellenistic finds at the Nabatean capital Petra are associated with scant architectural remains. Some use of stone architecture there certainly does not provide much base for the assumption that the Nabateans were not largely nomadic in this period.

Finally, while we have dealt here with societies that in evolutionary terms would be typed as tribes, chiefdoms or states, "hunter-gatherer" societies are now labeled complex. The term hunter-gatherer "implies nothing but that—a mode of subsistence" and "does not carry the unified conceptual weight it once did, and we have to ask ourselves why and how the concept of complex hunter-gatherers truly differs from pastoral tribes or agricultural chiefdoms" (Sassaman, 2004: 230). When considered together with many of the particular cases reviewed above, it is no longer tenable to tether a society's (lack of) potential for social complexity to its mode of subsistence.

Where does this leave us in terms of defining social complexity and applying this concept archaeologically? It is clear that there is not simply one social complexity; rather the ways that it can play out are truly myriad and with many internal variations and combinations of elements in any particular case. This holds even if one only considers those societies whose complexity is taken for granted, only increasing when one adds those societies in which mobility is important and material indicators like monumentality are not clearly central to the maintenance of political structure. Moreover, we contend, following the emphasis of post-processual and even Boasian thinking in this vein, that complexity has to be understood as something that is embedded within the native cultural complex of any particular society. It is not only that hierarchy or centralization can appear to different degrees and with different arrangements in any particular society, but that those degrees and arrangements are directly informed by cultural values and metaphors that structure and operationalize social, political and economic relationships. These relationships are themselves articulated and constrained within practical confines such as technology and social or physical geography. This is not to say that we advocate a theoretically anarchic approach in which there is no room to discuss what complexity might be cross-culturally or to compare, and more precisely to contrast, the complexity of different societies. Flannery's (1972) emphasis on the number of moving parts and their interconnections remain at the core of complexity, nor can complexity at a local level be understood without examining the manner and degree of centralization. We would only insist that these are starting points, and that the focus ought to be not so much on *whether or not* and *how much* they appear in any particular society, and how this compares to some Eurocentric ideal, but rather on *how* they appear, and how their appearance is embedded in and thus directly influenced by that society's social context *as well as* its environment. Instead of just thinking of wealth and power in terms of material goods, including (but not limited to) monuments, what about wealth in people? Diversity in the nature of complex political structures will also affect their recognition; how well equipped is our "conceptual toolkit" for recognizing rule by more horizontal structures like councils and assemblies (McIntosh, 1999)? We can only echo and endorse Nelson's argument to turn from asking "how complex were they?" to asking "how were they complex?" (1995: 599; Alt, 2010).

2.6 Ethnography and Comparison: Filling in the Gaps?

Before moving on from the above discussion, it is necessary to address the use of ethnography in the study of complex societies, given that it has been crucial to the construction of evolutionist stadial types and preconceptions of what is or is not a marker of social complexity (Trigger, 2006: 166). In addition to the ethnographic record of descriptions (scholarly or otherwise) of societies and cultures made within the modern world, we can also define a comparative record of historical societies and cultures falling within the same geographical region and approximate timeframe, which like the ethnographic record are often mined for evidence to aid in scholarly historical reconstructions and evaluations. For our case study, the United Monarchy of ancient Israel during the tenth century BCE, the relevant comparative record comes from the wider ancient Near East during approximately the third to first millennia BCE, but for some purposes is extended to southern Europe and North Africa. The justification behind this derives from the long-term and intensive cultural continuity among and interaction between ancient Near Eastern (and other Mediterranean) societies attested in both text and artifact, with the widespread Semitic language family as a major factor in this, as well as the shared geography and environment of the wider region.

In short, we contend that reliance on the ethnographic record, allowing it to dictate the way we reconstruct what historical societies did or did not do, or what they were or were not like, is a highly suspect practice. The "tyranny of the ethnographic record" imposes limitations on what is considered possible and has the potential to blind us to possibilities that lie outside the range of documentation, however wide, of ethnography (Belfer-Cohen & Goring-Morris, 2009; Wobst, 1978). There are a few reasons for this. First, it would be foolhardy to assume that the ethnographic record covers the complete breadth of human social experience and cultural practice, so we must assume that some, especially those in the past, lie outside of it. Second, we cannot ignore either the restricted and recent timeframe in which the ethnographic record has been put together, starting no further back than the nineteenth century, or the impact of European contact especially on so-called "primitive" societies. Thus, reliance on the ethnographic record means falling into a presentist fallacy that assumes the past looked something like the present. Eurocentrism can be considered an example of what we would call "bad ethnography," even if it is not usually thought of as such (Bernbeck, 2008: 49; Dunnell, 1980; Kohl, 2007: 11–12; Wobst, 1978; Yoffee, 2005: 188).

Third, for those working in the Middle East, Asia and Africa, that is a very large percentage of scholars, the specter of Orientalism (Said, 2003; see also the essay by Greenberg in this volume) hangs over any use of the ethnographic record, as much as in the very way the record was formulated in the first place as is in the way it is applied. This is especially the case for nomads and pastoralists. Coming from a world of practically full settlement, extensive urbanization and the marginalization of mobile groups (such as the Romani), European visitors to these continents, including those travelling to the "Holy Land" and its neighboring regions viewed the mobile lifestyle of groups they encountered there as exotic yet savage and primitive. One mid-nineteenth century traveler, expecting to see his romantic image of Near Eastern nomads fulfilled, instead "never saw among the wanderers of the desert any traits of character or any habits of life which did not make me prize and value more the privileges of civilization" (reproduced in van der Steen, 2013: 29). Commenting on some Turkic tribes encountered in the Ottoman realm, an earlier traveler observed:

> It would be difficult to subdue these tribes, as they are expert horsemen, and move from place to place with great celerity; and being moreover devoted to a roving life of freedom it would be found equally impracticable to give them a taste for settled habits. To induce them to become an industrious part of the community, to settle in villages and till the ground, would require a more efficient, more liberal, and a better regulated government than that of the Grand Seignior, whose authority in this part of his dominions is already tottering to its fall. (Kinneir, 1818: 77)

The Eurocentric biases here are hard to miss. Such views filtered down into older scholarship on the Near East. In their extensive socio-political history of the ancient Near East first published in 1923, Moret and Davey treat nomadic tribes as backward barbarian hordes who threatened emerging settled civilizations, "political, military, industrial, and agricultural organization in the midst of peoples who are still for the most part in a state of nomadism without a true civilization" (Moret & Davy, 1926: 169). Nomads were but "backward starvelings who knew not yet the labor of civilization, but wished to taste its fruits cheaply by plundering the fields and towns of the valley" (ibid.: 146). Orientalism fed into, if not downright instigated, the scholarly dichotomy between sedentism and nomadism and the sociological biases that go with it (Bernbeck, 2008). It is also not hard to see how Western observers and then Western scholars of the Near East would come to view tribalism and nomadism as the antithesis of social complexity, given that tribes throughout the Ottoman Empire went out of their way to resist the hegemony of the Sultan's administration, which often struggled to gain a foothold and impose control on them. In a few cases, however, some tribal leaders were able to put together complex confederations that practically acted as polities within a polity (van der Steen, 2009, 2013).

Although travelers encountered nomadic groups of different ethnicities, the one ethnographic image that truly took hold of the Western imagination through the writings of figures such as T. E. Lawrence (1935) was that of the Arab Bedouin, who ranged across the Ottoman Near East (including Egypt), who in their autonomous, desert-dwelling lifestyle were viewed both romantically and disparagingly as the antithesis of civilization. The romantic but dubious notion that the Bedouin illuminated the nature of society and culture of the Holy Land in the biblical era was prominent (Assi, 2018; van der Steen, 2013). The term "Bedouin" is frequently applied in a casual and uncritical manner to ancient nomadic and pastoral societies in the Near East, including in otherwise excellent scholarship on the kingdom of Mari discussed above (e.g., Durand, 1998; Rede, 2015). Even if used casually rather than with the intent of directly characterizing ancient nomads according to the nature of their modern counterparts, "Bedouin" is still a perilous and problematic term to use as such because it implicitly limits what possibilities are allowed, especially concerning social complexity and the relationship between mobility and sedentism (Ben-Yosef, 2019; Luke, 1965: 21–23). In writing about "Bedouin States," Knauf (1992) correctly rejects the ethnographic use of the term and its implications for nomads of the early period yet is quite content to apply it in the first millennium BCE, and so confederations of his "Bedouin" tribes in the this period could not achieve the same complexity as sedentary societies: "Bedouin states did not, however, acquire all the attributes of real states; at best they were ephemeral, unstable, and short-lived organizations, [so] a society ultimately has to cease being 'bedouin' in order for it to become fully a 'state.'"

What we have defined above as the comparative record that can be used for studying specific pre-modern societies provides safer ground, given that it is closer to the cultural, chronological and geographic context of the society in question, and for the ancient world especially if it was unaffected by modern interference. However, it should not be assumed that even the comparative record exhausts all possibilities, largely because it is often dependent on (discovered and published) textual sources, Mari being a good case in point. Where archaeological evidence is available, it must be remembered that "[a]rchaeology is, by and large, not the past tense of ethnography" (Pluciennik, 2005: 98); it does not speak directly to behavior in the same way as ethnographic descriptions or ancient texts. Mobile populations, for one, that left ephemeral remains and no textual sources will go unrepresented. The benefit of both the comparative and ethnographic records is that when considered in breadth, they can demonstrate the full variability in social, political, economic and cultural dimensions of life and their ideal and material manifestations, providing a warning against placing societies into artificial boxes or assessing them according to predictive presumptions about what this or that kind of society was or was not like or did or did not do. The enchainment of complexity to monumentality is exactly this. That is why we have cited many cases from world history and archaeology above, to demonstrate this variability and how it indicates the real and unavoidable possibility of complexity without monumentality, which is only reinforced when it is accepted that there may yet be more variations that reside outside what is recorded. Hence, while we agree with Arbuckle and Hammer's (2019) suspicion of the use of ethnography to dictate methodologies for reconstructing pastoral nomadism in the Near East before the first millennium BCE, this leads them to narrow the possibilities they are willing to consider, leaving insufficient room for exceptional cases.

3 Case Study: The United Monarchy in Ancient Israel

3.1 The Standard Methodology of Biblical Archaeology

The term "United Monarchy" is modern scholarly shorthand for the Israelite kingdom of David and his son Solomon, and its formation, history and dissolution (into the separate kingdoms of Israel and Judah) which is narrated primarily in the biblical books of 1–2 Samuel and 1 Kings (Fig. 1). The biblical text describes this kingdom as incorporating Israelite tribes who dwelt (settled or mobile) in the Galilee, in the Israelite heartland in the Central Hill Country, and down to what is now known as the northern Negev, eventually incorporating some regions such as the Jezreel

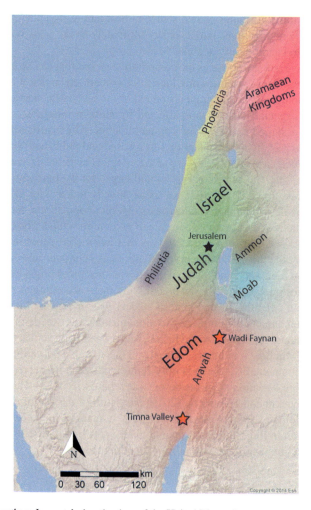

Fig. 1 The Southern Levant during the time of the United Monarchy

Valley that had been at the center of the network of Canaanite polities during the Late Bronze Age (sixteenth-early twelfth centuries BCE). The biblical text also records David as forcibly establishing a degree of domination over some of Israel's neighbors while establishing friendly diplomatic relations with others, a situation which persisted into Solomon's reign. While the exact length and start or end dates of David's and Solomon's reigns cannot be established with certainty, it is agreed that they occurred in the tenth century BCE, with David's reign perhaps beginning in the very late eleventh century. The United Monarchy is a famously, much-debated subject in biblical studies and biblical archaeology (the archaeology of the southern Levant as it relates to the Hebrew Bible), and while a prominent topic in these disciplines, much of this debate involves subjects and problems that are extensively discussed in the disciplines at large, including the dating of the composition and redactions of biblical texts and the relationship between the archaeological record and the history of the Israelites narrated in these texts. The use of the archaeological record to assess the historical veracity of individual parts of the biblical narrative is a core practice within the current methodology of these disciplines. As far as the United Monarchy goes, the debate has revolved around which chronological period of the archaeological record of the early Iron Age coincides with the reigns of David and Solomon; based largely on different assessments of a large body of ^{14}C dates from throughout Israel, some scholars locate the tenth century in the earlier part of the Iron Age IIA period, while others locate it in the later part of the preceding Iron Age IB period (Levy & Higham, 2005).

Scholars of the former persuasion tend to view the archaeology as supporting the basic historicity of the biblical narrative (e.g. Mazar, 2007), while those of the latter persuasion see it as undermined by the archaeology (Finkelstein, 2007), and argue that the biblical description of the United Monarchy is an invention of scribes working hundreds of years later on behalf of the Davidic dynasty as it continued to rule the small kingdom of Judah centered on the highlands around Jerusalem (Finkelstein & Silberman, 2001, 2006). The reasons behind this are evident in publications from the two different perspectives that present their contrasting historical assessments: the accepted archaeological indicators of complexity and state-formation, including monumentality, only appear in the Iron Age IIA and are absent in the Iron Age I. So, while there are differing assessments of the archaeological chronology, there is a basic, shared methodology that assumes that if the United Monarchy was a historical kingdom, it should have certain correlates in the archaeological record of the tenth century. This methodology is underpinned on the one hand by a positivistic bias towards settled communities and architecture as the visible agents of social complexity and political structure, and on the other by an etic, ethnocentric and vaguely-theorized idea of what kind of polity the United Monarchy would have been (Ben-Yosef, 2019; Thomas, 2018).

The synopsis above summarizes the methodological-theoretical landscape of the archaeology of Israel and biblical studies. In this case study we describe a reconstruction of the United Monarchy as a kingdom with a polymorphous settled-nomadic society and a complexity that did not hinge on monumentality. From our discussion in the first half of this paper it is evident that this would hardly make the

United Monarchy a novel or alien political formation within world history and world archaeology, but to understand why it appears so radical within research that focuses on ancient Israel it is necessary to discuss the methodological-theoretical landscape more fully. An irony of archaeology in Israel is that while it is at the forefront of archaeological fieldwork, publication and applications of the archaeological sciences in particular, it is far from the forefront of archaeological theory. Outside of very specific subjects such as the archaeology of ethnicity and ethnogenesis (e.g. Faust, 2006, 2010), sustained engagement with theory is minimal and typically left unexplicated, but when perspectives can be discerned they are often a mix of culture history, processualism and to a lesser extent post-processualism (Bunimovitz, 2007). This theoretical vagueness permeates much of the historical and archaeological scholarship on the United Monarchy; the most that can be said is that a nebulous neo-evolutionism coupled to a positivist, processualist focus on the materialization of complexity guides the analytical methodology, by which scholars conclude that the archaeology either supports the presence of a state or only some less-evolved entity like a chiefdom. Though one can find some older neo-evolutionary scholarship cited, more recent literature and critiques from post-processualism especially are effectively absent (Kletter, 2004; Thomas, 2018).

It is important to emphasize that this cuts across otherwise quite differing schools of thought in biblical archaeology and biblical historiography and different perspectives on the United Monarchy or tenth century BCE. Mazar (2007: 145) for instance posits that "reading the Hebrew Bible, one would expect archaeology to prove the existence of the strong, mature State of David and Solomon with a large city in Jerusalem, dense urban settlement throughout the country, and formal inscriptions and art," while Garfinkel directly tethers the material realization of state formation to the emergence of urbanism as marked by fortifications and consistent patterns of city planning during the Iron Age and the Iron Age IIA in particular (Garfinkel, 2017; Garfinkel et al., 2012, 2016, 2019). Garfinkel even views the archaeology of the tenth century BCE as backing up the biblical description of the United Monarchy's emergence under David because "the biblical text…describes state formation processes" in ancient Israel (Garfinkel, 2017: 127). His statement that if there was no urbanism until after David and Solomon's reigns then they "were not rulers of a kingdom but merely local tribal leaders" (Garfinkel et al., 2016: 32) reveals the binary in which he works. Finkelstein's views on state formation in ancient Israel are similarly pre-occupied with the presence or absence of monumentality, urbanism and changes in the settled world as supposedly requisite indicators of Israel's achievement of complexity (Finkelstein, 1999, 2005, 2007). Dever's (2017) more recent scholarship on the United Monarchy diverges somewhat, in that he accepts that the neo-evolutionism and ethnocentrism applied (if inarticulately) by others such as Finkelstein is no longer valid, and in his archaeological understanding of the United Monarchy he makes explicit his use of general systems theory, a processual, biologistic theory drawing much from the work of Binford and Flannery that envisions discrete socio-political entities as systems made up of interlocking sub-systems that function according to a set of rules that operate and maintain the larger system (Trigger, 2006: 419–422). As such, Dever ends up drawing upon many of the same archaeological traits according to the same preconceptions as Finkelstein and others, including a degree of urbanization, population size, a ranked settlement pattern and monumental and/or as part of an approach using a trait-list of archaeological correlates to identify the presence of a dichotomized elite-commoner social stratification with the centralization of authority, a state, in tenth century BCE Israel.

As David and Solomon's capital and the location of both the royal residence and temple of Israel's patron deity, the nature of Jerusalem during the tenth century BCE is a major focus. In keeping with the broader methodology, scholars of differing opinions still work from the premise that if it truly existed, the biblical United Monarchy, being a state by default, must have had a capital of a certain size, architecturally-visible population and monumentality (Finkelstein, 2007, 2010; Mazar, 2007, 2010; Ussishkin, 2003). Thus, Dever's (2017: 281) defense of tenth century Jerusalem as the capital of a state stands upon a maximizing estimation of the settlement's size and population and the population of its hinterland as based on surveys. In contrast, it is notable that Finkelstein's conclusion that Jerusalem was but the small stronghold of a local chief goes hand in hand with its rule over "sparsely settled territory with a few sedentary villages and a large pastoral population" (Finkelstein, 2003: 79, and see below). Monumentality typically is singled out as a marker of complexity and the imposition of authority by the ruling elite in Jerusalem over the domain that they controlled from there, being "part of a material language used by elite groups in their effort to consolidate social order and group identity" (Gadot & Uziel, 2017: 138). In a discussion that understands the political dynamics of the Iron Age I–IIA periods and the eleventh-tenth centuries BCE purely through developments related to settled communities, Sergi (2017, 2020) accepts the possibility of a polity centered on Jerusalem during the tenth century (though not in the form of the biblical United Monarchy), but only sees this as evident based on the existence of monumentality in Jerusalem at the time that he assumes imposed political hegemony over settled communities in the vicinity. And yet, Sergi (2020: 78–82) correctly identifies kinship as structuring socio-political relationships in the early monarchic period in Israel, which as we discuss below is the native conceptualization of such relationships through the active metaphor of the patriarchal household, and more demonstrable than monumentality in this role. Sergi's coupling of what is essentially a post-processual perspective to a processual materialist assumption about the nature and manifestation of political power in ancient Israel is thus quite an awkward, even incompatible one.

This methodology is not only found in scholarship relating to Israel itself during the tenth century BCE but also its neighbors, most notably the Philistines on the southern Levantine coastal plain. Maeir (2017a, b, 2020a, b; Maeir et al., 2013) has argued consistently that during the Iron Age I–IIA the Philistine polity of Gath was the dominant player among the other Philistine polities and that it was also in a dominant position over the nascent, highlands-based Israelite monarchy, whose power and ability to expand was thus curtailed. His basis for this argument is in the sheer size of the fortified city of Gath itself (modern Tell-es/Safi) during the Iron Age I–IIA, being the largest city in the southern Levant at this time, as well the important economic role of its regional trade connections, which contrasts sharply with any Israelite settlement. As the scholarship discussed above, Maeir's methodology is not situated within a well-drawn and current theoretical discussion but rather seems to be based on some very general, uncontextualized assumptions, derived from a vaguely processualist position about the nature of socio-political power and its necessary association with a certain materialization. Exactly what the mechanics were by which Gath's sheer size and connections endowed it with superior political power, or how these overcame mitigating factors such as geography or historical contingency, are not adumbrated. Similarly, Finkelstein and Lipschits's (2011) model for the initial emergence of a polity in Moab, one of Israel's Transjordanian neighbors, works from the premise that such a complex political entity can only have existed when it can be identified with settlements, as they do for a group of fortified settlements of the late Iron Age I sites (eleventh to late tenth centuries BCE by their chronology) on the Transjordanian plateau, on the implicit assumption that a complex polity must have a normative sedentary agricultural basis. Likewise, they dismiss the possibility of any earlier polity that is not visible archaeologically, such as one based on a nomadic population (Finkelstein & Lipschits, 2011: 147). Moreover, their reconstruction leaves an awkward gap between this hypothetical Moabite polity that came to an end with the termination of the aforementioned Iron Age I sites in the late tenth century and actual inscriptional evidence for the existence of a kingdom of Moab in the late Iron Age IIA, the late ninth century BCE, evidence which they acknowledge (Finkelstein & Lipschits, 2011: 149) without adequately explaining the gap. The kingdom of Moab whose existence during the ninth century is in fact known primarily through chance-find inscriptions, primarily the extensive (but incomplete) stela text of king Mesha found near his capital Dibon (Routledge, 2000; Smelik, 2003), while evidence for Moabite settlements in the late Iron Age IIA is hardly substantial enough to indicate the existence of a complex polity if settlement—and its monumentality—is the only factor in view (Dearman, 1989; Herr, 2012; Steiner, 2014).

We should also recognize the profound impact that archaeological debate over the United Monarchy and the Iron Age I–IIA has had on biblical studies and historiography on ancient Israel, an impact that is rooted in the tendency of many biblical scholars to allow archaeological scholarship, particularly that which is framed as "scientific" or "objective," to dictate the course of "critical" scholarship regarding the date, composition and historical veracity of the Hebrew Bible. The position represented by Finkelstein and others that the archaeology flatly contradicts the historicity of the biblical description of the United Monarchy, which must in turn be a later ideological invention, has been particularly influential in European and segments of Israeli biblical scholarship, to the point that it is accepted uncritically as gospel by many biblical scholars and limits their historical interpretations. A recent edited volume on the early monarchic period in Israel (Krause et al., 2020) provides good examples of this, though one does find there some tentative exceptions to this very critical position. The mentality at work here is that archaeology serves as the "High Court" for the history of Israel, in which the historical veracity of the biblical texts is judged on the basis of the archaeological record as an unimpeachable source for "what really was" in the past, so to speak (Pioske, 2019). Na'aman (2010) has challenged the uncritical acceptance that archaeology should have the status of a "High Court" even when hewing to the settled and visible, but when we consider the archaeologically-invisible, a substantial nomadic component of the population, as a central rather than marginal factor to the historical reality of ancient Israel, assigning archaeology such a vaunted status is methodologically unacceptable.

It should be noted that the existing differences in the methodologies of some of the scholars cited above, such as Garfinkel defining "urban" by the presence of fortifications (Garfinkel et al., 2016: 202) versus Dever (2017: 296) rejecting the necessity of fortifications for this definition, are negligible in the frame of the discussion at hand, for either way these methodologies are all beholden to sedentarocentrism (Bernbeck, 2008) and the conceptual tyranny of the monumental (McIntosh, 1999). Both of these can be seen as components in the "architectural bias" (Ben-Yosef, 2019) found throughout biblical archaeology, in which social complexity is understood as imbued in permanent, usually stone-built architecture (whether putatively monumental or prosaic) to the point that architecture is actually critical to social complexity. The corollary is that social complexity cannot exist where architecture is not archaeologically visible, so that which is archaeologically invisible, such as nomadic groups, is outside the bounds of complexity and therefore outside of the interest of archaeological research (in addition to the actual remains of walls, "architecture" is used here as shorthand for the archaeological richness of the sedentary, Ben-Yosef, 2019, 2020). The architectural bias is itself tied directly to the ingrained methodological positivism and a vaguely-defined, processual neo-evolutionism in biblical archaeology, in which social complexity and stages like the state can be identified in a supposedly scientific manner, through the presence of specified and objective archaeological correlates. Aside from the problem of how valid such an approach is considering the considerable amount of critique it has received, as discussed above, we do not see here any real engagement with either of two absolutely critical questions that we ourselves will consider below. First, were there any non-sedentary and therefore archaeologically-invisible components of the population of Israel during the tenth century? Second, what was the native model of the biblical kingdom, its structuration of authority relationships and the emic concepts and metaphors that informed them, and do notions like the state or monumentality have any relevance within this model?

3.2 Nomadism: Marginal or Central to Ancient Israelite Society?

What is striking about the architectural bias in biblical archaeology is not only how it limits the development of social complexity to sedentary life visible in the remains of settlements and their architecture, but also how scholars hold to this even when many accept that Israel and some of its neighboring people-groups had a nomadic background, and are aware of the long history of nomads within the social history of the Levant. In keeping with the basic evolutionary dichotomy between mobile/pastoral-nomadic/simple and settled/agricultural/complex, they only envision the formation of a socially complex polity in Israel, whether or not it is the biblical United Monarchy, with the sedentarization of an earlier nomadic population (Ben-Yosef, n.d.). The classic presentation of this appears in the edited volume, *From Nomadism to Monarchy*, in its very title no less than the papers therein (Finkelstein & Na'aman, 1994). While we contend that it would always be impossible to rule out the presence of a nomadic component to the population of Israel during the time of the United Monarchy, we present two positive reasons that it is not only possible but in fact quite probable that Israel had a significant nomadic component even during the tenth century: first, Israel's historical background in nomadism, and second, newer archaeological evidence for an unusually visible nomadic population at this time in Israel's neighbor Edom.

It is broadly accepted that the Hebrew Bible presents Israel as having a nomadic background primarily (but not exclusively) in the period leading up to its entrance into the land of Canaan and then the eventual establishment of monarchic rule. One need only think of wandering patriarch Abraham and his family, or the Israelite's steady migration through the Sinai and Transjordan into Canaan following the Exodus from Egypt. While the historicity *grosso modo* of these narratives is now seen as highly questionable at best by most scholars, still a nomadic background for Israel has remained a prominent view, even for those such as Sparks (2009) who stick to an evolutionist viewpoint in which nomads want to become sedentary. We can put this down to two initial factors: first, it is hard to understand why the biblical authors would claim that Israel was not autochthonous to the land of Canaan if it in fact was, and second because it better explains extra-biblical data, which would eventually include archaeology but also the appearance of the name "Israel," in an inscription recording a campaign in the Levant of the Nineteenth Dynasty Pharaoh Merneptah. The name "Israel" is accompanied there by a hieroglyphic modifier that identifies it as a people, perhaps because Merneptah encountered an Israel that was fully or partly non-sedentary (Benz, 2016; Na'aman, 1994). Additionally, Baily's (2018) much more recent study shows that much of the culture of the Israelites portrayed in the biblical text, including daily life, material culture, social practices and law, reflects the culture of Levantine nomadic peoples of the recent past. This is for us a more valuable use of ethnography as it makes cultural comparisons rather than limiting the potential social complexity of ancient nomads on the basis of modern nomads.

Efforts to understand the background of the people group Israel up to the formation of the monarchy (state formation according to those cited above) from the vantage of archaeology and anthropology in recent decades are centered on one particular phenomenon. During the Late Bronze Age, when Canaan was under the hegemony of New Kingdom Egypt, we know of very few settlements (or really farmsteads in some cases) in the highlands of Canaan, while the Iron Age I, which saw the end of Egyptian rule, saw a dramatic rise in the number of settlements, with a large number of small settlements appearing throughout the highlands, mostly in the more fertile areas north of Jerusalem. These settlements are overwhelmingly accepted as belonging to early Israelites, and there is no other realistic identification for them. Some of these Iron Age I sites have been excavated (e.g. Giloh, see Mazar, 1981) but the vast majority are known from surveys in the different geographical subunits of the highlands (Ilan, 2018; for the surveys see Finkelstein et al., 1997; Finkelstein & Magen, 1993; Frankel et al., 2001; Gal, 1992; Kloner, 2001; Ofer, 1993; Zertal et al., 2004–2022). Decades before these data had become available, Alt had argued that there must have been a low density of settlement in the highlands during the Late Bronze Age on the basis of the country's political divisions recorded in documents pertaining to Egyptian rule. He saw the early Israelites as nomads who had infiltrated peacefully the sparsely populated highlands of Canaan from the desert fringe east of the Jordan (Alt, 1986). Alt was followed in this regard by others such as Aharoni (1979) and Weippert (1971).

Following the availability of much of the survey data cited above, Finkelstein (1988, 1992b, c, 1994) argued that the phenomenon of Iron Age I settlements in the highlands was part of a long-term regional cycle between pastoral-nomadism and sedentarization. Nomads who had been present in the highlands during the Late Bronze Age sedenterized throughout the highlands, hence the large number of new, small settlements. In his view, the elliptical plan found at several of these sites with a belt of buildings enclosing a courtyard was a direct continuation of the layout of a camp of mobile herders. He also took sites that may have been campgrounds, with pottery but no architecture, as one indication that even during the sedentarization of the Iron Age I there was still a portion of the population the remained mobile, all the more so in Judah where this was coupled to a much lower density of Iron Age I settlement than in the northern highlands. This would become part of his argument that social complexity was not achieved in Judah until after the time of the United Monarchy, all the more so when placing much of the tenth century BCE within the Iron Age I (Finkelstein, 2003). Further to the north in the Upper Galilee, an Iron Age I stratum of pits accompanied by limited architecture at Hazor could be another indication of the (periodic or seasonal) use of the site by nomads (Ben-Ami, 2012; Finkelstein, 1988).

Some scholars have identified the nomadic populations that would come to be known as Israel with people groups that appear in textual sources relating to the period of New Kingdom Egyptian hegemony in the southern Levant, including Egyptian royal inscriptions and papyri in Egypt itself and the archive of fourteenth century BCE Akkadian-language correspondence between the Egyptian court and the Pharaoh's vassal rulers in the southern Levant found at el-Amarna (ancient Akhetaten). However, only one such group that still draws real interest in this regard, known in Egyptian as the $š{}^3sw$, usually transliterated as "Shasu," which may have an etymology meaning "to wander" or may come from a Semitic root meaning "to plunder." Whatever the etymology of the name, the textual sources indicate quite clearly that the Shasu were tent-dwelling mobile pastoralists, apparently divided into multiple socio-political units (tribes) affiliated with different names and places, in the southern Levant including the Transjordan where Egypt did not exercise hegemony. Unsurprisingly, one sometimes finds them described as Bedouin (e.g.

Giveon, 1971). As much as they seem to have been generally mobile the Shasu seemingly existed in some form of polymorphic social relationship with settled communities and may themselves have included settled (but not necessarily *permanently* settled) elements (Benz, 2016; Giveon, 1971; Hasel, 1998; Rainey & Notley, 2014; Ward, 1972). Rainey (2007) puts more emphasis on the early Israelites as Shasu nomadic pastoralists who came into the highlands west of the Jordan from the Transjordan than on those already in the former region as Finkelstein does.

Before moving on, we must briefly discuss the most prominent alternative explanation for the origin of the Israelite settlement phenomenon in the Iron Age I, which originated with Mendenhall (1962) and Gottwald (1979; see also Benz, 2016: 287–293). They argued that while there may have been a small group within early Israel that had migrated in from outside the region, the bulk of the population that moved into the highlands were peasants who had abandoned the oppressive Canaanite "city-states" (cf. Benz, 2016) of the lowlands. Mendenhall rejected explanations of the early Israelites as nomads who moved into the highlands from the desert; he believed this was based on a romantic view of the Bedouin and would have been unfeasible because the Israelites, unlike the Bedouin, would not have had domesticated camels for long-distance movement. He admitted that there were nomads around in the Bronze Age, "but they can, like the modern Bedouin, be safely regarded as statistically and historically negligible" (Mendenhall, 1962: 69), a rather outstanding example of an *a priori* bias against nomads as historical actors. We assume Mendenhall would have maintained this opinion even if he had modern survey data in hand as he otherwise insists that mobile pastoral populations are always associated with settled communities rather than sharply separated from them. However, the camel was not critical even for scholars like Albright (1942), who thought the Israelites had come across the Jordan from the desert (Benz, 2016: 287–288), and if a significant part of this nomadic population was already circulating into, out of or around the highlands during the Late Bronze Age, this would seem even less critical.

A new reconstruction by Gadot (2019) is somewhat similar in arguing for an origin of the Iron Age I settlers in at least part of the highlands (north of Jerusalem) in the lowland Canaanite "city-states," though he argues that the settlement phenomenon was the expansion of the same states that mostly continued to flourish in the Iron Age I, in effect colonizing a previously underpopulated region. This reconstruction also shows an architectural, sedentarocentrist bias. Some archaeological evidence marshalled in support of Mendenhall's basic idea, which would also work with Gadot's, has been proffered by a few scholars but especially Dever (1995, 2003, 2017), who has pointed to the strong continuities in ceramic forms between the Canaanite lowlands in the Late Bronze Age and the Israelite highlands in the Iron Age I. The significance of this has been challenged, however; aside from other differences in material culture, the repertoire of ceramic shapes in the highlands is much more limited than that of the lowlands (Finkelstein, 1988: 312–314), while many such shapes as well as other points of material culture can also be found in Late Bronze Age Transjordan (Rainey, 2007: 49–52).

This establishes the nomadic background of Israel within its own self-conception and the likelihood of the same in the available historical and archaeological evidence for the Late Bronze Age and Iron Age I. Evidence of nomads among the Canaanite and Israelite populations does tend to be indirect, in keeping with the usual archaeological invisibility of nomads discussed above. Research in recent decades in the Aravah region of southern Israel and Jordan has provided a case in which we see both an unusually high degree of the archaeological visibility of nomads and their activities and a complex and even interregionally important nomadic polity. This research has been discussed extensively in the scholarship cited here, and so we offer a synopsis of the most important points.

Excavations in the area in and around Wadi Faynan, Jordan by the Edom Lowlands Regional Project (ELRAP) and in the Timna Valley, Israel by the Central Timna Valley Project (CTV) have revealed extensive, industrial-scale copper mining and smelting activities in these two arid areas dating to the early Iron Age that are accompanied by a minimal amount of domestic architecture and no evidence of permanent year-round occupation. Some architecture is present in both Faynan and in Timna, but is either defensive in form or related to the metallurgical activities, and otherwise contemporary settlements near the copper production sites are absent even after extensive surveys. This indicates that the population responsible for these large-scale production activities were nomads, or perhaps more properly semi-nomads, who mined and smelted copper seasonally as part of their transhumance between the lowlands (the Aravah) and the highlands on either side, in the Negev to the west and Jordanian plateau to the east, camping at or near the sites in tents. Their lifestyle as well as the transportation of copper outside of the Aravah did not initially rely on domesticated camels, for which the earliest evidence in Faynan and Timna comes from the late tenth century BCE at the earliest (Sapir-Hen & Ben-Yosef, 2013). Though some copper production in Timna already took place under Egyptian auspices in the thirteenth century BCE, the main phase of copper production throughout the Aravah lasted from the twelfth to the ninth centuries BCE (see Ben-Yosef, 2016, 2018, 2019; Levy et al., 2014; Levy, 2009 with many further references). Some campsites and remains of tents that may belong to this period (their dating being difficult) have been found (Knabb et al., 2014; Workman, 2016) but the most direct evidence for these nomads comes from the cemetery of Wadi Fidan 40, one of several cemeteries identified in surveys. Chemical and isotopic investigation of some of the human remains indicated that some of the individuals interred were directly involved in the copper production activities (Beherec, 2011; Beherec et al., 2014, 2016).

The complexity of the nomadic society that undertook these activities is beyond a reasonable doubt, starting with the organization and co-ordination needed for the long-term, highly productive and technologically sophisticated copper production industry that had to be constantly supplied with fuel, and the workers who had to be provided with water and food that had to be brought from some distance away. This must have involved some degree of centralization starting at the local level in both Faynan and Timna but also quite likely at a higher level—that of a nomadic polity (Ben-Yosef et al., 2019; Ben-Yosef, 2010; Ben-Yosef & Levy, 2014; Cavanagh,

2016). This polity dominated the supply of copper between the twelfth and ninth centuries BCE, when bronze was still the primary metal in the Near East even with the transition to the "Iron" Age (Yahalom-Mack et al., 2014; Yahalom-Mack & Eliyahu-Behar, 2015; Yahalom-Mack & Segal, 2018). Metallurgical analyses have shown that copper from the Aravah reached as far as Greece and Egypt (Ben-Dor Evian et al., 2021; Kiderlen et al., 2016; Vaelske et al., 2019).

Being nomadic, it is clear that the archaeologically visible copper production centers are only one part of a polity with a larger geographical reach that included the highlands to the east and west (Ben-Yosef, 2021), and whose exact extent is inherently difficult to delineate archaeologically. In addition to the fact that the arid Aravah desert is the least hospitable area in the broader region and the reasonable assumption of subsistence practices based on transhumance, there is also some evidence for nomadic activities on the Jordanian plateau (Iron I sherds without architecture (Finkelstein, 1992a)), and direct evidence that the Negev Highlands were inhabited by the same people of the Aravah copper production centers (Martin et al., 2014; Martin & Finkelstein, 2013; Yahalom-Mack et al., 2015).

The extreme arid conditions of the Timna Valley have also allowed an unprecedented high level of preservation of organic remains, providing even more insights into the nomadic polity that orchestrated the mining and smelting activities there. Studies of the botanical, faunal and textile remains indicate that the metal producers were well-fed on meat and had access to plants and foods that had to be imported to the Aravah from distances as far away as the Mediterranean coast (Ben-Yosef et al., 2017; Muniz & Levy, 2014; Sapir-Hen et al., 2018; Sapir-Hen & Ben-Yosef, 2014). In addition to textiles dyed with plants brought from outside the Aravah, fragments of textiles dyed in "royal" purple with the *murex* snail, a practice associated with the Phoenician coast in northern Israel and Lebanon, were found in Timna (Sukenik et al., 2017, 2021). Connections with Arabia, perhaps an indication of some quite early form of Arabian trade into the Levant, are indicated by the presence of Qurayya Painted Ware (QPW), which was produced in the Hejaz (Saudi Arabia) and imported to the Levant in the Late Bronze Age until some point in the early Iron Age (Kleiman et al., 2017).

The best historical identification for this nomadic polity is the kingdom of Edom, one of Israel's neighbors during the tenth century BCE as well as earlier and later, known from the Hebrew Bible and some Assyrian and Babylonian sources. We will not dwell on the reasons for this identification aside from matching the general historical geography of Edom as it has been discussed elsewhere (see Ben-Yosef, 2019, 2020, 2021; Levy et al., 2014; Zucconi, 2007 and references there). The most important point for our purposes here is that the early Iron Age archaeology of the Aravah provides an example of an unusually visible population of nomads, and a population that formed a complex polity that was integral to the interregional economy at that. This kingdom of Edom may also have had a background in the Shasu encountered by the Egyptians; indeed one text names a group of pastoralists who were allowed into the Delta with their herds as the "Shasu tribes of Edom" (Rainey & Notley, 2014: 103). The Aravah copper industry came to an end in the late ninth century BCE with the destruction of Gath, one the copper trade's main outlets, and the resurgence of the copper industry in Cyprus, which had formerly been the dominant player during the Late Bronze Age (Ben-Yosef & Sergi, 2018). And yet in the very early eighth century BCE, Edom is recorded as paying tribute to the Assyrian king Adad-nirari III (Millard, 1992), at a time when there is little to no archaeological evidence for either nomads or settled communities in the region of Edom. Permanent settlement in Edom only appears from the late eighth century BCE, in the Transjordanian highlands, and following the architectural bias it had previously been thought that the kingdom of Edom only began at that time (Bienkowski, 1990, 1992). With the newer evidence from excavations in the Aravah in hand, it appears that the Edomite polity is much older than this but was predominantly nomadic and thus often invisible to archaeology. It became relatively visible during the twelfth to ninth centuries BCE under the very particular circumstances of its copper production activities, and once this ceased, the Edomites simply continued on with their mobile agropastoralist ways. The eventual sedentarization of the Edomites (or more likely some portion of their population) was probably a response to their role in the increasing Arabian trade, something that would later induce the Nabateans to settle and engage in architecture as well (Ben-Yosef, 2019, 2021).

A similar situation would appear to obtain in Moab, where a nomadic population adopted a degree of sedentism during the Iron Age I in response to some need for protection and defense, perhaps the protection of their position on a route of the copper trade from the Aravah that ran north through the Transjordanian plateau. The abandonment of the Iron Age I sites in Moab was simply a reversion of their population back to nomadic life (Ben-Yosef, 2021). One possible positive indication of a nomadic population in Moab is the Moabite temple dated to the Iron Age IIA at Khirbat 'Ataruz, which existed in its earliest phases in isolation from any domestic occupation (Ji, 2012, 2018; Ji et al., 2020), which would indicate that it was a cultic gathering place of nomads.

While we understand both Edom and Moab to have been polymorphic societies over the long term of a few centuries, demographically they seem to have been weighted more towards nomadism than Israel, which clearly underwent a sustained sedentarization of part of its population sooner than Edom or Moab. As such, we reconstruct the United Monarchy as a more fully polymorphic polity during the tenth century BCE. To begin tracing the implications of this, we discuss the culturally embedded socio-political structure of the kingdom from an emic perspective and how on the one hand this enabled the integration of communities that were settled, mobile, or perhaps somewhere in between, but on the other hand structured relationships of social integration and authority in a way that was not contingent upon monumentality.

3.3 *The Native Model of the Kingdom and Its Structure*

To begin at the methodological level, understanding the native socio-political model of the United Monarchy of ancient Israel means paying attention to how relationships of authority are structured, especially the relationship between the king, his patron deity and his people. *Contra* the processualist, materialist and vaguely evolutionist methodology often applied in studies relating to Israel in the tenth century, understandingthe reality of societies and polities in a particular ancient context cannot be achieved purely or even primarily on archaeological grounds. Rather, it is necessary for us to be led by the historical texts we have available, both texts of local relevance and from culturally related, cognate traditions. From this we can understand native linguistic expressions that structure relationships of authority and their ongoing operation at different levels. Significantly, they also help us to see what sort of factors are *not* embedded within such structuration. For the United Monarchy, this means first considering the Hebrew Bible—and fortunately the relevant books, 1–2 Samuel and 1 Kings, coupled with appropriate references from other books, are quite illuminating for this purpose. To add to this, we have a great amount of contextual material from the Bronze and Iron Ages in the Near East world around Israel. While no archaeologist or historian would claim that any of the kingdoms in the ancient Near East were identical in terms of their internal form and structure, it is nonetheless important to consider underlying patterns they share that are essential to the nature of their form and structure (Schloen, 2001: 53–54).

Ancient Near Eastern polities and particularly kingdoms in the time prior to the Hellenistic period can broadly be described as "patrimonial," that is, they were understood by their constituents through the active structuring metaphor of the patriarchal household and the household's internal relationships of authority. This metaphor operated at all levels, such that the king's position of supreme authority rested in his status as patriarch of one great household that included all those within his realm. As per the centrality of the household metaphor, socio-political structure at all levels in the patrimonial Near East had kinship in its essence, even if that kinship was (even predominantly) "fictive" rather than biological. Smaller kinship units were integrated into larger ones, including kingdoms, through bonds of biological or fictive kinship and authority operated dyadically between relative household positions, primarily the authority of the "father" or "lord" over his "sons," "daughters" and "(maid)servants" (Schloen, 2001). Patrimonialism was one of the ideal types of society developed in extensive detail by Weber (1978), a social form he saw as founded upon authority understood as inherently legitimate on the basis of tradition and social custom, as opposed to legitimate on some rational or objective basis.

The foundational study that demonstrated the patrimonial character of society and polity in the ancient Near East by Schloen (2001) focused primarily upon the Late Bronze Age kingdom of Ugarit in Syria, in which he made use of both the abundant textual sources as well as the archaeological record. Schloen also discussed the patrimonial nature of some other kingdoms like the Middle Assyrian kingdom (cf. Postgate, 2013) and Israel more briefly in the same volume, and subsequently others have reached very similar conclusions regarding other kingdoms, including Uruk-period Mesopotamia (Ur, 2014), Third Dynasty Ur (Garfinkle, 2008), the Hittite kingdom (Bilgin, 2018), New Kingdom Egypt (Lehner, 2000) and its Late Bronze Age vassals in Canaan (Benz, 2016). Schloen's (2001) "Patrimonial Household Model" is also similar to, though much more extensively elaborated than, the "tribal model" of Israel's neighboring kingdoms of Edom, Moab and

Ammon, which emphasized decentralized, polycentric tribal confederacy as fundamental to the structure of the these kingdoms (see in particular Bienkowski, 2009; LaBianca & Younker, 1998; van der Steen, 2004; Younker, 1997). Nonetheless, the tribes of Israel were most certainly fundamental to the United Monarchy and subsequent kingdoms of Israel and Judah. Stager (2003) and Master (2001) authored the initial studies on the United Monarchy as a patrimonial kingdom, noting that it both explained the biblical evidence and matched much better with tribal basis of polities and social complexity in the Near East in the *longue durée* than models that worked from a wholly etic, evolutionist basis. A more in depth study that also focused on implications for assessing the United Monarchy from an archaeological perspective was produced by Thomas (2019b, n.d.).

Israel's nomadic background and its tribal character are sometimes conflated (e.g., Petter, 2018) but these two characteristics were not dependent on each other. While the tribe is a problematic evolutionary type, as we have noted, the nature of the Israelite tribe is clear from the biblical text and it can in effect be considered the ur-tribe of Western thought. The kinship-based social structure of the Israelite tribe is laid out most directly in Josh 7:14–18, which shows the tribe (Hebrew שבט, lit. "staff, scepter") named for an initial ancestor (in this case Judah) who was himself the son of the ancestor of the people as a whole (Israel/Jacob), with the tribe divided into multiple clans (Hebrew משפחות) and clans divided into patriarchal households (Hebrew בתים), an individual household referred to as a House of the Father (Hebrew בית אב) (Stager, 1985). It is important to note though that in some places in the Hebrew Bible a tribe is also referred to as a house (Hebrew בית), as are royal dynasties. The name of the ruling house can also stand as one name for that kingdom as a whole in not only the Hebrew Bible but the ancient Near East more broadly, in keeping with the patrimonial model (Thomas, 2019a). The term "House of David" appears in reference to the kingdom of Judah in an Aramaic stela found at Tel Dan in northern Israel (Millard, 2003). The clans and tribes were led by what are most commonly referred to simply as "elders" (Hebrew זקנים), the male heads of households within the kinship unit.

It cannot be emphasized too greatly that the tribes and their leadership were critical to the formation and structure of the United Monarchy within the culturally-embedded conception of the biblical authors. David is first made king of Judah, his own familiar tribe, after giving gifts to the tribal elders (1 Sam 30; 2 Sam 2), and is then accepted as king by the other tribes of Israel (2 Sam 5). The description of Solomon's administrative system in his realm (1 Kings 4–5; 9) indicates clearly that it is focused on the tribes, most of which are named directly as one of the kingdom's administrative units (Thomas, 2019b). While some aspects of Solomon's reign are indicative of efforts to centralize power and control to the king and his immediate household, Solomon still had to maintain a proper, respectful relationship with tribal leadership. The construction of a temple (actually a בית "house") for YHWH, the patron deity of Israel and the House of David, next to the king's house in Jerusalem, cements that divinely-mandated, elect status of the House of David, but Solomon is sure to conduct the symbolic entrance of YHWH into his new house in the presence of the elders of the tribes of Israel, complete with sacrifices and feast (1 Kings 8).

Finally, the dissolution of the United Monarchy under Solomon's son Rehoboam once again demonstrates the critical role of the tribes and their own political volition in the very existence of the kingdom. The tribes gather at Shechem, a Late Bronze Age city in the northern highlands and an old place of assembly for the tribes of Israel (Joshua 24), to anoint Rehoboam king, where the northern tribes ask Rehoboam to lighten the burden that they had experienced under Solomon's administration. When he refuses, they simply leave and form a separate kingdom, leaving Rehoboam and the House of David to rule only the tribe of Judah once again (1 Kings 12) (Benz, 2016).

To properly complete the native model of the United Monarchy as a kingdom we also need to recognize two important points about what is *not* part of this model. First, there is no evidence that a qualitative distinction was made between settled and mobile components of Israel's population, at least in terms of socio-political structure. Some biblical references (see the following section) indicate tent-dwelling in pre-monarchic and monarchic Israel, but a sedentary, nomadic or semi-nomadic lifeway of persons and groups mentioned in the narrative is not generally remarked upon because, in our view, this was not remarkable to the biblical authors; rather it was something they took for granted. Nor is there solid evidence from the Hebrew Bible that Israelites at the time of the United Monarchy either had an emic category of architecture resembling our modern notion of monumentality or that the construction and maintenance of hierarchical, socio-political relationships were instituted by the construction and maintenance of architecture. Complexity within the specific cultural context of ancient Near Eastern patrimonial kingdom is not a characteristic that can be measured according to such independent variables; rather, complexity here is better defined as the degree of elaboration and interconnection of branching household relationships, such that a kingdom is a more socially complex entity because it incorporates and co-ordinates a larger network of patrimonial relationships. This network can likewise be broken down into "simpler" structures at the level of the tribe down to the level of the household and even the individual (Schloen, 2001).

The biblical text does describe various building projects under Solomon, including his own house and the house for YHWH his patron deity (1 Kings 6–8), but ultimately such constructions were "done by the divine or human ruler's servants in order to provide him or her with a house, in exactly the same way that any householder's dependents labored on his behalf to build and maintain his household" (Schloen, 2001: 266); they were not critical to the legitimization of Solomon's rule. Solomon's construction, or more likely refurbishment of defenses in the formerly Canaanite city of Jerusalem (1 Kgs 9:15, 11:27) can be explained prosaically as a simple concern for the defensibility of the capital. The element of Solomon's building projects that has attracted the most attention is the statement in 1 Kgs 9:15–18 that Solomon "built" (the text offers no more detail) Hazor, Megiddo, Gezer, Lower Beth-Horon, Baalath, and Tamar, with the focus being on the first three as these sites are the most well-known in terms of their archaeology and history. All three of these sites were of strategic importance as they guarded sensitive points along major routes through the southern Levant, including the main route between Egypt and

Syria/Mesopotamia, so again a prosaic defensive need is sufficient to explain Solomon's interest in building there (Rainey & Notley, 2014; Thomas, 2019b). In any event we should be wary of reading too much into the biblical text because it provides no detail whatsoever on what was built at any of these sites, which may be a very deliberate move on the part of the authors; scribes working on behalf of ancient Near Eastern kings were not above spinning relatively minor actions by the king into impressive achievements through the careful selection of their wording. So if Solomon did "build" at these sites, he may not have built very much at all, though importantly this would not contradict the biblical authors (Halpern, 2001; Thomas, 2022).

3.4 Reconceiving the United Monarchy as a Polymorphic, Patrimonial Kingdom

We propose that the United Monarchy needs to be reconceived as a patrimonial kingdom (as has been done already) with a polymorphic population made of communities (and even segments of communities) that were sedentary, nomadic, or a shifting mix of both. The social complexity of the kingdom, in terms of both its structure of legitimate authority and the contingent exercise of that authority (what it was used for) by the king and his subordinates was not maintained through the imposition of materializations of power like so-called "monumental" architecture. Instead, it was conceived and operationalized through the active metaphor of the patriarchal household, a metaphor that bound both sedentary and nomadic communities as kinship groups at various levels, from the local household through the clan to the tribe and ultimately the kingdom. We envision a landscape of sedentary, mobile and mixed-subsistence life throughout the regions in which the United Monarchy's communities lived, from the hills of the Galilee down to what is now the northern Negev at least. This would have been a landscape of constant interaction and undifferentiation in terms of lifestyle, to the point that tents stood next to stone-and-brick houses within the same household and clan, even for extended periods of time.

This polymorphism penetrated throughout social, political and economic life in tenth century BCE Israel and should influence how we see the kingdom reflected in the biblical text. When the Israelites of the northern tribes declare "to your tents, O Israel!" and thusly "Israel went to its tents" (1 Kgs 12:16), it is unnecessary to write this off as "out of place in the monarchical period, as the majority of the population are not tent-dwellers" and therefore archaic (Homan, 2002: 187–192), since it would appear that tent-dwelling remained a quite normal part of life in Israel. We also contend that when toponyms and communities appear in biblical books related to the United Monarchy, and also those that purport to narrate earlier periods in Israel's history (specifically the books of Joshua and Judges), modern readers are conditioned by their own cultural context to default to the assumption that the text refers to a fixed, permanent settlement, but if we accept that Israel was a polymorphic society then we should consider the possibility that the text has tent-based or even properly mobile habitation in view as well. This would have mostly been below the horizon of the biblical authors' interest, being to them an unremarkable element of life in ancient Israel. In particular the Hebrew term typically translated as "city," עיר, is likely to indicate a community composed fully or partly of tent dwellings in some instances (cf. Koehler & Baumgartner, 1994: 821), reflecting the similar situation in the Mari texts (see above).

The nomadic aspect most clearly surfaces the use of the phrase "to your tents, O Israel!" or a reference to the "Way of the Tent-Dwellers" in Judges 8. The latter route may have even played a role in Solomon's system of administrative divisions described in 1 Kings 4; one official's remit is centered on a place named Mahanaim (1 Kgs 4:14), which lay on this Way of the Tent-Dwellers, a seasonal transhumant route between the Jordan Valley and Transjordanian highlands (Hutton, 2006). Positing an official here would have made it ideal for the king to communicate with and extract from nomadic or pastoral Israelites. We also find in this system an official stationed in the northern Transjordan whose remit included the *Havvoth* of Jair, a descendant of the tribal ancestor Manasseh. The plural Hebrew term *Havvoth* (חות) is not a term for settlements but most likely means an encampment or stockade (Rainey, 1975), which more directly suggests that this official was responsible for a mobile clan within the tribe of Manasseh (Thomas, 2019a, b, n.d.).

On the expressly archaeological side, the nomadic component of the United Monarchy's population would represent an invisible or difficult-to-detect "x-factor" that confounds any attempt to form a comprehensive archaeological portrait of the kingdom. For any particular sphere we would wish to study, be it economics, politics, military organization, cult or otherwise, it will always be necessary to acknowledge that there is an archaeologically-elusive component to the dynamics, connections and resources involved. The complexity of the kingdom was not lessened by this factor; rather it is simply that archaeologically we are studying a complex socio-political entity whose internal workings are composed as much by the "dark matter" (Hämäläinen, 2013: 85) of the nomadic Israelites as by their sedentary brothers and sisters. Moreover, these brothers and sisters were not detached from the nomadic culture of their origin (and contemporary kin), in a way that their archaeology—although sedentary—should be investigated using an appropriate lens. Unlike the case of contemporary Edom discussed above, there was nothing that stimulated an exceptional archaeological visibility of the nomads of Israel at this time. At best there may be isolated instances of sites that could be related to nomads during the late Iron Age I and Iron Age IIA (which extends into the ninth century BCE), including sites with pottery but no architecture found in surveys as mentioned above. We could also point to the group of small sites with scattered pottery and fragmentary architecture called "Hazerim" (Gophna & Singer-Avitz, 1984) or the isolated temple next to the Nahal Patish (Nahashoni, 2009), both found in the northwestern Negev. Aside from the question of whether these sites actually relate to Israelites as opposed to the nearby Philistines, these sites do present the pitfalls that come with too rash an assignment of archaeological remains to nomads, as it is just as possible that these sites relate to the activities of pastoralists coming from settlements proper. The best archaeological indication for the substantial nomadic population of the United Monarchy/Iron Age IIA is the dramatic increase in the number of settled sites in Israel and Judah from the Iron Age IIA to IIB (from the tenth to the eighth centuries BCE), which cannot be explained by simple population growth (Faust, 2014; Livni, 2015), the simplest explanation being the large-scale sedentarization of the nomadic population. This fits well with the near absence of references to dwelling in tents in biblical texts relating to latter (eighth to early sixth) centuries of the kingdoms of Israel and Judah, though it is important to note that as late as the end of the seventh century BCE the prophet Jeremiah encounters a tent-dwelling, nomadic clan, the Rechabites, in Judah (Jeremiah 35).

An important microcosm of how a reconceptualized United Monarchy would play out is in Jerusalem. As noted above, scholars have generally been preoccupied with its size and monumentality in evaluating Jerusalem as the capital of whatever sort of political entity during the tenth century BCE. In a polymorphic and patrimonial kingdom, however, these factors have really no importance. To begin with, it is well-acknowledged that for a variety of reasons, especially the continuous and invasive later occupation history of the city, it is very hard to assess Jerusalem's character during the early Iron Age. The inaccessibility of the Temple Mount is a particular problem, as this would be the approximate location for the new constructions under Solomon, including the Temple itself (cf. Finkelstein et al., 2011). The role of Jerusalem as a regional center in the Late Bronze Age, which we know of from undisputable contemporaneous historical sources (the el-Amarna letters), could never have been reconstructed based on the scarce archaeological remains from this period (Na'aman, 2010). There is no need for the Jerusalem of David and Solomon to have been some great metropolis when its role from the position of the ruling dynasty was as a center of the regal and ritual functions held in special distinction from the everyday life of the population, where the conjunction of human ruler and divine patronage were expressed by the royal residence in colocation with the Temple (Stager, 2003; Uziel & Shai, 2007). While David and Solomon did reside in built structures within a fortified compound, עיר דוד, commonly but misleadingly translated as the "City of David" (see Hutzli, 2011), it is possible that many household of early Iron Age Jerusalem resided in tents.

On the basis of our review of other cases in world history and archaeology, and the local case of early Iron Age Edom, we have no grounds on which to assume that the early kingdom of Israel was lacking in social complexity only for the fact that it likely incorporated a substantial nomadic element within its population. Nor can we doubt its complexity from an absence of monumentality, if the relevance of this concept is even applicable. Notwithstanding the lack of any clear indication within the biblical text that monumentality was understood as critical to political relationships, it is questionable that a population that was either still largely nomadic or that had transitioned relatively recently from a nomadic lifestyle would likely build anything we would recognize as particularly "monumental." Consider that in 2 Samuel 7, Israel's patron deity YHWH acknowledges his residence in a tent as sufficient and resists the necessity of being housed in a permanent structure. In any event, Israel followed the pattern of its Near Eastern context, in which the active metaphor of the household served as the real, if largely intangible symbol that structured relationships of political authority and submission. What we have presented here as the anthropological reality in which the United Monarchy would have existed sits quite uncomfortably within the history of biblical and archaeological scholarship, for on the one hand it runs counter to the tendency to read out of the text a historical claim for an ancient political entity envisioned through the filter of Western biases about what a complex political entity must be, rather than one whose nature and literary presentation are deeply embedded and refracted by its cultural context.

On the other hand, and even more problematic for the approach of many of those scholars referenced above, it undermines the privileged status as the ultimate arbiter of the reality of tenth century BCE Israel and the historicity of the biblical text. Archaeological scholarship on the United Monarchy has been driven by a desire to say something decisive rather than equivocal and uncertain, and has had the confidence to do so because of the assumption that archaeology had all the necessary tools (the theory and concepts) and all of the relevant data with which to make a decisive judgment. Scholars have worked within a supposedly scientific framework, in which social complexity can be assessed based on the objective and testable presence or absence of material correlates, including monumentality, for a pre-defined, stadial evolutionary type of socio-political organization, the state. Especially for scholars who doubted the historicity of the biblical kingdom of David and Solomon, this allowed for the fabrication of a convenient "straw man" who could easily be knocked down, constructed out of simplistic and inaccurate assumptions about what the text claims, such as that it presents David and Solomon as ruling over an "empire" (cf. Hayes, 2015). The critical aspect of understanding the United Monarchy as polymorphic and structured through the active metaphor of the household and household relationships of authority is the incorporeality of much of the population and the manner of their socio-political structuration, which critically undermines archaeology's ability to test the existence of social complexity and thus the kingdom itself on the basis of purely material markers like monumentality.

4 Conclusion

In this paper we have presented a theoretical rationale for the existence of social complexity without monumentality, a direct contradiction to ingrained tendencies in scholarship that have variously been referred to as sedentarocentrism, the architectural bias and the tyranny of monumentality. The manner in which complexity occurs anthropologically and is manifested archaeologically is dictated by the nature of both the social reality of people who actually participate(d) in complexity and the cultural context in which their socio-political structuration occurs. In our case study we have presented a kingdom with a polymorphic (mixed nomadic-settled) population whose political structure and hierarchic relationships of authority did not depend on monumentality. The widely-accepted nomadic background for the core Israelite population and the understanding that also those who had gradually settled down necessarily retained aspects of nomadic culture, should mitigate against expectation that this population would automatically resort to monumentality to express political structure, while at the same time the case of neighboring Edom demonstrates that within this cultural context, nomadism itself was no barrier to social complexity. We see instead that it was the active, culturally-embedded metaphor of the household and its relationships of hierarchical authority that structured and operationalized the kingdom's complexity, not purely material symbols like monumentality. We are in the fortunate position of being able to see what was critical to the nature of social complexity in the United Monarchy (the household) and what was not critical (monumentality) because of the native linguistic expression found in texts, the Hebrew Bible and sources from other Near Eastern polities of the Bronze and Iron Ages. Yet still, these texts and a careful, culturally-sensitive appreciation of them are sidelined in favor of expressly archaeological evaluations of Israel during the tenth century BCE as this allows scholars to appear scientific rather than naively beholden to the religious and ideological perspective of the biblical authors. In turn, archaeological evaluations themselves have been confined to processualism and positivism for the same reason: adherence to what is considered the most "scientific" archaeology is the ultimate shield against claims of naiveté in the historical interpretation of the biblical text.

Rather than being revelatory, the prospect of complexity without monumentality in the world of ancient Israel and its neighbors concurs with other cases from world archaeology and history noted in this paper, in which we see that complexity can appear in many different variations and guises, both where archaeologically elusive mobile populations are involved but also in the case of properly sedentary societies. This stands in stark contradiction to the ways in which the history of archaeological and anthropological theory on social complexity, which has tended to limit its preconceptions of what social complexity is, what sort of societies are complex and how complexity must appear archaeologically. Social evolution, especially in the neo-evolutionist guise, has worked from a basic, Eurocentric dichotomy of primitive-civilized in which the apex of complexity is the modern state or some earlier form of it, defined by settlement and monumentality at the expense of more "primitive" mobility and kinship organization. Moreover, processualism embraced a scientific identity for archaeology, establishing societies as natural phenomena whose characteristics, including complexity, could be tested and evaluated according to objective (but truly ethnocentric) criteria. Monumentality was such a visible, discoverable correlate of complexity, and so what lay outside archaeology's vision was thus marginal and unimportant to the study of complex historical societies.

We offer a few important lessons for world archaeology deriving from this study, the most important of which is that archaeologists must consider that which is not immediately visible, what is intangible and what falls outside of the familiar when approaching the complexity of a complex society. Complexity should not be assumed to be absent just because it is not manifested in a material manner, or in a certain, predefined manner. Instead of beginning from an assumption about the necessary nature of social complexity as defined in universalizing evolutionist schemes, complexity should be treated as something whose nature and appearance is very much a product of the cultural context in which it occurs, including both the values and symbols and structure of socio-political relationships and the lifeways or backgrounds of the society, which may mitigate against easily perceptible forms in materialization. This ultimately means moving on from a positivistic, strictly scientific (but actually scientistic) approach to ancient society and admitting to the limitations inherent in archaeology. This is particularly relevant to a situation in which the archaeological record is poor, as this should no longer itself be a reason to resort to social evolutionism to fill in gaps in understanding or to assume that a lack of archaeological remains equates with a lack of a socially complex population. Likewise, where texts are not available, archaeologists and historians should be willing to admit that they therefore lack insight into the local cultural rules for socio-political structuration, rather than again resorting to the decontextualized predictions of social evolution. However rich or poor either the archaeological and textual records are, archaeologists should be wary of letting ethnography limit how they understand particular sorts of societies, especially those that fall outside the familiar Western experience of complexity, and instead ethnography, should serve to indicate what is possible, as a starting point, rather than what it only possible.

Acknowledgments This study was partially supported by the Institute of Archaeology of Tel Aviv University (through its Post-Doctoral Fellowship Program to ZT) and the Israel Science Foundation, grant #1880/17 to EB-Y.

References

Adams, R. M. (2001). Complexity in archaic states. *Journal of Anthropological Archaeology, 20*(3), 345–360.
Aharoni, Y. (1979). *The land of the Bible: A historical geography* (Rev. Ed.). Westminster.
Albright, W. F. (1942). *Archaeology and the religion of Israel*. The Johns Hopkins University Press.
Alden, J. R. (2015). Review of D.T. Potts. Nomadism in Iran: From antiquity to the modern era. *Antiquity, 89*, 996–997.
Alizadeh, A. (2010). The rise of the Highland Elamite state in Southwestern Iran. *Curent Anthropology, 51*(3), 353–383.
Alon, Y. (2005). The tribal system in the face of the state-formation process: Mandatory Transjordan, 1921–46. *International Journal of Middle Eastern Studies, 37*(2), 213–240.
Alt, A. (1986). *Essays on old testament history and religion*. JSOT Press.
Alt, S. M. (2010). Considering complexity: Confounding categories with practices. In S. M. Alt (Ed.), *Ancient complexities: New perspectives in Precolumbian North America* (pp. 1–7). University of Utah Press.
Arbuckle, B. S., & Hammer, L. E. (2019). The rise of pastoralism in the ancient Near East. *Journal of Archaeological Research, 27*, 391–449.
Assi, S. (2018). The original Arabs: The invention of the "Bedouin Race" in Ottoman Palestine. *International Journal of Middle Eastern Studies, 50*(2), 213–232.
Baily, C. (2018). *Bedouin culture in the Bible*. Yale University Press.

Barfield, T. J. (2001). The shadow empires: Imperial state formation along the Chinese-nomad frontier. In S. E. Alcock (Ed.), *Empires: Perspectives from archaeology and history* (pp. 10–41). Cambridge University Press.

Barth, F. (1967). On the study of social change. *American Anthropologist, 69*(6), 661–669.

Bawden, G. (1989). The Andean state as a state of mind. *Journal of Anthropological Research, 45*(3), 327–332.

Beherec, M. (2011). *Nomads in transition: Mortuary archaeology in the lowlands of Edom (Jordan)*. Unpublished PhD dissertation, University of California.

Beherec, M., Najjar, M., & Levy, T. E. (2014). Wadi Fidan 40 and mortuary archaeology in the Edom lowlands. In T. E. Levy, M. Najjar, & E. Ben-Yosef (Eds.), *New insights into the Iron Age archaeology of Edom, Southern Jordan* (Vol. 1, pp. 665–721). Cotsen Institute of Archaeology Press.

Beherec, M. A., Levy, T. E., Tirosh, O., Najjar, M., Knabb, K. A., & Erel, Y. (2016). Iron Age nomads and their relation to copper smelting in Faynan (Jordan): Trace metal and Pb and Sr isotopic measurements from the Wadi Fidan 40 cemetery. *Journal of Archaeological Science, 65*, 70–83.

Belfer-Cohen, A., & Goring-Morris, A. N. (2009). The tyranny of the ethnographic record, revisited. *Paléorient, 35*(1), 107–108.

Ben-Ami, D. (2012). The Iron Age I (Stratum "XII/XI"): Stratigraphy and pottery. In A. Ben-Tor, D. Ben-Ami, & D. Sandhaus (Eds.), *Hazor VI: The 1990–2009 excavations. The Iron Age* (pp. 7–51). Israel Exploration Society/Hebrew University of Jerusalem.

Ben-Dor Evian, S., Yagel, O., Harlavan, Y., Seri, H., Lewinsky, J., & Ben-Yosef, E. (2021). Pharaoh's copper: The provenance of copper in bronze artifacts from post-imperial Egypt at the end of the second millennium BCE. *Journal of Archaeological Science Reports, 38*, 103025.

Ben-Yosef, E. (2010). *Technology and social process: Oscillations in Iron Age copper production and power in Southern Jordan*. Unpublished PhD dissertation, University of California, San Diego.

Ben-Yosef, E. (2016). Back to Solomon's era: Results of the first excavations at "Slaves' Hill" (Site 34, Timna, Israel). *Bulletin of the American Schools of Oriental Research, 376*, 169–198.

Ben-Yosef, E. (2018). The central Timna Valley project: Research design and preliminary results. In E. Ben-Yosef (Ed.), *Mining for ancient copper: Essays in memory of Beno Rothenberg* (pp. 28–63). Eisenbrauns/Tel Aviv University.

Ben-Yosef, E. (2019). The architectural bias in current biblical archaeology. *Vetus Testamentum, 69*(3), 361–387.

Ben-Yosef, E. (2020). And yet, a nomadic error: A reply to Israel Finkelstein. *Antiguo Oriente, 18*, 33–60.

Ben-Yosef, E. (2021). Rethinking social complexity of early Iron Age nomads. *Jerusalem Journal of Archaeology, 1*, 155–179.

Ben-Yosef, E. (n.d.). A false contrast? On the possibility of an early Iron Age nomadic monarchy in the Arabah (early Edom) and its implications to the study of ancient Israel. In I. Koch, O. Lipschits, & O. Sergi (Eds.), *From nomadism to monarchy? Revisiting the early iron age southern levant* (pp. 235–262). The Institute of Archaeology of Tel Aviv University and Penn State University Press.

Ben-Yosef, E., & Levy, T. E. (2014). The material culture of Iron Age copper production in Faynan. In T. E. Levy, M. Najjar, & E. Ben-Yosef (Eds.), *New insights into the Iron Age archaeology of Edom, Southern Jordan* (Vol. 2, pp. 887–959). Cotsen Institute of Archaeology Press.

Ben-Yosef, E., & Sergi, O. (2018). The destruction of Gath by Hazael and the Arabah copper industry: A reassessment. In I. Shai, J. R. Chadwick, L. A. Hitchcock, A. Dagan, C. McKinney, & J. Uziel (Eds.), *Tell it in Gath. Studies in the history and archaeology of Israel essays in honor of Aren M. Maeir on the occasion of his sixtieth birthday* (pp. 461–480). Zaphon.

Ben-Yosef, E., & Thomas, Z. (2023). Complexity without monumentality in Biblical times. *Journal of Archaeological Research*. https://doi.org/10.1007/s10814-10023-09184-10810

Ben-Yosef, E., Langgut, D., & Sapir-Hen, L. (2017). Beyond smelting: New insights on Iron Age (10th c. BCE) metalworkers community from excavations at a gatehouse and associated livestock pens in Timna, Israel. *Journal of Archaeological Science: Reports, 11*, 411–426.

Ben-Yosef, E., Liss, B., Yagel, O., Najjar, M., Tirosh, O., & Levy, T. E. (2019). Ancient technology and punctuated change: Detecting the emergence of biblical Edom. *PLoS One, 14*. https://doi.org/10.1371/journal.pone.0221967

Benz, B. C. (2016). *The land before the kingdom of Israel*. Eisenbrauns.

Bernbeck, R. (2008). An archaeology of multisited communities. In H. Barnard & W. Wendrich (Eds.), *The archaeology of mobility: Old World and New World nomadism* (pp. 43–77). Cotsen Institute of Archaeology Press.

Bienkowski, P. (1990). Umm el-Biyara, Tawilan and Buseirah in Retrospect. *Levant, XXII*, 91–109.

Bienkowski, P. (1992). The beginning of the Iron Age in Edom: A reply to Finkelstein. *Levant, XXIV*, 167–169.

Bienkowski, P. (2009). 'Tribalism' and 'Segmentary society' in Iron Age Transjordan. In P. Bienkowski (Ed.), *Studies on Iron Age Moab and neighbouring areas in honour of Michele Daviau* (pp. 7–26). Peeters.

Bilgin, T. (2018). *Officials and administration in the Hittite world*. de Gruyter.

Binford, L. R. (1962). Archaeology as anthropology. *American Antiquity, 28*(2), 217–225.

Biran, M. (2015). Introduction: Nomadic culture. In R. Amitai & M. Biran (Eds.), *Nomads as agents of cultural change: The Mongols and their Eurasian predecessors* (pp. 1–9). University of Haawai'i Press.

Blakeley, J. W. (2021). The changing landscape of the Hesi region and its implications for archaeological research. *Journal of Eastern Mediterranean Archaeology and Heritage Studies, 9*(1–2), 135–163.

Blakolmer, F. (2019). No kings, no inscriptions, no historical events? Some thoughts on the iconography of rulership in Mycenaean Greece. In J. M. Kelder & W. J. I. Waal (Eds.), *From 'LUGAL.GAL' to Wanax. Kingship and political organisation in the late Bronze Age Aegean* (pp. 49–94). Sidestone Press.

Boas, F. (1896). The limitations of the comparative method of anthropology. *Science, 4*, 901–908.

Boas, F. (1920). The methods of ethnology. *American Anthropologist, 22*(4), 311–321.

Brooks, J. F. (2016). The southwest. In F. E. Hoxie (Ed.), *The Oxford handbook of American Indian history* (pp. 217–233). Oxford University Press.

Bunimovitz, S. (2007). Archaeological views: Children of three paradigms. *Biblical Archaeology Review, 33*(5), 30–80.

Cavanagh, M. (2016). *Sustainability of an industry on the fringe: A Dendroarchaeological investigation into fuel sources at the Iron Age copper smelting sites of the Timna Valley*. Unpublished MA thesis, Tel Aviv University.

Chapman, R. (2003). *Archaeologies of complexity*. Routledge.

Chapman, R. (2007). Evolution, complexity and the state. In S. Kohring & S. Wynne-Jones (Eds.), *Socialising complexity: Approaches to power and interaction in the archaeological record* (pp. 13–28). Oxbow.

Charpin, D., & Durand, J.-M. (1986). Fils de Sim'al: Les Origines Tribales des Rois de Mari. *Revue d'Assyriologie et d'archéologie orientale, 80*(2), 141–183.

Childe, V. G. (1936). *Man makes himself*. Watts & Co.

Childe, V. G. (1950). The urban revolution. *Town Planning Review, 21*(1), 3–17.

Clarke, D. (1973). Archaeology: The loss of innocence. *Antiquity, XLVII*, 6–18.

Cooper, J. (2018). Kushites expressing 'Egyptian' kingship: Nubian dynasties in hieroglyphic texts and a phantom Kushite king. *Ägypten und Levante, XXVIII*, 143–167.

Cooper, J. (2020). A nomadic state? The 'Blemmyean-Beja' polity of the ancient Eastern Desert. *Journal of African History, 61*(3), 383–407.

Cowgill, G. L. (2004). Origins and development of urbanism: Archaeological perspectives. *Annual Review of Anthropology, 33*, 525–549.

Cribb, R. (1991). *Nomads in archaeology*. Cambridge University Press.

Dan-Cohen, T. (2020). Tracing complexity: The case of archaeology. *American Anthropologist, 122*(4), 733–744.
Dearman, J. (1989). *Studies in the Mesha inscription and Moab* (A. ed.). Scholars Press.
Delitz, H., & Levenson, F. (2019). The social meaning of big architecture, or the sociology of the monumental. In F. Buccellati, S. Hageneuer, S. van der Heyden, & F. Levenson (Eds.), *Size matters: Understanding monumentality across ancient civilizations* (pp. 107–132). transcript Verlag.
Dever, W. G. (1995). Ceramics, ethnicity, and the question of Israelite origins. *Biblical Archaeologist, 58*(4), 200–213.
Dever, W. G. (2003). *Who were the early Israelites and where did they come from?* Eerdmans.
Dever, W. G. (2017). *Beyond the texts: An archaeological portrait of ancient Israel and Judah.* SBL Press.
Diaz-Andreu, M. (2007). *A world history of nineteenth-century archaeology: Nationalism, colonialism, and the past.* Oxford University Press.
Drompp, M. B. (2005). Imperial state formation in inner Asia: The early Turkic empires (6th to 9th centuries). *Acta Orientalia Academiae Scientiarum Hungaricae, 58*(1), 101–111.
Dunnell, R. C. (1980). Evolutionary theory and archaeology. *Advances in Archaeological Method and Theory, B*, 35–99.
Durand, J.-M. (1998). *Documents épistolaires du Palais de Mari, Tome II.* Éditions du Cerf.
Emberling, G. M. (2014). Pastoralist states: Towards a comparative archaeology of early Kush. *Origini, XXXVI*, 125–156.
Faust, A. (2006). *Israel's ethnogenesis: Settlement, interaction, expansion and resistance.* Equinox.
Faust, A. (2010). Future directions in the study of ethnicity in ancient Israel. In T. E. Levy (Ed.), *Historical biblical archaeology and the future: The new pragmatism* (pp. 55–68). Equinox.
Faust, A. (2014). Highlands or lowlands? Reexamining demographic processes in Iron Age Judah. *Ugarit-Forschungen, 45*, 111–142.
Feinman, G. M. (1998). Scale and social organization: Perspectives on the archaic state. In G. M. Feinman & J. Marcus (Eds.), *Archaic states* (pp. 95–133). School of American Research Press.
Feinman, G. M. (2017). Multiple pathways to large-scale human cooperative networks: A reframing. In R. J. Chacon & R. G. Medoza (Eds.), *Feast, famine or fighting? Multiple pathways to social complexity* (pp. 459–478). Springer.
Feinman, G. M., & Carballo, D. M. (2019). The scale, governance, and sustainability of central places in pre-Hispanic Mesoamerica. In L. R. Lozny & T. H. McGovern (Eds.), *Global perspectives on long term community resource management* (pp. 235–253). Springer.
Feinman, G. M., & Marcus, J. (Eds.). (1998). *Archaic states.* School of American Research Press.
Feinman, G. M., & Neitzel, G. (1984). Too many types: An overview of sedentary prestate societies in the Americas. *Advances in Archaeological Method and Theory, 7*, 39–102.
Finkelstein, I. (1988). *The archaeology of the Israelite settlement.* Israel Exploration Society.
Finkelstein, I. (1992a). Edom in the Iron I. *Levant, XXIV*, 159–166.
Finkelstein, I. (1992b). Invisible nomads – A rejoinder. *Bulletin of the American Schools of Oriental Research, 287*, 87–88.
Finkelstein, I. (1992c). Pastoralism in the highlands of Canaan in the third and second millenium B.C.E. In O. Bar-Yosef & A. Khazanov (Eds.), *Pastoralism in the Levant: Archaeological materials in anthropological perspectives* (pp. 133–151). Prehistory Press.
Finkelstein, I. (1994). The emergence of Israel: A phase in the cyclic history of Canaan in the third and second millennia BCE. In I. Finkelstein & N. Na'aman (Eds.), *From nomadism to monarchy: Archaeological and historical aspects of early Israel* (pp. 150–178). Yad Izhak Ben-Zvi.
Finkelstein, I. (1999). State formation in Israel and Judah: A contrast in context, a contrast in trajectory. *Near Eastern Archaeology, 62*(1), 35–52.
Finkelstein, I. (2003). City-states to states: Polity dynamics in the 10th–9th centuries B.C.E. In W. G. Dever & S. Gitin (Eds.), *Symbiosis, symbolism, and the power of the past: Canaan, ancient Israel, and their Neighbors from the late Bronze Age through Roman Palaestina* (pp. 75–83). Eisenbrauns.

Finkelstein, I. (2005). [De]formation of the Israelite state: A rejoinder on methodology. *Near Eastern Archaeology, 68*(4), 202–208.

Finkelstein, I. (2007). King Solomon's Golden Age: History or myth? In B. B. Schmidt (Ed.), *The quest for historical Israel: Debating archaeology and the history of early Israel* (pp. 107–116). Brill.

Finkelstein, I. (2010). A great united monarchy? Archaeological and historical perspectives. In R. G. Kratz & H. Spieckermann (Eds.), *One God – One Cult – One Nation* (pp. 3–28). de Gruyter.

Finkelstein, I., & Lipschits, O. (2011). The genesis of Moab: A proposal. *Levant, 43*, 139–152.

Finkelstein, I., & Magen, Y. (1993). *Archaeological survey of the hill country of Benjamin*. Israel Antiquities Authority.

Finkelstein, I., & Na'aman, N. (Eds.). (1994). *From nomadism to monarchy: Archaeological and historical aspects of early Israel*. Yad Izhak Ben-Zvi.

Finkelstein, I., & Perevolotsky, A. (1990). Processes of sedentarization and nomadization in the history of Sinai and the Negev. *Bulletin of the American Schools of Oriental Research, 279*, 67–88.

Finkelstein, I., & Silberman, N. A. (2001). *The bible unearthed: Archaeology's new vision of ancient Israel and the origin of its sacred texts*. Touchstone.

Finkelstein, I., & Silberman, N. A. (2006). *David and Solomon: In Search of the Bible's sacred kings and the roots of the Western tradition*. Simon & Schuster.

Finkelstein, I., Lederman, Z., & Bunimovitz, S. (1997). *Highlands of many cultures: The southern Samaria survey* (Vol. 2 vols). Tel Aviv University.

Finkelstein, I., Koch, I., & Lipschits, O. (2011). The mound on the mount: A possible solution to the "Problem with Jerusalem". *Journal of Hebrew Scriptures, 11*. https://doi.org/10.5508/jhs.2011.v11.a12

Fitzhugh, W. W., Rossabi, M., & Honeychurch, W. (Eds.). (2009). *Genghis Khan and the Mongol empire*. Dino Don/The Mongolian Preservation Foundation and Arctic Studies Center, Smithsonian Institution.

Flannery, K. V. (1972). The cultural evolution of civilizations. *Annual Review of Ecology and Systematics, 3*, 399–426.

Flannery, K. V. (1998). The ground plans of archaic states. In G. M. Feinman & J. Marcus (Eds.), *Archaic states* (pp. 15–58). School of American Research Press.

Fleming, D. E. (2004). *Democracy's ancient ancestors: Mari and early collective governance*. Cambridge University Press.

Fleming, D. E. (2009). Kingship of City and tribe conjoined: Zimri-Lim at Mari. In J. Szuchman (Ed.), *Nomads, tribes, and the state in the ancient Near East* (pp. 227–240). Oriental Institute.

Fowles, S. M. (2002). From social type to social process: Placing "tribe" in a historical framework. In W. A. Parkinson (Ed.), *The archaeology of tribal societies* (pp. 13–33). International Monographs in Prehistory.

Fowles, S. (2018). The evolution of simple society. *Asian Archaeology, 2*, 19–32.

Frachetti, M. D. (2012). Multiregional emergence of mobile pastoralism and nonuniform institutional complexity across Eurasia. *Current Anthropology, 53*(1), 2–38.

Frankel, R., Getzov, N., Aviam, M., & Degani, A. (2001). *Settlement dynamics and regional diversity in ancient upper Galilee: Archaeological survey of upper Galilee*. Israel Antiquities Authority.

Freikman, M., Ben-Shlomo, D., & Garfinkel, Y. (2021). A stamped sealing from middle chalcolithic Tel Tsaf: Implications for the rise of administrative practices in the Levant. *Levant, 53*, 1–12.

Frendo, A. J. (1996). The capabilities and limitations of ancient near eastern nomadic archaeology. *Orientalia, 65*(1), 1–23.

Fried, M. H. (1975). *The notion of tribe*. Cummings Publishing Company.

Gadot, Y. (2019). The Iron I settlement wave in the Samaria highlands and its connection with the urban centers. *Near Eastern Archaeology, 82*(1), 32–41.

Gadot, Y., & Uziel, J. (2017). The monumentality of Iron Age Jerusalem prior to the 8th century BCE. *Tel Aviv, 44*(2), 123–140.

Gal, Z. (1992). *Lower Galilee during the Iron Age*. Eisenbrauns.

Gallay, A. (1989). Logicism: A French view of archaeological theory founded in computational perspective. *Antiquity, 63*, 27–39.

Garfinkel, Y. (2017). The Iron Age City of Khirbet Qeiyafa. In O. Lipshits & A. M. Maeir (Eds.), *The Shephelah during the Iron Age: Recent archaeological studies* (pp. 115–132). Eisenbrauns.

Garfinkel, Y., Streit, K., Ganor, S., & Hasel, M. G. (2012). State formation in Judah: Biblical tradition, modern historical theories and radiometric dates at Khirbet Qeiyafa. *Radiocarbon, 54*, 359–369.

Garfinkel, Y., Kreimerman, I., & Zilberg, P. (2016). *Debating Khirbet Qeiyafa*. Israel Exploration Society.

Garfinkel, Y., Hasel, M. G., Klingbeil, M. G., Kang, H.-G., Choi, G., Chang, S.-Y., Hong, S., Ganor, S., Kreimerman, I., & Bronk Ramsey, C. (2019). Lachish fortifications and state formation in the biblical kingdom of Judah in light of radiometric Datings. *Radiocarbon, 61*, 695–712.

Garfinkle, S. J. (2008). Was the Ur III state bureaucratic? Patrimonialism and bureaucracy in the Ur III period. In S. J. Garfinkle & J. C. Johnson (Eds.), *The growth of an early state in Mesopotamia: Studies in Ur III administration* (pp. 55–61). Consejo Superior de Investigaciones Científicas.

Geertz, C. (1973). *The interpretation of cultures*. Basic Books.

Giddens, A. (1984). *The constitution of society*. Polity Press.

Ginat, H., Meeshly, D., Avner, U., & Langford, B. (2018). Evidence of past flood intensities in the Nahal Amram copper mines. In E. Ben-Yosef (Ed.), *Mining for ancient copper: Essays in memory of Beno Rothenberg* (pp. 188–198). Tel Aviv University.

Giveon, R. (1971). *Les Bédouins Shosu de Documents Égyptien*. Brill.

Glassner, J.-J. (2004). *Mesopotamian chronicles*. SBL.

Gophna, R., & Singer-Avitz, L. (1984). Iron Age I sites the the West of Tel Beer-Sheba. In Z. Herog (Ed.), *Beer-Sheba II: The early Iron Age settlements* (pp. 125–131). Ramot.

Gottwald, N. K. (1979). *The tribes of Yahweh: A sociology of the religion of liberated Israel, 1250–1050 B.C.E.* Orbis.

Graeber, D., & Wengrow, D. (2021). *The dawn of everything: A new history of humanity*. Allen Lane.

Graf, D. F. (2007). In search of Hellenistic Petra. In T. E. Levy, P. M. M. Daviau, R. W. Younker, & M. Shaer (Eds.), *Crossing Jordan: North American contributions to the archaeology of Jordan* (pp. 333–339). Equinox.

Graf, D. F. (2013). Petra and the Nabataeans in the early Hellenistic period: The literary and archaeological evidence. In M. Mouton & S. G. Schmid (Eds.), *Men on the rocks: The formation of Nabataean Petra* (pp. 35–56). Logos Verlag.

Halpern, B. (2001). *David's secret demons: Messiah, murder, traitor, king*. Eerdmans.

Hämäläinen, P. (2008). *The Comanche empire*. Yale University Press.

Hämäläinen, P. (2013). What's in a concept? The kinetic empire of the Comanches. *History and Theory, 52*(1), 81–90.

Hamilakis, Y. (2002). What future for the 'Minoan' past? Re-thinking Minoan archaeology. In Y. Hamilakis (Ed.), *Labyrinth revisited: Rethinking Minoan archaeology* (pp. 2–28). Oxbow.

Hardin, J. W., & Blakeley, J. W. (2019). Land use, regional integration, and political complexity: Understanding the Hesi region as pasturage during Iron Age IIA. *Strata, 37*, 61–94.

Hartshorne, R. (1950). The functional approach in political geography. *Annals of the Association of American Geographers, 40*(2), 95–130.

Hasel, M. G. (1998). *Domination and resistance: Egyptian military activity in the Southern Levant, ca* (pp. 1300–1185). B.C. Brill.

Hawkes, C. (1954). Archeological theory and method: Some suggestions from the Old World. *American Anthropologist, 56*(2), 155–168.

Hayes, C. B. (2015). Biblical claims about Solomon's kingdom in light of Egyptian "three-zone" ideology of territory. In T. E. Levy, T. Schneider, & W. H. C. Propp (Eds.), *Israel's exodus in transdisciplinary perspective* (pp. 503–515). Springer.

Herr, L. G. (2012). Jordan in the Iron I and IIA periods. In G. Galil, A. Gilboa, A. Maeir, & D. Kahn (Eds.), *The ancient Near East in the 12th–10th centuries BCE: Culture and history* (pp. 207–220). Ugarit-Verlag.

Herr, S. A., & Clark, J. A. (2002). Mobility and the organization of prehispanic southwest communities. In W. A. Parkinson (Ed.), *The archaeology of tribal societies* (pp. 123–154). International Monographs in Prehistory.

Hildebrand, E. A. (2013). Is monumentality in the eye of the beholder? Lessons from constructed spaces in Africa. *Azania, 48*(2), 155–172.

Hingley, R. (2013). Colonial and post-colonial archaeologies. In A. Gardner, M. Lake, & U. Soomer (Eds.), *Oxford handbook of archaeological theory (online)*. Oxford University Press. https://doi.org/10.1093/oxfordhb/9780199567942.013.008

Hodder, I. (1985). Postprocessual archaeology. *Advances in Archaeological Method and Theory, 8*, 1–26.

Hodder, I. (1992). *Theory and practice in archaeology*. Routledge.

Homan, M. M. (2002). *To your tents, O Israel! The terminology, function, form, and symbolism of tents in the Hebrew Bible and the ancient Near East*. Brill.

Honeychurch, W. (2013). The nomad as state builder: Historical theory and material evidence from Mongolia. *Journal of World Prehistory, 26*, 283–321.

Honeychurch, W. (2014). Alternative complexities: The archaeology of pastoral nomadic states. *Journal of Archaeological Research, 22*, 277–326.

Honeychurch, W., & Makarewicz, C. A. (2016). The archaeology of pastoral nomadism. *Annual Review Anthropology, 45*, 341–359.

Hutton, J. M. (2006). Mahanaim, Penuel, and Transhumance Routes: Observations on Genesis 32–33 and Judges 8. *Journal of Near Eastern Studies, 65*(3), 161–178.

Hutzli, J. (2011). The meaning of the term ʿîr Dawıd in Samuel and Kings. *Tel Aviv, 38*(2), 167–178.

Ilan, D. (2018). The "conquest" of the highlands in the Iron Age I. In A. Yasur-Landau, E. H. Cline, & Y. M. Rowan (Eds.), *The social archaeology of the Levant* (pp. 283–309). Cambridge University Press.

Jennings, J., & Earle, T. (2016). Urbanization, state formation, and cooperation: A reappraisal. *Current Anthropology, 57*(4), 474–485.

Ji, C.-H. (2012). The early Iron Age II temple at Hirbet ʿAtarus and its architecture and selected cultic objects. In J. Kamlah (Ed.), *Temple building and Temple cult: Architecture and cultic paraphernalia of temples in the Levant (2.–1. Mill. B.C.E.)* (pp. 203–222). Harrassowitz.

Ji, C.-H. (2018). A Moabite sanctuary at Khirbat Ataruz, Jordan: Stratigraphy, findings, and archaeological implications. *Levant, 50*, 173–210.

Ji, C.-H., Bates, R. D., Hawkins, R. K., & Schade, A. (2020). Khirbat ʿAtaruz 2015: A preliminary report. *Andrews University Seminary Studies, 58*, 85–104.

Joffe, A. H. (2018). Defining the state. In C. A. Rollston (Ed.), *Enemies and friends of the state: Ancient prophecy in context* (pp. 3–23). Eisenbrauns.

Johnson, M. (2020). *Archaeological theory: An introduction* (3rd ed.). Wiley.

Khazanov, A. M. (1994). *Nomads and the outside world* (2nd ed.). University of Wisconsin Press.

Kiderlen, M., Bode, M., Hauptmann, A., & Bassiakos, Y. (2016). Tripod cauldrons produced at Olympia give evidence for trade with copper from Faynan (Jordan) to South West Greece, c. 950–750 BCE. *Journal of Archaeological Science Reports, 8*, 303–313.

Killion, T. W. (2013). Nonagricultural cultivation and social complexity: The Olmec, their ancestors, and Mexico's Southern Gulf Coast lowlands. *Current Anthropology, 54*(5), 569–606.

Kim, H. J. (2016). *The Huns*. Routledge.

Kinneir, J. M. (1818). *Journey through Asia Minor, Armenia and Koordistan, in the years 1813 and 1814*. John Murray.

Kleiman, S., Kleiman, A., & Ben-Yosef, E. (2017). Metalworkers' material culture in the early Iron Age Levant: The ceramic assemblage from Site 34 (Slaves' Hill) in the Timna Valley. *Tel Aviv, 44*(2), 232–264.

Kletter, R. (2004). Chronology and united monarchy: A methodological review. *Zeitschrift des Deutschen Palästina-Vereins, 120*(1), 13–54.

Kloner, A. (2001). *Survey of Jerusalem: The Northeastern sector*. Israel Antiquities Authority.

Knabb, K. A., Jones, W. N., Najjar, M., & Levy, T. E. (2014). Patterns of Iron Age mining and settlement in Jordan's Faynan district: The Wadi al-Jariya survey in context. In T. E. Levy, M. Najjar, & E. Ben-Yosef (Eds.), *New insights into the Iron Age archaeology of Edom, Southern Jordan* (Vol. 2, pp. 577–626). Cotsen Institute of Archaeology Press.

Knauf, E. A. (1992). Bedouin and Bedouin states. In D. N. Freedman (Ed.), *Anchor bible dictionary* (Vol. 1, pp. 634–638). Doubleday.

Koehler, L., & Baumgartner, W. (Eds.). (1994). *The Hebrew and Aramaic Lexicon of the old testament* (Rev. Ed.). Brill.

Kohl, P. L. (2007). *The making of Bronze Age Eurasia*. Cambridge University Press.

Krader, L. (1978). The origin of the state among the nomads of Asia. In H. J. Claessen & P. Skalnik (Eds.), *The early state* (pp. 93–107). Mouton.

Kradin, N. N. (2006). Archaeological criteria of civilization. *Social Evolution & History, 5*(1), 88–107.

Kradin, N. N. (2013). Criteria of complexity in evolution: Cross-cultural study in archaeology of prehistory. *Social Evolution & History, 12*(1), 28–50.

Kradin, N. N., Kharinsky, A. V., Baksheeva, S. E., Kovychev, E. V., & Prokopets, S. D. (2016). Archaeology of Genghis Khan empire in Mongolia and Transbaikalia (in Russian). In N. D. Russev (Ed.), *Pax Mongolica and Eurasian Shocks in the 13th–14th centuries* (pp. 17–43). Stratum.

Kramer, C. (Ed.). (1979). *Ethnoarchaeology*. Columbia University Press.

Krause, J. J., Sergi, O., & Weingart, K. (Eds.). (2020). *Saul, Benjamin and the emergence of monarchy in Israel*. SBL Press.

Kristiansen, K. (1984). Ideology and material culture: An archaeological perspective. In M. Spriggs (Ed.), *Marxist perspectives in archaeology* (pp. 72–100). Cambridge University Press.

Kristiansen, K. (2007). The rules of the game: Decentralised complexity and power structures. In S. Kohring & S. Wynne-Jones (Eds.), *Socialising complexity: Approaches to power and interaction in the archaeological record* (pp. 60–75). Oxbow.

Kuper, A. (2005). *The reinvention of primitive society: Transformations of a myth*. Routledge.

Kupper, J.-R. (1957). *Les Nomades de Mésopotamie au temps des rois de Mari*. Société d'Édition Les Belles Lettres.

LaBianca, Ø. (2009). The poly-centric nature of social order in the Middle East: Preliminary reflections from anthropological archaeology. In P. Bienkowski (Ed.), *Studies on Iron Age Moab and neighbouring areas in honour of Michele Daviau* (pp. 1–5). Peeters.

LaBianca, Ø. (2021). Lenses on accumulative cultural production in the southern Levant: Toward a middle-range interpretive methodology. In T. Stordalen & Ø. LaBianca (Eds.), *Levantine entanglements: Cultural productions, long-term changes, and globalizations in the eastern Mediterranean* (pp. 46–77). Equinox.

LaBianca, Ø., & Younker, R. W. (1998). The kingdoms of Ammon, Moab and Edom: The archaeology of Society in Late Bronze/Iron Age Transjordan (ca. 1400–500 BCE). In T. E. Levy (Ed.), *Archaeology of society in the holy land* (pp. 399–415). Leicester University Press.

Lawrence, T. E. (1935). *Seven pillars of wisdom*. Jonathan Cape.

Lehner, M. (2000). Fractal house of Pharaoh: Ancient Egypt as a complex adaptive system, a trial formulation. In T. Kohler & G. Gumerman (Eds.), *Dynamics in human and primate societies* (pp. 275–353). Oxford University Press.

Lemche, N. P. (1985). *Early Israel: Anthropological and historical studies*. Brill.

Levy, T. E. (2009). Pastoral nomads and Iron Age metal production in ancient Edom. In J. Szuchman (Ed.), *Nomads, tribes, and the state in the ancient Near East* (pp. 147–177). Oriental Institute.

Levy, T. E., & Higham, T. (Eds.). (2005). *The bible and radiocarbon dating*. Equinox.
Levy, T. E., Najjar, M., & Ben-Yosef, E. (Eds.). (2014). N*ew insights into the Iron Age archaeology of Edom, Southern Jordan* (2 vols). Cotsen Institute of Archaeology Press.
Livni, J. (2015). Investigation of population growth of ancient Israel. *Ugarit-Forschungen, 46*, 213–134.
Luke, J. T. (1965). *Pastoralism and politics in the Mari period*. Unpublished PhD dissertation, University of Michigan.
MacWhite, E. (1956). On the interpretation of Archeological evidence in historical and sociological terms. *American Anthropologist, 58*(1), 3–25.
Maeir, A. M. (2017a). Philistine Gath after 20 years: Regional perspectives on the Iron Age at Tell es-Safi/Gath. In O. Lipschits & A. M. Maeir (Eds.), *The Shephelah during the Iron Age: Recent archaeological studies* (pp. 133–154). Eisenbrauns.
Maeir, A. M. (2017b). The Tell eṣ-Ṣâfi/Gath archaeological project: Overview. *Near Eastern Archaeology, 80*(4), 212–231.
Maeir, A. M. (2020a). Introduction and overview. In A. M. Maeir & J. Uziel (Eds.), *Tell Es-Safi/Gath II: Exacavations and studies* (pp. 3–52). Zaphon.
Maeir, A. M. (2020b). Memories, myths, and megalithics: Reconsidering the Giants of Gath. *Journal of Biblical Literature, 139*(4), 675–690.
Maeir, A. M., Hitchcock, L. A., & Horwitz, L. K. (2013). On the constitution and transformation of philistine identity. *Oxford Journal of Archaeology, 32*(1), 1–38.
Mahaney, W. C., et al. (2017a). Biostratigraphic evidence relating to the age-old question of Hannibal's invasion of Italy, I: History and geological reconstruction. *Archaeometry, 59*(1), 164–178.
Mahaney, W. C., et al. (2017b). Biostratigraphic evidence relating to the age-old question of Hannibal's invasion of Italy, II: Chemical biomarkers and microbial signatures. *Archaeometry, 59*(1), 179–190.
Marcus, J. (2003). Monumentality in archaic states: Lessons learned from large scale excavations of the past. In J. Papadopoulos & R. Leventhal (Eds.), *Theory and practice in Mediterranean archaeology: Old World and New World perspectives* (pp. 115–134). Cotsen Institute of Archaeology.
Marcus, J. (2008). The archaeological evidence for social evolution. *Annual Review of Anthropology, 37*, 251–266.
Martin, A. (2005). Agents in inter-action: Bruno Latour and agency. *Journal of Archaeological Method and Theory, 12*(4), 283–311.
Martin, M. A. S., & Finkelstein, I. (2013). Iron IIA pottery from the Negev highlands: Petrographic investigation and historical implications. *Tel Aviv, 40*(1), 6–45.
Martin, M. A. S., Eliyahu-Behar, A., Anenburg, M., Goren, Y., & Finkelstein, I. (2014). Iron IIA slag-tempered pottery in the Negev highlands, Israel. *Journal of Archaeological Science, 40*, 3777–3792.
Master, D. M. (2001). State formation theory and the kingdom of ancient Israel. *Journal of Near Eastern Studies, 60*(2), 117–131.
Mazar, A. (1981). Giloh: An early Israelite settlement site near Jerusalem. *Israel Exploration Journal, 31*(1–2), 1–36.
Mazar, A. (2007). The search for David and Solomon: An archaeological perspective. In B. B. Schmidt (Ed.), *The quest for historical Israel: Debating archaeology and the history of early Israel* (pp. 117–139). Brill.
Mazar, A. (2010). Archaeology and the biblical narrative: The case of the united monarchy. In R. G. Kratz & H. Spieckermann (Eds.), *One God – One Cult – One Nation: Archaeological and biblical perspectives* (pp. 29–58). de Gruyter.
McGuire, R. H. (1983). Breaking down cultural complexity: Inequality and heterogeneity. *Advances in Archaeological Method and Theory, 6*, 91–142.
McIntosh, S. K. (1999). Pathways to complexity: An African perspective. In S. K. MacIntosh (Ed.), *Beyond chiefdoms: Pathways to complexity in Africa* (pp. 1–30). Cambridge University Press.

Meir, A. (1988). Nomads and the state: The spatial dynamics of centrifugal and centripetal forces among the Israeli Negev Bedouin. *Political Geography Quaterly, 7*(3), 251–270.

Mendenhall, G. (1962). The Hebrew conquest of Palestine. *Biblical Archaeologist, 25*(3), 66–87.

Miglio, A. E. (2014). *Tribe and state: The dynamics of international politics and the reign of Zimri-lim*. Gorgias Press.

Millard, A. R. (1992). Assyrian involvement in Edom. In P. Bienkowski (Ed.), *Early Edom and Moab: The beginning of the Iron Age in Southern Jordan* (pp. 35–39). J.R. Collis Publications.

Millard, A. R. (2003). The Tell Dan Stele. In W. F. Hallo & K. L. Younger Jr. (Eds.), *The context of scripture, Vol. II: Monumental inscriptions from the biblical world* (pp. 161–162). Brill.

Miller, G. L. (2021). Ritual, labor mobilization, and monumental construction in small-scale societies: The case of Adena and Hopewell in the middle Ohio River valley. *Current Anthropology, 62*(2), 164–197.

Mithen, S. (1989). Evolutionary theory and post-processual archaeology. *American Antiquity, 63*, 483–494.

Moreland, J. (2001). *Archaeology and text*. Duckworth.

Moret, A., & Davy, G. (1926). *From tribe to empire: Social organization among primitives and in the ancient East*. Kegan Paul.

Muniz, A., & Levy, T. E. (2014). Feeding the Iron Age metalworkers at Khirbat en-Nahas Zooarchaeological data. In T. E. Levy, M. Najjar, & E. Ben-Yosef (Eds.), *New insights into the Iron Age archaeology of Edom, Southern Jordan* (Vol. 2, pp. 627–663). Cotsen Institute of Archaeology Press.

Na'aman, N. (1994). The "Conquest of Canaan" in the book of Joshua and in history. In I. Finkelstein & N. Na'aman (Eds.), *From nomadism to monarchy: Archaeological and historical aspects of early Israel* (pp. 218–281). Yad Izhak Ben-Zvi.

Na'aman, N. (2010). Does archaeology really deserve the status of a 'high court' in biblical historical research? In B. Becking & L. Grabbe (Eds.), *Between evidence and ideology: Essays on the history of ancient Israel read at the joint meeting of the Society for Old Testament Study and the Oud Testamentisch Werkgezelschap Lincoln, July 2009* (pp. 165–183). Brill.

Nahashoni, P. (2009). Naḥal Patish: Preliminary report. *Hadashot Arkheologiyot Excavations and Survey in Israel*. 121. https://www.hadashot-esi.org.il/report_detail_eng.aspx?id=1272&mag_id=115

Nelson, B. A. (1995). Complexity, hierarchy, and scale: A controlled comparison between Chaco Canyon, New Mexico, and la Quemada, Zacatecas. *American Antiquity, 60*, 597–618.

O'Shea, J. (1980). Mesoamerica: From village to empire. In A. Sherratt (Ed.), *The Cambridge encyclopedia of archaeology* (pp. 382–390). Cambridge University Press.

Ofer, A. (1993). *The highland of Judah during the biblical period*. Unpublished PhD dissertation, Tel Aviv University.

Osborne, J. F. (2014a). Monuments and monumentality. In J. F. Osborne (Ed.), *Approaching monumentality in archaeology* (pp. 1–19). SUNY Press.

Osborne, J. F. (2014b). Settlement planning and urban symbology in Syro-Anatolian cities. *Cambridge Archaeological Journal, 24*(2), 195–214.

Patterson, T. C. (2003). *Marx's ghost: Conversations with archaeologists*. Berg.

Pauketat, T. R. (2007). *Chiefdoms and other archaeological delusions*. AltaMira Press.

Pearson, J. E. (2011). *Contextualizing the Nabataeans: A critical reassessment of their history and material culture*. Unpublished PhD dissertation, University of California.

Petter, T. D. (2018). Tribes and nomads in the Iron Age Levant. In J. S. Greer, J. W. Hilber, & J. H. Walton (Eds.), *Behind the scenes of the old testament* (pp. 391–395). Baker Academic.

Pioske, D. (2019). The "High Court" of ancient Israel's past: Archaeology, texts, and the question of priority. *The Journal of Hebrew Scriptures, 19*. https://doi.org/10.5508/jhs.2019.v19.a1

Pluciennik, M. (2005). *Social evolution*. Duckworth.

Porter, A. (2012). *Mobile pastoralism and the formation of Near Eastern civilizations*. Cambridge University Press.

Possehl, G. L. (1979). Pastoral nomadism in the Indus civilization: An hypothesis. In M. Taddei (Ed.), *South Asian archaeology 1977* (pp. 537–551). Instituto Universaritario Orientale.
Possehl, G. L. (1998). Sociocultural complexity without the state: The Indus civilization. In G. M. Feinman & J. Marcus (Eds.), *Archaic states* (pp. 261–291). School of American Research Press.
Possehl, G. L. (1999). *Indus age: The beginnings*. University of Pennsylvania Press.
Possehl, G. L. (2002). *The Indus civilization: A contemporary perspective*. AltaMira Press.
Postgate, N. (2013). *Bronze age bureaucracy: Writing and the practice of government in Assyria*. Cambridge University Press.
Potts, D. T. (2014). *Nomadism in Iran: From antiquity to the modern era*. Oxford University Press.
Rainey, A. F. (1975). Notes on some proto-sinaitic inscriptions. *Israel Exploration Journal, 25*(2–3), 106–116.
Rainey, A. F. (2007). Whence came the Israelites and their language? *Israel Exploration Journal, 57*(1), 41–64.
Rainey, A. F., & Notley, R. S. (2014). *The sacred bridge* (2nd ed.). Carta.
Rede, M. (2015). Le palais bedouin a Mari: royaute urbaine et chefferie tribal. In C. Michel (Ed.), *Séminaire d'Histoire et d'Archéologie Des Mondes Orientaux (SHAMO), 2010–2013: De La Maison à La Ville Dans l'Orient Ancient* (pp. 139–147). CNRS.
Renfrew, C., & Bahn, P. (2019). *Archaeology: Theories, methods, and practice* (8th ed.). Thames & Hudson.
Ribeiro, D. (1968). *The civilizational process*. Smithsonian Institution Press.
Riehl, S. (2006). Nomadism, pastoralism and transhumance in the archaeobotanical record – Examples and methodological problems. In S. R. Hauser (Ed.), *Die Sichtbarkeit von Nomaden Und Saisonaler Besiedlung in Der Archäologie. Multidisziplinäre Annäherungen an Ein Methodisches Problem* (pp. 105–125). Orientwissenschaftliches Zentrum.
Rosen, S. A. (2017). *Revolutions in the desert: The rise of mobile pastoralism in the Southern Levant*. Routledge.
Rosen, S. A., & Lehmann, G. (2010). Hat das biblische Israel einen nomadischen Ursprung? Kritische Beobachtungen aus der Perspektive der Archäologie und Kulturanthropologie. *Welt des Orients, 40*(2), 160–189.
Ross, J. C., & Steadman, S. R. (2017). *Ancient complex societies*. Routledge.
Routledge, B. (2000). The politics of Mesha: Segmented identities and state formation in Iron Age Moab. *Journal of the Economic and Social History of the Orient, 43*(3), 221–256.
Routledge, B. (2004). *Moab in the Iron Age: Hegemony, polity, archaeology*. University of Pennsylvania Press.
Rowlands, M. (1984). Objectivity and subjectivity in archaeology. In M. Spriggs (Ed.), *Marxist perspectives in archaeology* (pp. 108–113). Cambridge University Press.
Rowlands, M. (1989). A question of complexity. In D. Miller (Ed.), *Domination and resistance* (pp. 28–39). Unwin Hyman.
Rowton, M. B. (1976). Dimorphic structure and the tribal elite. In *Al-Bahit: Festschrift Joseph Henninger* (pp. 219–257). Verlag des Anthropos-Instituts.
Sahlins, M. D. (1960). Evolution: Specific and general. In M. D. Sahlins & E. R. Service (Eds.), *Evolution and culture* (pp. 12–44). University of Michigan Press.
Said, E. (2003). *Orientalism*. Penguin.
Sanders, W. T., & Price, B. J. (1968). *Mesoamerica: The evolution of a civilization*. Random House.
Sapir-Hen, L., & Ben-Yosef, E. (2013). The introduction of domestic camels to the Southern Levant: Evidence from the Aravah valley. *Tel Aviv, 40*(2), 277–285.
Sapir-Hen, L., & Ben-Yosef, E. (2014). The socioeconomic status of Iron Age metalworkers: Animal economy in the 'Slaves' Hill, Timna, Israel. *Antiquity, 88*, 775–790.
Sapir-Hen, L., Lernau, O., & Ben-Yosef, E. (2018). The diet of ancient metalworkers: The late Bronze and early Iron Ages in the Arabah Valley (Timna and Feynan). In E. Ben-Yosef (Ed.), *Mining for ancient copper: Essays in memory of Beno Rothenberg* (pp. 64–80). Eisenbrauns/ Tel Aviv University.

Sassaman, K. E. (2004). Complex hunter–gatherers in evolution and history: A North American perspective. *Journal of Archaeological Research, 12*, 227–280.

Scheidel, W. (2013). Studying the state. In W. Scheidel & P. Fibiger Bang (Eds.), *The Oxford handbook of the state in the ancient Near East and Mediterranean* (pp. 5–58). Oxford University Press.

Schiffer, M. B. (1996). *Formation processes of the archaeological record*. University of Utah Press.

Schloen, J. D. (2001). *The house of the father as fact and symbol: Patrimonialism in Ugarit and the ancient Near East*. Eisenbrauns.

Schloen, J. D. (2017). Economic and political implications of raising the date for the disappearance of walled towns in the early Bronze Age Southern Levant. In F. Höflmayer (Ed.), *The late third millennium in the ancient Near East: Chronology, 14C and climate change* (pp. 59–72). University of Chicago.

Sergi, O. (2017). The emergence of Judah as a political entity between Jerusalem and Benjamin. *Zeitschrift des Deutschen Palästina-Vereins, 133*(1), 1–23.

Sergi, O. (2020). Saul, David, and the formation of the Israelite monarchy: Revisiting the historical and literary context of 1 Samuel 9–2 Samuel 5. In J. J. Krause, O. Sergi, & K. Weingart (Eds.), *Saul, Benjamin and the emergence of monarchy in Israel* (pp. 57–91). SBL Press.

Service, E. R. (1971). *Primitive social organization* (2nd ed.). Random House.

Service, E. R. (1975). *Origins of the state and civilization*. Norton.

Shaffer, J. G. (1982). Harappan culture: A reconsideration. In G. L. Possehl (Ed.), *Harappan civilization:A contemporary perspective* (pp. 41–50). Oxford and IBH/The American Institute of Indian Studies.

Shanks, M., & Tilley, C. (1987). *Social theory and archaeology*. University of New Mexico Press.

Silvia Castillo, J. (2005). Nomadism through the ages. In D. C. Snell (Ed.), *A companion to the ancient Near East* (pp. 126–140). Blackwell.

Sinopoli, C. M. (1994). Monumentality and mobility in Mughal capitals. *Asian Perspectives, 33*(2), 293–308.

Smelik, K. A. D. (2003). The inscription of King Mesha. In W. W. Hallo & K. L. Younger Jr. (Eds.), *The context of scripture: Monumental inscriptions from the biblical world* (pp. 137–138). Brill.

Smith, A. T. (2003). *The political landscape: Constellations of authority in early complex polities*. University of California Press.

Sneath, D. (2007a). The decentralised state: Nomads, complexity and sociotechnical systems in inner Asia. In P. L. Kohl & S. Wynne-Jones (Eds.), *Socialising complexity: Approaches to power and interaction in the archaeological record* (pp. 228–244). Oxbow.

Sneath, D. (2007b). *The headless state: Aristocratic order, Kinship Society & misrepresentations of Nomadic inner Asia*. Columbia University Press.

Souvatzi, S. (2007). Social complexity is not the same as hierarchy. In S. Kohring & S. Wynne-Jones (Eds.), *Socialising complexity: Approaches to power and interaction in the archaeological record* (pp. 37–59). Oxbow.

Sparks, K. L. (2009). Israel and the nomads of ancient Palestine. In G. N. Knoppers & K. A. Ristau (Eds.), *Community identity in Judean historiography* (pp. 9–26). Eisenbrauns.

Stager, L. E. (1985). The archaeology of the family in ancient Israel. *Bulletin of the American Schools of Oriental Research, 260*, 1–35.

Stager, L. E. (2003). The patrimonial kingdom of Solomon. In W. G. Dever & S. Gitin (Eds.), *Symbiosis, symbolism, and the power of the past: Canaan, ancient Israel, and their neighbors from the late Bronze Age through Roman Palaestina* (pp. 63–74). Eisenbrauns.

Stein, G. J. (1998). Heterogeneity, power, and political economy: Some current research issues in the archaeology of Old World complex societies. *Journal of Archaeological Research, 6*, 1–44.

Steiner, M. L. (2014). Moab during the Iron Age II period. In M. L. Steiner & A. E. Killebrew (Eds.), *The Oxford handbook of the archaeology of the Levant: C. 8000–332 BCE* (pp. 770–781). Oxford University Press.

Sukenik, N., Iluz, D., Amar, Z., Varvak, A., Workman, V., Shamir, O., & Ben-Yosef, E. (2017). Early evidence (late 2nd millennium BCE) of plant-based dyeing of textiles from Timna, Israel. *PLoS One, 12*. https://doi.org/10.1371/journal.pone.0179014

Sukenik, N., Iluz, D., Amar, Z., Varvak, A., Shamir, O., & Ben-Yosef, E. (2021). Early evidence of royal purple dyed textile from Timna Valley (Israel). *PLoS One, 16*. https://doi.org/10.1371/journal.pone.0245897

Swayam, S. (2006). *Invisible people: Pastoral life in proto-historic Gujarat*. BAR.

Tainter, J. S. (1988). *The collapse of complex societies*. Cambridge University Press.

Thomas, Z. (2018). A matter of interpretation: On methodology and the archaeology of the united monarchy. *Archaeology and Text, 2*, 25–51.

Thomas, Z. (2019a). *A patrimonial model of the united monarchy of ancient Israel*. Unpublished PhD dissertation, Macquarie University.

Thomas, Z. (2019b). Polycentrism and the terminology of polity in early Israel. *Bible Lands e-Review, S2*, 1–14.

Thomas, Z. (2021). On the archaeology of 10th century BCE Israel and the idea of the 'state'. *Palestine Exploration Quaterly, 153*(3), 244–257.

Thomas, Z. (n.d.). *This house that I have built: The patrimonial kingdom of David and Solomon*. SBL Press.

Thomas, Z. (2022). The political history of Megiddo in the early Iron Age and the ambiguities of evidence. *Journal of Ancient Near Eastern History, 9*(1), 69–94.

Thucydides. (2013). *The war of the Peloponnesians and the Athenians* (J. Mynott, Ed.). Cambridge University Press.

Toynbee, A. J. (1946). *A study of history: Abridgement of volumes I–VI*. Oxford University Press.

Trigger, B. G. (1974). The archaeology of government. *World Archaeology, 6*(1), 95–106.

Trigger, B. G. (1980). Archaeology and the image of the American Indian. *American Antiquity, 45*, 662–676.

Trigger, B. G. (1990). Monumental architecture: A thermodynamic explanation of symbolic behaviour. *World Archaeology, 22*(2), 119–132.

Trigger, B. G. (2003). *Understanding early civilisations*. Cambridge University Press.

Trigger, B. G. (2004). Settlement patterns in the postmodern world: A study of monumental architecture in early civilizations. In L. Vishnyatsky, A. Kovalev, & O. Scheglova (Eds.), *The archaeologist: Detective and thinker* (pp. 237–248). St. Petersberg University Press.

Trigger, B. G. (2006). *A History of Archaeological Thought* (2nd ed). Cambridge University Press.

Ur, J. (2014). Households and the emergence of cities in ancient Mesopotamia. *Cambridge Archaeological Journal, 24*(2), 249–268.

Ussishkin, D. (2003). Solomon's Jerusalem: The text and the facts on the ground. In A. G. Vaughn & A. E. Killebrew (Eds.), *Jerusalem in the Bible and archaeology: The first temple period* (pp. 103–116). SBL.

Uziel, J., & Shai, I. (2007). Iron Age Jerusalem: Temple-palace, Capital City. *Journal of the American Oriental Society, 127*(2), 161–170.

Vaelske, V., Bode, M., & Loeben, C. E. (2019). Early Iron Age Copper Trail between Wadi Arabah and Egypt during the 21st dynasty: First results from Tanis, ca. 1000 BC. *Zeitschrift für Orient-Archäologie, 12*, 184–203.

van der Steen, E. J. (2004). *Tribes and territories in transition*. Peeters.

van der Steen, E. (2009). Tribal societies in the nineteenth century: A model. In J. Szuchman (Ed.), *Nomads, tribes, and the state in the ancient Near East* (pp. 105–117). Oriental Institute.

van der Steen, E. (2013). *Near Eastern tribal societies in the nineteenth century*. Equinox.

van Driel, G. (2001). On villages. In W. H. van Soldt, J. G. Dercksen, N. J. C. Kouwenberg, & T. J. H. Krispijn (Eds.), *Veenhof anniversary volume: Studies presented to Klaas R. Veenhof on the occasion of his sixty-fifth birthday* (pp. 103–118). Nederlands Instituut voor het Nabije Oosten.

Ward, W. W. (1972). The Shasu "Bedouin": Notes on a recent publication. *Journal of the Economic and Social History of the Orient, 15*(1–2), 35–60.

Weber, M. (1978). In G. Roth & C. Wittich (Eds.), *Economy and society: An outline of interpretative sociology*. University of California Press.

Weippert, M. (1971). *The settlement of the Israelite tribes in Palestine*. SCM Press.

Wenke, R. J. (1981). Explaining the evolution of cultural complexity: A review. *Advances in Archaeological Method and Theory, 4*, 79–127.

Whallon, R. (1982). Comments on "explanation". In C. Renfrew & S. Shennan (Eds.), *Ranking, resource and exchange: Aspects of the archaeology of European society* (pp. 155–158). Cambridge University Press.

White, L. A. (1959). The concept of culture. *American Anthropologist, 61*(2), 227–251.

Wilkinson, T. J. (2000). Regional approaches to Mesopotamian archaeology: The contribution of archaeological surveys. *Journal of Archaeological Research, 8*, 219–267.

Wobst, H. M. (1978). The Archaeo-ethnology of hunter-gatherers or the tyranny of the ethnographic record in archaeology. *American Antiquity, 43*(2), 303–309.

Workman, V. (2016). *The fabric of copper production: The textile and cordage artifacts from Iron Age Timna*. Unpublished MA thesis, Tel Aviv University.

Yahalom-Mack, N., & Eliyahu-Behar, A. (2015). The transition from Bronze to Iron in Canaan: Chronology, technology, and context. *Radiocarbon, 57*, 285–305.

Yahalom-Mack, N., & Segal, I. (2018). The origin of the copper used in Canaan during the late bronze/iron age transition. In E. Ben-Yosef (Ed.), *Mining for ancient copper: Essays in memory of Beno Rothenberg* (pp. 313–331). Tel Aviv University/Eisenbrauns.

Yahalom-Mack, N., Galili, E., Segal, I., Eliyahu-Behar, A., Boaretto, E., Shilstein, S., & Finkelstein, I. (2014). New insights into Levantine copper trade: Analysis of ingots from the Bronze and Iron Ages in Israel. *Journal of Archaeological Science, 45*, 159–177.

Yahalom-Mack, N., Martin, M. A. S., Tirosh, O., Erel, Y., & Finkelstein, I. (2015). Lead isotope analysis of slag-tempered Negev Highlands pottery. *Antiguo Oriente, 13*, 83–98.

Yoffee, N. (1979). The decline and rise of Mesopotamian civilization: An ethnoarchaeological perspective on the evolution of social complexity. *American Antiquity, 44*(1), 5–35.

Yoffee, N. (1993). Too many chiefs? (Or, safe texts for the '90s). In N. Yoffee & A. Sherratt (Eds.), *Archaeological theory: Who sets the agenda?* (pp. 60–78). Cambridge University Press.

Yoffee, N. (2005). *Myths of the archaic state*. Cambridge University Press.

Younger, K. L., Jr. (2016). *A political history of the Arameans: From their origins to the end of their polities*. SBL.

Younker, R. W. (1997). Moabite social structure. *Biblical Archaeologist, 60*(4), 237–248.

Zertal, A., Bar, S., & Mirkam, N. (2004–2022). *The Manasseh Hill Country survey* (7 vols). Brill.

Zucconi, L. M. (2007). From the wilderness of Zin alongside Edom: Edomite territory in the eastern Negev during the eighth-sixth centuries B.C.E. In S. Malena & D. Miano (Eds.), *Milk and honey—Essays on ancient Israel and the Bible in appreciation of the Judaic Studies Program at the University of California, San Diego* (pp. 241–256). Eisenbrauns.

History Without Texts: Interdisciplinary Interpretive Methods for Understanding the Early Iron Age

Sarah Malena

Abstract The minimalist-maximalist debates in the 1990s and early 2000s shook the conventional foundations for historical inquiry of the southern Levant's early Iron Age. Scholars typically relied on biblical texts such as 1 and 2 Samuel to understand the period, but the debates called into question both the reliability of the biblical material and the underlying assumptions and methods of scholars who engaged with the texts. The biblical texts have played a significant role in research, in part because other historical evidence is scarce. Compared to the Late Bronze and later Iron Age, there are very few inscriptions that date to the early Iron Age and no monumental inscriptions until the ninth century BCE. Without the monuments, scholars argued, there were no states and little complexity. Levy's work in southern Jordan's Faynan region complicated this equation at a critical point in scholarly debates. The massive copper processing center at Khirbat en-Nahas defied the prevailing understanding of the region's social organization and resource exploitation prior to the era of Iron Age kings boasting of their exploits on steles. Even without contemporary historical documentation about consequential early Iron Age sites, this essay explores approaches that allow for new interpretive opportunities. A historical approach in conjunction with anthropological analytical frameworks enriches our understanding of the organization and leadership of societies that either did not produce written records or whose texts did not survive.

Keywords History of Southern Levant · Early Iron Age · Inscriptions · Hebrew Bible · Kingship in Early Iron Age · Elite culture

S. Malena (✉)
St. Mary's College of Maryland, St. Marys City, MD, USA
e-mail: slmalena@smcm.edu

© The Author(s), under exclusive license to Springer Nature Switzerland AG 2023
E. Ben-Yosef, I. W. N. Jones (eds.), *"And in Length of Days Understanding" (Job 12:12): Essays on Archaeology in the Eastern Mediterranean and Beyond in Honor of Thomas E. Levy*, Interdisciplinary Contributions to Archaeology, https://doi.org/10.1007/978-3-031-27330-8_23

1 Introduction

The main title of this essay bluntly states the reality that any historian of the southern Levant's early Iron Age faces. Despite mounting archaeological evidence that the centuries after the end of the Late Bronze Age were full of dramatic social and political change, historians have extremely little in the way of contemporary historical accounts to help us understand the period. Biblical narratives, such as the books of Samuel and Kings, while purporting to recount a detailed history of the era, cannot be relied on in toto because of complex compositional and redaction processes that shaped the texts over centuries. The region lacks lengthy epigraphic sources prior to the ninth century, and most written records from the eleventh and tenth centuries BCE consist of just a few letters making up a name or name formula on small objects. Without comprehensive, contemporary narrative accounts or monumental inscriptions—which are not attested as local products before the mid-ninth century BCE—the historian appears to be significantly disadvantaged or even irrelevant.

This essay explores some of the more significant challenges that have faced researchers of the ancient southern Levant. Despite the seemingly incompatible evidence among inscribed objects, biblical texts, and archaeological remains, I propose that some analytical frameworks, namely elite interaction spheres, allow for consideration of a diversity of evidence and facilitate a reconstruction of how elite leadership impacted the era. Critical to this perspective is an interdisciplinary approach because of the limitations in our evidence. A text-based focus provides an important perspective for new interpretation, but it is also necessary to work with a variety of sources of information and critical perspectives if we want to refine our understanding of early Iron Age histories and societies. Investigating this period will continue to be a dynamic enterprise as new analytical techniques are introduced into archaeological research and historians and biblical scholars continue to challenge previous interpretations from new perspectives.

1.1 The "Minimalist" Critique

The problem of investigating so-called "dark" periods is not new to today's researchers and is not exclusive to the southern Levant, but scholars' approaches to the problem have changed dramatically since the late twentieth century CE. The positivism and uncritical reliance on biblical sources that was characteristic of earlier scholarship received a thorough critique in the last decades of the twentieth century. During this time, scholars became more stringent in limiting historical reconstruction based on later sources, especially the Hebrew Bible, after academic debates called into question many traditional epistemological anchors, such as the reliability of biblical histories or "Solomonic" architecture in the region. The debates, commonly referred to as "minimalist" versus "maximalist," have their origins in the 1970s in the form of a critique of biblical scholarship regarding the use of patriarchal narratives in Genesis for historical inquiry (Thompson, 1974; Van Seters, 1975). By the late 1980s and throughout the 1990s, scrutiny centered on scholars' uncritical reliance on the biblical presentations of a United Monarchy of David and Solomon. The critique demanded that histories of the tenth century be rewritten and that archaeological anchors based in biblical accounts be reexamined. Israel Finkelstein's radical adjustment to Iron Age chronologies, in which he proposed lowering the absolute dates of archaeological stratigraphy in the region approximately a century, has had the most sweeping impact (for the initial proposal, see Finkelstein, 1996, see also 2005a; Finkelstein & Piasetzky, 2011). The consequences of the proposal reached beyond southern Levantine sites and initiated a reassessment of archaeology-based chronologies throughout the eastern Mediterranean (Fantalkin, 2001).

The so-called "minimalist" critique and Finkelstein's Low Chronology kicked off new interpretative approaches, both in reaction to and in embrace of these perspectives. In archaeological circles Amiḥai Mazar spearheaded a counter to Finkelstein in the form of the Modified Conventional Chronology, a more moderate reassessment of stratigraphy and absolute chronology (Mazar, 2005, 2011). Further refinements are increasingly nuanced especially in recognition of regional variation (e.g., Herzog & Singer-Avitz, 2004, 2006; Katz & Faust, 2014; Kleiman et al., 2019; Thomas, 2021). In biblical scholarship, it has become much more common that textual traditions are understood first and foremost as later idealizations or cultural memories and that early Iron Age material remains cannot be reliably interpreted vis-a-vis biblical texts. The shift is evident across historians' works and historically-oriented biblical scholarship of the last twenty years (e.g., Liverani, 2005; Miller & Hayes, 2006; Pioske, 2015; Wilson, 2017). The particular impact for a historical-critical approach to biblical texts describing early Iron Age states, namely the books of Samuel and Kings, has been a marginalization of history of the eleventh and tenth centuries. For example, if the biblical texts are unreliable concerning early Iron Age figures such as David or Solomon, one's focus must necessarily be on the *legacy* of such figures or on the later periods that were critical in the formation of their stories (e.g., Torijano, 2002; Finkelstein & Silberman, 2006; Kalimi, 2018). Nevertheless, biblical scholarship has persisted with fruitful studies involving textual, source, and redaction criticism, as well as epigraphic study, that has implications for historical questions about the early centuries of the Iron Age (e.g., Halpern, 2001; Sanders, 2009; Robker, 2012; Richelle, 2016a, b).

1.2 Khirbat en-Nahas and the Scholarly Climate

The high-profile publication of the initial results at Khirbat en-Nahas arrived at a critical point in these scholarly debates. In 2004, Levy, et al.'s "Reassessing the Chronology of Biblical Edom: New Excavations and 14C Dates from Khirbat en-Nahas (Jordan)" announced that the site, with its extensive copper processing operation, was active from the eleventh through ninth centuries BCE. The publication also suggested that a local polity, likely related to or influential in some way on the later highland Edomite kingdom, was responsible for the complexity at the site. In addition to the debates about the historicity of biblical texts, which had implications for interpreting the existence of kingdoms in the tenth century, the findings engaged other critical issues, including the increased use of radiocarbon dating for anchoring stratigraphic relationships to absolute chronologies and the identification and classification of social complexity. The scale of the site, especially in an early Iron Age chronological context, defied the prevailing understanding of the region's social organization prior to the era of later Iron Age kings and the arrival of the resource hungry Neo-Assyrian empire.

Critical responses to the initial publication highlight the scholarly tension of the moment. Finkelstein quickly published an interpretation of the new findings in *Tel Aviv* (Finkelstein, 2005b). He concluded his article by acknowledging that the remains at Khirbat en-Nahas were indeed important for understanding copper production, but also stated "[t]hey do not provide evidence for early, 10th century BCE state formation in Edom"; rather they "contribute to a better understanding of the Tel Masos chiefdom of the late Iron I and early Iron IIA" (Finkelstein, 2005b, p. 123). He also asserted that scholars should continue to look to Neo-Assyrian influence to understand changes in state-level complexity in the region—in effect casting doubt on the absolute dating in the Khirbat en-Nahas report and the potential for local innovation and complexity in southern Jordan. Similarly, exchanges in later volumes of *Antiquity* between Levy et al., and Eveline van der Steen and Piotr Bienkowski were especially heated (Levy et al., 2006; van der Steen & Bienkowski, 2006). The tension evident in these debates rested in a prevailing notion that there simply were not complex societies east of the Jordan Valley and in the Arabah during eleventh to ninth centuries. For those who took issue with the Khirbat en-Nahas report, Levy et al. appeared to be discussing complex resource exploitation that belonged to another time and place, not to the early Iron Age and the polity traditionally known as Edom. An important foundation for this understanding was the fact that the main archaeological evidence for an Edomite polity rested on the excavations of the region's highland sites, especially Tawilan and Busayra, which date to later in the Iron Age (Bennett & Bienkowski, 1995; Bienkowski & Balla, 2002). These results were influential for the understanding that an Edomite state was a late Iron Age, highland phenomenon.

2 Analytical Frameworks

2.1 *Social Organization and Political Complexity*

Differing understandings of social organization and political complexity are at the core of many disputes regarding the early Iron Age. In order to account for copper industry on the scale now known at Khirbat en-Nahas, one might expect a state or polity, but the Faynan lacked the presumed hallmarks of statehood (e.g., urban settlements, defensive architecture and fortifications, royal complexes and monumental architecture, or evidence of bureaucracy; for recent discussion of the challenges in defining and identifying states, see Joffe, 2018 and discussion and sources below). Although there is the well-known four-chambered gate and some sizeable structures, the site's overwhelming character is industrial. Consequentially for some scholars, the site did not produce written evidence of administrative practices, such as state-sponsored writing.

During the height of the "minimalist-maximalist" debates, the absence of writing became a critical issue in the determination of social and political complexity, a prerequisite for the label "state" or "kingdom." This emphasis stemmed from the influence of David Jamieson-Drake's 1991 book, *Scribes and Schools in Monarchic Judah*. A particular distillation of the book's thesis focused on the necessity of administrative writing for complex Iron Age states in the region. Supporters of this view declared that we could not posit the complexity of kingdoms in regions where such evidence of scribal institutions was not present; for how can one have a kingdom without scribes? No examples of the type of writing required by Jamieson-Drake's thesis are known in the eleventh and tenth centuries. As is often observed, the earliest southern Levantine monumental inscriptions, the Tel Dan and Mesha steles, date to the mid-ninth century and were not the product of Israelite or Judean scribes.

Scholars have long struggled with how to express the social and political organization of the region even during the periods when inscriptions attest to an institution of kingship. The search for appropriate models and language is evident during the entirety of the minimalist-maximalist debate years as reflections on the problem demonstrate (e.g., Master, 2001; Kletter, 2004; Routledge, 2004), and it continues to the present. Especially for the territories east of the Jordan River Valley, there are not lengthy periods of urban development or classic evidence of centralized states in the archaeological remains of the Iron Age, but language and imagery of kingship is evident in many Iron Age sources. Mesha's inscription, for example, states unequivocally that he was the king of Moab, that he succeed his father, the previous king, and that he directed key projects fitting of our modern notions of state-level complexity: building programs and care for state projects such as temples, fortifications, palace complexes, water supply systems, military campaigns, definition of territory, and of course, the documentation of these acts on a monument. Despite this evidence, researchers have sought alternative terminologies for states whose subsistence base was pastoral nomadic and where regional organization was not strongly centralized. Terminology such as "tribal kingdoms" (LaBianca & Younker, 1998), "complex chiefdoms," or "archaic state" (Levy et al., 2014a, p. 992) illustrate the difficulty scholars have faced fitting these societies into traditional characterizations. In contrast, Bruce Routledge's "hegemony" (2004) or Benjamin Porter's "communities" (2013) represent efforts to break from definitions associated with the social evolutionary framework. In yet another tack, Zachary Thomas advocates for retaining the language of the Iron Age societies (e.g., "king" and "kingdom") but without imposing assumptions stemming from modern concepts of the state (2021).

2.2 Pitfalls of Positive Evidence

The preference for positive evidence in our efforts to understand the early Iron Age is understandably grounded in the basic methods of historians and archaeologists. Despite the frequency with which the caveat "absence of evidence is not evidence of absence" is repeated, however, absence as evidence has been influential in the analysis of the age. The debates regarding writing and statehood are but one example. Recently Erez Ben-Yosef has highlighted another, an intellectual blind spot caused by researchers' architectural bias when assessing archaeological remains and describing complexity (2019, 2020). Similar to a preference for architectural proof in archaeology, there is a tendency (among historians, text scholars, and archaeologists) to work within an interpretive framework of known figures. Porter's critical review of the state of Levantine archaeological and historical research offers a similar critique. He notes, "Regardless of their intellectual position, however, all scholars broadly share a commitment to culture historical research paradigms in which archaeological evidence is used to narrate the histories of groups whose identities have been established a priori by extant written sources" (Porter, 2016, p. 376).

In terms of a political history of the early Iron Age, this preference results in the perpetuation of assumptions about ethnicities, identities, polities, and leadership that are rooted in historical evidence of the later Iron Age. Reconstructions rely heavily on known entities, rosters of states, monarchs, and assumptions about regional affairs. When a new structure, industrial complex, inscription, or other uncommon object is discovered, it is not long before an interpretation relating the new find to known names comes along, both among scholars and in popular media (e.g., Selk, 2018). The tendency is based in the assumption that all critical players and patterns are currently known to us, but it limits interpretive possibilities. In a period of limited writing, decentralized power, social upheaval, and considerable demographic change, we should assume rather that the chance of a new discovery being linked to a known entity would be quite small. Those early Iron Age figures whose epigraphic records did not survive, who did not commission scribes, or whose careers were not retained in cultural memory far less often receive consideration in historical reconstruction.

The Hebrew Bible plays a role in this tendency as well. The obvious examples are David and Solomon, whose names have been applied to countless features in archaeological remains and whose reputations absorbed the accomplishments of other figures (e.g., David receiving credit for the defeat of a Philistine warrior; Halpern, 2001, pp. 6–8). Even in efforts to deemphasize the biblical bias that favors a Davidic dynasty and Jerusalem-based power, the biblical record remains a resource for alternative candidates. It contains a wealth of names: places, people, and states. Somewhat ironically, the Bible influences the work of those who critique as well as those who favor the use of the biblical texts for historical questions. As will be evident from the discussion below, I maintain there is valuable information in the biblical record. The aim of the present critique is not to dismiss the biblical texts but to continue to think critically about their influence in reconstructions.

2.3 Elites in the Early Iron Age

In an effort to examine early Iron Age societies without extensive historical records, this discussion focuses on elites, a group whose activities tend to be accessible even with limited archaeological and historical evidence. For this period, the most conspicuous evidence comes from prestige material culture. Short possession inscriptions, imported vessels from the Aegean, feasting practices, and trade in Arabah copper via Mediterranean networks are a few examples of exceptional activities that are firmly established for the era. Aside from inscribed objects, these examples are also notable for their association with individuals and locations that are largely anonymous historically.

To provide an interpretive framework for the evidence (material and written), I rely on intercultural interaction models rooted in anthropological and archaeological investigations (for a larger-scale application of this approach, see Malena forthcoming). The concept of "interaction spheres" was first proposed by Joseph Caldwell to explain the appearance of shared cultural elements across distinct prehistoric North American sites, ranging from what is today the American Midwest to the Southeast (Caldwell, 1964; see also Struever, 1964). Caldwell proposed that the autonomous sites were connected by spheres of interaction–especially involving trade networks–through which disparate communities not only exchanged goods but also shared symbolic systems. Although based in analysis of North American cultures, Caldwell's idea has been applied to prehistoric Mesopotamia (Stein, 2010; Yoffee, 1994). In Gil Stein's application of the model to Ubaid cultural influences, he observes that the interaction sphere model does not require that subjects fit into a core-periphery hierarchy or other preconceived power relationships. In addition, the interaction sphere approach avoids overlooking local variation and innovation (Stein, 2010). These are attractive advantages for examining the early Iron Age southern Levant, where local distinction is prevalent in the archaeological record.

A complementary approach to Caldwell's interactions spheres comes from Mesoamerican archaeologists Edward Schortman and Patricia Urban. They employ a concept of "salient identities," which they define as "an affiliation or set of affiliations which are used more commonly than others and whose members, as a result, share a strong feeling of common purpose and support" (Schortman, 1989; Schortman & Urban, 1987). Schortman elaborates on this concept and describes a chain reaction that links identity, interaction activities, and societal change: local elites who are able to gain access to nonlocal goods, create the demand for interregional interaction. The interaction supports the development of a salient identity among participants that then solidifies the elites' role in the exchange network. The development of an elite group of exchange partners separates the elites from other members of their own communities and, despite their shared interests with their elite community, also creates competition and even warfare within the exchange network (1989, pp. 59–61).

By combining these approaches, we have an interpretive framework that supports exploration of the people involved in early Iron Age exchange systems and how their involvement may have impacted local and regional changes. In the explorations below, I demonstrate that this approach is fruitful with a variety of types of evidence including epigraphic, textual, and archaeological examples. In each of these types we can identify aspects of elite culture and interaction. I argue that rather than focus on kings and centralization, which would result in the absence-of-evidence pitfall, we should turn our attention to elites and resource control. This focus bears fruit and allows for a reconstruction of elite roles in early Iron Age societies.

3 Documents, Kings, and Polities

Because the earliest monumental inscriptions from Iron Age, southern Levantine kings date to the mid-ninth century, which is at the end of the period in question, the examples below draw from diverse sources: epigraphic, archaeological, and literary, and represent a range of locations and social organization. The interaction frameworks just described create a meeting point among what would normally be considered incompatible evidence, examples that are environmentally and politically distinct, and in the case of the biblical material, frequently more literary than historical. Nevertheless, these examples help to establish a proposal for leadership and interactions during the early Iron Age.

3.1 Byblos (and Egypt)

As points of comparison and reference, I begin with some brief observations regarding the rulers of Byblos, especially in relation to their Egyptian contemporaries. The purpose of such an excursion is to illustrate some expressions of leadership that conform to expectations for kingship and to note the difference among rulers who exhibited these qualities. Based on the limited information about these kings, their status was defined, at least in part, by their engagement in exchange networks and their demonstration of elite culture.

On the surface, Byblian kings of this era seem a far cry from their southern Levantine counterparts. Notably for the present conversation, they commissioned inscriptions: Ittobaʿal's inscription on the sarcophagus for his father, Aḥiram, and dedicatory inscriptions for the city's patron goddess from the kings Abibaʿal, Yeḥimilk, and Elibaʿal (Gibson, 1982, pp. 12–24). From the texts themselves, our first impressions of these figures seem to confirm conventional notions of kingship: they called themselves *mlk*, "king," typically emphasized dynastic lines, and supported local institutions like sanctuaries and scribes. They also engaged in long-distance exchange, or at least enjoyed being on the receiving end of it.

Two of these kings, Abibaʿal and Elibaʿal, made an exceptional show of this exchange by placing their messages on statues of Egyptian kings, their presumed contemporaries Shoshenq I and Osorkon I, respectively. The Byblian kings engaged in the same elite behavior of employing scribes to document their status and assert their legitimacy through these objects, but they did so on the previously inscribed monuments. It is possible that the Byblians were not in command of the resources necessary for constructing their own statuary and instead improvised through the appropriation of the Egyptian kings' dedications. Alternatively (or additionally) the Egyptian monuments may have been especially useful as a boost to the Byblians kings' prestige and a hearkening back to their Bronze Age predecessors' history of relations. In either case, there is a significant contrast in the material expressions of power and kingship between the evidence of Abibaʿal's reign and Shoshenq's or between Elibaʿal's and Osorkon's. (Although, admittedly, the evidence from the royal burials at Tanis are incomparable.) Despite apparent disparity in wealth and resources, these men relied on similar models of playing the role of being a ruler. In these examples, the models included public display of inscriptions and exchange with other elites, but we also see that "kings" were diverse in their command of resources and prestige.

3.2 Tel Rehov

The impressive site of Tel Rehov is unsurpassed in providing evidence of southern Levantine elite activity in the early Iron Age. It has many hallmarks of social complexity but has not yielded administrative or monumental inscriptions (although other signs of administrative infrastructure are present; Mazar, 2021). Excavations have, however, turned up numerous inscribed objects and many other indications of elite culture and interregional activity. Among the most obvious are imported goods from the Mediterranean and Egypt, evidence of feasting, and industrial activity, including a large-scale apiary. In addition, the material culture generally is distinct and defies a lumping together with other sites in the region (Mazar, 2021). There can be little doubt that Tel Rehov's physical location contributed to its prominence, scale, and prosperity. It is situated at the crossroads of the northern Jordan Valley and the easternmost extent of the Jezreel Valley. This position means that the site would not only have experienced unusual traffic and commerce but rulers of the site would also have been in a position to benefit from control of the crossroads, factors examined recently by Amiḥai Mazar and Nota Kourou (Mazar, 2021; Mazar & Kourou, 2019).

One of the most distinctive features of Tel Rehov's early Iron Age activities is the high concentration of short inscriptions found at the site; a dozen were recovered from Iron IIA strata (Mazar, 2021, pp. 252–54). The only other area to have produced more than one or two examples of writing at this time is the region of Tell es-Safi/Gath, another site situated at a critical location for exchange (Finkelstein & Sass, 2021). Scholars have suggested that both regions may have been engaged in some aspect with the copper exchange to be discussed below (Finkelstein & Sass, 2021; Mazar, 2021; Mazar & Kourou, 2019; Ben-Yosef & Sergi, 2018). Of the Tel

Rehov inscriptions, one from Stratum V (late tenth-early ninth century) bears a name, *nmš*, which has also been identified in an inscription at nearby Tel ʿAmal; both were inscribed in a possession formula, *lnmš*, on "hippo"-type storage jars. Mazar and Shmuel Aḥituv suggest that the Nimshi name in these inscriptions identifies an elite family that ruled in the region. They further propose that this Nimshi family may in fact be the same Nimshites known from Jehu's lineage detailed in 2 Kings 9 (Mazar & Aḥituv, 2011). It is intriguing that there may well be a connection between the short inscriptions and a prominent family known from other sources. Related or not, we must still pursue additional questions, particularly about whether there were other elite families at Tel Rehov and what kinds of relations existed among prominent families in the region. Tel Rehov's extraordinary resources must have been managed by some portion of the elite population. The archaeology also suggests that the elite segment of this city enjoyed banquets, displayed their prestige through imported pottery, luxury objects, and imported bees for the large apiary. Without question, they were among the most privileged of the entire southern Levant for some time.

3.3 Faynan

We return now to the topic of Khirbat en-Nahas in the Faynan, situated at the southern end of the Jordan Valley and northeastern edge of the Arabah. This site has also yielded extraordinary evidence for the period. Like Tel Rehov, it was intimately connected to trade routes, but in the case of Khirbat en-Nahas, the site's raison d'être was the copper industry. Final publication of the site shows not only the extensive copper production but also the architectural elements that were not yet evident at the time of the 2004 article (Levy et al., 2014b). Khirbat en-Nahas further stands out for the presence of monumental structures, particularly the Area A gatehouse and large structures of Areas R, T, and W (Levy et al., 2014b). Publication of the totality of the Edomite Lowlands project, of which the Khirbat en-Nahas work is a significant part, situates the site in the broader context of other early Iron Age Faynan evidence. The work documents cemeteries, smaller metallurgical sites, surveys of ancient routes, and evidence of mining activities, but not an extensive network of settlements to correspond to the intensity of resource exploitation (Levy et al., 2014a). This absence contributes to the excavators' proposal that pastoral-nomads were not only the labor force but also in command of the region.

The intensive production activity was concentrated in the centuries that are least known to us through contemporary historical sources and, controversially, centuries prior to the evidence for the highland Edomite polity known from epigraphic, archaeological, and biblical sources. In light of the Faynan evidence, however, we must posit some kind of coordinated exploitation of the region's resources to explain industry on the scale of Khirbet en-Nahas. Despite the fact that there are no local inscriptions or ostraca to provide names of elites, no administrative records, and no definitive evidence of non-local control of the site, there is unquestionably evidence of a command of natural and human resources. Evidence for an elite group at Khirbat en-Nahas comes in the form of prestige goods such as unusual jewelry and figurines, Cypriot Black-on-Red pottery, Qurayyah Painted Ware, and a significant number of Egyptian scarabs and amulets. In addition, the excavators make the case for elite architecture and activities at the site. The large, originally two-story structure of Area R provides the most compelling evidence. The nearby structures in Areas T and W are also suggestive of a stratified population (Levy et al., 2014b, pp. 169–232).

The reach of the southern Levantine copper and the exchange networks that carried it is much better understood following more recent analysis of slag-tempered (so called "Negebite") pottery and of copper objects discovered far from the Arabah. Regarding the "Negebite" pottery, petrographic analysis has demonstrated that the assemblages associated with Negev Highland sites of the Iron I-IIA consist of handmade, slag-tempered wares originating in the Arabah along with wheel-made vessels originating in the northern Negev, southern Levantine coast, and Shephelah (Martin et al., 2014; Martin & Finkelstein, 2013). Martin et al. argue that both the handmade and wheel-made pottery should be viewed as imports to the Negev Highlands, used by pastoral-nomadic communities who were instrumental to the workings of the Arabah copper trade. Alternatively, Ben-Yosef argues that a "supra-regional entity" encompassed the Negev Highlands, the Arabah, and the Edomite Plateau (Ben-Yosef, 2019). Either reconstruction reflects the fact that there was an intensively coordinated body (whether networked or political/ethnic) among the Faynan, Timna, and the Negev Highlands (if not farther). Additionally, we are learning how far the Arabah's copper traveled. Lead isotope analysis of prestige copper and bronze objects from Egypt's Delta, in the form of a high official's ushabti figurines, and tripod cauldrons from mainland Greece can be traced back to Arabah sources, which includes Khirbat en-Nahas/the Faynan as well as Timna in the southwest Arabah (Ben-Dor Evian et al., 2021; Kiderlen et al., 2016; Vaelske, 2019). Arabah copper is also present in bronze objects and debased silver recovered from the Levantine coast (Eshel et al., 2021). These findings make clear that despite the Khirbat en-Nahas' remote location in respect to the Mediterranean, people in charge of the site were deeply connected to some of the most important interactions of the period.

3.4 Hebrew Bible

In contrast to the contemporary early Iron Age examples discussed above, I finish this survey of evidence with a discussion of the later, literary depictions of the era's rulers. In contrast to the canonical line of first kings (i.e., Saul, David, and Solomon), we will focus on diversity in the biblical examples of elite leadership.

Frequently, discussion of potential rulers of sites like Khirbat en-Nahas or Tel Rehov leads us to examinations of named kings and states in the biblical and historical sources. For example, scholars have linked both sites with Shoshenq I's campaign (Levy et al., 2014a; Mazar, 2021); debate continues over which (or whether) Israelite kings succeeded in bringing Tel Rehov into the northern kingdom (Mazar, 2021, pp. 263–64); and there is strong disagreement about whether the Faynan should be considered Edomite in the tenth century (see above).

Biblical depictions of Iron Age leadership are prone to the same tendency. Although intensely debated as a historical reference, Genesis 36:31–40 remembers "kings" (מְלָכִים), along with a collection of "chiefs" (אַלּוּפִים), in the early generations of Esau/Edom. In material describing the early monarchic period, kings are named for many of Israel's neighbors including Edom (e.g., Hadad in 1 Kings 11:14). Although the biblical language of kings and kingdoms is not surprising considering the historical use of the title throughout the Iron Age, it is also important to note that there is no extrabiblical, historical evidence identifying an Edomite monarch prior to the eighth century (Crowell, 2021; Porter, 2004). I suggest here that looking for examples outside of the characterization of kings and kingdoms may introduce new interpretive possibilities, and the interaction models are compatible with this alternate approach.

In the biblical depiction of the early Iron Age, we have various examples of men of exceptional wealth, reputation, and influence. Although the depictions of these men do not include the title "king," they appear quite similar to the figures who are more familiar, namely Saul and David. If we set aside the notions of monarchy, we find that some of the purported contemporaries to "Israel's first kings" may be better described as peer elites than as subjects. The prominent men Nabal and Barzillai provide useful comparisons. Even though these individuals as we know them from the biblical texts are first and foremost literary in character, the stories may reflect a historical context of a broader community of elites in the region. In the least, the stories assume certain values that may help us think about leadership, wealth, and power struggles among local and regional elites.

Nabal, presented as the first husband of David's wife Abigail, is introduced in 1 Samuel 25. If there was once a historical figure at the core of this story, the man's name has been obscured by the nickname Nabal, meaning "fool." (There is a possibility he could be identified with Ithra of 2 Sam 17:25 (see Levenson & Halpern, 1980, pp. 511–12)). The figure Nabal is a prominent property holder, introduced as having three thousand sheep and a thousand goats, whose influence covered a strategic portion of southern Judah, near Hebron (1 Sam 25:2). The dramatic tension in the episode centers on Nabal's refusal to pay for protection that David claims he and his men provided for Nabal's shepherds. Although Nabal disregards David's request, his wife Abigail assembles a large payment of produce, prepared food, wine, and sheep for David, which further demonstrates the abundance of Nabal's holdings (1 Sam 25:18). Later in the episode, Nabal is described as enjoying an extravagant feast in his house, literally "like the king's feast" (1 Sam 25:36). Since the bias in the biblical narrative presumes that only one man can hold the title "king," Nabal cannot be a rival in title, but the reader should have no misunderstanding about the stakes involved in David's maneuvers. The episode works toward larger goals of the narrative, namely justifying David (and later his descendants) as king over "all Israel." This stage in that argument relies in part on David's taking possession of

Nabal's wife, household, and wealth. The claim only works if the significance of Nabal's wealth and influence is compelling. In other words, Nabal's position must be understood as on par with a ruler for David to have legitimacy in the south (Levenson, 1978; Levenson & Halpern, 1980).

Later in David's story, in the context of the Absalom's coup, there is yet another influential figure, the aged and very wealthy Barzillai of Gilead. In his first appearance in the narrative, Barzillai is one of several prominent figures who provide gifts and lavish provisions for David and his men at Mahanaim, just before the battle against Absalom (2 Sam 17:27–29). Following Absalom's death, Barzillai reappears, accompanying David to the Jordan River. In this case, there is a lengthy exchange between the two men. The scene is crafted to identify David as legitimate and unrivaled, but it also emphasizes Barzillai's status as wise and wealthy (2 Sam 19:32–39).

The parallels and contrasts between the Barzillai and Nabal figures are plentiful, and we can see that the savvy and stately Barzillai functions as a foil to the boorish Nabal (Hamilton, 2009, p. 529). Both stories are situated in contexts of coups related to David's career: Nabal as David rivals Saul; Barzillai when Absalom rivals David. Although both figures are wealthy and influential, the contrast in how they use their elite standing accentuates the extreme difference between them. Barzillai supports David, willingly provides for David's men, and volunteers a family member to join David's court. In contrast, Nabal famously belittles David, denies payment to his men, and loses members of his household to David. For these and many other reasons, not least of which are the literary intricacies of the dialogue and tensions in these stories, we cannot assume that these are reliable for historical reconstructions of precise events.

These stories are, however, an interesting study in depictions of elite power, especially outside of the characterization of kingship. Both Nabal and Barzillai are explicitly described as having great wealth, and they exert considerable influence in regional, political matters. While not overly emphasized in the stories, they appear to be prominent in nomadic or semi-nomadic territories. The men's households are secure enough to provide food for others (although unwittingly in Nabal's case), and they are each labeled אִישׁ גָּדוֹל, literally "great man" (1 Sam 25:2; 2 Sam 19:33), but notably not "king." Mark Hamilton, who examines these figures in terms of social-scientific and literary analysis, suggests we consider the phrase as a "rank" in society. He explains that in every use of the phrase, the person "(1) enjoys great wealth; (2) exercises dominion over large numbers of subordinates; and (3) has close access to the central power of the state in which he is located" (2009, p. 513, note 2). In Hamilton's analysis, Nabal and Barzillai "illustrate the complexity of the rhetoric of gift-giving in ancient Israel and the Levant" (2009, p. 520). Because of the political and theological goals of the Deuteronomistic History, there is no room for these figures to be rivals for the narrative's kings, but if we step outside of the text's biases, the figures are exceptional in their status, and they are far similar to the main characters, Saul and David, than the history lets on.

We can evaluate the "first kings" according to the characteristics noted above and separate from the later notion of centralized monarchy. Saul's leadership qualifications include having a prestigious pedigree, being striking and charismatic, and proving himself as a successful warrior (1 Sam 9:1–2). His power base was in a prime location, in the heart of the Benjaminite hill country, along the main road. He also gained the loyalty of some neighboring populations, which resulted in extended influence and status. We have a similar picture of David, described as a man of battle and a fine speaker (1 Sam 16:12, 18). According to the text, his strategic alliances and victories secured him a southern territory, with bases at a number of strategic sites. In the biblical depictions, these men had personal weaponry that set them apart (e.g., 1 Sam 13:22). They are also described as providing meals for others and offering gifts of food and wine (e.g., 1 Sam 16:20; 20:27). Like Nabal and Barzillai, they are noted for their elite status, attributed to factors like their wealth, pedigree, and commanding presence.

Saul and David appear to fall into a different elite class than Nabal and Barzillai, however. Saul and David are associated with the phrase גִּבּוֹר חַיִל. The label גִּבּוֹר is an intensified form of גֶּבֶר, "man," which is frequently used to describe a warrior or hero (Mobley, 2005, p. 35; Murphy, 2019, pp. 37–39) and is invoked a number of times in the books of Samuel in this sense (e.g., 2 Sam 20:7; 23:9). Steven McKenzie's rendering of the phrase as "powerful nobleman" provides additional food for thought, especially for his attention to interpretive options beyond the "warrior" characterization (2000, p. 51). He elaborates that even though the phrase is frequently equated with military might ("man of valor"), we should understand it in terms of social standing. David's description as a גִּבּוֹר חַיִל (1 Sam 16:18) likely references his family's wealth in livestock, but we should not make the mistake of conflating the later, kingship-oriented symbolism of the young, humble shepherd that the author uses to make David fit the bill of the soon-to-be king (McKenzie, 2000, pp. 47–51, 57). McKenzie uses the example of Saul's father, Kish, who is directly identified as a גִּבּוֹר חַיִל to elaborate on the title; he suggests we think in terms of a "'business man' rather than a military figure" (McKenzie, 2000, p. 57). In other words, Kish's strengths were in his acumen, perhaps in a number of arenas, military, social, political, and economic.

Gregory Mobley's acknowledgement of the economic implication of חַיִל is important to note:

> …it could mark a class of *gibbôrîm* who possessed land and who were firmly entrenched, with concomitant honors and responsibilities, in the traditional kinship networks, with the means to outfit themselves or others, in contrast to the small farmers and artisans who hastily beat plowpoints into swords, mustering into units under a leader. (Mobley, 2005, p. 35)

Mobley's efforts to understand another, contrasting title, אֲנָשִׁים רֵיקִים (Judg 9:4; 11:3; 2 Chr 13:7), which he ultimately translates "empty men," provides a point of comparison. He determines that the term refers to those who lacked "sturdy kinship attachments" or "a portion of the family estate, the *naḥalâ*"; they were "*worth*-less and un-*principal*-ed men, without a stake, who were not vested in the economy of primogeniture" (emphasis in original; Mobley, 2005, pp. 36–37). Although it is not uncommon to see this "landed gentry" characterization, it is perhaps more appropriate for the depictions of later times (e.g., 2 Kings 15:20 that Mobley also examines). For the early Iron Age figures and in relation to other aspects of the depictions of

David and Saul, we should consider other forms of wealth or "fullness," to contrast Mobley's "empty" imagery. This might come in the form of the ability to feed community members, due to accumulations in food stores and livestock, or the ability to protect households and neighbors from rival elites. These traits would be valuable in pastoralist and semi-pastoralist societies in the southern hill country and territories east of the Jordan.

In Porter's study of small-scale early Iron Age communities of west-central Jordan, he calls attention to the importance of food and feasting as symbols of wealth and demonstrations of leadership (2013, pp. 112–27). He focuses on "patrimonial and charismatic genres of authority" during the early Iron Age, which allows for recognition of broader expressions of elite status and leadership than the (likely anachronistic) biblical image of kingship (Porter, 2013, p. 109). Based on archaeological evidence, he makes the case for the importance of food, especially when shared in communal feasts, as a compelling demonstration of wealth and thus authority. The discussion of infrastructure related to the storage, protection, and preparation of food establishes how ingrained in social practices the connection between food and power must have been. Thus outside of the biblical evidence, we have a strong case for expressions of elite status and authority separate from hallmarks of kingship or kingdoms and in a variety of locations, in other words in a decentralized landscape of power.

From these explorations, it is reasonably clear that within the cultural worldview(s) that gave rise to the biblical narratives, there were varied titles for influential elites, and their paths to prestige involved more than the iconic selection and anointing rituals featured in royal justifications. We may not be able to capture all of the nuances in the different terminology, but in each case, expressions of wealth, social influence, charisma, and community care feature as of significant importance. Even Nabal's exception is illustrative as the contrast to Barzillai's idealized example. Although we cannot rely on the biblical figures as historical, there is a richness in the depiction of elite status and authority that is easily overlooked due to the prioritization of the monarchy's story in the Deuteronomistic History. Contrary to that perspective, these first biblical kings do not hold up to the common royal boast of being men without peers (cf. 1 Sam 10:24). They appear instead to be members of an established elite rank, embedded in certain norms of leadership.

4 Summaries and Reconstructions

The preceding examples provide a glimpse at several ways elite status and leadership found expression in the early Iron Age Levant and in the biblical depictions of the era. The Byblian kings and their Egyptian counterparts conform to certain aspects of the classic expectations of Levantine kingship: rulers created monumental inscriptions and legitimized their positions through dedications to patron deities and documentation of lineage and deeds. The Byblian kings who inscribed their dedications on Egyptian statuary also made clear that they were connected to other influential kings. At the same time, the character of the earlier inscriptions and the borrowing of statuary challenges our assumptions that contemporary "kings" should be held to common expectations in terms of command of resources and complexity of royal institutions.

The archaeological examples of two large-scale early Iron Age sites, Tel Rehov and Khirbat en-Nahas, demonstrate that some polities existed not only on a large scale but also with extraordinary wealth and significant organizational complexity. Although they have considerable differences—undoubtedly, life at urban Tel Rehov was quite distinct from the desert processing center of Khirbat en-Nahas—they have in common a number of key attributes that might be considered part of a similar or related elite interaction sphere. Both locations were situated on the north-south Jordan valley corridor that ultimately connected the southern Levant to Arabia and Syria, and both were connected to routes leading westward (for this relationship, see also Mazar, 2021, p. 256). Additionally, both sites were home to large-scale production of rare goods, honey in the case of Tel Rehov and copper at Khirbat en-Nahas. Although the sites are not similar in their overall cultural assemblages, there are distinctive wares, prestige objects, and architectural features at each site that suggest an elite presence, and imported goods further testify to each site's connections to long-distance networks. Paradoxically, for all that is known about these sites, neither can be confidently identified in terms of a historical polity or ethnic identity in large part because of a lack of lengthy, contemporary epigraphic or narrative sources.

Finally, in spite of the Deuteronomistic History's efforts to assert a narrow view of kingship, the books of 1 and 2 Samuel describe a number of figures who exhibit qualities that we would associate with leadership. They are identified through specialized terminology that marks them as elite. Nabal and Barzillai are each labeled as an אִישׁ גָּדוֹל. Similarly, David and Saul's father, Kish, are each referred to as a גִּבּוֹר חַיִל. Evaluating the stories about these figures introduces the notion that prior to the ideology of a singular king over the people, communities were led by elite individuals. These men achieved their positions of power in part due to their wealth and ability to care for those within the reach of their influence.

I contend that the interaction spheres models described in the beginning of this essay provide a structure for thinking about commonalities and connections across the differences in the early Iron Age evidence. In each of these categories, the analytical framework of elite interaction spheres enhances our possibilities for interpretation. Elites distinguished themselves through access to specialized goods and resources, which translates to wealth as well. The Byblian kings, local leaders of early Iron Age production and trade centers, and the biblical figures served similar roles in each of their contexts. In addition, elites interacted with counterparts across a substantial network, and their long-distance interactions further informed their distinctive status. Abibaʿal and Elibaʿal advertised a relationship with kings of the 22nd Dynasty by enhancing the Egyptian monuments. Imported goods at Tel Rehov and Khirbat en-Nahas attest to the unusual exchange that came to each site, and in both cases, the excavators report concentrations of special finds in areas that correspond to elite infrastructure. Finally, the exchanges between David and Barzillai in particular highlight a notion (or ancient form of historical reconstruction?) of exchange among peer elites whose cooperative interactions proved mutually beneficial and reinforced a code of proper behavior.

A focus on elite culture and resource control emphasizes that there were various locations in the region that operated as small, independent polities. They did not all have the characteristics of a state or an urban center, but some inhabitants were accumulating wealth and unusual goods and becoming an elite class. The elite participants were from diverse forms of social organization and presumably identities, ranging from pastoral nomads in the Arabah to urban, inland centers such as Tel Rehov. What investigations of the last 20-odd years have shown is that our archaeological evidence reaches beyond traditional concepts of kingdoms. Similarly a concentration on state-centric attributes in written sources misses more nuanced aspects of early Iron Age leadership.

Archaeological work at Khirbat en-Nahas, in particular, underscores that there were new, arguably independent and historically unknown players that had a tremendous impact on the transition from the Late Bronze to the early Iron Age. Our inability to link the archaeological remains to known historical figures and states has confounded interpretive efforts, leading to a polarization of reconstruction, pitting material evidence against textual, or subsuming one discipline to "handmaid" status in service of another. In this essay, I argue for an alternative perspective in which disparate evidence can contribute in concert to a reconstruction of the age: rising but potentially short-lived elite institutions emerged in the eleventh to ninth centuries. Their leadership was influential in shaping the political landscape of the era. Their combined network connections transformed interregional economies, as is now evident from the copper trade evidence and the excavations of Khirbat en-Nahas.

References

Ben-Dor Evian, S., Yagel, O., Harlavan, Y., Seri, H., Lewinsky, J., & Ben-Yosef, E. (2021). Pharaoh's copper: The provenance of copper in bronze artifacts from post-imperial Egypt at the end of the second millennium BCE. *JASREP Journal of Archaeological Science: Reports, 38*.

Bennett, C.-M., & Bienkowski, P. (Eds.). (1995). *Excavations at Tawilan in southern Jordan*. Published for the British Institute at Amman for Archaeology and History by Oxford University Press.

Ben-Yosef, E. (2019). The architectural bias in current biblical archaeology. *Vetus Testamentum, 69*(3), 361–387. https://doi.org/10.1163/15685330-12341370

Ben-Yosef, E. (2020). And yet, a nomadic error: A reply to Israel finkelstein. *Antiguo Oriente, 18*, 33–60. https://doi.org/10.1163/15685330-12341370

Ben-Yosef, E., & Sergi, O. (2018). The destruction of Gath by Hazael and the Arabah copper industry: A reassessment. In I. Shai, J. R. Chadwick, L. Hitchcok, A. Dagan, C. McKinny, & J. Uziel (Eds.), *Tell it in Gath: Studies in the history and archaeology of Israel, essays in honor of Aren M. Maeir on the occasion of his sixtieth birthday* (pp. 461–480) Zaphon.

Bienkowski, P., & Balla, M. (2002). *Busayra: excavations by Crystal M. Bennett 1971–1980*. Oxford University Press.

Caldwell, J. R. (1964). Interaction spheres in prehistory. In J. R. Caldwell & R. L. Hall (Eds.), *Hopewellian studies* (pp. 134–143). [s.n.].
Crowell, B. L. (2021). *Edom at the edge of Empire: A social and political history*. SBL Press.
Eshel, T., Gilboa, A., Yahalom-Mack, N., Tirosh, O., & Erel, Y. (2021). Debasement of silver throughout the Late Bronze-Iron Age transition in the Southern Levant: Analytical and cultural implications. *Journal of Archaeological Science, 125*, 1–24.
Fantalkin, A. (2001). Low chronology and Greek Protogeometric and Geometric pottery in the Southern Levant. *Levant, 33*(1), 117–125.
Finkelstein, I. (1996). The archaeology of the United Monarchy: An alternative view. *Levant, 28*(1), 177–187. https://doi.org/10.1179/007589196790216767
Finkelstein, I. (2005a). A low chronology update: Archaeology, history and bible. In *The bible and radiocarbon dating--Archaeology, text and science* (pp. 31–42). Equinox.
Finkelstein, I. (2005b). Khirbet en-Nahas, Edom and biblical history. *Tel Aviv, 32*, 119–125.
Finkelstein, I., & Piasetzky, E. (2011). The Iron Age chronology debate: Is the gap narrowing? *Near Eastern Archaeology, 74*(1), 50–54.
Finkelstein, I., & Sass, B. (2021). The exceptional concentration of inscriptions at Iron IIA Gath and Rehob and the nature of the alphabet in the ninth century BCE. In T. Römer, H. Gonzalez, L. Marti, & J. Rückl (Eds.), *Oral et écrit dans l'Antiquité orientale: les processus de rédaction et d'édition* (pp. 127–173). Peeters.
Finkelstein, I., & Silberman, N. A. (2006). *David and Solomon. In Search of the Bible's Sacred Kings and the roots of western tradition*. Free Press.
Gibson, J. C. L. (1982). *Textbook of Syrian semitic inscriptions III: Phoenician inscriptions including inscriptions in the mixed dialect of Arslan Tash*. Clarendon Press.
Halpern, B. (2001). *David's secret demons: Messiah, murderer, traitor, king*. W.B. Eerdmans.
Hamilton, M. W. (2009). At whose table? Stories of elites and social climbers in 1–2 Samuel. *Vetus Testamentum, 59*(4), 513–532.
Herzog, Z., & Singer-Avitz, L. (2004). Redefining the centre: The Emergence of State in Judah. *Tel Aviv, 31*(2), 209–244.
Herzog, Z., & Singer-Avitz, L. (2006). Sub-dividing the Iron Age IIA in northern Israel: A suggested solution to the chronological debate. *Tel Aviv, 33*(2), 163–195.
Joffe, A. (2018). Defining the state. In C. Rollston (Ed.), *Enemies and friends of the state: Ancient prophecy in context* (pp. 3–24) Eisenbrauns.
Kalimi, I. (2018). *Writing and rewriting the story of Solomon in ancient Israel*. Cambridge University Press.
Katz, H., & Faust, A. (2014). The chronology of the Iron Age IIA in Judah in light of Tel ʿEton Tomb C3 and other assemblages. *Bulletin of the American Schools of Oriental Research, 371*, 103–127.
Kiderlen, M., Bode, M., Hauptmann, A., & Bassiakos, Y. (2016). Tripod cauldrons produced at Olympia give evidence for trade with copper from Faynan (Jordan) to South West Greece, c. 950–750 BCE. *Journal of Archaeological Science: Reports, 8*, 303–313.
Kleiman, A., Fantalkin, A., Mommsen, H., & Finkelstein, I. (2019). The date and origin of Black-On-Red Ware: The view from Megiddo. *American Journal of Archaeology, 123*(4), 531–555.
Kletter, R. (2004). Chronology and United Monarchy: A methodological review. *Zeitschrift des Deutschen Palästina-Vereins, 120*, 13–54.
LaBianca, O. S., & Younker, R. W. (1998). The kingdoms of Ammon, Moab and Edom: The archaeology of society in Late Bronze/Iron Age Transjordan (ca. 1400-500 BCE). In T. E. Levy (Ed.), *The archaeology of society in the Holy Land* (2nd ed., pp. 399–415). Leicester University Press.
Levenson, J. D. (1978). I Samuel 25 as literature and as history. *The Catholic Biblical Quarterly, 40*(1), 11–28.
Levenson, J. D., & Halpern, B. (1980). The political import of David's marriages. *Journal of Biblical Literature, 99*(4), 507–518. https://doi.org/10.2307/3265190
Levy, T. E., Adams, R. B., Najjar, M., Hauptmann, A., Anderson, J. D., Brandl, B., Robinson, M. A., & Higham, T. (2004). Reassessing the chronology of Biblical Edom: new excavations and 14 C dates from Khirbat en-Nahas (Jordan). *Antiquity, 78*(302), 865–879. https://doi.org/10.1017/S0003598X0011350X

Levy, T. E., Higham, T., & Najjar, M. (2006). Response to van der Steen & Bienkowski. *Antiquity, 80*(307) http://antiquity.ac.uk/projgall/levy307/. Accessed 30 Dec 2021.

Levy, T. E., Najjar, M., Ben-Yosef, E., & Smith, N. G. (Eds.). (2014a). *New insights into the Iron Age archaeology of Edom, southern Jordan: Surveys, excavations, and research from the University of California, San Diego & Department of Antiquities of Jordan, Edom Lowlands Regional Archaeology Project (ELRAP)* (Vol. 1–2). The Cotsen Institute of Archaeology Press.

Levy, T. E., Najjar, M., Higham, T., Arbel, Y., Muniz, A., Ben-Yosef, E., et al. (2014b). Excavations at Khirbat en-Nahas, 2002–2009: An Iron Age Copper production Center in the Lowlands of Edom. In T. E. Levy, M. Najjar, E. Ben-Yosef, & N. G. Smith (Eds.), *New insights into the Iron Age archaeology of Edom, southern Jordan: Surveys, excavations and research from the University of California, San Diego & Department of Antiquities of Jordan, Edom Lowlands Regional Archaeology Project (ELRAP)* (pp. 88–245). The Cotsen Institute of Archaeology Press.

Liverani, M. (2005). *Israel's history and the history of Israel*. Equinox Pub.

Malena, S. (forthcoming). *Fertile crossroads: Elites and exchange in the Southern Levant's Early Iron Age*. Equinox Pub.

Martin, M., & Finkelstein, I. (2013). Iron IIA Pottery from the Negev highlands: Petrographic investigation and historical implications. *Tel Aviv, 40*, 6–45.

Martin, M., Eliyahu-Behar, A., Anenburg, M., Goren, Y., & Finkelstein, I. (2014). Iron IIA Slag-tempered Pottery in the Negev highlands. *Israel, Journal of Archaeological Science, 40*, 3777–3792.

Master, D. M. (2001). State formation theory and the kingdom of ancient Israel. *Journal of Near Eastern Studies, 60*(2), 117–131.

Mazar, A. (2005). The debate over the chronology of the Iron Age in the Southern Levant: Its history, the current situation and a suggested resolution. In T. E. Levy & T. Higham (Eds.), *The bible and radiocarbon dating--archaeology, text and science* (pp. 15–30) Equinox.

Mazar, A. (2011). The Iron Age chronology debate: Is the gap narrowing? Another viewpoint. *Near Eastern Archaeology, 74*(2), 105–111.

Mazar, A. (2021). The Beth Shean Valley and its Vicinity in the 10th century BCE. *Jerusalem Journal of Archaeology, 1*, 241–271.

Mazar, A., & Aḥituv, S. (2011). Inscriptions from Tel Rehov and their contribution to the study of writing and literacy during the Iron Age IIA. *Eretz-Israel, 30*, 300–316.

Mazar, A., & Kourou, N. (2019). Greece and the Levant in the 10th-9th centuries BC: A view from Tel Rehov. *Opuscula*. Accessed 29 Oct 2021

McKenzie, S. L. (2000). *King David: A biography*. Oxford University Press.

Miller, J. M., & Hayes, J. H. (2006). *A history of ancient Israel and Judah* (2nd ed.). Westminster John Knox Press.

Mobley, G. (2005). *The empty men: The heroic tradition of ancient Israel*. Doubleday.

Murphy, K. J. (2019). *Rewriting masculinity: Gideon, men, and might*. Oxford University Press.

Pioske, D. (2015). *David's Jerusalem: Between memory and history*. Taylor & Francis.

Porter, B. W. (2004). Authority, polity, and tenuous elites in Iron Age Edom (Jordan). *Oxford Journal of Archaeology, 23*(4), 373–395. https://doi.org/10.1111/j.1468-0092.2004.00216.x

Porter, B. W. (2013). *Complex communities: The archaeology of early Iron Age West-Central Jordan*. University of Arizona Press.

Porter, B. W. (2016). Assembling the Iron Age Levant: The archaeology of communities, polities, and imperial peripheries. *Journal of Archaeological Research, 24*(4), 373–420. https://doi.org/10.1007/s10814-016-9093-8

Richelle, M. (2016a). Elusive scrolls: Could any hebrew literature have been written prior to the eight century BCE? *Vetus Testamentum, 66*, 1–39.

Richelle, M. (2016b). Intentional omissions in the textual history of the books of kings: In search of methodological criteria. *Semitica, 58*, 135–157.

Robker, J. M. (2012). *The Jehu revolution: A royal tradition of the northern kingdom and its ramifications* (Beihefte Zur Zeitschrift Für Die Alttestamentliche Wissenschaft ; 435). De Gruyter.

Routledge, B. E. (2004). *Moab in the Iron Age: Hegemony, polity, archaeology.* University of Pennsylvania Press.

Sanders, S. L. (2009). *The invention of Hebrew.* University of Illinois Press.

Schortman, E. M. (1989). Interregional interaction in prehistory: The need for a new perspective. *American Antiquity, 54*(1), 52–65.

Schortman, E. M., & Urban, P. A. (1987). Modeling interregional interaction in prehistory. *Advances in Archaeological Method and Theory, 11*, 37–95.

Selk, A. (2018, June 9). A 3,000-Year-Old Glass Head Deepens One of the Bible's Oldest Mysteries: The Tiny Head Was Unearthed from One of the Last Major Biblical Sites Remaining to Be Excavated. It Just Might Be Jezebel's Husband. *The Washington Post.* https://www.washingtonpost.com/news/speaking-of-science/wp/2018/06/09/a-3000-year-old-glass-head-deepens-one-of-the-bibles-oldest-mysteries/?utm_term=.63c017c7b276

Stein, G. J. (2010). Local identities and interaction spheres: Modeling regional variation in the Ubaid horizon. In *Beyond the Ubaid: Transformation and integration in the late prehistoric societies of the middle east* (pp. 23–44). Oriental Institute of the University of Chicago.

Struever, S. (1964). The Hopewell interaction sphere in Riverine--Western Great Lakes culture history. In J. R. Caldwell & R. L. Hall (Eds.), *Hopewellian studies* (pp. 85–106). [s.n.].

Thomas, Z. (2021). On the archaeology of the 10th century BCE Israel and the idea of the "state.". *Palestine Exploration Quarterly, 153*(3), 244–257.

Thompson, T. L. (1974). *The historicity of the patriarchal narratives; the quest for the historical Abraham.* Walter de Gruyter.

Torijano, P. A. (2002). *Solomon the Esoteric King: From King to Magus.* Supplements to the Journal for the Study of Judaism 73. Brill.

Vaelske, V. (2019). Early Iron Age Copper Trail between Wadi Arabah and Egypt during the 21st dynasty: First Results from Tanis, ca. 1000 BC [with Michael Bode, DBM]. *Zeitschrift für Orient-Archäologie, 12*, 184–203.

van der Steen, E., & Bienkowski, P. (2006). Radiocarbon dates from Khirbat en-Nahas: A methodological critique. *Antiquity, 80*(07) http://antiquity.ac.uk/projgall/vandersteen307/. Accessed 30 Dec 2021

Van Seters, J. (1975). *Abraham in history and tradition.* Yale University Press.

Wilson, I. D. (2017). *Kingship and memory in ancient Judah.* Oxford University Press.

Yoffee, N. (1994). Mesopotamian interaction spheres. In *Early stages in the evolution of Mesopotamian civilization: Soviet excavations in northern Iraq* (pp. 257–270). University of Arizona Press.

What Is the Name of Our Discipline? Or, the Onomastic Stew That Is Archaeology in the Southern Levant

Zachary Thomas

Abstract It is remarkable that despite the long history of archaeological exploration in the southern Levant, it is hard to identify a single, consistent, and certainly an uncontroversial name for this discipline, akin to Classical archaeology, for example. Disciplinary boundaries are always subjective, but in the southern Levant they are practically political. Much of the problem revolves around the name "biblical archaeology" and efforts, never entirely successful, to move away from it as the discipline has matured, not to mention the problem of how to represent the relevance of all periods studied (prehistoric to Medieval), geographical constraints, and close associations with disciplines like Jewish studies. The history of the region and its place as a crossroads of cultures and empires adds yet another dimension. All these are factors that pull on how one chooses to name (or not name) the discipline. Rather than suggest a definitive solution, this paper will explore the many ways of naming the discipline and the complexities, advantages and limitations of each, as well as how different names relate to different conceptions of the discipline and its priorities.

Keywords Biblical archaeology · Levantine archaeology · Nomenclature · Classical archaeology · Islamic archaeology · Syro-Palestinian archaeology · Historical archaeology

---

My thanks to the editors of the volume, especially Erez Ben-Yosef for encouraging this paper, and to Ian Jones for advising on publications relating to Islamic archaeology. All views and any errors remain mine alone. It is my pleasure to dedicate this paper to Prof. Tom Levy and to write in his honor on a subject for which both he and his teacher Bill Dever have made important contributions.

Z. Thomas (✉)
Sonia and Marco Nadler Institute of Archaeology, Tel Aviv University, Tel Aviv, Israel
e-mail: thomasz1@mail.tau.ac.il

© The Author(s), under exclusive license to Springer Nature Switzerland AG 2023
E. Ben-Yosef, I. W. N. Jones (eds.), *"And in Length of Days Understanding" (Job 12:12): Essays on Archaeology in the Eastern Mediterranean and Beyond in Honor of Thomas E. Levy*, Interdisciplinary Contributions to Archaeology, https://doi.org/10.1007/978-3-031-27330-8_24

1 Introduction to the Problem

Around the beginning of my PhD at Macquarie University, I was explaining to a fellow doctoral candidate in my department that I was writing on the archaeology of the early monarchic period in Israel as its appears in the Hebrew Bible, and this eventually prompted her to ask what exactly my discipline was called. I honestly do not remember exactly what I said, but I remember that my answer consisted of some rushed, probably garbled explanation that there was disagreement over the discipline's identity these days, and I believe I settled on "Syro-Palestinian archaeology", probably because that sounded more modern and acceptable than just defaulting to "biblical archaeology". Perhaps it would have been better, if less specific, to say "Near Eastern archaeology"?

I am not sure several years later that I would find it any easier to give a straightforward answer to this question, because I do not believe that there is one (or one that is economical enough for your everyday conversation, even in academia). Several years ago, none other than William Dever noted this same difficulty, largely because he had at that point concluded that neither "biblical" or "Syro-Palestinian archaeology" were any longer very satisfactory or accurate, while Near Eastern archaeology was just the larger regional discipline. This was a serious problem as they have for a long time been the names that have approach the status of standard usage (Dever, 2003b). All these years later, I do not see that this problem is resolved, even if it has faded from the immediate attention of the discipline.

This situation is indeed frustrating. It is true that disciplinary definitions are always fuzzy and subjective up to a point, while the disciplinary identity one adopts is very much a personal decision. But they are important nonetheless, as they speak to a sense of coherence and a claim to ownership of a particular academic domain, a set field of expertise. A clear identity and consistent name say to other disciplines and to the public "this is our domain", and thus as a topic it is more than just a minor issue of semantics. It is also the case that a disciplinary name can be reflective of what the individual using it believes about their discipline's scope, priorities and even methodology (Holland, 1974).

I have to admit, therefore, that I have sometimes looked jealously over at friends and colleagues in the neighboring disciplines of Classical archaeology and Egyptology for instance, for even if they lack a strict definition these identities are nonetheless used consistently and their basic meanings are well established. How convenient it would be, I think to myself, if I similarly had a standard name for my discipline that I could provide. Obviously, I have used one possible candidate in the title of my paper, but I would not really consider "the archaeology of the southern Levant" very satisfactory, as I think that terms like this are better used as topical specifications, rather than disciplinary identities.

My aim in this paper is not to declare which name should be adopted outright as the clearly correct choice, for making another such pronouncement will not add anything useful. Nor is it to rehash earlier debates over the discipline's identity. Rather, it is simply to discuss the different names that are out there and their various problems of definition, scope, and how they reflect different research priorities. I hope that these considerations can prove useful to the discipline as debate over its identity continues to evolve. Though never intended to encompass the entirety of the discipline, my discussion also includes Islamic, Classical and prehistoric archaeology. As well as being useful for comparative purposes, each these are relevant for understanding the practice of archaeology in the southern Levant, yet are often overlooked in how it is named and defined. I begin with a closer description of the problem as I see it, and close by offering some comments on how we might proceed in the future.

2 The Nature of the Problem

An archaeologist such as myself who works actively in a country of the southern Levant and has a specific interest in this region has a multitude of different choices for the name they can adopt for their discipline, or what they understand as their discipline. The problem is that each of these names comes with either practical constraints or outright methodological problems, to go along with their merits. There are different bases behind names as well. Some are geographic, including "Syro-Palestinian", "Levantine", and "Near Eastern Archaeology", in contrast to a subjective focus like "biblical archaeology". I think it also important to consider more period-based names, namely "prehistoric", "Classical" and "Islamic", that are a disciplinary identity for some of our colleagues. While they are seemingly more limited in scope, these names have their own issues of definition and usage, and also bring complexities in how they fit in alongside or crosscut other names. What we have, ultimately, is a group of different names mixed together in stew that is archaeology in the southern Levant, bubbling away across the *lounge durée* of the region's history. It is a tasty stew to be sure, and the variety of different ingredients that go into it, representing the different perspectives and interests, are part of what makes the discipline so interesting and vibrant. And yet, the lack of widely recognized and easily deployable identity for the discipline can be frustrating.

I would put this situation down to two factors. The first is simply the long archaeological record of the southern Levant, coupled to the region's complicated and shifting political, social and cultural history over the *lounge durée*. The southern Levant's history has been defined as much at level of its local, stable populations as it has by the rule of great empires, a situation resulting from its geographical position as a bridge between Africa and Asia and between the Mediterranean and the mainland (Rainey & Notley, 2014; Stordalen & LaBianca, 2021). This would always have complicated any possibility of a unified and consistent disciplinary identity developing in the archaeology of the southern Levant. But this has only been complicated further by the second factor, that of the charged nature of debate within the discipline about what its scope, priorities, and methodologies should be. I refer of course to differences over whether the discipline's scope and priorities are oriented towards the biblical text, as per the name "biblical archaeology", or towards a more holistic, even scientific orientation working within a geographical scope and no chronological limitations, as per terms such as "Syro-Palestinian archaeology", to simplify a complex issue. The tension between what these different schools of though represent and a desire to try to find away between them remains at the heart of the problem of naming the discipline.

It is notable that in spite of their outwardly more solid disciplinary identities, even Egyptology and Classical archaeology are not without their problems when it comes to their internal definition and relationship to other disciplines. The name of Egyptology suggests that is simply interested in Egypt, whereas the term really refers only to ancient Egypt. Anything too early, before the Pharaonic period comes under prehistoric archaeology, while the end of Egyptology overlaps with Classics and Classical archaeology, but does not continue into the Islamic period. Egyptology also mixes together archaeology with the disciplines of history, philology, and certainly art history (Thompson, 2015: 2–3); in his way it resembles early biblical archaeology to an extent.

Classical (especially Greek) archaeology, meanwhile, has its own history of entanglement with and even enchainment to Classical texts, which have long loomed large in the agenda and practice of that discipline (Kotsonas, 2016; Morris, 1994). The desire to discern the historicity and background of Homer's works even resulted in a "Homeric archaeology" within the archaeological study of the Bronze and Early Iron Age Aegean world. Although this interest in Homer remains for some scholars, the study of the Bronze Age and Early Iron Age as "Aegean prehistory" has since emerged as a quite distinct and separate discipline, with a more anthropological orientation that now places it much closer to world prehistoric archaeology than to Classical archaeology (Bryce, 2010; Margomenou et al., 2005; Tartaron, 2008). This also recalls the earlier history of biblical archaeology in the Near East and even parallels the drift away from seeing the biblical narratives of the Patriarchs and early Israel as "historical", in the same sense that biblical texts relating to the Israelite and Judahite monarchies are understood as basically historical. Classical archaeology has also dealt with the issues of the whether the archaeological record can be associated with textually-attested historical developments and the challenge of integrating the approaches of the "New" or "processual archaeology" (Snodgrass, 1985a, b). Once again, these are issues familiar to the development of archaeology in the southern Levant in more recent decades. We can take comfort, then, in the fact that we are not alone in our difficulties.

3 Biblical Archaeology and Back Again

3.1 Biblical Archaeology

This is at once the most recognized and most contested name that has been applied to the discipline. Other names like those discussed below have often been presented as direct alternatives where "biblical archaeology" was thought to be insufficient. Its priority is quite clear, being the Bible, but what is its scope? William F. Albright's definition of biblical archaeology encompassed "all Biblical lands, from India to Spain and from southern Russia to South Arabia, and to the whole history of those lands from about 10,000 B.C. or even earlier, to the present time" (Albright, 1966: 13). His student G. Ernest Wright had a different definition; for him, biblical archaeology is concerned with an discovery "that throws a direct, indirect, or even diffused light upon the Bible" (Wright, 1947: 74). Albright's definition is obviously rather broad and covers a range of archaeology that need not be and is not only practiced in relation to the Bible. Nor does much of the geography and chronology that Albright included have a very clear relationship with the biblical world. Wright's definition, in contrast, cannot really stand as the definition for a discrete discipline, instead it is really a subjective interest, a research theme (Dever, 2003b: 58; Holland, 1974: 21). Despite the breadth of the definitions of these august scholars, "biblical archaeology" is inherently associated with archaeological practice in the southern Levant, particularly on the Cisjordanian side, though Albright did not write on this region solely under the rubric of biblical archaeology (Albright, 1960).

As discussed below, biblical archaeology as a name and a practice has been controversial and the subject of not little critique within the history of the discipline, and yet I notice that the name is used and adopted quite often today. This would appear to fulfill Trude Dothan's prediction that the name would come back into fashion (Shanks, 1993). It is even, I would argue, used in an often vague, expansive, and overly general way, even if that use is casual rather than programmatic. Ultimately, if the objective is to name the archaeology of the southern Levant, "biblical archaeology" is clearly not a sufficient name, considering the intellectual point at which the discipline has arrived. Much of the archaeology of the southern Levant is unrelated to the Bible except in the most tendentious sense of either prefiguring the biblical world (prehistory) or receiving the text (the Classical period onwards). Researchers should not be under any obligation to frame their research in terms of how it relates to the biblical text, even those working on the Bronze and Iron Ages, though this is not an excuse for ignoring the Bible when it is a relevant part of the evidence. Given that the borders of the world that provides the cultural and material context of the Bible lies well beyond the southern Levant, whether or not one pushes them as far as Albright, archaeology in the southern Levant can never be coterminous with biblical archaeology.

At this point in the discipline' development, biblical archaeology in its traditional conception is at best problematic as a field practice, so long as large the focus remains on the stratified tells and ruins that dot the landscape of the southern Levant.

Many of these sites include remains of later periods, generally post-Classical, that it has long been the practice to ignore or not treat with the same attention as the biblical periods. Fortunately, I am able to note that current expeditions in Israel now include the investigation of remains of local life in Ottoman and British Mandate Palestine as part of their research design.

3.2 Syro-Palestinian Archaeology

As Dever (2003b: 57) recognized, the name "Syro-Palestinian archaeology" that is so associated with his position on the identity of the discipline actually originated with Albright,[1] in a long review chapter by the latter on the then-current state of knowledge on the archaeology of Mandatory Palestine (including Transjordan) and Syria (including Lebanon), starting in the prehistoric period (Albright, 1938). Dever included most of this in his definition, but apparently not the northern part of Syria (Dever, 2001: 62). Syro-Palestinian archaeology is so associated with Dever because it is the identity that he long argued that the discipline needed to adopt, moving on from the parochialism and isolation of biblical archaeology to a more mature and professional practice (chronicled by Anderson, 2014).[2] He did not, however view Syro-Palestinian archaeology and biblical archaeology as synonymous, in view of how Albright and Wright had defined the latter (see above), but he viewed it as a more appropriate term in part because of its geographical specificity and a chronological breadth not restricted to "biblical" periods (Dever, 1985, 2003b) also Holland, 1974: 22–23). To this extent, Syro-Palestinian archaeology overlaps to a degree with "Levantine archaeology" as I have understood that name below.

The other part of Dever's motivation to shift the discipline's identity was his view that archaeology in the Levant needed to learn from the New Archaeology that had formed primarily in American academia, indeed that it needed to embrace the New Archaeology's anthropological and (putatively) scientific orientation in the way that research questions were posed and answered. This did not mean that Dever wanted archaeology completely sealed off from interaction with the Bible and the interests of biblical scholars, indeed he decried that. It was more that with Syro-Palestinian archaeology becoming a professional field rather than just something at the service of biblical studies these two disciplines needed to be understood first as independent entities before they can be in dialogue (Dever, 1981, 1985, 2003a: 523).

Looking at the field from the perspective of 2022, it is hard to miss the degree to which the discipline is "scientific" both in the regular practice of research and in the way that it reaches conclusions about the social, political, economic, and cultural aspects of the ancient southern Levant in an avowedly "scientific" manner. Here

---

[1] The terms "Palestinian archaeology" or "archaeology of Palestine", with a purely geographical sense, are also found in some older publications, including Albright's (e.g. Albright, 1960).

[2] See also Zevit, 2004 and Davis, 2004.

there is some difference in scholarship between Israel and North America, as the latter is more influenced by post-processual critiques. Nonetheless, a strongly positivistic predisposition and a corresponding suspicion of that which cannot be assessed in an objective manner through direct observation are pervasive in the discipline. The relationship between the biblical text, the archaeological record, and the writing of historical evaluations is a much discussed subject, but there is presently a strong tendency to treat archaeology as a source of objective, scientific knowledge that should dictate the historiographic interpretation of the biblical text and serve as the ultimate arbiter of historical truth (see variously Finkelstein, 2010; Na'aman 2010; Pioske, 2019). This is a position that Dever himself seems to have adopted (Dever, 2017). But the idea that the archaeological record provides a fully representative material impression of the reality of the ancient southern Levant and that it should therefore be used as an objective control in critical biblical scholarship has recently been called into question by Erez Ben-Yosef (2019, 2021) in his work on Iron Age nomads and the problem of their visibility. His debate with Israel Finkelstein (Ben-Yosef, 2020; Finkelstein, 2020) is indicative how unbending the positivistic scientific predisposition of the discipline has become.

How viable does "Syro-Palestinian" archaeology remain as a name for the discipline now? The answer to this depends in part on how much one weights it with the intellectual position with which it has come to be associated through Dever's work, and the degree to which one does or does not agree with that position. But in addition to this, there is the problem of the actual terms within the name. As Dever himself has noted, it seems to indicate a disciplinary unity across the countries involved that is not really apparent. Moreover, the name "Palestinian" cannot, unfortunately, hope to avoid association with how that term is used in the current political situation in the Middle East. It also brings the potential of confusion with archaeological work being done specifically by the Palestinians themselves (Dever, 2003b: 58–59).

Dever suggested (2003b: 60) "simply to adopt the current modern names of the various political entities in the region, however much we acknowledge their arbitrariness", so we would speak of the "archaeology of Israel" or "of Jordan" for instance. Although these terms are used at least casually, I am not sure they were ever likely to catch on as disciplinary names, given that the ancient entities we study just do not adhere well enough to these modern boundaries (the arbitrariness Dever noted). That said, I am sympathetic in the sense that I have always found the term "archaeology (and history) of ancient Israel" a better (if more unwieldy) name for my own specialization than "biblical archaeology", given that the Bible is a source for understanding ancient Israel, but does not address everything we might want to know about ancient Israel or everything that we can investigate through archaeology, epigraphy, and other Near Eastern sources.

3.3 Historical Biblical Archaeology

Thomas Levy introduced this name in 2010 in the opening chapter of his homonymous edited volume (Levy 2010a, b). There he lays out a conceptualization of biblical archaeology as a modern approach defined by the application of philosophical pragmatism, a problem and solution-oriented approach that seeks to apply available tools, sources and data (especially those using the latest technological methods) to attack problems for which we desire answers. It is these questions that frame the priority of historical biblical archaeology, rather than either archaeology or biblical studies specifically and any ingrained ideology or preconception that goes along with these. As per the name offered, Levy intends that historical biblical archaeology will therefore be but one manifestation of historical archaeology generally, in that it is concerned with a period, in this case the Bronze and Iron Ages, for which historical texts are available.[3] Importantly, Levy defines historical biblical archaeology as a "specialization" within Levantine archaeology (see below), the latter of which runs from prehistory up to and including the Islamic periods (Levy, 2010b: 8). Other scholars writing in this edited volume take up a similar approach, retaining the "biblical archaeology" identifier in some form but along the methodological lines proposed by Levy (esp. Bunimovitz & Faust, 2010; Maeir, 2010; cf. Burke, 2010).

I can only agree with Levy's methodological position, and I am encouraged by his insistence on engagement with theory and the contributions of post-processual archaeology (Levy, 2010b: 11). I also think that *if* one wishes to retain the term "biblical" in the name one applies, it is best used to refer to a specialist focus on the period and societies that are actually covered by biblical literature, rather than as the name of the entire discipline of archaeology in the southern Levant or even much of the ancient Mediterranean world. That said, if the biblical text is no longer setting the priorities of research but is rather serving as an aspect of the evidentiary base for answering research questions, is "biblical" still an appropriate modifier? Levy presents his work on Iron Age remains in the Faynan that can be associated with the biblical Edomites as an example of the pragmatic approach of historical biblical archaeology (Levy, 2010b: 13–31) and of course this demonstrates his methodology very well. But I would simply note that this demonstrates another nagging problem with the "biblical" modifier, for while the Edomites are mentioned in the Bible, it is not their literature. While the information on Edom in the Bible in invaluable, it presents an Israelite/Jewish perspective on a related but sometimes enemy society, which is not counterbalanced by any available Edomite text, though such a text may have existed.

---

[3] For a usual if not entirely unproblematic definition of "historical archaeology", see Hicks & Beaudry, 2006.

4 Geography-Based Names

4.1 Near Eastern Archaeology

I would submit that this is actually one of the least controversial names I discuss here, as I think it can be widely agreed that whatever individuals working in the southern Levant call their particular discipline, we can agree that we come under the larger umbrella of Near Eastern archaeology, like Mesopotamian archaeology does as well, for example. The Near East is, after widely understood to be a region synonymous with the modern "Middle East", and it therefore includes the countries of the southern (and northern) Levant. But still there are some issues; do we include Egypt? Egyptology is obviously a separate discipline of its own and yet it is hardly controversial to say the history of the ancient Near East and its peoples is incomplete without the inclusion of Egypt.[4] This is especially true for the southern Levant, being as it was literally under Egyptian hegemony during the New Kingdom period, leaving both Egyptian material culture and an intangible cultural legacy to later periods in the region. Moreover, the very term "Near East" is of course a Eurocentric term (Snell, 2005). In the current post-colonial, post-*Orientalism* milieu, the term "West(ern) Asia" is increasingly used where "Near East" might have been used before, though the former term properly incorporates a larger area.[5]

The advantage that Near Eastern archaeology has is that it can now be considered a very inclusive discipline in terms of geography, chronology, subject matter and methodology. Daniel Potts' two volume *Companion to the Archaeology of the Ancient Near East* covers the Paleolithic to Late Antiquity (Potts, 2012), while ASOR annual meeting and publications cover a chronological range right up to the modern period and geographical range from the Caucasus to southern Arabia. As such, it avoids some of the limitations of scope that other names discussed here have. But Near Eastern archaeology cannot stand as a name when it is specifically archaeology in the southern Levant that is in view, nor is it an appropriate synonym for the archaeology of the biblical world. A popular textbook published in 2003 is entitled *Near Eastern Archaeology: A Reader* (Richard, 2003), and was justifiably criticized for adopting such a title when it focused on the southern Levant (Mullins, 2006). The place of archaeology in the southern Levant within Near Eastern archaeology is undoubtedly a vital aspect of the former, but the latter has long since ceased to be a dominated by a purpose or priority of specifically illuminating the world of the Bible.

---

[4] Increasingly, this is also the case for Arabia.

[5] For example, the name of the International Association for Archaeological Research in Western & Central Asia, founded in 2020, with its geographic scope incorporating the Caucasus, western Central Asia and the Indus (https://arwa-international.org/archaeology/geographical-range/). Likewise, the term "Oriental" has been discarded as part of ASOR's recent official name change.

4.2 Levantine Archaeology

This name actually holds much potential, I think, as a name for the discipline. It covers a more-or-less distinct regional focus within Near Eastern archaeology and is not determined by any topical or chronological limitations, therein fitting better with the realities and standards of modern tell and survey-based archaeology currently practiced. At minimum, the Levant is widely acknowledged to include modern Israel, Jordan, the Palestinian territories, Lebanon, western Syria and the Amuq Valley in southmost Turkey, to which one can add the Sinai or part of it for some purposes. This covers much the same ground as that covered by "Syro-Palestinian" archaeology, but avoids possible political confusion of that term (Levy, 2010b: 8). As with Mesopotamia for instance, there are internal geographical and historical-cultural consistencies that can be considered bases for treating the Levant as a discrete unit of archaeological analysis (Gzella, 2013; Suriano, 2013), especially when the surrounding regions of Mesopotamia, Anatolia, Egypt and Arabia are studied within their own established disciplines.

It is true that the term "Levant" is a Eurocentric and historically-conditioned term, and that the idea of a "Levantine archaeology" is partly rooted in biblical archaeology (Routledge, 2017: 50–52). But even so, it simply makes more sense at this point for archaeology and archaeologists in the southern Levant to be part of discipline incorporating the whole Levant (Burke, 2010: 83). Just as with "Syro-Palestinian archaeology" or terms like "the archaeology of ancient Israel", this has not precluded direct engagement with the biblical text either for the purposes of illuminating its meaning and context, or for using it as a historical source. Consider the specialization of historical geography within our discipline; its practice as established by Yohanan Aharoni and his predecessors is very much rooted in biblical archaeology (Aharoni, 1979), but it has remained the same until today, mostly because it is impossible to do something like the identification of an ancient place name without both textual and archaeological knowledge (Suriano et al., 2021).

This raises a question: is there, at present, really a Levantine archaeology *in practice*? To some extent there is. The term has certainly gained in currency (Burke, 2010), indeed our honoree has established the Levantine Archaeology Laboratory at UC San Diego, a most important application of the name. Some archaeologists working today have excavated in both Israel and/or Jordan and Turkey. A limited number of works with a fully Levantine focus have appeared, including the comprehensive *Oxford Handbook of the Archaeology of the Levant* (Steiner & Killebrew, 2013),[6] the anthropologically-minded *Levantine Entanglements* (Stordalen & LaBianca, 2021), Benjamin Porter's recent essay on the region in the Iron Age (Porter, 2016) and James Fraser's volume on dolmens (Fraser, 2018). On the other

---

[6] I did not include Raphael Greenberg's recent volume *The Archaeology of the Bronze Age Levant* (Greenberg, 2019) as it mostly covers the southern Levant and is intended to compliment chapters on the Bronze Age in *The Archaeology of Syria* (Akkermans & Schwartz, 2003), though together they can be said to represent a fully Levantine approach.

hand, one does also find that publications whose titles indicate they are concerned with the Levant but are focused almost if not completely exclusively on the southern Levant, including the volume *The Social Archaeology of the Levant* (Yasur-Landau et al., 2018), though it is fair to acknowledge that said volume also covers a chronology from the Paleolithic to Islamic and Crusader times. The trend seems to be towards a properly Levantine archaeology, but it is still far from the dominant practice, and a divide between north and south, or even within these regions, remains quite prominent. As Porter (2016: 374–376) notes, this scholarly divide is very much a product of the modern political situation in the Middle East.

5 Period-Based Names

5.1 Islamic Archaeology

Here I use this name in reference to the archaeology of the period of the Islamic conquest of the Near East in the seventh century AD, including the southern Levant, up until the end of the Ottoman empire following the First World War (following Jones et al., 2014: 171–172). "Islamic archaeology" is also used to refer to the whole historical Islamic world, however.[7] Even limiting it the Near East, this is obviously quite a wide scope to place under one name. Not all of those who lived in the Levant or Near East during this period were Muslim, and so this definition by necessity subsumes subjects or sub-disciplines such as "Crusader archaeology", which intimately connects Islamic archaeology in the Near East with the medieval archaeology of Europe. This is not to mention the cultural variety and shifting politics of Muslim societies themselves. Then there is also the question of how much of the material culture of the Near East of this period is expressly "Islamic". Practitioners are well aware of these issues, and the name "Islamic archaeology" is used as a general term for the archaeology of the areas under Muslim elite rule (Jones et al., 2014: 171–173; Milwright, 2010: 6–8; Walker et al., 2020a: 2; Whitcomb, 1995: 48–49). That said, as with any other archaeological periodization, there is also the issue of fixing the transition from one period to another; in the southern Levant, the time immediately after the Islamic conquest saw considerable continuity in material culture from end of the Byzantine period there (Milwright, 2010: 29).

---

[7] Particularly in the recent *Oxford Handbook of Islamic Archaeology* (Walker et al., 2020b).

5.2 Classical Archaeology

Aside from the fact that it relates to Greco-Roman civilization generally, this name is only relevant to a specific slice of the chronology of the southern Levant, so those specializing in the Bronze and Iron Ages or before would not adopt it. On the other hand though, if Classical archaeology is what one does whenever surveying or excavating remains from the period following Alexander's conquest until the end of the Byzantine period, then much archaeological fieldwork in the southern Levant necessitates it. This is so even when one comes to a site with interests and research questions focused on an earlier period, as the expectation of professional fieldwork in our discipline is that all periods will be treated with equal archaeological care. In any event, modern archaeological projects on multi-periods tels in Israel often adopt a research model with a multidisciplinary team, including specialists for particular periods.[8]

Having said that, this does depend on exactly how one defines "Classical archaeology" in the Land of Israel specifically, given that the material culture of the region is, to oversimplify, a variously entangled or deliberately distinct mix of non-native influences from the Greco-Roman world and native cultures, including that of the Jews, Phoenicians and Nabateans. Indeed, it would be more than a little ironic to include remains relating to Jewish revolts against the Seleucids and Romans under the heading "Classical archaeology". Moreover, the appearance of Greek material culture in Israel far preceded the conquest of Alexander, reaching a head in the late Iron Age and Persian period (Fantalkin, 2006), which are traditionally seen as very separate from the time covered by classical archaeology there. All of this is simply to say that even Classical archaeology has its blurry edges in the southern Levant.

5.3 Prehistoric Archaeology

This name likewise is only relevant to a certain slice of the southern Levant's chronology and at the same time refers to a much wider discipline in both Old World and world archaeology. What is relevant here is the relationship of prehistoric archaeology to other names used in the discipline and the scopes with which they are associated, especially in view of Albright's desire to stretch the definition of "biblical archaeology" back to 10,000 BC. In spite of that, Steven Rosen has observed that prehistoric archaeology in Israel grew away from this and that there is now an overall degree of separation now between prehistoric archaeology and that of later periods that are of more direct relevance to the Bible (Rosen, 1991: 308, 2005).

That said, I would observe that the line between "prehistoric" and "historic" in the southern Levant is not entirely clear-cut. The most recent call for papers for the

---

[8] A parade example being the Tel Shimron excavations, see https://www.telshimronexcavations.com/staff

Journal of the Israel Prehistoric Society informs that the journal's remit covers "the prehistory and protohistory of the Levant, up to the Early Bronze Age".[9] If one takes the availability of texts as the basis for assigning a period as historical, as is usually the case, the southern Levant in and of itself was basically still prehistoric even into the Middle Bronze Age,[10] even though this is a period that otherwise belongs firmly in realm of the historically-minded archaeology of the Bronze and Iron Ages, by "biblical archaeology" or whatever other name.

This is a product of three factors: first, a "conservative" view of biblical history and the historicity of the Hebrew Bible that was once much more typical of the discipline sees the Middle and even the Early Bronze Ages as historical because the Patriarchal narratives belong to these periods. In spite of the discipline's move away from this, there is still a general sense that the Early and Middle Bronze Ages still appear historic in the sense of material progress. Raphael Greenberg has recently noted that the "Bronze Age…connotes an era during which the Levant was affected by the earliest movements toward urbanization, political centralization, and the coalescence of charismatically led kingdoms and empires" (Greenberg, 2019: 2). Second, because while there is an absence of historical texts from the southern Levant itself, the production of such texts was already well underway in Egypt, Syria and Mesopotamia in these periods. They sometimes shed light at a very basic level on the southern Levant, such as the names of places and rulers that appear in the Middle Kingdom Execration Texts (Ritner, 2003). Thus the term "protohistoric" might be extended down into the Middle Bronze Age.

6 Conclusions: And the Future?

None of the names currently available for the discipline of archaeology in the southern Levant are faultless or ideal. Each has its problems and limitations, whether on the methodological or practical side, and some are weighted with theoretical baggage. Again, I do not pretend to be able to posit a solution to this problem, and offer the above considerations only in aid of continued debate on the discipline's identity. In the spirit of our honoree's own scholarship on the issue, for now I ask what pragmatic approach can we take to this?

It is hard to avoid the suggestion that of all the options (with their pros and cons) available, "Levantine archaeology" may be a good one for the discipline to move its identity towards. This would mean admitting that "the archaeology of the southern Levant" must now be a regional sub-focus rather than a discipline unto itself. "Levantine archaeology" has the right geographical scope and represents it

---

[9] https://www.prehistory.org.il/wp-content/uploads/2020/02/JIPS-call-for-papers-instructions-2020-1.pdf

[10] The Middle Bronze Age date of even short alphabetic inscriptions found in the southern Levant is uncertain, see (Höflmayer et al., 2021). Proper cuneiform texts come only from Hazor, which was much more associated with Syria-Mesopotamia at this time, see (Horowitz et al., 2002).

neutrally enough, while covering the full chronological range that is actually researched, from prehistory to modernity. Given how Near Eastern archaeology (including Egypt here) is otherwise divided into geographic archaeological disciplines, Levantine archaeology slots in well. Those working on particular periods and topics can work under it, but it also provides the framework for seeing the region's archaeological history over the *lounge durée*. These are reasons that seem to have driven the increasing popularity of "Levantine archaeology" as a disciplinary identity, and I think the most pragmatic move would be to encourage this further.

A few problems remain to be overcome. First, as noted above, it is not clear that a properly Levantine archaeology yet exists, as a scholarly divide between north and south remains. But this divide is weakening. Though modern politics does sometimes intrude, scholars working in the northern and southern Levant respectively are able to interact and share results at conferences, while the availability of publications online make mutual knowledge of data and analyses easier than ever. While I may be overly optimistic, the present political situation especially in terms of relations between Israel and its neighbors may not last forever, so it makes sense for the discipline to prepare for an increase in communication in the future. Then there is the matter of how the period-specific prehistoric, Classical and Islamic archaeologies fit in. If we imagine Levantine archaeology as the long axis of regional history, these archaeologies meet it are right angles. They intersect with Levantine archaeology though not in sharply defined ways, as they are really larger disciplines of Near Eastern, Mediterranean and even Old World archaeology unto themselves.

And what of (historical) biblical archaeology? I have my misgivings about the "biblical" modifier, but it does seem that if it is going to be used, it is best used to designate the historical archaeology of the southern Levant in the Bronze and Iron Ages following Levy's suggestion. There is no reason why "historical biblical archaeology" could not continue as sub-discipline or research interest under the larger umbrella of Levantine archaeology. Given that what the name refers to is generally understood and the name's enduring usage, this is indeed the pragmatic choice.

References

Aharoni, Y. (1979). *The land of the Bible: A historical geography* (Rev. ed.). Westminster Press.
Akkermans, P. M. M. G., & Schwartz, G. M. (2003). *The archaeology of Syria*. Cambridge University Press.
Albright, W. F. (1938). The present state of Syro-Palestinian archaeology. In E. Grant (Ed.), *Haverford symposium on archaeology and the Bible* (pp. 1–46). Haverford College/ASOR.
Albright, W. F. (1960). *The archaeology of Palestine*. Penguin.
Albright, W. F. (1966). *Archaeology, historical analogy & early biblical tradition*. Lousiana State University Press.
Anderson, M. E. (2014). *Clearing the ground: William G. Dever and the reorientation of Palestinian archaeology*. unpublished PhD thesis, University of Melbourne.
Ben-Yosef, E. (2019). The "architectural bias" in current biblical archaeology. *Vetus Testamentum, 69*(3), 361–387.

Ben-Yosef, E. (2020). And yet, a nomadic error: A reply to Israel Finkelstein. *Antiguo Oriente, 18*, 33–60.

Ben-Yosef, E. (2021). Rethinking social complexity of Early Iron Age nomads. *Jerusalem Journal of Archaeology, 1*, 155–179.

Bryce, T. (2010). The Trojan war. In E. H. Cline (Ed.), *The Oxford handbook of the Bronze Age Aegean* (pp. 475–482). Oxford University Press.

Bunimovitz, S., & Faust, A. (2010). Re-constructing biblical archaeology: Toward an integration of archaeology and the Bible. In T. E. Levy (Ed.), *Historical biblical archaeology and the future: The new pragmatism* (pp. 43–54). Equinox.

Burke, A. A. (2010). The archaeology of the Levant in North America. In T. E. Levy (Ed.), *Historical biblical archaeology and the future: The new pragmatism* (pp. 81–95). Equinox.

Davis, T. W. (2004). *Shifting Sands: The rise and fall of biblical archaeology*. Oxford University Press.

Dever, W. G. (1981). The impact of the "new archaeology" on Syro-Palestinian archaeology. *Bulletin of the American Schools of Oriental Research, 242*, 15–29.

Dever, W. G. (1985). Syro-Palestinian and biblical archaeology. In D. A. Knight & G. M. Tucker (Eds.), *The Hebrew Bible and its modern interpreters* (pp. 31–74). Fortress Press.

Dever, W. G. (2001). *What did the biblical writers know and when did they know it? What archaeology can tell us about the reality of ancient Israel*. Eerdmans.

Dever, W. G. (2003a). Syro-Palestinian and biblical archaeology: Into the next millennium. In W. G. Dever & S. Gitin (Eds.), *Symbiosis, symbolism, and the power of the past: Canaan, ancient Israel, and their neighbors from the Late Bronze Age through Roman Palaestina* (pp. 513–527). Eisenbrauns.

Dever, W. G. (2003b). Whatchamacallit: Why it's so hard to name our field. *Biblical Archaeology Review, 29*(4), 56–61.

Dever, W. G. (2017). *Beyond the texts: An archaeological portrait of ancient Israel and Judah*. SBL Press.

Fantalkin, A. (2006). Identity in the making: Greeks in the eastern Mediterranean during the Iron Age. In A. Viling & U. Schlotzhauer (Eds.), *Naukratis: Greek diversity in Egypt: Studies on east Greek pottery and exchange in the Eastern Mediterranean* (pp. 199–208). British Museum.

Finkelstein, I. (2010). Archaeology as a high court in ancient Israelite history: A reply to Nadav Na'aman. *JHS*, article 19. https://jhsonline.org/index.php/jhs/article/view/11286

Finkelstein, I. (2020). The Arabah copper polity and the rise of Iron Age Edom: A bias in biblical archaeology? *Antiguo Oriente, 18*, 11–32.

Fraser, J. A. (2018). *Dolmens in the Levant*. Routledge.

Greenberg, R. (2019). *The archaeology of the Bronze Age Levant*. Cambridge University Press.

Gzella, H. (2013). Peoples and languages of the Levant during the Bronze and Iron Ages. In M. L. Steiner & A. E. Killebrew (Eds.), *The Oxford handbook of the archaeology of the Levant: c. 8000–332 BCE* (pp. 24–34). Oxford University Press.

Hicks, D., & Beaudry, M. C. (2006). Introduction: The place of historical archaeology. In D. Hicks & M. C. Beaudry (Eds.), *The Cambridge companion to historical archaeology* (pp. 1–9). Cambridge University Press.

Höflmayer, F., Misgav, H., Webster, L., & Streit, K. (2021). Early alphabetic writing in the ancient Near East: The 'missing link' from Tel Lachish. *Antiquity, 95*, 705–719.

Holland, D. L. (1974). "Biblical archaeology": An onomastic perplexity. *Biblical Aarchaeologist, 37*(1), 19–23.

Horowitz, W., Oshima, T., & Sanders, S. (2002). A bibliographical list of cuneiform inscriptions from Canaan, Palestine/Philistia, and the land of Israel. *Journal of the American Oriental Society, 122*(4), 753–766.

Jones, I. W. N., Najjar, M., & Levy, T. E. (2014). "Not found in the order of history": Toward a "medieval" archaeology of Southern Jordan. In S. D. Stull (Ed.), *From west to east: Current approaches to medieval archaeology* (pp. 171–254). Cambridge Scholars.

Kotsonas, A. (2016). Politics of periodization and the archaeology of early Greece. *American Journal of Archaeology, 120*(2), 239–270.

Levy, T. ed. (2010a). *Historical biblical archaeology and the future: The new pragmatism*. Equinox.

Levy, T. E. (2010b). The new pragmatism: Integrating anthropological, digital, and historical biblical archaeologies. In T. E. Levy (Ed.), *Historical biblical archaeology and the future: The new pragmatism* (pp. 3–42). Equinox.

Maeir, A. (2010). Stones, bones, texts, and relevance: Or, how I lost my fear of biblical archaeology and started enjoying it. In T. E. Levy (Ed.), *Historical biblical archaeology and the future: The new pragmatism* (pp. 295–303). Equinox.

Margomenou, D., Cherry, J. F., & Talalay, L. F. (2005). Reflections on the 'Aegean' and its prehistory: Present routes and future destinations. In J. F. Cherry, D. Margomenou, & L. E. Talalay (Eds.), *Prehistorians round the pond: Reflections on Aegean prehistory as a discipline* (pp. 1–21). Kelsey Museum of Archaeology.

Milwright, M. (2010). *An introduction to Islamic archaeology*. Edinburgh University Press.

Morris, I. (1994). Archaeologies of Greece. In I. Morris (Ed.), *Classical Greece: Ancient histories and modern archaeologies* (pp. 8–47). Cambridge University Press.

Mullins, R. A. (2006). Review of near eastern archaeology: A reader by Suzanne Richard. *Near Eastern Archaeology, 69*(1), 42–43.

Na'aman, N. (2010). Does archaeology really deserve the status of a 'high court' in biblical historical research? In B. Becking & L. Grabbe (Eds.), *Between evidence and ideology: Essays on the history of ancient Israel read at the joint meeting of the Society for Old Testament Study and the Oud Testamentisch Werkgezelschap Lincoln, July 2009* (pp. 165–183). Brill.

Pioske, D. (2019). The "high court" of ancient Israel's past: Archaeology, texts, and the question of priority. *Journal of Hebrew Scriptures*, Article 19. https://jhsonline.org/index.php/jhs/article/view/29393

Porter, B. W. (2016). Assembling the Iron Age Levant: The archaeology of communities, polities, and Imperial peripheries. *Journal of Archaeological Research, 24*(4), 373–420.

Potts, D. T. (Ed.). (2012). *A companion to the archaeology of the ancient near east*. Blackwell.

Rainey, A. F., & Notley, R. S. (2014). *The sacred bridge* (2nd ed.). Carta.

Richard, S. (Ed.). (2003). *Near eastern archaeology: A reader*. Eisenbrauns.

Ritner, R. K. (2003). Execration texts. In W. W. Hallo & K. L. Younger (Eds.), *The context of scripture, Vol. I: Canonical compositions from the biblical world* (pp. 50–52). Brill.

Rosen, S. A. (1991). Paradigms and politics in the terminal Pleistocene archaeology of the Levant. In G. A. Clark (Ed.), *Perspectives on the past: Theoretical biases in Mediterranean hunter-gatherer research* (pp. 307–321). University of Pennsylvania Press.

Rosen, S. A. (2005). Coming of age: The decline of archaeology in Israeli identity. *BGU Review – A Journal of Israeli Culture, 1*.

Routledge, B. (2017). Is there an Iron Age Levant? *Revista del Instituto de Historia Antigua Oriental, 18*, 49–76.

Shanks, H. (1993). The philistines and the Dothans: An archaeological romance, part 1. *Biblical Archaeology Review, 19*(5), 22–31.

Snell, D. C. (2005). Introduction. In D. C. Snell (Ed.), *A companion to the ancient near east* (pp. xviii–xix). Blackwell.

Snodgrass, A. M. (1985a). Greek archaeology and Greek history. *Classical Antiquity, 4*(2), 193–207.

Snodgrass, A. M. (1985b). The new archaeology and the classical archaeologist. *American Journal of Archaeology, 89*(1), 31–37.

Steiner, M. L., & Killebrew, A. E. (Eds.). (2013). *The Oxford handbook of the archaeology of the Levant: c. 8000–332 BCE*. Oxford University Press.

Stordalen, T., & LaBianca, Ø. S. (Eds.). (2021). *Levantine entanglements: Cultural productions, long-term changes, and globalizations in the eastern Mediterranean*. Equinox.

Suriano, M. J. (2013). Historical geography of the ancient Levant. In M. L. Steiner & A. E. Killebrew (Eds.), *The Oxford handbook of the archaeology of the Levant: c. 8000–332 BCE* (pp. 9–23). Oxford University Press.

Suriano, M. J., Shai, I., & Uziel, J. (2021). In search of Libnah. *Jounral of the Ancient Near Eastern Society, 35*(1), 152–182.

Tartaron, T. F. (2008). Aegean prehistory as world archaeology: Recent trends in the archaeology of Bronze Age Greece. *Journal of Archaeological Research, 16*, 83–161.

Thompson, J. (2015). *Wonderful things: A history of Egyptology, vol. 1*. American University in Cairo Press.

Walker, B. J., Insoll, T., & Fenwick, C. (2020a). Editor's introduction. In B. J. Walker, T. Insoll, & C. Fenwick (Eds.), *Oxford handbook of Islamic archaeology* (pp. 1–16). Oxford University Press.

Walker, B. J., Insoll, T., & Fenwick, C. (Eds.). (2020b). *Oxford handbook of Islamic archaeology*. Oxford University Press.

Whitcomb, D. S. (1995). Toward a common denominator: An archaeological response to M. Morony on pottery and urban identities. In I. A. Bierman (Ed.), *Identity and material culture in the early Islamic world* (pp. 47–66). Center for Near Eastern Studies, UCLA.

Wright, G. E. (1947). The present state of biblical archaeology. In H. R. Willoughby (Ed.), *The study of the Bible today and tomorrow* (pp. 74–97). University of Chicago Press.

Yasur-Landau, A., Cline, E. H., & Rowan, Y. M. (Eds.). (2018). *The social archaeology of the Levant*. Cambridge University Press.

Zevit, Z. (2004). The biblical archaeology versus Syro-Palestinian archaeology debate in its American institutional and intellectual contexts. In J. K. Hoffmeier & A. Millard (Eds.), *The future of biblical archaeology: Reassessing methodologies and assumptions* (pp. 3–19). Eerdmans.

"Their Voice Carries Throughout the Earth, Their Words to the End of the World" (Ps 19, 5): Thoughts on Long-Range Trade in Organics in the Bronze and Iron Age Levant

Aren M. Maeir

Im Anfang war das Gewürz
(Zweig 1938, 1)

Abstract Recent archaeological finds and analyses have changed our understanding of the geographic horizons and margins of connectivity in the Bronze and Iron Age southern Levant. Evidence of trade in materials to and from far-away regions, way beyond what was believed to be within the "worldview" of the ancient Levant, has implications for understanding issues relating to economy, connectivity, cultural influences, bio-diversity, etc. This suggests that ancient Levantine and Mediterranean cultures had a significant role in "global scale" trade – more than often assumed. In addition, recent finds and analyses indicate that "exotic" organic materials – often not surviving in the archaeological record – played a central part in this trade; this, as opposed to common assumptions, which focused on highly visible (and better preserved) finds.

Keywords Southern Levant · Trade · Bronze Age · Iron Age · Organics · Connectivity · Euroasia · Spheres of interaction · Globalization

Thanks to Ezra Marcus and Chris McKinny for their comments and J. Rosenberg for the maps. The biblical quote uses the JPS TANAKH translation.

A. M. Maeir (✉)
Bar-Ilan University, Ramat Gan, Israel
e-mail: arenmaeir@gmail.com

© The Author(s), under exclusive license to Springer Nature Switzerland AG 2023
E. Ben-Yosef, I. W. N. Jones (eds.), *"And in Length of Days Understanding" (Job 12:12): Essays on Archaeology in the Eastern Mediterranean and Beyond in Honor of Thomas E. Levy*, Interdisciplinary Contributions to Archaeology, https://doi.org/10.1007/978-3-031-27330-8_25

1 Introduction

Thomas Evan Levy, or Tom as we know him, has made seminal contributions to Levantine archaeology, and beyond. Among them, his work in the northern Negev (Levy, 1987, 2006), the Arabah (Levy et al., 2014), and the Mediterranean (Shtienberg et al., 2020; Yasur-Landau et al., 2021), has shed light on aspects relating to trade and connections in the ancient Near East and beyond. It is with pleasure and joy that I dedicate this paper to Tom, who I'm fortunate to consider a friend, a respected colleague, and a source of admiration!

Archaeological evidence for long-range connections between regions in the ancient world is well-known, with numerous studies covering different periods, regions, cultures, types of materials and their meaning, from multiple research perspectives.

In this paper, I don't intend to broadly review this topic, but rather focus on selected points on the study of trade and connectivity in the Bronze and Iron Age southern Levant.

2 Pre-modern Connectivity

Our interconnected world deeply effects how we understand the past. Perhaps due to today's extensive connectivity, seemingly based on modern technology, some doubt the existence of extensive long-range connections in the far past. Global trade and connectivity in the early modern period (Crowley, 2015; Smith, 2008; Zweig, 1938), Middle Ages (Abu-Lughod, 1989; Hansen, 2020; Park, 2012; Regert et al., 2008; Ritter, 2009) and Roman times (Cobb, 2018a, b; de Romanis, 1996; Grivas, 2018; Horton et al., 2021; Lischi et al., 2020; Lytle, 2016; Mango, 1996; Parker, 2002; Sidebotham, 2011; Tchernia, 2017; Thapar, 1992; Thorley, 1969; Tomber, 2000; Van der Veen & Morales, 2015) is well-known. But for earlier periods, many appear to believe that connectivity between regions in Eurasia (and beyond) was limited (Hansen, 2020; Haw, 2017; Knapp et al., 2021). More evidence and new analyses, along with reassessments of known finds, are slowly changing this picture (e.g., Beaujard, 2010, 2018; Ben-Yosef, 2019; Bourogiannis, 2022; Fischer, 2023; Kechagias, In press; Kristiansen, 2018; Warburton, 2020).

Archaeological evidence for long-range connectivity is substantially growing (Figs. 1 and 2). In the past it was thought that most of the connections between the Levant and the eastern Mediterranean during the Bronze and Iron Age was from the general Near Eastern region (more or less from the Aegean in the west and Iran in the East), with rare examples of trade outside of this sphere. However, more and more evidence points to a much broader spectrum of farther connections. While sporadic evidence of trade in natural resources and "prestige" objects – usually metal, stone, ivory, pottery (and other archaeologically more visible materials) – was known in the past, recent study only accentuates the extensive – and long-range character of these contacts. Cornish (Berger et al., 2019) and central Asian (Powell et al., 2020) tin, Iberian and other silver (Eshel et al., 2019, 2023; Wood et al., 2019, 2020), Baltic amber (Mukherjee et al., 2008; Gestoso-Singer 2016; Sabatini &

Fig. 1 Map of Eurasia with various sites and regions mentioned in text (see Fig. 2)

Melheim, 2017), Sardinian lead (Yagel & Ben-Yosef, 2022; Yahalom-Mack et al., 2022) and pottery (Bretschneider et al., 2021; Gradoli et al., 2020), and elephant and hippopotamus ivory from various parts of Africa and the Near East (Fischer et al., 2015; Lafrenz, 2004), have been reported from various sites and regions in the Bronze and Iron Age Levant.

Due to the visibility and preservation – and abundance – of the evidence for metal ores and metal objects from distant sources, the metal trade is seen as a cornerstone of the ancient economy, and underlying mechanism powering ancient long-distance trade (Beaujard, 2018; Kassianidou & Knapp, 2005; Ling et al., 2019; Radivojević et al., 2018; Sabatini & Lo Schiavo, 2020; Vandkilde, 2016, 2019, 2021). Without a doubt, trade in metal, and other non-organic "prestige objects" played a central role in ancient trade, and there was a complex social and ideological narratives associated with these objects (Boivin et al., 2012; Feldman, 2002, 2014; Hahn & Weis, 2013; Helms, 1988; Knapp, 2022; Kristiansen, 2018; Maran, 2011, 2013; Maran & Stockhammer, 2012; Ulf, 2014). That said, perhaps organic components of the long-distance trade have received insufficient attention.

It is long known that organic materials were traded between regions, as seen from ceramic transport containers found throughout early Mediterranean (Ben-Shlomo et al., 2011; Demesticha & Knapp, 2016; Grace, 1956; Haskell et al., 2011; McGovern & Harbottle, 1997; Raban, 1980; Robert, 2021; Serpico et al., 2003). Yet, the actual organic materials that were traded were less known, save for common agricultural produce and local products of the Mediterranean region (Salles, 1991; Haldane, 1993; Gitin, 1997; Holladay, 2001; Ward, 2003; Kelder, 2009; Monroe, 2009; cf. Knapp, 1991).

Fig. 2 Map of the Levant with sites and regions mentioned in text

In recent years, this has changed. With the implementation of a broad range of analytic techniques in archaeology, and evidence of organic materials, of foreign – and at times very distant – origins, found in second and first millennium BCE contexts in the Levant.

The long-range movement of botanical and faunal species throughout ancient Eurasia, Africa and beyond, clearly due to human-related vectors, is well-known (Boivin, 2017; Boivin et al., 2012, 2013, 2014, 2015; Boivin & Frachetti, 2018;

Campbell, 2016; De Langhe et al., 2019; Fuller, 2003; Fuller et al., 2011; Grimaldi et al., 2018; Hoogervorst & Boivin, 2018; Horton et al., 2021; Kennedy, 2008; Lejju et al., 2006; Long et al., 2017; Mbida et al., 2001a, b; Muthukumaran, 2014, 2016a, b; Neumann & Hildebrand, 2009; Perrier et al., 2019; Power et al., 2019; Prendergrast et al., 2017; Verdugo et al., 2019; Woldekiros & D'Andrea, 2016). This sets the stage to stress that transfer and trade of organic products to and from the Levant, was hardly an uncommon phenomenon. Finds from Middle and Late Bronze and Iron Ages southern Levantine sites demonstrate a broad range of imported organic materials for distant origin.

This includes:

- Organic residue analyses (=ORA) of "votive" cultic vessels from the Middle Bronze Age temple at Nahariya (ca. 1700–1500 BCE) identified ginger, patchouli oil, citrus, and myrtle/myrrh, species deriving from southeast Asia, Africa and other distant regions (Namdar et al., 2018).
- ORA of wine jars from the Middle Bronze palace at Kabri identified various additives in the wine (Koh et al., 2014), including, possibly, cinnamon, of southeast Asian origin.
- ORA of vessels from a royal tomb at Megiddo, dating to end of the Middle Bronze Age (ca. 1500 BCE; Linares et al., 2019), demonstrate the presence of vanilla, a plant deriving from either southeast Asia or east Africa (Linares et al., 2019, 81).
- ORA of early Iron Age ceramic flasks, from cultic, elite and quotidian contexts at Dor, from a temple at Tel Qasile, and quotidian and cultic contexts from Tel Kinrot (ca. 1100–900 BCE) were found to contain cinnamon (Gilboa & Namdar, 2015; Namdar et al., 2013), of southeast Asian origin.
- ORA of Iron Age II (ca. tenth cent BCE) chalices from a cultic repository pit in Yavneh, possibly indicating use of nutmeg and jasmin, of southeast Asian origin (Namdar et al., 2010).
- Proteomic and phytolith analyses of dental calculus (Scott et al., 2020) from an elite Middle Bronze tomb at Megiddo (ca. 1500 BCE), and a non-elite Iron IB burial from Tel Erani (ca. 1050 BCE), indicate consumption of exotic foods, including sesame, soy and turmeric from Megiddo, and millet, sesame and banana from Erani. These foods are all non-local, probably deriving from southeast Asia (save for banana, possibly from east Africa).[1] Notably, the finds from Erani indicate that materials of distant origins were in circulation even during times that were thought to have limited international connections, and from a non-elite context at a site of minimal importance.
- Analyses using ORA, of residues on two altars from the Iron IIB (eighth century BCE) shrine in the Judahite temple at Arad, identified cannabis and frankincense

---

[1] Banana quickly ripens and spoils, and is thus difficult to transport over long distances (and theoretically one could question whether it is possible that banana was traded in early periods), but traditional methods of preservation, such as drying, enable the edible parts of the fruit to survive for extended periods. See Lancaster & Coursey, 1984.

(Arie et al., 2020). Frankincense originates from east Africa, southern Arabia or the region of India (Bard & Fattovich, 2018; Ben-Yehoshua et al., 2012; Boivin & Fuller, 2009; Creasman & Yamamoto, 2019; Retso, 1991). Similarly, cannabis was not grown locally in the Levant at this time, probably imported from distant locations (Russo, 2014; Jiang et al., 2016; Long et al., 2017; Arie et al., 2020, 17).

- ORA of jars from late Iron IIC Jerusalem (ca. 586 BCE) indicate presence of wines flavored with vanilla (Amir et al., 2022), originating from east Africa or southeast Asia.
- Charred remains of non-local plants have been reported from sites in the southern Levant.[2] This includes: Spanish vetchling (*Lathyrus Clymenum*) from Middle Bronze Tel Nami (Kislev et al., 1993); Aegean fenugreek (*Trigonella foenumgraecum*) and Cyprus vetch (*Lathyrus ochrus*) from an elite context at Late Bronze IIA (14th century BCE) Tel Beth Shemesh (Weiss et al., 2019); various non-local plants from early Iron Age Philistia (Frumin et al., 2015); timber from various parts of the eastern Mediterranean from Bronze and Iron Age sites in Israel (Liphschitz, 2007, 116–131).[3]
- Evidence of the importation of Anatolian honeybees from Tel Rehov (Bloch et al., 2010; Mazar, 2020; Simon, 2014).
- Preserved fish, of Mediterranean and Red Sea origins, has been reported from various Late Bronze and Iron Age sites clearly arriving as the result of trade (Lernau, 2020a, b; Linseele et al., 2013; Routledge, 2014; Sisma-Ventura et al., 2018; Zohar & Artzy, 2020).
- European pigs were imported into the Southern Levant starting from the Middle Bronze Age, but more so in the early Iron Age, most likely connected to the appearance of the Philistine culture (Meiri et al., 2013, 2017). Similarly, fauna of eastern origin, such as the zebu cow (Amar, 2015; Verdugo et al., 2019) and the chicken (Mwacharo, 2016; Boivin et al., 2014, 553; Spiciarich, 2020, 62),[4] appear in second mill. BCE Levant and Egypt.[5]

---

[2] The earliest evidence of long-range imports of organic materials that I am aware of was recently reported from Chalcolithic Tel Tsaf in the Jordan Valley (ca. 5200–4700 BCE), where imported cotton fibers, originating from southeast Asia, were reported (Liu et al., 2022).

[3] Langgut et al., 2013 reported citron pollen, originating from citron trees in a garden in the Persian period palace at Ramat Rachel, most likely originating/imported from Persia. Earlier finds of citron, from Late Bronze Age Hala Sultan Teke (Hjelmqvist, 1979, 113–114) and seventh cent. BCE Italy (Pagnoux et al., 2013, 425; Mai & Girard, 2014, 173–174), indicate that this plant was imported to the Mediterranean region in the Bronze and Iron Ages as well. This is supported by ORA results from Narahiya (above; Namdar et al., 2018), where citron is also reported.

[4] Analysis of Middle Bronze Age Aegean-style wall paintings from Kabri (late 18th cent. BCE; Linn et al., 2018) indicate the use of egg yolks as an organic binder, although whether these eggs derived from chickens other birds (such as ostrich [see below]). Thanks to Ezra Marcus for mentioning this.

[5] Add to this evidence of the importation during the Early Bronze Age, from Egypt to the Levant, of donkeys and perhaps goats (Arnold et al., 2016, 2018; Arnold & Greenfield, 2017, 2018), as well as the suggestion that Egyptian cattle were imported as well (Sowada, 2016–2018). Note as well apparent mention of the importation of Egyptian donkeys to Iron II northern Syria (Simon, 2014).

This rapidly expanding list of organic imports into the Mediterranean region and the southern Levant during the second and first millennia BCE (Alberti & Sabatini, 2013; Aruz et al., 2008, 2014; Aubet, 2013; Broodbank, 2013; Hodos, 2020; Kristiansen et al., 2018; Marcus, 2007, 2019, 2022; Sherratt, 2017), dovetails nicely with other sets of evidence from the region:

- Evidence for long-range importations of metals mentioned above: Cornish tin (Berger et al., 2019), Iberian silver (Eshel et al., 2019; Thompson & Skaggs, 2013; Wood et al., 2019), Sardinian lead (Yagel & Ben-Yosef, 2022; Yahalom-Mack et al., 2022), and the complex trade routes that developed (Sabatini & Lo Schiavo, 2020).
- Importation of Baltic amber to the eastern Mediterranean in the Late Bronze and Iron Age (Gestoso Singer, 2016; Maran, 2013; Mukherjee et al., 2008; Sabatini & Melheim, 2017).
- Export during the Late Bronze Age of glass of Mesopotamian origin, reaching Egypt and central and northern Europe (Varberg et al., 2016).
- A cooking pot from northern Syria with Luwian style seal impressions, found at Hazor in a tenth century BCE context (Ben-Tor et al., 2017).
- Possible late Iron Age connections between Judah and southern Arabia, reflected through supposed south Arabian texts from Jerusalem (Sass, 1990; Shiloh, 1987) and ʿAroer (Thareani, 2011, 228), and the apparent mention of the Kingdom of Judah in a late seventh century BCE inscription from southern Arabia (Lemaire, 2012; but see Stein, 2017; Multhoff, 2019; Danielson, 2022).
- Bitumen chemically provenanced to the Dead Sea from early Iron Age Nubia (Fulcher et al., 2020).
- Copper from the Arabah from late Iron I/21st Dynasty Egypt (Ben-Dor Evian et al., 2021; Vaelske et al., 2019) and Late Protogeometric/Early Geometric Period Olympia Greece (Kiderlen et al., 2016).
- An early Iron Age bronze bowl from Spain may originate from the southern Levant (Zorea, 2018).
- Studies of the genomic history of the Bronze and Iron Age Levant now provide evidence of complex human connectivity throughout the Mediterranean and beyond (Agranat-Tamir et al., 2020; Feldman, 2020; Feldman et al., 2019; Ingman et al., 2021; Skourtanioti et al., 2020; Stockhammer et al., 2021; Zalloua et al., 2008).
- Suggestions for lexical contacts between Indian and SW Semitic languages in pre-Hellenistic contexts (Rabin, 1970, 1994; Weinstein, 2000).

To this one can add other arrays of evidence:

- Finds, both artifactual and textual, of botanical (and other) connections between Bronze and Iron Age Egypt and southeast Asia (Boivin et al., 2014; Gestoso Singer, 2007; Gilboa & Namdar, 2015; Marcus, 2002b, 2007, 2019, 2022; Moreno García, 2021; Muthukumaran, 2016a; Scott et al., 2020).
- Extensive trade in textiles throughout Eurasia (Gleba, 2015; Maeir, 2000; Marín-Aguilera et al., 2018; Wilkinson, 2014, 2018).

- Charred remains of cloves, grown only in Indonesia, from Late Bronze Terqa, Syria (Buccellati & Kelly-Buccellati, 1997/1998, 94, Buccellati & Kelly-Buccellati, 1983, 54; Smith, 2019).
- Exotic animals depicted in Egyptian and Neo-Assyrian art, particularly those brought to royal palaces (Foster, 1998, 2020; Mitchell, 2000).
- Apparent depictions of African and Asian monkeys in zoomorphic figurines and statuary from EB Elam (Urbani, 2021; Urbani & Youlatos, 2020).
- The suggestion that a south Indian monkey is depicted in a wall painting from late Middle Bronze Age Thera (Pareja et al., 2019, 2020; but see Binnberg et al., 2021; Urbani et al., 2021; Masseti, 2021 who believe it is a monkey of African origin).
- Trade in shells of Indo-Pacific origins in the Near East, the Mediterranean and beyond (Reese, 1991). In particular, the engraved *Tridacna squamosa* shells, originating from the Red Sea, Persian Gulf and the Indian Ocean, were seemingly brought to the Southern Levant, were they were worked in local workshops, and then widely distributed (Brandl, 1984; Caubet, 2014; Reese, 2009; Stucky, 1974).
- Ostrich eggs, found at many Bronze and Iron Age sites in the Mediterranean region, have been shown to originate from a broad geographical region (Gönster, 2014; Gorzalczany & Rosen, 2022; Hodos et al., 2020).
- Various textual evidence inform us that olive oil, wheat, and textiles, were extensively traded during the Iron Age, throughout the Mediterranean (Hodos, 2020, 136–141).
- Wide ranging iconographic representations, seen from the eastern Mediterranean to northwestern Europe, during the second and first millennia BCE (Vandkilde et al., 2021)
- The recent suggestion (Wertmann et al., 2021) that Assyrian-style armor was found in a seventh century BCE burial in Yanghai in northwestern China (see though Manning, 2021).

An important methodological note is warranted. Doubts have been raised on the identifications of plants of distant origins in the archaeological remains in the Levant (Haw, 2017; Villing, 2021, 9–10), or on the accuracy of the analytic methods used in these studies (regarding ORA, Whelton et al., 2021). However, the use of a broad range of types of independent analytic methods (analysis of charred botanical remains, ORA, phytoliths, proteomics, aDNA, etc.) together point to a variety of non-local organic products. While care to utilize proper methods is critical (Roffet-Salque et al., 2017; Whelton et al., 2021), the overall picture demonstrates that foreign "exotic" organic materials are identifiable in the Bronze and Iron Age southern Levant.

Thus, the materials from distant sources listed above (summarized in Table 1) provide compelling evidence of the extent and intensity of the trade and connectivity in the Bronze and Iron Age ancient Near East and Mediterranean in general, and the southern Levant in particular, and the significant representation that organic materials had among this.

Table 1 List of imported materials noted in text

Material	Site	Origin	Date
Ginger, patchouli oil, citrus, myrtle/myrrh	Nahariya	SE Asia, Africa	MB
Cinnamon	Kabri	SE Asia	MB
Vanilla	Megiddo	SE Asia or E Africa	MB
Cinnamon	Dor, Qasile, Kinrot	SE Asia	Iron I
Nutmeg, Jasmin	Yavneh	SE Asia	Iron II
Sesame, soy, turmeric	Megiddo	SE Asia	MB
Millet, sesame and banana	Erani	SE Asia or E. Africa	Iron I
Cannabis, frankincense	Arad	E. Africa, S. Arabia, India	Iron II
Vanilla	Jerusalem	SE Asia or E Africa	Iron II
Spanish vetchling	Nami	Aegean	MB
Aegean fenugreek, Cyprus vetch	Beth Shemesh	Aegean	LB
Various plants	Philistia	Near East	Iron I
Timber	Israel	Mediterranean region	Bronze and Iron Ages
Honeybees	Rehov	Anatolia	Iron II
Fish	Israel	Mediterranean, Red Sea	LB and Iron Ages
Pig	Philistia	SE Europe	Iron I
Zebu	Levant	India	MB, LB, Iron I
Tin	Levant	Cornwald	LB
Silver	Levant	Iberia	Iron I
Lead	Levant	Sardinia	LB
Amber	Eastern Mediterranean	Baltic	LB and Iron Ages
Glass	Egypt, C & N Europe	Mesopotamia	LB
Cooking pot	Hazor	N Syria	Iron II
S Arabian texts	Jerusalem, Aroer	S Arabia	Iron II
Bitumen	Nubia	Dead Sea	Iron I
Copper	Olympia	Arabah Valley	Iron I/II
Bronze bowl	Spain	S Levant	Iron I
Biological connectivity	Levant	Mediterranean, SW Asia	Bronze and Iron Ages
Lexical borrowings	SW Asia	India	Bronze and Iron Ages
Botanical	Egypt	SE Asia	Bronze and Iron Ages
Textiles	Eurasia	Eurasia	Bronze and Iron Ages
Cloves	Terqa, Syria	Indonesia	LB
Exotic animals	Egypt, Assyria	Various regions	Bronze and Iron Ages

(continued)

Table 1 (continued)

Material	Site	Origin	Date
Monkeys	Elam	Africa, Asia	EB
Monkeys	Thera, Greece	Indian or African	LB
Shells	Near East, Mediterranean, Europe	Indo-Pacific	Bronze and Iron Ages
Ostrich Eggs	Mediterranean Region	Africa, W Asia	Bronze and Iron Ages
Olive oil, wheat, textiles	Mediterranean Region	Mediterranean Region	Iron Age
Iconographic depictions of connections	E Mediterranean to NW Europe	E Mediterranean to NW Europe	Bronze and Iron Ages
Assyrian style armour (?)	Yanghai, China	Assyria	Iron II

3 Long Range Trade and Connectivity in the Bronze and Iron Age

Based on the evidence noted, we clearly need to ask what this informs us regarding the character of long-range trade and connectivity in these periods.

While much debated in the past, there is now almost unanimous agreement that globalization did exist in the Bronze and Iron Ages (Frank & Gills, 1993a; Sherratt, 2003, 2017; Gills & Thompson, 2006; LaBianca & Scham, 2006; Jennings, 2011; Wilkinson et al., 2011; Boivin et al., 2012, 2015; De Angelis, 2013; Chase-Dunn & Lerro, 2016; Vandkilde, 2016, 2019; Boivin, 2017; Beaujard, 2018; Boivin & Frachetti, 2018; Kristiansen et al., 2018; Hodos, 2017, 2020; Hirth, 2020; Horton et al., 2021; Warburton, 2020, 2021).[6] For the sake of this study, the existence of early phases of globalization, with ebbs and flows, throughout the Bronze and Iron Ages is important, but not the central issue. Rather, I believe stressing that the underlying structures and mechanisms that enabled the extended trade noted above, and in particular, that of organic materials, was the existence of a mosaic of overlapping spheres of interaction, spanning the entire Eurasian landmass and associated island regions (Fig. 3; for similar perspectives, Beaujard, 2010, 2018; Kohl, 2011; Vandkilde, 2016, 2019; Barjamovic, 2018).[7] This overlapping mosaic of "connective tissue" enabled the extensive and intensive connectivity, and the transfer of materials over long distances. While there is no doubt that the character and intensity of connectivity between these spheres of interaction went through changes over time (Beaujard, 2010, 2018; Kohl, 2011; Kristiansen, 2018; Vandkilde, 2016, 2019), it is important to note that even in periods of ebb, as during the Levantine early Iron Age, these connections didn't cease (Gilboa & Namdar, 2015; Scott et al., 2020; see below).

---

[6] Hansen, 2020 believes that true globalization occurred from ca. 1000 CE onwards. While earlier examples don't cover the entire globe, the extent of these early webs of connectivity, spanning continents and oceans, suffice to be considered phenomena of globalization.

[7] These spheres of interaction can be compared to Abu-Lughod's (1989) eight "circuits" of connectivity in medieval Mediterranean and Asia.

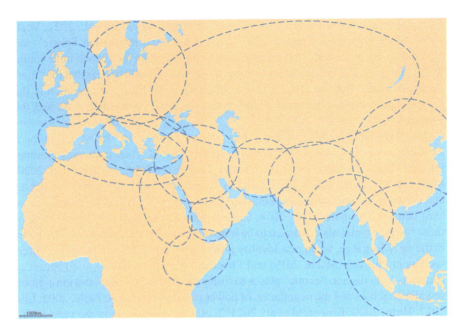

Fig. 3 Schematic representation of possible overlapping spheres of interaction in late Iron Age Eurasia (following Beaujard, 2018, 425, map II.4)

An important point to keep in mind is the character of the transportation technologies (terrestrial and maritime) available in the pre-Classical periods. The practical possibilities of long-range sailing, utilizing the maritime technologies of the Bronze and Iron Age world – even if not explicitly evidenced in earlier periods – should be not be denied (Marcus, 2002a, 2019; Wachsmann, 1998). For example, the broad extent of early maritime connectivity between mainland Asia and "Island Southeast Asia" (and beyond) is indicative of impressive long-range travel abilities (Bellina, 2022; Bellina et al., 2019; Bellwood, 2017; Hoogervorst, 2013; Mahdi, 2016; Rieth & Hunt, 2008; Spriggs, 2011). Another example, from later times, is the ninth century CE "Belitung Shipwreck" (Chong & Murphy, 2017). This ship, originating from the Persian Gulf, discovered off Belitung Island, Indonesia, was carrying a cargo (mainly ceramics) from Tang Dynasty China, and most probably sunk on its voyage back to the Persian Gulf (during the time of the Abbasid Caliphs in Iraq). While of a much later date, it can indicate the possibility, in theory at least, of such long journeys in earlier periods as well; the differences between the maritime technologies available during the early Middle Ages and in the Bronze and Iron Ages were not that great.[8] Even if very early direct connectivity between the Near East and Island Southeast Asia has not been demonstrated, maritime connections between Arabia and the Indian sub-continent likely began in the third millennium

---

[8] For a survey of maritime technologies in southeast Asia, see Manguin, 2016. I'm grateful to Ezra Marcus for discussing with me aspects of pre-Medieval maritime technology and navigation.

BCE (Beaujard, 2018; Frenez, 2019; Possehl, 1995; Schneider et al., 2021; Vogt, 1996). Since connections between the "South China Sea Interaction Sphere" and the "Bay of Bengal Interaction Sphere" started no later than the second millennium BCE (Bellina, 2022; Gupta, 2021; Hung et al., 2013), it would appear that the "maritime silk road" (Bellina, 2014, 2022) so to speak, was already in operation in the Bronze Age – connecting, even if indirectly, southeast Asia, south Asia and the Near East.[9]

The fact that organic materials from faraway places are found in southern Levantine early Iron Age contexts, supposedly a period when trade was minimal (Dothan, 1982; Liverani, 1987; cf. Frank & Thompson, 2006; Master, 2009, 2020; Master & Aja, 2020; Maeir, 2022a, 2022b, for evidence of Iron I trade[10]) indicates that even during times when the Eurasian world-system supposedly collapsed, or at least faltered (Beaujard, 2010, 2018; Chew, 2006; Vandkilde, 2007, 2019), some of these "exotic" materials continued to be transshipped over long distances.[11] Perhaps, in the early Iron Age, when new identity groups were being forged, emerging elites, such as in Philistia (Maeir, 2019) and Phoenicia (Lehmann, 2021), used access to materials from distant, "exotic" places to foster the crafting of inter- and intra-group social hierarchies and the negotiation of power (for other contexts: Earle, 2002; Liu, 2017; Hirth, 2020; Rosenfeld et al., 2021[12]), playing even a role in the very definition of these identity groups (Maeir, 2021a, 2021b). One can also wonder whether some of these materials can be connected to warriors/mercenaries (Maran, 2018) or cultures of piracy (Hitchcock & Maeir, 2014, 2016; cf. Knapp, 2020) which may have been factors in the Late Bronze/Iron Age transition.

As we have seen above, more and more evidence of the trade in organic materials, many of distant origins, is now available. This indicates that organics were an important – and perhaps even crucial – part of the international trade at the time – with perhaps significant social and ideological roles; not a minor derivative, that casually occurred along with the trade in metal and other prestige materials. There is no doubt that metal products played a central role in creating, fostering and development of inter-regional connectivity (Earle et al., 2015; Kristiansen, 2018; Ling et al., 2019; Sabatini & Lo Schiavo, 2020). That said, the extensive textual, and growing artifactual evidence of the importance of organic items in early trade and connectivity, including those of distant origins, were of central importance for Bronze and Iron Age Mediterranean societies, including those of the southern Levant (e.g. Hodos, 2020, 134).

---

[9] See Chase-Dunn et al., 2000 who show that the there was "synchronicity" in the rise and fall of political systems and expansion and contraction of economic systems, from the Mediterranean to east Asia from the mid-second millennium BCE onward.

[10] See Iacono et al., 2021 who note that interregional connectivity continued, although more limited in character, in the western Mediterranean, after 1200 BCE.

[11] Frank and Gills (1993b) stress that during phases of abatement in world systems (their "Phase B"), connections between these systems are often retained. In fact, these continuing connections serve as foundations for the expansions of connections in the following "Phase A" stages.

[12] See Routledge 2012 who suggests that Nile Perch was imported to Iron I sites in the Levant as a prestige objects for elites.

One should not consider these organics solely as "exotica" (Foster, 1998, 2020). Rather, these organic materials played an important role – and perhaps even one of the central motivations – for the long-range trade in the Bronze and Iron Ages. Metal was clearly of central importance, as were other materials such as ceramic and stone, but the organic materials, which up until now have been relatively invisible, may very well have been of cardinal importance as well.

I believe the pages above stress the need to view connectivity in the Bronze and Iron Age southern Levant – and beyond – in a much more complex and multifaceted manner. The entanglement of different spheres of interaction brings to mind perceptions on the past such as "Histoire Croisée" (Werner & Zimmermann, 2006), Subrahmanyam's (2005) "Connected history," or following Giraud and Lallement (2021), the need for "cross border" perspectives. In our case, to move beyond a limited frame of reference on connectivity with, between and beyond the Near East and Mediterranean spheres of interaction.

Similarly, the tension between *fragmentation* and *connectivity* as a primary underlying mechanism in the development of cultures in the Mediterranean region, brilliantly defined by Horden and Purcell (2000), perhaps should be extended to broader regions – that of the overlapping and entangled spheres of interaction mentioned above. While Pearson (2003) suggested using a Mediterranean perspective in the study of the Indian Ocean, I would argue that we have no choice but to integrate perspectives from much larger regions, and study them as fragmented and connected spheres of interaction. Otherwise, once again, we limit our horizons and interpretive possibilities.

By recognizing the broad and expansive horizon of the mosaic of connectivity in from the Bronze and Iron Age Levant, we should also be aware that these webs of connectivity most likely had a profound effect on the geographic "imaginary" (*sensu* Castoriadis, 1987)[13] of the peoples in the Levant during these periods. Thus, biblical narratives indicating long distance connections, such as the story of King Solomon and the Queen of Sheba (whether reflecting Iron Age realia [Lemaire, 2012; Finkelstein et al., 2021] or not [Stein, 2017; Multhoff, 2019]), the land of Tarshish (Celestino & López-Ruiz, 2016; Niehr, 2020) and the biblical passage in the title of this paper ("Their voice carries throughout the earth, their words to the end of the world" [Ps 19, 5]), seemingly embody awareness of the magnitude and scope of the connected world of these times (contra, e.g., Day, 2022).

In ending, I return to the opening quote of this paper (*Im Anfang war das Gewürz* [=in the beginning there was spice]), from Stefan Zweig's (1938, 1) biography of Magellan. While clearly only a distant mirror to the early periods covered above, nevertheless, one cannot but reflect on the centrality of organic materials – and in particular spices – in the early modern European trade, expansion and conquests, in southeast Asia and other parts of the world. The fact that up until recently the evidence for the importance of trade in organic materials during the Bronze and Iron Ages has been minimal, this may be due to the limits and constraints of

---

[13] For somewhat similar perspectives in other contexts, see: Said's (Said, 1979) "imaginative geography;" Marcus, 1995; Daniels, 2011; Yarrow, 2018; Samarawickrema, 2020.

archaeological research. I believe it is only a question of time until contemporary research, with its wide array of analytical methods, already revealing many exotic organic finds, from broad contexts (cultic/quotidian; elites/non-elites; central/non-central sites), that more data of these types will be discovered. These will further bolster the importance of this facet of ancient trade and connectivity – organic products – and broaden the horizon of our understanding of the ancient world and its surprisingly extensive and expansive spheres of interaction and connectivity.

References

Abu-Lughod, J. (1989). *Before European hegemony: The world system 1250–1350*. Oxford University.
Agranat-Tamir, L., Waldman, S., Martin, M. A. S., Gohkman, D., Mishol, N., Eshel, T., et al. (2020). The genomic history of the Bronze Age Southern Levant. *Cell, 181*, 1116–1157.
Alberti, M. E., & Sabatini, S. (Eds.). (2013). *Exchange networks and local transformations*. Oxbow.
Amar, Z. (2015). Zebu – Cattle with a Hump [In Hebrew with English abstract]. *Cathedra, 157*, 7–32.
Amir, A., Finkelstein, I., Shalev, Y., Uziel, Y., Chalaf, O., Freud, L., Neumann, R., & Gadot, Y. (2022). Residue analysis evidence for wine enriched with vanilla consumed in Jerusalem on the eve of the Babylonian destruction in 586 BCE. *PLoS ONE, 17*(3): e0266085.
Arie, E., Rosen, B., & Namdar, D. (2020). Cannabis and Frankincense at the Judahite Shrine of Arad. *Tel Aviv, 7*(1), 5–28.
Arnold, E. R., & Greenfield, H. J. (2017). Isotope analyses of early Bronze Age Fauna at Tell eṣ-Ṣâfi/Gath. *Near Eastern Archaeology, 80*(4), 261–263.
Arnold, E., & Greenfield, H. (2018). Understanding animal movement and urban provisioning through the integration of zooarchaeology and isotopic analyses: A case study from early Bronze Age Tell es-Safi/Gath, Israel. In I. Shai, J. R. Chadwick, L. Hitchcock, A. Dagan, C. McKinny, & J. Uziel (Eds.), *Tell it in Gath: Studies in the history and archaeology of Israel. Essays in honor of A. M. Maeir on the occasion of his sixtieth birthday* (pp. 816–838). Zaphon.
Arnold, E. R., Hartman, G., Greenfield, H. J., Shai, I., Babcock, & Maeir, A. M. (2016). Isotopic evidence for early trade in animals between Old Kingdom Egypt and Canaan. *PLoS One, 11*(6), e0157650. https://doi.org/10.1371/journal.pone.0157650
Arnold, E. R., Greenfield, H. J., Hartman, G., Greenfield, T. L., Shai, I., Carter-McGee, P. M., et al. (2018). Provisioning the Early Bronze Age city of Tell es-Safi, Israel: Isotopic analyses of domestic livestock management patterns. *Open Quaternary, 4*(1). https://doi.org/10.5334/oq.35
Aruz, J., Benzel, J., & Evans, J. (Eds.). (2008). *Beyond Babylon: Art, trade, and diplomacy in the second millennium B.C.* MOMA.
Aruz, J., Graff, S., & Rakic, Y. (Eds.). (2014). *Assyria to Iberia at the Dawn of the Classical Age*. MOMA.
Aubet, M. E. (2013). *Commerce and colonization in the ancient near east*. Cambridge University.
Bard, K. A., & Fattovich, R. (2018). *Seafaring expeditions to punt in the middle kingdom: Excavations at Mersa/Wadi Gawasis, Egypt*. Brill.
Barjamovic, G. (2018). Interlocking commercial networks and the infrastructure of trade in western Asia during the Bronze Age. In K. Kristiansen, T. Lindkvist, & J. Myrdal (Eds.), *Trade and civilisation: Economic networks and cultural ties, from prehistory to the early modern era* (pp. 113–112). Cambridge University.
Beaujard, P. (2010). From three possible iron-age world-systems to a single Afro-Eurasian world-system. *Journal of World History, 21*(1), 1–43.
Beaujard, P. (2018). *The worlds of the Indian Ocean: A global history, volume 1*.

Bellina, B. (2014). "Maritime Silk Roads" ornament industries: Socio-political practices and cultural transfers in the South China Sea. *Cambridge Journal of Archaeology, 24*(3), 345–377.

Bellina, B. (2022). Southeast Asian evidence for early maritime Silk Roads exchange and trade-related polities. In C. Higham (Ed.), *Oxford handbook of early Southeast Asia* (pp. 458–500). Oxford University.

Bellina, B., Faveeau, A., & Dussubieux, L. (2019). Southeast Asian early Maritime Silk Road trading polities' hinterland and the sea-nomads of the Isthmus of Kra. *Journal of Anthropological Archaeology, 54*, 102–120.

Bellwood, P. (2017). *First islanders: Prehistory and human migration in Island Southeast Asia.* Wiley-Blackwell.

Ben-Dor Evian, S., Yagel, O., Harlavan, Y., Seri, Lewinsky, J., & Ben-Yosef, E. (2021). Pharaoh's Copper: The provenance of copper in bronze artifacts from post-imperial Egypt at the end of the second millennium BCE. *Journal of Archaeological Science: Reports, 38*, 103025.

Ben-Shlomo, D., Nodarou, E., & Rutter, J. B. (2011). Transport stirrup jars from the southern Levant: New light on commodity exchange in the eastern Mediterranean. *American Journal of Archaeology, 115*(3), 329–353.

Ben-Tor, A., Cohen-Weinberger, A., & Weeden, M. (2017). A cooking pot from Hazor with Neo-Hittite (Luwian) sea impressions. In O. Lipschits, Y. Gadot, & M. J. Adams (Eds.), *Rethinking Israel: Studies in the history and archaeology of ancient Israel in honor of Israel Finkelstein* (pp. 29–45). Eisenbrauns.

Ben-Yehoshua, S., Borowitz, C., & Hanuŝm, K. I. (2012). Frankincense, Myrrh, and Balm of Gilead: Ancient spices of Southern Arabia and Judea. *Horticultural Reviews, 39*, 1–76.

Ben-Yosef, E. (2019). Archaeological science brightens Mediterranean dark age. *Proceedings of the National Academy of Sciences, 116*(13), 5843–5845.

Berger, D., Soles, J. S., Giumlia-Mair, A. R., Brügmann, G., Galili, E., Lockhoff, N., et al. (2019). Isotope systematics and chemical composition of tin ingots from Mochlos (Crete) and other Late Bronze Age sites in the eastern Mediterranean Sea: An ultimate key to tin provenance? *PLoS One, 14*(6), e0218326.

Binnberg, J., Urbani, B., & Youlatos, D. (2021). Langurs in the Aegean Bronze Age? A review of a recent debate on archaeoprimatology and animal identification in ancient iconography. *Journal of Greek Archaeology, 6*, 100–128.

Bloch, G., Francoy, T. M., Wachtel, I., Panitz-Cohen, N., Fuchs, S., & Mazar, A. (2010). Industrial apiculture in the Jordan Valley during Biblical Times with Anatolian Honeybees. *PNAS, 107*(25), 11240–11244.

Boivin, N. (2017). Proto-globalisation and biotic exchange in the old world. In N. Boivin, R. Crassard, & M. Petraglia (Eds.), *Human dispersal and species movement: From prehistory to the present* (pp. 349–408). Cambridge University.

Boivin, N., & Frachetti, M. D. (2018). *Globalization in prehistory: Contact, exchange, and the 'people without history'.* Cambridge University.

Boivin, N., & Fuller, D. O. (2009). Shell middens, ships and seeds: Exploring coastal subsistence, maritime trade and the dispersal of domesticates in and around the ancient Arabian Peninsula. *Journal of World Prehistory, 22*, 113–180.

Boivin, N., Fuller, D. Q., & Crowther, A. (2012). Old World globalization and the Columbian exchange: Comparison and contrast. *World Archaeology, 44*, 452–469.

Boivin, N., Crowther, A., Helm, R., & Fuller, D. Q. (2013). East Africa and Madagascar in the Indian Ocean world. *Journal of World Prehistory, 26*, 213–281.

Boivin, B., Crowther, A., Prendergast, M., & Fuller, D. Q. (2014). Indian food globalisation and Africa. *African Archaeological Review, 31*, 547–581.

Boivin, N., Fuller, D. Q., & Crowther, A. (2015). Old World globalization and food exchanges. In K. B. Metheny & M. C. Beaudry (Eds.), *Archaeology of food: An Encyclopedia* (pp. 350–356). Rowman & Littlefield.

Bourogiannis, G. (Ed.). (2022). *Beyond Cyprus: Investigating Cypriot Connectivity in the Mediterranean from the Late Bronze Age to the End of the Classical Period.* Athens University.

Brandl, B. (1984). The engraved Tridacna-shell discs. *Anatolian Studies, 34*, 15–41.
Bretschneider, J., Driessen, J., & Kanta, A. (2021). Cyprus and Ugarit at the end of the Late Bronze Age: Insights from Pyla-*Kokkinokremos*. In A. Matoïan (Ed.), *Ougarit, un Anniversaire: Bilans et Recherches en Cours* (pp. 607–638). Peeters.
Broodbank, C. (2013). *The making of the Middle Sea*. Oxford University.
Buccellati, G., & Kelly-Buccellati, M. (1983). Terqa: The first eight seasons. *Les Annales Archéologique Arabes Syriennes, 33*(2), 47–67.
Buccellati, G., & Kelly-Buccellati, M. (1997/1998). The Terqa archaeological project: First preliminary report. *Les Annales Archéologique Arabes Syriennes, 27–28*, 71–96.
Campbell, G. (Ed.). (2016). *Early Exchange between Africa and the Wider Indian Ocean World*. Palgrave Macmillan.
Castoriadis, C. (1987). *The imaginary institution of society*. MIT.
Caubet, A. (2014). Tridacna Shell. In J. Aruz, S. Graff, & Y. Rakic (Eds.), *Assyria to Iberia at the Dawn of the Classical Age* (pp. 163–166). Metropolitan Museum.
Celestino, S., & López-Ruiz, C. (2016). *Tartessos and the Phoenicians in Iberia*. Oxford University.
Chase-Dunn, C., & Lerro, B. (2016). *Social change: Globalization from the Stone Age to the present*. Paradigm.
Chase-Dunn, C., Manning, E. S., & Hall, T. D. (2000). Rise and fall: East-west synchronicity and Indic exceptionalism reexamined. *Social Science History, 24*(4), 727–754.
Chew, S. C. (2006). Dark Ages. In B. K. Gills & W. R. Thompson (Eds.), *Globalization and global history* (pp. 149–183). Routledge.
Chong, A., & Murphy, S. A. (2017). *The Tang Shipwreck: Art and exchange in the 9th century*. Asian Civilisations Museum.
Cobb, M. A. (2018a). Rome and the Indian Ocean trade from Augustus to the early third century CE.
Cobb, M. A. (Ed.). (2018b). *The Indian Ocean Trade in Antiquity: Political, cultural and economic impacts*. Routledge.
Creasman, P. P., & Yamamoto, K. (2019). The African incense trade and its impact in Pharaonic Egypt. *African Archaeological Review, 36*, 347–365.
Crowley, R. (2015). *Conquerors: How Portugal sized the Indian Ocean and forged the first global empire*. Faber & Faber.
Daniels, S. (2011). Geographical imagination. *Transactions of the Institute of British Geographers, 36*(2), 182–187.
Danielson, A. J. (2022). Trade, Kingdom, and Empire: Edom and the South Arabian Trade. *Journal of Ancient Near Eastern History*. https://doi.org/10.1515/janeh-2022-0007
Day, J. (2022). The table of the nations in genesis 10. In J. Day (Ed.), *From creation to Abraham: Further studies in genesis 1–11* (pp. 163–187). T & T Clark.
De Angelis, F. (Ed.). (2013). *Regionalism and globalism in antiquity*. Peeters.
De Langhe, D., Vrydahgs, L., Perrier, X., & Denahm, T. (2019). Fahien reconsidered: Pleistocene exploitation of wild bananas and Holocene introduction of Musa cultivars to Sri Lanka. *Journal of Quaternary Science, 34*(6), 405–409.
de Romanis, F. (1996). *Cassia, cinnamomo, ossidiana: Omini e merci tra Oceano indiano e Mediterraneo*. Bretschneider.
Demesticha, S., & Knapp, A. B. (Eds.). (2016). *Maritime transport containers in the Bronze–Iron Age Aegean and Eastern Mediterranean*. Studies in Mediterranean archaeology and literature, PB 183. Åströms Förlag.
Dothan, T. (1982). *The Philistines and their material culture*. IES.
Earle, T. (2002). *Bronze Age economics: The beginnings of political economics*. Westview.
Earle, T., Ling, J., Uhnér, C., Stos-Gale, Z., & Melheim, L. (2015). The political economy and metal trade in Bronze Age Europe: Understanding regional variability in terms of comparative advantages and articulations. *European Journal of Archaeology, 18*(4), 633–657.
Eshel, T., Erel, Y., Yahalom-Mack, N., Tirosh, O., & Gilboa, A. (2019). Lead isotopes in silver reveal earliest Phoenician quest for metals in the west Mediterranean. *Proceedings of the National Academy of Sciences, 116*(13), 6007–6012.

Eshel, T., Gilboa, A., Tirosh, O., Erel, Y., & Yahalom-Mack, N. (2023). The earliest silver currency hoards in the Southern Levant: Metal trade in the transition from the Middle to the Late Bronze Age. *Journal of Archaeological Science, 23*, 105705.

Feldman, M. H. (2002). Luxurious forms: Redefining a Mediterranean international style, 1400–1200 B.C.E. *The Art Bulletin, 84*, 6–29.

Feldman, M. H. (2014). *Communities of style: Portable luxury arts, identity, and collective memory in the Iron Age Levant*. University of Chicago.

Feldman, M. (2020). *Tracing past human mobility and disease in western Eurasia by the genetic analysis of ancient human remains*. Unpublished PhD, Friedrich-Schiller-Universität, Jena.

Feldman, M., Master, D. M., Bianco, R. A., Burri, M., Stockhammer, P. W., Mittnik, A., et al. (2019). Ancient DNA sheds light on the genetic origins of early Iron Age Philistines. *Science Advances, 5*(7), eaax0061.

Finkelstein, I., Gadot, Y., & Langgut, D. (2021). The unique specialised economy of Judah under Assyrian rule and its impact on the material culture of the kingdom. *Palestine Exploration Quarterly*. https://doi.org/10.1080/00310328.2021.1949531

Fischer, P. M. (2023). Interregional trade at Hala Sultan Tekke, Cyprus: Analysis and chronology of imports. *Journal of Archaeological Science: Reports, 47*, 103722.

Fischer, P. M., Bürge, T., & Al-Shalabi, M. A. (2015). The "Ivory Tomb" at Tell Irbid, Jordan: Intercultural relations at the end of the Late Bronze Age and the beginning of the Iron Age. *Bulletin of the American Schools of Oriental Research, 374*, 209–232.

Foster, K. P. (1998). Gardens of Eden: Exotic Flora and Fauna in the ancient near east. *Yale Forestry and Environmental Studies Bulletin, 103*, 320–329.

Foster, K. P. (2020). *Strange and wonderful: Exotic Flora and Fauna in image and imagination*. Oxford University.

Frank, A. G., & Gills, B. K. (Eds.). (1993a). *The world system: Five hundred years or five thousand*. Routledge.

Frank, A. G., & Gills, B. K. (1993b). World system cycles, crises, and hegemonic shifts, 1700 BC to 1700 AD. In A. G. Frank & B. K. Gills (Eds.), *The world system: Five hundred years or five thousand* (pp. 143–199). Routledge.

Frank, A. G., & Thompson, W. R. (2006). Early Iron Age economic expansion and contraction revisited. In B. K. Gills & W. R. Thompson (Eds.), *Globalization and global history* (pp. 127–148). Routledge.

Frenez, D. (2019). Cross-cultural trade and socio-technical developments in the Oman Peninsula during the Bronze Age, ca. 3200 to 1600 BC. *OCNUS, 27*, 9–49.

Frumin, S., Maeir, A. M., Horwitz, L. K., & Weiss, E. (2015). Studying ancient anthropogenic impact on current floral biodiversity in the southern Levant as reflected by the philistine migration. *Scientific Reports, 5*, 13308.

Fulcher, K., Stacey, R., & Spencer, N. (2020). Bitumen from the Dead Sea in Early Iron Age Nubia. *Scientific Reports, 10*, 8309.

Fuller, D. Q. (2003). African crops in prehistoric South Asia: A critical review. In K. Neumann, A. Butler, & S. Kahlheber (Eds.), *Food, fuel and fields: Progress in African archaeobotany* (pp. 239–271). Heinrich-Barth-Institut.

Fuller, D. Q., Boivin, N., Hoogervorst, T., & Allaby, R. (2011). Across the Indian Ocean: The prehistoric movement of plants and animals. *Antiquity, 85*, 544–558.

Gestoso Singer, G. (2007). *El Intercambio de Bienes entre Egipto y Asia Anterior*. Desde el reinado de Tuthmosis III hasta el de Akhenaton.

Gestoso Singer, G. (2016). Amber exchange in the Late Bronze Age Levant in cross-cultural perspective. *Aula Orientalis, 31*(2), 251–264.

Gilboa, A., & Namdar, D. (2015). On the beginnings of south Asian spice trade with the Mediterranean region: A review. *Radiocarbon, 57*(2), 265–283.

Gills, B. K., & Thompson, W. R. (Eds.). (2006). *Globalization and global history*. Routledge.

Giraud, O., & Lallement, M. (Eds.). (2021). *Decentering comparative analysis in a globalizing world*. Brill.

Gitin, S. (1997). The Neo-Assyrian Empire and its western periphery: The Levant, with a focus on Philistine Ekron. In S. Parpola & R. Whiting (Eds.), *Assyria 1995* (pp. 77–103). The Neo-Assyrian Text Corpus Project.

Gleba, M. (2015). Production and consumption: Textile economy and urbanisation in Mediterranean Europe 1000–500 BCE (PROCON). In K. Grömer & F. Pritchard (Eds.), *Aspects of the design, production and use of textiles and clothing from the bronze age to the early modern era* (pp. 25–34). Archaeolingua.

Gönster, Y. (2014). Straußeneier in Bewegung: ein Indikator für Kulturkontakte im Mittelmeerraum? *Frankfurter elektronische Rundschau zur Altertumskunde, 23*, 1–9.

Gorzalczany, A., & Rosen, B. (2022). Ostriches and people in archaeological contexts in the southern Levant and beyond. *Levant*. https://doi.org/10.1080/00758914.2021.2000709

Grace, V. R. (1956). The Canaanite jar. In S. Weinberg (Ed.), *The Aegean and the Near East: Studies presented to Hetty Goldman* (pp. 80–109). Augustin.

Gradoli, M. G., Waiman-Barak, P., Bürge, T., Dunseht, Z. C., Sterba, J. H., Lo Schiavo, F., et al. (2020). Cyprus and Sardinia in the Late Bronze Age: Nuragic table ware at Hala Sultan Tekke. *Journal of Archaeological Science: Reports, 33*, 102479.

Grimaldi, I. M., Muthukumaran, S., Tozzi, G., Nastasi, A., Boivin, N., Matthews, P. J., et al. (2018). Literary evidence for taro in the ancient Mediterranean: A chronology of names and uses in a multilingual world. *PLoS One, 13*(6), e0198333.

Grivas, C. (2018). Non-native herbal Materia Medica in Greek texts of the Roman period. *Medicina nei Secoli Arte e Scienza, 30*(2), 531–578.

Gupta, S. (2021). Early glass trade along the maritime silk route (500 BCE–500 CE): An archaeological review. In A. K. Kanungo & L. Dussubieux (Eds.), *Ancient glass of South Asia: Archaeology, ethnography and global connections* (pp. 451–488). Springer.

Hahn, H. P., & Weis, H. (Eds.). (2013). *Mobility, meaning and transformation of things*. Oxbow.

Haldane, C. (1993). Direct evidence for organic cargoes in the Late Bronze age. *World Archaeology, 24*(3), 348–360.

Hansen, V. (2020). *The year 1000: When explorers connected the world - and globalization began*. Penguin.

Haskell, H. W., Jones, R. E., Day, P. M., & Killen, J. T. (2011). *Transport stirrup jars of the Bronze Age and East Mediterranean*. INSTAP.

Haw, S. G. (2017). Cinnamon, Cassia, and ancient trade. *Journal of Ancient History and Archaeology, 4*(1), 5–18.

Helms, M. W. (1988). *Ulysses' Sail: An ethnographic odyssey of power, knowledge, and geographical distance*. Princeton University.

Hirth, K. (2020). *The organization of ancient economies: A global perspective*. Cambridge University.

Hitchcock, L. A., & Maeir, A. M. (2014). Yo-ho, Yo-ho, a Seren's life for me! *World Archaeology, 46*(3), 624–640.

Hitchcock, L. A., & Maeir, A. M. (2016). A pirates' life for me: The maritime culture of the sea people. *Palestine Exploration Quarterly, 148*(4), 245–264.

Hjelmqvist, H. (1979). Some economic plants and weeds from the Bronze Age of Cyprus. In *Hala Sultan Tekke 5* (pp. 110–133). Paul Åströms.

Hodos, T. (Ed.). (2017). *The Routledge handbook of archaeology and globalization*. Routledge.

Hodos, T. (2020). *The archaeology of the Mediterranean Iron age: A globalising world c. 1100–600 BCE*. Cambridge University.

Hodos, T., Cartwright, C. R., Montgomery, J., Nowell, G., Crowder, K., Fletcher, A. C., et al. (2020). The origins of decorated ostrich eggs in the ancient Mediterranean and Middle East. *Antiquity, 94*(374), 381–400.

Holladay, J., Jr. (2001). Toward a paradigmatic understanding of long-distance trade in the ancient near east: From the Middle Bronze II to early Iron II - a sketch. In P. Daviau, J. Wevers, & M. Weigl (Eds.), *The world of the Aramaeans: Biblical studies in honour of Paul-Eugène Dion* (Vol. II, pp. 136–198). Sheffield Academic Press.

Hoogervorst, T. (2013). *Southeast Asia in the ancient Indian Ocean world*. Archaeopress.

Hoogervorst, T., & Boivin, N. (2018). Invisible agents of eastern trade: Foregrounding Island Southeast Asian Agency in pre-modern globalisation. In N. Boivin & M. D. Frachetti (Eds.), *Globlisation in prehistory* (pp. 204–231). Cambridge University.

Horden, P., & Purcell, N. (2000). The corrupting sea: A study of Mediterranean history. .

Horton, M., Boivin, N., & Crowther, A. (2021). Eastern Africa and the early Indian Ocean: Understanding mobility in a globalising world. *Journal of Egyptian History, 13*(1–2), 380–408.

Hung, H. C., Nguyen, K. D., Bellwood, P., & Carson, M. T. (2013). Coastal connectivity: Long-term trading networks across the South China Sea. *Journal of Island and Coastal Archaeology, 8*, 384–404.

Iacono, F., Borgna, E., Cattani, M., Cavazzuti, C., Dawson, H., Galanakis, Y., et al. (2021). Establishing the Middle Sea: The Late Bronze Age of Mediterranean Europe (1700–900 BC). *Journal of Archaeological Research*. https://doi.org/10.1007/s10814-021-09165-1

Ingman, T., Eisenmann, S., Skourtanioti, E., Akar, M., Ligner, J., Ruscone, G., et al. (2021). Human mobility at Tell Atchana (Alalakh), Hatay, Turkey during the 2nd millennium BC: Integration of isotopic and genomic evidence. *PLoS One, 16*(6), e0241883.

Jennings, J. (2011). *Globalizations and the ancient world*. Cambridge University.

Jiang, H., Wang, L., Merlin, M., Clarke, R., Pan, Y., Zhang, Y., et al. (2016). Ancient cannabis burial shroud in a central Eurasian cemetery. *Economic Botany, 70*, 213–221.

Kassianidou, V., & Knapp, A. (2005). Archaeometallurgy in the Mediterranean: The social context of mining, technology, and trade. In E. Blake & A. Knapp (Eds.), *The archaeology of Mediterranean prehistory* (pp. 215–251). Blackwell.

Kechagias, A. E., (In press). Between China and the Mediterranean: Detecting intercultural communication before the silk road. In J. Wood, G. Herrera-Franco, A. Dłużewska, K. Al-Kodmany, & S. Kostopoulou (Eds.), *Proceedings of Science and Technology*. Springer Publishing.

Kelder, J. (2009). Royal gift exchange between Mycenae and Egypt: Olives as "greeting gifts" in the Late Bronze Age eastern Mediterranean. *American Journal of Archaeology, 113*(3), 339–352.

Kennedy, J. (2008). Pacific bananas: Complex origins, multiple dispersals? *Asian Perspectives, 47*(1), 75–94.

Kiderlen, M., Bode, M., Hauptmann, A., & Bassiakos, Y. (2016). Tripod cauldrons produced at Olympia give evidence for trade with copper from Faynan (Jordan) to South West Greece, c. 950–750 BCE. *Journal of Archaeological Science Reports, 8*, 303–313.

Kislev, M., Artzy, M., & Marcus, E. (1993). Import of an Aegean food plant to a Middle Bronze IIa coastal site in Israel. *Levant, 25*, 145–154.

Knapp, A. B. (1991). Spice, drugs, grain and grog: Organic goods in Bronze Age east Mediterranean trade. In N. Gale (Ed.), *Bronze Age trade in the Mediterranean* (pp. 21–67). Paul Åstrom.

Knapp, A. B. (2020). Piracy in the Late Bronze Age Eastern Mediterranean? A Cautionary Tale. In A. Gilboa & A. Yasur-Landau (Eds.), *Nomads of the Mediterranean: Trade and contact in the Bronze and Iron Ages: Studies in honor of Michal Artzy* (pp. 142–160). Brill.

Knapp, A. B. (2022). Bronze age Cyprus and the Aegean: 'Exotic currency' and objects of connectivity. *Journal of Greek Archaeology, 7*, 67–93.

Knapp, A. B., Russell, A., & van Dommelen, P. (2021). Cyprus, Sardinia and Sicily: A maritime perspective on interaction, connectivity and imagination in Mediterranean prehistory. *Cambridge Archaeological Journal*. https://doi.org/10.1017/S0959774321000330

Koh, A. J., Yasur-Landau, A., & Cline, E. H. (2014). Characterizing a Middle Bronze Palatial Wine Cellar from Tel Kabri, Israel. *PLoS ONE, 9*(8), e106406.

Kohl, P. (2011). World-systems and modelling macro-historical processes in later prehistory: An examination of old and a search for new perspectives. In T. C. Wilkinson, S. Sherratt, & J. Bennet (Eds.), *Interweaving worlds: Systemic interactions in Eurasia, 7th to 1st millennia BC* (pp. 77–86). Oxbow.

Kristiansen, K. (2018). The rise of Bronze Age peripheries and the expansion of international trade 1950–1100 BC. In K. Kristiansen, T. Lindkvist, & J. Myrdal (Eds.), *Trade and civilisation* (pp. 107–136). Cambridge University.

Kristiansen, K., Lindkvist, T., & Myrdal, J. (Eds.). (2018). *Trade and civilisation*. Cambridge University.
LaBianca, O. S., & Scham, S. A. (Eds.). (2006). Connectivity in Antiquity: Globalization as a long-term historical process.. Equinox.
Lafrenz, K. A. (2004). *Tracing the source of the elephant and hippopotamus ivory from the 14th century B.C. Uluburun shipwreck: The archaeological, historical, and isotopic evidence*. Unpublished PhD, University of South Florida, Tampa.
Lancaster, P. A., & Coursey, D. G. (1984). *Traditional Post-Harvest Technology of Perishable Tropical Staples*. Food and Agriculture Organization.
Langgut, D., Gadot, Y., Porat, N., & Lipschits, O. (2013). Fossil pollen reveals the secrets of the Royal Persian Garden at Ramat Rahel. *Jerusalem. Palynology, 37*(1), 115–129.
Lehmann, G. (2021). The emergence of early Phoenicia. State formation processes in the 10th century BCE Levant. *Jerusalem Journal of Archaeology, 1*, 272–324.
Lejju, B. J., Robertshaw, P., & Taylor, D. (2006). Africa's earliest bananas? *Journal of Archaeological Science, 33*(1), 102–113.
Lemaire, A. (2012). New perspectives on the trade between Judah and South Arabia. In M. Lubetski (Ed.), *New inscriptions and seals relating to the biblical world* (pp. 93–110). Society of Biblical Research.
Lernau, O. (2020a). Fish bones. In I. L. Stager, D. M. Master, & A. J. Aja (Eds.), *Ashkelon 7: The Iron Age I* (pp. 731–746). Eisenbrauns.
Lernau, O. (2020b). Chapter 50: Fish remains. In A. Mazar & N. Panitz-Cohen (Eds.), *Tel Reḥov, A Bronze and Iron Age City in the Beth -Shean Valley, volume V: Various objects and natural-science studies* (pp. 639–658). Institute of Archaeology.
Levy, T. (Ed.). (1987). *Shiqmim I: Studies concerning chalcolithic societies in the northern Negev desert*. Israel.
Levy, T. (2006). *Archaeology, anthropology and cult: The sanctuary at Gilat*. Israel.
Levy, T. E., Najjar, M., & Ben-Yosef, E. (2014). *New Insights into the Iron Age Archaeology of Edom, Southern Jordan* (Vol. 1–2). Cotsen Institute of Archaeology.
Linares, V., Adams, M. J., Cradic, M. S., Finkelstein, I., Lipschits, O., Martin, M. A. S., et al. (2019). First evidence for vanillin in the old world: Its use as mortuary offering in Middle Bronze Canaan. *Journal of Archaeological Science: Reports, 25*, 77–84.
Ling, J., Hjärthner, E., Grandin, L., Stos-Gale, Z., Kristiansen, K., Melheim, A. L., et al. (2019). Moving metals IV: Swords, metal sources and trade networks in Bronze Age Europe. *Journal of Archaeological Science Reports, 26*, 101837.
Linn, R., Bonaduce, I., Ntasi, G., Birolo, L., Yasur-Landau, A., Cline, E. H., et al. (2018). Evolved gas analysis-mass spectrometry to identify the earliest organic binder in Aegean style wall paintings. *Angewandte Chemie, 130*, 13441–13444.
Linseele, V., van Neer, W., & Bretschneider, J. (2013). The mysteries of Egyptian Nile perch (Lates niloticus). The case of Tell Tweini (Syria, Middle Bronze Age – Iron Age). In B. De Cupere, V. Linseele, & S. Hamilton-Dyer (Eds.), *Archaeozoology of the Near East X. Proceedings of the tenth international symposium on the archaeozoology of South-Western Asia and adjacent areas* (pp. 209–226) Peeters.
Liphschitz, N. (2007). *Timber in ancient Israel*. Emery and Claire Yass Publications in Archaeology.
Lischi, S., Odelli, E., Perumal, J. L., Lucejko, J. J., Ribechini, E. R., Lippi, M. M., et al. (2020). Indian Ocean trade connections: Characterization and commercial routes of torpedo jars. *Heritage Science, 8*, Article 76.
Liu, Y. (2017). Exotica as prestige technology: The production of luxury gold in Western Han society. *Antiquity, 91*(360), 1588–1602.
Liu, L., Levin, M. J., Klimscha, F., & Rosenberg, D. (2022). The earliest cotton fibers and pan-regional contacts in the near east. *Frontiers in Plant Science, 13*, 1045554.
Liverani, M. (1987). The collapse of the Near Eastern regional system at the end of the Bronze Age: The case of Syria. In M. Rowlands, M. Larsen, & K. Kristiansen (Eds.), *Centre and periphery in the ancient world* (pp. 66–73). Cambridge University.

Long, T., Wagner, M., Demske, D., Leipe, C., & Tarasov, P. E. (2017). Cannabis in Eurasia: Origin of human use and Bronze Age trans-continental connections. *Vegetation History and Archaeobotany, 26*, 245–258.

Lytle, E. (2016). Early Greek and Latin sources on the Indian Ocean and Eastern Africa. In G. Campbell (Ed.), *Early exchange between Africa and the wider Indian Ocean world* (pp. 113–134). Palgrave Macmillan.

Maeir, A. M. (2000). The political and economic status of MBII Hazor and MBII trade: An inter- and intra-regional view. *Palestine Exploration Quarterly, 132*(1), 37–58.

Maeir, A. M. (2019). Iron Age I Philistines: Entangled identities in a transformative period. In A. Yasur-Landau, E. H. Cline, & E. Rowan (Eds.), *The social archaeology of the Levant* (pp. 310–323). Cambridge University.

Maeir, A. M. (2021a). Identity creation and resource controlling strategies: Thoughts on Edomite ethnogenesis and development. *Bulletin of the American Society of Overseas Research, 386*, 209–220.

Maeir, A. M. (2021b). On defining Israel: Or, let's do the *Kulturkreislehre* again! *Hebrew Bible and Ancient Israel, 10*(2), 106–148.

Maeir, A. M. (2022a). Between Philistia, Phoenicia, and beyond: A view from Tell es-Safi/Gath. In U. Davidovich, S. Matskevich, & N. Yahalom-Mack (Eds.), *Material, method, and meaning: Papers in eastern Mediterranean archaeology in honor of Ilan Sharon* (pp. 185–194). Zaphon.

Maeir, A. M. (2022b). Jerusalem and the west – Via Philistia: An early Iron Age perspective from tell es-Safi/Gath. In F. Hagemeyer (Ed.), *Jerusalem and the coastal plain in the Iron Age and Persian periods: New studies on Jerusalem's relations with the southern coastal plain of Israel/Palestine (ca. 1200–300 BCE)* (pp. 7–21). Mohr Siebeck.

Mahdi, W. (2016). Origins of Southeast Asian shipping and maritime communication across the Indian Ocean. In G. Campbell (Ed.), *Early exchange between Africa and the wider Indian ocean world* (pp. 25–49). Palgrave Macmillan.

Mai, B. T., & Girard, M. (2014). Citrus (Rutaceae) was present in the western Mediterranean in Antiquity. In A. Chevalier, E. Marinova, & L. Peña-Chocarro (Eds.), *Plants and people: Choices and diversity through time* (pp. 170–174). Oxbow.

Mango, M. (1996). Byzantine maritime trade with the east (4th–7th centuries). *ARAM, 8*, 139–163.

Manguin, P. Y. (2016). Austronesian shipping in the Indian Ocean: From outrigger boats to trading ships. In G. Campbell (Ed.), *Early exchange between Africa and the wider Indian Ocean world* (pp. 51–76). Palgrave Macmillan.

Manning, S. (2021). *The Scale Armour from Yanghai.* www.bookandsword.com/2021/12/11/the-scale-armour-from-yanghai/

Maran, J. (2011). Lost in translation: The emergence of Mycenaean culture as a phenomenon of glocalisation. In T. C. Wilkinson, S. Sherratt & J. Bennet (Eds.), *Interweaving worlds: Systemic interactions in Eurasia, 7th to 1st Millennium BC. Papers from a conference in memory of Professor Andrew Sherratt – What would a Bronze Age World System Look Like? World system approaches to Europe and western Asia 4th to 1st millennia BC* (pp. 282–294). Oxbow.

Maran, J. (2013). Bright as the sun: The appropriation of amber objects in Mycenaean Greece. In H. P. Hahn & H. Weis (Eds.), *Mobility, meaning and transformation of things* (pp. 147–169). Oxbow.

Maran, J. (2018). Goliath's peers: Interconnected Polyethnic warrior elites in the Eastern Mediterranean of the 13th and 12th centuries BCE. In I. Shai, J. R. Chadwick, L. Hitchcock, A. Dagan, C. McKinny, & J. Uziel (Eds.), *Tell it in Gath: Studies in the history and archaeology of Israel. Essays in honor of A. M. Maeir on the occasion of his sixtieth birthday* (pp. 223–241). Zaphon.

Maran, J., & Stockhammer, P. W. (Eds.). (2012). *Materiality and social practice.* Oxbow.

Marcus, M. I. (1995). Geography as visual ideology: Landscape, knowledge, and power in neo-Assyrian art. In M. Liverani (Ed.), *Neo-Assyrian geography. Quaderni di Geographia Storica 5* (pp. 193–202). Università di Roma 'La Sapienza'.

Marcus, E. (2002a). The southern Levant and maritime trade during the Middle Bronze IIA period. In S. Ahituv & E. Oren (Eds.), *Aharon Kempinski memorial volume (pp. 241–263)*. Ben Gurion University.

Marcus, E. (2002b). Prehistoric and Protohistoric seafaring in the southeastern Mediterranean Sea. In E. Van den Brink & Levy (Eds.), *Egypt and the Levant: Interrelations the 4th through the early 3rd millennium BCE* (pp. 403–417). Leicester University.

Marcus, E. (2007). Amenemhet II and the sea: Maritime aspects of the Mit Rahina (Memphis) inscription. *Ägypten und Levante, 17*, 137–190.

Marcus, E. S. (2019). A maritime approach to exploring the Hyksos phenomenon. In M. Bietak & S. Prell (Eds.), *The Enigma of the Hyksos, Volume 1* (pp. 149–164). Harrassowitz.

Marcus, E. S. (2022). Middle kingdom Egypt and the eastern Mediterranean. In K. Radner, N. Moeller, & D. T. Potts (Eds.), *Oxford history of the ancient near east, Volume 2* (pp. 777–853). Oxford University.

Marín-Aguilera, B., Iacono, F., & Gleba, M. (2018). Colouring the Mediterranean: Production and consumption of purple-dyed textiles in pre-Roman times. *Journal of Mediterranean Archaeology, 31*(2), 127–154.

Masseti, M. (2021). An analysis of recent literature regarding the Minoan "blue monkeys" represented in Aegean Bronze Age art. *Journal of Anthropological Sciences, 99*, 153–156.

Master, D. M. (2009). The renewal of trade at Iron Age I Ashkelon. *Eretz Israel, 28*, 111*-122*.

Master, D. M. (2020). Petrographic analysis. In I. L. Stager, D. M. Master, & A. J. Aja (Eds.), *Ashkelon 7: The Iron Age I* (pp. 364–373). Eisenbrauns.

Master, D. M., & Aja, A. J. (2020). Conclusion: Uncovering philistines. In I. L. Stager, D. M. Master, & A. J. Aja (Eds.), *Ashkelon 7: The Iron Age I* (pp. 854–862). Eisenbrauns.

Mazar, A. (2020). Chapter 14E: Socioeconomic, historical and ethnographic aspects of the apiary. In A. Mazar & N. Panitz-Cohen (Eds.), *Tel Reḥov, A Bronze and Iron Age City in the Beth -Shean Valley, Volume II: The Lower Mount: Area A and the Apiary* (pp. 639–658). Institute of Archaeology.

Mbida, M. C., Doutrelepont, H., Vrydaghs, L., Swennen, R. L., Swennen, R. J., Beeckman, H., et al. (2001a). First archaeological evidence of banana cultivation in Central Africa during the third millennium before present. *Vegetation History and Archaeobotany, 10*, 1–6.

Mbida, M. C., Doutrelepont, H., Vrydaghs, L., Swennen, R. L., Swennen, R. J., Beeckman, H., et al. (2001b). The initial history of bananas in Africa. A reply to Jan Vansina. *Azania, 40*(1), 128–135.

McGovern, P., & Harbottle, G. (1997). "Hyksos" trade connections between Tell ed-Dab'a (Avaris) and the Levant: A Neutron Activation study of the Canaanite jar. In E. Oren (Ed.), *The Hyksos: New historical and archaeological perspectives* (pp. 141–157). University Museum.

Meiri, M., Huchon, D., Bar-Oz, G., Boaretto, E., Horwitz, L. K., Maeir, A. M., et al. (2013). Ancient DNA and population turnover in southern Levantine pigs- signature of the sea peoples migration? *Scientific Reports, 3*, 3035.

Meiri, M., Stockhammer, P. W., Marom, N., Bar-Oz, G., Sapir-Hen, L., Morgenstern, P., et al. (2017). Eastern Mediterranean mobility in the bronze and Early Iron Ages: Inferences from ancient DNA of pigs and cattle. *Scientific Reports, 7*, article 701.

Mitchell, T. C. (2000). Camels in the Assyrian Bas-Reliefs. *Iraq, 62*, 187–194.

Monroe, C. M. (2009). *Trade, tradition, and transformation in the eastern Mediterranean ca. 1350–1175 BCE*. Ugarit-verlag.

Moreno García, J. C. (2021). Markets, transactions, and ancient Egypt: New venues for research in a comparative perspective. In J. C. Moreno García (Ed.), *Markets and exchanges in pre-modern and traditional societies* (pp. 189–229). Oxbow.

Mukherjee, A., Rossberger, E., James, M., Pfälzner, P., Higgitt, C., White, R., et al. (2008). The Qatna lion: Scientific confirmation of Baltic amber in Late Bronze Age Syria. *Antiquity, 82*, 49–59.

Multhoff, A. (2019). Merchant and Marauder – The adventures of a Sabaean clansman. *Arabian Archaeology and Epigraphy, 30*, 239–262.

Muthukumaran, S. (2014). Between archaeology and text: The origins of Rice consumption and cultivation in the middle east and the Mediterranean. *Papers from the Institute of Archaeology, 24*(1), 1–7.

Muthukumaran, S. (2016a). *An ecology of trade: Tropical cultivars, commensals and Fauna between the Mediterranean, the near east and South Asia in the 1st millennium BC*. Unpublished PhD.

Muthukumaran, S. (2016b). Tree cotton (*G. arboreum*) in Babylonia. In E. Foietta, C. Ferrandi, E. Quirico, F. Giusto, M. Mortarini, J. Bruno, et al. (Eds.), *Cultural & Material contacts in the ancient near east* (pp. 98–105). Apice Libri.

Mwacharo, J. M. (2016). Intercontinental networks between Africa and Asia across the Indian Ocean: What do village chickens reveal? In G. Campbell (Ed.), *Early exchange between Africa and the wider Indian Ocean world* (pp. 255–274). Palgrave Macmillan.

Namdar, D., Neumann, R., & Weiner, S. (2010). In I. R. Kletter, I. Ziffer, W. Zwickel, & I. Yavneh (Eds.), *Residue analysis of chalices from the repository pit* (pp. 167–173).

Namdar, D., Gilboa, A., Newmann, R., Finkelstein, I., & Weiner, S. (2013). Cinnamaldehyde in early Iron Age Phoenician flasks raises the possibility of Levantine trade with South East Asia. *Mediterranean Archaeology and Archaeometry, 12*(3), 1–19.

Namdar, D., Cohen-Weinberger, A., & Zuckerman, S. (2018). Towards a new understanding of MB IIB cult practices: Analyses of seven-cupped bowls from the shrine of Nahariya. In I. Shai, J. R. Chadwick, L. Hitchcock, A. Dagan, C. McKinny, & J. Uziel (Eds.), *Tell it in Gath: Studies in the history and archaeology of Israel. Essays in honor of Aren M. Maeir on the occasion of his sixtieth birthday* (pp. 723–746). Zaphon.

Neumann, K., & Hildebrand, E. (2009). Early Bananas in Africa: The state of the art. *Ethnobotany Research and Applications, 7*, 353–362.

Niehr, H. (2020). Tartessos – Tarschisch. Von der Iberischen Region zur literarischen Landschaft im Alten Testament. In J. J. Krause, W. Oswald, & K. Weingart (Eds.), *Eigensinn und Entstehung der Hebräischen Bibel* (pp. 497–526). Mohr Siebeck.

Pagnoux, C., Celant, A., Coubray, S., Fiorentino, G., & Zech-Matterne, V. (2013). The introduction of Citrus to Italy, with reference to the identification problems of seed remains. *Vegetation History and Archaeobotany, 22*(5), 421–438.

Pareja, M. N., McKinney, T., Mahyew, J. A., Setchell, J. M., Nash, S. D., & Heaton, R. (2019). A new identification of the monkeys depicted in a Bronze Age wall painting from Akrotiri, Thera. *Primates, 61*, 159168.

Pareja, M. N., McKinney, T., & Setchell, J. M. (2020). Aegean monkeys and the importance of cross-disciplinary collaboration in archaeoprimatology: A reply to Urbani and Youlatos. *Primates, 61*, 767–774.

Park, H. (2012). *Mapping the Chinese and Islamic worlds: Cross-cultural exchange in pre-modern Asia*. Cambridge University.

Parker, G. (2002). Ex Oriente Luxuria: Indian commodities and Roman experience. *Journal of the Economic and Social History of the Orient, 45*(1), 40–95.

Pearson, M. (2003). *The Indian Ocean*. Routledge.

Perrier, Z., Jenny, C., Bakry, F., Karamura, D., Kitavi, M., Dubois, C., et al. (2019). East African diploid and triploid bananas: A genetic complex transported from South-East Asia. *Annals of Botany, 123*(1), 19–36.

Possehl, G. L. (1995). Seafaring merchants of Meluhha. *South Asian Archaeology, 1*, 87–97.

Powell, W., Frachetti, M., Pulak, C., Bankoff, H. A., Barjamovic, G., Johnson, M., Mathur, R., Pigott, V. C., Price, M., & Yener, K. A. (2020). Tin from Uluburun shipwreck shows small-scale commodity exchange fueled continental tin supply across Late Bronze Age Eurasia. *Science Advances, 8*(48), abq3766.

Power, R. C., Güdemann, T., Crowther, A., & Boivin, N. (2019). Asian crop dispersal in Africa and late Holocene human adaptation to tropical environments. *Journal of World Prehistory, 32*, 353–392.

Prendergrast, M. E., Buckley, M., Crowther, A., Frantz, L., Eager, H., Lebrasseur, O., et al. (2017). Reconstructing Asian faunal introductions to eastern Africa from multi-proxy biomolecular and archaeological datasets. *PLoS One, 12*(2), e0190336.

Raban, A. (1980). *The portable jar in the ancient near east: Typology, distribution and provenance*. Unpublished PhD, Hebrew University, Jerusalem [In Hebrew with English summary].

Rabin, C. (1970). Words in biblical Hebrew from Indo-Aryan languages of the Near East (in Hebrew). In S. Abramski, Y. Aharoni, H. Gvaryahu, & B. Luria (Eds.), *Shmuel Yeivin Volume* (pp. 462–497) Kiryat-Sepher.

Rabin, C. (1994). Lexical borrowings from Indian languages as carriers of ideas and technical concepts. In H. Goodman (Ed.), *Between Jerusalem and Benares* (pp. 25–32, 281–282). SUNY.

Radivojević, M., Roberts, B. W., Pernicka, E., Stos-Gale, Z., Martinón-Torres, M., Vandkilde, H., et al. (2018). The provenance, use, and circulation of metals in the European bronze age: The state of debate. *Journal of Archaeological Research, 27*, 131–118.

Reese, D. (1991). The trade of IndoPacific shells into the Mediterranean Basin and Europe. *Oxford Journal of Archaeology, 10*(2), 159–196.

Reese, D. (2009). On incised scapulae and *Tridacna*. *Eretz Israel (Ephraim Stern Volume), 29*, 188*–193*.

Regert, M., Devièse, T., Le Hô, A., & Rougeulle, A. (2008). Reconstructing ancient Yemeni commercial routes during the Middle Ages using a structural characterization of terpenoid resins. *Archaeometry, 50*, 668–695.

Retso, J. (1991). The domestication of the camel and the establishment of the frankincense road from South Arabia. *Orientalia Suecana, 40*, 187–219.

Rieth, T. M., & Hunt, T. L. (2008). A radiocarbon chronology for Samoan prehistory. *Journal of Archaeological Science, 35*, 1901–1927.

Ritter, N. C. (2009). Vom Euphrates zum Mekong: Maritime Kontakte zwischen Vorder- und Südostasien in vorislamischer Zeit. *Mitteilungen des deutschen Orientalischen Gesellschaft, 141*, 143–171.

Robert, M. (2021). *Reconstructing maritime networks in the Bronze and Iron Age eastern Mediterranean: A diachronic analysis of Canaanite and Phoenician maritime transport containers*. Unpublished PhD, University of Toronto.

Roffet-Salque, M., Dunne, J., Altoft, D., Casanova, E., Cramp, L. J. E., Smith, J., et al. (2017). From the inside out: Upscaling organic residue analyses of archaeological ceramics. *Journal of Archaeological Science: Reports, 16*, 627–640.

Rosenfeld, S. A., Jordan, B. T., & Street, M. E. (2021). Beyond exotic goods: Wari elites and regional interaction in the Andes during the Middle Horizon (AD 600–1000). *Antiquity, 95*(380), 400–416.

Routledge, B. (2014). A fishy business: The inland trade in Nile perch (Lates niloticus) in the Early Iron Age Levant. In T. Harrison, E. B. Banning, & K. Klassen (Eds.), *Walls of the Prince: Egyptian interactions with Southwest Asia in Antiquity. Essays in honour of John S. Holladay Jr* (pp. 212–233). Brill.

Russo, E. B. (2014). The pharmacological history of cannabis. In R. G. Pertwee (Ed.), *Handbook of cannabis* (pp. 23–43). Oxford University.

Sabatini, S., & Lo Schiavo, F. (2020). Late bronze age metal exploitation and trade: Sardinia and Cyprus. *Materials and Manufacturing Processes, 35*(13), 1501–1518.

Sabatini, S., & Melheim, I. (2017). Nordic-Mediterranean relations in the second millennium BC. In I. S. Bergerbrant & A. Wessman (Eds.), *New perspectives on the bronze age* (pp. 355–362). Archaeopress.

Said, E. W. (1979). *Orientalism*. Random House.

Salles, J.-F. (1991). Du blé, de l'huile et du vin (notes sur les échanges commerciaux en Méditerranée orientale vers le milieu du 1er millennaire av. J.-C.). In H. Sancisi-Weerdenburg & A. Kuhrt (Eds.), *Achaemenid history VI, Asia Minor and Egypt* (pp. 207–236) Nederlands Instuituut voor Het Nabije Oosten.

Samarawickrema, N. (2020). Elsewheres in the Indian Ocean: Spatio-temporal encounters and imaginaries beyond the sea. In S. Srinivas, B. Ng'weno, & N. Jeychandran (Eds.), *Reimagining Indian Ocean worlds* (pp. 89–102). Routledge.

Sass, B. (1990). Arabs and Greeks in late first Temple Jerusalem. *Palestine Exploration Quarterly, 122*, 59–61.

Schneider, A. W., Gill, E. C., Rajagopalan, B., & Algaze, G. (2021). A trade-friendly environment?: Newly reconstructed Indian summer monsoon wind stress curl data for the third millennium BCE and their potential implications concerning the development of early bronze age trans-Arabian Sea maritime trade. *Journal of Maritime Archaeology, 16*, 394–411.

Scott, A., Power, R. C., Altmann-Wendling, V., Artzy, M., Martin, M. A. S., Eisenmann, S., Hagan, R., Salazar-García, D. C., Salmon, Y., Yegorov, D., Milevski, I., Finkelstein, I., Stockhammer, P. W., & Warinner, C. (2020). Exotic foods reveal contact between South Asia and the near east during the second millennium BCE. *Proceedings of the National Academy of Sciences, 118*(2), e2014956117.

Serpico, M., Bourriau, J., Smith, L., Goren, Y., Stern, B., & Heron, C. (2003). Commodities and containers: A project to study Canaanite amphorae imported into Egypt during the New Kingdom. In M. Bietak (Ed.), *The synchronisation of civilisations in the eastern Mediterranean in the second millennium B.C. II* (pp. 365–375). Österreichischen Akademie der Wissenschaften.

Sherratt, S. (2003). 'Globalization' at the end of the second millennium B.C.E. In W. Dever & S. Gitin (Eds.), *Symbiosis, symbolism, and the power of the past* (pp. 37–62). Eisenbrauns.

Sherratt, S. (2017). A globalizing bronze and Iron Age Mediterranean. In T. Hodos (Ed.), *The Routledge handbook of archaeology and globalization* (pp. 602–617). Routledge.

Shiloh, Y. (1987). South Arabian inscriptions from the City of David, Jerusalem. *Palestine Exploration Quarterly, 119*, 9–18.

Shtienberg, G., Yasur-Landau, A., Norris, R. D., Lazar, M., Rittenour, T. M., Tamberino, A., et al. (2020). A Neolithic mega-tsunami event in the eastern Mediterranean: Prehistoric settlement vulnerability along the Carmel coast, Israel. *PLoS ONE, 15*(12), e0243619.

Sidebotham, S. E. (2011). *Berenike and the ancient maritime spice route*. University of California Press.

Simon, S. (2014). Remarks on the Anatolian background of the Tel Reḥov bees and the historical geography of the Luwian states in the 10th c. BCE. In Z. Csabai (Ed.), *Studies in the economic and social history of the ancient near east in memory of Pèeter Vargyas* (pp. 715–738). University of Pécs.

Sisma-Ventura, G., Tütken, T., Zohar, I., Pack, A., Sivan, D., Lernau, O., et al. (2018). Tooth oxygen isotopes reveal Late Bronze Age origin of Mediterranean fish aquaculture and trade. *Scientific Reports, 8*, Article number 14086.

Skourtanioti, E., Erdal, Y. S., Frangipane, M., Balossi Restelli, F., Yener, K. A., et al. (2020). Genomic history of Neolithic to Bronze Age Anatolia, Northern Levant, and southern Caucasus. *Cell, 181*, 966–968.

Smith, S. H. (2008). 'Profits sprout like tropical plants': A fresh look at what went wrong with the Eurasian spice trade c. 1550–1800. *Journal of Global History, 3*, 389–418.

Smith, M. L. (2019). The Terqa cloves and the archaeology of aroma. In S. Valentine & G. Guarducci (Eds.), *Between Syria and the highlands. Studies in honor of Giorgio Buccellati and Marilyn Kelly-Buccellati* (pp. 373–377). Arbor Sapientiae.

Sowada, K. (2016–2018). Hidden exports: A likely Early Bronze Age exchange in Egyptian cattle to the Levant. *Bulletin of the Australian Centre for Egyptology, 26*, 71–78.

Spiciarich, A. (2020). Birds in transition: Bird exploitation in the Southern Levant during the Late Bronze Age, Iron Age I, and Iron Age II. *Bulletin of the American Society of Overseas Research, 383*, 61–78.

Spriggs, M. (2011). Archaeology and the Austronesian expansion: Where are we now? *Antiquity, 85*, 510–528.

Stein, P. (2017). Sabäer in Juda, Juden in Saba. Sprach- und Kulturkontakt zwischen Südarabien und Palästina in der Antike. In U. Hübner & H. Niehr (Eds.), *Sprachen in Palästina im 2. und 1. Jahrtausend v. Chr* (pp. 91–120). Harrassowitz.

Stockhammer, P. W., Feldman, M., Artzy, M., Boaretto, E., Eisenmann, S., Faerman, M. et al. (2021). *Population dynamics in the Central and Southern Levant during the 2nd and 1st millennium BCE: Tell es-Safi and beyond* [Paper presented at ASOR Annual Meeting Chicago, December 2021].

Stucky, R. A. (1974). *The Engraved Tridacna Shells. Dédalo, 10*(19), 1–170.

Subrahmanyam, S. (2005). *Explorations in connected history: From the Tagus to the Ganges.* Oxford University.
Tchernia, A. (2017). *The romans and trade.* Oxford University.
Thapar, R. (1992). Black Gold: South Asia and the Roman maritime trade. *South Asia, 15,* 1–27.
Thareani, Y. (2011). *Tel 'Aroer.* Hebrew Union College.
Thompson, C. M., & Skaggs, S. (2013). King Solomon's silver? Southern Phoenician Hacksilber hoards and the location of Tarshish. *Internet Archaeology, 35,* 10.11141/ia.35.6.
Thorley, J. (1969). The development of trade between the Roman Empire and the east under Augustus. *Greece and Rome, 16*(2), 209–223.
Tomber, R. (2000). Indo-Roman trade: The ceramic evidence from Egypt. *Antiquity, 74*(285), 624–631.
Ulf, C. (2014). Rethinking cultural contacts. In R. Rollinger & K. Schnegg (Eds.), *Kulturkontakte in Antiken Welten* (pp. 507–563). Peeters.
Urbani, B. (2021). The primates of Susa: Depictions of monkeys in stone statuettes from Elam. *Ash-sharq: Bulletin of the Ancient Near East, 5*(1), 1–10.
Urbani, B., & Youlatos, D. (2020). On the earliest representations of chimpanzees (*Pan troglodytes*): Were African apes traded to Bronze Age Elam? *International Journal of Primatology, 41,* 654–663.
Urbani, B., Youlatos, D., & Binnberg, J. (2021). Galilei's mutter, archeoprimatology, and the 'blue' monkeys of Thera: A comment on Pruetz and Greenlaw (2021). *Primates, 62,* 879–886.
Vaelske, V., Bode, M., & Loeben, C. E. (2019). Early Iron Age Copper Trail between Wadi Arabah and Egypt during the 21st dynasty: First results from Tanis, ca. 1000 BC. *Zeitschrift für Archäologie, 12,* 184–203.
Van der Veen, M., & Morales, J. (2015). The Roman and Islamic spice trade: New archaeological evidence. *Journal of Ethnopharmacology, 167*(5), 54–63.
Vandkilde, H. (2007). *Culture and change in central European history, sixth to 1st millennium BC.* Aarhus University Press.
Vandkilde, H. (2016). Bronzization: The Bronze Age as pre-modern globalization. *Prähistorische Zeitschrift, 91*(1), 103–223.
Vandkilde, H. (2019). Bronze Age beginnings: A scalar view from the global outskirts. *Proceedings of the Prehistoric Society, 85,* 1–27.
Vandkilde, H. (2021). Trading and weighing metals in Bronze Age Western Eurasia. *PNAS, 118*(30), e2110552118.
Vandkilde, H., Matta, V., Ahlqvist, L., & Nørgaard, H. W. (2021). Anthropomorphised warlike beings with horned helmets: Bronze Age Scandinavia, Sardinia, and Iberia compared. *Prähistorische Zeitschrift.* https://doi.org/10.1515/pz-2021-2012
Varberg, J., Gratuze, B., Flemming, K., Haslund Hansen, A., Rotea, M., & Wittenberger, M. (2016). Mesopotamian glass from Late Bronze Age Egypt, Romania, Germany and Denmark. *Journal of Archaeological Science, 74,* 184–194.
Verdugo, M. P., Mullin, V. E., Scheu, A., Mattiangeli, V., Daly, K. G., Delser, P. M., et al. (2019). Ancient cattle genomics, origins, and rapid turnover in the Fertile Crescent. *Science, 365,* 173–176.
Villing, A. (2021). Spicing wine at the symposion: Fact or fiction? Some critical thoughts on material aspects of commensality in the early iron age and archaic Mediterranean world. *The Journal of Hellenic Studies, 141,* 1–30.
Vogt, B. (1996). Bronze Age maritime trade in the Indian Ocean: Harappan traits on the Oman peninsula. In J. E. Reade (Ed.), *The Indian Ocean in antiquity* (pp. 107–132). Kegan Paul.
Wachsmann, S. (1998). *Seagoing ships and seamanship in the Bronze age Levant.* Texas A & M University.
Warburton, D. A. (Ed.). (2020). *Political and Economic Interaction on the Edge of Early Empires.* eTopoi: Journal for Ancient Studies, Special Volume 7. Exzellenzcluster 264 Topoi.
Warburton, D. A. (2021). Globlisation for archaeologists. *Topoi, 9,* 142–192.
Ward, C. (2003). Pomegranates in eastern Mediterranean contexts during the Late Bronze Age. *World Archaeology, 34*(3), 405–427.

Weinstein, B. (2000). Biblical evidence of spice trade between India and the land of Israel: A historical analysis. *Indian Historical Review, 27*, 12–28.

Weiss, E., Mahler-Slasky, Y., Melamed, Y., Lederman, Z., Bunimovitz, S., Bubel, S., et al. (2019). Foreign food plants as prestigious gifts: The archaeobotany of the Amarna period palaces at Tel Beth-Shemesh, Israel. *Bulletin of the American Schools of Oriental Research, 381*, 83–105.

Werner, M., & Zimmermann, B. (2006). Beyond comparison: Histoire Croisée and the challenge of reflexivity. *History and Theory, 45*(1), 30–50.

Wertmann, P., Xu, D., Elkina, I., Vogel, R., Yibulayinmu, M., Tarason, P. E., et al. (2021). No borders for innovations: A ca. 2700-year-old Assyrian-style leather scale Armour in Northwest China. *Quaternary International.* https://doi.org/10.1016/j.quaint.2021.11.014

Whelton, H., Hammann, S., Cramp, L., Dunne, J., Roffet-Salque, M., & Evershed, R. (2021). A call for caution in the analysis of lipids and other small biomolecules from archaeological contexts. *Journal of Archaeological Science, 132*, 105397.

Wilkinson, T. C. (2014). *Tying the threads of Eurasia.* Sidestone.

Wilkinson, T. C. (2018). Cloth and currency: On the ritual-economics of Eurasian textile circulation and the 'origins' of trade, fifth to second millennia BC. In K. Kristiansen, T. Lindkvist, & J. Myrdal (Eds.), *Trade and civilisation: Economic networks and cultural ties, from prehistory to the early modern era* (pp. 25–55). Cambridge University.

Wilkinson, T. C., Sherratt, S., & Bennet, J. (Eds.). (2011). *Interweaving worlds: Systemic interactions in Eurasia, 7th to 1st millennia BC. Papers from a conference in memory of Professor Andrew Sherratt* (pp. 189–204). Oxbow.

Woldekiros, H. S., & D'Andrea, A. C. (2016). Early evidence for domestic chickens (*Gallus gallus domesticus*) in the Horn of Africa. *International Journal of Osteoarchaeology, 27*(3), 329–341.

Wood, J. R., Montero-Ruiz, I., & Matinón-Torres, M. (2019). From Iberia to the Southern Levant: The movement of Silver across the Mediterranean in the Early Iron Age. *Journal of World Prehistory, 32*, 1–31.

Wood, J. R., Bell, C., & Montero-Ruiz, I. (2020). The Origin of Tel Dor Hacksilver and the Westward Expansion of the Phoenicians in the Early Iron Age: The Cypriot Connection. *Journal of Eastern Mediterranean Archaeology and Heritage Studies, 8*(1), 1–21.

Yagel, O., & Ben-Yosef, E. (2022). Lead in the Levant during the Late Bronze and Early Iron Ages. *Journal of Archaeological Science: Reports, 46*, 103649.

Yahalom-Mack, N., Finn, D. M., Erel, Y., Tirosh, O., Galili, E., & Yasur-Landau, A. (2022). Incised Late Bronze Age lead ingots from the southern anchorage of Caesarea. *Journal of Archaeological Science: Reports, 41*, 103321.

Yarrow, S. (2018). Economic imaginaries of the global middle ages. *Past and Present, 238*(Supplement 13), 214–231.

Yasur-Landau, A., Shtienberg, G., Gambash, G., Spada, G., Melini, D., Arkin-Shalev, E., et al. (2021). New relative sea-level (RSL) indications from the Eastern Mediterranean: Middle Bronze Age to the Roman period (~3800–1800 y BP) archaeological constructions at Dor, the Carmel coast, Israel. *PLoS ONE, 16*(6), e0251870.

Zalloua, P. A., Platt, D. E., El Sibai, M., Khalife, J., Makhoul, N., Haber, M., et al. (2008). Identifying genetic traces of historical expansions: Phoenician footprints in the Mediterranean. *American Journal of Human Genetics, 83*(7), 633–642.

Zohar, I., & Artzy, M. (2020). The role of preserved fish: Evidence of fish exploitation, processing and long-term preservation in the Eastern Mediterranean during the Late Bronze Age (14th-13th Century BCE). *Journal of Archaeological Science: Reports, 23*, 900–909.

Zorea, C. (2018). Theories about the bronze bowl of Berzocana and the East Mediterranean in the 12th – 10th centuries B.C. *Complutum, 29*(2), 339–359.

Zweig, S. (1938). *Magellan. Der Mann und seine Tat.* Reichner.

The Site of Khirbet 'Aujah el-Foqa: Identifying Its Iron Age Architecture

David Ben-Shlomo

Abstract The site of Khirbet 'Aujah el-Foqa is an Iron II fortified town in the southern Jordan Valley, just north of Jericho. It was identified and surveyed by the Menasseh Hills Survey Project headed by the late Adam Zertal and is currently in the third season of excavation. The site is characterized by a casemate wall and other components, including large structures with massive straight walls that indicate fortification. Nevertheless, the more conspicuous surface remains are dozens of rounded one-room houses that stand up to 2 m high, built of stones robbed from the site's Iron Age walls, probably during the Mamluk-Ottoman period. What is left of the walls can be seen under these structures. The paper discusses the preliminary identification and reconstruction of the Iron Age structures and the nature of the Iron Age site according to the evidence from the survey, the results of the recent 2019–2021 excavations at two of the site's areas, and analysis of high-quality aerial photographs. One of the important questions arising considered is whether the internal structures are integrated into the casemate wall or are free-standing. The date, political affinity and function of the site are also discussed.

Keywords Jordan Valley · Iron Age · Aujah el-Foqa · Drone photographs · Fortifications

1 Introduction

The article discusses the site of 'Aujah el-Foqa in the Jordan Valley, an Iron II fortified town, and recent excavations at the site. Due to the arid environment the remains at this ancient site are well preserved and many walls are visible on the surface. The site was identified and extensively surveyed by the Menasseh Hills Survey Project

D. Ben-Shlomo (✉)
Ariel University, Ariel, Israel
e-mail: davben187@yahoo.com

© The Author(s), under exclusive license to Springer Nature Switzerland AG 2023
E. Ben-Yosef, I. W. N. Jones (eds.), *"And in Length of Days Understanding" (Job 12:12): Essays on Archaeology in the Eastern Mediterranean and Beyond in Honor of Thomas E. Levy*, Interdisciplinary Contributions to Archaeology, https://doi.org/10.1007/978-3-031-27330-8_26

headed by the late Adam Zertal (e.g., Bar & Zertal, 2016, 2019; Zertal & Bar, 2017, 2019). Zertal and others published the results of the survey and their interpretation of its plan, date, function and historic identification (Zertal et al., 2005, 2009). Recently, an excavation project was initiated at the site, and three seasons have been conducted thus far (2019–2021).

2 Khirbet 'Aujah el-Foqa

The Iron II period is relatively poorly known in the southern Jordan Valley (from Wadi Farʿah in the north to Jericho in the south) since few substantial archaeological excavations of Iron Age sites have been conducted in this region. The area is arid and marginal in relation to other areas of the southern Levant. The main source of archaeological information so far is the Manasseh Hill Country Survey headed by Adam Zertal (e.g., Bar & Zertal, 2016, 2019; Zertal & Bar, 2017, 2019). One of the important sites in the region identified and described in the survey is Khirbet ʿAujah el-Foqa, a large, well-preserved Iron II site identified by the survey approximately 11 km northwest of Jericho (Site 143; ITM 237908/650482; Zertal & Bar, 2019: 394–403; Zertal et al., 2005, 2009; Ben-Shlomo et al., 2020a, b, 2022). This site was not excavated prior to 2019.

Khirbet ʿAujah el-Foqa (Arabic for "Upper ʿAujah"), apparently a small, fortified town, is located on the summit of a hill south of and above Nahal Yitav (Wadi ʿAujah), 2 km west of Moshav Yitav. The site is on a high, stony hill isolated by steep slopes and is almost circular (110 m north-south and 85 m east-west), with a projection on its southeastern edge (Fig. 1). It rises about 100 m above its surroundings, with an elevation of up to 27 m asl. The total area of the ancient hilltop site, including the parts outside and around the preserved walls, is 1.5 ha. (15 dunam). The site is 1.5 km southeast of the large spring of ʿEn ʿAujah (Fig. 1 rear). The hill is not easily accessible due to a difficult climb from most directions. The southern and eastern slopes are steep and covered by hard flint rocks, while the northern slopes are slightly more moderate, with soft limestone outcrops; thus, access is easier from the north. The hilltop strategically controls the area of Nahal Yitav (ʿAujah) and the spring and this entire part of the Jordan Valley, including the Jericho plateau (Ben-Shlomo et al., 2020a: [Figs. 2 and 3]).

The site was first visited and reported by the British Survey in 1874, but was described as "a ruined village on a mound, apparently modern" (Conder & Kitchener, 1882: 391). This description was probably deduced from its good state of preservation, especially with respect to the remains of the later phase (see below). It was first surveyed intensively during the winter of 2003/2004 by Zertal and the Manasseh Hill Country Survey team (Zertal et al., 2005, 2009). Zertal demonstrated that the main occupation at the site dates from the Iron II (see below).

The Site of Khirbet ʿAujah el-Foqa: Identifying Its Iron Age Architecture 603

Fig. 1 The site and Wadi ʿAujah, looking north. (Drone photo taken by M. Freikman)

The visible remains at the site consist of several dozen stone structures observable on the surface; some are even preserved up to 1.5–2.0 m high (Fig. 2, see below) and a casemate wall is visible on the ground in several areas. Zertal and his team made a plan of the site that includes all the architectural elements visible on the surface (Fig. 2; Zertal et al., 2009: Fig. 2). They collected many pottery sherds and published some dating to the Iron II (Zertal et al., 2009: 110–117, Figs. 5, 6 and 7). Several robbery pits and earth piles testify that parts of the site were looted, mostly during a short period after the intensive survey. Although the results of Zertal's survey were published, the site was not excavated until 2019.

3 Excavations at the Site (2019–2021)

Three excavation seasons were conducted at the site between 2019–2021, directed by the author and Ralph Hawkins (Ben-Shlomo et al., 2020a, b; Ben-Shlomo & Hawkins, 2021; Ben-Shlomo et al., 2022).[1] So far two excavation areas have been

---

[1] The excavations were initiated as a part of the larger Jordan Valley Excavation Project (JVEP, www.jvep.org; see also Ben-Shlomo & Hawkins, 2017), and directed by David Ben-Shlomo from Ariel University and Ralph Hawkins from Averrett University. Permit Nos. 9-1-2019 (May–June 2019, 4 weeks), 3-1-20 (February 2020, 2 weeks) and 5-1-21 (February 2021, 2 weeks). The team included many dozens of volunteers from Israel, the US, and other countries. Michael Freikman was field supervisor, and assistance was provided by J. Rosenberg (surveying, plans, and graphics), Tal Rogovski (photographs of finds), and Olga Dubovsky (drawings).

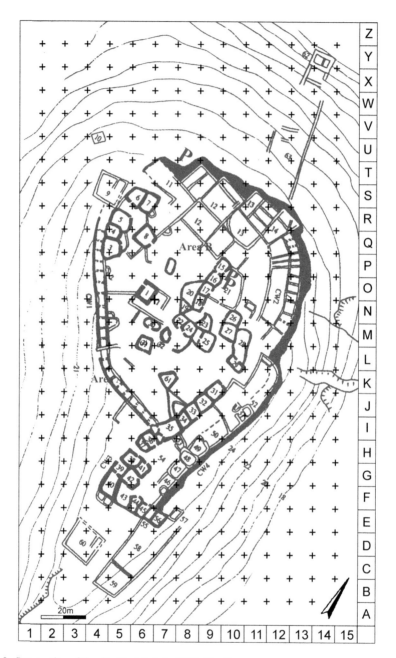

Fig. 2 Survey plan of the site (Zertal et al., 2009: Fig. 2)

Fig. 3 'Aujah el-Foqa: Area A excavations. (Drone photo taken by M. Freikman)

opened: Area A (2019) on the southwestern part of the site (Figs. 3, 4 and 5), and Area B (2020–2021) on the northern side of the site (Figs. 6, 7 and 8).

3.1 Architecture

3.1.1 Area A

Area A was opened on and adjacent to visible sections from the casemate wall (Figs. 3, 4 and 5). The main feature here is the casemate wall; three or four of the casemates were excavated down to floor level or bedrock (Figs. 3, 4 and 5). The fortification walls are generally 1.2–1.5 m thick, and the casemates measure about 1.2–1.8 × 4.0–5.5 m (inner dimensions), where excavated. The entrances to the casemates are located at the same northern corner on the inner wall, whereas north of Wall 120 they seem to be located on the opposite side (Fig. 4).[2] As the stones

---

[2] This is somewhat similar to the early Iron IIA casemate wall at Khirbet Qeiyafa (e.g., Garfinkel et al., 2016: 61–66).

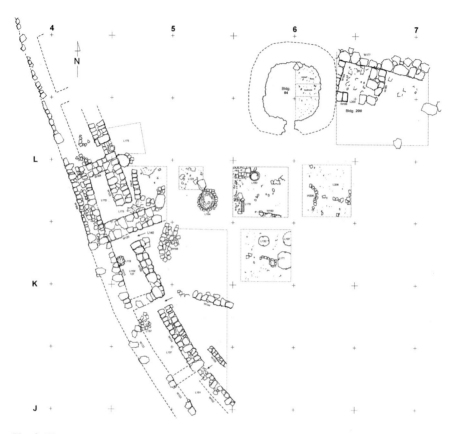

Fig. 4 The plan of excavations at Area A

Fig. 5 A section in the casemate wall, with a possible passage. (Field photo taken by author)

Fig. 6 Area B excavations. (Drone photo taken by M. Freikman)

from the walls were robbed from all but the lowest courses, the floor remains are often either on the surface, a few centimeters below it, or even, in several cases, completely eroded. The southern casemates in particular are badly eroded (Fig. 3).

A destruction layer rich in broken pottery was discovered, especially at the entrances to the middle casemates (Fig. 4: Loci 127, 137), on the inner side (Ben-Shlomo et al., 2020a: Fig. 10). The destruction was evidenced by both the crushed and intact vessels and ashy layers in several locations (Fig. 5) and by several iron arrowheads and a spearhead also discovered there (Ben-Shlomo et al., 2020a: Fig. 14: 2, 3). A stepped entrance to a casemate, or a small passageway, was excavated (Fig. 5).

Apparently, very few interior walls were found abutting the fortification. Either all such architecture was looted, or there were no structures abutting the casemate wall from the inside, at least in this section of the site. The squares excavated adjacent to the fortification wall on the inside yielded remains including floors, debris, pits, and various installations. This may have been an open area in the main Iron Age phase. A circular installation about 2 m in diameter and 1.1 m deep is probably a silo (Fig. 4: Locus 104, Ben-Shlomo et al., 2020a: Fig. 12). Similar silos are well known in the hill country of Israel, especially from the Iron II (e.g., Khirbet Marjameh [Mazar, 1995: 96, Fig. 14]; Tel Moza [Greenhut, 2009: 26–33, Figs. 2.25–2.33]), though most of them are larger and better built. Several pits were excavated in the adjacent square and one contained large amounts of restorable pottery, as well as some charcoal. Another floor layer here included a rounded *tabun*; a

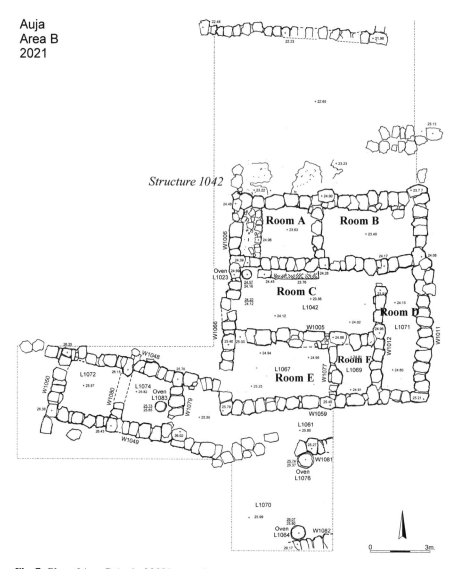

Fig. 7 Plan of Area B (end of 2021 season)

rectangular installation lined with stones and a rectangular installation or "bin" lined with a thin brick/mud wall were also uncovered.

A fragment of a structure was found in the northeastern part of the excavated area (Ben-Shlomo et al., 2020a: Fig. 8: Building 200). Although most of the walls were robbed it is clear from what remained that this had been a massive structure, with ca. 2 m-thick walls built of large stones (Fig. 4: Building 200). Sherds on the floor

The Site of Khirbet 'Aujah el-Foqa: Identifying Its Iron Age Architecture 609

Fig. 8 Smashed pottery vessels in Structure 1042, Room A. (Field photo taken by author)

date to the Iron IIA-B. This was very likely part of a large structure, possibly a fortress or a tower.

3.1.2 Area B

Area B was opened in 2020 and is located in an important part of the site (Figs. 6, 7 and 8). The northern slope of the site is less steep than the other slopes and is characterized by softer limestone exposures. This area likely included the pathway and entrance to the site and the town gate (Figs. 6, 7 and 8) and is also located on top of a series of "support" walls or structures (Fig. 2: Structures 62, 63, also Zertal et al., 2009: 109; Structure 62 is located on this pathway, delimited by a straight wall along the slope). An area relatively clear of late structures was chosen for excavation. Here, the area to the southern inner, side of the casemate wall was excavated; the fortification some 20–30 m to the north is roughly covered by some excavation debris, and will be cleared and excavated in the future, in an attempt to identify the town gate (see below) and to clarify whether the casemate wall was generally freestanding as noted in the section excavated in Area A, or whether structures were connected to it or combined with it.

One complete structure was excavated (Fig. 7; Ben-Shlomo et al., 2020b, 2022; "Structure 1042"), yet it seems to be part of a larger complex (see below, Fig. 12: Complex I). The structure contains six rooms, and its entrance was in the southwestern corner (Fig. 7, Room E), yet, this is not yet clear. To the north, there was an open area or a courtyard on top of the bedrock. Further excavations will determine whether this area may already have been part of the fortification and/or a gate complex (in particular an area measuring 8 × 11 m in the north, see Fig. 12: "tower?").

To the southwest, as noted. The structure is connected to or combined with another structure, from which only two units have thus far been excavated (Fig. 7). The southern part of the structure was overlain by a later structure (Figs. 2 and 6: Structure 15) which was completely removed in the 2021 season.

Structure 1042 contained six rooms of varying sizes (A–F; ca. 10 × 9.5 m. On the floor of two of the rooms (A and C) a clear and rich destruction layer was excavated containing reconstructable and intact vessels (Fig. 8, Ben-Shlomo et al., 2020b: Figs. 17, 18). This destruction is similar in date and nature to the one recorded in Area A (see above), and is dated according to pottery to the eighth century BCE (see below). While the other rooms contained fewer finds (Rooms B, D and E). The units to the southwest of the structure (Fig. 7) also contained this destruction layer, yet it is still only partly excavated. A small room (Room F) contained several mud loom weights, probably remains of an *in-situ* loom. The southern part possibly contained two sub-phases, with a later phase comprised of a bench, installation and/or thickening of the southern wall of the house (Fig. 7). Several *tabun*s were discovered in this area, one in Room C (Oven 1023: Fig. 7); another oven was located in a small room in the structure to the west (Oven 1083: Fig. 7) while two others (Ovens 1064 and 1081, Fig. 7) were located in a unit or room to the south of Structure 1042. Whether this is a domestic house, or part of a structure of a more administrative nature, related to storage or a combination of the above, is still unclear. The general outline of the house plan may resemble a four-room house, common during the Iron Age in the southern Levant, yet it is not clear whether the central area (Room C) is an open area or a columned courtyard, as in many houses of this kind. According to the finds, the main functions were both storage (jars) and cooking (*tabun*s); in fact, these details could fit a military barracks.

To the southwest Building 1042 is connected to or combined with another structure in which only two units have been partially excavated thus far. These are small and square, and one contains a tabun; the floor levels have not yet been reached. Just to the south of Wall 1049, several vessels were found, including a complete amphoriskos and a grinding stone. This area will be further excavated and expanded in future seasons.

3.2 Stratigraphy and the Late Phase

Three phases have thus far been identified at the site (Table 1), with Phase 2 denoting the main Iron II architectural phase and the fortified town; this phase possibly had two sub-phases. These remains were robbed and overlain with a much later settlement (Phase 1, Fig. 9), which clearly overlies the main Iron Age phase (Ben-Shlomo et al., 2020a: *18–*19). The width, shape, and orientation of the walls, and the size and shape of the structures are quite different from the lower phase; yet, in some cases, later walls and/or structures use the earlier more massive ones (see below). These structures have some accumulation in them, seemingly rather poor in artifacts, that may be debris from the period when they were constructed and used,

Table 1 Initial phasing at Khirbet ʿAujah el-Foqa

Phase	Main remains	Areas excavated	Date	Notes
1	Rounded and oval one-room houses	A, B	Mamluk/ottoman	Well-preserved houses, modern usage (Fig. 9)
2	Casemate wall, massive rectilinear structures	A, B	Iron II	Possibly two sub-phases (Figs. 11 and 12)
3	Poorly preserved walls	A	Iron I/II?	Empty floors

but also from occasional modern use. During the 2019 season, half of such a structure from this phase was excavated to bedrock (Ben-Shlomo et al., 2020a: Building 64, Figs. 6, 7, right; see also Fig. 2: Structure 64). The debris consisted mostly of Iron II sherds, but there was also later material (Roman–Byzantine, Mamluk, and Ottoman). A nearly complete vessel that can be dated to the Ottoman period was found on the floor in a burnt patch (Ben-Shlomo et al., 2020a: Fig. 14: 4). Therefore, the late phase of the site may date from the Mamluk or Ottoman period, yet these late structures were probably occasionally used by squatters during the modern period. Identification of the later phase of the site as a small administrative center seems plausible since the site controls the spring but lacks easy access to its water and to agricultural areas because of its hilltop location. It was probably constructed here due in part to the abundance of good building material (rubble stone) available from the Iron Age walls that had stood at the site until then (see Fig. 9).

There is also some evidence of a construction phase predating the main Iron Age phase and the fortification in Area A (Phase 3). This is attested by several walls and features in Squares L5c, K5a, K5b, and K5d (Fig. 4: Walls 162, 166, 144); these poorly preserved walls underlie the casemate walls and have a different orientation. A mud plaster floor layer relating to this phase was also unearthed but it was practically devoid of artifacts. Therefore, this phase cannot at this point be dated with any confidence. This phase, probably largely destroyed by the main Iron Age phase, could date from the Iron II as well, but may be earlier—perhaps the Iron I.

3.3 Finds

3.3.1 Pottery

A large amount of pottery was recovered, especially from some of the casemate spaces and Structure 1042 (Fig. 10: 1–6). So far only the pottery from Area A has been reconstructed (Fig. 10). Because the pottery has not yet been fully restored or analyzed, a more detailed discussion of it will be published separately. Representative vessels, mainly from the casemate area, indicate forms appearing during the late Iron IIA and early Iron IIB (ninth and eighth centuries BCE), with most parallels probably coming from northern Israelite sites (Ben-Shlomo et al., 2020a:*25–*27, Figs. 14, 15; Ben-Shlomo et al., 2020b: 153–157). Several sherds of imported Black

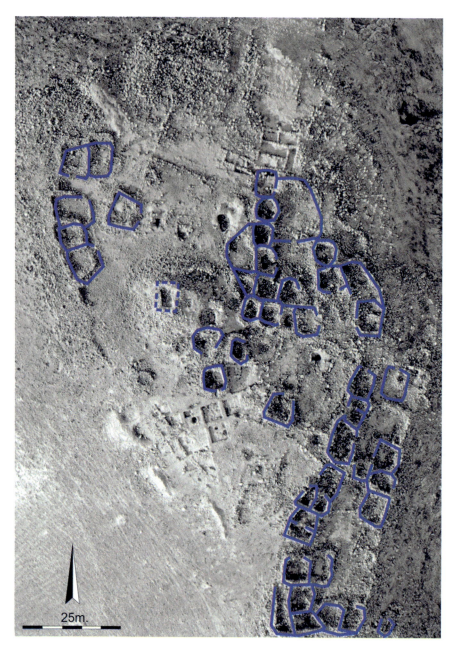

Fig. 9 Aerial photo and reconstructed plan of upper phase structures. (Drone photo taken by M. Freikman)

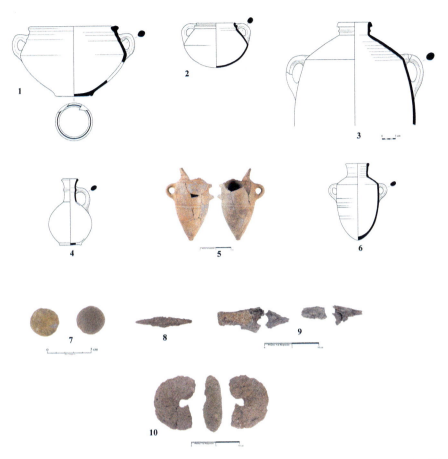

Fig. 10 Pottery and finds from Khirbet 'Aujah el-Foqa. (Artifacts photos were taken by Tal Rogovski)

on Red juglets were found, as were two fragments of strainer-spouted jugs. Southern, "Judahite" Iron II types, such as folded rim bowls and holemouth jars, are rare, as are red-slipped and burnished ware. To date, the quantity of bowls and other tableware at the site is relatively small. Although large kraters appear (Fig. 10: 1), the most common forms are closed vessels, such as storage jars and jugs (Fig. 10: 3–6). Most jar necks are similar to those of "hippo jars" (Fig. 10: 3). Cooking pots appear in several locations, including complete specimens in Casemate L110 (Fig. 10: 2). Especially interesting are amphoriskoi and a pyxis (Fig. 10: 5, 6, Ben-Shlomo et al., 2020a: Fig. 15: 8, 9), rare forms in this region. One amphoriskos is decorated with light red slip, vertical burnish, and red and white horizontal bands possibly linking the vessel to "Late Philistine Decorated Ware" (Fig. 10: 6, Ben-Shlomo et al., 2020a: *27).[3]

Rooms A and C in Structure 1042 contained several complete vessels, currently in reconstruction. These include storage jars of the typical "hippo" type, cooking pots, a chalice and jug and juglets (Fig. 8). In the area south of Structure 1042 an unusual and interesting vessel was uncovered: a large krater with an applied decoration depicting a snake or snakes.

3.3.2 Other Finds

The small finds assemblage is not rich and diversified. Most categories are groundstone tools, iron and other metal tools and weapons, and loom weights (Ben-Shlomo et al., 2020a: Fig. 16: 1–3). Notable finds are several complete "doughnut-shaped" loom weights or stoppers (Fig. 10: 10), several iron arrowheads, spearheads (Fig. 10: 8, Ben-Shlomo et al., 2020a: Fig. 16: 2, 3) and iron tools such as picks and an axe found in Area B (Fig. 10: 9). A large number of spherical flint or chert objects, 4–5 cm in diameter (Fig. 10: 7), may be tools—perhaps rubbers or slingshot stones. The arrowheads and possible slingshot stones fit in well with the interpretation of Khirbet ʿAujah el-Foqa as a military site. Some of these artifacts may be remnants of the battle that produced the destruction level. In addition, several of the lower pieces of the basalt grinding stones were found, two of them at the entrances to the casemates near the side wall. These may represent various activities that took place after the casemate had fallen out of use. Alternatively, these large, flat pieces may have been in secondary use in the entrances and may have already functioned as part of the thresholds during the main period of occupation of the site. Ground stone tools were also published from the survey (Eitam, 2007, 35 stone items).

4 Identifying Additional Iron Age Architecture at the Site

4.1 Survey Results

Since the archaeological remains at the site of ʿAujah el-Foqa are exposed and even well preserved on the surface, it was possible to outline many architectural features prior to excavation. This was naturally done, and to a large extent, by the survey team, creating a "complete" plan of the site (Fig. 2; Zertal et al., 2009). According

---

[3] Many of the published forms from the survey are more similar to Judahite types, such as folded rim bowls and kraters (Zertal et al., 2009: 110–113, Fig. 5: 1–7); they also have a later eighth-century BCE date. However, these types are very rare in the excavation so far. Perhaps they represent a later phase evident in other parts of the site.

to the description in the survey, the visible remains include the central tower, which measures 7.5 × 7.5 m in area (Fig. 2: Structure 1), standing inside a square court, and a section of the casemate wall on the west, 90 m long and 5 m wide, with more than 20 casemate rooms inside it (Zertal et al., 2009: 105). In the northwest, six structures can be identified in two clusters. Another section of the casemate wall, 45 m long, lies in the northeast; a section in the south is about 65 m long. According to Zertal, this last section consists of two chains of casemates (as opposed to one in other areas) with walls preserved up to 1.5 m high (Zertal et al., 2009: 107). A larger tower (12 × 15 m; Fig. 2: Structure 9) is located west of the wall; Zertal suggested it may have been part of an entrance/gate complex (Zertal et al., 2009: 106). Another tower (Fig. 2: Structure 62) is located about 50 m north of the site on a steep slope. It consists of two large rooms or units built of large boulders. This tower is attached to the site by two long walls on the slope, with several wide connecting walls in between, built for support or as a path foundation. The recent excavation in this tower (Area C, 2022 season) have in fact shown that this structure dates to the Middle Bronze Age IIB-C, yet, these results will be published elsewhere.

As will be shown below, the description and reconstruction above is problematic since the remains represent at least two stratigraphic phases and different periods and do not all belong to the same settlement.

4.2 Identifying and Reconstructing Architectural Units According to Air Photos

The survey employed aerial photos for reconstruction and mapping architectural remains (Zertal et al., 2009: Fig. 3), yet, as noted the remains of the two phases were combined.[4] In fact, it is easy to separate the two phases in most cases according to the shape and construction characteristics of the walls and structures (see above). After the excavation it was also possible to extrapolate from excavated areas to unexcavated ones regarding structures and complexes (Figs. 9, 11, 12, see also for this use Wiseman & El-Baz, 2007; Alexakis et al., 2012).

4.2.1 The Upper Phase

The uppermost phase includes over 40 structures distributed all over the site (Fig. 9, in blue, see above; the reconstructed plan illustrates 43 structures). Many of these are well-preserved, built stone structures. The structures are rounded, square, or oval in shape, have one entrance and no apparent inner divisions, and are roughly 6–9 m in diameter. Most structures are built in clusters, with the outer walls attached

---

[4] Drone photos were taken by M. Freikman with a Mavrick 2 Pro drone.

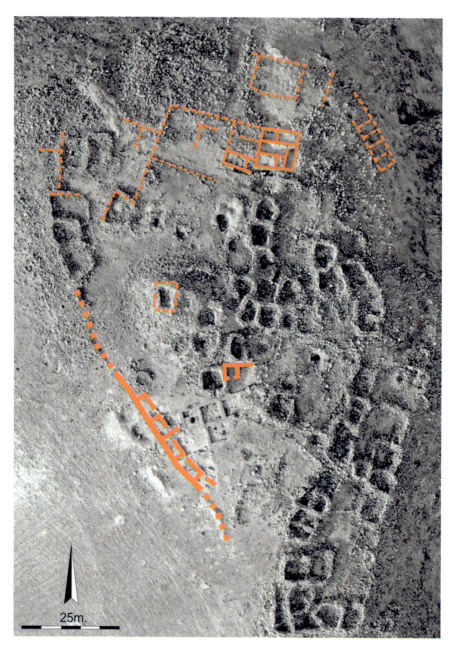

Fig. 11 Aerial photo and reconstruction of the main Iron Age phase structures. (Drone photo taken by M. Freikman)

The Site of Khirbet ʻAujah el-Foqa: Identifying Its Iron Age Architecture

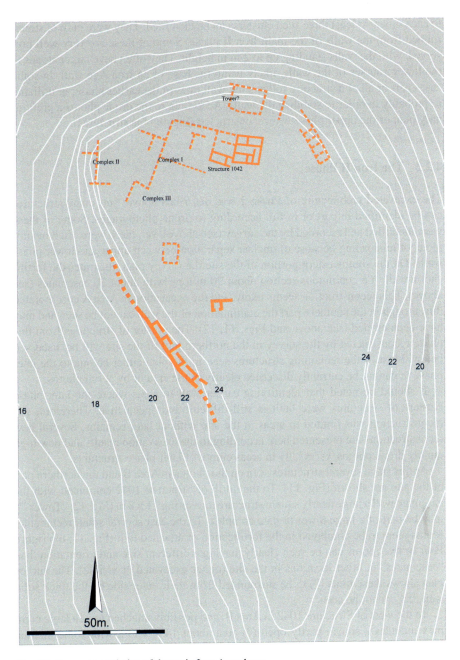

Fig. 12 Reconstructed plan of the main Iron Age phase

to each other. At least three such clusters can be identified. They were built of stones robbed from the walls of the main Iron II phase. Some of these are very well preserved, with the walls standing up to 2 m in height. They often have larger stones in the lower courses of the walls, likely using the base of an Iron Age wall. In some cases part or all of a structure follows the wall lines of the earlier phase, or utilizing it, probably in order to stabilize the walls. According to the drone photos a preliminary plan of the upper phase was reconstructed (Fig. 9, blue structures).

4.2.2 The Iron II Phase

The excavated architecture of Phase 2 was described above, yet, many structures can be identified in part or in full according to drone photographs. Some of these were identified and recorded by the survey (see above), yet, these were often incomplete, or misleading because of unclear separation between upper and lower phase walls. On the southwestern portion of the site the survey plan illustrates the fortification wall in a continuous section about 90 m long with about 20 casemates (see above). This reconstruction seems likely, and the excavation in Area A corroborated this, though in the southern part the continuation of the wall cannot be seen and may have been eroded (see above and Figs. 11, 12). The cluster of structures from this phase reconstructed by the survey in the northern part of the site will be discussed below. Most of the remaining structures seen in the plan either belong to the later phase or cannot be currently discerned clearly in the area or by aerial photos.

It should be noted that identifying earlier wall in areas where the later phase clusters of structures were built is still difficult and speculative. Therefore, our reconstruction was limited to areas in the site without later remains. Several new reconstructions are presented here according to the excavation results and new high quality drone photos, especially in areas empty of later phase structures.

At this stage several structures seen on the photos in Area B and the northern part of the site are shown (Fig. 11). To the north of Structure 1042 combined with the casemate wall a large nearly square structure measuring 11 × 8 m (Fig. 12: "Tower?") may be part of a large tower or gate complex. To the east several small rectangular rooms seem to be combined in the fortification or attached to it (Fig. 11: top right). Four or five rooms can be seen clearly, having a different size and orientation than "casemates" in other locations in the site (either excavated or visible). The survey plan shows these units (?) to be surrounded from their outer side by the thick solid wall, but cannot be seen.

To the west of Structure 1042 in Area B, and possibly attached to it, a large complex includes a square partly open (?) area about 14 × 15 m, with some internal divisions identified, possibly into at least six units. The size of this complex would be about 22 × 14 m (Complex I). This complex may have continued to the southwest as well, with another "empty" area defined by a thick wall (Fig. 12: Complex III). Further to the west, this complex continues possibly through to the fortification line

(Fig. 12: Complex II). This arrangement of large square areas divided into smaller units, with no visible entrance, could fit large storage structures.

Some of these walls were noted on the survey plan (Fig. 2: Structures 12–14; Zertal et al., 2009: 106), noting that: "The general nature of the northern part is not yet clear. It seems to contain public buildings including fortified towers." Zertal divided the area into three or four units, Nos. 12, 13 and 14; he even suggested that Structure 13 was a typical four-room house (Zertal et al., 2009: 106). Some of the walls noted there are shown in the current reconstruction while others are not. As suggested here the northwestern part of this complex may represent a gate and tower structure (No. 14), while most of the structures to the west and south may represent a large, possibly administrative structure with groups of store rooms; a domestic function is less likely, due to both the site and plan of the remains and their possible location near the entrance to the site.

Thus, while only a few Iron Age architectural remains within the settlement were excavated, and so far no structures have been seen to abut or join with the city wall, visible remains reconstructed according to aerial photographs in the northwestern part of the site show otherwise (Fig. 12). Also, the existence of a large structure with possible storage facilities would fit an administrative function of the site (see below).

5   Discussion: The Significance and Function of the Site of 'Aujah el-Foqa

5.1   Location

The location of the site of Khirbet ʿAujah el-Foqa as well as its fortified nature highlights its strategic and military function. Since the site is located on the top of a steep hill, access to agricultural fields would have been difficult, as would transporting water to the site from the spring about 1 km away. Moreover, below the site on the plain and river banks, agricultural activity could have been easier; possibly, a contemporary site was located in this area. Another part of the site may have extended to the north (Zertal & Bar, 2019: 404, site 143(1)). About 400 m to the northeast (ITM 238851/650082), below Khirbet ʿAujah el-Foqa, on the bank of the wadi (today inside the modern Bedouin settlement, Ras ʿEn el-ʿAujah), lies a smaller archaeological site known as the "Aujah Fortress" (Zertal, 2012: 380–385, Site 140; Zertal & Bar, 2019: 384–389, Site 140). An archaeological excavation was conducted here in 2012 by the Archaeology Staff Officer of the Civil Administration (Hizmi, pers. comm.; Zertal & Bar, 2019: 387). The primary remains here belong to a Byzantine-period monastery, but this may have been built on top of an Iron Age fortress linked with Khirbet ʿAujah el-Foqa (Zertal & Bar, 2019: 389).

As for the water supply on the hilltop site, if no water reservoir was constructed at the site (none has yet been identified), then the water must have been stored in jars and/or pithoi, as well as in skins. This situation, like the fortifications, seems, as noted, to point to a military function for the site, a function that raises questions about the number of inhabitants and their identity (for example, whether entire families or only soldiers and administrative personnel lived there). Moreover, if the site was also an administrative center of some sort, one would expect to find large storage structures. The excavation and identification of several additional structures at the site in the future may resolve these issues. Possibly a part of one of these structures was excavated in Area B.

5.2 Date

Zertal suggested that the site was founded during the Iron I, its main activity was during the Iron IIB and that it was deserted by the end of the Iron IIB, possibly in relation to Senacherib's campaign to Judah in 701 BCE (Zertal et al., 2009: 116–117). The excavations thus far have shown no evidence of the Iron I. The date of construction of the fortification will become clear only after the phase predating it is more securely established (Phase 3 that probably did not include a casemate wall). The pottery of the main phase dates to the Iron IIA and IIB. The main building remains including the casemate were thus constructed sometime during the Iron IIA, possibly the ninth century BCE. Zertal suggested two phases: one with the casemate wall, and a later one including uniformly constructed barracks (Zertal et al., 2009: 117). While the so-called later "barracks" are in fact Phase 1 rounded structures (e.g., Fig. 2: Structures 15–22) and are not related to the Iron Age, different, localized, sub-phases of the main building remains were noted in the excavation. Eventually, the site was destroyed, probably violently in battle, and not deserted as Zertal suggested, during a later stage of this period, somewhere in the eighth century BCE.

Whether the site was destroyed by the Assyrians during one of their campaigns at the end of the eighth century BCE as was suggested for nearby Khirbet Marjameh (Mazar, 1995: 101) is still an open question. Khirbet ʿAujah el-Foqa may have been destroyed earlier. This raises the question of the historical background of its destruction. One possibility, already suggested by Zertal (Zertal et al., 2009: 119), would be a conflict with the Ammonites, who ruled the region surrounding Jordan's present-day capital city, Amman. The "tribal kingdom" of Ammon had emerged in part to counter the mounting threat posed by the Israelites (LaBianca & Younker, 1995: 399), and the Bible recounts perpetual conflict between them (Tyson, 2014: 107–145). Naturally, the southern Jordan Valley would have featured in some of the battles, since both parties would have crossed the Jordan River there to engage each other (e.g., 2 Sam 10). Another possibility could be a destruction caused by the Arameans, whom the Bible claims conducted intermittent campaigns against Israel and Judah throughout the period of their national existence (see Zertal et al., 2009: 119; Younger Jr., 2016).

5.3 The Political Affinity of the Site (Judean or Israelite)

Zertal concluded that the site of 'Aujah el-Foqa was a Judean fortified center. He made this claim as a result of the pottery types found in the survey, his reconstruction of the ancient Israel-Judah border and the plan of the site with its casemate wall (Zertal et al., 2009: 118–120). The site was paralleled to Beersheba Stratum II (idem: 118). However, as will be shown, according to the recent finds, if a "political identity" for the site is sought, an Israelite affiliation is more likely.

Casemate walls from the Iron II are indeed a well-known feature in Judah. Possibly the best-known and clearly earliest example is Khirbet Qeiyafa (e.g., Garfinkel et al., 2016: 48–56, 68–72), where the wall was built according to a similar plan as at Khirbet 'Aujah el-Foqa, with similar casemate sizes and entrances. Yet, in most cases of this plan reported from Judah a "radial" plan is attested as some of the domestic houses are joined with the wall in a "belt," with the casemates serving as the rear rooms of the houses (the original city plan may have consisted of only the city wall), with other Iron IIB examples at Tel Beer-sheba, Tel Beit Mirsim, and Tel en-Nasbeh (e.g., Herzog, 1997: 237–249; Garfinkel et al., 2016: 207).[5]

The plan involving construction at the outset with a casemate wall may be a more universal functional design for military settlements throughout the southern Levant during the Iron Age; it appears in northern Israel as well (see, e.g., Zarzecki-Peleg, 2005:169–183, regarding Stratum XIV of the Iron IIA at Yoqneam).

The northern or "Israelite" parallels for the pottery from the destruction level were noted above (Ben-Shlomo, 2020b: 153–157). Since the material culture of our site (especially pottery) seems to be of a more northern or "Israelite" nature and its location was traditionally under the control of the northern kingdom according to biblical descriptions, as Jericho to the south was still on the Israelite side of the border (Josh 16:7; 1 Kgs 16:31), it may be tentatively seen as an Israelite site, at least during the late Iron II. The rather similar nearby site of Khirbet Marjameh was also identified by Mazar as Israelite (Mazar, 1995).

Zertal identified Khirbet 'Aujah el-Foqa as biblical 'Ataroth (Zertal et al., 2009: 120–121) mentioned in the description of the Manasseh-Ephraim boundary (Josh 16:6–7). Recently, Shmuel Ahituv and others (Ahituv et al., 2016) suggested identifying the site with Na'arath (נערתה) mentioned in the same list. While the biblical identification of the site is not the aim of this paper, Na'arath seems more likely since it is the closest site to Jericho according to the list (Ben-Shlomo et al., 2020b: 139) and thus 'Ataroth would be identified with the next Israelite town, Khirbet Marjameh to the west (Bar, 2021).

---

[5] Iron II sites in the Negev Highlands with a plan consisting of a rounded compound with cells and a gate have also traditionally been interpreted as Judahite or early Israelite fortified strongholds (e.g., Cohen, 1979; Cohen & Cohen-Amin, 2004; Zertal et al., 2009: 117, and references therein). Alternatively, this architectural plan may represent settlement compounds of semi-nomadic populations (e.g., Shachak-Gross et al. 2014), who probably lived in this area as well (e.g., Ben-Shlomo & Hawkins, 2017; Ben-Yosef, 2015).

5.4 The Function of the Site

Zertal already noted the multifaceted importance of the site: its control over the nearby important ʿAujah spring, its regional location as a border site, and its wider important location, facing the Amonite Kingdom and controlling the Jordan Valley road (Zertal et al., 2009: 118–119).[6] From a regional perspective, the main importance of Khirbet ʿAujah el-Foqa was control of nearby ʿEn ʿAujah, a major water source for the region from Jericho to Wadi Farʿah. Similarly, Khirbet Marjameh, 8 km to the northwest, near the upper section of Nahal Yitav, is another fortified town controlling another important spring, ʿEn Samiyeh (Mazar, 1995; Ben-Shlomo et al., 2018; note, though, it is located in a less arid region than ʿAujah).

The significance of the site may have been as a local border town between Israel and Judah as well. However, whether the site was on the Israelite or Judahic side of the border (or occasionally flipping sides during the period), it is not clear what the nature of the border between these political entities was both generally and in this marginal area during the Iron II (regarding Judean borders and material culture, see, e.g., Stern, 1993; Kletter, 1995). Was it an open, rather administrative, border defining mostly land ownership, was it a more supervised border due to variable political issues, or was it a more closed and fortified border reflecting periods of conflicts between the states? And thus, what would be the roles and characteristics of a "border town"? Therefore, the function and character of such Iron Age "border towns" as ʿAujah and Marjameh is still to be clarified.

Zertal defined these sites as "military base and presence sites" (Zertal et al., 2009: 118), suggesting also their important regional administrative role (Zertal suggested that ʿAujah may have been the administrative center for the entire Jordan Valley area south of Beth Shean). Notably, the Iron II remains at the important site of Jericho (Tell es-Sultan) are meager, according to the published data.[7] Thus, Khirbet ʿAujah el-Foqa may have been a small regional administrative center of the Jericho area and the southern Jordan Valley during some of this period.

Indeed, it may not be clear for what purpose these fortified sites were built and maintained in the first place: whether to protect the main water sources of the region from external (Ammonite? Assyrian?) or internal (Judahite?) enemies, aiding in territorial disputes, or to control the water sources and protect them from local semi-nomadic populations that may have been subdued or partly subdued by a central political power. These sites may have been part of an administrative and/or military system during the Iron Age, probably governing the local nomadic population, although, it is not clear whether they belonged to the kingdom of Israel or Judah. So far not much direct archaeological data as administrative and storage structures, or

---

[6] Note that Zertal suggested several "tower sites" along the Jordan Valley may reflect an "Amonite penetration" in this region (Zertal, 1995; Zertal et al., 2009: 119).

[7] While some substantial Iron II remains were mentioned at Jericho (Tel es-Sultan) (Marchetti et al., 2008: 587; Nigro, 2020: 204–206), these had not yet been published.

seals and sealings, has been found in the excavation, but walls identified in other areas may be promising, as the units excavated and reconstructed from aerial photos in Area B could represent storage facilities. The pottery assemblage is dominated by storage vessels as well. This issue may be clarified when more information about the site is available.

In the coming excavation seasons, therefore, additional areas within the site will be excavated in order to determine the interior architecture, as well as the architecture of some large, possibly administrative, structures. The entrance to the site and gate area will also be sought in Area B. This will be complemented by further analysis of aerial photographs on the un-excavated parts of the site. Hopefully, in the future, radiocarbon dates from well-stratified contexts will be attained as well. The need for further study of the site is clear both from the site's special location and from its well-preserved remains from the Iron Age and late antiquity in the southern Jordan Valley, a region relatively poorly understood in archaeological research, especially with respect to the Iron II.

References

Ahituv, S., Klein, E., & Ganor, A. (2016). "To Jerusalem": A seventh century BCE shipping certificate. *New Studies in the Archaeology of Jerusalem and Its Region, 10*, 239–251.

Alexakis, D. D., Agapiou, A., Hadjimitsis, D. G., & Sarris, S. (2012). Remote sensing applications in archaeological research. In B. Escalante-Ramirez (Ed.), *Remote sensing – Applications* (pp. 435–462). Intech.

Bar, S. (2021). *The eastern border between Manasseh and Ephraim and a new identification of Khirbet el-Marjame*. Lecture in ASOR Meeting.

Bar, S. & Zertal, A. (2016). *The Manasseh Hill country survey*, vol. 6: *The south-eastern Samaria shoulder (from Wadi Farʿah to Maʿaleh Efraim Junction)*, Haifa (Hebrew).

Bar, S. & Zertal, A. (2019). *The Manasseh Hill country survey*, vol. 7: *The eastern Samaria shoulder (from Wadi Rashash to Wadi ʿAujah)*, Haifa (Hebrew).

Ben-Shlomo, D., & Hawkins, R. K. (2017). Excavations at Khirbet el Mastarah, the Jordan Valley, 2017. *Judea and Samaria Research Studies, 26*, 49–82.

Ben-Shlomo, D., & Hawkins, R. K. (2021). ʿAuja el-Foqa. A desert fortress on ancient Israel's eastern frontier. *Biblical Archaeology Review, 47*(1), 58–64.

Ben-Shlomo, D., Freikman, M. & Hawkins, R.K. (2020a) New excavations at Khirbet ʿAujah el-Foqa and the Iron Age II settlement. *In the Highland's Depth* 10/1, 11–35.

Ben-Shlomo, D., Freikman, M. & Hawkins, R.K. (2020b). New excavations at Khirbet ʿAujah el-Foqa and the Iron Age II settlement. *Judea and Samaria Research Studies* 29/2, 133–166 (Hebrew).

Ben-Shlomo, D., Freikman, M., & Hawkins, R. K. (2022). Excavations at Khirbet ʿAujah el-Foqa: Results from the 2020–2021 seasons. *Judea and Samaria Research Studies, 31*(1), 31–68.

Ben-Shlomo, D., Tavger, A., & Har-Even, B. (2018). Back to Marjameh: The iron II Pottery of Khirbet Marjameh—Typology and Provenance Study. *Judea and Samaria Research Studies, 27*, 81–115.

Ben-Yosef, D. (2015). The Jordan Valley during the Iron Age 1: A first look, *Be-Ma'ave Hahar 5*, 34–59 (Hebrew).

Cohen, R. (1979). The Iron Age Fortresses in the Central Negev. *BASOR, 236*, 61–79.

Cohen, R., & Cohen-Amin, R. (2004). *Ancient settlement of the Negev highlands* (Vol. 2). The Iron Age and the Persian Period.

Conder, C. R., & Kitchener, H. H. (1882). *The survey of Western Palestine: Memoirs of the topography, orography, hydrography and archaeology* (Vol. 2). Samaria.

Eitam, D. (2007). The ground stone tools from Kh. Aujah el Foqa, daily life in an Iron Age Fortified City in the Jordan Valley. In S. Crawford, A. Ben-Tor, J. P. Dessel, W. G. Dever, A. Mazar, & J. Aviram (Eds.), *Up to the Gates of Ekron* (pp. 93–106). Seymour Gytin Festriftch, IES.

Forte, M., & Campana, S. (Eds.). (2016). *Digital methods and remote sensing in archaeology. Archaeology in the age of sensing*. Springer.

Garfinkel, Y., Kreimerman, I., & Zilberg, P. (2016). *Debating Khirbet Qeiyafa: A Fortified City in Judah from the time of king David*. Israel Exploration Society.

Greenhut, Z. (2009). The excavations: Stratigraphy and architecture. In Z. Greenhut & A. De Groot (Eds.), *Salvage excavations at Tel Moẓa* (pp. 9–60). The Bronze and Iron Age Settlements and Later Occupations.

Herzog, Z. (1997). *Archaeology of the city: Urban planning in ancient Israel and its social implications*. The University of Chicago Press.

Kletter, R. (1995). *Selected material remains of late iron age Judah in relation to its political Borders*. Ph.D. Dissertation, Tel Aviv University (Hebrew).

LaBianca, Ø. S., & Younker, R. W. (1995). The kingdoms of Ammon, Moab and Edom: The archaeology of Society in Late Bronze/Iron Age Transjordan (ca. 1400–500 BCE). In T. E. Levy (Ed.), *The archaeology of Society in the Holy Land* (pp. 399–411). Bloomsbury.

Lasaponara, R., & Masini, N. (Eds.). (2012). *Satellite remote sensing. A new tool for archaeology*. Springer.

Marchetti, N., Nigro, L., & Taha, H. (2008). In I. Thuesen (Ed.), *Preliminary report on the third and fourth seasons of excavations of the Italian-Palestinian expedition at Tell es-Sultan/Jericho, 1999 and 2000* (pp. 581–597). Proceedings of the Second International Congress on the Archaeology of the Ancient Near East, Copenhagen, 2000.

Mazar, A. (1995). Excavations at the Israelite town at Khirbet Marjameh in the hills of Ephraim. *Israel Exploration Journal, 45*, 85–117.

Nigro, L. (2020). The Italian-Palestinian expedition to Tell es-Sultan, ancient Jericho (1997–2015): Archaeology and valorisation of material and immaterial heritage. In R. T. Sparks, B. Finlayson, B. Wagemakers, & J. M. Briffa (Eds.), *Digging up Jericho: Past* (pp. 175–214). Present and Future.

Stern, E. (1993). The Jericho region and the eastern border of the Judean kingdom in its last days. *Eretz-Israel, 24*, 192–197. (Hebrew), 238* (English summary).

Tyson, C. W. (2014). *The ammonites: Elites, empires, and sociopolitical change (1000–500 BCE)*. Bloomsbury.

Wiseman, J., & El-Baz, F. (Eds.). (2007). *Remote sensing in archaeology*. Springer.

Younger Jr., K. L. (2016). A political history of the Arameans: From their origins to the end of their polities

Zarzecki-Peleg, A. (2005). Stratigraphy and architecture: The Iron Age IIA (Strata XVI–XIV). In A. Ben-Tor, A. Zarzecki-Peleg, & S. Cohen-Anidjar (Eds.), *Yoqneʿam II: The Iron Age and the Persian period: Final report of the archaeological excavations (1977–1988)* (pp. 90–168).

Zertal, A. (1995). Three iron age fortresses in the Jordan Valley and the origin of the ammonite circular towers. *Israel Exploration Journal, 45/4*, 253–273.

Zertal, A. (2012). *The Manasseh Hill country survey*, vol. 5: *The middle Jordan valley (from Wadi Fasael to Wadi ʿAuja)*, Haifa (Hebrew).

Zertal, A. & Bar, S. (2017). The Manasseh Hill country survey, vol. 4: *From Nahal Bezeq to the Sartaba*, Leiden.

Zertal, A. & Bar, S. (2019). The Manasseh Hill country survey, vol. 5: *The Middle Jordan Valley, from Wadi Fasael to Wadi ʿAujah*, Leiden.

Zertal, A., Ben-Yosef, D., & Cohen, O. (2005). Khirbet ʿAujah el-Foqa (ʿAtaroth): A fortified town from the Iron Age in the Southern Jordan Valley. *Judea and Samaria Research Studies, 14*, 11–34. (Hebrew).

Zertal, A., Ben-Yosef, D., Cohen, O., & Be'eri, R. (2009). Kh. ʿAujah el-Foqa (ʿAtaroth): An Iron Age Fortified City in the Jordan Valley. *Palestine Exploration Quarterly, 141*, 104–123.

Die Like an Egyptian: Burial Customs in Iron Age I Philistia

Shirly Ben Dor Evian and Mario A. S. Martin

Abstract The five tombs of the "Philistine lords" at Tell el-Far'ah (South) have been a focal point for the study of Philistine burial customs. This, despite the long recognized fact, that they are also highly Egyptianized and possibly earlier than the Philistine pottery within them. In the present study we point out the similarities between these tombs and Egyptian rock-cut chamber tombs from Egypt itself and suggest a different interpretation to the Philistine burial customs they represent.

Keywords Tell el-Far'ah (South) · Philistines · Burial practices

1 Introduction

The characteristic burial customs of southwest Israel during the early stages of the Iron Age have yet to be fully comprehended by modern day research. The accumulated evidence has thus far pointed to a mixture of burial forms, ranging from man-made caves,[1] to cremations, pit burials, brick-case tombs, jar burials, intramural

---

It is with great joy that we dedicate this article to Tom Levy, a dear colleague, an outstanding archaeologist with a passion for both the past and the future, and above all a true *mentsh*.

---

[1] For Tell 'Etun, see Edelstein & Aurant, 1992; for Tell es-Safi/Gath, see Faerman et al., 2011.

S. Ben Dor Evian (✉)
Department of Cultural Heritage and the Recanati Institute for Maritime Studies, University of Haifa, Haifa, Israel
e-mail: bdevian@gmail.com

M. A. S. Martin
Institute of Ancient History and Ancient Near Eastern Studies, University of Innsbruck, Innsbruck, Austria
e-mail: mario_antonio@hotmail.com

© The Author(s), under exclusive license to Springer Nature Switzerland AG 2023
E. Ben-Yosef, I. W. N. Jones (eds.), *"And in Length of Days Understanding" (Job 12:12): Essays on Archaeology in the Eastern Mediterranean and Beyond in Honor of Thomas E. Levy*, Interdisciplinary Contributions to Archaeology,
https://doi.org/10.1007/978-3-031-27330-8_27

infant interments[2] as well as rock-cut chamber tombs.[3] This diversification is often considered as the result of the varied ethnic groups that inhabited the land in the early Iron Age, most notably the Philistines and the Canaanites.

The varied burial forms have prompted attempts to find a correlation between certain mortuary practices and a specific ethnic group, but this has been difficult to pursue. Burials directly associated with the main early Philistine sites are few and include only a jar burial at Ashkelon, intramural infant interments at Ekron and the man-made multi-burial cave at Tell es-Safi/Gath.[4] A common practice is therefore difficult to establish. The larger burial grounds at Azor, Tell 'Etun and Tell el-Far'ah (South) are just as diversified and cannot be attributed to specific ethnic groups on the basis of the burials themselves.

Nevertheless, five tombs at Tell el-Far'ah (South) have been identified as Philistine burials (Petrie, 1930: 7, Pl. XIX, Tombs 544, 542, 552, 532, 562) on the basis of the Philistine Bichrome pottery found within them (a view maintained also by Dothan, 1982; Gonen, 1992). This however represents an out-dated approach to the question of "pots and people," one that has been questioned in regard to the Philistine pottery found within some of the Azor and 'Etun burials (Ben-Shlomo, 2008; Edelstein & Aurant, 1992). What then is the ethnic affiliation of these five unique tombs and their relation to Philistine burial practices? A new analysis of the tombs may provide an answer.

2 The Problem of The Philistine Burials at Tell el Far'ah (South)

Located in the northwestern Negev, the site was excavated during the years 1928–1929 and published in two reports (Petrie, 1930; Starkey & Harding, 1932). An Egyptian residency of the New Kingdom era was unearthed in the northern part of the mound and numerous tombs were excavated in its environs. Cemetery 900 in particular, was correlated with the Egyptian occupation of the site.

The subsequent Philistine phase was identified by the presence of Philistine Bichrome pottery found on top and above a cobbled courtyard to the south of the residency (Yannai, 2002). Additional such pottery was retrieved from various burials in Cemeteries 100, 200, 500, 600, and 800, but notably not from Cemetery 900 (Dothan, 1982: 29, n. 53).

Five of the rock-cut chamber tombs that contained Philistine pottery in Cemetery 500 were exceptional in their size and plan, hence titled by Petrie "tombs of the

---

[2] For Azor, see Ben-Shlomo, 2008; for Ashkelon, see Birney & Doak, 2011; for Ekron, see Gitin et al., 2006: 54–55.

[3] For Cemetery 500 at Tell el Far'ah (South), see Petrie, 1930; Starkey & Harding, 1932.

[4] The recently discovered cemetery in Ashkelon is later than the presently discussed period (Master & Aja, 2017).

lords of the Philistines" (Petrie, 1930: 7, Pl. XIX, Tombs 544, 542, 552, 532, 562). However, this designation, although widely cited, presents some major difficulties. Firstly, these "Philistine" tombs yielded such features that were also associated with the *Egyptian* burials of Cemetery 900, namely Egyptian-type pottery (Tombs 542, 552, 562, see Martin, 2011: 233, Table 112) and anthropoid clay coffins (Tombs 552, 562). Secondly, the same allegedly "Philistine" plan of the "tombs of the Philistine lords" in Cemetery 500, also occurred in *non*-Philistine tombs from Cemetery 900 (Starkey & Harding, 1932: Pls. LIX–LX, Tombs 905, 914, 920, 934, 935, 936; 960; Petrie, 1930: Pl. XIII, Tomb 902). Therefore, in both design and artefacts, Cemeteries 900 and 500 were more alike than apart.

This similarity was also noted by Gonen who commented that the two burial grounds could have been considered contemporaneous, were it not for the Philistine pottery and the anthropoid coffins within them (Gonen, 1992: 128).

As anthropoid coffin burials are no longer regarded as a sign of Philistine "Egyptianization," but rather as the coffins of Egyptian personnel who had died while stationed abroad, or at the very least, coffins of Canaanite personnel in Egyptian service (Oren, 1973: 139–141; Brug, 1985: 151–152; Bunimovitz, 1990: 216; Gonen, 1992: 28–30; Stager, 1995: 341–342; Yannai, 1996: 202–209; Morris, 2005: 701; Ben-Shlomo, 2010: 97),[5] the only Philistine aspect remaining in the 500 tombs is the Bichrome pottery (Dothan, 1982: 29–33).

Philistine Bichrome Ware is generally dated to the period following the end of Egyptian rule in Canaan, therefore, its appearance together with marked Egyptian traditions in Tombs 552 and 562 was interpreted as the result of on-going Egyptian influence at Tell el-Farʻah (South) well into the Philistine era (Petrie, 1930: 9; Dothan, 1982; Martin, 2011: 235).

However, we stipulate that this view is based on the presupposition that both Philistine and Egyptian-type assemblages in the tombs are contemporaneous, a notion that need not be retained in light of the state of the tombs upon their discovery. Tombs 542, 552 and 562 were discovered in disarray (Petrie, 1930: Pl. XIX; Oren, 1973: 141), having been disturbed in antiquity (Petrie, 1930: 8). Continuous use with multiple-layered burials was attested in many of the Tell el-Farʻah (South) tombs (Petrie, 1930: 8 on Tomb 542; Dothan, 1982: 30; Laemmel, 2003, 2013: 145 on Tomb 534) and especially in the "Philistine" chambers: "When new burials were

---

[5] Dothan hypothesized that these anthropoid clay coffins were linked to the interment of the so-called Sea-Peoples. Dothan's argument was based on the similarities between the head decoration of some of the Beth-Shean clay coffins and the Medinet Habu depictions of the Sea-Peoples. This hypothesis has since been widely rejected due to the geographical distribution of clay coffins, which can be found, among others, at the Jordanian sites of Pella, Amman, Sahab and Dibon (Cotelle-Michel, 2004: 205–207) and their chronological affiliation to thirteenth century BCE pottery-coffin burials at Deir el-Balaḥ (Dothan, 2008), thus pre-dating the arrival of the Philistine material culture to Canaan. On the possible connection between the head decoration on the anthropoid clay coffins from Beth-Shean and Aegean burials with similar headdress, see Yasur-Landau, 2013. For a different interpretation, associating the Beth-Shean depictions with *thr* warriors within the Egyptian empire before the advent of the Sea-Peoples, see Ben-Dor Evian, 2015.

made the remains of previous interments were apparently swept aside or placed in the rear chamber to make room for the new occupants" (Waldbaum, 1966: 334).

It therefore seems more likely that the Bichrome pottery was in fact another outcome of the disturbance of the burials in antiquity.

The above observations strengthen Gonen's hypothesis that the tombs of the "lords of the Philistines" were cut earlier than the Philistine pottery interred within them (Gonen, 1992: 128). In the following lines we shall present additional evidence for the contemporaneous execution and initial use of the rock-cut tombs in Cemeteries 500 and 900.

3 The Origin of the "Philistine" Tomb Plan

The rock-cut tombs in Cemetery 500 stand out due to their unique plan and large size. The tombs consist of a stepped entrance leading into a rectangular chamber. The chamber is divided into a central passageway with raised platforms on either side and the occasional addition of a back chamber. This layout stands in sharp contrast to the rectangular burial pits that constitute the majority of the tombs in the Tell el-Far'ah (South) cemeteries.

The unusual plan was initially compared to Mycenaean chamber tombs (Waldbaum, 1966) but an alleged continuity between the MB IIC (Hyksos) tombs at Tell el-Far'ah (South) and their Philistine counterparts has been used to suggest a mutual Cypriot origin dating to the Middle Bronze Age (Stiebing, 1970).[6] The link to Cypriot and/or local prototypes has since gained further support to the point of refuting the Aegean origin of the tombs (Bunimovitz, 1990: 216–217; Gonen, 1992: 24; Morris, 2005: 750).

Indeed, the plan of the so called Philistine tombs, although somewhat reminiscent of Mycenaean chamber tombs, differs from them in significant aspects: the stepped entrance, which is unlike the very long *dromos* of Mycenaean tombs (Gonen, 1992: 22–24); the roughly rectangular or trapezoidal form, which differs from the often rounded or varied shape of the Mycenaean chambers (Waldbaum, 1966: 335); the internal division into a main hall and side niches, a division completely lacking from the Mycenaean examples.

The alternatively suggested Cypriot origin is likewise questionable. Prehistoric Bronze Age Cypriot chamber tombs that have been associated with the MB IIC tombs at Tell el-Far'ah (South) are characterized by a *dromos* of varying depth and "a domed, irregular chamber roughly hewn into the bedrock" (Knapp, 2013: 311). These early examples of Cypriot tombs are often rounded and lack a back niche altogether and therefore differ considerably from the rectangular chambers of the Iron I. Moreover, it is difficult to argue for local continuity of the chamber tomb

---

[6] Bloch-Smith uses the term "bench-tombs" and views the Tell el Far'ah (South) tombs as the prototype of the later Iron Age tombs in Judah, while accepting Stiebing's MB Cypriot origin (Bloch-Smith, 1992: 44–47).

plan from the MB IIC to the LB II when chamber tombs are not represented at Tell el-Far'ah (South) at all between these two periods at the site, e.g. during the LB I–IIA.[7]

Later Protohistoric Bronze Age Cypriot tombs are highly diversified and mostly restricted to intramural burials, yet none can provide a good parallel for the Tell el-Far'ah (South) plan (Knapp, 2013: 381–383). Late Cypriot chamber tombs are generally rounded rather than rectangular or trapezoidal (Åström, 1972: Figs 25–27; Karageorghis, 1990: Fig. 11; Fischer & Bürge, 2017: Fig. 8). Therefore the possibility that the Tell el-Far'ah (South) chamber tombs were inspired by contemporary Cypriot tombs is not supported by the Cypriot prototypes.[8]

In contemplating the prototype for the Cemetery 500 rock-cut tombs, it is significant that the same "Philistine" plan also occurs in *non*-Philistine tombs from Cemetery 900 (Starkey & Harding, 1932: Pls. LIX–LX, Tombs 905, 914, 920, 934, 935, 936, 960; Petrie, 1930: Pl. XIII, Tomb 902). As Cemetery 900 exhibits many Egyptian characteristics in pottery (Tombs 934, 905, 902, see Martin, 2011: Pl. 63), architectural features (Gonen, 1992: 128, referring to a central pillar in Tomb 914), and burial equipment (Starkey & Harding, 1932: 25, regarding a fragment of an anthropoid clay coffin in Chamber Tomb 935), an Egyptian prototype for the tomb design should be considered.

We suggest that the rock-cut tombs in both Cemeteries 500 and 900 follow the basic plan of Egyptian rock-cut private tombs of the New Kingdom era (Fig. 1).[9] Such tombs consist of a narrow stepped entrance leading to a rectangular broad room and sometimes include a back chamber. Many Theban private tombs follow this most simple and basic plan, recognized as Types I and IIa in Kampp's typology (1996: 16–17). See for example TT302 from Dra Abu el-Naga (Kampp, 1996: 570, Fig. 463), with a roughly rectangular chamber and slightly rounded corners; TT205 and TT238, comprising a short entrance, broad room with a depression in the middle and a back niche (Kampp, 1996: 491, Fig. 384; 516, Fig. 410); TT176 (Fig. 1; *ibid*.: 464, Fig. 360; Calcoen, 2012: Pl. 22); TT54 with a division into two spaces

---

[7] For a comprehensive survey of all burial plans at Tell el-Far'ah (South) and their chronological affiliation, see Laemmel, 2003: 45–59.

[8] An unpublished dissertation by S. Laemmel suggests that various finds from Tell el-Far'ah (South) exhibit evidence for on-going relations with Cyprus during the Iron I (Laemmel, 2003: Chapter 7, p. 69–70), thus providing a possible scenario for the adoption of Cypriot burial practices at Tell el-Far'ah (South). Nevertheless, as shall be explained below, Laemmel, as do we, acknowledges a different origin for the plan of the chamber-tombs.

[9] The similarity was noted by Risser and Harvey in a short abstract, but the idea was apparently not pursued (Risser & Harvey, 1992). Consequently, Gilmour suggested that the Tell el Far'ah (South) tombs drew inspiration from three sources: Mycenaean, Cypriot and Egyptian (Gilmour, 1995: 161). Laemmel acknowledged the highly Egyptianized plan of the Tell el Far'ah (South) chamber tombs, noting: "In fact, structurally, these tombs are not totally unlike some of the rock-cut chamber tombs of New Kingdom Egypt. The steep access corridor, in particular, is in a way quite close to the shafts of the Egyptian tombs and the chamber, which was reopened several times for successive body depositions, is evocative of Egyptian family burial chambers. This Egyptian flavour in the local mortuary practices is further evidenced by the occasional presence of the clay anthropoid sarcophagi in the chamber graves" (2003: 79).

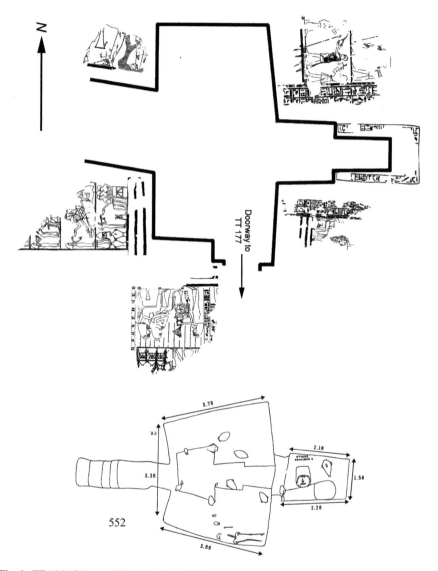

Fig. 1 TT 176 (Calcoen, 2012: Pl. 22) and Tell el-Far'ah (South) Tomb 552. (After Petrie, 1930: Pl. XIX, minor features removed), not to scale

(Kampp, 1996: 261, Fig. 152; Polz, 1997: 15, Fig. 2). Numerous examples attest to the popularity of these simple tombs in Thebes and beyond it.[10]

The Egyptian prototype of the Tell el-Farʿah (South) rock-cut tombs may also be traced through their dimensions. Some of the more symmetrical chambers are roughly square or rectangular in form and correspond to the Egyptian royal cubit system. Thus, Tomb 544 (Fig. 2) has two adjoining sides measuring 2.70 m each, which is the equivalent of five cubits (a royal cubit measures 52.3–52.5 cm). The entrance to the tomb also measures 2.70 m in length. The third side measures 1.62 m, roughly equivalent to three cubits, while the fourth side is clearly an attempt to correct the offshoot, measuring 1.80 m. The five cubits measure can also be observed in Tombs 914, 934 and 960 (Fig. 2). Tombs 532, 542, 552 and 562 seem to have been initially planned to measure seven royal cubits, as the side of the opening, which would logically have been dug first, ranges from 3.36 to 3.60 m in all of them (Figs. 3 and 4). The same measure is maintained on the perpendicular sides of both Tombs 532 and 552. The remaining published rock-cut Tombs 905, 935, 920 are too rounded to be measured, while Tomb 902 was not drawn to a known scale (Petrie, 1930: Pl. XIII).

4 Discussion

During the LB II, the site of Tell el-Farʿah (South) provides one of the best attestations of Egyptian presence as well as influence on local Canaanite culture. This includes the founding of a residency, considered to be the most accurately executed Egyptian architectural feature in Canaan (Morris, 2005: 745), associated with Egyptian-type pottery and prestige items (Fischer, 2011), that were likely used by the Egyptian inhabitants at the site (Morris, 2005: 537–538).

Mortuary practices also reflected Egyptian habits (Braunstein, 2011), as attested by the abundance of Egyptian-type pottery (Martin, 2011: 229–235) and amulets, as well as the use of anthropoid clay coffins in Cemetery 900, often associated with Egyptian residencies in the Levant (Beth-Shean, Lachish, Deir el-Balaḥ; see Morris, 2005: 701–702).

As argued above, Egyptian architecture was employed not only in the residency but also in the burial grounds around the settlement. While many of the interments were simple pit-burials, several large rock-cut chamber tombs in Cemeteries 900 and 500 were prepared in a distinct Egyptian fashion, common among New Kingdom private tombs.

It has generally been assumed that the two burial grounds were not contemporaneous. Cemetery 900, associated with the Egyptian phase of Tell el-Farʿah (South), was dated on both historical and typological grounds to the thirteenth–mid-twelfth

---

[10] Kampp, 1996: 16–17, Table 3 lists more than 50 tombs with the back chamber or niche Type IIA, Table 2 lists 50 of the square room Type I. For Saqqara compare the tomb plan in Martin et al., 2001: Pl. 3.

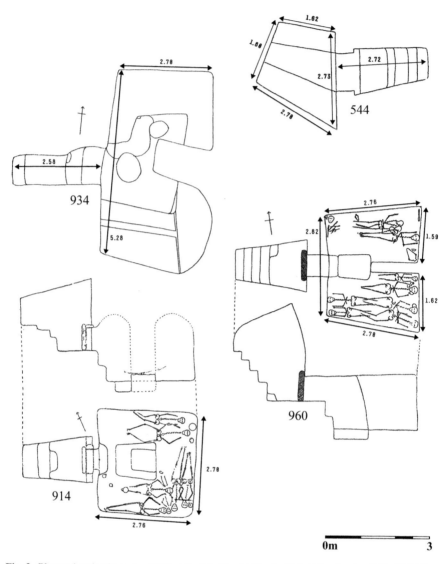

Fig. 2 Plan and major features of Tell el-Far'ah (South) Tombs 544. (After Petrie, 1930: Pl. XIX), 934, 960 and 914. (After Starkey & Harding, 1932: Pls. LIX–LX), minor features removed

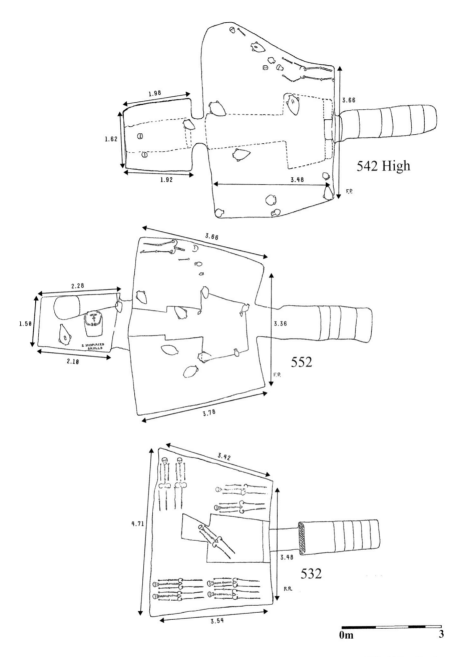

Fig. 3 Plan and major features of Tell el-Far'ah (South) Tombs 542, 552 and 532. (After Petrie, 1930: Pl. XIX), minor features removed

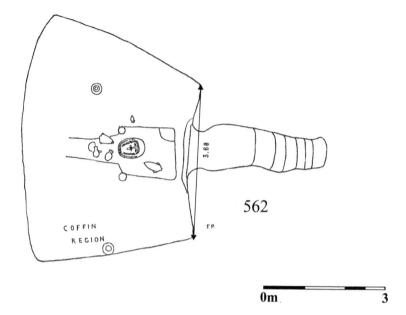

Fig. 4 Plan and major features of Tell el-Far'ah (South) Tomb 562. (After Petrie, 1930: Pl. XIX), minor features removed

centuries BCE (Martin, 2011: 229–234; see already Goldwasser, 1999; Morris, 2005; Fischer, 2011), while Bichrome Ware dated the Cemetery 500 Philistine tombs to ca. 1150–1100 BCE (Dothan, 1982: 290, Table 2; or even later, see McClellan, 1979). However, the fact that rock-cut chamber tombs in both cemeteries follow the same Egyptian plan, and that in both cases the burials included clay coffins and Egyptian-type pottery, suggests otherwise.

It seems that under Egyptian rule, rock-cut tombs were prepared in both Areas 900 and 500 following several Egyptian mortuary practices:

1. Both burial grounds were oriented towards the west: Cemetery 900 was dug into the western slope of the tell and Cemetery 500 lies to the west of the mound, although the entrances to the 500 tombs faced the east and the 900 tombs faced the west.
2. The tomb plan followed basic Egyptian prototypes and measurements: the 900 tombs revolved around the five royal cubits Egyptian measure, while the 500 tombs were larger, measuring seven royal cubits.

3. Burial goods included anthropoid clay coffins, Egyptian-type pottery and amulets. The Egyptian-type pottery predominantly comprised of locally produced vessels of Egyptian shape and technology.[11]

Following the end of Egyptian rule, a new occupation of the site began during the Iron I. This phase was characterized by the appearance of Philistine Bichrome Ware in both the settlement and the burials around it (Cemeteries 100, 200, 500, 600, and 800). It was during this time that Cemetery 500 was reused and expanded (Morris, 2005: 751; Ben-Shlomo, 2010: 96). Evidence for re-use was recorded in Petrie's description of the tombs. Moreover, the position of the clay coffins within the tombs, found in the back chamber of Tomb 552 and along the sidewall of Tomb 562, attests to their earlier deposition in the tombs. The Philistine pottery was therefore another sign of disturbance and not the marker of the initial burial.

Notably different was the condition of Tomb 532, the only undisturbed tomb of the "Philistine lords." Nine skeletons were found in articulation together with Philistine pottery. However, no Egyptian-type pottery or any anthropoid coffins were found in this tomb (Oren, 1973: 141-142) and a Ramesses X scarab attested to the later date of this interment (Petrie, 1930: 7, Pl. XXII: 202).[12] The layout of this tomb is no different than the other "Philistine" tombs, making it likely that the Iron I occupants either imitated the Egyptian plan or, even more likely, used an empty chamber tomb left unused from the Egyptian era. Such an empty, unused rock-cut chamber tomb was found nearby—Tomb 544—which was tagged as "Philistine" merely for its plan.

The evidence from the burial grounds therefore does not support a contemporaneous presence of Philistine and Egyptian populations at Tell el-Far'ah (South) but opts for a reuse of the original Egyptian rock-cut chamber tombs during the time that Philistine Bichrome pottery became popular in southwestern Canaan.[13] This partiality towards Egyptian burial customs can be detected at other Iron I burial sites exhibiting Egyptian motifs associated with the protection of the dead. These include a jar burial from Ashkelon inscribed with an Anubis/Wepwawet figure (Birney & Doak, 2011), and the inclusion of lotus decorations on Bichrome pottery within funerary contexts at Azor and Tell 'Etun (Ben-Dor Evian, 2012).

---

[11] Personal observation of one of us in the Rockefeller Museum (courtesy of the Rockefeller Museum, Jerusalem). Note also that the Egyptian forms appearing at Tell el-Far'ah (South) are typically Egyptian Nile clay shapes; in the southern Levant these forms were by and large locally manufactured (cf. Martin, 2011: 91 for the correlation between shape and fabric).

[12] The seal was first published by Petrie as a Ramesses XI scarab, later identified as Ramesses X by Brandl (1982: 383) and later as an Amun-Re cryptogram by Uehlinger (1988: 25, n. 80). In any event, the typological features of the scarab suggest a late Ramesside date.

[13] The presence, if at all, of Philistines at Tell el Far'ah (South) is beyond the scope of the present article.

5 Conclusions

The Egyptian prototype for the Tell el-Far'ah (South) rock-cut tombs is closer in shape, time and geography than the previously suggested Mycenaean or Cypriot origin. The nature of Tell el-Far'ah (South) under Egyptian rule provides a reasonable historical background for the execution of Egyptian-type tombs at the site.

The similarities between the rock-cut tombs of Cemeteries 500 and 900 are remarkable. Not only do both tomb groups display highly Egyptianized burial practices, *i.e.* type of offerings, use of anthropoid clay coffins and western orientation, but they also share the most common tomb design of New Kingdom Egypt.

The overall evidence of the tomb plan, the anthropoid clay coffins and the Egyptian-type pottery all point to the Egyptian, rather than Philistine, execution of Tombs 532, 542, 544, 552 and 562.

Some of these Egyptian-type tombs were later intruded upon and reused by the new occupants of the site. The identity of these new occupants cannot be conclusively identified. Philistine Bichrome Ware cannot, on its own, be used to determine a Philistine, rather than Canaanite identity. It is however interesting to note that Philistine Bichrome Ware has been unearthed at other formerly Egyptian sites of the western Negev (Tell el-'Ajjul [Dothan, 1982: 35], Tell Jemmeh [*ibid.*: 33–35; Ben-Shlomo, 2014], Deir el-Balaḥ [Brandl, 2010: 107–108] and Qubur el-Walaydah [Lehmann et al., 2010: 149–151]) attesting to the reuse of the deserted Egyptian residencies by the local and/or new populations of southwest Canaan. The presence of Philistine Bichrome pottery within the Egyptian burials of Tell el-Far'ah (South) may be the result of a similar process by which newcomers associated themselves with the land through the reoccupation of its past centers of power. Alternatively, this can be seen as a further manifestation of the "entangled" identity of the early Iron Age inhabitants (Maeir & Hitchcock, 2017), mixing Egyptian tombs with Philistine, Canaanite and Egyptianized objects.

References

Åström, P. (1972). *The Swedish Cyprus Expedition. Volume IV. Part 1C. The late Cypriot Bronze Age architecture and pottery*. The Swedish Cyprus Expedition.

Ben-Dor Evian, S. (2012). Egypt and Philistia in the Iron Age I: The case of the Philistine lotus flower. *Tel Aviv, 39,* 20–37.

Ben-Dor Evian, S. (2015). "They were thr on land, others on sea…" The etymology of the Egyptian term for "Sea-Peoples". *Semitica, 57,* 57–75.

Ben-Shlomo, D. (2008). The cemetery of Azor and early Iron Age burial practices. *Levant, 40,* 29–54.

Ben-Shlomo, D. (2010). *Philistine iconography: A wealth of style and symbolism* (Orbis Biblicus et Orientalis 241). Academic.

Ben-Shlomo, D. (2014). Decorated Philistine pottery. In D. Ben-Shlomo & G. W. van Beek (Eds.), *The Smithsonian institution excavation at Tell Jemmeh, Israel, 1970–1990* (pp. 721–731). Smithsonian Contributions to Anthropology 50.

Birney, K., & Doak, B. R. (2011). Funerary iconography on an infant burial jar from Ashkelon. *Israel Exploration Journal, 61*, 32–53.

Bloch-Smith, E. (1992). *Judahite burial practices and beliefs about the dead* (JSOT Supp 123). JSOT Press.

Brandl, B. (1982). The Tel Masos scarab: A suggestion for a new method for the interpretation of royal scarabs. *Scripta Hierosolymitana, 28*, 371–405.

Brandl, B. (2010). The stratigraphy of the settlement. In T. Dothan & B. Brandl (Eds.), *Deir el Balaḥ: Excavations in 1977–1982 in the cemetery and settlement* (Qedem 49) (pp. 63–249).

Braunstein, S. L. (2011). The meaning of Egyptian-style objects in the late Bronze cemeteries of Tell el-Farʿah (South). *Bulletin of the American Schools of Oriental Research, 364*, 1–36.

Brug, J. F. (1985). *A literary and archaeological study of the Philistines*. BAR International Series 265.

Bunimovitz, S. (1990). Problems in the "ethnic" identification of Philistine material culture. *Tel Aviv, 17*(2), 210–222.

Calcoen, B. (2012). *TT176. The Tomb Chapel of Userhat* (GHP Egyptology 16). Golden House Publications.

Cotelle-Michel, L. (2004). *Les sarcophages en terre cuite en Égypte et en Nubie: de l'époque prédynastique à l'époque romaine*. Faton.

Dothan, T. (1982). *The Philistines and their material culture*. Yale University Press.

Dothan, T. (2008). Deir el-Balaḥ: Uncovering an Egyptian outpost in Canaan from the time of the exodus.

Edelstein, G., & Aurant, S. (1992). The Philistine tomb at Tell ʿEitun. *ʿAtiqot, 21*, 23–41.

Faerman, M., Smith, P., Boaretto, E., Uziel, J., & Maeir, A. M. (2011). "… in their lives, and in their death …": A preliminary study of an Iron Age burial cave at Tell eṣ-ṣāfī, Israel. *Zeitschrift des Deutschen Palästina-vereins, 127*(1), 29–48.

Fischer, E. (2011). *Tell el-Farʿah (Süd): Ägyptisch-levantinische Beziehungen im späten 2. Jahrtausend v. Chr*. Orbis Biblicus et Orientalis 247.

Fischer, P. M., & Bürge, T. (2017). Tombs and offering pits at the Late Bronze Age metropolis of Hala Sultan Tekke, Cyprus. *BASOR, 377*, 161–218.

Gilmour, G. (1995). Aegean influence in Late Bronze funerary practices in the southern Levant. In S. Campbell & A. Green (Eds.), *The archaeology of death in the ancient Near East* (pp. 155–170). Oxbow Monograph 51.

Gitin, S., Meehl, M. W., & Dothan, T. (2006). Occupational history – Stratigraphy and architecture. In M. W. Meehl, T. Dothan, & S. Gitin (Eds.), *Tel Miqne-Ekron. Excavations 1995–1996, Field INE East Slope: Late Bronze II–Iron I* (pp. 27–69). The early Philistine city, Tel Miqne-Ekron 8.

Goldwasser, O. (1999). Hieratic fragments from Tell el Farʿah (South). *Bulletin of the American Schools of Oriental Research, 313*, 31–38.

Gonen, R. (1992). *Burial patterns and cultural diversity in late Bronze Age Canaan* (ASOR dissertation series 7). Eisenbrauns.

Kampp, F. (1996). *Die Thebanische Nekropole. Zum Wandel des Grabgedankens von der XVIII. bis zur XX. Dynastie*. Theben 13.

Karageorghis, V. (1990). *Tombs at Palaeopaphos: 1. Teratsoudhia 2. Eliomylia*. A.G. Leventis Foundation.

Knapp, A. B. (2013). *The archaeology of Cyprus. From earliest prehistory through the Bronze Age*.

Laemmel, S. (2003). *A case study of the late Bronze and early Iron Age cemeteries of Tell el-Farʿah (South)*. Dissertation, University of Oxford.

Laemmel, S. (2013). A few tomb groups from Tell el-Farʿah south. In A. E. Killebrew & G. Lehmann (Eds.), *The Philistines and other "Sea Peoples" in text and archaeology* (pp. 145–189). SBL.

Lehmann, G., Rosen, S. A., Berlejung, A., et al. (2010). Excavations at Qubur al-Walaydah, 2007–2009. *Die Welt des Orients, 40*(2), 137–159.

Maeir, A. M., & Hitchcock, L. A. (2017). Rethinking the Philistines: A 2017 perspective. In O. Lipschits, Y. Gadot, & J. M. Adams (Eds.), *Rethinking Israel – Studies in the history and archaeology of ancient Israel in honor of Israel Finkelstein* (pp. 247–266).

Martin, M. A. S. (2011). *Egyptian-type pottery in the Late Bronze Age southern Levant.* Österreichische Akademie der Wissenschaften: Denkschriften der Gesamtakademie 69.

Martin, G. T., van Dijk, J., Raven, M. J. et al (2001). The tombs of three Memphite officials: Ramose, Khay and Pabes.

McClellan, T. L. (1979). Chronology of the "Philistine" burials at Tell el-Far'ah (south). *Journal of Field Archaeology, 6*(1), 57–73..

Morris, E. F. (2005). *The architecture of imperialism: Military bases and the evolution of foreign policy in Egypt's New Kingdom.* Probleme der Ägyptologie 22.

Oren, E. D. (1973). The northern cemetery of Beth Shan. Leiden.

Petrie, F. (1930). *Beth-Pelet I (Tell Fara)* (BSAE 48).

Polz, D. (1997). *Das Grab des Hui und des Kel: Theben 54.* Archäologische Veröffentlichungen 74.

Risser, M. K., & Harvey, S. P. (1992). A reexamination of chamber tombs at Tell el-Far'ah (South). *American Journal of Archaeology, 96*(2), 344.

Stager, L. E. (1995). The impact of the Sea Peoples in Canaan (1185–1050 BCE). In T. E. Levy (Ed.), *The archaeology of society in the Holy Land* (pp. 332–348).

Starkey, J. L., & Harding, L. (1932). *Beth Pelet II* (BSAE 52).

Stiebing, W. H. (1970). Another look at the origins of the Philistine tombs at Tell el-Far'ah (S). *American Journal of Archaeology, 74*(2), 139–143.

Uehlinger, C. (1988). Der Amun-Tempel Ramses' III. In p3-Kn'n, seine südpalästinischen Tempelgüter und der Übergang von der Ägypter- zur Philisterherrschaft: Ein Hinweis auf einige wenig beachtete Skarabäen. *Zeitschrift des Deutschen Palästinavereins, 104*, 6–25.

Waldbaum, J. C. (1966). Philistine tombs at tell Far'ah and their Aegean prototypes. *American Journal of Archaeology, 70*(4), 331–340.

Yannai, E. (1996). *Aspects of the material culture of Canaan during the Egyptian 20th dynasty (1200–1130 BCE).* Dissertation, Tel Aviv University (Hebrew).

Yannai, E. (2002). A stratigraphic and chronological reappraisal of the "Governor's residence" at Tell el-Far'ah (South). In S. Ahituv (Ed.), *Ahron Kempinski memorial volume: Studies in archaeology and related disciplines* (Beer-Sheva 15) (pp. 368–376). Beer Sheva.

Yasur-Landau, A. (2013). The "feathered helmets" of the Sea Peoples—Joining the iconographic and archaeological evidence. *Talanta, 44*, 27–40.

Philistine Rural Temple Economy: The Early Iron Age Fauna from Nahal Patish

Edward F. Maher and Pirhiya Nahshoni

Abstract Excavations at the site of Nahal Patish in the northwestern Negev have revealed an Iron-Age Philistine temple that dates to the end of the eleventh – early tenth century BCE. The non-domestic status of one area of the site as a functioning temple complex is suggested by features that include architectural layout, an altar, a standing stone, benches, *favissa* pits, and ritual paraphernalia that consists of chalices, stands, and a lion-headed drinking cup. The faunal sample from the temple precinct provides an opportunity to investigate the role animals played in a ritual context in terms of species selection, culling schedules, body part representation, symmetry bias, and other details. Relatively little data on Philistine cultic proceedings are known from rural occupations; what exists is primarily derived from urban centers. This study offers an opportunity to further document the expression of early Philistine cult as performed in a boundary zone at the periphery of southeastern Philistia.

Keywords Iron Age · Philistine · Zooarchaeology · Fauna · Animal sacrifice · Temple

1 Introduction

Ancient economies centered on different core purposes. Some related to secular themes involving domestic and palatial agendas or fluctuating political climates that either forged independence or led to vassalage. Other causes like the requirements

E. F. Maher (✉)
Northeastern Illinois University, Chicago, IL, USA
e-mail: efmaher@hotmail.com

P. Nahshoni
Independent Scholar, Beer-Sheva, Israel
e-mail: npirhiya@post.bgu.ac.il

© The Author(s), under exclusive license to Springer Nature Switzerland AG 2023
E. Ben-Yosef, I. W. N. Jones (eds.), *"And in Length of Days Understanding" (Job 12:12): Essays on Archaeology in the Eastern Mediterranean and Beyond in Honor of Thomas E. Levy*, Interdisciplinary Contributions to Archaeology, https://doi.org/10.1007/978-3-031-27330-8_28

imposed by sacred rituals in the form of offerings also interfaced with a community's economic structure. Understanding the relationship between sacred and secular demands on local economic assets demonstrates how the needs of both were met. Defining how such contexts were maintained economically also defines which assets were used, the frequency of their usage, and how they were utilized. Isolating usage then becomes a method by which to better highlight the decisions made by owners and managers of the assets in question.

Philistine economies are best known from major urban centers such as Tel Miqne-Ekron (Dothan, 1995, 1998; Dothan & Dothan, 1992; Gitin, 1989, 1995, 1997; Gitin & Dothan, 1987; Hesse, 1986; Lev-Tov, 2000, 2006; Maher, 2014; Maher & Hesse, 2016, 2017), Tell es-Safi/Gath (e.g., Eliyahu-Behar et al., 2012; Akermann et al., 2014; Hitchcock et al., 2015; Lev-Tov, 2012), Ashdod (Dothan & Ben-Shlomo, 2005; Maher, 2005) and Ashkelon (e g., Hesse et al., 2012; Stager et al., 2020; Weiss & Kislev, 2004). With the exception of a few sites like Tel Batash/Timnah (Kelm & Mazar, 1995) and perhaps Qubur al-Walaydah (Lehmann, 2011; Lehmann et al., 2018; Maher, 2010), Philistine rural economies are less understood. Not surprisingly, when temple economies are drawn into focus, it is the data from the cities that form the bulk of the evidence while the temple economies of the countryside, with one exception at Tell Qasile (Mazar, 1980), remain largely unknown. Comparing and contrasting how temple economies worked between Philistine cities and villages advances our understanding on how such economies operated in large urban hubs as opposed to more isolated settlements with reduced population density. To complicate the issue, several of the rural communities were situated some distance from the urban centers. It is altogether possible that their political or ideological influence was muted or at least less pronounced. Settlements positioned far enough away from the core cultural territories might have occupied an interface between two different and sometimes opposing polities. This area of interface, a liminal zone, is where communities might adopt and/or select elements of competing cultural cores without taking on all the subtle nuances of each, thus forging their own unique expression of identity. Although these elements, which could include material culture (architecture, pottery) or concepts regarding ethnicity and belief systems, may have been less structured, they still would have held symbolic meaning to community members (Tappy, 2008: 16–26). A group's choice of foods could constitute an ethnic marker, as cuisine represents a relatively conservative cultural element that underscores a key component in constructing and projecting self-identity (Hesse & Wapnish, 1998: 124). Barth (1969: 15) suggested that cultural boundaries even facilitate the means by which a group can be defined.

This paper details a zooarchaeological analysis of the site of Nahal Patish, a rural Philistine community that was located on the southeastern edge of Philistia. This moderately-sized archaeofaunal assemblage totaled nearly 1000 fragments (Table 1). The sample collected was studied in Israel during the summer of 2012. Although field excavations explored three main areas of the site (see below) no fauna was found in Area A. Only Area B (over 800 fragments) and Area C (more than 50 fragments) yielded suitable osteological material for study.

Table 1 Faunal abundance by locus type and occupation phase

Locus type	Occupation level				Total
	Phase 1	Phase 2	Phase 3	mixed	
Accumulation on floor	39	269			308
Baulk	1			2	3
Bench, dismantle		51			51
Bin of stone and clay		14			14
Debris	40	135	8		183
Debris on floor	1				1
Defining podium		1			1
Floor	16	20			36
Floor makeup	22				22
Floor with tabun	1				1
Hearth		56			56
Mudbrick debris		46			46
Opening in Wall 6		1			1
Pit	9	8	46		63
Pit fill	72	32			104
Probe		2			2
Stone collapse	14	23			37
Surface		21			21
Topsoil				18	18
Wall		3			3
Total	215	682	54	20	971

2 The Archaeology of Nahal Patish

The site (Fig. 1), which was excavated for three seasons (2006–2008), is located on the southern bank of Nahal Patish, a tributary of Nahal Grar, ca. 12 km west of modern Beer-Sheva. It lies within a 200 mm rain zone, suitable for grazing and grain agriculture, especially in rainy winters. The site spreads over an estimated area of about 3 acres on the escarpment facing the *wadi*. The nearest major sites which were inhabited during the same period are Tel Sera, about 9 km to the north, and Tel Haror, about 9 km to the northwest.

Excavations conducted in three areas (Fig. 2) uncovered three occupational phases (Fig. 3), all of which occurred within a relatively brief window of time. Founded at the end of the eleventh century BCE, Phase 3 was exposed only in a few spots. It preceded the building constructions of Phase 2 and only included ash layers and a few installations. In Phase 2 the site underwent intensive building construction during which major structures (209, 249 and 365) were erected. Activity continued at the site in Phase 1 but in a much-reduced capacity until its eventual abandonment at the beginning of the tenth century BCE.

In the first season of excavations (2006) scant architectural remains were found in Area A, and ash layers and refuse pits were found in Area C. However, part of a

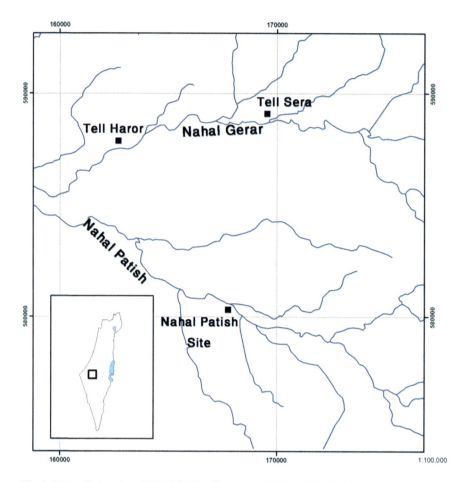

Fig. 1 Map with location of Nahal Patish. (Courtesy of the Israel Antiquities Authority)

built complex was unearthed in Area B (Fig. 2). Excavations eventually centered on Area B, covering ca. 200 m² (Fig. 3) where it became clear that the complex was comprised of two main structures (209 and 249) and another (365) partly excavated structure. Of note is that the architectural elements of the cult place, including its bent axis, indirect access to the sanctuary, and the benches around the walls, is reminiscent of Temple 131 from Stratum X at Tell Qasile X (Mazar, 1980). All three occupation phases are evident in Area B.

2.1 Area B Phase 3

Living surfaces with ash layers covered the slope in the east and accumulated in depressions and pits (Loci 310 and 361). A stone paved area (Locus 328) was found underlying the storeroom's floor and the northwestern wall (Wall 23) and a stone installation (Locus 356) was exposed underlying the floor of the mudbrick walls (Walls 28 and 37) of Structure 365.

Philistine Rural Temple Economy: The Early Iron Age Fauna from Nahal Patish

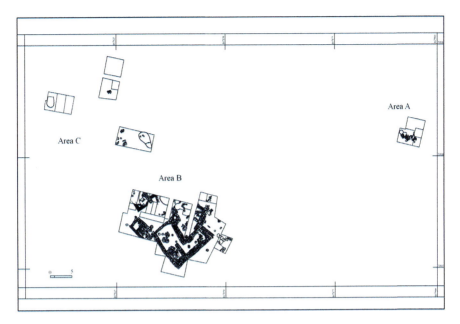

Fig. 2 Areas of excavation at Nahal Patish. (Natalia Zak, courtesy of the Israel Antiquities Authority)

Fig. 3 Nahal Patish shrine: ground plan of excavation in Area B. (Natalia Zak, courtesy of the Israel Antiquities Authority)

2.2 Area B Phase 2

Structure 209, built on the higher part of the slope facing the *wadi*, was comprised of two small contiguous rooms in the west (Loci 238 and 241). Room 238 (2.6 × 1.7 m) was stone paved, and the finds included ash and pottery sherds. An opening in Room 238 led to a courtyard (Locus 209) with a *tabun* placed next to the southeastern end of Wall 17, near the entrance. Room 241 (1.6 × 1.15 m) had an earthen floor and may have been a storeroom as indicated by three storage jars standing in the eastern corner. This room yielded a rare lion-headed cup decorated with typical black and red Philistine motifs (Fig. 4; Meiberg & Nahshoni, 2020). Most of the lion-headed vessels, known thus far, have been uncovered at Philistine sites or sites attributed to other Sea Peoples and share typical Philistine decorative motifs and dimensions. Moreover, several lion-headed cups, including ours, have been uncovered in ritual contexts, yet their exact cultic symbolism remains unclear (Meiberg & Nahshoni, 2020).

Structure 249 was built southeast of the earlier Structure 209. This well-planned L-shaped structure was built onto the slope after it had been partly cut away, in order to create a leveled surface, ca. 1 m lower than the floors of Structure 209. The walls, constructed of pebbles and fieldstones of various sizes, were preserved to a height of 1.0–1.6 m. Revetment Wall 15 was built in the northwest, delineating the courtyard (Locus 249).

The courtyard (Locus 249) was a rather small enclosure (4.5 × 4.0 m) with a stone bench built along eastern Wall 6 and another short mudbrick and stone bench built against southern Wall 23. A sacrificial, nearly square, altar (1.1 × 1.2 × 0.2 m) built of three undressed large stones and supported by small stones was situated in the center. A pit (Locus 260) was found southwest of the altar. A thick ash layer covered most of the floor. A small, rounded hearth (Locus 266) was cut into the natural loess east of the altar. Three small *favissa* pits (Loci 352, 353, and 364) cut into the courtyard floor contained pottery and stone vessels.

The finds in the courtyard included many grinding and pounding stone vessels; several storage jars smashed by collapsed rubble were found along the walls and a group of cylindrical loom-weights (spools) was found near the southern wall. This concentration of pinched loom-weights (spools) represents a new weaving technology that appears in various Philistine sites, as well in some other Iron Age sites, yet is unknown in the Late Bronze Age southern Levant (Mazow, 2006/2007; Lehmann, 2011; Maeir et al., 2019).

A unique figurative cultic stand, possibly fallen from a higher shelf, was found within the collapsed mud bricks (Figs. 5 and 6; Nahshoni & Ziffer, 2010). It is a rare clay imitation of a bronze offering stand. Bronze stands were manufactured in Cyprus in the eleventh century BCE and were also imported into the Levant, possibly by Philistine independent entrepreneurs (Sherratt, 1998). Various clay imitations of offering stands are known from other cult-related Iron Age sites, exhibiting Philistine traits, especially in the cult repository at Yavneh (Kletter, 2010; Ziffer, 2010). The locally made stand from Nahal Patish is decorated in a typical Philistine

Fig. 4 Nahal Patish lion-headed cup, view of the front. (Clara Amit, courtesy of the Israel Antiquities Authority)

style with red horizontal bands on a white-washed surface. The surviving three figures (out of four) include an anthropomorphic head, a ram's head (Fig. 6) and a palmette that were attached to the circular base between the offering stand's legs, demonstrating cultural traits that can be found in the local Philistine iconography, Iron Age Cypriote iconography, and also in earlier Canaanite iconography (Nahshoni & Ziffer, 2010: 548–550).

The storeroom (Locus 261, 2.0 × 2.8 m) was entered from the enclosed courtyard. A stone bench (0.9 × 1.1 × 0.4 m) and a bin built of stone and clay (Locus 311, 0.9 × 1.0 × 0.68 m) were built along its southern wall. Part of the floor was paved with large stones. This paving (Locus 328) preceded the construction of the walls, filling up an existing depression and leveling the surface in preparation for the construction of Structure 249. The finds in the room included many food-preparation and serving pottery vessels, stone vessels and one fragment belonging to the figurative cultic stand from the courtyard. The finds inside the stone and clay bin (Locus 311, Fig. 7) included parts of a restorable cooking pot, a bowl, assorted animal bones (see below), and a piece of a bronze object. The bin may have served as a *favissa* since it was intentionally filled with earth and stones.

Fig. 5 The offering stand. (Clara Amit, courtesy of the Israel Antiquities Authority)

The sanctuary/cult room (Locus 211) was an elongated room (2.0 × 5.2 m) in which two phases were discerned. The indirect access was from the enclosed courtyard. The eastern wall had probably been built of mudbricks; its collapse was attested by brick material covering the floor. The earthen floor was plastered with clay and presumably white-washed, extending as far as the benches which were built next to the long walls.

A stepped platform was found in the eastern end. The lower step was made of packed earth and the higher one was then added, by cutting into the lower platform and inserting three courses of single bricks. A standing stone was inserted into the platform next to the higher step (Fig. 8).

Fig. 6 Close-up of ram head portraiture on offering stand. (Clara Amit, courtesy of the Israel Antiquities Authority)

2.3 Area B Phase 1

While most of the Phase 2 buildings lay in ruins in Phase 1, only the sanctuary was restored. A new earthen floor (Locus 251) and a column post were laid on top of the leveled Phase 2 ruins. It remains unclear where the access to the cult-room was in this phase, since the courtyard fell out of use. Cooking operations continued in open-area living surfaces with *tabun*s that were found east (Loci 316, 317, and 230) and west (Locus 244) of the sanctuary. A Phase 1 living surface was also traced overlying Structure 209, where it was badly preserved due to modern activities.

Fig. 7 Bottom of stone and clay bin (Locus 311) in the storeroom of structure 249. (Photo by Pirhiya Nahshoni)

Fig. 8 Sanctuary room within structure 249 facing northeast, Wall 25 in foreground. (Photo by Pirhiya Nahshoni)

3 Methods of Faunal Analysis

Retrieval of the excavated materials was carried out by employing a selective recovery program that combined hand collection with sifted layers passed through a 5 × 5 mm mesh screen. These efforts resulted in an assemblage scattered between 11 excavation units (5 × 5 m). The actual studied assemblage is somewhat smaller than what was discovered since some contexts were excluded due to their problematic stratigraphic nature (see below). After field collection, the fauna was carefully cleaned with wet brushes to better expose surfaces, a procedure that revealed diagnostic characteristics that assisted identification. Bones and teeth were temporarily dampened but never allowed to soak overnight. Wet remains were kept out of direct sunlight in shaded or enclosed areas, so they would not dry too quickly and potentially break. They were bagged only when completely air-dried. All cleaned faunal material was inspected under 3× magnification.

Species identification was assisted by publications routinely used for such purposes (Boessneck, 1969; Halstead & Collins, 2002; Lister, 1996; Payne, 1985; Prummell & Frisch, 1986; Schmid, 1972; Zeder & Lapham, 2010; Zeder & Pilaar, 2010). Because of the similar morphology and size of sheep and goats, many of their remains were combined into a pooled ovicaprine category whenever precise taxonomic distinction between the two could not be determined. The identification of problematic remains was verified by consulting the modern comparative zoological skeletal specimens at the National Natural History Collections, Institute of Earth Sciences, Institute of Archaeology at The Hebrew University of Jerusalem. For the remains that did not allow for species identification, a size-based taxonomy comprising three classes was used: small, medium, and large mammals. Fauna in such advanced states of breakage that could not be assigned to an appropriate size-based division were considered unidentifiable.

Determining the age at death for the animals provides a means of assessing their value and the kinds of products and services targeted by their human handlers. Age at death was estimated by using post-cranial epiphyseal fusion rates (Silver, 1969) and dental attrition scores (Payne, 1973; Zeder, 1991: 93). Aging data were combined for sheep and goats. Although this served to augment the sample size which produced more interpretable datasets, pooling them into one category potentially obscures or masks sheep or goat-specific slaughter schedules. Measurements taken on bones and teeth, done in accordance with von den Driesch (1976), assisted in species identification.

The fauna was quantified by counting the number of bone and tooth fragments and intact elements for each species which are expressed as an NISP value (number of identifiable specimens), further abbreviated as 'n' in the text. Body part representation is key to any faunal analysis and should be investigated on large enough samples that allow for it. Bovid body part breakdowns are expressed as a ratio that compares non-meat bearing to meat bearing limb bones to demonstrate whether entire and presumably living animals occurred at specific locations on a site or if they were mainly introduced as cuts of meat having already been slaughtered elsewhere (Redding, 1994; Zeder, 1991). Approaches to establishing bovid body part division also assess the nutritional yield of certain anatomical portions (Hellwing & Gophna, 1984; Horwitz, 1999, 2000) by tabulating types of carcass debris (butchery vs. slaughter offal), comparing the proportions of upper, middle, or lower limb segments, and considering the relative abundance of fore and hind limbs.

The analysis attempted to document evidence for butchery, burning, carnivore access, and pathologies. Binford (1981) indicates various stages of anatomical reduction that include dismemberment (transverse cut marks on or near articulating joints), defleshing or skinning (cut marks facilitating hide removal), and filleting (characterized by a series of short chevron or obliquely grouped cut marks or as longitudinal butchery marks relative to the bone shaft). Cut mark location and orientation on the bones were matched, whenever possible, to this system that corresponds to different butchering procedures. Demonstrated under experimental conditions, burned bone color reflects firing temperatures, where brown and black fragments are ascribed to relatively cooler temperatures compared to more intensely heated bones colored white or blue gray (Nicholson, 1993; Shipman et al., 1984). To reduce subjective reporting, the color of every burned bone was coded using a Munsell Soil Color Chart as it provides a standardized and replicable means of description. Carnivores feeding on soft tissue attached to bones leave behind distinct marks from gnawing, biting, and patterned erosional wears due to partial digestion (Horwitz, 1990; Kerbis-Peterhans & Horwitz, 1992, Maher unpublished manuscript A) and are easily recognizable when present in an archaeofaunal sample.

4 The Faunal Assemblage and Associated Chronology

Near Eastern zooarchaeological studies are particularly challenged because determining their temporal association is sometimes problematic. Unlike material culture such as pottery or lithics whose approximate date of manufacture and use can be estimated via defined sequences of development, the morphology of animal remains is not as typologically sensitive to the passage of time as there have been no significant changes to their skeletal and dental anatomies for the past several thousand years (Davis, 1987a, b: 31; Hesse & Rosen, 1988: 118). As this reality renders the same dating technique inapplicable to historic and protohistoric period fauna in the region, establishing dates for archaeofaunal collections becomes highly dependent on their demonstrated contextual and stratigraphic associations with artifacts and architectural features.

Although faunal remains from all contexts were recorded (Table 1), not all loci bearing animal remains were included in the final analysis. Levels with a mix of artifacts from layers of topsoil, accumulations of mud bricks, or stone walls were excluded because of the high likelihood that they represent temporal mixing.

Additional examples of contexts that feature probable temporal contamination include the reuse of architectural materials or excavation procedures that trimmed baulks.

Primary contexts assumed to be the most stratigraphically secure, like surfaces and floors, and secondary deposits such as debris layers, pit contents, or installations were included in the present study. Although the systematic exclusion of certain contexts is warranted, it cannot promise absolute immunity from temporal contamination for the remaining material. After selectivity reducing the overall sample size, the remaining assemblage is assumed to be more indictive of ancient decisions involving animal management.

5 Areas of Excavation and Associated Occupation Phases

The fauna from Nahal Patish comes from three distinct phases of occupation, all of which date to the late eleventh to early tenth century BCE. While Phase 1 represents the latest (youngest) and Phase 3 the earliest (oldest) occupational horizon at the site, most of the fauna belongs to the middle period during Phase 2 (Table 2).

Table 2 Species abundance and diversity by occupation phase in Areas B and C

Species list	Area B Phase 1 NISP	Area B Phase 1 NISP %	Area B Phase 2 NISP	Area B Phase 2 NISP %	Area B Phase 3 NISP	Area B Phase 3 NISP %	Area C Phase 1 NISP	Area C Phase 1 NISP %	NISP Total
Cattle (*Bos taurus*)	6	11.5%	11	8.7%	1	20.0%	3	21.4%	21
Deer (Cervidae)			1	0.8%					1
Dog (*Canis familiarus*)	1	1.9%	1	0.8%					2
Donkey (*Equus asinus*)	1	1.9%							1
Fish (Osteichthyes)			1	0.8%					1
Fox (*Vupes vulpes*)	7	13.5%			1	20.0%			8
Hare (*Lepus capensis*)			9	7.1%					9
Ovicaprine (*Ovis aries/ Capra hircus*)	37	71.2%	103	81.7%	3	60.0%	11	78.6%	154
Small mammal			6						6
Medium mammal	86		340		5		7		438
Large mammal	13		15				4		32
Unidentified	8		143		44		30		225
Total	159		630		54		55		898

5.1 Area B: Phase 3

The faunal assemblage from the Phase 3 occupation (Table 2) represents the smallest temporally specific sample from Nahal Patish. Some of the sample was excluded due to the probable temporal mixture (see above). The remaining sample is comprised of 54 bones, of which only five (9.3%) were identified. Most of the fragments ($n = 46$, 85.2%) were found in a pit while the rest were collected from debris layers.

The Phase 3 fauna mainly consists of domestic animals that include sheep and goats ($n = 3$) and cattle ($n = 1$). One red fox (*Vulpes vulpes*) forelimb (radius) was also identified. It is plausible that most if not all of the bones classified as medium-sized mammals are in fact ovicaprines.

Only three bones provided age-related data based on species-specific long-bone fusion rates. Two proximal ends of an ovicaprine second phalanx were unfused, indicating the animal's death before 13–16 months old. One fused distal scapula from cattle was at least 7–10 months old.

There is a lack of cultural and natural modification on the animal bones. This includes no evidence for burn or butchery marks, carnivore feeding or digestion, rodent gnawing, or pathologies or healed traumas.

5.2 Area B: Phase 2

The faunal assemblage from the Phase 2 occupation (Table 2) represents the largest temporally specific sample from Nahal Patish. Some of the collection was excluded due to the probable mixture of contemporary and earlier materials. The remaining sample exceeds 600 bones and teeth, of which 126 (20%) were taxonomically identified. Most of the fragments ($n = 567$, 90%) were found on floors/surfaces, in debris layers, and installations (bin, hearth, podium). Additional remains from pit, probe and stone collapse loci were also recovered.

The Phase 2 fauna is dominated by domestic species, mainly sheep and goats ($n = 103$, 81.7%), where sheep remains ($n = 10$) outnumber those of goats ($n = 3$). Although interpreting the sheep to goat ratio is often done in zooarchaeological studies to estimate herding strategies (Redding, 1984), it is problematic in this case for two reasons. First, the sample is too small ($n = 13$) to be considered truly representative of the period. Second, the sheep to goat ratio may not accurately reflect the local economy and instead may better illustrate only those animals chosen for temple use. Cattle ($n = 11$, 8.7%) were also exploited but to a much lesser extent. Non-domesticated species such as deer (Cervidae) and hare (*Lepus capensis*), represented only in this phase, exemplify how wild animals were occasionally hunted/snared and may have diversified the local diet. Exploiting a wider resource base is further illustrated by the lone fish bone in the collection, represented by the mandible of the common sea bream (*Pagrus ceruleostictus*). Its non-local origin (see Sect. 6.10) underscores the operation of commercial networks to which Nahal Patish was connected.

The lone Cervid (deer) bone, being one of the toes (first phalanx), warrants additional comment. As it did not show wear typically associated with carnivore consumption (e.g., Horwitz, 1990; Maher, 2006/07), its introduction to the site is assumed to be associated with cultural rather than natural agency. Bones from the lower extremities, such as carpals, tarsals, and phalanges are commonly left inside an animal's hide once separated from the carcass (see Perkins & Daly, 1968 for their discussion of the "schlep effect"). The deer may have been partially processed at a distant kill site, skinned there, then disarticulated further as choice meaty parts were transported back to the site and wrapped in the animal's own hide. The deer phalanx may therefore be a remnant of that procedure.

A small sample of bones provided age-related data based on species-specific long bone fusion rates, most of which represent sheep and goats ($n = 24$). The fusion data are grouped by similar fusion schedules (Table 3) which is converted into a mortality profile (Fig. 9). Cull rates (lower register) that include juveniles and sub-adults likely indicate that meat was a valued commodity. Dental evidence for young sheep/goats is evident by small and isolated incisors as well as one second lower molar from a 6–12 month old individual. Mature animals were also present, some of which had survived beyond the latest fusion stage at 42 months. Older milk-producing females would have been kept alive, as would wool and hair-producing members of both sexes. The loom weights in the courtyard of Structure 249 may complement the harvest of sheep wool or goat hair. Since these exploitable products do not require the animal's death to acquire, the procedures could be maintained repeatedly until their production levels dipped below profitable margins. None of the cattle remains provided age-based data.

Aging data were also recorded for two additional species. One fused distal end of a third metatarsal of a dog was from an individual older than 10 months. Fusion data were noted on four hare bones, all of which were metatarsals (second, third, fourth, and fifth). Based on their common find-spot (see below) and fused state, they may have once belonged to a single individual. Five hare hind phalanges were also clustered with the hare metatarsals. As all hare remains come from a hind foot from the right side, the bones likely represent the same individual specimen. The fused distal metatarsal ends, as well as their size, indicates the hare was at least a sub-adult or adult at death.

A small sample of four bones featured evidence for butchery. Transverse cut marks across the proximal end of a sheep metacarpal (MCp-1 according to Binford, 1981) were inflicted during the dismemberment process. Cut marks on an ovicaprine proximal radius (RCp-6 according to Binford, 1981) are indicative of meat removal during filleting procedures. Cut marks were also identified along a rib fragment of a medium-sized mammal. A short row of three definite notches, with perhaps one or two additional notches appearing on one end of the row, was carved onto the unidentified limb bone of a medium-sized mammal (Fig. 10). The possible significance of this is addressed further in Sect. 6.8.

A total of 19 bones were burned and located across five different kinds of loci. Eleven bones associated with surfaces (Loci 174, 206, 211, 248, 249, 336) include two black (10YR 2/1) medium mammal limbs, two gray (10YR 5/1 and 10YR 6/1)

Table 3 Ovicaprine fusion data from Area B Phase 2

Element	Quantity	Rate of fusion	Age range
Fused scapula	1	Greater than 6–8 months	6–10 months
Unfused scapula	2	Less than 6–8 months	
Fused distal humerus	1	Greater than 10 months	
Unfused distal humerus	1	Less than 10 months	
Fused proximal radius	2	Greater than 10 months	
Number fused	4		
Number unfused	3		
Fused proximal phalanx	1	Greater than 13–16 months	13–16 months
Unfused proximal phalanx	5	Less than 13–16 months	
Number fused	1		
Number unfused	5		
Fused distal metapodial		Greater than 18–28 months	18–28 months
Unfused distal metapodial	1	Less than 18–28 months	
Fused distal metacarpal		Greater than 18–24 months	
Unfused distal metacarpal	1	Less than 18–24 months	
Fused distal tibia	1	Greater than 18–24 months	
Unfused distal tibia	1	Less than 18–24 months	
Fused distal metatarsal		Greater than 20–28 months	
Unfused distal metatarsal		Less than 20–28 months	
Number fused	1		
Number unfused	3		
Fused calcaneum		Greater than 30–36 months	30–36 months
Unfused calcaneum		Less than 30–36 months	
Fused proximal femur		Greater than 36 months	
Unfused proximal femur		Less than 36 months	
Fused distal radius	1	Greater than 36 months	
Unfused distal radius		Less than 36 months	
Fused ulna	2	Greater than 36 months	
Unfused ulna	2	Less than 36 months	
Number fused	3		
Number unfused	2		
Fused proximal humerus		Greater than 36–42 months	36–42 months
Fused distal femur		Greater than 36–42 months	
Unfused distal femur		Less than 36–42 months	
Fused proximal tibia	1	Greater than 36–42 months	
Unfused proximal tibia	1	Less than 36–42 months	
Number fused	1		
Number unfused	1		

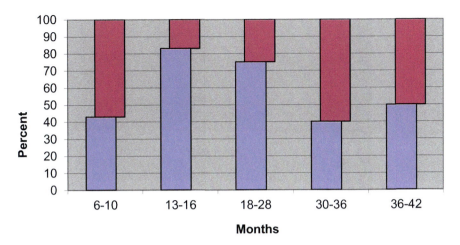

Fig. 9 Ovicaprine mortality profile based on bone fusion from Area B Phase 2. (Upper register: survivorship rate; lower register: cull rate)

medium mammal limb shafts, two gray (GLEY1 6/0 and 10YR 6/1) and one black (10YR 2/1) medium mammal rib fragments, two gray (10YR 6/1) unidentified bone fragments, one white (10YR 8/1) medium mammal limb, and one white (10YR 8/1) ovicaprine first phalanx. Three bones found in a hearth (Locus 320) included brown (10YR 5/2) and bluish-gray (GLEY 2 7/1) medium mammal limb shafts and one black (10YR 2/1) medium mammal rib fragment. Two bones from pits (Loci 163 and 260) included a bluish-gray (GLEY 2 6/1) medium mammal limb shaft and a brown (10YR 5/3) ovicaprine humerus. Two bones from a probe (Locus 216) included black (10YR 2/1) unidentified bone fragments. One bone from an area with collapsed stone (Locus 202) included one black (10YR 2/1) cattle metapodial. Nine bones (brown and black) were likely related to meal preparation since they were associated with relatively cooler temperatures. They were from the main courtyard, sanctuary, and the open area. The remaining burnt sample is associated with hotter temperatures and may be the result of refuse management or charring animal offerings. The Phase 2 faunal sample bore no evidence of any carnivore feeding and digestion or rodent gnawing nor was there any indication of pathologies or healed traumas.

5.3 Area B: Phase 1

The faunal assemblage from the Phase I occupation (Table 2) represents the second-largest temporally specific sample from Nahal Patish. Some of the collection was excluded due to the probable mixture of layers. The remaining sample is comprised of 159 bones, of which 52 (32.7%) were identified. Most of the fragments ($n = 118$, 74.2%) were associated with floors and debris layers. Additional remains came from pits and collapsed stone areas.

Fig. 10 Incised bone from Phase 2 floor of sanctuary room in structure 249. (Photo by Edward. F. Maher)

Fig. 11 Fox upper jaw (maxilla) with teeth from Phase 1 surface makeup in the Northeast Courtyard of structure 249. (Photo by Edward F. Maher)

The Phase 1 fauna is dominated by domestic species, mainly ovicaprines ($n = 37$, 71.2%). Only four bones could be specifically identified as sheep, whereas goats were not identified. Cattle were also exploited but at a reduced frequency. Small equids would have provided a means of hauling loads of supplies and equipment throughout the area. The only non-domesticate in the sample (Fig. 11) is represented by the maxilla (upper jaw) and associated teeth of a red fox (*Vulpes vulpes*).

Only six bones provided age-related data based on their long bone fusion rates, all of which are identified as sheep and goats. One unfused distal scapula was from a juvenile specimen less than 6–8 months old. Three bones from a slightly older animal(s) include a fused distal scapula (greater than 6–8 months) and two fused proximal second phalanges (more than 13–16 months old). A sub-adult or market-aged animal (older than 18–24 months) is represented by a fused distal tibia. One mature specimen (exceeding 36 months) was identified by a fused proximal ulna.

Three burned bones came from two different kinds of loci. One medium mammal limb from a debris layer (Locus 304) was white (10YR 8/1). Two other burned medium mammal limbs from stone collapse contexts (Locus 154 and 246) were light gray (5YR 7/1) and white (10YR 8/1). All colors reflect higher firing temperatures that facilitate faunal reduction due to exposure to intense heat, and as such, may suggest refuse disposal rather than cooking activities.

Other than burn marks, there is a lack of cultural and natural modification on the animal bones. This includes no evidence of any cut marks, carnivore feeding or digestion, rodent gnawing, or pathologies and healed traumas.

5.4 Area C: Phase 1

The entire faunal collection from Area C comes from Phase 1. This sample (Table 2) includes 55 bones, of which 14 (25.5%) were identified. All but one bone came from fills in pits (Loci 115 and 116). Most of the identifiable remains ($n = 11$) were from ovicaprines. Three cattle bones were also recovered.

Data on aging was limited to only a few ovicaprine bones and teeth. One juvenile was identified based on an unfused distal humerus from an individual less than 10 months of age. Older specimens were indicated by the fused proximal ends of a radius (older than 10 months) and second phalanx (at least 13–16 months). These may in fact belong to the same individual from which dental attrition scores identified a sheep aged 12–24 months. One individual of more advanced age is demonstrated by a fused distal ulna (older than 36 months).

Only two bones were burned. One cattle second phalanx was burned black (10YR 2/1) while the limb shaft of a medium mammal was burned light bluish-gray (GLEY 2 8/1). They likely represent different burning events since black is associated with a relatively cooler temperature range than hotter temperatures that tend to produce bones in the blue and gray color registers. Their placement in pit fills indicate redeposition after removal from their original area(s) of combustion.

No butchering marks were found on any of these bones. In addition, none of the bones in this sample bore signatures for pathology or healed trauma, nor was there any evidence of carnivore feeding and digestion or rodent gnawing.

6 Discussion

The faunal assemblage from Nahal Patish reflects site formation processes and a range of decisions pertaining to animal management from a small village site and allows us to better understand early Philistine economics. Perhaps, most importantly, it sheds light on a structured Philistine temple economy in a rural borderland settlement.

6.1 Faunal Preservation

Taphonomic processes that displace, fragment, and destroy faunal remains (Davis, 1987a: 17) constantly exerted their influence on the buried zooarchaeological assemblage at Nahal Patish. Considering the rates of taxonomic identification, grouped by occupation phase, helps identify notable cross-chronological variations. Elevated rates of species identification typify less fragmentary and more intact samples. The same inverse relationship is evident in suppressed rates of species identification that illustrate a more fragmented sample that rendered taxonomic recognition more problematic. The rate of species identification for each occupation phase and area is grouped as follows: Area B Phase 3 (9.3%), Phase 2 (20%), Phase 1 (32.7%); Area C Phase 1: 25.5%. The range in identification rates from Areas B and C in Phase 1, even though derived from different sample sizes, varies by only 7.2%. Similar rates of identification from different occupation phases suggest that the taphonomic agents interacting with the remans had an approximately equal effect. Identification rates progressively deteriorate into the deeper and earlier deposits, which may relate to multiple factors. Lower rates of identification in Area B Phase 3 may simply reflect its small sample size. Variation may also be linked to erosional agents in the environment that may have been more active and intense in certain periods. These agents may have impressed a differential effect on the stratified remains at the site, resulting in a more detrimental effect on the earlier (deeper) levels while its influence was minimized on the material from the later (higher) layers. Eroded areas of the site were noted during field excavations, which seem evident in the contemporary fauna. Another way to explain the varying species identification is that different cultural activities, resulting in further bone fragmentation, were more commonly carried out in Phase 3 than in Phases 1 and 2. Perhaps the apparent rapid and purposeful burial and leveling of the deposits (see carnivore access in Sect. 6.11) exposed the remains to mechanical stresses resulting in heightened fragmentation. It is plausible that all or a combination of these models contributed, in varying degrees, to the preserved state of the fauna.

6.2 Species Range

Most of the remains were identified as sheep and goats, with a more pronounced reliance on sheep. A ceramic three-legged ring-based stand with additional columns topped with portraits was found in the main courtyard of the temple area (Sect. 2.2). One of the animal portraits features a zoomorphic head and face with snout and horns clearly visible; its form is consistent with an adult sheep or goat (Fig. 6), thus emphasizing the importance of ovicaprines to the shine which is in turn supported by their dominance in the faunal record.

Domestic animal use in a temple area is meaningful. An offering was owned by the person or group making it, which implies some level of personal value and cost to the offerer and an attachment between them (Firth, 1972: 325–327). As items of human property, the act of willingly sacrificing animals equates to the surrender of one's possession to a divine cause (Burkert, 1979: 56). Temple rituals are based on the assumption that the offerees willingly relinquish a portion of their personal goods (Durkheim, 1995: 347) thus the sacrifice of a true economic asset (Grant, 1984: 224). The greater its value to the offeree, the greater its regard as an acceptable sacred gift (Tylor, 1970: 484). Due to the intimate nature embedded in the offering ritual, sacrificing domestic animals was more commonly practiced and seemed to carry greater weight of appropriateness because their loss would be felt more by its owner than the sacrifice of a wild animal. Wild game has no meaningful association with humans in terms of rearing, feeding, and protection, and as such, were probably a less valued though not forbidden animal offering.

Primary reliance on domestic animals also relates to animal availability. Referenced by Firth (1972: 332) as "rational calculation," the management of animal resources played a role in temple economies. Since ritual slaughter can include unproductive or surplus animals (Grant, 1984: 225–226), the requirements of the temple economy can be met while simultaneously maintaining the integrity of the overall herd structure. Thus, sheep and goats were chosen for temple rituals because they were commonly raised and the most readily available species. Although the sample is too small and fragmentary to make any definitive claims about sexual dimorphism based on metric data, most of the young animals identified in the mortality profiles (see Sect. 6.3) were probably males. Eliminating young males early underscores an effective strategy to ensure they do not compete later for resources with more productive females (birthing and dairy). Offering males would also satisfy ideological orientations since male deities were often the central supernatural figure around whom rituals were intended to venerate. Thus, the sheep and goats incorporated into the temple economy at Nahal Patish could have simultaneously met the needs of the secular economy while striking a complementary ideological and practical balance between them.

6.3 Mortality Profile

Temple economies often include the ritual slaughter of juvenile specimens (see Maher, 2004), which reflects the strategy at Nahal Patish. Based on long bone epiphyseal fusion and dental attrition, unfused bones from juvenile sheep and goats constitute over half of the ageable remains. Even bones that fuse early in life could have come from an animal that died relatively young. Meat-producing economies with sheep characteristically cull the young, especially males, in their second or third year of life, with only a few surviving to maturity for breeding programs intended to maintain herd viability (Payne, 1973: 281). Once growing animals have achieved optimal weight gain, any added bulk acquired becomes disproportionate to the amount of fodder required. The slaughter schedule then represents an economic consideration, as it seeks balance between the greatest achieved bulk of the animal and the least amount of food needed to reach it. The slaughter of young animals indicates that meat acquisition was a prime consideration for the temple ceremonies. Ritual offerings of meat would have represented the basis for communal meals that would maintain common bonds of beliefs, shared heritage, kinship, and friendship.

6.4 Culture and Cuisine

Linkages have been made between early Philistine culture and their consumption of canids (Lev-Tov et al., 2018; Maher, 2017; Wapnish & Hesse, 1999) and elevated amounts of pork (Faust & Lev-Tov, 2011, 2014; Finkelstein, 1996, 1997; Hesse, 1990, 1995; Hesse & Wapnish, 1997, 1998; Horwitz et al., 2017; Killebrew & Lev-Tov, 2008; Lev-Tov, 2006, 2010; Maeir et al., 2013; Meri et al., 2013; Sapir-Hen et al., 2013, 2015; Stager, 1995; Uziel, 2007). Although fox and dog remains were found at Nahal Patish, none of them showed signs of butchering (cutmarks) or bore any evidence of meal preparation (burning). In addition, pig (*Sus scrofa*) remains were not identified in the faunal assemblage. Even though pork consumption was already on the decline by the mid to late eleventh century BCE, their complete absence seems to run counter to how early Philistine culture is classically understood. What plausibly accounts for their absence? Hogs require a high water intake compared to other domesticated species (Hesse & Wapnish, 1998: 125). Although located in the northern Negev, Nahal Patish, a tributary of Nahal Grar, extends just to the immediate north and east of the site (Meiberg & Nahshoni, 2020). Locals and the animals they reared would have had access to water, thus eliminating environmental factors as explanations for pig avoidance. This premise is supported by the very presence of cattle and sheep in the assemblage which both prefer well-watered zones (Horwitz & Tchernov, 1990: 290). The low occurrence of goats may also reflect the local climate since they are better suited for hot arid regions (Redding, 1984: 233).

The absence of pigs at Nahal Patish may therefore have centered on economic concerns. Agricultural producers occupying rural areas may have been less keen to raise pigs. As omnivores, pigs would have been in direct competition with humans for the same crops, thus a potential threat to profits. Perhaps elevated pig consumption for the Philistines may have been a uniquely urban phenomenon. City dwellers, regarded primarily as consumers instead of producers, were largely removed from direct animal production operations. Pigs in urban centers would not only have represented readily available sources of protein, but they would also have been considered helpful in waste management by consuming food that had been discarded or found unsuitable for humans.

Other than economic strategies, cultural dynamics may also be proposed as an explanatory model for the lack of a hog operation at Nahal Patish. The site lies on the southeastern fringe of Philistia, located some distance from the essential core elements of Philistine culture that were probably associated with large urban centers like Tel Miqne-Ekron, Tell es-Safi/Gath, Ashkelon, Ashdod, and Gaza. Occupying a peripheral, and perhaps even liminal zone, may have strained affiliative orientations with their parent cultural core, freeing them to construct their own unique sense of unity and identity by adopting elements from multiple competing cultural cores, mainly Philistia to the west and non-Philistine groups to the east (see Tappy, 2008: 12–26). Estimating the frequency of pig exploitation can be assessed by comparing the number of pig remains relative to the rest of the assemblage from which it is derived. Thus, pig use from neighboring contemporary Judean and Philistine sites (Croft, 2004; Lev-Tov, 2012; Maher, 1998; Maher & Hesse, 2016) socially contextualizes the lack of interest in pork products at Nahal Patish. Philistine pig bones from the eleventh to tenth century BCE at Tel Miqne-Ekron (11.1%) make up a small portion of the identifiable animals and is similar to a slightly later sample from the tenth to ninth century BCE at Tell es-Safi/Gath (13.4%). These proportions far outnumber those dating to contemporary or near-contemporary levels from Judean settlements at Lachish (0.3%) and Tel Harasim (0%). The borderland site at Tel Zayit, lying in the Judean western foothills located just 8 km south of Tell es-Safi/Gath (Tappy et al., 2006: 5) did not raise any pigs in the tenth century BCE (Maher, In preparation). In this light, it can be seen that while the lack of pigs from the late eleventh/early tenth century BCE occupations at Nahal Patish diverges from the Philistine norm, it not only aligns well with Judean sensibilities but also with another neighboring borderland settlement (Tel Zayit) that likely encountered similar cultural and political challenges.

The residual influence of their interactions with non-pork producing non-Philistine groups from neighboring areas may not only explain why pigs were not raised and consumed at Nahal Patish, but it could also address the lack of evidence for canid consumption, a distinctly Philistine culinary pursuit presently unknown in Iron Age Judah. The semi-permeability of select elements from competing core cultures is evident in the apparent incorporation of non-Philistine foodways, yet other elements of material culture (pottery, temple architecture, cultic stands) are reminiscent of Philistine traditions, thus illustrating the fluctuating cultural influences that trickled into the borderlands. This underscores the complexity of life in a boundary zone where a community is displaced from its cultural core. The material expression of the culture that featured a disparate mix of traits did not comfortably fit under the same intense institutional scrutiny directed by the core group and was thus regarded as more acceptable when forged in peripheral areas.

6.5 Body Part Representation

The differential distribution of animal carcass parts in Area B was examined to determine animal use and access as they related to temple proceedings. This methodological approach is adopted since patterns in animal body part representation can be a defining feature of a sacred area (Horwitz, 1999: 63). An analysis of body parts can address the arrival of whole animals or if animal parts were introduced as processed cuts of meat. This method, based on Zeder (1991: 96–97) and Redding (1994: 287), predicts that non-meat bearing bovid bones are twice as abundant as those bearing meat if the entire animal had been present. The ratio of the archaeological sample is then compared to the relative frequency of the bones as they occur in the living animal. Body part representation was only calculated for ovicaprines since sheep and goats were the most common species. The Area B data for Nahal Patish (Table 4, Column A) indicate more meat-bearing than

Table 4 Sheep and goat body part representation by occupation phase in Area B

	Column A			Column B		Column C		Column D		
	Non-meat and meat-bearing bones			Refuse type		Limb front/back		Limb section		
	Non-meat	Meat	Non-meat: Meat ratio	Consumption	Slaughter	Fore	Hind	Lower	Middle	Upper
Phase 1	3	11	0.27:1	14 (56%)	11 (44%)	8 (73%)	3 (17%)	3 (23%)	8 (54%)	3 (23%)
Phase 2	20	33	0.61:1	45 (62%)	28 (38%)	31 (74%)	11 (26%)	13 (28%)	18 (39%)	15 (33%)
Phase 3	1	1	1 to 1	2 (67%)	1 (33%)	1 (100%)	0	0	0	1 (100%)

non-meat-bearing bones. The resultant ratios illustrate that ovicaprines were most likely brought to the area as parcels of meat that had been processed in a different but likely nearby work area, and not as whole and presumably living specimens.

Wapnish and Hesse (1991: 45) considered how an animal bone assemblage associated with temple use could be understood in terms of slaughter and consumption refuse. An abundance of consumption refuse would suggest animals were killed at a point some distance away, where the slaughter debris remained. Slaughter debris is characterized by skulls, mandibles, and toe bones, while consumption elements consist of meat-bearing sections: ribs, vertebrae, and limbs (Horwitz, 1999: 65; Hellwing & Gophna, 1984: 51). The Area B data for Nahal Patish (Table 4, Column B) indicate more consumption than slaughter refuse, suggesting sheep and goats were killed and butchered away from the temple precinct.

One can also determine if there was a tendency to emphasize elements of relatively greater meat yield. One way to examine this is to consider the proportion of forelimbs to hindlimbs since forelimbs carry more meat (Wapnish et al., 1977: 60). The Area B data from Nahal Patish (Table 4, Column C) demonstrate that the ovicaprine assemblage featured more meat bearing forelimbs, which illustrates a focus on meatier portions of the animal. The relative amounts of meat associated with different limb sections can also be examined. Following Horwitz (2000), limb sections are defined as upper (scapula, humerus, pelvis and femur), middle (radius, ulna, tibia, astragalus, and calcaneum), and lower (metapodials). The Area B data for Nahal Patish (Table 4, Column D) indicate more meat-bearing upper and middle limb sections than non-meat-bearing lower leg elements. This too demonstrates an emphasis on meatier portions.

Taken collectively, each of the four methods outlined above that investigate body part representation, are in general agreement with one another. Sheep and goats were killed and processed elsewhere, and their meatier portions were delivered to the temple precinct. The demand for meat likely supported a communal meal at or near the temple for worshipers and officiants alike. The predilection for meat is substantiated by the mortality profile that identified the presence of young sheep and goats of high meat quality. The focus on meaty meals is also suggested by filleting marks that removed meat from the bone, the presence of serving pottery vessels, and cooking areas equipped with *tabuns*.

6.6 Spatial Distribution

Another method of estimating area function via zooarchaeological material is to note any conspicuous spatial clustering of faunal material, as such concentrations may point to specific activities relating to animal use in a temple area (Buitenhuis, 1985: 143). When considering all three phases together (Table 5) most of the fauna from the temple precinct was located in the northeast courtyard ($n = 234$) and the sanctuary ($n = 219$). The Phase 3 fauna was found only in the storeroom. Most of the juvenile aged animal remains were from the main courtyard ($n = 5$) and the

Table 5 Spatial distribution of the fauna from Area B in all phases

	Occupation level			
Spatial zone	Phase 1	Phase 2	Phase 3	Total
Open area	22	29		51
Cattle	1			1
Large mammal		3		3
Medium mammal	11	21		32
Sheep/goat	6	1		7
Small mammal		2		2
Unidentified	4	2		6
Structure 209	2	13		15
Northern room	2	2		4
Medium mammal	2	2		4
Southern room		11		11
Sheep/goat		1		1
Unidentified		10		10
Structure 249	123	535	53	711
Main courtyard	6	160		166
Cattle		7		7
Large mammal	1	4		5
Medium mammal	4	103		107
Sheep/goat	1	31		32
Unidentified		15		15
NE courtyard	92	142		234
Cattle	3	2		5
Dog	1			1
Fish		1		1
Large mammal	10	7		17
Medium mammal	43	90		133
Sheep/goat	24	26		50
Unidentified	4	16		20
Fox	7			7
Sanctuary	25	194		219
Cattle	1			1
Dog		1		1
Large mammal	2			2
Medium mammal	16	90		106
Sheep/goat	6	29		35
Small mammal		4		4
Unidentified		70		70
Store room		39	53	92
Cattle		1	1	2
Hare		9		9
Medium mammal		9	5	14

(continued)

Table 5 (continued)

	Occupation level			
Spatial zone	Phase 1	Phase 2	Phase 3	Total
Sheep/goat		10	2	12
Unidentified		10	44	54
Fox			1	1
Structure 365	10	2	1	13
Cattle	1	1		1
Large mammal		1		1
Donkey	1			1
Medium mammal	8			8
Sheep/goat			1	1
Total	157	579	54	790

sanctuary ($n = 5$). The burned bone assemblage (Table 6) is small ($n = 22$) with most of the remains associated with Structure 249. Eight came from the main courtyard, four from the sanctuary, and two from the northeast courtyard. Another eight bones came from hearths in the open space near the main temple which probably served as a roasting area. Thus, certain parts of the temple grounds had varying degrees of interactions with animal products.

Additional spatial distributions on the temple grounds can also be noted. Although a much smaller space, yet still considered part of the temple precinct, 15 bones came from Structure 209. Only four bones, all from medium mammals consisting of two limb shafts and two rib fragments, were found in Structure 209's northern room. All of these are regarded as consumption refuse elements. Found in the same room as the lion-headed drinking cup (Sect. 2.2), perhaps meals were eaten here. An opening in Wall 6 (Locus 366), the easternmost wall of the main courtyard, contained one medium mammal limb shaft fragment. The maxilla (upper jaw) of a fox along with associated teeth were found in the Phase 1 floor makeup of the Northeast courtyard. Its early inclusion within the foundational levels of the temple structure may represent some form of dedication ceremony. The only bones identified as hare in the entire collection come from a Phase 2 stone and clay bin (Locus 311) from the storeroom in Structure 249. Hare metatarsals were also recovered from an Iron Age I installation at Mt. Ebal (Horwitz, 1986/87: 176), a site with possible cultic orientations.

6.7 Symmetry

A notable bias in the distribution of body part symmetry is assumed to represent a unique feature of temple faunal assemblages. Since taphonomic agents are expected to exert equal influence on elements from both sides of the body, one side should not be more abundant than the other. Clear symmetry bias suggests some manner of human choice and ritualized manipulations instead of the randomness of

Table 6 Spatial distribution of burned bones in Area B

Spatial context	Occupation level Phase 1	Phase 2	Total
Open area		8	8
Medium mammal		6	6
Limb		2	2
Rib		2	2
Unidentified		2	2
Unidentified		2	2
Unidentified		2	2
Structure 249	3	11	14
Main courtyard	1	7	8
Cattle		1	1
Metapodial		1	1
Medium mammal	1	5	6
Limb	1	3	4
Rib		2	2
Sheep/goat		1	1
1st phalanx		1	1
NE courtyard	1	1	2
Medium mammal	1		1
Limb	1		1
Sheep/goat		1	1
Humerus		1	1
Sanctuary	1	3	4
Medium mammal	1	3	4
Limb	1	3	4
Total	3	19	22

preservation and resultant taphonomic loss. The sided remains listed for Phases 1 and 2 in Area B clearly show that most of the material is from the right side of the body (Table 7). Pronounced evidence comes from the temple's sanctuary in Structure 249 where rights are twice as abundant as lefts. The storeroom only housed rights and no elements at all were identified from the left side. The ratio of rights to lefts in Phase 2 (2.1: 1) is similar to that in Phase 1 (2.3: 1), suggesting similar tactical decisions. The focus on the right side of the body extended to multiple species, both wild and domestic, terrestrial and aquatic, as right elements were identified for cattle, dog, sheep, goat, fox, hare, and even fish.

It is unclear why rights were selected for use more often. One clue may lie with the lion-headed cup found in Phase 2 of Building 209. While raising the cup when holding its lone handle in the right hand to drink, the imbiber's face would have appeared as a lioness to an onlooker (Meiberg & Nahshoni, 2020: 300–301). The effect is lost if one holds the handle in the left hand to raise the cup as it would unnecessarily invert the lioness's face to an onlooker. Thus, lifting the cup in the right hand is a requirement for the imbiber to temporarily transition their face to that

Table 7 Spatial distribution of sided remains in Area B

Species and context	Phase 1 Left	Phase 1 Right	Phase 2 Left	Phase 2 Right	Phase 3 Left	Total
Open area	1	1				2
Sheep/goat	1	1				2
Structure 209				1		1
Southern room				1		1
Sheep/goat				1		1
Structure 249	7	15	20	37	2	81
Main courtyard		1	10	8		19
Cattle			1			1
Sheep/goat		1	9	8		18
NE courtyard	5	13	6	7		31
Dog	1					1
Fish				1		1
Sheep/goat	4	6	6	6		22
Fox		7				7
Sanctuary	2	1	4	9		16
Dog				1		1
Sheep/goat	2	1	4	8		15
Store room				13	2	15
Hare				9		9
Sheep/goat				4	1	5
Fox					1	1
Structure 365		2		1		3
Cattle		1				1
Donkey		1				1
Sheep/goat				3		3
Total	8	18	20	42	2	90

of an animal. Perhaps the right side was then symbolically linked to the notion of transition as expressed in performative rituals carried out in the temple area that remain partially evident in the abundance of right-sided animal remains. It may also be important to note that contemporary lion-faced drinking cups from Tell Zeror, Megiddo, and Megiddo also feature single handles affixed to the right side of the vessel (see Dothan, 1982: 230, 232–233).

6.8 Incised Bone

Incised animal bones, most notably scapulae (shoulder blades), are associated with Philistine cult in the Iron I and early Iron IIA at Tel Miqne and Tell es-Safi/Gath (Dothan, 1998: 155: Zukerman et al., 2007: 64). They have also been found at other northern sites from Dor (Stern, 1994, 1997, 2000, 2006), Tell Abu Hawam (Reese, 2002: 194), and Tel Kinrot (Marom et al., 2006). The short incisions are usually uniformly oriented and parallel to one another. Their placement on the scapula and their unnecessary depth renders an unlikely linkage to common butchery procedures. Although the precise function of these objects is presently unknown, speculation ranges from their use as a rudimentary calendar system (Redman, 1973: 258); musical instrument (Dothan, 1995: 48; Karageorghis, 1990), tallies for record keeping (Zuckerman et al., 2007: 74), thread separators on a loom (Zuckerman et al., 2007: 71), or for oracular purposes involving scapulomancy (Stern, 1994: 6; Webb, 1985: 324–327). It is entirely possible that these artifacts had multiple functions.

Although the faunal sample from Nahal Patish did not yield any incised scapulae, it did include one limb shaft fragment from a medium-sized mammal, possibly a sheep or goat, that featured three short but deep parallel incisions (Fig. 10). Found on the floor of the sanctuary in the temple (Structure 249), this object bears similarity to other incised bones from sites in Philistia (Maher, unpublished manuscript B). For example, at least six other bones from Philistine sites, designated as unidentified medium mammal limbs, also bear a row of deep parallel incisions. A dozen other incised animal bones from Philistia sport ten or fewer incisions. The row of three incisions on the object from Nahal Patish measures 6.47 mm in length, resulting in an average interval of 2.16 mm (number of incisions divided into length of incision row). While most of the average interval of incised bone objects in Philistia fall between 3–5 mm in length, there are three other objects with average intervals that fall between 2–3 mm, an interval which corresponds to the object now reported from Nahal Patish.

6.9 Pathology

None of the animal remains from Nahal Patish, including those from the temple area, exhibited any evidence of pathology or healed trauma. As sacred offerings in a temple context, either as food for the gods or food for the people, animals may have needed to be perfect and without blemish. Since disease may have been attributed to supernatural agents (Baker & Brothwell, 1980: 189), the presentation of a healthy faultless animal may have been a basic requirement of the rite (Robertson-Smith, 1901: 361). If so, it follows that diseased animals may have been unsuitable and thus not selected for the ceremony. Given the number of remains from young animals in the temple, one may suspect the reason they did not bear pathological development was because they died before they had contracted anything. However, several diseases are confined to juveniles, and in many instances, adults seem immune to certain parasites and bacteria (Baker & Brothwell, 1980: 27). While some infectious agents can modify an animal's skeleton, the presence of others cannot be readily identified via skeletal inspection (Baker & Brothwell, 1980: 12). Afflictions in their latter stages of development may also be undetectable (Hesse & Wapnish, 1985: 82). The lack of diseased elements is not surprising since infected animals may not even bear the imprint of a given condition. Thus, the animals used in the rites at the Nahal Patish temple may have been carefully selected based on their general state of good health.

6.10 Trade

One bone, found in Phase 2 of the Northeast Courtyard, was identified as a fish. This bone is a right mandible (jaw) from a member of the Sparidae family known as the common sea bream (*Pagrus*). Sparidae occupy murky sand-laden bottoms and are found in relatively shallow water (Reese, 1981: 238). Their dietary regime has led to the development of specialized oral adaptations that facilitate their taxonomic classification, including enlarged flattened molars for grinding calcareous items regularly encountered in their natural habitat (Lernau, 2000a: 466). While Sparidae can achieve a size of 70 cm in length, most average size ranges occur between 20–40 cm (Lernau, 2000b: 235). Captured in nets or by angling, Sparidae meat has been popular since ancient times (Lepiksaar, 1995: 187). As a salt-water marine species, Sparidae could have been taken from the open waters in the Mediterranean or the shallower depths of a lagoon (Sisma-Ventura et al., 2018; Lernau & Golani, 2004: 2461; Reese, 1981: 238). No matter the original source, the presence of *Pagrus* at Nahal Patish represents faunal evidence for local involvement with trade networks.

6.11 Carnivore Access

There was no evidence of carnivore feeding or partial digestion on any of the bones from Nahal Patish, which is of particular interest since canids (dog and fox) are known in contemporary levels. The lack of carnivore modified animal bones suggests that relatively little time had passed between occupation phases. Had the fauna been exposed for any length of time, one would expect more bones to have been ravaged by rodents or opportunistic scavenging carnivores. Perhaps the reason for the relatively rapid burial of each occupation level related to the sacred status of the temple complex as an area of worship. Quickly burying and leveling the area over may have been a method by which they sought to seal in the essence or energy believed to be associated with the temple's holy space and may indicate the remnant of a closing ritual where the temple complex was retired. Using carnivore damaged faunal remains as a means of estimating elapsed time was also applied to the tenth to eighth century BCE destruction levels at Tel Zayit (Maher, In preparation) and to Philistine Ekron on the eve of a Babylonian invasion led by Nebuchadnezzar at the end of the seventh century BCE (Maher, 2006/07).

7 Comparison with Tell Qasile and Tell Qiri

To examine how the temple economy at Nahal Patish compares to other contemporaneous assemblages, samples from two other sites were selected. The Philistine site of Tell Qasile (Davis, 1985; Mazar, 1980) and the Canaanite occupation at Tell Qiri (Ben-Tor, 1979: 111–113; Davis, 1987b) both feature sacred areas dating to the Iron I. Their different cultural affiliation broadens our view of the economic accommodations allowed for sacred proceedings. Although these faunal analyses are preliminary in nature, they are sufficient to provide some details against which the sample from Nahal Patish can be considered.

Lying near the Mediterranean coast just north of Jaffa, Tell Qasile is a small 4-acre town located along the northern side of the Yarkon River. Three successive temples were assigned to Strata XII-X, with the bent axis architectural design of Temple 131 from Stratum X, mid-11th century BCE, resembling that of Nahal Patish. The faunal report from Tell Qasile does not mention specific spatial contexts and may include material from both sacred and secular areas. The sample is dominated by domestic species such as sheep, goats, cattle, and to a lesser extent pigs. One unique feature of the fauna is the appearance of hippopotamus. Sheep ($n = 212$) outnumber cattle ($n = 35$) by a ratio of 6.1:1. Sheep ($n = 25$) also outnumber goats ($n = 12$) by a ratio of more than 2:1. Mortality based on dental attrition scores for ovicaprines show that young animals were important, as 38 of 73 mandibles (52%) were from animals less than 36 months old.

Tell Qiri is a small town near the Jezreel Valley in the foothills of the Carmel range, and the site was occupied continuously throughout the Iron Age. Overall, the assemblage mainly consists of domestic species that include sheep, goats, cattle, and a few pigs. Sheep ($n = 793$) outnumber cattle ($n = 142$) by a ratio of 5.5:1. Sheep and goats are equally abundant. Young sheep and goats were commonly exploited as indicated by nearly one-quarter of the bone fusion and almost two-thirds of the mandibles were from animals that died less than 36 months old. The most important early Iron Age area for the present discussion centers on a Stratum VIII structure dating to the eleventh century BCE. Although its general architectural design suggested a domestic area, one room in particular, perhaps a small shine in the building, may have been reserved for cultic activities based on the presence of incense burners, stands, and double vessels for libations. The available ovicaprine faunal data from five of the loci in this room straddle different strata and phases of occupation (Gilmour, 1995: 44–45): Stratum IX (Locus 1146), Stratum VIII C (Loci 1065 and 1074), and Stratum VIII B (Loci 1044 and 1064). The assemblage mainly consists of forelimbs (Table 8, Column A) and a clear preference for upper and middle limb sections (Table 8, Column B), which firmly attests to the importance of meat. Also evident is the preponderance of bones from the right side of the body (Table 9). Combining the data from all five loci, sheep and goat bones from the right side outnumber those from the left by a ratio of 13.7:1 (192 right, 14 left). Although these tabulations are based on Davis (1987b: 251, Table 24), they slightly vary here since they exclude cattle bones. Also, the third phalanx was not included in the

Table 8 Sheep and goat body part representation by select Iron I loci from Tell Qiri

	Column A Limb front/back		Column B Limb section		
	Fore	Hind	Lower	Middle	Upper
Stratum VIII B Loci: 1044, 1064	41 (95%)	2 (5%)	1 (2%)	16 (36%)	27 (61%)
Stratum VIII C Loci: 1065, 1074	138 (93%)	11 (7%)	3 (2%)	33 (22%)	114 (76%)
Stratum IX Locus 1146	14 (88%)	2 (12%)	1 (6%)	3 (18%)	13 (76%)
Total	193	15	5	52	154

Adapted from Davis (1987b: 251, Table 24)

Table 9 Sheep and goat sided remains by select Iron I loci at Tell Qiri

	Symmetry		
	Left	Right	Total
Stratum VIII B Loci: 1044, 1064	0	43	43
Stratum VIII C Loci: 1065, 1074	13	134	147
Stratum IX Locus 1146	1	15	16
Total	14	192	206

Adapted from Davis (1987b: 251, Table 24)

calculations since it is better suited to indicate foot portion (medial or lateral) rather than body side (left or right).

Both above faunal assemblages bear some similarities to that of Nahal Patish. All three economies relied heavily on the sacrifice of domestic species rather than wild game, sheep and goats in particular. Pigs were not found at Nahal Patish yet were identified in small numbers at Tell Qasile and Tell Qiri. Ovicaprines outnumber cattle by a 7.3:1 margin at Nahal Patish, which exceeds ovicaprine to cattle ratios from Tell Qasile and Tell Qiri. Sheep were more abundant than goats at Nahal Patish and Tell Qasile. Mortality data based on rates of long bone fusion and dental wear from Nahal Patish indicate 53% (18/34) of the remains came from specimens aged less than 36 months, which is nearly identical to the proportion from Tell Qasile. Young animals are also reported from Tell Qiri. The selection of meatier limbs and limb sections at Nahal Patish mirrors the same selective strategies employed at Tell Qiri. The preference for rights over lefts at Nahal Patish and Tell Qiri also illustrates similar decision-making. The Tell Qasile and Tell Qiri reports make no mention of bones with evidence of disease, which may have been beyond the scope of those preliminary works. However, if none were found, it too would align with the faunal data from Nahal Patish.

Ritual offerings of animals were practiced in similar (yet not identical) ways between Philistine and Canaanite cultures which underscores how some of the basic and fundamental approaches to the practice extended cross-culturally. While they undoubtedly drew on well- known traditions that reached back into the Bronze Age, aspects of these rituals continued in practice well into the later centuries of the Iron II.

8 Conclusion

The faunal record from Nahal Patish represents the animals that interfaced with those that occupied a small rural borderland settlement in the Negev region. While much of what is known about Philistine cultic orientations comes from large urban centers, the faunal sample from Nahal Patish informs us about the nature of the local temple economy. The zooarchaeological attributes shared between Nahal Patish and other contemporary sites demonstrate that similar decisions were followed when supplying animals for ritual slaughter. The construction of cultural identity along Philistia's southeastern border is also evident.

The temple economy at Nahal Patish relied heavily on offerings of domestic animals, mainly consisting of sheep and goats. While the body part distribution indicate the acquisition of meat as the primary goal, the young ages of the animals at death ensured high quality. Further selective processes are suggested in that no temple animals bore any evidence of pathology or healed fracture. It may have been a requirement to offer animals without any obvious imperfections, thus avoiding branding the offering as inferior and risking divine wrath. The predilection for animal parts from the right side represents another indication of selectivity and may have been symbolically linked to ideological concepts central to the temple rituals. The fact that elements of the animal offerings share similar traits cross-culturally suggests there were common approaches to the rituals and that similar decisions were made regardless of heritage.

The cultural identity of those at Nahal Patish is suggested in the archaeological data. The architectural elements of the sanctuary and Structure 249 as a whole resembles the Philistine shrine at Tell Qasile Stratum X. The cultic paraphernalia from the site, the figurative stand, and the lion-headed cup in particular exhibit clear Philistine traits. Ritual and cultic activities involving pinched loom-weights are a kind of loom found mostly at Philistine sites. The expression of cultural affiliation is also suggested in the faunal collection. The selective non-use of certain species represents deliberate choices made by community members. Those decisions, such as the apparent avoidance of pork and canid consumption, may align with core non-Philistine cultural sensibilities. However, the incised bone found in the sanctuary of the temple is similar in character to those known from other Philistine contexts. In addition, some of the features of the zooarchaeological assemblage are evident at Philistine Tell Qasile. This mix of features is also seen in the pottery repertoire, where local Canaanite forms appear together with Philistine shapes and hybrid styles. Such entangled features reflect the reality of a peripheral community living on the border of a core cultural territory.

The lack of animal bones devoid of carnivore ravaging suggests that each occupation phase at Nahal Patish was punctuated by the relatively rapid burial of the deposits, along with all associated items. Sealing the temple precinct, then, may have been a way to contain the energetic essence of the ceremonies that were once performed there, in effect, evoking a temporary retirement of the temple. Perhaps covering the temple precinct was part of a closing ceremony of sorts, not at the conclusion of the ritual, but perhaps signaled by other unknown factors (e.g., changes in local political or religious leadership). It was perhaps these kinds of changes that led to the permanent retirement of the temple complex and general abandonment of the site in the early decades of the tenth century BCE.

Acknowledgments It is our pleasure to contribute to this volume in honor of Professor Thomas Levy whose many significant contributions throughout his long and distinguished career have allowed us to better understand so many varied aspects of the ancient world. Maher would like to thank Pirhiya Nahshoni for the opportunity to study the faunal remains from Nahal Patish. Rivka Rabinovich kindly provided access to the comparative faunal collections at the Hebrew University of Jerusalem. Our thanks to the editors of this volume for their understanding, patience, and flexibility.

References

Ackermann, O., Greenbaum, N., Bruins, H., Porat, N., Bar-Matthews, M., Almogi-Labin, A., Schilman, B., Ayalon, A., Horwitz, L. K., Weiss, E., & Maeir, A. M. (2014). Palaeoenvironment and anthropogenic activity in the southeastern Mediterranean since the mid-Holocene: The case of Tell es-Safi/Gath, Israel. *Quaternary International, 328–329*, 226–243.

Baker, J., & Brothwell, D. (1980). *Animal diseases in archaeology*. Academic.

Barth, F. (1969). *Ethnic groups and boundaries: The social organization of culture difference*. Little.

Ben-Tor, A. (1979). Tell Qiri: A look at village life. *Biblical Archaeologist, 42*, 105–113.

Binford, L. R. (1981). *Bones: Ancient men and modern myths*. Academic.

Boessneck, J. (1969). Osteological differences between sheep (*Ovis aries* Linne) and goat (*Capra hircus* Linne). In D. Brothwell & E. S. Higgs (Eds.), *Science in archaeology* (2nd ed., pp. 331–358). Thames and Hudson.

Buitenhuis, H. (1985). The animal remains from tell Sweyhat, Syria. *Paléorient, 25*, 131–144.

Burkert, W. (1979). Structure and theory in Greek mythology and ritual. In *Sather classical lectures 47*. University of California Press.

Croft, P. (2004). Archaeozoological studies – Section A – The osteological remains (mammalian and avian). In D. Ussishkin (Ed.), *The renewed archaeological excavations at Lachish 1973–1994* (pp. 2254–2350). Emery and Claire Yass Publications in Archaeology.

Davis, S. J. M. (1985). The large mammal bones, appendix 5. In A. Mazar (Ed.), *Excavations at Tel Qasile II. The philistine sanctuary: Various finds, the pottery, conclusions, appendixes* (Vol. 20, pp. 148–150). The Hebrew University.

Davis, S. J. M. (1987a). *The archaeology of animals*. Yale University Press.

Davis, S. J. M. (1987b). The faunal remains from tell Qiri. In A. Ben-Tor & Y. Portugali (Eds.), *Tell Qiri: A village in the Jezreel valley (Qedem 24)* (pp. 249–251). The Hebrew University of Jerusalem.

von den Driesch, A. (1976). *A guide to the measurement of animal bones from archaeological sites*. Peabody Museum Bulletin I.
Dothan, T. (1982). *The philistines and their material culture*. Israel Exploration Society.
Dothan, T. (1995). Tel Miqne-Ekron: The Aegean affinities of the sea peoples' (philistines') settlement in Canaan in the iron age I. In S. Gitin (Ed.), *Recent excavations in Israel – A view to the West* (pp. 41–56). Dubuque.
Dothan, T. (1998). Initial philistine settlement: From mitigation to coexistence. In S. Gitin, A. Mazar, & E. Stern (Eds.), *Mediterranean peoples in transition: Thirteenth to early tenth centuries BCE (pp. 148–161)*. Israel Exploration Society.
Dothan, T., & Dothan, M. (1992). *People of the sea: The search for the philistines*. Macmillan Publishing Company.
Dothan, M., & Ben-Shlomo, D. (2005). Eds., *Ashdod VI, excavation of areas H and K*, Report No. 24. Israel Antiquities Authority.
Durkheim, E. (1995). *The elementary forms of religion*. (K. E. Fields, Trans.). The Free Press.
Eliyahu-Behar, A., Yahalom-Mack, N., Shilstein, S., Zukerman, A., Shafer-Elliott, C., Maeir, A. M., Boaretto, E., Finkelstein, I., & Weiner, S. (2012). Iron and bronze production in Iron Age IIA Philistia: New evidence from Tell es-Safi/Gath, Israel. *Journal of Archaeological Science, 39*, 255–267.
Faust, A., & Lev-Tov, J. (2011). The constitution of philistine identity: Ethnic dynamics in twelfth to tenth century Philistia. *Oxford Journal of Archaeology, 30*, 13–31.
Faust, A., & Lev-Tov, J. (2014). Philistia and the philistines in the iron age I: Interaction, ethnic dynamics and boundary maintenance. *HIPHIL Novum, 1*, 1–24.
Finkelstein, I. (1996). Ethnicity and the origin of the Iron I Settlers in the highlands of Canaan: Can the real Israel stand up? *Biblical Archaeologist, 59*, 198–212.
Finkelstein, I. (1997). Pots and people revisited: Ethnic boundaries in the Iron Age I. In N. Silverman & D. Small (Eds.), *The archaeology of Israel: Constructing the past, interpreting the present* (pp. 216–237). Academic.
Firth, R. (1972). Offering and sacrifice: Problems of organization. In W. A. Lessa & E. Z. Vogt (Eds.), *Reader in comparative religion: An anthropological approach* (pp. 324–333). Harper and Row.
Gilmour, G. H. (1995). *The archaeology of cult in the Southern Levant in the early Iron Age: An analytical and comparative approach*. DPhil dissertation, University of Oxford.
Gitin, S. (1989). Tel Miqne-Ekron: A type site for the inner coastal plain in the Iron Age II period. In S. Gitin & W. G. Dever (Eds.), *Recent excavations in Israel: Studies in Iron Age archaeology* (pp. 23–58). Eisenbrauns.
Gitin, S. (1995). Tel-Miqne-Ekron in the 7th century B.C.E.: The impact of economic innovation and foreign cultural influences on a neo-Assyrian vassal city-state. In S. Gitin (Ed.), *Recent excavations in Israel-a view to the west* (pp. 61–79). Dubuque.
Gitin, S. (1997). The neo-Assyrian empire and its Western periphery: The Levant, with a focus on philistine Ekron. In S. Parpola & R. M. Whiting (Eds.), *Assyria 1995* (pp. 77–104). University of Helsinki.
Gitin, S., & Dothan, T. (1987). The rise and fall of Ekron of the philistines. Recent excavations at an urban border site. *Biblical Archaeologist, 50*, 197–199.
Grant, A. (1984). Survival or sacrifice? A critical appraisal of animal burials in Britain in the iron age. In C. Grigson & J. Clutton-Brock (Eds.), *Animals and archaeology: 4. Husbandry in Europe* (pp. 221–227). BAR International Series 227.
Halstead, P., & Collins, P. (2002). Sorting the sheep from the goats: Morphological distinctions between the mandibles and mandibular teeth of adult *Ovis* and *Capra*. *Journal of Archaeological Science, 29*, 545–553.
Hellwing, S., & Gophna, R. (1984). The animal remains from the early and middle bronze ages at Tel Aphek and Tel Dalit: A comparative study. *Tel Aviv, 11*, 48–59.
Hesse, B., & Wapnish, P. (1985). *Animal bone archaeology – From objectives to analysis*. Taraxacum.

Hesse, B. (1986). Animal use at Tel Miqne-Ekron in the bronze age and iron age. *Bulletin of the American Schools of Oriental Research, 264*, 17–27.

Hesse, B. (1990). Pig lovers and pig haters: Patterns of Palestinian pork production. *Journal of Ethnobiology, 10*, 195–225.

Hesse, B. (1995). Husbandry, dietary taboos and the bones of the ancient near east: Zooarchaeology in the post-processual world. In D. B. Small (Ed.), *Methods in the Mediterranean: Historical and archaeological views on texts and archaeology* (pp. 197–232). Brill.

Hesse, B., Fulton, D. N., & Wapnish, P. (2012). Animal remains. In L. E. Stager, D. Schloen, & D. Master (Eds.), *Ashkelon III: The seventh century B.C* (pp. 615–643). Eisenbrauns.

Hesse, B., & Rosen, A. (1988). The detection of chronological mixing in samples from stratified archaeological sites. In R. E. Webb (Ed.), *Recent developments in old and new world archaeology* (pp. 117–129). BAR International Series 416.

Hesse, B., & Rosen, A. (1997). Can pig remains be used for ethnic diagnosis in the ancient near east? In N. A. Silberman & D. Small (Eds.), *The archaeology of Israel: Constructing the past, interpreting the present (JSOT supplemental)* (pp. 238–270). Sheffield.

Hesse, B., & Rosen, A. (1998). Pig use and abuse in the ancient Levant: Ethno-religious boundary-building with swine. In S. M. Nelson (Ed.), *Ancestors for the pigs: Pigs in prehistory* (pp. 123–135). (MASCA Research Papers in Science and Archaeology 15). University of Pennsylvania Museum of Archaeology and Anthropology.

Hitchcock, L. A., Horwitz, L. K., Boaretto, E., & Maeir, A. M. (2015). One Philistine's trash is another's treasure: Feasting at Iron Age I tell es-Safi/Gath. *Near Eastern Archaeology, 78*, 12–25.

Horwitz, L. K. (1986/87). Faunal remains from the early Iron Age site on mount Ebal. *Tel Aviv, 13–14*, 173–189.

Horwitz, L. K. (1990). The origin of partially digested bones recovered from archaeological contexts in Israel. *Paleorient, 16*, 97–106.

Horwitz, L. K. (1999). The contribution of Archaeozoology to the identification of ritual sites. In S. Pike & S. Gitin (Eds.), *The practical impact of science on near eastern and Aegean archaeology* (pp. 63–69). Archetype Publications.

Horwitz, L. K. (2000). Animal exploitation – Archaeozoological analysis. In Z. Gal & Y. Alexandre (Eds.), *Horbat Rosh Zayit: An iron age storage fort and village* (pp. 221–232). Israel Antiquities Authority.

Horwitz, L. K., Tchernov, E., & Dar, S. (1990). Subsistence and environment on Mount Carmel in the Roman-Byzantine and mediaeval periods: The evidence from Kh. Sumaqa. *Israel Exploration Journal, 40*, 287–304.

Horwitz, L. K., Gardeisen, A., Maeir, A. M., & Hitchcock, L. A. (2017). A contribution to the iron age philistine pig debate. In J. Lev-Tov, P. Hesse, & A. Gilbert (Eds.), *The wide lens in archaeology: Honoring Brian Hesse's contributions to anthropological archaeology* (pp. 92–116). Lockwood Press.

Karageorghis, V. (1990). Miscellanea from Late Bronze Age Cyprus II. A bronze age musical instrument? *Levant, 23*, 159.

Kelm, G. L., & Mazar, A. (1995). *Timnah*. Eisenbrauns.

Kerbis-Peterhans, J. C., & Horwitz, L. K. (1992). A bone assemblage from a striped hyaena (*Hyaena hyaena*) den in the Negev Desert, Israel. *Israel Journal of Zoology, 37*, 225–245.

Killebrew, A. E., Lev-Tov, J. (2008). Early Iron Age feasting and cuisine: An indicator of philistine-Aegean connectivity? In L. A. Hitchcock and R. Laffineur (Eds.), *Dais: The Aegean Feast. Proceedings of the 12th International Aegean Conference* (pp. 339–346). University of Liege.

Kletter, R. (2010). The typology of the cult stands. In R. Kletter, I. Ziffer, & W. Zwickel (Eds.), *Yavneh I: The excavation of the 'Temple Hill' repository pit and the cult stands* (pp. 25–45). Fribourg and Göttingen.

Lehmann, G. (2011). Cooking pots and loomweights in a 'Philistine' village: Preliminary report on the excavations at Qubur el-Walaydah, Israel. In V. Karageorghis & O. Kourka (Eds.), *On cooking pots, drinking cups, loomweights and ethnicity in bronze age Cyprus and neighboring regions: An international archaeological symposium held in Nicosia, November 6th–7th, 2010* (pp. 387–314). A.G. Leventis Foundation.

Lehmann, G., Rosen, S. A., Berlejung, A., Naumeier, B.-A., & Niemann, H. M. (2018). Excavations at Qubur al-Walaydah. *Die Welt des Orients, 48*, 137–159.

Lepiksaar, J. (1995). Fish remains from Tel Hesban, Jordan. In O. S. LaBianca & A. von den Driesch (Eds.), *Hesban 13* (pp. 169–210). Andrews University Press.

Lernau, O. (2000a). Fish bones. In I. Finkelstein, D. Ussishkin, & B. Halpern (Eds.), *Megiddo III – The 1992–1996 seasons* (pp. 463–477). Emery and Claire Yass Publications in Archaeology.

Lernau, O. (2000b). Fish bones from Ḥorbat Rosh Zayit. In Z. Gal & Y. Alexandre (Eds.), *Ḥorbat Rosh Zayit: An Iron Age storage fort and village* (pp. 233–237). Israel Antiquities Authority.

Lernau, O., & Golani, D. (2004). Section B: The osteological remains (aquatic). In D. Ussishkin (Ed.), *The renewed archaeological excavations at Lachish 1973–1994* (pp. 2456–2489). Emery and Claire Yass Publications in Archaeology.

Lev-Tov, J. S. E. (2000). *Pigs, philistines, and the ancient animal economy of Ekron from the Late Bronze Age to the Iron Age II*. PhD. Dissertation, University of Tennessee.

Lev-Tov, J. S. E. (2006). The faunal remains: Animal economy in the Iron Age 2006. In M. W. Meehl, T. Dothan, & S. Gitin (Eds.), *Tel Miqne-Ekron excavations 1995–1996: Field INE east slope Iron Age I (early philistine period)*. (Final Report Series 8, pp. 207–234). The Hebrew University of Jerusalem.

Lev-Tov, J. S. E. (2010). A plebeian perspective on empire economies: Faunal remains from Tel Miqne-Ekron, Israel. In D. Campana, A. Choyke, P. Crabtree, S. D. de France, & J. Lev-Tov (Eds.), *Anthropological approaches to Zooarchaeology: Colonialism, complexity and animal transformations* (pp. 90–104). Oxbow Books.

Lev-Tov, J. S. E. (2012). A preliminary report on the late bronze age and iron age faunal assemblages from tell es-Safi/Gath. In A. M. Maeir (Ed.), *Tell es-Safi/Gath I: The 1996–2005 seasons part I* (pp. 589–611). Harrassowitz Verlag.

Lev-Tov, J., Killebrew, A., Greenfield, H., & Brown, A. (2018). Puppy sacrifice and Cynophagy from early philistine Tel Miqne-Ekron contextualized. *Journal of Eastern Mediterranean Archaeology & Heritage Studies, 6*, 1–30.

Lister, A. M. (1996). The morphological distinction between bones and teeth of fallow deer (*Dama dama*) and Red Deer (*Cervus elaphus*). *International Journal of Osteoarchaeology, 6*, 119–143.

Maeir, A. M., Hitchcock, L. A., & Horwitz, L. K. (2013). On the constitution and transformation of philistine identity. *Oxford Journal of Archaeology, 32*, 1–38.

Maeir, A. M., Ben-Shlomo, D., Cassuto, D., Chadwick, J. R., Davis, B., Eliyahu-Behar, A., Frumin, S., Gur-Arieh, S., Hitchcock, L. A., Horwitz, L. K., Manclossi, F., Rosen, S. A., Verduci, J., Weiss, E., Welch, E. L., & Workman, V. (2019). Technological insights on philistine culture: Perspectives from Tell es-Safi/Gath. *Journal of Eastern Mediterranean Archaeology and Heritage Studies, 7*, 76–118.

Maher, E. F. (1998). Iron Age Fauna from the Tel Harasim excavations (1996). In S. Givon (Ed.), *The eighth season of excavation at Tel Harasim (Nahal Barkai) 1997* (pp. 13–25). Bar-Ilan University.

Maher, E. F. (2004). *Food for the Gods: The identification of philistine rites of animal sacrifice*. PhD dissertation, University of Illinois.

Maher, E. F. (2005). Faunal Remains. In M. Dothan & D. Ben-Shlomo (Eds.), *Ashdod VI, excavation of areas H and K* (pp. 283–290). Israel Antiquities Authority.

Maher, E. F. (2006/07). Imminent invasion: The abandonment of philistine Ekron. *Scripta Mediterranea, 27–28*, 323–337.

Maher, E. F. (2010). Late Iron Age faunal remains from Qubur al-Walaydah. *Die Welt des Orients, 40*, 268–272.

Maher, E. F. (2014). Lambs to the slaughter: Cultic orientations at Philistine Ekron in the 7th century BCE. In J. R. Spencer, A. J. Brody, & R. A. Mullens (Eds.), *Material culture matters: Essays on the archaeology of the Southern Levant in honor of Seymour Gitin* (pp. 111–130). American Schools of Oriental Research.

Maher, E. F. (2017). Flair of the dog: The philistine consumption of canines. In J. Lev-Tov, P. Hesse, & A. Gilbert (Eds.), *The wide lens in archaeology: Honoring Brian Hesse's contributions to anthropological archaeology* (pp. 117–147). Lockwood Press.

Maher, E. F. (n.d.-a). (Unpublished manuscript A). *The analysis of modern striped Hyaena (Hyaena hyaena) scats from Israel and their archaeological significance*. Unpublished manuscript based on a study conducted at the Field Museum in Chicago.

Maher, E. F. (n.d.-b. (Unpublished manuscript B). *Notched animal bones from Philistia*.

Maher, E. F. (In preparation). *Border-town Animal Exploitation: The Late Ottoman Period – Iron Age Fauna from Tel Zayit*.

Maher, E. F., & Hesse, B. (2016). The middle Bronze Age II and Iron Age I faunal remains. In S. Gitin (Ed.), *The Tel Miqne-Ekron excavations 1985–1988, 1990, 1992–1995: Field IV lower – The elite zone volume 9/1 part 1: The Iron Age I early Philistine City* (pp. 515–570). Eisenbrauns.

Maher, E. F., & Hesse, B. (2017). The Iron Age II faunal remains. In S. Gitin (Ed.), *The Tel Miqne-Ekron excavations 1985–1988, 1990, 1992–1995: Field IV lower – The elite zone volume 9/2 part 2: The iron age I early Philistine City* (pp. 357–363). Eisenbrauns.

Marom, N., Bar-Oz, G., & Munger, S. (2006). A new incised scapula from Tel Kinrot. *Near Eastern Archaeology, 69*, 37–40.

Mazar, A. (1980). *Excavations at Tell Qasile, part 1: The Philistine Sanctuary: Architecture and cult objects (Qedem* 12) Jerusalem.

Mazow, L. B. (2006/2007). Producing a philistine: The philistine textile industry and its implications for reconstructing philistine settlement. *Scripta Mediterranea, 27–28*, 53–80.

Meiberg, L., & Nahshoni, P. (2020). A philistine lion-headed cup from Nahal Patish. In B. Gür & S. Dalkiliç (Eds.), *Anadolu Prehistoryasına Adanmış Bir Yaşam Jak Yakara Armağan* (pp. 297–307). A Life Dedicated to Anatolian Prehistory – Festschrift for Jak Yakar.

Meiri, M., Huchon, D., Bar-Oz, G., Boaretto, E., Horwitz, L. K., Maeir, A. M., Sapir-Hen, L., Larson, G., Weiner, S., & Finkelstein, I. (2013). Ancient DNA and population turnover in southern Levantine pigs – Signature of the sea peoples migration? *Nature-Scientific Reports, 3*, 3035.

Nahshoni, P., & Ziffer, I. (2010). Caphtor, the throne of his dwelling, Memphis, the land of his inheritance. The pattern book of a philistine offering stand from a shrine at Nahal Patish (with an appendix on the technology of the stand by Elisheva Kamaisky). *Ugarit-Forschungen, 41*, 543–580.

Nicholson, R. A. (1993). A morphological investigation of burnt animal bone and an evaluation of its utility in archaeology. *Journal of Archaeological Science, 20*, 411–428.

Payne, S. (1973). Kill-off patterns in sheep and goats: The mandibles from Asvan kale. *Anatolian Studies, 23*, 281–303.

Payne, S. (1985). Morphological distinctions between the mandibular teeth of young sheep, *Ovis*, and goats, *Capra*. *Journal of Archaeological Science, 12*, 139–147.

Perkins, D., & Daly, P. (1968). A hunter's village in Neolithic Turkey. *Scientific American, 219*, 397–106.

Prummell, W., & Frisch, H. J. (1986). A guide for the distinction of species, sex, and body side in bones of sheep and goat. *Journal of Archaeological Science, 13*, 567–577.

Redding, R. W. (1984). Theoretical determinants of a Herder's decisions: Modeling variation in the sheep/goat ratio. In J. Clutton-Brock & C. Grigson (Eds.), *Animals and archaeology 3. Early herders and their flocks* (pp. 223–241). BAR International Series 202.

Redding, R. W. (1994). The vertebrate Fauna. In S. C. Herbert (Ed.), *Tel Anafa I – final report on ten years of excavation at a Hellenistic and Roman settlement in northern Israel* (pp. 279–322). University of Michigan.

Reese, D. S. (1981). Notes on the fish identified from the cisterns. In J. H. Humphrey (Ed.), *Excavations at Carthage 1977* (Vol. VI, pp. 238–241). University of Michigan.

Reese, D. S. (2002). On the incised cattle scapulae from the East Mediterranean and near East. *Bonner Zoologiscie Beitrage, 50*, 183–198.

Redman, C. L. (1973). Early village technology: A view through the microscope. *Paléorient, 1*, 249–261.

Robertson-Smith, W. (1901). *Religion of the Semites*. Adam and Charles Black.

Sapir-Hen, L., Bar-Oz, G., Gadot, Y., & Finkelstein, I. (2013). Pig husbandry in Iron Age Israel and Judah: New insights regarding the origin of the taboo. *ZDPV, 129*, 1–20.

Sapir-Hen, L., Meiri, M., & Finkelstein, I. (2015). Iron Age pigs: New evidence on their origin and role in forming identity boundaries. *Radiocarbon, 57*, 307–315.

Schmid, E. (1972). *Atlas of animal bones*. Elsevier Publishing Company.

Sherratt, S. (1998). 'Sea people' and the economic structure of the late second millennium in the Eastern Mediterranean. In S. Gitin, A. Mazar, & E. Stern (Eds.), *Mediterranean peoples in transition-thirteenth to early tenth centuries in honor of professor Trude Dothan* (pp. 292–313). Israel Exploration Society.

Shipman, P., Foster, G., & Schoeninger, M. (1984). Burnt bones and teeth: An experimental study of color, morphology, crystal structure, and shrinkage. *Journal of Archaeological Science, 11*, 307–325.

Silver, A. (1969). The aging of domestic animals. In D. Brothwell & E. S. Higgs (Eds.), *Science in archaeology* (2nd ed., pp. 283–302). Thames and Hudson.

Sisma-Ventura, G., Tütken, T., Zohar, I., Pack, A., Sivan, D., Lernau, O., Gilboa, A., & Bar-Oz, G. (2018). Tooth oxygen isotopes reveal late Bronze Age origin of Mediterranean fish aquaculture and trade. *Scientific Reports, 8*, 1–10.

Stager, L. E. (1995). The impact of the sea peoples in Canaan (1185–1050 B.C.E.). In T. E. Levy (Ed.), *The archaeology of Society in the Holy Land* (pp. 332–348). Leicester University Press.

Stager, L. E., Master, D. M., & Aja, A. J. (2020). *Editors, Ashkelon 7: The Iron Age I (final reports of the Leon Levy expedition to Ashkelon)*. Eisenbrauns.

Stern, E. (1994). A Phoenician-Cypriote Votive Scapula from Tel Dor: A maritime scene. *Israel Exploration Journal, 44*, 1–12.

Stern, E. (1997). Discoveries at Tel Dor. In N. A. Silberman & D. Small (Eds.), *The archaeology of Israel: Constructing the past-interpreting the present* (pp. 128–143). (Supplementary Series 237). Sheffield Academic.

Stern, E. (2000). *Dor, ruler of the seas: Nineteen years of excavations at the Israelite-Phoenician Harbor town on the Carmel coast*. Israel Exploration Society.

Stern, E. (2006). The sea peoples cult in Philistia and northern Israel. In A. M. Maeir & P. de Miroschedji (Eds.), *"I will speak the riddles of ancient times": Archaeological and historical studies in honor of Amihai Mazar on the occasion of his sixtieth birthday* (pp. 385–398). Eisenbrauns.

Tappy, R. E., McCarter, P. K., Lundberg, M. J., & Zuckerman, B. (2006). An abecedary of the mid-tenth century B.C.E. from the Judean Shephelah. *Bulletin of the American Schools of Oriental Research, 344*, 5–46.

Tappy, R. E. (2008). Tel Zayit and the Tel Zayit abecedary in their regional context. In R. E. Tappy & P. K. McCarter (Eds.), *Literate culture and tenth-century Canaan: The Tel Zayit abecedary in context* (pp. 1–44). Eisenbrauns.

Tylor, E. B. (1970). *Religion in primitive culture*. Harper and Row.

Uziel, J. (2007). The development process of philistine material culture: Assimilation, acculturation, and everything in between. *Levant, 39*, 165–173.

Wapnish, P., Hesse, B., & Ogilvy, A. (1977). The 1974 collection of faunal remains from Tell Dan. *Bulletin of the American Schools of Oriental Research, 227*, 35–62.

Wapnish, P., & Hesse, B. (1991). Faunal remains from Tel Dan: Perspectives on animal production at a village, urban and ritual center. *Archaeozoologia, 4*, 9–86.

Wapnish, P., & Hesse, B. (1999). *Iron I: A problem of identity. Near Eastern Archaeology* 62: Editorial on inside of cover page.

Webb, J. M. (1985). The incised scapula. In V. Kargeorghis (Ed.), *Excavations at Kition V, the pre-Phoenician levels (part II)* (pp. 317–330). Nicosia.

Weiss, E., & Kislev, M. E. (2004). Plant remains as indicators for economic activity: A case study from Iron Age Ashkelon. *Journal of Archaeological Science, 31*, 1–13.

Zeder, M. A. (1991). *Feeding cities: Specialized animal economy in the ancient near-East*. Smithsonian Institution Press.

Zeder, M. A., & Pilaar, S. E. (2010). Assessing the reliability of criteria used to identify mandibles and mandibular teeth in sheep, *Ovis*, and goats, *Capra*. *Journal of Archaeological Science, 37*, 225–242.

Zeder, M. A., & Lapham, H. A. (2010). Assessing the reliability of criteria used to identify postcranial bones in sheep, *Ovis*, and goats, *Capra*. *Journal of Archaeological Science, 37*, 2887–2905.

Ziffer, I. (2010). The iconography of the cult stands. In R. Kletter, I. Ziffer, & W. Zwickel (Eds.), *Yavneh I: The excavation of the 'Temple Hill' repository pit and the cult stands* (pp. 61–104). Fribourg and Göttingen.

Zukerman, A., Horwitz, L. K., Lev-Tov, J., & Maier, A. M. (2007). A bone of contention? Iron IIA notched scapulae from Tell es-Safi/Gath, Israel. *BASOR, 347*, 57–81.

The Hesi Region: A Regional Perspective on Interaction and Integration Processes During the Iron I/II Transition

James W. Hardin

Abstract Following a careful examination of the excavation and survey data of the Hesi region, and after studying its history and analyzing its soil characteristics, rainfall, malacology and botany, Jeff Blakely and I suggested that during the Iron Age the region was used largely as a pasturage and not for agriculture. What follows builds on this work as I try to understand better how the Iron Age sites of the Hesi region interacted with, and were integrated into, larger regional networks appearing in the southern Levant at the end of the Iron I and the beginning of the Iron II.

Keywords Iron Age · Hesi · Archaeological survey

1 Introduction

Over the last several decades, a number of studies have advanced our understanding of many regions of the southern Levant during the Iron I/II transition. However, some of these regions, such as Hesi, have been misunderstood, and this has complicated our understanding of trends more generally in the larger southern Levant (Fig. 1). Recently, Jeff Blakely and I attempted to correct some of the misconceptions related to the Hesi region specifically (Hardin & Blakely, 2019). We suggested that during the Iron Age it was used largely as a pasturage rather than primarily for agriculture. What follows builds on this work as I try to gain a better understanding of how the Hesi region interacted with, and was integrated into, larger regional networks in the southern Levant at the end of the Iron I and the beginning of the Iron II.

J. W. Hardin (✉)
Mississippi State University, Mississippi State, MS, USA
e-mail: jwh1@ra.msstate.edu

© The Author(s), under exclusive license to Springer Nature Switzerland AG 2023
E. Ben-Yosef, I. W. N. Jones (eds.), *"And in Length of Days Understanding" (Job 12:12): Essays on Archaeology in the Eastern Mediterranean and Beyond in Honor of Thomas E. Levy*, Interdisciplinary Contributions to Archaeology, https://doi.org/10.1007/978-3-031-27330-8_29

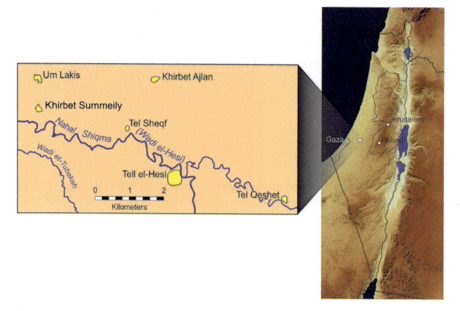

Fig. 1 Location map showing the Hesi region and other significant sites discussed in the article. (Created by William Isenberger in consultation with Jeffrey Blakely and the author)

2 The Hesi Region

Following the work of Edward Robinson in the 1830s and until recently, the Hesi region has been understood as an agricultural hinterland largely associated with Judah (Hardin & Blakely, 2019). When Robinson visited the greater Hesi region in May of 1838, he wrote (1841: 44), "The region…is filled with deserted sites and ruined villages; there not being one of them inhabited." But he explained that (1841: 45–46), "The soil of all the plain through which we passed is good; as is proved by the abundant crops of grain we saw…" in the flood plain to the west of Tell [this is spelled both Tell and Tel throughout; I have changed all spellings to Tell as per Arabic] el-Hesi (quoted in Hardin & Blakely, 2019: 64). Josias L. Porter, who visited the region in the 1850s, emphasized the same fact (1858, 1865) as did Charles Warren, who mapped the Hesi region in 1867 (Warren, 1871: 82–83; Hardin & Blakely, 2019: 64).

These two observations, that (1) the soil is good and (2) the land was inhabited in the past, formed the basis for understanding the region for the past 175 years (e.g., Smith, 1894: 79–80 and 83–84, 1931: 72 and 74; Stager, 1971; Finkelstein, 1996; Dever, 1996: 39; Faust & Weiss, 2005: 78–79, Fig. 1). When sites in the Hesi region were no longer identified directly with Judahite settlements, many scholars associated the area with Philistia but continued to understand it as an agricultural hinterland. Over the next century, excavation and surveys were carried out periodically in the region and its agricultural hinterland identity continued.

However, in 2004 and 2008, the Hesi Regional Project sponsored by the Cobb Institute of Archaeology at Mississippi State University conducted a systematic pedestrian survey of the 100 sq km of the Ruhama Quad – roughly centered on Tell el Hesi. One of the primary reasons for undertaking the survey was to provide a better understanding of the greater Hesi region through broader time, but also so that the various settlements at Tell el-Hesi itself could be understood better on the same scale. Under the direction of Jeffrey A. Blakely and myself, we recorded all observed archaeological remains in the area from the earliest of times to 1947. We were particularly interested in how people at various times articulated themselves across, and interacted with, the regions' specific climatic, geologic, topographic, and environmental regimes (Hardin & Blakely, 2019). Ultimately, it was from this broader temporal perspective, with considerations for soil, rainfall, malacology, and botanical evidence; historical observations and archaeological survey and excavation that we derived what we believe is a better understanding of the region at particular times and in general.

2.1 Soil

An understanding of the soils of the Hesi region has improved dramatically since the pioneering work of Picard and Solomonica (1936). The newest geological and soils map of the greater Hesi region shows it to be dominated by three basic units: loessal units (Q1 and Qr), kurkar (Qk), and various depositional and erosional units found in and along floodplains (e.g., A1, undifferentiated Holocene alluvium; or NQp, Pleshet formation) (Sneh, 2008; Sneh & Rosensaft, 2008a, b). The most expansive units are loessal (Fig. 2). These units are not common, eroding into sometimes dramatic features. The erosion is powered by a characteristic of the soil which absorbs some water quickly, but rapidly saturates, causing significant runoff and dangerous and powerful flash floods. Much of the rain ends up in the wadis flowing toward the sea and/or being absorbed into the lower-lying gravelly and sandy wadi bed below the loessal layers, meaning that it is unavailable for agriculture (Hardin & Blakely, 2019: 64–66).

2.2 Rainfall

Recording of regional rainfall in a manner sufficient to draw annual precipitation maps began only during the British Mandate. The greater Hesi region is around the 350 mm isohyet line but the actual amount can vary rather broadly. Local farmers tell us that precipitation drops off dramatically as one moves from north to south through the region, a point hinted at by Conder and Kitchener who stated that farming ceased as one passed south of Wadi el-Hesi (1883: X). The modern farmers also tell us that even with modern improved traits in the traditional wheat and barley grains, that crops fail about 3 years in ten (Hardin & Blakely, 2019: 66). How does the modern situation compare with the past?

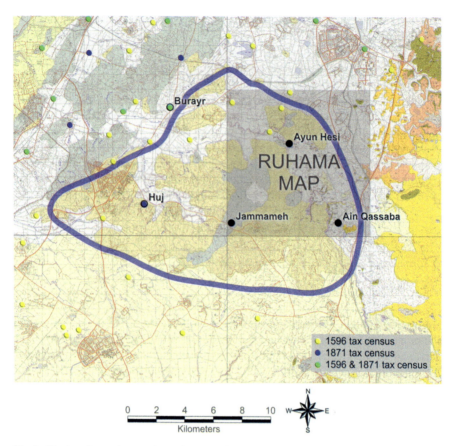

Fig. 2 The location and approximate borders of the greater Hesi region where potential agriculture is adversely impacted by the character of the Ruhama loess and *kurkar* is inside the blue circle. The location of the Ruhama Map (97) and our survey is named and shaded. The location of hamlets, villages, towns, and cities based on the 1596 and the 1871 tax lists placed over a base map showing the Quaternary geology of the region. The sites Huj, Jemmameh, Ain Qassaba, and Ayun Hesi are the locations of deep wells or springs, and only Huj was occupied (Hütteroth & Abdulfattah, 1977; Grossman, 2004: 234–257; Sneh, 2008; Sneh & Avni, 2008; Sneh & Rosensaft, 2008a, b). (Image created by William Isenberger in consultation with Jeffrey Blakely and the author)

2.3 Malacological and Botanical Considerations

Snails are excellent indicators of climate. Recently Blakely and Ktalav published an analysis of the snails excavated at Tell el-Hesi and Khirbet Summeily as well as those collected today (2017). The snails currently inhabiting the greater Hesi region are an almost unique combination of Mediterranean and desert snails. Interestingly the exact same species dominate the land snail corpus in the Early Bronze III, Late Bronze, Iron I/II transition, Iron II, and Persian periods (Hardin & Blakely, 2019:

67). However, the Early Bronze III materials from Tell el-Hesi also include some species suggesting a higher water table and flowing stream (Blakely & Ktalav, 2017). In the early 1970s, Stewart examined the floral species in uncultivated fields and along wadis in the Hesi region (1978). He compared these with archaeological specimens of seeds taken from flotation samples at Tell el-Hesi and found continuity with today (Hardin & Blakely, 2019: 68). Taken together the malacological and botanical evidence suggests that for the past five millennia the long-term climate dynamics of the greater Hesi region have been largely constant, albeit probably with significant short-term ups and downs. This interpretation is in general agreement with that provided years ago by Goodfriend (1990).

2.4 Historical Observations

In the thirteenth and fourteenth centuries, a wide variety of Western travelers described the region in their diaries. Examples include Georgio Gucci in 1384, Bertrandon de la Brocquiere in 1432, and Felix Fabris in 1483. Unless they passed the region in early spring the description was universally one of desolation. A survey of historical sources provides no evidence of usage of the Hesi region as agrarian farmland during any pre-Modern period (Hardin & Blakely, 2019: 70).

Hardin and Blakely used a tax list for Palestine that dates to about 1871 along with the nearly contemporary Survey of Western Palestine that covers the Hesi region (Grossman, 2004: 239–243; Conder & Kitchener, 1880: Sheets XIX, XX, and XXI, 1883) to plot all occupied settlements in and around the greater Hesi region during the 1870s with precision while using the geological map as a base (Fig. 3). They similarly used a 1596 Ottoman tax document for the region that was translated and published by Hütteroth and Abdulfattah who also mapped many of the sites (1977). Blakely and Huster identified more sites (2016) and it was possible to plot these sites from this same time in and around the greater Hesi region with precision while using the geological map as a base (Fig. 4).

No sites are found on the loess or in the kurkar of this region except for Huj, a poor village that only existed because the mayor of Gaza dug a 200-foot deep well to provide it with water (Robinson, 1841: 385–386; Khalidi, 1992: 103). From the earlier map, Malagues and Ajlan are two settlements that appear to be on the loess, but in reality, they are located in the floodplain without the deep overburden of loess. Still the greater Hesi region was devoid of sedentary occupation; pasturage seems likely. At these times, sedentary life did not occur in this region. In fact, Diqs (1967), Teichman (1921), Bliss, Petrie, Conder and Kitchener, and Robinson all viewed the region as a pasturage (Hardin & Blakely, 2019: 68). Gaza ware is found across the landscape; we suggest, however, that this is indicative of Bedouin herding activities.

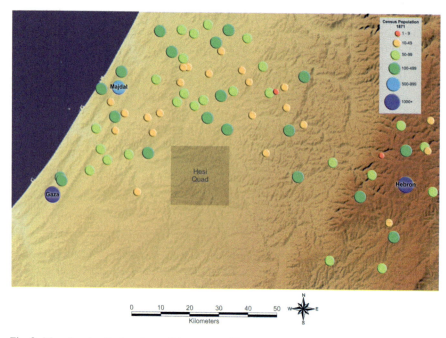

Fig. 3 Map showing the locations of the towns, villages, and hamlets in the entire region of Gaza that were enumerated in the tax census of about 1871. (Data from Grossman (2004); Our map prepared by William Isenberger in association with and Jeffrey Blakely and the author)

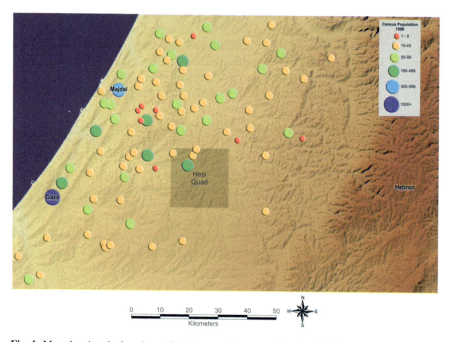

Fig. 4 Map showing the locations of the towns, villages, and hamlets in the entire region of Gaza that were enumerated in the tax census of 1596/7. (Data from Hütteroth and Abdulfattah (1977); Our map prepared by William Isenberger in association with Jeffrey Blakely and the author)

2.5 Hesi Archaeological Survey

Archaeological surveys have been carried out in the greater Hesi region for the past several decades. Gophna did extensive work in the greater region at one level in the 1950s (Gophna, 1963, 1981). Dagan surveyed to the east and northeast of the Hesi region (Dagan, 1992, 2006), Huster surveyed to the northwest and the west (Huster 2015), and Blakely and I have surveyed the 100 sq. km basically centered on the site of Tell el-Hesi. From the Chalcolithic period onward, only during the Roman and Byzantine periods is there a presence of towns and villages across the landscape. This is a moister period (this also suggested by Sperber [1974] who looked at historical data for the same period), with possibly a higher water table, which might have allowed for sedentary agriculture for a few centuries. The work of Orland and others at Sorek Cave has provided qualified support for more moisture in this specific period (Orland et al., 2009). However, for most other periods the survey shows a far sparser occupation in the region (Hardin & Blakely, 2019: 70–71).

3 The Hesi Region During the Iron I and Iron IIA

3.1 Iron Age Environmental Reconstruction for the Hesi Region

While the work of Langgut, Finkelstein and others provides an overview for this period, other works provide more detail (e.g., Langgut et al., 2013, 2015; Finkelstein et al., 2017). Neumann and Sigrist (1978a, b) and Neumann and Parpola (1987) noted that the climate at the end of the thirteenth century and the whole of the twelfth century BCE was generally not good in the Fertile Crescent. Reculeau did not see this as a sudden change, but rather a long-term decline reaching its nadir (2011: esp. 67–69). These interpretations are similar to Bookman and others who saw a low Dead Sea representing a dry event in the period 1440–1120 BCE (2004: 565–566; but see Neumann & Others, 2007: 1487–1488 for slightly earlier dates). In Judah it seems that this was a warm dry event that was followed by a relatively short, cooler and moister period that probably began in the tenth century BCE, if not in the previous century, and may have continued into the ninth century before returning to a more normative dryer period (Kaniewski et al., 2019: 72).

To summarize the above, it appears that over much of the past four and a half millennia, the Hesi region would have been a grassland and functioned as pasturage. With specific regard to the region during the late Iron I and early Iron II, the period of concern here, the environment may have been a bit moister than today and, over the following century or so, it slowly dried to reach an environment more or less like today.

3.2 Iron Age Archaeological Remains from the Hesi Region

During the time that Blakely and I worked in the Hesi region, we tried to understand its role in the broader region, and how Iron Age settlements at sites such as Khirbet Summeily and Tell el-Hesi could help us to understand the processes that culminated in the small tribal or territorial kingdoms typical of the Iron IIB and onward. Following is a brief review of the Iron Age remains at Khirbet Summeily and Hesi, as well as several other sites in the broader region that are functionally different but that may shed light on changing regional interactions and processes of integration in the late Iron I and early Iron II.

3.2.1 Khirbet Summeily

Khirbet Summeily is a small, very late Iron I – early Iron II site roughly 3–4 km west of Tell el- Hesi (Fig. 1). It is a smaller part of the larger Ottoman and Mandate site of Horvat Soreqa. Its immediate surrounding is an arid borderland with the Philistine heartland lying to the west and Judean heartland to the east. Borderland as used here follows Parker's understanding as "regions around or between political or cultural entities where geographic, political, demographic, cultural and economic circumstances or processes may interact to create borders or frontiers" (2006: 80). While a border cannot be demonstrated in the Hesi region until later in the Iron II (Blakely et al., 2014), its identification as a frontier is fitting. Frontiers are zones that separate various types of political or cultural units and may also consist of empty areas where no such units exist or where there is no direct physical contact (Parker, 2006: 79, adapted from Elton, 1996; Rosler & Wendl, 1999; and others). Elton understands these as zones of various overlapping political, economic, and cultural boundaries (1996: 3–9). I would add geographic/ecological overlaps as well.

When Blakely and I decided to begin excavations at Khirbet Summeily in 2011, we expected to find a hamlet or rural farmstead that dated to the early Iron II and we planned to investigate households. While we had the dates more or less correct, the area of the site where we focused our excavations turned out *not* to be farm-like, or domestic, at all, but more in the vein of administrative, evidenced by the remains of a large building rebuilt several times. To date, we have identified four archaeological strata (Phases 5–2) all dating to the Iron Age. Phase 5 is the earliest of the Iron Age strata and it has been reached only in a few areas. These remains consist mainly of stone foundations and mudbrick superstructures of several walls as well as a small patch of cobblestone surfacing. On one wall there are three small circular rock installations that likely served as bases for pillars.

On the other end of the occupational sequence, Phase 2 is the latest of the Iron Age strata. It is a smaller occupational horizon, at least based on exposures in the area of the site excavated. It is limited to only a couple of areas and appears to date to the early eighth century BBCE. It was abandoned in the early eighth century BCE and the mound was never again used by a sedentary population. The remains unearthed between Phases 5 and 2 are identified as Phases 4 and 3 (Fig. 5), and provide the best-preserved and most complete phases found to date at the relatively short-lived settlement. Both preserve the remains of a large architectural complex. Phase 4 is quite limited in its exposure but appears to be a well-planned building with mudbrick walls built on wadi and fieldstone foundations. Based on a limited collection of ceramics found thus far, archaeomagnetic samples, and this phase's relationship to Phase 3, it appears to date to the early to mid-tenth century BCE.

Immediately above Phase 4 is Phase 3, the best understood of the site's phases since it was the first architectural phase to be encountered in most of the excavated areas (Fig. 5). It consists of the rebuilt walls of Phase 4 at a higher level and with raised floors in some of the rooms. There are six clear structural units or rooms, all connected architecturally. A room understood by the team as a cult room includes a series of thin white plaster floors, a structural jar stand with a large oil stain in front of it, a *kurkar* altar, a chalice, and a large, terra cotta zoomorphic head, likely a lion, all from Phase 3. We believe the earlier Phase 4 incarnation of the room was also for cult purposes. In that phase, we identified a large oil stain on the floor with a sump beneath. A central large wadi stone was embedded in the floor, almost directly under the altar found in Phase 3, and collections of loom weights and astragali were found in it as well.

Other remains from Phases 3 and 4 include several ceramic vessels left on floors and a number of Egyptian artifacts. Multiple scarabs with standard Egyptian motifs (e.g., falcon, ankh, mace) were recovered as well as faience pendants (including Ptah Sokar; Ludvik, 2020) and figurines (including an Asherah plaque figurine; Hallote, 2014). To date, we have not recovered a single seed, pit or grain or the like

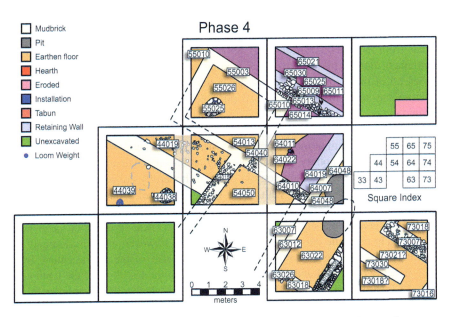

Fig. 5 Plan of Phase 3 at Khirbet Summeily, which dates to the second half of the tenth century. The room in the southwest half of Area 44 is a cult room. (Plan prepared by William Isenberger in association with Jeffrey Blakely and the author)

preserved in a primary context – this even with 100% sifting of all materials and flotation of at least samples of all loci. We found large quantities of ash and bits of wood charcoal.

One key to understanding the administrative function of Summeily was the discovery of at least seven burned an epigraphic bullae, probably associated with packages, documents, or cargo, that were at the site as a normal course of activity (Hardin et al., 2014). Two bullae have complete seal impressions, two have fragmentary seal impressions, and the others lack any remains of seal impressions at all. Most are made of the local soils, however at least one derives from Egypt, made from Nile silt. All were found in the sifting screens, and none were derived from floors or some similar context. But stratigraphically, they derive from one of the earlier strata, Phases 5–3, probably early in the Iron IIA. This would put them in the same general period as Tell el-Hesi's three large tripartite buildings from Bliss' City V, which I will turn to momentarily.

Other supporting evidence of the administrative nature of Summeily comes from oxygen, carbon, and strontium isotope analysis of ruminants from the site in its Iron IIA strata (Phases 4 and 3). Stable isotope work provides evidence of sheep and goats living their early life in one place and then being brought to the Summeily region after the forming of their third molar (Larson, 2020, 2022; Larson et al., 2022). This is suggestive of provisioning. Sheep and goat remains not native to the area had connections with more arid regions (the Arabah, Egypt?) and the Shephelah but not the coastal plain (Larson et al., 2022). In addition, Maher has identified Nile perch in the faunal assemblage (2014). Other remains include a relatively large quantity of Egyptian scarabs and amulets mentioned above, likely prestige goods associated with social status. The senior staff of our project sees these materials as the possible beginnings of a renewed regional contact with larger geographical areas from the Mediterranean Coast to Egypt. All of these suggest a function of settlement during these two phases beyond subsistence farming or herding and when all of these lines of evidence are combined, they further attest to the site's interactions with distant regions and possible integration into a larger socioeconomic system.

The most significant work towards dating Phases 4 and 3 came from the Center for Rock Magnetism at the University of Minnesota, where Dr. Michele Stillinger dated some of the pottery and tabuns using archaeomagnetism (Stillinger, 2018). More work with this methodology is planned, hopefully correlating our archaeomagnetic intensity samples with those from Ben-Yosef's published work from Timna (2018). His project's numerous radiocarbon dates and accompanying archaeomagnetic intensity samples deriving from excellent stratigraphic sequences should help us refine our dating further. Currently, however, and based largely on Stillinger's work, we date Phase 3 to the second half of the tenth century BCE before being destroyed and abandoned sometime in the last third of the tenth century BCE (Stillinger, 2018: 160). An open question is whether this destruction might be attributable to Pharaoh Shoshenq. We date Phase 4 on stratigraphic grounds and archaeomagnetism to the earlier half of the tenth century BCE.

3.2.2 Tell el-Hesi

Tell el-Hesi's geographical situation is very similar to Khirbet Summeily's. Its immediate surrounding is an arid borderland with the Philistine heartland lying to the west and the Judean heartland to the east; however it sits on the best water source in the entire region (Fig. 1). In addition, similar to Summeily, Hesi's late Iron I/early Iron II iteration is a non-agricultural settlement with at least three large tripartite buildings – certainly suggesting that this site, like Summeily, served a function beyond subsistence.

Tell el-Hesi's Iron Age history has been investigated since 1890, first by Petrie, continued by Bliss, and then finally by the Hesi Joint Project in the 70 s and 80 s. Early Iron Age remains include Petrie's Pilaster Building and "Large House" of Bliss's City IV (Hesi Joint project's Str. X). Both were terminated in a conflagration and then likely abandoned for a time. Although *in situ* remains were limited within the Pilaster Building, an Aegean cooking bowl and a LHIIIC1b bowl were found on its floor, providing evidence of a date somewhere after the mid-twelfth century BCE (Fig. 4.08; Petrie, 1891, Pl. 8:128; Matthers, 1989: 61–62, Fig. 13; Blakely, 2000, 2018: 277–78). If the destruction of Hesi occurred at the same time as the destruction of Lachish's Level VI, a destruction around 1140 or 1130 BCE is further supported. Tell el-Hesi is the sole site known to be occupied in the Hesi region in the twelfth century. With its destruction, the region appears to have been abandoned, probably for just over a century.

It is worth noting here that Blakely and Hardin understand that from the fourteenth to the twelfth centuries BCE, Hesi housed a rural Egyptian garrison that provided observation, protected the roads, controlled the best local water, and patrolled the pasturage on behalf of Imperial Egypt through ca. 1130 BCE (2022: 79–81; see also Blakely, 2018). This understanding is based on models developed more recently by Egyptologists that emphasize the workings and goals of Imperial Egypt in its overseas empire (e.g., Higginbotham, 2000; Morris, 2005, 2018). This City IV iteration of Hesi (Bliss's terminology) may provide insight into Hesi's function in the later Iron I and early Iron IIA.

In the Autumn of 1891 Bliss identified, above the level of his City IV remains, "roughly parallel lines of isolated stones and mud-brick wallings, worn down to 2 or 3 feet above their base …" (1894: 90), the main structures of his City V (Fig. 6). He was unsure what they were, and called them a "fascinating structure of parallel walls and stones" (1894: 12). In describing the stones, he wrote, "They are of rough sandstone very roughly squared, the surfaces bearing the marks of a tool with a broad thin edge at one end, while the other end was small and rounded" (1894: 92). The stones are rough but basically uniform in size, "30 inches × 15 inches by 15 inches" set on their side and perpendicular to their inferred line (Bliss, 1894: 92). Bliss is describing the first three tripartite pillared buildings ever excavated in the southern Levant, which he described and illustrated as his City V (Fig. 6). Above City IV, Bliss provided a plan of his City V (the Joint project's Stratum IX), and his illustration shows the Joint project's Stratum VIII fortification wall system (Bliss's

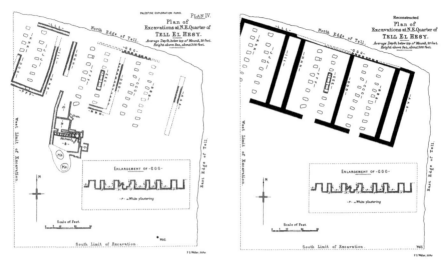

Fig. 6 Plan of the three tripartite pillared buildings that Bliss excavated at Tell el-Hesi in 1891, the first ever excavated, his City V (Bliss, 1894). (This plan had extraneous features removed and was prepared by William Isenberger in association with Jeffrey Blakely and the author)

City VI), which is massive, sitting over the tripartite pillared buildings (Fig. 7). Bliss describes a destruction and two phases of use before the buildings were buried by the construction of his City VI, or the Joint Project's Stratum VIII. When the Joint Hesi Project excavated next to "Bliss's cut," they did not encounter his City V remains. Instead, they found that his City VI (their Stratum VIII) fortification construction efforts entirely removed their Stratum IX (his City V remains) (Blakely et al., 2023). The residual pottery from Stratum VIII constructional fill – that is fill predating Stratum VIII, was carefully analyzed and supports a date for the construction and usage of the tripartite buildings of City V/Stratum IX in the late eleventh or tenth centuries BCE (Blakely et al., 2023).

It is significant that no known site in the southern Levant has either as many or more tripartite pillared buildings in tenth-eleventh century contexts as Tell el-Hesi. Blakely and I have argued that the three large tripartite buildings were in fact stables/administrative buildings and that a significant road and probable trade route passed the site due to its proximity to excellent water (Blakely and Hardin, 2023). The broader discussion of tripartite buildings is extended and extensive and will not be rehashed here, except to say that at least three of these buildings at Hesi demonstrate an effort to integrate this area into a larger network, likely economically.

3.2.3 Other Contemporary Settlements in the Hesi Region

Other than Khirbet Summeily and Tell el-Hesi, there are few Iron I and IIA sites in the Hesi region at all. Only the sites "Khirbert Umm el-Baqar," slightly east of Hesi and Summeily, and Ḥaṣer 3 a little south of Hesi and Summeily, are identified

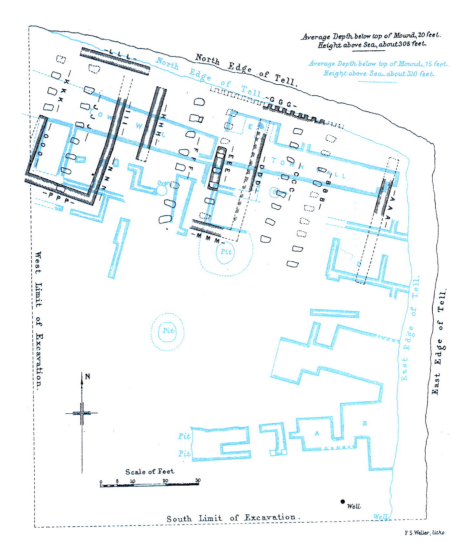

Fig. 7 Plan of Bliss' City VI (Hesi Joint Project Stratum VIII – in blue) superimposed over Bliss' City V (shown in black) proving that the tripartite pillared buildings predate the ninth century fort (Bliss, 1894). (This plan was prepared by William Isenberger in association with Jeffrey Blakley and the author)

(Fig. 7; also Fig. 1). Only the edge of umm el-Baqar has been investigated as part of salvage work associated with Highway 6. Therefore, it is difficult to determine the size and function of the settlement although perhaps agricultural settlement may be suggested. It was dated to the late eleventh and tenth centuries BCE by the excavators (Nahshoni & Talis, 2008, 2015). Gophna excavated Ḥaṣer 3, located just south of the Hesi quad, in 1960 and identified it as an agrarian settlement. While the remains of a couple of Iron I sherds were unearthed, the site's main use was dated to the Iron IIA, or the tenth century BCE (Gophna, 1963, 1981). Both sites were settled at about the same time as Summeily and Hesi and may have survived for a century or so before they were abandoned. While it is possible or perhaps likely that Umm el-Baqar and Haṣer 3 were agricultural, Khirbet Summeily and Tell el-Hesi seem to have been non-agricultural sites with occupation commencing at the end of the Iron I and continuing through the Iron IIA.

Ultimately, it appears that the building of settlements with an administrative, rather than a subsistence function, occurred as part of the interaction of those in the Hesi region with even broader areas. The term "interaction," has a wide variety of uses in archaeology. Parkinson and Galaty suggest modeling it along two separate but intertwined analytical dimensions when analyzing social organization: "Units of integration" and "Degrees of interaction." They suggest that the term integration is "helpful in referring to processes that incorporate individuals into specific organizational units." For them, interaction refers to a more diffuse process that "operates between these units" (Parkinson & Galaty, 2009: 10). Thus, "societies can be envisioned as integrating various social units – households, villages, polities – and interaction can be measured between various units at different scales" (Parkinson & Galaty, 2009: 10).

4 Other Iron I/II Sites of the Broader Region

The challenge then is to identify how different social units interacted over space and time. Thus, in this case, which is spatially and temporally quite narrow, how did the people of the Hesi region interact with others inside and outside of their general area in the late eleventh and tenth centuries BCE? And who were they interacting with? Were they Egyptians? Tribal/nomadic groups from the south or elsewhere? People from urban centers like those of the Philistine plain to the west and the north? Or perhaps other more tribal/egalitarian groups living in hamlets and villages (a nascent Israel?), or even town and city folk to the East? If it can be determined who people in the Hesi region were interacting with, and the nature of their interaction, then perhaps this will shed light on who they were and what their "units of integration" and "degrees of interaction" were. This could help identify the processes leading to greater complexity (i.e., integration) in the late eleventh/early tenth century BCE in the Hesi region. Perhaps it would be useful here to look at other settlements in nearby regions where similar patterns of greater regional interaction (and possibly integration) may be occurring that typify the same pattern observed at both Tell el-Hesi and Khirbet Summeily – settlements such as those at Qeiyafa, Lachish, and Khirbet er-Raii in the southern Shephelah just to the north and east of the Heis region, Tell Masos in the Beer Sheva Basin, the Negev Highland fortresses – an area also traditionally typified as a marginal farming area, the arid sites of Feinan in Jordan and Timna in the south, and a brief mention of the settlements of the Coastal Plain/Philistine Centers (Fig. 8).

The Hesi Region: A Regional Perspective on Interaction and Integration Processes... 695

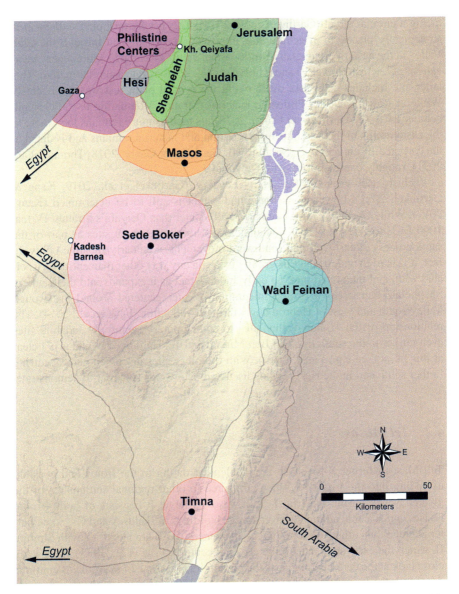

Fig. 8 Map showing a number of the settlements discussed in this chapter. (Map prepared by William Isenberger in association with Jeffrey Blakely and the author)

4.1 Khirbet Qeiyafa, er-Ra'i, Lachish, and the Trough Valley

Khirbet Qeiyafa sits 2 km east of Azekah just above and north of the Elah Valley. Garfinkel's excavations provide a well-dated, late Iron I/early Iron IIA planned settlement with a casemate enclosure wall associated with built-in pillared houses facing a circular street (Garfinkel et al., 2014). This briefly occupied settlement is strategically placed to affect/monitor movement east and west through the Elah Valley in the eastern Shephelah. A little farther south, Garfinkel's more recent excavations at Lachish (Level V) and Khirbet er-Ra'i demonstrate a similar picture. This latter site includes a fortress overlooking the coastal plain just west of Lachish. While er-Ra'i has earlier Philistine material (Stratum VIII dating to the eleventh century BCE, see Garfinkel & Ganor, 2018), its tenth century remains look more to the eastern hills in their architectural tradition and material remains and is dated to the early tenth century BCE (Stratum VII, Garfinkel & Ganor, 2018; Thomas et al., 2021), roughly contemporary with Qeiyafa IV.

Lachish itself was fortified in its Level V (Garfinkel et al., 2019; Kang & Garfinkel, 2021), however, its horizontal extent is still to be determined (Kang, 2017). While Garfinkel dates Lachish Level V later than Qeiyafa's Stratum IV (ca. 1000 BCE for Qeiyafa), it is nonetheless possible to see both sites as part of the same process of eastward and southward movement of an early Judahite polity. In fact, it is hard to understand this group of sites in any way other than entities associated with, and integrated into, an early Judah/Israel as it expands into the southern Shephelah. Faust sees a similar integration of sites centered around the Trough Valley south and west of Hebron down through Tell Aitun (Faust et al., 2014). The relationship of the Trough Valley sites to contemporary seemingly Judahite sites even farther to the south like Tell Beit Mirsim and Tel Halif and beyond is not clear at this point (see e.g., Faust, 2019). With the other sites discussed here occurring farther south and in the Hesi region, discussed below, this is harder to demonstrate.

4.2 Tel Masos

Tell Masos/Khirbet el-Meshash is a settlement dating to the Iron I and possibly extending into the Iron IIA. When compared to other regional settlements of the greater Negev during the Iron I, Tell Masos is large. It consists of both 4-room houses and sizeable administrative/storage buildings in Fields A and C – some better planned than others (chronological differences?). All are identified with Stratum II, which the excavators date to the eleventh century (Fritz et al., 1983), however, a close look at the ceramics suggests the possibility that some of the remains continue down into the Iron IIA. The location of Masos at the north end of the desert routes where the east-west route along the wadi Beer Sheva meets the international north-south routes that, together, allow access to Egypt, the Mediterranean coast, and the Judean Hills, attest to its importance along a major arterial in this area and helps explain its size and its implication in long-distance trade activities (Fig. 8). Holladay and Klassen called Masos, along with Beer Sheva/Tell es-Saba a caravan city with a detachment of chariots, further implicating its significance for long-distance trade (Holladay & Klassen, 2014). Perhaps this is also the nature of Hesi with its multiple examples of tripartite buildings from roughly the same period.

Finkelstein also understood the significance of Tel Masos in the southern regions, but his attempt to associate it with the enclosures of the Negev Highlands (discussed below) as the seat of a small chiefdom – his Tel Masos Chiefdom (Finkelstein, 1995, 2020; Martin & Finkelstein, 2013) – is unconvincing. Masos appears earlier than the Negev Highland settlements and it sits in a different geographic zone (Beer Sheva basin vs. the Negev Highlands), its metallurgical associations are perhaps overstated (Yahalom-Mack, 2009: 272–273), and it has a different architectural tradition than other regions in the south. It also lacks the hand-made pottery so prevalent in the Highlands sites (where it is up to 50%; Mazar, 2010: 31). The apparent but subtle chronological difference is significant, likely placing the copper working at Tel Masos in the Iron I (Gottleib, 2018: 448–451). Perhaps it is simply the earliest iteration known to this point of the type of increasing frontier regional connectivity or interaction that this article addresses.

Finkelstein's attempts also to associate the expanded settlements at Arad (str. XII) and Beer Sheva (str. VII) are problematic as well, based on differing metallurgical traditions (follows Yahalom-Mack, 2009) and lack of camel bone (Gottleib, 2018: 449), and, once again they appear to be a little later. Tel Masos likely served as a gateway community (Finkelstein, 1995; Martin & Finkelstein, 2013: 10; Fantalkin & Finkelstein, 2006) distributing goods to urban centers, north, west possibly including the Philistine seaports (although see comment from Herzog & Singer-Avitz, 2011 above). Interestingly, Parker has noted the significance that such communities in borderlands can play in ethnogenesis through processes of hybridization (2006: 86–88). I follow Ben-Yosef et al. in *not* assuming that both regions are part of the same political or social entity (Ben-Yosef et al., 2010).

4.3 *Negev Highland Enclosures*

Regarding the Negev Highland enclosures investigated decades ago by Cohen (1979) and now others, the best explanation of these settlements remains a directed, or at least concerted, attempt to settle and control the region sitting across important crossroads and through the Negev Highlands (Fig. 8). These perhaps reflect a cultural symbiosis – in the words of A. Mazar (2010: 31) – of people from what later becomes Judah, the southern coastal plain (tying this area to ours), and local desert nomads. A little more recently, Martin and Finkelstein (2013) added very important corroborative evidence strongly connecting these sites to the Arabah copper producing regions with petrographic studies of both handmade and wheel-made ceramic vessels from a number of the southern and northern Highland Enclosures. Based largely on these analyses they identified three petrographic groups that demonstrate a southern origin, likely in the Arabah for both hand and wheel-made vessels. A fourth group of materials is further divided into two smaller groups deriving from (1) the northwestern Negev (Nahal Besor area) and the southern Philistine coast as far north as Ashkelon and (2) the central northern Negev (Beer Sheva Valley) and the southern Shephelah. So basically, the northern Negev extending into the southern coastal plain and the southern Shephelah. Additional fabrics were identified as terra rosa and other wares from the lower Shephelah and the northern valleys of Israel, as well as "moza ware" from the Hill Country (Martin & Finkelstein, 2013: 27–28; Fig. 5).

While Martin and Finkelstein rightly note the significance of their study for demonstrating what many have suspected for some time – a strong connection between the copper districts of the Arabah and the Negev Highland enclosures – there is no similar significance attributed to the large quantities of pottery coming from the north. In fact, more wheel-made pottery comes from the fourth group, from the areas of the Negev beyond the Negev Highlands to the north and northwest, than any other area (Martin & Finkelstein, 2013: 29). It makes up a larger portion of the petrographic data than the pottery from the Arabah. For this reason, their somewhat cumbersome dichotomized choice of a "Copper Network A" or "Copper Network B" (Martin & Finkelstein, 2013) does not appreciate the nuanced approach of Mazar whose suggestion of an area of cultural symbiosis better explains the observed phenomena.

As to nomads in general, using the Negev Highland sites as animal enclosures, Bruins made a strong argument for dismissing this understanding (Bruins, 2017). And, as pointed out to me by Ben-Yosef, the high percentage of handmade pottery in the Highland enclosures suggests (and corroborated by Martin & Finkelstein, 2013) that their associations with more southerly directions, possibly with the metal trade as copper moved from the producing areas/mines/smelting sites of the south and east to distant markets (Blakely et al., 2023: 83).

With regard to the copper-producing areas to the south and east, new data have come to light in the last decade, especially related to the work of teams led by Tom Levy in the Wadi Feinan of Jordan and Erez Ben-Yosef in the Timna Valley of Israel (Levy et al., 2008; Ben-Yosef et al., 2010). Based on Levy's and Ben-Yosef's glut of ^{14}Carbon dates and Ben-Yosef's extensive use of archaeomagenetism, we now know that much of the mining activity in these regions dates to the Late Iron I, Iron IIA, and the beginning of the Iron IIB, with a height of activity in the Iron IIA (Ben-Yosef et al., 2012). Remains include, in addition to the abundant evidence of mining activity, the remains of a large "citadel" and large buildings at Feinan and a large fortified enclosure identified as "Slave's Hill" at Timna – a fortified smelting camp in the center of the Valley (Ben-Yosef et al., 2012; Levy et al., 2014; Ben-Yosef, 2018). The mining activities in both locations were extensive and productive, with nomadic expeditions extracting the metal and producing thousands of tons of slag. The scarcity of Cypriote copper at this same time and the appearance of copper from the southern Levant as far away as Olympia. in Greece attests to the greater regional impact of the exploited resource (Kiderlin et al., 2016; Ben-Yosef & Sergi, 2018). Levy's and Ben-Yosef's work to identify further the miners is providing a view of nomadic folk often obscured, or mostly missing, or simply overlooked in the archaeological record (Ben-Yosef, 2019).

So not addressing the significance of these areas in conjunction with the broader activities going on in most of the regions discussed here dramatically impacts our understanding of regional dynamics in the later Iron I and early Iron II more generally. Based on the extent of these mining activities, two relatively marginal areas become new sources of great wealth. The resource is traded north (up the plateau), through Masos (Holladay & Klassen, 2014) or the Negev Highland areas (Martin & Finkelstein, 2013) and then farther north and west or east. Some copper could have been moved directly west to Egypt from Timna on an Egyptian road marked earlier by the armies of Ramesses III (Somaglino & Tallet, 2013), or it could have been moved directly north. Likewise, there is the possibility of trade to the southeast, at about the same time, to South Arabia.

4.4 South Arabia

In addition to copper from Timna and Feinan, there is growing evidence of contact between the southern Levant and South Arabia, indicating the emergence of the incense trade route occurring near the end of the second millennium BCE (including isotopic data from camel teeth enamel and ceramics; Jasmin, 2006). This would have been facilitated by domestication of the camel. Grigson (2012) suggests that evidence for the domesticated camels at Timna is as early as the eleventh – tenth century BCE which fits reasonably well, with Magee's results (2011) in South Arabia. Sapir-Hen and Ben-Yosef suggest that domestication occurred several decades later. By the ninth – eighth centuries, documents and stele from the Assyrians attest to how extensive and varied this trade network had become, with monetary toll gifts – wealth – passing in each direction. According to Hodder (1965), followed by Holladay (2006), markets arose after trade routes. The sequence is trade routes, then markets established on trade routes, then subsidiary markets developing around the main market as transportation networks develop (Holladay & Klassen, 2014: 38) (perhaps Hesi and Summeily should be seen in this last light). So, the markets were established on trade routes, and they do not arise from purely local demand. They are a result of the division of labor and the varied location of desired goods.

4.5 The Coastal Plain/The Philistine Centers

The ports of Philistine Gaza and Ashkelon, and others on up the Levantine coast during the Iron I and II, make much more sense when understood as participating in the forwarding of the "distilled wealth" of South Arabia, East Africa, Egypt, and further afield. We can now add to this a focus more locally that includes the resources produced in the Feinan and Timna. The local resources of Gaza and Ashkelon were quite limited, and the absence of Egyptian support upon their withdrawal from the region may explain Philistine movements and incursions to the East (Master, 2019, 2021; see also Holladay & Klassen, 2014: footnote 12). Herzog and Singer-Avitz (2011) believe the coast was not sufficiently prosperous in the Iron IIA to argue for its participation in a thriving international market. However, non-local trade networks would have been pivotal in providing resources for their continual existence as well as providing lucrative opportunities for indigenous inhabitants, maybe even those in frontier regions. Gath, on the other hand, seems to have thrived in the late Iron I and Iron IIA.

4.6 Regional Summary

But, as to the larger region, we have good evidence now for a number of different types of settlements interacting across even broader regions than was previously the case. What are the driving factors behind this changing interaction and increasing integration? It certainly is possible, or even likely, that the shifting populations at the end of the Bronze Age played a role. However, I believe economics driven by shifting resources and opportunities must certainly have played a major part in regional integration of the southern areas of the Levant. As Holladay and Klassen point out, "major changes in social organization above the village or city level are hardly, if ever, gradual or "organic" but almost always invariably occur as "tipping points"" (2014: 31). I would especially implicate the role played by economics associated with overland trade, among other things, serving as the basis for one of these "tipping points." Attempts to benefit from this trade could drive the expansion and diversification of settlements in the south leading to interaction at greater distances and increased regional integration of sites and regions across the landscape as part of the early processes ultimately leading to territorial and/or tribal kingdom formation typical of the Iron II by the ninth century BCE.

5 Expanding Interaction and Increasing Integration

With regard to the specific processes, how are these areas integrated through trade into a larger regional framework that promotes interaction with those even further afield? Would it begin with an initial contact phase characterized by the feeding of specific goods from larger into smaller systems targeting emerging hierarchical figures leading to the acquisition of exotics and other desirables setting in motion a process that eventually alters the economic base and socio-political landscape? Or is it beginning internally? Imports or wealth accrued from trade could legitimize power based on local connotations and may actually change very little of the social underpinnings of society. The processes whereby these Iron II kingdoms formed are not well known. How did certain lineages or groups obtain power? How were territories and people integrated, and what was the nature of their interaction with others, whether peer groups identified as "other" or more powerful core states farther away? What were the roles played by trade/exchange, competition, networking, belligerence, and other factors?

The Late Bronze Age was a time of competitive networked city-states identified, from a World-systems perspective as semi-peripheral cores adjunct to older, larger central core states (e.g., Egypt, Anatolia, Mesopotamia) (Galaty et al., 2009: 35–36). The local client city-states in the southern Levant interacted especially with Egypt which maintained a presence consisting of garrisoned troops, observation, road protection, providing provisions and creating economic benefits (Higginbotham, 2000; Morris, 2018). This was followed by a period of staggered collapse that affected most regions of the eastern Mediterranean and Aegean and especially resulted in the disruption of the movement of many high-end goods throughout the region and even ended or dramatically lessened for a time the production of copper on Cyprus (Yahalom-Mack & Segal, 2018: 213–316, 326). This collapse negatively affected some but undoubtedly led to opportunity for others and, in the region of the southern Levant, resulted in demographic shifts and changing political and social systems during the Iron I, likely with less political integration and more social mobility. During these shifts, certain lineages or other groups could coalesce and obtain power used to integrate more people and larger territories. These political systems ultimately evolved into a network of territorial states dominated by political capitals in the Iron IIB (ca. ninth century BCE).

Prior to the processes that led to the rise of the Iron II kingdoms, the economics of the southern Levant were subsistence-based with few non-herding or agrarian natural resources, and little ability to accumulate capital or wealth. The role played by subsistence crops, including cereals, wine, raisins, and other dried fruits, honey, olives/olive oil and greasy wool (or perhaps even higher processed wool) has been appreciated (all named by Holladay & Klassen, 2014: 35). But in the south at the end of the Iron I and beginning of the Iron IIA, new sources for income included tolls on long-distance trade heading for Mediterranean ports or perhaps the raiding of these same trading ventures and diminishing one's competition (Holladay & Klassen, 2014: 36). Thus, the large-scale copper smelting activity in the Feinan and Timna regions, especially with the diminished role of Cypriote copper, along with the growing evidence of contact between the southern Levant and South Arabia that indicates the emergence of the incense trade route, undoubtedly occurring at about this same time, creates new sources of wealth associated with this network.

The non-local trade networks were thus pivotal in the changing regional complexity, site functionality, and had a very direct impact on the micro-regional systems like those of the Hesi and Summeily region. But who shaped the nature of the interaction and integration of these regional networks during the Iron I and Iron II transition? I would appeal to agency to help answer this question as numerous opportunities would have been created for various groups and individuals by changing political and social fortunes on the heels of the Late Bronze Age collapse. Leaders with exceptional charisma, luck, and opportunity can quickly create a powerful, even if small, military and control of relatively expansive geographical territory for short periods of time, and ethnohistoric and textual/historic examples abound.

6 Agency and Charismatic Leaders

van der Steen provides two nineteenth century examples of tribal leaders who, through ability and charisma, briefly alter the political landscape of the southern Levant and Arabian Peninsula (2009). Akila was the youngest son of an Egyptian mercenary who deserted his Egyptian army post, changed sides to the local fellahin, attracted a group of followers and started successfully robbing and pillaging. In a very short time, he became the sheikh of a powerful tribe controlling the whole of the Galilee for much of the rest of his life (van der Steen, 2009).

Abdallah, Tlal and Mohammad Rashid created an expansive Shammar emirate in the Arabian Peninsula that lasted for several decades. They rose to, and consolidated power in their own tribe through adroit political maneuvering with a good handful of murders thrown in. They then began attracting other tribes by successfully raiding and directing caravan traffic through their territories until they became paramount sheiks among the Shammar. Their base of operations, the Oasis of Hayil, grew into one of the largest trade centers of the region (van der Steen, 2009: 112), ultimately becoming a capital that acted as a service center for the population and focus of power. A standing army was even created to maintain law and order throughout their territories. After Mohammad's death the Shammar emirate collapsed, and power retrenched among the Saudis and Riyad (van der Steen, 2009).

van der Steen herself rightly provides a cautionary tale to applying such examples to the deeper past. Both of these examples have a tribal structure embedded in nineteenth-century power relations, technology, and religious and social norms – and their own relations with territory, territorial competition, economic responses to things in the natural and political environment, intertribal power structures, and tribal autonomy within hierarchical structure to name a few (van der Steen, 2009). But these examples can be used to make sense where underlying structures are similar. Additionally, elements of these stories have intriguing similarities that can be found in the deeper past. Examples are numerous, including the Bronze Age Labayu of Shechem mentioned in the Amarna letters, persons mentioned in texts from the kingdom of Mari, and Idrimi of Alalakh.

The biblical text's description of Saul's and David's unification of tribes into a monarchy is another example. Sergi, examines the role played by such texts in state formation. He understands the kingdoms of Saul and David beginning through a process of "extending political power by integrating different territories, communities, and political formations under centralized rule" (2015: 57). For him, once political hegemony over settled territories was established, the political actors were constantly involved in attempts to expand their territory for strategic and economic purposes. Sergi understands the role texts played in this formation as intellectual property and the texts like those describing David's battles with the Philistines and the accounts of Mesha's battles with the Omrides as narrating events of the past in order to reconstruct (or construct) a shared memory that conveys socio political claims and brings to the fore religious concepts in an attempt to establish the royal cult as the official religious practices throughout the newly formed territorial kingdom (Sergi, 2015: 57–59).

Aren Maeir has begun to explore the role of charismatic leaders in Philistine society (2019: 310). He sees the Philistines as an "entangled transcultural society, comprised of various groups deriving from the eastern and central Mediterranean" (with Mycenaean, Minoan, Cypriot, Anatolian, and other connections), "along with local Canaanites – all joining in to form a unique culture" (2019: 311). Notably, this process would have started just a little before the period of discussion here. Maeir suggests that the various groups coalesced under charismatic leaders, the so-called "seren leaders" of the biblical Philistines – whose name may be connected with the Luwian term "tarwanis," understood as "warlord" (Maeir & Hitchcock, 2017). Sometime after the early Iron Age, the charismatic "seren" slowly took on more and more characteristics of the local Canaanite ruling traditions. Biblical and Assyrian texts indicate that by the Iron IIB, the leaders of the Philistines were seen as local kings, of what Maeir and Shai describe as "patronage kingdoms" composed of a petty king who had a web of connections with local leaders, and below that, wide strata of urban and rural peasants (Maeir, 2019: 320; Maeir & Shai, 2016).

All of these examples demonstrate how situations with less political integration and more social mobility provide opportunities for strong charismatic leadership to change quickly the political and economic fortunes over large (relatively speaking) areas and integrating large groups of people, and many different types of settlements into a single political unit. With regard to different types of settlements, all of the archaeological sites discussed above provide evidence of increasing patterns of integration evidenced by settlement specialization and, in some cases, construction. Settlements in the Hesi region, including both Tell el-Hesi and Khirbet Summeily, provide strong evidence of political, or at least, economic integration and extra-regional interactions or both. As we look at the sites and the Hesi borderland region in the late Iron I and IIA, what are the driving factors behind this changing interaction and increasing integration? Here I have suggested that economics must have played a significant role in the regional integration of the southern areas of the Levant, leading to increasing regional integration and complexity. While I have focused on trade/economics and described the possible role of charismatic leaders, what were the roles played by competition, networking, belligerence, and other factors? While many or perhaps all of these factors undoubtedly played a part in the changing dynamics of the late Iron I and early Iron II, I believe the new sources of wealth from the south continues to be understated.

7 Some Concluding Comments on Sites in the Hesi Region

In the Hesi region, Tell el-Hesi, sitting on the best source of sweet water in the greater region, was re-occupied in the late Iron I or early Iron IIA. The new settlement included at the very least three large tripartite buildings. These can only be understood as facilities associated with large-scale storage and or stabling, or some related activity (barracks/housing?) that required larger buildings and administrative activity than was necessitated by local resource production and consumption. I would associate this settlement with the same type of activities undertaken by the Egyptians in Petrie's Pilaster Building a century earlier. However, unlike this earlier iteration, there is much less evidence (e.g., architectural traditions or material culture) for direct involvement or control from outside of the southern Levant (i.e. Egypt). This settlement at Hesi remained well-positioned to control the pasturage resources in the region and to move goods as part of a regional trade network through the area between the coastal plain and the Shephelah as well as north and south.

With regard to Summeily, establishing a settlement in addition to Hesi (if indeed the two settlements are contemporary) with an administrative function, is further evidence of the integration of the Hesi region into a larger regional entity/entities or network. Summeily could be what Hodder called a station along trade networks supplying subsidiary markets. The surrounding pasture or grassland could well have provided "meat on the hoof" for a variety of political entities while maintaining the movement of goods through the area. And resources, evidenced by bullae and stable isotope analyses of sheep/goat, were supplied to the settlement from the greater region, but not the coastal plain. This resource integration is not simply the incorporation of rural farmers/herders into a more complex socio-political entity, but a more deliberate attempt to establish *de novo* control, or at least, occupation, of a marginal area agriculturally speaking – a borderland or frontier – likely associated with a larger trade network.

The centers/cores with which the outposts and networks of the Hesi region were associated are hard to identify from this perspective. Using historical continuity, one could suggest that they are part of Philistia, or a nascent Judah or Israel, or Egypt. Or perhaps it is even possible that an otherwise unknown or unidentified entity that existed outside of any contemporary historical or later biblical or extra biblical textual tradition is responsible. Regardless, it seems that many of the complex processes often associated with increasing interaction and increased regional integration that typify the later Iron Age southern Levantine kingdoms of the ninth and eighth centuries BCE are evident quite early during the late Iron I and early Iron II in the regions discussed above. This early date for these processes makes sense when they are associated with the eleventh – ninth century exploitation of copper in the rift valley regions of Feinan and Timna and the beginnings of the spice trade from regions even further south. This renewed regional copper exploitation created significant sources of wealth and new opportunities in the form of mining, metal processing, and especially distribution. In the absence of direct political and economic control of the southern Levant from the outside by the once powerful Late Bronze Age imperial cores, I would suggest that local players maneuvered, organized, and coalesced, and were the primary actors in the activities leading to new elite formation and the more integrated occupations at all the settlements discussed or mentioned above. I would further implicate these same processes contributing to the formation of local southern Levantine kingdoms of the Iron IIB where we can see better evidence of border maintenance and territoriality (Blakely et al., 2014). So, what we are seeing in the greater Hesi region is early evidence for increased interactions and regional integration that must have a played a role in the early formations to the Iron II kingdoms of the southern Levant.

In the Hesi region, the late Iron I and early Iron II occupations at Hesi and Summeily provide evidence of the changing economic and political landscapes of the southern Levant on the heels of the Late Bronze Age collapse. They do so on a very local scale and demonstrate how these changing landscapes can have a very direct impact on micro-regional systems, affecting interactions, regional dynamics, and settlement functionality in borderland or frontier regions. And a nuanced approach and study of settlements in peripheries, such as the one here, demonstrates the potential of these types of regions for providing a better understandings of greater regional dynamics and evolving socio-political and economic landscapes than is sometimes appreciated.

References

Ben-Yosef, E. (Ed.). (2018). *Mining for ancient copper: Essays in memory of Beno Rothenberg*. Eisenbrauns.

Ben-Yosef, E. (2019). The architectural bias in current biblical archaeology. *Vetus Testamentum, 69*(3), 361–387.

Ben-Yosef, E., & Sergi, O. (2018). The destruction of Gath by Hazael and the Arabah copper industry: A reassessment. In I. Shai, J. R. Chadwick, L. Hitchcock, A. Dagan, C. McKinny, & J. Uziel (Eds.), *Tell it in Gath: Studies in the history and archaeology of Israel. Essays in Honor of A. M. Maeir on the occasion of his sixtieth birthday* (Ägypten und Altes Testament 90) (pp. 461–480). Zaphon.

Ben-Yosef, E., Higham, T., Levy, T. E., Najjar, M., & Tauxe, L. (2010). The beginning of iron age copper production in the Southern Levant: New evidence from Khirbat al-Jariya, Faynan, Jordan. *Antiquity, 84*, 724–746.

Ben-Yosef, E., Shaar, R., Tauxe, L., & Ron, H. (2012). A new chronological framework for Iron Age copper production at Timna (Israel). *Bulletin of the American Schools of Oriental Research, 367*, 31–71.

Blakely, J. A. (2000). Petrie's pilaster building at Tell el-Hesi. In L. E. Stager, J. A. Greene, & M. D. Coogan (Eds.), *Archaeology of Jordan and beyond: Essays in Honor of James A. Sauer* (pp. 66–80). Eisenbrauns.

Blakely, J. A. (2018). Tell el-Hesi: A type site for reevaluating so-called "Egyptian governors' residencies" of the South. *Palestine Exploration Quarterly, 150*(4), 271–295.

Blakely, J. A. & Hardin, J. W., with Banks, R., Ellis, G., Farrow, D., Hatfield, B., Ludvik, G. E., Morrow, M., Schadeberg, J. L., & Zwang, D. (2023). Dating the joint archaeological expedition's phantom stratum (IX): Bliss's City V at Tell el-Hesi. In J. A. Blakely, J. W. Hardin, & J. Spencer (Eds), *Tell el-Hesi VI. Bronze and Iron Age research in the Hesi region* (pp. 79–111). Penn State University.

Blakely, J. A., & Huster, Y. (2016). The Wadi el-Hesi region in 1256/7: An interpretation of John of Ibelin's contract with the Hospital of Saint John. *Crusades, 15*, 35–53.

Blakely, J. A., & Ktalav, I. (2017). Identifying and understanding residuality in Hesi's archaeological record: The malacological evidence. In J. Lev-Tov, A. Gilbert, & P. W. Hesse (Eds.), *The wide lens in archaeology: Honoring Brian Hesse's contributions to anthropological archaeology* (pp. 3–29). Society of Biblical Literature.

Blakely, J. A., Hardin, J. W., & Master, D. (2014). Expenditure of human capital on the southern/western borders of Judah in the 9th century as evidence of Judahite statehood. In J. R. Spencer, R. A. Mullins, & A. J. Brody (Eds.), *Material culture matters: Essays on the archaeology of the Southern Levant in Honor of Seymour Gitin* (pp. 33–51). Eisenbrauns.

Bliss, F. J. (1894). *A mound of many cities*. Macmillan.

Bookman, R., Enzel, Y., Agnon, A., & Stein, M. (2004). Late Holocene Lake levels of the Dead Sea. *Geological Society of America Bulletin, 116*, 555–571.

Bruins, H. J. (2017). *Late Bronze and Iron Age I dates of terraced wadi agriculture: Amalek lives in the land of the Negev?* Paper presented at International Workshop entitled, Archaeology and Life Science and Environment, Ariel University, Israel, 14 June 2017.

Cohen, R. (1979). The Iron Age fortresses in the Central Negev. *Bulletin of the American Schools of Oriental Research, 236*, 61–79.

Conder C. R., & Kitchener, H. H. (1880). *Map of Western Palestine. Scale 1:63,360, 26 sheets.*

Conder, C. R., & Kitchener, H. H. (1883). *The survey of Western Palestine: Memoirs of the topography, orography, hydrology, and archaeology* (Vol. 3). Judaea.

Dagan, Y. (1992). *Archaeological survey of Israel: Map of Lakhish (98)*. Israel Antiquities Authority.

Dagan, Y. (2006). *Archaeological survey of Israel: Map of Amazya (109)* (2 Vols). Israel Antiquities Authority.

Dever, W. G. (1996). The Tell: Microcosm of the cultural process. In J. D. Seger (Ed.), *Retrieving the past: Essays on archaeological research and methodology in Honor of Gus W. Van Beek* (pp. 37–46). Eisenbrauns.

Diqs, I. (1967). *A Bedouin Boyhood*. Allen and Unwin.

Elton, H. (1996). *Frontiers of the Roman empire*. Indiana University.

Fantalkin, A., & Finkelstein, I. (2006). The Sheshonq I campaign and the 8th-century BCE earthquake – More on the archaeology and history of the South in the Iron I-IIA. *Tel Aviv, 33*(1), 18–42.

Faust, A. (2019). The inhabitants of Philistia: On the identity of the Iron I settlers in the periphery of the philistine heartland. *Palestine Exploration Quarterly, 151*(2), 105–133.

Faust, A., & Weiss, E. (2005). Judah, Philistia, and the Mediterranean world: Reconstructing the economic system of the seventh century B.C.E. *Bulletin of the American Schools of Oriental Research, 338*, 71–92.

Faust, A., Katz, H., Ben-Shlomo, D., Sapir, Y., & Eyall, P. (2014). Tēl ʿĒtōn/Tell ʿĒtūn and its interregional contacts from the Late Bronze Age to the Persian-Hellenistic period: Between highlands and lowlands. *Zeitschrift des Deutschen Palästina-Vereins, 130*(1), 43–76.

Finkelstein, I. (1995). *Living on the fringe: The archaeology and history of the Negev, Sinai, and neighboring regions in the Bronze Age and the Iron Ages* (Monographs in Mediterranean archaeology, Vol. 6). Sheffield University Press.

Finkelstein, I. (1996). The philistine countryside. *Israel Exploration Journal, 46*, 225–242.

Finkelstein, I. (2020). The Arabah copper polity and the rise of Iron Age Edom: A bias in biblical archaeology? *Antiguo Oriente, 18*, 11–32.

Finkelstein, I., Langgut, D., Meiri, M., & Sapir-Hen, L. (2017). Egyptian imperial economy in Canaan: Reaction to the climate crisis at the end of the Late Bronze Age. *Ägypten und Levante/Egypt and the Levant, 27*, 249–259.

Fritz, V., Kempinski, A., Mittmann, S., & Weippert, M. (1983). *Ergebnisse der Ausgrabungen auf der Ḥirbet el-Mšāš (Tēl Māsōś) 1972–1975* (3 Vols). Harrassowitz.

Galaty, M., Parkinson, W., Cherry, J., Cline, E., Kardulias, P. N., Schon, R., Sherratt, S., Tomas, H., & Wengrow, D. (2009). Interaction amidst diversity: An introduction to the Eastern Mediterranean Bronze Age. In W. Parkinson & M. Galaty (Eds.), *Archaic state interaction: The Eastern Mediterranean in the Bronze Age* (pp. 29–51). School for Advanced Research Press.

Garfinkel, Y., & Ganor, S. (2018). Khirbet al-Ra'i near Lachish. In I. Shai, J. R. Chadwick, L. Hitchcock, A. Dagan, C. McKinny, & J. Uziel (Eds.), *Tell it in Gath: Studies in the history and archaeology of Israel. Essays in Honor of A. M. Maeir on the occasion of his sixtieth birthday* (Ägypten und Altes Testament 90) (pp. 943–955). Zaphon.

Garfinkel, Y., Ganor, S., & Hasel, M. G. (2014). *Khirbet Qeifaya, vol 2. Excavation report 2009–2013: Stratigraphy and architecture (Areas A, C, D, F)*. Old City Press.

Garfinkel, Y., Hasel, M. G., Klingbeil, M. G., Kang, H. G., Choi, G., Chang, S. Y., Hong, S., Ganor, S., Kreimerman, I., & Bronk Ramsey, C. (2019). Lachish fortifications and state formation in the Biblical Kingdom of Judah in light of radiometric datings. *Radiocarbon, 61*(3), 695–712. https://doi.org/10.1017/RDC.2019.5

Goodfriend, G. A. (1990). Rainfall in the Negev Desert during the Middle Holocene, based on C13 of organic matter in land snail shells. *Quaternary Research, 34*, 186–197.

Gophna, R. (1963). "Haserim" settlements in the Northern Negev. *Yediot, 27*, 173–180. (Hebrew).

Gophna, R. (1981). The Border between Judah and the Kingdoms of Gaza and Ashkelon Kingdoms in the light of the Archaeological Survey of Nahal Shiqma. In D. Krone (Ed.), *Proceedings of the Seventh World Congress of Jewish Studies: Held at the Hebrew University of Jerusalem, 7–14 August 1977, under the Auspices of the Israel Academy of Sciences and Humanities, vol. 2: Studies in the Bible and the Ancient Near East* (pp. 49–52). World Union of Jewish Studies.

Gottlieb, Y. (2018). Judah of iron vs. copper of Israel: The metalworking development in the land of Israel and its historical implications. In E. Ben-Yosef (Ed.), *Mining for ancient copper: Essays in memory of Beno Rothenberg* (Monograph series of the Sonia and Marco Nadler Institute of Archaeology) (pp. 435–454). Tel Aviv University.

Grigson, C. (2012). Camel, copper and donkeys in the Early Iron Age of the Southern Levant: Timna revisited. *Levant, 44*, 82–100.

Grossman, D. (2004). *Arab demography and early Jewish settlement in Palestine: Distribution and population density during the late Ottoman and early Mandate periods*. Transaction.

Hallote, R. (2014). A new suggestion regarding plaque figurines and a new figurine from Khirbet Summeily. *STRATA: Bulletin of the Anglo-Israel Archaeological Society, 32*, 37–47.

Hardin, J. W., & Blakely, J. A. (2019). Land use, regional integration, and political complexity: Understanding the Hesi region as pasturage during Iron Age IIA. *STRATA: Bulletin of the Anglo-Israel Society, 37*, 53–81.

Hardin, J. W., Rollston, C. A., & Blakely, J. A. (2014). Iron Age Bullae from Officialdom's periphery: Khirbet Summeily in broader context. *Journal of Near Eastern Archaeology, 77*(4), 299–301.

Herzog, Z., & Singer-Avitz, L. (2011). Iron Age IIA occupational phases in the coastal plain of Israel. In I. Finkelstein & N. Na'aman (Eds.), *The signal fires of Lachish: Studies in the archaeology and history of Israel in the Bronze Age, Iron Age, and Persian Period in Honor of David Ussishkin* (pp. 159–174). Eisenbrauns.

Higginbotham, C. R. (2000). *Egyptianization and elite emulation in Ramesside Palestine: Governance and accommodation on the Imperial periphery*. Brill.

Hodder, B. W. (1965). Some comments on the origins of traditional markets in Africa South of the Sahara. *Transactions and Papers, Institute of British Geographers, 36*, 97–105.

Holladay, J. S., Jr. (2006). Hezekiah's tribute, long-distance trade and the wealth of nations ca. 1000–600 B.C.: A new perspective ("Poor little [Agrarian] Judah" at the end of the eighth century B.C.: Dropping the first shoe). In S. Gitin, J. E. Wright, & J. P. Dessel (Eds.), *Confronting the past: Archaeological and historical essays on ancient Israel in Honor of William G. Dever* (pp. 309–331). Eisenbrauns.

Holladay, J. S., Jr., & Klassen, S. (2014). From bandit to king: David's time in the Negev and the transformation of a tribal entity into a nation state. In J. M. Tebes (Ed.), *Unearthing the wilderness: Studies on the history and archaeology of the Negev and Edom in the Iron Age* (Ancient Near Eastern studies 45) (pp. 31–45). Peters.

Huster, Y. (2015). *Ashkelon 5: The land behind Ashkelon*. Eisenbrauns.

Hütteroth, W. D., & Abdulfattah, K. (1977). *Historical geography of Palestine, Transjordan and Southern Syria in the late 16th century* (Erlanger Geographische Arbeiten Sonderband 5). Frankische Geographische Gesellschaft.

Jasmin, M. (2006). The emergence and first development of the Arabian trade across the Wadi Arabah. In P. Bienkowski & K. Galor (Eds.), *Crossing the rift: Resources, routes, settlement patterns and interaction in the Wadi Arabah* (Levant supplementary series) (Vol. 3, pp. 143–150). Oxford University Press.

Kang, H. -G. (2017). *The city gate of Tel Lachish Level V: Where is it?* Paper presented at the Annual Meeting of the American Schools of Oriental Research, Boston, 16–19 November.

Kang, H.-G., & Garfinkel, Y. (2021). The fortifications of areas CC and BC at Tel Lachish. State formation processes in the 10th century BCE Levant. *Jerusalem Journal of Archaeology, 1*, 352–374. https://openscholar.huji.ac.il/jjar

Kaniewski, D., Marriner, N., Bretschneider, J., Jans, G., Morhange, C., Cheddadi, R., Otto, T., Luce, F., & Van Campo, E. (2019). 300-year drought frames Late Bronze Age to Early Iron Age transition in the Near East: New palaeoecological data from Cyprus and Syria. *Regional Environmental Change*. https://doi.org/10.1007/s10113-018-01460-w

Khalidi, W. (Ed.). (1992). *All that remains: The Palestinian villages occupied and depopulated by Israel in 1948*. Institute for Palestine Studies.

Kiderlen, M., Bode, M., Hauptmann, A., & Bassiakos, Y. (2016). Tripod cauldrons produced at Olympia give evidence for trade with copper from Faynan (Jordan) to South West Greece, c. 950–750 BCE. *Journal of Archaeological Science: Reports, 8*, 303–313.

Langgut, D., Finkelstein, I., & Litt, T. (2013). Climate and the late bronze collapse: New evidence from the Southern Levant. *Tel Aviv, 40*, 149–175.

Langgut, D., Finkelstein, I., Litt, T., Neumann, F. H., & Stein, M. (2015). Vegetation and climate changes during the Bronze and Iron Ages (~3600-600 BCE) in the Southern Levant based on palynological records. *Radiocarbon, 57*, 217–235.

Larson, K. M. (2020). *Meat on the Hoof: A zooarchaeological isotopic investigation into administrative and cultic herd management at Khirbet Summeily*. MA thesis, Mississippi State University.

Larson, K. M. (2022). Meat on the Hoof: A zooarchaeological and isotopic investigation into administrative herd management at Khirbet Summeily. In J. R. Spencer, J. W. Hardin, & J. A. Blakely (Eds.), *Hesi after 50 and 130 years: Beginning a new generation of Hesi research, Tel el-Hesi 6* (pp. 141–160). Eisenbrauns.

Larson, K. M., Elizabeth, A., & Hardin, J. W. (2022). Resource allocation and rising complexity during the Iron Age IIA: An isotopic case study from Khirbet Summeily, Israel. *Quaternary International*. https://doi.org/10.1016/j.quaint.2022.03.022

Levy, T. E., Higham, T., Bronk Ramsey, C., Smith, N. G., Ben-Yosef, E., Robinson, M., Munger, S., Knabb, K., Schulze, J.P., Najjar; M., & Tauxe, L. (2008). High-precision radiocarbon dating and historical Biblical Archaeology in southern Jordan. *Proceedings of the National Academy of Sciences, 105*, 16460–16465.

Levy, T. E., Majjar, M., & Ben-Yosef, E. (2014). *New insights into the Iron Age archeology of Edom, southern Jordan*. Cotsen Institute of Archaeology.

Ludvik, G. E. (2020). A faience amulet of Pataikos/Ptah-Sokar from the Iron Age IIA border site of Khirbet Summeily, Israel. *Strata: Bulletin of the Anglo-Israel Archaeological Society, 38*, 11–30.

Maeir, A. M. (2019). Iron Age I Philistines: Entangled identities in a transformative period. In A. Yasur-Landau, E. H. Cline, & E. Rowan (Eds.), *The social archaeology of the Levant: From prehistory to the present* (pp. 310–323). Cambridge University Press.

Maeir, A. M., & Hitchcock, L. A. (2017). The appearance, formation, and transformation of philistine culture: New perspectives and new finds. In P. Fischer & T. Burge (Eds.), *The sea peoples up-to-date: New research on the migration of peoples in the 12th Centure BCE, Denkschriften der Gesamtakademie 81c contriuction for the chronology of the Eastern Mediterranean 35* (pp. 149–162). Austrian Academy of Sciences.

Magee, P. (2011). Shifts in ceramic production and exchange in late prehistoric Southeastern Arabia and the introduction of domesticated Camelus Dromedarius. In M. J. Conrad, P. Drechsler, & A. Morales (Eds.), *Between sand and sea: The archaeology of human ecology of Southwestern Asia* (pp. 213–226). Kerns Verlag.

Maher, E. F. (2014). Economy and exchange: Preliminary remarks on the Iron Age Fauna from Khirbet Summeily, 2011 season. *Journal of Near Eastern Archaeology, 75*, 33.

Maier, A. M., & Shai, I. (2016). Reassessing the character of the Judahite Kingdom: Archaeological evidence for non-centralized, kinship-based components. In S. Ganor, I. Kreimerman, K. Streit, & M. Mumcouglu (Eds.), *From Sha'ar Hagolan to Shaaraim: Essays in Honor of Professor Yosef Garfinkel* (pp. 323–340). Israel Exploration Society.

Martin, A. S., & Finkelstein, I. (2013). Iron IIA pottery from the Negev Highlands: Petrographic investigation. *Tel Aviv, 40*(1), 6–45.

Master, D. (2019). *Philistines in the highlands, the impetus for 10th century BCE centralization*. Paper presented at The First International Conference on the Archaeology of Judah: State Formation Processes in the 10th Century BCE Levant, Jerusalem, 7–8 April 2019.

Master, D. (2021). The philistines in the highlands: A view from Ashkelon. State formation processes in the 10th century BCE Levant. *Jerusalem Journal of Archaeology, 1*, 203–220. https://openscholar.huji.ac.il/jjar

Matthers, J. W. (1989). Excavations by the Palestine exploration Fund at Tell el-Hesi 1890–1892. In K. Dahlber & G. O'Connell (Eds.), *Tell el-Hesi: The site and the expedition, excavation reports of the American Schools of Oriental Research, Tell el-Hesi 4* (pp. 37–67). Eisenbrauns.

Mazar, A. (2010). Archaeology and the biblical narrative: The case of the united monarchy. In R. G. Kratz & H. Spieckermann (Eds.), *One god – One cult – One nation: Archaeological and biblical perspectives* (Beihefte zur Zeitschrift für die alttestamentliche Wissenschaft 405) (pp. 29–58). Walter de Gruyter.

Morris, E. F. (2005). *The architecture of imperialism: Military bases and the evolution of foreign policy in Egypt's new kingdom*. Brill.

Morris, E. F. (2018). *Ancient Egyptian imperialism*. Oxford University Press.

Nahshoni, P., & Talis, S. (2008). Khirbat Umm el-Baqar (Nahal Adorayim). *Hadashot Arkheologiyot, 120*.

Nahshoni, P., & Talis, S. (2015). An Iron Age site at Khirbat Umm el-Baqr (Nahal Adorayim). *'Atiqot, 81*, 69–105, 122*–123* [Hebrew].

Neumann, J., & Parpola, S. (1987). Climatic change and the eleventh-tenth century eclipse of Assyria and Babylonia. *Journal Near Eastern Studies, 46*, 161–182.

Neumann, J., & Sigrist, R. M. (1978a). Harvest dates in ancient Mesopotamia as possible indicators of climatic variations. *Climatic Change, 1*, 239–252.

Neumann, J., & Sigrist, R. M. (1978b). Harvest dates in ancient Mesopotamia as possible indicators of climatic variations: Addendum. *Climatic Change, 1*, 253–256.

Neumann, F. H., Kagan, E. J., Schwab, M. J., & Stein, M. (2007). Palynology, sedimentology, and palaeoecology of the Late Holocene Dead Sea. *Quaternary Science Reviews, 26*, 1476–1498.

Orland, I. J., Bar-Matthews, M., Kita, N. T., Matthews, A., & Valley, J. W. (2009). Climate deterioration in the Eastern Mediterranean as revealed by ion microprobe analysis of a speleothem that grew from 2.2 to 0.9 ka in Sorek Cave, Israel. *Quaternary Research, 71*, 27–35.

Parker, B. J. (2006). Toward an understanding of borderland processes. *American Antiquity, 71*(1), 77–100.

Parkinson, W. A., & Galaty, M. L. (2009). Introduction: Interaction and ancient societies. In W. A. Parkinson & M. L. Galaty (Eds.), *Archaic state interaction: The Eastern Mediterranean in the Bronze Age* (pp. 3–28). School for Advanced Research Press.

Petrie, W. M. F. (1891). *Tell el Hesy (Lachish)*. Palestine Exploration Fund.

Picard, L., & Solomonica, P. (1936). On the geology of the Gaza-Beersheva District. *Journal of the Palestine Oriental Society, 16*, 180–223.

Porter, J. L. (1858). *A handbook for travellers in Syria and Palestine*. J. Murray.

Porter, J. L. (1865). *Giant cities of Bashan*. J. Murray.

Reculeau, H. (2011). *Climate, environment and agriculture in Assyria*. Harrassowitz Verlag.

Robinson, E. (1841). *Biblical researches in Palestine, Mount Sinai and Arabia Petræa* (2 Vols). J. Murray.

Rösler, M., & Wendl, T. (1999). Frontiers and borderlands: The rise and relevance of an anthropological research genre. In M. Rösler & T. Wendl (Eds.), *Frontiers and borderlands: Anthropological perspectives* (pp. 1–30). Peter Lang.

Sergi, O. (2015). State formation, religion and "collective identity" in the Southern Levant. *Hebrew Bible and Ancient Israel, 4*, 56–77.

Smith, G. A. (1894). *The historical geography of the Holy Land*. Hodder and Stoughton.

Smith, G. A. (1931). *The historical geography of the Holy Land*, 25th revised ed. Hodder and Stoughton.

Sneh, A. (Ed.). (2008). *Geological map of Israel: 1:50,000: Qiryat Gat 10-IV*. Geological Survey of Israel.

Sneh, A., & Avni, Y. (Eds.). (2008). *Geological map of Israel: 1:50,000: Mishmar HaNegev 14-II*. Geological Survey of Israel.

Sneh, A., & Rosensaft, M. (Eds.). (2008a). *Geological map of Israel: 1:50,000: Ashqelon 10-III*. Geological Survey of Israel.

Sneh, A., & Rosensaft, M. (Eds.). (2008b). *Geological map of Israel: 1:50,000: Netivot 14-I*. Geological Survey of Israel.

Somaglino, C., & Tallet, P. (2013). A road to the Arabian Peninsula in the reign of Ramesses III. In F. Förster & H. Riemer (Eds.), *Desert road archaeology in ancient Egypt and beyond* (Africa praehistorica 27) (pp. 511–518). Heinrich Barth Institut.

Sperber, D. (1974). Drought, famine and pestilence in Amoraic Palestine. *Journal of Social and Economic History of Palestine, 17*, 272–298.

Stager, L. E. (1971). A problem of ancient topography: Lachish and Eglon. Appendix: Climatic conditions and grain storage in the Persian period. *Harvard Theological Review, 64*(2/3), 448–450.

Stewart, R. B. (1978). Archeobotanic studies at Tell-El-Hesi. *Economic Botany, 32*, 379–386.

Stillinger, M. D. (2018). *Archaeomagnetism as a geochronological tool: Dating a Levantine Iron Age conflagration*. Dissertation, University of Minnesota, Minneapolis.

Teichman, O. (1921). *The diary of a Yeomanry M. O.: Egypt, Gallipoli, Palestine and Italy*. T. Fisher Unwin.

Thomas, Z., Keimer, K. J., & Garfinkel, Y. (2021). The Early Iron Age IIA ceramic assemblage from Khirbet al-Ra'i. State formation processes in the 10th century BCE Levant. *Jerusalem Journal of Archaeology, 1*, 1–15. https://www.jjar.huji.ac.il

van der Steen, E. (2009). Tribal societies in the nineteenth century: A model. In J. Szuchman (Ed.), *Nomads, tribes and the state in the Ancient Near East: Cross-disciplinary perspectives, oriental institute seminars* (Vol. no. 5, pp. 105–118). Oriental Institute University of Chicago Press.

Warren, C. (1871). The plain of Philistia. *Palestine Exploration Fund Quarterly Statement, 1871*, 82–96.

Yahalom-Mack, N. (2009). *Bronze in the beginning of the Iron Age in the land of Israel production and utilization in a diverse ethno-political setting*. Hebrew University Press.

Yahalom-Mack, N., & Segal, I. (2018). The origin of the copper used in Canaan during the Late Bronze/Iron Age transition. In E. Ben-Yosef (Ed.), *Mining for ancient copper: Essays in memory of Beno Rothenberg* (pp. 313–331). Eisenbraun.

Agricultural and Economic Change in the Iron II Judean Shephelah as a Result of Geopolitical Shifts: A View from Tel Burna

Itzhaq Shai

Abstract Major geopolitical and social changes took place in the Southern Levant during the Iron II including the establishment of territorial states, and subsequently, the intervention of the Assyrian and Babylonian empires in local economies. These geopolitical shifts affected local economic and agricultural practices, along with other aspects of daily life and subsistence. This paper presents and analyzes changes in the economic practices of the people living in the Iron II site of Tel Burna in light of the geopolitical changes that occurred throughout the period.

Keywords Agriculture · Shepehlah · Iron Age II · Economy · Judah · Assyria and Babylonia

1 Introduction

The Shephelah is one of the four districts of the biblical Kingdom of Judah (e.g., Josh 15: 21–62). The region was intensively settled in the Iron II and was politically affiliated with the Kingdom of Judah, which is supported by the archaeological material (survey – Dagan, 2000; and excavations, e.g., Lachish – Ussishkin, 2004; Garfinkel et al., 2019; Beth Shemesh – Bunimovtiz & Lederman, 2016; Tel Burna – Shai et al., 2014; Shai, 2017; Tel Zayit – e.g., Tappy, 2008) along with the historical and biblical records (e.g., Hardin et al., 2012; Na'aman, 2013). In the last few decades, many ancient sites have been excavated in the Shephelah and multiple studies have dealt with different research topics on aspects such as state formation,

---

The research presented here on Tel Burna was funded by grants of the Israel Science Foundation (Grants No. 522/16; 257/19).

I. Shai (✉)
Ariel University, Ariel, Israel
e-mail: shai.itzick@gmail.com

© The Author(s), under exclusive license to Springer Nature Switzerland AG 2023
E. Ben-Yosef, I. W. N. Jones (eds.), *"And in Length of Days Understanding" (Job 12:12): Essays on Archaeology in the Eastern Mediterranean and Beyond in Honor of Thomas E. Levy*, Interdisciplinary Contributions to Archaeology, https://doi.org/10.1007/978-3-031-27330-8_30

borders, material culture, and historical and political changes (e.g., Mazar, 1985; Bunimovitz et al., 2009; Tappy, 2008; Lehmann & Niemann, 2014; Faust, 2020).

In a recent article, Finkelstein et al. (2021) examined the ancient economy of the Kingdom of Judah in light of its geographic and geo-political location. Yet, as the data regarding the different sites grows to include fauna, botanical remains, pottery, etc., archaeologists are beginning to gain a more complex understanding of the economy and the daily life of ancient peoples in the Iron II. Furthermore, the *longue durée* view (of the Iron II) enables us to examine correlations between geopolitical status and economic changes. Tel Burna, a Judahite site located in the western Shephelah, provides an excellent case study for conducting such research as it offers well-stratified evidence from the early Iron IIA through to the end of the Iron IIC with rich archaeological finds. Thus, this paper presents the finds from the various strata at Tel Burna, emphasizing the economic and agricultural evidence. Additionally, it discusses and suggests an explanation for aspects of both continuity and change in the economy of the region in light of geopolitical modifications.

2   The Shephelah in the Biblical Narrative

The economic and agricultural role of the Shephelah is well demonstrated in the biblical narrative. For example, in Jacob's blessing to Judah, he emphasized the importance of wine in the economy of the tribe (Gen 49: 11). The Chronicler also mentions other industry and manufacturing in the Shephelah region such as pottery (e.g., 1 Chr 4: 23) and textile production (e.g., 1 Chr 4: 21). In light of this, it was previously suggested (Demsky, 1966; Shai & Maeir, 2003) that *LMLK* pottery workshops were located in the Shephelah, and the region may have been a production center dating back to the Iron IIA.

3   The Archaeological Remains from Tel Burna

3.1   The Site

Tel Burna is located in the southern Shephelah along the northern banks of the Nahal Guvrin stream (Fig. 1). The site was first settled in the Early Bronze Age and occupation continued through to the Persian period (Uziel & Shai, 2010). The site reached its apex in the Late Bronze II and Iron II (Uziel & Shai, 2010; Shai & Uziel, 2014). Annual rainfall in the Iron II was approximately 430–510 mm per year (Bar-Matthews & Ayalon, 2004: Fig. 12), and was therefore sufficient for rain-fed agriculture (Orendi et al., 2017: 168).

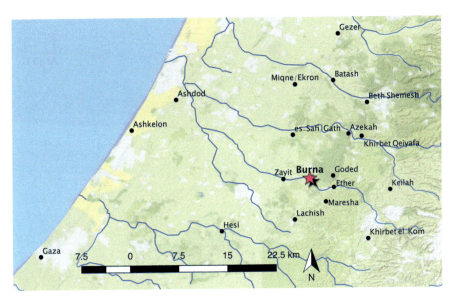

Fig. 1 Map showing the location of Tel Burna

To date, six areas have been excavated over 12 excavation seasons (Fig. 2), with substantial Iron Age remains uncovered in Areas A1, A2, B2, C, and G. The finds from these areas have been recovered from several strata well dated to the Iron II.

3.1.1 Early Iron IIA (Fig. 3)

This phase was exposed in Areas A1 and B2, and it appears that during this phase the summit was not yet enclosed by the casemate fortifications. In both areas there is evidence that the domestic buildings suffered heavy fire damage and destruction. Areas A1 and B2 sit on opposite sides of the summit approximately 70 metres apart, which suggests a widespread destruction as opposed to a localized or accidental fire event. In Area B2 the finds include dozens of smashed *in-situ* complete vessels well assigned to the early Iron IIA. While it is tempting to relate this destruction to Shoshenq's campaign, it is too early to correlate this destruction with a specific historical event.

3.1.2 Late Iron IIA (Fig. 4)

It was in this phase that the casemate wall on the summit was established (Shai et al., 2012). Since the fortification seals the Early Iron Age IIA destruction it is clear that this should be dated later than Kh. Qeiyafa (see also in the discussion). The fortification enclosed an area of 70 × 70 m, yet the settlement was not limited only to the enclosed area. Therefore, it was not a fortified town or a city but rather a

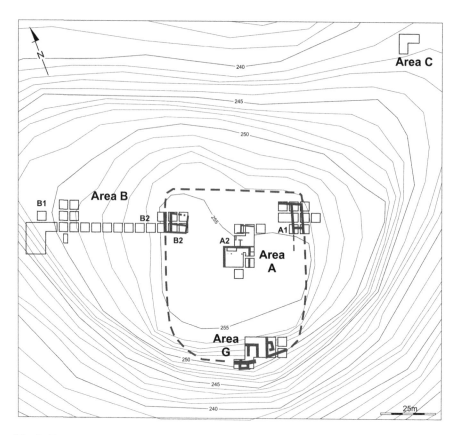

Fig. 2 Site plan with the excavation areas

fortress/stronghold on the summit with a small town surrounding it. The small summit that was enclosed by the wall was most probably used as a fortified stronghold. It has a clear view towards the north (i.e., to Philistine Gath), and it controlled the road running west-east through the Guvrin Valley and the adjoining diagonal route that connected the Sorek, Elah, Guvrin, and Lachish Valleys (see also Shai, 2017: 55). A large well-constructed multi-phase building was uncovered in Area A2. Although only fragments of the building were exposed that date to the Late Iron IIA, the plan of the building remained more or less the same in the subsequent Iron IIB phase (Shai, 2017: 48–49). Thus, there is a clear continuation in the town planning from the Late Iron IIA through the Iron IIB, as the casemate wall also shows the same pattern of continuation. Loom weights and an installation found in Area A1 reflect homemade textile activity in this period (Shai et al., 2012: 147).

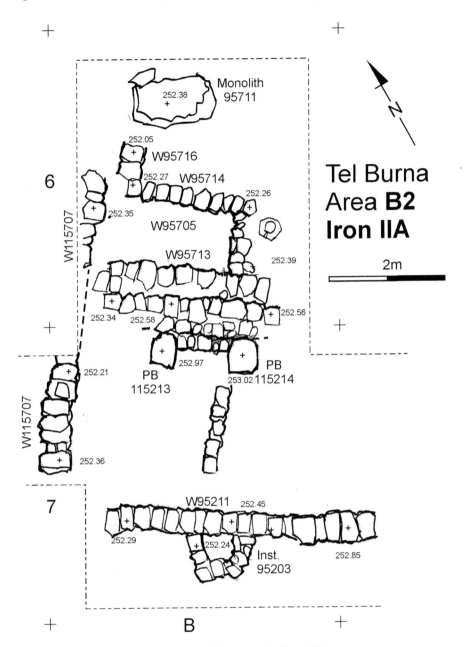

Fig. 3 Plan showing the remains of the early Iron Age IIA (Area B2)

3.1.3 Iron IIB (Fig. 5)

As mentioned above, the fortification wall continued to be in use during this period,

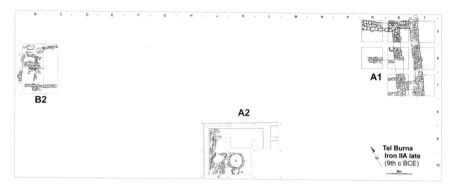

Fig. 4 Plan showing the remains of the late Iron Age IIA (A1, A2, B2)

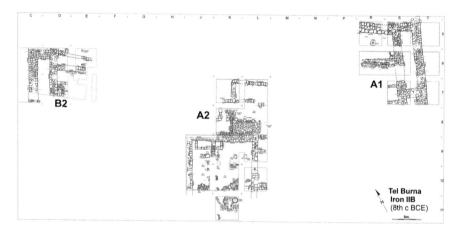

Fig. 5 Plan showing the remains of the Iron Age IIB (Areas A1, A2, B2, C)

although a glacis was added in order to support the wall along the western face (Shai & McKinny, 2020; Janovisky et al., 2020). In Area A2, a large new building was constructed on top of the earlier one along with additional features including the pavement and the courtyard north of the building. In the courtyard, a textile production installation was exposed where dozens of loom weights were found near two stones covered with plaster (Shai, 2017). In Area B2 a small domestic structure containing *in-situ* loom weights was discovered inside the fortification wall. A similar surface/structure abuts the inner wall in Area A1 and suggests that domestic structures within and against the fortification wall was part of the use of space and the layout of the town during the Iron IIB. This stratum exhibits evidence of a violent destruction that should be tentatively attributed to Sennacherib in the late eighth century BCE. The agricultural installations (cup marks, wine presses) in Area C were found both on the surface and through excavation. The excavated installations are dated to the eighth century BCE (Sharp et al., 2020).

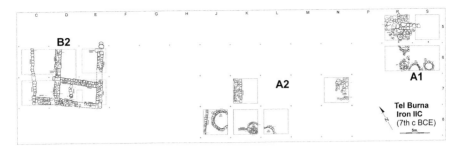

Fig. 6 Plan showing the remains of the late Iron Age (Areas A1, A2, B2, G)

3.1.4 Iron IIC (Fig. 6)

The Iron IIC is the final phase of the Iron Age. Several changes in architecture and use of space occurred in this final period. The town plan of a 70 × 70 m fortified summit was kept and the outer casemate wall continued to be in use, however, the inner wall went out of use (Shai et al., 2014: 147–148). Silos were also found across the summit, with a total of ten excavated to date. The main large (public?) building in A2 was not rebuilt as it was in previous periods, and instead had multiple silos built into the previous structure. The final phase of the gate structure on the south face of the fortification (Area G) is also dated to this period. Earlier phases of the gate are suspected although have not yet been excavated. Therefore, the archaeological evidence shows continued habitation throughout the entirety of the Iron II despite multiple destructions and fire events. It can be summarized that the site was still inhabited in the seventh century BCE, the town plan of a 70 × 70 m fortified summit was kept, yet the main large (public?) building that was constructed in the Iron Age IIA was not re-built and a series of silos appeared alongside private domestic houses.

3.2 *The Economic Background of the Site Through the Iron II*

Botanical remains indicate that the fields around Tel Burna were cultivated for various crops (Orendi et al., 2017: 166). Within the late Iron Age silos, the remains of grains, lentils, and olives were identified (Orendi et al., 2017: 176–177). As precipitation in the region of Tel Burna was sufficient for rain-fed agriculture (Riehl & Shai, 2015: 531), the cultivation of grapes was possible. The presence of presses clearly indicates that grapes were processed at Tel Burna (Riehl & Shai, 2015: 529–530), which also supports the theory that grapes were cultivated in the area. We hypothesize that the vineyards were present to the northeast of the Tel, which is the closest cultivation area to the installations and wine presses (Area C).

Textile activity is well attested at Tel Burna from a combination of both weaving tools (loom weights) and weaving plant material (linseeds/flax). The earliest indirect evidence is a large concentration of linseeds found in the Iron IIA destruction phase of Area B2. Slightly later in the Iron IIA, we see direct evidence for weaving in Area A1 with an installation and multiple loom weights. In the Iron IIB, another installation and dozens of loom weights were once again recovered from Area A2. A separate concentration of loom weights dated to the Iron IIB were also recovered from Area B2.

The lack or scarcity of imported vessels is evident throughout all the Iron II phases. This may reflect limited contact between the local community of Tel Burna with foreigners and, in turn, limited outside cultural influence on the local material culture. For example, very few LPDW vessels were found at Tel Burna, while in Jerusalem this decoration is well attested (Cohen-Weinberger et al., 2017). Interestingly, a lack, or limited number of imported vessels is also a phenomenon seen at nearby Philistines sites.

The presence of the pre-*LMLK*, *LMLK*, concentric and *rosette* stamped handles shows that the site was incorporated into the Judahite administration system. This is also supported by a private stamped handle found at Tel Burna bearing the name of EZR/HGI, which is a name that appears on handles found at other sites (Shai et al., 2014: 130).[1]

4 Discussion and Conclusions

Combining evidence from the botanical remains, agricultural installations, general layout of the site and weaving evidence from Tel Burna gives us the opportunity to gain a clearer understanding of the daily life of the local population during the Iron II. From a geopolitical point of view, it is clear that at least from the late Iron IIA the summit was enclosed by the casemate wall and that the site was a Judahite fortress (see Shai et al., 2012; Shai, 2017). The fortification was established not early than the late tenth century BCE, that means the site was fortified at least a few decades after the destruction of Kh. Qeiyafa (Shai et al., 2012; Shai, 2017).[2] The identification of Tel Burna as a Judahite site is based on various aspects of the material culture, including the ceramic assemblage, administration system (i.e., the pre-*LMLK-LMLK-Rosette* stamped handles[3]), the Judean pillar figurines, as well as the architecture and layout of the site. The location of Tel Burna between the main Philistine political center, Tell es-Safi/Gath, and the main Judahite administration city in the region, Lachish, as well as the strategic view from the summit of Tel Burna,[4] explains why the summit was fortified and the importance of this town in

---

[1] For the role of these stamped handles as a Judahite administration tools, see recently: Lipschits 2021; for a discussion on the date of the stamped handles, see also: Lipschits et al. 2010.

[2] For the debate on the dating of Kh. Qeiyafa, see for example: Garfinkel et al. 2012 and Finkelstein and Piasetzky 2015.

[3] For the pre-*Lmlk* type see: Shai and Maeir 2003 and Gitin 2006.

[4] To the west – all the coastal plain from Ashdod in the north to Gaza in the south; to the east the Hebron hills.

the Iron II. However, the site not only functioned as a garrison or a fortress, but it also seems that it was a small town with a local population that based its economy and daily life on the fields surrounding the Guvrin stream. Domestic buildings found in Area A1 and G outside of the fortification supports this conclusion. The presence of linseeds and multiple concentrations of loom weights within late Iron IIA and Iron IIB domestic structures suggests that domestic weaving production may have helped support the local economy at Tel Burna.

Olive oil production is well attested in the Shephelah by the late Iron IIA (e.g., Maeir et al., 2021; Finkelstein et al., 2021: 9–10), and continued to be one of the main sources of economic income in this region (Finkelstein et al., 2021: 9–10). In late Iron Age Philistine Ekron, over 115 olive presses were exposed and the city was the largest olive oil production center in the Levant (e.g. Gitin, 1997; Eitam, 1996). Changes in the local economy at Tel Burna appears to fit the changes required as a result of the Assyrian campaigns and tribute policy. This tribute policy likely forced Judah to adopt the regional specialized economy (see Finkelstein et al., 2021: 12–13 for the details on the specialization of each region).

The local community at Tel Burna were active producers of both primary and secondary agricultural products within the Shephelah (grain, olive oil, wine, textile, etc.). Interestingly the limited presence of imported ceramic vessels (both large and small closed vessels, serving vessels, and prestige vessels) may indicate low amounts of trade activity. However, Tel Burna's role in the local economy of the Kingdom of Judah and in the Shephelah in particular is well attested archaeologically, and the presence of Judahite administration tools (i.e., the stamped handles) shows that the site was integrated within the local Judahite administration and economic systems. It is clear that the site's main function was as a Judahite security and defense location. Yet, the material culture indicates that the local inhabitants had limited interactions outside of their immediate surroundings and managed a fairly closed local economic system with limited trade and foreign relationships.

References

Bar-Matthews, M., & Ayalon, A. (2004). Speleothems as climate indicators, a case study from Soreq Cave located in the Eastern Mediterranean Region, Israel. In R. W. Battarbee, F. Gasse, & C. Stickley (Eds.), *Past climate variability through Europe and Africa* (pp. 363–391). Kluwer Academic Publishers.

Bunimovitz, S., & Lederman, Z. (2016). *Tel Beth-Shemesh – A border community in Judah renewed excavations 1990–2000: The Iron Age* (Vol. 34). Penn State University Press.

Bunimovitz, S., Lederman, Z., & Manor, D. W. (2009). The archaeology of border communities: Renewed excavations at Tel Beth-Shemesh, Part 1: The Iron Age. *Near Eastern Archaeology, 72*, 114–142.

Cohen-Weinberger, A., Szanton, N., & Uziel, J. (2017). Ethnofabrics: Petrographic analysis as a tool for illuminating cultural interactions and trade relations between Judah and Philistia during the Iron Age II. *Bulletin of the American Schools of Oriental Research, 377*, 1–20.

Dagan, Y. (2000). *The settlement in the Judean Shephela in the second and first millennium B.C. – A test-case of settlement processes in a geographic region.* Unpublished PhD dissertation, Tel Aviv University. (Hebrew).

Demski, A. (1966). The 'House of Achzib' (A critical note on Micah 1:l4b). *Israel Exploration Journal, 16,* 211–215.

Eitam, D. (1996). The olive oil industry at Tel Miqne-Ekron during the Late Iron Age. In D. Eitam & M. Heltzer (Eds.), *Olive oil in antiquity: Israel and neighbouring countries from the Neolithic to the early Arab period* (pp. 167–198). Sargon.

Faust, A. (2020). Between the highland polity and Philistia: The united monarchy and the resettlement of the Shephelah in the Iron Age IIA, with a special focus on Tel ʿEton and Khirbet Qeiyafa. *Bulletin of the American Schools of Oriental Research, 383,* 115–136.

Finkelstein, I., & Piasetzky, E. (2015). Radiocarbon dating Khirbet Qeiyafa and the Iron I-IIA phases in the Shephelah: Methodological comments and a Bayesian model. *Radiocarbon, 57,* 891–907.

Finkelstein, I., Gadot, Y., & Langgut, D. (2021). The unique specialised economy of Judah under Assyrian rule and its impact on the material culture of the kingdom. *Palestine Exploration Quarterly,* 1–19. https://doi.org/10.1080/00310328.2021.1949531

Garfinkel, Y., Streit, K., Ganor, S., & Hasel, M. G. (2012). State formation in Judah: Biblical tradition, modern historical theories, and radiometric dates at Khirbet Qeiyafa. *Radiocarbon, 54,* 359–369.

Garfinkel, Y., Hasel, M. G., Klingbeil, M. G., Kang, H., Choi, G., Chang, S., Hong, S., Ganor, S., Kreimerman, I., & Bronk Ramsey, C. (2019). Lachish fortifications and state formation in the biblical kingdom of Judah in light of radiometric datings. *Radiocarbon, 61,* 695–712.

Gitin, S. (1997). The Neo-Assyrian empire and its western periphery: The Levant, with a focus on Philistine Ekron. In S. Parpola & R. Whiting (Eds.), *Assyria 1995: Proceedings of the 10th anniversary symposium of the Neo-Assyrian Text Corpus Project (September 7–11)* (pp. 77–103). Neo-Assyrian Text Corpus Project.

Gitin, S. (2006). The LMLK jar-form redefined: A new class of Iron Age II oval-shaped storage jar. In A. M. Maeir & P. De Miroschedji (Eds.), *I will speak the riddles of ancient times* (Archaeological and historical studies in honor of Amihai Mazar on the occasion of his sixtieth birthday) (Vol. 2, pp. 505–524). Eisenbrauns.

Hardin, J. W., Rollston, C. A., & Blakely, J. A. (2012). Biblical geography in Southwestern Judah. *Near Eastern Archaeology, 75,* 20–35.

Janovský, M., Horák, J., Ackermann, O., Tavger, A., Cassuto, D., Šmejda, L., Hejcman, M., Anker, Y., & Shai, I. (2020). The contribution of POSL and PXRF to the discussion on sedimentary and site formation processes in archaeological contexts of the southern Levant and the interpretation of biblical strata at Tel Burna. *Quaternary International, 618,* 24–34. https://doi.org/10.1016/j.quaint.2020.11.045

Lehmann, G., & Niemann, H. M. (2014). When did the Shephelah become Judahite? *Tel Aviv, 41,* 77–94.

Lipschits, O. (2021). *Age of empires: The history and administration of Judah in the 8th–2nd centuries BCE in light of the storage-jar stamp impressions.* Penn State University Press.

Lipschits, O., Sergi, O., & Koch, I. (2010). Royal Judahite jar handles: Reconsidering the chronology of the lmlk stamp impressions. *Tel Aviv, 37*(1), 3–32.

Maeir, A. M., Welch, E. L., & Eniukhina, M. (2021). A note on olive oil production in Iron Age Philistia: Pressing the consensus. *Palestine Exploration Quarterly, 153,* 129–144.

Mazar, A. (1985). Between Judah and Philistia: Timnah (Tel Batash) in the Iron Age II. *Eretz Israel, 18,* 300–324. (Hebrew).

Na'aman, N. (2013). The Kingdom of Judah in the 9th century BCE: Text analysis versus archaeological research. *Tel Aviv, 40,* 247–276.

Orendi, A., Smejda, L., McKinny, C., Cassuto, D., Sharp, C., & Shai, I. (2017). The agricultural landscape of Tel Burna: Ecology and economy of a Bronze Age/Iron Age settlement in the Southern Levant. *Journal of Landscape Ecology, 10,* 165–188.

Riehl, S., & Shai, I. (2015). Supra-regional trade networks and the economic potential of Iron Age II sites in the southern Levant. *Journal of Archaeological Science: Reports, 3*, 525–533.

Shai, I. (2017). Tel Burna – A Judahite fortified town in the Shephelah. In O. Lipschits & A. M. Maeir (Eds.), *"...as plentiful as sycamore-fig trees in the Shephelah" (I Kings 10:2) recent archaeological research in the Shephelah of Judah: The Iron Age* (pp. 45–60). Eisenbrauns.

Shai, I., & Maeir, A. M. (2003). Pre-lmlk jars: A new class of Iron Age IIA storage jars. *Tel Aviv, 30*, 108–123. https://doi.org/10.1179/tav.2003.2003.1.108

Shai, I., & McKinny, C. (2020). Canaanite votive offerings and their significance within their context at Tel Burna. *Israel Exploration Journal, 70*, 1–17.

Shai, I., & Uziel, J. (2014). Addressing survey methodology in the southern levant: Applying different methods for the survey of Tel Burna. *Israel Exploration Journal, 64*, 172–190.

Shai, I., Cassuto, D., Dagan, A., & Uziel, J. (2012). The fortifications at Tel Burna: Date, function, and meaning. *Israel Exploration Journal, 62*, 141–157.

Shai, I., Dagan, A., Riehl, S., Orendi, A., Uziel, J., & Suriano, M. (2014). A private stamped seal handle from Tel Burna, Israel. *ZDPV, 130*, 121–137.

Sharp, C., Šmejda, L., McKinny, C., Nicoll, K., Orendi, A., & Shai, I. (2020). Bedrock installations used and reused outside Tel Burna. *Judea and Samaria Research Studies, 29*(1), 5–24.

Tappy, R. (2008). Historical and geographical notes on the "lowland districts" of Judah in Joshua xv 33-47. *Vetus Testamentum, 58*, 381–403.

Ussishkin, D. (Ed.). (2004). *The renewed archaeological excavations at Lachish (1973–1994)*. Tel Aviv University Press.

Uziel, J., & Shai, I. (2010). The settlement history of Tel Burna: Results of the surface survey. *Tel Aviv, 37*, 227–245.

Gezer Destructions: A Case Study of a Border City

Steven M. Ortiz

Abstract The Lanier Center for Archaeology Tel Gezer excavations has recently concluded 10 seasons of excavations at Tel Gezer, Israel. This project has excavated five major destructions from the Late Bronze III to Iron Age IIB (thirteenth–eighth centuries BCE). These destructions have been associated with military campaigns from outside (e.g. Egyptian, Assyrian). This paper will present an overview of the nature of these destructions, the preservation of the archaeological record, and possible historical reconstructions. Discussion of the Gezer destructions in light of recent methodological and theoretical approaches to defining destruction layers in the archaeological record will be presented. Emphasis will be placed on a contextual approach to the identification of destructions in the archaeological record.

Keywords Gezer · Late Bronze Age · Iron Age · Shoshenq I

1 Introduction

It is an honor to contribute to Tom Levy's festschrift. Tom was an undergraduate student when he excavated at Tel Gezer with William Dever. This was the start of his archaeological career. It was not until many years later that Tom was able to visit the tel. This second visit was as the director of the Committee of Archaeological Policy of the American Schools of Oriental Research.[1] It was fun to reminisce with Tom about his time at Gezer as a student, as well as the academic program at the University of Arizona.

---

[1] Now called the American Society of Overseas Research.

S. M. Ortiz (✉)
Lanier Center for Archaeology at Lipscomb University, Nashville, TN, USA
e-mail: sortiz@lipscomb.edu

The archaeology of the Ancient Near East relies on the various destruction levels found in most multi-layered sites. The history of the region is written by various kings and empires marching through vast landscapes in search of resources and the expansion of power. Archaeologists quickly coordinated their stratified layers with historical events—mostly military. The collation of artifacts within these destruction layers was the main method for associating artifacts with a chronological datum. The various destruction layers were seriated across the cultural landscape as they were assigned to Egyptian, Assyrian, or Babylonian military campaigns. It was based on a simplistic model of: [conqueror] + destruction = archaeological correlate.

The attempt to define the parameters of "Destructions in the Archaeological Record" is a recent phenomenon, which is ironic since the southern Levant should have already developed a robust theory of destructions. This past decade has seen edited volumes attempting to define destructions within their larger social and historical contexts that focus on the Ancient Near East (Berlejung, 2012; Driessen, 2013b; Nigro, 2014). This is a welcome theoretical development as previous studies have focused on destructions within specific historical contexts (e.g. Hasel, 1998; Fiaccavento, 2014a, b; Höfflmayer, 2014).

Jan Driessen has noted that destructions are "so frequent that they must have formed part of normal life (2013a: 5)." He notes that crisis and destruction are commonplace—whether the agency is manmade such as outside invaders or local battles, or natural such as earthquakes, volcanoes, floods, and tsunamis. Three domains of destruction within archaeological inquiry and interpretation are defined. The first is the scale found within destruction levels in the archaeological record. Destructions can be found at all spatial and temporal levels; such as an attack on a city or earthquake, a single structure, or over a prolonged period of time such as a period of Assyrian or Babylonian conquests. This last scale is typical in the archaeology of the southern Levant as scholars discuss the effects of the thirteenth century collapse and the Egyptian campaigns of the New Kingdom. The second domain is destruction deposits that are residues of events—whether a natural crisis, conflict, or purposeful such as the destruction of objects for a ritual. The third domain is the Pompeii Premise. Driessen notes that this event has influenced our way of looking at archaeological contexts as circumstances that are "hermetically sealed and hence completely reflect the moment preceding the destruction." (2013a: 12).

Cunningham (2013) also attempts to place archaeological destructions within a theoretical framework. He discusses three domains as well: Destructions…*in archaeology, for archaeology, and by archaeology.* Like Driessen, Cunningham acknowledges that the nature of the archaeological data is mostly destructions. He notes paradoxically that the process of destructions leaves deposits, which when preserved, serve as the framework for archaeological reconstructions. His second domain focuses on human behavior and how destructions are innate in humans. He provides examples from modern life and notes that civilization consists of a cycle of building, demolition, and rebuilding (2013: 53), implying that destruction is part of the process of creating. The third domain discussed is the fact that the nature of excavations is also destructive. He posits that we need to think of excavation as a "form of displacement rather than destruction, [where] we find ourselves back in the continuum of contextualization linked both to the 'past' as represented by the artifactual record and to the future as that record is reconfigured and projected to its various audiences (ibid, 55)."

2 Methodology: Typology of Destructions in the Southern Levant

As most have acknowledged that destruction is a dominant paradigm within the archaeological record, scholars have shifted their focus to try and develop models of 'types' of destructions. The debate is not whether or not we have evidence of a destruction; but how do we define the destruction (whether it is human activity or natural); how do we contextualize remnants of destruction (distribution of weapons, dead bodies); and attempts at a historical reconstruction of the 'event' that is represented by the destruction.

Current research has addressed the following: (1) Identification of destructions (Finkelstein, 2009), (2) Scale of Destructions (Finkelstein, 2009), (3) and how to differentiate between a manmade vs. natural destruction (i.e. Earthquakes) (Cline, 2011; Dever, 1992a; Edelman, 2012; Nur & Cline, 2000). Igor Kreimerman (2016) in several studies has attempted to define the nature of destructions by conflict. He has delineated destructions by conflict and siege warfare according to the distribution and analysis of long-range weapons (e.g. arrowheads, sling projectiles). He isolates some principles. First, that the destruction of cities should be separated from the actual conquest event. Some cities were destroyed even if the city capitulated without any armed resistance to the invading army. He posits that evidence of siege warfare is not necessarily a destroyed city but evidence of long-range weapons found in the destruction. He also notes that there were only five sites with destruction layers predating Iron Age IIB that had evidence of siege. In a later article he expands on this pattern and concludes that siege warfare was not practiced in the Late Bronze or Iron Age I. Kreimerman also focused on evidence of casualties in Middle Bronze—Iron Age destructions (2017b). He notes that human skeletons are very rare in destruction contexts in the southern Levant. This phenomenon is rather surprising to the public as the effect of the *Pompeii premise* is widely accepted and it is assumed that there would be evidence of battle casualties. Every effort was made to remove bodies from the destruction debris. If skeletons remained it was because (1) the skeletons were not found soon after death, (2) they were buried under thick debris and their recovery was difficult, (3) the site was abandoned, or (4) they were left intentionally as a punishment (Kreimerman, 2017a: 24). Other studies have emphasized the nature of mudbrick collapse; discerning geoarchaeological patterns of mudbrick detritus (Shahack-Gross, 2017; Shahack-Gross et al., 2018) or using experimental archaeology to test the nature of the pattern of mudbrick collapse due to fire (Forget et al., 2015; Forget & Shahack-Gross, 2016; Kreimerman & Shahack-Gross, 2018).

2.1 Models for Destructions in the Archaeological Record

Several scholars have recently proposed typologies for identifying destructions in the archaeological record. Finkelstein has proposed three identifying features for a destruction, and suggests that we need at least two of them to define a stratum as a destruction (Finkelstein, 2009: 113). In the same article he analyzes the destructions at Megiddo in light of other destructions and proposes at least three scales of destruction—from partial destruction to complete annihilation, such as Megiddo VIA (ibid, pp. 120–121). Contrary to Finkelstein's analysis, Eric Cline (2011) proposes that there was a destruction at Megiddo VIA—but the culprit was an earthquake and not human invaders. Hence attempts to find earthquakes in the archaeological record entered the debate (see discussion below). Kreimerman (2017a) has focused on the material correlates of destruction events, and indirectly variables of agency as it patterns the destructions.

2.1.1 Megiddo Destruction Scale

Israel Finkelstein (2009) has developed a model ("The Megiddo Destruction Scale") to determine the extent of a destruction at a site. He uses Megiddo strata for his model development: Stratum VIIA (Late Bronze) and Iron Age Strata VIA and VA-VB. He coalesces the results of the previous excavations (e.g. University of Chicago, Schumacher Excavations, and Yadin's Excavations) with the current Tel Aviv University excavations. He notes that "a real destruction of a settlement" should consist of two of the following features (2009: 113):

1. A black layer with charcoal, representing burnt beams, on the floor, usually overlaid with a thick ashy layer.
2. A thick accumulation of collapse—of bricks or stones—on the floor. This accumulation can at times be as much as one meter or more deep. In the case of bricks and a strong fire, the bricks may turn red or even white.
3. In most cases, an accumulation of finds, mainly broken pottery vessels, on the floors.

A second component of his method, is a tri-level scale of destruction (2009: 120). He notes that ancient cities could be destroyed in military raids by a local neighboring power or an outside campaign (e.g. Egypt, Assyria, Aram). The degree of destruction depends on the aims of the *destroyer*.

Scale 1—partial destruction of a city with no occupational gap following it.
Scale 2—A more severe destruction, with evidence for conflagration and/or collapse, sometimes followed by a short abandonment.
Scale 3—complete annihilation of a settlement with evidence for a heavy conflagration, wall and roof collapse, and large assemblages of finds on the floors. An occupational gap of some sort follows.

Based on these various levels he defines four major destructions of Megiddo using his scale and provides an historical reconstruction for each of the destruction events of the site in relation to other sites within the northern region. Basically, Finklestein's model attempts to determine the goals of the conqueror, whether it is only to subjugate the populace or replace the elite with a new administrative apparatus. He notes that total annihilation of a settlement (Scale 3) is unusual and only occurred in Stratum VIA at Megiddo.

2.1.2 Integrative Paradigm Model

Michael Hasel (2016) also offers a typology of destruction; his model is focused on agency. He proposes an integrative paradigm that incorporates archaeological and historical correlates. His model emphasizes four domains of inquiry: focus, extent, means, and content of destruction. He raises the problem of various scholars dating the same destruction to different conquerors and proposing different historical reconstructions. Hasel uses the example of a destruction layer at Gezer traditionally assigned to the Egyptian king of 1 Kings 9: 16 (Siamun?) and Finkelstein's redating it to Sheshonq (Finkelstein, 1996: 183, 2000, but see Ortiz & Wolff, forthcoming). He illustrates the lack of clear procedures among Near Eastern Archaeologists to develop clear archaeological correlates for connecting specific destructions to historical events. The *focus of destruction* is the scale of the campaign—was it against a single city or a region of the country. The *extent of destruction* addresses questions concerning a particular site and how much of it was destroyed (this would correspond with Finkelstein's three-tiered scale model). The *means of destruction* assesses the physical correlates present in archaeological contexts. He isolates these correlates as architectural features (wall and ceiling conditions), material culture, and extent of burning. The *content of destruction* refers to "the destruction of the life-support system of the enemy." (2016: 214). This is a bit more difficult to determine archaeologically. Hasel points out the various written sources that discuss the fields, orchards and crops that were destroyed or confiscated. He states that this must also be taken into account when we define destructions in the archaeological record. Lastly, Hasel discusses the effect of destruction on the inhabitants and the continuity or discontinuity of life at a given site. Hasel's model emphasizes the nature of destruction from a historical perspective.

2.1.3 Typology of Destruction Layers

The third model is developed by Kriemerman (2017a) who has studied destruction in the archaeological record from various perspectives. He provides a typology of destruction based on the Late Bronze—Iron Age IA period in the southern Levant. One of the features of Kriemerman's model is that it accounts for previous excavation reports which would be more descriptive versus adopting a theoretical model to interpret the archaeological correlates. His model starts first with defining *destruction* layers (similar to Finkelstein's model). He posits that a destruction layer must fulfill at least one of the following two criteria (2017a: 176).

- The layer must contain abundant finds and especially *de facto refuse* on many of the floor levels. The finds should consist of complete or broken pottery vessels, metal objects and prestige items. Among the pottery vessels, relatively light objects that could easily be carried should also be present.
- There is evidence for conflagration in places other than cooking or industrial area.

After defining a destruction layer in the archaeological record, the next phase is to determine whether it is caused by a primary or secondary correlate. A primary correlate refers to human agency—either an abandonment or devastation process. Abandonment refers to actions of the inhabitants such as concealing of hoards or curation of objects while devastation refers to the actions of the destroyer such as looting, intentional mutilation of objects and architectural features as well as burning the site. A component of primary correlates is the outcome of the destructions (quick reoccupation, reconstruction following a new plan, or a hiatus of at least a few decades). Kriemerman notes that secondary correlates are not less important than the primary but that they are less commonly reported or require a great deal of interpretation (2017a: 179). Secondary correlates are *crisis architecture*,[2] termination rituals, presence of long-range weapons (evidence of warfare), evidence for earthquakes, and intentional mutilation of objects.

Like Hasel, an aspect of Kriemerman's model is the destruction within its spatial context. He notes that the data is partial and misleading in many reports. Most will describe a destruction but not the extent across a site. The second issue is that many sites are multi-layered and the later layers can alter earlier layers of destruction. A third issue is that modern excavations are slowly and meticulously excavated and only a small percentage of a site is uncovered, hence a reconstruction of a site is based on partial data. Similar to Finkelstein's model he proposes four types (scale) of destruction (2017a: 182–184):

1. Complete Burning of an Entire City
2. Signs of Fire only in the Public Buildings
3. Signs of Fire by the Fortifications
4. No signs of Fire
5. Other destructions

These types are similar to Finkelstein's model based on the scale of destruction with the exception of defining the location of the destruction within a city.

---

[2] Adopted from Driessen who defines crisis architecture as specific and sudden short term architectural changes to come as a response to situations of social crisis (Driessen, 1995: 66).

2.2 Earthquakes

Several scholars have attempted to discern between an earthquake and human agency. The Megiddo Stratum VIA destruction has prompted the debate whether this destruction is attributed to a military campaign or an earthquake (Marco et al., 2006). Finkelstein has proposed that the destruction is part of a military campaign (2009) while Cline (2011) proposes that the destructions are due to an earthquake. There have been several studies on earthquakes in the biblical and historical texts (e.g. Dever, 1992a; Edelman, 2012) as well as earthquakes to explain the Late Bronze Age collapse (Jusseret & Sintubin, 2012; Nur & Cline, 2000). The earthquake debate was influential in Kreimerman developing a model that added a typological model that differentiated between human agency and natural disasters.

3 The Lanier Center for Archaeology- Tel Gezer Excavation Project[3]

Gezer is located at Tell Jezer (Tell Jazari), 8 km (5 mi.) south-southeast of Ramleh. It is located in the Aijalon Valley overlooking the southern coastal plain. The Aijalon Valley is a broad basin covered with rich alluvium, it is an excellent plain for grain. The Aijalon Valley is the northern limit of the Judean Foothills (Shephelah) which serves as a natural border between the hill country and the coastal plain. The Shephelah was known for its olives and sycamore trees (1 Chron. 27: 28; 1 Kings 10: 27). Annual rainfall averages 400–500 mm (16–22 in). The intersection of the international and regional highways, along with the confluence of the two coastal regions (southern coastal plain and Sharon plain), the hill country, and the Shephelah, make this area an important regional hub. The geographical location is significant because of its proximity to the major north-south international coastal highway (so-called Via Maris), from Egypt to Mesopotamia. It also guards the junction of the coastal highway with the principal highway from the coast up to the hill country via the Beth Horon ascent.

Tel Gezer is a 33-acre rectangular shaped mound and situated at 225 m above sea level. The tel consists of a western and eastern hill with a valley between forming a saddle. The western hill is higher and where the acropolis is located. To the southeast of the eastern hill is a natural spring.

---

[3] The project was sponsored by the Tandy Institute for Archaeology at Southwestern Baptist Theological Seminary from 2006 to 2017. This institute and the associated academic program were dissolved by a new administration in 2020. The Lanier Center for Archaeology (LCA) was established at Lipscomb University where a new academic program as well as a research institute was established in 2021. The LCA has now assumed the research and field projects of the previous Tandy Institute.

Two major excavations were conducted from 1902 to 1909 by R.A.S. Macalister (Macalister, 1912) and another from 1964 to 1973 by William G. Dever and Joe D. Seger (Dever et al. 1974; Dever et al., 1970, 1986; Gitin, 1990; Seger et al., 1988). Several smaller excavations were led by Raymond Weill (1913, 1923), Maeir (2004), Zelwer-Silberberg (1942), Alan Rowe (1934, 1935a, b), Dever (1984, 1985, 1986, 1990) and Dever and Younker (1990). The Tandy Institute for Archaeology have conducted 10 seasons of excavations from 2006 to 2017. This last excavation of Gezer was located on the southern part of the tel within the saddle between the western and eastern hills, west of the so-called "Solomonic" or six-chambered gate[4] and east of HUC's Fields VII and X (Fig. 1). The excavations are designed to unite the Iron Age architectural elements and cultural horizons of Field VII and Field III of the HUC excavations with our renewed excavations, thus allowing for optimal reconstruction of the growth and expansion of the Iron Age city as well as artifact distributional patterns.

3.1 Gezer Destructions

To date, the Tandy excavations have 14 major strata (see Table 1), of these there is evidence for five major destructions as well as rebuilding that might correspond to earthquake destruction. This is similar to the HUC excavations.[5] Summaries of

Fig. 1 Gezer Aerial: Overview of excavations (2006–2017)

---

[4] R.A.S. Macalister's 'Maccabean Castle', Hebrew Union College's Field III.

[5] A noticeable difference is that they have evidence for destruction in certain areas of the site while in another field, they might not have evidence. This suggests that either there was destruction due to military attacks/human invaders only in particular sections of the city, or the evidence was only preserved in particular contexts. We will discuss this below.

Table 1 Tel Gezer stratigraphic table

Strata	Dates	Description	HUC excavations
1	Modern	HUC dump: excavation trenches, dumps, rock piles	
2	Modern (ca. 1800–1950)	Bergheim Estate, Abu Shusheh, Macalister ackfill and trenches	
3	Hellenistic	Domestic buildings, walls (some reused IA), kilns, silo, several pits above Four Room House; *HUC:* reused gate	Strata IIA-C, III
4	Persian	Ceramic, Retaining wall (A4/5), Dog burials, pits	IV
5	Late Iron Age IIc	Small building, Silos, wall stubs, pits	V
	Destruction: 734 Assyrian Destruction (Tiglath Pileser III)		
6A	IA IIB 9th–8th	This phase represents minor building/construction modifications Enlarging south wall of 4 Room House, Rebuild of Industrial Building C	VI
6B		Public: Administrative Buildings A-B, Industrial Building C (Oil Production?); Rebuilt fortification walls, 4 room house, courtyard, street; *HUC:* domestic buildings (Field VII)	
	Destruction		
7	IA IIA (10th/early 9th)	Domestic: Units A-E [Unit E =rebuild of Building 52136, enlarged and strengthened], Dog burials. *HUC:* 4-chambered gate	VII
	Destruction: Sheshonq I		
8	IA IIA Mid-10th	Public: Central Administrative Courtyard Building, Fortifications: Casemate city-wall, monumental flagstone pavement, *HUC:* 6 chambered Gate (Field III), Buildings 52136, 52057: larger walls plus cobble floor and tabun, Fortifications: Single-line City-wall and rebuild glacis. *HUC:* 6-chambered gate	VIII
9	IA Ic (10th)	Rectangular Building with Tabun 62067, courtyard with Tabun 82007	
	Destruction: Siamun		
10A	IA Ib 11th/10th	Isolated walls beneath casemate, Complex of Building Units, City wall, Glacis and curb	IX
10B		Complex of building units, city wall	XI
11	IA Ia/b (12th)	Complex of building units, city wall	XIII–XII
12A	LB IIB (LB III/IAIA)	Repair, rebuild of 12B buildings	XIV
	Destruction-Merenptah		
12B	LB IIB	Patrician House, various wall stubs	XV
13	LBIIA	W94123, 94127 (massive building)	XVI
14	MB IIC	Walls and Glacis	XVIII

these excavations and full descriptions of the destructions have been published in detail elsewhere (Ortiz & Wolff, 2017, 2019, 2021).

3.1.1 Stratum 12

The excavations by the Tandy Institute for Archaeology have revealed a large patrician house typical for this period (Fig. 2). This building sat on the southern slope of the western hill where about 2 meters of the building eroded down the slope. The building complex consists of multiple rooms. There is a large rectangular main room leading into an industrial room (A), and two southern rooms (B and C). There is a courtyard with a bin (E), and an auxiliary western room or another building (F).

Industrial Room A is about 10 × 5 m with entrances to Units B and C to the south and two entrances to Unit D to the north. This room is only partially excavated as a later Iron Age I wall was built over this LB building and the wall line remains in situ. This room had several installations. There was a vat in the NE corner of the room with a circular disc-shaped stone installation. The stone was not sunk into the surface but sat on top of the surface. It is also smoothed on top, apparently well-worn from the activity. About 2 m southwest of this installation was a cylindrical roller, probably used in conjunction with the stone installation. Remnants of a cobble surface were found in this room as well as a third installation consisting of a line of stones forming a trough possibly to support storejars and a large pithoi. Several small finds such as scarabs and cylinder seals were also found within this destruction (Rooms B and C).

The Main Room (Unit D), ca. 10 × 5 m was north of the industrial room. It was at a slightly higher elevation as it sat higher up the slope of the western hill. About half the room was removed by later pits. We have remnants of cobble surfaces as well as a central wall running east-west with engaged pillars serving as a support wall for the ceiling and a room divider wall. This room had two entrances from

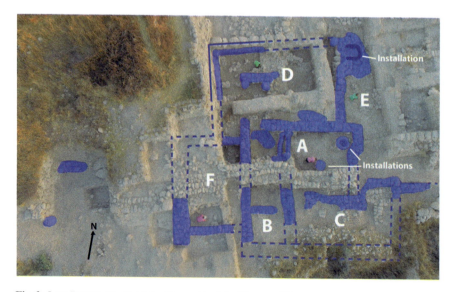

Fig. 2 Late Bronze Age Patrician House (Aerial of Stratum 12)

Units A–C to the south and an exterior entrance in the SE corner into Unit E. Inside this room was found a bifacial rectangular faience plaque. It had a barrel-shaped top with a cartouche of Thutmose III flanked by a truth feather on each side. This is a typical XIX Dynasty product commemorating the name of the great pharaoh of the XVIII Dynasty. Unit D led out to Unit E, which is probably a paved courtyard with a bin. While this Unit was also disturbed by a later pit and foundation deposit, several complete storage jars were found in destruction debris. Based on a comparison of other Late Bronze Age buildings—this is a large residency, perhaps an elite residency.

This building was destroyed in a fierce conflagration. In the summer 2017 excavations, we found the remains of three individuals, two adults and one child. In Room A among the installations was an adult lying on their back with hands over their head. Next to them was a youth. Both of these bodies were badly burnt—most of the bones were decomposed. As we were closing down for the season, we found the remains of a well-preserved third individual (Fig. 3). This adult was curled up in a fetal position, probably shielding themselves from the collapse of the building as several stones and mudbrick debris were found on the skeleton. Based on the pottery, the stratigraphic context, and the glyptic material, the destruction of this building dates to the thirteenth century BCE. It is likely associated with the Merneptah campaign.

Fig. 3 Human skeleton in southwest corner of Room D of Late Bronze Age Patrician House

3.1.2 Stratum 11, 10

Our Strata 11–10 were constructed above the Late Bronze Age Stratum 12 (Fig. 4). There was a major phase with a building complex (Stratum 11), which contained Philistine bichrome (Phil 2). This building complex was rebuilt in Stratum 10, which also had a major remodel. The last phase of this series of buildings consists of a pillared room complex with five storage rooms built up against an exterior city wall (see Fig. 4). Evidence of destruction was found throughout the building, but especially in two major rooms; the pillared room and one of the storerooms. This destruction is dated to the mid tenth century BCE.[6] One of the unique finds was a group of mushroom clay stoppers, one of them stamped with glyptics associated with Siamun—a pharaoh of the 21st Dynasty, who some scholars propose had a campaign in the Southern Levant.

Stratum 11 was built directly on the remnants of the Late Bronze Age building, as some of the founding levels of Iron Age I walls sat on Late Bronze Age floors and destruction. The builders were evidently aware of the earlier building, but nevertheless the settlement was built on a completely new plan. The Stratum 11 settlement consists of a major building with several units between it and the series of storage units forming the perimeter wall. The excavations uncovered only the southeast corner of the building. It is constructed from large boulders. South and west of this building were several units that contained installations, sunken storage jars, and a

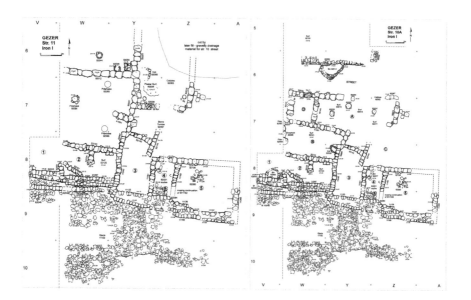

Fig. 4 Iron Age I: Plans of Stratum 11 and 10A

---

[6] See Ortiz and Wolff (2021) for discussion of dating.

tabun, and featured various surfaces such as cobbles, plaster, and beaten earth. There were three foundation deposits, all variations of the typical lamp-and-bowl deposit of this period. Of the three, one featured three bowls and a lamp between the bowls; another had two "Gezer bowls" with a lamp between them; and the third comprised a chalice, a bowl, and two unfired bowls (a feature described by Macalister, 1912: 436) with a lamp between them. Another interesting element of this phase was the seemingly intentional burial of juglets by walls. The Stratum 11 plan went out of use without leaving any evidence of destruction, except for the stone debris uncovered in the main building (Unit A).

The Stratum 10 city continued to use the series of rooms along the perimeter wall, but the rest of its plan was very different, although a few of the same wall lines were used in the building of the new walls. This plan was modified in the stratum's last phase (Fig. 4), perhaps as a shift to a cultic pillared building with three pillars. The finds included a spearhead, a miniature rattle, the six-toed foot of a ceramic figurine, and three storage jars that were found partially sunken beneath the floor level in the west of the building. Almost every room yielded at least one restorable storage jar. Unit 3 (the largest of the storerooms built against the wall) contained nearly half a meter of ash and destruction. This room contained two storage jars and a multi-handled krater, along with seven mushroom-shaped clay stoppers. One of these stoppers was stamped with a pre-Early Iron Age mass-produced seal (Münger et al., forthcoming).

The series of superimposed buildings in this area are public, unlike the typical Iron Age I courtyard houses that were excavated on the acropolis (Field VI of HUC). All the surfaces were either beaten earth or plastered. The pottery is typical Iron Age I with minimal Philistine Bichrome pottery (it is more common in Stratum 11). Most of the complete vessels were storage jars, lamps, bowls, and juglets, with the occasional chalice and multi-handled krater. The last phase of Stratum 10 was violently destroyed; almost every unit and room contained evidence of this destruction. The HUC excavations attributed this to the Egyptian Pharaoh who gave the city to Solomon as a dowry (Dever et al., 1970: 61, 1974: 59). Since the HUC excavations, however, evidence for Egyptian 21st Dynasty activity has accumulated (Münger, 2003). The end of this phase is dated to the mid tenth century BCE (Fig. 5).

3.1.3 Stratum 8

The next chapter in Gezer's history saw a radical change in the city plan.[7] A new fortification system with an administrative complex was built in the saddle and stratigraphically on top of the Iron Age I destruction (Fig. 6). A casemate city wall was built along with a six-chambered gate. This fortification was known from previous excavations and the gate has become infamous as the 'Solomonic Gate.' The

---

[7] Stratum 9 represents an ephemeral phase constructed on top of stratum 10. It consists of foundation remnants of a single domestic structure.

Fig. 5 Stratum 10A destruction

Fig. 6 Administrative quarter: Iron Age IIA (Stratum 8)

administrative quarter was west of the six-chambered gate and consisted of a large administrative building (ca. 20 × 25 m), monumental stairway, and fortification system. The building is the typical courtyard administrative building earlier referred to as *Bit Hilani*-type; now Lateral-Access Podium (LAP) Structures or Central Hall Tetra-Partite residencies (Sharon & Zarzecki-Peleg, 2006; Lehmann & Killebrew,

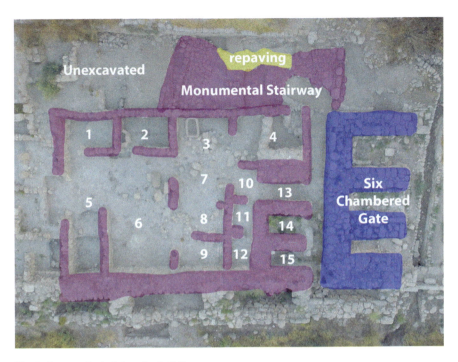

Fig. 7 Stratum 8 administrative building

2010). Our Administrative Central Hall Building has features of these types of structures and fits this Iron Age tradition of large administrative buildings (e.g. Megiddo Palace 10,000).[8]

The Administrative Building (Fig. 7) was built mostly of large, rough, field stones with the corners of the buildings containing ashlar stones. The building has two entrances (east and west), two long central halls/courtyards that are surrounded by various rooms and units. At least 15 distinct rooms and areas (called units below) can be delineated within this building. The two central courtyards, ca. 9 m in length, contained well-preserved plastered surfaces, extending from the casemate wall in the south to the entrances to two rooms in the northwest corner of the building. Associated with the eastern courtyard were three tabuns, as well as a small concave stone feature set into the plaster and surrounded by a ring of small cobbles. This stone feature may have been a grinding installation, or perhaps a post-hole for some sort of temporary covering.

The Administrative Building was destroyed in a significant and violent event. The destruction debris from the building buried the floors and walls in up to 1.50 m

---

[8] Note that Dever (1985) found parts of this building, which he identified as Palace 10,000. He recognized that this was a large administrative/elite building based on the construction (e.g. ashlar masonry) and partial plan, he did not know that it was one of these typical *Bit Hilani*-type structures.

Fig. 8 Stratum 8 destruction debris. Toppled stone architecture in Room 2 of administrative building

of debris. This debris was mostly deteriorated mudbrick, but certain areas within the structure, typically to the immediate west of a wall, contained high concentrations of large boulders and ashlars. From the distribution of these boulders, it appears that when the building was destroyed, most of the walls fell toward the west. Perhaps this represents a destructive force moving westward from the area of the city gate.

The Stratum 8 administrative building was destroyed around the third quarter of the tenth century (Fig. 8), most likely by Pharaoh Sheshonq (biblical Shishak) as part of his military campaign in the region (ca. 925 BCE). Prior to this destruction, the building was emptied of its contents, either by its occupants, who likely abandoned it and fled, or by its conquerors, who may have looted the building during its final hours. Very little was discovered on the floors. In the whole building, we only found a game board, pounding stones, gaming pieces (3), a spindle whorl, sling stones, bronze bracelet, projectile points, and a couple of figurines. A rattle, black juglet, and cooking pot were the only complete ceramic artifacts found. The few ceramic finds available are consistent with a tenth-century date for the use and destruction of the building.

3.1.4 Stratum 7

The administrative quarter drastically shifted from a public administrative quarter to a domestic quarter during the ninth century BCE (Fig. 9). This chapter of the city's history shows a major realignment. The casemate fortifications were rebuilt, and the

Gezer Destructions: A Case Study of a Border City

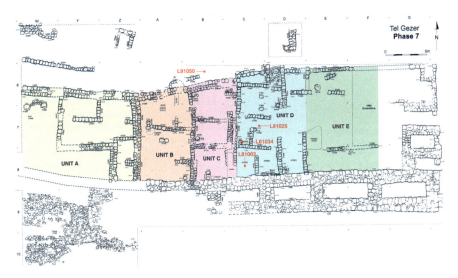

Fig. 9 Stratum 7 Plan with overview of domestic units built over Stratum 8 architecture

gate apparently became a four-chambered gate. Instead of rebuilding the administrative center, a series of domestic buildings were constructed, some abutting the still-standing inner (northern) wall of the casemate fortification. The builders were aware of the plan of the earlier administrative building, reusing some of the walls and maintaining their orientation. A unique feature was two canine burials here, each located in front of a different unit. We have defined five domestic structures built up against the north face of the casemate city wall.

We have a complete plan for only one of the five complexes (Fig. 10). This building is about 12 × 8 m in dimensions. It is built on top of the destroyed Stratum 8 and reused some of the Stratum 8 administrative building walls. The surfaces are beaten earth with some cobble and flagstone areas. This domestic building is not a typical four room house. It consists of a main pillared room with a storage room to its north. Flanking this room to the east were cobbled steps that led up to an elevated tabun and an entrance. To the south was a central area with a tabun room and evidence of household industry. To the south were two rooms. This building has evidence of a violent destruction found in almost all the rooms.

This domestic house was not a typical Israelite four-room house, but rather a segmented building with single-row fieldstone walls added to divide the living area into smaller spaces. A pillared segment (Rooms 1, 2, 10) contained several storage jars. The next segment (Rooms 4 and 5, and perhaps 6) was possibly an open courtyard; this segment also contained several storage jars, along with a tabun in a corner and sunken plaster-lined installations. This led to the third segment (Rooms 7 and 8), which was accessed via the central space with entrances allowing access only to the room in the back corner and then to Room 8. Room 7 contained a bench and Room 8 produced restorable pottery of various forms, including several juglets and two chalices. It appears that Room 8 was utilized as a storage room for items that

Fig. 10 Stratum 7: Domestic Unit D

were infrequently used, or perhaps were of some importance to the household and hence were kept out of primary activity areas.

The builders were aware of the plan of the earlier administrative building, reusing some of the walls and maintaining their orientation. Two canine burials were uncovered here, each located in front of a different unit. This city was violently destroyed. We previously associated this destruction with Hazael's campaign (Ortiz & Wolff, 2017: 95), but based on radiocarbon dates (Ortiz & Wolff, 2021; Webster et al., forthcoming) and an initial reading of the pottery, we now date it to the late tenth/early ninth centuries BCE, which would predate Hazael's campaign (Fig. 11).

3.1.5 Stratum 6A

Stratum 6 resulted in a major phase of rebuilding, the Stratum 7 city was drastically changed. The domestic structures abutting the line of the casemate wall went out of use and three major administrative buildings were built, changing the area west of

Fig. 11 Stratum 7 Destruction debris. South end of Room 6, Unit D. Note the depth of destruction debris is over half a meter

the gate back into an administrative quarter. The domestic quarter was relocated to the northwest. Most of the archaeological data was removed by Macalister leaving only the remnants of the foundation of the wall lines. All the pottery was mixed with Iron Age and Hellenistic sherds. To the north of this building the project was fortunate that Hellenistic buildings prevented Macalister from penetrating to the Iron Age levels; in which we found a large four-room house with over a meter of destruction.

Iron Age Four Room House

The four-room house consists of three long rooms (a central room flanked by parallel northern and southern rooms), separated by large limestone pillars (average dimensions $0.50 \times 0.50 \times 1.00$ m) with a broadroom to the back (west), which was subdivided into two smaller rooms (Fig. 12). The area of the house as a whole is estimated at 135 m^2, considerably larger than typical four-room houses found previously at Gezer and at other urban sites. The back rooms contained several types of storage jars. The central room had a few tabuns and contained pottery vessels (mainly storage jars), grinding stones, and loom weights. The side rooms were both divided into two areas and the surfaces were either plastered or cobbled. The side rooms also contained many vessels and artifacts. The building and its contents were sealed by burnt mudbrick destruction debris, testimony to a considerable conflagration. The portable finds from the building included basalt grinding stones, loom weights and a sizeable ceramic assemblage, consisting primarily of restorable storage jars with lesser numbers of bowls and kraters (over 30 whole vessels). Other finds include glyptic objects, jewelry, and a cosmetic palette. The ceramic assemblage and small glyptic finds date to the eighth century BCE and are associated with the destruction of the site by Tiglath-Pileser III in 734 BCE (Wolff, 2021).

3.1.6 Stratum 6B

Stratum 6B represents an earlier phase of Stratum 6A (Fig. 12b). This phase represents single wall rebuilds of structures that we postulate are due to walls that became unstable and had to be rebuilt. The 1990 excavations by Dever did find evidence of walls leaning and off their foundations which they interpreted as evidence for the eighth century earthquake (Dever, 1992a, b; Younker, 1991). We do not have any destruction associated with the earthquake. We have evidence in two, possibly three, separate buildings of walls within a building that went out of use and were rebuilt. The four-room house has evidence that the southern exterior wall was rebuilt and extended about a meter to the south. The rebuild (Stratum 6A) constructed the new outer wall with a single row of boulder sized stones. Near the gate was a series of three administrative buildings. In tripartite building A, the northern exterior wall was rebuilt. In Building C we have evidence of an industrial building that changed its plan. A large olive press and vat went out of use and a wall was built directly on top of the press and the vat was flipped over and reused in this wall. This third example might not be due to an earthquake but a repurposing of the function of the building. These rebuilds during the eighth century appear to be re-stabilization of existing walls. Any evidence of destruction (e.g. burning, collapsed walls, etc.) would have been cleared away by the residents and select walls would be rebuilt and the buildings would have continued in use until their final destruction of 6A.

4 Theory and Gezer Destructions

The current phase of research is focusing on how we define destructions in the archaeological record by applying theoretical approaches. I have coalesced the three models (Megiddo Destruction, Integrative Paradigm, and Kriemerman's typology of destruction layers) into a discussion of the Gezer destruction layers (Table 2). I have grouped the models into five groups of archaeological correlates. *Evidence of Destruction* are the physical correlates found in the archaeological record: destroyed buildings, burnt mudbricks or mudbrick detritus, evidence of burning (layers of ash, etc.), collapsed walls and an abundance of artifacts found within the destruction debris. Most of these are from the Megiddo destruction typology and Hasel's *means* of destruction. The second group discusses the *Extent of Destruction* (Megiddo's 3-point scale and Hasel's *extent of destruction*). *Historical record/Texts* refers to texts that mention military campaigns as well as the *focus* of destruction. The third

Gezer Destructions: A Case Study of a Border City

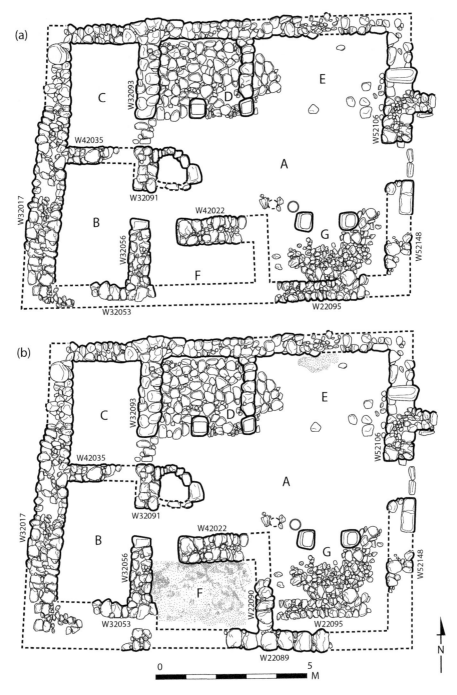

Fig. 12 Stratum 6 eighth century BCE Four-Room House. (**a**) Stratum 6B. (**b**) Stratum 6A. Note the expansion and rebuild of the southern exterior wall due to earthquake damage

Table 2 Tel Gezer: Destruction data

Destruction Stratum	12	10A	8	7	6B	6A
Archaeological period	LB	IA I	10th	10th/9th	8th	8th
Evidence of destruction (means): Physical correlates							
Destroyed buildings	+	+	+	+	+	+
Burnt mudbrick	+	+	?	+	+	+
Layers of burnt residue	+	+	–	–	–	++
Collapsed walls (stone)	–	–	+	–	–	–
Artifacts in situ	+	+	–	+	+	–
Extent of destruction							
Extent of destruction	Patrician House	50%	30% (10% total)	1 of 5 buildings	+/–	4 room house 10%
Scale of destruction	3	2	3	2/3	–	3
Content of destruction	?	?	?	?	?	?
Destruction of life support system (e.g. surrounding countryside: Crops, forests, etc.)							
Historical record/text: (e.g. campaigns)							
Military campaigns	Direct	Indirect	Campaign	Campaign	Direct	Indirect
Focus [region or city]	Region	?	Region	City	None	Region
Material correlates: Warfare							
Long range weapons	–	–	–	–	–	NA
Human skeletal remains	+++	–	–	–	–	NA
Construction (siege)	–	–	–	–	–	NA
Post-depositional + = destroyed features were rebuilt in the following stratum, – = no evidence of rebuilding							
Rebuilt buildings/walls	+	–	+	–	+	+
Fills/leveling	+	–	+	–	+	–
Pits	+	–	+	–	–	–
Earthquake evidence							
	–	–	–	–	+	–

group contains artifacts that reflect evidence of warfare (from Kreimerman's model). The last two groups are post-depositional evidence of rebuilding and response to destruction, as well as evidence for earthquakes.

4.1 Evidence of Destruction: Structures and Artifacts

Most of our evidence for destruction comes from collapsed architecture (e.g. mudbrick detritus, collapsed walls) and artifacts in situ. This is seen in our LB, Iron Age I, tenth century, ninth, and eighth century strata. The preservation of the mudbrick collapse was based on later leveling activity of the rebuilt occupation on top of the destruction. Our LB (Stratum 12) destruction was mostly preserved in Rooms A, F, and the southern half of Room D. Not much mudbrick debris was found in Rooms B, C, or courtyard E. Rooms B and C were downslope and most evidence would have eroded away, while the mudbrick detritus accumulation was shallow in courtyard E as the later Stratum 11 cleared most due to leveling. The HUC excavations only found evidence of the Stratum 12 (= HUC Stratum XIV) in their Field II sounding, which is also on the south side of the tel.

In the later Stratum 10A, destruction was only found in Unit 3, although complete storage jars were found mostly in Rooms A, B, and 3. We have the same phenomenon of only certain rooms or sections in a building containing evidence of destruction in Stratum 8 and 7. The HUC excavations also found this destruction (HUC Stratum IX) on the southside of the western hill (Field II), on the acropolis, and in Field VI (adjacent to the new Tandy excavations). Dever notes that "Everywhere they were investigated, these levels [e.g. Stratum X–IX] came to an end in a violent destruction, which may be correlated with the campaigns of the Egyptian pharaoh who according to 1 Kgs. 9: 15–17 had 'captured Gezer and burnt it with fire' before ceding it to Solomon (Dever, 1992b: II 1001)."

Stratum 8 is associated with the Sheshonq I campaign. We have a large administrative building near the gate that was destroyed. Rooms and courtyards had evidence of mudbrick detritus, but the main destruction was in rooms filled with massive collapsed stone destruction. In Rooms 1, 2, and courtyard 6, we have stone walls (some with ashlars) tipped from east to west. There were few finds in the building. We postulated that the inhabitants knew of the impending attack and cleaned out the building. It is also possible that the city surrendered and the city gate and the administrative building next to it were destroyed by the Egyptians as a statement that they were in control. In Stratum 7 we have five domestic structures, yet only one, Unit D, had evidence of a massive destruction. The walls were preserved in some places for a meter, while the other four domestic structures had only the remnants of the lower course or even just the foundation line. Perhaps this pattern of preservation was due to later builders (e.g. Stratum 6), who wanted a level surface to build large public buildings. They leveled most of the other buildings and intentional left Unit D untouched (with the exception of a deep foundation wall) because it was down slope. The post depositional rebuild does not provide any information as to whether all the structures were destroyed or if they intentionally only destroyed Unit D because it was the house of someone important. The HUC excavations did not find evidence of this destruction (Stratum 7) in any of their excavation fields. Stratum 6A is a different story. There was massive evidence of site wide destruction.[9] We have extensive burning, collapsed walls and an abundance of artifacts in situ. There is no question that this destruction was extensive and covered most of the city. The HUC excavations also found massive destruction (Field VII adjacent to our excavations).

---

[9] This destruction was also defined by the HUC excavations.

The Tandy excavations confirmed most of the destruction layers that the HUC excavations discerned (although this was not the goal), yet each excavation found various degrees of destruction. Both found that the Assyrian destruction (Stratum 6A, HUC = Stratum VI) was extensive throughout the site. The Siamun destruction was extensive according to the HUC excavations, yet we only found one room with more than one variable of destruction (e.g. smashed pottery, burnt layers, collapsed mudbrick) while other rooms had only smashed pottery. The Sheshonq destruction was also evident in most excavation fields of the HUC project, yet extensive destruction was only found in one area of the city (e.g. the gate [HUC] and the large administrative building [Tandy] built adjacent to the gate). The gate was rebuilt so if there was any evidence of a fierce destruction it was removed by the rebuilding of a later phase. We found limited smashed pottery, collapsed mudbrick and burnt layers in the administrative building, yet each room had massive stone architectural destruction. It appears that each destruction level had different patterns of evidence. This phenomenon has been found at other excavations throughout the Southern Levant, hence scholars have attempted to define models that incorporate the extent of destruction.

4.2 Extent of Destruction

Finkelstein has proposed a three-level scale model for the Megiddo destructions based on severity. This would not work for Gezer. If you look at Table 2, we could classify each destruction as Scale 3 (complete annihilation) based on the evidence of destruction, but not every destroyed occupation experienced a period of abandonment, except for Stratum 6A. Yet if we incorporate the HUC excavations, we know that they found evidence of destruction for Strata 12, 10, and 6 (HUC Strata XV, X–IX, and VIII) where we had an immediate rebuild of the city (hence the 2 rating). If we look at the extent of the destruction as to how much of the area was destroyed we get a different picture of the severity of the destruction. It is probable that the post-depositional activity altered the evidence for severity of the destructions. Also our tenth century building had evidence for an extreme destruction—but if we look at the artifacts left on the floor and the amount of ash—we would not classify this as a destruction according to the model.

Another factor is the chance discovery of a destruction layer. The HUC excavations did not record a destruction for their Stratum VII (Stratum 7 of the new excavations). This is a 'newly discovered' destruction that was not known. Also, the HUC excavation noted at least three destruction layers on the acropolis (Field VI) during the Iron Age I. The Tandy excavations also had multiple strata of the Iron Age I period (e.g. Stratum 11, 10B, 10A) yet we discerned only one destruction layer (Stratum 10A). In our excavations we have 'peaceful' transitions during the Iron Age I with the last ending in a destruction. On the acropolis, the HUC excavations found that the Iron Age I period was turbulent with multiple destructions. It is clear that the acropolis experienced the brunt of any attack while the part of the city we excavated did not experience any destructive behavior. The extent of the destructions during Iron Age I were only focused on the acropolis—the elite zone of the city, while other parts of the city did not experience any destructive action on other buildings. The HUC excavations did not discern a destruction of their Stratum VII, yet for the same occupation layer we found a major destruction (Stratum 7).

4.3 Material Correlates of Warfare

The only evidence we have of warfare are the human bodies found in our LB Patrician House. Any other weapons of warfare or construction (e.g. siege, etc.) have not been found (except the occasional arrowhead, etc.). According to Kreimerman,[10] there are approximately 58 skeletons found in wholesale destructions of Late Bronze and Iron Age sites in the southern Levant (5 in localized destruction). Eleven date to the LB IIA/III, hence the Gezer three represents nearly a 30% increase. We excavated an area of over 200 square meters; we left 10 meters of balk in this area and one of the individuals we uncovered happened to be in the balk. One less day of excavation and we would have changed the outcome by 10%. While I agree with Kreimerman's premise that every attempt was made to remove bodies in destruction, there is still an element of chance of discovery. I propose the same is true for the recycling of weapons.

4.4 Other Factors for Material Correlates of Destruction

One of the main issues in using destruction debris as a factor in defining the extent and evidence of destructions is whether or not these debris layers have been altered. This could be similar to Kriemerman's definition of secondary correlates. While he defined these correlates as part of the destruction event, post-destruction activity (processes associated with clean-up, rebuilding, abandonment, scavenging, etc.) greatly alters the destructions. Archaeologists might be developing a typology based on post-destruction human activity versus the actual destruction event. Hence I propose that we need to account for post-depositional activity that would influence the evidence left for the evidence of destruction, and in determining the extent (or severity) of the destruction.

5 Conclusion

Gezer is a key site to isolate variables in any attempt to build models for discerning and defining destructions in the Southern Levant. The Tandy excavations delineated five strata with evidence of man-made destruction and one that has evidence of

---

[10] Kreimerman (2017b).

earthquake damage. My contribution to the discussion is to propose that we incorporate the post-depositional activity into any theory development of destruction as it (1) patterns the remnants of destruction, which in turn (2) affects the interpretation of the nature of the specific destruction. Also, the human activity in response to destruction aides in placing the destruction in its context. Finkelstein's and Kreimerman's models are beneficial as they provide criteria for focusing on the material correlates as found in the archaeological record. Yet the models must be used as guides vs. definitive types. All of the Gezer destructions were the result of military campaigns—yet only one would fit Kreimerman's model. Hence I am supportive of Hasel's model of an integrative paradigm—as the emphasis should be on the assumption that any remnants of destruction are based on human agency (with the exception of natural disasters). This is easily done when we have historical sources that can be juxtaposed with the archaeological record. At Gezer the Assyrian destruction of the eighth century was very intense, where the city was burnt and completely destroyed, while the Sheshonq I campaign appears to have conquered the city with minimal destruction, purposefully toppling the stone walls of the city gate and administrative building. Thus it seems appropriate to approach the identification of destructions in the archaeological record within the framework of a behavioral archaeology model, where the nature of the destruction preserved in the archaeological record is determined to be formed in the act of the initial destruction or altered during the post-depositional context.

The Gezer region continues to play an important role in history. The geographical dynamics and strategic location in the Aijalon Valley makes this site a contested border and prized city for the various local polities in the area as well as major states who wished to dominate the southern coastal plain. In addition, archaeological research of the site continues to influence historical reconstructions and theoretical models of the past as well as biblical interpretation.

Any theoretical models of destruction need to account for post-depositional activity. It is this activity that alters how much of a destruction remains for the archaeologists to excavate. While I fully agree with the models that have been recently proposed; and use them to assist in the interpretation of the Gezer destructions, I do not think we can develop general laws of how to define 'destruction in the archaeological record.' The evidence from Gezer illustrates that no two destructions are alike.

References

Berlejung, A. (Ed.). (2012). *Disaster and Relief Management/Katastrophen und ihre Bewältigung*. Mohr Siebeck.

Cline, E. H. (2011). Whole Lota Shakin' going on: The possible destruction by earthquake of Stratum VIA at Megiddo. In I. Finkelstein & N. Na'aman (Eds.), *The fire signals of Lachish: Studies in the archaeology and history of Israel in the Late Bronze Age, Iron Age, and Persian Period in honor of David Ussishkin* (pp. 55–70). Eisenbrauns.

Cunningham, T. (2013). Deconstructing destructions: A contextual approach to methodology and meaning in archaeology. In J. Driessen (Ed.), *Destruction: Archaeological, philological and historical perspectives* (pp. 51–59). Presses universitaire de Louvain.

Dever, W. G. (1985). Solomonic and Assyrian period 'Palaces' at Gezer. *Israel Exploration Journal, 35*(4), 217–230.

Dever, W. G. (1986). Late Bronze Age and Solomonic defenses at Gezer: New evidence. *Bulletin of the American Schools of Oriental Research, 262*, 9–34.

Dever, W. G. (1992a). A case study in biblical archaeology: The earthquake of ca. 760 BCE. *Eretz-Israel, 23*, 27–35.

Dever, W. G. (1992b). Gezer. In D. N. Freedman (Ed.), *Anchor bible dictionary*. Doubleday.

Dever, W. G., & Younker, R. W. (1990). Tell Gezer, 1990. *Israel Exploration Journal, 41*, 282–286.

Dever, W. G., Lance, H. D., & Wright, G. E. (1970). *Gezer I: Preliminary report of the 1964–66 seasons*. Annual of the Hebrew Union College Biblical and Archaeological School in Jerusalem I. Nelson Glueck School of Biblical Archaeology.

Dever, W. G., Lance, H. D., Bullard, R. G., Cole, D. P., & Seger, J. D. (1974). *Gezer II: Report of the 1967–1970 seasons in Fields I and II*. Annual of the Hebrew Union College/Nelson Glueck School of Biblical Archaeology II. Nelson Glueck School of Biblical Archaeology.

Dever, W. G., Lance, H. D., & Bullard, R. G. (1986). *Gezer IV: The 1969–71 seasons in Field VI, the "Acropolis"*. Nelson Glueck School of Biblical Archaeology.

Driessen, J. (1995). Crisis architecture? Some observations on architectural adaptations and immediate responses to changing socio-cultural conditions. *Topoi, 5*, 63–88.

Driessen, J. (2013a). Time capsules? Destructions as archaeological phenomena. In J. Driessen (Ed.), *Destruction: Archaeological, philological and historical perspectives* (pp. 5–23). Presses universitaire de Louvain.

Driessen, J. (Ed.). (2013b). *Destruction: Archaeological, philological and historical perspectives*. Presses universitaire de Louvain.

Edelman, D. V. (2012). Earthquakes in the Ancient Southern Levant: A literary Topos and a problem requiring architectural solutions. In A. Berlejung (Ed.), *Disaster and Relief Management/Katastrophen und ihre Bewältigung* (pp. 205–238). Mohr Siebeck.

Fiaccavento, C. (2014a). Destructions as historical markers towards the end of the 2nd and during the 1st millennium BC in Southern Levant. In L. Nigro (Ed.), *Overcoming Catastrophes. Essays on disastrous agents characterization and resilience strategies in pre-classical Southern Levant* (ROSAPAT 11—PRIN 2009-The Seven Plagues).

Fiaccavento, C. (2014b). Destructions as historical markers towards the end of the 2nd and during the 1st millennium BC in Southern Levant. In L. Nigro (Ed.), *Overcoming Catastrophes: Essays on disastrous agents characterization and resilience strategies in pre-classical Southern Levant* (Rome "La Spienza" Studies on the Archaeology of Palestine & Transjordan, pp. 205–259). Dipartimento di Scienze dell'Antichità.

Finkelstein, I. (1996). The archaeology of the united monarchy: An alternative view. *Levant, 28*, 177–187.

Finkelstein, I. (2000). The campaign of Shoshenq I to Palestine. *Zeitschrift des Deutschen Palästina-Vereins, 118*, 109–135.

Finkelstein, I. (2009). Destructions: Megiddo as a case study. In J. David Schloen (Ed.), *Exploring the Longue Durée: Essays in Honor of Lawrence E. Stager* (pp. 113–126). Eisenbrauns.

Forget, M., & Shahack-Gross, R. (2016). How long does it take to burn down an Ancient Near Eastern City? *Antiquity, 90*, 1213–1225.

Forget, M., Regev, L., Friesem, D., & Shahack-Gross, R. (2015). Physical and mineralogical properties of experimentally heated sun-dried mud bricks: Implications for reconstruction of environmental factors influencing the appearance of mud bricks in archaeological conflagration events. *Journal of Archaeological Science: Reports, 2*, 80–93.

Gitin, S. (1990). *A ceramic typology of the Late Iron II, Persian and Hellenistic periods at Tell Gezer: Based on a stratigraphic analysis of Field VII West*. Hebrew Union College-Jewish Institute of Religion.

Hasel, M. (1998). *Domination and resistance: Egyptian military activity in the Southern Levant, 1300–1185 BC*. Brill.
Hasel, M. (2016). The archaeology of destruction: Methodological desiderata. In S. Ganor, I. Kreimerman, K. Streit, & M. Mumcuoglu (Eds.), *From Sha'ar Hagolan to Shaaraim: Essay in Honor of Prof. Yosef Garfinkel* (pp. 205–228). Israel Exploration Society.
Höfflmayer, F. (2014). Dating Catastrophes and collapses in the Ancient Near East: The end of the first urbanization in the Southern Levant and the 4.2 ka BP event. In L. Nigro (Ed.), *Overcoming Catastrophes. Essays on disastrous agents characterization and resilience strategies in pre-classical Southern Levant* (pp. 117–140) (ROSAPAT 11—PRIN 2009—The Seven Plagues).
Jusseret, S., & Sintubin, M. (2012). All that rubble leads to trouble: Reassessing the seismological value of archaeological destruction layers in Minoan Crete and beyond. *Seismological Research Letters, 83*, 736–742.
Kreimerman, I. (2016). Siege warfare, conflict and destruction: How are they related? In S. Ganor, I. Kreimerman, K. Streit, & M. Mumcuoglu (Eds.), *From Sha'ar Hagolan to Shaaraim: Essay in Honor of Prof. Yosef Garfinkel* (pp. 229–245). Israel Exploration Society.
Kreimerman, I. (2017a). A typology for destruction layers: The Late Bronze Age Southern Levant as a case study. In T. Cunningham & J. Driessen (Eds.), *Crisis to collapse: The archaeology of social breakdown (Aegis 11)* (pp. 173–203). Presses Universitaires de Louvain Louvain-la-Neuve.
Kreimerman, I. (2017b). Skeletons in Bronze and Iron Age destruction contexts in the southern Levant: What do they mean? *West and East, II*, 13–30.
Kreimerman, I., & Shahack-Gross, R. (2018). Understanding conflagration of one-story mud-brick structures: An experimental approach. In *Archaeological and anthropological sciences*. Springer. https://doi.org/10.1007/s12525-018-0714-7
Lehmann, G., & Killebrew, A. (2010). Palace 6000 at Megiddo in context: Iron Age central hall tetra-partite residencies and the *Bit-Hilani* building tradition in the Levant. *Bulletin of the American Schools of Oriental Research, 359*, 13–33.
Macalister, R. A. S. (1912). *The excavation of Gezer, 1902–1905 and 1907–1909, Volumes 1–3*. Palestine Exploration Fund.
Maeir, A. M. (2004). *Bronze and Iron Age Tombs at Tel Gezer, Israel: Finds from Raymond-Charles Weill's excavations in 1914 and 1921* (BAR international series 1206). Archaeopress.
Marco, S., Agonon, A., Finkelstein, I., & Ussishkin, D. (2006). Chapter 31: Megiddo earthquakes. In *Megiddo VI* (pp. 568–575). Tel Aviv University.
Münger, S. (2003). Egyptian stamp-seal amulets and their implications for the chronology of the Early Iron Age. *Tel Aviv, 30*, 66–82.
Münger, S., Ortiz, S., & Wolff, S. (forthcoming). *A seal impression on a clay stopper from Tel Gezer*.
Nigro, L. (Ed.). (2014). *Overcoming catastrophes: Essays on disastrous agents characterization and resilience strategies in pre-classical Southern Levant* (Rome "La Spienza" studies on the archaeology of Palestine & Transjordan). Dipartimento di Scienze dell'Antichità.
Nur, A., & Cline, E. H. (2000). Poseidon's horses: Plate tectonics and earthquake storms in the Late Bronze Age Aegean and Eastern Mediterranean. *Journal of Archaeological Science, 27*, 43–63.
Ortiz, S., & Wolff, S. (2017). Tel Gezer excavations 2006-2015: The transformation of a Border City. In O. Lipschits & A. M. Maeir (Eds.), *"...as plentiful as sycamore-fig tress in the Shephelah" (1 Kings 10:27) recent archaeological research in the Shephelah of Judah: The Iron Age* (pp. 61–102). Eisenbrauns.
Ortiz, S., & Wolff, S. (2019). A reevaluation of Gezer in the Late Bronze Age in light of renewed excavations and recent scholarship. In A. M. Maeir, I. Shai, & C. McKinny (Eds.), *And the Canaanite was in then in the land (Gen. 12:6): Canaanites in Southern Canaan during the Late Bronze and Early Iron Ages. Proceedings of the Ackerman Family Workshop in Biblical Archaeology, Bar-Ilan University, April 15th–16th, 2015* (pp. 62–85). DeGruyter.

Ortiz, S., & Wolff, S. (2021). New evidence for the 10th century BCE at Tel Gezer. In A. Faust, Y. Garfinkel, & M. Mumcuoglu (Eds.), *State formation processes in the 10th century BCE Levant* (Jerusalem Journal of Archaeology) (Vol. 1, pp. 221–240).

Ortiz, S., & Wolff, S. (forthcoming). *The Sheshonq Redemption: An Analysis of the Current and Previous Excavation Results of the 10th Century BCE Destruction at Tel Gezer.*

Rowe, A. (1935a). Excavations at Gezer. *Palestine Exploration Fund Quarterly Statement, 67,* 19–33.

Rowe, A. (1935b). Gezer. *Quarterly of the Department of Antiquities in Palestine, 4,* 198–201.

Seger, J. D., Lance, H. D., & Bullard, R. G. (1988). *Gezer V: The Field 1 caves*. Nelson Glueck School of Biblical Archaeology.

Shahack-Gross, R. (2017). Rethinking destruction by fire: Geoarchaeological case studies in Tel Megiddo and the importance of construction methods. In O. Lipschits, Y. Gadot, & M. J. Adams (Eds.), *Rethinking Israel: Studies in the history and archaeology of Ancient Israel in Honor of Israel Finkelstein* (pp. 125–130). Eisenbrauns.

Shahack-Gross, R., Shaar, R., Hassul, E., Forget, M., Nowacyk, N., Marck, S., Finkelstein, I., & Argnon, A. (2018). Fire and collapse: Untangling the formation of destruction layers using archaeomagnetism. *Geoarchaeology, 33,* 513–528.

Sharon, I., & Zarzecki-Peleg, A. (2006). Podium structures with lateral access: Authority ploys in royal architecture in the Iron Age Levant. In S. Gitin, J. E. Wright, & J. P. Dessel (Eds.), *Confronting the past: Archaeological and historical essays on Ancient Israel in Honor of William G. Dever* (pp. 145–167). Eisenbrauns.

Webster, L., Ortiz, S., Wolff, S., et al. (forthcoming). *The chronology of Gezer from the late Bronze Age crisis to Iron Age II: A meeting point for radiocarbon, archaeology, egyptology and the Bible.*

Wolff, S. R. (2021). The date of destruction of Gezer Stratum VI. *Tel Aviv, 48*(1), 73–86.

Younker, R. (1991). A preliminary report of the 1990 season at Tel Gezer: Excavations of the "Outer Wall" and the "Solomonic" gateway (July 2 to August 10, 1990). *Andrews University Seminary Studies, 29*(1), 19–60.

Zelwer-Silberberg, P. (1942). *Les Tombes du Bronze et du Premier Age du Fer de Tell Gezer Mobilier et Typologie: Memoire d'après les fouilles de Raymond Weill 1913–1914 et 1923–1924 accompagné d'un Tableau des classements des tombes de Gézer.* Pubished by ancienne élève de l'École du Louvre, 2012.

Jerusalem's Settlement History: Rejoinders and Updates

Israel Finkelstein

Abstract The article offers critical reviews on several recent publications, which deal with the archaeology of Jerusalem: The location of the Bronze and Iron Age mound, the Middle Bronze remains, the pre-eighth century finds, the results of the excavations in the Ophel and the Persian and Hellenistic finds in the Givati Parking Lot. It then presents an update on the settlement history of the city between the Middle Bronze and the Hellenistic period.

Keywords Jerusalem · City of David · Temple Mount · Ophel · Gihon Spring · Givati Parking Lot · Middle Bronze · Iron IIA · Persian period · Hellenistic period

In recent years I have published several articles that deal with the settlement history of Jerusalem from the Middle Bronze to the late Hellenistic period (among others, Finkelstein et al., 2011; Finkelstein, 2008, 2012). Research in Jerusalem is exceptionally dynamic; accordingly, a series of recent publications require attention. This article is divided into two parts. The first includes rejoinders to new publications, both field results (Gadot & Uziel, 2017; Shalev et al., 2020; Regev et al., 2017; Winderboim, 2021) and discussion of past remains (Ussishkin, 2016; Geva & De Groot, 2017; Mazar, 2020). The second offers a brief updated reconstruction of the settlement history of the city.

I. Finkelstein (✉)
Tel Aviv University, Tel Aviv, Israel

Haifa University, Haifa, Israel
e-mail: fink2@post.tau.ac.il

© The Author(s), under exclusive license to Springer Nature Switzerland AG 2023
E. Ben-Yosef, I. W. N. Jones (eds.), *"And in Length of Days Understanding" (Job 12:12): Essays on Archaeology in the Eastern Mediterranean and Beyond in Honor of Thomas E. Levy*, Interdisciplinary Contributions to Archaeology,
https://doi.org/10.1007/978-3-031-27330-8_32

1 The Archaeology of Jerusalem: Rejoinders

Though seemingly dealing with different periods and themes, the studies reviewed below are all related, having to do with the layout and settlement history of Jerusalem from the Middle Bronze Age to the Hellenistic period.

1.1 The Location of the Ancient Mound of Jerusalem

The location of the ancient mound of Jerusalem is a pivotal issue in any discussion of the settlement history of the city. Over 10 years ago, together with colleagues, I argued, following Knauf (2000), that the ancient mound of Jerusalem in the Bronze Age and early phases of the Iron Age should be sought on the Temple Mound rather than on the City of David ridge (Finkelstein et al., 2011).[1] The main arguments were:

- Long periods in the history of Jerusalem, which are backed by real-time textual material, such as the Late Bronze Age and the Persian and early Hellenistic (Ptolemaic) periods, are not represented on the City of David ridge, at least not by significant remains.
- In all pre-Roman periods except for the Iron IIB-C and the late Hellenistic (Hasmonean) period, evidence for activity on the City of David ridge is limited mainly to the eastern flank of its central sector – above and around the Gihon Spring – with no indication for occupation in the northern, southern and western parts of the ridge.
- The City of David ridge is dominated on the east, west and north by higher grounds and is therefore located in topographic inferiority, which would seem odd for the hub of a Bronze Age city-state and an Iron Age territorial kingdom. Moreover, the City of David ridge does not have the profile of a mound. In addition, most mounds in the highlands are located on hills that dominate their vicinity; for instance Kiriath-jearim, Mizpah and Gibeon. In fact, very few are situated on a slope.
- The temple of the Davidic Dynasty was located on the Temple Mount (the palace too, to the best of my understanding). The instinctive tendency is to reconstruct the layout of this area in the Bronze and Iron Ages according to what we see today (the Harem el-Sharif) or what we know about Herodian times: A large open space with a single building in its center. Yet, in hubs of Bronze Age city-states and capitals of Iron Age territorial kingdoms the royal compound was an integral part of town, with no such large empty space around it.
- Three fortification systems dating to the Middle Bronze, Iron IIB-C and late Hellenistic (Hasmonean) period were traced on the eastern slope of the City of

---

[1] Here and below, I use the term City of David as a modern-research geographical indication for the ridge located to the south of the Temple Mount, also known in some publications as "the southeastern ridge." For a discussion of the biblical toponym, City of David, see Hutzli, 2011.

David ridge. If this had been a *tell*, the western side would undoubtedly also have been fortified. Yet, no city-wall has ever been found there.
- The Temple Mound has sufficient space to accommodate a large tell the size of the major mounds in the highlands, such as those in Shechem and Kiriath-jearim.

Jerusalem researchers quickly rejected this proposal, with the most detailed rebuttal published by Geva and De Groot (2017). Below I relate to their arguments:

1. In trenches dug in the eastern side of the Temple Mound (one of the places referred to is in fact located near the peak of the hill) bedrock was exposed close to the surface, with finds not earlier than the Iron II and with no mound accumulation. Yet, nothing else is expected in highland tells because of erosion. Bedrock is exposed at the summit of most mounds in the region, for instance at Tell en-Nasbeh (Mizpah), Shiloh and Kiriath-jearim. Moreover, in the specific case of Jerusalem, much of the ancient mound must have been erased during the large-scale construction operation of leveling and laying fills in the days of Herod the Great. Incidentally, Geva and De Groot agree that the Temple was located on the Temple Mount starting in the Iron IIA. If so, how is it that no Iron IIA and Persian period sherds were detected in trenches cut on the hill and its slopes?
2. The fill debris taken from the front of the northern façade of "Solomon's Stables" produced pottery dating not earlier than the Iron II. Geva and De Groot negate the possibility that this debris was brought from the City of David because in that case earlier pottery should be expected in it (this is a circular argument because they take it for granted that the mound of Jerusalem should be sought there). They also argue that the quantity of earth in this debris is too massive to have originated entirely from the Temple Mount and negate the possibility that it came from valleys within the city. Geva and De Groot conclude that the debris must have originated from the eastern slope of the Temple Mount. Yet, there is no modern-archaeology evidence for the nature of the accumulation outside of the eastern wall of the Herodian compound and the bottom of the Kidron is too far away to supply reliable evidence. This is a redundant discussion as there is no way to know where this fill came from.
3. Geva and De Groot's description of the intensity of activity on the City of David ridge is misleading. This is best demonstrated in their treatment of the Middle Bronze and Persian period remains. They see the Middle Bronze fortifications around the Gihon Spring as major evidence against the mound on the Temple Mount theory. Yet, these fortifications do not continue to the north or south (more below) and as mentioned above, there are no fortifications on the western side of the City of David ridge. For the Persian period they state that the "few clear remains … attest to settlement during that period extending over the entire hill" (2017: 41). This is not the case; the evidence for this period is limited to stray pottery sherds (including stamped handles) in the area around the Gihon Spring and a few poor remains, probably representing squatters, in two other spots (more below).
4. Asserting that a mound on the Temple Mount would be distant from the water source and hence "uncharacteristic of settlements in ancient times, which were

founded as near as possible to a water source" (Geva & De Groot, 2017: 42) is no argument. Important mounds in the highlands have no spring in their immediate periphery; it is enough to cite the cases of Samaria, Shiloh and Kiriath-jearim.
5. Geva and De Groot state that 2 Chronicles and 1 Maccabees see the City of David as separated from the Temple Mound. This too is no argument: These texts are centuries later than the Iron Age and therefore one should ask if their authors knew the meaning and location of the Iron Age City of David.

Finally, and no less important, Geva and De Groot did not answer any of the major issues listed above, involved with the identification of the City of David as the mound of Jerusalem.

1.2 Middle Bronze Jerusalem

Ussishkin (2016) reviewed the evidence for Middle Bronze fortifications along the eastern slope of the City of David ridge and proposed that all elements in fact date to the Iron IIB-C. I agree with some of his conclusions and oppose others.

I agree with Ussishkin (also Reich & Shukron, 2010: 150) that Wall 3 (Kenyon's Wall NB; Steiner, 2001: 10–12) in mid-slope above the Gihon Spring should probably be understood as a terrace or revetment rather than a fortification (for the phenomenon of terraces on the eastern slope of the City of David ridge, see Bocher, 2021). I also agree that the sherds retrieved from the narrow trench between Wall 3 and the rock scarp to its west provide only a *terminus post-quem* for its dating. I oppose the idea that the wall can be dated (to the Iron II) according to the pottery found in the debris thrown against its eastern face, on the side of the slope. This debris could have been put there to support the wall when it was built or added to an existing wall in order to reinforce it; it only provides this operation with a *terminus post-quem*. All that can be said is that the wall abuts Wall 108 (rather than is incorporated into it – contra Gadot & Uziel, 2017: 129) – the northern of the two parallel cyclopean walls which run from west to east and connect to the Spring Tower (Reich & Shukron, 2010: 149; Ussishkin, 2016: 5; more below). Despite the few large boulders (Gadot & Uziel, 2017: Fig. 4), the quality of Wall 3 is inferior to Wall 108 (Reich & Shukron, 2010: 149). Wall 3 is "trapped" in a time-slot between the construction of Wall 108 in the Middle Bronze (see below) and Wall 1 (which was built over it) of the Iron IIB.

Shiloh (1984: 26; De Groot, 2012: 147) described Wall 285 in Area E as a city-wall, which was reused in the Iron Age (Wall 219). Ussishkin is correct in seeing both as terraces on the slope and in proposing that the former is later than the Middle Bronze remains found to its west (see Reich, 2011: 260–261, who interpreted the two as one architectural element).

I do not agree with Ussishkin's proposal to date Walls 108 and 109 and the Gihon Spring Tower to the Iron Age. Reich and Shukron (2010) dated this monumental construction to the Middle Bronze. They interpreted the two parallel walls as a fortified passage leading to the spring and the Spring Tower as a system aimed to defend the water source. The pottery found in relation to Walls 108 and 109 – even if originating from fills – dates to the Middle Bronze. To differ from the case of Wall 3, there are enough find spots there to argue that if the wall had been built in the Iron Age, a few sherds from this period would have been found. No less important, the construction with cyclopean boulders is similar to at least two other sites in the highlands – Shechem and Shiloh (for the latter, see Finkelstein & Lederman, 1993);[2] I am not aware of Iron II construction of this type, certainly not in the highlands.[3]

A year after Ussishkin's article, Regev et al. (2017) published radiocarbon determinations for samples extracted under the eastern wall of the Spring Tower. The two latest results fall in the ninth century BCE. Regev et al. raised two possible interpretations for these results: (1) Construction in the Middle Bronze and repair of the wall in the Iron II; (2) construction in the Iron II. The former solution is the one to accept, because repair of the original wall can in fact be observed in the area from which the samples were taken (Regev et al., 2017: Figs. 3–4; for other arguments against the second option, see Reich, 2018). The two radiocarbon determinations which fall in the ninth century provide the earliest possible date for the repair.[4]

1.3 The Intensity of the Pre-Eighth Century BCE Remains on the City of David Ridge

Gadot and Uziel (2017) and A. Mazar (2020) listed places on the City of David ridge with what they consider as pre-eighth century BCE monumental remains. I agree with both regarding at least some of these locations, but not necessarily about the precise dating of the remains.

Gadot and Uziel speak about five "anchors":

Anchor 1: Wall 3 above the Gihon Spring. See my discussion above. Chronologically, Wall 3 is "trapped" between the Middle Bronze (Wall 108) and the Iron IIB-C (Wall 1).

Anchor 2: Building 2482 and the fortified passage. The latest items in the sherd collections retrieved from the make-up between bedrock and the floor of Building 2482 and from the floor itself (Uziel & Szanton, 2015: Figs. 7–8) belong to the Iron IIB.

---

[2] To demonstrate similar construction in the Iron Age, Ussishkin (2016, in details 2021) proposed to down-date the cyclopean wall of Hebron (Tell el-Rumeidah) from the Middle Bronze to the Iron Age. Yet, his theory is based on pottery retrieved from the glacis which supports the wall, an element that may have been part of restoration in the Iron Age of the older Middle Bronze system.

[3] Note how different the construction method of the Gihon walls is from that of the Iron Age fortification unearthed just a few meters to the south (Vukosavovic et al., 2021: Fig. 4).

[4] The date of the Gihon complex is indirectly related to the nature and date of the Rock-Cut Depression unearthed immediately to the south of Wall 109; I will discuss this issue below.

Anchor 3: The rock-cut feature (the Rock-Cut Depression below) south of the fortified passage dates to the ninth century. This is indeed a strong possibility to which I will relate below.

Anchor 4: The radiocarbon dates from the eastern wall of the spring tower. See my comments above; the collapsed part of the wall could have been repaired in the ninth century BCE or later.

Anchor 5: Wall 219 in Area E was built prior to Stratum 12a of the Iron IIB. This is a viable possibility, which would put the wall in the early phase of the Iron IIB or slightly earlier. In any event, we are probably speaking about a terrace (Ussishkin, 2016).

Gadot and Uziel offer two more observations: First, the Warren Tunnel and the southern sector of Channel II near the Gihon Spring predate the cutting of the Siloam Tunnel. Second, Monumental pre-eighth century construction can be seen in Area G and the Ophel.[5] I accept these observations and will elaborate on both below.

A. Mazar (2020) describes four locations with pre-eighth century monumental remains: Around the Gihon Spring, the Stepped Stone Structure and Large Stone Structure above the spring, the Ophel south of el-Aqsa Mosque and the Temple Mount. I agree about three of them, possibly even all four (more below) and indeed described them long ago as evidence for the first leap forward in the expansion of Jerusalem from the Temple Mount to the south and west (e.g., Finkelstein, 2012). I do not agree with A. Mazar about the exact date of construction of these elements within the early phases of the Iron Age.

1. The Temple Mount: There can be no doubt that the palace and Temple of the Davidic Dynasty were located on the Temple Mount, but without excavation it is impossible to verify the exact history of these buildings.
2. The Ophel: The earliest monumental structures in the Ophel (e.g., Mazar, 2015a: 459–474, 2018: 315–324) possibly date to the Iron IIA, in my opinion to the late Iron IIA in the ninth century BCE (details below), though a slightly later date cannot be disregarded (more below).
3. Around the Gihon Spring: In the area of the Gihon Spring we are dealing with reconstruction of a Middle Bronze wall in the ninth century BCE or later (radiocarbon dating – see above).
4. The Stepped Stone Structure and the Large Stone Structure: I agree with E. Mazar (2015b: 169–172) and with A. Mazar (2020), that the two structures could have originally belonged to one monumental architectural complex – an elaborate building on the ridge and a support system on the upper slope. I also agree with A. Mazar that the *terminus post-quem* for the construction is the Iron I, as remains dating to this period were found under both structures (Steiner, 1994; Finkelstein, 2011 respectively). Yet, I do not agree about A. Mazar's *termini ad-quem*, as he cites material in fills (much of which has not been published). I repeat past comments (e.g., Finkelstein, 2011), that Iron IIA sherds were retrieved from the stone mantle of the Stepped Stone Structure and proba-

---
[5] In this case too I am using the term (Ophel) in its modern-archaeology sense.

bly also from below the Large Stone Structure. A. Mazar dates the construction of the two structures "towards the end of Iron Age I (11th–early 10th cent. B.C.E.) or during the Early Iron Age IIA (main part of 10th cent. B.C.E.)" (Mazar, 2020: 146).[6] I date them to the late Iron IIA in the ninth century BCE.

1.4 The Date of the Monumental Architecture in the Ophel

Winderboim (2021) has recently analyzed the pottery from E. Mazar's excavations in the eastern sector of the Ophel (Mazar, 2015a: 459–474, 2018: 315–324). Following a meticulous study, he concluded that the first monumental construction at this site belongs to Horizon IIIb, which dates to the end phase of the early Iron IIA. Winderboim acknowledges that this horizon is mainly composed of fills and that it is not clean of later intrusions. Still, he asserts that this monumental phase "refutes ... the claims that Jerusalem of the Early Iron Age IIA was a small and unimpressive village" (2021: 450).

The end phase of the early Iron IIA dates in the very late tenth century BCE (e.g., Finkelstein & Kleiman, 2019), a period with no trace of monumental building activity in Judah. The first attestation in this direction comes from well-dated late Iron IIA layers of the ninth century BCE (Lachish IV, Beth-shemesh III, Beer-sheba V, Arad XI). The same holds true for Israel (the Northern Kingdom – the Megiddo VA-IVB horizon).[7] An *uniqum* in Jerusalem – the capital of the demographically depleted and culturally marginal Judah – is perhaps possible, but unlikely. In order to consider this possibility a strong case must be presented. I refer to clean pottery assemblages of complete vessels (or at least a significant sherd collection) on floors, which can be affiliated with a secure relative ceramic horizon, and with these floors clearly connected to the monumental architectural features. The system cannot stand alone; it must be compared to well-stratified sites in Judah, especially Lachish.

This is not the case in the eastern sector of the Ophel:

1. The main monumental element there is Mazar's "Straight Wall," which probably dates to the Iron IIB (Finkelstein, Forthcoming).
2. The eastern sector of the Ophel exhibits only patches of floors which are difficult to associate with the main architectural elements.
3. Winderboim speaks about seven horizons (11 sub-phases – 2021: 58). Nowhere have they been unearthed in a stratigraphic sequence; in fact, the reader gets the impression that these horizons were decided according to pottery analysis.

---

[6] Based on a large number of radiocarbon determinations at Megiddo and elsewhere, including Tel Rehov, I date the Iron I/II transition to sometime in the middle of the tenth century and the early Iron IIA to the second half of that century (e.g., Toffolo et al., 2014; Finkelstein & Kleiman, 2019 respectively).

[7] Early appearance of significant architecture in Level Q-5, which dates ca. 900 BCE (Finkelstein & Kleiman, 2019).

4. There are no pottery assemblages of restorable vessels on floors in the eastern Ophel, in fact except for one locus (more below), not even a collection of large enough sherds. Most of the pottery fragments in this area are small, sometimes tiny.
5. Distinction between early and late Iron IIA is difficult even in the case of an assemblage of complete vessels (e.g., Herzog & Singer-Avitz, 2004: 210), let alone in the case of tiny sherds.
6. Most of the pottery assemblages discussed by Winderboim originated from fills. Even in cases of patches of plaster, with no tight stratigraphy one does not know if the sherds belong to the floor or to the fill laid above it in preparation for later construction. The following citation summarizes the situation: "very few floors were found with pottery lying upon them, with the few floors that did have in-situ pottery on them yielding only small amounts of indicative pottery" (Winderboim, 2021: 8).
7. In any collection of small sherds, especially in fills, the latest items decide the date of the assemblage, as old sherds may originate from earlier earth debris, bricks, etc. This is well demonstrated in several cases:

   (a) The holemouth jar in Fig. 7.9: 2 is described as representing Horizon II (Winderboim, 2021 I: 380; II: 235), dated to the Iron I/II transition. As far as I can judge this item cannot date earlier than the later phase of the late Iron IIA, preferably slightly later.

   (b) The only locus with large parts of vessels is L12-223c, a concentration of broken storage jars found immediately on bedrock (Winderboim, 2021 II: Pl. 4). Winderboim affiliates this assemblage with Horizon IIIA, in his opinion dating to the early phase of the early Iron IIA. Yet, four of the pithoi (Mazar, 2015a: 468) appear only in the later phase of the late Iron IIA (detailed discussion in Kleiman, 2021). In other words, what looks like one of the earliest context in the eastern sector of the Ophel cannot date before the late ninth century BCE (not to mention that the broken vessels could have been part of a fill).

   (c) The cooking pot in Fig. 6.8: 10 represents Horizon IIIB, dated to the second half of the early Iron IIA. This typically Iron IIB vessel may appear in the final phase of the late Iron IIA, but not in the early Iron IIA.

   (d) The cooking pot in Fig. 7.2: 19 is described as representing Horizon III of the early Iron IIA. There are no such cooking pots in this phase of the Iron Age; they appear for the first time in the later phase of the late Iron IIA and are typical of the Iron IIB.

Winderboim dealt with the eastern sector of the Ophel. The situation in the western sector (Mazar & Mazar, 1989; Mazar, 2011) is clearer. This complex includes first and foremost the Royal Structure and the "Gatehouse" (Buildings C and D in Mazar & Mazar, 1989, probably representing a single administrative building – Finkelstein, Forthcoming). The pottery associated with the final use of these structures dates to the Iron IIC. According to E. Mazar, an early floor of these structures, found close to bedrock, dates to the Iron IIA. Yet, the latest sherds from the fills between bedrock and the supposed early floors date to the Iron IIB-C (Finkelstein, Forthcoming).[8]

To summarize, it is reasonable to date the earliest significant structures in the eastern sector of the Ophel to the late Iron IIA, but impossible to give them a precise date within this period (and impossible to dismiss a slightly later date). Placing these remains in the late Iron IIA is supported by the broader situation in Judah; I refer to the appearance of monumental structures in places such as Lachish, Beth-shemesh, Beer-sheba and Arad. The structures in the western sector of the Ophel were added in the Iron IIB. The buildings in the west continued to function until the destruction of Jerusalem in 586 BCE; the poor preservation of the structures in the east does not allow tracing their history in the Iron IIB-C.

1.5 Is There Evidence in the Givati Parking Lot Excavations for Continuous Activity Between the Iron IIC and the Late Hellenistic Period?

Shalev et al. (2020) have recently published a preliminary report on the excavation of Iron IIC-to-late Hellenistic remains in Area 10 in the Givati Parking Lot. They describe four layers, dating to the Iron IIC, Persian, early Hellenistic (Seleucid) and late Hellenistic (Hasmonean) periods. The first and third of the four are represented by superimposed public buildings.

The Persian period is represented by a few poor wall stabs and a pit which cut into the destruction debris of the Iron IIC. The Ptolemaic period is absent here. Next comes a large Seleucid structure (Building 110) constructed into the ruins of Iron IIC Building 100. A coin of Antiochus III dated between 198 and 187 BCE found under its floor gives the *terminus post-quem* for the construction. There is nothing significant between the Iron Age and Seleucid remains (walls of Building 110 were constructed directly over walls of Building 100), showing that there was almost no activity here for about four centuries, between 586 and the early second century BCE.

Previous excavations in the Givati Parking Lot south of Area 10 revealed pottery from the Persian period with no architectural remains associated with it (Ben-Ami, 2013: 4) and several remains from the Hellenistic period (idem: 19–22), dated by Sandhaus (2013) to the second half of the second century BCE. Sandhaus added: "Based on the appearance of earlier Hellenistic ceramic types in the assemblage, we suggest that some activity took place in the immediate vicinity during the third century BCE" (Sandhaus, 2013: 98). Freud (2017: 100, 2018: 252–254) proposed that a few sherds from Ben-Ami's poorly built Strata X and IX date to the Persian period (accepted by Shalev et al., 2020: 160). If so, it may be understood as another

---

[8] Pottery from debris found against the outer (southern) face of the structures are not discussed here; the earth could have been brought from any location and hence these sherds have lesser chronological value.

post-destruction squatter activity. An ashlar-built structure and the fortification system unearthed in the eastern sector of the excavation dates to the first half of the second century BCE (Ben-Ami & Tchekhanovets, 2015, 2016).

To summarize, it seems that the excavation in the Givati Parking Lot supports the broader picture for the four centuries between ca. 586–200 BCE in the City of David ridge (Finkelstein, 2008): A few poor remains (mainly pottery sherds), representing squatters and activities related to the nearby spring.

2 An Updated Settlement History

Table 1 summarizes my understanding of the situation in the different parts of the City of David ridge.

The table is sufficient to show that the mound of Jerusalem cannot be identified in the City of David Ridge, which lacks evidence for settlement activity in much of the Middle Bronze-to-late Hellenistic sequence, including periods well-attested textually. The only solution is that the old mound was located on the Temple Mount. This was the sole location of the settlement except for two phases: the (late?) ninth-to-early sixth centuries and the late second century BCE (and later).

A point to clarify before I continue: Isolated buildings are frequently found near tell sites (e.g., Peersmann, 2006 for Megiddo). In the case of Jerusalem, with the spring slightly distant from the mound on the Temple Mount and cultivation plots in the Kidron Valley, discovery of isolated houses along the eastern slope of the City of David ridge should not come as a surprise. The intensity of excavations along this line indeed facilitated such discoveries. In other words, a single structure in a given period, with no similar evidence in the many other areas dug along the ridge, cannot be interpreted as representing a settlement – village or town.

2.1 From the Middle Bronze to the Iron I

Middle Bronze remains are restricted to two areas: Monumental construction near and around the spring and some activity to the south of the spring (Areas E and J for the latter, see Reich & Shukron, 2021). This is so despite the fact that in many places excavations reached bedrock. Hence there is no way to speak about a Middle Bronze town on the City of David ridge. The two parallel monumental walls (Walls 108 and 109) should probably be interpreted as a fortified passage leading to the fortified spring (Reich & Shukron, 2010). If so, a fortress must have existed on the ridge, similar to the second century BCE Hellenistic fortification that has recently been interpreted as part of the Akra (Ben-Ami & Tchekhanovets, 2016). The domestic structures in Areas E and J are related to the spring and cultivation in the Kidron Valley.

Table 1 Remains in the different sectors of the City of David ridge (stray sherds not included)

	Ophel	Area G and Visitors' Center	Givati Parking Lot	Gihon Spring area	South (Area E)
Middle Bronze	–	–	–	Walls 108, 109 and Spring Tower; quarry?	Several structures
Late Bronze	–	–	–	–	–
Iron I (until ca. 950)	–	A few remains under the SSS and the LSS	–	–	?
Early Iron IIA	?	–	–	–	–
Late Iron IIA	Significant remains	The early phase of the SSS and the LSS	Structures on the western slope	Repair of Middle Bronze Spring Tower; Rock-Cut Depression?	Several remains
Iron IIB	Monumental buildings	?	V	Fill and building	V
Iron IIC	Monumental building	Buildings over the SSS	Public building; destruction layer	?	V
Persian	–	–	Squatters	–	Scanty remains
Early Hell (Ptolemaic)	?	?	–	–	Scanty remains
Early Hell (Seleucid)			Fortifications and public buildings		
Late Hell (Hasmonean)	?	Fortification	V	–	Terraces and burials

SSS Stepped Stone Structure, *LSS* Large Stone Structure

Evidence for activity on the City of David ridge in the Late Bronze Age is limited to stray sherds, almost always found in later debris. These are found above the spring and in its vicinity and hence seem to represent activity near the water source. Evidently, this does not fit the textual evidence from the Amarna tablets, for Jerusalem being the hub of a city-state which ruled over the southern highlands and was involved in affairs in other parts of the country (on Jerusalem in the Amarna period, see Na'aman, 1996;[9] on activity of Jerusalem in areas to its west, Finkelstein, 2014). The Iron I is slightly better represented; remains of structures were found both under the terraces on the slope (Steiner, 1994) and under the Large Stone

---

[9] Na'aman saw this as a demonstration that sometimes archaeology provides negative evidence for places which are attested in textual materials. At least in this case I interpret the finds in an opposite way: Since the evidence from the City of David ridge – intensively excavated in the last century – is negative, the mound should be sought elsewhere – on the Temple Mount.

Structure on the ridge (Mazar, 2009: 59–60; see Finkelstein, 2011). Still, this testimony too is restricted to the area above the spring.

2.2 The Iron IIA

For now, there is no clear testimony for activity on the City of David Ridge in the early Iron IIA.

The first activity on the City of David ridge not restricted to the area of the spring dates to the late Iron IIA. All significant remains are located in the northern and central part of the ridge. I refer to buildings in the eastern sector of the Ophel immediately to the south of el-Aqsa Mosque (Mazar, 2015a: 459–474, 2018: 315–324), the early phase of the Stepped Stone Structure and the Large Stone Structure above the Gihon and domestic buildings on the western slope of the Givati Parking Lot (Ben-Ami, 2013: 8–10, 2014). I would interpret the Large Stone Structure (and its support – the Stepped Stone Structure) as an administrative building related to the activity in and around the spring. Attention to the spring is evident from the radiocarbon results for samples extracted under the eastern wall of the Spring Tower, which attest to renovation of a collapsed segment of the tower.

Another late Iron IIA activity spot, related to the spring, can be theorized for the Rock-Cut Depression unearthed immediately to the south of Wall 109, near the Gihon Tower. Evidently, being higher than the spring, this feature cannot be interpreted as a pool. Gill (2012; followed by Ussishkin, 2016) suggested explaining it as a quarry, probably for the large boulders used in the construction of Walls 108 and 109 and the Gihon Spring Tower. Yet, the well-cut smooth rock walls of the depression do not fit a quarry (and do not preserve indication for this interpretation, hence the boulders found inside the depression cannot be understood as left-overs from a quarry). A possible hint for the original use of the depression is the Round Chamber located at its bottom, in its northeastern corner, which at a certain stage received water from the Gihon Spring via Channel II and Tunnel III. I am aware of the fact that the cutting of the rock in the Round Chamber is of a lower quality than in the Rock-Cut Depression. Still, it seems to me that what follows is the only logical history of this area, which squares with most of the evidence.

Of course, there could have been a quarry here in the Middle Bronze for boulders used in the construction of Walls 108 and 109 and the Spring Tower; but there are no clear indications for this theory. What we see today is a nicely cut depression; I suggest that it was meant to provide access to the water, similar to the pool at Gibeon (Pritchard, 1961). There are two possibilities here: (1) The idea was to reach the water (to be fed by a tunnel) in the full space of the bottom of the depression, but at a certain point work was stopped and the water was reached only in the Round Chamber. (2) A system of a rectangular depression and a deeper round approach to the water was planned from the outset. At Gibeon too we see a nicely cut round depression and a lesser-quality stepped tunnel continuing from its bottom. The Rock-Cut Depression dates before the latest sherds in the debris which filled it (late ninth century BCE according to De Groot & Fadida, 2011, or late eighth century according to Singer-Avitz, 2012), and by logic before the cutting of the Siloam Tunnel and probably also the Warren system. A date in the Iron IIA or the early Iron IIB seems the most probable. The large-scale activity in this part of the City of David ridge in the Iron IIA, including reconstruction of the Spring Tower (according to the radiocarbon evidence) seem to point to the Iron IIA, in the ninth century BCE.

When the Siloam Tunnel was hewn (or before, when the Warren Tunnel was cut) there was no longer any use for this water system. In the Iron IIB it was filled and a building was constructed over the fill. The boulders at the bottom of the depression could have been part of the fill (pushed down from Wall 109?), or may represent a phase of neglect and collapse from Wall 109 – perhaps during the earthquake of ca.760 BCE.

Above I discussed four pieces of evidence for late Iron IIA activity in the northern and central part of the ridge. Together, they seem to represent the first expansion of Jerusalem from the mound on the Temple Mount toward the spring. There is no indication for a fortification in this new sector of the city. Judging from central Judahite towns in the Shephelah and the Beer-sheba Valley (e.g., Lachish and Beer-sheba) and from the clue in the chronistic verse of 2 Kings 14:13, the mound itself must have been fortified.

When exactly in the framework of the late Iron IIA did this expansion take place? With sherds rather than restorable floor assemblages and with no radiocarbon results from reliable contexts, this is difficult to establish. Broader historical reasoning may hint at the second half of the century. I refer to the possibility that the expansion of Judah to the Shephelah (Lachish IV, Beth-shemesh III) and Beer-sheba Valley (Beer-sheba V and Arad XI) and prosperity in Jerusalem took place under the auspices of Damascus in the days of Hazael.

2.3 The Iron IIB-C

Starting in the Iron IIB, Jerusalem extended over the entire area of the City of David ridge and the southwestern hill (the Armenian and Jewish Quarters of the Old City). This expansion was rapid; in the late eighth century the city was already surrounded by a massive fortification. Elsewhere I suggested linking the unprecedented demographic and geographic expansion of Jerusalem with the fall of the Northern Kingdom and the incorporation of Judah into the Assyrian imperial system (Finkelstein, 2015). If so, the process can be even further restricted chronologically – to the last third of the eighth century BCE.

2.4 The Persian and Hellenistic Periods

There is no indication for permanent settlement activity along the City of David ridge in the Persian and early Hellenistic (Ptolemaic) periods. Pottery sherds, including stamped handles, found in the vicinity of the Gihon Spring and above it may indicate some activity near the water source. Squatter activity was detected over the ruins of Building 100 in the Givati Parking Lot excavation (Shalev et al., 2020) and in Area E (De Groot, 2012: 173–177). Textual sources (the Elephantine and Zenon papyri) indicate that Jerusalem was inhabited in these centuries and hence the inevitable conclusion is that the settlement shrank back to the original mound on the Temple Mount; the meager number of pottery sherds from this period found in soundings around the Temple Mount shows that it was a modest settlement. The first indication for renewed expansion to the City of David ridge can be traced in the Seleucid period in the first half of the second century BCE. Evidence comes from the Givati Parking Lot: The fortification in its eastern sector (Ben-Ami & Tchekhanovets, 2016) and two public buildings nearby (Building 110 in Shalev et al., 2020 and another structure in Ben-Ami & Tchekhanovets, 2015). The fortification may be interpreted as belonging to a fort built above the spring, somewhat similar to what I described above for the Middle Bronze and Iron IIA. Jerusalem expanded back to the entire area of the City of David ridge and the southwestern hill in Hasmonean times in the late Hellenistic period, starting in the second half of the second century BCE.

3 Summary

The original mound of Jerusalem was located on the Temple Mount. From there in times of prosperity the settlement expanded to the south and west and in periods of decline receded. In two periods – in the Iron Age and the Hellenistic period – expansion is characterized by two stages: First to the area of the Gihon Spring, with a fort or administrative building above the water source, and then to the entire City of David ridge and the southwestern hill.

In the era discussed here this would mean:

- Settlement restricted to the mound on the Temple Mount: Late Bronze, Iron I, probably early Iron IIA, Persian and early Hellenistic (Ptolemaic) periods.
- Expansion, to the area of the Gihon Spring: Middle Bronze, late Iron IIA (and early Iron IIB?), and the early Hellenistic (Seleucid) period.
- Full expansion to the City of David ridge and the southwestern hill: late Iron IIB and Iron IIC and the late Hellenistic period.

References

Ben-Ami, D. (2013). *Jerusalem: Excavations in the Tyropoeon Valley* (Givati Parking Lot) (IAA Reports 52). Israel Antiquities Authority.

Ben-Ami, D. (2014). Notes on the Iron IIA settlement in Jerusalem in light of excavations in the northwest of the City of David. *Tel Aviv, 41*, 3–19.

Ben-Ami, D., & Tchekhanovets, Y. (2015). The gaps closed—The Late Hellenistic Period in the City of David. *Eretz-Israel, 31*, 30–37. (Hebrew)

Ben-Ami, D., & Tchekhanovets, Y. (2016). 'Then they built up the City of David with a high, strong wall and strong towers, and it became their citadel' (I Mac 1:33). *City of David Studies of Ancient Jerusalem, 11*, 19*–29*.

Bocher, E. (2021). The fortifications on the Eastern Slopes of the City of David in Areas A and J: A reappraisal. *New Studies in the Archaeology of Jerusalem and its Region, 14*, 39–52. (Hebrew)

De Groot, A. (2012). Discussion and conclusions. In A. De Groot & H. Bernick-Greenberg (Eds.), *Excavations at the City of David 1978–1985 Directed by Yigal Shiloh*, Vol. VIIA: *Area E: Stratigraphy and architecture* (Qedem 53) (pp. 141–184). Hebrew University.

De Groot, A., & Fadida, A. (2011). The pottery assemblage from the Rock-Cut Pool near the Gihon Spring. *Tel Aviv, 38*, 158–166.

Finkelstein, I. (2008). Jerusalem in the Persian (and Early Hellenistic) Period and the Wall of Nehemiah. *Journal for the Study of the Old Testament, 32*, 501–520.

Finkelstein, I. (2011). The "Large stone structure" in Jerusalem: Reality versus yearning. *Zeitschrift des Deutschen Palästina-Vereins, 127*, 1–10.

Finkelstein, I. (2012). L'archéologie et l'histoire de Jérusalem (1000 à 700 av. J.C.). *Comptes rendus de l'Académie des Inscriptions & Belles-Lettres*, 827–858.

Finkelstein, I. (2014). The Shephelah and Jerusalem's western border in the Amarna period. *Egypt and the Levant, 24*, 265–274.

Finkelstein, I. (2015). Migration of Israelites into Judah after 720 BCE: An answer and an update. *Zeitschrift für die Alttestamentliche Wissenschaft, 127*, 188–206.

Finkelstein, I. (Forthcoming). *The "Ophel" complex in Jerusalem: A critical analysis.*

Finkelstein, I., & Kleiman, A. (2019). The archaeology of the days of Baasha? *Revue Biblique, 126*, 277–296.

Finkelstein, I., & Lederman, Z. (1993). Area H-F: Middle Bronze III fortifications and storerooms. In I. Finkelstein (Ed.), *Shiloh: The archaeology of a biblical site* (Monograph series of the Institute of Archaeology, Tel Aviv University 10) (pp. 49–64). Tel Aviv University.

Finkelstein, I., Koch, I., & Lipschits, O. (2011). The mound on the mount: A solution to the "Problem with Jerusalem"? *Journal of Hebrew Scriptures, 11*, Article 12.

Freud, L. (2017). Production and widespread use of Holemouth vessels in Jerusalem and its environs in the Iron Age II: Typology, chronology and distribution. *New Studies in the Archaeology of Jerusalem and Its Region, 11*, 93–110. (Hebrew)

Freud, L. (2018). *Judahite pottery in the transitional phase between the Iron Age and the Persian Period: Jerusalem and its environs*. PhD. thesis, Tel-Aviv University. (Hebrew with an English abstract)

Gadot, Y., & Uziel, J. (2017). The monumentality of Iron Age Jerusalem prior to the 8th century BCE. *Tel Aviv, 44*, 123–140.

Geva, H., & De Groot, A. (2017). The City of David is not on the Temple Mount after all. *Israel Exploration Journal, 67*, 32–49.

Gill, D. (2012). Controversial issues in understanding the water supply systems in the City of David: The 'Rock-Cut Pool', 'Round Chamber', Channels III, IV, V and VI and the feeding of the Siloam Channel. *New Studies on Jerusalem, 18*, 31–74. (Hebrew)

Herzog, Z., & Singer-Avitz, L. (2004). Redefining the centre: The emergence of state in Judah. *Tel Aviv, 31*, 209–244.

Hutzli, J. (2011). The meaning of the expression 'ir dawid in Samuel and Kings. *Tel Aviv, 38*, 167–178.

Kleiman, A. (2021). The date of the Ophel Pithos inscription: An archaeological perspective. *Zeitschrift des Deutschen Palästina-Vereins, 137*, 167–179.

Knauf, E. A. (2000). Jerusalem in the Late Bronze and Early Iron Ages: A proposal. *Tel Aviv, 27*, 75–90.

Mazar, E. (2009). *The Palace of King David, excavations at the summit of the City of David, preliminary report of seasons 2005–2007*. Shoham Academic Research and Publication.

Mazar, E. (2011). *Discovering the Solomonic Wall in Jerusalem*. Shoham Academic Research and Publication.

Mazar, E. (2015a). *The Ophel excavations to the South of the Temple Mount 2009–2013: Final reports volume I*. Shoham Academic Research and Publication.

Mazar, E. (2015b). *The summit of the City of David excavations 2005–2008: Final reports volume I*. Shoham Academic Research and Publication.

Mazar, E. (2018). *The Ophel excavations to the South of the Temple Mount 2009–2013: Final reports volume II*. Shoham Academic Research and Publication.

Mazar, A. (2020). Jerusalem in the 10th cent. B.C.E.: A response. *Zeitschrift des Deutschen Palästina-Vereins, 136*, 139–151.

Mazar, E., & Mazar, B. (1989). *Excavations in the South of the Temple Mount: The Ophel of Biblical Jerusalem* (Qedem 29). Hebrew University.

Na'aman, N. (1996). The contribution of the Amarna letters to the debate on Jerusalem's political position in the tenth century B.C.E. *Bulletin of the American Schools of Oriental Research, 304*, 17–27.

Peersmann, J. (2006). Area N (The 1999 season). In I. Finkelstein, D. Ussishkin, & B. Halpern (Eds.), *Megiddo IV: The 1998–2002 seasons* (Monograph series of the Institute of Archaeology, Tel Aviv University 24) (pp. 81–86). Tel Aviv University.

Pritchard, J. B. (1961). *The water system of Gibeon*. University Museum, University of Pennsylvania.

Regev, J., Uziel, J., Szanton, N., & Boaretto, E. (2017). Absolute dating of the Gihon Spring fortifications, Jerusalem. *Radiocarbon, 59*, 1–23.

Reich, R. (2011). *Excavating the City of David; where Jerusalem's history began*. Israel Exploration Society.

Reich, R. (2018). The date of the Gihon Spring Tower in Jerusalem. *Tel Aviv, 45*, 114–119.

Reich, R., & Shukron, E. (2010). A new segment of the Middle Bronze fortification in the City of David. *Tel Aviv, 37*, 141–153.

Reich, R., & Shukron, E. (2021). Area J, stratigraphy and architecture. In R. Reich & E. Shukron (Eds.), *Excavations in the City of David, Jerusalem (1995–2010): Areas A, J, F, H, D and L, final report* (pp. 171–214). University Park.

Sandhaus, D. (2013). The Hellenistic period. In D. Ben-Ami (Ed.), *Jerusalem: Excavations in the Tyropoeon Valley (Givati Parking Lot)* (IAA reports 52) (pp. 83–108). Israel Antiquities Authority.

Shalev, Y., Shalom, N., Bocher, E., & Gadot, Y. (2020). New evidence on the location and nature of Iron Age, Persian and Early Hellenistic Period Jerusalem. *Tel Aviv, 47*, 149–172.

Shiloh, Y. (1984). *Excavations at the City of David I: 1978–1982: Interim report of the first five seasons* (Qedem 19). Hebrew University.

Singer-Avitz, L. (2012). The date of the pottery from the Rock-Cut Pool near the Gihon Spring in the City of David, Jerusalem. *Zeitschrift des Deutschen Palästina-Vereins, 128*, 10–14.

Steiner, M. L. (1994). Re-dating the terraces of Jerusalem. *Israel Exploration Journal, 44*, 13–20.

Steiner, M. L. (2001). *Excavations by Kathleen M. Kenyon in Jerusalem 1961–1967, volume III; the settlement in the Bronze and Iron Ages*. Sheffield Academic Press.

Toffolo, M. B., Arie, E., Martin, M. A. S., Boaretto, E., & Finkelstein, I. (2014). Absolute chronology of Megiddo, Israel, in the Late Bronze and Iron Ages: High-resolution radiocarbon dating. *Radiocarbon, 56*, 221–244.

Ussishkin, D. (2016). Was Jerusalem a fortified stronghold in the Middle Bronze Age? An alternative view. *Levant, 48*, 135–151.

Ussishkin, D. (2021). The date of the Cyclopean Wall at *Tell er-Rumede/Tel Hevron*. *Zeitschrift des Deutschen Palästina-Vereins, 137*, 125–136.

Uziel, J., & Szanton, N. (2015). Recent excavations near the Gihon Spring and their reflection on the character of Iron II Jerusalem. *Tel Aviv, 42*, 233–250.

Vukosavovic, F., Chalaf, O., & Uziel, J. (2021). "And you counted the houses of Jerusalem and pulled houses down to forfity the wall" (Isaiah 22:10): The fortifications of Iron Age II Jerusalem in light of new discoveries in the City of David. *New Studies in the Archaeology of Jerusalem and its Region, 14*, 1*–16*.

Winderboim, A. (2021). *The Iron IIA pottery assemblages from the Ophel excavations and their contribution to the understanding of the settlement history of Jerusalem*. PhD. thesis, Tel Aviv University, Tel Aviv.

The Interconnections Between Jerusalem and Samaria in the Ninth to Eighth Centuries BCE: Material Culture, Connectivity and Politics

Yuval Gadot, Assaf Kleiman , and Joe Uziel

Abstract The relations between Israel and Judah are often described in contemporary research as extremely unbalanced, with the latter being portrayed as thriving in the shadow of its stronger and more influential northern neighbor, most likely as its vassal. In this study, we examine this common hypothesis from an archaeological perspective, assuming that close relations between the two kingdoms would have stimulated the flow of objects and ideas across the highlands and thus be reflected in the material culture. We suggest that the archaeological record of Jerusalem, the Benjamin Plateau and southern Samaria reflects a low level of connectivity across the highlands in the ninth to eighth centuries BCE prior to the downfall of the Northern Kingdom, thus challenging the conventional understanding of the power relations in this region. In our view, Judah was an independent socio-political entity for most of its existence with Jerusalem as its capital.

Keywords Jerusalem · Omride dynasty · Israelite kingdom · Kingdom of Judah · Samaria · Material culture · Contact zones

1 Introduction

Historical reconstructions of the geopolitical map of the southern Levant in the ninth and eighth centuries BCE have frequently discussed the unbalanced relations between Israel and Judah, with the latter usually being depicted as the smaller and

Y. Gadot (✉)
Tel Aviv University, Tel Aviv, Israel
e-mail: ygadot@gmail.com

A. Kleiman
Ben-Gurion University of the Negev, Beer-Sheva, Israel
e-mail: assafkle@bgu.ac.il

J. Uziel
Israel Antiquities Authority, Jerusalem, Israel
e-mail: joeuziel@gmail.com

© The Author(s), under exclusive license to Springer Nature Switzerland AG 2023
E. Ben-Yosef, I. W. N. Jones (eds.), *"And in Length of Days Understanding" (Job 12:12): Essays on Archaeology in the Eastern Mediterranean and Beyond in Honor of Thomas E. Levy*, Interdisciplinary Contributions to Archaeology, https://doi.org/10.1007/978-3-031-27330-8_33

less regionally-connected polity (e.g., Finkelstein, 2013: 162–164). It was even suggested that Judah was Israel's protégée for relatively long periods: at first, during the days of the Omride kings in the first half of the ninth century, and again, during the reign of Jeroboam II in the first half of the eighth century BCE, possibly even until the fall of the Kingdom of Israel in 720 BCE.[1] For the most part, these suggestions are based on biblical traditions and scarce extra-biblical sources, such as the Tel Dan stele, rather than archaeological finds (and see, e.g., Na'aman, 2019: 17–18, who contests the idea of Israelite domination of Judah, apart from a short window of time during the rule of Joash). In theory, it makes sense to think that if Judah was indeed under the political hegemony of the Kingdom of Israel for long periods, these relations would be manifested in the material culture, as objects and ideas are likely to flow in such conditions between Samaria and Jerusalem. Nevertheless, this assumption was never put to the archaeological test: Were there trade relations between the two cities? And if so, how intensive were they? Furthermore, can we document a flow of ideas between the two entities based on the material culture alone?

In this article, we wish to explore possible evidence for connectivity between Samaria and Jerusalem in the ninth and eighth centuries BCE as manifested in the material culture, particularly on pottery, other clay objects such as bullae, and architecture. We chose to focus the discussion mostly on Jerusalem and the contact zone between the two kingdoms (i.e., southern Samaria and the Benjamin Plateau) since it is not entirely clear whether the Judahite kings were already able at this early stage to affect settlements located beyond the immediate vicinity of the city such as Beth-Shemesh, Lachish or Beersheba (for the non-centralized nature of Judah in the ninth and eighth centuries BCE, see Shai & Maeir, 2018; for a map with the sites mentioned in this paper, see Fig. 1).

On a personal note, the research presented here is based on the analysis of finds from Jerusalem, of which Thomas E. Levy has been a consistent, enthusiastic supporter (and see recently Levy, 2021). It is, therefore, with great pleasure that we offer this contribution in his honor.

2 Israel's Expansion to the Northern Valleys and Its Reflection in the Material Culture

Before turning our attention to the highlands, it is important to take a close look at how the north-Israelite kings imposed their political authority over the northern valleys and at the expression of this domination in the local settlement system and material culture. Notwithstanding the different environmental conditions in the

---

[1] See, e.g., Miller & Hayes, 2006: 286, 303–304, 316, 352–357; Sergi, 2013: 232–237; Finkelstein, 2013: 162–164; Frevel, 2018: 190–191, 234–235; Ska 2021; Knauf & Niemann, 2021: 189–190, 223–225; and see especially Finkelstein & Römer, 2020.

Judean Hills, the case of the northern valleys should provide us with a general idea of what we should expect to find in Jerusalem, which as mentioned before, was assumed to have been dominated by the Kingdom of Israel as well.

Attempts to identify the political control of a highland polity in the material culture of northern Israel were made quite early in the research, for instance, Yadin's (1970, 1972: 147–164) famous interpretation of the six-chambered gates unearthed in Hazor, Megiddo, and Gezer as the building projects of King Solomon as described in 1 Kgs 9:15. More recently, Finkelstein (2000, 2013: 85–105) proposed that these gates, as well as other monumental contemporaneous building projects, should be understood as a materialistic expression of the territorial expansion of the Kingdom of Israel in the days of the Omride kings (see also Finkelstein & Lipschits, 2010).[2] Among the listed features, predominantly identified in Samaria and Tel Jezreel, are podium structures, casemate walls, six-chambered gates, and earthworks, e.g., rock-cut quarries, moats, and ramparts.[3] In addition, it is possible to add to this list Ussishkin's (1990: 77) observation that the use of ashlar masonry (and especially the discovery of masons' marks) may suggest cultural and political affiliation with the Northern Kingdom, whereas this construction technique is rare in the south before the late eighth century BCE (see a review of the data in Shiloh, 1979: 50–59).[4] As for the ceramic evidence, it is generally agreed that there is a relatively high degree of morphological uniformity in the pottery traditions of north-Israelite sites, along with some small-scale regional differences (Arie, 2013; Singer-Avitz, 2018).[5]

---

[2] Needless to say, the date of many of these monuments is still debated. Beyond the common disagreements regarding their possible tenth century BCE date (e.g., Mazar, 2014: 355–358), a post-Omride date has also been considered for some of them. This is the case of the casemate wall revealed at Samaria (Franklin, 2004: 189–202; Sergi & Gadot, 2017: 106), as well as of the six-chambered gate exposed at Megiddo (e.g., Ussishkin, 1980, 2020). Noteworthy as well is that the date and political affiliation of some of the fortresses that were listed in the past as Omride strongholds were recently contested (Katz, 2021 [for Har Adir]; Sergi & Kleiman, 2018: 3–5 [for Tel 'Ein Gev]).

[3] Due to the exceptional human and physical resources invested in the construction of the features mentioned above, as well as their impact on the layout of the sites in which they were built and surroundings, they are often considered one of the ideological products of the Kingdom of Israel (see, e.g., Finkelstein, 1999; Sergi & Gadot, 2017). For the social background of the constructions of the Bronze Age ramparts, see Bunimovitz, 1992.

[4] An alleged exception for this rule is Building 101 at Tel 'Eitun. Even though the ceramic assemblages originated from the destruction of the structure were dated to the second half of the eighth century BCE (Katz & Faust, 2012), and that no substantial stratification or Iron Age IIA pottery was found in it, Faust and Sapir (2018) argued that it was built in the early tenth century BCE. For a critique of this suggestion, see Shai & Maeir, 2018: n. 6; Finkelstein, 2020: 86–87. Recently, Faust and Sapir (2021) responded to this critique and continued to date the structure to the tenth century BCE, although this is still questionable.

[5] Such local variances are especially apparent in sites that reflect strong cultural continuity from the second millennium BCE, such as Tel Rehov in the Beth-shean Valley (Mazar, 2020). Morphological uniformity of mundane items in northern Israel, as opposed to objects with evident administrative aspects (e.g., the hippo and holemouth jars), probably reflect the close cultural and/or economic contacts between the local communities, regardless of political affiliation. For a detailed discussion on the relations between material culture and political entities, see Kletter, 1999.

Several vessel types, such as hippo and holemouth jars, are particularly indicative for the territories controlled by the Northern Kingdom and are assumed to reflect the existence of cross-regional administrative and economic networks (Alexandre, 1995; Butcher et al., 2022; Kleiman, 2017). Lastly, we can mention that the north-Israelite kings also acted to change the local settlement hierarchies of the northern valleys in a significant way through the establishment of agricultural estates such as Horvat Tevet (Sergi et al., 2020), the construction of new royal centers, such as Jezreel and Megiddo (Sergi & Gadot, 2017) or through the restoration of prominent sites that were sparely settled in the Iron Age I, such as Hazor (Kleiman, 2019: 305).

From this brief overview, we can conclude that Israel's territorial expansion in the ninth century BCE, from the Samaria Highlands to the lowlands below, manifested itself mainly through the establishment of a network of newly shaped political and agricultural centers and tightening their interconnections through the use of dedicated containers (e.g., hippo storage jars).

3 Objects on the Move? Evidence for Trade Relations Between Samaria and Jerusalem

Conventionally, tracing cross-regional trade through material culture is limited to the identification of tangible objects that might have been exchanged due to their exceptional properties (e.g., Philip & Badreshany, 2020 and further references therein).[6] When it comes to connections between two neighboring highland entities such as Jerusalem and Samaria, there are very few natural resources that might have been exclusively available or produced at one site and entirely missing at the other site, and so there is little motivation for the development of intensive trade relations. However, it is important to note that economic exchange is usually interwoven with the consolidation of political relations and that in these cases, we may expect to see reciprocal relations between elite groups in Samaria and Jerusalem (see, e.g., Faust, 2019). In order to examine this issue, we focus on the following paragraphs on two categories of objects found in large numbers in Jerusalem.

3.1 Pottery

Recent ceramic studies, including both typological (Uziel et al., 2019; Singer Avitz, 2019; Winderbaum, 2021) and petrographic (Cohen-Weinberger et al., 2017; Ben-Shlomo, 2018, 2019) analyses, provide an opportunity to examine the level of

---

[6] Residue analysis, a method of discovering intangible trade relations (Weiner, 2010: 23–30), has only just began. While future research in this field will certainly contribute to this discussion, as of now the data is still too limited.

interaction between Judah and Israel in general and Jerusalem and Samaria in particular. Morphologically, several ceramic types stand out as "northern" or "southern" in the local pottery traditions (Amiran, 1969, more recently Singer-Avitz, 2018). Some examples are the closed cooking pots (Uziel et al., 2019: 75–77), 'Ajrud-type pithoi (Kleiman, 2021: 168–173) and early lmlk and lmlk type storage jars (Gitin, 2006; Sergi et al., 2012; Shai & Maeir, 2003), which are quite common in sites in the south including Jerusalem, but generally do not appear in the north. In contrast, northern types which do not appear, or are rare in the south, including Jerusalem, are hippo (Alexandre, 1995) and torpedo (Lehmann, 1996: 433–435) storage jars, thin-walls and densely burnished bowls ("Samaria Ware"), which most likely originated from Phoenicia (Stern, 2015: 436–437), and open vessels of the Cypriot Black-on-Red Ware (Schreiber, 2003: 34, Map 7; Gilboa, 2015: 487).

A more precise evaluation of trade relations can be reached through petrography. Recent works conducted by Cohen-Weinberger et al. (2017), and subsequently, Ben-Shlomo (2018, 2019; see also Ben-Shlomo & Mommsen, 2018), stress the use of microscopic ceramic analysis in recreating relationships involving trade and cultural influence. Especially important is Ben-Shlomo's comprehensive study, which is based on the examination of over 400 clay vessels that were found in various excavations in Jerusalem (Ben-Shlomo, 2019: 126–165, Table 6.1). His results demonstrate that very few of the vessels found in Jerusalem were imported from the Samaria Highlands in the Iron Age II—only five items out of 451 examined vessels (Ben-Shlomo, 2018: Table 2; 2019: Table 9.1). Remarkably, most of the imported ceramics were produced in Philistia (as also shown by Cohen-Weinberger et al., 2017), especially during the Iron IIA. This is a surprising result considering the assumed political ties between Israel and Judah, as well as the fact that a major highway connected between their capitals (the Jerusalem-Nablus Road, see Dorsey, 1991: 132–136, Map 7).

3.2 Bullae

One of the most outstanding finds of Iron Age Jerusalem is the large number of bullae. These finds are roughly divided into two groups: the earlier, iconographic bullae and the later, epigraphic bullae. Bullae were not directly traded, but if their clay proves to not from other places then Jerusalem, then they attest to the movements of containers or documents. Once again, the petrographic studies conducted on these finds seem to indicate their local production (see, e.g., Goren & Gurwin, 2013; Goren et al., 2014). The local nature of these finds seems to signify the realm in which Jerusalem's economy was based, within its more direct vicinity. From an iconographic perspective, special attention has been given to a few of the bullae that display symbols that are associated with northern entities, most notably the depiction of a Phoenician ship and the presence of Proto-Aeolic capitals on several bullae found in a secondary deposition in the rock-carved installation southwest of the Gihon Spring (Reich et al., 2007; Keel, 2017). Still, it is important to mention that these only consist of a small portion of the entire collection. The presence of the volute capitals on bullae is also notable, as the actual stone-made capitals only seem to appear in Judah from the late eighth century BCE (at the earliest) onward (Lipschits, 2011). However, as noted above, to date, all evidence of the production of these bullae indicates that they were locally made, including the earlier, iconographic examples (Goren & Gurwin, 2013).[7] Therefore, despite the presence of a small amount of northern symbolism, the bullae, in fact, indicate a much more localized trade network revolving around the direct region of Jerusalem. In this respect, it is interesting to note that many of the bullae discussed above were found in a fill that also contained thousands of fish bones (Adler & Lernau, 2021: Table 3). While it is clear that the bullae are local and therefore not necessarily connected with the fish, the bones are an important indication for importing fish that originated from distant sources, including the Mediterranean Sea, the Red Sea, the northern lakes, and the Egyptian Nile.

4 Set in Stone? Evidence for Northern Influences on the Architectural Style of Jerusalem

Based on the evidence for the north-Israelite expansion from the Samaria Highlands to the north and to the southeast (as presented above), the relations between Israel and Judah, and especially the assumed political superiority of the former, could also, in theory, be expressed in northern influence on the local architectural traditions of Jerusalem, specifically in monumental buildings built before the late eighth century BCE (Gadot & Uziel, 2017).

The architecture of Jerusalem is deeply related to its physical attributes and limitations, particularly the deep valleys that surround its hills, and the steep slopes leading down to these valleys. Of no less importance is the location of the city's water source, which drew the settlement, to begin with, to one of the site's most difficult slopes, just above the Kidron Valley. The local architecture is primarily built of stone natural to the local vicinity, i.e., the limestone formations (*malake, mizzi hilu*) that form the upper geological layers, and to a limited extent in early periods, the harder dolomite layers (*mizi ahmar*) underlying the limestone (see, e.g., Gill, 1996). In order to facilitate construction along the slopes, several tactics can be denoted, including the building of support structures, the stepped carving of the bedrock, and occasionally, the construction of platforms for the leveling of an area. Despite the constant settlement of the area and the damage caused to earlier layers, there are many structures that still stand to great heights and provide solid information for the architectural syntax common in Jerusalem of the Iron Age IIA–B.

---

[7] Unfortunately, the preliminary publications of these bullae and the petrographic analysis conducted do not present the specific bullae sampled, making it difficult to know whether the specific bullae bearing Israelite or Phoenician iconography were sampled. That said, the sample size seems to be quite encompassing, with 120 out of 170 bullae sampled.

When searching for elements that may signal northern influence predating the late eighth century BCE, they are hard to come by. First and foremost, evidence for the use of ashlar masonry only appears in Jerusalem in the late eighth century BCE (Shiloh, 1979: Table 6), in the area of the Ophel (Mazar & Mazar, 1989; Winderbaum, 2021) and in the City of David (Vaknin et al., 2020). Earlier elements of public architecture are not built of ashlar masonry, rather from a range of small fieldstones to large, uncut boulders. A fine example of this is the fortifications surrounding the spring, which were constructed/renovated in the ninth century BCE of large, uncut boulders (Regev et al., 2017). Comparable monuments seem to be found to the west of Jerusalem, in the Judean Shephelah. Interestingly, recent excavations in the lower city of Tell es-Safi/Gath have revealed a massive fortification in the lower city (for the preliminary report, see Dagan et al., 2018). Maeir (2020a), who dates the fortification to the late Iron Age I and Iron Age IIA, suggests that the biblical traditions of Anakim from Gath could be linked to the large, roughly cut boulders used to build this fortification. Remarkably, this architectural style for fortifications seems to closely parallel the construction of Jerusalem's spring fortifications.

In addition, it should be stressed that hitherto there seems to be no evidence for the use of volute capitals prior to the late eighth century BCE (Lipschits, 2011). The fragments found by Kenyon (1963: 16, Pl. 8: b; 1967: 59, Pl. 20) and later by Ben-Ami and Tchekhanovets (2015) can be understood in light of the more secure dating of the buildings at Ramat Rahel, and more recently the excavations in Armon Hanatsiv (Billig et al., 2021). Both sites are certainly not predating the terminal years of the eighth century, and more likely belonging to the seventh century BCE.

5 The Contact Zone: Benjamin Plateau and Southern Samaria

In order to further evaluate our observations, it will be interesting to focus our attention also on the contact zone between two kingdoms, the Benjamin Plateau and southern Samaria, mainly in order to see if indications for the flow of ideas and products can be found there.

In terms of material culture, there is little doubt that the Iron Age IIB settlements excavated in the Benjamin Plateau throughout the years were influenced by the cultural traditions that prevailed in the Kingdom of Judah rather than those of the north (Na'aman, 2009: 216–217). The ceramic assemblages originated from the excavations of Gibeon (Pritchard, 1964), Tell el-Ful (Lapp, 1981), Khirbet el-Burj (Weinberger-Stern, 2015) and Kiriath-Jearim (Finkelstein et al., 2018; McKinny et al., 2018) do not include any clear indication for northern traditions. Especially instructive is the absence of red-slipped and densely burnished bowls with exceptionally thin walls (e.g., Tappy, 2015: 194–195; Pl. 2.3.12: 1–3), red-slipped and burnished jugs with a trefoil rim (ibid.: 193; Pls. 2.3.9: 7; 2.3.10: 1) and, especially, ridged storage jars with a swollen body (ibid.: 192; Pl. 2.3.6: 10–11). Putting it differently, the pottery traditions of these sites are exactly what one would expect to find in a Judean settlement of the eighth century BCE. Only at Tell en-Nasbeh, the northernmost settlement in this region, are there a few vessels that are possibly connected to the north (e.g., Wampler, 1947: Pls. 18: 303–312; 19: 313–321).

A somewhat opposite trend was observed in a few excavated Iron IIB settlements located just to the north of the Benjamin Plateau, in the vicinity of Nahal Shiloh.[8] Excavations carried out in Rosh Ha'ayin, Khirbet Hudash and Qla', retrieved only isolated Judahite ceramic forms, and the material culture of these sites, as a whole, is closely related to that of sites located in northern Israel (Riklin, 1997: 41; Torga & Avner, 2018: 54; Eitam & Lederman, forthcoming).[9] While the few pottery figures which were published from the Iron IIB stratum at Shiloh do seem to reflect Judahite traditions (Bunimovitz & Finkelstein, 1993: Fig. 6.66), recent excavations at the site exposed larger ceramic assemblages with closer affinities to the material culture of the north (e.g., Livyatan Ben Arie, 2021: Figs. 3.4: 8–9; 3.9: 17–19, but for a few other Judahite-style vessels, see ibid.: Figs. 3.4: 4, 11; 3.9: 20).

A few sites located north of the contact zone do show some degree of connectivity with Judah. The pottery exposed at Khirbet Marjameh, about 26 km to the north of Jerusalem, features a mix of north-Israelite and Judahite traditions with some local variants (Mazar, 1995: 114). Mazar particularly referred to the presence of neckless pithoi with an outfolded rim and lamps with a disk base (ibid.: Fig. 21: 2–4, 15–16). Petrographic analysis of the pithoi in question suggests that they were not produced from the Moza formation as were most of the southern examples (e.g., Mommsen et al., 1984: 107–109), but rather from Lower Cretaceous which can be found in eastern Samaria or near Tell en-Nasbeh (Ben-Shlomo et al., 2018, 109*; see also Buzaglo & Goren, 2006: 387). Depending on the exact location of the workshops that produced these pithoi, the possibility that north-Israelite potters imitated a limited number of Judahite-style vessels cannot be excluded.

Perhaps the most interesting case here is that of Bethel, unquestionably one of the most important sites of the Northern Kingdom (e.g., 1 Kgs 12:25–33). It is located less than 20 km to the north of Jerusalem. Due to the problematic nature of the old excavations carried out at the site (for the results, see Kelso, 1968), it is difficult to trace the exact context of the published sherds. In this light, Finkelstein and Singer-Avitz (2009) examined the pottery from a strictly typological perspective and noted the scarcity of ceramic material from the Iron IIA and Iron IIC vis-à-vis the abundance of finds from the Iron IIB. Estimating the cultural orientation of the site in the latter period is impossible with the data at hand, as there is no way to know whether the ceramic assemblages post-date the destruction of the Northern Kingdom or not. We can only note, then, that ridged storage jars, certainly a

---

[8] To-date, the only secure Iron Age IIA ceramic assemblage excavated in southern Samaria originated from a tomb near Khirbet Bir el-Kharayib (Shawamra & Cappela, 2020). The finds are rooted in the cultural traditions of northern sites such as Hazor, Megiddo and Samaria, even if some generic forms do find sufficient parallels in the south.

[9] For additional Judahite vessels found in southern Samaria (e.g., Finkelstein et al., 1997: Figs. 8.233: 6; 8.240: 37).

northern feature, are prominent among the published sherds (e.g., Kelso, 1968: Pls. 66: 14–15; 67: 1–6, 10–19) and that Judahite pottery can also be identified (e.g., ibid.: Pls. 62 [small bowls with an outfolded rim]; 67: 9 [a neckless pithos] and 65: 21[a lamp with a disk base]). Perhaps the situation at Bethel was more similar to that observed in Khirbet Marjameh (see above).

It seems that the inspection of sites located in the contact zone further supports the meager evidence for connectivity between Samaria and Jerusalem. It must be remembered that although items made in Judah or in Judahite tradition were unearthed in sites such as Tell el-Far'ah North (e.g., Chambon, 1984: Pls. 53: 13 [cooking jug]; 59: 15 [lamp][10]) and even in the Beth-Shean Valley (Mazar, 2006: 355–356: Pl. 39: 3 [neckless pithos]), these were isolated artifacts. Furthermore, some of the artifacts that are of Judahite origin/influence (such as inscribed weights, pillar figurines and burial caves – Kletter, 1996: 45–46, Fig. 16; 1998: 57; Fig. 6; 1999: 29; Figs. 4, 7; Yezerski, 1999) seem to date to the seventh century BCE, after the fall of Israel (Kletter, 1998: 45–46, 154–155). Therefore, they are not of relevance to the discussion on Israelite-Judahite interconnections.

6 Discussion and Conclusions

At the beginning of this article, we stressed that the relations between Israel and Judah were mostly determined based on the biblical texts rather than on archaeological evidence. Our review of the data from Jerusalem and from the contact zone (i.e., the Benjamin Plateau and southern Samaria) now adds an important piece to the puzzle. It shows that during the ninth to eighth centuries BCE, connectivity across the central hill country was extremely low and that Jerusalem was actually more interconnected through trade to the west, specifically, to Philistine Gath (already Cohen-Weinberger et al., 2017; Ben-Shlomo, 2018, 2019; see also Na'aman, 2013: 264). Even in terms of monumental architecture, Jerusalem seems to be connected more to the lowlands in the west rather than to the traditions that prevailed in the north (e.g., the use of ashlar masonry).

Before moving on, two important factors must be acknowledged: (1) admittedly, our observations regarding trade and other types of contacts are limited to objects that survived in the archaeological record, and theoretically, perishable items could have been exchanged between Samaria and Jerusalem (e.g., wooden items or fabrics); and (2) some forms of cultural contacts may not be expressed directly in the material culture, for example, language and belief (e.g., Finkelstein & Römer, 2020: 183). Even marriages between royal courts, in our case, the marriage between Athaliah (the daughter of King Ahab) and Jehoram of Judah, is an expression of such gift exchange (for other possible examples of gift-exchange between elites in

---

[10] While this item was associated with Stratum VIId, dated to the second half of the eighth century BCE, its high base actually recalls the lamps of the seventh century BCE. In this light, an intrusion from Stratum VIIe cannot be excluded.

the ninth century BCE, see, e.g., Niemann, 2008; Nam, 2012; Mazar & Kourou, 2019: 386–387).[11] Yet, if such archaeologically-invisible connections really existed, and especially if they were as meaningful as leading to the artificial shaping of the landscape, as argued, for instance, for Kiriath-Jearim (Finkelstein et al., 2018; Finkelstein & Römer, 2020), then the expectation is that these relations will stimulate the exchange of more mundane objects such as pottery, or encourage the imitation of architectural styles, at least among elite groups. As our review of the evidence showed, this is clearly not the situation in Jerusalem, and as a matter of fact, even in the contact zone between the two kingdoms, not much interaction is visible. We are left, then, with quite straightforward archaeological evidence for weak connectivity between Samaria and Jerusalem, and the question is, of course, what are the implications of this observation.

In our view, the meager interactions observed across the highlands undermines many of the conventional assumptions regarding the *absolute* superiority of the Northern Kingdom over Judah (e.g., Finkelstein, 2013: 162–164), as well as suggestions, in both archaeological and theological literature, that the two kingdoms formulated in one or more points of times one socio-political entity: either in the early days of the monarchy (e.g., Blum, 2021; Weingart, 2019) or even during Jeroboam II's reign in the first half of the eighth century BCE (e.g., Finkelstein, 2019; Finkelstein & Römer, 2020: 183). Needless to say, we fully acknowledge that the environmental and demographic conditions of the Northern Kingdom were better than those of Judah, as well as the textual sources that hint at some political ties between the royal families of Samaria and Jerusalem (2 Kgs 8:18, 26), the execution of joint military campaigns against nearby kingdoms (1 Kgs 22:4), or the supremacy of Israel in international affairs (Na'aman, 2019). At the same time, we argue that unlike settlements in the northern valleys (e.g., Hazor, Jezreel and Megiddo), Judah was an independent socio-political entity for most of its existence (Na'aman, 2007: 402–403; 2019: 18), and kept to a minimum its contacts with the north while maintaining its more natural interactions with the west. Indeed, the comparison of our finds with archaeological manifestations for interactions between Jerusalem and Gath, a centralized polity that seems to dominate the Judean Shephelah during the tenth and ninth centuries BCE (Maeir, 2020b: 21–34 and earlier bibliography therein), indicates that the Jerusalem elites did not choose to isolate themselves from surrounding cultures. Relations between Jerusalem and Gath are expressed in the import of pottery vessels and the adoption of their decoration style by local producers. In addition to these, they are also expressed in a common building style, found both at Tell es-Safi/Gath and in the fortifications by the spring.

Curiously, it was only after the collapse of the Kingdom of Israel (or slightly before) that northern traditions began influencing Jerusalem in a more meaningful way, hinting that the earlier absence of such impact on the material culture of the residents of the city resulted from something deeper than just preference for

---

[11] Note that in ancient societies, women, as well as slaves, were sometimes regarded as commodities with exchange values, specifically in marriage contexts (e.g., Appadurai, 1986: 15).

products and style originating from the west. Such traditions, especially those related to ideologically-charged architecture, could be associated with the general negative attitude towards northern practices (e.g., cult or foodways), profoundly expressed in various biblical materials. It could be conjectured, then, that the collapse of the Northern Kingdom vis-à-vis the gradual emergence of pan-Israelite ideologies in Judah of the late monarchic period removed certain social barriers, enabling the intensification of movement of ideas across the highlands.

References

Adler, Y., & Lernau, O. (2021). The Pentateuchal dietary proscription against finless and scaleless aquatic species in light of ancient fish remains. *Tel Aviv, 48*, 5–26.

Alexandre, Y. (1995). The 'hippo' jar and other storage jars at Hurvat Rosh Zayit. *Tel Aviv, 22*, 77–88.

Amiran, R. (1969). *Ancient pottery of the holy land: From its beginnings in the neolithic period to the end of the Iron Age*. Massada Press.

Appadurai, A. (1986). Introduction: Commodities and the politics of value. In A. Appadurai (Ed.), *The social life of things. Commodities in cultural perspective*. Cambridge University Press.

Arie, E. (2013). The Iron IIA pottery. In I. Finkelstein, D. Ussishkin, & E. H. Cline (Eds.), *Megiddo V: The 2004–2008 seasons* (Monograph Series of the Institute of Archaeology of Tel Aviv University 31) (pp. 668–828). The Institute of Archaeology of Tel Aviv University.

Ben-Ami, D., & Tchekhanovets, Y. (2015). A new fragment of proto-Aeolic capital from Jerusalem. *Tel Aviv, 42*, 67–71.

Ben-Shlomo, D. (2018). Trade contacts, economy and administration in Iron Age Jerusalem. *Ugarit-Forschungen, 49*, 29–65.

Ben-Shlomo, D. (2019). *The Iron Age pottery of Jerusalem: A typological and technological study* (Ariel University Institute of Archaeology Monograph Series 2). Ariel University Press.

Ben-Shlomo, D., & Mommsen, H. (2018). Pottery production in Jerusalem during the Iron Age: A new compositional profiling. *Geoarchaeology, 33*, 349–363.

Ben-Shlomo, D., Tavger, A., & Har-Even, B. (2018). Back to Marjameh. The Iron II pottery of Khirbet Marjameh – Typology and provenance study. *Judea and Samaria Research Studies, 27*, 81–115.

Billig, Y., Freud, L., & Bocher, E. (2021). A lavish royal estate from the first temple period in Armon haNatziv. *New Studies in the Archaeology of Jerusalem and Its Region, 14*, 77–100.

Blum, E. (2021). The Israelite tribal system: Literary fiction or social reality? In J. J. Krause, O. Sergi, & K. Weingart (Eds.), *Saul, Benjamin, and the emergence of monarchy in Israel: Biblical and archaeological perspectives* (Ancient Israel and its literature 40) (pp. 201–222). Society of Biblical Literature.

Bunimovitz, S. (1992). The Middle Bronze Age fortifications as a social phenomenon. *Tel Aviv, 19*, 221–234.

Bunimovitz, S., & Finkelstein, I. (1993). Pottery. In I. Finkelstein (Ed.), *Shiloh: The archaeology of a biblical site* (Monograph Series of the Institute of Archaeology of Tel Aviv University 10) (pp. 81–196). The Institute of Archaeology of Tel Aviv University.

Butcher, M., Covello-Paran, K., Waiman-Barak, P., Lipschits, O., Bezzel, H., & Sergi, O. (2022). The late Iron IIA cylindrical holemouth jars and their role in the royal economy of early monarchic Israel. *Tel Aviv, 49*, 205–229.

Buzaglo, Y., & Goren, Y. (2006). Petrographic study of selected Iron Age pottery. In A. Mazar (Ed.), *Excavations at Tel Beth-Shean 1989–1996, I. From the Late Bronze Age IIB to the*

Medieval Period (The Beth-Shean Valley Archaeological Project Publication 1) (pp. 385–391). Israel Exploration Society.
Chambon, A. (1984). *Tell el-Far'ah I: L'Âge du Fer ("Mémoire" 31)*. Éditions recherché sur les Civilisations.
Cohen-Weinberger, A., Szanton, N., & Uziel, J. (2017). Ethnofabrics: Petrographic analysis as a tool for illuminating cultural interactions and trade relations between Judah and Philistia during the Iron Age II. *Bulletin of the American Schools of Oriental Research, 377*, 1–20.
Dagan, A., Eniukhina, M., & Maeir, A. M. (2018). Excavations in area D of the lower city: Philistine cultic remains and other finds. *Near Eastern Archaeology, 81*, 28–33.
Dorsey, D. A. (1991). *The roads and highways of ancient Israel*. The John Hopkins University Press.
Eitam, D. & Lederman, Z. (forthcoming). *Qla': A royal oil and wine production centre in the kingdom of Israel*. Tel Aviv.
Faust, A. (2019). A social archaeology of the kingdom of Judah: Tenth to sixth centuries BCE. In A. Yasur-Landau, E. H. Cline, & Y. M. Rowan (Eds.), *The social archaeology of the Levant from prehistory to the present* (pp. 337–353). Cambridge University Press.
Faust, A., & Sapir, Y. (2018). The "governor's residency" at Tel 'Eton, the united monarchy, and the impact of the old-house effect on large-scale archaeological reconstructions. *Radiocarbon, 60*, 801–820.
Faust, A., & Sapir. (2021). Building 101 at Tel 'Eton, the low chronology, and the perils of a bias-perpetuating methodology: A response and a proposal for the study of all the phases in the history of buildings. *Palestine Exploration Quarterly, 153*, 304–334. https://doi.org/10.108 0/00310328.2021.1975071
Finkelstein, I. (1999). State formation in Israel and Judah: A contrast in context, a contrast in trajectory. *Near Eastern Archaeology, 62*, 35–52.
Finkelstein, I. (2000). Omride architecture. *Zeitschrift des Deutschen Palästina-Vereins, 116*, 114–138.
Finkelstein, I. (2013). *The forgotten kingdom: The archaeology and history of northern Israel* (Ancient Near Eastern Monographs 5) (pp. 105–108). Society of Biblical Literature.
Finkelstein, I. (2019). First Israel, core Israel, united (northern) Israel. *Near Eastern Archaeology, 82*, 8–15.
Finkelstein, I. (2020). Iron Age chronology and biblical history rejoinders: The Late Bronze/Iron Age transition, Tel 'Eton and Lachish. *Palestine Exploration Quarterly, 152*, 82–93.
Finkelstein, I., & Lipschits, O. (2010). Omride architecture in Moab: Jahaz and Ataroth. *Zeitschrift des Deutschen Palästina-Vereins, 126*, 29–42.
Finkelstein, I., & Römer, T. (2020). The historical and archaeological background behind the old Israelite ark narrative. *Biblica, 101*, 161–185.
Finkelstein, I., & Singer-Avitz, L. (2009). Reevaluating Bethel. *Zeitschrift des Deutschen Palästina-Vereins, 125*, 33–48.
Finkelstein, I., Bunimovitz, S., & Lederman, Z. (1997). *Highlands of many cultures: The southern Samaria survey* (Monograph Series of the Institute of Archaeology of Tel Aviv University 14). The Institute of Archaeology of Tel Aviv University.
Finkelstein, I., Römer, T., Nicolle, C., Dunseth, Z. C., Kleiman, A., Mas, J., & Porat, N. (2018). Excavations at Kiriath-Jearim near Jerusalem, 2017: Preliminary report. *Semitica, 60*, 31–83.
Franklin, N. (2004). Samaria: From the bedrock to the Omride palace. *Levant, 36*, 189–202.
Frevel, C. (2018). *Geschichte Israels*. Kohlhammer.
Gadot, Y., & Uziel, J. (2017). The monumentality of Iron Age Jerusalem prior to the 8th century BCE. *Tel Aviv, 44*, 123–140.
Gilboa, A. (2015). Iron Age I–II Cypriot imports and local imitations. In S. Gitin (Ed.), *The ancient pottery of Israel and its neighbors: From the Iron Age through the Hellenistic period* (pp. 483–507). Israel Exploration Society.
Gill, D. (1996). The geology of the City of David and its ancient subterranean waterworks. In D. T. Ariel & A. De Groot (Eds.), *Excavations at the City of David 1978–1985 directed by Yigal*

Shiloh. Volume IV. Various reports (Qedem 35) (pp. 1–28). The Institute of Archaeology of the Hebrew University of Jerusalem.

Gitin, S. (2006). The lmlk jar-form redefined: A new class of Iron Age II oval shaped storage jar. In A. M. Maeir & P. de Miroschedji (Eds.), *"I will speak the riddles of ancient time": Archaeological and historical studies in honor of Amihai Mazar on the occasion of his sixtieth birthday* (pp. 505–524). Eisenbrauns.

Goren, Y., & Gurwin, S. (2013). Royal delicacy: Material study of Iron Age bullae from Jerusalem. *The Old Potter's Almanac, 18*, 2–9.

Goren, Y., Gurwin, S., & Arie, E. (2014). Messages impressed in clay: Scientific study of Iron Age Judahite bullae from Jerusalem. In M. Martinón-Torres (Ed.), *Craft and science: International perspectives on archaeological ceramics* (UCL Qatar Series in Archaeology and Cultural Heritage 1) (pp. 143–149). Bloomsbury Qatar Foundation.

Katz, H. (2021). Mount Adir: An Iron I polity in the upper Galilee? *Tel Aviv, 48*, 171–198.

Katz, H., & Faust, A. (2012). The Assyrian destruction layer at Tel 'Eton. *Israel Exploration Journal, 62*, 22–53.

Keel, O. (2017). *Corpus der stempelsiegel-amulette aus Palästina/Israel von den anfängen bis zur Perserzeit. Katalog band V: Von Tell el-Idham bis Tel Kitan* (Orbis Biblicus et Orientalis. Series Archaeologica). Vandenhoeck Ruprecht Verlage.

Kelso, J. L. (1968). *The excavation of Bethel (1934–1960)* (Annual of the American Schools of Oriental Research 39). The American Schools of Oriental Research.

Kenyon, K. M. (1963). Excavations in Jerusalem, 1962. *Palestine Exploration Quarterly, 95*, 7–21.

Kenyon, K. M. (1967). *Jerusalem: Excavating 3000 years of history*. Thames & Hudson.

Kleiman, A. (2017). A North Israelite royal administrative system and its impact on late monarchic Judah. *Hebrew Bible and Ancient Israel, 6*, 354–371.

Kleiman, A. (2019). Invisible kingdoms? Settlement oscillations in the northern Jordan valley and state formation in southwestern Syria. In A. Berlejung & A. M. Maeir (Eds.), *Researches on Israel and Aram: Autonomy, interdependence and related issues. Proceedings of the first annual RIAB center conference, Leipzig, June 2016* (Orientalische Religionen in der Antike 34) (pp. 293–311). Mohr Siebeck.

Kleiman, A. (2021). The date of the Ophel pithos inscription. An archaeological perspective. *Zeitschrift des Deutschen Palästina-Vereins, 137*, 167–179.

Kletter, R. (1996). *The Judean pillar-figurines and the archaeology of the Asherah* (BAR International Series 636). Archaeopress.

Kletter, R. (1998). *Economic keystones. The weight system of the kingdom of Judah* (JSOT Supplement Series 276). Sheffield Academic Press.

Kletter, R. (1999). Pots and polities: Material remains of Late Iron Age Judah in relation to its political borders. *Bulletin of the American Schools of Oriental Research, 314*, 19–54.

Knauf, E. A., & Niemann, H. M. (2021). *Geschichte Israels und Judas im altertum*. De Gruyter.

Lapp, N. L. (1981). *The third campaign at Tell el-Fûl: The excavations of 1964* (Annual of the American Schools of Oriental Research 45). The American Schools of Oriental Research.

Lehmann, G. (1996). *Untersuchungen zur späten Eisenzeit in Syrien und Libanon: Stratigraphie und keramikformen zwischen ca. 720 bis 300 v. Chr* (Archäologische Studien zur Kultur und Geschichte des Alten Orients 5). Ugarit-Verlag.

Levy, E. T. (2021). Interpreting Jerusalem: Science, politics, identity, and conflict converge in investigations of the city of peace. *Science, 374*(6573), 1330. https://doi.org/10.1126/science.abn0362

Lipschits, O. (2011). The origin and date of the volute capitals from the Levant. In I. Finkelstein & N. Na'aman (Eds.), *The fire signals of Lachish. Studies in the archaeology and history of Israel in the Late Bronze Age, Iron Age, and Persian period in honor of David Ussishkin* (pp. 203–225). Eisenbrauns.

Livyatan Ben Arie, R. (2021). *Shiloh in the Iron Age 2 (1000–700 BC): Updated Archaeological Review* (M.A. thesis, Ariel University). Ariel.

Maeir, A. M. (2020a). Memories, myths and megaliths: Reconsidering the giants of Gath. *Journal of Biblical Literature, 139*, 675–690.

Maeir, A. M. (2020b). Introduction and overview. In A. M. Maeir & J. Uziel (Eds.), *Tell es-Safi/Gath II: Excavations and studies* (Ägypten und Altes Testament 105) (pp. 3–52). Zaphon.

Mazar, A. (1995). Excavations at the Israelite town at Khirbet Marjameh in the hills of Ephraim. *Israel Exploration Journal, 45*, 85–117.

Mazar, A. (2006). The Iron Age II pottery from Areas S and P. In A. Mazar (Ed.), *Excavations at Tel Beth-Shean 1989–1996. Volume I: From the Late Bronze Age IIB to the medieval period* (The Beth-Shean Valley Archaeological Project 1) (pp. 313–384). Israel Exploration Society.

Mazar, A. (2014). Archaeology and the bible: Reflections on historical memory in the Deuteronomistic history. In C. M. Maier (Ed.), *Congress volume Munich 2013* (Supplements to Vetus Testamentum 163) (pp. 347–369). Brill.

Mazar, A. (2020). The Tel Reḥov excavations: Overview and synthesis. In A. Mazar & N. Panitz-Cohen (Eds.), *Tel Reḥov: A Bronze and Iron Age city in the Beth-Shean valley, volume I (Qedem 59)* (pp. 69–140). The Institute of Archaeology of the Hebrew University of Jerusalem.

Mazar, A., & Kourou, N. (2019). Greece and the Levant in the 10th–9th centuries BC. A view from Tel Reḥov, *Opuscula, 12*, 369–392.

Mazar, E., & Mazar, B. (1989). *Excavations in the south of the temple mount: The Ophel of biblical Jerusalem (Qedem 29)*. The Institute of Archaeology of the Hebrew University of Jerusalem.

McKinny, C., Schwartz, O., Barkay, G., Fantalkin, A., & Zissu, B. (2018). Kiriath-Jearim (Deir el-ᶜÂzar): Archaeological investigations of a biblical town in the Judaean hill country. *Israel Exploration Journal, 68*, 30–49.

Miller, J. M., & Hayes, J. H. (2006). *A history of ancient Israel and Judah* (2nd ed.). Westminster John Knox Press.

Mommsen, H., Perlman, I., & Yellin, J. (1984). The provenience of the "lmlk" jars. *Israel Exploration Journal, 34*, 89–113.

Na'aman, N. (2007). The northern kingdom in the late tenth–ninth centuries BCE. In H. G. H. Williamson (Ed.), *Understanding the history of ancient Israel* (Proceedings of the British Academy 143) (pp. 399–418). Oxford University Press.

Na'aman, N. (2009). Saul, Benjamin and the emergence of "biblical Israel". *Zeitschrift für die alttestamentliche Wissenschaft, 121*, 211–224.

Na'aman, N. (2013). The kingdom of Judah in the 9th century BCE: Text analysis versus archaeological research. *Tel Aviv, 40*, 247–276.

Na'aman, N. (2019). Samaria and Judah in an early 8th-century Assyrian wine list. *Tel Aviv, 46*, 12–20.

Nam, R. S. (2012). Power relations in the Samaria ostraca. *Palestine Exploration Quarterly, 144*, 155–163.

Niemann, H. M. (2008). A new look at the Samaria ostraca: The king-clan relationship. *Tel Aviv, 35*, 249–266.

Philip, G., & Badreshany, K. (2020). Discussion and conclusions: Ceramics, society and economy in the northern Levant. *Levant, 52*, 278–296.

Pritchard, J. B. (1964). *Winery, defenses and soundings at Giveon*. University Museum, University of Pennsylvania.

Regev, J., Uziel, J., Szanton, N., & Boaretto, E. (2017). Absolute dating of the Gihon spring fortifications, Jerusalem. *Radiocarbon, 59*, 1171–1193.

Reich, R., Shukron, E., & Lernau, O. (2007). Recent discoveries in the City of David, Jerusalem. *Israel Exploration Journal, 57*, 153–169.

Riklin, S. (1997). An Iron Age IIB site at Beit Aryeh. *'Atiqot, 32*, 7–20.

Schreiber, N. (2003). *The Cypro-Phoenician pottery of the Iron Age* (Culture and History of the Ancient Near East 13). Brill.

Sergi, O. (2013). Judah's expansion in historical context. *Tel Aviv, 40*, 226–246.

Sergi, O., & Gadot, Y. (2017). Omride palatial architecture as symbol in action: Between state formation, obliteration, and heritage. *Journal of Near Eastern Studies, 76*, 103–111.

Sergi, O., & Kleiman, A. (2018). The kingdom of Geshur and the expansion of Aram-Damascus into the northern Jordan valley: Archaeological and historical perspectives. *Bulletin of the American Schools of Oriental Research, 379*, 1–18.

Sergi, O., Karasik, A., Gadot, Y., & Lipschits, O. (2012). The royal Judahite storage jar: A computer-generated typology and its archaeological and historical implications. *Tel Aviv, 39*, 64–92.

Sergi, O., Bezzel, H., Tsur, Y., & Covello-Paran, K. (2020). In K. Covello-Paran, A. Erlich, & R. Beeri (Eds.), *Horvat Tevet in the Jezreel valley: A royal Israelite estate* (pp. 31–48). New Studies in the Archaeology of Northern Israel.

Shai, I., & Maeir, A. M. (2003). Pre-LMLK Jars: A new class of Iron Age IIA storage jars. *Tel Aviv, 30*, 108–123.

Shai, I., & Maeir, A. M. (2018). Reassessing the character of the Judahite centralized kingdom: An updated archaeological view. *In the Highlands' Depth, 8*, 29–45. (Hebrew).

Shawamra, A., & Cappella, F. (2020). *An Iron Age II tomb with Phoenician items at Khirbet Bir el-Kharayib, central Palestine* (Vol. 24, pp. 27–55). Vicino Oriente.

Shiloh, Y. (1979). *The proto-Aeolic capital and Israelite ashlar masonry (Qedem 11)*. The Hebrew University of Jerusalem: The Institute of Archaeology of the Hebrew University of Jerusalem.

Singer-Avitz, L. (2018). The Iron IIB pottery: On typological differences between the regions of Judah and Israel. In I. Shai, J. R. Chadwick, L. Hitchcock, A. Dagan, C. McKinny, & J. Uziel (Eds.), *Tell it in Gath. Studies in the history and archaeology of Israel. Essays in honor of Aren M. Maeir on the occasion of his sixtieth birthday* (Ägypten und Altes Testament 90) (pp. 663–679). Zaphon.

Singer-Avitz, L. (2019). Typological comparison of the Judahite Iron Age IIB pottery assemblages from Jerusalem, Lachish and Tel Beer-Sheba. In D. Ben-Shlomo (Ed.), *The Iron Age pottery of Jerusalem: A typological and technological study* (Ariel University Institute of Archaeology Monograph Series 2) (pp. 103–126). Ariel University Press.

Stern, E. (2015). Iron Age I–II Phoenician pottery. In S. Gitin (Ed.), *The ancient pottery of Israel and its neighbors: From the Iron Age through the Hellenistic period* (pp. 435–482). Israel Exploration Society.

Tappy, R. (2015). Iron Age IIA–B: Samaria. In S. Gitin (Ed.), *The ancient pottery of Israel and its neighbors: From the Iron Age through the Hellenistic period* (pp. 189–211). Israel Exploration Society.

Torga, H., & Avner, R. (2018). Qurnat Haramiya (Rosh Ha-'Ayin): Remains of a settlement from the Iron Age and the Persian–Hellenistic periods. *Hadashot Arkheologiyot, 130* (online publication).

Ussishkin, D. (1980). Was the "Solomonic" city gate at Megiddo built by king Solomon? *Bulletin of the American Schools of Oriental Research, 239*, 1–18.

Ussishkin, D. (1990). Notes on Megiddo, Gezer, Ashdod, and Tel Batash in the tenth to ninth centuries B.C. *Bulletin of the American Schools of Oriental Research, 277*(278), 71–91.

Ussishkin, D. (2020). The 'Solomonic', six-chambered gate 2156 at Megiddo once again. *Tel Aviv, 47*, 246–255.

Uziel, J., Dan-Goor, S., & Szanton, N. (2019). The development of pottery in Iron Age Jerusalem. In D. Ben-Shlomo (Ed.), *The Iron Age pottery of Jerusalem: A typological and technological study* (Ariel University Institute of Archaeology Monograph Series 2) (pp. 59–102). Ariel University Press.

Vaknin, Y., Shaar, R., Gadot, Y., Shalev, Y., Lipschits, O., & Ben-Yosef, E. (2020). The earth's magnetic field in Jerusalem during the Babylonian destruction: A unique reference for field behavior and an anchor for archaeomagnetic dating. *PLoS One, 15*, Article e0237029. https://doi.org/10.1371/journal.pone.0237029

Wampler, J. C. (1947). *Tell en-Naṣbeh II: The pottery*. The American Schools of Oriental Research.

Weinberger-Stern, M. (2015). *Khirbet el-Burj (Ramot 06) and its place in the hinterland of the Benjamin region* (M.A. thesis, Tel Aviv University). Tel Aviv.

Weiner, S. (2010). *Microarchaeology: Beyond the visible archaeological record*. Cambridge University Press.

Weingart, K. (2019). "All these are the twelve tribes of Israel": The origins of Israel's kinship identity. *Near Eastern Archaeology, 82*, 24–31.

Winderbaum, A. (2021). *The Iron IIA pottery assemblages from the Ophel excavations and their contribution to the understanding of the settlement history of Jerusalem*. Ph.D. dissertation, Tel Aviv University.

Yadin, Y. (1970). Megiddo of the kings of Israel. *Biblical Archaeologist, 33*, 65–96.

Yadin, Y. (1972). *Hazor: The head of all those kingdoms (Joshua 11:10), with a chapter on Israelite Megiddo*. The Schweich Lectures of the British Academy.

Yezerski, I. (1999). Burial-cave distribution and the borders of the kingdom of Judah toward the end of the Iron Age. *Tel Aviv, 26*, 253–270.

Tel Beth-Shean in the Tenth–Ninth Centuries BCE: A Chronological Query and Its Possible Archaeomagnetic Resolution

Yoav Vaknin ⓘ, Amihai Mazar ⓘ, Ron Shaar ⓘ, and Erez Ben-Yosef ⓘ

Abstract In this article, we show how an archaeomagnetic study can help resolve a chronological dilemma related to the correlation and the relative and absolute dating of Iron IIA strata in two adjacent sites: Tel Beth-Shean and Tel Reḥov, located 5 km apart in the Beth-Shean Valley in northern Israel. The excavations at Tel Reḥov revealed three Iron IIA strata (VI-IV), two of which (V-IV), attributed to the late Iron IIA, yielded rich identical ceramic assemblages. These strata cover a time range from the late tenth century to the mid-to-late ninth century BCE, based on a significant number of radiocarbon dates, comparative studies and historical considerations. At Beth-Shean, massive structures of a public nature were found in Stratum S-1a, with pottery similar to that of Tel Reḥov V and IV, but it was difficult to provide a tighter dating. An archaeomagnetic study of burnt mudbricks and a burnt beehive at Tel Reḥov showed a clear difference between Stratum V and Stratum IV. The destruction of Stratum IV corresponded to the destructions of other sites, all attributed to Hazael's military campaign (s) to the region in the second half of the ninth century BCE. The magnetic signal recorded in the destruction of Stratum S-1a at Beth-Shean corresponded with that of the destruction of the apiary of Stratum V at Tel Reḥov (late tenth to early ninth centuries BCE) and is significantly different from that of Stratum IV at Tel Reḥov. These results, pointing to an earlier date of the destruction of Stratum S-1a at Beth-Shean, are significant for resolving chronological and historical questions

Y. Vaknin (✉)
Tel Aviv University, Tel Aviv, Israel

The Hebrew University, Jerusalem, Israel
e-mail: yoavvaknin@mail.tau.ac.il

A. Mazar · R. Shaar
The Hebrew University, Jerusalem, Israel
e-mail: mazar@huji.ac.il; ron.shaar@mail.huji.ac.il

E. Ben-Yosef
Department of Archaeology and Ancient Near Eastern Cultures,
Tel Aviv University, Tel Aviv, Israel
e-mail: ebenyose@tauex.tau.ac.il

© The Author(s), under exclusive license to Springer Nature Switzerland AG 2023
E. Ben-Yosef, I. W. N. Jones (eds.), *"And in Length of Days Understanding" (Job 12:12): Essays on Archaeology in the Eastern Mediterranean and Beyond in Honor of Thomas E. Levy*, Interdisciplinary Contributions to Archaeology,
https://doi.org/10.1007/978-3-031-27330-8_34

relating to northern Israel in the Iron IIA, a period which stands at the heart of the continued debate concerning the historicity of biblical narratives.

Keywords Archaeomagnetism · Tel Rehov · Beth-Shean · Iron Age · Biblical archaeology · Dating · Hazael

1 Introduction

1.1 Background

This article demonstrates how archaeomagnetism can help resolve a chronological debate related to three Iron Age IIA strata in Tel Beth-Shean and Tel Rehov, located 5 km apart in the Beth-Shean Valley. The possible synchronization between two different late Iron Age IIA strata in Tel Rehov and one stratum at Tel Beth-Shean has been debated since they were excavated. The Iron IIA period stands at the heart of a continued debate concerning the interface between archaeology and biblical narratives, mainly those related to the alleged kingdoms of David and Solomon and the early history of the independent kingdoms of Israel and Judah. Resolving chronological issues related to this period is essential for the utilization of archaeological finds in the reconstruction of the cultural and political development in this period. The following is a contribution to this issue, dedicated to our friend and colleague Thomas Levy, whose work at Faynan was groundbreaking for understanding this period.

1.2 Defining the Archaeological Query

Several Iron Age strata yielding rich material culture assemblages have been revealed at both Tel Beth-Shean and Tel Rehov. Our interest here is in the Iron IIA period, which covers a time range in the tenth and ninth centuries BCE based on a significant number of radiocarbon dates, comparative studies and historical considerations (Mazar, 2016, 2020, 2021). The period is divided into early Iron IIA and late Iron IIA (Herzog & Singer-Avitz, 2006).

Tel Beth-Shean. Levels V and IV in the University Museum of the University of Pennsylvania excavations during the 1920s belong to the Iron II period (James, 1966). Level V covers a wide chronological range in the Iron IIA and perhaps the early part of the Iron IIB. A well-planned quarter was exposed on the summit of the mound, yet the stratigraphic resolution is too vague to enable precise dating of these finds. Renewed excavations directed by A. Mazar from 1989 to 1996 revisited the Iron Age strata in two excavation areas, P and S (Mazar, 2006). In Area P it was possible to excavate a substantial residential building of the Iron IIB (eighth century

BCE); earlier phases were examined there only in narrow probes. In Area S, on the summit of the mound, the previous excavations had removed the Iron IIB remains and also exposed the top of structural remains of the Iron IIA. In the new excavations, these remains were further exposed and Iron I strata were excavated below them so that a refined stratigraphic sequence from Iron I to Iron II was achieved. Two architectural phases belonging to the Iron IIA were identified, both with similar pottery. The earlier phase, denoted Stratum S-1b, is known only from a limited excavated area (Mazar, 2006: 174–180). Only a small amount of pottery from this phase was available (Mazar, 2006: 398–403, Plates 6–8). This pottery assemblage is typical of the Iron IIA but due to the limited number of examples, it is difficult to determine whether it should be attributed to the early or late phases of the Iron IIA. However, two of the items from this assemblage appear to be characteristic of the late Iron IIA (Mazar, 2006: 401, 4012, Plates 7: 5 and 8: 14).

The later phase, denoted Stratum S-1a, yielded remains of four massive structures of public nature, called Buildings A-D (Fig. 1) (Mazar, 2006: 180–196). These buildings had wide walls with large basalt stone foundations, supporting mudbrick superstructures. In some locations wooden beams were placed on the stone foundations, creating a leveled and flexible foundation for the mudbrick superstructure. Only parts of these buildings were preserved; other parts had been removed during the earlier excavations or eroded. All these buildings were destroyed by severe fire that caused bricks to melt into white powder. In Building A the mudbricks were fired to a hard, reddish matrix recalling fired pottery (Fig. 2). In the publication it was suggested that these buildings had been part of the well-planned complex of Level V excavated by the University Museum expedition farther west (Mazar, 2006: 193, Fig. 7.5). The rather large collection of pottery from these buildings is typical of the late Iron IIA. A concentration of "Hippo" type storage jars was found in a destruction level in one of the rooms in Building A (Room 88721). The assemblage also includes red slipped bowls and imported Cypriot Black on Red pottery, all typical of the late Iron IIA and similar to the pottery assemblage of Tel Reḥov Strata V and IV (Mazar, 2006: 404–415, Plates 9–14). For the absolute date of this assemblage see below. Two radiocarbon dates were obtained from wooden beams used during the construction of the buildings in Stratum S-1a. One of these dates is approximately two centuries later than the other. The later date, which is 2955 BP calibrated to 1050–920 Cal. BCE in 68.2% probability, may be taken as providing a *terminus post quem* for the construction of the buildings, but it could also be contemporary or very close to the construction date. In any case, neither date contributes significantly to the absolute dating of the buildings' destruction (Mazar, 2006: 723).

Tel Reḥov The Iron IIA period is the main period excavated in this large mound. It was exposed in several excavation areas and yielded an exceptionally rich assemblage of pottery and artifacts (for the final report, see Mazar & Panitz-Cohen, 2020). In each of the excavation areas local stratigraphic sequence was established and correlation between the areas resulted in the definition of three major Iron IIA strata: Stratum VI of the early Iron IIA and Strata V and IV of the late Iron IIA (Figs. 3 and 4). These latter two strata yielded similar pottery assemblages. In certain parts of the

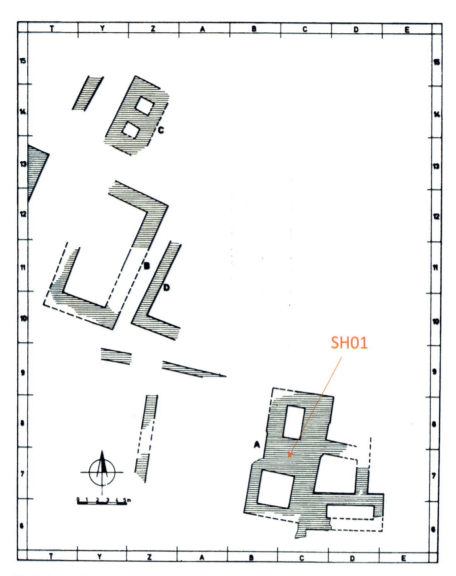

Fig. 1 Schematic plan of Buildings A-D in Stratum S-1a at Beth-Shean. (From Mazar, 2006: 182 Fig. 7.2). The location of the archaeomagnetic samples (SH01) is marked in red

excavation (in particular the apiary zone in Area C) Stratum V was destroyed in a conflagration, while in other areas the transition from V to IV was a peaceful one, with buildings continuing to be in use with some modifications. Stratum IV came to an end in a great conflagration, attributed to a conquest by Hazael, King of Aram Damascus, probably ca. 840–830 BCE (Mazar, 2016, 2020). A large number of radiocarbon dates from Strata VI-IV were published and Bayesian models were constructed (Bruins et al., 2003; Mazar et al., 2005; Mazar & Streit, 2020). These

Tel Beth-Shean in the Tenth–Ninth Centuries BCE: A Chronological Query...

Fig. 2 View of Building A in Beth-Shean Stratum S-1a, looking southwest. The stone foundation is visible in the northern part of the structure and the mudbrick superstructure is visible in the southern part. The location of the archaeomagnetic samples (SH01) is marked in red, where flat mudbricks are located in their original position. The collapsed mudbrick material which can be seen to the west of SH01 was removed prior to the archaeomagnetic sampling. The mudbrick walls west of Building A belong to Strata S-2 and S-3 of the Iron Age I period. (Photo: Mazar, 2006: 181, Photo 7.9)

have provided a range of dates in the tenth century BCE for Stratum VI, in the late tenth and early ninth centuries BCE for Stratum V and in the ninth century BCE for Stratum IV. Table 1 shows the results of the Bayesian models, suggesting relatively tight dating for the different strata. Yet, close examination of the actual dates and taking into consideration the late 9th century BCE dates from Area E show a more complex picture (Mazar & Streit, 2020).

A major question concerning these two archaeological sites is the destruction date of Building A (as well as B and C) at Beth-Shean Stratum S-1a. In the publication the issue was presented as follows:

> This pottery [of Stratum S-1A] resembles to a large extent… the assemblages found at nearby Tell el-Ḥammah, Tel Reḥov Strata VI–IV [so in the original; can now be refined to V-IV] and Tel 'Amal and those from Megiddo Strata VB and VA-IVB and Rosh Zayit Strata 2–3. The absolute date of this assemblage is the subject of current debate. It could belong to the tenth century BCE, in which case the buildings could be related to the United Monarchy administration and the destruction to the campaign of Shoshenq I (biblical Shishak), who mentions Beth-Shean among the cities he conquered. However, as demonstrated at Jezreel and Tel Reḥov, the same pottery continued in use well into the ninth century—this level, therefore, could also belong to the Omride period. This question

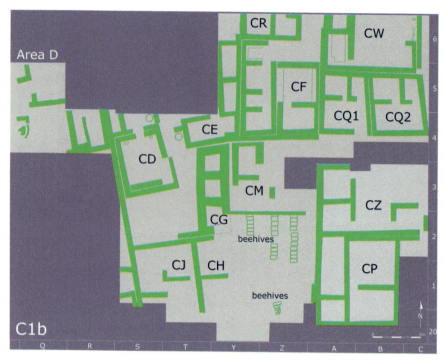

Fig. 3 Schematic plan of Stratum V in Area C at Tel Reḥov. (Tel Reḥov Expedition, Drawing: J. Rosenberg)

remains unresolved at Beth-Shean, due to the lack of sufficient stratigraphic phases, such as those excavated at Tel Reḥov. (Mazar, 2006: 32)

In the final publication of Tel Reḥov excavations this issue was discussed again and it was suggested that Beth-Shean Stratum S-1a had come to an end at the same time as Tel Reḥov Stratum IV, perhaps at the hands of Hazael in ca. 840/830 BCE (Mazar, 2020: 113–114 and Table 4.2). A difference of almost 100 years between the two possible dates for this destruction resulted from the identical pottery types found at Tel Reḥov Strata V and IV and in Beth-Shean Stratum S-1a. The two alternative scenarios are presented in Table 2.

1.3 Archaeomagnetism

The direction and intensity of Earth's magnetic field are constantly changing. People have been directly measuring the direction of the field for the past ca. 400 years and its intensity for the past ca. 190 years. Paleomagnetism deals with the reconstruction of the magnetic field in periods that predate direct measurement. In order to do so, paleomagnetists measure the magnetic field recorded in different materials, mainly

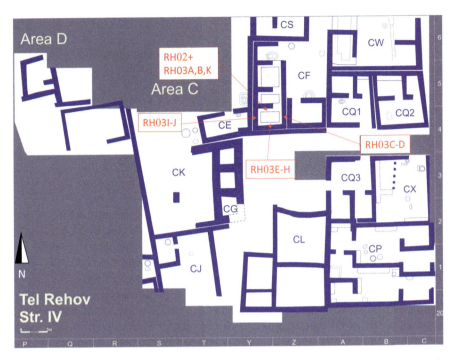

Fig. 4 Schematic plan of Stratum IV in Area C at Tel Reḥov. The locations of the archaeomagnetic samples (RH02, RH03) are marked in red. (Tel Reḥov Expedition, Drawing: J. Rosenberg with additions by authors)

Table 1 Results of a Bayesian model for secure dates from Areas C + D and B at Tel Reḥov in 1σ, 68% probability) and 2σ (95.4% probability) CalBC showing dates for Strata VI–IV (not including unmodeled dates from Area E; Compiled from Mazar & Streit, 2020: 486–487, Tables 4.87, 4.88)

	Areas C + D		Area B	
	1σ CalBC	2σ CalBC	1σ CalBC	2σ CalBC
End of IV	904–863	910–817	906–838	914–822
Transition V–IV	911–896	916–886	916–861	922–848
Transition VI–V	919–916	925–902	948–896	985–851
Beginning of VI	936–911	962–907		

geological ones. In the interdisciplinary field of archaeomagnetism the ancient magnetic field is measured from archaeological materials, such as burnt features or pottery. Archaeomagnetism is mutually beneficial to archaeology and geophysics. On the one hand archaeomagnetists use geophysical tools in order to answer archaeological questions. On the other hand, geophysicists use well-dated archaeological materials in order to reconstruct spatial and temporal variations of the geomagnetic field. This reconstruction sheds light on the mechanisms responsible for the changes in the field.

Table 2 Iron IIA strata at Beth-Shean and Tel Reḥov, with two optional correlations between the sites and suggested dates

Period	Tel Reḥov general stratum	Beth-Shean correlation option 1	Beth-Shean correlation option 2	Date (BCE) as suggested in publication (modified chronology)
Late Iron IIA	IV	–	S-1a	Early 9th century until 840-830
	V	S-1a	S-1b	Late 10th to early 9th centuries
Early Iron IIA	VI	S-1b (?) Gap (?)	Gap (?)	From ca. 980/960 to ca. 920?

In order to understand how archaeological finds can help reconstruct the ancient geomagnetic field, one needs a basic understanding of how archaeological materials record the field. Many archaeological materials, such as clay objects, contain ferromagnetic minerals (such as magnetite Fe_3O_4). On the atomic level one can imagine the magnetic signal of these minerals as a tiny needle of a compass. As long as the needle is free to move it will "prefer" to align with the magnetic field around it. Similarly, the magnetic signal of ferromagnetic minerals can also sometimes change its direction but, unlike the compass needle, this ability depends on the temperature. Above the 'Blocking Temperature' (T_B), which depends on both the mineralogy and the grain size, the magnetization of a ferromagnetic mineral can change its direction and therefore it tends to align with Earth's magnetic field. Below T_B the magnetic signal is fixed. Archaeological materials that have not been burnt often contain ferromagnetic minerals but the magnetic signals of the different minerals are randomly oriented and their total magnetic signal is very weak. However, when archaeological materials have been heated to high temperatures (at least several hundred degrees) the magnetic signals of the different minerals align in the direction of the geomagnetic field. When these materials cool down, their magnetic signals become "locked." The total magnetic signal, which is the sum of the magnetic signals of all the different minerals within a sample, is a vector that can be defined by its direction and intensity. The intensity of the vector depends on the intensity of the ambient magnetic field and the direction of the vector is parallel to the field. Therefore, measuring the recorded signal in a sample enables reconstruction of the direction and intensity of the ancient geomagnetic field. In order to demonstrate the archaeomagnetic method, one can think of an ancient kiln that was used for firing pottery vessels. Ferromagnetic minerals are usually found both in the vessels and in the furnace walls. After the firing, while the furnace cooled down, the furnace and the vessels recorded the geomagnetic field. In order to reconstruct the direction of the geomagnetic field during the fire the archaeological materials must be sampled in the orientation in which they had cooled down. If the furnace walls are unearthed in their original position, they can be used in order to reconstruct the direction of the field. Once the pottery vessels have been taken out of the furnace, they cannot be used for reconstruction of the direction of the field. Both the furnace and the vessels can be used in order to reconstruct the intensity of the field.

Since the geomagnetic field is sometimes characterized by local anomalies, the geomagnetic field during a certain period needs to be reconstructed separately in different parts of the world (a 1000 km radius is commonly used). The dating of the archaeological materials is based on the common dating methods (historical sources, radiocarbon, ceramic typology, etc.). However, a large and well-dated database of archaeomagnetic data from a certain region can enable reconstruction of the changes in the geomagnetic field over time and can be used for dating. In the southern Levant, the growing archaeomagnetic database (Ben-Yosef et al., 2017; Shaar et al., 2011, 2016, 2018, 2020, 2022; Vaknin et al., 2020, 2022) can be used as a basis for developing an archaeomagnetic dating tool. A large percentage of the southern-Levant archaeomagnetic dataset represents the Iron Age. Many of the data points from this period are very well dated, thanks to extensive archaeological research focused on the chronology of this period. Besides chronological applications (e.g., Ben-Yosef et al., 2010; Peters et al., 2017; Vaknin et al., 2022) archaeomagnetism can be used as a useful tool for reconstructing site formation processes. For example, it can determine whether archaeological materials have been burnt, determine whether they had cooled down in the orientation in which they were unearthed and shed light on the firing temperature (Shahack-Gross et al., 2018; Vaknin et al., 2020).

2 Materials and Methods

For a full description of the methods and acceptance criteria used for this research, see previous publications (Shaar et al., 2022; Vaknin et al., 2022).

2.1 Archaeomagnetic Features and Groups and Their Ages

We define here an 'archaeomagnetic group' as a collection of burnt materials which presumably recorded the magnetic field at a certain point in time and is used for reconstructing the intensity of the ancient field (termed hereafter "archaeointensity"). An "archaeomagnetic feature" is defined as a burnt archaeological find (such as a kiln, tabun or a burnt mudbrick wall) which is sampled in the orientation in which it cooled down and enables reconstruction of both the direction and intensity of the field. Table 3 lists the studied archaeomagnetic groups and features from Tel Reḥov and Beth-Shean, along with other published archaeological sites (Vaknin et al., 2022) dated to the same period of time and thus relevant to the chronological discussion. The age range assigned to every group and feature is based on the different dating methods (radiocarbon, ceramic typology, historical considerations).

Table 3 The archaeomagnetic groups and features studied for archaeointensity and archaeomagnetic direction[a]

Archaeomagnetic group for archaeointensity	Archaeomagnetic feature for archaeomagnetic direction	Location, stratum/level and archaeological feature	Assigned age (BCE)[b]	Age range (BCE)[c]
Bet_Shean_destr	**Beth-Shean_structure**	**Tel Bet-Shean, Stratum S-1a, Building A**	**900**	**940–820**
Reḥov_str_IV_destr	**Reḥov_structure**	**Tel Reḥov, Stratum IV, Building CF**	**830**	**870–820**
Reḥov_str_V_destr		**Tel Reḥov, Stratum V, apiary and related structures**	**900**	**930–880**
Gath_destr	Gath_structure	Gath (Tell es-Safi)_Strata A3 and M1.	830	845–815
Tevet_level_V_destr	Tevet_kiln	Ḥorvat Tevet, Level V	830	900–800
Tevet_level_VII_destr	–	Ḥorvat Tevet, Level VII	900	940–840
Zayit_level_XIII_destr	–	Tel Zayit, Level XIII	830	870–790

[a]The groups and features that are the focus of this paper are marked in bold. Published data from other archaeological sites used as reference are mentioned as well

[b]These assigned ages were set by the authors arbitrarily, according to different chronological considerations including the archaeomagnetic results presented here. These ages are not part of the prior data for the archaeomagnetic dating model. For details see: Vaknin et al. (2022)

[c]These age ranges are part of the prior data for the archaeomagnetic dating model. These age ranges are based on radiocarbon data and/or historical constraints when applicable. They are also based on other archaeological considerations. Non-analytic archaeological age ranges are generally wider and include all the possible corrections to absolute timescales. The archaeomagnetic results are not considered in the prior ages to prevent circular reasoning. For details see: Vaknin et al. (2022)

2.2 Archaeomagnetic Directions

Archaeomagnetic directions from Stratum S-1a at Beth-Shean were obtained from a burnt mudbrick wall in building A (SH01. Figures 1, 2, 5). From Stratum IV at Tel Reḥov archaeomagnetic directions were obtained from a burnt layer of mud plaster covering a mudbrick wall in Building CF (RH02. Figures 4, 6, 7). In order to ensure that the sampled walls in both features had not shifted since they were burnt, we measured the orientation of their outer surfaces. The top surfaces of the bricks in SH01 were horizontal and the outer surfaces of the bricks (in SH01) and the plaster (in RH02) were vertical. From Stratum V at Tel Reḥov we were not able to sample any burnt material in its original position and thus could not reconstruct the archaeomagnetic direction (Figs. 5 and 6).

In order to create flat surfaces, we polished the outer surface of the bricks prior to sampling. On the flat surfaces we marked horizontal lines (Figs. 5, 7) and

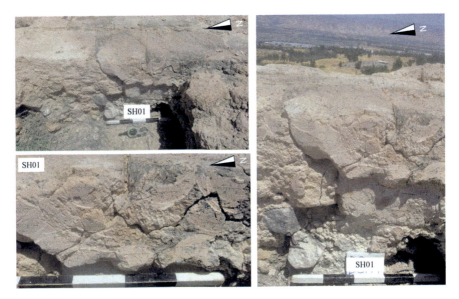

Fig. 5 Sampling burnt mudbricks from Stratum S-1a at Beth-Shean (SH01) for archaeomagnetic direction

measured their field orientation relative to the geographic north. These oriented samples were cut into specimens in the laboratory while the field orientation measurements were maintained. We then measured the magnetic signal recorded in every specimen. In order to make sure that the recorded magnetic signal was stable and was recorded during a single event, we carried out demagnetization experiments in which the magnetization of each specimen was gradually erased in a series of demagnetization steps. After each demagnetization step the remaining signal was measured. During demagnetization experiments the magnetic vector of each specimen weakens gradually but in cases in which the magnetic signal was recorded during one event, the directions of gradually-demagnetized vectors remain similar. After measuring the direction recorded in each oriented specimen, we used statistical tools in order to calculate the mean direction of every archaeomagnetic feature and its corresponding statistical error.

2.3 Archaeointensity

In order to reconstruct the intensity of the ancient field (archaeointensity) we sampled materials which had been burnt during destruction events from all relevant strata. For archaeointensity measurements from Tel Reḥov Stratum IV, we sampled one sample which had been sampled for direction (RH02E) and 9 additional unoriented samples (RH03A-I) from the 4 walls of Room 5444 in Building CF (Fig. 8). We prepared 3–7 specimens from each of these samples. From Stratum S-1a at

Fig. 6 View of Building CF at Tel Reḥov, looking south. The locations of the archaeomagnetic samples (RH02, RH03) are marked in red. (Note that only the upper parts of the walls belong to Stratum IV. The picture was taken after the excavation had reached the levels of Strata V and VI)

Beth-Shean we used 5 samples for archaeointensity from the same bricks used for archaeomagnetic direction and prepared 3–4 specimens from every sample. From Stratum V at Tel Reḥov we used one sample for archaeointensity (RH05C): a mud beehive which had been burnt during the destruction of the apiary (Fig. 9). Three unoriented specimens from this sample were demagnetized in order to make sure that the magnetization was strong and unified, which is critical for the success of the archaeointensity experiments. We prepared 15 specimens from this sample for archaeointensity experiments, an exceptionally large number of specimens, due to the small number of samples.

2.4 Rock Magnetism

Several additional experiments were carried out in order to shed light on the nature of the magnetic minerals and the temperature of the fire (For technical details regarding these experiments see: Vaknin et al., 2020).

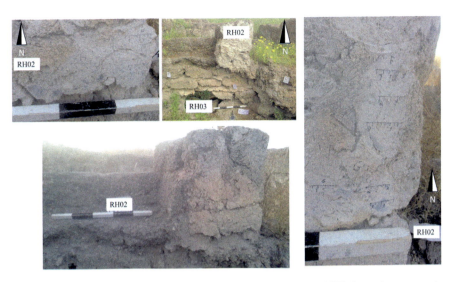

Fig. 7 Sampling burnt mudbricks from Stratum IV at Tel Reḥov (RH02) for archaeomagnetic direction. The locations of some of the samples for archaeointensity (RH03A, B. K) are marked as well

Fig. 8 The sampling of burnt mudbricks in Stratum IV at Tel Reḥov (RH03) for archaeointensity

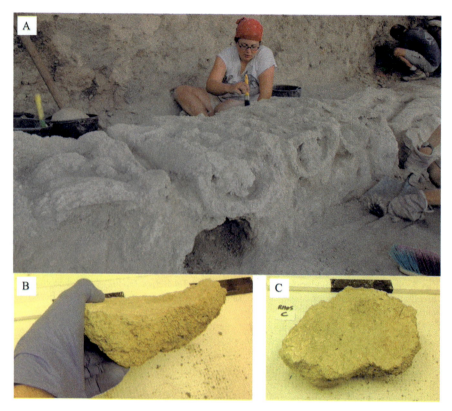

Fig. 9 Mud beehives from Stratum V at Tel Reḥov (**a**) The unearthed beehives during the excavations. (**b**, **c**) sampling a mud beehive (RH05C) for archaeointensity in the laboratory

3 Results

3.1 Archaeomagnetic Direction

The archaeomagnetic direction results from Beth-Shean, Tel Reḥov and other previously published archaeological sites from the same period are displayed in Fig. 10b, c. All 26 specimens from Tel Beth-Shean Stratum S-1a, all 26 specimens from Stratum IV at Tel Reḥov and all three preliminary specimens from the beehive unearthed in Stratum V at Tel Reḥov yielded a strong magnetic signal. The direction of the recorded field in all these specimens remained nearly unchanged during the demagnetization steps (Fig. 11). These results, graphically expressed as straight lines converging to the origin in Fig. 11, reinforce the archaeological observation that all these materials were burnt to high temperatures and that the magnetic information recorded in each of them represents one heating event.

All 26 specimens from Reḥov Stratum IV yielded well-clustered directions. From Tel Beth-Shean Stratum S-1a, 25 specimens yielded directions clustered

Tel Beth-Shean in the Tenth–Ninth Centuries BCE: A Chronological Query...

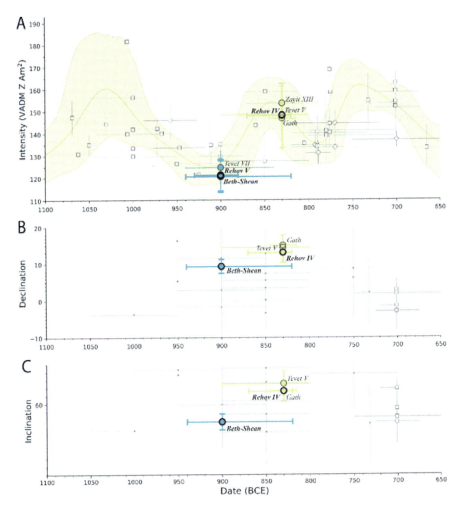

Fig. 10 Archaeomagnetic results: (**a**) Intensity. (**b**) Declination. (**c**) Inclination. The destruction layers mentioned in the text are marked with colored circles. Other previously published data from Israel (squares) and Syria (diamonds) are marked in grey. The destruction layers from Tel Reḥov and Tel Beth-Shean are highlighted in bold

together and one specimen (SH01D05a) with a different direction was rejected as an outlier. These results are displayed in Table 4 along with published results from two other archaeological sites: the destruction of Gath (Tell es-Safi) attributed to Hazael by the excavator (Maeir, 2020) and most other scholars and a kiln which presumably went out of use during the destruction of Level V at Ḥorvat Tevet in about the same period (Sergi et al., 2021). The calculated direction of the field is represented by the angle between the horizontal component of the paleomagnetic vector and the geographic north (Declination) and the angle between the paleomagnetic vector and the horizontal plane (Inclination). The statistical parameter k (Fisher, 1953)

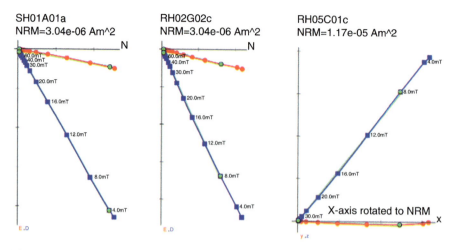

Fig. 11 Representative results from the demagnetization experiments. (**a**) Beth-Shean, Stratum S-1a. (**b**) Tel Reḥov Stratum IV. (**c**) Tel Reḥov Stratum V. Each subplot represents a demagnetization experiment of one specimen. Since the magnetic signal is a 3-dimensional vector, it is displayed by 2 lines (red and blue), each representing the projection of the vector on a different plane. The original magnetization is gradually erased by an increasingly strong magnetic field (4.0 mT, 8.0 mT etc.) All three graphs display a strong magnetic vector (natural remanent magnetization – NRM) and straight lines converging to the origin indicating stable magnetization

Table 4 Direction results

Archaeomagnetic feature	Stratum, structure	Age (range)	n specimens (out of measured specimens)	Dec	Inc	k	α_{95}	CSD
Beth-Shean_structure	**Stratum S-1a, Building A**	900 (940–820)	25 (26)	9.3	59.1	847	1.0	2.8
Reḥov_str_IV_structure	**Stratum IV, Building CF**	830 (870–820)	26 (26)	13.1	62.2	496	1.3	3.6
Gath_structure	Stratum A3	830 (845–815)	62 (62)	15.1	61.5	189	1.3	5.9
Tevet_kiln	Level V	830 (900–800)	20 (22)	14.7	63.2	420	1.6	4

represents the degree of scatter around the mean paleomagnetic direction. A cutoff value of k ≥ 50 is used here as a selection criterion. The α_{95} and Circular Standard Deviation (CSD) represent the angular error around the mean direction. The relatively high k and low α_{95} and CSD imply that the results from both archaeomagnetic features reliably represent the direction of the geomagnetic field at the time of the destruction of each of these ancient sites.

3.2 Archaeointensity and Thermomagnetic Curves

The archaeointensity results from Beth-Shean, Tel Reḥov and other previously published archaeological sites from the same period are displayed in Fig. 10a as the Virtual Axial Dipole Moment (VADM). From Stratum S-1a at Tel Beth-Shean we measured 17 specimens from 5 different samples (mudbricks). Sixteen of the specimens met the specimen acceptance criteria. One sample (SH01B) out of the 5 did not meet the sample acceptance criteria and was rejected. From Stratum IV at Tel Reḥov we measured 45 specimens from 9 samples (mudbricks). Forty specimens and 8 samples met the acceptance criteria. All 15 specimens from the beehive from Reḥov Stratum V (RH05C) met the specimen acceptance criteria. All the intensity results of the samples which passed the criteria are presented in Table 5. The results from these samples were used in order to calculate the mean intensity result of each group and the standard deviation, as presented in Table 6 along with results from other published archaeological sites.

In order to reconstruct the intensity of the ancient field we gradually erased the original magnetic signal (which had been recorded during the conflagration—marked in blue in Fig. 12a, c) and recorded a new magnetic signal in a controlled environment in the lab (marked in red in Fig. 12a, c). The erasing and recording steps were carried out by heating the specimens to increasingly high temperatures. In the vast majority of specimens from the two strata at Tel Reḥov and from Stratum S-1a at Beth-Shean the original magnetic signal was almost entirely erased between 300 °C and 400 °C. Therefore, these samples were heated during the conflagration

Table 5 Intensity results (according to samples)

Archaeomagnetic group	Stratum, archaeological feature	Sample/s	n specimens	Mean (µT)	Standard deviation (µT)	Lower error bound (µT)	Higher error bound (µT)
Beth-Shean_destr	Stratum S-1a, Building A	SH01A	3	69.3	1.6	65.1	73.6
		SH01C	4	62.2	0.4	57.7	68.7
		SH01D	3	62.4	1.3	58.3	65.6
		SH01E	3	60.9	0.6	55.8	65.2
Reḥov_str_V_destr	Stratum V, apiary	RH05C	15	64	3.8	57.5	71.1
Reḥov_str_IV_destr	Stratum IV, Building CF	RH02E	5	83.1	2.4	74.4	90.1
		RH03A	4	74.1	0.2	70.6	81.1
		RH03C	5	77	1.2	74.6	84.5
		RH03D	7	88.9	3.2	77.2	99.7
		RH03E	5	84.6	5.8	84.6	84.6
		RH03F	4	68.6	4.5	62	74.5
		RH03G	3	67.9	0.8	64.1	76.1
		RH03H	4	85.2	0.3	76.9	95.2
		RH03I	3	73.6	0.1	67.1	78.9

Table 6 Intensity results (according to archaeomagnetic groups)

Archaeomagnetic group	Stratum, archaeological feature	Age	N samples	n specimens	Mean field (μT)	Standard deviation(σ)	VADM (ZAm^2)	VADM_sigma
Beth-Shean_destr	Stratum S-1a, Building A	900 (940–820)	4	13	63.7	3.8	120.6	7.1
Reḥov_str_V_destr	Stratum V, apiary	900 (930–880)	1	15	64	3.8	121.2	7.1
Reḥov_str_IV_destr	Stratum IV, Building CF	830 (870–820)	9	40	78.1	7.6	148	14.4
Gath_destr	Stratum A3, Stratum M1	830 (845–815)	12	44	76.7	7.6	146.7	14.5
Tevet_level_VII_destr	Level VII	900 (940–840)	2	8	66	3.9	124.7	7.4
Tevet_level_V_destr	Level V	830 (900–800)	6	24	78.5	2.9	148.4	5.5
Zayit_level_XIII_destr	Level XIII	830 (870–790)	5	28	80.2	2.4	153.6	4.5

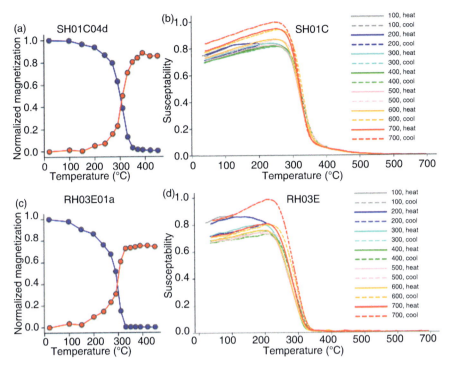

Fig. 12 Representative results of the archaeointensity experiments and thermomagnetic curves. (**a**, **b**) Beth-Shean Stratum S-1a. (**c**, **d**) Tel Reḥov Stratum IV. In graphs (**a**) and (**c**) the Y-axis represents the magnitude of magnetization normalized according to the primary magnetization (recorded during the conflagration). The blue line represents the original magnetization, starting at 1.0 by definition, and decreasing as the temperature steps rise, until it is completely erased. The red line represents the magnetization "recorded" in the lab, starting at 0 by definition, and increasing as the temperature steps rise, until it reaches its maximum. Graphs (**b**) and (**d**) display the magnetic susceptibility (Y-axis) according to temperature (X-axis). The magnetic susceptibility was measured in repeated heating cycles at progressively elevated peak temperatures (every color represents one cycle)

to at least 300–400 °C. At temperature steps higher than this range the samples gained no substantial magnetic signal in the lab. In addition to the archaeointensity results (Fig. 12a, c) Fig. 12 displays representative thermomagnetic curves from Beth-Shean (Fig. 12b) and Tel Reḥov (Fig. 12d). Each color represents one heating and cooling cycle. The thermomagnetic curves are nearly reversible, i.e., every time the sampled material reached a certain temperature its susceptibility was similar to the susceptibility previously measured at that temperature. This demonstrates little alteration of the magnetic minerals during this experiment, which indicates stability of the magnetic minerals up to 600 °C and often 700 °C. In the vast majority of specimens from Tel Reḥov and Tel Beth-Shean the main and final drop in susceptibility occurred between ca. 300 °C to ca. 400 °C. Thus, the magnetic properties displayed in the archaeointensity experiments and in the thermomagnetic curves indicate that in the mudbricks in these two archaeological sites and in the mud beehives at Tel Reḥov the Curie temperature (T_c- the temperature above which the magnetic minerals lose their magnetic properties) of the main magnetic component is ca. 300 °C to ca. 400 °C. Interestingly, in the vast majority of burnt mudbricks sampled in 15 other archaeological sites in the southern Levant the main and final drop in susceptibility occurred at much higher temperatures, between ca. 550 °C to ca. 580 °C, indicating the presence of magnetite (Vaknin et al., 2022). It seems likely that the unique magnetic properties of the samples from Beth-Shean and Tel Reḥov are related to the composition of the mud used for construction in these two neighboring archaeological sites in the Beth-Shean Valley.

4 Discussion and Conclusions

Choosing between the two alternatives presented in Table 2 has significant historical implications. The archaeomagnetic study contributes to resolving at least part of this query. The archaeointensity analysis showed a clear difference between the burnt beehive from Stratum V and burnt bricks from Stratum IV at Tel Reḥov (Fig. 10). According to the archaeointensity and archaeomagnetic direction results, the destruction of Stratum IV showed outstanding correspondence with the destructions of other archaeological sites and, in particular, Tell es-Safi (Gath), safely attributed to Hazael in the second half of the ninth century BCE, thus supporting the hypothesis that Stratum IV at Tel Reḥov also fell prey to Hazael's conquests (Mazar, 2016: 107–112; 2020: 126–127). In contrast both the intensity as well as the direction of the geomagnetic field recorded in the destruction of Stratum S-1a at Beth-Shean are significantly different from those of Stratum IV at Tel Reḥov, while the intensity corresponds with that of the destruction of the apiary of Stratum V at Tel Reḥov (as previously mentioned, no direction could be measured from this context). These results imply a correlation between Beth-Shean Stratum S-1a and Reḥov Stratum V and indicate a considerable chronological gap that separated the destructions of these two strata from that of Stratum IV at Tel Reḥov. Based on this result and the radiometric dates from Stratum V at Tel Reḥov it would mean that the public buildings at Beth-Shean S-1a as well as Stratum V at Tel Reḥov predated the Omride Dynasty in Israel. One option is that these two strata corresponded with the first kings of the Northern Kingdom of Israel, the most significant of whom, according to the biblical narrative, is Baasha. Our archaeomagnetic study thus supports the assumption that the late Iron IIA started in northern Israel in the last quarter of the tenth century BCE, corresponding with the early days of the northern kingdom (Mazar, 2011: 107; 2020: 113, Table 4.2, 119–122). Another, more radical, option is to attribute these buildings at Beth-Shean to the Solomonic era, which remains one of the most controversial issues in the history and archaeology of the Iron Age. We have to recall that the topographic list of Shoshenq I (biblical Shishak) following his military raid in ca. 920 BCE mentions Beth-Shean and Reḥov side by side. Is it possible to identify these two cities with Beth-Shean Stratum S-1a and Tel Reḥov

Stratum V? The latter possibility was suggested by the excavators in light of the results of the first four excavation seasons at Tel Reḥov (Bruins et al., 2003) but was taken with reservation in the final publication (Mazar, 2020: 123–124; for a more hesitant statement that leaves this possibility open see: Mazar, 2021: 261–263). The archaeomagnetic dating of the destruction of Stratum S-1a at Beth-Shean may revive this suggestion (Fig. 13. For details, see Vaknin et al., 2022). This dating is based on the archaeointensity results from Beth-Shean Stratum S-1a, from the other strata discussed here and from other previously published results (Shaar et al., 2022). Besides these results the input for our model is the age range of every group (Table 6). For instance, in the case of Beth-Shean the prior date is 940–820 BCE. The result of the archaeomagnetic dating must be, by definition, within this range. Within this age range, the archaeomagnetic model "prefers" the dates for which the intensity results from Beth-Shean "agree" with the model of archaeointensity changes (light green area in Fig. 10a). For the full description of the archaeointensity model and the dating according to this model, see Shaar et al. (2022) and Livermore et al. (2018).

While the archaeomagnetic dating of the destruction of Stratum S-1a at Beth-Shean points to 935–900 BCE (68.2% probability), most of the radiocarbon dates from Tel Reḥov V, as well as the results of the Bayesian models, appear to point to a slightly later date. Furthermore, the attribution of destruction levels to Shoshenq is highly debatable (Mazar, 2020: 123–124; 2021: 261–263 for extended discussion).

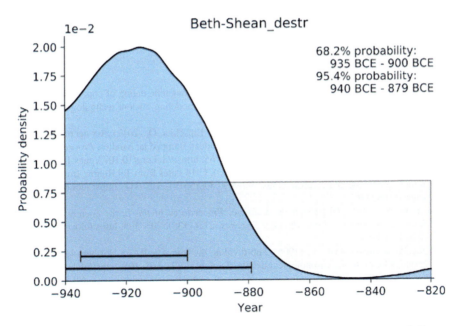

Fig. 13 Archaeomagnetic dating of the destruction of Building A in Stratum S-1a at Beth-Shean

The results of this study suggest that the late Iron IIA public buildings, reflecting central administration, were constructed at Beth-Shean either during the Solomonic era or during the pre-Omride phase in the history of the Northern Kingdom of Israel and were destroyed violently during this same time range. The reason for the destruction cannot be determined with any certainty. Our results may point to the raid of Shoshenq I, but the severe destruction could also be a result of a historical or natural event in the following decades, either at the end of the tenth or the beginning of the ninth centuries BCE. Stratum V at Tel Reḥov with its apiary must have existed during this same time range. Since both these contexts can be safely attributed to the late Iron IIA, these conclusions are significant regarding the debate concerning Iron Age chronology of the tenth–ninth centuries BCE as well as the emergence of the early state in Israel. They support the conclusions reached at Tel Reḥov (based on radiometric dates) that the transition between the early and late Iron IIA occurred during the last third or quarter of the tenth century BCE, that during this time Tel Reḥov was a well-planned town, including the unique apiary, and suggest that the monumental architecture at Beth-Shean Stratum S-1a was constructed during this time and most probably destroyed prior to the rise of the Omride dynasty.

As this article is published in a volume in honor of Tom Levy, we should mention the fact that the period under discussion here corresponds to the peak of copper production at Faynan and Timna. One of us (A. Mazar) has suggested that some of the copper trade was carried out through Transjordan and the Jordan Valley towards the Phoenician coast, where the copper was traded with far-off destinations like Greece. It has also been suggested that Tel Reḥov and perhaps also Tel Beth-Shean were part of this trading system (Mazar, 2020: 103, 105; 2021: 263).

References

Ben-Yosef, E., Tauxe, L., & Levy, T. E. (2010). Archaeomagnetic dating of copper smelting site F2 in Timna Valley (Israel) and its implication on modeling ancient technological developments. *Archaeometry, 52*(6), 1110–1121.

Ben-Yosef, E., Millman, M., Shaar, R., Tauxe, L., & Lipschits, O. (2017). Six centuries of geomagnetic intensity variations recorded by royal Judean stamped jar handles. *Proceedings of the National Academy of Sciences, 114*(9), 2160–2165. https://doi.org/10.1073/pnas.1615797114

Bruins, H. J., van der Plicht, J., & Mazar, A. (2003). C-14 dates from Tel Rehov: Iron-Age chronology, pharaohs, and Hebrew kings. *Science, 300*(5617), 315–318. https://doi.org/10.1126/science.1082776

Fisher, R. A. (1953). Dispersion on a sphere. *Proceedings of the Royal Society of London. Series A. Mathematical and Physical Sciences, 217*(1130), 295–305. https://doi.org/10.1098/rspa.1953.0064

Herzog, Z., & Singer-Avitz, L. (2006). Sub-dividing the Iron Age IIA in Northern Israel: A suggested solution to the chronological debate. *Tel Aviv, 33*(2), 163–195. https://doi.org/10.1179/tav.2006.2006.2.163

James, F. W. (1966). *The iron age at Beth Shan*. University Museum, University of Pennsylvania.

Livermore, P. W., Fournier, A., Gallet, Y., & Bodin, T. (2018). Transdimensional inference of archeomagnetic intensity change. *Geophysical Journal International, 215*(3), 2008–2034. https://doi.org/10.1093/gji/ggy383

Maeir, A. (2020). Introduction and overview. In A. Maeir & J. Uziel (Eds.), *Tell es-Safi/Gath II: Excavations and studies* (pp. 1–52). Zaphon.

Mazar, A. (2006). *Excavations at Tel Beth-Shean 1989–1996: Volume 1 – From the Late Bronze Age IIB to the Medieval Period.* Israel Exploration Society and The Hebrew University of Jerusalem.

Mazar, A. (2011). The Iron Age chronology debate: Is the gap narrowing? Another viewpoint. *Near Eastern Archaeology, 74*(2), 105–111. https://doi.org/10.5615/neareastarch.74.2.0105

Mazar, A. (2016). Culture, identity and politics relating to Tel Reḥov in the 10th–9th centuries BCE. In O. Sergi, M. Oeming, & I. J. de Hulster (Eds.), *In search for Aram and Israel: Politics, culture and identity* (pp. 89–120). Mohr Siebeck.

Mazar, A. (2020). The Tel Reḥov excavations: Overview and synthesis. In A. Mazar & N. Panitz-Cohen (Eds.), *Tel Reḥov: A Bronze and Iron Age city in the Beth-Shean Valley I* (pp. 69–140). Institute of Archaeology, Hebrew University of Jerusalem.

Mazar, A. (2021). The Beth Shean Valley and its vicinity in the 10th century BCE. *Jerusalem Journal of Archaeology*, 241–271.

Mazar, A., & Panitz-Cohen, N. (2020). *Tel Reḥov: A Bronze and Iron Age city in the Beth-Shean Valley.* Institute of Archaeology, Hebrew University of Jerusalem.

Mazar, A., & Streit, K. (2020). The radiometric dates from Tel Reḥov. In A. Mazar & N. Panitz-Cohen (Eds.), *Tel Reḥov, a Bronze and Iron Age city in the Beth-Shean Valley.* The Institute of Archaeology, the Hebrew University of Jerusalem.

Mazar, A., Bruins, H. J., Panitz-Cohen, N., & van der Plicht, J. (2005). Ladder of time at Tel Reḥov: Stratigraphy, archaeological context, pottery and radiocarbon dates. In T. E. Levy & T. Higham (Eds.), *The bible and radiocarbon dating. Archaeology, text and science* (pp. 193–255). Equinox.

Peters, I., Tauxe, L., & Ben-Yosef, E. (2017). Archaeomagnetic dating of Pyrotechnological contexts: A case study for copper smelting sites in the central Timna Valley, Israel: Copper smelting sites in the central Timna Valley, Israel. *Archaeometry, 60*, 554–570. https://doi.org/10.1111/arcm.12322

Sergi, O., Bezzel, H., Tsur, Y., & Covello-Paran, K. (2021). Ḥorvat Ṭevet in the Jezreel Valley: A Royal Israelite Estate. In K. Covello-Paran, A. Erlich, & R. Beeri (Eds.), *New studies in the archaeology of northern Israel* (pp. 31–48). The Israel Antiquities Authority. https://doi.org/10.2307/j.ctv1rr6ddq.5

Shaar, R., Ben-Yosef, E., Ron, H., Tauxe, L., Agnon, A., & Kessel, R. (2011). Geomagnetic field intensity: How high can it get? How fast can it change? Constraints from Iron Age copper slag. *Earth and Planetary Science Letters, 301*, 297–306. https://doi.org/10.1016/j.epsl.2010.11.013

Shaar, R., Tauxe, L., Ron, H., Ebert, Y., Zuckerman, S., Finkelstein, I., et al. (2016). Large geomagnetic field anomalies revealed in Bronze and Iron Age archaeomagentic data from Tel Megiddo and Tel Hazor, Israel. *Earth and Planetary Science Letters, 442*, 173–185.

Shaar, R., Hassul, E., Raphael, K., Ebert, Y., Segal, Y., Eden, I., et al. (2018). The first catalog of archaeomagnetic directions from Israel with 4000 years of geomagnetic secular variations. *Frontiers in Earth Science, 6*, 164. https://doi.org/10.3389/feart.2018.00164

Shaar, R., Bechar, S., Finkelstein, I., Gallet, Y., Martin, M. A. S., Ebert, Y., et al. (2020). Synchronizing Geomagnetic Field Intensity Records in the Levant Between the 23rd and 15th Centuries BCE: Chronological and Methodological Implications. *Geochemistry, Geophysics, Geosystems, 21*(12), e2020GC009251. https://doi.org/10.1029/2020GC009251

Shaar, R., Gallet, Y., Vaknin, Y., Gonen, L., Martin, M. A. S., Adams, M. J., & Finkelstein, I. (2022). Archaeomagnetism in the Levant and Mesopotamia reveals the largest changes in the geomagnetic field. *Journal of Geophysical Research: Solid Earth, 127*, e2022JB024962.

Shahack-Gross, R., Shaar, R., Hassul, E., Ebert, Y., Forget, M., Nowaczyk, N., et al. (2018). Fire and collapse: Untangling the formation of destruction layers using archeomagnetism. *Geoarchaeology, 33*, 513–528. https://doi.org/10.1002/gea.21668

Vaknin, Y., Shaar, R., Gadot, Y., Shalev, Y., Lipschits, O., & Ben-Yosef, E. (2020). The Earth's magnetic field in Jerusalem during the Babylonian destruction: A unique reference for field behavior and an anchor for archaeomagnetic dating. *PLoS One, 15*(8), e0237029. https://doi.org/10.1371/journal.pone.0237029

Vaknin, Y., Shaar, R., Lipschits, O., & Ben-Yosef, E. (2022). Reconstructing biblical military campaigns using geomagnetic field data. *PNAS, 119*(44), e2209117119.

Time and Paradigm at Tel Megiddo: David, Shoshenq I, Hazael and Radiocarbon Dating

Hendrik J. Bruins

Abstract The tenth century BCE synchronism between Pharaoh Shoshenq I, the founder of the 22nd Dynasty in Egypt, and the biblical Shishak is widely accepted. However, various paradigms exist regarding the understanding of biblical texts and their possible association with archaeological strata. The nineteenth century Wellhausen paradigm theorized that the Law is younger than the Prophets, thereby initiating a Low Chronology and mythologizing much of Israel's biblical history. Thomas Levy advocated throughout his career an open-minded approach concerning biblical texts and archaeology in the southern Levant. The present paper focuses on the radiocarbon dating results of Tel Megiddo, an Iron Age site of major importance and its possible relationships with biblical texts. The paper evaluates the influence of various scholarly paradigms on chronology, followed by an assessment of Tel Megiddo's radiocarbon dates, using the latest IntCal 20 calibration curve. Based on nuclear physics, ^{14}C dating results provide inherently unbiased numbers, unaffected by human paradigms and literary theories, whether liberal, conservative or postmodern. The radiocarbon evaluations of Tel Megiddo do *not* support chronological correlation of a destruction layer with the Shoshenq Campaign, neither the Stratum VIA destruction (former Finkelstein paradigm), nor the Stratum VA-IVB destruction (Yadin and Mazar paradigm). Stratum VB has two radiocarbon dates covering the tenth century BCE, supporting Yadin, who associated Megiddo V with the United Monarchy of Solomon. However, the destruction layer of Stratum VA-IVB dates to the ninth century BCE, supporting Finkelstein who related this devastation to Hazael's Campaign. The radiocarbon dating results imply that Megiddo V and VA-IVB cover both the tenth century BCE (United Monarchy) and a large part of the ninth century BCE (Omride Dynasty of the Northern Kingdom of Israel). The historical break between the United Monarchy and the Divided Monarchies at Megiddo was apparently not accompanied by a distinct archaeologi-

H. J. Bruins (✉)
Jacob Blaustein Institutes for Desert Research, Swiss Institute for Dryland Environmental & Energy Research, Ben-Gurion University of the Negev, Sede Boker Campus, Beer-Sheva, Israel
e-mail: hjbruins@bgu.ac.il

© The Author(s), under exclusive license to Springer Nature Switzerland AG 2023
E. Ben-Yosef, I. W. N. Jones (eds.), *"And in Length of Days Understanding" (Job 12:12): Essays on Archaeology in the Eastern Mediterranean and Beyond in Honor of Thomas E. Levy*, Interdisciplinary Contributions to Archaeology, https://doi.org/10.1007/978-3-031-27330-8_35

cal break. Ceramic studies appear to have difficulties distinguishing between the tenth and the ninth centuries BCE, as judged by the radiocarbon dating results. The stratigraphy and periodization of Megiddo VIA, VB, and VA-IVB should be reassessed in much more detail with radiocarbon dating to sort out the chronology and archaeological history across the tell.

Keywords Tel Megiddo · Destruction layers · Iron Age · Synchronisms · Biblical associations · Paradigms · Radiocarbon dating

1 Introduction

Professor Thomas E. Levy has been at the forefront of research regarding the vexed problems at the interface of archaeology and biblical texts in the southern Levant, stimulating multi-disciplinary investigations and scientific dating. The excavations at Khirbat en-Nahas (Levy et al., 2008) and his books (for example, Levy & Higham, 2005a, b; Levy, 2010; Levy et al., 2015) bear witness to his approach and thinking on these matters.

My contribution to this *Festschrift* in honor of his career relates to some of the issues that came up in the important conference he organized in 2004 with Thomas Higham at the Oxford Centre for Hebrew and Jewish Studies. The conference focused on Radiocarbon Dating and the Iron Age of the Southern Levant, highlighting the two principal and conflicting paradigms: the Traditional Chronology (Mazar, 2005) and the Low Chronology (Finkelstein, 2005).

The conference resulted in the book, *The Bible and Radiocarbon Dating: Archaeology, Text and Science*, edited by Levy and Higham (2005a, b). On page 10 of their introductory article, a schematic cross-section is shown of Tel Megiddo (Figs. 1 and 2), highlighting Strata VI, V, IV and III with three intervening destruction layers. Figure 2 summarizes principal dating differences between the conventional archaeological age assessment and the low chronology age assessment. The traditional scheme of the conventional dating paradigm, as described by Mazar (2005), related these three destruction levels respectively to David's Campaigns (ca. 1003 BCE), Shishak's Campaign (ca. 926 BCE) and the Assyrian Conquest (732 BCE). On the other hand, Finkelstein's Low Chronology paradigm (1996, 2005; Finkelstein & Silberman, 2001) associated these three destruction layers to Shishak's Campaign (ca. 926 BCE), Hazael's Campaign (ca. 835 BCE), and the Assyrian Conquest (732 BCE). Hence, there is only mutual consensus concerning the uppermost destruction layer between Megiddo Stratum IV and III, related to the Assyrian Conquest. Yet, paradigms may be modified, based on new data sets. Finkelstein changed his interpretation concerning Megiddo Stratum VI, unlinking its destruction with the Shishak Campaign, as additional radiocarbon dates showed this stratum to be too old for possible association with the latter Pharaoh (Finkelstein & Piasetzky, 2006: 58).

Time and Paradigm at Tel Megiddo: David, Shoshenq I, Hazael and Radiocarbon Dating

Fig. 1 Tel Megiddo, looking east over the Jezreel Valley; on the horizon from left to right Mount Tabor, Mount Moreh, and Mount Gilboa. (© Shutterstock 1530716327)

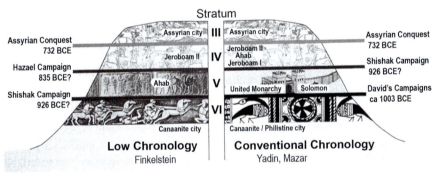

Fig. 2 Schematic cross-section of Tel Megiddo showing the principal differences in archaeological interpretation and dating between the Conventional Chronology (Yadin, 1970; Mazar, 2005) and the Low Chronology (Finkelstein, 2005). (Modified after Levy and Higham (2005a, b: 10), cross-section image courtesy of Israel Finkelstein, who later (Finkelstein & Piasetzky, 2006: 58) changed his view concerning the destruction of Stratum VI, unrelating it with the Shishak Campaign)

A useful overview of the history of archaeological excavations at Tel Megiddo (Finkelstein et al., 2008), as well as definitions and correlations of its various strata, is given by Cline (2020). The ambiguities and difficulties to relate archaeological strata at Early Iron Age Megiddo with political history is evaluated by Thomas (2022). The latest excavation results and interpretations of Tel Megiddo were published in Megiddo VI (Finkelstein & Martin, 2022), comprising 61 chapters, totaling 1924 pages. This massive volume came out at the time of writing of this paper and only newly published radiocarbon dating results of the strata evaluated could be incorporated in the text and tables.

Association of different archaeological destruction layers at Tel Megiddo with the military campaign of Shoshenq I (biblical Shishak) played an important part in the controversy (Levy & Higham, 2005a, b: 10) between the alternative schemes (Fig. 2). Hence, a concise update is given of recent viewpoints by Egyptologists on possible historical time options for the reign of Shoshenq I, based on Egyptian literary data.

Whether one likes it or not, biblical texts also play a significant role in the "dating" of the above three archaeological destruction layers at Tel Megiddo. Therefore, yet another paradigm pertaining to the "dating" of the Hebrew Bible and its various books is briefly evaluated. The "historical-critical" German school, which developed during the nineteenth century, well before the inception of Near Eastern archaeology, attained considerable influence on archaeological interpretation concerning issues related to the Hebrew Bible.

The basic theme of this paper, radiocarbon dating, is highlighted as an impartial time basis for chrono-stratigraphy, well-known in the geological sciences, but less common in "historical" Near Eastern archaeology. Radiocarbon dating is intrinsically independent of both archaeological age assessment, biblical texts and other literary sources. A measurement of time based on nuclear physics is obviously not influenced by human opinion. However, Bayesian statistics of a sequence of radiocarbon dates (Bronk Ramsey, 2009), a valuable approach when used properly, may also be skewed or "cooked" in desired directions by manipulation of the model parameters. Moreover, the use of average radiocarbon dating results that may not properly represent the perceived archaeological strata involved may cause distortions (Bruins et al., 2011), as also mentioned in a reply to Fantalkin et al. (2011). Concerning the use of Greek pottery in dating, also at Megiddo (Fantalkin et al., 2015), new radiocarbon dates on stratified animal bones from Sindos (northern Greece) concerning the Protogeometric and Geometric periods indicate a surprisingly high chronology (Gimatzidis & Weninger, 2020). The authors concluded that their stratified ^{14}C results imply the need for a revised understanding of the Greek archaeological periodization system. These complex issues in relation to the Greek Iron Age are beyond the scope of the present study.

A re-assessment is made of available radiocarbon dates of Tel Megiddo, published after the 2004 Oxford Conference, in relation to Strata VIA, VB, and VA-IVB. Possible associations with David, Shoshenq I and Hazael, suggested in the two conflicting paradigms (Fig. 2) are evaluated in terms of time coincidence between suggested historical dates and radiocarbon dating, using the latest IntCal20 calibration curve (Reimer et al., 2020). The results are surprising, as detailed below.

2 Time and Paradigm

Time is a crucial factor in archaeological interpretation because it forms the principal basis for placing data from different sources (archaeology, geology, geography, ancient texts) on the same 4th dimension level: synchronicity. In fact, the lack of ability in the nineteenth century to measure time in relation to antiquities led to the development of the first paradigm in archaeology: the Three Age System. Attempting to bring chronological order to the arrangement of antiquities for the Royal Museum of Nordic Antiquities in Copenhagen (Denmark), the Stone Age, Bronze Age, and Iron Age were introduced by Thomsen. This division was based on the succession of technological advances through time regarding the production of weaponry and tools (Heizer, 1962). The system is still with us today, even though the actual usage through time of stone, bronze and iron is obviously far more complex, as illustrated for example by the title of the book, *Lithics after the Stone Age,* written by Rosen (1997).

So what is the meaning today of "the Iron Age of the southern Levant" (Levy & Higham, 2005a, b: 3–14)? It has usually little to do with iron. The adoption of iron metallurgy in the region occurred gradually and inconsistently (Gottlieb, 2010) and does not form the basis for the respective divisions between and within Iron I, Iron II and Iron III. Mazar (2005) presented an overview of the development of scholarly viewpoints concerning the Iron Age in Israel in terms of archaeological periods, suggested time boundaries, and possible correlations with regional history and biblical texts. He also described the rationale for his Modified Conventional Chronology. Finkelstein (2005) gave an informative update at the 2004 Oxford Conference concerning his logic to explain the Low Chronology of the Iron Age in the southern Levant.

What is the difference between Iron I and Iron II? This question relates directly to the "biblical" dimension of archaeology. The Iron I archaeological period is usually associated with initial Israelite settlement in the country after the Late Bronze Age "Egyptian domination." The Iron IIA is related to the first appearance of monumental architecture, associated in the Traditional scheme with the United Monarchy of Solomon, and in the Finkelstein Low Chronology with the Omride Dynasty of the Northern Kingdom of Israel (Fig. 2). However, the designation at Megiddo concerning the critical Strata V and IV, in this respect, had a confusing history in the course of the successive expeditions, as described by Yadin (1970: 68–72).

The time boundaries for Iron I were traditionally placed in the time range 1200–1000 BCE (Mazar, 2005). However, Finkelstein (1996), in his Low Chronology paradigm, rejected the biblical United Monarchy and enlarged the Iron I archaeological period to also include the tenth century BCE until ca. 900 BCE. "Consequently, the tenth century is represented by Stratum VIA at Megiddo" (Finkelstein, 1996: 177), a statement evaluated below in the context of radiocarbon dating. Evidently, ancient biblical texts play a larger role than iron in the Iron Age archaeology of the southern Levant.

A controversial textual dating paradigm of the Hebrew Bible, advanced by German theologians, developed during the nineteenth century, based on critical exegetical analysis. This theoretical hypothesis resulted in sweeping chronological changes in relation to the biblical narrative of ancient Israel, deconstructing much into a myth or fairy story prior to King Josiah in the seventh century BCE. A major development of this new paradigm was proposed in 1805 by Wilhelm Martin Leberecht de Wette, who presented at the University of Jena his *Dissertatio critico-exegetica qua Deuteronomium...*, a thesis written in Latin (De Wette, 1805) and consisting of only 14 pages (Paul, 1988). The full title in English reads as follows: "Critical and exegetical dissertation wherein it is shown that Deuteronomy is a work different from the earlier books of the Pentateuch and by a different author, of a more recent age" (translated by Harvey & Halpern, 2008). Time is clearly involved.

De Wette based his theories on 2 Kings 22–23, which describe events during the reign of King Josiah. The "book of the law," found by Hilkiah the high priest in the Temple, was assumed by De Wette to be Deuteronomy. This was his *first assumption*. The Hebrew Masoretic text uses the general term "2) "ספר התורה" Kings 22: 8). The *second assumption* he made presumed that Deuteronomy was written shortly before the reign of Josiah. The historical time of Josiah is currently understood to be ca. 640–609 BCE (Kahn, 2013). Therefore, De Wette "dated" the "book of the law," without any external evidence, to the seventh century BCE. Subsequently, De Wette (1806) published his two volume *Beiträge zur Einleitung in das Alte Testament* in 1806 and 1807. He dealt in the first volume with the Book of Chronicles, which did not fit in with his emerging theory. Hence, he concluded that Chronicles is not a reliable source for the history of ancient Israel. Likewise, De Wette expressed little trust in the historicity of Exodus, Leviticus, Numbers, Deuteronomy, Joshua, and Judges (Paul, 1988: 218–219).

Though the influence of De Wette was very important, it is Julius Wellhausen (1883), who further developed and spread the emerging *paradigm*. He "dated" the Pentateuch *later* than the Prophetic books of the Bible. His dating process was remarkably laconic, as emphasized by Weinfeld (2004: 15). In the year 1876, Wellhausen was informed about Karl Heinrich Graf's hypothesis (1866), placing the Law later than the Prophets. He instantly adopted this dating "almost without knowing his reasons" (Weinfeld, 2004: 15). The original statement by Wellhausen (1905: 3–4) in German in the 6th edition of his famous book *Prolegomena zur Geschichte Israels* reads as follows:

> Da erfuhr ich gelegentlich im Sommer 1867, daß Karl Heinrich Graf dem Gesetze seine Stelle hinter den Propheten anweise, und beinah ohne noch die Begründung seiner Hypothese zu kennen war ich für sie gewonnen: ich durfte mir gestehn, daß das hebräische Altertum ohne das Buch der Thora verstanden werden könne (Wellhausen, 1905: 3–4).

Evidently, the historical-critical paradigm developed by De Wette and Wellhausen favored a "low chronology" for what in their interpretations remained of the history of ancient Israel. Wellhausen did not specifically address the issue of Shishak and the synchronism with Solomon, Jeroboam and Rehoboam in his book *Prolegomena*. But he made some comments about the reign lengths of the Kings of Judah and

Israel, which he considered artificial *künstlichen Zahlenverhältnisse* (Wellhausen, 1905: 271). He also suggested that the synchronisms were added later and did not belong to original sources: "daß die Synchronismen ursprünglich nicht dazu gehören" (Wellhausen, 1905: 271). Such "higher criticism" appears for the "uninitiated" more a play with assumptions and statements, rather than robust research based on thorough external evidence.

Moshe Weinfeld (2004) published a critical study about the *Prolegomena* and its author. The negative prejudice of Wellhausen towards the Jewish people was expressed in a letter he wrote to his friend Ferdinand Justi (dated March 5, 1893):

> The Jews of old are not very likeable, but they are to be respected. They perished in war against the Romans, but in a manner quite different from the Athenians and Spartans – although of military matters they comprehended nothing and knew no discipline. To be sure, they did not perish at all, but rather triumphed, despite everything, over Rome. *One may lament this fact*, but it must be recognized (Weinfeld, 2004: 3, citing Boschwitz, 1968: 58, emphasized part of the last sentence in italics).

It is rather perplexing that the Wellhausen paradigm, which arose in the nineteenth century, well before the serious development of Near Eastern archaeology, still forms an important factor in the *interpretation of archaeological findings* in the southern Levant. This is acknowledged by Finkelstein (2007: 9–10):

> The major proposals of the higher-critical scholars of the nineteenth to twentieth centuries have, in my opinion, withstood the test of time… no convincing paradigms have been offered that can replace these models… In the early days, conservative scholars deployed archaeology to help defeat the higher criticism of scholars such as Julius Wellhausen….

3 The Shoshenq I/Shishak Synchronism

3.1 Texts and Time

Shishak, king of Egypt, is mentioned in 1 Kings 11: 40 together with Solomon and Jeroboam, who later became king of the Northern Kingdom of Israel. After the death of Solomon, the campaign of Shishak against Jerusalem "in the fifth year of king Rehoboam" is briefly described in 1 Kings 14: 25. A more extensive account of his campaign against Jerusalem, as well as its military nature, is written in 2 Chronicles 12: 1–9. A recent translation of Chronicles in English with commentary was written by Levin (2017). The following are a few verses from this translation (2 Chr. 12: 2–4, 9; Levin, 2017: 17):

> And it came to be in the fifth year of King Rehoboam, Shishak king of Egypt came up against Jerusalem, because they had been unfaithful to the Lord. With one thousand two hundred chariots and sixty thousand horsemen, and there was no counting the people who came with him from Egypt–Libyans, Sukkites and Kushites. And he captured the fortified cities of Judah and came as far as Jerusalem…. And Shishak king of Egypt came up against Jerusalem; he took the treasures of the house of the Lord and the treasures of the house of the king, he took everything; he took the shields of gold that Solomon had made.

The fact that Chronicles mentions Libyans as part of the Egyptian army is remarkable, because Shoshenq I was of Libyan descent. Such information points to an original textual source close to the time of the campaign, as also suggested by Mazar (1986). Josephus wrote about Shoshenq (written in Greek as Ἴσωκον Isok) in his Antiquities:

> As the avenger of his outrages against him, God sent Isok, the king of the Egyptians, about whom Herodotus is in error when he attributes his exploits to Sesostris. For this Isok, in the fifth year of Roboam's kingship, launched a campaign against him with many ten thousands. For he had following him 1,200 chariots, 60,000 horsemen, and 400,000 foot soldiers. The majority of those he brought with him were Libyans and Ethiopians (Judean Antiquities 8: 253–254, Brill's Scholarly Editions platform, Flavius Josephus Online).

Nearly 2000 years ago, Josephus apparently had literary sources similar to the medieval Masoretic version of Chronicles. The figures for chariots and horsemen are the same. In addition, Josephus used the more specific term "foot soldiers" and their numbers, which are mentioned in Chronicles only in general terms.

Some scholars date Chronicles as late as 350–300 BCE (McKenzie, 2004). Here one should make a distinction between the final compilation of the book and original text sources (*Urtext*). For example, if the *Urtext* of 2 Chronicles 12: 3 would date to the fourth century BCE, it seems doubtful that the writer could have imagined the tenth century BCE with Libyan soldiers in Shishak's army. The subject of an *Urtext* regarding the biblical books is discussed in detail by Emanuel Tov (2001: 164–180):

> [T]he assumption of a single original text cannot easily be proven or refuted and its correctness depends primarily on its probability. Nevertheless, it should be noted that the known textual evidence points in the direction of one original text, since most of the known textual variation, in major as well as minor details, should be viewed as genetic, supporting the assumption of textual development in one direction only, that is linear development (Tov, 2001: 172).

The situation today is that only a few ancient biblical texts have survived the tooth of time. Therefore, the process of text transmission *through time*, from generation to generation, is largely unknown before the medieval manuscripts of the Masoretic text. Hence, there is much room for speculation and "higher criticism" such as that developed by De Wette and Wellhausen.

Most scholars agree that Shishak, king of Egypt, mentioned in the Hebrew Bible, is the same as Pharaoh Shoshenq I, the founder of the 22nd Dynasty in Egypt, who reigned at some time during the tenth century BCE. Finkelstein, too, has agreed that the biblical Shishak refers to Shoshenq I in the tenth century BCE. However, he added, apparently in relation to his Low Chronology: "But the vicious circle of dating the campaign according to 1 Kgs 14, 25 and dating Solomon and Rehoboam according to the campaign must be eliminated" (2002: 110).

Concerning the actual chronological position of Shoshenq I within the tenth century BCE, there are several possible historical methodologies and calculations. Kitchen, in his monumental work on the Third Intermediate Period in Egypt (1986), dated the reign of Shoshenq I to 945–924 BCE. However, it is not known from Egyptian sources when Shosheng's campaign took place. Using biblical chronological information, Kitchen (1986) calculated a date of 925 BCE for the Shishak campaign, i.e., 1 year before the end of his reign.

Several alternative historical dates for the reign of Shoshenq I, based on analyses of ancient Egyptian literary sources, have been published in recent years. Shortland (2005) presented during the Oxford Conference a study concerning the reign of Shoshenq I, based only on Egyptian records. He concluded that the minimum date for the accession of Shoshenq I is 941 BCE, only 4 years less than the accession year of 945 BCE, calculated by Kitchen (1986). If the campaign took place in year 20 of his reign, often suggested by scholars but *not* specified in Egyptian writings, then 921 BCE would be an option, according to the evaluation by Shortland (2005).

A detailed study about the cumulative chronology of the New Kingdom and the Third Intermediate Period was conducted by Schneider (2010). He concluded that most historical uncertainties from within Egyptian records are situated around 900 BCE. Variable chronological options of ±25 years exist around this time, which cannot be solved at present. Evaluating various possibilities, he suggested the period 962–941 BCE for the reign of Shoshenq I (Schneider, 2010: 401), which is 23 years older than Kitchen's calculation (1986).

Another detailed chronological study by Krauss (2015) covered the period from Ramesses II through Shoshenq III, including lunar dates of Thutmoses III. His methodology led him to calculate three possible accession years for Shoshenq I: 954, 943, or 929 BCE (Krauss, 2015: 342–343). The range of 25 years fits remarkably well the degrees of chronological uncertainty of ±25 years expressed by Schneider (2010). Evaluating the various options, Krauss (2015: 351) considered the accession year of 929 BCE less likely. He retained the two other possible options within his methodology, whereby 943 BCE is very close to the 945 BCE by Kitchen (1986) and the minimum date of 941 BCE by Shortland (2005). The older option, 954 BCE, is only 8 years younger than the date of 962 BCE favored by Schneider (2010).

3.2 Shoshenq's Campaign: Devastation or Subjugation?

A vast amount of literature and scholarly viewpoints exist regarding the nature and route(s) of the campaign by Shoshenq I in the southern Levant. The Egyptian evidence is inscribed in the temple at Karnak, on the southwestern wall of the Bubastite gate constructed by Shoshenq. His triumphal relief contains a unique list of about 150 topographical names, carved in hieroglyphic script, using a style independent of conventions common during the 18th, 19th, and 20th Dynasties (Simons, 1937). Translation of these place names and association with known sites is a complex undertaking (Simons, 1937; Mazar, 1986; Kitchen, 1986; Rainey & Notley, 2006). Unfortunately, quite a number of name-ovals have been obliterated or partially defaced, while others convey place names unknown today, which should not be a surprise some 3000 years after the campaign. A detailed list of all name-ovals with translation and possible association has been published by Rainey and Notley (2006: 185–189).

Ben-Dor Evian (2011) emphasized the need to consider the entire composition of the Karnak relief in its Egyptian context and not only the topographical list of place names. She reviewed the smiting scenes in Egyptian royal art, which evolved to include topographical lists of conquered enemies. The smiting scene of Shoshenq is typical for a triumphal relief. Two unique aspects were highlighted by Ben-Dor Evian (2011: 13–19), the white crown and the building inscription within the triumph hymn. The hymn itself can be regarded as an original composition, not a mere copy of older examples (Kitchen, 1999: 433; Ben-Dor Evian, 2011: 15).

Concerning possible archaeological associations, the Shoshenq relief does not tell us whether a place name in the list was conquered by destruction or conflagration, or subdued to surrender without damage. The account given by Josephus is instructive in this respect (Judean Antiquities 8: 255–258, Brill's Scholarly Editions platform, Flavius Josephus Online):

> Advancing then against the country of the Hebrews, he captured the most solidly fortified cities of Roboam's kingdom without a fight. Having secured these, he finally marched against Hierosolyma… Isok got possession of the city without a fight, Roboam having admitted him out of fear. He [Isok] did not, however, stick to the agreements he had made. Rather, he plundered the sacred precinct and emptied the treasuries of God and those of the kings; he carried off countless quantities of gold and silver and left nothing whatever behind. He likewise took away the golden small shields and the large shields that King Solomon had constructed. Nor did he leave untouched the golden quivers that David had dedicated to God after taking them from the king of Sophene. Having done this, he returned to his own country.

We do not know the textual sources Josephus had at his disposal in the first century CE, but he clearly mentions that the fortified cities of the Judean Kingdom were taken by Shishak *without* a fight. If these sources are correct, then archaeology would not be able to find destruction layers in relation to Shishak's Campaign, at least regarding the Judean Kingdom.

Finkelstein (2009) wrote an instructive article about destruction layers, focused on Megiddo. His field observations regarding destruction layers, gained during many years of archaeological excavations at various sites, can be summarized as follows. An ashy layer found in a dig is not necessarily a destruction layer. The extent of destruction by an enemy may be limited and does not always involve a conflagration. Much depends on the aim of the enemy. The objective may be the total annihilation of a settlement, which would probably result in large-scale destruction accompanied by fire. A punitive campaign would likely result in much smaller damage to a settlement, as the enemy may want dominion with taxes to continue without destroying the economy of the settlement and its surroundings. Yet another objective may be a takeover to establish a new administration, possibly involving only the destruction of the elite quarter of a town. Alternatively, an enemy may be interested in inheriting a settlement and cooperate with its elite groups, leaving public buildings undamaged (Finkelstein, 2009: 113, 121).

A real destruction of a settlement should be defined by the presence of at least two of the following features:

1. A black layer with charcoal, representing burnt beams, on the floor, usually overlaid with a thick ashy layer.
2. A thick accumulation of collapse – of bricks or stones – on the floor. This accumulation can at times be as much as one meter or more deep. In the case of bricks and a strong fire, the bricks may turn red or even white.
3. In most cases, an accumulation of finds, mainly broken pottery vessels, on the floors (Finkelstein, 2009: 113).

4 Tel Megiddo and Shoshenq I

Among the archaeological sites in Israel, Megiddo has a particularly robust connection with Shishak. First, Megiddo is mentioned in the topographical list of Shoshenq I in the Upper Register of his Karnak inscription, written on the third line in name-oval 27 (Rainey & Notley, 2006: 186).

Second, during excavations at Megiddo by the Oriental Institute of the University of Chicago in 1926, part of a stela with Egyptian hieroglyphs was found by one of the workmen in a dump from the previous German excavations, conducted by Schumacher during 1903–1905. James Henry Breasted, who visited Megiddo in 1926 during the excavations by Fisher (1929), was the first Egyptologist to decipher the hieroglyphs (Fig. 3) on the stone fragment of the stela (Breasted, 1929: xi): "It was with considerable satisfaction on the first sunny day after the rains had diminished that I was able to make out the name Shishak or Sheshonq I, in hieroglyphs very dimly glimmering from a badly weather-worn and almost illegible inscribed stone surface." Based on his experience, Breasted (1929: xi–xii) suggested that the fragment may have been part of a large round-topped victory stela about 5 feet wide and some 10 feet high. The Megiddo excavations by the University of Chicago lasted until 1939. After the establishment of the State of Israel, Yigal Yadin (Hebrew University) conducted excavations during the 1960s and 1970s. Subsequently, Israel Finkelstein (Tel Aviv University) and his colleagues have excavated Megiddo since 1992. Unfortunately, so far, no additional fragments of the Shoshenq stela have been found at the site.

Several destruction layers at Megiddo were associated with the Shoshenq I Campaign, as summarized by Finkelstein (2002) in a detailed overview of scholarly opinions. Describing optional scenarios, he considered the violent destruction by fire of Megiddo VIA as a possible candidate for association with the Shoshenq Campaign in the tenth century BCE. According to a second scenario he suggested the possibility of a peaceful takeover, whereby "Shoshenq erected his stele in the settlement of Megiddo VB" (Finkelstein, 2002: 122). Another key difference between the Low Chronology and the Traditional Chronology relates to Stratum VA-IVB. Finkelstein relates Stratum VA-IVB to the ninth century BCE as the

Fig. 3 Facsimile drawing of the stone fragment of the Shoshenq stela found at Tel Megiddo, published in Fisher (1929: 13)

administrative city of the Omrides, subsequently destroyed by Hazael's Campaign, which probably took place around 835 BCE. However, in the conventional dating scheme (Mazar, 2005), shown also in Fig. 2, Stratum VA-IVB is associated with the United Monarchy of Solomon in the tenth century BCE, whereby its destruction layer is linked to the Shoshenq Campaign (Yadin, 1970) later in the tenth century BCE. Megiddo VIA is considered a Canaanite-Philistine city in the Traditional Chronology, probably destroyed by David around 1003 BCE (Yadin, 1970: 95).

5 Tel Megiddo and Radiocarbon Dating of Iron Age Strata

Radiocarbon dating brought about a revolution how archaeologists view Central and Western Europe, as certain archaeological structures, thought to be younger than their supposed Near-Eastern forerunners, were in fact older, as dated by radiocarbon. The related archaeological theories had to be almost completely rewritten (Renfrew, 1973). Concerning the southern Levant, most archaeologists considered archaeological dating based on pottery and associations with the historical calendars of Egypt and Mesopotamia more reliable and precise than radiocarbon dating. Moreover, it is easier and cheaper to date with a paradigm than to consider dry radiocarbon numbers that may turn out to be nasty flies in the precious ointment of seemingly clever hypotheses.

During his work in the early 1980s with the Negev Emergency Survey and the excavations at Tell el-Qudeirat, I became convinced of the necessity to use radiocarbon dating as an independent physical measurement of time *also* in the "historical periods" of the Near East (Bruins, 1986, 2001; Bruins & Mook, 1989; Van der Plicht & Bruins, 2001, 2005; Bruins & Van der Plicht, 2005; Van der Plicht et al., 2009; Bruins et al., 2011).

Concerning Megiddo, radiocarbon dating results of Iron Age strata, published by Boaretto (2006, 2022), Sharon et al. (2007), Gilboa et al. (2013), Toffolo et al. (2014, 2022), Fantalkin et al. (2015) and Kleiman et al. (2019), are evaluated here with the latest IntCal20 calibration curve. The rationale in the context of this paper is to determine which of the strata proposed for possible correlation with the Campaign of Shoshenq I (Fig. 2) may fit in terms of time coincidence between historical dating and radiocarbon dating. Suggested associations of destruction layers at Megiddo with David and Hazael (Fig. 2) are also taken into consideration.

5.1 *Tel Megiddo and Radiocarbon Dating: Stratum VIA*

Megiddo Stratum VIA is a key example how archaeological age assessment by different archaeologists may differ significantly, including the political agent responsible for its destruction. The oldest archaeological age assessment was made by the Chicago Expedition, attributing an age of 1150–1100 BCE for Stratum VIB and VIA combined. Yadin (1970) lowered the assumed date for Stratum VIA and its destruction by about a century to 1050–1000 BCE (Shiloh, 1993), while relating its devastation to David's Campaigns around 1000 BCE (Fig. 2). An even younger archaeological date in the tenth century BCE was suggested by Finkelstein (1996: 177) for Stratum VIA in the context of his Low Chronology paradigm, considering Shoshenq a candidate for its violent destruction (Finkelstein, 2002), a viewpoint he later changed (Finkelstein & Piasetzky, 2006).

Many radiocarbon dates of Stratum VIA, based on short-lived charred seeds, usually olive pits, have been published (Boaretto, 2006, 2022; Sharon et al., 2007; Gilboa et al., 2013; Toffolo et al., 2014, 2022; Fantalkin et al., 2015). Concerning the publication by Sharon et al. (2007), 21 individual radiocarbon dates from Level K-4 (associated with Stratum VIA) were previously evaluated by Bruins et al. (2011). The dates display large time differences. Additional dates (Gilboa et al., 2013; Toffolo et al., 2014, 2022) from different areas, levels and loci, all associated with Stratum VIA, show a similar pattern. The average dates for each locus (Table 1) range from 2940 ± 20 BP to 2763 ± 28 BP. Such a large time difference cannot relate to a *single* destruction horizon. Three different radiocarbon time groups (Table 1) can be distinguished for Stratum VIA destruction debris: 2900+ BP dates, 2800+ BP dates, and 2700+ BP dates (see also Bruins et al., 2011).

Table 1 Megiddo Stratum VIA[a]

Stratum VIA area level, locus and archaeological context	Average ^{14}C date (year BP) Lab #	Calibrated age 1σ (68.3% probability) cal BCE	Calibrated age 2σ (95.4% probability) cal BCE	Calibrated median cal BCE
Loci with 2900+ BP dates				
Level K-4, 00/K/034 Pre-destruction floor	2907 ± 26 (2) RTT-3946	1155–1149 (3.3%) **1126–1046** (60.0%) 1030–1020 (5.0%)	1205–1140 (21.4%) 1134–1012 (74.1%)	1094
Level K-4, 98/K/032 Destruction debris	2921 ± 25 (4) RTT-3944	1193–1176 (9.9%) 1159–1145 (9.5%) **1129–1054** (48.9%)	1213–1044 (91.8%) 1032–1018 (3.6%)	1117
Level M-4, 04/M/46 Destruction debris	2900 ± 16 (6) RTT-5089	**1119–1049** (68.3%)	1192–1176 (3.5%) 1158–1146 (2.6%) 1128–1012 (89.3%)	1082
Level M-4, 04/M/055 Destruction level, olive pits in jar (affiliation?)	2940 ± 20 RTT-5077	**1206–1118** (68.3%)	1217–1055 (95.4%)	1153
Loci with 2800+ BP dates				
Level K-4, 00/K/008 Pre-destruction floor	2882 ± 30 (2) RTT-3945	**1112–1013** (68.3%)	1198–1172 (4.1%) 1163–1143 (3.2%) 1131–975 (85.6%) 954–934 (2.6%)	1062
Level K-4, 98/K/043 Destruction debris	2846 ± 20 (4) RTT-3942	1047–1027 (15.7%) **1021–977** (41.4%) 951–936 (11.1%)	1107–1096 (1.8%) 1082–1068 (2.3%) 1056–925 (91.4%)	1003
Level K-4, 98/K/031 Destruction debris	2853 ± 28 (2) RTT-3943	**1054–974** (57.4%) 955–933 (10.9%)	1114–927 (95.4%)	1016
Level H-9, 08/H/4 Pre-destruction floor	2881 ± 26 (4) RTK-6273	**1111–1013** (68.3%)	1193–1176 (2.4%) 1159–1146 (1.8%) 1129–978 (89.6%) 950–936 (1.7%)	1059
Level H-9, 08/H/5 Destruction debris	2866 ± 30 (4) RTK-6274	**1111–995** (68.3%)	1184–1181 (0.3%) 1126–927 (95.2%)	1037
Level H-9, 06/H/50 Destruction debris	2837 ± 16 (6) RTT-5496	**1016–972** (47.6%) 956–933 (20.7%)	1048–927 (95.4%)	989
Level H-9, 06/H/56 Destruction debris	2835 ± 16 (6) RTT-5497	**1014–972** (46.6%) 956–933 (21.7%)	1047–925 (95.4%)	986
Level Q-7c, 14/Q/145 Olive pit	2843 ± 22 RTD-8052	1046–1030 (11.5%) **1020–975** (42.1%) 953–934 (14.7%)	1107–1096 (1.7%) 1082–1068 (2.2%) 1057–922 (91.6%)	998
Level Q-7c, 14/Q/79 Olive pit	2834 ± 22 RTD-8046	**1015–967** (44.2%) 960–931 (24.0%)	1054–913 (95.4%)	985

(continued)

Table 1 (continued)

Stratum VIA area level, locus and archaeological context	Average ¹⁴C date (year BP) Lab #	Calibrated age 1σ (68.3% probability) cal BCE	Calibrated age 2σ (95.4% probability) cal BCE	Calibrated median cal BCE
Level Q-7a, 14/Q/163 Olive pit	2824 ± 21 RTD-8053	1008–968 (40.7%) 959–931 (27.6%)	1047–1029 (4.7%) 1021–912 (90.8%)	974
Loci with 2700+ BP dates			
Level K-4, 98/K/037 Destruction debris	2767 ± 25 (3) RTT-3940	968–960 (4.8%) **931–895** (36.9%) 875–839 (26.6%)	988–832 (95.4%)	907
Level K-4, 98/K/036 Destruction debris	2763 ± 28 (2) RTT-3939	**931–892** (34.5%) 880–836 (33.8%)	987–829 (95.4%)	902

[a]See Boaretto (2006, 2022), Arie (2006, 2013), Sharon et al. (2007), Gilboa et al. (2013), Toffolo et al. (2014, 2022), Fantalkin et al. (2015), Kleiman et al. (2019) and Finkelstein and Martin (2022) for radiocarbon dating info and archaeological context. The calibrated age ranges are based on the IntCal20 calibration curve (Reimer et al., 2020) and OxCal 4.4.4 (Bronk Ramsey, 2009, 2021). The bold calibrated sub-ranges within the 1σ range have the highest relative probability (shown in percentages). Note that in a number of cases, two age ranges have rather similar probability percentages, rendering the results more ambiguous

In my opinion, radiocarbon dating is in most cases *not* the problem; stratigraphic resolution is. Archaeological excavations may deal with individual loci that are difficult to differentiate and "date" according to archaeological criteria, while possibly containing mixed material from different periods. Hence, radiocarbon dating should be used in my opinion also to sort out stratigraphic issues and correlation between the different areas, levels and loci of Tel Megiddo. Indeed, additional dates published by Boaretto (2022) from Area Q, Level Q-7a and Level Q-7c, associated with Stratum VIA, are similar and consistent, belonging to the group of 2800+ BP dates. Chrono-stratigraphy is widely used in geology and prehistory, but much less in Near Eastern "historical" archaeology, where stratification is based primarily on pottery.

Unlike Sharon et al. (2007), the later publications by Gilboa et al. (2013), and Toffolo et al. (2014) published only the average dates for each locus. This constitutes a lack of transparency, because the readers cannot know and evaluate the individual dates on which the averages are based. For example, the destruction debris in Level K-4, Locus 98/K/036, yielded three radiocarbon dates (Sharon et al., 2007: 28): 2910 ± 45 BP, 2790 ± 40 BP, 2735 ± 40 BP (RTT-3939). Combining the three dates is not supported by the chi-squared test: fails at 5% – df = 2 T = 8.7 (5% 6.0). However, Sharon et al. (2007) did use the average value of 2804 ± 24 cal BCE, which was subsequently also used by Gilboa et al. (2013) and Toffolo et al. (2014, 2022: 1426). Removing the oldest date (2910 ± 45 BP) results in an average of 2763 ± 28 BP, which is accepted by the chi-squared test: df = 1 T = 0.9 (5% 3.8). This average is used here (Table 1).

Table 1 shows the radiocarbon dating results of 16 different loci from Area K, Area M, Area H, and Area Q, which are all associated by the excavators with Stratum VIA. Three loci represent pre-destruction floors, whereas 10 loci represent destruction debris. The calibrated dates for the "same" destruction event range in terms of the respective median calibrated values of each locus (Table 1) from 1117 cal BCE (98/K/032) to 902 cal BCE (98/K/036). Locus 04/M/055 has an even older calibrated median value (1153 cal BCE), measured on charred seeds from within a jar (!), but later the archaeological context was considered unclean or unsafe "due to new evaluation of the loci after stratigraphic study and restoration of the pottery (I. Finkelstein, personal communication)", quoting Gilboa et al. (2013: 1117).

In any case, the destruction event, which terminated Stratum VIA at Tel Megiddo, has calibrated radiocarbon ages of different areas and loci from the twelfth century BCE to the ninth century BCE (Table 1). This is impossible for the *same* destruction horizon! So, what is wrong here? The various radiocarbon dating results seem to be acceptable, based on multiple individual dates for each locus. Concerning Area K, the great majority of radiocarbon dates within each locus are coherent (Sharon et al., 2007), with few exceptions as mentioned above. Concerning Areas M and H, the individual dates have not been published. Area Q is represented by high-quality individual dates (small standard deviation) for each locus (Boaretto, 2022: 1441). However, let us assume that the respective authors (Gilboa et al., 2013; Toffolo et al., 2014, 2022) took care that each average is based on a coherent set of dates. Then the problem can only be situated within the stratigraphic resolution of the archaeological excavations, whereby, apparently, *different* destruction layers from *different time periods* from *different areas, levels and loci*, were all considered to represent the *same* termination event of Stratum VIA.

Mazar (1990) correlated Megiddo VIA with Tel Dan Stratum V, and so does Finkelstein (1999: 67), as these strata from the two sites have similar pottery assemblages. However, Mazar (1990) "dated" Megiddo VIB-VIA and Dan V to ca. 1150–1000 BCE, whereas Finkelstein (1999) "dated" these strata to the tenth century BCE, according to his Low Chronology paradigm. Biran (1994: 11), the excavator of Tel Dan, assigned an older age of 1200–1050 BCE to Stratum V and Ilan (1999: 137) favored the period 1150–1050 BCE.

Considering radiocarbon dating, the four loci with 2900+ BP dates of Megiddo VIA (Table 1) match well with the radiocarbon dates of Tel Dan Stratum V (Bruins et al., 2005, 2011). The short-lived sample of charred olive pits (GrA-9624, 2930 ± 50 BP) in destruction debris on a tamped earth floor in Dan Stratum V has a 1σ calibrated age range of 1210–1053 cal BCE (68.3%) and a calibrated median value of 1132 cal BCE, using the IntCal20 (Reimer et al., 2020) calibration curve. These results fit very well with the archaeological age assessment of Biran (1994) for Stratum V: 1200–1050 BCE.

Regarding the various dating schemes by the respective excavators of Tel Megiddo, the radiocarbon results of the four loci in Area K and M with 2900+ BP dates match only with the archaeological age assessment of 1150–1100 BCE by the Chicago Expedition! On the other hand, these radiocarbon results are too old for both Yadin's Traditional Chronology (Mazar, 1990, 2005) and Finkelstein's Low Chronology (1996, 1999).

Concerning the 2800+ BP dates of Megiddo VIA (Table 1), the pre-destruction floors in Area K (Locus 00/K/008) and Area H (Locus 08/H/4) have a similar radiocarbon date. Their highest relative probability (1σ) is in the range 1112–1013 (68.3%) cal BCE, while their respective median values are 1062 cal BCE and 1059 cal BCE. Additional dates from Area Q, Level Q-7a and Level Q-7c, associated with Stratum VIA (Table 1), published by Boaretto (2022) show consistent results with median calibrated values of 998, 985, and 974 cal BCE. Hence these dates fall within the archaeological age assignment favored by Yadin (1970) and Mazar (1990, 2005), associated with the possible time of David's Campaigns. The five destruction debris dates in this group (Table 1) are also derived from Area K (Loci 98/K/043 and 98/K/031) and Area H (Loci 08/H/5, 06/H/50, and 06/H/56). All these five calibrated dates (Table 1) are too old for time association with the Campaign of Shoshenq I. Even Finkelstein acknowledged, contrary to his previous opinion (Finkelstein, 1996, 2002, see also Fig. 1), that a Shoshenq destruction of Megiddo Stratum VIA "may be somewhat too late for the date of this devastation, which has recently been determined by radiocarbon studies" (Finkelstein, 2009: 122; see also Finkelstein & Piasetzky, 2006). However, the above eight destruction dates in the 2800+ BP group (Fig. 2) would fit in time with *David's Campaigns* (Fig. 1), as suggested by Yadin (1970) and Mazar (2005). Megiddo is not specifically mentioned in the biblical narratives concerning the military battles conducted by David (1 and 2 Samuel). The site does appear in the administrative regions ruled by Solomon (1 Kings 4: 12).

Regarding the 2700+ BP dates of Megiddo "VIA" (Table 1), both radiocarbon dates are from Area K (Loci 98/K/037 and 98/K/036). The results are almost the same. The highest relative probabilities of the calibrated dates range from 931 to 836 cal BCE. The time range may theoretically relate at the upper margin to Shoshenq or to Hazael at the lower margin, but the median calibrated values, 907 and 902 cal BCE, indicate that these options are borderline. Needless to say, Locus 98/K/037 and Locus 98/K/036 in Area K are too young for Stratum VIA. The archaeological "dating" of these loci requires reevaluation and revision.

5.2   *Tel Megiddo and Radiocarbon Dating: Strata VB and VA-IVB*

Megiddo Stratum VB is represented by four radiocarbon dates (Table 2) from Area H (Level H-7) and Area Q (Level Q-6). The same areas provided five radiocarbon dates for Stratum VA-IVB, Level Q-4 and Level H-5, respectively (Table 2). Excavations by Tel Aviv University in Area Q produced four radiocarbon dates from charred seeds in Level Q-5 (Fantalkin et al., 2015: 29; Kleiman et al., 2019; Boaretto, 2022). Initially Level Q-5 was associated with Stratum VB (Fantalkin et al., 2015). However, in a later study Level Q5 became to be considered a separate stratum, not identified by the University of Chicago excavations, stratigraphically ranked by

Table 2 Megiddo Stratum VB, Level Q5, and Stratum VA-IVB[a]

Stratum area level, locus and archaeo context	14C date (year BP) Lab #	Calibrated age 1σ (68.3% probability) Cal BCE	Calibrated age 2σ (95.4% probability) Cal BCE	Calibrated median (cal BCE)
Stratum VB Level H-7, 06/H/78 Floor	2808 ± 27 (2) RTT-5498	**998–925** (68.3%)	1048–898 (95.4%)	961
Stratum VB Level Q-6a, 12/Q/94 Olive pit	2780 ± 45 RTK-6755	**991–897** (54.4%) 871–841 (13.9%)	1046–1030 (2.0%) 1020–820 (93.4%)	928
Stratum VB Level Q-6a, 14/Q/50 Olive pit	2740 ± 22 RTD-8045	905–891 (14.2%) **881–834** (54.1%)	927–822 (95.4%)	869
Stratum VB Level Q-6b, 12/Q/120 Olive pit	2700 ± 45 RTK-6753	898–864 (29.8%) **850–809** (38.4%)	967–960 (0.7%) 931–794 (94.7%)	858
Level Q-5 10/Q/73 Olive pits	2848 ± 28 (4) RTK-6403	**1051–973** (55.4%) 955–933 (12.8%)	1111–925 (95.4%)	1008
Level Q-5 10/Q/95 Wheat	2779 ± 29 (4) RTK-6404	983–946 (24.3%) **941–898** (35.6%) 866–849 (8.3%)	1006–891 (75.7%) 882–835 (19.8%)	925
Level Q-5 10/Q/95 Wheat	2806 ± 32 (3) RTK-6405	**1002–921** (68.3%)	1048–896 (91.4%) 873–843 (4.0%)	959
Level Q-5 10/Q/96 Olive pits	2716 ± 28 (4) RTK-6406	**898–864** (35.4%) 853–822 (32.8%)	911-809 BC (95.4%)	861
Stratum VA-IVB Level Q-4, 10/Q/163 wheat	2786 ± 29 (4) RTK-6286	**986–901** (68.3%)	1011–891 (81.6%) 881–836 (13.8%)	936
Stratum VA-IVB Level Q-4, 10/Q/112 Olive pits	2706 ± 52 RTK-6408	**898–811** (68.3%)	981–947 (5.0%) 940–793 (90.4%)	865
Stratum VA-IVB Level Q-4, 12/Q/22 Wheat	2700 ± 45 RTK-6760	898–864 (29.8%) **850–809** (38.4%)	967–960 (0.7%) 931–794 (94.7%)	858
Stratum VA-IVB Level H-5, 98/H/79 Destruction debris	2695 ± 50 RTT-3948	898–862 (29.2%) **853–808** (39.1%)	971–956 (1.7%) 932–791 (93.7%)	857
Stratum VA-IVB Level H-5, 98/H/62 Destruction debris	2708 ± 32 (3) RTK-6429	898–867 (32.2%) **848–814** (36.1%)	914–806 (95.4%)	858

[a]See Boaretto (2006, 2022), Sharon et al. (2007), Gilboa et al. (2013), Toffolo et al. (2014, 2022), Fantalkin et al. (2015), Kleiman et al. (2019) and Finkelstein and Martin (2022) for radiocarbon dating info and archaeological context. A number between brackets in the second column after the radiocarbon date indicates a weighted average date, as well as the number of 14C dates involved. Calibrated age ranges are based on the IntCal20 calibration curve (Reimer et al., 2020) and OxCal v4.4.4 (Bronk Ramsey, 2021). The bold calibrated sub-ranges within the 1σ range have the highest relative probability (shown in percentages). Note that in a number of cases, two age ranges have rather similar probability percentages, rendering the results more ambiguous

Kleiman et al. (2019: 535) between Strata VB and VA-IVB. Level Q-5 is represented by four radiocarbon dates (Boaretto, 2022).

The radiocarbon dating results of Stratum VB are not uniform. RTT-5498 (Level H-7) and RTK-6755 (Level Q-6a) cover mainly the tenth century BCE. On the other hand, RTD-8045 (Level Q-6a) and RTK-6753 (Level Q-6b) are situated in the ninth century BCE. Therefore, Stratum VB levels may be associated in terms of chronostratigraphy with Solomon's United Monarchy and also with the Divided Northern Kingdom. Moreover, the older dates of Stratum VB also coincide with Shoshenq I, whose 21-year reign may be positioned within the time range of 962–920 BCE, according to Egyptological assessments (Shortland, 2005; Schneider, 2010; Krauss, 2015), as detailed above. Finkelstein (2002: 122) proposed that Stratum VB might be associated with a peaceful takeover by Shoshenq I, since no destruction layer appears in this stratum. Thus, Shoshenq may have erected his victory stela (Fig. 3) in the settlement of Megiddo VB.

Concerning the younger Stratum VA-IVB, four of its five radiocarbon dates are similar, all of them covering the ninth century BCE (Table 2): RTK-6408 and RTK-6760 from Level Q-4, as well as RTT-3948 and RTK-6429 from Level H-5. Evidently, these dates are *too young* for association with the Shoshenq Campaign, a key component of the Yadin paradigm (Yadin, 1970) and the Traditional Chronology (Mazar, 2005). However, the radiocarbon dated destruction debris of Stratum VA-IVB fits very well with the Hazael Campaign (Fig. 1), as suggested by Finkelstein (2009: 118):

> But circumstantial archaeological considerations, such as the similarity in building techniques between Megiddo VA-IVB and Samaria (Franklin, 2005), the similarity between the pottery assemblages of Megiddo VA-IVB and the Jezreel compound (Zimhoni, 1997: 38–39), led me to the conclusion that this wave of destructions took place in the middle of the ninth century, and that they were inflicted by Hazael of Aram-Damascus (Na'aman, 1997).

The comparatively new archaeological Level Q-5 in Area Q was archaeologically classified by Kleiman et al. (2019: 535) as Late Iron IIA and politically related to the pre-Omride period. Its chronology was suggested to hover around 900 BCE (late tenth/early ninth century BCE). The authors presented Level Q-5 as a new stratigraphic phase, which was not identified by the University of Chicago expedition, placing it stratigraphically between Strata VB and VA-IVB. However, looking at the four radiocarbon dates of Level Q5 (Kleiman et al., 2019: 547; Boaretto, 2022), recalibrated here with IntCal20 (Table 2), it is clear that three dates (RTK-6403, RTK-6404, RTK-6405) are significantly older, covering the entire tenth century BCE and even part of the eleventh century BCE. The so-called old wood factor cannot be utilized here as an excuse, because the dates are based on short-lived seeds. These three dates would fit very well chronologically with the two older radiocarbon dates of Stratum VB (RTT-5498, RTK-6755).

The youngest date of Level Q-5 (RTK-6406) is similar to the four dates of Stratum VA-IVB (RTK-6408, RTK-6760, RTT-3948, RTK-6429), discussed above. Hence, the question arises whether Level Q-5 is indeed a genuine stratigraphic level sandwiched in time between Strata VB and VA-IVB? Perhaps Level Q-5 incorporates parts of both Stratum VB (Fantalkin et al., 2015: 29) and Stratum VA-IVB?

Pottery time assessment of Iron IIA at Tel Megiddo, traditionally the prime basis of archaeological stratigraphy, does not match quite well with chrono-stratigraphy, based on radiocarbon dating (Table 2). Level Q-6a and Q-6b, both associated with Stratum V have the same radiocarbon age in the ninth century BCE (RTD-8045 and RTK-6753) as four dates of Stratum VA-IVB (RTK-6408, RTK-6760, RTT-3948, RTK-6429). Antiquities in general, including pottery, undoubtedly carry the mark of time. However, the time resolution sensitivity of ceramics in the tenth and ninth century BCE may not be sufficiently precise to make an unequivocal distinction between these two centuries. Radiocarbon dating ought to be the prime basis of chronology and archaeological stratigraphy in Iron IIA, as well as in other periods (Bruins & Mook, 1989).

6 Conclusions

6.1 Megiddo Stratum VIA

The archaeological associations of different levels in different areas of Tel Megiddo with *one destruction event* that terminated Stratum VIA is *not* supported by radiocarbon dating. The radiocarbon results can be divided into three age groups (uncalibrated): 2900+ BP, 2800+ BP, and 2700+ BP. Therefore, the archaeological stratigraphic associations require revisions. More than one destruction event exists in relation to Stratum VI. The very definition of Stratum VI requires a reassessment, based on chrono-stratigraphy and refined archaeological criteria.

The 2900+ BP group of radiocarbon dates fits best with the age assessment of the Chicago Expedition for Stratum VIA (1150–1100 BCE), as well as with radiocarbon dates of Tel Dan Stratum V (Bruins et al., 2005). This destruction event is much too old for association with Shoshenq I (Finkelstein, 1996, 2002) and also too old for association with David's Campaigns (Yadin, 1970; Mazar, 2005).

The 2800+ BP group of radiocarbon dates represent, in terms of chronology, another destruction event, younger in time than the previous destruction horizon. The five average destruction dates in the 2800+ BP group (Fig. 2) from Loci 98/K/043, 98/K/031, 08/H/5, 06/H/50, 06/H/56, as well as the three radiocarbon dates from Area Q (Levels Q-7a and Q-7c) would fit in time with *David's Campaigns* (Fig. 2), as suggested by Yadin (1970) and Mazar (2005). However, also these radiocarbon dates are too old for association with the Campaign of Shoshenq I, as previously proposed by Finkelstein (1996, 2002), who later changed his view concerning Stratum VIA (Finkelstein & Piasetzky, 2006).

The 2700+ BP group of radiocarbon dates (Loci 98/K/037 and 98/K/036) relate to yet another younger destruction event that took place some time during the calibrated age range of 931–836 cal BCE. Evidently, this destruction debris is not related to Stratum "VIA."

6.2 Megiddo Stratum VB and Level Q-5

The four radiocarbon dates associated with Stratum VB can be divided (Table 2) in two age groups: (a) The tenth century BCE is represented by Level H-7, Locus 06/H/78 (RTT-5498) and by Level Q-6a, Locus 12/Q/94 (RTK-6755); (b) The ninth century BCE is represented by Level Q-6a, Locus 14/Q/50 (RTD-8045) and by Level Q-6b, Locus 12/Q/120 (RTK-6753). Therefore, the archaeological criteria to call a certain layer Stratum VB, usually on the basis of ceramics, seem not well established. It seems better to base the archaeological stratigraphy on radiocarbon dating. The archaeological layers dated to the tenth century BCE would fit in terms of chronology with both the United Monarchy of Solomon and the reign of Shoshenq I. The archaeological layers, associated with Stratum V, dated by radiocarbon to the ninth century BCE might fit the Northern Kingdom of Israel. The question is whether these latter associations are correct? If so, it would seem to blur the temporal distinction between Stratum VB and Stratum VA-IVB?

Norma Franklin (2006) made a detailed archaeological study of Megiddo V and she concluded that "the Stratum V city was a long-lived, multi-phased city with two monumental palaces. It was continuously maintained and rebuilt, and not destroyed" (Franklin, 2006: 109). The radiocarbon results also accommodate the proposal by Finkelstein (2002: 122) for a peaceful takeover of the Megiddo VB settlement by Shoshenq I and the setting up of his victory stela (Fig. 3). This would apply of course only to those Levels and Loci dated by radiocarbon to the tenth century BCE.

The insertion of Level Q-5 in between Stratum VB and Stratum VA-IVB, as suggested by Kleiman et al. (2019), makes the phasing in time of archaeological defined layers even more crowded. Kleiman et al. (2019) define Level Q-5 as pre-Omride around 900 BCE. Looking at the four radiocarbon dates of Level Q-5 (Table 2), three of them are significantly older than 900 BCE, i.e. Locus 10/Q/73 and Locus 10/Q/95. These dates (RTK-6403, RTK-6404, RTK-6405) cover the tenth century BCE and are similar to two dates of Stratum VB (Level H-7, Locus 06/H/78, RTT-5498 and Level Q-6a, Locus 12/Q/94, RTK-6755). On the other hand, the youngest radiocarbon date of Level Q-5 (Locus 10/Q/96, RTK-6406) has the same time signature as four of the five dates of Stratum VA-IVB (Loci 10/Q/112, 12/Q/22, 98/H/79, 98/H/62).

6.3 Megiddo Stratum VA-IVB

The destruction horizon of Stratum VA-IVB was dated by radiocarbon (Table 2) to the ninth century BCE, as supported by four dates (1σ range). This is too young for a destruction by the Shoshenq Campaign (Fig. 2), according to the Yadin paradigm (Yadin, 1970; Mazar, 2005). However, the radiocarbon dates fit very well with the suggestion by Finkelstein (Fig. 2) to relate the Stratum VA-IVB destruction to the Hazael Campaign in the ninth century BCE (Finkelstein, 2009: 118).

I would suggest that the radiocarbon dating results may imply that Stratum VB and Stratum VA-IVB covered the tenth century BCE (United Monarchy) and the ninth century BCE (Northern Kingdom of Israel), until the destruction by Hazael around 835 BCE. A historical change of rulers, caused by a division of the Kingdom, did not result in significant archaeological change. Solomon's United Monarchy rule in Megiddo was followed by the Northern Kingdom of Israel without a distinct "archaeological break." Ceramic studies appear to have difficulties distinguishing between the tenth and the ninth centuries BCE, as judged by the above radiocarbon dating results (Table 2).

Yadin (1970) described the confusing archaeological excavation history regarding Strata IV and V of Tel Megiddo. Moreover, archaeology is not always able to investigate the duration of use of certain buildings, as explained in detail by Faust and Sapir (2018). They suggested that monumental buildings may have been used for a much longer time than indicated by the surviving latest occupation characteristics. Likewise, the two palaces in Megiddo V may have served both the United Monarchy and the Omride Dynasty. Franklin (2006) noted that the Stratum V city was long-lived. The stratigraphy and periodization of the above strata should be investigated in much more detail with radiocarbon dating to sort out the chronology and archaeological history.

6.4 The Campaign by Shoshenq I

What was the nature of Shoshenq's Campaign in the southern Levant, devastation or subjugation, as posed with a question mark in the title of Sect. 3.2? The written evidence evaluated in this paper, particularly 2 Chronicles 12: 2–4, 9 (Levin, 2017: 17) and Judean Antiquities 8: 253–254 (Brill's Scholarly Editions platform, Flavius Josephus Online) indicate a non-destructive campaign by Shoshenq I. A comprehensive study by Na'aman (1998) led to a similar conclusion.

The radiocarbon dating evaluation of Tel Megiddo indicates the same result. Two different destruction horizons at Tel Megiddo, at the close of Stratum VIA and at the end of Stratum VA-IVB, were proposed for association with the Campaign of Shoshenq I, respectively by Finkelstein (1996, 2002) and by Yadin (1970; Mazar, 2005). However, none of these strata fits, in terms of radiocarbon dating, with the historical time interval for the Shishaq Campaign somewhere in the third quarter (ca. 1050–1021 BCE) of the tenth century BCE.

Therefore, subjugation of places listed in Shoshenq's Triumphal Relief at Karnak, including Megiddo, rather than destruction, seems the more realistic scenario resulting from this study. The suggestion by Finkelstein (2002: 118) of a peaceful take-over of Megiddo VB by Shoshenq and the placing of his victory stela in this settlement is certainly possible in terms of chrono-stratigraphy, based on radiocarbon dating. However, more ^{14}C dates from Megiddo Strata VB and VA-IVB are necessary to obtain a more robust chronological basis.

Finally, how do the radiocarbon dates of Tel Rehov Stratum V, previously published as a candidate for association with the Shoshenq Campaign (Bruins et al., 2003; Mazar et al., 2005), fit into the above context? Rehov is also listed at Karnak (Rainey & Notley, 2006) in the topographical list of names, even above Megiddo, in the second line of the Upper Register, name-oval 17, after Beth-shean (no. 16). There was only "partial destruction by fire of Stratum V in Areas C and perhaps B" (Mazar et al., 2005: 253). The weighted average radiocarbon dates for each locus of Stratum V are as follows (Bruins et al., 2003): Area B (Locus 4218) 2786 ± 22 BP, Area C (Locus-2422) 2771 ± 8 BP, (Locus-2425) 2788 ± 14 BP, (Locus-2441) 2776 ± 9 BP. The dates, measured in Groningen, are very coherent indeed and their combined average is 2776 ± 5 BP. Using the latest calibration curve IntCal 20 (Reimer et al., 2020) and OxCal 4.4.4 (Bronk Ramsey, 2009, 2021), the 1σ calibrated range, having the highest relative probability, is 931–901 cal BC (68.3%). Within the 2σ range the most probable calibrated range is 940–896 (73.9%) cal BCE. Therefore, a chronological correlation of Rehov Stratum V with the Shoshenq Campaign remains viable in terms of time coincidence, even though the latter campaign was probably not destructive, as discussed above.

Acknowledgments The comments by two anonymous reviewers are very much appreciated.

References

Arie, E. (2006). The Iron Age I pottery: Levels K-5 and K-4 and an intra-site spatial analysis of the pottery from Stratum VIA. In I. Finkelstein, D. Ussishkin, & B. Halpern (Eds.), *Megiddo IV: The 1998–2002 seasons* (pp. 191–298). Monograph Series of the Institute of Archaeology of Tel Aviv University.

Arie, E. (2013). Area H: Levels H-9 to H-5. In I. Finkelstein, D. Ussishkin, & E. H. Cline (Eds.), *Megiddo V: The 2004–2008 seasons* (pp. 247–274). Monograph Series of the Institute of Archaeology of Tel Aviv University.

Ben-Dor Evian, S. (2011). Shishak's Karnak relief – More than just name-rings. In S. Bar, D. Kahn, & J. J. Shirley (Eds.), *Egypt, Canaan and Israel: History, imperialism, ideology and literature* (pp. 11–22). Brill.

Biran. (1994). *Biblical Dan*. Israel Exploration Society.

Boaretto, E. (2006). Radiocarbon dates. In I. Finkelstein, D. Ussishkin, & B. Halpern (Eds.), *Megiddo IV: The 1998–2002 seasons* (pp. 550–557). Monograph Series of the Institute of Archaeology of Tel Aviv University.

Boaretto, E. (2022). Radiocarbon dating. In I. Finkelstein & M. A. S. Martin (Eds.), *Megiddo VI: The 2010–2014 seasons* (pp. 1438–1446). Eisenbrauns.

Boschwitz, F. (1968). *Julius Wellhausen: Motive und Mass-stäbe seiner Geschichtsschreibung*. Dissertation, Marburg (1938). Reprinted 1968 Darmstadt.

Breasted, J. H. (1929). Foreword. In C. S. Fisher (Ed.), *The excavation of Armageddon* (pp. vii–xiii). University of Chicago Press.

Bronk Ramsey, C. (2009). Bayesian analysis of radiocarbon dates. *Radiocarbon, 51*(1), 337–360.

Bronk Ramsey, C. (2021). *OxCal v4.4.4 research lab for archaeology*. Oxford University. https://c14.arch.ox.ac.uk/oxcal.html

Bruins, H. J. (1986). *Desert environment and agriculture in the Central Negev and Kadesh-Barnea during historical times*. Published PhD dissertation. Wageningen University/Stichting Midbar Foundation, The Netherlands/Nijkerk.

Bruins, H. J. (2001). Near East chronology: Towards an integrated ^{14}C time foundation. *Radiocarbon, 43*(3), 1147–1154.

Bruins, H. J., & Mook, W. G. (1989). The need for a calibrated radiocarbon chronology of Near Eastern archaeology. *Radiocarbon, 31*(3), 1019–1029.

Bruins, H. J., & Van der Plicht, J. (2005). Desert settlement through the Iron Age: Radiocarbon dates from Sinai and the Negev highlands. In T. E. Levy & T. Higham (Eds.), *The bible and radiocarbon dating: Archaeology, text and science* (pp. 349–366). Equinox.

Bruins, H. J., Van der Plicht, J., & Mazar, A. (2003). ^{14}C dates from Tel Rehov: Iron Age chronology, pharaohs, and Hebrew kings. *Science, 300*, 315–318.

Bruins, H. J., Van der Plicht, J., Ilan, D., & Werker, E. (2005). Iron-Age ^{14}C dates from Tel Dan: A high chronology. In T. E. Levy & T. Higham (Eds.), *The bible and radiocarbon dating: Archaeology, text and science* (pp. 323–336). Equinox.

Bruins, H. J., Nijboer, A. J., & Van der Plicht, J. (2011). Iron Age Mediterranean chronology: A reply. *Radiocarbon, 53*(1), 199–220.

Cline, E. H. (2020). *Digging up Armageddon: The search for the lost city of Solomon*. Princeton University Press.

De Wette, W. M. L. (1805). *Dissertatio critico-exegetica. qua Deuteronomium a prioribus Pentateuchi libris diversum, alius cuiusdam recentioris auctoris opus esse monstratur*. Publice defendet auctor Guilielm Martin Leberecht de Wette, Jena.

De Wette, W. M. L. (1806). *Beiträge zur Einleitung in das Alte Testament* (Vol. 1 (1807), Vol. 2). Schimmelpfennig.

Fantalkin, A., Finkelstein, I., & Piasetzky, E. (2011). Iron Age Mediterranean chronology: A rejoinder. *Radiocarbon, 53*, 179–198.

Fantalkin, A., Finkelstein, I., & Piasetzky, E. (2015). Late Helladic to Middle Geometric Aegean and contemporary Cypriot chronologies: A radiocarbon view from the Levant. *Bulletin of the American Schools of Oriental Research, 373*, 25–48.

Faust, A., & Sapir, Y. (2018). The "Governor's residency" at Tel 'Eton, the United Monarchy, and the impact of the old-house effect on large-scale archaeological reconstructions. *Radiocarbon, 60*(3), 801–820.

Finkelstein, I. (1996). The archaeology of the united monarchy: An alternative view. *Levant, 28*, 177–187.

Finkelstein, I. (1999). Hazor and the North in the Iron Age: A low chronology perspective. *Bulletin of the American Schools of Oriental Research, 314*, 55–70.

Finkelstein, I. (2002). The campaign of Shoshenq I to Palestine: A guide to the 10th century BCE polity. *Zeitschrift des Deutschen Palästina-Vereins, 118*(2), 109–135.

Finkelstein, I. (2005). A low chronology update: Archaeology, history and bible. In T. E. Levy & T. Higham (Eds.), *The bible and radiocarbon dating: Archaeology, text and science* (pp. 31–42). Equinox.

Finkelstein, I. (2007). Digging for the truth: Archaeology and the bible. In I. Finkelstein, A. Mazar, & B. B. Schmidt (Eds.), *The quest for the historical Israel: Debating archaeology and the history of early Israel*. Society of Biblical Literature.

Finkelstein, I. (2009). Destructions: Megiddo as a case study. In D. J. Schloen (Ed.), *Exploring the Longue Durée: Essays in Honor of Lawrence E. Stager* (pp. 113–126). Eisenbrauns.

Finkelstein, & Martin (Eds.). (2022). *Megiddo VI: The 2010–2014 seasons*. University Park, PA.

Finkelstein, I., & Piasetzky, E. (2006). The Iron I-IIA in the highlands and beyond: ^{14}C anchors, pottery phases and the Shoshenq I campaign. *Levant, 38*, 45–61.

Finkelstein, I., & Silberman, N. (2001). *The bible unearthed: Archaeology's new vision of ancient Israel and the origin of its sacred texts*. The Free Press.

Finkelstein, I., Ussishkin, D., & Halpern, B. (2008). Megiddo. In *The new encyclopedia of archaeological excavations in the Holy Land* (Vol. 5, pp. 1944–1950). Israel Exploration Society.

Fisher, C. S. (1929). *The excavation of Armageddon*. University of Chicago Press.
Franklin, N. (2005). Correlation and chronology: Samaria and Megiddo redux. In T. E. Levy & T. Higham (Eds.), *The bible and radiocarbon dating: Archaeology, text and science* (pp. 310–322). Equinox.
Franklin, N. (2006). Revealing Stratum V at Megiddo. *Bulletin of the American Schools of Oriental Research, 342*, 95–111.
Gilboa, A., Sharon, I., & Boaretto, E. (2013). Radiocarbon dating of the Iron Age levels. In I. Finkelstein, D. Ussishkin, & E. H. Cline (Eds.), *Megiddo V: The 2004–2008 seasons* (pp. 1117–1127). Institute of Archaeology of Tel Aviv University.
Gimatzidis, S., & Weninger, B. (2020). Radiocarbon dating the Greek protogeometric and geometric periods: The evidence of Sindos. *PLoS One, 15*(5), e0232906. https://doi.org/10.1371/journal.pone.0232906
Gottlieb, Y. (2010). The advent of the Age of Iron in the land of Israel: A review and reassessment. *Tel Aviv, 37*, 89–110.
Graf, K. H. (1866). *Die Geschichtliche Bücher des Alten Testaments. Zwei Historisch-kritische Untersuchungen*. Weigel.
Harvey, P. B., Jr., & Halpern, B. (2008). W.M.L. de Wette's "Dissertatio Critica.... ": Context and translation. *Zeitschrift für Altorientalische und Biblische Rechtsgeschichte, 14*, 47–85.
Heizer, R. (1962). The background of Thomsen's three-age system. *Technology and Culture, 3*(3), 259–266.
Ilan, D. (1999). *Northeastern Israel in the Iron Age I*. Tel Aviv University, PhD thesis unpublished.
Josephus (ben Matityahu). Judean Antiquities 8: 253–254, Brill's Scholarly Editions platform, Flavius Josephus Online.
Kahn, D. (2013). Revisiting the date of king Josiah's death. In A. F. Botta (Ed.), *In the shadow of Bezalel: Aramaic, biblical, and Ancient Near Eastern studies in honor of Bezalel Porten* (pp. 255–264). Brill.
Kitchen, K. A. (1986). *The third intermediate period in Egypt (1110–650 B.C.)* (2nd ed. with supp.). Aris and Phillips.
Kitchen, K. A. (1999). *Poetry of Ancient Egypt*. Documenta Mundi/Aegyptica. I. Jonsered/Paul Åström.
Kleiman, A., Alexander, F., Mommsen, H., & Finkelstein, I. (2019). The date and origin of Black-on-Red Ware: The view from Megiddo. *American Journal of Archaeology, 123*, 531–555.
Krauss, R. (2015). Egyptian chronology: Ramesses II through Shoshenq III, with analysis of the Lunar Dates of Thutmoses III. *Ägypten und Levante/Egypt and the Levant, 25*, 335–382.
Levin, Y. (2017). *The chronicles of the kings of Judah; 2 Chronicles 10–36: A new translation and commentary*. Bloomsbury Publishing.
Levy, T. E. (Ed.). (2010). *Historical biblical archaeology and the future: The new pragmatism*. Equinox.
Levy, T. E., & Higham, T. (Eds.). (2005a). *The bible and radiocarbon dating: Archaeology, text and science*. Equinox.
Levy, T. E., & Higham, T. (2005b). Introduction: Radiocarbon dating and the Iron Age of the Southern Levant: Problems and potentials for the Oxford conference. In T. E. Levy & T. Higham (Eds.), *The bible and radiocarbon dating: Archaeology, text and science* (pp. 3–14). Equinox.
Levy, T. E., Higham, T., Bronk Ramsey, C., Smith, N. G., Ben-Yosef, E., Robinson, M., Münger, S., Knabb, K., Schulze, J. P., Mohammad Najjar, M., & Tauxe, L. (2008). High-precision radiocarbon dating and historical biblical archaeology in southern Jordan. *PNAS, 105*(43), 16460–16465.
Levy, T. E., Schneider, T., & Propp, W. H. C. (Eds.). (2015). *Israel's exodus in transdisciplinary perspective: Text, archaeology, culture, and geoscience*. Springer.
Mazar, B. (1986). Pharaoh Shishak's campaign to the land of Israel. In B. Mazar (Author), S. Ahituv & B. A. Levine (Eds.), *The early biblical period, historical studies* (pp. 139–150). Israel Exploration Society.
Mazar, A. (1990). *Archaeology of the land of the bible: 10,000–586 B.C.E.* Doubleday.

Mazar, A. (2005). The debate over the chronology of the Iron Age in the Southern Levant: Its history, the current situation, and a suggested resolution. In T. E. Levy & T. Higham (Eds.), *The bible and radiocarbon dating: Archaeology, text and science* (pp. 15–30). Equinox.

Mazar, A., Bruins, H. J., Panitz-Cohen, N., & Van der Plicht, J. (2005). Ladder of time at Tel Rehov: Stratigraphy, archaeological context, pottery and radiocarbon dates. In T. E. Levy & T. Higham (Eds.), *The bible and radiocarbon dating: Archaeology, text and science* (pp. 193–255). Equinox.

McKenzie, S. L. (2004). *I & II chronicles: Abingdon old testament commentaries*. Abingdon Press.

Na'aman, N. (1997). Historical and literary notes on the excavations of Tel Jezreel. *Tel Aviv, 24*, 122–128.

Na'aman, N. (1998). Shishak's campaign to Palestine as reflected by the epigraphic, biblical and archaeological evidence. *Zion, 63*, 247–276. (Hebrew).

Paul, M. J. (1988). *Het Archimedisch Punt van de Pentateuchkritiek*. Published PhD thesis, University of Leiden, The Hague, Boekencentrum (Dutch).

Rainey, A. F., & Notley, R. S. (2006). *The sacred bridge: Carta's atlas of the biblical world*. Carta.

Reimer, P., Austin, W. E. N., Bard, E., Bayliss, A., Blackwell, P. G., Bronk Ramsey, C., Butzin, M., Cheng, H., Lawrence Edwards, R., Friedrich, M., Grootes, P. M., Guilderson, T. P., Hajdas, I., Heaton, T. J., Hogg, A. G., Hughen, K. A., Kromer, B., Manning, S. W., Muscheler, R., Palmer, J. G., Pearson, C., van der Plicht, J., Reimer, R., Richards, D. A., Scott, E. M., Southon, J. R., Turney, C. S. M., Wacker, L., Adolphi, F., Büntgen, U., Capano, M., Fahrni, S. M., Fogtmann-Schulz, A., Friedrich, R., Köhler, P., Kudsk, S., Miyake, F., Olsen, J., Reinig, F., Sakamoto, M., Sookdeo, A., & Talamo, S. (2020). The IntCal20 Northern Hemisphere radiocarbon age calibration curve (0–55 cal kBP). *Radiocarbon, 62*(4), 725–757. https://doi.org/10.1017/RDC.2020.41

Renfrew. (1973). *Before civilization: The radiocarbon revolution and prehistoric Europe*. Cape.

Rosen, S. A. (1997). *Lithics after the Stone Age*. AltaMira Press.

Schneider, T. (2010). Contributions to the chronology of the new kingdom and the third intermediate period. *Ägypten und Levante/Egypt and the Levant, 20*, 373–403.

Sharon, I., Gilboa, A., Jull, A. J. T., & Boaretto, E. (2007). Report on the first stage of the Iron Age dating project in Israel: Supporting a low chronology. *Radiocarbon, 49*(1), 1–46.

Shiloh, Y. (1993). Megiddo. The iron age. In *The new encyclopedia of archaeological excavations in the Holy Land* (Vol. 3, pp. 1012–1024). Israel Exploration Society.

Shortland, A. (2005). Shishak, king of Egypt: The challenges of Egyptian calendrical chronology in the Iron Age. In T. E. Levy & T. Higham (Eds.), *The bible and radiocarbon dating: Archaeology, text and science* (pp. 43–54). Equinox.

Simons, J. J. (1937). *Handbook of the study of Egyptian topographical lists relating to Western Asia*. Brill.

Thomas, Z. (2022). The political history of Megiddo in the early Iron Age and the ambiguities of evidence. *Journal of Ancient Near Eastern History, 9*(1), 69–94.

Toffolo, M. B., Arie, E., Martin, M. A. S., Boaretto, E., & Finkelstein, I. (2014). Absolute chronology of Megiddo, Israel, in the late bronze and iron ages: High-resolution radiocarbon dating. *Radiocarbon, 56*(1), 221–244.

Toffolo, M. B., Arie, E., Martin, M. A. S., Boaretto, E., & Finkelstein, I. (2022). Absolute chronology of Megiddo, Israel, in the late bronze and iron ages: High-resolution radiocarbon dating. In I. Finkelstein & M. A. S. Martin (Eds.), *Megiddo VI: The 2010–2014 Seasons* (pp. 1418–1437). Eisenbrauns.

Tov, E. (2001). *Textual criticism of the Hebrew Bible* (Second revised ed.). Fortress Press/Assen/Royal Van Gorcum.

Van der Plicht, J., & Bruins, H. J. (2001). Radiocarbon dating in Near-Eastern contexts: Confusion and quality control. *Radiocarbon, 43*(3), 1155–1166.

Van der Plicht, J., & Bruins, H. J. (2005). Quality control of Groningen ^{14}C results from Tel Rehov: Repeatability and intercomparison of proportional gas counting and AMS. In T. E. Levy & T. Higham (Eds.), *The bible and radiocarbon dating: Archaeology, text and science* (pp. 256–270). Equinox.

Van der Plicht, J., Bruins, H. J., & Nijboer, A. J. (2009). The Iron Age around the Mediterranean: A high chronology perspective from the Groningen radiocarbon database. *Radiocarbon, 51*(1), 213–242.

Weinfeld, M. (2004). *The place of the law in the religion of ancient Israel*. Brill.

Wellhausen, J. (1883). *Prolegomena zur Geschichte Israels* (2nd ed.). Reimer; (1905) (6th ed.). Reimer.

Yadin, Y. (1970). Megiddo of the kings of Israel. *The Biblical Archaeologist, 33*(3), 65–96.

Zimhoni, O. (1997). *Studies in the Iron Age pottery of Israel: Typological, archaeological, and chronological aspects*. Institute of Archaeology, Tel Aviv University.

The Buqeiʿa Plateau of the Judean Desert in the Southern Levant During the Seventh to Early Sixth Centuries BCE: Iron Age Run-off Farmland or a Pastoralist Rangeland?

Shimon Gibson, Rafael Y. Lewis, and Joan E. Taylor

Abstract Previous archaeological studies of Iron Age IIC/III settlements in the Buqeiʿa plateau, situated in the north-eastern part of the Judean Desert, suggest they were operated as permanent paramilitary farming establishments with their primary subsistence based on run-off farming in the alluvial soils of nearby tributary wadis. Using a landscape archaeology approach and data from archives, an alternative interpretation is presented in this paper, identifying the Buqeiʿa plateau as a rangeland for the grazing of livestock (sheep/goats), with the bounded alluvial lands next to the settlements serving as green pasturage. This allows for a different model for understanding the Iron Age inhabitants as specialized transhumant pastoralists.

The original version of the chapter has been revised. A correction to this chapter can be found at https://doi.org/10.1007/978-3-031-27330-8_83

This paper is dedicated with appreciation to Professor Thomas E. Levy. His scholarly approach to the study of ancient human landscape dynamics in the arid and desert environments of southern Israel and Jordan, has been exceptional and ground-breaking. Our thanks to the editors, Professors Ian Jones and Erez Ben-Yosef, for their invitation that we submit our paper on the Buqeiʿa to this volume.

S. Gibson (✉)
Department of History, University of North Carolina at Charlotte, Charlotte, NC, USA
e-mail: sgibso34@uncc.edu

R. Y. Lewis
Department of Land of Israel Studies, Ashkelon Academic College, Ashkelon, Israel

University of Haifa, Haifa, Israel
e-mail: rafilewiss@gmail.com

J. E. Taylor
Department of Theology and Religious Studies, King's College London, London, UK
e-mail: joan.taylor@kcl.ac.uk

© The Author(s), under exclusive license to Springer Nature Switzerland AG 2023, corrected publication 2023
E. Ben-Yosef, I. W. N. Jones (eds.), *"And in Length of Days Understanding" (Job 12:12): Essays on Archaeology in the Eastern Mediterranean and Beyond in Honor of Thomas E. Levy*, Interdisciplinary Contributions to Archaeology, https://doi.org/10.1007/978-3-031-27330-8_36

Keywords Judean Desert · Buqeʿah plateau · Pastoralism · Field systems · Road systems · Iron Age · Agriculture · Shepherds · Nomads · Desert agriculture · Landscape archaeology · Qumran · Sheep · Goats · Pasturage (green) · Animal pens · Lookout towers · Buqeiʿa plateau · Iron Age II · Transhumant pastoralists

1 Introduction

At the time of Fr. Roland de Vaux's 1954 season of excavations at Khirbet Qumran, famous for its association with the Dead Sea Scrolls, the remains of a much earlier enclosed compound was detected dating from the Iron Age IIC/III, with walls situated directly beneath the foundations of the later Hasmonean and Early Roman settlements (periods I-II) (de Vaux, 1973). The Iron Age remains at Qumran intrigued two of the scholars working at the site that same year, Frank Moore Cross and Józef Tadeusz Milik, and this led them to undertake additional reconnaissance work in the Buqeiʿa region, situated a short distance above and west of Qumran, noting Iron Age pottery scattered on the slopes of three rocky knolls: Khirbet Abu-Tabaq, Khirbet es-Samrah and Khirbet el-Maqari (Cross & Milik, 1956; Cross, 1993). They reached the conclusion that these settlements were of the same "pattern" as the one de Vaux exposed at Qumran. This ultimately led to exploratory soundings at the Buqeiʿa sites conducted by Cross and Milik in 1955. Further exploration was made at these same sites by Lawrence E. Stager for his doctoral research in 1972, which also included the study of the earlier work from the 1950s (Stager, 1974, 1975, 1976). Stager reached the conclusion that in the Iron Age II (seventh to early sixth centuries BCE) "paramilitary" farmers were practicing a form of desert agriculture for cereal production, based on flood-water and/or run-off farming, in the tributary wadis near the three Iron Age sites of the Buqeiʿa.[1]

Our own observation of the region of Qumran and the Buqeiʿa plain was made, with intermittent visits from 2005 to 2019, with the intention of understanding the connectivity between the two regions in the Iron Age II, and to determine the

---

[1] The Buqeiʿa project was undertaken in 1972 by the late Lawrence E. Stager (1943–2017). It was undoubtedly a pioneering step toward the development of Landscape Archaeology in Israel/Palestine. It was carried out at a time when Stager could "find hardly a soul interested in the topic" (letter to Gibson of 20 December 1985). Stager never fully published the major work he did in the Buqeiʿa, but in an e-mail of 16 December 2008, he wrote to Gibson saying he intended to bring out a book of essays, with a reprint of his 1976 essay on the Buqeiʿa sites, and that he would be adding to it an excursus with detailed plans of the sites and pottery plates. On another occasion, Gibson had an interesting and friendly debate on the interpretation of the Buqeiʿa sites at a memorable dinner held at the house of the late Professor Trude Dothan. Stager knew about the writing of the present paper, but unfortunately, he passed away before he could read a draft or comment upon it. Although we are presenting alternative views in this paper, this does not imply any disrespect to Stager's memory and accomplishments. Without Stager's precise recording and acute observations, our knowledge of the Buqeiʿa in the Iron Age would be severely limited and this analysis would not have been possible.

appearance and function of the sites.[2] Firstly, we were able to clarify that the pathway systems around Qumran, including those ascending to the Buqeiʻa, were fundamentally Iron Age II in terms of their basic template and character, and that all later traffic used the same network of paths and tracks already established in the Iron Age (Gibson & Taylor, 2008; Taylor & Gibson, 2011). Secondly, we determined that the Iron Age settlement at Qumran (0.15 ha) had a rectangular enclosure with a central courtyard, a separate domestic unit, a round water system, and an industrial area with two pottery kilns (Taylor & Gibson, 2020), and that it was not an insignificant cluster of "huts" as has recently been suggested (Magen & Peleg, 2018). Pastureland existed next to the settlement and it was on land that was leveled and watered at times of flooding during the winter months. Close by, just south of Qumran, we looked at a very large rectangular enclosure at Khirbet Irneh (0.37 ha) that would have been used to contain the livestock (sheep/goats) of the main settlement, with pasturage extending all the way toward Ain Feshkha. It appears that pastoralism was a significantly important facet of the economy of Qumran in the Iron Age, and not just a sideline. This led us to make a reappraisal of the Iron Age IIC/III sites on the Buqeiʻa plateau.

We visited the Buqeiʻa plateau on a number of occasions to further our knowledge and to clarify problems that could not be resolved except in the field. The sites previously investigated by Stager, at Khirbet Abu-Tabaq, Khirbet es-Samrah and Khirbet el-Maqari, were in a very bad state of preservation owing primarily to current military training activities conducted in the region, as well as recreational joy-riding of four-wheel drive vehicles (Fig. 1).[3] While our visits were not intended to be field surveys, the ever-growing levels of destruction we observed led us to gather as much information as we could on every visit. Our purpose was to re-examine the architectural layout of the three main settlements, their water sources, ancient paths and tracks, and the extent of the areas of bounded alluvium in the adjacent wadi tributaries that were identified by Stager as farmland. The pottery visible on the surface of these sites was largely from the Iron Age IIC/III (seventh to early sixth

---

[2] Visits to observe the sites and pathways (not for surveying) made by the co-authors of this paper to the Qumran and Buqeiʻa regions at times between 2005–2019. Our visits involved no survey or excavations work and was purely observational. We are grateful for the participation of Norma Franklin and Louise Hitchcock during one of our visits to the region in 2009. Our thanks to Mareike Grosser who participated in the visits to Buqeiʻa, and who also read and improved this manuscript. A number of papers based on our observations have already appeared (Gibson & Taylor, 2008; Taylor & Gibson, 2011; Taylor & Gibson, 2020).

[3] The drastic changes and destruction made to the Iron Age sites of the Buqeiʻa by military activities is overwhelming. A recent visit in December 2019 shows that almost nothing has survived of Khirbet Abu-Tabaq, except for two segments of its western enclosure wall. The Khirbet es-Samra enclosure is still visible, but heavy military vehicles have gradually encroached on the limits of the site. Khirbet el-Maqari still exists, but it is situated immediately to the east of a significant area of modern earthworks and there is little chance of it surviving. Moreover, the entire Buqeiʻa landscape has been chopped up and scarred by weekend joy-riders practicing with their four-wheel drive vehicles and creating a palimpsest of tire marks, moving around oblivious to the original beauty of the landscape. None of these sites are fenced or marked in any way by the authorities in charge, which is troubling.

Fig. 1 Aerial view of the Buqeiʿa valley looking north in the early 1970s, with the compound of Khirbet Abu-Tabaq (right) and with the enclosure wall of the D1 field system seen below the site (in the lower right of the picture). (Photo: courtesy R. Cleave and Rohr Productions)

centuries BCE), with smaller quantities from the Early Roman period (first to early second centuries CE), confirming earlier chronological observations made by Cross and Milik, and Stager.[4]

An examination of the collated data led us to ask the following question: Could it be that the Buqeiʿa plateau in the Iron Age II was not inhabited by quasi-military farmers primarily practicing run-off cereal agriculture, as previously supposed by Stager, but that the region had been populated instead by pastoralists using the land as rangeland for livestock and practicing transhumance during the summer months?

This is the key question we intend to answer in this paper.

2 Description of the Buqeiʿa Plateau

The Buqeiʿa plateau (or the Hyrcania Valley) is situated on the lower north-eastern side of what is referred to today as the Judean Desert, and it is isolated on its west by a steep range of hills (the el-Muntar ridge) and on its east by low undulating hills

---

[4] Since we were not conducting an official survey, all potsherds seen were recorded on the spot and left at the sites. The records we made include photographs and some profile drawings of the diagnostic artifacts for comparative purposes.

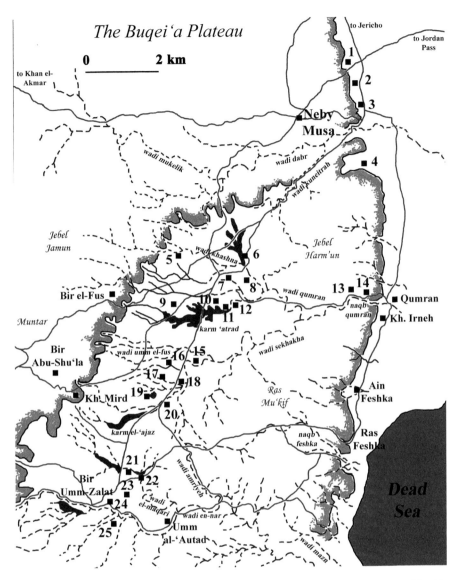

Fig. 2 Map of the Buqei'a Valley showing the three principal sites from the Iron Age: No. 10: *Khirbet Abu-Tabaq*; No. 20: *Khirbet es-Samrah*; and No. 21: *Khirbet el-Maqari*. For a full description of the numbered sites, see Table 1. (Drawing: Gibson)

cut by gullies and sharp water courses, with an escarpment of cliffs running along its edge forming the western side of the Rift Valley (Fig. 2). It was identified by Noth as the biblical "Valley of Achor" (Joshua 7:24), and many scholars follow this suggestion (Noth, 1955; King, 1988: 26–27; Barmash, 2012: 99), though this is questionable, given Eusebius (*Onom.* 19:17–20; 84:17–20) strongly associates it with Jericho. The three principal Iron Age sites in the plateau were thought to be biblical Middin (Abu-Tabaq), Secacah (es-Samrah), and Nibshan (el-Maqari) mentioned in Joshua 15: 61–62 (Cross & Wright, 1956: 224; see also the comments in Cross, 1997: 110, note 57), which, if correct, based on the pottery evidence from the sites (see below), would push back the composition date for the province list to the second half of the seventh century BCE at the earliest, i.e. to the time of Josiah (Na'aman, 1991). However, such identifications are far from certain. Biblical texts refer to the *Midbar Yehudah*, "the Wilderness of Judah" (Judg. 1:16; Ps. 63:1), which should not strictly be understood as indicating "desert." While the biblical Hebrew term *midbar* refers to a "wilderness" in a variety of geographical contexts, it defines uncultivated land rather than desert, especially potential "pasturelands." It derives from the root *dbr*, "drive", referring to "driving" sheep and goats. The plateau was used as the grazing lands of the Sawahireh Bedouin on its north side and by the Ibn 'Ubed Bedouin to the south, until it was transformed into a military zone in the mid-twentieth century.

The basin-like plateau itself is crescent-shaped, with a length of about 9 km from north-east to south-west, and a breadth of 3 km, with a range of hills running on the east side of the plateau, parallel to the eastern shore of the Dead Sea. The northern boundary of the plain corresponds with the lower extension of Wadi Mukellik/Wadi ed-Dabr, and its southern boundary by Wadi en-Nar. In lithological terms, the chalk and marl layers of the Buqeiʻa plain are fairly young, of Senonian age, and belong mainly to the Ghareb formation.[5] The erosion of the soft powdery chalk layers on the plateau creates a vulnerable landscape, with surfaces that easily become scarred, particularly by army vehicles using this zone for military training (Savage et al., 2017). The locally developed soils in the plain have little agricultural potential and support only very sparse natural vegetation. The only soil of value is the washed down alluvium spreading out in the shallow beds of the meandering wadis, of which there are five tributaries running from west to east across the plateau: Wadi Khashna, Wadi Qumran, Wadi Umm el-Fus, Wadi Abu Shuʻlah, and Wadi el-Maqari. The climate is arid, with an annual rainfall of no more than 156 mm during a limited period in winter (December–February), and with a water-less and dry period, over the rest of the year.[6]

3 Connectivity in the Buqeiʻa

A surfaced road extends along the length of the plateau. It serves as the main artery of communication running from north-east to south-west, approximating the overall geological structure of the region. Modern surfacing follows the line of an old road attested on maps going back to the nineteenth century. The antiquity of this road has

---

[5] Roth, *Wadi el-Qilt Map: Structural Map*, Sheet 12-I, Geological Survey of Israel, 1970, scale 1:50,000.

[6] The up-to-date rainfall statistics for this region are based on 39 years of records (see: Morin et al., 2009: 1067, Table 1). The annual rain depth averages at 156 mm, with a mean number of 40 rainy days, mostly in December to February.

not been proven, but since no other ancient road is visible connecting the ancient sites we will be discussing, we may safely assume it must have had an ancient antecedent, most likely going back to the Iron Age (Dorsey, 1991: route A2). Ancient paths and tracks extend from this road into the interior parts of the plateau, and to other ancient settlements as well.

The road and track system of the Buqeiʿa was first clearly delineated on the map of the Survey of Western Palestine (henceforth SWP) prepared by Palestine Exploration Fund explorers in 1873 (Conder & Kitchener, 1883: Sheet XVIII) (Fig. 3). An improved map of the region was published in the early Mandate period. The explorer E. G. W. Masterman describes travelling along the main road in 1902 from the Kidron in the south-west (Masterman, 1903: 264). This began as a winding road running along the sides of Wadi en-Nar (Kidron) reaching from the upper highlands east of Bethlehem and Mar Saba monastery, along the wadi. The road entering the plateau, began at Bir Umm Zalat and climbed to the north-east, toward Mughair el-Maqari, whereas the Wadi en-Nar road continued to the east, passing Kh. Umm al-ʿAutad, and descending toward the Dead Sea.

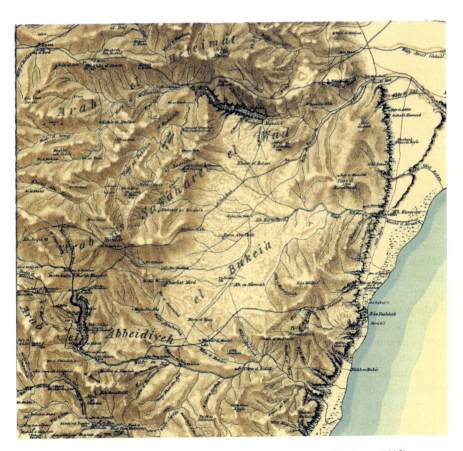

Fig. 3 The SWP Map of the Buqeiʿa valley – Sheet XVIII. (Conder & Kitchener, 1883)

The road extending through the plateau runs to the north-east almost on a straight line for 6 km, passing the sites of Khirbet es-Samrah and Khirbet Abu-Tabaq. At Wadi Khashna, the main road has a fork, with one branch running diagonally toward the north-east via Wadi Kuneitrah to Wadi ed-Dabr (el-Kueiserah). This road gave access at its north-eastern end to the outlet of Wadi ed-Dabr/Wadi Mukelik which debouches into the plain just south of Jericho (Nahal Og), and connects up with an ancient road seen running in two directions: northwards to Jericho, and southwards to Qumran, Ain Feshkha and the Dead Sea. Importantly, there is some evidence that this road was in use in the Iron Age, and a cluster of eight Iron Age animal pens and structures for herders was found east and south of Kibbutz Almog (Cross, 1997: 110, note 57; Bar-Adon, 1972: Sites Nos. 80, 82, 83 and 85).

The second branch of the main road at Wadi Khashna runs to the north where it crosses Wadi Mukelik, extending through a hilly range, passing the Maqam er-Ra'i, and reaching Neby Musa. Eventually this main road links up with the Jerusalem to Jericho road, which is an important highway for traffic that undoubtedly existed from as early as the Iron Age, and it may even be the one referred to as *Derekh ha-Arabah* (Jer. 39: 4; 52–7-8; 2 Kings 25: 4: 2 Samuel 4:7) (Dorsey, 1991: 204–205: J32). From Nebi Musa a track runs toward the west, parallel and to the north of Wadi Mukelik, and it extends as far as Khan el-Ahmar. Another path runs along the banks of Wadi Mukellik (Nahal Og), toward the west. It was much frequented in the Byzantine period at which time there was a burgeoning of monasticism in the region (Patrich, 1994:10*), but there is no evidence it was in use in the Iron Age.

The main road at Wadi Khashna also links up with another road running diagonally toward the south-west and this stretch is marked as an "ancient road" on the SWP map (Sheet XVIII). At Bir Umm el-Fus it veers off to the hills west of the plateau, ascending next to the reservoir Bir es-Sûk, and then passing west of Khirbet el-Mird (the fortress of Hyrcania) it ran toward the el-Muntar ridge, and then on to Jerusalem (Conder & Kitchener, 1883: 188). Another track leads from the main road near Khirbet Abu-Tabaq and extended in a south-westerly direction toward Khirbet el-Mird. An additional track runs from Khirbet el-Mird toward the south-east, where it joins the main road in the southern Buqeiʿa near es-Samra. Hyrcania was an important site controlling the Buqeiʿa, but this connection is likely to be linked to the principal periods of the occupation of the site, namely in the Hasmonean-Roman and Byzantine periods.

A few paths from the north-west side of the Dead Sea, climb the cliffs precariously to the plateau, and some of these eventually continue westwards into the Judean highlands, but none appear to have been significant thoroughfares in the Iron Age, or even later. The shortest track from the Buqeiʿa to the Dead Sea is from Khirbet Abu-Tabaq via Wadi Qumran. It was traversed by Masterman in 1902, who described it as an "exceedingly rough path down which a horse can only be led with difficulty" (Masterman, 1903: 266–267). Cross and Milik thought it might be an Iron Age road (Cross & Milik, 1956: 7, note 4). Stager also investigated this path in 1972, noting Iron Age pottery scattered on the summit of a promontory just east of Abu-Tabaq, which he thought may have served as a look-out post above the track (Stager, 1975: 213). The road runs for about 6 km towards the east. In 2007, we followed this track, noting along the way a Byzantine period structure, and a plastered cistern, which had evidently been in use until modern times. At the top of the pass are the remains of a small stone heap, strategically positioned, perhaps the base of a tower, with scattered Iron Age II pottery around it (Taylor & Gibson, 2011: 26). At the center of the piled heap of stones (9.35 m in diameter) was a square pit (1.90 × 1.70 m). This is likely to be the same location where Siegfried Schulz spotted Iron Age pottery during his investigation of the area in 1959, and it is probably Bar-Adon's Site No. 93 (Schulz, 1960: 58, with map in Fig. 3; Bar-Adon, 1972: 121). Eventually, the descent to the Iron Age settlement at Qumran could be achieved via a steep path with a series of hairpin turns, as described by Schulz (1960: 58, Pl. 7A), and this was in the rocky cliff behind Qumran and north of the outlet of Wadi Qumran. We also climbed this path, but from the opposite direction, from Qumran to the Buqei'a, noting at one point structural remains, perhaps a look-out tower, and scattered pottery from the Iron Age II, including one bowl rim with ring-burnishing (Taylor & Gibson, 2011: 24).

Another track extends from the southern Buqei'a, via paths leading from both Khirbet es-Samrah and Khirbet el-Maqari, down to the pass of Ras Feshhka (Nakb Feshkha) and then on to Ain Feshkha. It was traversed by Masterman during his 1902 trip and by Schultz in 1959, the latter reporting on the difficulties of access for beasts of burden.

4 History of Research

The Buqei'a Plateau was briefly visited by a number of travelers and explorers in the nineteenth century, notably by two teams of the SWP in November 1873 (Conder & Kitchener, 1883)[7] (Figs. 4 and 5). This was followed by Masterman's visit of 1902 (Masterman, 1903). In the spring of 1954, Cross and Milik conducted a survey of the three main ruins on the plateau: Kh. Abu-Tabaq, Kh. es-Samrah, and Kh. el-Maqari. A more extensive survey was made with limited excavations in August 1955. During their survey, six Iron Age sites were recorded near Abu-Tabaq and close to the road, including towers and building complexes, and another five sites north of Khirbet es-Samrah, of which two small towers were of definite Iron Age date (Cross & Milik, 1956: 9, notes 9–10, 12, note 17). A map of the Buqei'a showing the position of the main sites was prepared by William R. Farmer in that same year.[8] In 1959 the Iron Age sites of the plateau were also visited by Schulz owing to his general interest in the region next to Qumran (Schulz, 1960: 59–60).

---

[7] We are grateful to Felicity Cobbing, Executive Secretary and Curator at the Palestine Exploration Fund in London, for providing us with scans of the original manuscript maps of the SWP maps for the Buqei'a region: PEF Archives/M/WS/137 (map of central and northern Buqei'a, dated 9–10 Nov. 1873, signed by C. R. Conder R.E.); PEF Archives/M/WS/138 (map showing the southern Buqei'a, dated Nov. 1873, signed by James Brophy, Lance Corporal R.E.).

[8] An original map of the Buqei'a (scale 1:20,000) is located in the archives of the Albright Institute of Archaeological Research in Jerusalem. It is signed by William R. Farmer of Drew University and dated July 1955. We are grateful to the former Director of the Albright Institute of Archaeological Research in Jerusalem, Seymour Gitin, for allowing us access to this map in 2009.

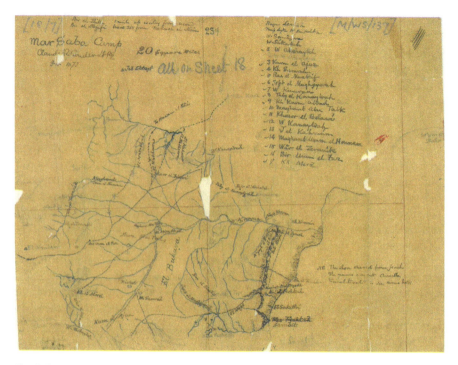

Fig. 4 Draft SWP map of the central and northern Buqei'a Valley from November 1873. (Courtesy PEF archives/M/WS/137)

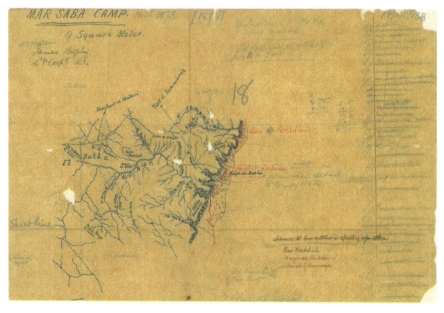

Fig. 5 Draft SWP map of the southern Buqei'a Valley and Wadi en-Nar from November 1873. (Courtesy PEF archives/M/WS/138)

A comprehensive archaeological survey was eventually made of the region in 1967–1968 by Pessah Bar-Adon and it resulted in the identification of a total of seventeen Iron Age II sites, only some of which had previously been named and marked on maps (Bar-Adon, 1972: 114, 117). At the behest of Cross and G. Ernest Wright, the investigation of the Buqeiʿa was resumed by Lawrence E. Stager in November 1972, and he was also asked to study the earlier material from the mid-1950s work toward publication (Stager, 1975: 160, note 2). Stager's research ultimately appeared as a doctoral thesis which was submitted to Harvard University in January 1975 (Stager, 1975). A short article on the results of his work appeared the following year in 1976, but his thesis was never published. The Buqeiʿa region was surveyed once again in 1981–82 by Joseph Patrich for the Archaeological Survey of Israel, and it included the examination of 15 Iron Age sites (Patrich, 1994: 44* ff).

There seems to be some confusion regarding the correspondence of place names and their exact situation on maps.[9] First of all, Khirbet Abu-Tabaq (map ref. 1886/1276) is also known by the name Khirbet Kurm/Karm ʿAtrad (Schulz, 1960), but Cross and Milik state that this second name should only be used in reference to the field system (D1) next to the site (Cross and Milik 1956: 6, note 2). However, Kh. Kurm ʿAtrad distinctly appears as the name of the main site on the SWP map, with a cave (Mugharet Abu-Tubk) close by. In the SWP memoirs it is described as a place with the "remains of rude drystone walls, which are traditionally supposed to have belonged to former vineyards by the Arabs," which sounds like the field systems in the nearby wadi (Conder & Kitchener, 1883: 211). The SWP also refers to another site (Kurm Abu-Tubk) as having "scattered stones, said to be the remains of a vineyard, and a small cave of the same name" (Conder & Kitchener, 1883: 213), and their map (Sheet XVIII) clearly indicates that this site is some distance to the south-west of the main site later excavated by Cross/Milik and Stager. In 1902, Masterman appears to have misheard the name of the site as Umm Tabaq, when his guide probably meant Kurm Tabaq, though he had obviously arrived at Khirbet Abu-Tabaq and not Kurm Abu-Tabaq (Masterman, 1903: 264). On a map published at the beginning of the British Mandate period (1924) the site of Kh. Karm Abu Tabaq is indicated slightly north of where it is placed in the SWP survey map, but otherwise Mgt. Abu Tabaq (the cave) is similarly marked on the north side of the ruin called Kh. Karm ʿAtrad.

Hence, Khirbet Abu-Tabaq (i.e. Kurm Atrad) refers to the Iron Age settlement and it differs from the location Kurm Abu-Tabaq which is situated further south-west. The Arabic word *kurm* (plural *kurûm*, meaning "vineyards") was used by Bedouin to designate places with fenced areas of alluvial soils in the Buqeiʿa (Conder & Kitchener, 1883: 231). This led Cross and Milik to suggest the name Khirbet Abu-Tabaq had been incorrectly marked on the SWP map, since at this

---

[9] For purposes of clarification, we are using in this paper the ICS (Israel Cassini Soldner) grid, or "old Israel grid," and this is because the map references to the sites provided by earlier investigators were linked to that system, rather than with the ITM (Israel Transverse Mercator) grid which is now customary on modern maps of sites: https://zvikabenhaim.appspot.com/software/ITM.

western location there was only a small Iron Age tower (map ref. 18745/12760) (Cross & Milik, 1956: 6, note 2). In January 1928, J. Ory, an Inspector of the Mandatory Palestine Department of Antiquities, arrived at Kurm Abu-Tabaq, providing its situation (map ref. 187/128), to the south of Kurm el-'Atrad, and he describes "long foundations of stone of irregular plan said to be the remains of vineyards."[10] However, Stager indicates that his Site 6 is probably to be identified with the site the SWP was referring to (map ref. 1864/1275), i.e. it was situated near the foot of the hills to the west (Stager, 1975: 119).

Khirbet es-Samrah appears in the Mandatory Palestine Department of Antiquities' *Schedule of Sites* spelled as es-Samira and in maps of that period as Karm es-Samra. In the SWP map it was indicated as Khurbet es-Sumrah, though on the original draft map it is marked as Khirbet Samrah, and Conder describes it as a place with "scattered stones and terrace walls, said to be the remains of vineyards by the Arabs" (Conder & Kitchener, 1883: 213). The SWP map indicates a pool immediately to the north-west of es-Sumrah. According to Stager, the D4 field system next to Khirbet es-Samrah was known as Kurum el-'Ajuz (map ref. 1864/1248), and this is also how it is shown on modern maps. However, the SWP map indicates Kurm el-'Ajaz as located some 1.5 km to the south of es-Samrah (Conder & Kitchener, 1883: 213).

The name Khirbet el-Maqari is a new name provided by Cross and Milik to designate the southernmost Iron Age site which they investigated in the Buqei'a, since it appears nameless on maps (Cross & Milik, 1956: 6). Immediately to the north-west of this site, on the SWP map, there is a cave system named Mughair el-Makari, which is also known on some maps as Maghayir (or Mughr) et-Tabaqa.

5 The Sites

The plateau is dominated by three main Iron Age settlements, and they are located on the same main trajectory next to the main road, with Khirbet Abu-Tabaq in the north, Khirbet es-Samrah some 3 km further south-west, and Khirbet el-Maqari another 2 km to the south-west.[11] The close physical proximity these three sites have, and the fact they were chronologically contemporaneous with each other (seventh to early sixth centuries BCE), suggest they share a common purpose. Each settlement might have controlled a territory of about 12 km² within the plateau. Many smaller Iron Age structural features are scattered in the plateau as well, and they cluster

---

[10] We are grateful to Aryeh Rochman-Halperin, formerly head of the IAA archives at the Rockefeller Museum, for granting us permission in January 2009 to access the files relating to the Buqei'a sites from the British Mandate period: Palestine Department of Antiquities Archive volumes Nos. 120 and 168. Ory's report from 18 January 1928 is labeled Report No. S.316.

[11] We are grateful to Richard Cleave of Rohr Productions (Cyprus) for providing us with excellent aerial coverage of the Buqei'a sites. A new set of aerial views of the Iron Age sites was made with a drone by one of the authors (Lewis) in December 2019.

within the territories of the three main settlements. These include small round or square structures, perhaps watch-towers or look-out posts, to protect and overlook the road and water sources. Seven were situated in the plateau, three at Naqb Qumran, one near Wadi en-Nar to the south and at the base of Wadi Mazn, and another close to Tel Muhalhil in the north-east where Wadi Dabr enters the Jordan Valley. They might also have been been used for signaling and surveillance (Yekutieli, 2006). There were also enclosed animal pens with built shelters for herders, stone quarries, and open area locations with pottery scatters. Other features include seasonal water pools, cisterns, and areas of open and enclosed pasture. Many of these remains were close to the main road traversing the plateau and others were in its general proximity. Some of these sites were recorded by Cross and Milik in 1955,[12] as well as by Bar-Adon during his 1967–1968 survey,[13] others by Stager in 1972, who referred to them as "outlier" sites,[14] and finally by Patrich in 1981–82[15] (Table 1).

5.1   Khirbet Abu-Tabaq (Kh. Kurm 'Atrad; Map Ref. 1886/1276)

This is a rectangular compound (31 × 59 m) with walls of stone (1.16–1.30 m thick), situated on a chalky knoll (0.18 ha) and rising 15 m above the surrounding area (Stager, 1975: 40 ff.)[16] (Figs. 6 and 7). J. Ory, Inspector for the Mandatory Palestine Department of Antiquities, visited the site in January 1928, took measurements and described it as "square strong building… possibly a fortress."[17]

Outside the compound, on the south-east, are curvilinear enclosures with walls of stone, and Masterman, in 1902, refers to the lower enclosed level as covering an area of 12 × 12 m. Patrich, who surveyed the site in 1981–82, is much more precise, indicating six enclosures covering an area of 25 × 40 m, with a possible tower on a stone pile at its center (Patrich, 1994: 48*: Site 35). While they were of similar construction to the walls of the compound, Stager suggested these enclosures, as well as similar structures seen outside Samrah, had to be "later, if not recent, constructions for the Bedouin for their tents and animals" (Stager, 1975: 43). Our examination of these enclosures suggests they are actually Iron Age in date and contemporary with the main buildings and enclosed fields at the sites.

---

[12] Sites Nos. BC2; BC3, BC7, B10, BC16: Cross and Milik (1956).

[13] Sites Nos 89a; 89c; 91; 92b; 92c; 92e; 93; 94; 95c; 99; 100c; 102; 104; 106; 108a: Bar-Adon (1972).

[14] Information on these sites appears in Stager (1975: 180–181, 186).

[15] Sites Nos. 18; 19; 21; 33; 34; 36; 37; 52; 56; 71; 72; 73; 91; 101; 111; 112; 121: Patrich (1994).

[16] The measurements given here for Kh. Abu-Tabaq and later for Kh. es-Samrah are those provided by Stager (1975), but with a few corrections and additions based on our own measurements which were taken while visiting the two sites.

[17] Palestine Department of Antiquities Archive: Ory's report from 18 January 1928 is labeled Report No. S.315 (see above, Note 10).

Table 1 Iron Age sites in the Buqei'a Valley and vicinity (from north to south) (see Fig. 2)

Site no.	Name or location	Map ref.	SWP 1873 & Early Travellers	Bar Adon 1967–68	Cross & Milik/Stager 1972	Patrich 1981–82	Comments
1	No name	1921/1342		Site 80: Curvilinear enclosure (88 × 40 m) with 2-roomed tower.			Probable animal pen. IA pottery
2	No name	19232/13383 19233/13373		Site 82a: Two curvilinear enclosures (diameters: 30 m; 20 m) and structures. Site 82b: Curvilinear enclosure (34 × 38 m) and structure.			Probable animal pens. 82a: IA and later pottery 82b: IA and later pottery
3	Tel Muhalhil	1919/1334 1919/1331 19211/13332 1921/1331		Site 83a: Curvilinear enclosure (33 × 25 m) and structures. Site 83b: Curvilinear enclosure (45 × 18 m) and structures. Site 83c: Circular tower. Site 83d: Curvilinear enclosure (40 × 50 m) and structures.			Probable animal pens. 83a: IA pottery 83b: IA and earlier pottery 83c: IA and later pottery. 83d: IA pottery
4	No name	1927/1313		Site 85: Curvilinear enclosure (30 × 40 m) and structures.			Probable animal pen. IA and earlier/later pottery
5	Tributary of Wadi Khashna	18755/12892				Seasonal pool (70 m diam.). Dry in summer. Located SE of site 9.	Located 1.6 km NW of Kh. Abu Tabaq.

Site no.	Name or location	Map ref.	SWP 1873 & Early Travellers	Bar Adon 1967–68	Cross & Milik/ Stager 1972	Patrich 1981–82	Comments
6	Tributary of Wadi Khashna	18931/12890			Site BC3: enclosure with round towers. IA pottery Cross and Milik (1956: 9, note 9).	Site 19; dam wall spanning Wadi tributary	Located 2.2 km NE of Kh. Abu-Tabaq. Probable animal pen, and alluvial soil in Wadi.
7	Ard el-Gharabi, S of Wadi Khashna	18893/12855 18899/12852		Site 89a: Five square towers. IA pottery. Site 89b: Structure. IA and later pottery		Site 18: Square structure/ tower: IA and later pottery.	900 m N of Khirbet Abu Tabaq. Overlooks main road, 300 m to its W.
8	Ard el-Gharabi	18940/12830		Site 89c: Curvilinear enclosure (25 × 15 m). IA pottery		Site 21: Enclosure wall 40 m long; structure: IA pottery.	Located 1 km NE of Kh. Abu-Tabaq
9	Kh. Karm Abu-Tabaq	18743/12761		Site 91: Structure. IA pottery		Site 33: Rectangular tower on knoll (substantial modern damage): IA pottery	Located 1.1 km west of Kh. Abu-Tabaq
10	Kh. Abu-Tabaq/Kh. Karm 'Atrad/ Magharat Abu-Tabaq	Site 34: 18848/12770 Site 35: 18855/12767		Site 92b: (18848/12770) curvilinear structure & Bedouin cemetery. IA and later pottery. Site 92a: Rectangular fortress and cistern on north.		Site 34: Bedouin cemetery. IA and later pottery Site 35: IA fortress; curvilinear animal pens to E with remains of tower at center; cistern at N foot of hill.	The cemetery is located 100 m to NW of Kh. Abu-Tabaq.

(continued)

Table 1 (continued)

Site no.	Name or location	Map ref.	SWP 1873 & Early Travellers	Bar Adon 1967–68	Cross & Milik/ Stager 1972	Patrich 1981–82	Comments
11	Kh. Abu-Tabaq/Wadi Qumran	18870/12750		Site 92e: Enclosure wall and semi-circular structure. IA and later pottery.	D1: Farm	Site 36: Farming complex with enclosure walls, dams, and one semi-circular tower. IA and later pottery.	Located immediately S of Kh. Abu-Tabaq.
12	Wadi Qumran	18893/12758		Site 92c: Circular enclosure (19 m diam). IA and later pottery.	Lookout	Site 37: Circular enclosure (19 m diameter). IA and earlier and later pottery	On SE spur of Abu-Tabaq hill. Probably animal pen and not "threshing floor" as Patrich suggested. A rock-cut cistern was examined nearby by Gibson and others.
13	Wadi Qumran	1921/1278		Site 93: Rectangular lookout tower on N bank of Wadi. IA pottery			Schults; Taylor and Gibson
14	Naqb Qumran	19288/12772		Site 94: Two rectangular structures. IA pottery			
15	Nahal Sekaka	18804/12610		Site 95c: Rectangular structure with circular interior room. IA and later pottery.		Site 56: Tower structure. IA and later pottery	

Site no.	Name or location	Map ref.	SWP 1873 & Early Travellers	Bar Adon 1967–68	Cross & Milik/ Stager 1972	Patrich 1981–82	Comments
16	Nahal Sekaka	18727/12603		Site 96: Enclosure (106 × 76 m); walls of stone with entryways on west side; cistern on S side with diversion channels. Identified as Roman camp.	1956: 12; D2: Roman camp	Site 52: Enclosure with walls 1.2 m wide. Believes it may originally be IA.	
17	Nahal Sekaka	18720/12560		Site 100b: Two stone-built pools west of road: One rectangular (34 × 32 m), the second rounded (34 m diam.)		Site 72: Two pools (32 × 34; 34 × 34 m) in Wadi damaged by floodwaters.	Located 0.7 km to the N of es-Samrah.
18	Nahal Sekaka	18755/12558		Site 100c: (18755/12558) circular structure. IA and later pottery.		Site 73: Circular tower. IA and later pottery.	Located 0.75 km to the NE of es-Samrah.
19	Nahal Sekaka	18680/12517		Site 99: Curvilinear enclosure (140 × 130 m) with opening to east; with rock-cut cistern. IA and later pottery.		Site 71: Oval enclosure (130 × 140 m) between tributaries. IA and later pottery.	Located 0.5 km to the NW of Khirbet es-Samrah. Drone photos taken in December 2019.
20	Khirbet es-Samrah/ Kurm el-'Ajaz	18720/12493		Site 102: Fortress with additional enclosures to E and S. near site are a number of dams for irrigation. IA pottery		Site 91: IA fortress. Eight enclosures on the E; two enclosures to S. open reservoir to SW (18 × 22 m). IA pottery Site 91: Enclosure wall (95 m long) connected to alluvial soil in Wadi east of es-Samrah.	Drone photos taken in December 2019.

(continued)

Table 1 (continued)

Site no.	Name or location	Map ref.	SWP 1873 & Early Travellers	Bar Adon 1967–68	Cross & Milik/ Stager 1972	Patrich 1981–82	Comments
21	Khirbet el-Maqari/ Maghayir et-Tabaqa	18624/12300		Site 104: Fortress. IA and later pottery; pool E of fortress surrounded by earthen walls (25 m diam.; 2 m deep). IA and later pottery.	Cross and Milik: IA fortress; Wadi el 'Eidharawi: Field systems with dams	Site 101: IA fortress. Site 101: (18625/12320) pool 200 m N of fortress, surrounded by earthen ramp. IA and later pottery. Wadi el 'Eidharawi (18460/12360): Extensive field system 1.5 km W of fortress. Maghayir et-Tabaqa: (18612/12318): Pair of cisterns on slope 200 m NW of K. el-Maqari. IA and later pottery	Drone photos taken in December 2019.
22	Wadi el-Maqari	18643/12295				Site 111: Cistern and small dam	
23	Wadi el-Maqari	18610/12248		Site 106c: One large curvilinear enclosure and two smaller ones and one rectangular structure		Site 112: Structures S of Wadi el-Maqari. IA pottery, Persian and Hellenistic.	Defined during our visit as "Maqari south". Drone photos taken in December 2019.
24	Bir umm-Zalat						Cistern at junction of Wadi en-Nar road and the southern Buqeiʻa road.
25	Wadi en-Nar/ Nahal Kidron	18565/12173		Site 108a: Various structures and one IA potsherd. Nearby ancient paved road (3 m maximum breadth) leading S.		Site 121: IA jug frag.	

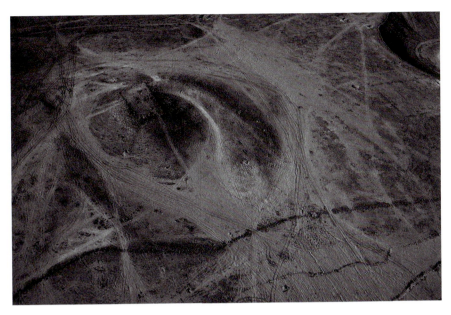

Fig. 6 Aerial view of Khirbet Abu-Tabaq from the early 1970s towards the north-east. Note the northern enclosure wall of the D1 field system, with a small "tower" incorporated into it, near the bottom of the picture. (Photo: courtesy R. Cleave and Rohr Productions)

Fig. 7 Khirbet Abu-Tabaq from the south in a photograph taken in 2007. (Photo: Gibson)

In addition, at a distance of less than 200 m to the south, Stager identified a substantial U-shaped enclosure wall containing an area of alluvial soil within a tributary wadi, which he identified as remnants of an ancient farm (D1) (see below). Stones used for the construction of the walls of the settlement came from quarries on the ridges to the east of the settlement. We inspected one such quarry on a ridge next to the path in Wadi Qumran. The quarry extended over an area of 40 × 20 m, and next to the extraction areas were piles of roughly-cut rectangular stones ready for transportation.

At the foot of the hill on the north side of the site is a very large tunnel-like rock-hewn cistern (Mugharet Abu-Tabaq) which Cross and Milik explored, and found that it extended for 34.7 m towards the south-south/east. They believed it ran beneath the north wall of the Iron Age compound (Cross & Milik, 1956: 8; Cross, 1956: 15, Fig. 9).[18] Our measurements however show that the inner end of the cistern falls short of the north wall.

The original excavators, Cross and Milik, made a number of soundings (Areas A–D) along the north wall of the compound, in an area where rooms were visible. Stager also excavated two soundings on the north (Areas 4–5), but he also sank a trench within the wall in the south (Area 3), and two additional trenches along the west wall (Areas 1–2) (Fig. 8).

The stratigraphic results from Area A were largely unproductive, with debris seen descending down (0.10 m) to the chalky living surface of the central courtyard of the compound. However, in Areas 1–2 an ashy layer was encountered along the inner face of the western compound wall, but it disappeared at a distance of 2.25 m to the east, suggesting to Stager that a parallel wall must once have existed there. The ashy deposit had a few intrusive Early Roman sherds, but most of the pottery was from the Iron Age. The external compound wall at this point was 1.25 m thick. The southern half of the enclosed courtyard slopes to the south. The area of the southern wall had been badly disturbed by military trenching, but Stager managed to obtain a good stratigraphic sequence against the interior compound wall in Area 3, finding seven superimposed living surfaces of ashy appearance which he believed were made out of "burnt dung," descending with different phases to bedrock (Stager, 1975: 48, Fig. 12). The lowest of these ashy floors contained Iron Age pottery and the charred humerus of a young dog. In the intermediate layers of the sequence of floors, Stager encountered partly-fired clayey material contained chaff and resembling mud brick, but it is more likely to have been tamped down consolidation materials (Stager, 1975: 54–55). Apart from Iron Age pottery, a charred grape seed was found in one of the surfaces, an olive pit and sheep/goat vertebrae in another, and a sheep/goat molar and a long bone of a large ungulate. The compound wall at this point was 1.10 m thick, and the courses of fieldstones were visibly laid in a slaked lime mortar. The function of this southern part of the compound in the Iron Age, according to Stager, was as a sheep or goat fold, but individual coprolites were not visible, and the ashes may be the result of fire fumigation to get rid of

---

[18] Masterman also mentioned a small cemetery "evidently of antiquity" at the site (1903: 264), and it may be the same Bedouin cemetery with trench graves which Patrich later investigated about 100 m to the north-west of Kh. Abu-Tabaq (Patrich, 1994: 47*: Site 34). Today, none of these tombs are visible.

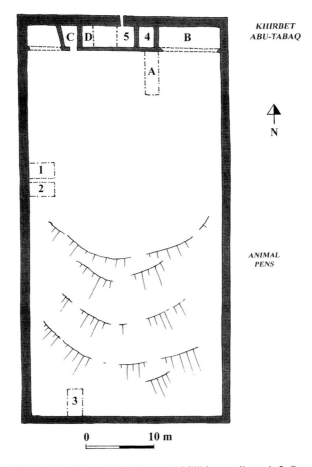

Fig. 8 Map of Khirbet Abu-Tabaq: A–D: Cross and Milik's soundings; 1–5: Stager's soundings. (Drawing: Gibson, partly based on a schematic map in L. E. Stager, 1975)

unnecessary insects and vermin (Stager, 1975: 67–68). The surface fills included intrusive Early Roman potsherds, and a polished stone pendant, leading Stager to suppose that the Early Roman occupation was brief and that it did not include a rebuilding of the compound wall (Stager, 1975: 66).[19]

The row of 'casemate' rooms built inside the interior wall on the northern side of the compound, had been cleared by Cross and Milik in places down to bedrock (B, C and D). Stager identified the fills which were excavated by the earlier team as representing eroded occupational debris derived from the top of the courtyard (Stager, 1975: 69). He decided, therefore, to seek undisturbed deposits by excavating one room in its entirety (Area 4) and half of an adjacent room (Area 5). The

---

[19] During our 2007 visit to the site, one diagnostic Iron Age II bowl with a folded-rim of a reddish-brown ware with ring burnishing was seen lying on the surface of the compound, as well as a rim of a cooking pot from the first century or early second century CE.

strata in these two areas included two phases from the Iron Age and two from the Early Roman period. Stager surmised that the outer wall (1.50 m thick), which had a foundation of stones preserved to a height of three courses, must originally have had a superstructure built of mudbrick, and this would have been true for walls of the adjoining rooms as well (Stager, 1975: 70). The room exposed in Area 4 (2.25 × 3.25 m) had narrow partition walls (0.65 m thick). The original floor of the room was the leveled chalk surface of the hill, slightly cobbled. Iron Age pottery and one grain of wheat was found on this floor. In the fill sequence above this, occupational debris included pottery, a ceramic disk-like stopper, unidentified bones, dung ash and fragments of fired mud bricks (Stager, 1975: 44–75, Fig. 12). On top of this debris was a badly built wall of Early Roman date (Stager, 1975: 78, Fig. 12: No. 5). Within the surface fill was an Iron Age scaraboid seal inscribed in Hebrew in two registers: *lbdyhw bn m...* ("belonging to Badyahu son of M...") (Stager, 1975: 79–80, Fig. 15). The Iron Age archaeological materials from this area suggested to Stager that this part of the site was in use for a short term only (Stager, 1975: 75).

Stager's work inside the eastern half of the broad-room (7.75 × 3.50 m) in Area 5 revealed a stratigraphic sequence that was similar to the one seen in Room 4, with two phases from the Iron Age and two phases from the Early Roman period. In the earlier excavation by Cross and Milik, a small trench (Area D) was excavated on the western side of the same room that Stager later dug as Area 5. They too detected two main levels from the Iron Age and Early Roman periods.

The original floor of the room uncovered in Stager's excavations was the flattened chalk surface of the hill leveled off with a cobbling of small stones. A narrow doorway (0.80 m wide) existed at this point in the outer compound wall and it led into the room in Area 5, but strangely it did not provide access to the compound as a whole (Stager, 1975: 84). This doorway goes against an identification of the compound as a military fort, because it would have opened up vulnerability for attack from outside. It may however have provided the occupant of this specific room direct access to the vertical shaft leading into the large water reservoir, on the slope at a distance of 18 m from the north wall of the enclosure.

The debris inside this room (Area 5) included Iron Age pottery, dung ash, a premolar of a sheep/goat, a barley grain, and a cotyledon of a pea. Unfortunately, later Early Roman intrusions were seen extending down into the upper Iron Age phase. A pocket of animal bones was identified next to the blocked interior doorway of the room, containing the remains of sheep/goat, and young gazelle, which are native to the area, which would most likely have been hunted by the inhabitants of the site (Stager, 1975: 86–87).

Area C was a small room to the west of the broad room and it was uncovered during the earlier work made by Cross and Milik at the site. The doorway into the courtyard shown on Stager's map of the site is surmised and the gap there may be the result of stone having been robbed out at a later date (Stager, 1975: 95). An ashy deposit was found overlying a leveled chalk floor, and it contained Iron Age pottery. Immediately above this was the Early Roman level which included cooking pot fragments and a complete lamp of the first century CE (Cross & Milik, 1956: 7, note 5).

Area B comprises the interior north-east corner of the compound and it too was excavated by Cross and Milik, with the discovery of two strata; the earliest ascribed to the Iron Age and it containing a nearly complete cooking pot (Stager, 1975, Pl. 4:21). The layer above it contained a large collection of Early Roman cooking pot and storage jar fragments (Stager, 1975: Pl. 2: 28–29, 32–40).

The site was clearly originally built as a rectangular walled compound in the Iron Age, with a series of rooms at the northern end, described by Stager as "a perimetric series of rustic rooms" of casemate appearance, which could house no more than 9 or 10 people if used as dwellings (Stager, 1975: 99, 102). The rooms must have been accessed from inside the compound but doorways were not visible. They may have been inserted into the walls at a higher level, with a few stones serving as steps, but these have not been preserved; alternatively, wooden ladders may have been used. In any case, higher thresholds would have prevented water from running straight into the rooms during heavy winter rainfalls. The rooms on the north side are described by Stager as "dwellings," but it is more likely they were used for primary storage (e.g. for equipment, basketry, bedding, fodder, dung-cakes, etc.), with the inhabitants spending much of their time in tents within the central courtyard which slopes to the south. Stager suggests cooking activities in the southern part of Room 4, but the evidence for this is meager. The Iron Age pottery assemblage was dominated by bowls, followed by cooking pots, and a very small number of closed vessels and storage jars (Stager, 1975: 102–103). A jar handle with a worn stamp impression of the two-winged *lmlk* type was found on the surface of the site in 2007[20] (Fig. 9).

Fig. 9 Stamped storage jar handle of *lmlk* type from the surface of Khirbet Abu-Tabaq. (Photo: Gibson)

---

[20] Our thanks to Oded Lipschits (Tel Aviv University) who examined a photograph of the handle and gave us his comments.

A very large open space or courtyard occupied much of the interior of the compound (53 × 28 m), the southern half sloping towards the south, and Stager identified possible animal pens at the southern end, but the evidence he gave for this is questionable. Firstly, dung ashes were found at both ends of the compound and so they were not exclusive to this one location. Secondly, the compacted clayey areas appear to represent the consolidation of living surfaces, intentionally made in order to protect the floor of the southern part of the compound from water-pooling during the winter rains. Indeed, it is quite possible that at the southern end of the compound, which was not excavated, there was a shallow water hole, similar to the one visible at Samrah or smaller (see below). There may also have been additional lean-on rooms or structures built against the western interior wall, as suggested based on the evidence from Stager's work in Areas 1–2.

The Early Roman re-use of the site was in the first century CE or early second century CE and this was probably contemporary with the Period III settlement at Qumran through to the Bar Kokhba revolt (Taylor, 2006). Some of the rooms on the north side of the compound appear to have been occupied at this time, albeit on a very temporary basis, but while some of the Iron Age layers were disturbed in the Early Roman period, no attempt was made to clear away the underlying Iron Age fills down to the chalky surface of the hill.

Additional damage to the site appears to have occurred during the encampment of Bedouin in the nineteenth century, but the worst destruction has been the direct result of military training activities conducted there since the mid-twentieth century (Savage et al., 2017). Devastating changes took place at the site following our visits in 2007 and 2009. In 2019 we observed that hardly anything architectural had survived of the site. This includes substantial destruction to the D1 field system in the wadi to the south of the site.

5.2 *Khirbet es-Samrah (Map Ref. 1873/1251)*

This is a second rectangular compound (39 × 69 m; 0.26 ha) with walls of stone, situated on a chalky knoll, 3 km to the south-west of Khirbet Abu-Tabaq (Stager, 1975: 137 ff, Fig. 25), and with a large central courtyard at its center (30 × 52 m) (Figs. 10 and 11). A series of "casemate" rooms were identified running along the interior of the northern, southern and western compound walls, and 14 narrow chambers were seen built against the interior eastern wall. A gate was seen at the eastern end of the northern wall. During our visit in 2009 we noticed the blocked opening to a cave (cistern?) situated just outside this gate; it is presumably the same as the "large cave" in which illicit digging was taking place in May 1934, as reported by D. C. Baramki, an inspector of the Mandatory Palestine Department of Antiquities.[21]

---

[21] Palestine Department of Antiquities Archive: Baramki's report from 30 May 1934 is labeled Report ATQ/207 (see above, Note 10). He reports on the illicit digging as follows: "They [the names of four individuals are then provided] dug a few trenches to the south of the site near an

Fig. 10 Aerial drone shot of Khirbet es-Samrah in 2019. (Photo: Lewis)

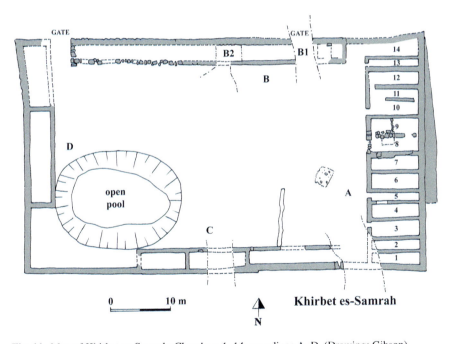

Fig. 11 Map of Khirbet es-Samrah: Chambers 1–14; soundings A–D. (Drawing: Gibson)

An elliptical depression (21 × 16 m) is visible within the south-east quadrant of the compound. Since it was perceived to have destroyed part of the casemate wall to its south, Stager suggested it was probably cut by soldiers in modern times as a gun emplacement (Stager, 1975: 137, 169, note 54).[22] However, Cross and Milik believed this to be an ancient open cistern (Cross & Milik, 1956: 11), and we concur, though the term "open reservoir" is perhaps a more apt term for this depression. Indeed, it had already been observed by J. Ory, an inspector of the Mandatory Palestine Department of Antiquities, having visited the site in January 1928 before any of the military damage, and he wrote: "The wall [of the compound] enclosed also a depression in the ground which is probably a *birkeh*..." The reservoir is also visible in a photograph Ory took at the time of his visit[23] (Fig. 12). It would definitely not have contained water throughout the year, owing to high summer evaporation rates, but the impermeability of the underlying chalk meant the depression probably retained water at least until the spring months. At the time of our visit to the site, we could find no evidence that the open reservoir undercut the walls of the rooms running along the southern wall of the compound, as Stager seemed to have thought.

Outside the compound, on a lower terrace to the east, are six curvilinear enclosures with well-built walls of stone (60 × 65 m), which Stager attributed to Bedouin origin, but we think these are likely to have been contemporary with the Iron Age settlement. We think they were used as leveled areas for the pitching of tents. A curvilinear enclosure that was definitely used as an animal pen exists immediately to the south of the compound (16 × 35 m) (Patrich, 1994: 66*: Site 91) (Fig. 13). At a short distance from the site, were areas of terraced fields in the tributary wadis (D3 and D4) (see below).

A number of soundings were made at the site by Cross and Milik, followed by additional work by Stager.[24] A small trench excavated in Area A, near chamber 5, on the east side of the compound, revealed a few modern sherds; this was probably the position of a Bedouin grave. A wall running north from the southern "casemate" wall may also date from that time. In 2009, some trench graves covered with stones, one with an upright stone marker still in place, were visible on the slope just outside the southern wall of the compound. However, Cross and Milik reported they did

---

ancient wall, striking an ancient foundation. But, apparently, finding nothing there, they transferred their operations to a very large cave to the north of the site. There they dug trenches in three different places, one as deep as three meters."

[22] There can be no doubt that currently the reservoir has a military function. A track was cut through the southern wall of the compound at some point, to allow for military vehicular access to the interior of the reservoir. Moreover, the site continues to suffer damage from military activities, with a track cut through the northern wall of the compound between 2007 and 2009, destroying the gate excavated by Stager. This same track extends through the southern wall, close to the south-eastern corner, damaging the edge of some of the Iron Age rooms. In one of the narrow rooms on the east side of the compound, one can see the Hebrew name "Gad" written in red paint on one of the walls.

[23] Palestine Department of Antiquities Archive: Ory's report from 18 January 1928 is labeled Report No. S.317 (see above, Note 10).

[24] A series of photographs showing the site of es-Samrah under excavation, made by Marc Hoyle Lovelace, in c.1963 (Accession Nos. LV 210 – 3891 to LV 238 – 3921), is available in the collection of the Southern Baptist Historical Library and Archives, Nashville, TN.

Fig. 12 The reservoir of Khirbet es-Samrah within the south-eastern angle of the site, seen looking towards the west, in a photograph taken by Ory in 1928, as compared to a recent photograph taken from the same angle in 2007. (Photos: courtesy Israel Antiquities Authority archives; Gibson)

Fig. 13 The animal pen on the south side of Khirbet es-Samrah. (Photo: Gibson)

uncover an ashy layer (0.30 m thick) which contained Iron Age pottery above a chalky bedrock floor at this same general location (Cross & Milik, 1956: 11).

Three Iron Age "casemate" rooms were visible along the interior southern wall, and at least one along the interior western wall. Area B comprised the area of "casemates" on the northern side of the compound and two trenches were dug there by Cross and Milik. The first was in the area of a wide break in the wall (B1) and it transpired that this was a gate leading into the compound (4.25 m wide), which has since been destroyed. Another gate may have existed at the western end of the northern wall (3.00 or 4.00 m wide). The northern compound wall was 1.10 m thick. The ashy deposits within the area of the gate brought to light Iron Age pottery and a stamped jar handle of the *lmlk* type, perhaps of the *mmsht* series.[25] Cross and Milik also came across a high-base lamp (Cross & Milik, 1956: 11), which is a rarity in the Iron Age pottery assemblage at sites in the Buqei'a. The second trench in Area B was dug by Stager to the west of the gate (B2) and it was intended to provide information on the stratigraphy within one of the "casemate" rooms (Stager, 1975: Fig. 27). Owing to the small size of the sounding, the separation walls between the rooms could not be seen, and only the south wall of one of the rooms was detected (0.60 m thick). The floor consisted of leveled chalk bedrock (phase 1), and above it was an ashy deposit (0.25 m thick) which was identified as occupational debris (phase 2). Stager suggested this was dung ash originating from a fireplace (Stager, 1975: 141). The pottery assemblage included bowls, and cooking pots, but also a few decanters and storage jars, and five small fragments of a substance identified as sulphur (Stager, 1975: 143). In addition there were 58 bones of sheep/goat, and part of one kernel of barley, a date pit, and two parts of pomegranate peel.

The excavation of two of the long rooms (8.20 m interior length, 2.25 m wide) on the east side of the compound in Areas 8–9 (internal walls were 0.60–0.70 m thick), was disappointing (Fig. 14). Stager does not mention doorways. Gaps now visible in the wall in front of rooms 3, 5, 8, 10 and 13, may represent doorways, or are the result of displaced stones from later damage made to the walls. The eastern wall of the compound was supported by a terrace or buttress wall. A layer of grey chalky fill was found in both rooms above the leveled chalk floors. The finds include pottery typical of the Iron Age II, with cooking pots, but lacking in soot marks. Stager suggested this was because they were used as storage containers rather than for cooking.[26] Indeed, they could have been used as containers to hold fermented (soured) full milk, or even as churns for making butter and other by-products (see Degen, 2007: 8). The floor of room 9 provided a *lmlk* stamped handle, with an added incised concentric circle mark (Stager, 1975: 147, Fig. 29). Two indeterminate ani-

---

[25] Cross and Milik (1956: 11, Fig. 2); Stager (1975: 140). Based on the published photograph it appears only the *mem* of *mmsht* may be visible on the handle. G. M. Grena disagrees with this interpretation, see: http://lmlk.blogspot.com/2006/05/stager-samrah-light-of-milik.html. See now: Lipschits et al., 2010: 14–15, note 20.

[26] During our 2009 visit to the site, three diagnostic Iron Age II rims were found on the surface of the site: one bowl with a folded-rim of red-brown ware, with a few white grits, and without burnishing; one bowl with a folded-rim of yellow-brown ware with ring burnishing; and one storage jar with a simple thickened rim (c.10 cm in diameter).

Fig. 14 Chamber 9 on the east side of Khirbet es-Samrah in 2007. (Photo: Gibson)

mal bones were also found. The 14 rooms along the east side of the compound are interpreted by Stager as "storage magazines," and their shape and size would certainly suggest this, but nothing was actually found in them that might confirm this assumption (Stager, 1975: 146–147). Hence, caution is needed in regard to Stager's overall assertion about this being the place of the "granary" of the settlement (Stager, 1975: 146) (Fig. 15).

5.3 Khirbet el-Maqari (Map Ref. 1862/1231)

The third site is situated just north of Wadi el-Maqari, which flows into the Wadi en-Nar at a distance of 2 km to the south-east (Stager, 1975: 156–159). This walled enclosure was square (31.72 × 32.30 m; 0.10 ha), with "casemate" rooms built along the north-western wall of the compound (1.0 m thick), and with an open central courtyard, like those seen at Abu-Tabaq and es-Samrah (Fig. 16). The internal wall of the casemate rooms has a width of 0.70 m, with internal divider walls 0.50 m wide. Cross and Milik conducted excavations there in 1955 (Cross & Milik, 1956: 12–14, Figs. 3–6), but Stager made only a cursory visit to the site during his Buqeiʿa work (Stager, 1975: 156), and no plan of the site was ever published.

A trench was excavated against the west wall of the enclosure (Area A) and it was then extended southwards to expose a room at the south-west of the

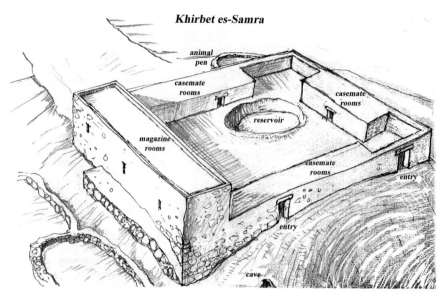

Fig. 15 A reconstruction of the Khirbet es-Samrah compound towards the south-west. (Drawing: Gibson)

enclosure. An ostracon was found with two chisel-incised letters: *lamed* and *aleph,* but the rest of the inscription is not preserved (Cross & Milik, 1956: Fig. 5). At the north-west corner of the compound (Area B), Cross and Milik unearthed two adjoining "casemate" rooms. A number of building phases were detected, which date to the seventh century BCE, based on the pottery finds. A basalt mortar for grinding purposes was found sunken into the floor and it belonged to the earlier phase (Cross, 1956, 16, Fig. 10). Nearby was found a round pounding stone of flint (9 cm in diameter). Complete, shattered, pottery vessels (cooking pots and bowls) were found belonging to the earlier phase of the site (Cross & Milik, 1956: Fig. 4; Stager, 1975: Fig. 34). The upper phase included a plaster floor and an ashy layer.

On the northern slope of the site, at a distance of 92 m, are twin cisterns (Maghayir et-Tabaqa), tunneled into the lower part of the ridge which were likely used by those living at the walled enclosure, and at a distance of 73 m in the wadi directly to the north-east is an open pool (*birkeh*) which may also have originated in the Iron Age (see below). About a kilometer south of the site is a small area of scattered stones and wall remnants – which we have labeled "Maqari South."[27]

---

[27] This is Bar-Adon's Site No. 106c and Patrich's Site No. 112. Our visit in October 2007 indicated not just Iron Age II potsherds but also Early Roman (first century to early second century CE) potsherds on the surface of the site, including the rim of a krater. During our visit in December 2019 we noticed signs of illegal excavations. On the south side of the site we saw in October 2007 the remains of a cemetery with at least two Bedouin trench graves covered with piled stones having

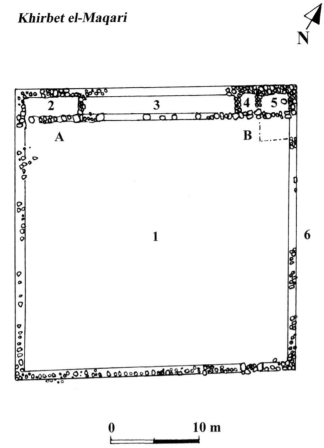

Fig. 16 Map of Khirbet el-Maqari: A–B: soundings by Cross and Milik; 1: courtyard; 2–5: casemate rooms; 6: possible entry. (Drawing: Gibson)

6 The Economy of the Settlements

On the basis of the faunal remains recovered from Khirbet Abu-Tabaq, it was deduced that in addition to other agricultural activities flocks of sheep were herded by the inhabitants of that site (Stager, 1975: 87, Appendix B). A similar picture was obtained based on the faunal remains obtained at Khirbet es-Samrah. Stager pointed out that no indisputable goat bone was identified at either of these two sites excavated in the Buqeiʿa (Stager, 1975: 141), but one has to recognize that the morphological separation of some of the bones of these two species (*Ovis aries* and *Capra*

---

a general NW to SE direction. Scattered on the surface were black Gaza ware (BGW) *ibriq* fragments, and glass bracelet fragments of late Ottoman appearance. These tombs were no longer visible in December 2019.

hircus) is particularly difficult. It may mean that specialized sheep rearing was conducted at these places, though traditionally pastoralists tend to shepherd more than one species of livestock (Redding, 1984; Degen, 2007: 8; Sasson & Greenfield, 2014: 213). Alternatively, it may mean that when meat was consumed, on religious or special occasions, the inhabitants preferred eating sheep rather than goat, which could explain the appearance of the bones of only the latter in their middens. In any case, pastoralists do not usually want to deplete their flocks by eating meat on a regular basis (Marx, 1992: 256–257).[28] Hence, if we are correct in identifying the inhabitants as pastoralists and not farmers, then meat consumption in their diet would have been limited, with a concentration on the consumption of secondary products such as milk and cheese, butter, and dried curds (Degen, 2007: 10–12). The gazelle bones found at Abu-Tabaq may suggest occasional hunting as well.[29] The dog femur at that same site might imply dogs were regularly kept in the encampments for protection and to help with the herding (Borowski, 1998: 133–140). Judging by ethno-historical data it would appear that the sale of animals, by exchange or barter at the marketplace, was the primary way by which these Iron Age communities supported themselves.

Curvilinear enclosures protected by stone fences are clearly identifiable adjacent to the compounds of the sites of Khirbet Abu-Tabaq and Khirbet es-Samrah, and they are also known in the vicinity of Khirbet el-Maqari. The stone fences of these enclosures have a similar construction style as the walls of the three settlement compounds, and are therefore likely to be contemporary. Based on the behavior of pastoral communities, some of these enclosures would have served to corral the animals during the day when they were not being let out to graze, or as milking pens; others would have been used as storage facilities for fodder, and/or as leveled areas for pitching tents. Owing to the importance of sheep rearing in such communities, the holding pens were vital and they would have had to have been in the immediate proximity of the settlements. At night time the livestock would have been shifted into the interior courtyards of the compounds for protection, and then let out in the morning. Since the enclosures attached to the compounds had multiple uses and were not always used just as animal pens, we believe the best way to estimate the sizes of animal herds at these sites, is to look at the size of the internal courtyards where the animals were protected at night, using the co-efficient density of one animal per 2 m^2 for estimating the spacing of animals in holding pens.[30]

---

[28] Amongst pastoralists, older animals are slaughtered on an annual basis for meat and are then replaced with young males subsequently introduced into the herd: Sasson (1998: 10).

[29] A gazelle bone was also found at the contemporaneous Iron Age II site of Vered Yeriho: Horowitz et al. (2018: 979).

[30] This co-efficient calculation of one sheep per 2 m^2 is based on our observation of herding practices of transhumant Bedouin communities at el-'Aujah in the lower Jordan Valley, north of Jericho. Haiman uses a similar co-efficient for the spacing of animals in animal pens at Iron Age sites in the western Negev highlands, concluding that an Iron Age family there possessed no more than 20 animals per herd (Haiman, 1994: 51). On general aspects relating to the co-efficient density of animals in holding pens (Hutson, 1984).

The internal courtyard of Khirbet Abu-Tabaq has an area of 0.12 ha of space, taking into consideration the evidence from Stager's excavations, which suggest casemate rooms built not just along the northern wall of the compound but along the western wall as well. This space would allow the herding of some 624 animals at night. However, if there were tents and storage facilities taking up space in one-half of the courtyard, this would reduce the average number of animals that might be accommodated in that space to only 312 animals. Indeed, the six external pens situated outside the compound (25 × 40 m), where animals were housed during the day, would allow for no more than 250 animals, and this when one excludes from the calculation the area taken up by the extant bisecting stone fences and tower. Hence we may conclude that some 250–624 animals could conceivably have been herded at Abu-Tabaq.[31]

Khirbet es-Samrah has 0.15 ha of space inside the courtyard, but we have to exclude from this equation the area of its open pool. The remaining space (0.11 ha) could have housed 585 sheep. The external animal pen situated immediately to the south of the compound covers an area of 16 × 35 m, i.e. a total area of 0.05 ha, providing a holding area suitable for no more than 250 animals. The enclosures on the east side of the settlement appear to have been used as areas for the storage of fodder, and perhaps also for pitching tents, but not as animal folds. Hence we may conclude that some 250–585 animals could conceivably have been herded at es-Samrah.

The plan of Khirbet el-Maqari consists of a walled enclosure with casemate rooms along one side. Excluding these, the interior courtyard has a space of 0.09 ha, which could conceivably have housed 225–450 animals.

In general, a minimum sustaining herd of sheep/goats of about 25–60 animals has been estimated for pastoralists in the Near East (Beaumont et al., 1976: 154; Perevolotsky et al., 1989:155), but traditionally-based Bedouin currently active in the Negev are known to own between 50 and 250 head of sheep (Stavi et al., 2006). Abu Rabi'a's research in that same region has shown that the herding of a flock of 200 sheep requires the overall labor of an entire extended family (Abu-Rabi'a, 1990; cf. Marx, 1992: 256). Added to this is our own observation of the practices of transhumant pastoralists of Bedouin extraction at el-Aujah in the lower Jordan Valley, where an average family of ten individuals subsists on a herd of 250 sheep. This is confirmed by Avitsur who estimated that 25 animals were needed to sustain the energy requirements of each individual living in a marginal environment (Avitsur, 1975–76: 94), though Sasson has suggested reducing this number to 10 animals (Sasson, 1998: 46; see also Avni, 1996: 70).[32]

If we accept a possible minimum herd size of c. 250 livestock per settlement in the Buqei'a, with a family of ten herders each, then a total of about 750 animals

---

[31] At el-Aujah, in the lower Jordan Valley, based on our personal observations, an average Bedouin family comprising of around ten individuals will subsist on a herd of 250 sheep. Out of this herd 10–15 of the older animals are sold for meat every year at market, as well as 50% of the lambs (mostly male).

[32] A very different co-efficient average of 2.2 animals essential to sustain one person has been estimated for pastoralists at villages practicing mixed farming in the highland regions (Sasson, 1998: 36).

might have been put out to graze in the overall pasturage of that region in the Iron Age. This would imply an overall population of no more than 30 pastoralists in the plateau, and each one of the three main Iron Age sites probably would have had a rangeland territory of about 12 km². It may be that the carrying capacity of the Buqeiʿa therefore is to be estimated as having no more than one herdsman per square kilometer, which is much less than the estimate of six herdsmen per square kilometer for the Bedouin in the Negev (see on this: Grossman, 1992: 95). Additional animal pens are known at a greater distance from the settlements in the Buqeiʿa, and these sometimes have attached to them semi-circular or roughly square stone shelters/huts for the use of the herdsmen.

Animal pens have been recorded in the vicinity of Abu-Tabaq. One animal pen is situated about a kilometer to the north-east of Abu-Tabaq and it could have held 187 animals. Another animal pen (mistakenly identified as a threshing floor) was identified on the south-east spur of the Abu-Tabaq hill, and it could have corralled 180 animals. Two others exist near the site but their sizes were not recorded: one is situated 1.2 km to the north-east of the site, and another much smaller animal pen just 100 m to the north-west. Interestingly, based on size, the contemporary Iron Age enclosure at Khirbet Irneh, just south of Qumran, might have held a flock of close to 2000 animals, and the animal pens near Tel Muhalhil, near where Wadi Dabr debouches into the Jordan Valley, had herding areas which conceivably could have held 1760, 650, 646, 648, 412, 405, 1000, and 600 animals respectively.[33]

The few carbonized seeds, found at Khirbet Abu-Tabaq and Khirbet es-Samrah, are helpful only in so far as they tell us what was consumed at these sites. They do not tell us what might have been cultivated in the Buqeiʿa, if at all. The carbonized seeds retrieved from Abu-Tabaq, including one wheat grain and one barley grain, certainly do not justify concluding, as Stager has, that cereal staples (barley and wheat) were an important part of the overall diet of the inhabitants at that site (Stager, 1975: 87).[34] Similarly, Samrah only produced one kernel barley fragment. Hence, Stager's statement that "cereals were grown in the Buqe'ah, not imported" (Stager, 1975: 196), is an assertion that cannot be sustained, or at least not based on the sparse archaeo-botanical finds provided. Sacks of grain could have been brought to the site from outside the region as a result of trade or barter with farmers; certainly the presence of a few seeds cannot by itself be taken to imply local cereal cultivation. Round silos were notably absent at the sites. Sickle blades made of metal or flint were not found, and Stager suggests this may be because the cereals were harvested by being pulled out of the ground by their stalks (Stager, 1975: 90). The supposed "granary" at Samrah, however, was found empty and not one seed confirming this identification was found. The single charred grape seed, an olive pit and a cotyledon of a pea found at Abu-Tabaq, and the pomegranate peel fragments

---

[33] Sites 80, 82a, 83a, 83c, 85 (Bar-Adon, 1972; Sites 83–84: Sion, n.d.).

[34] One should note that Stager's use of flotation procedures for the careful retrieval of carbonized plant remains was truly exceptional in his day (1972) when such materials were hardly being collected at archaeological excavations in Israel and Jordan.

and the single date pit from Area B at Samrah, were probably also obtained by the inhabitants through external contacts.

Pottery making was evidently not an industrial pursuit of the people living in the Buqeiʿa during the Iron Age, or at least we may assume this to be the case on the basis of the evidence provided from the three excavated sites. The pottery assemblage was relatively the same at all three sites, with common wares consisting largely of bowls and cooking pots, with smaller quantities of decanters and storage jars, and only one high-base lamp (Stager, 1975: Abu-Tabaq: Pls. 1, 2 and 3: 1–5; Samrah: Pl. 3: 6–40, and Pl. 4; Maqari: Pl. 5), and typologically the assemblage belongs to the second half of the seventh century BCE.[35] This pottery greatly resembles the ceramic assemblage obtained from Iron Age Qumran (Yezerski, 2018). However, there is a chronological problem: the presence of three *lmlk* stamped handles found at Abu-Tabaq and Samrah, would seem to push back the date of the assemblage to at least the *earlier* part of the seventh century BCE (Vaughn, 1999: 108; see discussion in Lipschits et al., 2010, 2011: Table 1, Fig. 2; Lipschits, 2012).

What about the end date for these sites? If the sites were abandoned in 587 or 586 BCE, or perhaps slightly later in 582 BCE, at the time of Nebuchadnezzar's campaign to Ammon and Moab in Transjordan (Herr, 1999), this would suggest the Buqeiʿa settlements were in existence for at least a century. However, as Stager rightly points out, the uncomplicated phasing of the occupational debris as reflected at the excavated sites, suggests they were short-lived settlements and they likely survived for no longer than half a century, at the most (Stager, 1975: 175, 250). This then rules out the possibility that the stamped handles are residuals, for earlier eighth to early seventh century BCE strata have not been identified at the Buqeiʿa sites.[36] The *lmlk* stamped handles at Abu-Tabaq and Samrah appear as part of a pottery assemblage dating to no earlier than the mid-seventh century BCE, and this is paralleled at Qumran, which also had two *lmlk* stamped handles (Yezerski, 2018; Taylor & Gibson, 2020) and at Horvat Shilhah which had one *lmlk* stamped handle (Mazar et al., 1995: 207, 208–209).

Stager surmised that the pottery vessels were brought into the Buqeiʿa by caravan from the west (Stager, 1975: 77, 212 ff.), and subsequent petrographic work made by Daniel Master has confirmed this, but he was also able to show that "a surprising amount of the domestic pottery was made locally…" (Master, 2009: 308, Figs. 1–3).[37] Two pottery kilns from the Iron Age were excavated at Qumran (L.66) and these may very well have been the source for this "local" pottery (Taylor &

---

[35] The plates of the pottery from the sites investigated by Stager appear in his unpublished Ph.D. thesis. For the general characteristics of these wares: Gitin, 2015.

[36] Contra Ussishkin, 2011: 227. Stager in a private letter to David Ussishkin seems to agree that the pottery from Khirbet es-Samrah had to be either eighth or seventh centuries BCE in date (Ussishkin, 2011: 227; cf. Master, 2009: 308), but in our opinion the pottery shown in Stager's thesis (1975) provides a clear seventh century BCE date.

[37] For further information on Master's petrographic work: www.levantineceramics.org/contributors/231-daniel-master

Gibson, 2020); alternatively the pottery was brought to the Buqeiʻa from other pottery manufacturing sites at Jericho or nearby.

Contact with the Dead Sea region is also emphasized by the discovery of small fragments of sulphur at Khirbet es-Samrah Stager (1975: 143), and these were probably used for lighting fires.

7 Did Desert Farming Exist at the Buqeiʻa Sites?

On the basis of the limited seasonal rainfall (c.150 mm) and high temperatures prevalent in the Buqeiʻa plateau, Stager suggested that only areas of permeable alluvium in the wadi tributaries could conceivably be farmed, and that these therefore could only have been winter crops. By the efficient harnessing of floodwaters, through irrigation by gravity-flow, the farmer was thus able to increase productivity of the land (Stager, 1975: 22–23). Stager parallels this with the patch cultivation practiced by the Sawahira Bedouin before 1948, in the area of the *kurum* alluvial lands (Stager, 1975: 181). Master in his re-assessment of the Buqeiʻa sites describes them as "farmsteads," that were involved in the local cultivation of cereals and legumes, and possibly even grapes; he also discusses the possible total wheat yield there at just under 8000 kg (Master, 2009: 307–308).

But what evidence do we have for Iron Age farming in the Buqeiʻa?

7.1 The Abu-Tabaq Field System (D1)

On the south side of the hill of Khirbet Abu-Tabaq, within a southern tributary of Wadi Qumran, is an area of alluvial soil, covering an area of about 10 ha, surrounded by an enclosure wall of stones, and with six (visible) terrace check-dams bisecting the wadi with a north-to-south axis (Cross & Milik, 1956: 8–9) (Figs. 17 and 18). There were probably additional check-dams and especially between dams C and D, with Stager estimating that there were up to ten in total (Stager, 1975: 111). This area of check dams has misleadingly been described as a "farm" (Stager, 1975: 104, Fig. 16), when in fact it would be more correct to define it as a "field system." This system is referred to as U-shaped in appearance, owing to the fact that at some point a large section of the southern wall was dismantled or intentionally destroyed; obviously the entire area was originally planned as one self-contained unit surrounded by a continuous stone fence.[38] On the west side of the system, the enclosure wall (A) was built of upright blocks of stone, and it served to impede the floodwaters from the west. The velocity of the floodwaters would have

---

[38] The D1 field system has suffered substantially owing to military activities in the area. When we examined this field system in October 2007 very little had survived, except for segments of the northern enclosure wall (0.70–0.90 m thick).

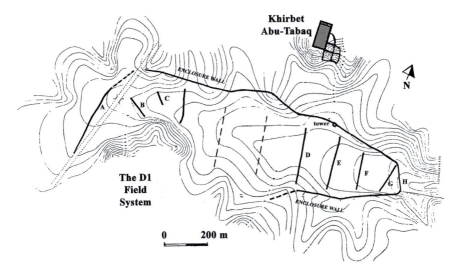

Fig. 17 The D1 field system at Khirbet Abu-Tabaq. (Drawing: Gibson, partly based on L. E. Stager, 1975)

Fig. 18 The enclosure wall on the north side of the D1 field system at Khirbet Abu-Tabaq, towards the east. (Photo: Gibson)

been regulated by sluice gates for efficiency, allowing water to spread evenly across the surfaces of the terraced dams, adapted with a slight gradient (B-G). The soil thus absorbed the water to allow for vegetal growth, with any surplus discharged into the narrow defile further to the east (H).

Stager was puzzled by the need for enclosure walls on the north and south sides of the system (Stager, 1975: 106, 132, 136), but this we suggest was to prevent livestock from moving unimpeded from one grazing ground to another, and to a lesser extent it was to prevent grazing gazelle from gaining access to the fields at night. Importantly, Stager was unable to identify features that are common to the run-off systems in the Negev, such as diversion channels, conduits and stone heaps ("tuleilat el-'anab") or spillways in the dams (Stager, 1975: 110), which strengthens our suggestion that these fields were not used for farming purposes but as areas of enhanced pasturage for grazing purposes (see below).

7.2 The Samrah Field Systems (D2, D3 and D4)

The D2 site is an enclosure (54 × 82.5 m) containing a good amount of collected alluvial soil (0.44 ha), situated in a northern tributary of Wadi Abu Su'lah 1.15 km to the north of Khirbet es-Samrah[39] (Fig. 19). The enclosure was surrounded by a stone fence and bisected into two parts by a stone cross wall. While topographically it was not located in the best position for flooding purposes, Cross and Milik thought it was constructed to "slow and spread the winter torrent" (Cross & Milik, 1956: 12). In any case, regardless of flooding, rainwater would constantly collect and pool within the area in the winter months. Stager thought it was a Roman camp, but we think this unlikely since it had no obvious defensive or military strategic value. No pottery whatsoever was found during Stager's survey of the site (Stager, 1975: 152), and so the date of the enclosure remains open. This plot would have made for excellent grazing ground, and the two parts could have been be utilized at different times.

The D3 site (Kurm es-Samrah) is an area of alluvial soil west of Samrah (map ref. 1869/1249), on a northern branch of Wadi Abu Su'lah before it reaches the main bed, which has been badly damaged by erosion, covering an area of 0.81 ha. One cross-dam terrace wall was examined at the site (Cross & Milik, 1956: 6; Stager, 1975: 152, Fig. 31). Immediately to the north is a large natural depression (130 × 140 m) surrounded by a stone enclosure wall; surface flow of rainwater is trapped within this depression and the area thus could have served as green pasturage (Table 1:15 and Fig. 20).

The D4 site is situated not too far away from the previous site, to the south-west of the Iron Age compound, and on the Wadi Abu Su'lah, and its alluvial soils cover an area of c. 1.21 ha (Stager, 1975: 152–156). This place is known on maps as Kurm el-'Ajuz or 'Ajaz (map ref. 1864/1248). It was pointed out as a "vineyard" to the

---

[39] According to Patrich the enclosure measures 76 × 106 m (Patrich, 1994: 52*: Site No. 52).

Fig. 19 D2: The so-called "Roman camp" (Table 1:16) north of Khirbet es-Samrah. (Photo: courtesy R. Cleave and Rohr Productions)

Fig. 20 Flat enclosed area to the NW of Khirbet es-Samrah (Table 1:19) used for green pasturage. (Photo: Gibson)

explorers of the SWP in the nineteenth century (Conder & Kitchener, 1883: 213). The terraced dam which retained the alluvial soil, crosses the wadi at this point, and has a length of 57.5 m. A protective enclosure wall built of stone was established on both sides of the wadi.

During Patrich's survey of 1981–82, an enclosure wall (95 m in length) connected to an area of alluvial soil, was investigated to the east of es-Samrah (Patrich, 1994: 66*: Site 91).

7.3 The Maqari Field System (D5)

The D5 site (map ref. 1846/1236) is situated 1.5 km west of the site of Khirbet el-Maqari. The field system was not mapped, and it included "...the remains of an enormous dam complex (D5) on a northern tributary of Wadi el-Maqari. Three 'flows' of water are broken by two large traverse dams, and a smaller traverse dam. These traverse walls in turn are related to each other by complicated side walls in an irregular patterns, involving a total of more than 1000 m. of walls, including destroyed sections" (Cross & Milik, 1956: 14).

8 Pasturage

Stager employs ethnographic parallelism for the reconstruction of the needs of the Iron Age people who settled the Buqeiʻa, by investigating modern-day Bedouin use of the area in terms of the exploitation of wild plant resources, for food and medicinal needs, and as opportunistic pasturage (Stager, 1975: 24 ff.) (Fig. 21). Setting aside the various culinary and advantageous uses such plants might provide, we shall now discuss the Bedouin use of plants for pasturage.

Pasturage was undoubtedly possible in the Buqeiʻa and in the nearby hills, as it is today. It was sparse, but as Stager notes a number of plants do make for good foraging for livestock, notably the *Salsola vermiculata* and the *Suaeda asphaltica* dwarf shrubs, and the more limited saltbush *Atriplex halimus* (Stager, 1975: 32). But there are limits in terms of the carrying capacity of the area for grazing livestock, which would certainly have been sufficient for the occasional needs of the local modern Bedouin, but somewhat limiting for the large-scale specialized herding we envisage pastoralists of the Buqeiʻa engaging in during the Iron Age. A study made on the voluntary ingestive behaviour governing the daily herbage intake made by sheep while grazing, has shown that sheep in smaller groups spend less time grazing than sheep in larger groups (Penning et al., 1993), which means shepherding larger flocks of sheep in the Buqeiʻa in the Iron Age would have been a much more labor intensive activity, requiring the constant shifting of herds from one pasturage to another in the rangeland and beyond. Herders would have had to constantly re-evaluate the grazing potential of the area they were using in terms of available herbage.

Fig. 21 Green pasturage with grazing goats on the north side of the Buqei'a in December 2019. (Photo: Lewis)

Hence, the alluvial soils in the tributaries of the wadis would have been utilized *fully* for enriched green pasturage, and great care would have been taken to avoid overgrazing. Accessibility and timing would have been critical when taking advantage of this rangeland for pasturage. One assumes that the three main Iron Age settlements in the plateau, divided up the pasturage of their rangeland equally three ways – unless of course they all belonged to the same clan – with an estimated 12 km^2 of territory given over to each settlement. The alluvial soil was washed down from the west into the shallow meandering wadi beds, where it spread out into the tributaries of Wadi Khasnah, Wadi Qumran, Wadi Umm el-Fus, Wadi Abu Shu 'lah and Wadi el-Maqari, and it has been estimated at 170 ha of potentially exploitable land (Stager, 1975: 194). Following the winter growth of shrubs and grasses, the first areas to be exploited would have been at the very edges of the outlying Iron Age territory, with the itinerary of exploitation moving gradually closer to the areas in the immediate proximity of the settlements, and especially as the summer months approached. Eventually, grazing was transferred to the enclosed and protected fields adjacent to the settlements, which may be estimated at 12 ha of land.

Following the winter rains, the growth of the annual short grasses on the plots near the settlements could be enhanced when intermingled with intentionally scattered grain, wheat or barley, on the wet and roughly plowed surfaces (for similar practices in the northern Negev: Nevo, 1991: 103) (Fig. 22). This prime pasturage, situated immediately next to the settlements, would have been grazed very carefully in rotation, and perhaps plot by plot, which may explain the necessity for the

Fig. 22 Bedouin plowing for pasturage in the Buqei'a in the early 1960s in a photograph taken by John M. Allegro. (Photo: courtesy Judith Brown & the Allegro Estate)

building of surrounding boundary walls, such as those seen at Abu-Tabaq and Samrah. However, eventually, once the local grazing possibilities for the herds had been exhausted in the plateau, the pastoralists then must have turned to transhumance, shifting their flocks to better summer pasturage, further up in the highlands to the west and at some distance from their home settlements located in the Buqei'a.

9 Water Sources

There can be no doubt that availability to water was important not just for the daily needs of the inhabitants of the Iron Age settlements in the Buqei'a, but it was essential for the watering of the herds of animals. During our visits to the Buqei'a in 2007 and 2009, we examined the water installations at the three main Iron Age sites.

At the foot of the northern slope of Abu-Tabaq, at a distance of 43 m, is the entrance to a large horizontal rock-cut cistern (Mugharet Abu-Tabaq) (Figs. 23 and 24). It was explored by Masterman in 1902 (1903: 264), and by Cross and Milik in 1955 (Cross & Milik, 1956: 8; Cross, 1956: 15, Fig. 9). Masterman provided the following measurements: 35.3 m in length, 5.33 wide and 6.00 m in height, and wrote: "At the extreme inner end there is a hole at the top of the accumulated dirt which may lead into an inner part. My man put his gun in as far as he could without touching rock. The right side of the cave shows tool-marks where the walls have been smoothed, and at two places there are recesses for lamps. Close to the entrance on this side of the cave

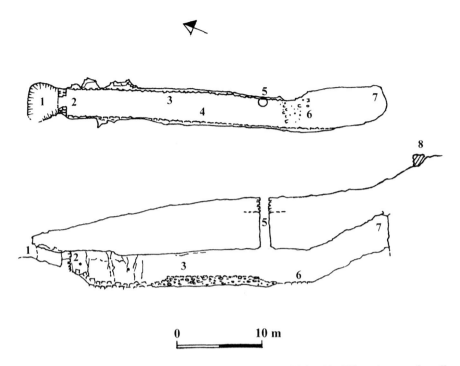

Fig. 23 Map and section of the Iron Age rock-cut cistern at Khirbet Abu-Tabaq: 1: entry; 2: wall with doorway; 3–4: stone-built side-walls; 5: vertical shaft in ceiling; 6: cobbled floor; 7: hole in ceiling; 8: enclosure wall. (Drawing: Gibson)

there is a place where my Bedawin guide declared the Arabs had cut away an inscription – or what they took for an inscription. There are signs that something has been cut away…" (Masterman, 1903: 264). Masterman's description is fairly detailed, but he neglected to mention the vertical circular shaft visible in the ceiling (0.90 m in diameter), rock-cut except for its upper part (1.78 m in height) which is stone-lined[40] (Fig. 25).

The cave of Mugharet Abu-Tabaq is elongated and tunnel-like in appearance (41.50 m in length; 3.70–5.00 m wide; 3.83 m in height). A wall (0.90 m thick) was built at the mouth of the cave, with roughly-squared stones built in courses (0.15–0.25 m high), and with a gap providing access to the interior. Patrich at the time of his 1981–82 survey noticed the doorway had ashlar jambs and the remains of a metal hinge for a wooden door, with steps leading down into the interior of the cave (Patrich, 1994: 48*: Site 35). None of these are visible today. Dry-built walls of small stones were built to clad either side of the chamber (1.44 m in height), presumably in order to protect the eroding side walls of the chamber. No tooling or plaster was obvious on the walls. Two small niches for lamps were observed in the

---

[40] This shaft is presumably the same as the one Patrich observed at a distance of 18 m from the cave entrance (1994: 48*: Site No. 35).

Fig. 24 The interior of the rock-cut cistern at Khirbet Abu-Tabaq, looking south. (Photo: Gibson)

side walls. A patch of stone paving was obvious at one point in the floor of the cave. The interior of the cave slopes upwards, presumably towards the compound of the settlement, and a small hole is visible at this point -- which had already been seen by Masterman (see above). The capacity of the large cistern at the northern foot of the hill, would have sufficed for the needs of the inhabitants of Abu-Tabaq, and they could easily have accessed the water for drinking purposes via the vertical shaft close to the top of the hill.

The Abu-Tabaq cistern when it was full, i.e. to a depth of 2 m, could have provided the inhabitants of the site with 222,000 l of water. This means each person living at the site would have had enough for a daily allowance of water throughout the year, and additional water sufficient to water the herd of animals as well.

Fig. 25 Shaft in the ceiling of the cistern at Khirbet Abu-Tabaq. (Photo: Gibson)

However, there were also additional cisterns on the slopes of the site and in the vicinity. One such rock-hewn cistern (7 × 5 m) is situated on the lower slope on the eastern side of the D1 field system at Abu-Tabaq, with evidence that winter rainwater could have been diverted into it from the run-off during the flooding of the field system (Figs. 26 and 27). Water would have been drawn from the cistern via a circular vertical shaft (0.80 m in diameter) in the ceiling. This cistern could have provided an additional 70,000 l of water.

To the north-west of Abu-Tabaq at a distance of 1.5 km is a large open seasonal pool. It contained water until the summer, and would have been a target for the herders grazing their flocks in that vicinity. It resembles the open seasonal pools in the Negev highlands which are generally dated to the Iron Age (Haiman, 1989: Avni, 1996: 32).

The Iron Age enclosure at Khirbet es-Samrah has a large elliptical open reservoir (21 × 16 m) within the south-east quadrant of the courtyard, which could have supplied 336,000 l of water on a seasonal basis. During the summer months it would have been dry owing to the extreme heat and high evaporation rates. The antiquity of this pool has been questioned owing to the military damage done there in the 1950s (Stager, 1975: 137, 169, note 54). Its antiquity is assured however since it had already been recorded as an ancient *birkeh* (open water pool) in 1928, long before the military activities began at the site. In 2009 a blocked shaft opening to a rock-hewn cave, was observed just outside the gate of the Iron Age compound on the north-east slope, and we believe this was to a cistern. [41] Based on the description provided by

---

[41] The vertical shaft is no longer visible when we visited the site in December 2019.

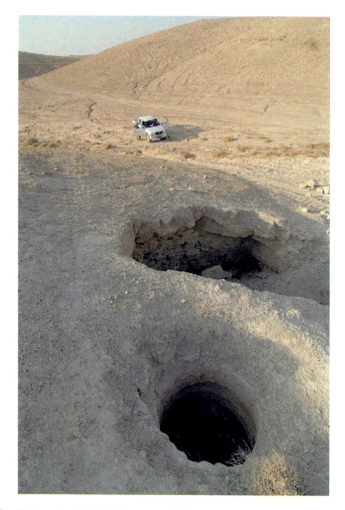

Fig. 26 Small cistern in the D1 field system at Khirbet Abu-Tabaq. (Photo: Gibson)

D. C. Baramki from 1934, this cave was quite large, but he did not provide measurements, and access to the cave is no longer possible. At a distance of 0.7 km to the north-west of es-Samrah are two open seasonal pools, one of which was noted by the SWP on their map as a "birket" (Conder & Kitchener, 1883: Sheet XVIII).

The excavations at Khirbet el-Maqari did not reveal cisterns within the enclosure, but this does not mean there were none in the unexcavated areas. Two very large "twin" cisterns are situated on the north-western slope of the site (Magawir et-Tabaqah), at a distance of 92 m from the enclosure, and Cross and Milik believed they would have been used by the Iron Age inhabitants of the site (Cross & Milik, 1956: 13–14)[42] (Figs. 28, 29 and 30). These cisterns are indicated on the SWP map from the 1873 exploration of the region. The cisterns are tunneled into

---

[42] According to Cross and Milik one of the cisterns had a length of 14.8 m and the other 13.6 m.

Fig. 27 Small cistern in the D1 field system at Khirbet Abu-Tabaq. (Drawing: Gibson)

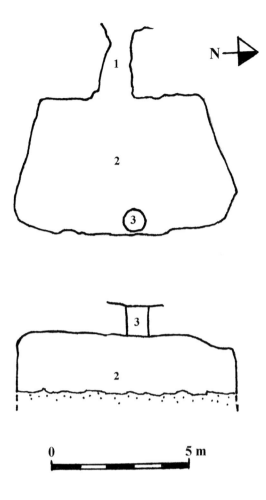

the side of the lower part of a rocky ridge, and water was diverted from the adjacent wadi into an oval area in front of the two cistern openings. One cistern has a length of 13.90, a breadth of 4.80 and a height of 2.05 m from floor to ceiling, the other a length of 10.90 m, a breadth of 5.60 m, and a height of 2.10 m from floor to ceiling, and the joint wall between the adjoining cisterns is 2.50 m wide. Together these cisterns could have provided 26,495 l of water, when full to capacity, The entrances and front parts of the cisterns are blocked by soil, and they have rough walls (0.50 m) built of small stones (clearly of later date). In front of the second cistern is a small water-catchment basin (1.50 × 1.15 m) with a rock-cut channel extending into the cave. Another niche visible in the side wall (0.50 m wide and 1.90 m deep) is of uncertain function. The walls of the cave were extremely well-cut, but tooling was not visible, and in the interior of the cave patches of a light brown plaster (5 cm thick) were discernible coating the wall surfaces.

Fig. 28 Aerial drone view of the entrances to the twin cisterns at Khirbet el-Maqari. (Photo: Lewis)

At a distance of 73 m to the north-east of the Iron Age site (map ref. 18625/12320) is a large open pool (*birkeh*) which may have been utilized in the Iron Age, but, according to Cross and Milik (1956: 13), it was also functioning in the Roman, Byzantine, and Ottoman periods, and was still being used by the Bedouin in the twentieth century. It was clearly used as a seasonal pool for use during the winter and spring months, but at the time of our visits in October 2007 and December 2019 it was completely dry (Figs. 31 and 32). It was established in a tributary leading to Wadi el-Maqari. It is roughly square (27.50 × 23.80 m) and was cut into the ground to a depth of 2.60 m. The walls of the pool consist of heaped earth (7–13 m wide), and the south-eastern side also has a dam wall built of stones (30 m in length and 1.28 m wide) bisecting the wadi. Along the south-western side of the *birkeh* is a small stretch of a plastered wall (0.18 m thick), which may represent part of a diversion channel leading to a rectangular plastered tank within the southern angle.[43] Very few potsherds were visible on the surface, except for a few dating from the late Hellenistic or Early Roman periods. In a survey conducted at the site by Patrich in 1981–82 he noted Iron Age pottery, as well as potsherds from the Hellenistic, Roman and early Islamic periods (Patrich, 1994: 91*: Site 101). When full of water, the large pool could have contained 1,701,000 l of water.

---

[43] The north-west angle of this tank was recently exposed in clandestine excavations at the site. Walls are seen coated with white plaster. This illegally dug pit was first noticed on a visit to the site in December 2019.

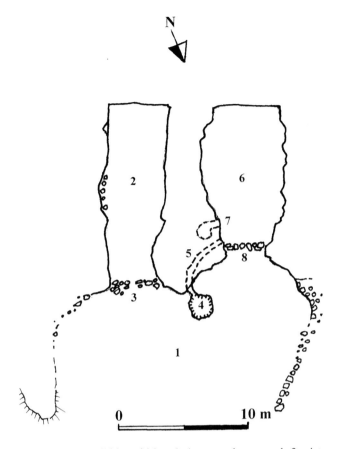

Fig. 29 The twin cisterns at Khirbet el-Maqari: 1: external courtyard; 2: cistern; 3: wall at entrance; 4: silting basin; 5 channel to cistern; 6: cistern; 7 niche in wall; 8: wall at entrance. (Drawing: Gibson)

In structure and purpose this pool resembles the micro-catchment rainwater harvesting systems known in the badia of Jordan (Oweis, 2017: 143), and the "liman" earthwork basins of which there are hundreds in the Negev Desert (Grossman, 1992: 97–98). Indeed, two very large limans are situated in Wadi en-Nar as it descends to the Dead Sea. Primarily for watering purposes, these limans when once dry can be used for grazing owing to the persistence of their special micro-climates.

10 Conclusions

A summary of the archaeological evidence from the three main Iron Age IIC/III sites on the Buqeiʿa Plateau supports our proposal that in the seventh and early sixth centuries BCE this region was inhabited by specialist transhumant pastoralists using

Fig. 30 The interior of the eastern of the twin cisterns at Khirbet el-Maqari. (Photo: Gibson)

it as rangeland for grazing livestock (sheep, and perhaps goats),[44] and not by quasi-military farmers practicing run-off desert agriculture for cereal cultivation, with some pastoralist activities, as was previously believed.

On ecological grounds, the people who lived in the Buqeiʿa in the Iron Age must have had a restricted and tough way of life. This was because of the harsh climate, the poor quality of available land and limited access to water. Obviously, however, the basic sustainability of this marginal environment did allow for the management of livestock, with the herding of sheep and possibly also goats, and this became the primary economic concern and way of life for the inhabitants living at the three main Iron Age sites on the plateau: Kh. Abu-Tabaq, Kh. es-Samrah, and Kh. el-Maqari. The close proximity between these sites and their position next to the main road, suggest shared common economic goals. The position of some of the small towers allowed for signaling to take place along the road and between settlements.

---

[44] For definitions of terms such as "nomadic pastoralists," "mobile pastoralists," "transhumant pastoralists," and "agro-pastoralists" (see: Levy, 1983; Borowski, 1998: 40; Degen, 2007, 8). There is still much discussion and disagreement on terminology, and on correlating the nuances of such terms with the myriad of ancient societies as reflected in the archaeological record (Chang & Koster, 1986; Bar-Yosef & Khazanov, 1992: 2–3; Marx, 1992: 255–256; Meadow, 1992; Kardulias, 2015; Biagetti & Howe, 2017). For the spatial organization of pastoral systems and a definition of terms (Chang, 1992: 67). For astute remarks concerning cyclical nomadic-sedentary relations in the Negev, and on the problem of simplistic generalizations (Rosen, 2009). On the social complexity of mobile nomadic groups which deviate from the "Bedouin model," and on the impact they had on state formation processes in the early Iron Age (see: Ben-Yosef, 2021).

Fig. 31 Aerial drone view of the pool to the north-east of Khirbet el-Maqari. (Photo: Lewis)

The Iron Age pastoralists of the Buqeiʿa very likely practiced a degree of transhumance, particularly with the onset of the dry summer months, when the carrying capacity for grazing in this area was pushed to its absolute limit. This meant the movement of shepherded flocks to better grazing destinations further west upland, and this would have been undertaken on a seasonal basis every year. The three Iron Age settlements on the plateau were probably fixed assets that were maintained on a sedentary basis by the stationary members (male and female) of the pastoralist community on a year-round basis. The younger male members were likely put in charge of moving the herds in the summers toward the west, to better pastures at fixed and identifiable upland locations, and then back again to the Buqeiʿa in late fall. It is difficult to be certain about the number of inhabitants per settlement, because some members of these communities may have lived in tents, and others in outlier structures (towers and small enclosures) which dot the plateau, but we may safely assume there was at least one extended family per settlement, consisting of at

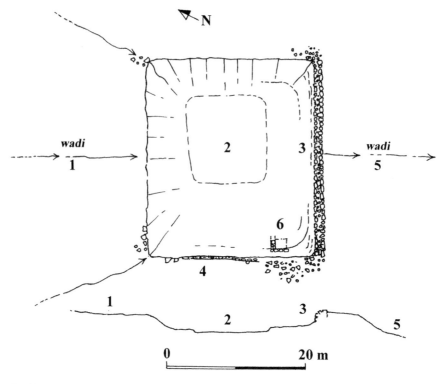

Fig. 32 Plan and section of the pool to the north-east of Khirbet el-Maqari: 1: original wadi bed; 2: pool; 3: stone dam wall; 4: plastered channel; 5: wadi bed beyond the earthen embankment; 6: corner of plastered tank. (Drawing: Gibson)

least ten adult individuals, though the extended family will also have had dependents such as children.

The pastoralists of the Buqeiʿa plateau improved their grazing zones in the tributary wadis near their settlements by creating well demarcated green pastures. The improvement of these lands was made by leveling areas of alluvial soil, surrounding them with stone fences, and building sluice gates for irrigation. This was a serious investment of labor. It allowed for the efficient spreading and dispersal of flood waters across the plots during episodes of intense rainfall in the winter months. Whether these activities were done solely to stimulate the growth of natural wild grasses in the fields, or whether this was further facilitated by the sowing of seed by hand, is unknown. The arid environmental conditions of this region, with its limited water resources and with soil that was largely lacking in sustainable fertility, would not have permitted sustainable cultivation. The Buqeiʿa plateau fits perfectly the environmental definition of "marginal" land, which is an area unsuitable for major farming pursuits, such as the sustained cultivation of grain crops, vineyards or orchards (Legge, 2004; Berger & Juengst, 2017). The grazing of livestock was undoubtedly possible and green pasturing further allowed for an even greater sustainability when it came to maintaining larger flocks.

The general architectural layout of the three Iron Age sites in the Buqei'a suggests an arrangement and permanency that would have been particularly suitable for people involved in animal husbandry. As such, they differ from encampments used by nomads. Traditionally, nomads take up temporary abode in tents and not in buildings or rectilinear compounds.[45] They leave behind very few artifacts when they move, which does not however render them "invisible" in the archaeological spectrum (Rosen, 1993), but the remains left behind are still sparse consisting mostly of boundary walls, fire-pits, random artifacts, etc. Nomads have a mobile existence and tend to follow an irregular pattern of grazing for their livestock. They are capable of adapting to changing climatic fluctuations fairly rapidly, and will move their grazing lands quickly from one location to another, sometimes over great distances, in pursuit of better watering holes. Unlike nomads, transhumant pastoralists have a greater dependency on fixed mobility patterns in regard to the immediate availability of pasture for their flocks, and will practice regular seasonal transhumance from their home bases (LaBianca, 1990: 36).

The template of an Iron Age pastoralist settlement, as it emerges from our examination of sites in the Buqei'a, comprises a hill-top location with an enclosed compound with sufficient space for livestock and tents, storage rooms, a seasonal open water pool, cisterns, external holding pens for animals, and permanent well demarcated fields for pasturage in the tributary wadis round about. All of this implies they possessed land ownership/property rights, not just for the settlement, but also for the land round about (see also Faust, 2017). Boundaries would have been asserted to ensure they would not encroach upon the adjacent territories of neighbors, and a proximity to a road was vital for establishing connectivity. As mentioned above, the grazing zone surrounding a settlement was parceled into individual plots, and these were likely irrigated consecutively during episodes of winter flooding. The dam walls might indicate divided ownership, but it is much more likely they were established to ensure staggered access for animals to grazing land for forage, with availability constantly shifting from plot to plot during the spring months. External curvilinear animal pens were built to contain and protect the livestock, but the surrounding walls also ensured that the animals did not encroach on the grazing areas when untended. Manure collected from within the holding pens could be scattered in the fields to revitalize pasturage (Broderick & Wallace, 2016). The size of the internal courtyard at each one of the settlements, was such, that at nights the flock was moved inside for safety, and then let out into the holding pens in the mornings. Land ownership would also have included access rights to water holes and cisterns as well, especially since without water their herds would not have survived. While hardier goats might be watered just once every 2–4 days, sheep required a much more constant supply of water on a regular basis. The small cubicle-like rooms

---

[45] A nomadic site which illustrates this point well was investigated by SWP explorers at Umm el-'Autad, situated to the south-east of the Iron Age site of Khirbet el-Maqari, and close to the point where Wadi el-Maqari enters Wadi en-Nur, and they describe it as follows: "Ruins of a Bedawin camp, the stones arranged round the tents and cooking-places remaining; hence the name 'Mother of Tent-pegs'" (Conder & Kitchener, 1883: 227).

within the compound walls might have been used for the storage of tools and for food, and other commodities that were imported from outside the plateau.

In general terms, the economic activity at these Iron Age settlements may be defined as a specialized form of pastoralism for one part of the year and with transhumance over the dry summer months.[46] Their inhabitants practiced a well-thought out survival strategy, that was attuned to changes in the availability of water and grazing resources. Meat was a major resource for trade, with wool and leather products as well. Daily subsistence would have been based on the consumption of secondary by-products such as milk, yoghurt, butter and dried curds. Tanned skins, woolen garments and rugs were probably also produced, which could be exchanged at markets, such as at Jericho, or at other smaller Iron Age settlements in the general region. The sulphur fragments found at Khirbet Abu Tabaq obviously implies direct contact with the area of the Dead Sea, perhaps via the Iron Age settlement at Qumran, which was also able to supply pottery vessels from its kilns. Drought, drastic climatic fluctuations, and disease to animals, were potentially devastating to specialized transhumant pastoralists, such as those living in the Buqeiʿa, and sometimes it could lead to impoverishment and even death (Moritz et al., 2011). It was evidently a fragile lifestyle which required them to be constantly responsive to climatic changes, and in making risk-management assessments, much more so perhaps than their nomadic counterparts, who enjoyed a greater mobility (Grossman, 1992: 96).

The origin and identity of the pastoralists who came to inhabit the Buqeiʿa in the Iron Age is unknown. One option is that this land was formerly used by nomads but that they came to be displaced, and that the plateau was eventually reclaimed for specialized pastoralism by people originating from outside the region in the early part of the seventh century BCE, but no evidential material exists that might confirm this. There has been a suggestion that some of these people may have been refugees who flooded parts of Judah in the late eighth century BCE, following the conquest of Samaria by the Assyrians (Magen & Peleg, 2018: 101–104), but this view has been seriously questioned (Na'aman, 2014). The seventh century was undoubtedly a time of prosperity, and it clearly impacted on settlement in the Judean Desert fringe and in the Buqeiʿa as well (Faust, 2008: 170; Faust & Weiss, 2011: 190, Fig. 15.1). Those living in the plateau at that time were certainly not isolationists, and their economy was not autarkic. They clearly interacted with travelers passing along the road. The pottery at the three sites clearly identifies them as people who maintained a Judahite ceramic culture. At the southern end of the plateau, the Iron Age settlers were linked via road to Wadi en-Nar, which led to places up in the highlands to the west, such as Bethlehem and Hebron. On the north there was direct access to the Jerusalem to Jericho road. Cereals, olives and fruits were brought in from markets outside the plateau, and the pastoralists will have had some bartering maneuverability. Some living in this region were literate, if we accept the evidence of the inscribed ostracon from Maqari. The discovery of the personal seal of

---

[46] For comparative purposes, one should point out that pastoralism rather than agriculture was the overall primary pursuit at sites in the Negev Highlands from as early as the Iron Age IIA: Shahack-Gross & Finkelstein, 2015: 257. For an alternative view: Bruins, 2012: 37.

Badyahu at Khirbet Abu-Tabaq, must imply some Judahite status for at least one of its settlers, though being a leader in charge of the herding of small ruminants was generally regarded as a low status activity in antiquity. One possibility is that Badyahu was the head of the local clan, and that all three settlements were under his dominion. While the people of the Buqeiʿa were definitely not cereal farmers, as we have shown, it is highly probable that the inhabitants of these sites had some association or affiliation with the Judahite military of that time, perhaps receiving patronage in return for help in protecting the security of the eastern border of the Kingdom of Judah (Stern, 1994). Stager suggested that the inducement to settle in the Buqeiʿa was made through initial governmental incentive derived from Jerusalem, at the time of the rule of Josiah (c.639 BCE), when the eastern borders of his kingdom were being strengthened, which certainly seems a reasonable scenario (Stager, 1975: 213), but in our opinion this was as pastoralists not cereal farmers. If the settlements of the Buqeiʿa were abandoned in 587/586 BCE, or alternatively in 582 BCE, this means they were only in use for half a century or so, which matches perfectly the pottery evidence from the sites. This therefore extends the possible use (or re-use) of jars of *lmlk* type to as late as the mid-seventh century BCE (Lipschits et al., 2010: 8).

Some Iron Age settlements in the Judean Desert, such as Horvat Shilhah and Vered Yeriho (Eitan, 1983), appear to have had a military function as outposts, but the use of the term "fort" for these sites is restrictive and unhelpful. Even "military center" is problematic (Horowitz et al., 2018: 966), since many of the inhabitants were most likely not soldiers. Such places appear to have served at times as caravanserai or supply/trade depots. Architecturally these two sites, Horvat Shilhah and Vered Yeriho, are not at all like the three settlements in the Buqeiʿa, except for the general existence of the architectural template of the "enclosed courtyard." It is conceivable that the inhabitants of these settlements formed alliances with the Buqeiʿa pastoralists, perhaps as additional suppliers of meat and by-products.[47] They might also have provided protection services along the road, at least for non-military travelers. Such alliances made more sense than working with nomads, who

---

[47] The faunal assemblage at Vered Yeriho was dominated by sheep, goat and cattle, with the remains appearing to be the residue of the dietary activities of the inhabitants, based on evident butchery marks and burning (Horowitz et al., 2018: 971). In regard to the sheep/goat it is unclear whether the meat was brought to the site as pre-prepared or almost complete carcasses, or whether animals were brought alive to be butchered there in their entirety. The absence of lower hind-and fore-limbs was noticed, and the wide range of meat cuts goes against choice portions of meat having been transported into the site. The evidence of bones of newborn lambs/kids would seem to indicate animals were being raised on-site, since the young animals provide little or no meat and thus their carcasses would ostensibly have been of little value (Horowitz et al., 2018: 995). However, their appearance there could have been the result of specific cultural preferences or dietary practices that are still unknown to us. Hence, Vered Yeriho may very well have been supplied with animals provided by external pastoral groups, perhaps similar to those groups active in the Buqeiʿa. It should be noted that fish bones from the Mediterranean Sea at Vered Yeriho does attest to the fact that food was being brought into the settlement from great distances. Indeed, the authors agree that "it cannot…be discounted, that animals (live or slaughtered) were obtained from farms and rural settlements near the site" (Horowitz et al., 2018: 997). The Buqeiʿa sites may have been one such source.

were not so dependable owing to their long-distance mobility and possible banditry. Hence, the Buqeiʿa pastoralists in the Iron Age, between the mid-seventh and early sixth centuries BCE, may very well have played a significant role as a dependable entity of people living on the eastern outskirts of the Kingdom of Judah. They were visible along the paths and roads leading between major settlements in the lower eastern Judean Desert, and may very well have provided protection services for the caravans of traders taking salt, sulphur and bitumen from the area of the Dead Sea to Jerusalem.

References

Abu-Rabi'a, A. (1990). *The bedouin of the Negev and sheep-rearing*. Ph.D. thesis. Tel Aviv University.
Avitsur, S. (1975–76). *Daily life in Eretz Israel in the XIX century*. Rubenstein (Hebrew).
Avni, G. (1996). *Nomads, farmers, and town-dwellers. Pastoralist-sedentist interaction in the Negev highlands, sixth-eighth centuries CE*. Israel Antiquities Authority.
Bar-Adon, P. (1972). The Judaean Desert and plain of Jericho. In M. Kochavi (Ed.), *Judaea, Samaria, and the Golan: Archaeological survey 1967–1968* (pp. 91–149). The Archaeological Survey of Israel (Hebrew).
Barmash, P. (2012). Reimagining exile through the lens of the Exodus: Turning points in Israelite history and texts. In J. J. Ahn & J. Middlemas (Eds.), *By the irrigation canals of Babylon: Approaches to the study of the Exile* (pp. 93–106). T & T Clark.
Bar-Yosef, O., & Khazanov, A. (1992). *Pastoralism in the Levant: Archaeological materials in anthropological perspectives* (Monographs in world archaeology no. 10). Wisconsin.
Beaumont, P., Blake, G. H., & Wagstaff, J. M. (1976). *The Middle East: A geographical study*. Wiley.
Ben-Yosef, E. (2021). Rethinking the social complexity of early Iron Age nomads. In A. Faust, Y. Garfinkel, & M. Mumcuoglu (Eds.), *State formation processes in the 10th century BCE levant (Jerusalem Journal of Archaeology, 1)* (pp. 155–179). https://doi.org/10.52486/01.00001.6. https://openscholar.huji.ac.il/jjar
Berger, E., & Juengst, S. L. (2017). Humans in marginal environments: Adaptation among living and ancient peoples. *American Journal of Human Biology, 29*, e23022. https://doi.org/10.1002/ajhb.23022
Biagetti, S., & Howe, T. (2017). Variability is the key. Towards a diachronic view of pastoralism. *Nomadic Peoples, 21*, 167–172.
Borowski, O. (1998). *Every living thing. Daily use of animals in ancient Israel*. Walnut Creek.
Broderick, L. G., & Wallace, M. (2016). Manure: Valued by farmers, undervalued by zooarchaeologists. In L. G. Broderick (Ed.), *Perspectives and studies in ethnozooarchaeology* (pp. 34–41). Oxbow books.
Bruins, H. J. (2012). Ancient desert agriculture in the Negev and climate-zone boundary changes during average, wet and drought years. *Journal of Arid Environments, 86*, 28–42.
Chang, C. (1992). Archaeological landscapes: The ethnoarchaeology of pastoral land use in the Grevena province of northern Greece. In J. Rossignol & L. Wandsnider (Eds.), *Space, time, and archaeological landscapes* (pp. 65–89). Plenum Press.
Chang, C., & Koster, H. A. (1986). Towards an archaeology of pastoralism. *Advances in Archaeological Method and Theory, 9*, 97–148.
Conder, C. R., & Kitchener, H. H. (1883). *The survey of western Palestine. Memoirs of the topography, orography, hydrography, and archaeology. Vol. III: Sheets XVII-XXVI, Judaea*. Palestine Exploration Fund.

Cross, F. M. (1956). A footnote to biblical history. *The Biblical Archaeologist, 19*(1), 12–17.
Cross, F. M. (1993). El-Buqei'a. In E. Stern (Ed.), *New encyclopedia of archaeological excavations in the Holy Land* (Vol. I, pp. 267–269). Israel Exploration Society.
Cross, F. M. (1997). *Canaanite myth and Hebrew epic. Essays in the history of the religion of Israel* (9th ed.). Harvard University Press.
Cross, F. M., & Milik, J. F. (1956). Explorations in the Judaean Buqe'ah. *Bulletin of the American Schools of Oriental Research, 142*, 5–17.
Cross, F. M., & Wright, G. E. (1956). The boundary and province lists of the kingdom of Judah. *Journal of Biblical Literature, 75*(3), 202–226.
de Vaux, R. (1973). *Archaeology and the Dead Sea scrolls*. The Schweich Lectures 1959. (revised ed.). Oxford University Press.
Degen, A. A. (2007). Sheep and goat milk in pastoral societies. *Small Ruminant Research, 68*, 7–19.
Dorsey, D. A. (1991). *The roads and highways of ancient Israel*. The John Hopkins University Press.
Eitan, A. (1983). Vered Jericho. *Excavations and Surveys in Israel, 2*, 106–107.
Faust, A. (2008). Settlement and demography in seventh-century Judah and the extent and intensity of Sennacherib's campaign. *Palestine Exploration Quarterly, 140*(3), 168–194.
Faust, A. (2017). The bounded landscape: Archaeology, language, texts, and the Israelite perception of space. *Journal of Mediterranean Archaeology, 30*(1), 3–32.
Faust, A., & Weiss, E. (2005). Judah, Philistia, and the Mediterranean world: Reconstructing the economic system of the seventh century B.C.E. *Bulletin of the American Schools of Oriental Research, 338*, 71–92.
Faust, A., & Weiss, E. (2011). Between Assyria and the Mediterranean world: The prosperity of Judah and Philistia in the seventh century BCE in context. In T. C. Wilkinson, S. Sherratt, & J. Bennet (Eds.), *Interweaving worlds. Systemic interactions in Eurasia, 7th to 1st millennia BC* (pp. 189–204). Oxbow.
Gibson, S., & Taylor, J. (2008). Roads and passes round Qumran. *Palestine Exploration Quarterly, 140*, 225–227.
Gitin, S. (2015). Iron Age IIC: Judah. In S. Gitin (Ed.), *The ancient Pottery of Israel and its neighbors from the Iron Age through the Hellenistic period* (Vol. 1, pp. 345–364). Israel Exploration Society.
Grossman, D. (1992). *Rural process-pattern relationships. Nomadization, sedentarization, and settlement fixation*. Praeger.
Haiman, M. (1989). *Herders and farmers in the Kadesh Barnea region*. Society for the Protection of Nature (Hebrew)..
Haiman, M. (1994). The Iron Age II sites of the western Negev highlands. *Israel Exploration Journal, 44*(1), 36–61.
Herr, L. G. (1999). The Ammonites in the late Iron Age and Persian period. In B. MacDonald & R. W. Younker (Eds.), *Ancient Ammon* (pp. 219–237). Brill.
Horowitz, L. H., Tchernov, E., & Lernau, O. (2018). The archaeozoology of Vered Yericho, an Iron Age II fortified structure in the kingdom of Judah. In I. Shai, J. R. Chadwick, L. Hitchcock, A. Dagan, C. McKinny, & J. Uziel (Eds.), *Studies in the history and archaeology of Israel. Essays in honor of Aren M. Maier on the occasion of his sixtieth birthday* (pp. 966–1007). Zaphon.
Hutson, G. D. (1984). Spacing behaviour of sheep in pens. *Applied Animal Behaviour Science, 12*(1–2), 111–119.
Kardulias, P. N. (2015). Introduction: Pastoralism as an adaptive strategy. In P. N. Kardulias (Ed.), *The ecology of pastoralism*. University of Colorado.
King, P. J. (1988). *Amos, Hosea, Micah – An archaeological commentary*. Westminster Press.
LaBianca, Ø. S. (1990). *Sedentarization and nomadization. Food system cycles at Hesban and vicinity in Transjordan* (Hesban 1). Andrews University Press.
Legge, A. J. (2004). Margins and marginality. In M. Mondini, S. Munoz, & S. Wickler (Eds.), *Colonisation, migration, and marginal areas* (pp. 118–120). Oxbow.
Levy, T. E. (1983). The emergence of specialized pastoralism in the southern Levant. *World Archaeology, 15*(1), 15–36.

Lipschits, O. (2012). Archaeological facts, historical speculations and the date of the lmlk storage jars: A rejoinder to David Ussishkin. *Journal of Hebrew Scriptures, 12*(4).

Lipschits, O., Sergi, O., & Koch, I. (2010). Royal Judahite jar handles: Reconsidering the chronology of *lmlk* stamp impressions. *Tel Aviv, 37*, 3–32.

Lipschits, O., Sergi, O., & Koch, I. (2011). Judahite stamped and incised jar handles: A tool for studying the history of late monarchic Judah. *Tel Aviv, 38*, 5–41.

Magen, Y., & Peleg, Y. (2018). *Back to Qumran: final report (1993–2004)* (Judea and Samaria Publications 18). Israel Antiquities Authority.

Marx, E. (1992). Are there pastoral nomads in the Middle East? In O. Bar-Yosef & A. Khazanov (Eds.), *Pastoralism in the Levant: Archaeological materials in anthropological perspectives* (Monographs in world archaeology no. 10) (pp. 255–260). Madison.

Master, D. (2009). From the Buqê'ah to Ashkelon. In J. D. Schloen (Ed.), *Exploring the longue durée. Essays in honor of Lawrence E. Stager* (pp. 305–317). Eisenbrauns.

Masterman, E. W. G. (1903). Notes on some ruins and a rock-cut aqueduct in the Wady Kumran. *Palestine Exploration Fund's Quarterly Statement, 35*(3), 264–267.

Mazar, A., Amit, D., & Ilan, Z. (1995). Hurvat Shilhah: An Iron Age site in the Judean desert. In J. Seger (Ed.), *Retrieving the past: Research and methodology in honour of Gus Van Beek* (pp. 193–211). Cobb Institute of Archaeology.

Meadow, R. H. (1992). Inconclusive remarks on pastoralism, nomadism, and other animal-related matters. In O. Bar-Yosef & A. Khazanov (Eds.), *Pastoralism in the Levant: Archaeological materials in anthropological perspectives* (Monographs in world archaeology no. 10) (pp. 261–269). Madison.

Morin, E., Jacoby, Y., Navon, S., & Bet-Halachmi, E. (2009). Towards flash-flood prediction in the dry Dead Sea region utilizing radar rainfall information. *Advances in Water Resources, 32*, 1066–1076.

Moritz, M., Giblin, J., Ciconne, M., Davis, A., Fuhrman, J., Kimiaie, M., Madzsar, S., Olson, K., & Senn, M. (2011). Social risk-management strategies in pastoral systems: A qualitative comparative analysis. *Cross Cultural Research, 45*(3), 286–317.

Na'aman, N. (1991). The Kingdom of Judah under Josiah. *Tel Aviv, 18*, 3–72.

Na'aman, N. (2014). Dismissing the myth of a flood of Israelite refugees in the late eighth century BCE. *Zeitschrift für die alttestamentliche Wissenschaft, 126*(1), 1–14.

Nevo, Y. D. (1991). *Pagans and herders. A re-examination of the Negev run-off cultivation systems in the byzantine and early Arab periods*. IPS.

Noth, M. (1955). Das deutsche evangelische institut für altertumswissenschaft des heiligen landes, Lehrkursus 1954. *Zeitschrift des Deutschen Palästina-Vereins, 71*, 42–55.

Oweis, T. Y. (2017). Rainwater harvesting for restoring degraded dry agro-pastoral ecosystems: A conceptual review of opportunities and constraints in a changing climate. *Environmental Reviews, 25*, 135–149.

Patrich, J. (1994). *Archaeological survey in Judea and Samaria. Map of Deir Mar Saba (109/7)*. Israel Antiquities Authority (Hebrew, with an English summary on the sites).

Penning, P. D., Parsons, A. J., Newman, J. A., Orr, R. J., & Harvey, A. (1993). The effects of group size on grazing time in sheep. *Applied Animal Behaviour Science, 37*(2), 101–109.

Perevolotsky, A., Perevolotsky, A., & Noy-Meir, I. (1989). Environmental adaptation and economic change in a pastoral mountain society: The case of the Jabaliyah bedouin of the Mt. Sinai region. *Mountain Research and Development, 9*(2), 159–164.

Redding, W. R. (1984). Theoretical determinants of a herder's decisions: Modelling variation in the sheep/goat ratio. In J. Clutton-Brock & C. Grigson (Eds.), *Animals and archaeology* (BAR International Series 202) (pp. 223–241). Archaeopress.

Rosen, S. A. (1993). A Roman-period pastoral tent camp in the Negev, Israel. *Journal of Field Archaeology, 20*(4), 441–451.

Rosen, S. A. (2009). History does not repeat itself: Cyclicity and particularism in nomad-sedentary relations in the Negev in the long term. In J. Szuchman (Ed.), *Nomads, tribes, and the state in the ancient Near East: Cross-disciplinary perspectives* (pp. 57–86). Oriental Institute University of Chicago.

Sasson, A. (1998). The pastoral component in the economy of hill country sites in the Intermediate Bronze and Iron Ages: Archaeo-ethnographic case studies. *Tel Aviv, 25*(1), 3–51.

Sasson, A., & Greenfield, H. J. (2014). The second revolution of secondary products: Do mortality profiles reflect herd management or specialised production? In J. H. Greenfield (Ed.), *Animal secondary products* (pp. 206–218). Oxbow.

Savage, S. H., Johnson, A., & Levy, T. E. (2017). TerraWatchers, crowdsourcing, and at-risk world heritage in the Middle East. In M. Vincent, V. B. López-Menchero, M. Ioannides, & T. Levy (Eds.), *Heritage and archaeology in the digital age. Quantitative methods in the humanities and social sciences*. Springer.

Schulz, S. (1960). Chirbet kumran, 'en feshcha und die Buke'a: Zugleich ein archäolodischer Beitrag zum Felsenaquädukt und zur Strasse durch das Wadi Kumran. *Zeitschrift des Deutschen Palästina-Vereins, 76*, 50–72.

Shahack-Gross, R., & Finkelstein, I. (2015). Settlement oscillations in the Negev highlands revisited: The impact of microarchaeological methods. *Radiocarbon, 57*(2), 253–264.

Sion, O. (n.d.). *The map of Kalia*. Archaeological Survey of Israel/Israel Antiquities Authority. http://www.antiquities.org.il/survey/newmap_en. Accessed on 29 Oct 2019.

Stager, L. E. (1974). Chronique archéologique: El-Bouqei'ah. *Revue Biblique, 81*, 94–96.

Stager, L. E. (1975). *Ancient agriculture in the Judaean desert: A case study in the Buqe'ah valley in the Iron Age*. Ph.D. thesis, Harvard University.

Stager, L. E. (1976). Farming in the Judean desert during the Iron Age. *Bulletin of the American Schools of Oriental Research, 221*, 145–158.

Stavi, I., Kressel, G., Gutterman, Y., & Degen, A. A. (2006). Flock use among bedouin in 'spontaneous' settlements in the Negev desert, southern Israel. *Nomadic Peoples, 10*, 53–69.

Stern, E. (1994). The eastern border of the kingdom of Judah in its last days. In M. D. Coogan, J. C. Exum, & L. E. Stager (Eds.), *Scripture and other artifacts. Essays on the Bible and archaeology in honor of Philip J. King* (pp. 399–409). John Knox Press.

Taylor, J. E. (2006). Kh. Qumran in period III. In K. Galor, J.-B. Humbert, & J. Zangenberg (Eds.), *Qumran, the site of the Dead Sea scrolls: Archaeological interpretations and debates* (pp. 133–146). Brill.

Taylor, J. E., & Gibson, S. (2011). Qumran connected: The paths and passes of the North-Western dead sea. In J. Frey & C. Claussen (Eds.), *Qumran und Archäologie – Wechselseitige Perspektiven* (pp. 1–51). Mohr Siebeck.

Taylor, J. E., & Gibson, S. (2020). Qumran in the Iron Age in comparison with the Hasmonean to Early Roman periods: A cross-temporal study. In J. Ebeling & P. Guillaume (Eds.), *The woman in the pith helmet: A tribute to archaeologist Norma Franklin* (pp. 177–224). Lockwood Press.

Ussishkin, D. (2011). The dating of the *lmlk* storage jars and its implications: Rejoinder to Lipschits, Sergi and Koch. *Tel Aviv, 38*, 220–240.

Vaughn, A. G. (1999). *Theology, history and archaeology in the chronicler's account of Hezekiah*. Society of Biblical Literature.

Yekutieli, Y. (2006). Is someone watching you? Ancient surveillance systems in the southern Judean desert. *Journal of Mediterranean Archaeology, 19*(1), 65–89.

Yezerski, I. (2018). Iron Age III pottery vessels from the renewed excavations in Qumran. In Y. Magen & Y. Peleg (Eds.), *Back to Qumran: final report (1993–2004)* (Judea and Samaria Publications 18) (pp. 179–338). Israel Antiquities Authority.

Recognizing Ceramic Traditions: Moabite Painted and Decorated Wares

P. M. Michèle Daviau

Abstract The discovery of painted pottery at Khirbat al-Mudayna (Thamad) by Nelson Glueck and his publication of these sherds as Moabite painted ware set the stage for future research. Although several styles were apparent in his assemblage, it was not clear if all or only some of these sherds were locally produced. The recovery of a rich assemblage of pottery from excavation of town sites in Edom by C.-M. Bennett during the years 1960–1980 revealed a Transjordanian painted repertoire that was distinct from Glueck's Moabite sherds. More recent excavation of Iron Age sites in northern and central Moab has now yielded a rich repertoire of pottery providing the basis for recognizing locally produced pottery and distinguishing it from Ammonite and Edomite styles as well as from imported wares. This study, in honour of and appreciation for the contribution of Thomas E. Levy to the archaeology of Jordan, presents a description of the dominant styles of Iron Age II decorated pottery at Mudayna Thamad as well as the criteria for distinguishing several related potting traditions reflected in the various styles of regional and imported decorated wares.

Keywords Moab · Red slip · Technology · Imports · Cypro-Phoenician · Workshop

1 Introduction

In 1932, Nelson Glueck began his historic survey of Eastern Palestine, identifying more than 1000 sites. Starting in Mafraq in the north during the winter and surveying the Eastern Desert as far as Kilwa, he initiated a subsequent survey in the spring of 1933 from ʿAmman to Wadi ath-Thamad (Fig. 1a), where he visited sites

P. M. M. Daviau (✉)
Wilfrid Laurier University, Waterloo, ON, Canada
e-mail: micheledaviaudion@yahoo.ca

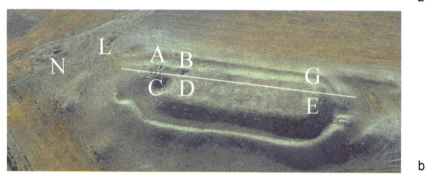

Fig. 1 (**a**) Central Transjordan and Palestine during Iron Age II; (**b**) mound of Khirbat al-Mudayna Thamad with excavation areas

previously identified by travelers in the late nineteenth and early twentieth centuries.[1] A unique aspect of his survey work involved the collection and study of pottery sherds from the surface in order to determine the settlement history of each site. Khirbet el-Medeiyineh on Wadi eth-Themed, now spelled Khirbat al-Mudayna, was Glueck's site 68. In his report, there remains a certain amount of confusion regarding the pottery attributed to "Khirbet el-Medeiyineh" because there are six sites with this name in Jordan (Miller, 1989). However, his reference to the dump on the eastern slope of the mound does point to Mudayna Thamad as the source of much of the painted pottery in his report, since this dump is still a source of ceramic sherds and discarded artefacts.[2] In fact, Glueck (1934, 15) says explicitly that the sherds he describes in his report come from el-Mudeiyineh on Wadi Themed unless otherwise specified.[3]

Glueck identified the decorated sherds he collected from the east dump at Mudayna Thamad as Moabite pottery similar to those first identified by Albright at Karak (1924, 10–11). Along with a juglet "related to" the Cypro-Phoenician style (Glueck, 1934, 14; fig. 5), Glueck chose to highlight red slipped and polished sherds and those with bands of "slip" bordered with dark narrow bands. Indeed, these are the types of sherds one notices on the dump because they stand out against the ash-stained windblown soil. Given their distribution at a number of sites both north and south of Wadi Mujib (Arnon), Glueck identified these sherds as Moabite ware.[4] However, it is not now possible to examine these sherds to evaluate the composition of the fabric and the paint colours[5] for comparison with pottery found during more recent survey on the Karak plateau and in excavation at Baluʿ (Worschech, 2014), the largest Iron Age II site south of Wadi Mujib. Ceramic assemblages from excavation at contemporary sites on the Dhiban plateau closer to Mudayna Thamad include those from Dibon (Winnett & Reed, 1964; Tushingham, 1972), ʿAroʿer (Olávarri, 1965, 1969), Lahun (Steiner, 2013) and WT-13 (Daviau, 2017; Steiner, 2017). Smaller assemblages have been published from ar-Rumayl (WT-18; Daviau, 2017) and tomb WT-200 (Chadwick, 2017). Other excavated sites in the region are in the initial phases of publication, such as Tall Madaba (Harrison et al. 2003) and ʾAtarus (Ji, 2011, 2012), as well as surface survey collections from the Dhiban plateau (Ji & Lee, 1998, 2000), and from survey at Libb and Zarqa Maʿin north of the Wadi Thamad. Now, after 14 seasons of excavation at Mudayna Thamad, ceramic

---

[1] Previous visitors who identified Khirbat al-Mudayna on Wadi Thamad include Tristram in 1873 (1874), Brünnow and von Domaszewski in 1897 and 1898 (1904–1905), and Musil in 1896 (1907).

[2] A final count from the 1995 Wadi Thamad Project surface survey at Mudayna Thamad numbered 2830 sherds collected in 32 pottery pails at various points on and around the site, including the eastern dump.

[3] *pace* Brown (1991, 202) who attributed these sherds to Khirbat al-Mudayna Muʿarradjeh, south of Wadi Mujib, although subsequent excavation did not yield any notable painted sherds (Olávarri, 1977–1978, fig. 2; 1983, fig. 6).

[4] As was typical of the time, Glueck's ceramic identification assigned an early Iron I through early Iron II date to these sherds (1934, 14).

[5] The pottery from Glueck's survey was located for a time at The Nelson Glueck School of Biblical Archaeology; however, its current location is not confirmed (E. van der Steen, personal communication).

analysis has begun to reveal the complexity of the ceramic corpus and the various local, regional and foreign sources of the repertoire.

This study presents an initial description of the dominant local wares and their painted motifs as well as criteria for distinguishing pottery produced in various workshops in the region. An attempt is also made here to identify imported pottery, although the actual production centres of these wares may be difficult to locate at this time. A second task of creating appropriate terminology that can be applied by scholars working in the region to clarify the differences between pottery found in Moab and pottery made in various workshops throughout Moab and the surrounding area, and more broadly at other Levantine centres, will follow additional analysis in future.[6]

The site of Mudayna Thamad is located at the northeastern extremity of what we consider to be the Iron Age kingdom of Moab, south of the Ammonite site of Jalul and on the fringe of the desert. The mound is small, less that one hectare, hidden from view below the surrounding hills but was well fortified with an Iron Age chambered gate and casemate fortification system (Fig. 1a, b). Inside the walls were houses, industrial and administrative buildings, and a small temple (Daviau & Steiner, 2000). Outside the gate was a series of stone-lined silos filled with broken pottery and fragments of clay ovens adjacent to a small plaza with standing stones. It was here in the silos and in all the buildings excavated to date inside the town that Iron Age II painted pottery was found.

2 The Ceramic Corpus

2.1 Plain Wares at Mudayna Thamad

An initial observation of the various vessel types, forms, fabrics, firing techniques and surface treatments in the Mudyana Thamad ceramic repertoire immediately highlighted the contrast with the better-known Ammonite pottery at ʿAmman, Tall ʿUmayri, Tall Jawa, Saḥab and Tall Ḥisban.[7] For example, vessels with red slip at Mudayna Thamad constitute 5.1% out of 6103 colour-coded registered sherds,[8] a degree of occurrence that stands in stark contrast to the Ammonite site of Tall Jawa (Daviau, 2020), where red slip equals 19.3% of 15,871 coded sherds.[9] Given these

---

[6] This study is made possible by the generous grant by the Department of Antiquities of Jordan to the Department of Archaeology and Heritage Studies of Wilfrid Laurier University, Waterloo, ON, Canada, of the broken pottery from each excavation season and by the initial research of Margreet L. Steiner and Loe Jacobs at the Ceramic Laboratory of the University of Leiden (Steiner, 2009).

[7] Final reports with parallels to earlier publications include Daviau 2020 and Herr 2012.

[8] Altogether there are more than 19,000 diagnostics, including mends, and nearly 100.000 total sherds.

[9] In both assemblages, mended sherds with individual registration numbers were not counted individually; only the sherd with the lowest registration number is considered as the representative of a mended vessel.

data, it appears that slipped and painted pottery was not common at Mudayna Thamad, although this was the type of pottery highlighted by Glueck in his 1934 publication. This study begins with a brief introduction to certain plain wares for comparison with painted wares and then continues with various styles of painted and decorated vessels; in the catalogues accompanying each illustration, only a small sample of the most distinctive styles of decoration are described and illustrated.

While vessel type may be directly related to daily domestic activities, certain special functions, or the specific nature of a given site, enough of the full range of ceramic wares is represented at Mudayna Thamad to recognize the unique features of the assemblage. Notable by their frequency in the assemblage are plain ware kraters with two or four handles (Fig. 2:1–3), jugs, various styles of storejar, amphorae, bottles and utilitarian basins. Deep kraters with an incurving thickened or triangular rim served as utilitarian vessels that were not chosen for ornamentation, although smaller, handleless kraters are among the painted wares.

Catalogue[10]

P2004 (Fig. 2:1; B1/37.4). Krater, rim to base, rim D 26.5, H 27.5 cm; light reddish brown (2.5YR 7/4) fabric, light red (10R 6/6) exterior.

P3005 (Fig. 2:2; D42/23.1). Krater, rim to base; rim D 28.0, H *ca.* 31.0 cm; very pale brown (10YR 7/3) fabric, very pale brown (10YR 8/3) exterior; broken.

P4045 (Fig. 2:3; G9/44.9). Krater, rim to base; rim D 37.0, H 37.5 cm; reddish yellow (5YR 6/6) fabric, very pale brown (10YR 8/2) slip(?); MT 3676.

P3046 (Fig. 2:4; D82/42.5). Tall jug, rim to base, rim D 5.0, H 35.0 cm; very pale brown (10YR 8/2) fabric and exterior; broken.

P1134 (Fig. 2:5; C96/129.1). Jug, rim to base; rim D 8.0, H 26.6 cm; grayish brown (10YR 5/2) exterior; complete; MT 3505

P3035 (Fig. 2:6; D71/23.1). Jug, rim to base; rim D 5.5, H 28.0 cm; pink (5YR 7/4) fabric, very pale brown (10YR 8/2) exterior; broken.

P3004 (Fig. 2:7; D42/16.1). Amphora, rim to base; rim D 6.0, H 38.0 cm; light reddish brown (2.5YR 6/4) fabric and exterior; broken.

P2003 (Fig. 2:8; B1/39.9). Storejar, 3 handles; rim D 5.7, H 48.5 cm; light red (2.5YR 6/6) fabric, very pale brown (10YR 8/2) slip; colour variable; broken.

P140 (Fig. 2:9; C94/11.2). Storejar, 4 handles; rim D 8.0, H 52.0 cm; pink (5YR 7/4) fabric, very pale brown (10YR 8/2) exterior, white wash; broken.

Greater variety is seen in the fabric of amphorae and storejars (Fig. 2:7–9) but that is to be expected since these jars with their contents may have come to Mudayna from neighboring sites or through long distance trade. At the same time, 3-handled and 4-handled bag-shaped jars appear to be characteristic of Moabite assemblages. Storejars also have greater longevity than vessels used daily, such as bowls and

---

[10] Each sherd is registered with its Field+Square/pottery pail · sherd number (A4/35·2); mended sherds and restored or complete vessels also receive a pot number (P136); those retained by the Department of Antiquities also received an object number. Diameter records the interior measurement of the rim/opening.

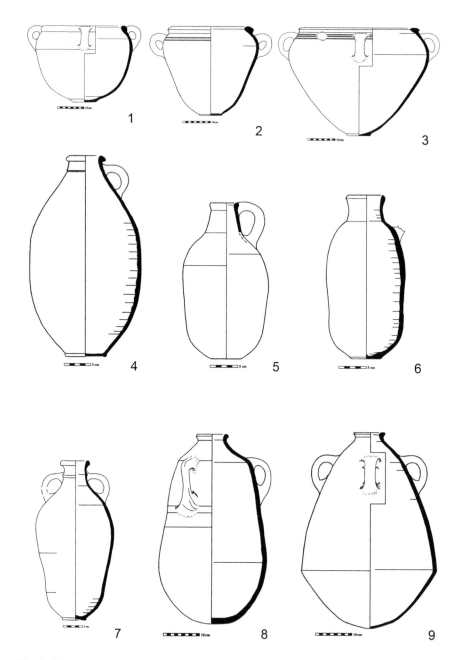

Fig. 2 Plain Wares: kraters, (*1*) P2004; (*2*) P3005; (*3*) P4045; jugs, (*4*) P3046; (*5*) P1134; (*6*) P3035; amphora, (*7*) P3004; storejars, (*8*) P2003; (*9*) P140

cooking pots, adding to the diversity in certain long-lived forms. At Mudayna Thamad, it is among unslipped jugs and kraters that we find painted wares that suggest a local workshop for vessels in these two classes. The second largest group consists of small painted bowls, which are quite distinct in fabric composition.

2.2 Unslipped Painted Wares

The careful work of mending broken vessels is a significant component of our research on painted vessels because several forms, especially among jugs and juglets, were not painted on the rim and neck but only on the body.[11] All painted body sherds were registered and kept for future study and possible restoration, even if only enough sherds could be mended to identify the type of vessel. Mending greatly facilitated our ability to identify painted vessels and their decorative styles; this was certainly the case where a number of sherds could be assigned to a single vessel, P3022.

2.2.1 Jugs

The corpus of jugs shows variety in decorative style from broad painted bands on an unslipped surface to slipped, burnished and carefully painted jugs and amphoriskoi. The unslipped painted jugs are medium size vessels, 20–30 cm in height, and the dominant shape is cylindrical with a thickened rim and round or low ring base. Typically, these unslipped jugs are thick-walled, fully oxidized vessels with calcite inclusions. Beginning with the simplest style of broad bands on the shoulder and body, variation occurs in the use of red paint alternating with a band of white wash (Fig. 3:1, 2).

A more elaborate design is found on certain jugs with red and white painted bands framed by narrow black or dark reddish brown bands (Fig. 3:3, 4). Only on rare occasions is there a red band on the rim (Fig. 3:5). More complex is the design consisting of reddish brown horizontal bands separated by one or even two broad white bands, each with four dark narrow bands under the white wash (P4016). The technique of covering the dark bands with white wash was a feature already noted by Glueck (1934, 15).

Catalogue

P3037   (Fig. 3.1; D82/44.4). Rim to base; light reddish brown (2.5YR 6/4) fabric, pink (5YR 7/4) exterior; dark red (2.5YR 3/6) paint.

---

[11] I am deeply grateful to Heather-Jane Maurice, who has diligently mended innumerable vessels through the difficult years of the 2019 pandemic and Marianne Kraft who prepared the colour codes.

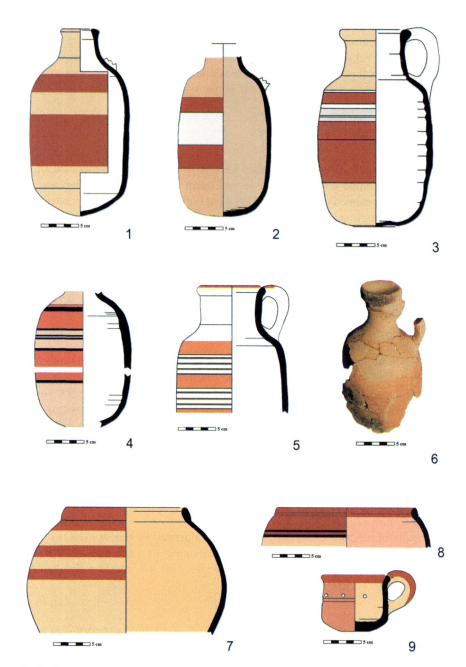

Fig. 3 Simple painted wares: jugs, (*1*) P3037; (*2*) P4044; (*3*) P4041; (*4*) P3022; (*5*) P4016; (*6*) P4012; kraters, (*7*) P134; (*8*) C94/68.12; cup, (*9*) P1091

P4044 (Fig. 3.2; E99/77.2). Neck to base; pink (5YR 7/4) fabric and exterior, dark gray (5YR 4/1) and red (10R 4/6) paint, white (2.5YR 8/1) wash; broken.

P4041 (Fig. 3.3; E97/27.1). Rim to base; light red (2.5YR 6/8) fabric and exterior; dark gray (5YR 4/1) and red (2.5YR 5/8) paint, white (10YR 8/1) wash; broken.

P3022 (Fig. 3.4; D81/74.1). Shoulder to base; pinkish white (7.5YR 8/2) fabric, dark gray (5YR 4/1) and red (10R 5/6) paint; broken.

P4016 (Fig. 3.5; E89/45.3). Rim to lower body; very pale brown (10YR 7/3) fabric and exterior; very dark gray (N 3/), red (2.5YR 5/6) paint, pinkish white (7.5YR 7/2) wash; broken.

P1107 (Not shown; C96/22.1) Body; light reddish brown (5YR 6/4) fabric, yellowish red (5YR 5/6) slip, white (7.5YR 8.5/) wash, dark gray (7.5YR 4/1) paint; sherds.

P4012 (Fig. 3.6; E78/63.1). Rim+body, neck ridge; reddish yellow (5YR 7/6) fabric, red (2.5YR 5/8) paint; broken.

Parallels

The unslipped and unburnished painted wares in the classes of jugs described above appear to share the same fabric composition as the plain wares. In the large corpus of jugs, the shape of the painted jugs is consistently cylindrical, whereas the shape of unpainted jugs is more varied; ovoid, globular, piriform, and decanter style, several of which are elongated and not yet seen in the repertoires of other sites in central Jordan. Jug P4012 appears to be from another potting tradition with features more common on unpainted decanters; this vessel has a rectangular rim, a neck ridge and a large area of the body painted in an irregular band, while the rim, neck, handle and most of the shoulder remains unpainted (Fig. 3.6). Among jugs of this style, the handle springs from the neck ridge instead of from the rim.

2.2.2 Kraters

While jugs are dominant among painted wares, other vessel forms include small to medium size handleless kraters and a perforated cup. Among piriform kraters with a thickened rim and broad shoulder are two decorative styles, the simplest of which consists of broad red bands on the rim and shoulder, usually ending at midbody (P134; Fig. 3.7), while the second style also has broad red to reddish brown bands along with narrow bands in dark brown or gray paint (Fig. 3:8), closer in style to the decoration on small bowls.

Catalogue

P134 (Fig. 3:7; A4/119.4). Krater; very pale brown (10YR 7/3) fabric and exterior, red (2.5YR 5/6) paint.

C94/68.12 (Fig. 3:8). Rim; pink (5YR 7/4 and 7.5YR 8/3) fabric and exterior, red (10R 5/6) and black (2.5Y 2.5/1) paint.

P1091 (Fig. 3:9; A28/38.1). Cup; reddish yellow (5YR 7/6) fabric and exterior, red (10R 5/8) paint.

Parallels

Painted kraters have parallels in the region, principally at Dibon (Tushingham, 1972, figs. 22:11, 13; 24:26), Tomb WT-200 (Chadwick, 2017, fig. 3.4:4–5), Madaba Tomb B (Piccirillo, 1975, pl. II:10, fig. II:3) and Tomb 20 at Nebo, which yielded a number of handleless kraters with painted bands and other designs including a band of net pattern along with one vessel decorated with diagonal pendant lines (Saller, 1966, figs. 24:14–23, 26:1, 2, 44, 5). Although the handleless painted krater is found at sites in Ammon (Daviau, 2020: fig. 4.13:1–8) and at WT-200 (Chadwick, 2017, fig. 3.4:6), these are red slipped and burnished and painted on the shoulder and rim.

2.2.3 Cups

Cup P1091 is distinct from the well-known undecorated tripod footed cups with multiple rows of perforations seen in Moab at WT-13 and Dibon, as well as at sites throughout Palestine and Transjordan (Daviau, 2017, fig. 7.1). One thick-walled painted cup from Mudayna Thamad has a flat base, a single row of perforations and red paint on the rim and handle (Fig. 3:9; see above).

2.2.4 Variant Painted Designs

While the vessels discussed above all appear to be the product of a single workshop or decorative tradition, one amphoriskos and two kraters are unique in their surface treatment and or fabric composition. Amphoriskos P132 has a porous fabric with heavy calcite inclusions, is covered with a light-colored slip and painted with dark bands on the shoulder and midbody (Fig. 4.1). The design consists of a register of narrow bands flanked by slightly broader bands, as seen on Cypriot barrel flasks and on Ammonite white slipped amphorae, jugs and juglets. In contrast to the vessels at Tall Jawa to the northeast of the Madaba Plain (Daviau, 2013, fig. 3), P132 has unpainted strap handles rather than loop handles decorated with horizontal strokes, a surface treatment seen at Ammonite, Israelite and Syrian sites (Daviau, 2013), but rarely in Moab.

Among the kraters are sherds made of a compact crisp ware, a fabric that is rare among kraters but with the typical design of broad painted bands flanked by narrow dark borders (Fig. 4.2). One vessel with a porous fabric, thin reddish slip in patches on the surface and an unusual design is the largest example of a painted krater (Fig. 4:3). Immediately below the rim is a dark gray band with a second band lower on the shoulder. Between these bands is a series of diagonal lines, each one begins at the upper band and extends to or slightly beyond the lower horizontal band, possibly representing streamers or tassels while forming a pattern of triangles.

Recognizing Ceramic Traditions: Moabite Painted and Decorated Wares 909

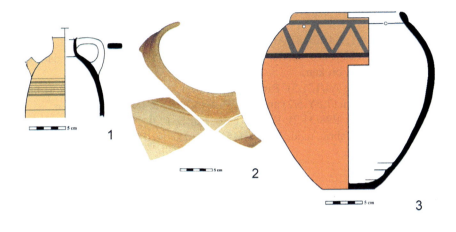

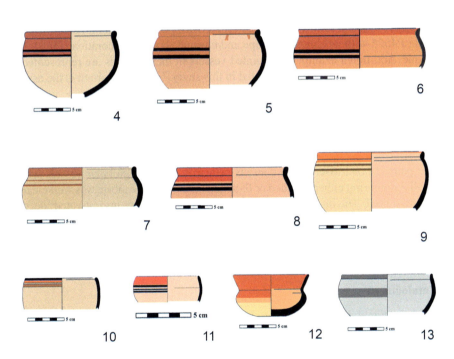

Fig. 4 Unique wares: white slipped amphoriskos, (*1*) P132, crisp ware krater, (*2*) P107; oversize krater, (*3*) P4055; painted bowls, (*4*) P124, (*5*) P123, (*6*), P125, (*7*) P126, (*8*) C93:30.9; (*9*) P1037; miniature bowls, (*10*) C93/29.1; (*11*) C93/20.2; (*12*) P3087; (*13*) A25/24.4

Catalogue

P132   (Fig. 4:1; A4/124.8). Amphoriskos; body and handles; body D *ca.* 11.0 cm; reddish yellow (5YR 6/6) fabric, very pale brown (10YR 8/2) slip, very dark gray (7.5YR 3/1) paint; broken.

P107   (Fig. 4:2; A4/121.5). Rim+shoulder; very pale brown (10YR 8/3) fabric and exterior, brown (7.5Y 5/2) and reddish brown (5YR 4/4) paint; broken.

P4055   (Fig. 4:3: E98/35.2). Rim to base; rim D 14.0, H 23.5 cm; light reddish brown (5YR 6/4) fabric, reddish brown (5YR 5/4) and red (10R 5/6) slip/wash; dark gray paint; broken.

Parallels

For these vessels, there are no parallels within the Mudayna corpus processed as of 2021. The single white slipped and painted amphoriskos (Fig. 4:1) appears to be unique but its surface treatment does have parallels at Tall Jawa and sites to the north and west of Ammon (Daviau, 2013). Although distinct in this assemblage, Krater P107 with its crisp fabric and precise painted bands (Fig. 4:2) is comparable to a vessel found at Jalul 5 km to the north (Rivas, personal communication), while krater P4055 with its elongated shape and unusual shoulder decoration (Fig. 4:3) is unique. Additional examples of painted vessels in these classes are represented in the sherd material but are not included in this study.[12] More important is the assemblage of small painted bowls.

2.2.5 Small Bowls

The painted bowl assemblage consists primarily of small globular vessels with a small upright rim, either rounded or flattened on the lip. The fabric was well cleaned and hard fired. The interior was carefully smoothed but remains untreated; decoration occurs on the exterior and interior of the rim and on the upper body. It consists of a broad painted band, either with narrow bands of the same colour (Fig. 4:7) on the upper body or with dark narrow bands on the painted band itself (Fig. 4:4–6) or immediately below it (Fig. 4:8, 9).

Catalogue

P124   (Fig. 4:4; C93/11.2). Rim D 14.0 cm; very pale brown (10YR 8/2) fabric and exterior, red (2.5YR 5/6) paint, black (5YR 2.5/1) bands.

P123   (Fig. 4:5; C93/8.8). Rim D 13.0 cm; light gray (10YR 7/2) fabric and exterior, reddish yellow (5YR 6/6) paint, dark gray (10YR 4/1) bands.

P125   (Fig. 4:6; C93/22.5). Rim D 16.0 cm; light brown (7.5YR 6/4) fabric and exterior, red (10R 5/8) paint, very dark gray (5YR 3/1) bands.

P126   (Fig. 4:7; C93/15.20). Rim D 14.5 cm; very pale brown (10YR 8/2) fabric, light gray (10YR 7/1) exterior, brown (7.5YR 5/2) paint.

---

[12] Each sherd is classified, typed and colour coded in the database designated for its excavation field; these databases will be available online when documentation is complete.

C93/30.9   (Fig. 4:8). Rim D 14.0; pink (5YR 7/4) fabric and exterior, light red (10YR 6/6) paint, dark gray (N 4/) bands.
P1037   (Fig. 4:9; A25/59.1). Rim D 14.0 cm; pink (7.5YR 7/4) fabric and exterior, red (10R 5/8) paint, reddish brown (5YR 5/4) bands.

Parallels
The small painted bowls are restricted to a common form, round bodied with small upright or slightly flaring rim (Fig. 4:4–9). The clay used to make the vessels in this assemblage was distinct from that in thick-walled plain ware bowls and was somewhat granular in texture. These bowls have some features in common with the small hemispherical painted bowl at Tyre (Bikai, 1978, pl. 1:4) and with the red slipped hemispherical bowls with black bands at Busayra (Bienkowski, 2002: fig. 9.23:2, 3). Small bowls with a small upright rim and narrow painted bands on the outer surface of the rim itself and at midbody were also found at Rumj Hamra Ifdan (Smith & Levy, 2014, fig. 4.27:2; 29:5) and at Tawilan in Edom (Bienkowski, 1995, fig. 6.8:1, 2, 4).

2.2.6   Very Small and Miniature Bowls

Two miniature hemispherical bowls (Fig. 4:10, 11), each with a simple rim, are similar to the painted tradition of the larger bowls. One of these very small bowls is carinated in shape, with a tall rim and paint or slip on the upper body and rim (Fig. 4:12). A fourth example is a small bowl with a hemispherical body and a cyma-shaped rim that is distinct in its fabric composition and colouring (Fig. 4:11). The only decoration is dark gray bands on a light gray granular surface that is rough to the touch.

Catalogue

C93/29.1   (Fig. 4:10). Miniature; very pare brown (10YR 7/3) fabric and exterior, yellowish red (5YR 5/8) and very dark gray (N 3/) bands.
C93/20.2   (Fig. 4:11). Miniature bowl; pink (7.5YR 7/4) fabric, very pale brown (10YR 8/3) exterior, red (2.5YR 5/8) paint. Dark gray (2.5YR 4/1) bands.
P3087   (Fig. 4:12; D51/45.3). Miniature bowl; light reddish brown (2.5YR 6/4) fabric, light red (2.5YR 6/6) paint/slip; broken.
A25/24.4   (Fig. 4:13). Small bowl; light gray (10YR 7/2) fabric and exterior; dark gray (7.5YR 4/1) paint; sherd.

Parallels
The same lack of exact parallels is also true for several of the miniature bowls that share similarities with the small painted bowls but represent various bowl forms (Fig. 4:10–13). These are comparable to the tiny bowls at Busayra as well as a small painted bowl (Bienkowski, 2002, figs. 9.23:10–18; 9.29:15).

3 Miscellaneous Painted Styles

A number of sherds testify to additional vessels with painted patterns similar to what has been discussed above, as well as vessels with unique designs. These include a sherd with alternating red and white bands (C93/22.18), a jug with a slipped surface painted with dark narrow bands that were subsequently covered by a white wash (P1107), and another sherd with alternating black and red bands from the neck of a krater (E79/29.1). Two sherds with a net pattern on an unslipped exterior (C93/11.10, C94/68.9) were found in adjoining silos in front of the gate but may not have come from the same vessel. The net pattern had a long tradition in Palestine and is seen in Jordan on the shoulder of kraters from Tomb 20 at Nebo (Saller, 1966, 24:15–23), in sherd material at Ḥisban (Herr, 2012, fig. 2.10:23, and on the neck of a jug at Khirbat en-Nahas in Edom (Smith & Levy, 2014, fig. 4.5:12). Other sherds represent the face of a flask with concentric circles (C93/16.2) and bowls with an inverted triangular rim painted only on the upper surface of the rim (P133), or with random strokes across the rim and down the side (A25/16.10). Such strokes in groups were found on bowls and cups at Tall Jawa in Ammon (Epler & Daviau, 2020, fig. 7.1:11, 12), in Edom at Khirbat en-Nahas (Smith & Levy, 2014, fig. 4.4:12, 13), and Kadesh Barnea in Judah (Bernick-Greenberg, 2007, pl. 11.63:5, 65:4, 5). More unusual is a carinated, vertical rim bowl (D52/137.2) with a dark, weak red coloring in broad bands in the tradition of Edomite pottery (Smith & Levy, 2014, fig. 4.28:212; Herr, 2017, fig. 10.8:9, 10).

4 Other Decorative Traditions

4.1 Red Slipped Bowls

A special collection of decorated vessels consists of a group of red slipped bowls. Unlike the use of red slip on dinner ware at Tall Jawa (Daviau, 2020, figs. 4.1:1–5, 7–10, 12–14; 4.3, 4.4, 4.5, 4.8), red slip was an unusual surface treatment at Mudayna Thamad. Here it was found on bowls formed of a well sorted compact fabric distinct from that used for the small painted bowls. The firing of these vessels was consistent throughout resulting in an unusual pink–reddish brown fabric colour. The slip is medium to dark red in value and burnished to a high polish except for one perforated cup and two lamps (Fig. 5:9, 10) that were slipped but not burnished. The range of shapes for these bowls also reflects a very different mental template not seen in plain wares, including paper-thin fine wares and thick-walled vessels not seen in the unslipped repertoire. For the most part, vessels in this assemblage were found in the silos outside the gate and in a basement storeroom located between the gate and the outer wall (R135), although occasional finds from houses and industrial buildings across the site are also included in this category. Certain of these vessels were registered as objects[13] and are in the Madaba Museum of the Department of Antiquities of Jordan.

Catalogue

P2092 (not shown; A30/68.1). Conical; reddish brown (2.5YR 5/4) fabric, red (2.5YR 4/8) slip.

P1069 (Fig. 5:1; A25/55.1). Small bowl; pink (7.5YR 8/3) fabric, red (10R 4/8) slip; MT 3649.

P1078 (Fig. 5:2; A25/33.11). Thin walled; light brown (7.5YR 6/3) fabric, red (10R 5/6) slip; MT 3658.

P1079 (Fig. 5:3; A25/37.12). Fine ware; red (10R 4/6) fabric and slip; incised on base; MT 3677.

P1082 (Fig. 5:4; A25/33.1). Deep saucer; light red (2.5YR 6/6) fabric, red (10R 4/6) slip; MT 3660.

P102 (Fig. 5:5; A4/125.25). Everted rim; reddish brown (2.5YR 5/4) fabric and slip; broken.

P1073 (Fig. 5:6; A25/33.15), Bent-sided; pink (5YR 7/3) fabric, red (2.5YR 5/6) slip; MT 3653.

P1038 (Fig. 5:7; A25/37.6). Conical; light reddish brown (2.5YR 6/4) fabric, red (10R 5/6) slip, MT 3670.

P1100 (Fig. 5:8; A25/63.20). Footed bowl, light red (10R 6/6) fabric, red (10R 5/8) slip; MT 3681.

P1080 (Fig. 5:9; A25/55.7). Perforated cup; pinkish white (7.5YR 8/2) fabric, light red (10R 6/6) slip; MT 3678.

P1039 (Fig. 5:10; A25/37.13). Lamp; pink (5YR 7/4) fabric, red (10R 4/6) slip; MT 3671.

Parallels

The repertoire of red slipped bowls (Fig. 5) reflects different bowl styles and represents various traditions when compared to local bowls and is possibly derived from Ammon, Syria or even from among the fine ware plates of Phoenicia (Bikai, 1978, pl. XCI). This is seen most clearly in the one-of-a-kind vessels, especially the shallow thin-walled bowls with polished slip (Fig. 5:2, 3) and the thumb-footed tripod bowl (Fig. 5:8). Examples of everted rectangular rim bowls with a bent-sided body and tall ring base coated in red to reddish brown slip were present in both Tomb 20 and Tomb 84 at Mount Nebo (Saller, 1966: figs, 18:17–19; 41:3). Closer to Mudayna is a bowl with the same features from Tomb WT-200 (Chadwick, 2017: fig. 3.4:3). Formal parallels are found at Dibon, although these are white slipped (Tushingham, 1972: fig. 2:17), while at Busaya in Edom various Edomite painted styles are represented (Bienkowski, 2002: figs. 9.6:1–18; 9.7:1–8). At Samaria, bowls with similar

---

[13] Objects were registered sequentially in the range of 1–3700, and each item received a Site + individual number code (MT 345). Finds from survey sites were registered with WT + site + item number (WT-13 465).

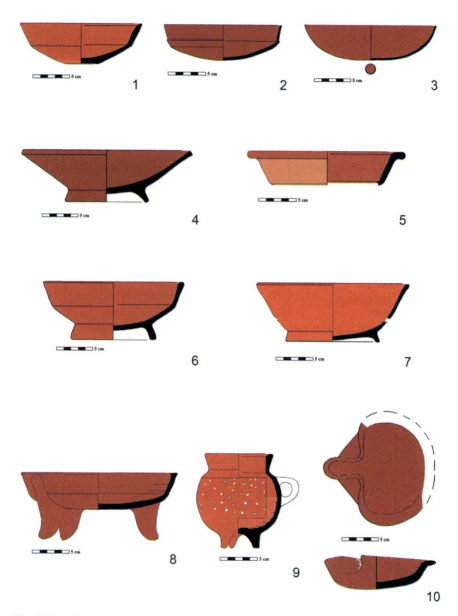

Fig. 5 Red slipped vessels: bowls, (*1*) P1069, (*2*) P1078; (*3*) P1079, (*4*) P1082, (*5*) P102, (*6*) P1073, (*7*) P1038; footed bowl, (*8*) P1100; cup, (*9*) P1080; lamp, (*10*) P1039

formal features were black slipped and burnished (Crowfoot, 1957: fig. 14:13), but the fabric is not reduced as was seen in the Ammonite black bowl repertoire (Daviau & Graham, 2009).

4.2 Levantine Production

Unique vessels are more difficult to locate within the landscape of potting traditions in central Jordan. The best example is a small amphora (Fig. 6:1; P2010) made of a finely mixed, levigated clay with an elaborate design, consisting of slip and burnish on the body, thin dark bands bordering a broad light red band on the shoulder and a variation of this motif on the body. The rim, neck and handles of P2010 are unslipped. This vessel is distinct not only in its refined fabric composition and surface decoration but also in its narrow neck with twin handles springing from the mid-neck ridge. Amphora P2010 stands on a disc base, another distinct feature in a corpus dominated by flat and ring bases. A second small amphora (Fig. 6:2; P3028) was also formed of a compact levigated clay that fired light red–reddish yellow; in this case, the vessel was thick-walled, comparable to two vessels from Tall Jawa that were also unique in the late Iron II corpus (Daviau, 2020, fig. 5.21:15, 16).

5 Foreign Influence and Imports

The two largest groups of decorated vessels with clear evidence of foreign origin are the Assyrian imports and the so-called Cypro-Phoenician juglets/amphoriskoi. In smaller numbers are the miniature juglets from Cyprus itself.

5.1 Assyrian/Syrian Imports

At Mudayna Thamad the Assyrian imports include one large, pointed bottle painted with narrow horizontal bands (P2032) on the neck, shoulder and at mid- and lower body (Fig. 6:3) and two ceramic glazed bottles (Fig. 6:4), possibly multi-coloured but now faded. Although small, pointed bottles were common in Ammon, the large, elongated bottle has its twin among the bottles at Nimrud and a more ornately painted parallel at Assur (Hausleiter, 2010, FL 6.4, FL 6.3). Glazed bottles were produced in Assyria proper where they had a wide distribution at sites in the Assyrian heartland, such as Assur (Anastasio, 2010, pl. 60:3), and in the Nineveh area at Khirbat Khatuniyeh (Curtis & Reade, 1995, fig. 38:161) and Qasr Shamamuk (Anastasio, 2010, pl. 50:18). Such small bottles were also produced in northern Syria (see for discussion, Peltenburg, 1969). Parallels throughout northern Mesopotamia and as trade goods as far east as Zawiye (Peltenburg, 1997, 312–313) and War Kabud in Iran (Haerinck & Overlaet, 2004, 31; fig. 9), and across the Mediterranean to Etruria in the west, have been noted previously (Daviau & Klassen, 2014, 102, 104).

A smaller group of probable imports consists of white polished and painted vessels that may have their origin in Syria or Mesopotamia. One sherd of finely

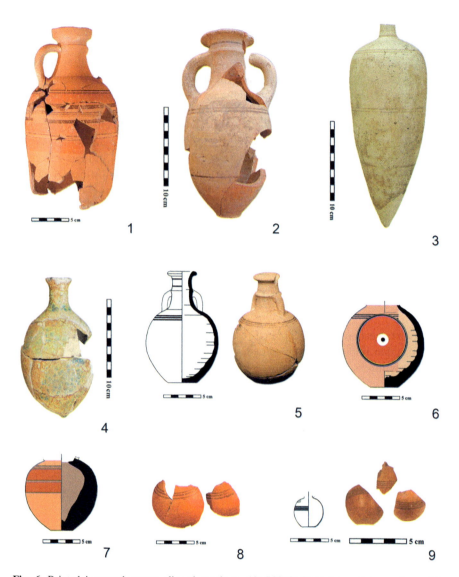

Fig. 6 Painted imported wares: slipped amphora, (*1*) P2010; Phoenician style amphora, (*2*) P3028; Assyrian bottles, (*3*) P2032; glazed bottle, (*4*) P4029; Cypro-Phoenician juglets/amphoriskoi, (*5*) P1034; (*6*) P3017; (*7*) 4068; Black-on-Red, (*8*) P1094, miniature BoR, (*9*) P1110

levigated clay with a white polished slip (E89/30.4) is from a small, closed vessel decorated with two thin brown painted bands, similar in style to the decoration seen on imported Assyrian pointed bottles.

Catalogue

P2010 (Fig. 6:1; B11/33.2). Amphora; rim to base; rim D 5.9, body D 13.5, H 26.5 cm; reddish brown (2.5YR 5/4) fabric, light red (2.5YR 6/8) slip, very dark gray (N 3/) paint, red (10R 5/8) paint; broken.

P3028 (Fig. 6:2; D71/109.1). Amphora; rim to base; rim D 7.0, H 23.0 cm; light red (2.5YR 7/6) fabric, very pale brown (10YR 8/2) slip, dark brown (7.5YR 3/3) paint; broken.

P2032 (Fig. 6:3); B22/82.7 = MT 2778). Assyrian pointed bottle; levigated clay; int D of neck 0.96, D of body 8.85, H 23.6 cm, Wgt 567.7 g; white (10YR 8/1) fabric, pale yellow (2.5Y 8/2) exterior, yellowish brown (10YR 5/4) paint; rim missing (Daviau & Klassen, 2014, fig. 6:1).

P4029 (Fig. 6:4; G9/60.4 = MT 3096).[14] Ovoid bottle; neck D 2.92, max body D 10.04, H ca. 17.39, wall T 1.08 cm; pale brown (2.5Y 8/3) fabric, pale green (5Y 8/3) glaze, dark bluish green (7.5 BG 3/4–4/4) glaze remaining in patches; broken (Daviau & Klassen, 2014, fig. 3:1).

P4030 (not shown; G8/39.8 = MT 3043).[15] Glazed bottle, rim, shoulder and base; D 6.03, preserved H 8.02 cm; yellow–pale brown (2.5Y 8/2) fabric, sherds (Daviau & Klassen, 2014, fig. 3:2).

Imports and imitations reflect the diversity of contacts and influences at Mudayna Thamad, especially the thin-walled painted amphora, without known parallels, and the thick-walled everted rim amphora (Fig. 6:1–2) that has parallels to its fabric at Tall Jawa in Ammon. To date, the workshops that produced these vessels have not been located in the region. Direct imports from Assyrian territory in the form of a pointed bottle and two ceramic glazed bottles (Fig. 6:3, 4) are better documented at sites extending from northwestern Iran to central Syria but are rare in the Southern Levant.

5.2 Cypro-Phoenician Style and Cypriot Imports

5.2.1 Cypro-Phoenician

Juglets and amphoriskoi modeled on the globular Cypriot Black-on-Red (BoR) juglet with a flat base are typically identified as Cypro-Phoenician juglets. The best example of the Cypriot proto-type in Moab was found at WT-13 in the form of an imported vessel of which the rim and neck are preserved. It features a thinned lip, a

---

[14] When found, the sherds of the glazed bottles were not recognized as such with the result that each sherd was registered individually. Only when one bottle was partially restored (MT 3096) was it assigned to its diagnostic sherd number (Field+Square: locus/pail number). For example, MT 3096 mends with MT 3122, MT 3125, MT 3127 and together form vessel P4029.

[15] MT 3043 mends with MT 3044 and MT 3072; These may be the same vessel as base sherd MT 3538 recovered 2 year later (2012) in the same square.

flaring simple rim, a neck ridge and a handle springing from the ridge. This sherd is painted on the lip, has black bands around the neck, diagonal strokes across the join of the handle at the ridge and a vertical stroke down the outer surface of the handle itself (Daviau, 2017, fig. 7.2:1).

The form of the southern Levantine vessel is a blend of Cypriot and Phoenician features, seen most clearly in the shape of the profiled everted rim and small, or in some cases, compressed handles. Unlike the miniature Cypriot BoR juglets found at WT-13 west of Mudayna (Daviau, 2017, fig. 7.2:1–3), the juglets from Moabite tombs and from Mudayna Thamad consist of standard size (11–17 cm tall) relatively thick-walled, globular or piriform vessels with a small flat base, narrow neck with a neck ridge, and thickened profiled rim. Juglets without handles, those with one handle and amphoriskoi with twin handles (P1034; Fig. 6:5) were burnished on the body and base and painted with two or three dark narrow bands on the neck and shoulder, although the paint is faded in most cases. Alternate designs are seen in the examples of juglets with a "shield" design with concentric circles filled with a red disc and a central bull's eye (P3017, Fig. 6:6; Steiner, 2020, fig. 3). The shield design derives from the concentric patterns of Cypriot BoR juglets and is found on juglets in the tombs at Dibon (Tushingham, 1972, fig. 16:6, 12), WT-200 west of Mudayna Thamad (Chadwick, 2017, fig. 3.5:6), and Tomb 20 at Nebo (Saller, 1966, fig. 22:10), as well as in Stratum II at WT-13 (Daviau 2017, fig. 7.2:4).

Glueck (1934, fig. 5) described a burnished juglet with broad painted bands from Qasr Saliyeh as a related style that may be grouped with a juglet from Dibon (Steiner, 2020, fig. 2 lower left) and one from Mudayna Thamad (Fig. 6:7). Another related style, similar in shape, is a juglet from Dibon (Steiner, 2020, fig. 2 lower right) with a wide band divided in two and framed on the top and bottom by one or more dark narrow bands. This same style is found at Mudayna Thamad in the sherd material (A4/119.7; C93/21.4). Painted juglets with a bag-shaped or ovoid body with a round base are classed as local wares, distinct from the Cypro-Phoenician flat-based vessels. In her study, Steiner (2020, 285) counted 20 complete or partial vessels at Mudayna Thamad; altogether there are now known to be more than 75 registered sherds from vessels of this type.

Catalogue

P1034 (Fig. 6:5; A18/97.1). Amphoriskos; rim to base, rim D 3.0, H 14.4 cm; reddish yellow (5YR 7/6) fabric and exterior, very dark gray (N 3/) paint. Broken.
P3017 (Fig. 6:6; D72/29.2). Juglet; body+base; body D 10.5, H 10.0+ cm; light red (2.5YR 7/6) fabric and exterior, very dark gray (N 3/) and red (10R 5/8) paint; shield design; broken.
P4068 (Fig. 6:7; E88/59.1) Amphoriskos; body+base; body D 9.5, H 9.6 cm; pink (5YR 7/4) fabric, light reddish brown (5YR 6/4) exterior, dark gray (N 4/) and light red (2.5YR 6/6) paint; broken.

At Mudayna Thamad, the vessels which are identified as Cypro-Phoenician juglets and amphoriskoi were found in the street, the houses and industrial buildings, the temple (Daviau & Steiner, 2000, fig. 12:5), and the gatehouse. These

Cypro-Phoenician style juglets and amphoriskoi with narrow painted bands as well as those with a large shield design are more numerous than local round-bottomed juglets. The concentration of these vessels at Mudayna Thamad, Dibon, and Nebo is unusual when compared to the small numbers in Edom (Smith & Levy, 2014, figs. 4.2: 20, 21; 4.24:5), although these Edomite vessels appear to be earlier than the thick-walled Moabite juglets. In view of these factors, Steiner (2020, 289) suggests that Cypro-Phoenician juglets were produced in local production centers. On the other hand, a small number of actual Cypriot imports (Fig. 6:8–9) appear to be unique at Mudayna Thamad.

5.2.2 Cypriot Imports

Closer in surface treatment to Cypriot juglets are three partially mended sherds of a red slipped and burnished juglet with dark bands on the shoulder (Fig. 6:8). Since the neck is missing and petrographic analysis has not yet been undertaken, we cannot confirm that these sherds belonged to an imported vessel. But we can identify an actual Cypriot import, most notably, three sherds which were all part of a miniature BoR juglet, P1110 (Fig. 6:9). The levigated clay of the paper-thin body wall was decorated with polished red slip, fine black bands on the upper body and concentric circles on the shoulder.

Catalogue

P1094 (Fig. 6:8; A15/22.2). Juglet; body D *ca.* 8.0 cm; pale red (10R 6/4) fabric, red (2.5YR 5/8) slip, dark gray (5YR 4/1) paint; sherds.

P1110 (Fig. 6:9; A25/54.13). Miniature; neck to base; body D 3.8, base D 1.8, H 4.0+ cm; light red (2.5YR 7/6) fabric, red (2.5YR 5/8) slip, gray (5YR 4/1) paint; broken.

Although direct imports from Cyprus are few, numbering less than a dozen sherds, their presence along with Assyrian glazed bottles indicates that Madayna Thamad was integrated in an extensive trade network.

6 Summary and Reflections

When we compare the painted ceramic corpus found at Mudayna Thamad with pottery from other regions in central Jordan, we find that this decorated assemblage has parallels from several sites on the Karak pleateau as well as in the north at Nebo. Glueck himself compared his assemblage from Mudayna Thamad to sherds from Saliya, Baluʿ, Jemeil and Qasr Zaʿfaran I (1934, pls. 22, 23). His description of painted ware as finely made pottery covered with slip and painted bands does not take into account the diverse corpus of unslipped painted wares found during our excavations at Mudayna Thamad. More recently, Brown (1991, 198) noted considerable diversity among fabrics from the various classes of vessels represented in the Karak Plateau Survey material. However, when we compare the decorated pottery at Mudayna Thamad with that from the Karak plateau the number of close parallels is limited. Among the 62 Iron II sherds published from the survey assemblage, Brown illustrates nine decorated sherds (1991, sherds 248, 280–287), three of which may be from the same vessel. The excavated corpus from al-Baluʿ consists of 419 illustrated sherds, of which three Iron Age sherds from Area A and eight from Area E are painted (Worschech, 2014). Most notable are the designs on small bowls that include painted horizontal bands with painted strokes on the rim and down the side (Worschech, 2014: E 060, E 061) rather than painted horizontal bands.

This preliminary study of the decorated wares at Mudayna Thamad opens the way for more detailed examination, especially for petrographic analysis that can compare the clay sources with finds from sites north of the Dhiban plateau and from Edom, where such studies have already been undertaken (Smith et al., 2014). To date, no Iron Age kilns or pottery workshops have been identified on the Dhiban plateau to assist in our investigation of the production centers and distribution patterns of Moabite ceramics. The search for clay beds in the Jordan Valley may be an avenue to consider given the fine clay beds in the valley foothills (Daviau, 2016, 471). Additional preparation of the ceramic corpus from Mudayna Thamad will expand our knowledge of both the plain wares and the decorated pottery in this small but rich site on the northern edge of the Dhiban plateau.

References

Albright, W. F. (1924). The archaeological results of an expedition to Moab and the Dead Sea. *Bulletin of the American Schools of Oriental Research, 14*, 1–12.

Anastasio, S. (2010). *Atlas of the Assyrian pottery of the Iron Age* (Subartu XXIV). Brepols.

Bernick-Greenberg, H. (2007). The ceramic assemblages and the wheel-made pottery typology. In R. Cohen & H. Bernick-Greenberg (Eds.), *Excavations at Kadesh Barnea (Tell el-Qudeirat) 1976–1982* (IAA Reports 34/1, 2) (pp. 131–185). Israel Antiquities Authority.

Bienkowski, P. (2002). *Busayra. Excavations by C.-M. Bennett 1971–1980* (British Academy Monographs in Archaeology, No. 13). Oxford University Press.

Bikai, P. M. (1978). *The pottery of Tyre*. Aris & Phillips Ldt.

Brown, R. (1991). Ceramics from the Kerak plateau. In J. M. Miller (Ed.), *Archaeological survey of the Kerak Plateau* (America Schools of Oriental Research, No. 1) (pp. 169–279). Scholars Press.

Brünnow, R. E., & von Domaszewski, A. (1904–1905). *Die Provincia Arabia auf Grund zweier in den Jahren 1897 und 1898 unternommenen Reisen und der Berichte früherer Reisender, I, II*. Karl J. Trübner.

Chadwick, R. (2017). A newly discovered Iron Age II Cave Tomb near Khirbat al-Mudayna on the Wadi ath-Thamad. In M. Neeley, G. A. Clark, & P. M. M. Daviau (Eds.), *Walking through Jordan: Papers in honor of Burton MacDonald* (pp. 25–38). Equinox.

Crowfoot, G. M. (1957). Israelite pottery, general list. In J. W. Crowfoot, G. M. Crowfoot, & K. M. Kenyon (Eds.), *The objects from Samaria* (Samaria III) (pp. 134–198). Palestine Exploration Fund.

Curtis, J. E., & Reade, J. E. (Eds.). (1995). *Art and empire: Treasures from Assyria in the British Museum*. The British Museum Press.

Daviau, P. M. M. (2013). Imports, imitations or local production? The white painted ware from Tall Jawa. In *Studies in the history and archaeology of Jordan XI* (pp. 625–637). Department of Antiquities.

Daviau, P. M. M. (2016). Traditional methods of cooking: The evidence from ethnography and experimental archaeology. In J. R. Battenfield, P. M. M. Daviau, et al. (Eds.), *Excavations at Tall Jawa, Jordan, Jordan. Volume V: Survey, zooarchaeology and ethnoarchaeology* (Culture and History of the Ancient Near East 11/5) (pp. 462–478). Brill.

Daviau, P. M. M. (2017). *A wayside shrine in Northern Moab. Excavations in the Wadi ath-Thamad* (Wadi ath-Thamad Project I). Oxbow Books.

Daviau, P. M. M. (2020). *Excavations at Tall Jawa, Jordan: Vol. 3. The Iron Age pottery* (Culture and History of the Ancient Near East, 11/3). Brill.

Daviau, P. M. M., & Graham, A. J. (2009). Black slipped and burnished pottery. A special 7th century Technology in Jordan and Syria. *Levant, 41*, 41–59.

Daviau, P. M. M., & Klassen, S. (2014). Conspicuous consumption and tribute: Assyrian glazed ceramic bottles at Khirbat al-Mudayna on Wadi ath-Thamad. *Bulletin of the American Schools of Oriental Research, 372*, 115–138.

Daviau, P. M. M., & Steiner, M. (2000). A Moabite sanctuary at Khirbat al-Mudayna. *Bulletin of the American Schools of Oriental Research, 320*, 1–21.

Epler, P., & Daviau, P. M. M. (2020). Surface treatment and decorative traditions. In P. M. M. Daviau *Excavations at Tall Jawa, Jordan: Vol. 3. The Iron Age pottery* (Culture and History of the Ancient Near East, 11.3) (pp. 318–322). Brill.

Glueck, N. (1934). *Explorations in Eastern Palestine, I* (AASOR XIV). American Schools of Oriental Research.

Haerinck, E., & Overlaet, B. (2004). *The Iron Age III graveyard at war Kabud, Pusht-i Kuh, Luristan* (Luristan Excavation Documents 5, Acto Iranica 42). Centre International d'études Indo-Iraniennes.

Harrison, T. P., Foran, D., Graham, A., Griffith, T., Barlow, C., & Ferguson, J. (2003). The Tall Mâdabâ archaeological project: Preliminary report of the 1998–2000 field season. *Annual of the Department of Antiquities of Jordan, 47*, 129–148.

Hart, S. (1995). The pottery. In C.-M. Bennett & P. Bienkowski (Eds.), *Excavations at Tawilan in Southern Jordan* (British Academy Monographs in Archaeology, No. 8) (pp. 53–66). Oxford University Press.

Hausleiter, A. (2010). *Neuassyrische Keramik im Kerngebiet Assyriens* (Abhandlungen der Deutschen Orient-Gesellschaft, 27). Harrassowitz Verlag.

Herr, L. G. (2012). The Iron age. In J. A. Sauer & L. G. Herr (Eds.), *Ceramic finds: Typological and technological studies of the pottery remains from Tell Hesban and vicinity* (Hesban 11) (pp. 9–172). Andrews University Press.

Herr, L. G. (2017). The Iron Age pottery from Burton MacDonald's last three surveys in the highlands of Southern Jordan. In M. Neeley, G. A. Clark, & P. M. M. Daviau (Eds.), *Walking through Jordan: Papers in honor of Burton MacDonald* (pp. 151–182). Equinox.

Ji, Ch-H. (2011). Khirbat ʿAtaruz: An interim overview of the 10 years of archaeological architectural findings. *Annual of the Department of Antiquities of Jordan, 55*, 561–579.

Ji, Ch-H. (2012). The early Iron II Temple at Ḥirbet ʿAtārūs and its architecture and selected cultic objects. In J. Kamlah (ed.), *Temple building and Temple cult: Architecture and cultic paraphernalia of temples in the Levant (2.-1. Mill. B.C.E.)*. Abhandlungen des Deutschen-Palästina-Vereins 41 (pp. 203–221). Harrassowitz Verlag.

Ji, C.-H., & Lee, J. K. (1998). Preliminary report on the survey of the Dhiban Palteau, 1997. *Annual of the Department of Antiquities of Jordan, 47*, 549–571.

Ji, C.-H., & Lee, J. K. (2000). A preliminary report on the Dhiban plateau survey project, 1999: The Versacare expedition. *Annual of the Department of Antiquities of Jordan, 49*, 493–506.

Miller, J. M. (1989). Six Khirbet el-Medeinehs in the region east of the Dead Sea. *Bulletin of the American Schools of Oriental Research, 276,* 25–28.
Musil, A. (1907). *Arabia Petraea I. Moab.* Alfred Holder.
Olávarri, E. (1965). Sondages à ʿAroʿer sur l'Arnon. *Revue Biblique, 72,* 77–94.
Olávarri, E. (1969). Fouilles à ʿAroʿer sur l'Arnon. *Revue Biblique, 76,* 230–259.
Olávarri, E. (1977–1978). Sondeo Arqueologico en Khirbet Medeineh junto a Smakieh (Jordania). *Annual of the Department of Antiquities of Jordan, 22,* 136–149.
Peltenburg, E. J. (1969). Al Mina glazed pottery and its relations. *Levant, 1,* 73–96.
Peltenburg, E. J. (1997). Vitreous materials: Artifacts of the Bronze and Iron Ages. In E. M. Meyer (Ed.), *The Oxford encyclopedia of archaeology in the Near East* (pp. 309–314). Oxford University Press.
Piccirillo, M. (1975). Una tomba del Ferro I a Madaba (Madaba B – Moab). *Liber Annuus, 25,* 199–224. Pls. 49–67.
Saller, S. (1966). The Iron Age tombs at Nebo, Jordan. *Liber Annuus, 16,* 165–298.
Smith, N. G., & Levy, T. E. (2014). Iron Age ceramics from Edom: A new typology. In T. E. Levy, M. Najjar, & E. Ben-Yosef (Eds.), *New insights into the Iron Age archaeology of Edom in Southern Jordan* (pp. 297–459). The Cotsen Institute of Archaeology Press, University of California.
Smith, N. G., Goren, Y., & Levy, T. E. (2014). The petrography of Iron Age Edom: From the lowlands to the highlands. In T. E. Levy, M. Najjar, & E. Ben-Yosef (Eds.), *New insights into the Iron Age archaeology of Edom in Southern Jordan* (pp. 461–491). The Cotsen Institute of Archaeology Press, University of California.
Steiner, M. L. (2009). Khirbat al-Mudayna and Moabite pottery production. In P. Bienkowski (Ed.), *Studies on Iron Age Moab and Neighbouring areas in honour of Michèle Daviau* (Ancient Near Eastern Studies, Supplement 29) (pp. 145–164). Peeters.
Steiner, M. L. (2013). The Iron I Pottery of Khirbat al-Lāhūn. *Annual of the Department of Antiquities of Jordan, 53,* 519–533.
Steiner, M. L. (2017). WT-13 pottery and the Central Jordan tradition. In P. M. M. Daviau *A wayside shrine in Northern Moab: Excavations in Wadi ath-Thamad* (pp. 171–178). Oxbow Books.
Steiner, M. L. (2020). The case of the "Cypro-Phoenician" Juglets in Moab. In J. Ebeling & P. Guillaume (Eds.), *The woman in the pith helmet: A tribute to archaeologist Norma Franklin* (pp. 279–281). Lockwood Press.
Tristram, H. B. (1874). *The land of Moab: Travels and discoveries on the east side of the Dead Sea and the Jordan.* Harper.
Tushingham, A. D. (1972). *The excavations at Dibon (Dhībân) in Moab. The third campaign 1952–53* (AASOR 40). The American Schools of Oriental Research.
Winnett, F. V., & Reed, W. L. (1964). *The Excavations at Dibon (Dhībân) in Moab, Part 1: The first campaign, 1950–1951; Part 2: The second campaign, 1952* (Annual of American Schools of Oriental Research 36–37 for 1957–1958). American Schools of Oriental Research.
Worschech, U. (2014). *Ceramics from el-Bālūʿ.* Beiträge zur Erforschung der antiken Moabitis (Arḍ El-Kerak), 7. PL Academic Research.

The Qasr at Balu'a

Kent Bramlett, Monique Roddy, Craig Tyson, and Friedbert Ninow

Abstract The Qasr al-Balu'a is a monumental Iron Age structure located at the highpoint of Khirbat al-Balu'a, a 16-ha multi-period settlement with extensive Iron Age II-period remains. Overlooking the Wadi Balu'a, the *qasr* stands prominent on the horizon of the site. This paper would provide a brief review of the history of exploration and theories of interpretation surrounding the *qasr*. In 1930 a yet-undeciphered inscribed stele, the Balu'a Stele, was found and excited interest in the structure and in its possible contributions to understanding state formation in the Moabite region. Current excavations by the Balu'a Regional Archaeological Project (BRAP) against the exterior northern wall of the *qasr* have preliminarily clarified its construction phases, including defining the pre-structure preparation surfaces and initial construction in the Iron Age down to its reuse in the Nabatean period. Pottery and radiocarbon dates assist in anchoring the construction and use of this building.

Keywords Balu'a · Moab · Crowfoot · Glueck · Iron Age

K. Bramlett
La Sierra University, Riverside, CA, USA
e-mail: kbramlett@lasierra.edu

M. Roddy (✉)
La Sierra University, Riverside, CA, USA

Walla Walla University, College Place, WA, USA
e-mail: mroddy@lasierra.edu

C. Tyson
D'Youville University, Buffalo, NY, USA
e-mail: tysonc@dyc.edu

F. Ninow
La Sierra University, Riverside, CA, USA

Theologische Hochschule Friedensau, Möckern, Germany
e-mail: fninow@lasierra.edu

© The Author(s), under exclusive license to Springer Nature Switzerland AG 2023
E. Ben-Yosef, I. W. N. Jones (eds.), *"And in Length of Days Understanding" (Job 12:12): Essays on Archaeology in the Eastern Mediterranean and Beyond in Honor of Thomas E. Levy*, Interdisciplinary Contributions to Archaeology,
https://doi.org/10.1007/978-3-031-27330-8_38

I (Monique) first met Tom in Paris at the 11th International Conference on the History and Archaeology of Jordan (ICHAJ) in 2010. This was my first ICHAJ and spending several days listening to fellow archaeologists talk about their research in Jordan was a formative experience for a young graduate student. Tom Levy, with his passion for new ways of approaching archaeological research, stood out at that event, and in the coming years I watched some of those new methods, developed by Levy and his students, take hold in the project I worked with at the time, the Madaba Plains Project at Tall al-ʿUmayri. Now, working at Khirbat al-Baluʿa, we use many of those same methods to capture our daily work, and when I sort through the 2012 season grinding stones back at the Center for Near Eastern Archaeology, it's the bar codes created for the ELRAP that tag each item. The authors here would like to express our appreciation for Tom's efforts in the field and for sharing his tech and staff with us in Jordan as our new project got off the ground.

1 Background on Khirbat al-Baluʿa

Khirbat al-Baluʿa is located on the Karak Plateau next to the Wadi Baluʿa, which feeds ultimately into the Wadi Mujib (Fig. 1). In this location, Baluʿa was able to control a major north-south route in the pre-Classical periods, acting as gatekeeper to the Central Karak Plateau. Baluʿa spreads across nearly 16 ha with some periods inhabiting distinct areas, such as the Iron Age settlement at the core of the site and the medieval Islamic remains to the southwest.

The site of Baluʿa is possibly to be identified with "Ar of Moab," a place mentioned in the biblical narrative (Numbers 21:15, 28; 22:36; Deuteronomy 2:9, 18, 29; Isaiah 15:1) as being on the border of Moab close to the Arnon/Mujib, the main drainage basin close to Baluʿa. The word Ar is closely related to the Hebrew word for city, and hence calling a place "Ar of Moab" may well be saying it is the *main* city of Moab. Baluʿa's size, central location, and proximity to the Arnon/Mujib fit these parameters though there are other possibilities (for more on the historical geography, see Gaß, 2009: 182–183). Even if this identification is ultimately disproven, the size and position of Baluʿa at an entrance to the Wadi Mujib make it a key site for considering the Moabite kingdom of the Iron Age.

Excavations at Baluʿa began in the 1930s by the Department of Antiquities under Crowfoot (1934) and then from the 1980s to 2000 under Udo Worschech and Friedbert Ninow (Worschech et al., 1986; Zayadine & Worschech, 1988; Worschech, 1989, 1990, 1991, 1992, 1995, 1997, 2000, 2006; Worschech & Ninow, 1992), and under Ninow from 2008 to 2012 (Ninow, 2008). While the earlier excavations concentrated on the Iron Age strata, the focus of the renewed work under Ninow was on the overall occupational history of the site. The 2010 and 2012 GPS surveys and test excavation probes laid the groundwork for the Baluʿa Regional Archaeological

The Qasr at Baluʿa

Fig. 1 Khirbat al-Baluʿa with distinct areas of habitation highlighted and visible architecture outlined

Project (BRAP), which started officially in 2017 under the direction of Friedbert Ninow, Kent Bramlett, and Monique (Vincent) Roddy (Vincent et al., 2014; Bramlett et al., 2018, 2020). Excavations have identified Roman, Nabatean, Hellenistic, Iron Age, Middle Bronze, and Early Bronze sherds south of the wadi and Early Bronze Age sherds to its north.

The goals of the BRAP, to cover five seasons of excavation from 2017 to 2025, include: (1) building a ceramic typology of the Baluʿa region with a specific focus on the Iron Age ceramic sequence for Moab, (2) understanding the political and economic history of a large site on a major route (the prominent location of Baluʿa near the Wadi Mujeb is likely related to its success in multiple periods), (3) establishing the sequence and expanse of settlements at Baluʿa through excavation (survey pottery has indicated a wide range of occupational periods, but some have yet to be detected stratigraphically), (4) survey and excavate test squares at regional survey sites from multiple periods (our inclusion of "regional" in the project's name was intentional – to build a larger social and environmental picture of the use and development of this region over time), and (5) we are also interested in the long-term preservation and development of the site, for which we have begun tracking looting pits seasonally (the rural nature of the site has made it difficult to guard and our excavation areas, though backfilled, always attract inter-seasonal attention).

1.1 The Iron Age Settlement

The Iron II settlement covers approximately 13.5 ha based on GPS surveys and test excavations of the visible outline of the defenses. A casemate wall surrounds the original settlement to the west, which was built on a promontory overlooking the wadi. One entry has been found so far on a path down into the wadi east of the Qasr. Later in the Iron II period an extension of the settlement was constructed eastward along the wadi edge and a new casemate wall added to protect the extension. The interior of the settlement is formed of densely clustered, multi-phased domestic structures in the older part of the settlement and less dense, single-phased structures in the eastern extension. Excavations in the Iron Age settlement in 2017 and 2019 focused on three main areas of excavation designated by their primary feature: (1) the Qasr, the monumental structure at the highest part of the site, (2) the House, a large domestic structure at the heart of the settlement, and (3) the Wall, a part of the fortification line dividing the main settlement from its later, eastern expansion (Fig. 2).

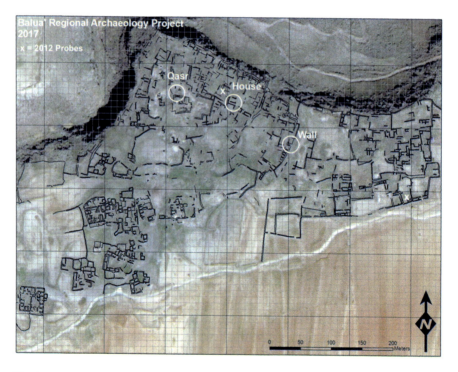

Fig. 2 BRAP excavation areas at Baluʿa

1.2 The Qasr

Archaeological interest in the Qasr at Baluʿa, and in the site more generally, arose with the discovery of the Baluʿa Stele by the outer northern side of the Qasr in 1930 (Crowfoot, 1934: 81; Horsfield & Vincent, 1932, Fig. 3). Crowfoot claims that it was discovered top down in the rubble of the structure that he excavated to the north of the Qasr and suggests that it might have been in secondary use in the construction of the Qasr and had then tumbled down from the Qasr wall along with the many other walls stones that litter the area (Crowfoot, 1934: 81–83; similarly Routledge & Routledge, 2009: 73–74). As we will see, the pottery readings from the current excavations also suggest that the Baluʿa Stele predates the Qasr, especially if the generally accepted date range for the Baluʿa Stele from the Late Bronze Age to Iron I is accepted (Routledge & Routledge, 2009: 83).

After the discovery of the Baluʿa Stele, Glueck visited the site in July of 1933 to collect sherds for his Survey of Eastern Palestine. The majority of the surface sherds that he collected were dated from the end of the Early Bronze period to the Middle Bronze period (ca. 3000–1550 BCE) and to the Iron Age (1200–500 BCE) (Glueck, 1934: 53–56). Crowfoot followed in November of 1933 to complete several soundings on behalf of the Committees of the Palestine Exploration Fund and the British School of Archaeology in Jerusalem (Crowfoot, 1934). Crowfoot executed three soundings at the site, two in relation to the Qasr. The sounding on the eastward-facing opening of the Qasr discovered an entrance of sorts that he suggests was built or repaired in the first century CE. The other sounding outside of the northern wall of the Qasr found a structure 4.9 m × 2.85 m with 0.80 m thick walls founded on the limestone bedrock. The structure had two doorways and three large pithoi were found in it. At the time, the pithoi were hard to date, though Crowfoot dated other pottery to the Middle Iron or later. Closer to the Qasr another wall paralleling the northern Qasr wall was found, and a line of stones between that wall and the Qasr made it difficult to excavate further. Consequently, Crowfoot was not able to reach the foundation of the Qasr and therefore not able to assign a date with any accuracy (Crowfoot, 1934: 80–83).

Glueck and Crowfoot also explored the Nabataean remains in relation to the Qasr. Glueck's visual study of sherds and architecture led him to believe that an eastern extension built against the Qasr's main walls should be dated to the Nabataean period (Glueck, 1933–34: 54). Crowfoot's clearing of this same extension discovered a doorway with a threshold – roughly 1.70 m across – with a long limestone slab which may have served as a lintel. For dating this extension, he found "under and between the rough stones of the threshold some late sherds from the same period… This part of the building at least was, therefore, built or repaired about the 1st century A.D." (Crowfoot, 1934: 81). During his survey of the Kerak plateau Max Miller noted in his report that they found a considerable amount of Nabataean sherds at the site (Miller, 1991: 43). Ninow's 2008 excavations of an area disturbed by illicit digging to the east of this extension and doorway revealed a stone structure of rectangular shape that has been interpreted as an altar platform. A closer examination revealed various building phases expanding on an original stone and plaster platform measuring 3.20 × 3.20 × 3.30 × 3.10 m. Based on the pottery associated with the structure it could be dated to the first century C.E. (Schmid's Phase 3, c. 20 – 100 C.E.; see Schmid, 2007: 314–316). Various parallels at Petra, Khirbet et-Tannur, and other places attest to this type of Nabataean altar platform (see, e.g., Tholbecq, 2007; Reyes & McKenzie, 2013). J. H. Healey notes that "the main temples of the Nabataean period share the same period of construction or reconstruction, the late 1st century B.C. to the 2nd century A.D., and have in common the feature of an elevated platform in the *cella* of the temple reached by steps" (Healey, 2001: 74). It is possible that on these platforms images were exhibited (Tholbecq, 2007: 115).

An addition on the western side of this platform included a fragmentary, carved basalt stone reused from an earlier architectural context. Comparison with similar carved stones indicated it had once formed part of a volute capital. This fragment preserves the left side of the central triangle that is formed by two parallel lines and a double base line. Since the Baluʿa volute fragment was found in secondary use we are left to date it typologically, which puts it somewhere in the eighth–seventh century B.C.E. Such a date fits comfortably with the Iron Age II remains that have been documented on the site. This volute fragment adds another exemplar to the corpus of Moabite volute capitals (Tyson & Ninow, 2019).

1.3 BRAP's Work at the Qasr

Recognizing that establishing a date for the founding of the Qasr is critical to understanding the history of the site, the Baluʿa Regional Archaeological Project decided to open up an excavation square on the north side of the Qasr in 2017. The choice to excavate on the north side was significantly influenced by the relative ease of access to the area and the desire to test Crowfoot's excavations in the same area. Viewing the Qasr from across the Wadi Baluʿa, its north wall has a visible gap between two piles of fallen wall stones (Fig. 3). It is this gap that we assume represents the place where Crowfoot excavated. To access what we hoped would be undisturbed strata, a front loader was brought in from the nearby town of Qasr to remove the large wall stones tumbled from the northwestern corner of the Qasr (visible as the pile toward the west of the Qasr in Fig. 3). This work was done under the auspices of the Director General of the Department of Antiquities and by arrangement of the local directorate. Once removed, a fan of dirt and smaller stones was exposed. This is where we marked out an initial 3.0 × 3.0 m probe in 2017 (Area 24.42) with the explicit goal of reaching and dating the foundation of the Qasr. This probe was expanded and completed in 2019.

The Qasr at Baluʿa

Fig. 3 The Qasr as viewed from the north, from across the Wadi Baluʿa

2 The Qasr: Stratigraphy (Area 24.42)

The BRAP's excavations (2017–2019) at the Qasr currently cover a 4.0 m × 4.0 m probe against the exterior of the north wall, which has been excavated to bedrock (though this probe narrows to less than 3.0 m at its base). The probe exposed the foundations of the structure, which allowed for a brief presentation of the architectural phases in order from earliest to latest.

2.1 Phase 1: Evidence for Pre-Iron II Occupation

The Qasr is the first evident architecture above bedrock in this area. If earlier architecture existed here, it was removed during the process of preparing this area for the stone boulders that created the founding level of the Qasr. The bedrock, a mix of limestone and basalt, is rough and pitted with natural holes. Most of the architecture at Baluʿa is made of a mix of basalt or limestone boulders. A thick, hard-packed earth layer covers the bedrock. This earth layer included a range of pottery sherds, from the Early Bronze Age – hole-mouth jar rims, flat bases, and a ledge-handle – to the predominant Iron I and early Iron II periods. A sampling of mostly later pottery forms are presented here (Fig. 4). This layer may have been laid down in the Early

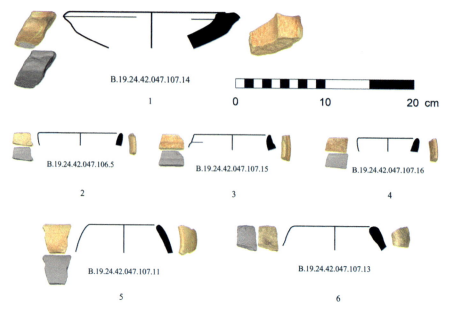

Fig. 4 Qasr pottery rim profiles, Phase 1

Iron II period to level the bedrock in preparation for the Qasr, though a large basalt mortar installed in its surface seems to indicate it was part of an earlier occupational phase whose architecture was lost in the construction process for the Qasr. Alternatively, the mortar could be used secondarily here as building material, in which case these layers would need to be seen as part of the construction phase of the Qasr and not its predecessor (Fig. 5).

2.2 Phase 2A: Iron IIB: Constructing the Qasr

The northern wall of the Qasr was built directly on top of the Phase 1 earth layer, running right over the mortar installation. The preparatory phase of this wall is represented by two to three courses of small and medium boulders (Fig. 6). A further three courses of very large boulders sit on top of the lowest courses and likely represent a later phase. The seamless integration of the phases of the Qasr wall suggests that from the earliest phase this wall was associated with a monumental structure that underwent renovation over the following centuries, but this will only be confirmed with further exposure.

At the same level as the second course of stones in the Qasr wall a single layer of large stones was laid parallel to the north. We have interpreted these stones as an intentional pavement, contra Crowfoot, who identified a similar layer of stones in his excavations to the east as a fill layer in a foundation trench; however, he admitted

Fig. 5 The mortar built into the base of the Qasr, either a remnant of Phase 1 occupation or part of construction efforts in Phase 2A. (Photo B19.24.42.131)

Fig. 6 Phase 2A of the Qasr's north wall. (Photo B19.24.42.114)

the dense architecture made it difficult to determine the stratigraphy in the area (Crowfoot, 1934: 82–83). With a larger exposure, it seems more likely that these stones were part of a pavement disrupted by later construction efforts.

The pottery from this phase is presented here (Fig. 7). Bowl forms included simple bowls (Fig. 7.1, 7.3, and 7.4), slightly carinated forms (Fig. 7.2), and varieties with offset rims (Fig. 7.6) or thickened rims (Fig. 7.5 and 7.8). Red-slip is frequent (Fig. 7.1, 7.4, 7.5, 7.6, and 7.7) and where burnishing is apparent, appears to

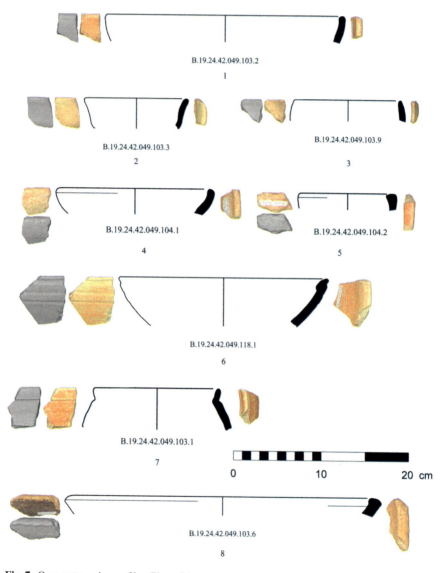

Fig. 7 Qasr pottery rim profiles, Phase 2A

be mostly hand burnishing (Fig. 7.1 has vertically oriented burnishing streaks on the interior; Fig. 7.6 has non-parallel burnishing streaks on the interior; and additional body sherds exhibited obvious hand burnishing over red-slip). The Fig. 7.5 bowl is potentially the latest form and was found lying flat on top of the preparatory earth layer for the stone pavement, providing a date for this phase and thus for the construction of the Qasr. The fragment is small, chipped, and worn on the exterior, but has a fine red slip and smooth burnish that suggests a date not earlier than the ninth century BCE. Given the preponderance of eleventh–tenth century forms, but with some probable later sherds, we cautiously suggest the current evidence points to a date early in the Iron IIB period for the construction of the Qasr, with the caveat that this phase has limited exposure and further excavation may provide additional clarity.

2.3 Phase 2B: Iron IIB: Domestic Additions

A new wall, Wall 11, laid close and parallel to the Qasr's northern wall (less than 1.0 m away) formed a domestic space to the north (Fig. 8). This room was partially paved with a cobble surface and had three stone pillar bases running parallel to the main wall. Animal bones and a number of groundstone tools provide one possible

Fig. 8 Phase 2B domestic structure with Wall 11 less than a meter from the north wall of the Qasr, visible in the upper right background of the image. The domestic structure is defined by Wall 11, the cobble stone surface, a north-south wall just visible in the east balk, and three pillar bases, two of which are visible in the lower left part of this image. (Photo B19.24.42.080)

Fig. 9 A complete Pataikos figurine excavated from the Phase 2B domestic surface to the north of the Qasr. (Photo B190014D)

interpretation of this space as a food preparation area. A complete Pataikos figurine (Fig. 9) found on the room's surface was only matched in interest by the phytolith remains of possible woven textiles in the collapse on top of the surfaces. This room was sealed in with destruction debris and later wash layers.

Pottery from the surfaces and destruction debris of this phase date to the Iron IIB (Fig. 10). Bowl forms and kraters are buff-slipped and not burnished, or red-slipped and wheel-burnished. The Fig. 10.2 bowl has a fine red slip and smooth burnish very similar to the Fig. 7.5 bowl discussed above. The large basin (Fig. 10.7) had chaff inclusions and was fired all the way through.

2.4 Phase 3: Iron IIC: Domestic Structure

The inhabitants of the following occupational phase dug a foundation trench for a new wall, Wall 6, running parallel to the Qasr and to the north of earlier Wall 11 (Fig. 11). A second wall was built to abut Wall 6 from the north, creating a new domestic space above the ruins of the Iron IIB structure. An earth surface covered thick preparatory fill layers and sealed against the walls. In the southeast corner of the room a large pithos, intact though cracked, had been buried in a pit under the

The Qasr at Balu'a

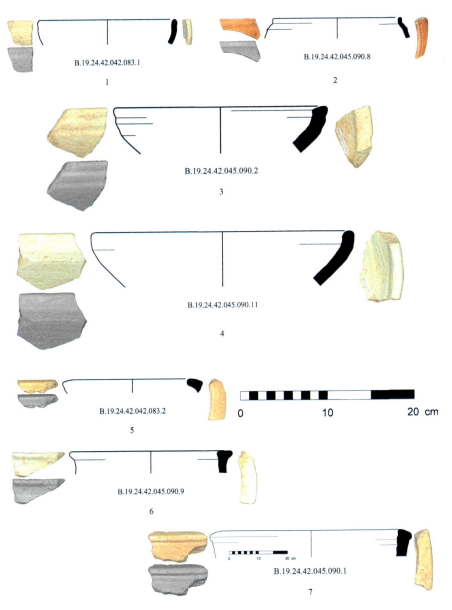

Fig. 10 Qasr pottery rim profiles, Phase 2B

level of the surface with only the rim likely visible to the room's occupants (Fig. 12). Preliminary analysis of some of the samples from this pithos by Geoffrey Hedges-Knyrim indicates it contained cereals, both wheat and barley, and legumes as well as wild grasses. This domestic structure was abandoned without a destruction event, with stone tumble and windblown earth slowly filling the space above the surface.

Fig. 11 The Phase 3 Wall 6 (center) running parallel to Phase 2B Wall 11 (behind Wall 6) and the Qasr's north wall (upper back of image). The pithos was found in the lower left hand corner of the image, its view blocked here by the north balk, its rim roughly at the level of the earth depicted. (Photo B19.24.42.028)

Fig. 12 The pithos excavated in the location where it had been buried under the Phase 3 house floor. The east wall of the domestic structure is just visible in the background, above and behind the pithos. (B19.24.42.056_5July)

The fill of the pit and the pithos, as well as the surface around the top of the pithos, contained Iron IIC pottery, a date that fits with the pithos itself (Fig. 13). The Fig. 13.3 cooking pot has double-ridges reduced to little more than a groove and inverted rim. Bowls (Fig. 13.1 and 13.2) and kraters (Fig. 13.5 and 13.6) are mostly unslipped. The pithos (Figs. 12 and 13.7) has the typical Late Iron II inverted rim reduced to practically a hole-mouth form. In the northeast corner of a room Crowfoot excavated to the east of ours, he found three large pithoi nearly identical to this new pithos (Crowfoot, 1934: 81–81, Pl. III, figs. 1–2). Our interpretation of the architecture and stratigraphy do differ from Crowfoot's significantly, possibly due to our larger exposure, made possible by two seasons of excavation.

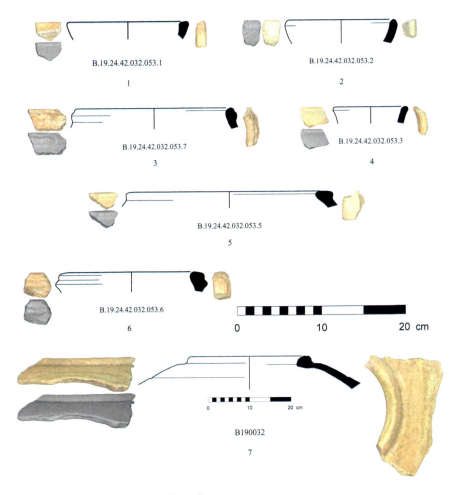

Fig. 13 Qasr pottery rim profiles, Phase 3

2.5 Phase 4: Roman/Nabataean Reuse

The final occupational phase identified in this area is attributed to the Roman/Nabataean period, though it consists of topsoil and debris layers with only one clear paved surface. This fragmentary pavement, built of boulders set on their edges and plastered into place, measures 2.25 × 1.4 m against the north wall of the Qasr (Fig. 14). The hard plaster seals against the Qasr. An inscribed sherd excavated with this pavement in 2017 notes a measurement of oil, "šmn 10." Pottery from the mixed debris layers above and around the pavement range from Early Bronze to Nabataean and Roman periods, suggesting a date for its construction and use that could be contemporary with the above-mentioned Nabataean platform (Ninow, 2008). Boulders tumbled from the Qasr and other possible architecture in the area obscure this later stratigraphy. The Qasr's building stones, including more limestone than used in the original Iron Age basalt construction, doubled the height of the Qasr at some point, though when is not yet clear from these exterior excavations.

2.6 Qasr Phasing Comments

Taking the associated architecture into account alongside a complete view of the north Qasr wall courses, we can suggest two main phases of use for the Qasr at Baluʿa (Fig. 15). The Qasr was constructed in the Early Iron II period, our Building

Fig. 14 The fragment of the Phase 4 cobbled stone pavement sealing against the north wall of the Qasr. The plaster is visible where the pavement meets the wall stones. (Photo B17.24.42.004)

Fig. 15 The completed exposure of the Qasr's north wall, with two visibly distinct phases of construction. (Photo B19.24.42.141_30July)

Phase 2A, as a monumental structure with possibly four main courses to its north wall, consisting of very large basalt boulders. Two main Iron Age domestic occupations made use of the space to the north of the Qasr, consisting of our Building Phases 2B and 3. The Qasr was then reused in the Nabataean/Roman period, Building Phase 4, adding several more courses of boulders, now mostly of very large limestone boulders with the occasional basalt boulder. This later phase consolidated the top row of remaining Iron Age boulders before reusing them as the base for their new courses. This preliminary understanding of the phasing will be tested by further excavation in this area in future seasons.

3 Concluding Remarks

While more work needs to be done to confirm and refine the dating of the Qasr, a date in the Iron IIB fits comfortably with other architectural finds at Baluʿa, including a large casemate perimeter wall and an extensive domestic area. The date also fits with other hints of an elite culture at the site, even if they date slightly later to the Iron IIC. These include: (1) a partially preserved inscription on the rim of a basalt fragment that is possibly restorable to [b]t mlk, "the daughter of the king" – found in secondary context, Zayadine dated it paleographically to the eighth century BCE (Worschech et al., 1986: 302–304); (2) an inscription on a small basalt mortar reading "We made the pestle for the chief [of]/[the] sons of the spring, the firstborn with his house" (Worschech, 2006); (3) a statue fragment that preserves feet on a pedestal base that is possibly Iron Age (found near the Nabatean podium/altar; Keller & Tuttle, 2010: 530–531), and (3) the above-mentioned basalt volute fragment that most likely dates to the eighth or seventh century BCE (Tyson & Ninow, 2019). Taken together, the architecture and other finds point to Baluʿa's connection to the broader sociopolitical intensification occurring across the southern Levant in the Iron IIB and IIC related to long-distance trade, powerful regional polities, such as Israel and Damascus, and then the Neo-Assyrian and Neo-Babylonian empires (for detailed discussion of Moab's history and place during the Iron II, see Gaß, 2009; Routledge, 2004; Timm, 1989; Vera Chamaza & Galo, 2005). This is not particularly surprising given Baluʿa's position at an important access point to the Wadi Mujib drainage basin that almost certainly means Baluʿa was engaged in managing overland trade moving north-south.

Many details about the Qasr, the site more generally, and how it relates to other sites in Moab and beyond remain to be discovered and teased out. What was the function of the Qasr? Who built it? When did the Qasr go out of use? Was the construction of the Qasr connected with Moab's strengthening under Mesha in the ninth century BCE? As the largest Iron Age site in the area, what role did Baluʿa play as a center of political and economic power? Did this role change from the preceding period in which Baluʿa might have been the most powerful site in the region (see Finkelstein & Lipschits, 2011: 146–147 for one suggestion)? How did the regional and supra-regional contexts affect the inhabitants of Baluʿa?

For now, these questions remain to be answered with real clarity. The dating of the Qasr to the Iron IIB does, however, begin to direct our focus and provide a foundation on which to build a more robust and precise understanding of Baluʿa.

Acknowledgments The BRAP is sponsored by La Sierra University and Theologische Hochschule Friedensau, is supported by Walla Walla University, and has received grants from the Versacare Foundation to support the 2017 and 2019 seasons. We especially appreciate the partnership of the Department of Antiquities of Jordan and the support of ACOR while we are in Jordan. We want to thank all those who have participated in the project over the years.

References

Bramlett, K., Vincent, M. D., & Ninow, F. (2018). Khirbat al-Baluʿa. *Archaeology in Jordan Newsletter: 2016 and 2017 Seasons*, pp. 61–62.
Bramlett, K., Vincent, M. D., & Ninow, F. (2020). Khirbat al-Baluʿa. *Archaeology in Jordan Newsletter: 2018 and 2020 Seasons*, pp. 119–121.
Crowfoot, J. W. (1934). An expedition to Baluʿah. *Palestine Exploration Quarterly, 66*(2), 76–84.
Finkelstein, I., & Lipschits, O. (2011). The genesis of Moab: A proposal. *Levant, 43*, 139–152.
Gaß, E. (2009). *Die Moabiter*. Geschichte und Kultur eines ostjordanischen Volkes im 1. Jahrtausend v. Chr. Harrassowitz
Glueck, N. (1933–1934). *Explorations in Eastern Palestine I* (The annual of the American Schools of Oriental Research 14). The American Schools of Oriental Research.

Healey, J. F. (2001). *The religion of the Nabataeans: A conspectus*. Brill.
Horsfield, G., & Vincent, H. L. (1932). Une stèle Égypto-Moabite au Balouʿa. *Revue Biblique, 41*, 417–444.
Keller, D. R., & Tuttle, C. R. (2010). Archaeology in Jordan, 2008 and 2009 seasons. *American Journal of Archaeology, 114*, 505–545.
Miller, M. (Ed.). (1991). *Archaeological survey of the Kerak Plateau*. American Schools of Oriental Research.
Ninow, F. (2008). Khirbat al Baluʿ excavation project 2008. *Munjazat, 9*, 86–87.
Reyes, A. T., & McKenzie, J. S. (2013). The Altars. In *The Nabataean Temple at Khirbet et-Tannur, Jordan. Vol. 2: Cultic offerings, vessels, and other specialist reports – Final report on Nelson Glueck's 1937 excavation. The annual of the American Schools of Oriental Research 68*. The American Schools of Oriental Research, pp. 51–72.
Routledge, B. (2004). *Moab in the Iron Age: Hegemony, polity, archaeology*. University of Pennsylvania Press.
Routledge, B., & Routledge, C. (2009). The Baluʿa stela revisited. In P. Bienkowski (Ed.), *Studies on Iron Age Moab and neighboring areas in honour of Michèle Daviau* (pp. 71–95). Peeters.
Schmid, S. G. (2007). Nabataean fine-ware pottery. In D. P. Konstantinos (Ed.), *The world of the Nabataeans: Volume 2 of the international conference "The World of the Herods and the Nabataeans" held at the British Museum, 17–19 April 2001*. Franz Steiner Verlag.
Tholbecq, L. (2007). Nabataean monumental architecture. In K. D. Politis (Ed.), *The world of the Nabataeans. Vol. 2 of the International Conference The World of the Nabataeans held at the British Museum, 17–19 Apr 2001*. Oriens et Occidens 15, 103–143.
Timm, S. (1989). *Moab zwischen den Mächten: Studien zu historischen Denkmälern und Texten*. Harrassowitz.
Tyson, C. W., & Ninow, F. (2019). A Basalt Volute Fragment from *el-Bālūʿ*, Jordan. *Zeitschrift des Deutschen Palästina-Vereins, 135*, 158–167. Tafeln 21–22.
Vera Chamaza, & Galo, W. (2005). *Die Rolle Moabs in der neuassyrischen Expansionspolitik*. Ugarit-Verlag.
Vincent, M. D., Vincent, M. L., & Ninow, F. (2014). Baluʿa regional archaeology project. In J. Corbett et al., (Eds.), Archaeology in Jordan, 2012–2013 seasons. *American Journal of Archaeology, 118*(4), 649–650.
Worschech, U. (1989). Preliminary report on the second campaign at the ancient site of el-Baluʿ in 1987. *Annual of the Department of Antiquities of Jordan, 33*, 111–121.
Worschech, U. (1990). Ergebnisse der Grabungen in el-Baluʿ 1987: Ein Vorberichte. *Zeitschrift des Deutschen Palästina-Vereins, 106*, 86–113.
Worschech, U. (1991). Eine keilalphabetische Inschrift von el-Balu? *Ugarit Forschungen, 23*, 395–400.
Worschech, U. (1992). El-Baluʿ: A Moabite City in Central Jordan. In S. Kerner (Ed.), *The near East in antiquity: German contributions to the archaeology of Jordan, Palestine, Syria, Lebanon and Egypt, volume III* (pp. 9–17). Goethe-Institut, German Protestant Institute for Archaeology, Al Kutba.
Worschech, U. (1995). City planning and architecture at the Iron Age City of al-Baluʿ in Central Jordan. *Studies in the History and Archaeology of Jordan, V*, 145–149.
Worschech, U. (1997). Baluʿ. In E. Meyers (Ed.), *The Oxford encyclopedia of archaeology in the near east. Volume 1: ABBA-CHUE* (pp. 269–270). Oxford University Press.
Worschech, U. (2000). Rectangular profiled rims from el-Baluʿa': Indicators of Moabite occupation? In L. Stager, J. Greene, & M. Coogan (Eds.), *The archaeology of Jordan and beyond: Essays in Honor of James A. Sauer* (Studies in the archaeology and history of the Levant 1) (pp. 520–524). Eisenbrauns.
Worschech, U. (2006). An inscription from al-Baluʿ (Ard al-Karak). *Annual of the Department of Antiquities of Jordan, 50*, 99–106.

Worschech, U., & Ninow, F. (1992). Preliminary report on the third campaign at the ancient site of el-Baluʿ in (1991). *Annual of the Department of Antiquities of Jordan, 36*, 167–174.

Worschech, U., Rosenthal, U., & Zayadine, F. (1986). The fourth survey season in the north-west Ard el-Kerak, and soundings at Baluʿ 1986. *Annual of the Department of Antiquities of Jordan, 30*, 285–310.

Zayadine, F., & Worschech, U. (1988). Khirbet el-Baluʿ (1986–1987). *Syria, 65*, 415–419.

The Case for Jalul as Biblical Bezer

Randall W. Younker

Abstract Tall Jalul is the largest tell in central Jordan. Its size and central location dominate the Madaba Plains, indicating that it was doubtless a site of some importance. This article reviews past proposals of its ancient identity, along with an analysis of geographical, textual, and archaeological data (based on the author's excavations over the last 20 years), with the aim of determining its most likely identity. The article concludes that based on available evidence, the most likely identity for Jalul is Bezer, a Levitical city of refuge mentioned in Deuteronomy 4:43; Joshua 20:8; Joshua 21:36.

Keywords Jalul · Bezer · Madaba Plains · Heshbon · Levitical city · Moabite plateau · King's highway

1 The Identity of Ancient Jalul

One of the challenges that many scholars face is ascertaining the ancient identity of the site they are excavating. This is no less true of Tall Jalul, a large, centrally located site (5 km east of Madaba) in the middle of the Madaba Plains. Its size and location, along with its long occupational history, suggest that it played an important role in the region in antiquity. At 74 dunams (74,000 sq. m or 18 acres) and occupying the highest point in the Madaba Plains (830 m asl) it is the most imposing archaeological site in the locale. Moreover, its settlement history runs (with some interruptions) from the latter part of the Early Bronze Age to the Ottoman period (see below)—nearly 5000 years of occupational activity. It is virtually inconceivable that such a large, occupied site in so dominating a position did not play a major role in the regional political, cultural and social history of the Madaba Plains. Its

R. W. Younker (✉)
Institute of Archaeology Andrews University, Berrien Springs, MI, USA
e-mail: younker@andrews.edu

© The Author(s), under exclusive license to Springer Nature Switzerland AG 2023
E. Ben-Yosef, I. W. N. Jones (eds.), *"And in Length of Days Understanding" (Job 12:12): Essays on Archaeology in the Eastern Mediterranean and Beyond in Honor of Thomas E. Levy*, Interdisciplinary Contributions to Archaeology, https://doi.org/10.1007/978-3-031-27330-8_39

ancient identity, therefore, must be among those significant places known for this region from ancient sources. But which one?

Its modern name, Jalul, has not provided many clues. Ibrahim Zabn, a Jordanian archaeologist who excavated part of the Islamic village at Jalul, suggested that the name Jalul comes from an Arabic word *Jaljul,* which mean luck. He also suggests that *Jaljul* in Aramaic means the high slope (Zaben, 2002). Unfortunately, he provides no references or support for his suggestions, nor does he tie the name to any ancient site.

Various scholars have suggested several possibilities for the identity of Jalul during Bronze and Iron Age times. These suggestions have included Heshbon (Num 21) (Horn, 1979a, b; Geraty, 1994), Jahaz, and Bezer (Dearman, 1989a, b; MacDonald, 2000: 177–178), the latter being one of the cities of refuge located in Transjordan (Josh 20:8). As we shall show, of these three proposals, recent views have been moving towards identifying Jalul with Bezer. At the same time, however, many earlier scholars, working from the Biblical references to Bezer have proposed other sites as ancient Bezer with Umm al 'Amad being the most common. We shall return to their suggestions below.

1.1 Is Jalul Biblical Heshbon?

At one point in my thinking, I favored identifying Jalul with Sihon's Heshbon (Num 21:21–35, Deut 2:24 and 29:7)—following up on the suggestions by Horn and Geraty. Support for this identification seemed to come from the discovery of a water system in Jalul which included a large reservoir and a water channel that seemed to run from the reservoir to a series of pools outside the city wall to the south. We thought that the water reservoir and the extramural pools might be the pools of Heshbon mentioned in the Song of Solomon (7:4). However, further study showed that the channel seems to have been constructed in the seventh century BCE (too late for Solomon) and does not seem to connect with the earlier (tenth–ninth century BCE) reservoir as originally thought. Moreover, there is less certainty that the water channel carried fresh water as opposed to sewage. Thus, it seems unlikely that the Jalul water channel fed the pools of Heshbon. Moreover, recent re-evaluation of the reservoir at Tall Hesban suggests that the large square reservoir/pool there does indeed date to the tenth century BCE, and thus remains a viable candidate for being at least one of the pools of Heshbon (Sauer, 1994: 241–243; Ray, 2001). These factors have led me to question whether Heshbon is a viable candidate for the ancient identity of Jalul.

Of the other proposals that have been made, the equation of Jalul with Bezer (as proposed by Dearman, 1989a, b) seems to make the most sense presently (Dearman has adequately dealt with Jahaz in his articles—see discussion below).

Before exploring the arguments that favor identifying Jalul with ancient Bezer, it is important to note that scholars have proposed other sites in the Madaba Plains region as ancient Bezer. The most commonly proposed candidate for Bezer as been

Umm al- 'Amad, a large site about 400 meters in diameter, located beside the Amman/Madaba road about 11 kms northeast of Madaba. Some Iron Age I, II, and IIB/Persian sherds have been found at the site (Ibach, 1987: 24). A few wall stubs found on the site are probably from recent nineteenth century occupation.

The earliest proposal that Bezer be located here was by the French geographer Félix-Marie Abel (1938: II, 264). He does not give a specific justification for this identification. Abel was followed by Ludwig Köhler (1953), Jan Jozef Simons (1959: 207), Albertus H. Van Zyl (1960: 91–92), and Yohanan Aharoni (1979: 339, 432). None of these scholars provided much justification for this identification except that Umm al—'Amad was large and in the eastern part of the tablelands of the Madaba Plains region not far from the eastern desert, meeting the Biblical requirement that Bezer was located on the tableland and the desert—generally understood to be on the border between the plain and the desert.

One exception to locating Bezer at a place other than Umm al- 'Amad was that of Zecharia Kallai who suggested Qaṣr Sāliyyeh instead (1986: 441) although without much justification. The Qaṣr Sāliyyeh proposal has not gained much support. Indeed, it has been proposed as an alternate site by several scholars for Kedemoth (see MacDonald, 2000: 94 for references).

As we will show below, the most detailed geographic analysis of the location of Bezer is that of Andrew Dearman who concluded that the best candidate for Bezer is Tall Jalul. We will argue that there are three lines of evidence that seem to support Jalul's identity with ancient Bezer: (1) geographic considerations; (2) historical/archaeological correlations; (3) and finally, some linguistic considerations.

1.2 Which Bezer?

Before looking at the geographical evidence in the Hebrew text for the location of Bezer, it is important to note that there are actually *three* placenames that are located in Jordan which have very similar names to biblical Bezer: (1) Bozrah of Moab/Bezer of Reuben; (2) Bozrah of Edom and; (3) Bozrah/Bosor of Gilead (Haurān). Naturally, we are interested in the Bezer located in Moab—so, which of our Hebrew texts describe Bezer of Reuben/Moab?

There is no doubt that the Bozrah of Isaiah 34:6; 63:1; Amos 1:12; Micah 2:12; Jeremiah 49:13, 22 is the name of the Edomite capital and properly equated with the ruins at Bouseira, Jordan, located 20 km south of Tafilah; the Arabic Bouseira, or course, still echoes the ancient Edomite name.

However, the Bozrah mentioned in Jeremiah 48:24 appears to be Bezer of Reuben; it is listed as a city of refuge in the wilderness (*midbar*) on the plateau (*mishor*) within the territory of the Reubenites (Deut 4:43; Josh 20:8), as well as a Levitical city within the same tribal territory (Josh 21:36; 1 Chr 6:78). Most interesting is that it seems to be the same town as *Bezer* mentioned in the Mesha Inscription (MI Line 27; ANET 320–321) where it is described as a ruined city that Mesha rebuilt. This Bezer of Reuben and Moab seems to have continued to be occupied during the talmudic period, since queries originate during this time as to whether Bezer belonged to Israel—an important question in that the answer affected whether or not Jewish occupants of Bezer were obligated to pay tithe on their agricultural produce.

Bezer of Reuben is sometimes confused with Bosra in the land of Gilead (the Haurān, located in what is now southwestern Syria and northwestern Jordan). The site today, located in southwestern Syria, is known in Arabic as بصرى or *Buṣrā/Bosra* (although Frants Buhl identified the ancient site with a site known in his time as Buṣr el-Bariri—see Buhl, *Geographie des Alten Palästina*, 1896: 253); historically, it has also sometimes been called Bostra, Busrana, Bozrah, Bozra, Busra ash-Sham and *Nova Trajana Bostra*). This city is mentioned in 1 Maccabees 5:26, 36 as a place conquered by Judas Maccabees. Josephus also makes reference to this battle (Antiquities 12.8.3). The confusion of Bosrah in Gilead with the more southern towns of the same name is noted in Lightfoot's *The Talmud and Hebraica* (1859: 177): "In the Jews we read, 'Trachon, which is bounded at Bozra.' Not Bozrah of Edom, Isaiah 63:1; nor Bezer of the Reubenites, Joshua 20:8; but another, to wit, Bosorra, or Bosor, in the land of Gilead," (concerning which see Josephus, and the First Book of Maccabees, 5:26).

Beyond their clarification of the three Bozrahs, the references in the Talmud are important in that they seem to suggest that Bezer in Moab (Reubenite Bezer) was still occupied between the third and sixth centuries CE. This point can be helpful in identifying Reubenite Bezer with the appropriate archaeological site (below).

1.3 Reubenite/Moabite Bezer

Having identified those Hebrew and extra-biblical texts that are talking about Reubenite/Moabite Bezer, we can now consider identifying archaeological sites that best fit the biblical description. Probably the best study in attempting to locate Reubenite Bezer is that of Andrew Dearman (1989a, b). After a brief review of text critical analysis of those passages that refer to Reubenite and Levitical cities in Transjordan, Dearman proceeds to the question of the geographical location of these sites. Dearman first notes that both Kedemoth and Jahaz are said to be located in the *midbar*—the wilderness or open steppe land of the Moabite plateau—north of the Arnon River and east of the King's Highway (which runs south past Heshbon and Madaba). Dearman then directs us to the description of Israel's battle with Sihon (Deut 2: 26–32) which shows that Jahaz must be located south or southeast of Heshbon, and Kedemoth is located south or southeast of both of them.

Next, Dearman discusses the locations of Bezer and Mephaath. Like Kedemoth and Jahaz, Bezer is also said to be located in the *midbar*. Mephaath has been reliably identified with Umm er-Rasas via inscriptional and ceramic evidence—placing it also in the *midbar* (Younker & Daviau, 1993). Thus, all four of these cities are located in the *midbar*—the eastern section of the Transjordanian plateau and east of the main settlement line along the King's Highway. Various prophetic references also indicate that Bezer, Jahaz and Mephaath eventually became Moabite cities, suggesting that they could not be north of the Madaba Plains region (which would take us into the hill country of Ammon); rather, these cities are likely to be located towards the southern end of the Transjordanian plateau.

Dearman then turns to the Mesha inscription and notes that Bezer is mentioned there as well—as one of the cities that Mesha rebuilt. Dearman also points out that *none* of the settlements mentioned by Mesha are located north of Madaba. For example, Heshbon or Elealah—both, north of Madaba—are *not* mentioned in the Mesha Inscription. Since Bezer is said to be in the *midbar*, and it is *not* north of Madaba, near Heshbon or Elealah, it must be located in the steppe lands east or southeast of Madaba.

Finally, Dearman discusses the other two Israelite sites mentioned by Mesha—Ataroth and Jahaz (which also appear in the conquest account—noted above). Both of these sites are described as *bnh*—built up towns—during the time of Mesha. This would be an appropriate and expected description of fortified Israelite towns along the Moabite/Israelite border. There are actually two (or three towns) named Ataroth in the Hebrew Bible—one (or two) west of the Jordan River and one to the east. The eastern Ataroth has been securely identified with *Khirbet 'Aṭarus* on the Wadi Heidan—a northern tributary of the Mujib—the traditional northern border of Moab. This would mean Ataroth was the most southwesterly border city of Israel on the plateau, facing Moab. Due east of Ataroth, on the *Wadi eth Themed*—also on a tributary of the Mujib, is another fortified site known today as *Khirbet Medeiniyeh*. This site is located in the eastern steppe country or *midbar* and thus makes a suitable candidate for the Israelite site of Jahaz (Dearman, 1989a, b). Since Jahaz is on the most southeasterly border of the Israelite Transjordan plateau—the Israelite *midbar*—then Bezer must be located *north* of this location. Hence, one should look for ancient Bezer east or southeast of Madaba and north of Jahaz, Mephaath, and Ataroth. The only significant ancient site in that area is Tall Jalul.

1.4 The Bezer Tableland/Desert Boundary

A final point we might add is in reference to one of the main arguments for Umm al-'Amad being Bezer—the fact that Umm al-'Amad is located on the border between the tableland and the desert. It is interesting that if one looks at a satellite image of the Madaba Plains region (see Google map or Google earth at a resolution that zooms in so that Madaba is on the west, the Alia Airport on the east, and Umm al-'Amad at the north—one can easily see that Umm al-'Amad in the northeast part of the plain, is still within a well-watered agricultural belt that runs in a northeast direction from Madaba to some 7 kilometers past Umm al-'Amad. Indeed, Umm al-'Amad is just a few kilometers south of the southwest to northeast range of hills that defined the southern boundary of Amman for much of its history. These southern hills received more rainfall and while the rainfall rapidly diminished south of the hill country, cites like Umm al-'Amad still received enough to sustain agricultural activity. In short, while it is near the desert region to the east, Umm al-'Amad is not really on the border of the desert.

Tall Jalul, on the other hand (5 km east of Madaba), is obviously in a more arid area, southwest of Umm al- 'Amad, and east of Madaba with less rainfed agriculture. The agriculture that does exist around Jalul today is because of modern irrigation systems that have been set up near the site. But it is clearly less productive than the area immediately around Umm al- 'Amad. Again, this is clear not only from personal observation, but also from satellite images that show that the land immediately east Jalul is much drier and more desert like than is the land around Umm al 'Amad. Thus, even though Jalul is more west than Umm al- 'Amad, Jalul better fits the description of being on the border between the tableland of the Madaba Plain and the desert to the east. Some observers make the mistake of assuming that the border between the tableland and the desert runs in a straight north-south direction—roughly along the "desert highway." In reality, the geo-physical boundary between tableland and desert runs from the northeast to the southwest—roughly south of the Madaba-Umm al 'Amad-Amman highway. Thus, the desert moves to the west the more south one goes. Jalul is on the boundary.

2 Historical/Biblical Considerations

In addition to the geographic information that can be found in the ancient texts (biblical, Mesha and Talmud) about Bezer, there is also significant historical information that can assist in determining whether Bezer can be equated with the archaeology of Jalul. Ancient references to Bezer can be found in the following sources—the Hebrew Bible, the Mesha Inscription, possibly in the Transjordanian (Moab) itinerary of Ramesses II, and the Talmud. When literary references to Bezer are brought together, the following reconstruction of Bezer's history emerges:

2.1 A Levitical City Within the Territory of Reuben

Bezer appears in the Hebrew text as an early Israelite settlement town within the territory of the tribe of Reuben; it is designated by lot as a **Levitical city** (one of 48 such cities), a place of residence of the children of **Merari** of the Levite tribe (Josh 21:36; 1 Chronicles 6:63, 78); it is also designated as one of three cities of refuge in Transjordan (Deut 4:43; Josh 20:8, 21:36; 1 Chron 6:78, 7:37). These cities of refuge in Transjordan—north to south—were Golan (Land of Manasseh), Ramoth Gilead (Land of Gad), and Bezer (Land of Reuben) (Josh 20: 1–9).

As a city of refuge and a Levitical city, Bezer would have been occupied by Levites (see above; in this case the Merarites); it possibly had a sanctuary of some sort (1 Kings 12:31; see Mazar, 1992: 140); it would have had good roads leading to it for easy access (Deut 19:3); likely it was strategically located—again for easy access; it served as a provincial administrative center (Mazar, 1992: 142); and was also likely a well-fortified site since its function included not only protecting its inhabitants, but also protecting the eastern frontier of the Transjordan tribes (Mazar, 1992: 142–144; Lipiński, 2006: 327).

2.2 A Levitical City Within the Territory of Gad

During the time of Saul, it appears likely that the Reubenites abandoned their territorial holdings in the Madaba Plains region for better lands in eastern Gilead—apparently leaving their former territory to their sister tribe, Gad (for a review and critique of the history of the Reubenites see Oller, 1992, V: 692–693). Specifically, 1 Chronicles 5: 18–22, recounts an event during the time of King Saul in which the Reubenites, Gadites, and half of the tribe of Manasseh in Gilead formed an allied army of 44,760 to battle with the Hagrites in east Gilead. The Hagrites (sometimes spelled Hagarite) were an offshoot of the Ishmaelites mentioned in the Bible, and were the inhabitants of the regions of Jetur, Naphish and Nodab, located east of Gilead. Their name is understood to be derived from Hagar (Ps 83:7 [6]). The Transjordan tribes successfully defeated the Hagarites. As a result of the battle, the Reubenites captured the Hagrite lands as well as 50,000 camels, 250,000 sheep, 2000 donkeys. Finally, the Reubenites captured 100,000 Hagrites, including men, women and children, and held them as captives. Reuben is then said to have occupied the Hagrite tents, suggesting they abandoned their holdings in the Madaba Plains region (not too dissimilar from the migration of the tribe of Dan (for alternate views on what happened to Reuben see Oller, 1992: 693).

The migration of Reuben from the Madaba Plains region to eastern Gilead is not particularly significant in historical terms except for the interesting fact that later, in the Mesha inscription, Mesha (line 10) mentions confronting only Gadites (at Ataroth, southwest of Madaba)—not Reubenites—as the Moabites moved across the Arnon (Mujib) River north into the Madaba Plains (Jackson, 1989: 97). It is likely that as a result of the Reubenite migration, Bezer also fell within Gadite territory. However, the migration does raise the question of whether it would have had any effect on Bezer's material culture. My assumption is that there would have been little if any effect. For example, if Bezer had been a Levitical city, how would their material culture have differed (if at all) from that of Reubenites and Gadites? And if Bezer had been occupied by Levites, would they not likely have continued to occupy Bezer and not participated in the Reubenite migration north? This would suggest that the material culture of Bezer would have continued uninterrupted (apart from normal gradual evolutionary changes) from its initial settlement by the Israelites until its takeover by the Moabites during the latter part of the ninth century BCE (below).

2.3 A Moabite City

Line 27 of the Mesha Inscription describes the destructipn of Bezer (presumably by the Dibonites) and its acquisition and rebuilding by the Moabites (Jackson, 1989: 98). This would have taken place towards the latter part of the ninth century BCE, sometime between 840 and 820 BCE.

2.4 An Ammonite City

During the late eighth century BCE, Bezer came under Ammonite control. While the biblical text does not specifically mention Ammon's conquest of Bezer, there are a ew texts that indicate that during the time of Assyrian domination, Ammon was able to expand north into Gilead (Amos 1) and south into Heshbon and the lands of Gad (Jer 49)—which would conceivably include Bezer.

2.5 A Byzantine Settlement in Talmudic Times

As noted above, Bezer appears in later talmudic sources in the context of clarifying where Bezer/Bosrah of the Reubenites was located during talmudic times. Additional references in the Talmud concerning Bezer deal with its function as a city of refuge and the obligation of paying taxes on territory tied to Bezer. Also, as noted, these references in the Talmud are significant because they seem to suggest that Bezer in Moab (Reubenite Bezer) was still occupied between the third and sixth centuries CE (see Lipiński, 2006: 327). If so, we would expect archaeological evidence for occupation during these centuries (which seems to be the case at Jalul, as shown below).

3 Occupational History of Jalul

After tentatively identifying Bezer with Jalul based on geographic and historic references in ancient texts, we now turn to Jalul's archaeological findings to see if such an identification is plausible in terms of archaeology.

As noted in the introduction, Tall Jalul at 18 acres (74 dunams or 74,000 sq. m) is the largest tell site in the central Jordan plateau and occupies the highest point in the immediate region around Madaba, making it a most imposing feature on the western side of the Madaba Plain It is located 5 km due east of the town of Madaba and due west of Queen Alia International Airport. The tell is almost square in outline with a high, flat acropolis occupying the southwest quadrant. Several rocky hills on the tell are suggestive of badly eroded ruins of ancient buildings. Two broad depressions in the southeast quadrant indicate the presence of elements of ancient water systems—a cistern on the north and a reservoir to the south. The ruins of a large Byzantine/Islamic settlement is located immediately south of the tell. Surface surveys and excavations of both the tell and the settlement to the south have revealed an occupational history for Jalul that runs (with a few interruptions) from the Early Bronze Age to the end of the Ottoman period in the early twentieth century (see below).

Of special interest is the evidence of Iron Age occupation—the time of the Moabites, Israelites and Ammonites who alternately dominated the region around Jalul. Excavations at Jalul have revealed architectural remains from the Iron Age IA, Iron Age IIA, IIB, IIC, Persian etc. Byzantine, as well as Islamic periods (Younker et al., 2011: 58–63).

3.1 Early, Middle and Late Bronze Ages

The earliest materials that have been recovered from Jalul include an Early Bronze Age wall in Field W2, as well as some Middle Bronze Age and Late Bronze Age sherds that have appeared in fills beneath the Iron Age II buildings in Field A. Forms include various MB/LB White slip wares, Chocolate-on-White ware, Late Bronze Bichrome Ware, biconical jugs, and triangular rimmed cooking pots. No architecture has as yet been found in association with these fills or ceramics. Possibly these fills are outside the city wall of the MB and LB periods.

3.2 Early Iron Age IA (Thirteenth–Twelfth Centuries BCE (1250–1100 BCE)

Remains from the early Iron IA have now been recovered and identified from Fields A, B, C, D, E and G at Jalul.

The ceramics from the Iron Age IA occupational phase include carinated bowls, so-called Manasseh bowls, cooking pots with elongated triangular rim, and collared rim store jars. Some LB forms were present as well, such as Chocolate on White, triangular rimmed cooking pots, etc. Some pots exhibit Iron I painted designs. A preliminary comparison with similar materials found at nearby Tall Umayri, suggests the two corpi of Umayri and Jalul are the same. Herr has dated the Umayri materials to the late thirteenth century BCE, making Umayri one of the earliest Iron I settlements in Cis- and Transjordan (Herr, 2000). Tall Jalul would seem to have been occupied during the same period. Iron IA bowls at Umayri, Hesban (Ray, 2001: 43–45; (Herr, 2012: 18–26) and Jalul seem identical to the so-called Manasseh bowls on the west side of the Jordan. Herr (1999) has suggested these early forms may reflect a Reubenite presence in this region at the beginning of the Iron Age. The date for the latter part of this period in the twelfth century was confirmed by an Egyptian seal found in Field E. The hieroglyphics read "Amun-Re, Re of the Two Lands" and dates to the time of Ramesses III of the 20th Dynasty (c. 1187–1156 BCE). The architectural remains from this period include a courtyard building in Field D and a four-room pillared house in Field C—the presence of such a house, along with ceramics often associated with the early Israelite settlement period support Herr's suggestion of a Reubenite presence in this part of Transjordan at this time. This would also fit the reference in Joshua 13:15–23 that the tribe of Reuben occupied this area during the earliest settlement period.

3.3 Iron Age IB (Eleventh–Tenth Centuries BCE; 1100–980 BCE)

This phase was dated by associated ceramics—typical cooking pots and collared rim jars of the eleventh and tenth centuries were common. The Jalul corpus for this phase is essentially identical to that of nearby Hesban Strata 20 and 19 (see Ray, 2001: 45–49, 80–99; Herr, 2012: 26–53). There is no reason to think that this occupational phase does not represent the continued presence of the tribe of Reuben seen in Iron Age IA (see Ray, 2001: 79, 99, 110).

The architectural features of the Iron IA continued in use in the Iron Age IB—the courtyard building in Field D and the four-room house in Field C. Ashy lenses associated with the end of this phase suggest parts of Jalul were destroyed by fire, perhaps early in the tenth century BCE. The cause of the fire is uncertain, but one wonders about evidence attesting to Ammonite oppressive attacks against Reubenites and Gadites early in Saul's reign (see Oller, 1992: 693).

3.4 Iron Age IIA (Tenth–Ninth Centuries; 980–840/830 BCE)

Several strata from the Iron IIA have been excavated at Jalul. The earliest has been provisionally dated to the tenth–ninth centuries BCE (Iron IIA). Ceramics of the Iron IIA again reflect the Hesban corpus for Iron IIA—Stratum 18. These include collared pithoi, but they now have short vertical necks. Cooking pots include a unique form—high ridged cooking pots but with a vertical neck (later in the Iron IIB, the neck appears inverted) (see Ray, 2001: 49–53).

The Iron IIA architecture is represented by a modification of the four room pillared house to a three room pillared house in Field C. The approach ramp to the city gate in Field B was paved with flagstones in a manner similar to that seen at Cisjordan sites such as Dan and Beersheba. A patch of paving stones within the inner gatehouse as well as the pylons for the inner gatehouse also date from this period. The interior of the outer gatehouse was surfaced with small pebbles. In the area of the outer gatehouse was found an Iron II stamp seal with a stylized depiction of an ibex.

This occupation may represent the Gadites rather than the Reubenites based on both biblical texts (e.g. 2 Sam 24:5–6 where David's census mentions only Gad north of the Arnon) and the Mesha inscription which also mentions only Gad in this region. This would be a modification of Ray's suggestion that Reubenites were still living in the area (2001: 110).

3.5 Iron IIB (Ninth–Eighth Centuries BCE; 840/830– 732/701 BCE)

The Iron IIB pottery corpus for central Transjordan (including the heart of the Madaba Plains region) has been well documented by the Iron IIB house at Tall al-Umayri (Herr & Bates, 2011), Hesban Stratum 17 and 16B (Ray, 2001: 53–57; Herr, 2012: 101–118). Essentially the same corpus has been found a little more south at Madaba and now Jalul. It includes cooking pots with double grooved rims, pierced tripod cups, and angle-rimmed kraters and bowls.

What is unique about Jalul (and Madaba) is the presence of some Iron IIB wares and forms that are commonly found at Moabite sites to the south of Jalul. This includes square rim cooking parts (Worschech, 2000). There are also decanters, similar to those found in the Madaba Plains region, but those found at Moabite sites, but the painted line patterns are a little different in Moab than farther north (Worschech, 2000). *Worschech* has suggested this pattern is reflective of Moabite styling. Light colored slip typical on Moabite ceramics was was found in this field. The date Iron IIB date for this pottery coincides with the time of the Moabite incursion into the southern part of the Madaba Plains region as described in the Mesha Inscription which is dated from the middle to late ninth century (ca. 840 BCE). We would suggest that the Moabite pottery found at Jalul is reflective of Mesha's takeover and rebuilding of Bezer.

One architectural feature that is dated to this period is the pillared building found in Field G. Most of the Moabite styled decanters, wares and squared rim cooking pots were found in this building. The approach road to the eastern gatehouse was completely rebuilt at this time. Architectural remnants from this period was also found in Field A (only the corner of a building), and later phases of the pillared house in Field C and the courtyard house in Field D also date to this period. Interestingly while the associated pottery from the structures in Field A, C and D was clearly from the Iron Age IIB, not distinctive Moabites forms have been found there. Was only part of the site occupied by Moabites? Perhaps, a garrison to maintain control of the conquered site?

3.6 Iron IIC (Eighth-Early Sixth Centuries BCE 732/701 BCE–605/586/BCE)

Based on parallels for the ceramics of this stratum, as well as a number of inscriptional finds (described below), such as an Ammonite seal fro the seventh century (e.g. Younker, 1999 and Ammonite Ostracon from the sixth century (Gane, 2008), we have provisionally dated this phase to the seventh–sixth centuries BCE—specifically to the years 732/701 BCE to 605/586 BCE following Mazar's modified chronology (Mazar, 2005). The ceramics are typical Ammonite forms, including some with distinctive painted designs (see Ray, 2001: 126–137; Herr, 2012: 111–118). This points to an expansion of Ammon into formerly Moabite territory. The presence of an Assyrian bowl provides support to literary sources that Ammon was under Assyrian hegemony during this time of expansion.

The architectural remains include a tripartite building against the city wall (Field A), the rebuilding of the inner gatehouse of Field B; the pillared house in Field C was modified as was the courtyard building in Field D. In Field G, the pillared house was rebuilt. The city wall continued in use.

In Field B, the inner gatehouse area was repaved with flagstones. No evidence of this repaving appeared in the outer gatehouse or the approach road, so it is assumed the ninth–eighth century pavement continued in use in these areas.

In Field C the pillared house continued in use with some modifications. A seal from this room was found in the sift pile. It was carved out of a red-brown limestone and was divided into three registers—the middle depicted a winged griffin while the upper and lower registers contained an inscription, "belonging to 'Aynadab son of Zedek 'il." The paleography is typical of late seventh century Ammonite (Younker, 1998). A couple of other Ammonite inscriptions sating to the seventh–sixth centuries—a bulla and a seal—were found in Field D (Goulart & Gane, 2012). These inscriptions along with distinct Ammonite ceramics and objects support the occupation of Jalul by the Ammonites in the seventh–sixth centuries.

3.7 Iron IIC/Persian. (Early Sixth-Fifth Centuries BCE; 605/586 BC–331 BCE)

Jalul's Iron IIC-Iron IIC/Persian pottery closely parallels that of Hesban Stratum 16 and 15 (Ray, 2001: 57–61; 138–150) and Stratum 16A and Stratum 15 (Herr, 2012: 118–157).

The ceramics, objects, and inscriptional evidence point to occupation during the Iron IIC/Persian period. Iron IIC ceramics continue for the most part, and an Ammonite ostracon, Jalul Ostracon I, (Gane, 2008) containing an Ammonite inscription, dates the earlier part of this occupational phase to this period (sixth century BCE. It contains six lines of texts and deals with distributions of some commodity (probably grain) to or from certain individuals. However, a few Persian period forms, including Attic ware and a small Persian stone incense stand (see Stern, 1982: 182–195) appear with the earlier Iron IIC forms, pointing to a transition into the Persian period for the Ammonite occupants of the site during the latter part of this phase. Future work may provide more clarity on the transition into the Persian period and the latter part of its occupational phase.

The architecture of this period includes a semicircular wall in Field A, a patch of pavement in the inner Gatehouse in Field B; a street and two large buildings in Field C that appear to have administrative functions and a large domestic structure with several rooms in Field D.

3.8 Byzantine Occupation

Finally, it should be noted that immediately to the south of the tell in the area we refer to as the "Islamic Village," remains have been found from the Byzantine and early Islamic periods. This is possibly significant because of talmudic references to Bezer—the talmudic periods dated to between the third and sixth centuries A.D. (noted above; Reeg, 1989: 134–35). The extent of the Byzantine settlement at Jalul (Bezer?) is not yet fully known. Ceramics have been recovered during surface surveys; a Christian gravestone was found in Field A as was part of a wall of a building. In Field C, part of a mosaic floor and various architectural elements (such as column drums) of a Christian church were found under the ruins of an Ottoman period house.

4 Linguistic Considerations for Bezer (Hebrew, Egyptian, Arabic)

Finally, an interesting discussion that equates Bezer with Jalul is found in a recent study by Lipiński (2006). He notes that the Hebrew word בֶּצֶר (*bezer*) means "fortress." The adjectival form (*btrt*—Qal imperfect feminine plural) is usually translated as a "fenced" or "fortified" city (e.g. בְּצוּרוֹת Eze 36:35; בְּצֻרוֹת Num 13:28; בְּצוּרֹת Deut. 1:28, Nehemiah 9:25; בְּצֻרֹת Deut. 3:5, 9:1). Similarly, the name *bozrah* means a fortified place (see Gray, 1902: 3317; Borée, 1968: 51, 108). Lipiński notes that the Arabic *bẓr* means "to be inaccessible" and, thus, similarly reflects the meaning of a fortified place (Lipiński, 2006: 327). Therefore, while not absolutely determinative, it is not unreasonable to assume that Bezer's name had something to do with the fact that it was a well-fortified site. As noted above, part of the Iron Age city wall has been found at the southeast corner of the site in Field G testifying to the fact that Jalul was a fortified city during part of its occupational history (part of the city wall of the eighth and seventh centuries was also found on the north side of the site in Field A).

Lipiński also argues that Bezer may appear in the itinerary of the Egyptian pharaoh, Ramesses II. The relevant inscription appears in the Upper Egyptian Temple of Luxor, at the north end of the east wall of Ramesses II's court. The inscription dates to the ninth year of the pharaoh's reign, c. 1270 BC. It is a topographical list with a section describing Moab as well as some key cities there, including *Ti-bu-nu* and a place called *Bu-tá-r-tá*:

> A city which the mighty arm of Pharaoh, blessed be he, conquered in the land of Moab (*Mú-'a-bu*), Butarta (*Bu-tá-r-tá*).

> A city which the mighty arm of Pharaoh, blessed be he, [captured], of Dibon (*Ti-bu-nu*).

The place name *tpn/tbn* is generally identified with Dibon (modern Dhiban)—capital of the Moabites (Kitchen, 1964, 1992).

As for locating and identifying B[w]trt, Kenneth A. Kitchen (1992) argued that this site should likely be equated with the south Transjordanian toponym Raba Batora which appears in the Byzantine gazetteer *Taubla Peutingeriana* (Peutinger Table); Kitchen further equated Raba Batora with the modern site of ar-Rabba (Areopolis/Rabbat Mo'ab), south of the Wadi Mujib. However, other scholars believe that Raba Batora is better identified with the Betthoro of the *Notitia Dignitatum* (Or. XXXVII, 22), the latter of which is indisputably equated with the modern site of Lajjun, (see Lipiński, 2006: 319). If so, this leaves the identification of *B[w]trt* open.

However, Lipiński (2006: 327) has recently proposed a linguistic connection between the Hebrew Bezer and the Egyptian toponym *b[w]trt* in the Ramesses II Moabite itinerary. First of all, Lipiński notes that in Hebrew *bzr* is typically translated as a "fortification" while the Arabic cognate, *bzr*, means to be inaccessible—which reflects a similar sense as the Hebrew. Based on this, Lipiński proposes that *btrt* (apparently referring to the Hebrew bezer in its adjectival form and which means "fortified") is reflected in the Egyptian *B-t-r-t* (*B-w-t-i-r-t-i*) from the topographical list of Ramesses II (Lipiński, 2006: 327; cf. Kitchen, 1969–70: 180.2). Lipiński also notes that another form of the word בָּצְרָה, (*bṣrh*) as seen in Jer 48:24, is reflected in later rabbinic (talmudic) texts which discuss the town of Bosrah (see Reeg, 1989: 134–135 and below). Based on this, Lipiński argues that Ramesses II's *b[w]trt* is none other than biblical Bezer! Elsewhere, he argues that Jalul is the best candidate for this site (ibid.).

Routledge (2004: 59) has conveniently summarized some important aspects of this text. First, he notes that Moab is written with the determinative sign for a foreign land or hilly country. Following Gardner (1957), Routledge goes on to say that this sign marks a spatial totality—a geographical or political entity, rather than a regional subdivision or a group of people. Routledge further points out (following Kitchen) that the settlement *b[w]trt* is described as a *dmi* (town) the largest type of settlement the Egyptian would recognize in foreign countries—a true city (*niwt*) was reserved for Egyptians only (see Redford, 1997: 211 n.5). The *dmi* was typically understood to be a central settlement (actual scale relative to its territorial context) while a *wḥywt* (village/hamlet) would be a smaller, dependent settlement.

In view of the above observations, Routledge (2004: 60) summarizes the Ramesses II inscription concerning *b[w]trt* as follows:

> Ramesses II campaigns against a Levantine walled town (as opposed to a village or a Nubian settlement), inhabited by "Syrians" (as opposed to "Shasu nomads, "Hitties," or "Libyans"), ruled by a *wr* (as opposed to an '3) in a territory (as opposed to an *ethné*, or province) named Moab.

This all points to *b[w]trt* as a rather significant city in terms of the Transjordanian context. In terms of sheer size, Jalul is the largest site in central Jordan, even beyond Dhiban—it would not at all be surprising that these two sites were the very ones that would have attracted Ramesses II's attention on his foray into northern Moab. Equating Jalul with *b[w]trt* based on this criterion alone would make sense. If Lipiński's linguistic arguments are valid, then the case that Jalul is ancient Bezer is even stronger. Ramesses II's relief of this site would also provide us with an actual (albeit stylized) picture of Jalul!

5 Conclusion

In this article we have proposed that Tal Jalul be identified with the Biblical site of Bezer. Arguments in favor of this proposal are its geographical location, its prominence as large, fortified city, and its occupational history. Jalul fits the geography for Bezer based on the Bible and Mesha Inscription. It is south of Hesbon, *not* north of Madaba, north of Ataroth and Jahaz— and it is on the border of the plain and in the wilderness (desert). This is particularly obvious when one compares the water availability for rain-fed agricultural productivity for the two leading candidates for Bezer—Umm al- 'Amad and Jalul. Whereas Umm al- 'Amad is well within an agriculturally productive zone to the northeast, Jalul is literally on the border of the desert which encroaches westward towards Madaba in the central part of the Madaba Plains region.

The occupational history of Jalul, established by recent excavations by Andrews University, fits that of Bezer—Jalul was continuously occupied from the thirteenth century (settlement period for the Transjordan Israelite tribes) to the sixth/fifth centuries. Artifactual evidence, including ceramics and inscriptions support the alternate presence of Israelite, Moabite, and Ammonite, occupations, harmonizing nicely with Biblical and extra-Biblical sources. Jalul continued to be occupied in the Christian period (in the area immediately south of the tall) and thus supports references to Bezer in Talmudic sources.

The physical characteristics of Jalul seem to fit the requirements of Bezer as a city of refuge. Jalul is a large site, centrally located on the highest point in the central Madaba Plains and can be seen from every direction. This would make it easy to find for anyone seeking refuge. It was on the border of the wilderness to its immediate east and often served as a southern border site for northern occupiers (Israelite and Ammonite) and experienced incursions from the Moabites to the south. Besides being perhaps the largest site in the region, excavations reveal it was protected by strong city walls (seen in Fields A and G). All these factors taken together—its geographic location, its occupational history, its fortified walls, make Jalul a preferred candidate for Biblical Bezer.

References

Aharoni, Yohanan. 1979. The land of the Bible: A historical geography. .
Borée, W. (1968). Die alien Ortsnamen *Palästinas*. 2. Auflage. Leipzig 1930. Olms, Boren-Borenstein.
Buhl, F. (1896). *Geographie des alten Palästina*. J.C.B. Mohr.
Dearman, A. (1989a). Levitical cities of Reuben and Moabite Toponymy. *Bulletin of the American Schools of Oriental Research, 276*, 55–66.
Dearman, A. (1989b). *Studies in Moab and the Mesha inscription*. American Schools of Oriental Research.
Gane, R. E. (2008). Jalul Ostracon I. *Bulletin of the American Schools of Oriental Research, 351*, 73–84.
Gardner, A. (1957). *Egyptian grammar* (3rd ed.). Oxford University Press.
Geraty, L. T. (1994). Why we dug at tell Hesban. In D. Merling & L. Geraty (Eds.), *Hesban after 25 years* (p. 51). Andrews University.
Goulart, C. J., & Gane, R. E. (2012). Three epigraphic finds from Tall Jalul. *Bulletin of the American Schools of Oriental Research, 365*, 27–32.
Gray, G. B. (1902). Place names. In T. K. Cheyne & J. S. Black (Eds.), *Encyclopaedia Biblica* (Vol. 3, pp. 3307–3320). Adam and Charles Black.
Herr, L. G. (1999). Tall al-'Umayri and the Reubenite hypothesis. *Eretz Israel, 26*, 64–77.
Herr, L. G. (2000). The settlement and fortification of Tell al-'Umayri in Jordan during the LB/Iron I transition. In *The archaeology of Jordan and beyond: Essays in honor of James A. Sauer* (pp. 167–179). Eisenbrauns.
Herr, L. G. (2012). The Iron Age. In J. A. Sauer & L. G. Herr (Eds.), *Hesban 11, ceramic finds: Typological and technological studies of the pottery remains from Tell Hesban and vicinity* (pp. 9–172). Andrews University.
Herr, L. G., & Bates, R. D. (2011). The Iron IIB pottery from a stratum 8 house at Tall al-'Umayri, Jordan. *Eretz Israel, 30*(Amnon Ben-Tor Volume), 18–32.
Horn, S. (1979a). Heshbon. In S. Horn (Ed.), *Seventh-day Adventist Bible dictionary* (p. 484). Review and Herald Publishing Association.
Horn, S. (1979b). Reuben. In S. Horn (Ed.), *Seventh-day Adventist Bible Dictionary* (pp. 936–937). Review and Herald Publishing Association.
Ibach, R. D. (1987). *Hesban V: Archaeological survey of the Hesban Region*. Andrews University.
Jackson, K. P. (1989). The language of the Mesha' inscription. In *Studies of the Mesha inscription and Moab* (pp. 96–130). American Schools of Oriental Research.
Kallai, Z. (1986). *Historical geography of the Bible: The tribal territories of Israel*. Brill.
Kitchen, K. A. (1964). Some new light on the Asiatic Wars of Ramesses II. *Journal of Egyptian Archaeology, 50*, 47–70.
Kitchen, K. A. (1969). *Ramesside Inscriptions II*. B.H. Blackwell.
Kitchen, K. A. (1992). The Egyptian evidence on ancient Jordan. In P. Bienkowski (Ed.), *Early Edom and Moab: The beginning of the Iron Age in Southern Jordan* (pp. 21–34). Collis.
Lightfoot, J. (1859). *Horæ hebraicæ et talmudicæ;* Hebrew and Talmudical exercitations upon the Gospels, the Acts, some chapters of St. Paul's Epistle to the Romans, and the First epistle to the Corinthians (Oxford) (originally published in 1658).

Lipiński, E. (2006). *On the skirts of Canaan in the Iron Age: Historical and topographical researches*. Peeters.

MacDonald, B. (2000). *East of Jordan: Territories and sites of the Hebrew scriptures*. American Schools of Oriental Research.

Mazar, B. (1992). *Biblical Israel: State and people*. Israel Exploration Society.

Mazar, A. (2005). The debate over the chronology of the Iron Age in the southern Levant: Its history, the current situation and a suggested resolution. In T. E. Levy & T. Higham (Eds.), *The Bible and radiocarbon dating: Archaeology, text and science* (pp. 15–30). Equinox.

Oller, G. H. (1992). Reuben. In D. N. Freedman (Ed.), *The Anchor Bible Dictionary V* (pp. 692–692). Doubleday.

Ray, P. (2001). *Tell Hesban and vicinity in the Iron Age*. Andrews University.

Redford, D. (1997). The ancient "City": Figment or reality? In W. Aufrecht, N. Mirau, & S. Gauley (Eds.), *Aspects of urbanism in antiquity: From Mesopotamia to Crete* (JSOT supplement 244) (pp. 210–220). Sheffield Academic Press.

Reeg, G. (1989). Die Ortsnamen Israels nach der rabbinischen Literatur. *Biehefte zur Tubinger Atlas des Vorderen Orients, B/51*, 134–135.

Routledge, B. (2004). *Moab in the Iron Age: Hegemony, polity, archaeology*. University of Pennsylvania Press.

Sauer, J. A. (1994). The Pottery at Hesban and its Relationships to the history of Jordan: An interim Hesban pottery report, 1993. In D. Merling & L. T. Gearaty (Eds.), *Hesban after 25 years*. Andrews University.

Stern, E. (1982). *Material culture of the land of the Bible in the Persian period (538–331 BC.)*. Aris & Phillips.

Van Zyl, A. H. (1960). *The Moabites*. Brill.

Worschech, U. (2000). Rectangular profiled Rims from el-Balu': Indicators of moabite occupation? In L. E. Stager, J. A. Greene, & M. D. Coogan (Eds.), *The archaeology of Jordan and beyond: Essays in Honor of James A. Sauer* (pp. 520–524). Eisenbrauns.

Younker, R. W. (1998). An Ammonit, Seal from Tall Jalul, Jordan: The Seal of 'Aynadab son of Zedek 'il. In B. Levine (Ed.), *Eretz Israel* (Frank M. Cross Volume) (pp. 221–224). Israel Exploration Society.

Younker, R. W., & Daviau, P. M. M. (1993). Is Mefa'at to be found at Tell Jawa (South)? *Israel Exploration Journal, 43*, 249–251.

Younker, R. W., Gane, C. C., & Al-Shqour, R. (2011). In D. R. Clark, L. G. Herr, O. S. LaBianca, & R. W. Younker (Eds.), *The Madaba Plains project: Forty years of archaeological research into Jordan's past*. Equinox Publishers.

Zaben, I. (2002). The excavation and survey Jalul Village. *Munjazat, 3*, 74–75.

Remarks on the Typology and Chronology of Iron Age and Persian Period Winepresses

Samuel Richard Wolff

Abstract Industrial installations from Tel Gezer, Lod, Tel Hamid and Tel Megadim are discussed in this article. Each one adds to our understanding of the typology and chronology of Iron Age and Persian period winepresses. The built examples from Gezer, whose dates range from Iron Age I to Iron Age IIA, have recently been classified as olive oil presses. This interpretation is questioned here. These installations are the earliest ones to feature a large circular collecting vat, whether it was used for wine or olive oil. The sheer number of such installations suggests that the industry, whether it be wine or olive oil production, was beyond the norm for purely domestic usage. The winery from Lod, probably dated to Iron IIA, features built vats which may have been used both for pressing and collecting. The built double press from Tel Hamid, probably dated to Iron Age IIB, features treading floors and spouts leading to a rectangular collecting vats that had two built steps, forerunners of what was to become standard features in winepresses. The rock-cut installations from Megadim, probably dated to the Persian period, continues the tradition of treading floors and spouts leading to rectangular collecting vats. The predominance of shell in the plaster matrix of the Lod, Hamid and Megadim installations confirms their Iron Age and Persian period dates.

Keywords Winepress · Olive oil press · Tel Megadim · Tel Hamid · Lod · Tel Gezer

I discuss in this article some issues regarding the typology and chronology of winepresses, I choose to refer to these installations as winepresses rather than wineries or treading installations (Frankel 1997: 73, n. 2; 1999: 51; Fantalkin 2005), even if the grapes are "pressed" by foot or with the aid of rollers. "Winery" is a business that manufactures wine, or a building or property where wine is produced, not an

S. R. Wolff (✉)
W.F. Albright Institute of Archaeological Research, Jerusalem, Israel
e-mail: samwolff024@gmail.com

© The Author(s), under exclusive license to Springer Nature Switzerland AG 2023
E. Ben-Yosef, I. W. N. Jones (eds.), *"And in Length of Days Understanding" (Job 12:12): Essays on Archaeology in the Eastern Mediterranean and Beyond in Honor of Thomas E. Levy*, Interdisciplinary Contributions to Archaeology,
https://doi.org/10.1007/978-3-031-27330-8_40

installation itself. The complex from Lod described below or, on a much larger scale, the recently published complex from Tel Yavne (Hadad et al., 2021), to list two examples, can be considered wineries composed of several winepresses. This article is based on installations that were excavated decades ago (some by me but all connected to sites where I excavated) but were never fully published. The installations are from the sites of Tel Gezer, Lod, Tel Hamid and Tel Megadim (Fig. 1). The first three are built installations which date to the Iron Age while the last is rock-cut

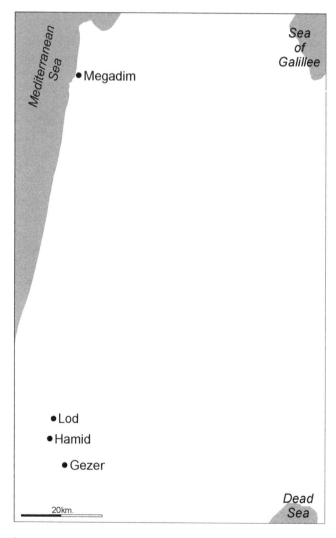

Fig. 1 Map of sites mentioned in the text

and most likely dates to the Persian period. They are discussed in chronological order (earliest to latest).[1]

1 Tel Gezer

In the 1972 season of the Hebrew Union College excavation, soon after Tom Levy participated in excavations at the site, an installation was revealed in Field X (Fig. 2). This installation, interpreted by the excavators as a winepress, was mentioned in a preliminary report (Seger, 1973: 251) but was never published in full. The recent Tandy excavations at Gezer re-excavated this installation in order to understand its context in relation to the stratigraphy in the newly excavated adjacent field.[2] The installation, Locus 1017, measures 2.00 m. in diameter at the top, 1.70 m. in diameter on the pressing stone and 0.80–0.84 m. in height (capacity: c. 2155 liters). The pressing stone itself was c. 30 cm thick and featured a sump which measured 0.55 × 0.46 × 0.28 m. At some point in time in antiquity the pressing stone cracked into two pieces and clay-like material was inserted into the crack. The walls were

Fig. 2 Gezer Field X installation. (Photograph courtesy of J.D. Seger)

---

[1] It is my great privilege to participate in this festschrift in honor of Tom Levy, my friend and colleague from at least as far back as his tenure as Professor at Hebrew Union College, Jerusalem and as Assistant Director of the Albright Institute of Archaeological Research, Jerusalem.

[2] Arbino (2018) pointed out that this same installation was first discovered by R.A.S. Macalister, making it thrice excavated.

described in the unpublished locus sheet as being plastered not with hydraulic plaster but rather an "unbaked mudbrick material," probably the same as the "red mud mortar mixed with marl" (Dever et al., 1970: 25) or "rendzinate field clay" (Dever, 1986: 53, 98) lining similar installations from Gezer. A foundation trench was dug to enable the construction of the vat. Despite having no surfaces associated with it, this vat, then, was either partially freestanding or totally built below the ancient surface. The HUC and Tandy excavators phased this installation to the early Iron I.

The base of a similar installation, also with sump, was found in the Tandy excavation in secondary use (Locus 41038; Fig. 3). It was roughly circular in shape and measured 1.30–1.33 m. in diameter and 0.31 m. in thickness. The sump, cut at its extremity, measures c. 0.34 m. in diameter and c. 0.20 m. in depth.

This type of installation is well-known at Gezer. Almost identical examples were excavated by HUC in Field I (Locus 1016; Dever et al., 1970: 25 and Pl. 7B) and Field VI Loci 13043, 18049 and 17020 (Dever, 1986: 47–48) and Pl. 83A–B; 98 and Pl. 103B; 124–126 and Pls. 113B and 114A) and range in date from LB II to Iron IIA. In the first publication mentioning such installations, they were described as being freestanding (Dever et al., 1970: 25), but in a later publication they were interpreted as having been "partially sunken into a foundation trench, but it must also have been partially freestanding, like all the other LB II-Iron I vats excavated elsewhere at Gezer" (Dever et al., 1986: 124). Vat 13043 was certainly related to Surface 13047 which adjoined its uppermost (preserved) course of stones (Dever et al., 1986: Plan V). Thus, while some installations were partially freestanding others may have been constructed with a surface reaching its uppermost course. Beeri (2008) noted that all of the Gezer installations were partially set into the ground

Fig. 3 Gezer Tandy excavations, installation base *ex situ*. (Photograph by Samuel Wolff)

with the exception of Locus 1016 which was freestanding (the latter following Dever et al., 1970: 25).

In addition to the examples mentioned above, it has been claimed that c. 43 of these installations were excavated at Gezer by Macalister (Arbino, 2018; for the base of one example see Macalister, 1912: 62, Fig. 255). This is based on counting the number of times that the letter "M" (representing "fruit presses") appears on Macalister's plans (Macalister, 1912: 60). Needless to say, it is impossible to date these installations with certainty.

A similar installation but with two sumps, dated to the twelfth century BCE, was found at Lachish Stratum VI (Barkay & Ussishkin, 2004: Fig. 8.45; Ussishkin, 2014: 171, Fig. 8: 26).

The Gezer installations and similar ones from elsewhere (e.g. Lachish, Tel Miqne) were among the earliest to feature a large constructed collecting vat (which may have functioned as a treading installation as well; cf. Ayalon, 1994)[3] as opposed to a small sunken stone vessel or ceramic jar as was the custom in the Late Bronze Age, extending into the Iron Age II (references to the latter in Onozuka, 2012: appendix to which add Macalister, 1912: 66, Fig. 260). The question is whether they functioned as winepresses or olive oil installations. Beeri (2008) and later Onozuka (2012: 74) argued that the Gezer installations, which belong to Beeri's Types 1.2 and 1.3, were olive presses and not winepresses. While this interpretation is certainly possible, I would not disregard the possibility that the Gezer installations functioned as winepresses. Reasons adduced against identifying them as winepresses include that (1) it is more efficient to locate winepresses in vineyards rather than within the settlement; (2) that they were too small to have been efficient winepresses; and (3) that such a heavy stone base is unnecessary in winepresses. I would suggest in response that (1) vineyards could have been adjacent to the tell, perhaps even on the slope of the tell like the ones that exist today, less than 100 m. from the Iron Age gate. In the Byzantine period, evidence at the site of Avdat indicates that vineyards were located in the terraced wadis while elaborate winepresses were located at the site (Erickson-Gini, 2012); (2) installations with smaller capacities than the Gezer installations have been identified as winepresses (see, e.g., Arbel, 2009; Fantalkin, 2005: 5, Locus 146); (3) given the alternatives (hydraulic plaster had not yet been utilized in winepresses), a solid stone disk measuring 1.70 m in diameter and 0.30 m thick does seem unrealistic. I would add that it would have been superfluous had the builders constructed sidewalls of 80 cm. or higher for an olive press installation, assuming that the olives were trodden on the vat's stone surface (Frankel, 2006: 624–625; Onozuka, 2012: 81); either the operators were knee-deep in olive oil, which seems unlikely, or the olives were crushed elsewhere and the oil was collected

---

[3] This stands in contrast to Middle Bronze Age rock-cut winepresses that featured treading floors independent from collection vats (cf. Getzov & Covello-Paran, 2011). This arrangement is found in rock-cut installations that were located near the vineyards and not within settlements. The two-part press (treading floor and collecting vat) was eschewed at Gezer, only to appear somewhat later, in the Iron Age IIA at Tel Aphek and Tel Michal, and in the Iron IIB at Tel Hamid (see below). Dating the Tel Aphek winepresses to the Iron Age IIA (Kleiman, 2015: 201, n. 14) and not to the Late Bronze Age (Frankel et al., 2009) is a convincing suggestion; typologically there are no parallels from the Late Bronze Age.

in the installation, for which there is no evidence. One could make the same argument for wine pressing, but it seems more reasonable for wine to be trodden and collected in a vat rather than olives being trodden and/or the resultant oil collected. It would be worth attempting organic residue analysis on the plastered lining of such installations in order to shed light on this issue (cf. Pecci, 2021).

If the total number of these installations at Gezer is close to being accurate, it attests to an intensity of wine (or olive oil) production unparalleled at any other site (contra Beeri, 2008: 163). As an analogy, one could say that wine (or olive oil) production at Tel Gezer in the Iron I and IIA (c. 1200–1000 BCE) was what olive oil production was to Tel Miqne in the seventh century BCE. Unlike Miqne, however, these installations were distributed throughout the tell and were not confined to an industrial quarter. It is difficult to believe that such a large number of installations were strictly a domestic concern. Rather, the product, whether it be wine or olive oil, might have been produced at a household level in order to be collected and then commercially marketed through a wider distribution system administered through a central authority or private initiative, either way something unattested for the period in question (cf. Eisenberg, 2012, 17*).

2 Lod

A salvage excavation was conducted at the ancient site of Lod in 2000 (Yannai, 2008; Yannai & Marder, 2000), Only one area (F) yielded remains dated to the Iron Age. These remains consisted of four plastered installations—perhaps two couples like at Tell Qasile and other coastal plain sites—cut into virgin sand (Fig. 4; Wolff, 2023). These installations should be interpreted as winepresses. The installations averaged 1.20 m. in diameter and 1.20 m. in depth (capacity: c. 1357 l). A sedimentation pit or sump, averaging 0.70 m. in diameter and 0.50 m. in depth (capacity: c. 190 l), was cut into the eastern portion of the floor of each installation. The walls of the installations were lined with pebbles covered by numerous layers of white plaster, in places forming a coating up to 10 cm. thick. Two small plastered basins (one between Installations 1 and 2, the other between Installations 3 and 4) were found to the east of the installations, c. 0.40 m. in diameter and 0.20 m. deep. The upper portions of all of the installations were apparently shaved off, and no treading surfaces were found in the vicinity. The installations contained pottery dated to the Iron IIA (tenth/ninth centuries BCE) so they should be dated to that period or slightly earlier.

If we assume that the small plastered basins served as intermediate settling vats and that any means of communication with either the large plastered vats or the purported treading floors was sliced off, then the treading floors should have been located immediately to the east of these basins. This assumes, however, that these installations had treading floors. In fact, almost all of the contemporary parallels[4] to

---

[4] Parallels are listed in Fantalkin (2005: 18–20) and in Orsingher et al. (2020:6, 8, 9). Additional winepresses were published from Rishon LeZiyyon (Arbel, 2009) and Tel Qana (van den Brink, 2007, 2020).

Fig. 4 Lod Field F installations

the Lod installations lack treading floors. Were the treading floors not preserved (as most excavators believe) or did these installations not have treading floors? It could be that treading and collecting occurred in the same installation, much like the installations discussed above from Gezer (cf. Ayalon, 1994, summarized in English in Fantalkin, 2005: 18–19). The contemporary complexes from Tel Michal (Derfler, 2005; Herzog, 1989a) and Tel Aphek (Frankel et al., 2009)[5] preserve the earliest treading floors known to date in a constructed winepress.

3 Tel Hamid

In 2002 a salvage excavation was conducted c. 200 m. west of Tel Hamid, a tell located 3 km. southeast of Ramla and c. 11 km. south of Tel Gezer. Excavations on the slopes of the tell yielded several strata of occupation, the most impressive dating to the ninth and eighth centuries BCE (Wolff & Shavit, 2008). Excavations revealed a winepress or, to be more exact, a double winepress; that is, two adjacent treading surfaces with two adjacent rectangular collecting vats (Figs. 5, 6 and 7).[6] The preserved portion of Floor 1 measures 2.5 × 2.3 m. Floor 2 was only partially excavated

---

[5] See note 2 above.

[6] Side-by-side but not identical treading floors and collecting vats were also found at Tel Michal (Derfler, 2005; Herzog, 1989a) and at Tel Yavne (Haddad et al., 2021).

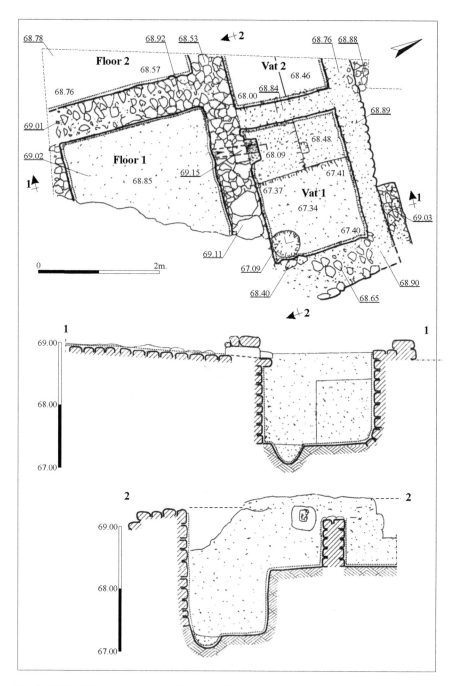

Fig. 5 Tel Hamid winepress, plan and sections. (Based on original drawing prepared by Avi Hajian)

Fig. 6 Tel Hamid winepress, treading floor. (Photograph by Tsila Sagiv)

(2.5 × 1.0 m); it continued into the west balk. The plastered floors were c. 8 cm thick and were set on a foundation of small cobble-size stones. The main constituent of the plaster matrix was crushed shell, a feature that characterizes Iron Age II (and later—see Megadim below and Shapira & Asscher, 2021)) installations (e.g., Tel Aphek, Tell Qasile, Rishon LeZiyyon, Jaffa and Tel Michal). Floor 2 is situated approximately 25 cm lower than Floor 1.

A channel was constructed through the wall separating Floor 1 from Vat 1 (Fig. 5); this channel terminated in a spout (hewn from a single stone?) that protruded into the vat (Fig. 6). This is the earliest example of a spout in a winepress; for a similar but not identical spout see collecting vats F and G from Tel Yavne, dated to the Persian period (Haddad et al., 2021: Fig. 11). Vat 1 (Figs. 3 and 6), whose total capacity was c. 4600 l, measured 2.3 × 1.6 m at the top, tapering slightly

Fig. 7 Tel Hamid winepress, collection vat. (Photograph by Tsila Sagiv)

towards the bottom. It was plastered with two layers of plaster. In Vat I, opposite the spout, were two steps, the lower step being closer to the spout than the higher step; the steps filled the entire width of the vat. The higher step measured c. 0.85×0.75 m, the lower step c. 0.84×0.84 m. The depth from the top of Vat 1 to the center of its floor is c. 1.56 m; from the top of the uppermost step to the floor, 1.14 m, and from the top of the lowermost step to the floor, 0.75 m. These steps are wider than those that appear in Classical period winepresses, their width coming at the expense of the capacity of the collecting vat; hence, comfortable entry into the vat(s) had higher priority over maximizing the capacity of expressed juice.[7] A small settling basin was found at the bottom of the vat, in the southeast corner; it measured c. 0.40 m in diameter and was c. 0.33 m deep. Vat 2 (1.55 × 0.95 m exposed, depth unknown), like Vat 1, had two similar steps (Fig. 3, right); only a portion of its two steps and none of its collecting vat were exposed, lying, as they were, beyond the western border of the excavation. Its capacity was presumably similar to that of Vat 1.

The alluvial soil that covered the installation contained pottery sherds that date to the Iron IIB (eighth century BCE, comparable to Strata VI and V on the tell). Thus, the press should probably be dated to the eighth century or somewhat earlier.

This press anticipates many of the features that will become standard in later periods; that is, a square or rectangular treading floor connected to a collection vat by a channel; a spout at the end of the channel; rectangular (as opposed to circular or oval) collection vats; and steps leading down into the collection vat.

4 Tel Megadim

Three rock-cut winepresses were discovered on the bank of the adjacent Wadi Khesib, some 60 m south of the southern perimeter wall of the Persian period settlement at Tel Megadim (official name: Tel Sahar; Broshi, 1967:278; Ronen & Olami, 1978:25 [Site 56]). One was excavated in its entirety and consists of a receiving vat (of some 12,000-liter capacity, according to Broshi's calculation; c. 10,800 according to my calculations) with three pressing floors around it (Figs. 8 and 9). The pressing floor opposite the settling basin measures 4.85 × 4.90 m (23.7 m^2); the ones to the side, being less well-preserved, measure 4.35 × 4.30 m (18.7 m^2) and 4.10 × 3.50 m (14.3 m^2). The receiving vat measures 2.75 × 2.70 × 1.3–1.5 m, with a sump (c. 0.75 in diameter and of unknown depth) set into a squarish settling basin (c. 1.0 × 1.0 × 0.40 m). Channels (only one visible in the photograph but all three indicated on the plan) conduct the expressed grape juice from the treading floors into the collection vat. Since three treading floors would produce too much juice to be contained in the collecting vat, one must consider the possibility that the two side floors were not treading surfaces but rather where grapes were left out in the sun, three days after which the choice sweet wine was pressed (cf. Frankel, 1999: 204, section A.2.2.1.8.3).[8] The entire installation is well plastered (up to three layers), with many shells in the plaster matrix, and was very well preserved.

---

[7] For a step in a vat from Ashkelon that dates slightly later (seventh century BCE) (see Stager et al., 2011: 18).
[8] I am grateful to E. Ayalon for this suggestion.

Fig. 8 Tel Megadim winepress. (Photograph courtesy of the Magen Broshi archives)

Rock-cut winepresses are notoriously difficult to date. The morphology of this press is not so different from Roman or Byzantine presses. The fact that the plaster contained much shell argues, however, for an earlier date. Shell-tempered plaster, as mentioned above, is typical of almost all Iron Age II winepresses and of the Persian period winepresses at Tel Yavne (Shapira & Asscher, 2021). Given that there was no Iron Age, Hellenistic or Roman period occupation at Tel Megadim but that there was a strong Persian period presence, I suggest that the presses date to the Persian period. If this is so, they would be among the very few Persian period winepresses that we know of, filling a gap between those from the Iron Age II and the Hellenistic period.[9]

---

[9] The most notable example of Persian period winepresses is found in the winery from Tel Yavne (Haddad et al., 2021); others were identified at the Nesher Quarry at Ramla (Avrutis, 2015: 8–11, 199), Tel Michal (Herzog, 1989b: 110), Southern Samaria (Tavgar, 2018: 414), and Khirbet Khaddash (Eitam, 1992). The above description, plan and photographs of the Megadim presses appear courtesy of the Magen Broshi archives; the author never observed the installations. It is unknown to me if they still exist. If they do, they would be in the small triangular area between the railroad tracks and the coastal highway, 60 m. east of the southern perimeter wall of the Persian period site. It is likely, however, that they were discovered in the course of construction of either the tracks or the highway and were subsequently destroyed.

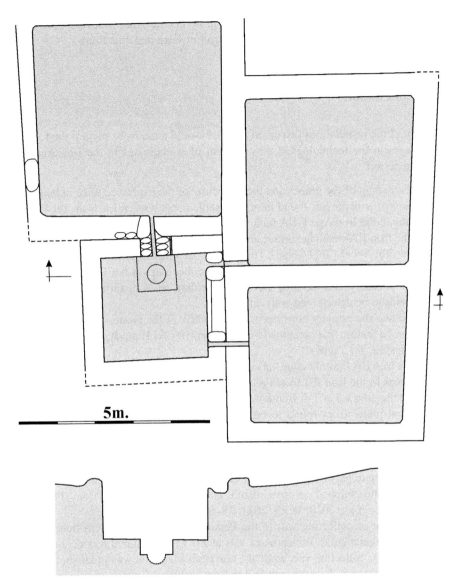

Fig. 9 Tel Megadim winepress, plan and section. (Based on a drawing from the Magen Broshi archives)

Since winepresses are usually located in or not far from vineyards, we must assume that the alluvial soil east of Tel Megadim sustained viticulture.

5 Conclusion

In light of the installations discussed above, I would tentatively suggest the following stages in the technological development of winepresses in the Iron Age and Persian period:

1. The treading of the grapes and the collecting of the expressed juice in built (not rock-cut) winepresses found in or near settlements (Gezer, Lachish, Tel Miqne) dating to the Iron Age I–IIA took place in one and the same installation.
2. In the Iron IIA treading surface and the collecting vat were separated from each other (Tel Aphek, Tel Michal). This feature became the norm in subsequent centuries. Those installations that preserve a collecting vat but lacking a treading floor probably had treading floors before they were disturbed, although this remains to be determined with certainty.
3. Shell was the primary constituent in the matrix of the plaster in Iron IIA installations, a feature that continued into the Iron IIB (Tel Hamid) and Persian period (Megadim, Tel Yavne).
4. In the Iron IIA the collecting vats were rounded in shape (Tel Aphek, Tel Michal), whereas in the Iron IIB rectangular vats began to appear (Tel Hamid). The Iron IIB collecting vat at Tell Burak was semi-circular, being an example of the transitional phase from round to rectangular. Steps inside the collecting vat and spouted channels that conducted expressed grape juice from the treading floor to the collecting vat first appeared in Iron IIB at Tel Hamid; such features did not reappear until the Hellenistic period. It was during the Iron IIB that commerce in wine began to play a significant role in the eastern Mediterranean economy, with wine being shipped in specialized containers, especially from Phoenicia (Orsingher et al., 2020; Wolff, 2021: 78–81).
5. The shape of collecting vats in the Persian period was still transitioning from round to rectangular. Winepresses vats at Tel Yavne featured round, square and rectangular collecting vats while the one from Megadim was squarish, the latter a feature that will become standard in later centuries.

The proposed developmental stages are based on scanty evidence; more well-dated presses are necessary to confirm the development outlined here.

Acknowledgments I am grateful to Gary Arbino for sharing the results of his research with me regarding installations from Tel Gezer and to Etan Ayalon and Alexander Fantalkin for their valuable comments and references. I remain responsible for any errors, Thanks to J. Rosenberg for preparing Figs. 1, 5 and 9.

References

Arbel, Y. (2009). *Rishon Le-Ziyyon sand dunes.* Hadashot Arkheologiyot/Excavations and Surveys in Israel 121. http://www.hadashot-esi.org.il/report_detail_eng.aspx?id=1243&mag_id=115

Arbino, G. P. (2018). *One square, three digs: Excavating HUC Field X at Gezer.* Lecture presented at American Schools of Oriental Research Annual Meeting.

Ayalon, E. (1994). Iron Age winepresses around Tell Qasile. In *Israel—People and land* (Eretz Israel Museum Yearbook New Series 7-8, 53–66) (pp. 10–11). Hebrew, English summary.

Barkay, G., & Ussishkin, D. (2004). Area S: The Late Bronze Age strata. In D. Ussishkin (Ed.), *The renewed archaeological excavations at Lachish (1973–1994)* (I (Monograph Series of the Institute of Archaeology of Tel Aviv University 22, pp. 316–407)). Emery and Claire Yass Publications in Archaeology.

Beeri, R. (2008). Round oil presses of the 13th–10th centuries BCE in Palestine and their implications: Chronology, function and geographical distribution. *Palestine Exploration Quarterly, 140,* 159–167.

Broshi, M. (1967). Tel Megaddim. *Israel Exploration Society, 17,* 277–278.

Derfler, S. (2005). The wine industry, the Sharon plain and Tel Michal. *ARAM, 17,* 83–94.

Dever W. G. (1986). *Gezer IV: The 1969–71 seasons in Field VI, the "Acropoli."* Annual of the Nelson Glueck School of Biblical Archaeology IV.

Dever, W. G., Lance, H. D., & Wright, G. E. (1970). *Gezer I: Preliminary report of the 1964–66 seasons.* Annual of the Hebrew Union College Biblical and Archaeological School in Jerusalem I.

Eisenberg, E. (2012). Khirbat Zaʻkuka: An Iron Age I site between Jerusalem and Bethlehem. *'Atiqot, 71,* 1–20.

Eitam, D. (1992). Khirbet Khaddash – Royal industry village in ancient Israel. *Judea and Samaria Research Studies, I,* 161–182. (Hebrew; English summary, pp. XVIII–XIX).

Erickson-Gini, T. (2012). Nabatean agriculture: Myth and reality. *Journal of Arid Environments, 86,* 50–54. https://doi.org/10.1016/j.jaridenv.2012.02.018

Fantalkin, A. (2005). A group of Iron Age wineries from ancient Jaffa (Joppa). *Salvage Excavation Reports, 2,* 3–26.

Frankel, R. (1997). Presses for oil and wine in the southern Levant in the Byzantine period. *Dumbarton Oaks Papers, 51,* 73–84.

Frankel, R. (1999). *Wine and oil production in antiquity in Israel and other Mediterranean countries.* JSOT/ASOR Monograph Series 10.

Frankel, R. (2006). Two installations for the production of olive oil. In I. Finkelstein, D. Ussishkin, & B. Halpern (Eds.), *Megiddo IV: The 1998–2002 seasons volume II* (Monograph Series of the Institute of Archaeology of Tel Aviv University 24, pp. 618–629). Emery and Claire Yass Publications in Archaeology Institute of Archaeology, Tel Aviv University.

Frankel, R., Gadot, Y., & Bachi, G. (2009). Late Bronze Age winepresses. In Y. Gadot & E. Yadin (Eds.), *Aphek-Antipatris II. The remains on the acropolis: The Moshe Kochavi and Pirhiya Beck excavations* (Monograph Series of the Institute of Archaeology of Tel Aviv University 27, pp. 72–83). Emery and Claire Yass Publications in Archaeology Institute of Archaeology, Tel Aviv University.

Getzov, N., Covello-Paran, K., & Tepper, Y. (2011). The "Taanakh winepress"—Evidence of the Middle Bronze Age wine industry in the Jezreel Valley. *Eretz Israel, 30,* 145–155. (Hebrew: English summary p. 149).

Haddad, E., Nadav-Ziv, L., Elisha, Y., Tal, G., Rauchberger, L., & Sandhaus, D. (2021). *Tel Yavne, area A.* Hadashot Arkheologiyot/Excavations and Surveys in Israel 133. http://www.hadashot-esi.org.il/report_detail_eng.aspx?id=25883&mag_id=133

Herzog, Z. (1989a). A complex of Iron Age winepresses (strata XIV–XIII). In Z. Herzog, G. Rapp Jr., & O. Negbi (Eds.), *Excavations at Tel Michal, Israel* (Publications of the Institute of Archaeology of Tel Aviv University 8, pp. 73–75). University of Minnesota Press and The Sonia and Marco Nadler Institute of Archaeology, Tel Aviv University.

Herzog, Z. (1989b). Persian period stratigraphy and architecture (strata XI–VI). In Z. Herzog, G. Rapp Jr., & O. Negbi (Eds.), *Excavations at Tel Michal, Israel* (Publications of the Institute of Archaeology of Tel Aviv University 8, pp. 88–114). University of Minnesota Press and The Sonia and Marco Nadler Institute of Archaeology, Tel Aviv University.

Kleiman, A. (2015). A late Iron IIA destruction layer at Tel Aphek in the Sharon plain. *Tel Aviv, 42*, 177–232.

Macalister, R. A. S. (1912). *The excavation of Gezer, 1902–1905 and 1907–1909*. II. John Murray.

Onozuka, T. (2012). Keeping up with the demand for oil? Reconsidering the unique oil presses from Late Bronze Age IIB to Iron Age IIA in the southern Levant. *Orient, 47*, 67–90.

Orsingher, A., Amicone, S., Kamlah, J., Sader, H., & Berthold, C. (2020). Phoenician lime for Phoenician wine: Iron Age plaster from a wine press at Tell el-Burak, Lebanon. *Antiquity*. https://doi.org/10.15184/aqy.2020.4

Pecci, A. (2021). Wine production, trade and consumption in the Roman world: organic residue analysis. In *Vine-growing and wine making in the Roman world: An International conference in honour of Jean-Pierre Brun 27–29 October, 2021*. Abstracts.

Ronen, A., & Olami, Y. (1978). *Atlit map (26)*. Archaeological Survey of Israel.

Seger, J. D. (1973). Notes and news: Tel Gezer. *Israel Exploration Society, 23*, 247–251.

Shapira, I., & Asscher, Y. (2021). *Appendix: Analysis of plaster from the winepress complex at Tel Yavne*. Hadashot Arkheologiyot/Excavations and Surveys in Israel 133. http://www.hadashot-esi.org.il/images//Yavne-8520-hangasha.pdf

Stager, L. E., Master, D. M., & Schloen, J. D. (2011). The winery in grid 38. In L. E. Stager, D. M. Master, & J. D. Schloen (Eds.), *Ashkelon 3: The seventh century B.C* (pp. 13–29). Eisenbrauns.

Tavger, A. (2018). *South Samaria during the Iron Age II and the Persian period: An archaeological view*. Ph.D. dissertation, Ariel University (Hebrew).

Ussishkin, D. (2014). *Biblical Lachish: A tale of construction, destruction, excavation and restoration*. Israel Exploration Society and Biblical Archaeology Society.

van den Brink, E. V. C. M. (2007). Tel Qana. *Hadashot Arkheologiyot/Excavations and Surveys in Israel, 119*. http://www.hadashot-esi.org.il/report_detail_eng.aspx?id=672&mag_id=112

van den Brink, E. V. C. M. (2020). A Late Bronze Age II cist grave at Tel Qana in the Sharon Coastal Plain. *'Atiqot, 99*, 67–84.

Wolff, S. R. (2021). The date of [the] destruction of Gezer Stratum VI. *Tel Aviv, 48*, 73–86.

Wolff, S. (2023). An iron age IIA winery and other remains from Tel Lod. Lod: "Diospolis—City of God". *Journal of the History, Archaeology and Heritage of Lod, 9*, 9–33 (Hebrew, English abstract, p. 11).

Wolff, S., & Shavit, A. (2008). Ḥamid, Tel. In E. Stern (Ed.), *The new encyclopedia of archaeological excavations in the Holy Land* (pp. 1762–1763). Supplementary Volume 5.

Yannai, E. (2008). Tel Lod. In E. Stern (Ed.), *The new encyclopedia of archaeological excavations in the Holy Land* (pp. 1913–1915). Supplementary Volume 5.

Yannai, E., & Marder, O. (2000). Lod. *Hadashot Arkheologiyot/Excavations and Surveys in Israel, 112*, 63–65.

My Heart Is To …: Some Cruxes in Identity Formation in Iron I Israel?

Baruch Halpern

Abstract Israelite identity is accessed through proxies, abstract as well as physical, but its socialization, activation and propagation were conceptual and complex in effect. Its nature defies static definition, and the later, royally-imparted narratives of its development, and the development of its parts, can only be understood *as narratives* against the background of the early landscape and how it was remembered. Key moments of conflict involving Israelite coalitions register in Judges 5–9. From the latter begins a thread on ethnic conflict that forms a secondary, peripheral plot line through 1 Kings. In both episodes, however, the identity serving as literary proxy for collective actions is the tribe. A general Iron I background accommodates both, and as a curated artefact, the Song of Deborah permits the localization of several tribes. In doing so, it speaks to the nature of Israelite identity, and its implied history, in ways complementary to Judges 9. It suggests that Israel before the Conquest did not define itself as a polity, but as an ethnic group, defined by allegiance to Yhwh of Sinai, with likely sociological implications.

In the texts, Deborah hovers like the mother of a fresh consciousness, a framework for the identity, and her role remains underappreciated. Key contrasts involve: an Israel with/without a Conquest; with/without a land; with/without entanglements in local politics; administrative systems versus labor; emblems versus value. But above all, thought about Israel: what was "folly in Israel" when there was no land of Israel? Israel as a culture versus Israel as a polity. At the least, we can trace a line notionally from Deborah and Abimelek to Saul and David, and the inaugural state-building process.

Keywords Israelite identity · Judges · Kings · Yhwh · Israelite religion

B. Halpern (✉)
University of Georgia, Athens, GA, USA
e-mail: bxh13@psu.edu

1 The Land of Israel Didn't Just Happen?

Heraclitus, we are told, relayed a tale that Homer was stumped when some boys confronted him with the riddle, "What we found and caught, we left behind. What we did not catch, we carried away." The solution? Lice.

Our nits, like Heraclitus', are intellectual. Words can betray, the dirt divulge ephemera that texture our ancient landscapes. The philosophical puzzle of superposition compounds our riddle (Halpern, 2022b). An imaginary collage of the past determines how we build scaffolds in our evidence. If the past is layered, our mind's representations are even more so. And deep stains bleed through those layers in every direction.

No scholar has demonstrated more ably or with more brio than Tom Levy that historical imagination has a crucial role to play in mediating the reductionist epistemologies of philology and unpredictably-biased sample of material remains. The community of opinion sticks as it shifts because we can never fully articulate, let alone document, the lost interconnectedness we sense. In consequence, we lug around socialized doctrine, the ingrown fragments of toddler imaginations. Adjusting to new realities – to a non-monumental power concentration in Iron IIA Edom, for example – means expunging relict assumptions, but also demands thoroughgoing recalculation of relations in our dataset. It means reimagining our dungeons.

My object here is to stimulate thought about identity as a process, and how we approach its parts. Not so much environmental identity like locations or consequences such as dialect or connubium or conflict resolution. – More, affective identity, varied and variable consciousness of what distinguishes Israelite deportment, articulated by attitudes in small groups and in contact between small groups; an intermittent consciousness of a version of a common Israelite narrative. Symbol systems serve for activation, but their mana comes from the moment.

To get at countryside Israelite identity leads toward a history of Israel's formations. Archaeological advances over the last 50 years lead to increasingly sophisticated historical probes engaging distinction in detail. In latter years, they examine levels of transaction that permit a sociological resolution unimagined only decades ago (Faust, 2006; Sergi, 2019).

When did a part of western Asia – in anyone's literature or even imagination – become *"the land of Israel"*? (Shalmaneser III's is the first securely-dated attestation.) This rubric question has a twin: when does the idea of a Conquest arise?

These questions break down the question of identity, or consciousness. For, the history of an identity is more complex than the histories of such single ideas. Before there was an Israelite territory, what did "Israel" mean to anyone?

The approach joins a conversation, to which Tom and his students have contributed immensely, about more granular consideration of site clusters, which is the burden of this contribution. The implications, I hope, will exercise others.

2 Kulturgeschichte

Cultural history sometimes uncovers successive horizons of shared consciousness, with a common awareness of conventions, rhetorical and social. Cultures form around practical components, to facilitate intercourse. But where does a society without institutions (and so says Judges) exhibit meaningful public consciousness?

Here, conscious of their contexts and judging them for content alone, the Abimelek story and the Song of Deborah (hereafter **J5**, for Judges 5) are brought into dialogue with Iron I human geography in the central hills, today's Samaria. The treatment uses many terms, like Deborah, Judges (the book), Hivite or Israel, as convenient incarnations of complex vectors and forces and not as purely concrete elements – functionally, they are Israelite social constructions, literary or historical. The stories of those constructions can be examined as a sort of ethnographic palimpsest for information pertinent to questions of identity – at medium-resolution the categories of exclusive group from the tribe to the gods. Mindful of hermeneutical concerns about physical evidence and about social frameworks imposed on traditions in textual evidence, historical inference wins information by interpreting the latter in light of the former and using the former to discuss the social construction of the latter. You can't understand the language as referential without reading the environment. You can only understand the words used to describe the environment. You can't understand the ideation without understanding how the language works in describing its referents. A point that holds today.

3 Abimelek

Recently (2022), I have argued that, in the narrative of Judges 9, Shechem is not part of Israel.

3.1 *Abimelek's Story*

Judges 9 follows the career of Gideon's ambitious half-Shechemite son, who takes control of two constituencies, evidently with the goal of establishing a condominium in Shechem's traditional territory. Abimelek's kingship is the price for maintaining Shechem's independence: his campaign platform is, Shechem, and Hamor, face submission to the Sons of Jerubbaal (9:2; 9:16–17 also imply Manassite superiority). His affines arrange for kingship in Shechem, and Shechem's treasury buys him warlordship (*wyśr*) in "Israel". Unchecked when it takes up piracy, Shechem graduates to nativism: its shareholders drunkenly resolve to depose the half-breed and restore the city's traditional old family council. Abimelek, king and strongman, levels and anathematizes Shechem and attacks two sites, taking no prisoners. He dies in the second beleaguerment, at Thebez (Zertal, 2004:106).

Abimelek's campaign may have been motivated by a need to pay his troops. It reads, but only between the lines, like ethnic war on Hivites. Notably, the conflict has a political, not religious, origin and explanation – theology comes as commentary explaining karma, some of it from an editor in the eighth–sixth century.

3.2 Dating

The outcomes that structure the Judges 9 narrative are neither invented nor reported. They are explained. The explanation stews chunks of memory, stereotype, canard – it is a history. Arguably, the note that Shechem was sown with salt (9:5) antedates its 10th-c. resettlement. Especially, the story *assumes* addressees know that Shechem's residents were Hivite: their dominant clan are "the sons of Hamor" (9:28; Gen 34). In the story, they are avoiding Israelite domination (9:2,16–17). The historiographic context does not belie the assumption: Alt noted, in *the* classic treatment of the settlement process, we lack conquest claims for Amarna Shechem's territory.

3.2.1 Theme: Non-fraternization

The story's contexts in Judges reflect its content. In the book's overall scheme, Abimelek is the poster-child for non-fraternization, and a narrator introduces the book's only prophet (6:7–10) to make the point.

3.2.2 Danger Outside Shechem

Judges 1–3:5 incorporates Judges' latest framing structure (Richter, 1964 for relative dating). Yet, on Joshua's death, it declares, polises controlled the lands on which Israelites settled. Shechem goes unmentioned (literary continuity; non-monarchic government; geographic position; evaluation of the history). Still, the populations remained: even after Shechem's depopulation, Jacob flees the district's now hostile population (Gen 34). It is this life *among* others, on land governed by others, that still in the Abimelek story threatens danger, and inevitably precipitates crisis.

3.3 Coexistence and Feud

This ancient view sits squarely in a popular Mediterranean historical topos. Herodotus begins with a prime instance: he explores the roots of the feud between Greeks and Phoenicians, summarizing a series of stratified folk tales (like JE and Joshua 9) before reporting concrete interactions. Likewise, Judges 9 describes the turning-point in Hivite-Israelite relations. The topic is an ongoing element of the Jerusalem historical canon into Solomon's reign. Judges 9 starts the strand off by describing the start of a feud, of which the audience shares some memory.

3.3.1 Feudal Origins

Once the conflict is explained based on mercurial nativism, Abimelek's ongoing campaign indicates, some elements continue to identify with Shechem, and are connected to fortifications. In a sadly plausible wrinkle, it is a recent accession to Shechem's polis who inflames the city's nativism. Gual (so Josephus) ben-Ebed bears a patronymic, "son of slave", that in traditional Arab villages distinguishes those whose family only recently integrated into a hamula (Cohen, 1965). So construed, "son of a slave" stamps Gual as a zealot of convenience (9:26 *bṭḥ*). Comparably, a Swiss acquaintance once explained that her house lay at the edge of town because the family arrived only in the fourteenth century. Memories of Iron I homesteading must also have persisted in villages of the early monarchy, as a status: the living old clan network can have been more conservative and more cohesive than we typically imagine.

3.3.2 Memories and Narrative

The hinterland hamlets that Judges 9 envisions were an imprint Egypt left, in a process extending from MB III forward, in the more broken landscapes—from Cilicia to Samaria, especially. City-states in such regions sometimes made a virtue of necessity, treating with mobile populations through leaders of groups of bands (EA 254, e.g.), which translate as hamulas (*ḥamūla/-āt*), an association of extended families. Here, tribe formation was an administrative desideratum. These habiru, under empire and after, were displaced persons—multi-generational vagrants, transients, hut-, cave-, and tent-dwellers, illegals. But unending presence in neighbors' environments also affected material culture.

These transients followed the pattern of villagers in pre-industrial Near Eastern societies, particularly where housing stock was cheap. In times of relative security, several hamulas form a village. The village, as a chartered corporation, holds lands.

These are distributed to the hamulas by the collective, and periodically redistributed inside the hamula as demographics dictate. When imposts are high, it is the hamula that pulls up stakes and takes to unsettled spaces (Cohen, 1965, 2–9).[1] Their lack of structure and capacity for evasion frustrated administrators, and do today. But with greater security from state predation, dispossessed elements, outside of nomadic political structures, revert to living where they harvest.

The ethos, at least, of this population, infuses Israel in Judges 9. Unlike a city-state playing out its role deserted by the empire that shaped it, Abimelek's Israel has no royalty, no defined membership, no territory. It has no formal institutions. Weber, of course, described the reality intimately in his discussion of charismatic succession; but he also inherited a habit of treating Israel as a whole. Abimelek's Israel is a mercenary army and anyone they can enlist. The narrative supposes that Gideon's House itself held a dominant position through martial strength.

Abimelek's program ends with his death. There is no hint of a territorial conquest, but there certainly is the portrayal of an attempt to achieve it. And a feud begins for which, in Judges 9, Hivites are principally to blame. The narrator attributes tension between Abimelek and Shechem to divine displeasure, but the objects of sympathy are Abimelek's brothers.

3.3.3 Scapegoats Faction by Faction

Judges 9 depicts condominium as a cauldron of disaster. Other texts address the same basic issue. Joshua 9 – Joshua's treaty with Gibeon – presents accommodation with central hills Hivites as a binding obligation contracted under misrepresented circumstances. J's more folkloristic explanation for the conflict also attributes the origin of the problem to the Hivites. But, like Joshua, Genesis 34 largely exculpates them: Shechem agree to and fulfill the amends agreed on for an abduction, and Jacob's sons wipe them out. And in Genesis 49 (J, below), Jacob repudiates the anti-Shechem zealots Simeon and Levi – "In their mysteries ("sect"), let my Soul never join" precludes ancestral communion. In Judges, the Hivites are devious (9:23 *bgd*), in Joshua negotiators (9:22 *rmh*) whose clothes – the narrator associates the concept of a garment, *bgd*, with the same point –contribute to their deception. In J, sons of Jacob – the only name used for the figure in Gen 34 (despite "folly in Israel" in 34:7) – are treacherous (*bmrmh*, 34:13; cf. 27:35, J). Israel's least acculturated elements scorn compensation for dishonor in favor of a deceit baldfaced enough to shame trickster Jacob. The statement is strong.

In E, conversely (Gen 33:18–20), Israel purchases sacred ground at Shechem from Hamor (cf. David's threshing-floor; on P's cave, Halpern, 2003, 334–336). The conformity to polis niceties implicitly acknowledges continuity in land tenure difficult to reconcile with a theory of title rooted in divine gift and scorched earth.

---

[1] See esp. EA 288:24–32; for epitome of the discussion, ABD 3.6–10; cf. BH "wide, wide-armed" for secure lands.

Such reflections have traveled through different prisms, and arrived in the text by different routes. The obvious contrasts reflect faction in the monarchic era – probably before the eighth century, judging from the distribution of passages engaging historical relations with Hivites.

3.3.4 Temporal Milieu

In J's folktale, Hamor proposes permanent Israelite land tenure, ratified by connubium, in a region of its Hivite polis (Gen 34:9–10). Even after Shechem's devastation, the central hills down to Bethel (Gen 35) fall under Hivite control. The loss of that control also occupies Judges 9. The story presents Abimelek as an experiment in synoecism (cf. Gen 34).

Regardless, the later involvements of Saul, Ishbaal, David and Solomon with the Gibeonites indicate that the theme of the story was germane for at least a time to the state's constitution. We have an etiology of the later politics, unremarkably, perspectival, detailed and realistic about the politics of the city, an important stop in the Judges narrative as an explanation for aspects of developments in 2 Samuel. The themes, as well as assumptions, of Judges 9 carry with them traces of Iron I Canaan.

4 Tradition and Ruins

Judges 9 speaks its version to a practical, historically-minded audience. Modern response has ranged mainly from respect to credence.

The destruction of Shechem XI has been identified as Abimelek's work since the 1950's. The layer is continous from LB Stratum XII, but Iron I rural forms, collar-rim jars and cooking pots, first appear in XI. The excavators inferred a peaceable Israelite takeover in Stratum XI just in time for Abimelek's onslaught (Finkelstein, 2006). The takeover matched their assumption that Abimelek destroyed an Israelite city.

The historical situation of Shechem XI was more probably the one also represented at Megiddo VIA. There, collar-rims led Douglas Esse (1992) to infer the kind of exchange Hamor proposes in Genesis 34: connubium and commensality. Survey data make it clear, the groups inhabited complementary ecological niches, as is usually the case with a transient population whose custom it is to minimize encounters with authority. In a historical analysis divorced from Judges-Samuel, one would conclude that one force impelling the Israelites toward statehood was efficiency in making local costs predictable by limiting polises' right to regulate traffic. Another, of course, was a population swollen by surplus young males in an uplands environment (Halpern, 1983).

5 Proximity to Iron I Landscapes

The literary picture comports with Gershon Galil's (2021) suggestion of a series of early monarchic histories. This historiography is attentive to conflict and collaboration with Hivites or their umbrella culture, Amorites. In Judges 9 the issue takes center stage because it was crucial to state and literary formations. Later, Israelite ascendancy reduced its political and narrative weight.

5.1 The Conquered

Confronting the assumption that from the outset the wilderness bands functioned collectively or even shared a pipedream reopens a question pertinent to the world of the Song of Deborah: The historical anachronism about unconquered enclaves is not non-Israelites. It is the idea that they were residual, enclaves inside a territorial Israel, from the writer's perspective starting from Joshua's day (9, *bqrb*; cf. Judg 1:32–33; 3:5; Halpern, 2021, 116–117, 124). Royal chanceries filed fragments of early history in a framework built from Iron II state aspirations.

George Mendenhall and Norman Gottwald were right to stress early antipathy to kings. But they wed that distaste to fervid proselytization. The same evidence might arise from pressures on groups avoiding polis radar, uninterested in recruits.

Regardless, the idea of a deeded country is a historical development. Early Israel had no national projects because it had no national institutions, no payroll, like the ideal commune of anarchist and Marxist eschatology. Israel was not a state, country, territory or people. It was a loosely-defined culture with a flag.

5.2 LB Sociologies

Scholars recognize, the idea of a conquest exhibits variant forms, including its completion by David, when Yhwh's peregrinations end. Where does the ideal of a conquest begin?

Also widespread is a view of seasonally-itinerant, corvee-averse bands exploiting empty spaces as havens. Amarna documents that especially off the coast, city rulers, like the procurator Biriawaza (EA 195), sometimes drew on such groups as tactical assets. Texts from LB Alalakh also document their taxation and conscription.

Novelties in Iron IA were the breadth of the Habiru networks, and increased sedentarization at a remove from the practices and requirements of the city. Cities' policies were sensitive to economic, political, personal and emotional circumstance.

Our picture of the highlands formations improves if we consider the inevitable interplay: bands might be represented as geographic or as lineage aggregates to decision-makers in local market centers or the city.

But those first homesteaders, however maladjusted, hadn't it in their head to attach Shechem's territory to an Israel. Judges 9 seems to know about this world and explains, at a remove, how it was shattered.

5.3 Historiographic Context

Pertinent to Abimelek is the story that precedes. Gideon's exploits, and armed force, make Ophrah a center for the Wadi Fara homesteading cluster. It remained a ritual and oracular venue into the monarchy (Judg 6:24; 1 Sam 13:17).

Gideon is one of the most underrated figures in the study of Israelite literary culture, as a subject, a producer or both. His call narrative is the definitive vocation. Close review – of the genre's application, of the language and of the integration in context, suggests his vocation and diligent double-checking of oracular results furnish the model for JE's call of Moses, and, significantly, Saul's call in 1 Samuel 9 (A source). What forms *the* pervasive Israelite myth of leadership (Halpern, 1981), the basis of Yhwh's liturgy, has its fullest and most down-to-earth human expression with Gideon.

5.3.1 Gideon's Story's Home

The story of Gideon collecting gold to fashion an icon for his shrine also finds an imitator, in the Exodus calf. The writerly frame dimly intimates that Abimelek was the comeuppance for the "ephod". The shrine, the wording would allow, may have lost lustre through or after Abimelech's failure. But in the implied narrator's day, it stood as a shrine still.

6:11–24 is its fairy story. The Cheshire Angel christens a tree (Asherah) by Gideon's altar for phyllomancy, divination by rustling leaves. Gideon checks and rechecks the results by other childlike tests. These workaday occultisms create a script for docents to exhibit features and artifacts to festival crowds ("and here's the crock in which Gideon served the bouillon"). The Gideon account incorporates the Ophrah legend's dictions: hence the linguistic and cultural oddities that famously freckle the account. Similarly, the story makes demands on its audience that, later, state folklore seems to contradict: prior knowledge must supply ethnic or political affiliations for Succoth and Penuel. There are also indications that Judges 6–8 were joined to J5, and thus re-embedded, by the early monarchy: scholars acknowledge various suggestive intertwinings whose collective subtlety defies attribution to the late monarchic compilers of DtrH.[2]

In all, the Gideon story shows signs of familiarity with Iron I conditions, the political semiotics of tribal recruitment, and fissures among tribes in relation to polises in the central hills and Jordan Valley. Conceivably, in some form it graced the plaster of a chapel at Ophrah into the monarchy.

5.4 Politics in the Story

The story brings allies to this omen-and-command center. Elements from Manasseh, Asher, Zebulun and Naphtali, importantly, donate to the shrine. Each of these names conjured up in the storyteller's mind a past Iron I landscape, a cluster of camps and farms in the hills. Gideon's reach across the Jezreel compares to Deborah's.

Strikingly, Gideon's invitation omits especially Issachar and Ephraim. Only a near-contemporary could decipher the politics. But listeners even a century removed would recognize that the news carried implications of mutual hostility, entailments with cities and towns, or other issues opaque to us, but with reflexes in competing cultural centers, like Ophrah and Shiloh. Significantly, Jerusalem promotes Shiloh as the ark's home, trumpeting continuity with the Ephraimite sect.

Gideon's legacy was Abimelek's war with Hivites. Tribal policies in the conflict are largely opaque to us. While implicating Abimelech in fratricide, Judges leaves us Abimelech's image as a warrior whose intensity ruptured the chance for an Israelite territory. Saul would extend the policy to the Hivites of the south, in Benjamin. Jerusalem took a more conciliatory line: David leads the ark to Jerusalem, where he commits it to a Shilonite's care, from Kiriath-Jearim, a Hivite town, among other things (Halpern, 2001:306–313, 367–371).

5.5 Genres and Themes: Origins of Conquest

The substance of the narratives fits expectations from non-royal, rumor-based historiography. As Susan Ackerman has seen, most pre-monarchic tradition was incubated and curated by establishments like those at Shiloh and Ophrah. The interpretive framework was renegotiated as it passed through kings' and possibly later hands. Ophrah, with its history reanalyzed as a war on an ethnos, has a direct connection to Saul, Ephraim and Issachar, with Shiloh, to the Hivite-friendly David. The seemingly incidental theme in Judges, however, is a fact. In base narrative structure, Abimelech

---

[2] Judg 8:18 Tabor >4:12–14. 5:8 $lḥm\ š‘rym$ > 7:13. 5:15.8:5 $brgl$ > 4:10,15,17 [cf. 5:26–27 $byn\ rglyh$], in various senses.

changes the dynamic in the direction of a Conquest, one that originally fruited under monarchs.

6 Deborah

Most of our oldest literature presupposes or promotes the conquest ideal – the unified entry of Exodus 15, for example. But that expresses monarchic aspiration to mobilization. Before Abimelech and what can be portrayed as ethnic warfare, what *is* the idea of Israel?

How can one describe its institutions, its functional identity, and its internal transactions in the premonarchic era. We think in terms of a territorial fight, ethnic polarization; and Abimelech enjoys freedom of the countryside alongside Nahal Tirzah and up to Shechem. The consciousness implicit in that story therefore has a background, dimly though we may glimpse it, and is not entirely a monarchic imposition.

For profitable comparison, the most promising lever, and one of the most interesting perspectives we have is in J5. The poem repays reading as a cultural artifact of Iron I by adding its own cognitive dimension in turn. Deborah's song provides a challenging but largely intact survival from the period.

6.1 Sociological Assumptions

J5 portrays Israelite war before standing armies. Nor, historically, does it stand entirely in isolation. Related and independent archaic language and sociology in the narratives running forward from J5 indicate that stories and even parts of pre-state accounts have survived – if to serve state ends.

6.2 Content Antiquity

Language and poetic conventions distinguish various passages from the Jerusalem-chancery literary dialect of the ninth–sixth centuries that dominates the ancient Hebrew corpus. J5's high antiquity among this literature is widely defended in a vast literature. Contrary representations uniformly depend on hypotheticals as positive evidence.

Philologists see J5's antiquity in vocabulary, morphology and style. Mark Smith's wide-ranging linguistic overture assembles features whose comparable attestations evaporate by the ninth century. He proposes, our version dates to the tenth century (2012; 2014:220–224, and e.g. n 95 on 5:8).

The philological nether limit cites silence mainly to show that later dates are less probable than earlier. It claims no exaggerated mathematical certainty. So in a way, the philology has had to answer to a generalized skepticism about Bible composition more than about J5.

The *historical* arguments for J5's age, of which, in our technic, we lose sight, are forceful. Here, we need mention only a few.

6.2.1 Tribes

Deborah's ten-tribe list has its own unique order; but this may be governed by poetic demands (below). A case against "updating" starts from the tribal registers, which feature Gilead and Machir, and omit Simeon, Levi, Judah, Gad, Manasseh, and Joseph.

6.2.2 Situation

Socially, the Song gives no sign of attachment even to a type of location, or any center other than the Israelite band ("gate", Halpern, 2021). It is diagnostic that the poem identifies Yhwh's residence as Sinai, beyond the sown, and does not imply that an equivalent locus can be found among the tribes (below).

6.2.3 Genre

The verse is a twist on heroic lyric, with women triumphant and women defeated. Aaron Koller (2020) offers an apt comparison in motif to Bedouin epic, and an alternative comparison to motifs in Ramesside battle poems (for evaluation, Notarius, 2017:85–89). In either case, Deborah stands out, especially for irony and twists on baked-in cultural conventions.

The Bedouin song is itself a cultural marker. Yigael Yadin used to tell the story of his first meeting in Amman in 1947. At it, King Abdullah introduced his cabinet, one man at a time: "This is so-and-so, minister of A; he's an Arab. This is such-and-such, minister of B; he's not an Arab." And the king provided the same three pieces of information to introduce a bevy of men seated around a table. At the end, Yadin confessed that he was puzzled on what basis His Majesty had divided his ministers into Arabs and not-Arabs. And Abdullah drew himself up and announced, "An Arab is someone who speaks like this," and launched into poetry that Yadin did not recognize. However, Yadin *had* taken a course from S. D. Goitein, in which students had to memorize one Bedouin poem. So he responded, "You mean, like this?" and recited a few lines. At which point Abdullah beamed, embraced him, and exclaimed, "Ya Yadin! You're an Arab!"

Less spectacularly, ample testimony sorts melodies, rhythms and genres in Archaic Greece with distinctive regional cultures (e.g., Plutarch, *On Music;*

Athenaeus, *Deipnosophistae*). Music marks cultural space – the end of *The Jazz Singer* still resonates. It is effective as a modern, but incomparable as an ancient vehicle for social messaging.

The congeners to J5 have vanished from Israel's canons except in tiny fragments; the laments over Saul and Abner are the closest we come. But such literary ephemera more likely survived into the monarchy than stemmed from it: this is folk literature, quick and clever. Perhaps such songs attached to David's heroes, but there is no sure sign of them.

6.2.4 Path of Preservation

The context of J5's preservation differs from that of the other, later tribal litanies (Halpern, 1983:117–159): Deuteronomy 33 exhibits only marginally less archaic usage but although composed for a ritual occasion may be adapted to a later E. Psalm 68 now places Yhwh in Jerusalem. Genesis 49, with little proprietary archaic language, was adapted for or written by J. Yet there is no positive indication that kings adapted J5:1–13, and Smith admits the possibility only.

6.2.5 Limits on Unity

But how far can one go when the semantics and significations are densely obscure? Physical context offers some entry. On the ground is a cultural community of sites whose members dwell in small bands. The bands cluster in regions, separated by distance, natural features, and borders. Yet when tribes collect, Zebulunites "pull a scribe's rod (*šēbeṭ*)."[3]

The context suggests a role for writing. But more important, Machir's *mḥqqym*, too, have roles and status. Issachar has commanders.

There are roles, but within the clusters. There is no state, and no collective purse, like that of the Shechemite state in Judges 9.

7 Social and Socialized Contexts

J5 connects a sequence of stage scenes with a story, some of which is untold. The scenes combine the pragmatic and symbolic into a time-bound world. The ingredients reach us, but more as fragments, as their world, their combined vibrancy dissipates. Our

---

[3] *mšk b-* denotes: stretching, as with the bow; dragging, as oxen the plough; or pulling on a trumpet. The prose version applies the verb twice, for sounding assembly, then for drawing Sisera to the battlefield (Judg 4:6–7): vocabulary redeployed from unused segments of written sources, endemic in Chr, poses a challenge to many models and a door to compositional aesthetics (crucial to process) in Biblical criticism.

exercise is to emulate an audience somewhat conversant with the period in which the scenes take place. While many questions are unresolved, like the politics of interclan relations, or coalitions with other polities, the atmosphere helps triage possibilities.

7.1 Other Times, Other Gods

J5:6 starts the story with a time-frame, inspiring Judg 3:31. From this point forward, we are in a continuous narrative, chronological in order, with an occasional retrospective remark.

In the time of Shamgar ben-Anat, in the time of Jael,
Expeditions had left off, and those who (habitually) travelled main avenues were taking winding routes.

Sizes, kinds and ranges of group travel remain vague: the audience grasps a significance now uncertain. But the disruption of group travel marks the situation described as problematic: as in Anzu, Enuma elish or Genesis 2, before Deborah stirs, stasis reigns.

5:7
Perazon (*pĕrāzôn*) refrained,
from *Israel*, they refrained
until when I arose, Deborah,
when I arose, a Mother in Israel

Perazon are the object of recruitment, constitute the backbone of the militia: "Yhwh's victories" (5:11). They held back (Lewis, 1985) "*b-*" Israel (cf. 5:2,7,8,11). Malbim, reading "among Israel", infers, others had perazon of their own. But it seems likelier that these authors of "Yhwh's victories, the victories of his perazon *b*-Israel", were shirking expectations of mutual aid.

Perazon is usually understood as peasantry (as Stager, 1988). An ancient alternative, leaders, would mean **heads of extended families or even bands**, who mobilize dependents like Joab's "lads" or Spartan helots. This is a question of nuance (below, 11.0). The phrasing excludes bedouin – Jael is a "tent-woman", and Deborah's target culture excludes Kenite bands (as Judg 8:11).

Caravans weren't setting forth to migrate, fight, traffic, visit. Perazon weren't serving their purpose – whether that was production (Judg 9:9–13) or, as fits the song's sculpted ideals, battle (kidnapping, plundering travelers?). The perazon's idling, not the travellers', produces a ponderous couplet – terse, blunt, the verbs repeated, the words perazon and Israel weighted. Their resuscitation is Deborah's mission. So, she elaborates the difficulty of reviving them:

7.2 The Challenge

5:8[4]
Yibḥar 'ĕlōhîm ḥădāšîm
'āz lāḥem šĕ'ārîm...
People chose new gods.
Then, conflict of bands.
Would shield appear, or spear,
in forty thousand(s) in Israel?"

The question hangs on Deborah's call to arms. Would the perazon of the previous verse, still the subject of discourse, turn out to fight?

7.3 The Tone

The question has its roots in the first part of the quatrain.

Fighting, says the singer, ensued on new gods. What about the new gods led to fighting? The Deuteronomist wraps his answer in a fluffy theological blanket. He supplies an angel to decry Israel's arrangements with its Amorite neighbors (Judg 1:36–2:3). Agreements with these authorities lead to chasing the baals. And chasing the baals incites Yhwh to unleash oppressors on Israel (Judg 1:1–3:6: on whose logic, Halpern, 1988:131–137). Segments of Judg 1–3:6 still claim that Galilean tribes (1:32–33) and Israelites (3:5) lived under others' jurisdiction. But other passages (1:29–30; Josh 9:7–22; 13:13; 16:10) reverse the view, in consonance with the superimposed historical panorama.

This narrative structure more than encompasses the song: "some chose new gods" becomes, Israel pursued baals and ashtarot. "Yhwh subjected them to" foreign domination generalizes J5's "fighting of the gates". In Judg 5:7–8, medieval exegetes saw enemy raids propelling farmers into walled towns. (States often base origin stories on insecurity.)

Deborah's emphasis differs from Judges': for Deborah, "new gods" says new politics. David uses the same code (1 Sam 26:19): exiling him is an injunction, "Serve other gods." David complies by enlisting at Gath (27:1).

Deborah displays a similarly nakedly transactional attitude toward religious idiom: she recommends and reports singing Yhwh's prowess as a tactic to whip up mobs (5:2–5,10); she assigns, the context will disclose, not just material benefit from, but concrete credit for Yhwh's victories to the perazon (5:11).

Here, too, we can see movement across a rhetorical spectrum from the barely encoded J5:8: anticipating Abimelech (Judg 6:7–10), Yhwh reminds a prophet's

---
[4] Space limitations compel me to reserve extensive philological comment on the passages cited to a separate treatment.

hearers that he had expelled the Amorites, given Israel their land, and demanded, "Don't fear the gods of the Amorite, in whose land you are dwelling." At Shechem, Joshua offers Israel the option of such integration – of serving "the gods of the Amorite in whose land you are dwelling" (24:15). There, "choosing" local Amorite gods is an open and casual code for assimilating into local political structures. "Choosing" gods in Josh 24:15 is legalization; and although the passage presupposes a conquest, and portrays Amorites as "your oppressors", it projects from the tradition of J5:8.

These texts are candid that, in the realm of human history and of historical action, polity gods are totems, pennants of a bond. Such a stance (cf. Herodotus 7.129,189) is practical: even Thucydides and others, who score Herodotus as superstitious, maintain a committed belief in divine intervention through natural forces (Dover, 1973:41). They are instead diffident about reliable interpretation, and, like Israel's prophets earlier, the efficacy of the cult (with Jordan, 1986).

The same holds for the more profound historiography in the Former Prophets. Like Judges 5 and 9, 2 Samuel exposes an intricate chain of human causation whose stages and outcomes are divinely determined (Halpern, 2001; cf. famously the Joseph story; in a karmic vein akin to Judges 9, and to Jacob: Friedman, 1986). These stories explore politics and psychology rather than, under government, encrypting them: like the demonstrative piety disfiguring Asshurbanipal's annals, political classes bid for halos in a theater of sanctimony that Athens skewers in the Melian dialogue. With no king, Athenians dispense with the fritters.

In Deborah's dialect, choosing other gods has objective meaning: recognizing a government, joining a community, whose god is not Yhwh. The actual sense was never lost – it remains the sense of the first commandment – only obscured: even in the latest framework of the stories of the major judges (Richter, 1964), astute readers may have seen the baals as gods – as the Joshua-Judges context dictates – of city-states. Adopting those gods, they infer, resulted in political disunity across regions.

This clarifies the role of empty roads, which engages a motif attested from Pap. Anastasi I into royal inscriptions of the Iron Age, like Azitawad's – that of unsafe conditions (Schloen, 1993). Hazard and anarchy are always associated with land beyond pockets of social order – the forest in *The Scarlet Letter*. Deborah inverts its logic, as she does so many stereotyped expectations: free intercourse or epic raids or visits dwindled because of political associations – hardly because of city-based military enforcement – and Israelite identity atrophied.

This is not a naïve transposition of superstition into political reportage – rallying together was choosing Yhwh, but peaceable conditions promoted sedentarism, and local horizons — indifference to Israelite identity and relations with neighbors. (Both Shechem versions invoke the issue of Hivite-Israelite connubium, like Herodotus' opening.) The referent is simply nearer the surface of the metaphor.

Whether rightly or not, mainstream scholarship never considers that Judges 2 is decrying Israelites having truck with a spectrum of established states – or that the implicated baals might come to blows. Judges thickens linguistic convention: in

Deuteronomistic rhetoric, including Jeremiah's, the baals are traditional Israelite clan gods attributed to the Canaanites, or, at least, that is how the matter has appeared to me (1991, 1996); I suspect that for Josiah those gods were the patrons of civic festivals, as in Deuteronomy (2022).

The Judges explanatory framework, regardless, derives from the ethos in the Song.

7.4 An Israel Deborah Confronts

Judges' framework elaboration generalizes a point that especially maps to the Iron IA landscape. There, new rural sites reflexively identified with later Israel – rightly, proleptically, or wrongly – sat on the turf of cities whose rulers were, by the time of our lyric, formerly pharaonic agents.

Among these relic states, Shechem, perhaps Gibeon, and likely Pella, appear to have been welcoming, judging from surveyed long-term camps and homes. Texts – Judg 1:34–35; 17–18 – suggest that Gezer prevented settlement in its district. (1:27, like 1:32–33, permits integration.)

7.4.1 Life Behind Verse

In Deborah's geography, Israelites were at home in the spaces marginal to a polis. Even Iron I homesteads tolerated by the polis, however, did not fit administrative categories: they sat, scattered, in the wilds. Some lacked permanent houses. Most groups lived in regular contact with livestock – both topography and extended mobility raise caprids' value in herding calculations, but contextualizing the increment requires unprocurable data.

Some Iron I settlers enjoyed enough security to plan a middle-term future. The stone and brick houses found and even excavated at some of the rural sites represent a substantial expenditure. They repay the expenditure by protecting assets, including human. The initial outlay, like that for terracing, required collaboration, and thus more debt. It also demanded a ready store of wealth in different forms including especially labor.

Homeowners on these farmsteads were bonded to one another, as in Judges 18, where "the men whose houses were together with Micah's" join the chase after Danite spies. Any given group of cooperating farms, however, also faced the prospect of treating with the polis, since their residence was now stable, and they asserted claims to land use at least. Most of their dealings will have been through rural centers, and their farming communities.

Why did these migrants stake claims, from which housebuilding followed? Perhaps they felt secure in defending a checkerboard of farming communes, as in Judges 18: the siting added a vertical layer of defense, terrain expensive to police:

in the eleventh century, readers may recall, the hills remained an effective refuge even from modern armies, summoning forth Tiglath-Pileser's military reforms. At Amarna, Gezer's ruler complains about a warlord charging higher ransom than kidnappers in the hills, whose price was standard (esp. EA 292:48–51; 294:16–24). For settlers, peripherality was fortification on the cheap.

But the investment in infrastructure has a more likely explanation: the settlers enjoyed peaceable relations with local centers on the primary roads, and through them with the polis center. Perhaps that context of formalized local exchange, even dues-paying, best explains the occasional Iron I conical seal, representing a group of smallholders. For all we know, some even registered legal possession of their sections.

7.4.2 Social Gods?

The local story of Iron I is of rural settlements steadily increasing in wealth, invested in children. They developed and eventually imposed their own legal and political practices, first on the central hills hinterland, then on former seats of authority. Before such prospects dawned, the logical recourse for long-term settlers committing to houses and terraces was to secure the polis's acknowledgement by mutual blessing before venturing to build communes. That sort of commitment also entails the kind of joint action to repel other itinerant communities – Judges 6–8's Midian – from the niche local Israelites occupied; or, to carve the lands under cultivation out of the normal paths of migration and transhumance of the preceding centuries. Settlement creates its own sense of local territoriality.

For the dormancy of Israel's perazon, Deborah blames political ties they had formed. These entailed commitment by Israelite bands to parties to their own conflicts. Deborah's settlers had integrated into diverse existing polities and their markets. Unsubsidized by imperial political economy, the traditional administrative centers developed into market hubs or atrophied.[5] Unconstrained by Egyptian armies, competition made them liable to outbreaks of hostilities. Even in Amarna's theoretically policed environment, outlying polis towns suffer constant agitation and regular military pressure to defect to neighboring polities. These are the mahazi of EA 272:1–17 (AEMW "market towns"), for example (Baalshipti's remit involved commitments outside Gezer). Similar Amarna-era shenanigans, of the sort that come to light from Rib-Addi's correspondence from Byblos, as well, are documented as far as Ugarit (van Soldt, 2005:52–55, 2016).

In these operations, habiru were a potential tactical asset, and habiru with sunk costs – like Israelites – more readily enlisted. The Alalakh texts that document their

---

[5] Off the coast, Mario Martin (2017) has shown, Megiddo VIIA (ends 1125–1050 judging from Finkelstein et al., 2017); especially Megiddo VIA with all its Egyptianizing trinkets.

conscription distinguish them from archers, suggesting specialist skills, such as tracking, scouting or logistics. But their services are reckoned as the contribution of a regional administration inside the kingdom, where, as in Deuteronomy, dues payments are filed with the annual delivery of livestock from the provinces to the capital (von Dassow, 2008:224–225).

Especially after Egypt's drawdown in the reigns of Ramses IV to VI, any of these entities could choose, as Megiddo VIIA and VI eventually would (per Martin), to coopt leaders among local settlers and enter into ventures with them.

Deborah's presentation, then, can cohere with another interpretation: Deborah needed to call on ethnic solidarity *because* the Israelites were distributed across polises. Settlement clusters chose distinct new gods, is the singer's way of saying it.

7.5 Israel and Not Israel

As a rule, our literature hides the tribes' several connections to the old city-states as a source of sectional conflict. Help from allies usually vanishes and always dims behind penny-pinching political morals. Opponents' reliance on allies casts them in a dim light.

7.5.1 Crossing Lines

Undisputed archaeological connection at Megiddo (VIIA-VIA) and Shechem (XI) is probably the tip of an iceberg. Among texts, too, Judges 9 is one of only a handful of episodes in which Israelites collaborate against compatriots. In Judges, Judahites give up Samson to Philistines (for fear of persecution, like Jacob after Genesis 34). In Samuel, David works for Gath (and Kenites disaffiliate from Amalek without taking sides). Conflict arises among settled populations – Gideon in confrontation with Ephraim, Jephthah and Ephraim, and, in a different case, Gideon with Succoth and Penuel, which, however, early audiences might recognize as non-Israelite; and the Wars over Benjamin to and beyond David and Ishbaal. But for the most part, intertribal conflict involving urban partners is hidden behind the writerly rhetoric of a homogeneous, coordinated Israel, represented as a whole by any of its parts.

Nevertheless, regional involvement with the polis finds indirect expression beyond Judges 9 or indeed Gideon seeking aid at secondary centers, or Joab at Abel Maacah (cf. Josh 13:13).

Issachar's Lot

Issachar is particularly fruitful on this question. Its collaboration with Shechem is a focus in Jacob's "Blessing", J's doublet for Deuteronomy 33 (49:14–15). Here, Issachar is content, recumbent among the cooking-fires, presumably of an encampment (as J5:16). They agree to collaborate with a polis, putting their shoulder, Shechem, to corvée.

Issachar and Rehov

Relations with Rehov, though complex, are also palpable. The Iron IIA city of Stratum V there hosts an extraordinary apiary, dated to the later 10th c.When destroyed, it contained a jar inscribed with the name, Nimshi, Jehu's clan. The same name is attested in a 9th-century stratum, as well as elsewhere (Ahituv-Mazar, 2016:#5–6).

Tantalizingly, another sherd also yielded an incision that has been read, Nimshi. Its (surface) find-spot, Khirbet Tannin (Zertal, 2004:#59), was close by the "Bull Site" (#61), Dhahrat et-Tawileh, below Gilboa (Mazar, 1982).

Shmuel Ahituv has rightly questioned the *mem*, which can only be read on allowance for the general execution: *nm(!)š*. Still, the Tannin ostracon reflects a hinterland script (Lemaire, 2004:552–554) differing from Iron II exemplars.

The bee nexus is suggestive. The Issacharian Deborah's name, and the song's occasional swarm diction (see appended translation), are weak, and perhaps merely paronomastic, hints of a bee connection for Issachar. Still, the apiary layers are associated with a corporation, Nimshi, for a reason. The industry achieves industrial scale in odd architecture at 10th c Rehov (V), contemporary with and culturally comparable to Megiddo VA. A partnership between Issachar's hillside apiculturists – irrespective of the Tannin sherd – and Rehov's merchants and architects seems a natural joint commercial venture as Israel's entrepreneurs reached out for credit and liquid capital to lowland elites.

Bees for Deborah's Kin

This hypothesis has an incidental explanatory force that warrants its consideration: the phenomenon of displaced countryside bands can furnish an otherwise invisible transfer mechanism for the otherwise problematic transport of swarms of Anatolian bees 500+ km to the city. For an ancient town to set apiculture at its heart and import swarms from that distance is more easily conceivable in the context of a neo-Assyrian empire (cited by Mazar and Panitz-Cohen, 2020:2.654). Across multiple commercial boundaries, it is a serial investment requiring resources, licensing, and the education of neighbors, that suggest sponsorship beyond the level of one town.

On the other hand, beekeeping is an occupation to which squatters resort as a moveable risk-spreading strategy. Anatolian bees may have reached the Rehov region not in one (smuggled?) shipment, but through a daisy-chain of transfers and cultivation probably down the Beqaa, ending with colonies in Issachar. Mazar and

Panitz-Cohen consider a variant on this model, which they call transhumant beekeeping (Mazar and Panitz-Cohen,. 2020:2.654–655). Their most powerful argument against it is a concern with hybridity. Its degree, though, is unknown. Other factors are also pertinent: the industry's planned introduction inside Rehov in the later 10th c., in a mudbrick architectural environment (like that of Megiddo VIA?), involved costs in real estate, not just plant, and in social engineering; and, the apiary's localized destruction in Stratum V might originate with neighbors, or from possible competing wasp infestations in the mudbrick. (Not to mention litigants invoking the goring ox principle, or possible cases of anaphylaxis.) Indirect association with the motif of hornets expelling Israel's predecessors, as with Deborah, both in Issachar, will not have escaped notice.

We should even consider a provocative rendition for the 9th-c. Rehov IV legend, *lšq 6 nmšy* – beside "For the cupbearer," based on a later Aramean legend at Hazor (and then in Phoenician-like orthography at Rehov), "For the apiary (< *šqq/šwq*, swarm, teem, as Isa 33:4; Joel 2:9), *6*, Nimshi." (Reading 6 after a suggestion raised by Ada Yardeni, *apud* Aḥituv, 2020).

7.5.2 Filtering Lots

Regardless of the world of interesting possibilities, and whatever the (fluid) background of Rehov's relations with Issachar and Machir, the later apiary venture involves an Israelite collaboration with other associations, and that suggests earlier commerce. What our monarchic, and in the end Jerusalemite sieve filters out, if the Israelites' mobile band culture hadn't already done so, is the extent to which the regional bands collaborated with polities like Shechem and Megiddo in Iron I, against other bands in the service of or combining with rival polities. This, I am arguing, is Deborah's concern.

7.6 *Lessons from Tradition History*

The concerns behind the monitions in the Pentateuch, Judges 1–3 about indigenes' gods and hallows and connubium seem a little different in earlier prose as well.

7.6.1 Hivites in the Rear

Dtr generalizes issues related to Hivites and Gibeonites (Josh 9; 2 Sam 21:2). 1 Sam 7:14, for example, reports conciliation between Israel and the Amorites. In 1 Kgs 9:20–21, Solomon subjects only Amorite populations (enumerated in apposition to that rubric) to corvée labor (Israel, in the narrative, having earned exemption by building Solomon's temple and palace, 5:27–30). This text differs in particulars from Dtr: it accepts forced labor in place of banishment in the highlands; it omits Canaanites, in Dtr's ethnography, lowlanders, as subject populations.

Dtr's view, or interpretation, was long in formation. Its evolution, like that of the Conquest, is not limited by what is hidden behind the materials that inspire it. Alliances and balances – Gideon for example, or even Abimelek, between Rehov, Megiddo and Shechem – Abimelek may easily have attracted allies elsewhere for his central hills program; Israelites may have been among the defenders of Migdal Shechem, if it is the el-Burnat site.

Silence leaves us with possibility. It will not do to forget what 1 Sam 21:11–15 (A source) denies and 1 Sam 29–2 Sam 1 (B source) try to conceal – David's done deals with Gath against Saul's Israel. Other partners – Gibeon, Nahash – pop up incidentally. Assuming the same protocols shaped records in the early monarchy, we glimpse the development of rhetoric about Canaan's ethnoi mainly in the broken silences of the text.

7.6.2 History to Tradition and Conquest

Later literary contexts, then, call for complete eviction. Still, in some texts, "to expel the Amorite" may target the political establishment rather than all non-Israelites. More explicitly, passages (1 Kgs 9:20–21; Josh 9:19; 17:12) that concede inability to expel populations differ from claims in Judges 1–3 which blame Israel for integrating with locals (Halpern, 1992). Both emphases recognize ongoing native political control of territories, and both embrace an ideal of supplanting rather than subjecting the populations. But the historiographic navigation is subtle. Diachronically-minded readers see inconsistency in Judges 1 itself: notices on Judah and Dan allow that lowland powers defied Conquest (1:19,34). On the other hand, Judges 1 suppresses Joshua's claim (17:12) that Manasseh was *unable* to take certain cities. In some cases, Canaanites lived among Israelites, and in others Israelites among Canaanites. These texts seem satisfied with political subordination as Conquest. That is, the Conquest of complete expungement is a later generalization, from a period when political rhetoric painted non-conformity as reversion to extinguished identities.

E, D, Dtr and P present traffic and *connubium* with prior populations as a national original sin. In doing so, they reinterpret a received concern with fraternization that was originally practical: if Israelites settled into existing states, into the polises, if they accepted existing administrative structures, they would be powerless to act in one another's interest, in the interest of Israel.

The process of distillation preserves distinct echoes of a past experienced mainly in the central hills. Thus, even Judges matches the conclusion derived through Yuval Gadot's discussion (graciously shared in manuscript) of Israel's relation to its landscape: the settlement cluster along the Wadi Tirzah, he infers, integrated into the regime of a neighboring urban center, in the instance perhaps Rehov. The association draws further support from the apparent integration of Iron I Issachar into Iron IIA Rehov, and the success of the Nimshi corporation.

The earlier intellectual layers in Judges reflect a struggle to construct Israel as a community and to overcome the effects of such integrative realities – Shechem, Megiddo, to begin – on affective identities.

8 Tribes in Place

Deborah's Israel appears after her call to arms in 5:9–12, and the troops arriving for war (5:13) are enumerated in her muster, in 5:14–18.

5:14
Then the survivors were conducted against the overlords –
The People of Yhwh were conducted to me against the veterans:
From out of Ephraim, whose root is in Amaleq -
Behind you is Benjamin, among your contingents.
From out of Machir, came down marshals,
And from Zebulun, those who draught with the scribe's rod,
5:15
And my commanders among Issachar (came down) to Deborah.
And Issachar was ready; as for Baraq, he was committed to the valley in his command.
    minor caesura
(BUT)
5:16
In Reuben's (voting) divisions(?), resolutions were grandiose:
    exhortation by hqqym
"Why would you sit around the campfires,
to hear the bleatings of flocks?"
Reuben's conclaves had grandiose deliberations.
5:17
Gilead, (who) abides across Jordan,
And Dan – why does he squat *'nyt*?
Asher, (who) settles at the seashore,
and abides along its inlets.
    minor caesura
5:18
Zebulun is a people that taunted itself to die,

And Naphtali, on the rises of the field.

    Caesura

8.1 Categorizing Realities

The role of parallelism in verse prejudices this sort of enumerative sequence toward ladders and contrasts. Tania Notarius notes some of Deborah's progressions (2013:126): Seir, field of Edom, earth, heaven, mountains (5:3), among others. We have encountered two series of travelers. Jael's scene teems with scaled triplets — women:Kenites:tent-dwellers:: water:milk:ghee:: pound:crush:cleave-pierce; and, the sequential actions, kneel, fall, lie down...*šādūd;* and finally, wombs:colors:dyes (v 30). Words resurface in sequence as well: v 24 calls for the blessing that follows, echoing Yhwh's blessing, in a different sense, from 5:2,9 (Notarius, 2017). 5:26f *hlm,* "pound" + object echoes 5:22 hooves. 5:18 *npšw* echoes in *npšy,* v 21. Sometimes the repetitions come in sequence: 5:16–17 proceed

Reuben	*yšb*		
Gilead		*škn*	
Dan			*ygwr*
Asher	*yšb*		
		yškwn	

What semiosis the patterns (aspect/root) have – as comment on kinds of dwelling – eludes us.

Of course, this is song, and aside from immediate repetitions (*mdhrt dhrt 'byryw* hastens to mind), some for meaning but most for effect, we expect wordplay, again often low-hanging fruit (*Deborah dabbĕrī*), rising to thematic (5:13,25 *'dyrym*), perhaps eisegetical, levels (5:23 Meroz, 5:3 *ha'ăzīnū rōzĕnîm,* e.g.). These features would multiply with regular performances. Marks of literate *sensibilities* in technique would speak to performance venues.

Repetitive wordplay also marks emphases. *Yrdw* (yarad[ū]), qal plural of *yrd,* "descend" (J5:11,14), brackets paired occurrences (5:13) of *yrd,* the piel singular of *rdh,* "direct, drive." The sequence introduces an aspect of guidance in a continuum from recruitment to the muster.

The singer particularly revels in reminders of those on whom her attention was focused, and whom Notarius (2017) plausibly identifies as her addressees in 5:2. She announces (5:9), "My attention turned to *ḥqqy* Israel." They play a role in raising volunteers (5:2,9). But play on the root (*ḥ/ḥḍḍ*) continues beyond the effective muster (5:10 *mḥṣṣym,* 15 *mḥqqym,* 16 *ḥqqy lb.* Finally, Jael's blessing reciprocates all the blessing of the *ḥqqym,* in combining the two dialectal realizations of /ḍ/ in 5:26 *mḥqh mḥšh rqtw.* At each occurrence, of a different form of the root, there is a further semantic play, in 5:15, between Machir's "stone-engravers," a subject for separate treatment, and Zebulun's letter-writers. When Deborah begins her campaign by announcing, "My mind is on *ḥqqy yśr'l,*" she's not kidding.

But perazon likewise is repeated, and *'rḥwt*, and categories of roads and travelers are grouped, and indeed, set into ladder sequences. While capping the echoes of *ḥqq*, the singer proceeds through a corporal sequence as well: cup (modifier repeated from earlier); stake//pounder (repeated); hand: head::*rqh*:feet, as the action starts high and ends below.

The tribal litany combines progressions. Geographically, the plot offers two fixed points toward which the currents rush. The foes clash near Taanach, with the Kishon flowing down from Megiddo to play its historical or, likelier, metaphoric role. The other point, where troops rendezvoused with Deborah, was probably a regional hallow, in Issachar or Zebulun. The bivouac may have been as close as the ridge running north of the Dothan Valley. So the plot moves us from field, road or house to the disparate gates, and from the gates to the staging-ground (vv 11–17). Finally, we reach the battlefield in v 18.

8.2 Hinterland Moves

The tribal geography, as noted, differs from later ideas. Machir is Cisjordanian; Gad may not yet have turned Israelite – its population are not Israelites under Mesha, or probably in Gideon's story.

Such shifts are characteristic of materials usually thought antique for other reasons entirely. And they tell some important stories. So, Zebulun in early monarchic Deut 33:18–19 draws profit from the sea, but as probably by trade as by fishing. It sacrifices inland. J's Gen 49:13 puts Zebulun on the seashore, verging on Sidon, and describes Zebulun by compressing the words that characterize Asher in J5:17 (Z. *lḥwp ymym yškn*). Asher leaves the coast.

Whatever underlies the aberrations (the Cabul barter?), Zebulun remains tied to Issachar: its population never shift even in the text. Joshua then moves Zebulun back inland, reaching to Galilee (esp. 19:27), and puts Asher back on the coast. Whatever their intent, these formulations mean, monarchs named administrative territories after more local tribal associations. The same process is witnessed in the appearance of archaic clan jurisdictions, and thus fixed territories, especially in Samuel.

8.3 Rachel

On siting Deborah's first two tribes, consensus obtains: the clusters on the Benjamin plateau and near Shiloh constitute the heartlands of Benjamin and Ephraim (as Finkelstein, 2020). Ephraim's "root in Amaleq" refers to the Amaleqite Hills in which the last of the "minor judges", Abdon, dwelt at Pirathon (not plainly Far'ata, Samarian Chronicle Ophrah).

8.3.1 Machir

As to the third Rachel tribe, in the hills astride the lower Wadi Far'a, sites spread around Sartab to the south and up the Jordan Valley. In an unpublished treatment, which he generously shared with me, of Iron I relations and perceptions at a level progress requires, Yuval Gadot posits the unity of these sites, and, importantly, suggests their integration into the political landscape, enjoying accommodation with a city, perhaps Rehov. On a related front, of integration, Gadot also points out that ceremonial fires atop Ebal, at el-Burnat, would be visible to the sites down the Wadi Far'a: there is a ceremonial link, a signal of some sort, from the one to the other. Its visual effect on community can only be gauged when we can identify the parties at Ebal. Dhahrat et-Tawileh (Mazar, 1982) likewise overlooks the Wadi Malih, without signs of Iron I settlement there (Zertal, 2008). The roasting fires from site cluster centers, especially where dense west of Wadi Far'a, would also contribute visually to a sense of community. This cluster probably represents Deborah's Machir, a set of clans: Edward Lipiński's proposal that Bet Shan's ancient city god, hieroglyphic *m'-k3-r,* gave Machir its name (see Levy, 2018a, b) dovetails with Gadot's link to Rehov.[6]

In the Judges context, Gideon next mobilizes the region east of Bethel, and attracts support from other clans, but, pointedly, not Ephraim, and not Benjamin.

8.4 North of Rachel

Two further tight groupings in the central hills, one in the Samaria hills and down the Wadi Shechem, and, the Dothan Valley, mentioned by Gadot, also offer themselves. Such clusters represent separate collectives, though it is not predictable if or when *Israelite* identity was paramount or, like the perazon, dormant – Meroz, cursed for non-participation, is more than a hilltop hamlet, likely a group, or a village, not necessarily Israelite. As like as not, the clusters represent the loci of Issachar and Zebulun, the next tribes enumerated.

8.4.1 Literary Location: Samaria

The Song suggests that the first five combatants occupy the central hills. It does so by grouping the five in its centerpiece, the muster. Ephraim//Benjamin, Machir//Zebulun and Issachar answered readily (5:14 f.). Reuben, Gilead//Dan and Asher did not (5:16 f.).

---

[6] On Lipiński's proposal, see E. Levy 2018a. Other tribes, too – Gad, Asher, Zebulun – share divine names or epithets.

The muster closes without any sign of help from across the Jordan or the Jezreel. 5:18 transitions listeners from assembly to battleground. We return to Zebulun, taking the field: next, one expects Issachar again, locus of the battle. But no — Naphtali! Only *after* battle is joined in the lyric does the sixth combatant, Naphtali, arrive (5:18).

The surprise reveal of an identity can be directed to the audience (even when anticipated), or to participants in the mindset of witnesses to the drama.[7] Here, the rest of the colon predictable, Naphtali's place at muster's realized climax expresses elation at a contribution from across the barrier of the Jezreel. The other participant-tribes lie apart.

8.4.2 Issachar

The northernmost cluster in Mt. Ephraim is a ribbon along the rim of the Jezreel north of the Dothan Valley, running east south of Jenin down to Dhahrat et-Tawileh and the southern reaches of Gilboa. It bids fair to be Issachar. Monarchs, Judges 1 and the list of Levitical cities concur, made Manasseh Samaria's seat, the administrative category for the line of Jezreel fortresses from En-Gannim/Ibleam to Megiddo. That region, Joshua nonetheless acknowledges, belongs to Issachar (17:11 f.; 19:21,29). The choice depends on categoric frameworks.

Another of Deborah's organizing sequences, in human geography, points to the same location. The sequence of five positive respondents runs from farthest to nearest the battle. Ephraim and its appendage Benjamin are directed to Deborah's staging point. Machir, bordering Issachar along the Wadi Far'a, and Zebulun, nearest Issachar, "descended" to it. Issachar and Baraq were ready, in the valley. Simultaneously, the first two units supply undifferentiated warriors, Manasseh marshals (*mḥqqym*), and Zebulun (*mškym bšbṭ spr*) specialists in some organizational function. Issachar produces "my commanders" and Israel's general. The ladder of roles seems to ascend as the troops from the highlands descend. All this suggests that Issachar furnished the theater of action, on Taanach's ground.

The location also coheres with Jacob's *pronouncement* (Gen 49:14 f.):

Issachar is a donkey gnawing (*grm*),
recumbent around the campfires,
Who saw a home, that it was good,
and the countryside, that it was arcadian,
And so set his shoulder to heavy lifting,

---

[7] My accidental list of surprise reveals, a common and ancient literary tool, includes the "incidental" disclosure of Atrahasis's name, for Utnapishtim, at the end of SB Gilgamesh XI (called to my attention by Tyler Kelley), as well as various classical stories ending, "that was the man who...". Judges itself climactically reveals to its audience the ancestry of Micah's priest (18:30), and to actors the character of angels (6:22; 13:16–21). Kings, only at the end of Josiah's history, names Moses as author of his literary find (2 Kgs 23:25).

and became conscript labor.

Likening a tribe to a donkey has struck readers as off-color. But the choice is dictated by the stanza's point, that the tribe contracted for land rights, specifically with Shechem. The polis's name suggests the stock image of shouldering loads, and the connection crystallizes as the shoulder, šikmô, of v 15. The donkey is ḥămōr, the city's founding clan. Even "gnawing" (grm) may be chosen as a homeophone for squatting, *gwr.

Ibleam and En Gannim and their hinterland were, historically, less liable to league with Shechem than with Rehov or Bet Shan. Still, one could imagine the sites west and east of En Gannim as distinct regional "segments", with variable entanglements, those in the Gilboa freest to remain aloof. Both Tola and Puah, the name and patronym of the first "minor judge" (10:1), are administrative clans; the judge is "man of Issachar", entombed in Shamir (G: Samaria) in Mt. Ephraim – Shamir may be the seat of a third Issacharite clan (of four), Shimron.[8]

Finally, Seti I claims to have campaigned against mobile populations, habiru and sutu (the distinction between squatters and nomads) from the Bet Shan and nearby regions. The weak link between Issachar and Rehov, mentioned above, deserves exploration.

In this tentative picture, although the logic of the poem is the sole positive indication, Zebulun constitutes the site cluster concentrated around Samaria and down the Wadi Shechem. It is the hinterland catchment, in any case, most likely to have availed itself of the hallow on Ebal. However, Burnat can also be modeled as a site for regional Hivite, or Hivite-Israelite, communion: its destruction repudiates condominium. As I write, press reports announce a Yahwistic (yhw) execration tablet from al-Burnat. This would probably confirm J. A. Soggin's suggestion that al-Burnat was Migdal-Shechem (Soggin, 1988; Halpern, 2022a). Publication will no doubt overtake this paper, but no resolution of the reports promises to unravel the historical intricacies.

8.5 *Images of Process*

The clusters in the central hills match the structure of Deborah's muster. The flow of warriors is suggested by Deborah's earlier focus on overland travel: her establishing image of deserted roads now opens onto a kinetoscope of isolated parties departing small sites, joining up where farmhouse and camp pathways feed busier defiles, columns waxing as more roads converge between mountain crests. Parts come together, separately but in unison, wheels grind into motion – the process of a people dedicating itself.

---

[8] Joshua 19:15's Shimron in Zebulun arises from paleo-Hebrew *resh-ayin* exchange for **šim'ōn*: G sumoōn, Amarna Shamhuna.

9 Wider Lenses

Before the battle scene (5:17–22), Deborah balances the heartland muster by surveying the peripheries. The survey begins with a long segment on Reuben, followed by a staccato of three tribes in four bicolons. Whereas the first five tribes swing into motion, the peripheral are static, like a gallery of separate stills.[9] Reuben is at least urged to abandon its peaceful encampments. The others follow almost colorlessly (the hemistich on Dan is obscure), the implications similar. Mount Ephraim is abuzz with activity, including the fight. Life around it, though an impulse to join is there, proceeds undisturbed.

9.1 Sizing the Event

Deborah's crisis may have been as politically significant as an attempt to dislodge encampments or even hamlets from the hills between the Dothan Valley and Taanach. It might be a response to a raid on goods, livestock, people. Taanach could be an ally under attack or, more likely, a launch pad against Israel. Perhaps an overlord at Megiddo (VIIA) regarded the migrants, with which some of its inhabitants trafficked (Martin, 2017), as agents of a competing power. In the verse, an unexpected turnout routs the infantry, with no real pursuit.

The politics are simplified to promote identification with Israel. Issachar beseeched comrades for aid. What we know about the region at the time comfortably accommodates the reading.

9.2 Deborah's Overview

When we envision Deborah's tribes as clusters of rural bands, the song's *plot* starts with absence "in Israel" – not as a territory, but as a society. Nothing suggests that Israel had ever assembled even in name – on her historical horizon, certainly. Deborah pleads a *moral* obligation of joint action. And so, she quickens at the first responses.

When she comes to tribes that did not contribute, Deborah scintillates: the brother-groups were called upon, and the choice to mobilize or abstain a complex one. Reuben wrestles with great intentions; the relevant factors, though, involved distance and obstacles, as with Gilead, and otherwise comfortable living conditions, as with Asher. Deborah sets an inviting, hopeful tone for their participation, their

---

[9] Smith, 2014 persuasively rejects Cross's (and my own) case that the peripheral tribes participated, which is based on Meroz' curse for abstaining. He takes the verbs (*yšb, škn, gwr*) as, "stay (away)". The sense is functionally the same but the nuance marginally less charitable than I imagine (below).

belonging, holding the invitation open even now. And, prudently, she reserves the real reproof: in the end, their own disappointment lies in not having fought "upon Saint Crispin's day".

Deborah's tack appeals less to shame, still less to guilt, as to envy – of others' glory. The song owes its dissemination to its effect, and it owes its effect to its compass.

9.3 Hearing Deborah

The noise we hear is Deborah restoring common enterprise, calling agrarians to mobilize. Previously, different groups accommodated with established polities and cast the Israelite project into doubt. Instead, Deborah called on them to unite for Israel under Yhwh's flag, to come to her assistance, from their every distinctive region. More important, her example propels her project into future consciousness, as an ideal always in search of embodiment.

Judges as a narrative finds a sequence: Deborah is indeed Israel's mother. She operationalizes its identity, and sets a tone for conjoint defensive actions. Before her, Israel may never have been a political identity.

Despite national ambitions, after all, Deborah never refers to institutions that transcend locality. The communications network depends on travellers, not professional messengers. Those so inclined gathered at multiple locations. The recruiters (*ḥqqym*) somewhat resemble the profile of Archaic rhapsodes. The latter were, themselves, compared to polis law-givers, partly for their familiarity with tradition, and the association of song with measures, from which some rhapsodic compositions took their name, *nomoi*. Those of repute were sometimes invited from abroad to conduct ceremonies especially of purification and healing.[10] With hooded robe and a long staff, they were legatees of regional genre-melody traditions (Thracian laments, etc.), and probably conducted rituals at magnet settlements, like Samuel at Ramah in 1 Samuel 9–10. Early poetry associates the *ḥqqym* and their role (*mḥqq*, po'lel) with patrons and volunteers (consider Nu 21:18 with J5:2). Under kings, subsidized guilds like Levi succeed these free-lance ceremonial specialists in texts (see Ackerman, 2011). In the Song, though, the *mḥqqym* of Manasseh make a natural lead-in to the *spr* of Zebulun. Here, they are the singers of Israelite identity. Theirs is the crucial role in Deborah's scheme. From the start, Deborah sings a song about singing, trumpeting its role, like that of Bedouin epic, in identity formation. Her song identifies for us the canon of Israel's infancy, the stuff of the later books of Yhwh's Wars (the conquest, below) and of Jashar.

What Deborah's account suggests is a chain of contacts and exchanges up and down the territories where members of the ethnic association, invested in realty or

---

[10] E.g., Aelian *Varia Historia* 12.50, with Thales of Gortyn called to Sparta by Lycurgus, or Terpander as arbitrator there. On the centralized institution, see Burkert, 1987; Collins, 2004.

not, were to be found. Within the rubric, Israel, their internal divisions, in part cultural, were magnified by settlement, by geographic stabilization.

Thus, their shared identity was organic, not structured by common institutions. In resisting external invaders, uplanders would melt away to avoid line battle (like other mobile peoples, famously Scyths), and pounce opportunistically (generally, Blome, 2020). Coordinating action was a challenge.

In contrast to LB, Iron I leaves marks of permanent encampment in landscapes inviting to the habiru. Their small bands, even when adopting a particular landscape as home, inclined to evade the demands and to deride the increasingly hollow hierarchy of the city.

These settlers included, as Israel Finkelstein has long held (1983), remote descendants of populations from all over the region who were dislocated first in MB III and then joined by the survivors of Egyptian pillage in evading administrative demands through LB II. Those rejecting polis architecture even after Egypt's disappearance were a mix of elements the region over. But in some enclaves, they established permanent homes, and trafficked with incorporated polis towns. By Gideon's time, we hear, they were combining to defend their niches against competitors for their resources.

But these elements were excluded from polis festivals, like those of the Sons of Hamor at Shechem. The transients were vagrants, whose separate cults were debased, unstructured, irregular. The gods of tent-folk were primitive, ignorant of protocol, collectively austere. Their exclusion from state ceremony fed a conditioned cultural fear of being uprooted and chased off. The cycle was real enough, and of course rebounded on those who would expel them – or did drive them off, from land held by Gezer, for example, or, earlier, in raids sponsored by imperial authorities.

We might with some confidence surmise that the Canaanite disease of LB II also tilted the demographics. Numbers and value shifted away from the cities and in some cases disposed market towns as well to integrate with the low culture. The value of labor climbed. Cultural contrast both within Israel and with countryside outsiders faded as the appeal of divisive political affiliations diminished.

10 Conquest

Deborah's Taanach donnybrook most probably involved defending encampments or homes against a predictable series of raids meant to break them up (resistance to corvée is less likely, in light of the anticipation of war-brides). The song is silent about territory, remarkable in a farming population. Her Israel lacks not just institutions, but physical boundaries beyond the immediate footprint of its bands. Israelites squat on isolated patches assigned to cities by Egyptian administration.

10.1 Conquest and Identity

The story goes, Abimelek comes along after parts of the Taanach coalition establish superiority over Shechem. His mercenary force turns on Ophrah, and next on Shechem and Hivites. Defense shades into offence. There is a territory to police, to protect commerce and migrants (9:25). Abimelek's is a chapter in the struggle to oust others from an increasingly cartographic Israel. In the chapter, all that results is a warlord's short-lived fiefdom.

Still, on its own terms, Abimelek's story starts the thread in which Israelite identity is counterposed specifically to Hivite identity, a point later addresssed in Joshua. It is the inception of ethnic conflict over Cisjordan.

Again, the traditional understanding tracks very close. Judges translates it into generally worshipping baals, elaborating the simpler idiom of the song, choose, into a farther-reaching metaphor. In Deborah's world, Israelites accommodated with city-states, though some (Gezer, Bet Shean, Philistia) repulsed them. In the later tradition, with a geographic domain as the goal, accommodation is not just a casual question of new gods. It is an interiorized renunciation of Israelite identity. The difference is, in Dtr, *identities* are exclusive, whereas in other writings (including Judges 1), they are compounded.

10.2 A Conquest Narrative

One, older, version of a conquest, widely acknowledged by both exegetes and scholars, permeates stories in Judges and Samuel. In it, Saul and David establish a territorial government that supersedes the authority of, and incorporates, Canaanite cities.

That narrative begins in the central hills. The historiography matches history, in that the unification of this bloc as a habiru polity extended or reinforced subscription to the god, Yhwh, in wider regions, reaching as far as Luash. Elsewhere, the conquest remains incomplete in Asher and Naphtali even on the time-horizon (proleptic in other cases) of Judges 1.

Early societal boundary markers and interstitial lifestyle explain the appeal of a god resident not just beyond worshipers' settlement, but at a remove from *any* enduring encampment. (E and P turn the mountain into a taboo zone, whereas Exod 24:9–11 and 1 Kings 19 countenance privileged access.) Yhwh is not in a polis, cannot be worshiped in a town. He is a peripatetic in Canaan, a visitor (Halpern, 1991:68), like his adorers.

He makes house calls for the same sociological reasons. In the Covenant Code and the early monarchic Deuteronomy 33, Yhwh comes to devotees wherever they are. Yhwh has no acropolis temple, nor even an intramural one. In that respect, he is closer to what in scholarly convention is an El-type-god, like Shechemite El Berit in extramural Migdal Shechem (Halpern, 2022a; cf. 1978), than to a city god, like Baal Berit, with his temple in Shechem (both Judges 9).

The disposition of the habiru cultural emblem in a niche isolated from order is also why we have no conquest tradition for the central hills – because the clans frequented the central hills before there was a conquest – explicit claims about *unconquered* regions are in broad agreement with the distribution of "Israelite"-looking Iron I architecture.

The conquest, the first conquest, was the assumption of political control in the central hills. That was the Wars of Canaan, or Wars of Yhwh, when Jacob became Jeshurun, the crooked the straight (Jashar, as in the book). It was the crucible from which a national identity flowed across the hillsides and wadi banks of the promised land. It looks as though there was no such aspiration until the monarchy. Deuteronomy 33 suggests, the early monarchy.

11 Toward Historical Processes

The Israelites are a loose, occasional society of *collectively* landless transients, whose normal communal interactions are limited to encounters between small groups. When undisturbed in a landscape in the hill country, they remain in bands, or in small groups of bands. They spread out (and this may be the sense of perazon, namely, invested bands). They share a culture without organization or institutions. Of them, individual bands and even groups of bands affiliate with populations observing the customs of civilization: formal, civic cult, paid officialdom, display propped on the backs of its targets, none of it was worth a whit to transients (still, Issachar). Too, they engaged other transients with distinct identities, whether a habiru coalition (Ammon, Moab) or ideological nomads (Kenites). Israelites begin as a network, since the opposite idea is an historical absurdity, and Israel became nothing more than the sum of the Israelites. When, thus, Merneptah encounters Israel, it must be a population of such bands already squatting in particular regions.

The image of Tiglath-Pileser I's 57 expeditions against the Ahlamu-Arameans holds a mirror to landless habiru in the west. The term is real enough – the habiru or Ahlamu are in a sociological sense ethnic. But there is no reality to the identity, politically. Only subgroups are capable of self-organization. Organizing one another poses more of a challenge.

11.1 Turf

Deborah makes a threat to a tribal cluster a threat to Israelites. They come to defend the homes, the crop patches, of their kin and to achieve a reputation for courage *in common cause*. (The role and reach of social debt in Israel in any period deserves detailed evaluation.) They hope, too, for widespread celebrity through their rhapsodes – the point of the Song of Deborah is to commend its own recital (in 5:2–5) as a means to swell public-mindedness – in the lingo, to edify the people. What she *has* done is make turf occupied by Israelites, but peripheral to the city-state, a question of wider concern.

When, via Gideon's league, Abimelek dominates Shechem's territory, that town's last gasp of nativism (Judg 9:28) ignites Israelite chauvinism. By Saul's day, ethnic targeting explodes, and it is a fair assumption that it was not asymmetrical. The Hivite Question even flings fragments back into Genesis and Joshua. Part of the reason for its ubiquity is its importance to the politics of coalition-building. It is, however, an issue that the monarchic writers leave disconnected, peripheral to the Conquest, again, because Saul's is principally another failed pursuit of the first conquest, and success in it preceded kings; and because David resolved the conflict in favor of a mutually profitable collaboration.

11.2 Territory

The extension of Israelite identity to territory leaves its first literary mark with the story of Saul at Jabesh (1 Sam 11), for which Jephthah's correspondence orients readers (Judg 11) in another complex literary arrangement. Subscription grew with military success. And where charisma and industry had created power centers, warlords either envisioned broader political control or adopted a more local perspective. The former, at least, paid ritual specialists, such as rhapsodes, to forward their agenda – at well-attended festivals.

We have a plot theme of the forging of relations between the central hills and central Transjordan, culminating in Saul's day. This pairs with precedent at Amarna, where one of Lab'aya's sons rules Pella. And again we have territorial authorities who harbor rural and migrant bands, and integrate them into the local economy. But in the minds of those who earliest propagated stories of a Conquest, it began with Deborah's defiance of governments who later, through a Saulide lens and perhaps on the model of Philistines rather than the reverse, morphed from old, quarrelsome centers into an undifferentiated ethnic adversary.

Deborah's role was to have rallied recruits from across all the tribal divides of the central hills. She joined to the later Leah tribes in the northern Ephraimite hills the later Rachel in the south, somewhat surprisingly given everyone's difficulties with Ephraim. To these, she added Naphtali, a new regional population. How is Deborah "a mother for Israel"? She birthed a sense that one group's security – Issachar, Zebulun – was a question of Israel's pride. So far as we know, she birthed Israel's cognitive national identity.

References

Ackerman, S. (2011). Who is sacrificing at Shiloh? The priesthoods of ancient Israel's regional sanctuaries. In M. Leuchter, J. Hutton, & S. Ackerman (Eds.), *Levites and priests in history and tradition* (pp. 25–44). Brill.

Ahituv, S. (2020). *The inscriptions.* Pp. 2.415–439 in Mazar & Panitz-Cohen 2020.

Ahituv, S., & Mazar, A. (2016). The inscriptions from Tel Reḥov and their contribution to the study of script and writing during the Iron Age IIA (revised). *MAARAV, 20,* 205–246.

Blome, D. A. (2020). *Greek warfare beyond the polis: Defense, strategy, and the making of ancient federal states.* Cornell University.

Burkert, W. (1987). The making of Homer in the sixth century B.C.: Rhapsodes versus Stesichoros. In M. True (Ed.), *Papers on the Amasis painter and his world* (pp. 43–62). Malibu, CA.

Cohen, A. (1965). *Arab border-villages in Israel. A study of continuity and change in social organization.* Manchester University.

Collins, D. (2004). *Master of the game : Competition and performance in Greek poetry.* Center for Hellenic Studies, Harvard University.

Dover, K. J. (1973). *Thucydides.* Oxford.

Esse, D. L. (1992). The collared Pithos at Megiddo: Ceramic distribution and ethnicity. *Journal of Near Eastern Studies, 51*(2), 81–103.

Faust, A. (2006). *Israel's Ethnogenesis: Settlement, interaction.* Expansion and Resistance.

Finkelstein, I. (1983). *The archaeology of the Israelite settlement.* Israel Exploration Society.

Finkelstein, I. (2006). Shechem in the Late Bronze Age. In E. Czerny et al. (Eds.), *Timelines: Studies in honour of Manfred Bietak* (pp. 349–356).

Finkelstein, I. (2020). The earliest Israel: Territorial history in the highlands of Canaan. In A. Azzoni, A. Kleinerman, D. A. Knight, & D. I. Owen (Eds.), *From Mari to Jerusalem. Assyriological and biblical studies in honor of Jack Murad Sasson* (pp. 404–412). Eisenbrauns.

Finkelstein, I., Arie, E., Martin, M. A. S., & Piasetzky, E. (2017). New evidence on the late bronze/iron I transition at Megiddo: Implications for the end of the Egyptian rule and the appearance of philistine pottery. *Egypt and the Levant, 27,* 261–280.

Friedman, R. E. (1986). Deception for deception. *Bible Review, 2*(22–31), 68.

Gadot, Y. (unpub). *Iron I settlements in the Samaria highlands (1).* Draft manuscript.

Galil, G. (2021). The formation of Judges and Samuel and the Deuteronomistic composition. *Vetus Testamentum, 71*(4–5), 566–590.

Halpern, B. (1981). *The constitution of the monarchy in Israel* (Harvard Semitic monographs, 25). Scholars.

Halpern, B. (1983). *The emergence of Israel in Canaan* (SBL Monographs). Scholars.

Halpern, B. (1988). *The First Historians: The Hebrew Bible and History.* San Francisco: Harper & Row.

Halpern, B. (1991). Jerusalem and the lineages: Kinship and the rise of individual moral liability. In B. Halpern & D. W. Hobson (Eds.), *Law and ideology in monarchic Israel* (Journal for the study of the old testament supplements 124) (pp. 11–107). Sheffield Academic.

Halpern, B. (1992). Settlement of Canaan. In D. N. Freedman (Ed.), *Anchor Bible Dictionary* (pp. 1120–1143). Doubleday.

Halpern, B. (2001). *David's secret demons: Messiah, murderer, traitor, king* (The bible in its world). Eerdmans.

Halpern, B. (2003). Late Israelite Astronomies and the Early Greeks. In S. Gitin & W. G. Dever (Eds.), *Symbiosis, symbolism, and the power of the past* (American Schools of Oriental Research Centennial) (pp. 352–393). Eisenbrauns.

Halpern, B. (2021). What does Deuteronomy centralize? In D. Edelman, B. Rossi, K. Berge, & P. Guillaume (Eds.), *Deuteronomy in the Making: studies in the production of Debarim* (Beihefte zur Zeitschrift für die Alttestamentliche Wissenschaft, 533) (pp. 97–162). Walter de Gruyter.

Halpern, B. (2022a). Touch of Ebal. Tesselated ethnicity on the historical frontier of iron I. In C. Rollston, S. Garfein, & N. Walls (Eds.), *Biblical and ancient near eastern studies in honor of P. Kyle McCarter, Jr* (Ancient near eastern monographs) (pp. 00–00). Atlanta, GA.

Halpern, B. (2022b). The weight of the past. *Biblische Notizen*, 138, 71–88.

Jordan, B. (1986). Religion in Thucydides. *Transactions of the American Philological Association, 116*, 119–147.

Koller, A. (2020). Composing the Song of Deborah: Empirical models. *TheTorah.com*. https://thetorah.com/article/composing-the-song-of-deborah-empirical-models

Lemaire, A. (2004). Inscriptions found by the Manasseh Hills survey. pp. 548–555 in Zertal 2004.

Levy, E. (2018a). A fresh look at the Mekal stele. *Egypt and the Levant, 28*, 359–378.

Levy, E. (2018b). A fresh look at the Mekal stele. *Ägypten Und Levante / Egypt and the Levant, 28*, 359–378.

Lewis, T. J. (1985). The Songs of Hannah and Deborah: HDL-II. *Journal of Biblical Literature, 104*, 105–108.

Martin, M. A. S. (2017). The fate of Megiddo at the end of the late bronze IIB. In O. Lipschits, Y. Gadot, & M. J. Adams (Eds.), *Rethinking Israel, studies in the history and archaeology of ancient Israel in honor of Israel Finkelstein* (pp. 267–286). Eisenbrauns.

Mazar, A. (1982). The 'bull site:' An Iron Age I open cult place. *BASOR, 247*, 27–42.

Mazar, A., & Panitz-Cohen, N. (2020). *Tel Reḥov. A Bronze and Iron Age City in the Beth-Shean Valley* (Vol. 4 vols. Qedem 59–62). Institute of Archaeology, Hebrew University.

Notarius, T. (2013). *The verb in archaic biblical poetry: A discursive, typological, and historical investigation of the tense system* (Studies in Semitic languages and linguistics 68). Brill.

Notarius, T. (2017). Lexical isoglosses of archaic Hebrew: פְּלִילִים (Deut 32:31) and כֵּן (Judg 5:15) as case studies. *Hebrew Studies, 58*, 81–98.

Richter, W. (1964). *Die Bearbeitung des "Retterbuches" in der deuteronomischen Epoche* (Bonner Biblische Beiträge). P. Hanstein.

Schloen, J. D. (1993). Caravans, Kenites, and Casus belli: Enmity and Alliance in the Song of Deborah. *Catholic Biblical Quarterly, 55*, 18–38.

Sergi, O. (2019). The formation of Israelite identity in the Central Canaanite highlands in the Iron Age I–IIA. *Near Eastern Archaeology, 82*(1), 42–51.

Smith, M. S. (2012). Why was 'Old Poetry' used in hebrew narrative? historical and cultural considerations about judges 5. In M. J. Lundberg, S. Fine, & W. T. Pitard (Eds.), *Puzzling Out the Past Studies in Northwest Semitic Languages and Literatures in Honor of Bruce Zuckerman* (Culture and History of the Ancient Near East 55) (pp. 97–212). Brill.

Smith, M. S. (2014). *Poetic heroes: The literary commemorations of warriors and warrior culture in the early biblical world*. Eerdmans.

Soggin, J. A. (1988). The Migdal Temple, Migdal Šekem, Judg 9 and the Artifact on Mount Ebal. In M. Augustin & K.-D. Schunck (Eds.), *Wunschet Jerusalem Frieden* (IOSOT Congress Volume, Jerusalem, 1986) (pp. 115–120). Peter Lang.

Stager, L. E. (1988). Archaeology, ecology, and social history: Background themes to the Song of Deborah. In J. A. Emerton (Ed.), *Congress volume Jerusalem 1986* (Vetus Testamentum supplements 40) (pp. 221–234). Brill.

van Soldt, W. H. (2005). *The Topography of the City-State of Ugarit* (Alter Orient und Altes Testament 324). Ugarit-Verlag.

van Soldt, W. H. (2016). The Orontes Valley in texts from Alalaḫ and Ugarit during the Late Bronze Age, ca 1500–1200 bc. *Syria* [En ligne], IV | 2016, mis en ligne le 01 décembre 2018, checked 4 Mar 22. https://doi.org/10.4000/syria.5121

Von Dassow, E. (2008). *State and Society in the Late Bronze Age. Alalaḫ under the Mittani Empire* (Studies on the civilization and culture of Nuzi and the Hurrians 17). CDL Press.

Zertal, A. (2004). *The Manasseh hill country survey. I. The Shechem syncline. Culture and history of the ancient near east, 21.1*. Brill.

Zertal, A. (2008). *The Manasseh Hill country survey. II. The eastern valleys and the fringes of the desert. Culture and history of the ancient near east, 21.2*. Brill.

Merenptah and Amenmesse – Egyptian Rumors Concerning the Exodus

Michael Bányai

Abstract The hypothesis at the core of this paper was published in a much larger work by the author in *JEgH* 12 2019. Due to its focus on Egyptological matters, that article reached a small circle of specialists, and its ramifications for the biblical scholarship have largely gone unnoticed. The present paper fills this gap – pointing as often as possible to the more extensive discussion of the previous paper's evidence.

Recent archaeological evidence invalidates previous chronological solutions for the reign of Amenmesse: edging him between the reigns of Merenptah and Sethos II or allowing a partial overlap between Sethos II and Amenmesse's early reigns. His reign's time and geographical base must be rethought and identified within the regnal period of Merenptah.

This reconstruction looks strikingly similar to the late narratives (Manetho, Apion, Potter's Oracle, The Lamb Oracle) concerning a revolt, Merenptah's flight to Ethiopia, his return to Egypt, and his defeat of the contender. The late narratives' association of Amenmesse's rule with the Israelites is understandable against the historical background of a stock of Israelite prisoners brought by Merenptah to Egypt from his previous campaigns.

Due to this historical context, the literature of the time offers several hidden references to Israel. The *Tale of Two Brothers*, the political manifesto of the revolt, is an etiological story of the relations between Egypt and Israel using eponymic patterns as in the story of Danaos and Aigyptos. A Ramses V dated parodistic retelling of the tale, pChassinat III, introduces allusions later picked up by Manetho's characters of Moses and Joseph (Barbotin, Revue d'égyptologie 50:5–26, 1999; Bányai, J Egypt Hist 12:36–103, 2019, n. 153).

A discussion of the literary material from this period demonstrates the necessity of a new approach to Early Israel and its possible relations to Retenu, a term designating an Asiatic neighbor of Egypt.

M. Bányai (✉)
Independent Scholar, Stuttgart, Germany
e-mail: scholarmichael.banyai@t-online.de

Keywords Early Israel · Retenu · Merenptah · Amenmesse · Israel Stele · pHarris I · Tale of Two Brothers

1 Amenmesse's Place Within the 19th Dynasty

From the viewpoint of an Israel-historian, Merenptah's reign must be considered a kind of watershed event both because of the famous Israel-Stele and because of the earliest signs of Israelite settlement in the Hill Country sometime after his reign. One should also remember that the late Manetho and Chairemon historiographies referring to Merenptah's reign introduce some oblique mentions of the Exodus and the Israelites. One of the problems with the objective interpretation of the enumerated evidence stems from the still-controversial position of Amenmesse, Merenptah's contemporary, relative to this latter's reign. The lacking historical context infringes on the results of any period discussion.

Two different approaches to Amenmesse's obscure reign dominated until shortly the scholarly discourse. Kitchen and Helck regarded Amenmesse's reign as separating Merenptah and his designated heir, Sethos II. The second approach, proposed by Krauss and Dodson, maintained that upon the death of Merenptah, Amenmesse and Sethos II became rival kings, with the domain of Amenmesse confined to the south.

New and hitherto overlooked evidence concerning this obscure period led to the recent formulation of a third chronological approach by Bányai (2019). This new approach contributes to a better understanding of Amenmesse's reign and, incidentally, to solving significant problems that deal with the transition from the 19th to the 20th dynasty. This solution partially relates to Early Israel.

According to this new chronological approach, Amenmesse's revolt disrupts the reign of Merenptah. Manetho's account of Merenptah's rule (operating under the erroneous name Ammenôphis, like in several versions of his Epitome)[1] tells the story of the flight of Merenptah to Nubia, driven out of Egypt by a former Heliopolitan priest identified by Manetho for propagandistic reasons with Moses (Amenmesse), and of pharaoh's later return. The evidence of the 19th–20th dynasties corroborates this narrative.

Trying to offer just a sketchy presentation of the main lines of the underlying historical reconstruction and introduce new points of talk instead, I will point to Bányai (2019) for questions of detail.

Kha-em-ter's Stela (Habachi, 1978), Amenmesse's southern vizier, shows Amenmesse in control of Upper Egypt, where he is not supposed to appear, according to Krauss and Dodson. The Stela celebrates Amenmesse's achievements in the north: "*Ret]enu (does not [...] the Asiatics are not seen (anymore) on the (city)*

---

[1] Helck (1956a, b: 64, 70), Beckerath (1980: 551) identify Ammenôphis as a frequent misspelling of the name of Merenptah in late antique literature alongside with all the garbled attested forms *Ammenephthês/Ammenephthis > Amenôphath > Amenôph > Ammenôphis*. It features within the Epitome as the name of a king of the 19th dynasty, obviously Merenptah.

walls, and the (Libyans(?))[2] *cannot (anymore) come forward....*" The northern extent of his suggested domain precludes a parallel reign to Sethos II. A stereotypic use of the formula is a weak option since one must first generally consider the practice of stereotypical stock phrases during the New Kingdom, which is instead a practice of the late period. Inscriptions attesting Amenmesse in the north are rare due to the archaeological circumstances in the Delta. Kitchen (1987) pointed to a vase with the royal titles of Merenptah found in Riqqeh, 45 km south of Memphis. At the same time, Sethos II's second regnal year is well-attested in the south deep in Nubia (Gilmour & Kitchen, 2012: 6). A parallel reign of ca. 3 years between regnal years 2 and 5 of Sethos II's reign is thus an impossibility.

The discovery of a short-lived workmen's village in front of KV10, Amenmesse's tomb usurped for the royal wives Takhat and Baketwerel (Schaden & Ertman, 1998; Schaden, 2009), and the royal years attested here led to synchronization problems for every conventional approach to Amenmesse.

Workmen's villages in the Valley were erected temporarily just for the work at tombs in their next proximity, and none other except KV10 lends itself to such a purpose during the attested lifetime of the village. An ostracon found in the village offering the dimensions of the main corridor of KV10 strengthens the causal connection between the village and KV10 (ostracon discovered in the 2003 campaign in the workmen's village, mentioned in Schaden 2009 (online publication without page numbering). "*No specific reference to Amenmesse has been found to date in the hut's areas, but one small ostracon gives dimensions matching the corridor width and height of KV-10.*")

There exists a coordination problem between the ostraca attesting to the 9th and 10th year of a ruler (probably Merenptah) and a year 1 (probably Sethos II, since Amenmesse appears in Thebes just in his later years) in the village with the activity within KV10. There exists nothing in the tomb to justify the existence of a workers' village before Amenmesse's reign since Amenmesse's activity within the tomb antedates its later desecration and transformation for the Queens Takhat and Baketwerel.

Despite a lacking identification of the rulers, whose regnal years appear in the workmen's village, there is no alternative to their identification with Merenptah and Sethos II. Since the existence of such a workmen's village in the Valley of the Kings was restricted to a short period as intensive work occurred at a tomb (example provided by oCairo CGC 25,581 – KRI IV, 151:5–152:1), this would have been demolished as soon as the work was fulfilled. The attestation of the year dates 9th, 10th, and 1st can, therefore, mean only a royal succession following closely upon the first's 10th year. None of the kings of the 20th dynasty conforms to this requirement. On the same grounds, one must also exclude the later kings of the 19th dynasty, leaving us only with Merenptah and Sethos as choices.

---

[2] The name is entirely ruined in the original text and can only be tentatively proposed as Libyans based on our knowledge concerning the ethnic groups tormenting Egypt under Merenptah. Being a negative statement, "*... cannot come forward,*" its intention is only to convey the feeling of security at the inception of the reign of Amenmesse, similar to the message of the Israel Stele concerning the situation following the victory over the Libyans.

Evidence from the village leads to the conclusion that the tomb was decorated for Amenmesse before Merenptah's ninth regnal year since the wall decoration for the later royal wives' burial plasters over reliefs made for Amenmesse. An activity under Merenptah (as suggested by the year-dates found outside the tomb, in the workmen's village) before Amenmesse would be unexplainable since there is nothing before happening at the tomb. The succession of events in and out of KV10 reconstructs as follows:

1. Anonymous royal tomb created for Ramses II's son, suggested by the existence at this spot of an earlier workmen's village. Its date provides a docket naming User-Maat-Re (Ramses II). Its original owner may be identified with Seth-her-khepeshef (also known as Amun-her-khepeshef), the designated crown prince of Ramses II, son of his first royal wife, Nefertari. Seth-her-khepeshef was (probably despite preparations for an own separate tomb) buried because of his violent early death in the tomb of the sons of Ramses II, with the tomb left unfinished. O. Louvre N 2221 lists Amenmesse attending the burial of a prince Sethos, son of Seth-her-khepeshef. He seems thus to have belonged to the Nefertari clan, too, removed from power by the Isisnofret family branch to which Merenptah belonged (Bányai, 2020: 51–53).
2. Decoration of the tomb for Amenmesse before year 9 of Merenptah.
3. Removal of the evidence for Amenmesse and usurpation of the tomb for the royal wives Takhat and Baketwerel between years 9 of Merenptah and the 1st year of Sethos II.

Dodson (1987) and Krauss (1984) identified Takhat as a queen of Sethos II,[3] thus synchronizing her death with the activity perceived in front of the tomb. She must have died before the attestation of Tewosret as a great royal wife by the second year of Sethos II (oCM JE72452 instruction to "*start upon the tomb of the King's Great Wife Tewosret*", which is sure to belong to the reign of Sethos II). A note at Deir el-Medina, oCM CG25560, concerning the visit made by Sethos II on II *Aḫt*, Year 1, to the Theban Necropolis must be connected with Takhat's burial and that year's activity in front of the KV10.

It is unknown, despite the work of Dodson (1987) on this issue, whose queen Baketwerel was. The only fact concerning Baketwerel, which can be securely extracted from the tomb evidence, is that she postdated Amenmesse since the tomb decoration was made by plastering over the deep-relief decoration of Amenmesse (see for this, for example, Dodson, 1985: 9: "*the poor plastering and painting stands in stark contrast to the fine relief employed by Amenmesse, and, on available data may well overlie the erased decoration of the king, of which the cartouche mentioned above may have formed a part.*"). Schaden and Ertmann's (1998) stylistic discussion of Baketwerel's tomb scenes (attributed by Dodson to the period of Ramses IX) corrects Dodson's impression and re-dates them to the 19th dynasty:

---

[3] There also exists a probably unrelated Takhat mother of Amenmesse. Given the frequency of the dynastic name, it is not necessary to assume the common identity of the two women.

"The fragments of the KV10 scene of Queen Baketwerel share a trait with some figures in the tomb of Queen/King Tawosret and Queen Nefertari, where crowns cut into or overlap with borders or upper decorations of scenes. This visually links these queenly depictions and implies a late 19th dynasty date for Baketwerel's portrayal."

However, the burial of Baketwerel must have antedated Takhat's. Given the position of her burial deep within the tomb in Room F, her funeral furnishings ought to otherwise have passed the narrow Room E, already crammed with the burial of Takhat, which is not exactly an easy feat. Under these circumstances, both queens' burials must have occurred during the short existence period attested to the workmen's village.

The deletion of the names of Merenptah by Amenmesse studied by Brand (2009: 31) in the Cour de la Cachette in Karnak demonstrates a *damnatio memoriae* perpetrated by Amenmesse against Merenptah. Evidence for Sethos II's monuments effaced/overwritten by Amenmesse is lacking. Evidence for the effacement of the names of Merenptah and his crown prince, Prince Sethy-Merenptah, was also provided by Brand (2009, 2010).

Dodson (2010: 25, 26, 63) observes an *"upheaval in the ranks of senior officialdom, with the vizier Panehsy and the treasurer Tjay, certainly superseded"* during the years 7/8 of Merenptah, which could, according to our scenario, illustrate the problems with which the late reign of Merenptah had to struggle.

An attestation gap between Sethos II's second and fifth regnal years at Deir el-Medina required by the Krauss and Dodson reconstruction to insert the Theban Amenmesse data is contested by Gilmour and Kitchen (2012: 6).

The date of Amenmesse can be similarly reconstructed based on the time gaps in the workmen's lists at Deir el-Medina village between those lists and dates attributable to Merenptah, thus, allowing the insertion of Amenmesse's dates. The Amenmesse data (oGard 174, oCG 2780, oCG 25783, oCG 2784) run from a *3. prt, 23. day* (of the 3rd year of an anonymous reign unanimously identified as that of Amenmesse) to a *3. šmw, 29. day* (of the 4th year of another anonymous reign identified as Amenmesse's). These can be inserted between Merenptah's *8th Year, 2. ꜣḫt, 20. day* (last date on the ostraca oCG 25504) and *9th Year, 3. šmw, 18. day* (oZouche H2). The date of pAnastasi VI 3 may reduce this rather large gap by its date within year 8, day 5 of [the birth of] Seth, the epagomenal days. However, the document is highly dubious.[4]

---

[4] pAnastasi VI 3 is just a pupil's joke. Enene (the scribe responsible for the writing of papyrus d'Orbiney, and pSallier II) poses as if reporting to his teacher Qagab about his border activity and recording the immigration of a Bedouin tribe (Caminos, 1954: 293).

This is a fiction since pAnastasi VI is part of a larger papyrus collection, beginning with pAnastasi IV, titled "[*Beginning of the instruction of letter-writing made by the scribe of the treasury Qagab for*] *his apprentice Enene in the regnal-year 1* (*of Sethos II*), *fourth month of Shomu, day 15*" (Caminos, 1954: 125). Qagab would, under normal circumstances, not have received official reports of this kind since he was sitting in the wrong department.

Most of the other texts seem to follow closer to a real model. Morris, 2005: 486–487, arrives at similar conclusions about the text.

There are exceedingly few year-dates pertaining to Merenptah from the period supposed to cover the reign of Amenmesse in Upper-Egypt. A year 8, 3. *prt*, often attributed to Merenptah, oDEm 594 must be re-attributed instead to Tewosret (Bierbrier, 1975; contra Krauss, 1976: 165). The workman *P3-nb* appearing in this ostracon lacking any higher titles must be instead identified with the son of the Deir-Medineh foreman of the same name. PBologna 1094 with a date in the 8th year 3. *prt* 29 (Caminos, 1954: 33–34) must be ignored since the transportability of the medium, written wherever the pharaonic court stayed, renders it irrelevant for the present discussion.

2 A Historical Reconstruction

One must look very deeply into the reign of Merenptah to identify the original grounds for Amenmesse's revolt. It must be surmised that Amenmesse had some entitlement to the throne since he rose, without having previously occupied, so far as we know, any position of power in the pharaonic administration. Without a critical situation compromising Merenptah and convincing parts of the Egyptian ruling class to rally around Amenmesse, there would have been no possibility of challenging a ruling pharaoh.

Merenptah's misfortune seems to have started during his 3rd year (judging by the notices of the "Grenztagebuch," pAnastasi III, attesting his presence in Canaan at this time)[5] trying to suppress a local revolt, which kept him occupied perhaps into his fourth year[6] in Asia.

It is irrefutable that the war brought Asian war prisoners to Egypt, some of them possibly Israelites. PBologna 1086, dating to the 3rd year of Merenptah, notices Asiatic slaves, as well as pAnastasi IV 16, 4 (year 1. Sethos II.) or pAnastasi V. pAnastasi III vs. 5,5, the *Grenztagebuch*, notices a messenger passing the border with

---

[5] Helck's (1971) treatment of the *Grenztagebuch* caused an involuntary setback compared to Breasted's translation and commentary (Vol. II, 1906). By replacing a single missing preposition in the *Grenztagebuch* assumed by Breasted as 'for' by 'from,' Helck reversed the messenger's travel direction to "*the place where the king is*" in the document. As long as one read about *Ḥʿj*, the captain of infantry being in *Ḫ3rw* during the 15th day of the ninth month, one had to assume that the presence of the same *Ḥʿj*, in the place where the king is, during the same month, determined Merenptah's presence in Syria.

Formerly thought to indicate Merenptah at war in Canaan, this was consequently modified to an irrelevant text. Naming the recipient of messages passing *Tjaru*/Sile was necessary because it entitled a messenger to border passage at Tjaru/Sile in the recipient's direction. After all, these are copies from the address dockets and must have in the first line offered exact information regarding the address of the recipient and the recipient. Caminos (1954: 108–109) follows on this issue Breasted: "*(for) where the king was, (for) the captain of infantry Ḥʿj.*"

[6] The Lachish bowl 3 with receipts of wheat in payment of taxes dated to a year 4 attributable to Merenptah was found in the LBA destruction stratum (Wright, 1961: 212). It thus dates to the insurgents' destruction of this Egyptian holding.

letters from (!) the "*[property of] Merenptah, the settlement of war prisoners,*[7] *which is in the district of irm*" on the way to the place in Canaan "*where the king was*".

irm in pAnastasi III cannot be corrected following Helck (1960: 12) to Amurru (Amurru being Hittite) but represents the district of Irem in Upper Nubia, the southernmost border of Egypt between the 4th and the 5th Nile cataract (Kahn, 2013: 19). It may have been even further to the south on the Atbara, according to O'Connor (1987: 101).

Male prisoners were sent according to the Egyptian practice to the opposite ends of the empire – for example, the *apiru*-prisoners to Kush (Kâmed el-Lôz letter KL 69:277).

This war seems to have ended with an Egyptian Pyrrhic victory, candidly admitted by Merenptah in his great Karnak inscription, explaining away his inactivity during the later Sea-People's crisis, with the unavailability of archers and military forces within the Egyptian army, Karnak 8–9: "*[Egypt was as (?)] that which was not defended. It was abandoned as pasture for cattle because of the Nine Bows. It was stormy in the vicinity of the ancestors, with the result that all the kings sat in their pyramids [...The dead] Lower Egyptian kings were opposite their town, isolated by the Seshemu-tawy (possibly a poetic name for the Nile) through a lack of military forces. They had no archers to champion them.*" (Manassa, 2003: 16; Kitchen, 2003). This situation lasted several months, during which all Egyptian cities barricaded themselves against raids of the allied Libyans and Sea-Peoples, the Nile providing their only defense (Karnak 19): "*Into the fields of Egypt have they entered. It was the [Great] River which opposed itself to them, with the result that they spent days and months dwelling [within it...].*"

Destructions at Beth-Shean VII (Mazar, 2010: 252–253), Lachish VII (Ussishkin, 1985: 240–267, and N. 6 in this paper), Aphek (Guzowska & Yasur-Landau, 2007), possibly Tel Dan (Meitlis, 2008), and the final destruction of Hazor (Kitchen, 2003) hint at a significant civil war tormenting Palestine. All the cities mentioned above were the usual Egyptian allies in the region. These destructions should not be attributed to Egyptian activity but to the local Asiatic anti-Egyptian insurgents. Kitchen (2003: 25–28) points to high-ranking hostages from some of these cities raised at the Egyptian court, ensuring the loyalty of their relatives in Canaan. Destructions are also identifiable on the other side, like Gezer. Recently found human rests of two adults and a child in Gezer by Ortiz attest to heavy destruction at the site. The site seems to have been re-used years later under Sethos II (Gilmour & Kitchen, 2012: 2).

Karnak 8–9 and 12 hints at the desolate state of the Egyptian army after the Asian war of Merenptah. The military weakness made the way free in Merenptah's fifth year to Egypt's first invasion since the expulsion of the Hyksos by an ad-hoc coalition of Libyans and Sea-Peoples. Merenptah and his generalissimo and designated

---

[7] Helck (1960: 12): "*(Eigentum) des Merenptah, die Kriegsgefangenensiedlung, die sich im Bezirk von irm (vielleicht verschrieben für Amurru) befindet.*" Helck's translation of the term *nḫtw* roughly meaning '*stronghold*,' conforms to the meaning '*mercenary camp*' in pHarris I 76, 8; 77, pointing at the employment of the Asiatic prisoners as military in the far south.

heir, prince Sethos (the later Sethos II), wasted months until the first groups of invaders advancing against Memphis at Per-Barset (identified by Manassa, 2003: 14 by Bubastis) forced the Egyptians to engage the Sea Peoples.

The isolation imposed by the foreign invasion over Egypt's nomes and cities might have enhanced the centrifugal ambitions of the Egyptian elites. The first revolt started in far-off Wawat, Lower Nubia, at the same time that the pharaoh engaged the Libyans and Sea-Peoples at Per-Ire. Merenptah conceded the rebellion just a year later on the Amada stela (and parallel texts found in Amarah-West) celebrating its suppression: *"His Majesty was informed (that) the fallen one of Wawat had transgressed in the south. (Now) it happened [in] Year 5, 3rd Month of Shomu, Day 1, corresponding to when the valiant army of his Majesty came to overthrow the despicable ruler of Libu...."* (Davies, 1997).

Lacking for the past 300 years before a local ruler in Wawat, anyone called *"the fallen one of Wawat"* must be identified as the head of the local Egyptian administration itself. The term is no equivalent to his official titles: it appeals to literary terminology drawn from the past. Apart from this consideration, the replacement of the King's Son of Kush, Kha-em-ter, with Messuwy in Kush occurred at the same juncture as a reflex to the revolt (Yurco, 1997: 50, 56).

The King's Son of Kush in charge at this point was Kha-em-ter, who later became the southern vizier of Amenmesse. His existence became known relatively late because his monuments have been effaced by the agents of Merenptah and Sethos II. He was replaced by a Messuwy, retaining these titles till late in the reign of Sethos II. By the sixth year of Merenptah, Messuwy was effectively in charge in the south, celebrating with understandable delay Merenptah's victories of the previous years due to the resistance one met in Kush. This left enough time for Kha-em-ter, who never declared himself a pharaoh but saw himself as the main target of Merenptah, to transfer allegiance to Amenmesse, crowned as a king in Lower Egypt, in monuments erected at Abu-Simbel, Amarah-West.

A stela from Buhen dedicated by Kha-em-ter illustrated in Dodson (2010: Fig. 26) as possibly showing Sethos II worshipping Horus, Lord of Buhen, must probably be coined on Amenmesse A lack of documents attesting Kha-em-ter at the side of Sethos II, excludes an original attribution (at the moment of carving) of the monument to Sethos II. The cartouche erasure conforms to the treatment accorded to the other monuments of Amenmesse. Habachi (1978) thinks that *"this prenomen must have been engraved on that of Amenmesse."*

Dodson tries to reverse by this the established order of the King's Sons of Kush: Kha-em-ter, Messuwy. He must ignore for this purpose all references to *Ms.j* in pSalt 124, identified with Messuwy by Krauss (1976, 1977, 1997).[8]

How can we understand the report to the court about the "revolt" of Kha-em-ter? Papyrus d'Orbiney, The *Tale of Two Brothers,* is the protocol of hearsay snapped by informants (*"what this concerns, one relates following..."*), checked by high

---

[8] Bányai (2019: 43 ff) agrees with Krauss's identification of Messuwy and ms.j, comparing the situation with the one under Ramses XI as the King's Son of Kush, Panehesy, was a military governor of the Thebaid.

officials of the treasury and subsequently presented to the prince Sethos (the designated heir), whose name appears on the verso as recipient: "*The fan bearer of the king, secretary of the chief, the elder royal son, Seti-Merenptah.*" The tale is identified as a highly secret state matter by the closing formula of the tale obliging confidentiality: "*Whoever speaks about this papyrus roll, may Thoth be a hostile adversary.*"[9] In short: the tale is identified as a state affair.

The text has been one-sidedly treated as a folktale, ignoring all the warning details of its handling as a secret state matter and its sole attestation in the highest political circles of the court. Also, the synthetic character of the story necessitating the knowledge of contemporary Semitic religious beliefs goes far beyond the horizon of Egyptian folktales. A new approach emerged only recently with Wettengel (2003), the first to point to the confidentiality formula, which has no place in Egyptian folktales. Schneider (2008), recognized here, later claims to reverse the throne-succession order, replacing the designated throne-heir, the narrative's Anubis/*Jnpw*, with a King's Son of Kush.

It is sufficient to say that the latter part of the narrative deals with the fate of the son of Bata (but born to the pharaoh), becoming a King's Son of Kush (!) and later following on the throne. Anubis, his brother, accedes to the throne upon the death of Bata. The political allusion was unescapable to the contemporary Egyptians since Anubis/*Jnpw* was the habitual designation for the designated crown prince (Schneider, 2008: 7). Such a succession is entirely unusual for the New Kingdom, especially for the 19th dynasty. This leads Schneider (2008: 5–6) to assume the tale's role in legitimizing a new model of royal succession. Lacking an identifiable historical context, Schneider's proposal didn't receive the deserved recognition.

The narrative thus proposes that the current crown prince, the *Jnpw*, therefore prince Sethos, the later Sethos II, to whom the papyrus is addressed, be replaced in succession with the present King's Son of Kush, Kha-em-ter (replaced in the sixth year of Merenptah in context with the Wawat rebellion) probably due to Sethos' incompetence defending Egypt. This allusion was a veiled way to let people know and test the support for Kha-em-ter.

A tale declared a state secret, addressed to the future Sethos II (who was by then the crown prince) and dealing with the replacement of the heir by a King's Son of Kush, roughly at the moment of a revolt in Wawat, revealed in Merenptah's monuments only a year later, makes the supposition of an existing connection between the two events unavoidable.

News about the "revolt" could have arrived after the two weeks required for the travel between Wawat and the northern residence (Krauss, 1984: 222), by the 14th day of the third month *šmw*, after the victorious battle against the Sea-Peoples and Libyan alliance. Amenmesse seems to have retroactively counted his reign beginning with the arrival of news concerning the revolt in the South.

---

[9] A similar formula appears in pSallier IV. The usually proposed completion "*speaks (bad)*" in the translations lacks a justification. See Wettengel (2003: 23).

Helck's (2002) observation of a change in the counting of the years in the Deir el-Medina record occurring during the 3. *šmw* month serves to date the crowning of Amenmesse between the 12th and the 14th day of that month.

One must rely on guesses and later narratives concerning the evolution of Amenmesse's revolt. Merenptah's burnt residence in Memphis (Sourouzian, 1989: 44) may, under the circumstances, attest to turmoil in Lower Egypt. In pAnastasi IV, 3, in the first year of Sethos II Qagab, one of the high officials authenticating the *Tale of Two Brothers* (Papyrus d'Orbiney) reports on the progress of the construction of the new Memphite palace (Helck, 1958: 410–411, Caminos, 1954: 220–221).

The flight of Merenptah (Ammenôphis) to Nubia is attributed in all late antique narratives (discussed below) to a prophetic act rather than a lost war against Amenmesse.

One could tentatively link this prophetic act to the Karnak decree of Sethos II, threatening drastic consequences to the higher clergy of Amun should it try to influence the bearers of the bark of Amun. Dembitz (2007) supposed a causal link between Sethos II's decree and the succession problems after Merenptah. The porters of the bark played an essential role in the oracular decisions met in the sanctuary. The bark's stops and movements during the Opet feast answered oracular questions (Fukaya 2012). Sethos' decree was probably published during his visit to Karnak for the Opet feast during the 10th–12th days of the second month of Akhet, Year 1, reflecting the changes in Thebes (Helck, 1956a, b: 86).

Priests influenced political decision-making by controlling the porters of the bark. To Merenptah's Theban date *8th Year, 2. ȝḫt, 20. day* (oCG 25504) follows the large record gap allowing an Amenmesse-Theban interlude. This last date of Merenptah in Thebes is three days ahead of the Opet festival (*2. ȝḫt, 23. day*), involving the presentation of the bark, which may have led to his banishment from Egypt. This evidence could attest to a large wave of elite support for Amenmesse within Egypt. Sourouzian (1989) lists monuments up to those celebrating Merenptah's victory over the Libyans and Sea-Peoples in Upper Egypt and Middle Egypt, thus, none of which could overlap with the period attributed here to Amenmesse's reign.

The High Priest of Amun Rome-Roy profited from the political confusion to name his son Bakenkhons as successor in the office without asking for pharaonic approval, without even calling a pharaoh in his inscription: "*My son is in my place, my office is in his hand, in hereditary succession, forever.*" Rome-Roy's succession was never to be. Sethos II's decree in Karnak was a shot at the high Theban clergy. The figure of Bekenkhons and his name were chiseled out of the monument, and he never succeeded his father. Rome-Roy seems to have soon disappeared, replaced by a new Bakenkhons, recently revealed by Boraik (2007). This Bakenkhons was the son of a nobody, of a certain Amenemopet, Chief-scribe of recruits of the Domain of Amun, chosen due to the name similarity to demonstrate Sethos II's power over the local hereditary priesthood. The new HPA died in the 4th year of Sethnakht, thus some 17 years later. He was still remembered in his funerary inscription for redressing the statues of former kings (probably statues of Merenptah vandalized in the temple under Amenmesse) upturned "*by the hands of poor people*" as the central act of his tenure.

One may also add to this Bietak's (2003, 2015) identification of typical Israelite four-room houses discovered among Hölscher's (1939: 68–72) finds within the court of the Mortuary Temple of the pharaohs Ai and Horemheb. Since domestic structures within the temple area are unexpected, Bietak thought these may have belonged to the workers demolishing the Mortuary Temples under Ramses IV. These could, however, have been erected as well during the civil war years between Amenmesse and Merenptah. Even if not designed for this purpose, the temple's walls offered excellent protection for the Asiatic households of some short-lived garrison during those troubled times. Under normal circumstances, such constructions would have been inconceivable within the temple area.

In Palestine, on the other hand, follows a segregation between the Egyptian-controlled Canaanite region and the Hill Country, now an obviously Israelite region. The Hill Country slowly returns to sedentarism while also being largely cut off from the circulation of international goods in which the Canaanites are still playing an important part.

3 Related Texts

3.1 The Israel Stela

This text has become a wide range of interpretations. My commentary will, therefore, focus only on the ones relevant to the current discussion. The stela deals with the recent Libyan war of Merenptah; a previous Asiatic victory that mentions Israel is alluded to only retrospectively.

This war still partially resounds in the title, *"one who subdues Gezer, Baienre Meramun,"* on stelae erected in Amada, Amarah-West, Wadi es-Sebua, and Aksha. These stelae no longer mention Israel, perhaps exchanged against the term, Retenu, lacking in the Israel Stela. Interestingly, Gezer and Yeno'am, in the Israel stela, cover the south-north extent of Upper Retenu (Bányai 2020: 15, 34 N. 83).

Yurco (1986) recognized in the south wall scenes of the Hypostyle Hall at Karnak an illustration of Merenptah's war scenes, previously attributed to Ramses II. This was later confirmed in the field report of the 2004–2005 season by Brand's (2010) detailed analysis. One of the cities appearing in the Israel Stela, Ashkelon, is unmistakably identified by an inscription naming it in the scene (Brand, 2010: 7), while two other unnamed towns are indirectly surmised from the Stela.

The singular mention of Israel in an Egyptian text is certainly not due to the sudden discovery of a new ethnic group under Merenptah. It is rather the consequence of the use of quoted speech. The quotes are attributed either to the vanquished Libyans or the Israelites, leading to the occasional verbatim use of Semitic words in the Egyptian text. Speech of the Libyans: "'*A chief, ill-fated and evil-plumed*' – so said all those of his town about him....' Such (literally 'it') has not been done to us since (the Time of) Pre, so says every old man, talking to his son. (It is) disastrous for the Libyans... Speech of the Asian rebels: "*The princes prostrate themselves, saying: 'šlm!'*" (Davies, 1997: 173–187; Hoch, 1994: 285–286).

One shouldn't attach, therefore, excessive historical importance to the singular mention of Israel in this text. Obviously, the Egyptians possessed their own term or terms for the region never replaced even with the advent of historical Israel. The word Israel is rather incidental, like the rare replacement of the exonym Germany by Deutschland in an English newspaper.

The sentence: "*Israel is wasted without seed, Ḫ3rw is made a widow for Egypt*" may thus represent the partly quoted speech of the Israelites themselves, building a compositional parallel to the one of the Libyans. This supports the observation of Hjelm and Thompson (2002: 14) that Israel, Ḫ3rw and Egypt in this text may represent eponymic figures interacting like real-life persons. This interpretation was criticized by Kitchen (2004) since Egyptian literature lacked a comparable use of eponymic figures. Treating the sentence as a literary quote of the speech of the vanquished Israelites solves this problem.

The expression, "*Israel is wasted without seed*," identifies Israel as the man-part and the leading contender in the conflict over the possession of the woman Ḫ3rw/Canaan, obviously identified as his widow. One must refute the literal interpretation of the expression (Hasel, 1994, 1998: 76–80) as a lack of grains. Rainey (2001) criticized this approach and explained the term "seed" as meaning progeny. This shows the occasional lack of precision of the Egyptian scribes in using determinatives since the human semen is additionally determined by a penis determinative, which is lacking here.

Ramses III's inscriptions (Breasted, 1906, vol IV: 28) describe him as: " *overthrowing the Temeh, slain in their places in heaps before his horses, causing that they cease their opposition in their land, whose sword has overthrown their seed by the might of his father, Amon, in all lands together, Lord of the Two Lands, Ramses III.*" Other textual parallels within the context of Ramses III's first Libyan war come even closer to the Israel Stele (Breasted, 1906, vol. IV: 33): "*I laid low the land of Temeh, their seed is not.*" Since Egypt provided the stage for Ramses III's first Libyan war, and the Libyans are said to have just trespassed the borders (Redford, 2018: 1–10), this statement and similar ones cannot relate to the destruction of Libyan crops by Ramses III.

The meaning of the expression is explicit in another of Ramses III's Medinet-Habu first Libyan war inscriptions (Redford, 2018: 9): "*I felled the land of Temehu and [now] it has no seed, the Meshwesh, they conceive through fear of me!*" Having no seed may mean losing one's manliness, not playing the masculine part in the conception process, and pushing in extremis one ethnic group into a "passive" conceiving feminine role.

The menage a trois between the three ethnic groups described in the Israel Stele as an interaction between eponymic figures also obtained a late expression in biblical stories. These concern the Israelite eponyms Abraham, Sarah,[10] and the pharaoh

---

[10] PVandier borrows narrative patterns from the *Tale of Two Brothers*. The magician Merire, a cheated husband, is sent to the land of the dead by a fictional pharaoh, Si-Sebek, who marries his widow. The magician Merire appears to speak in the Netherworld with a pharaoh Meneptah (sic!), probably the historical Merenptah.

(Gen 12:10–20), Isaac, Rebekah, and the pharaoh (Gen 46:1–8).[11] This menage a trois is continued in the *Tale of Two Brothers* about the failed matrimony between the hero, Bata (emasculating himself in the precedent episode), and the wife created by the gods for him in Lebanon, how she betrayed him and chose the pharaoh for a husband instead.

The production of aetiological narratives added to the patriarch stories trying to explain Israel's delicate position between Canaanites and Egyptians seems a Merenptah period phenomenon, both apogee and moment of decline of the Egyptian involvement in the region.

The generally acknowledged presence of at least one of the standard Israel tribes, Asher,[12] in its later biblical location, in pAnastasi I 25, 2ff, questions the possibility of reaching relevant results on an approach to Early Israel chronologically based on the Israel Stela, which massively postdates it. The humoristic scene described in pAnastasi I in context with the chief of Asher *Qdrdj*[13] (or Qatsra-yadi, Hallo, vol. III, 2001: 13) "*as the she-bear (?) found him in the 'bikàa' tree*" is illustrated at Luxor (Fig. 1) in context with Ramses II's conquest of *śá-tu-na* identified with Shatin (some 15 km southwest of Bsharri, Lebanon) according to Helck (1971: 211, 495). Sidon (regularly written in the Amarna correspondence, etc. with ṣ, Ṣadi), the northwestern border corner of Asher according to the Bible (Josh 19:28, Jud 1:31), is probably just confusion for *śá-tu-na* (written with š, Shin). Given the evidence for both terms in context with Asher and its northern border, the assumption of confusion is compelling despite the difference in spelling. One may assume that knowledge about *śá-tu-na* no longer existed at the time as some scribe tried to make sense of the name, likening it to Sidon.

The northern frontier of Canaan prominently passes by Lebo-Hamath[14] on the same north latitude as Shatin. This line creates one of the two known historical northern borders of Israel (Josh 1:4; Num 13:21, 34:8; 1 Kings 8:65; 1 Chron 13:5; 2 Kings 14:25; Amos 6:14; Ezek 48:1). At the same time, this border line existed

---

[11] A late attempt to replace the Egyptian figure in the biblical narrative by the Philistine Abimelech probably originates in the more Egyptian-friendly Northern Kingdom. The line of border-places convened between the "Philistine" king of Gerar and Abraham: Gerar, Esek, Sitnah, Rehoboth, and Beersheba represents a real historical border but existing between Israel and Egypt in the Negev, partly along the Besor, "the river of Egypt," attested even in Neo-Assyrian texts.

[12] Asher also appears in an even earlier inscription dating to Sethos I in his temple of Redeshiya (Müller, 1893: 237), placed within a geographical sequence between Kadesh and Megiddo.

[13] The name seems to ironically mean קְצַר־יָד, thus, qtṣry yad = short of power/i.e., powerless. The expression is attested in 2 Kings 19:26 and Isaiah 37:27. It probably transforms in pAnastasi I, a typical Egyptian derogatory designation of the enemy, as the powerless chief of Asher, to a proper Semitic name.

[14] Lebo is identical to *lebwe*, a station of Ramses II on the road to Kadesh (identified as Laboueh, in Lebanon, by Helck, 1971: 202; Na'aman, 1999) precisely on the same northern latitude as *śá-tu-na*.

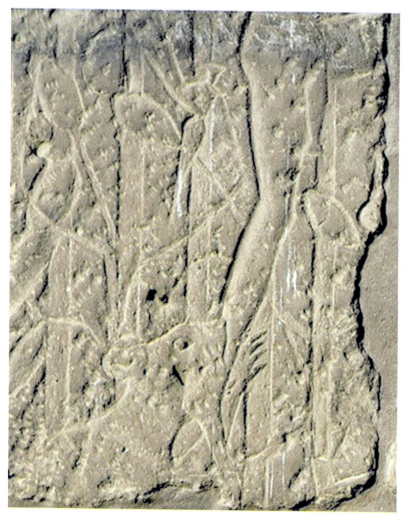

Fig. 1 The chief of Asher Qḏrdj in the 'bikàa' tree. (Photo credit kairoinfo4u)

since at least the MBA[15] between Canaan and any of its northern neighbors Qatna, Yamhad, etc. It was obviously passed over to every later state that managed to conquer the northeastern province of Canaan, named in AT 58, 15–22 (Kienast, 1980: 57–58), "the country Labān" and during the 18th dynasty R^c-mn-n, thus Lebanon. It must be concluded that this became the territory of the northernmost Israelite

---

[15] Mari texts M.7714 and A.3552 (Durand (1987: 219–220), Charpin (1992: 4 N.20–21)) record an early confrontation between Qatna and the "Canaanites" at the common border running by *Râḥiṣum* (the later *Ruḫizzi* appearing in the later Amarna correspondence). This is a place likewise at the border to the territory controlled first by Qatna, and later by Kadesh.

tribe, Asher, sometime before the 19th dynasty.[16] The weathered scene shows a person looking for refuge in the crown of a pine tree (the relief hints at pine needles and a bear pulling him by the leg) (Fig. 1).

The, term *bikàa* tree must be a second name for the pine tree (the primary one being ꜥš), explained by Rendsburg (1997: 448) as derived from the place-name where this kind of tree grew. Hoch (1994: 112–113) lists a *bikàa* fruit, appearing in pHarris I along with pomegranates and grapes. It is also a source for oil delivered as a tribute of Lebanon to the times of Sethos I. The stylization of the trees in Luxor (Fig. 1) allows for identifying the big *bikàa* fruits looking upwards from the branches only with pinecones. One can still recognize traces of the representation of pine needles in the relief.

3.2 Literature of a Revolt: The Tale of Two Brothers and the Hymn to the King in His Chariot

The interest in the historical discussion of superficially-seen literary texts stems from the sliding transition between the literary and the political sphere in ancient Egypt. What the Egyptian scribe cannot directly say, he hides as allusion or in the form of a roman á clef. These insinuations were easily understood, and a delight to their contemporaries but are difficult to fathom for succeeding generations that lack the context needed to understand the text's intentions.

The texts discussed here are the earliest attestation of the story of Bata and the only ones to present the hero in a positive light throughout. One must assume that the polarization of the subject and its later overall negative publicity were due to the revolt of Kha-em-ter and later Amenmesse, adopting these as programmatic texts.

I offer here a brief abstract of the *of Two Brothers*. The story, set in Egypt, involves two brothers: Anubis, the elder and the married of the two, and Bata, the younger, single and living in the household of his older brother. Anubis' wife tries unsuccessfully to seduce Bata. Following this, she accuses Bata of having assaulted her. In his fury, Anubis tries to kill Bata, who flees thereupon Egypt. Anubis is just short of catching Bata as the brothers reach the Egyptian border with Asia. But a miracle by the god Re saves Bata; he creates a crocodile-filled river separating them. Once secure, Bata tells his brother the truth of what happened and also announces he will live from now on in the Pine Valley, where he will hang his heart on a tree. The brothers are reconciled. Before his brother leaves, Bata tells Anubis the signs by which he will know something evil has happened to him and how to revive him in the event of his death.

---

[16] Another alternative traditional northern border was set by Dan. Generally speaking, borders can variate as well in "discrete" steps and "continuous" ones, with the fall of a neighbor state or due to war about provinces.

Bata settles in the Pine Valley, where the gods create a wife for him. He advises his wife to stay out of the sea, but she disregards his advice. While bathing, she loses a lock of hair, falling into the water. It floats to Egypt, and it is presented to the pharaoh. The pharaoh falls in love with the owner of the perfumed lock of hair and sends messengers seeking after her. Bata kills the messengers, but the pharaoh is tenacious. He will do anything to overcome Bata and thus get the woman for himself. Bata's wife betrays him by revealing the secret of his immortality to the pharaoh. The pharaoh orders that the pine on which Bata's heart hangs be felled. Bata dies. Anubis receives signals of his brother's death. He hurries to Lebanon to revive him. He manages to revive Bata, who now takes the shape of a handsome bull, upon which Anubis returns to Egypt.

Once in Egypt, Bata discloses his true nature to his former wife, who lets the pharaoh kill the bull. Beta is now reborn as a pair of Persea trees at the gate of the pharaoh's palace. After discovering his identity, his former wife orders the trees to be cut down. This time a tree-splinter manages to impregnate her, and she thus gives birth to a son from Bata. The pharaoh names Bata's son a King's Son of Kush. Upon the pharaoh's death, he inherits the throne and reveals his true identity as the reborn Bata. He lets the wife be judged and killed. After a 30-year reign, he is followed on the throne by his brother Anubis.

The tale miraculously survived almost in the original form known from the Papyrus d'Orbiney in Southern Arabia (Müller, 1902: 69–91). Peust (2001: 150): *„...(es) bestehen so viele Motivparallelen zum Zweibrüdermärchen, dass ein wie auch immer gearteter genetischer Zusammenhang kaum bestreitbar erscheint."* He is sure that due to the huge number of parallels between both versions, there is some genetic relation between both narratives, an impression I share. The most significant modification to the text, appearing in the Southern Arabian version, no more obliged to an allusive language, is the identification of the brothers as ethnic eponymic figures. The main hero's, Bata's, identity is revealed as the "*Son of the Abyssinian woman*" (wald al-ḥabašiyya), and the other brother is called "*Son of the Arab woman*," (wald al ʿarbiyya).

Hints about the different ethnicity of the eponymic Bata offers the *Hymn to The King in his Chariot*. Manassa (2012: 146): "*The sides (bt) of your chariot: Bata, lord of Saka, while he is the staff of the son of Bastet (Maahes), as one exiled to every foreign land.*" The term *bt* equivalated with Bata is Semitic related to Akkadian *bītu'* container, repository, housing. Schneider (2008) identifies this Semitic touch as primary because of Bata's abode in the Pine Forrest in Lebanon and because his name is written, unlike the name of the Egyptian god of Saka, regularly in group script, reserved for the transcription of foreign names. Schneider (2008: 7): "*Without doubt, the name of the tale's hero was pronounced 'Biti' or 'Bêti,' or just 'Bêt,' and this is confirmed by a pun in the poem on the king's chariot O. Edinburgh 916, 7–8 where the name of the Upper Egyptian deity Bata rhymes with Semitic bít/bêt, "(house =) case, box.*""

The parallels between the Joseph/Potiphar and Bata stories (Hollis, 1990, 2015) are as little circumstantial as other biblically loaded allusions in the text. Therefore, we must conclude that the identification of Bata with the namesake Egyptian deity is secondary, done to address an Egyptian cultural milieu.

There are more details of the story with solid biblical resonance. Thus, for example, the following narrative segment: Bata's wife loses a lock of her hair to the sea > the hair arouses the pharaoh's sexual desire > Bata's wife divulges to the pharaoh the secret for Bata's invincibility and advises him to fell the pine on which Bata's heart hangs > the hero dies.

The plot is merged in the Samson story: cutting the hero's side-locks leads directly to the hero's defeat. The number of two women fatal to Bata and Samson is a further plot parallel. Samson is an eponymic personification of Israel, Greenstein (1981: 247). The 30 bridegrooms following him probably represent the subservient 30 Canaanite kingdoms defeated by Joshua.

The Egyptian flavor of the Samson narrative may result from its mixed cultural milieu of inception. This is apparent in the Horus-themed solar symbolism of the hero's name, the importance given to his Horus side locks (payot conform to Lev. 19:27 and Num.6:5), and the loss of his eyes – recalling the quarrel between Horus and Seth in the course of which Horus lost his left eye.

Thus, for example, the little-understood riddle of Samson concerning the bees inhabiting the carcass of the lion killed by the hero plays on the known title of the Egyptian pharaoh, *nswt-bjtj*, 'of the Sedge and Bee.' The title seems to have been well-known to biblical writers. For example, Jes. 36,6 is a wordplay on the first part of this pharaonic title, the sedge (bulrush). The corpse of the lion plays on the hieroglyphic writing of *Ḫ3rw* (Canaan) as lotus plant + reclining lion. A comparable pun on the name of *Ḫ3rw* appears on the Amada Stela of Merenptah, calling the pharaoh "*a lion against Ḫ3rw.*" Such literary games must have been current during the intensive cross-cultural dissemination moment between the Egyptians and Hebrews under Merenptah and Amenmesse. One can explain, as a conclusion, that the riddle alludes to the soon-to-come defection of the Canaanites to the Egyptians.

The Bata-Samson parallels are much more profound than suggested by the few coincidences enumerated. One must take account of the late editorial level of the Samson narratives reaching us to understand why, for example – the implication of the Egyptian pharaoh as the rival in Samson's marital exploits – is preserved only as a kind of "palimpsest" after its erasure from the story.

To the details resonant with a Bible reader belongs the miracle of Re, creating a river infested with crocodiles separating Bata from his older brother Anubis who intended to kill him at the border of Asia, not-so-vaguely recalling the wonder of the sea. The water is iconographically identified as the border channel infested with crocodiles separating Egypt from Asia in some of Sethos I's reliefs, but as well over the names given to it "Waters of Pre" (used by Merenptah for the Pelusiac Nile arm running by Sile/Tjaru), whence the miracle or Re, or simply "Great River" (pHarris I 77, 1–77, 2 or the Karnak Victory Inscription of Merenptah, discussion Manassa 2003: 28–31).

Another turn of the tale narrates how Bata, in the Pine Valley, hung his heart in the crown of a pine for protection. This is a hilarious combination of 19th dynasty motives, known from the pAnastasi I, used for the instruction of the scribes, about the chief of Asher *Qḏrdj* "*as the she-bear (?) found him in the bikàa tree*," and reliefs of the period. One can recognize in one of Ramses' II Luxor reliefs (Fig. 1) with the scene of the chief of Asher climbing in the bikàa tree with a she-bear grappling his foot a similarity between the fruits in this tree and a heart. The place where *Qḏrdj* climbed the bikàa tree to save himself from the bear is the same where Bata, looking for protection, hung his heart high in the crown. The *'š* (pine) tree, in the Pine Valley, in the Bata narrative, must have been a slightly veiled allusion to the mock story of the chief of Asher, which belonged to the curriculum of scribal circles of the time. Even more interesting for the perceived general Asiatic identity of the Bata is the association of his abode with the territory of Asher, known from a biblical perspective as an Israelite tribe.

One conclusion based on the discussion of the biblical texts from the patriarch stories to the Samson tale is that the events at the time of Merneptah have probably contributed to curbing the production of etiological narratives trying to explain the ever-changing position of Israel in the quarrel over the control of Canaan. A lengthy political divide in the Egyptian colonial Asiatic realm showed that regular conflicts between the Asiatics were a constant feature through the Late Bronze Age, mostly involving the same parts on both sides (Bányai, 2020).

One may conclude, therefore, that the *Tale of Two Brothers* consists of two parts: an etiological tale explaining the past historical relations between the Egyptians and the Asiatics, personified by Bata, and a second part transporting the political demands of the King's Son of Kush Kha-em-ter, stressing both his connection to the royal house and the Asiatics represented by Bata.

We must assume that Kha-em-ter, looking by this tale only for a nomination as a crown prince in the place of Sethy, had a Ramesside family background. The propagandistic allusion to vague ethnic relations to the Asiatics deported to the south by Merenptah, making him a rebirth of Bata, may have had some factual basis allowing him to win over the deportees and to recruit them against the Sea Peoples. The Ramses family originated in the Delta, and its forebears were, as communicated by the 400-year-stela, hereditary priests of Baal/Seth in Avaris, a temple erected before the Hyksos dynasty (Bietak, 1990).

3.3 *Historical Reflections of the Merenptah-Amenmesse Conflict in the Later Ramesside Texts*

The turbulent situation in Egypt during the 20th dynasty is evident from the Elephantine-stela of Sethnakht, the first ruler of the dynasty. However, the date of the celebrated victory over the enemies (Altenmüller 1982) in Sethnakht's 2nd regnal year *šmw* is problematic. The order of the events in the stela places them before the beginning of his reign and not during his second regnal year: first suppressing the rebels within Egypt, then cleaning the throne of Egypt (obviously occupied previously by an illegitimate king), next becoming a pharaoh on the throne of Atum (probably in Heliopolis or Memphis).[17]

There is, therefore, a fair probability that this 2nd year designated the setting of the Elephantine Stela itself while essentially postdating the events into which Sethnakht may have once participated on the side of Merenptah.

Alternatively, identifying Tewosret (Altenmüller, 1982) with the illegitimate pharaoh fought by Sethnakht, a proposition which Altenmüller (2011) has in the meanwhile abandoned, is untenable for the reasons mentioned above but also because the royal dates in Tewosret's last year go beyond a 2. *šmw* (the date of the stela). A hieratic inscription on a foundation stone of the mortuary temple of Tewosret dated securely to her reign seems to allude to Sethnakht (Demarée, 2011: 126) positively: "*Year 8, 1. šmw, Day 24, [...] nice like Sethnakht.*" Finds at Qantir, Heliopolis, Memphis, and Hermopolis attest to Tewosret's presence in the north.

There is thus little to corroborate an enmity between Sethnakht and Tewosret, especially since pHarris I's Irsw, the *H3rw*, who must have been Sethnakht's actual enemy, defies any identification under Tewosret.

The same is true of the recently discovered stela of the HPA Bakenkhons, Son of Amenemopet. Dated to the 4th year of Sethnakht (Boraik, 2007), it deals with redressing some overthrown statues of earlier kings following a civil disturbance period. The title, "justified," added to Bakenkhons, qualifies him, however, as dead and his stela as celebratory of his death in the 4th year of Sethnakht and not as the date of the mentioned civil disturbances. Since he must have been installed as HPA in the first year of Sethos II, the inscription can refer to a restoration dating to the beginning of his incumbency as HPA in Thebes, the apex of his career, soon after the revolt of Amenmesse.

Other alternatives within the late 19th dynasty must be excluded on similar grounds. Siptah, for example, was present during his last year in the south for the installment of the new King's Son of Kush, Hori II, son of Kama. He thus had hardly any problems at that time in the Delta. Hori II, probably a trusted supporter of Siptah, kept his position under Ramses III and was succeeded by his son, Hori III.

The Elephantine-stela states that the enemy looked for support from Asia: "*[ennem]ies fall in his front because fear has filled their hearts. They flee back [like little birds] when the falcon pursues them. They let [fa]ll silver, gold [and copper, the property of] Egypt, which they intended to give these Asiatics, to send them the mh3tyw (northerners)*[18] *[as chie]fs of Egypt, as their (hostile) intentions had no success and their menaces didn't fulfill*" (Drenkhahn, 1980: 80).

---

[17] Altenmüller (1982): „er (Sethnacht) schlachtete die Rebellen, welche in dem Lande Ägypten waren und reinigte den großen Thron von Ägypten, er (Sethnacht) war/wurde Herrscher auf dem Thron des Atum."

[18] Amenhotep II, Amada stele, *dr ntt iti.n.f. rsyw wʿf.n.f mhtyw*: "*since he had seized the Southerners and he had subdued the Northerners*" (Helck, 1955: 1297–1298).

One can not regard his stela as a literal description of the situation at the death of Bay, Siptah, or Tewosre. It, therefore, made sense to admit the possibility that Sethnakht felt entitled to the throne simply due to his former participation in the dynastic wars against Amenmesse.[19]

PHarris I provides interesting information concerning the period before Ramses III. In his monumental translation of this text (1994, vol. II: 228) Grandet expresses his stupor to discover a situation surprisingly close to Manetho's description of the situation under Merneptah: *"Notons – en passant – que l'on peut, à titre d'hypothèse, poser la question de savoir si l'épisode de la « guerre des impurs », chez Manéthon…malgré la suspicion qui entoure la valeur historique de ce texte… ne se référait pas en partie aux mêmes événements."*

It is hard to demonstrate whether or not the Manethonic narratives are related to these events. The historical reconstruction of the events themselves is still remarkably close to both.

The historically relevant text of pHarris I was translated by Grandet as follows:

> The country of Egypt had been abandoned by flight.[20] Each followed his own laws, (the people) had no ruler, and many years followed (thus) ….
>
> Nevertheless, the country of Kemet was (in the hands of) princes and city mayors, (ea) ch (of them whether) great or small, (did not cease) to kill his fellows, and another (of his) parents, to inherit him.
>
> During (a time) of empty (?) years, Irsw, the $\underline{H}rw$, was their ruler (wr) because he had placed the entire country under his control (literally: under control before him).
>
> One closed an alliance with the other (literally: his partner), that their possessions were confiscated. And the gods were not treated differently (than) people because one did not sacrifice offerings within the temples anymore.
>
> However, as the gods turned back (again) to peace, to make the country be precisely in its original state, they established the son of their flesh as [king] of the entire country at their great place, Sethnakht….

The same key sentence concerning the abandonment of Egypt by its ruler appears at Medinet-Habu (Edgerton & Wilson, 1936: 52, n. 15a): *"Egypt was a fugitive, she had no shepherd, while they bore woes because of the Nine Bows."*

Another Ramses III Medinet-Habu text refers to the same events (Edgerton & Wilson, 1936: 23):

> The Asian and Libyan enemies are carried off who were (formerly) ruining Egypt so that the land lay desolate and in complete destruction since (previous) kings, while they persecuted the gods as well as everybody, and there was no hero to receive them when they rebelled. Now there exists a youth like a griffon (Ramses III)…."]….

We see Ramses III substituting himself for Sethnakht in the same way that Sethnakht interloped himself in the role of the pharaoh, defeating Amenmesse.

---

[19] This narrative seems to have found resonance in a detail of Manetho's garbled story of the events under Merenptah (Josephus I.28): *"This leader, Manetho adds, sent to Jerusalem inviting the people to join in alliance with him."*

[20] Grandet (1994 vol. II : 217–218) explains this key term as: „*abandonner (un pays) en fuyant, en (le) quittant.*"

Amenmesse's possible use of Asiatic soldiers against Merenptah does not make him somehow different from his enemy. The Egyptian army of the period was, to a significant part, mercenary, consisting of Sherden, as addressed in the speech of Ramses III in pHarris I.

The *"Hymn to the King in His Chariot"* explains the adoption of these Asiatics as allies as a fundamental reshaping of the earlier ruinous Egyptian foreign policy, which Amenmesse now attempted. Bata, the paragon of an Asiatic, is entrusted the part of the chariot the pharaoh would typically take place within: *"The sides (bt) of your chariot: Bata, lord of Saka, while he is the staff of the son of Bastet (Maahes), as one exiled to every foreign land."* From now on, he is enforcing Egypt's interests within its Asiatic empire.

Irsw, the name of the ruler in pHarris I, was explained by Schneider (2003: 138) as a numeral, in my view meaning *"(the one) of the 6th (regnal year of Merenptah),"* a way for Merenptah loyalists to avoid Amenmesse's name, thus explaining the loyalist emptiness of years of pHarris I. Later, this method was picked up by the *Potter's Oracle* and the *Oracle of the Lamb*, appropriating ancient prophetic material in the service of Ptolemaic-period conflicts. The Oracle of the Lamb paraphrases the conflicting pharaohs as *"the one for fifty-five,"* *"the one for two years"* (Thissen, 2002), while the Potter's Oracle names *"the one of the two (years),"* *"the one of the fifty-five (years)"* (Koenen, 2002).

This propagandistic slant about *Irsw* being a *H3rw* was introduced only late by Ramses III since Merenptah, Amenmesse, Sethos II, and Khaemtre were probably close relatives, members of the Ramses II family clan. This would have caused such chauvinistic accusations, under the 19th dynasty, to backfire. Not even Sethnakht dared to name his enemy Asiatic but merely implied he would have appealed for the help of the Asiatics.

The widespread support for Amenmesse and the hatred for the dynastic branch represented by Merenptah and Sethos II must have been far higher than the official propaganda version. A case of lèse-majesté, ending with the sentencing to death of an involved Deir el-Medina worker, is protocolled in the 5th year of Sethos II in oCGC 25.256: *"he [Hay] said: away with Sethos II."*

3.4 Reflections of the Tale of Two Brothers in Later Ramesside Literature

A political roman à clef such as the *Tale of Two Brothers* had to steadily adapt to changing circumstances to retain relevance. The initially absent Amenmesse character (the revolt starting first in Ethiopia with quite a different political agenda) had to be retrospectively identified in the story. The only option for this was his later identification with Anubis, said in the tale (Papyrus d'Orbiney) to have succeeded Bata on the throne.

One observes the result of this switch only in the later parody of the *Tale of Two Brothers*, pChassinat III (Ramses V), a negative recension of the tale told from the victors' position in the conflict. One observes a more explicit connection between the tale's characters and the historical events under Merenptah reminiscent of those of the late antique works of Manetho and Apion.

Anubis's name in the earlier tale is modified from *Jnpw* to *Mi-pw*, a sarcastic pun explained by Barbotin (1999: 15) as "like who?" or "it's entirely like" (thus: guess who is meant by the name?). It is, nevertheless, recognizable as the Anubis character by his identification as the brother of Bata. This is the kind of allusion expected for the character of a *roman à clef*.

He is described as born in the Heliopolitan scepter nome, his city being Heliopolis, and as one on whose back would sit the temple servants. All these sarcastic details become elements of the later Manetho and Apion writings calling the leader of the revolt against Merenptah, a former priest of Heliopolis.

Another detail concerning Anubis/*Mi-pw* has later biblical connotations. One cannot tell which was the author's intention of pChassinat III introducing this detail. However, this detail may be responsible for the later identification of this character with Moses in Manetho and consorts (and thus also for Amenmesse's identification with Moses in these polemical writings), whether intentional or not by the late Ramesside author. Barbotin (1999: 9, l. 9): "*you were born in the scepter nome, you are thrown into the water (tw.k ḫȝ.tw r pȝ mw), you will not die, you will live by a life....*"

It is rather improbable that any of the biblical authors knew pChassinat III. Therefore, either the author of pChassinat III had some knowledge of the Moses legend, or the similarity is fortuitous. In this case, only the late Egyptian authors in the following of Manetho, constructed from this a revolt-leader, Amenmesse, turned to Moses in their polemic writings against the Jews.

The papyrus ends with *Mi-pw* being apprehended and brought away by the troop commanders "*il amena le fils (?) lubrique [...] la troupe des commandants (?) l'amena.*"

3.5 Late Egyptian Echoes in the Hellenistic Historical and Prophetic Literature

There is a shared historical kernel between the anti-Jewish historical narratives of Manetho, Chaeremon, Lysimachos, and Apion, and the famous Oracles of the Lamb and that of the Potter, which escaped the attention of modern scholars. This common historical kernel is drawn from the civil war between the supporters of Merenptah and Amenmesse. I will tabulate the narrative parallels between the two last oracles and the Alexandrine historiographies.

Narrative stages, according to Manetho	Narrative stages, according to the Prophecies
First stage: under Amenophis III	**First stage: Potter's Oracle**
King Amenophis (Amenophis III) wishes to see the gods. Amenophis, the Son of Hapu, replies that he will see the gods only if he cleanses the land of leppers and other polluted persons. Amenophis predicts the conquest of Egypt by them and their allies, following which he dies, leaving a written account of the future catastrophic events in Egypt	King Amenophis (Amenophis III) wishes to visit the temples of Isis and Osiris. A potter blocks the king's way and carries out a symbolic ritual handling of emptying the oven, foretelling the future of the emptying of Egypt of foreigners. The potter dies after making his prophecy, and the king lets his prophecy be written in a book named "[everything] that will occur in Egypt," which is deposited in the treasury
Second stage: under Merenptah	**Second stage: Oracle of the Lamb**
Merenptah prepares to confront the enemy in the "City of the Shepherds" (probably the same city previously called the Belt-Wearers'-City or the City-by-the-Sea in the Potter's Oracle). These all initially represent different names for Pi-Ramesses. The enemy is led by a Heliopolitan priest, as called in the prophecy of Amenophis, the Son of Hapu. Upon this, he decides to quit Egypt for Ethiopia for the time ruled by the prophecy	The scribe Psenyris discovers a book called "the b]ook of the days, which [...] will occur in Egypt" (thus the previously mentioned book). A later scene introduces the lamb, who explains to Psenyris the meaning of the prophecy contained in the book. Following this, the lamb dies. The lamb and the potter are personifications of Khnum (represented as a potter or a ram). Psenyris brings the message of the ram to king Bokchoris (!) and confirms that the curse would be fulfilled during his reign and foreigners would conquer Egypt. Col. III.7–8: "*one read the book in front of the pharaoh. The pharaoh said to them: 'Will all these evil things happen to Egypt?' Psenyris said, 'Before even you will be dead, these will occur'*"

The detailed analysis of the Ptolemaic period prophetic material (Bányai, 2019) shows that this represents recycled older literary material adopted as political propaganda first under Ptolemaios I and later under Ptolemaios VIII.

The initial propagandistic use of the prophecies was to legitimize the rule of Ptolemaios I. His return of the "*holy images of the gods of Egypt, which one found in Asia, together with cult instruments and all the holy scrolls of the temples of Upper and Lower Egypt*" (Satrap Stela) followed the Battle of Raphia (312 BCE). The same is echoed in the Oracle of the Lamb as the second sign of the return of divine grace to Egypt: "*One will find in Syria the chapels of the gods (and return them to Egypt).*"

Bokchoris' name in the tradition preserved by the Oracle of the Lamb is spurious, as demonstrated by the narrative parallels and the 900 years that elapsed according to it between the period of disaster in Egypt under "Bokchoris" and the return of grace to Egypt under Ptolemaios I (312 BCE), which points chronologically to the first year of Merenptah at the onset of the curse.[21] Whether Amenophis

---

[21] 1212 BCE that is 312 BCE (the Battle of Raphia) + 900 years.

(as indicated in N. 1) or Bokchoris, the ruler's names must be primarily understood as late-antique Greek garbled forms for Merenptah.

The still later instrumentalization of the prophecies under Ptolemaios VIII accounts for their turn to a rabid Jew hatred. Due to the support offered by the Jews and the Greeks of Alexandria to his wife and sister Cleopatra II, Ptolemaios Physkon (known in Alexandria as Kakergetes, the "malefactor") had to flee to Cyprus. This background of the prophecy-recycling explains references in Potter's Oracle to an island formerly called Helios (a mistranslation of the original name of Cyprus known by the Egyptians, Alasyia, as Helios) from where the messianic king, Ptolemaios VIII, would return to Egypt: *"Then will Egypt grow powerful, when 'the one for fifty-five years'[22] the merciful king will come from Helios."* The prophecies thus prepare the return of this evil king from Cyprus by proclamations made to the Egyptians to take sides with him against his wife.

The ahistorical inclusion of Joseph in the Manetho narrative dealing with the conflict between Merenptah and Amenmesse is due to the slant given to the corresponding character in the *Tale of Two Brothers* as a roman à clef. While Bata's relation in the narrative to the figure of Joseph did not escape modern scholars, the identification of Anubis, his brother, with Moses was introduced first in pChassinat III during the 20th dynasty either by accident or design. It didn't belong in the initial context of the tale. This reflects an evolution of the narrative translating the roman à clef to terms closer to the propaganda needs of each side in the civil war. Art is shaped by reality; reality is shaped by art.

The late prophecies, dealing with the coming of a messianic king, seem to go back to an indefinite prophetic text from the days of the Hyksos. Already Hatshepsut at Speos Artemidos appears to quote from an earlier text, adapted for her purposes, identifying her with the messianic king, defeating the Hyksos. The same Speos Artemidos indirect quote Allen (2002) is recognizable still in the late *Prophecy of the Lamb*: *"They ruled without the Sun, and he did not act by god's decree down to my (own) uraeus-incarnation... I have come as Horus, the sole uraeus spitting fire at my enemies."* *"Es wird geschehen, wenn ich ein Uräus am Haupte Pharaos bin (der Heilsherrscher), der in Vollendung von 900 Jahren sein wird"* Thissen (2002: 118).

The Israel stele discovered 1896 by Petrie was not yet there, as Manetho's propagandistic narratives had already laid the ground for an Exodus scenario short before Merenptah. Wellhausen (1904: 12) based his guess about an Exodus date still just on the Alexandrian stories. Despite the rejection of Manetho's narratives, here we are still discussing Merenptah-based scenarios of an Exodus, which according to some scholars, was never historical.

---

[22] The evidence for the length of the reign of Ptolemaios VIII (54 yerars) is fuzzy, allowing even the assumption of a 55-year rule. See discussion in Bányai, 2019: n. 117. No Nilotic island called the island of Re exists – an Egyptian equivalent of a Greek Helios Island.

4 Israel and Retenu

Should the study of the Merenptah – Amenmesse period contribute anything to the discussion on the Exodus, it is firstly the realization that the Egyptians held an extensive record of their history during the thirteenth and twelfth centuries. A record of the historical Exodus occurring at this time (!) obviously did not belong to any of these recollections.

There are frequent veiled allusions in the Amenmesse literature, to which I have already pointed, to an Exodus happening in times immemorial, involving the departure of Bata to Asia. This part of the Tale of Two Brothers is an ethnic aetiological narrative. Therefore details regarding Bata's flight to Canaan or the river created by Re's miracle between the brothers saving Bata's life must be an essential part of an early Israelite tradition, shaped to please a late 19th dynasty Egyptian audience.

There is also the link between Bata's retreat in Canaan in the Valley of the Pine in the Tale of Two Brothers and the tribe of Asher, dwelling at this very place since at least Sethos I (n. 16), in which it also features in the lists of Josh 19:28 and Jud 1:31.[23] Bata's hanging of his heart in a pine for protection resonates with the contemporary story of the chief of Asher, *Qdrdj*, fleeing to a pine.

It is difficult, if not impossible, to explain this early evidence based on a conventional historical approach to the Exodus and the Conquest/Settlement.

The scholarly consensus about the Exodus/Conquest dates this supposedly historical event either into the late thirteenth century BCE, in the 19th dynasty (the Albright-Wright theory), or into the twelfth century. This later date, submitted by Rendsburg (1997) represents an approach initially based on the Deut. 2:23 association between the Israelite Conquest and the arrival of the Cretans, supposedly identical with the Sea-Peoples-Philistine migration wave.[24,25]

Arguably the main reason for the Albright-Wright hypothesis about Conquest/Settlement are offering the extensive city destructions in Canaan held to represent

---

[23] Van der Veen (2022: 29–30) pleas for a 19th-dynasty location of the tribe of Reuben in a position close by its later attested historical one. He also points (2022: 30–32) at the Qom el-Hettan list of Amenhotep III preserving the name of *šꜣ-kꜣr'*, which he compared with the one of Issachar, somewhere in the southern Lebanon or northern Palestine.

[24] Deut. 2:23 is the traditional reason for placing the Conquest in the thirteenth century BCE. It is mostly discussed in association with the parallel enumeration of the Philistines and Cretans in Am. 9:7 and Jer. 47:4–5, assumed as a statement of identity between both groups.

Rendsburg appeals to reinforce the same chronological conclusions by hinting at the Exod 13: 17 mention of a "Road of the Land of the Philistines." This is perceived as an anachronism by most scholars.

[25] As shown most recently by Bányai (2022), the Cretans settled in the Levant during the Middle Bronze Age. The Kasluhites, from whom the Philistines descend, as described by Ge 10:14 and 1 Chr 1:12 (Bányai, 2021–2022: 10), are firmly identified on the territory of Alalakh as Ḫa-zi-lu-uḫ-e (Wiseman, 1953: nos. 161, 207, 303). This town later belonged to Palasatini, the Iron Age follower state of Alalakh and the name-sake of Philistine. There is, therefore, no argument for a thirteenth-century date for Exodus and Conquest in Deut. 2:23 or Exod 13: 17.

the result of the Israelite Conquest. As one may have observed, these destructions probably belong within the context of Merenptah's war in Retenu. However, the correspondence between archaeologically dated city destructions and such attributed to the Conquest by the biblical texts, which the first should supposedly corroborate, is abysmal (see the damning list in Dever, 1992: 545–558). Retrospectively seen is the Albright-Wright hypothesis, only a further elaboration in the steps of Wellhausen (1904), replacing his Apion and Manetho-based guess concerning the Exodus with archaeological arguments for arriving at the same result.

Some scholars would have, at this point, asked what was wrong: Is the biblical text false, or instead, the initial chronological assumption on which the Albright-Wright Conquest theory rested? Instead of an answer came alternative sociological (Mendenhall, 1962; Gottwald, 1979) or pastoral sedentarization models (Alt, 1925; Noth, 1950; Weippert, 1971, etc.), not even bothered by questions of chronology. While transferring the discussion to immaterial issues, following the Conquest hypothesis's failure to produce the expected evidence,[26] they offered no valid reason for the preserved original chronological choice.

However, the methodology behind the Albright-Wright hypothesis was not entirely dedicated to identifying the Israelites in these regional destructions and their exclusion in earlier cases (honestly said, an impossible task). It involved instead the perception of a line of cultural continuity leading straight from the Merenptah period into the Israelite period. It was, thus, the perception of a cultural divide between the Late Bronze Age Canaan and Iron Age Israel, interrupting the *longue durée* processes characterizing the previous periods. This methodological approach must be retained even after the fall of the Albright-Wright theory.

From this perspective, the most notable thought impulses came, by any measure, from Finkelstein (1988, 1994, 1995). Intended as an archaeological contribution to the sedentarisation model, one must instead read his contribution instead as a serious challenge to the chronological basis of the Albright-Wright theory and all other ensuing "models." As Finkelstein points out, the *longue durée* perception starting according to the Albright-Wright theory, only in the thirteenth century BCE, perceived as a kind of watershed moment, was wrong.

Finkelstein suggested a cultural continuity in the Hill Country, the kernel of Early Israel, between the MBA and the Iron Age I. This continuity involved using an identical pottery assemblage (1988, 1994: 166, ill. 11, 1995: 359), exemplified by his finds at Shilo. The cultic continuity he observed in regions within the Hill Country, Ebal, Shiloh, Giloh, and the Bull Site, between the MBA and the Early Israelite period, looks even more exciting. Finkelstein (1994: 164) also notices the similarity between the Middle Bronze II domestic architecture at Emeq Rephaim and Manahat and the later Israelite "four-room houses."

---

[26] See Dever's (1992: 545) commentary on these models:" *All of these models make some use of the archaeological data, but only the first (Albright's Conquest model) is heavily dependent upon such evidence. Yet because these are models developed and employed mainly by biblical historians, the pertinent archaeological data have not always been adequately evaluated.*"

Another Finkelstein observation concerns the transformation of the Hill Country from a mainly urban society during the MBA to a pastoral one during the LBA. He finds this process also reflected by the changed ratio in cattle vs. sheep/goat bones left at the sites. That is: former urbanites from the Hill Country turn to a pastoral lifestyle within the same region. Middle Bronze Age sites were abandoned, and the population turned to nomadism. This phenomenon was once more reversed in the Manasseh Hill Country (but also in the Hill Country of Judah) during the transition to the Iron Age.

Most important, according to Finkelstein, is that the Iron I re-settlement phenomenon is not explainable as an expansion of land-hungry demographic surpluses from the lowlands. The material features of the Hill Country remain local (Finkelstein, 1995: 355): *"The pace of growth in the total built-up area in all sites of the Land of Ephraim from early Iron Age I to late Iron Age I cannot be explained by natural population growth. Rather, it shows that new elements, either from outside the region or from a pastoral background, continued to settle down during the twelfth-eleventh centuries BCE. The second possibility seems to be preferable (!) since, in the previous Late Bronze Age, a large number of pastoral groups was active in the hill country."*

The hypothesized Iron Age re-sedentarisation of the local pastoralist groups (Finkelstein, 1988: 345) was never translated by Finkelstein into terms of a relation between Early Israel and Retenu, the two political entities responsible for the archaeological record in the Hill Country, a link, which looks essential from the viewpoint of this paper. According to the suggestions of Helck (1971: 268), the term Retenu would best apply to the Hill Country during the Late Bronze Age: *"wobei vielleicht Ober-Rtnw den gebirgigen östlichen Streifen bezeichnet."*

One must notice that. Retenu is the only term used in Egyptian historical sources allowing us to delve sufficiently deep into the LBA and MBA without abusing the unattested name of Israel. A short survey of the Egyptian Retenu evidence will show whether it is helpful to introduce Retenu in this context. Despite all possible parallels, I insist on the difficulty of deciding the extent to which the term Retenu would overlap with our modern understanding of Israel.

The large-scale immigration of Asiatics to Egypt started during the latter part of Sesostris III's reign. Before that, one can observe Retenu steadily wandering southwards since its first mention under Sesostris I (Sinuhe). It is first identified by the geographic height of Byblos. Later under Sesostris III (Hw-$Śbk$), it was close to Shechem (*Sekmem*), with which it closed an alliance. Once more, later, under Amenemhet III, Retenu offered protection and labor to the Egyptians in the Sinai.

The settlement of Retenu-Asiatics at the end of the reign of Sesostris III may explain the fresh official interest in the Sinuhe story under Amenemhet IV as a proclamation of the earlier existing bonds between Egypt and Retenu. The evidence allows identifying the Asiatics in Egypt before the 15th dynasty with the Retenu.

The seal impression of the *"Ruler of Retenu, greatest of the great, Ipy-Shemu..."* (Kopetzky & Bietak, 2016: 359 and 369) made in local clay found at Tell el-Dab'a, demonstrates that the rulers of Retenu resided during the 13th dynasty in Avaris and that they probably directed the Asiatic interests of Egypt from there. Even a second amethyst scarab belonging to a ruler of Retenu was found at Tell el-Dabʿa with the fragmentary title: *[ḥq3 n] Rtnw* (Kopetzky & Bietak, 2016: 371).

Forstner-Müller (2010: 129) concludes about the loss of connection of the subsequent 15th (Hyksos) dynasty to Palestine, a juncture as one must look for Retenu once again in Asia: "*Significantly, there is no unity in material culture with southern Palestine. A spread—if ever there was one—of the Hyksos empire into Palestine is thus not traceable in the archaeological record.*"

Supposedly, Retenu was the Egyptian exonym for the Asiatics living in Egypt before the 15th dynasty. In that case, their subsequent emergence in Asia, where we identify Retenu later, could point to migration.

There also exists circumstantial evidence of Asiatics leaving Egypt roughly at this time. Thus, the earliest examples of Proto-Canaanite script, hitherto confined to Egypt and the Sinai, appear on tablets of the Schøyen collection (1st dynasty of the Sealand ca. 1600–1500 BCE). The signs are arguably the alphabetic signature of Semites featuring in the same cuneiform tablets (Colonna d'Istria, 2012; Hamidović, 2014; Koller, 2018). According to Dalley (2009, 2013), these same tablets would also offer the first attestation of the divine name *ia-ú* used in three personal names.[27]

There is another essential point that must be addressed in the paper. It concerns Zertal's observation that the supposed Early Israelite settlement in the region occurred as a three-stage sedentarisation process starting in the east of the Manasseh Hill Country, rolling only gradually to the west, obviously starting from Transjordan. He arrived at this observation after filtering the archaeological record of more than 200 Iron Age sites for the evolution of three types of cooking pots found in the Manasseh territory. Relevant to our discussion is not the apparent cultural difference between this Early Israel and its Canaanite neighbors in the plains, but rather the fact that this settlement didn't irradiate starting from the main population regions in the west but from the opposite side of the Hill Country.

Hawkins (2008) opined that the westward expansion movement identified by Zertal reflected the coming of the Israelites from the Transjordan as described by the Conquest narratives. However, I beg to differ on this issue.

The westward push of the Iron Age I Israelite settlements starting from Transjordan is just the reversed tide for the previous pull of Retenu to the east from within the same Manasseh Hill Country region towards Transjordan during the Late Bronze Age. The main territorial Retenu state in the Manasseh Hill Country region of the Amarna age, the principality of Lab'ayu of Shechem, moved a generation later its seat to Piḫilu in Transjordan. A remote position, out of the reach of the Egyptians interested of control over the Via Maris, was an essential argument for relocating across Jordan. Shechem/Piḫilu was in a permanent clash with the colonial administration and constantly allied with other trouble-makers, such as Ashtaroth/Yeno'am and Gezer, both recurring on the Israel stele of Merenptah. Still a generation later, Sethos I discouraged another alliance led by the same Piḫilu and Yeno'am (controlled by the king of Ashteroth), acting from Transjordan, trying to

---

[27] Expectedly, the opinions about the final interpretation of the possibly earliest Tetragrammaton attestation diverge. Zadok (2014) declares it a hypocoristic suffix, while Krebernik (2017: 61–63) offers a rather positive reception.

conquer the cities in the Beth-Shean Valley, separating their realms within Palestine (Beth-Shean stela). A generation later, Ramses II campaigned in Transjordan to root out the last sources of opposition against the Egyptian colonial rule nested in that remote region, never visited before by a pharaoh. His stela, found in Sheikh Saad, formerly Karnaim, is a mere four-kilometer distance from Tell Ashtara/Ashtaroth. Another Ramesses stela, in aṭ-Ṭurra, was located 25 km north of the first. Probably the same campaign led the Pharaoh to Moab (Haider, 1987), targetting, in reality, the primary trouble source, Piḫilu, which had allied this time with the Hittites.

This movement, away from Egypt's regional focus, to the east of Retenu, while leading to an almost complete depopulation of the Manasseh Hill Country, contributed to a settlement growth in central and northern parts of Transjordan in the Late Bronze II (van der Steen, 1996: 62–63). According to Ji (1998): "*sedentarization reached its apex during LB II and early Iron I in the Transjordan plateau and the Jordan Valley.*" Contrary to this are the conclusions drawn by Finkelstein (1998). His decision to overturn the findings of the Kerak plateau survey, reporting a record number of 109 Late Bronze Age settlements, replaced by his own arbitrarily set numbers, diminishes the value of his paper.

I give, therefore, priority to the conclusions presented by Ji (1998), identical to those of the Kerak plateau survey (Miller, 1991), the Jordan valley survey (Ibrahim et al., 1976, 1988), and the Wadi el-Yabis survey (Palumbo et al., 1990). For the south of the Jordan valley, the last survey mentioned above produced even higher results than for the Early Iron Age.

These results are understandable against the melting number of settlements on the other side of Jordan. Western Retenu and Eastern Retenu possibly worked in the manner of communicating chambers, with the population moving out from one to the other depending on the political circumstances and leaving behind only the pastoral fraction of the former local population.

Van der Steen (1996: 61) even observed a shared ceramic repertoire between sites west and east of the Jordan (Mount Ebal, the Bull Site, Shilo, and the Deir ʿAlla region).

The return of the population to the Manasseh Hill Country was possible again after the Egyptian grasp in Retenu deteriorated under the later reign of Merenptah. This population consisted probably of the same refugees once moving eastward within the region. Observing the overwhelming frequency of reoccupation of previous LBA family burial caves or cemeteries by the Iron IA settlers whenever they settled at previous LBA sites could suggest similar conclusions (Bloch-Smith, 2004; Kletter, 2001).[28]

---

[28] Kletter (2001: 34): "*There are almost no new burials in this period, but at the most, a continuation of a few LB burials.*" This model offers a good reason for the largely lacking burials associated with the new Iron Age I settlements. The Israelite ideal to rest with his fathers, attested by countless biblical references, may have led some (or most) of these settlers to bury their dead in Bronze Age family burial caves at still abandoned Highland sites far from their present homes. A small number of Iron Age IA inhumations at abandoned sites could fail archaeological identification. These first settlements have a provisional character and are abandoned as soon as return to remoter LBA sites becomes possible. This phenomenon of abandonment of first-wave settlements without an associated sign of destruction was observed during Iron Age I.

It remains undoubtedly challenging to fathom the degree to which there was an identity between the Retenu and the Israelites. The complete disregard for this term in the Hebrew Bible – as surprising as it may sound, since the "later" Israelites occupied, after all, the former core region of Retenu, the Hill Country – makes one wonder whether this name was used by anybody other than the Egyptians themselves. Herewith I bring the paper to a conclusion, appealing along with Dever: Will the real Retenu please stand up?

References

Alt, A. (1925). *Die Landnahme der Israeliten in Palästina* (Territorialgeschichtlkiche Studien). Druckerei der Werkgemeinschaft Leipzig.
Altenmüller, H. (1982). Tausret und Sethnacht. *The Journal of Egyptian Archaeology, 68*, 107–115.
Altenmüller, H. (2011). Die Fiktion von Sethnacht als dem Sohn Sethos' II. In Z. A. Hawass (Ed.), *Scribe of justice. Egyptological studies in honour of Shafik Allam* (Supp. Aux Annales du Service des Antiquités de l'Égypte 42) (pp. 59–69). Conseil Suprême des Antiquités de l'Egypte.
Allen, J. P. (2002). The Speos Artemidos Inscription of Hatshepsut. *Bulletin of the Egyptological Seminar, 16*, 1–17.
Bányai, M. (2019). Merenptah und Amenmesse : Entwurf einer alternativen Chronologie. *Journal of Egyptian History, 12*, 36–103.
Bányai, M. (2020). Retenu: Between the fifteenth and the nineteenth dynasties, with an appendix on the chronology of Tell el-Dab'a. *Journal of Ancient Egyptian Interconnections, 28*, 1–36.
Bányai, M. (2021–2022). The Northern Philistines reconsidered. *Journal of the Ancient Near Eastern Society "Ex Oriente Lux", 48*, 9–27.
Bányai, M. (2022). Cretans in the Levant. *Journal of Ancient Egyptian Interconnections, 34*, 1–28.
Barbotin, C. (1999). Le Papyrus Chassinat III. *Revue d'égyptologie, 50*, 5–26.
Beckerath von, J. (1980). Königsnamen. In W. Helck & E. Otto (Eds.), *Lexikon der Ägyptologie III* (pp. 540–556). Harrassowitz.
Bierbrier, M. L. (1975). *The late kingdom in Egypt (c. 1300–664 B.C.): A genealogical and chronological investigation*. Aris and Philips.
Bietak, M. (1990). Zur Herkunft des Seth von Avaris. *Ägypten und Levante/Egypt and the Levant, 1*, 9–16.
Bietak, M. (2003). Israelites found in Egypt, four-room house identified in Medinet Habu. *Biblical Archaeological Review, 29*(5), 40–47, 82–83.
Bietak, M. (2015). On the historicity of the exodus: What egyptology today can contribute to assessing the Sojourn in Egypt. In T. E. Levy, T. Schneider, & W. H. C. Propp (Eds.), *Israel's exodus in transdisciplinary perspective* (pp. 17–37). Springer.
Bloch-Smith, E. (2004). Resurrecting the Iron I dead. *Israel Exploration Journal, 54*, 77–91.
Boraik, M. (2007). Stela of Bakenkhonsu,High Priest of Amun-Re. *Memnonia, 18*, 119–127.
Brand, P. (2009). Usurped Cartouches of Merenptah at Karnak and Luxor. In P. Brand & L. Cooper (Eds.), *Causing his name to live – Studies in Egyptian epigraphy and history in memory of William J. Murnane* (pp. 29–48). Brill.
Brand, P. (2010). *The Karnak Hypostyle Hall Project. Field Report 2004–2005*. Retrieved under https://www.memphis.edu/hypostyle/project/pdfs/report_2004-2005.pdf
Breasted, J. H. (1906). *Ancient record of Egypt* (Vol. II). University of Chicago Press.
Caminos, R. A. (1954). *Late-Egyptian miscellanies*. Oxford University Press.
Charpin, D. (1992). Mari entre l'est et l'ouest : politique, culture, religion. *Akkadica, 78*, 1–10.
Collona D'Istria, L. (2012). Épigraphes alphabétiques du pays de la Mer. *Nouvelles Assiriologiques Bréves et Utilitaires, 3*, 61–63.

Dalley, S. (2009). *Babylonian tablets from the first Sealand dynasty (CUSAS 9)*. CDL Press.

Dalley, S. (2013). Gods from northeastern and northwestern Arabia in cuneiform texts from the First Sealand Dynasty and a cuneiform inscription from Tell en-Naṣbeh, c.1500 BC. *Arabian Archaeology and Epigraphy, 24*(2), 177–185.

Davies, B. (1997). *Egyptian historical inscriptions of the nineteenth dynasty (Documenta Mundi, Aegyptiaca, No 2)*. Jonsered.

Demarée, R. J. (2011). Hieratic texts. In R. H. Wilkinson (Ed.), *The Temple of Tausret, The University of Arizona Egyptian Expedition, Tausret Temple Project, 2004–2011* (pp. 121–130). The University of Arizona.

Dembitz, G. (2007). The Decree of Sethos II at Karnak: Further thoughts on the succession problem after Merenptah. In K. Endreffy & A. Gulyás (Eds.), *Proceedings of the fourth central European conference of young egyptologists. 31 August–2 September 2006, Budapest* (Studia Aegyptiaca 18) (pp. 91–108) Budapest.

Dever, W. G. (1992). Archaeology and the Israelite 'Conquest'. In D. N. Freedman (Ed.), *The anchor Bible dictionary* (Vol. 3, pp. 545–558). Doubleday.

Dodson, A. (1985). The Tomb of Amenmesse: Some observations. *Discussions in Egyptology, 2*, 7–11.

Dodson, A. (1987). The Takhats and some other royal ladies of the Ramesside period. *The Journal of Egyptian Archaeology, 73*(1), 224–229.

Dodson, A. (2010). *Poisoned legacy. The decline and fall of the nineteenth Egyptian dynasty*. The American University in Cairo Press.

Drenkhahn, R. (1980). *Die Elephantine-Stele des Sethnacht und ihr historischer Hintergrund*. Harrassowitz.

Durand, J.-M. (1987). Villes fantômes de Syrie et autres lieux. Mari. *Annales de Recherches Interdisciplinaire, 5*, 199–234.

Edgerton, W. F., & Wilson, J. A. (1936). *Historical records of Ramses III – The texts in Medinet Habu*. The University of Chicago Press.

Finkelstein, I. (1988). *The archaeology of the Israelite settlement*. Israel Exploration Society.

Finkelstein, I. (1994). The emergence of Israel: A phase in the cyclic history of Canaan in the third and second millennium BCE. In I. Finkelstein & N. Na'aman (Eds.), *From nomadism to monarchy* (pp. 152–178). Yad Ben-Zvi.

Finkelstein, I. (1995). The great transformation: The 'conquest' of the highlands frontiers and the rise of the territorial states. In T. E. Levy (Ed.), *The archaeology of society in the Holy Land* (pp. 349–362). Leicester University Press.

Finkelstein, I. (1998). From sherds to history: Review article. *Israel Exploration Journal, 48*(1/2), 120–131.

Forstner-Müller, I. (2010). Tombs and burial customs at Tell el-Dab'a during the late Middle Kingdom and the second intermediate period. In M. Marée (Ed.), *The second intermediate period (Thirteenth–seventeenth dynasties): Current research, future prospects* (pp. 127–141). Peeters.

Fukaya, M. (2012). Oracular sessions and the installations of priests and officials at the Opet festival. *Orientalia, 47*, 191–212.

Gilmour, G., & Kitchen, A. K. (2012). Pharaoh Sety II and Egyptian political relations with Canaan at the end of the late Bronze Age. *Israel Exploration Journal, 62*(1), 1–21.

Gottwald, N. K. (1979). *The tribes of Yahweh: A sociology of the religion of liberated Israel, 1250–1050 B.C.E.* Orbis Books.

Grandet, P. (1994). *Le Papyrus Harris I* (Vol. I–II). Institut Français.

Greenstein, E. (1981). The riddle of Samson. *Prooftexts, 1*(3), 237–260.

Guzowska, M., & Yassur-Landau, A. (2007). The Mycenaean Pottery from Tel Aphek: Chronology and patterns of trade. In M. Bietak & E. Czerny (Eds.), *The synchronisation of civilisations in the Eastern Mediterranean in the second millennium B.C. III* (pp. 537–546). Verlag der Österreichischen Akademie.

Habachi, L. (1978). King Amenmesse and Viziers Amenmose and Kha'emtore: Their monuments and place in history. *Mitteilungen des Deutschen Archäologischen Instituts, 34*, 57–67.
Haider, P. W. (1987). Zum Moab-Feldzug Ramses' II. *Studien zur Altägyptischen Kultur, 14*, 107–123.
Hallo, W. W. (2001). *The context of scripture*. Brill.
Hamidović, D. (2014). Alphabetical inscriptions from the Sealand. *Studia Mesopotamica, 1*, 137–155.
Hasel, M. (1994). Israel in the Merenptah Stela. *Bulletin of the American Schools of Oriental Research, 296*, 45–62.
Hasel, M. (1998). *Domination and resistance*. Brill.
Hawkins, R. K. (2008). The survey of Manasseh and the origin of the Central Hill Country settlers. In R. Hess, G. A. Klingbeil, & P. J. Ray (Eds.), *Critical issues in early Israelite history* (pp. 165–180). Eisenbrauns.
Helck, W. (1955). *Urkunden der 18. Dynastie. Abteilung IV, Heft 18: Biographische Inschriften der Zeitgenossen Thutmosis III. und Amenophis II.*
Helck, W. (1956a). *Untersuchungen zu Manetho und den ägyptischen Königslisten*. Akademie Verlag.
Helck, W. (1956b). Zwei thebanische Urkunden aus der Zeit Sethos II. *Zeitschrift für Ägyptische Sprache und Altertumskunde, 81*, 82–87.
Helck, W. (1958). *Zur Verwaltung des Mittleren Reiches und Neuen Reiches*. Brill.
Helck, W. (1960). Die ägyptische Verwaltung in den syrischen Besitzungen. *Mitteilungen der Deutschen Orient-Gesellschaft zu Berlin, 92*, 1–15.
Helck, W. (1971). *Die Beziehungen Ägyptens zu Vorderasien im 3. Und 2. Jahrtausend v. Chr.: 2., verbesserte Auflage* (Ägyptologische Abhandlungen). Harrassowitz.
Helck, W. (2002). *Die datierten und datierbaren Ostraka, Papyri und Graffiti von Deir el-Medineh*. Harrassowitz.
Hjelm, I., & Thompson, T. L. (2002). The victory song of Mernephtah, Israel, and the People of Palestine. *Journal for the Study of the Old Testament, 27*(1), 3–18.
Hoch, J. E. (1994). *Semitic words in Egyptian texts of the new kingdom and third intermediate period*. Princeton University Press.
Hollis, S. (1990). *The ancient Egyptian "Tale of Two Brothers"*. David Brown Book Company.
Hollis, S. (2015). Out of Egypt: Did Israel's exodus include tales? In T. E. Levy, T. Schneider, & W. H. C. Propp (Eds.), *Israel's exodus in transdisciplinary perspective* (pp. 209–222). Springer.
Hölscher, U. (1939). *The excavation of Medinet Habu, vol. 2: The temples of the eighteenth dynasty* (OIP, vol. 41). University of Chicago Press.
Ibrahim, M., Sauer, J., & Yassine, K. (1976). The East Jordan Valley Survey, 1975. *Bulletin of the American Schools of Oriental Research, 222*, 41–66.
Ibrahim, M. M., Sauer J. A., & Yassine, K. (1988). The East Jordan Valley Survey, 1975 (Part one). In K. Yassine (Ed.), *Archaeology of Jordan: Essays and reports* (pp. 159–187).
Ji, C.-H. C. (1998). Archaeological survey and settlement patterns in the region of 'Iraq Al-'Amir, 1996, A preliminary report. *Annual of the Department of Antiquities of Jordan, XLII*, 586–608.
Kahn, D. (2013). History of Kush – An outline. In F. Jesse & C. Vogel (Eds.), *The power of walls – Fortifications in ancient Northeastern Africa. Proceedings of the International workshop held at the University of Cologne 4th-7th August 2011* (Colloquium Africanum 5) (pp. 17–31). Heinrich-Barth-Institut.
Kienast, B. (1980). Die Inschrift der Statue des Königs Idrimi von Alalah. *Welt des Orients, 11*, 35–63.
Kitchen, K. (1987). Amenmesses in Northern Egypt. *Göttinger Miszellen, 98*, 23–25.
Kitchen, K. (2003). An Egyptian inscribed fragment from late Bronze Hazor. *Israel Exploration Journal, 53*, 20–28.
Kitchen, K. (2004). The victories of Merenptah, and the nature of their record. *Journal for the Study of the Old Testament, 28*(3), 259–272.

Kletter, R. (2001). People without burials? The lack of Iron I burials in the central highlands of Palestine. *Israel Exploration Journal, 52*, 28–48.

Koenen, L. (2002). Die Apologie des Töpfers an König Amenophis oder das Töpferorakel. In A. Blasius & B. U. Schipper (Eds.), *Apokalyptik und Ägypten: eine kritische Analyse der relevanten Texte aus dem griechisch-römischen Ägypten* (pp. 139–188). Peeters.

Koller, A. (2018). The diffusion of the alphabet in the second millennium BCE: On the movements of scribal ideas from Egypt to the Levant, Mesopotamia, and Yemen. *Journal of Ancient Egyptian Interconnections, 20*, 1–14.

Kopetzky, K., & Bietak, M. (2016). A seal impression of the Green Jasper workshop from Tell El-Dabʿa. *Ägypten und Levante/Egypt and the Levant, 26*, 357–375.

Krauss, R. (1976). Untersuchungen zu König Amenmesse (1. Teil). *Studien zur Altägyptischen Kultur, 4*, 161–199.

Krauss, R. (1977). Untersuchungen zu König Amenmesse (2. Teil). *Studien zur Altägyptischen Kultur, 5*, 131–174.

Krauss, R. (1984). Reisegeschwindigkeit. In W. Helck & E. Otto (Eds.), *Lexikon der Ägyptologie, Band V*. Harrasowitz.

Krauss, R. (1997). Untersuchungen zu König Amenmesse (Nachträge). *Studien zur Altägyptischen Kultur, 24*, 161–184.

Krebernik, M. (2017). The beginnings of Yahwism from an assyriological perspective. In J. Oorschot & M. Witte (Eds.), *The origins of Yahwism* (pp. 45–66). De Gruyter.

Manassa, C. (2003). *The Great Karnak inscription of Merenptah: Grand strategy in the 13th century BC*. Yale Egyptological Institute.

Manassa, C. (2012). The chariot that plunders foreign lands: 'The Hymn to the King in his Chariot'. In A. J. Veldmeijer & S. Ikram (Eds.), *Chasing chariots* (pp. 143–156). Sidestone Press.

Mazar, A. (2010). Tel Beth-Shean: History and archaeology. In R. G. Kratz, H. Spieckermann, et al. (Eds.), *One God – One Cult – One Nation. Archaeological and biblical perspectives* (Beihefte zur Zeitschrift für die alttestamentliche Wissenschaft (405)) (pp. 239–271). De Gruyter.

Meitlis, Y. (2008). A re-analysis of the archaeological evidence for the beginning of the Iron Age I. In A. Fantalkin & A. Yasur-Landau (Eds.), *Bene Israel – Studies in the archaeology of Israel and the Levant during the Bronze and Iron Ages in honour of Israel Finkelstein* (pp. 105–113). Brill.

Mendenhall, G. E. (1962). The Hebrew conquest of Palestine. *Biblical Archaeologist, 25*, 66–87.

Miller, J. M. (1991). *Archaeological survey of the Kerak plateau*. Scholars Press.

Morris, E. F. (2005). *The architecture of imperialism*. Brill.

Müller, M. (1893). *Asien und Europa nach Ägyptischen Denkmälern*. Verlag von Wilhelm Engelmann.

Müller, D. H. (1902). *Die Mehri und Soqoṭri Sprache*. Bd. I.

Na'aman, N. (1999). Lebo-Hamath, Ṣubat-Hamath, and the northern boundary of the land of Canaan. *Ugarit Forschungen, 31*, 419–441.

Noth, M. (1950). *Geschichte Israels*. Vandenhoeck & Ruprecht.

O'Connor, D. (1987). The location of Irem. *The Journal of Egyptian Archaeology, 73*, 99–136.

Palumbo, G., Mabry, J., & Kuijt, I. (1990). The Wadi el-Yabis Survey: Report on the 1989 field season. *ADAJ, 34*, 95–118.

Peust, C. (2001). Das Zweibrüdermärchen. In O. Kaiser, M. Dietrich, K. Hecker, & I. Kottsieper (Eds.), *Texte aus der Umwelt des Alten Testaments* (pp. 147–165). Mohn.

Rainey, A. F. (2001). Reviewed work: Domination and resistance; Egyptian military activity in the Southern Levant Ca. 1300–1185 B. C. by Michael G. Hasel. *Journal of the American Oriental Society, 121*(3), 489–490.

Redford, D. B. (2018). *The Medinet-Habu records of the foreign wars of Ramses III*. Brill.

Rendsburg, G. (1997). The early history of Israel. In G. D. Young, M. W. Chavalas, & R. E. Averbeck (Eds.), *Crossing boundaries and linking horizons: Studies in honor of Michael C. Astour on his 80th birthday* (pp. 433–453). CDL Press.

Schaden, O. (2009). The Amenmesse Project, season of 2006. *Annales du Service des antiquités de l'Egypte, 82*, 231–260.

Schaden, O., & Ertman, E. (1998). The Tomb of Amenmesse. (KV.10): The first season. *Annales du Service des antiquités de l'Egypte, 73*, 116–155.

Schneider, T. (2003). Siptah und Beja. *Zeitschrift für Ägyptische Sprache und Altertumskunde, 130*, 134–146.

Schneider, T. (2008). Innovation in literature on behalf of politics: The tale of the two brothers, Ugarit, and 19th dynasty history. *Ägypten und Levante/Egypt and the Levant, 18*, 315–326.

Sourouzian, H. (1989). *Les Monuments du roi Merenptah*. Zabern.

Thissen, H. J. (2002). Das Lamm des Bokchoris. In A. Blasius & B. U. Schipper (Eds.), *Apokalyptik und Ägypten: eine kritische Analyse der relevanten Texte aus dem griechisch-römischen Ägypten* (pp. 113–138). Peeters.

Ussishkin, D. (1985). Levels VII and VI at Tel Lachish and the end of the late Bronze Age in Canaan. In J. N. Tubb (Ed.), *Palestine in the Bronze and Iron Ages, papers in honour of Olga Tufnell* (pp. 213–230). Routledge.

Van der Steen, E. J. (1996). The Central East Jordan Valley in the late Bronze and early Iron Ages. *Bulletin of the American Schools of Oriental Research, 302*, 51–74.

Veen van der, P. (2022). Israel and the Tribes of Asher, Reuben and Issachar. In S. Wimmer & W. Zwickel (Eds.), *Ägypten und Altes Testament, Studien zu Kultur und Religion Ägyptens und des Alten Testaments, 100* (pp. 25–36). Zaphon.

Weippert, M. (1971). *The settlement of the Israelite Tribes in Palestine*. Alec R. Allenson.

Wellhausen, J. (1904). *Israelitische und Jüdische Geschichte. Fünfte Ausgabe*. Reimer.

Wettengel, W. (2003). *Die Erzählung von den beiden Brüdern: Der Papyrus d'Orbiney und die Königsideologie der Ramessiden* (Orbis Biblicus et Orientalis 195). Vandenhoek & Ruprecht.

Wiseman, D. (1953). *The Alalakh Tablets*. British Institute of Archaeology.

Wright, G. E. (1961). Review: Lachish IV. The Bronze Age by Olga Tufnell. *Journal of Near Eastern Studies, 20*(3), 210–212.

Yurco, F. J. (1986). Merenptah's Canaanite campaign. *Journal of the American Research Center in Egypt, 23*, 189–215.

Yurco, F. J. (1997). Was Amenmesse the Viceroy of Kush, Messuwy. *Journal of the American Research Center in Egypt, 34*, 49–56.

Zadok, R. (2014). On population groups in the documents from the time of the first Sealand dynasty. *Tel Aviv, 41*(2), 222–237.

Moses the Egyptian? A Reassessment of the Etymology of the Name "Moses"

Thomas Schneider

Abstract Moses scholarship has long held that the name "Moses" is one of the irreducible elements of the Moses narrative and would be an essential link to the exodus tradition, if it indeed is derived from the Egyptian root *mśy*, "to be born". This article reassesses the long-held Egyptian etymology of the name "Moses", constituting the first comprehensive treatment of the question since J.G. Griffiths' 1953 article, *The Egyptian Derivation of the Name Moses, Journal of Near Eastern Studies* 12: 225–31. This contribution adds to the debate an evaluation of the name's vocalization which is a major, hitherto unnoticed problem, and discusses ancient and modern hypotheses relating to Exod 2:10. The article concludes that an Egyptian etymology of the name "Moses" is difficult to maintain and that the debate about the name's, presumably Semitic etymology needs to be reopened.

Keywords Moses · Exodus story · Personal name · Onomastics · Egyptian morphology/phonology · Semitic morphology/phonology

T. Schneider (✉)
Department of Ancient Mediterranean and Near Eastern Studies,
The University of British Columbia, Vancouver, BC, Canada
e-mail: thomas.schneider@ubc.ca

© The Author(s), under exclusive license to Springer Nature Switzerland AG 2023
E. Ben-Yosef, I. W. N. Jones (eds.), *"And in Length of Days Understanding" (Job 12:12): Essays on Archaeology in the Eastern Mediterranean and Beyond in Honor of Thomas E. Levy*, Interdisciplinary Contributions to Archaeology,
https://doi.org/10.1007/978-3-031-27330-8_43

1 Introductory Remarks[1]

Debates about the historical background of the Moses figure have been prominent since antiquity. In Manetho, Moses is identified with a rebellious Egyptian priest Osarseph as the leader of lepers, maybe in an Anti-Semitic motivation.[2] Chaeremon gives for both Joseph and Moses Egyptian names: while Joseph is called *Peteseph*, Moses' Egyptian name is given as *Tisithen*,[3] a name that has so far received hardly any academic scrutiny. The debate has continued since the beginnings of Biblical scholarship, but as Rudolf Smend diagnosed in 1995, 'the history of Moses research is comprised of a sequence of subtractions' ("die Geschichte der Moseforschung besteht aus einer Folge von Subtraktionen"; Smend, 1995: 5). Among the very few elements of the textual tradition that are widely seen as irreducible elements of an original, historically genuine layer, the name "Moses" (מֹשֶׁה, *mōšǽ*) itself figures most prominently. Jörg Jeremias has emphasized that the Egyptian name is one of the fundamentals of the Moses narrative (Jeremias, 2015: 85–86; also Blum, 2012: 49). Most scholars agree that this name has an Egyptian origin and goes back to a form of the Egyptian root *mśy*,[4] "to be born" (e.g., Hoffmeier, 1999: 140–141; Dijkstra, 2006: 18–20; Frevel, 2018: 59). The personal name would thus represent an essential piece of historical information and implicitly also link Moses to the Exodus tradition. I quote again Rudolf Smend: 'We can most likely exclude later invention [of the name] because how could Israel possibly have given the man whom it regarded as its founder a name precisely in the language of those from whose oppression he had saved the people?' ("Spätere Erfindung dürfte auszuschließen sein; wie sollte Israel dem Mann, den es als seinen Begründer ansah, einen Namen gerade in der Sprache derer beilegen, aus deren Hand er das Volk gerettet hatte?" Smend, 1995: 15–16). The consensus among Biblical scholars has reached such a degree that Thomas Römer goes as far as to say that the name is 'undisputably of Egyptian origin' ('indiscutablement d'origine égyptienne'; Römer, 2015: 75). This is certainly not true; doubts about the name have indeed often been raised. However, as Erhard Blum has concluded, the wide-spread acceptance of the derivation of the name from the root *mśy* is due to the simple fact that no convincing alternative has ever been proposed (Blum, 2012: 38). It is the purpose of the following remarks to

---

[1] Earlier versions of this contribution were presented at the 2016 annual meeting of ASOR in San Antonio, Texas, and at the Hebrew University in Jerusalem in December 2018. I would like to thank the Halbert Centre for Canadian Studies for having hosted me at the Hebrew University, and Orly Goldwasser to have facilitated my visit. I am grateful to the audience of these two lectures as well as Ronald Hendel (Berkeley) for feedback on the ideas expressed herein. Hanna Jenni (University of Basel) was kind enough to provide me with an offprint of her pertinent article.

[2] For different views on this question, see Schäfer, 1997; Assmann, 2002; Römer, 2008; Thonhauser, 2009; Moore, 2015.

[3] Barclay, 2007: 341–350 (Appendix 3: Exodus Narratives in Cultural Context); Cook, 2004: 29 and 120; see also Gager, 1972: 121.

[4] For the sake of coherence, I use here <y> as a transcription symbol for IIIy verbs in both Egyptian and Northwest Semitic where scholarship also uses <j> and for Egyptian, <i>.

present a critical summary of the conventional etymology of the name and some recent literature on the topic, which will call that etymology into question, and to call for a reassessment of the name.

2 The Egyptian Name Forms: Meanings and Phonology

As a starting point, let me first provide some clarification on the conventional Egyptian etymology, proposed as early as 1849 by Richard Lepsius (1849: 325–326 n.5). The clarification is needed not only because many scholars provide mistaken translations of the Egyptian equivalents but also because my critique will address two major phonological objections to this proposal of which only one has so far been addressed. The standard explanation sees in *Mōšǽ* the Hebrew rendering either of an abbreviated name such as "Thutmose", or of the noun *mśw*, "child". Many participants of the debate have not understood the first of these alternatives correctly which in turn is essential for its vocalization and the phonological issues.

2.1 Egyptian Names Containing mśy: Meaning and Vocalization

2.1.1 Names of the Type "Thutmose" (Divine Name + Stative)

Names like "Thutmose" or "Ramose" need to be kept separate from names such as "Ramses".[5] The latter, correctly R^c-*mśy-św*, is a nominal sentence name comprising an initial noun, an active past participle and the pronominal object *–św* of the third person singular masculine, with the meaning "(the sun god) Re is the one who has 'born' = engendered him" (the newborn boy). By contrast, a name such as Ramose, correctly R^c-*mśy.w*, contains the divine name followed by an Egyptian stative, with a literal meaning "(the sun god) Re is born". This does not refer to the physical birth of the deity but is a feast name (Ranke, 1952: 217) which can be better paraphrased as "(a statue of) Re has been created = manufactured". The boy was born during a festival to the sun god and name after the consecration event of a divine statue during that festival.

A name like Thutmose does therefore *not* mean "son of Thoth" (Dozeman, 2009: 81–82; Baden 2019: 11), or "Thoth has born" (Albertz, 2012: 60), nor is it possible to understand a name such as "Ptahmose" as either "Ptah is born" or "Ptah has engendered", as Greifenhagen (2002: 63) and similarly Geertz (2002: 10) maintain – only the first translation is correct. Such a sentence name could be shortened to just the verbal element, the stative of the verb *mśy*.

---

[5] The name "Moses" cannot be an abbreviation of either of these names, as Jenni, 2016: 158 states (with an incorrect identification and translation of the name forms).

The vocalization of the stative of the third person singular masculine of third weak verbs can be reconstructed; it was (Paleo-Coptic[6]) CăCĭ˘w > CăCiy (New Kingdom). The stressed vowel ắ underwent a regular shift to ŏ between c. 550 and 450 BCE (Schenkel, 1990: 87), while the final syllable became /e/. I give two examples for which this pattern can be reconstructed: *čắsiy > (Coptic) [L] ⲭⲁⲥⲓ/ⲉ čắsi/e, [S] ϫⲟⲥⲉ čŏse 'to be exalted', *tắḫiy > [S] ⲧⲁϩⲉ tắḫe 'to be drunk' (where /a/ is preserved before the velar /ḫ/) (Peust, 1999: 151 and 236).[7] Accordingly, and in agreement with name forms preserved in Greek transcriptions such as *Ptahmose, Ahmose, Thutmose,* we have mắsiy > [S] mŏse 'born'.

2.1.2   One-Word Name with the Noun mśw, "Child"

The other suggested Egyptian form is the noun *mśw*, "child", preserved in Coptic as [SB] ⲙⲁⲥ *mas* and [S] ⲙⲁⲥⲉ *mase*,[8] used in this late phase primarily for young animals and birds. This late form goes back to a form *mĕs (Schenkel, 1983: 185; Osing, 1976: 228). ĕ itself in stressed syllables is the successor to either Paleo-Coptic ĭ or ŭ; the shift to ĕ occurred between the time of Ramses II and the Neo-Assyrian conquest (Schenkel, 1990: 87). In consequence, the noun was either *mĭs or *mŭs under Ramses II. This reconstruction of the vocalization of the suggested verbal or nominal forms that are believed to be reflected in the name "Moses" leads to the first, not fully acknowledged (Griffiths, 1953: 228–229; Görg, 2000: 23) problem presented by this equation: the vocalization pattern.

2.2   *The Phonological Problems: Vocalization and Sibilants*

The vocalization pattern in both possible forms of origin is different from the one in the name Moses, *mōšǽ*. The proposed nominal derivation from monosyllabic mĕs "child" or its possible pre-forms mĭs and mŭs do not provide any resemblance to the Biblical name. In turn, the verbal derivation mắśiy is bisyllabic but dissimilar to *mōšǽ*; the similarity is a late phenomenon of the Persian Period when we can assume that the pronunciation had shifted to a form *mŏse. Even at this time, the position of stress of the two terms was different. Intriguingly, if we purport the name *mōšǽ* to be an active Hebrew participle, its historically older form during the Late Bronze Age would have been *māšiyu, similar in appearance to the pre-sixth century Egyptian stative form *mắśiy "born". We will return to this observation below.

---

[6] "Paleo-Coptic" is a term used since William F. Edgerton (1947) for a (theoretical) stage of earlier ancient Egyptian when the sound developments that led to the Coptic phonological system had not yet taken place.

[7] The uppercase sigla "L" and "S" refer to the Lycopolitan and Saidic dialects of Coptic.

[8] The uppercase sigla "S" and "B" refer to the Saidic and Bohairic dialects of Coptic.

The different vocalization adds to the second problem on which so far most scholarly attention has focused: the different sibilants. In this respect it is important to underline that the precise phonological nature of Egyptian <śl> is unclear; in transcriptions of the New Kingdom (1530–1070 BCE) it is mostly used to render Semitic /ś/ and /ṯ/ (while Egyptian /š/ is the regular equivalent of Semitic /š/ (Hoch, 1994: 402–405; 409–410). The reverse situation is not clear, due to the lack of Egyptian-Semitic transcriptions.[9] Scholars advocating for the Egyptian derivation of the name Moses posit that Egyptian <śl> would have been rendered by the voiceless interdental /ṯ/ in Semitic, and that this would have produced /š/ as a result of the regular internal phonetic shift in Hebrew (Quack, 2000; reiterated by Breyer, 2019: 65–66). However, other scholars have maintained that the transcription of Egyptian /ś/ by Hebrew /š/ is not regular. Yoshiyuki Muchiki has for this very reason ruled out that the name "Moses" could be Egyptian (Muchiki, 1999: 217; criticized by Noonan, 2019, 277 with n. 13 who considers the equivalence possible), and scholars like Kenneth Kitchen (2003: 296–297) and James Hoffmeier (2016: 19–20) have again expressed doubts. Alternatively, a rendering of Egyptian <śl> by Semitic /š/ appears possible in principle and is suggested by a borrowed term for ship, Hebr.* *śᵉkiyyā* (or **śᵉkît*; only the plural form is attested in Isa 2:16) < Eg. *śk.tî* (as opposed to > Ugaritic *ṯkt*) (Muchiki, 1999: 255; 315; Breyer, 2019: 165; Noonan 2019: 205–6).[10] In this case (and disregarding the vocalization pattern), the Hebrew name should thus be **mōśǽ* and not *mōšǽ*, with Hebrew Sin and not Shin. In the first millennium BCE, the Semitic equivalent of Egyptian /ś/ is Samek, as shown by the rendering of "Ramses" as רעמסס in Ex 1:11 – a clear indication that this cannot be a historical reminiscence from the New Kingdom (according to Redford, 2009: 175, not earlier than end of the eighth c. BCE).[11]

A number of attempts have been made to explain the different sibilants, on the assumption that the Hebrew-Egyptian identification is valid. John Gwyn Griffiths postulated a difference between a temporary borrowing and a permanent adoption of a name (Griffiths, 1953: 229–230). Manfred Görg suggested that the explanation of the name by the root *mšy* in Exodus 2 could have induced a sibilant change in the Biblical text (Görg, 2000: 23). Other scholars (e.g., James Hoffmeier) claimed dialectal differences for the rendering of /ś/ by /š/, maintaining that "these considerations show that we cannot always expect sibilants going between Egyptian and

---

[9] On account of this situation of Egyptian-Semitic transcriptions, the frequently encountered view whereby the alleged rendering of Egyptian /ś/ by Hebrew /š/ in the name Moses is proof of the name's 2nd millennium date (Schipper, 2009, 1156; cf. Gertz's, 2008 statement: 'Additionally, the name's writing points to its old age since the Hebrew rendering of the Egyptian S-sound reflects the phonetics of the 2nd millennium BCE' ["Zudem spricht die Schreibweise für ein hohes Alter des Namens, da sich in der hebräischen Wiedergabe des ägyptischen S-Lautes die Phonetik des 2. Jt.s v. Chr. spiegelt"]) is not correct.

[10] Noonan adduces the possible loan words *mæsî* (2019: 149–50) and *taḥaš* (2019: 218–9) in support of a sound correspondence Egyptian /ś/ = Hebrew /š/; in both cases, the meaning of the Hebrew terms cannot be derived easily from the Egyptian ones (cf. Breyer, 2019: 143 and 174).

[11] Note that Hebrew Sin and Samekh coalesced in the later first millennium BCE – according to Bosker, 2013: 558, as late as the second century BCE.

Semitic languages conform to rigid rules set by modern linguists" (Hoffmeier, 1999: 141). I would contend that Egyptian phonology does net set abstract rules but tries to analyze the preserved evidence, which in this case does not readily support the equivalence. At any rate, in addition to the sibilant problem (2), the vocalization divergence (1) would need to be solved.

3 Exodus 2:10: Speculations About מְשִׁיתִהוּ *mᵉšîtihû*

3.1 Interpretations Relating to the Idea of "Drawing (A Child) from the Water"

On the assumption that *mōšǽ* is a transcription of an Egyptian verbal form or noun derived from the root *mśy*, many authors have advanced the hypothesis according to which the author of Exodus 2 (to some scholars, also the readers) knew of this etymology of the name. E.g., Andrzej Strus (1978: 64) and I. Willi-Plein (1991) have surmised that the root ילד "to give birth; child" which appears often in Exod 1:15–2:10, is a covert allusion to the Egyptian meaning of the name; an idea reiterated in many recent commentaries (Albertz, 2012: 60; Dozeman, 2009: 81–82; cf. also Jenni, 2016: 158). However, in a birth narrative, the omnipresence of the root ילד seems evident without the additional motivation of a covert explication of a name. In this respect, it is conspicuous to observe that no single Jewish or Christian author in the reception history of Exodus in antiquity – when the forms (Egyptian) *mōse* and (Hebrew) *mōšǽ* had at last almost fully converged phonetically – actually associated the two name forms with each other. In a detailed study, Heinz-Josef Thissen reviewed the antique speculation about the name Moses which focused on the Greek variants of the name, Μωσης, Μωυσης and Μουσης (Thissen, 2004). The ancient etymologists[12] interpreted the Greek forms as "saved from the water", identifying the first element with Egyptian *mw* (in Komposita, μου-), and the second most likely with –σης < ṯȝy, 'taken' (thus = 'water-taken').

Some scholars skeptical of the derivation of the Moses name from Eg. *mśy* have instead pointed to the explanation provided in Ex 2:10 (-וַתִּקְרָא שְׁמוֹ מֹשֶׁה וַתֹּאמֶר כִּי מִן הַמַּיִם מְשִׁיתִהוּ): 'And she called his name "Moses" and said: because from the water I have drawn him'. In their view, the root *mšy* 'to draw' would not be a folk etymology but instead provide the correct root underlying the name *mōšǽ* (Muchiki, 1999: 217; Kitchen, 2003: 296–297). However, from a Hebrew perspective, the name is an active and not a passive participle (Hoffmeier, 1999: 142; Jenni, 2016: 158). Given that the root appears only once more in the Hebrew Bible in a psalm ascribed to David (2 Sam 22:17 = Ps 18:17) where it denotes drawing from water

---

[12] Thissen lists Ezekiel Tragicus; Philo, De vita Moysis; Clemens Alexandrinus, Stromata; Flavius Josephus, Antiquitates Iudaicae and Contra Apionem; Cyril of Alexandria, Glaphyra on Exodus; (Pseudo-)Eustathius of Antioch, Commentary on the Hexaemeron.

as a metaphor for saving, could one possibly argue that the name is an abbreviated form of a theophoric personal name, "(DN) is a saviour"? Or does the name anticipate Moses' saving of his people from bondage through the waters of the Red Sea (Jenni, 2016: 158)?

3.2 Hanna Jenni's 2016 Proposal

This avenue, however, does not exist, either, according to a recent study by Hanna Jenni (2016). She has mounted the entire Semitic lexical repertoire to demonstrate that a root *mšy* "to draw (from water)" is a lexicological phantom. An Arabic root *masā* "to pull out" is attested exclusively in the specialized vocabulary of bedouin camel breeders where it is used with regard to the cleaning of the uterus of a female camel. A root *mšy* is well attested in Aramaic, Syriac and Arabic with the meaning "to wipe, sweep, take away, gather up"; but this verb was not used in any of the Aramaic, Syrian and Arabic translations of Ex 2:10 for the Hebrew מְשִׁיתִהוּ *mešîtihû*. Evidently, the translators did not associate it with the Hebrew verb and also did not deem it a translation semantically suitable for the described action. This leaves the question open of how to then explain the verbal form מְשִׁיתִהוּ *mešîtihû*.

Hanna Jenni advances an ingenious new explanation. She regards not only the name "Moses" but also the verbal form as derived from the Egyptian root *mśy*; מְשִׁיתִהוּ *mešîtihû* would thus be an inflected Hebrew form of the Egyptian verb *mśy*. This means that the author, knowledgeable of the derivation of the name מֹשֶׁה "Moses" from (purportedly) the root *mśy* "to give birth, engender", would have used the same Egyptian root to explain the personal name. For the sake of demonstration, we can use a French equivalent in English to exemplify this strategy: "And she called his name *enfant* and said: because from the water I have *enfanted* him". Since the Egyptian word *mw* "water" can also mean "semen", Jenni further argues that the verse could actually implicate conceiving a child from divine semen, an idea she then contextualizes within the Egyptian institution of the God's Wife of Amun. Such a God's Wife of Amun, an unmarried princess assuming political control in Upper Egypt, would have adopted the Moses child and understood it within the theological concept of the divine birth of royal princes.

While Jenni's approach is novel and ingenious, it is based on the assumption that both מֹשֶׁה *mōšǽ* and מְשִׁיתִהוּ *mešîtihû* can be derived from Egyptian *mśy* and that this involves regular sound correspondences. This is far from clear, as could be demonstrated above.

4 Etymological Scenarios: Reopening the Debate

In summary, there are two alternatives we face in assessing the name *mōšǽ*:

1. The name represents a borrowing of the Egyptian stative form *mā́śiy* from the period of Iron Age I/II but underwent in its new (Israelite) linguistic context the shift of vowel *qualities a-i > o-e* like the similar Northwest Semitic active participle, in addition to a change of the vowel *quantity* (short to long /a/), the *sibilant* (/ś/ > /š/; alternatively adopted into Hebrew as /ṭ/ and then undergoing the internal shift > /š/) and the *position of the stress* (first syllable to second syllable). The question arises whether such a scenario is likely for a borrowed name, and whether the name of a legendary hero would be modified rather than retained unchanged?[13] If we assume a takeover of the name after the vowel shift occurred in ancient Egypt (c. sixth century BCE), we can avoid the secondary vocalization change although the sibilant rendering and the stress position would still be incorrect. This would implicate a similarly late date for the figure of Moses and appears too late with regard to currently proposed dates for the origins of the Moses tradition.[14]

2. Alternatively, the name reflects an active participle of a Northwest Semitic root *mšy*; however, such a root is no longer attested in Northwest Semitic onomastics. Since the Canaanite vowel shift ā > ō occurred gradually after the fifteenth century BCE (Gzella, 2011: 434), the name מֹשֶׁה *Mōšǽ* could be the genuine form of a name originating in the Iron Age I period – or later. This hypothesis avoids the complex assumptions necessary in scenario 1 (see the end of this paragraph for a proposal).

Given this situation of the linguistic evidence, the conclusion is all but inescapable that the name "Moses" is not likely of Egyptian origin, which means yet another subtraction in the history of subtractions in Moses scholarship (to use Smend's imagery quoted at the beginning of this article), 170 years after Richard Lepsius proposed the idea of an Egyptian etymology. This would further invalidate the claim of a genuine historical association of Moses with Egypt[15] – "Moses the Egyptian" would indeed be a later construct.

Instead, the name "Moses" would most probably constitute a Northwest Semitic personal name, of uncertain etymology. Thus, it will be mandatory to reopen the debate on its meaning and the significance of the root מֹשֶׁה in Exod 2:10 and 2Sam 22:17 = Ps 18:17. From the Semitic inventory, a satisfactory semantic option for the text passages might be offered by Syriac *mšy* "to collect, to glean" (Ex. 2,10:

---

[13] Cf. here the interesting parallel debate regarding the – Latin or Celtic? – etymology of the name of the legendary king Arthur (Green, 2009: 18–9).

[14] Gertz, 2002: 14–5 proposes a historical anchor for the origin of the Moses tradition (with the use of older elements) after the end of the Northern kingdom of Israel. Many of the elements seen as genuinely old in the Moses tradition – e.g., the relation to Midian – have been put into doubt by recent scholarship (see, e.g., the contributions by Christoph Berner and Henrik Pfeiffer in van Oorschot & Witte, 2017).

[15] Cf. Blum, 2012: 42 where he emphasizes: 'Thus, the historical implications of the name "Moses" cannot be dissociated from the history of the exodus tradition' ("Die historischen Implikationen des Mose-Namens lassen sich mithin von der Geschichte der Exodustradition nicht lösen."). If the name is not Egyptian, this nexus between the figure and the Exodus tradition vanishes.

"From the waters I collected/gleaned him"); the name מֹשֶׁה *Mōšǽ* would then be the equivalent of Syriac *mšwy (māšōy)* "gleaner, collector" (cf. CAL s.v.).

I am delighted to offer these gleanings from reflections about the figure of Moses and the exodus narrative to Tom Levy who has been a friend and colleague for many years – particularly in grateful memory of our joint work on the 2013 Exodus conference at his home institution UC San Diego and the subsequent 2015 volume of proceedings (Levy et al., 2015). His research has led scholarship out of the bondage of many preconceived ideas and into the promise of new academic territory.

References

Albertz, R. (2012). *Exodus 1–18. Zürcher Bibelkommentare*. Theologischer Verlag.
Assmann, J. (2002). Antijudaismus oder Antimonotheismus? Hellenistische Exoduserzählungen. In D. Borchmeyer & H. Kiesel (Eds.), *Das Judentum im Spiegel seiner kulturellen Umwelten. Symposium zu Ehren von Saul Friedländer* (pp. 33–54). Mnemosyne Edition.
Baden, J. S. (2019). *The book of Exodus: A biography*. Princeton University Press.
Barclay, J. M. G. (2007). *Flavius Josephus: Against Apion. Translation and commentary*. Brill.
Blum, E. (2012). Der historische Mose und die Frühgeschichte Israels. *Hebrew Bible and Ancient Israel, 1*, 37–63.
Bosker, H.-R. (2013). Sibilant consonants. In G. Khan (Ed.), *Encyclopedia of Hebrew language and linguistics* (Vol. 3, P–Z, pp. 557–561). Brill.
Breyer, F. A. (2019). *Ägyptische Namen und Wörter im Alten Testament. Ägypten und Altes Testament 93*. Zaphon.
CAL = *Comprehensive Aramaic Lexicon*. http://cal.huc.edu/
Cook, J. G. (2004). *The interpretation of the Old Testament in Greco-Roman paganism. Studien und Texte zu Antike und Christentum* (Vol. 23). Mohr Siebeck.
Dijkstra, M. (2006). Moses, the Man of God. In R. Roukema & K. Spronk (Eds.), *The interpretation of exodus: Studies in honour of Cornelis Houtman* (pp. 17–36). Peeters.
Dozeman, T. B. (2009). *Commentary on Exodus. The Eerdmans critical commentary*. Eerdmans.
Edgerton, W. F. (1947). Stress, vowel quantity, and syllable division in Egyptian. *Journal of Near Eastern Studies, 6*, 1–17.
Frevel, C. (2018). *Geschichte Israels. Kohlhammer Studienbücher Theologie* (Second, Enlarged and Revised Edition). Kohlhammer.
Gager, J. G. (1972). *Moses in Greco-Roman paganism* (Society of Biblical Literature, Monograph series) (Vol. 16). Society of Biblical Literature.
Gertz, J. C. (2002). Mose und die Anfänge der jüdischen Religion. *Zeitschrift für Theologie und Kirche, 99*, 3–20.
Gertz, J.C. (2008). *Mose*. Retrieved January 4, 2022, from http://www.bibelwissenschaft.de/stichwort/28069/
Görg, M. (2000). Mose – Name und Namensträger. Versuch einer historischen Annäherung. In E. Otto (Ed.), *Mose. Ägypten und das Alte Testament. SBS 189* (pp. 17–42). Verlag Katholisches Bibelwerk GmbH.
Greifenhagen, F. V. (2002). *Egypt on the Pentateuch's ideological map: Constructing biblical Israel's identity*. Sheffield Academic Press.
Green, C. R. (2009). The historicity and historicisation of Arthur. In C. R. Green (Ed.), *Arthuriana: Early Arthurian tradition and the origins of the legend* (pp. 3–46). The Lindes Press.
Griffiths, J. G. (1953). The Egyptian derivation of the name Moses. *Journal of Near Eastern Studies, 12*, 225–231.
Gzella, H. (2011). Northwest Semitic in general. In S. Weninger (Ed.), *The Semitic languages. An international handbook* (pp. 425–451). De Gruyter.
Hoch, J. E. (1994). *Semitic words in Egyptian texts of the New Kingdom and the Third Intermediate Period*. Princeton University Press.

Hoffmeier, J. K. (1999). *Israel in Egypt. The evidence for the authenticity of the exodus tradition.* Oxford University Press.
Hoffmeier, J. K. (2016). Egyptian religious influences on the early Hebrews. In J. K. Hoffmeier, A. R. Millard, & G. A. Rendsburg (Eds.), *'Did I not bring Israel out of Egypt?' Biblical, archaeological, and Egyptological perspectives on the exodus narratives* (pp. 3–35). Eisenbrauns.
Jenni, H. (2016). Fragen zum Verb *mšj* in der Kindheitsgeschichte Moses (Ex 2,10). In H. Jenni & M. Saur (Eds.), *Nächstenliebe und Gottesfurcht. Beiträge aus alttestamentlicher, semitistischer und altorientalistischer Wissenschaft für Hans-Peter Mathys zum 65. Geburtstag* (pp. 151–175). Ugarit Verlag.
Jeremias, J. (2015). *Theologie des Alten Testaments.* Vandenhoeck & Ruprecht.
Kitchen, K. A. (2003). *On the reliability of the Old Testament.* Eerdmans.
Lepsius, C. R. (1849). *Die Chronologie der Aegypter. Einleitung und erster Theil: Kritik der Quellen.* Nicolaische Buchhandlung.
Levy, T. E., Schneider, T., & Propp, W. H. C. (Eds.). (2015). *Israel's exodus in transdisciplinary perspective: Text, archaeology and geoscience* (Qualitative methods in the humanities and social sciences). Springer.
Moore, S. (2015). *Jewish ethnic identity and relations in Hellenistic Egypt: With walls of iron?* Brill.
Muchiki, Y. (1999). *Egyptian proper names and loanwords in Northwest Semitic.* Society of Biblical Literature.
Noonan, B. J. (2019). *Non-Semitic loanwords in the Hebrew bible. A lexicon of language contact.* Eisenbrauns.
Osing, J. (1976). *Die Nominalbildung des Ägyptischen* (Vol. 2 vols). Von Zabern.
Peust, C. (1999). *Egyptian phonology. An introduction to the phonology of a dead language.* Peust & Gutschmidt.
Quack, J.F. (2000). Review of Y. Muchiki, Egyptian proper names and loanwords in Northwest Semitic (1999). *Review of Biblical Literature* http://www.bookreviews.org
Ranke, H. (1952). *Die altägyptischen Personennamen. Bd. 2: Einleitung. Form und Inhalt der Namen. Geschichte der Namen. Vergleiche mit anderen Namen. Nachträge und Zusätze zu Band I. Umschreibungslisten.* J.J. Augustin.
Redford, D. B. (2009). The land of Ramses. In P. J. Brand & L. Cooper (Eds.), *Causing his name to live. Studies in Egyptian epigraphy and history in memory of William J. Murnane* (pp. 175–178). Brill.
Römer, T. (2008). Moses outside the Torah and the construction of diaspora identity. *Journal of Hebrew Scriptures, 8*(15), 1–12. https://doi.org/10.5508/jhs.2008.v8.a15
Römer, T. (2015). *Moïse en version originale: Enquête sur le récit de la sortie d'Egypte.* Bayard.
Schäfer, P. (1997). *Judeophobia: Attitudes toward the Jews in the ancient world.* Harvard University Press.
Schenkel, W. (1983). *Zur Rekonstruktion der deverbalen Nominalbildung des Ägyptischen.* Harrassowitz.
Schenkel, W. (1990). *Einführung in die altägyptische Sprachwissenschaft.* Wissenschaftliche Buchgesellschaft.
Schipper, B. U. (2009). Ägypten und Israel. Erkenntnisse und Perspektiven. *Theologische Literaturzeitung, 134,* 1153–1164.
Smend, R. (1995). Der geschichtliche Mose. *Historische Zeitschrift, 260,* 1–20.
Strus, A. (1978). *Nomen – Omen: La stylistique sonore des noms propres dans le Pentateuque.* Biblical Institute Press.
Thissen, H. J. (2004). Zum Namen Moses. *Rheinisches Museum für Philologie, 147,* 55–62.
Thonhauser, J. (2009). Das Unbehagen am Monotheismus. Ein Rekonstruktionsversuch der Debatte um Jan Assmann's Thesen zur 'Mosaischen Unterscheidung'. In J. Kügler & U. Bechmann (Eds.), *Biblische Religionskritik: Kritik in, an und mit biblischen Texten* (pp. 229–259). LIT Verlag.
van Oorschot, J., & Witte, M. (Eds.). (2017). *The origins of Yahwism.* De Gruyter.
Willi-Plein, I. (1991). Ort und literarische Funktion der Geburtsgeschichte des Mose. *Vetus Testamentum, 41,* 110–118.

Heraclitus' Law and the Late Period Shaft Tombs of Abusir

Miroslav Bárta

Abstract The Late Period of Egyptian history (525–332 BCE) offers evidence for several critical factors that caused the collapse of the ancient Egyptian state. The state was losing the ground under its feet and changes were coming in sudden leaps, mutually reinforcing their impact. As stated in Heraclitus' law, the same factors that instigated its rise were now causing its decline. The elites were becoming increasingly dysfunctional, and what once was represented as a set of widely shared and acknowledged symbolical values and ideas began to disappear. The country lacked resources and the latest technologies, and it was failing to adapt to new geopolitical and economic conditions.

In this contribution, the particular case under scrutiny represents Egypt's Late Period, in which the country was repeatedly defeated by foreign armies, controlled by the Kushite kingdom or the Persian empire and, as a consequence, lost ground and an identity that had been built and maintained for centuries on the petrified centristic Nile-based model of civilization and kingship. As a consequence, Egypt and the Egyptian elites were desperately looking for new and indigenous means to regain and re-establish their uncompromised and unique identity.

This study will also demonstrate how innovations in culture are not always necessarily linked with the leading elite of the society. Quite the contrary, the lesser nobility is in fact usually more at liberty to depart from traditional means of expression and look for new, more appropriate ways to demonstrate their cultural, symbolical and intellectual preferences and mindsets. In this particular case, these are not new, but, represent antique elements based on the predynastic and Old Kingdom periods.

For editing the English text of this article I tender thanks to my colleague, Marianne Tames-Demauras.

M. Bárta (✉)
Czech Institute of Egyptology, Charles University, Prague, Czechia
e-mail: miroslav.barta@ff.cuni.cz

© The Author(s), under exclusive license to Springer Nature Switzerland AG 2023
E. Ben-Yosef, I. W. N. Jones (eds.), *"And in Length of Days Understanding" (Job 12:12): Essays on Archaeology in the Eastern Mediterranean and Beyond in Honor of Thomas E. Levy*, Interdisciplinary Contributions to Archaeology, https://doi.org/10.1007/978-3-031-27330-8_44

Keywords Heraclitus Law · Abusir · Late period · Shaft tombs · Saqqara

Dear Tom: I hope you find this piece of archaeological reflection worthy of interest. One of the perspectives that archaeology provides is the manner in which past civilizations rose, collapsed, transformed, or searched for their identity, and disregards their level of complexity or age. Below, I offer a specific example of such a process that took place shortly after the dawn of the Axial Age (Jaspers, 1949). I am certain that, were it not for our discussions over the years in San Diego, Wadi Feynan, Prague and various other locations, I would not have been able to travel back in time the way I have. I am very grateful not only for this but also for being one of your friends and colleagues.

In this contribution, I will demonstrate the specific impact of the so-called Heraclitus Law. This law, one of seven laws along which civilizations develop, thrive, and eventually collapse, states that the factors that originally instigated the rise of systems, are the same that eventually contribute to their decline and collapse (Bárta, 2018, 2019b). The particular case that I will focus on represents the Late Period. During this time period, Egypt was repeatedly defeated by foreign armies that were in turn controlled by the Kushite kingdom or Persian empire. As a result, Egypt lost ground and the identity that it had built and successfully maintained for centuries on the fixed centrist Nile-based model of civilization and kingship. Consequently, Egypt and the Egyptian elites were desperately looking for new and indigenous means to regain and re-establish their uncompromised and unique identity (see Assmann, 1988a).

I will also demonstrate that innovations in culture are not always necessarily linked with the leading elite of the society. Quite the contrary. In fact, the lesser nobility usually enjoys greater "freedom" to depart from traditional means of expression and search for new, innovative and more appropriate ways to demonstrate their cultural, symbolical and intellectual preferences and mindsets. In this particular case, these are not new, but on the contrary, antique expressions based on predynastic and Old Kingdom elements that include symbolic animal burials during the Predynastic period (such as in Hierakonpolis) or monumental architecture of the complex of Djoser at Saqqara (Assmann, 1988b).

The seven-law theory of civilizations was in full swing during the Late Period of Egyptian history; ancient Egypt was approaching the denouement of her dramatic past despite having once basked in the glory of unsurpassed monuments, such as pyramids of the Old and Middle Kingdoms, or the New Kingdom temple complexes of Karnak and Luxor (Bárta, 2019a). The state was losing the ground under its feet and changes were taking place in sudden leaps. The same factors that instigated her rise were now causing her decline. The elites were becoming increasingly dysfunctional, and what once represented a set of widely shared and acknowledged symbols and ideas disappeared. The country lacked resources and the latest technologies, and it was perilously failing to adapt to new geopolitical and economic conditions.

1 Geopolitical Setting

Looking at the history of ancient Egypt, one notices how, as a result of sudden or punctuated change, tradition and innovation take on a new twist as is the case during the Late Period (in general, see Bárta, 2015; Ben-Yosef et al., 2019). This particular era, especially the events of the seventh and sixth centuries BCE, provide unique evidence for cultural transformations of a society facing a major crisis of identity and undergoing a substantial transformation under external cultural and political pressure. For centuries, Egyptians considered themselves and their world order as inherited directly from the gods in which the mortal king took on the role of intermediary between his peoples and the divine sphere. Egyptians called themselves "people," a concept rooted in the idea of their being the *chosen nation*. The king, semi-divine and selected by the gods, was deemed to be invincible and always capable of defending his country, his nation, and maintaining the world's divine order given by the gods, the so-called Maat, and the driver off of the evil forces (Assmann, 1990). All this became heavily compromised and put in jeopardy during the Late Period. Evidently, the consequences were severe.

Incredible achievements that took place during the Nubian Twenty-fifth Dynasty (722–655 BCE) were based on their military and political supremacy covering large territories of ancient Egypt. This was possible due to a continual weakening of the Egyptian state, which paved the path for the suffering and recurring competition between the state's profane and priestly powers, and the regional powers. Originating from the south (modern day Sudan), Nubian kings ruled the majority of Egypt for several decades. This certainly meant a deep blow to the ancient Egyptian concept of her identity and self- perception, not to mention the kingship itself. By this time, Egypt had been attempting for more than 2000 years of its long history, to contain with a varying degree of success, the Nubian chiefdoms, and execute military and political control over the Nile cataracts. Now the opposite was happening—for the first time ever the Nubians were ruling Egypt.

However, despite their ambitions, the Kushite kings were not able to maintain the rule over Egypt's vast territory that stretched from the depths of Africa, all the way up north to the Mediterranean coast. The Assyrians, viewing contemporary Egypt as easy prey and an attractive source of riches, invaded in 667 BCE under the kings Esarhaddon and Ashurbanipal. The ruling Kushite king, Taharqo, was pushed back to Nubia by the Assyrian forces, and the local Egyptian ruler Necho (I) of Sais was put in charge of Egypt by the Assyrians (Kitchen, 1968; Taylor, 2000).

In 672 BCE, Necho I became ruler of the Delta city of Sais and adopted the traditional titulary of Egyptian kings. The Assyrian king Esarhaddon, who established his control over large parts of Egypt a year later, accepted Necho as his deputy-ruler over the Egyptian territory as far south as Memphis. Following a new Kushite aggression against the Delta, in 666–665 BCE Esarhaddon's successor, Ashurbanipal, managed to push Taharqo back to Thebes. Slightly later, Necho I was killed near Memphis during a counter-offensive led by another Kushite king, Tantamani. As a result, Necho's son Psamtek had to flee to Assyria. He returned in the company of the Assyrian troops in 664–663 BCE, and regained supremacy over the Delta and Memphis, and subjugated Thebes as well. This series of events on the part of foreign forces eventually led to a fragile reunification of Egypt under Psamtik's formal rule. While busy with re-establishing his power, Psamtik had to also form a military alliance with the Lydian king Gyges, who sent him troops to support his reign. Not long after, the ruling king, Apries, upon his return from a lost battle in Libya, was ousted from the country due to the escalating conflicts in the army between Egyptian and Greek soldiers. Popular military leader, Amasis, claimed the throne for himself. He was succeeded by one of the last indigenous rulers of Egypt, Amasis II. Amasis II died in 526 BCE and his son and successor Psamtik III, who had enjoyed a brief rule for about 6 months, was defeated in a battle near Pelusium by the Persian King Cambyses II. His alleged suicide in Susa nearly ended millennia-long indigenous tradition of the Egyptian pharaohs (Lloyd, 2000; Dodson, 2012).

Is it any wonder that the first-hand experience the majority of the Egyptian population faced by being defeated either by the Kushite kings, Assyrian rulers, or national collaborators such as kings of the Twenty-sixth Dynasty, had so extraordinary a negative impact? The indigenous Twenty-Sixth Dynasty (664–525 BCE) saw no other way to resurrect Egyptian identity and self-esteem than to harken back to predynastic and Old Kingdom traditions, which were in turn manifested in the increasingly popular sacred animals cults, archaic language, decorative style and architecture (Manuelian, 1994).

2 Living in the Past

Every society under pressure seeks to identify its former elements of success, instill them with updated meanings and reuse them. In the case of Egypt's Late Period, this penchant took on the form of returning to the very roots of Egyptian civilization. This is discernible in different domains. We can initially observe this by a sudden and very strong increase in animal cults as remarked by various Greek and Roman authors, starting with Herodotus (for predynastic symbolic animal burials, see Adams, 2000). These cults proliferated particularly at Saqqara, the principal necropolis of the time period. There, in the so-called North Saqqara area, various different temples and rock-cut galleries date to the reign of King Amasis (570–526 BCE). Much later, during the Thirtieth Dynasty, King Nakhtnebef (Nectanebos I, 380–362 BCE) enlarged the enclosures and built additional temples. This trend of mummifying sacred animals, such as hawks, ibises, cats, dogs or bulls, and building ostentatious burials for them, became of national importance (Ikram, 2005). Despite the fact that the precise final resting place of Imhotep is not known, it is believed that it must be somewhere in North Saqqara. This is also the reason why virtually all sacred animal necropolis of the Late Period were built in this region of Saqqara.

The principal sacred animal worshipped by the Egyptians since the foundation of their state was the sacred bull, Apis. The first attestations of his cult date to the third millennium BCE. Yet his burials are attested only from around 1300 BCE, when the precursor of the much later Serapeum had been established in the same area by the New Kingdom kings. During the Late Period, the cult of the Apis bull was associated with the one of Osiris, the god of the Egyptian Netherworld, and every sacred bull kept alive in the temple of the Memphite deity, was buried with high honors in the Serapeum galleries (Voss, 1992).

During the sixth century BCE, his mother was also worshipped as a divine entity, and became associated with the goddess Isis, the mythical sister of Osiris, and who gave birth to their son Horus. At a later stage, mummified baboons and ibises began to be buried at North Saqqara; they were considered to be the sacred animals of the god of wisdom, and the father of Isis, Thoth (Ray, 1978, 152). Similarly, one can observe this with the galleries created for the hawks, which were in turn considered embodiments of the god Horus. At some distance, in a southeast direction, on the eastern side of the North Saqqara promontory, galleries were established specifically for dogs, the cult animal of Anubis, protector of the necropolis. Further towards the south, a temple complex, known as the Bubasteion, was built in honor of the cat goddess Bastet. Hundreds of thousands of intrusive cat mummies are still being discovered every year in different tombs dating to the New Kingdom and Late Period.

It was also precisely during the Late Period, starting with the Twenty-sixth Dynasty, that Imhotep was deified as the first Egyptian sage, associated with wisdom, medicine and writing. As the architect of Djoser's pyramid (he most likely also constructed the pyramid of Sekhemkhet), he was considered to be the founder of building in stone (Wildung, 1977). He became so respected that, even during the reign of his Lord, King Netjerykhet, Imhotep was given the previously unheard of privilege of being mentioned by name and titles on a statue base of Djoser. He is featured on the base of this statue as "Chancellor of the king of Lower Egypt, the first after the king of Upper Egypt, administrator of the great palace, hereditary lord Greatest of Seers, Imhotep, the builder, the sculptor, the maker of stone vases (Ikram, 2005, 44–45)."

3 Shaft Tombs as a Specific Means for Modeling Old-New Identity

For more than 30 years, the Czech mission working at Abusir's pyramid field has been exploring the so-called *shaft tombs* located in the western part of the archaeological concession. This type of tomb was built specifically and predominantly in the Abusir-Saqqara area (Fig. 1). Each tomb consisted of a principal shaft at the bottom of which a stone-built burial chamber containing the burial of the tomb owner was constructed. The size of the biggest shafts could reach a ground plan of 14 × 14 m and a depth of almost 30 m. Among the shaft tombs that have been excavated in Abusir Western Cemetery so far, the large tombs of Udjahorresnet (Bareš et al., 1999), Iufaa (Bareš et al., 2008) and Menekhibnekau (Bareš & Smoláriková, 2011), as well as the smaller tomb of Padihor (Coppens et al., 2009), were only used

Fig. 1 General view of the shaft tombs in Abusir with Old Kingdom pyramids at the background. (Archive of the Czech Institute of Egyptology, M. Zemina)

for the burials of their owners. In some cases, minor subterranean galleries and burial chambers were added for other family members. The main shaft was, at least in one case (Udjahorresnet), surrounded by a deep trench. The evidence for superstructures with the cult function is rather sparse. In some cases, however, there have been remains of a mudbrick or limestone enclosure wall decorated with niches. The shaft tombs discovered and explored at Abusir so far are essentially contemporaneous and were built during the very last stages of the Twenty-sixth Dynasty, between 530 and 525 BCE, perhaps with some later additions and extensions within a decade or two (Stammers, 2009).

It is the above characteristics, the deep main shaft with the burial chamber and a burial at the bottom, a surrounding trench, and a niched wall around the shaft opening, which call for a comparison with the complex of Netjerykhet Djoser built about two millennia earlier (Smoláriková, 2008). Netjerykhet Djoser was considered, as far as tradition goes, to be the real founder of the Old Kingdom state. He was a ruler who built, for the first time in history, a truly monumental burial complex out of limestone blocks (Baud, 2002). His burial was placed at the bottom of a gigantic shaft in a burial chamber built out of enormous red granite blocks that had been transported from Aswan on the southern border of the country (Fig. 2). This shaft was probably cleared in the Twenty-sixth Dynasty during the reign of Psammtek I (Firth et al., 1935, 5–6). His pyramid complex was enclosed by a massive limestone wall decorated with niches, and the entire perimeter of his burial site was surrounded by a huge ditch hewn out of bedrock. Many rulers that followed, no matter the

Heraclitus' Law and the Late Period Shaft Tombs of Abusir

Fig. 2 The shaft and the burial chamber of Djoser built at its bottom, Saqqara. (M. Bárta)

time-period, made explicit statements regarding their symbolical relationship with Djoser. This was done by placing their monuments in the vicinity of his pyramid, or by using visual connections with his monument (Bárta, 2016). The famous Imhotep, who devised the idea of Djoser's complex, and converted it into a real three-dimensional complex built entirely out of limestone blocks, was most probably buried in North Saqqara.

It is therefore not surprising that the high officials of the Twenty-sixth Dynasty decided to emulate his complex. The reason for this was most likely in order to demonstrate their symbolic connection with the famous king who built the first empire of the ancient Egyptians. This particular type of tomb became a trend only in Giza, Abusir and Saqqara, and remained popular from the early sixth century BCE down to the beginning of Persian rule (Darius I). There is evidence of 14 shaft tomb owners with a burial chamber built at the bottom of the shaft, while another four shaft tombs have sarcophagi placed at the bottom and lack proper burial chamber construction (Bareš, 2006, 3–5) (Fig. 3).

In order to detect the social status of the shaft tomb owners, one can use as information the size of their tombs, decoration and burial equipment inside (surviving only in some rare cases), as well as the choice and quality of the texts. However, the best-preserved evidence in terms of its completeness are the titles of the individuals, which are available for 17 owners in total. Amongst them, 70 different titles are attested. The highest number, a total of 27, were held by the Abusir "overseer of the army," Menekhibnekau. The titles held by the shaft tombs owners can be divided into four major categories: ranking, military, administrative and priestly. The ranking titles indicate that their holders belonged to the higher level of the society; however, not to the top elite of the state. The most frequent of these were titles belonging to the administrative category. For example, responsibilities for financial matters, judiciary, and personal service to the king have been attested. None of the shaft

Fig. 3 The shaft and the burial chamber of Iufaa in Abusir. (Archive of the Czech Institute of Egyptology, M. Balík)

tomb holders are attested as a vizier, which is a title parallel to our modern concept of the prime minister. Seven of the owners held various military titles. Four of them were admirals, which is not surprising since Memphis, a major city of the ancient Egyptian state, was situated east of Abusir and Saqqara, and served as a major marine facility with a vast and famous harbor. The last category of titles, the priestly ones, are also relatively few. Only Abusir tomb owners Menekhibnekau and Udjahorresnet held titles including all four categories. Close scrutiny of their titles, carried out by Ladislav Bareš, has illustrated quite a heterogeneous picture in which no specific category of officials can be established (perhaps with one exception of admirals) (Bareš, 2006). Similarly, no relationship between the social status of an owner and the size or decoration of his tomb could be reconstructed.

4 Conclusion

The shaft tombs of Abusir represent a genuine, short-lived (ca. 530–500 BCE) testimony on how a relatively limited and specific elite group of the country attempted to establish a new, tradition-inspired means to demonstrate its identity. It was the emulation of the first stone monumental burial ever built: ceremonial complex of Djoser at Saqqara. This was due to the continual decline and relativization of traditional Egyptian concepts of the state given to the Egyptians by the gods, and the idea of kingship and its divine representative—the Egyptian king, to say nothing about once omnipresent monumental constructions which embodied the power and unity between the country, the king and the divine sphere. Resources became critically limited, and this in turn compromised the expected divine forces of the king when confronted with the powers rising behind Egyptian borders.

With regard to the Saite Twenty-sixth Dynasty and her collapse, an interesting new explanatory factor has recently been proposed based on analysis of the Seshat Database of several dozen civilizations.[1] According to Shin and his team, some civilizations/complex societies fail/collapse/implode because they become unable to develop sufficient information-processing capacities. This leads to a civilizations' lack of effective responses and performance because it misses external connectivity and internal social contract. Moreover, due to the lack of energy, resources and leadership, these failing societies find themselves unable to compete with civilizations that dispose of superior information-processing abilities, which in turn favor them in mutual competition and conflicts (Shin et al., 2020, 7; see also Bárta, 2019a). In fact, if we look at the period under scrutiny, we can see that the Egyptians, based on their concept of rule, Nilo-centric perspective attitudes towards the world and the kingship were most probably not equipped to deal with the significantly quicker advancing world in most of its aspects—socio-political, geopolitical, economic and technological.

---

[1] Seshatdatabank.info

Fig. 4 Inscribed eastern wall in the burial chamber of Iufaa. (Archive of the Czech Institute of Egyptology, M. Frouz)

Thus, the Abusir shaft tombs, built within a few decades at the end of the sixth century BCE, represent a brand-new tomb type that embodied the preferences of the historical period during which the ancient Egyptian civilization came into being. Their architecture, decoration, and texts, represent a vivid testimony of how a small and heterogeneous group of high officials reacted, and how they creatively converted the challenges of their time. Although they were certainly not members of the state's top elite, the shaft tomb owners probably enjoyed a higher degree of freedom and did not have to comply with all strict requirements of the official decorum. This in turn offered them the unique opportunity to look for material forms and expressions on how to demonstrate their specific priorities, which almost certainly included political legitimacy within the region where they operated (i.e., wider region of Memphis), as well as their ample ability to preserve the *status quo* to which all members of their wider households adhered. The shaft tombs of the Late Period can thus be considered as one of the last forms of indigenous expressions of ancient Egyptian sacral architecture, testimony of which we attempt to understand and decontextualize to these days (Fig. 4).

References

Adams, B. (2000). *Excavations in the Locality 6 cemetery at Hierakonpolis, 1979–1985*. ADAMS.
Assmann, J. (1988a). *Kollektives Gedächtnis und kulturelle Identität*. Suhrkamp.

Assmann, J. (1988b). *Stein und Zeit: das "monumentale" Gedächtnis der altägyptischen Kultur.* Suhrkamp.

Assmann, J. (1990). *Ma'at: Gerechtigkeit und Unsterblichkeit im alten Ägypten.* C. H. Beck.

Bareš, L. (2006). The social status of the owners of the large Late Period shaft tombs. In M. Bárta, F. Coppens, & J. Krejčí (Eds.), *Abusir and Saqqara in the year 2005* (pp. 1–17). Czech Institute of Egyptology.

Bareš, L., & Smoláriková, K. (2011). *Abusir XXV. The shaft tomb of Menekhibnekau.* Czech Institute of Egyptology.

Bareš, L., Smoláriková, K., & Strouhal, E. (1999). *Abusir IV. The shaft tomb of Udjahorresnet at Abusir.* Czech Institute of Egyptology.

Bareš, L., Smoláriková, K., & Balík, M. (2008). *Abusir XVII. The shaft tomb of Iufaa.* Czech Institute of Egyptology.

Bárta, M. (2015). Ancient Egyptian history as an example of punctuated equilibrium: An outline. In P. D. Manuelian & T. Schneider (Eds.), *Towards a new history for the Egyptian Old Kingdom. Perspectives on the Pyramid Age* (pp. 1–17). Brill.

Bárta, M. (2016). Abusir paradigm' and the beginning of the fifth dynasty. In I. Hein, N. Billing, & E. Meyer-Dietrich (Eds.), *The pyramids. Between life and death, proceedings of the workshop held at Uppsala University* (pp. 51–74). Acta Universitatis Upsaliensis, BOREAS—Uppsala Studies in Ancient Mediterranean and Near Eastern Civilizations.

Bárta, M. (2018). Heraclitus Law, punctuated equilibria and the dynamics of contemporary world. *Terrorism. An Electronic Journal and Knowledge Base, VII*(3), 7–14.

Bárta, M. (2019a). Introduction. Why to deal with a collapse? Considerations of Seven laws underlying dynamics of civilizations. In M. Bárta & M. Kovář (Eds.), *Civilizations: Collapse and regeneration. Addressing the nature of change and transformation in history* (pp. 19–29). Academia.

Bárta, M. (2019b). The Heraclitus Law. In M. Bárta & M. Kovář (Eds.), *Civilizations: Collapse and regeneration. Addressing the nature of change and transformation in history* (pp. 245–268). Academia.

Baud, M. (2002). *Djéser et la IIIe dynastie.* Pygmalion.

Ben-Yosef, E., Brady, L., Yagel, O. A., Tirosh, O., Najjar, M., & Levy, T. E. (2019). Ancient technology and punctuated change: Detecting the emergence of the Edomite Kingdom in the Southern Levant. *PLoS One, 14*(9), e0221967. https://doi.org/10.1371/journal.pone.0221967

Coppens, F., Smoláriková, K., Ondráš, F., & Strouhal, E. (2009). *Abusir XX: Lesser late period tombs at Abusir: The tomb of Padihor and the anonymous tomb R3.* Czech Institute of Egyptology.

Der Manuelian, P. (1994). *Living in the past: Studies in archaism of the Egyptian twenty-sixth dynasty.* Kegan Paul International.

Dodson, A. (2012). *Afterglow of empire. Egypt from the fall of the new kingdom to the Saite renaissance.* American University in Cairo Press.

Firth, C. M., Quibell, J. E., & Lauer, J. P. (1935). *The step pyramid* (Vol. I). IFAO.

Ikram, S. (2005). *Divine creatures: Animal mummies in ancient Egypt.* American University in Cairo Press.

Jaspers, K. (1949). *Vom Ursprung und Ziel der Geschichte.* R, Piper & Verlag.

Kitchen, K. (1968). *The third intermediate period in Egypt (1100–650 B.C.).* Aris & Phillips.

Lloyd, A. B. (2000). The late period (664–332 BC). In I. Shaw (Ed.), *The Oxford history of ancient Egypt* (pp. 369–394). Oxford University Press.

Ray, J. D. (1978). The world of North Saqqara. *World Archaeology, 10*(2), 149–157.

Shin, J., et al. (2020). Scale and information-processing thresholds in Holocene social evolution. *Nature Communications, 11*(1), 2394. https://www.ncbi.nlm.nih.gov/pmc/articles/PMC7224170/pdf/41467_2020_Article_16035.pdf

Smoláriková, K. (2008). The step pyramid—A constant inspiration to the Saite Egyptians. In M. Bárta, F. Coppens, & J. Krejčí (Eds.), *Abusir and Saqqara in the year 2005. Proceedings of the conference held in Prague (June 27 – July 5, 2005)*, Prague, pp. 42–51.

Stammers, M. (2009). *The elite late period Egyptian tombs of Memphis* (BAR international series 1903). Archaeopress.

Taylor, J. (2000). The third intermediate period (1069-664 BC). In I. Shaw (Ed.), *The Oxford history of ancient Egypt* (pp. 330–368). Oxford University Press.

Voss, R. L. (1992). *The Apis embalming ritual—P. Vindob. 3873*. Peeters.

Wildung, D. (1977). *Egyptian saints: Deification in Pharaonic Egypt*. New York University Press.

Hala Sultan Tekke, Cyprus. Trade with Egypt in the Bronze Age

Peter M. Fischer

Abstract Thirteen seasons of Swedish excavations at the Bronze Age harbor city of Hala Sultan Tekke on the southern coast of Cyprus confirm far-reaching trade contacts during the lifespan of the city, i.e., Late Cypriot I to IIIA or approximately 1630–1150 BCE. Commodities were imported from an area which comprises at least Sardinia to Afghanistan/India, and the Baltic Sea to Egypt/Nubia. Tons of copper slag and ore provide evidence of large-scale urban metallurgy. Tools to produce textiles, together with heaps of murex shells and installations for dyeing, confirm the production of purple-dyed textiles. Owing to the presence of one of the best sheltered harbors, these and other products were traded in exchange for imported commodities including ceramics and their contents, precious metals and stones, and ivory. This paper discusses evidence of contacts with Egypt mainly based on the results from recent field work.

Keywords Trade · Cyprus · Egypt · Gold · Scarabs · Faience · Ivory

1 Introduction

Hala Sultan Tekke is the modern name of the Bronze Age harbor city situated on the southeastern coast of Cyprus west southwest of the Larnaca Salt Lake and close to the international airport of Larnaca (Fig. 1). This modern name for the ancient city was taken from the homonymous famous mosque of Hala Sultan Tekke, which was originally built in the seventh century CE in an area where, according to a local tradition, Umm Haram, a relative or nurse of the prophet Mohammed, died (Fischer, 2019a). The ancient city has suffered from a long period of illegitimate digging and extremely badly recorded excavations especially in the nineteenth century CE

P. M. Fischer (✉)
University of Gothenburg, Gothenburg, Sweden
e-mail: peter@fischerarchaeology.se

© The Author(s), under exclusive license to Springer Nature Switzerland AG 2023
E. Ben-Yosef, I. W. N. Jones (eds.), *"And in Length of Days Understanding" (Job 12:12): Essays on Archaeology in the Eastern Mediterranean and Beyond in Honor of Thomas E. Levy*, Interdisciplinary Contributions to Archaeology,
https://doi.org/10.1007/978-3-031-27330-8_45

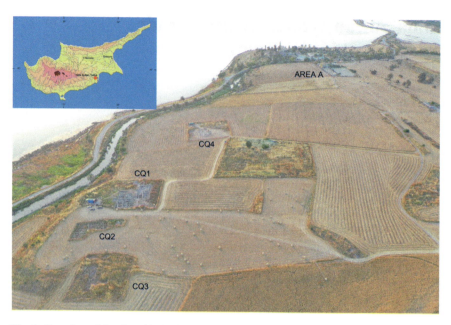

Fig. 1 Overview of the site with the four partly exposed city quarters (CQ1-4), and the cemetery (Area A) just in front of the mosque on the shore of the Larnaca Salt Lake

(Fischer, 2012a). It was not until the 1970s that a Swedish team started regular excavations (Åström, 1976). Since 2010, during 13 seasons, the present author directed excavations which were carried out in the settlement area and cemetery (see, e.g., the major report in Fischer & Bürge, 2018b).

Geophysical surveys with georadar and magnetometers of an area of ca. 25 hectares demonstrated regularly arranged subsurface anomalies in the entire surveyed area, which pointed to man-made structures. Over an additional approximately 25 hectares, mainly south of the surveyed area, surface finds of Bronze Age material suggest an even larger extension of the city.

The excavations that followed focused on four areas, City Quarters (CQ) 1–4 where stone structures belonging to domestic and industrial compounds were exposed (Fig. 1). On the magnetometer map there are also indications of a city wall with a moat surrounding the center of the city which occupies an area of approximately 15 hectares (Fischer & Bürge, 2020: 90–91). In addition, the magnetometer surveys of the area to the east of the city (Area A) indicated numerous, roughly circular anomalies ("pits"). These pits' vertical gradient ΔZ of the earth's magnetic field is close to -8 nT whereas that of the surrounding soil is up to $+8$ nT.[1] Thus the pits are clearly visible on the magnetometer map. The entire Area A is extremely endangered by farming because modern ploughs disturb the soil to a depth of ca. 25 cm. This depth corresponds to the uppermost level of many tombs and offering

---

[1] nT is the unit of magnetic flux density equal to 10^{-9} tesla.

pits as shown in subsequent excavations. Trial excavations of a few of these geophysical anomalies exposed tombs with multiple burials, associated offering pits without any skeletal remains, abandoned and later reused wells, and a rich array of objects from many different cultures (Fischer & Bürge, 2017c; Fischer, 2019 [2020]: 192–193).

The material evidence supported by radiocarbon dates has verified that the city was founded in the second half of the seventeenth century BCE, at the beginning of the Late Cypriot I period[2] (see Table 1), on the shoreline of a Mediterranean bay which cut deep into the island, thus providing a well-protected harbor. Over time, the city occupied an area of at least 25 hectares and flourished for approximately 500 years, after which it was abandoned around the mid-twelfth century BCE (Late Cypriot IIIA). The abandonment of one of the largest cities on Cyprus is a long-discussed conundrum for which several explanations have been put forward (Fischer, 2017). One suggests that destructions all over the eastern Mediterranean, including the final destruction of Hala Sultan Tekke, were caused by the "Sea Peoples phenomenon.", viz. as a result of one of several causes, including a large-scale migration of peoples triggered by worsening climatic conditions (Fischer & Bürge, 2017a; Kaniewski et al., 2020). Another hypothesis proposes that tectonic uplift which did not stabilize earlier than approximately 3000 BP caused the city's abandonment (Devillers et al., 2015): the harbor became a shrinking lagoon cut off from the open sea and, therefore, useless for direct anchorage, which had serious trade-related consequences and forced foreign ships to anchor elsewhere (Iacovou, 2013). The second hypothesis, however, does not take into account that the city was destroyed before it was abandoned.

The heyday of the city, when interregional contacts thrived, falls in the period from the 15th to 13th centuries BCE (Late Cypriot IIA–C). In this period, copper was produced on a large scale in intra-urban workshops at Hala Sultan Tekke, as indicated by furnaces and tons of mainly copper slag but also ore. In addition, purple-dyed textiles – certainly one of the most labor intensive and therefore expensive goods in the Bronze Age – were manufactured. Both products were produced in excess of local needs and surplus became the basis for trading coveted goods. This merchandise, together with the city's favorable position in the central part of

Table 1 Comparative chronology and approximate absolute dates

Cyprus	Egypt	Levant	Approximate dates BCE
LC IA1–2	Hyksos	MB III	1630–1560
LC IB	Early 18th Dyn. – Tuthmosis III	LB IA/B	1560–1450
LC IIA–B	Tuthmosis III – Late 18th Dyn.	LB IB– C	1450–1300
LC IIC1–2	End 18th Dyn. – 1st half 19th Dyn.	LB II	1300–1200
LC IIIA1–2	2nd half 19th Dyn. – 20th Dyn.	LB II/IA I	1200–1100

---

[2] There is ceramic evidence which points to a possible foundation in the Middle Cypriot period (MC III).

the eastern Mediterranean and the presence of one of the island's best sheltered harbors, transformed the city into an important trade hub.

The current paper presents the material evidence of contacts with Egypt and related cultures. The focus is on the imports found in the city and the extra-urban cemetery in Area A as a result of the past 13 seasons of renewed excavations at Hala Sultan Tekke. In a very few cases important finds from the old excavations directed by Paul Åström will be referred to, since a final excavation report presenting the stratigraphy of the previously exposed areas and relevant finds does not yet exist.[3]

Table 1, adapted to the Cypriot sub-periods, should be consulted for the proposed synchronization between Cyprus and Egypt, and suggested absolute dates. The synchronization with the southern Levant is also included since this area was dominated by Egypt at the time when the 18th and 19th Dynasties ruled (cf. the discussion in Fischer, 2019b). Note that the division of the periods is floating, and the absolute dates are rounded up or down in order to synchronize approximately the three areas in a single table.

2 Genuine and Probable Imports from the Egyptian Sphere of Culture

The presentation of diverse materials and objects as genuine or possible imports from Egypt concentrates on items of gold, to some extent alloyed with silver, scarabs, ivory, faience/composite/glass, pottery, precious stones, fish, and ostrich eggshells.

2.1 Gold and Scarabs (Figs. 2, 5)

The 100 objects of gold from the new excavations come from contexts which are dated mainly to the second half of the Late Cypriot period. They comprise beads (75), earrings (15), diadems (3), gold-mounted scarabs (2), pendants (3), a finger ring and the cap of a cylinder seal (selection in Fig. 2). Provenance studies of objects containing mainly gold, primarily alloyed with silver, represent a problem since these valuable and durable metals were certainly recycled and most likely re-alloyed. Most of the gold objects from the current excavations at Hala Sultan Tekke were analyzed by XRF to determine the degree of alloying with silver and, to a minor extent, other metals. The silver content varies between 17% and 47% ± 0.5% (Fischer & Bürge, 2015, 52; Table 2 in this paper).[4]

---

[3] In 2008, the year of Paul Åström's passing, this task was taken over by Karin Nys.

[4] My sincere thanks to Vasiliki Kassianidou and Andreas Charalambous for the XRF analyses of gold objects including one of the diadems, four ear rings and nine beads (see Table 2). Additional XRF-analyses in Fischer & Bürge, 2015: 52.

Fig. 2 Objects of gold, stone and faïence

The interment of a 4–5-year-old child from a fourteenth century context contained earrings, a diadem, many small beads, and a large central bead. According to the proportion of gold, three groups could be separated by XRF: the earrings (92.3–92.4 wt%), the diadem and the small beads (80.8–82.1 wt%), and the large central bead (70.6 wt%). This may point to different workshops or at least to three

Table 2 XRF of selected objects of gold from the interment of a 4-5-year-old child

Object	Chemical composition (wt% ± std)						
	Au	Ag	Cu	Sn	Fe	Pb	Bi
Diadem	82.0 ± 0.8	16.6 ± 0.5	0.3 ± 0.03	0.2 ± 0.02	0.2 ± 0.02	Traces (below 0.1%)	0.6 ± 0.05
Necklace							
Bead – Amorphous, in the middle	70.6 ± 0.7	26.2 ± 0.5	1.9 ± 0.1	0.3 ± 0.03	0.3 ± 0.03	Traces	0.55 ± 0.05
Bead 4 – Left side	81.9 ± 0.1	17.0 ± 0.1	n.d	0.3 ± 0.01	0.1 ± 0.01	Traces	0.6 ± 0.01
Bead 5 – Left side	81.5 ± 0.1	17.5 ± 0.1	n.d	0.3 ± 0.01	0.3 ± 0.01	Traces	0.5 ± 0.01
Bead 9 – Left side	81.4 ± 0.1	17.4 ± 0.1	n.d	0.3 ± 0.01	0.2 ± 0.01	Traces	0.6 ± 0.01
Bead 13 – Left side	81.6 ± 0.1	17.3 ± 0.1	n.d	0.3 ± 0.01	0.1 ± 0.01	Traces	0.6 ± 0.01
Bead 27 – Left side	82.1 ± 0.1	16.8 ± 0.1	n.d	0.3 ± 0.01	0.1 ± 0.01	Traces	0.6 ± 0.01
Bead 7 – Right side	80.8 ± 0.1	18.1 ± 0.1	n.d	0.3 ± 0.01	0.1 ± 0.01	Traces	0.6 ± 0.01
Bead 14 – Right side	81.4 ± 0.1	17.6 ± 0.1	n.d	0.3 ± 0.01	0.1 ± 0.01	Traces	0.5 ± 0.01
Bead 20 – Right side	80.7 ± 0.1	18.0 ± 0.1	n.d	0.3 ± 0.01	0.25 ± 0.01	Traces	0.6 ± 0.01
Earrings							
A	92.4 ± 0.4	6.5 ± 0.2	n.d	0.2 ± 0.02	0.15 ± 0.01	Traces	0.6 ± 0.05
B	92.5 ± 0.3	6.5 ± 0.1	n.d	n.d	0.2 ± 0.02	Traces	0.65 ± 0.05
C	92.6 ± 0.3	6.4 ± 0.2	n.d	0.15 ± 0.01	0.15 ± 0.01	Traces	0.6 ± 0.05
D	92.6 ± 0.3	6.3 ± 0.1	n.d	0.15 ± 0.01	0.15 ± 0.01	Traces	0.65 ± 0.05

different batches of alloyed gold. The latter may relate to the desired properties of the alloyed gold which were adapted to the manufacturing process of specific objects.

There are no significant sources of gold in Cyprus or the Levant. Although other sources are known, for instance in Anatolia, the Cycladic islands of Siphnos and Thasos in the Aegean, Macedonia, Thrace, Italy and western Europe (cf. Kassianidou & Knapp, 2005: 229), the author suggests that the majority of the 100 objects with gold as the major constituent were imported from Egypt, where gold mining has been carried out for millennia in the eastern deserts of Egypt and Nubia (Klemm & Klemm, 2013). Gold could have been imported from Egypt, for instance, in exchange for copper, tableware or purple-dyed textiles from Hala Sultan Tekke.

There is no proof at the site of gold imported as raw material and the evidence for the recycling of gold is scanty. One possible hoard of scrap(?) gold and silver derives from the destruction layer of Stratum 2 in CQ2 (LC IIIA1; Fig. 2: 8). It contains, inter alia, a silver amulet, a gold earring with an attached profiled plate of gold with a possible representation of a bull, a silver earring with a gold pendant and a sheet of silver which was attached to the item, two gold earrings and a melted lump of corroded silver in which another gold ring is embedded (Fischer & Bürge, 2015: 37, Fig. 12). Nevertheless, it cannot be excluded that this hoard represents a collection of personal jewelry which was exposed to fire, and not raw material for the production of new jewelry.

Among the genuine Egyptian imports at Hala Sultan Tekke are scarabs. Some are gold mounted and show the cartouches of pharaohs of the 18th (Tuthmosis III, Fischer & Bürge, 2017c; Fig. 2: 1) and 19th Dynasties (Ramesses II).[5] One of the former, which comes from Tomb X, is of steatite with the remains of blue glaze on the surface. The blue glaze was certainly applied in order to imitate lapis lazuli of which there are several objects at the site. To the left is the depiction of the pharaoh, clad in a kilt, walking to the right. He wears the "blue crown" (ḫprš), the uraeus on the forehead, and carries the ḥq-scepter in the bent front hand. The other hand is straight behind the body. To the right is a cartouche, which reads Mn-ḫpr-rʿ/Men-kheper-(ka)-Re ("Lasting are the manifestation and the spirit of Re"), corresponding to the throne name of Tuthmosis III. The substantial gold mounting suggests the secondary use of the scarab as a ring bezel.

There is another gold-mounted scarab of steatite from the same tomb (Tomb X; Fig. 2: 2). It shows the uraeus and a reed leaf (j-shape) or a Maat feather. We have suggested a date in the thirteenth century corresponding to the 19th Dynasty (Fischer & Bürge, 2017c). A third scarab from Tomb X is also of steatite (Fig. 2: 3). Horizontally arranged is the dd-pillar, which is flanked by two uraei. We suggest a date in the thirteenth century, during the 19th Dynasty. Another scarab, from Tomb RR, is of white enstatite and decorated with a four-leaf rosette with a rhomboid-shaped central node and an outward-facing uraeus in each spandrel.[6] The style of the motif is under discussion. The earliest item of this type dates to the Middle Bronze Age. The latest suggests a date in the second half of the 18th Dynasty or 1400–1300 BCE.

Scarabs of composition from Tomb RR include a bluish-white example with the base inscribed with the hieroglyphs *ankh* and *nfr*, a small (sun) disc and three short vertical lines between the signs. The inscription can be interpreted as "[all] good, [all] life."[7] Similar scarabs with this inscription come, e.g., from Gat Karmel.[8] However, the sign for *nb*, "all," seems to be missing on our scarab and we suggest

---

[5] The scarab with the cartouche of Ramesses II is from the old excavations (Martin, 1983).
[6] Keel (1997: § 208, Fig. 145, §494, §523,).
[7] I would like to thank Jürg Eggler for the interpretation and the parallels.
[8] Keel (2013: 124–125, no. 4).

that the three vertical signs should be interpreted as *nb*. A date within the later part of the 18th Dynasty, i.e., the second half of the fourteenth century BCE, is proposed. Another scarab of white composition from Tomb RR shows the divine name *Jmn-rꜥ* "Amun-Re" flanked by two vertically placed nb-hieroglyphs.[9] This type appears in the 18th–19th Dynasties, approximately 1400–1200 BCE. Still another scarab from the same tomb is of white composition with a deliberately blackened surface. It depicts a lion with an open mouth and tail bent over the back running to the right with a papyrus plant between the legs. Running lions on scarabs are very rare and they are typically depicted as striding, lying, seated, or mounting an animal from behind. Roaring lions are likewise unusual. A date in the 19th Dynasty, approximately 1300–1200 BCE, is proposed.

Conclusions about the provenance of other objects of gold are based on production techniques and design. A lotus flower pendant of gold with cloisonné of carnelian and faience is certainly an Egyptian import (Fig. 2: 7). An example of this type of pendant was found in Tomb KV 55, Thebes, Valley of the Kings, which is dated to the 18th Dynasty/Amarna Period (Davis, 1910: Pl. 21; Aldred, 1971: Pl. 71).[10] It was part of a *usekh* collar which is a broad collar depicted in figurative art, for instance on the wall paintings in the tomb of Nebamun and Ipuki (TT 181) at Thebes (date ca. 1390–1349 BCE/Amenhotep III–IV; de Davies, 1925: Pl. XI; see also the discussion in Paule, 2018). The remainder of the gold objects – beads (75), earrings (13; Fig. 2: 4,5), diadems (3; Fig. 2: 6), pendants (2), a finger ring and the cap of a cylinder seal – are probably of local production and design using imported and recycled items of gold.

2.2 Ivory (Fig. 3)

The 54 objects of ivory are also from contexts which are dated mainly to the second half of the Late Cypriot period. They comprise decorated boxes of which the lids and the bases are preserved (Fig, 3: 1), a pommel (Figure 3: 2), distaffs (Fig. 3: 3, 4), the shaft of a bronze knife (Fig. 3: 5), plain discs, spindle whorls, a comb, a plaque, several beads, a pendant, and numerous fragments of worked objects.

This prestigious material comes either from elephants or hippopotami. It was traded from both Africa and Asia/India in the Late Bronze Age (see, e.g., Caubet & Poplin, 2010; Fischer et al., 2015). The Late Bronze Age shipwreck from Uluburun from the late fourteenth century BCE contained, for instance, unworked hippo and elephant tusks in addition to worked ivory objects (e.g., Pulak, 2008). There is, however, at present no evidence of an ivory workshop at Hala Sultan Tekke.

---

[9] E.g., Keel (1997: Tell el-Ajjul).

[10] I would like to thank Anna Paule for pointing out this parallel.

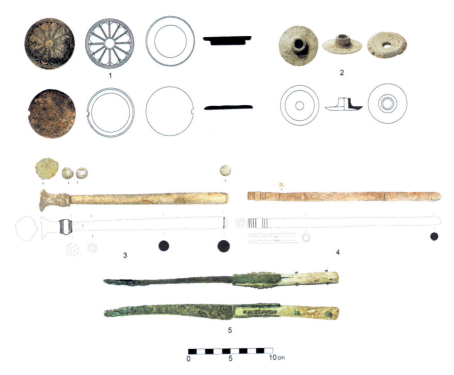

Fig. 3 Objects of ivory including a bronze knife with a handle of ivory

It has been claimed that there were herds of elephants in the northern part of the Levant around the beginning of the first millennium BCE (Miller, 1986; Moorey, 1994; Krzyszkowska & Morkot, 2000: 322). Hippopotamus skeletal remains have been found at various north Levantine Late Bronze Age coastal sites, such as Tell Sukas (Riis, 1970: 30), Minet el-Beida, and Ugarit (Caubet & Poplin, 1987, 2010), and at sites along the Orontes River (Gachet-Bizollon, 2007: 16). The presence of hippopotami in the southern Levant during the Bronze Age is suggested by Liora Kolska Horwitz and Eitan Tchernov (1990), although only dental remains have been found there. Hippopotami inhabited the Nile until the nineteenth century CE, and it is therefore likely that hippopotamus tusks were also imported from Egypt.

In the major report by David Reese (2018: 34, 35) dealing with the results of the current project at Hala Sultan Tekke up to 2017, the vast majority of the investigated finds of ivory are from elephants. In the same publication, Reese reported 18 pieces of ivory, mainly elephant, from the old excavations. Consequently, we can state that most of the ivories from Hala Sultan Tekke are from elephants. A good candidate for the source of our objects is Africa, from which they were imported via Egypt.

2.3 Faience/Composite and Glass (Figs. 4, 5)

There are 23 objects or groups of objects made of faience from the new excavations. They comprise amulets, beads, bowls, a cylinder seal, a scarab, a flask, a goblet, a button, and a possible cup.

Some items of this material might have been locally produced. A greater proportion of the Late Bronze Age faience objects, however, appears to have been imported from Egypt, and even the locally produced items frequently show Egyptian influences (cf. Maniatis et al., 2008). In contrast to earlier periods, the variety of faience objects increased significantly during the Late Bronze Age in Cyprus and include a wide variety of vessels. There exists no consensus regarding the extent to which this Late Bronze Age faience was imported from Egypt or the Levant, and the extent to which it was made locally under Egyptian and other influences.

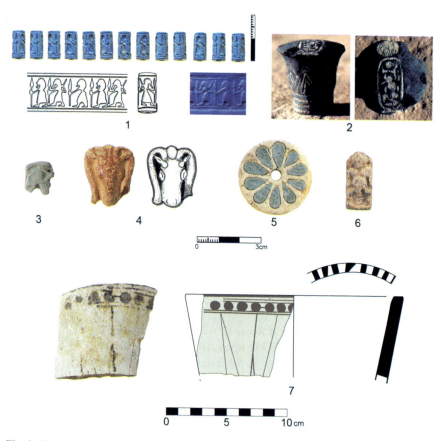

Fig. 4 Objects of faïence

Among the most significant of our faience items is a vase from a thirteenth century context (Stratum 3A) in CQ1 (Fischer & Bürge, 2020: 97; Fig. 4: 7). It is of greenish-white paste with black decoration: there are multiple strokes on the rim, dots enclosed by horizontal lines just below the rim and vertical lines on the body. Such vases are common finds of the Tuthmoside period. Consequently, our vase represents an heirloom. Other Egyptian-imported vessels of faience comprise small vases (Fischer, 2012b: 93–94, Fig. 3: 14) and bowls (Fischer & Bürge, 2013, 49, Fig. 18).

There are amulets and pendants depicting, variously, an eye symbol (Fischer & Bürge, 2015; Fig. 4: 3), the god Bes (Fischer & Bürge, 2016; Fig. 4: 6), a ram's head (Fischer & Bürge, 2020; Fig. 4: 4) and a female figurine (Fischer & Bürge, 2015). In addition to the scarabs described above, there are other scarabs of composite (Fischer & Bürge, 2015), a cylinder seal of Egyptian blue (Fischer & Bürge, 2013; Fig. 4: 1) and a bichrome button (Fig. 4: 5), all of which are imports from Egypt. From the old excavations, a blue scepter with the cartouche of Horemheb in white color, the last pharaoh of the 18th Dynasty, and traces of an ivory rod should be mentioned (Åström, 1979; Fig. 4: 2). The scepter is an heirloom found in an LC IIIA1 context, i.e., approximately 100 years after Horemheb's reign. Objects of obviously Egyptian glass are mainly multi-colored beads (Fig. 5: 2 center and above).

2.4 Pottery

Imported Egyptian pottery vessels are not uncommon at Hala Sultan Tekke but occur in far fewer numbers than Mycenaean, Minoan and Anatolian vessels, and most often in the second part of the city's life span. Ceramic containers include, for instance, an Egyptian imported jar of marl clay (Fischer & Bürge, 2017b) from a LC IIIA1 context. It has a rim type that has good parallels in the 19th and 20th Dynasties, i.e., roughly in the period Ramesses II–III (see e.g., Aston, 2004: 189–198). There are additional jars of related types, mainly found in Late Cypriot IIIA contexts (Fischer & Bürge, 2018a, 2019: 291).

2.5 Stone (Fig. 5)

Forty-two objects are of precious stones. There are beads of turquoise, a copper-phosphate mineral that has been mined at several locations on the Sinai Peninsula. The two most important are the Wadi Maghara and Serabit el-Khadim (Mansour, 2014). Other objects are of carnelian, the most common precious stone at Hala Sultan Tekke, amethyst, steatite and enstatite (the latter in Fig. 5: 1). The latter two were used for scarabs. Some of these stones were probably mined in Egypt and imported as raw material for further processing.

Fig. 5 Objects of stone, gold and glass

2.6 Fish and Shells

Remains of fish found at Hala Sultan Tekke come from habitats in the Nile. Various species include Nile perch (*Lates niloticus*), North African or Nile catfish (*Clarias gariepinus*), Nile (or Levant) fresh-water fish (family *Cichlidae*), naked catfish (family *Bagridae*) and Barracuda (*Sphyraena jello*).[11] Nile River shells (*Chambardia rubens arcuate*) were also imported (Reese, 2008).

---

[11] Publication by D. Reese and O. Lernau forthcoming.

2.7 Ostrich Eggshells

Ostrich eggshells were imported from either North Africa/Egypt or the Levant (Reese, 2008).

3 Discussion and Conclusions

Considering Hala Sultan Tekke's easy access to the Mediterranean and unlimited fishing opportunities, it comes as a surprise to find Egyptian-imported fish in contexts at Hala Sultan Tekke. It is possible that the Cypriots had a predilection for Nile fish and therefore imported it dried or salted. It is more likely, however, that Nile fish arrived with Egyptian ships or Cypriot vessels returning from Egypt carrying coveted goods.

Most of the imported objects can be dated to the second half of the Late Cypriot period. Objects of gold, ivory, precious stones, faience/composite/glass and pottery, in that order, are the most frequently found items, the majority of which were probably imported from Egypt and Nubia. The author believes that it is highly unlikely that the Egyptians exported gold as a raw material. Instead, they were no doubt aware of the larger profit in trading worked objects. Among the 100 objects of gold are several that beyond any doubt were imported from Egypt. These include the gold-mounted scarabs and the lotus flower pendant. The diadems, the ear- and finger rings, simple pendants, the caps of cylinder seals[12] and the numerous beads are most probably of Cypriot manufacture. Since gold seems not to have been imported from Egypt as raw material, it is suggested that these items were produced of recycled jewelry of varied provenance but mainly imported from the Egyptian cultural sphere. The alloying of gold with imported silver during the recycling process might have been carried out in Cyprus.

It is also suggested that the bulk of the objects of ivory (54), most of which were elephantine, were imported from Egypt. These include distaffs and other items related to the production of textiles, boxes with decorated lids, pommels and several other worked items.

The majority of objects of faience/composite and glass are certainly of Egyptian provenance. Several vessels of faience, amulets and pendants, scarabs and the Horemheb scepter were produced in Egyptian workshops. There are also ceramic containers of Egyptian marl clay. Organic residue analyses of Egyptian-imported pottery are in progress to define the vessels' original contents.

What was exported from Cyprus to Egypt in return, for instance, for the very expensive gold which was produced in a time- and labor-consuming process especially in Nubia? Copper, which was refined on a large scale at Hala Sultan Tekke, is the most likely traded merchandise. Another product was purple-dyed textiles, also

---

[12] There are more gold-capped cylinder seals from the old excavations.

the result of a time- and labor-consuming procedure. Before the large-scale spread of Mycenaean pottery in the Mediterranean, which began in LH IIIA (ca. 1400 BCE), Cypriot ceramics were the most popular foreign pottery in the Hyksos period and the first half of the 18th Dynasty, and also continued to be imported after 1400 BCE. It is highly probable that these Cypriot ceramics were stockpiled and exported from the harbor city of Hala Sultan Tekke to Egypt (and other cultures).

Acknowledgments This paper is dedicated to my colleague Tom Levy, who shared my research interests for many years. I would like to forward my sincere thanks to the editors of this volume, to Teresa Bürge, my very devoted collaborator in Cyprus and Jordan during the past 13 years, to Jenny Webb who checked the text for inconsistencies, and the Swedish Torsten Söderberg Foundation which provided the necessary funds. I am also thankful to the Department of Antiquities of Cyprus for the necessary permits.

References

Aldred, C. (1971). *Jewels of the Pharaohs. Egyptian jewellery of the dynastic period*. Thames and Hudson.
Aston, D. A. (2004). Amphorae in new kingdom Egypt. *Egypt and the Levant. International Journal for Egyptian Archaeology and Related Disciplines, 14*, 175–214.
Åström, P. (1976). Excavations in 1971: Trench 3. In P. Åström, D. M. Bailey, & V. Karageorghis (Eds.), *Hala Sultan Tekke 1: Excavations 1897–1971* (Studies in Mediterranean Archaeology, 45:1) (pp. 112–119). Åström.
Åström, P. (1979). *A faience scepter with the Cartouche of Horemheb* (Studies Presented in Memory of Porphyrios Dikaios) (pp. 46–48). Nicosia.
Caubet, A., & Poplin, F. (1987). Les objets de matière dure animale: Étude du matériau. In M. Yon (Ed.), *Ras Shamra-Ougarit III: Le centre de la ville, 38.–44. campagnes (1978–1984)* (Éditions Recherche sur les civilisations Mémoire 72) (pp. 273–306). Éditions Recherche sur les civilisations.
Caubet, A., & Poplin, F. (2010). Réflexions sur la question de l'éléphant Syrien. In H. Kühne (Ed.), *Dūr-Katlimmu 2008 and Beyond* (Studia Chaburensia 1) (pp. 1–9). Harrassowitz.
Davis, T. M. (1910). *The tomb of queen Tîyi*. Constable and Co., Ltd..
de Davies, N. G. (1925). *The tomb of two sculptors at Thebes*. Metropolitan Museum of Art.
Devillers, B., Brown, M., & Morhange, C. (2015). Paleo-environmental evolution of the Larnaca Salt Lakes (Cyprus) and the relationship to second millennium BC settlement. *Journal of Archaeological Science: Reports, 1*, 73–80.
Fischer, P. M. (2012a). SIMA and the new Swedish Cyprus expedition at Hala Sultan Tekke. In J. M. Webb & D. Frankel (Eds.), *Studies in Mediterranean archaeology: Fifty years on* (Studies in Mediterranean Archaeology, Vol. 137) (pp. 73–80). Åström.
Fischer, P. M. (2012b). The new Swedish Cyprus expedition 2011: Excavations at Hala Sultan Tekke: Preliminary results. *Opuscula. Annual of the Swedish Institutes at Athens and Rome, 5*, 89–112.
Fischer, P. M. (2017). The 12th century BCE destructions and the abandonment of Hala Sultan Tekke, Cyprus. In P. M. Fischer & T. Bürge (Eds.), *Contributions to the chronology of the Eastern Mediterranean* (Vol. 35, pp. 177–206). Austrian Academy of Sciences.
Fischer, P. M. (2019 [2020]). The occupational history of the Bronze Age Harbour City of Hala Sultan Tekke, Cyprus. *Egypt and the Levant. International Journal for Egyptian Archaeology and Related Disciplines, 29*, 189–230. https://doi.org/10.1553/AEundL29s188.

Fischer, P. M. (2019a). Hala Sultan Tekke, Cyprus: A Late Bronze Age trade metropolis. *Near Eastern Archaeology, 82*(4), 236–247.

Fischer, P. M. (2019b). The Transjordanian Jordan Valley in the Late Bronze Age: Under Egyptian control? In A. M. Maeir, I. Shai, & C. McKinny (Eds.), *The Late Bronze and early Iron Ages of Southern Canaan* (Archaeology of the Biblical Worlds) (pp. 217–232). De Gruyter.

Fischer, P. M., & Bürge, T. (2013). The New Swedish Cyprus expedition 2012: Excavations at Hala Sultan Tekke: Preliminary results. *Opuscula. Annual of the Swedish Institutes at Athens and Rome, 6*, 45–79.

Fischer, P. M., & Bürge, T. (2015). The New Swedish Cyprus expedition 2014: Excavations at Hala Sultan Tekke. Preliminary results. *Opuscula. Annual of the Swedish Institutes at Athens and Rome, 8*, 27–79.

Fischer, P. M., & Bürge, T. (2016). The New Swedish Cyprus expedition 2015: Excavations at Hala Sultan Tekke. Preliminary results. *Opuscula. Annual of the Swedish Institutes at Athens and Rome, 9*, 33–58.

Fischer, P. M., & Bürge, T. (Eds.). (2017a). *Contributions to the chronology of the Eastern Mediterranean* (Vol. 35). Austrian Academy of Sciences.

Fischer, P. M., & Bürge, T. (2017b). The New Swedish Cyprus expedition 2016: Excavations at Hala Sultan Tekke (The Söderberg Expedition). Preliminary results. With contributions by L. Recht, D. Kofel and D. Kaniewski, N. Marriner & C. Morhange. *Opuscula. Annual of the Swedish Institutes at Athens and Rome, 10*, 50–93.

Fischer, P. M., & Bürge, T. (2017c). Tombs and offering pits at the Late Bronze Age Metropolis of Hala Sultan Tekke, Cyprus. *Bulletin of the American Schools of Oriental Research, 377*, 161–218. https://doi.org/10.5615/bullamerschoorie.377.0161

Fischer, P. M., & Bürge, T. (2018a). The New Swedish Cyprus expedition 2017: Excavations at Hala Sultan Tekke (The Söderberg Expedition). Preliminary results. *Opuscula. Annual of the Swedish Institutes at Athens and Rome, 11*, 29–79.

Fischer, P. M., & Bürge, T. (Eds.). (2018b). *Two Late Cypriot City Quarters at Hala Sultan Tekke: The Söderberg expedition 2010–2017* (Studies in Mediterranean Archaeology) (Vol. 147). Åström.

Fischer, P. M., & Bürge, T. (2019). The New Swedish Cyprus expedition 2018: Excavations at Hala Sultan Tekke (The Söderberg Expedition): Preliminary results. *Opuscula. Annual of the Swedish Institutes at Athens and Rome, 12*, 287–326.

Fischer, P. M., & Bürge, T. (2020). The New Swedish Cyprus expedition 2019: Excavations at Hala Sultan Tekke (The Söderberg Expedition): Preliminary results. *Opuscula. Annual of the Swedish Institutes at Athens and Rome, 13*, 73–111.

Fischer, P. M., Bürge, T., & Al-Shalabi, M. (2015). The "Ivory Tomb" at tell Irbid, Jordan: Intercultural relations at the end of the Late Bronze Age and the beginning of the Iron Age. *Bulletin of the American Schools of Oriental Research, 374*, 209–232.

Gachet-Bizollon, J. (2007) Les ivoires d'Ougarit et l'art des ivoiriers du Levant au Bronze récent. Ras Shamra-Ougarit 16; Publications de la Mission archéologique française de Ras Shamra-Ougarit. : Éditions Recherche sur les civilisations.

Iacovou, M. (2013). Aegean-Style material culture in late Cypriot III: Minimal evidence, maximal interpretation. In A. E. Killebrew, & G. Lehmann (Eds.), *The philistines and other "Sea Peoples" in text and archaeology* (Archaeology and Biblical Studies, Vol. 15, pp. 585–618). Society of Biblical Literature.

Kaniewski, D., Marriner, N., Cheddadi, R., Fischer, P. M., Otto, T., Luce, F., et al. (2020). Climate change and social unrest: A 6,000-year chronicle from the eastern Mediterranean. *Geophysical Research Letters*. https://doi.org/10.1029/2020GL087496

Kassianidou, V., & Knapp, A. B. (2005). Archaeometallurgy in the Mediterranean: The social context of mining, technology, and trade. In E. Blake & A. B. Knapp (Eds.), *The archaeology of Mediterranean prehistory* (pp. 215–251). Wiley-Blackwell. https://doi.org/10.1002/9780470773536.ch9

Keel, O. (1997). *Corpus der Stempelsiegel-Amulette aus Palästina/Israel. Von den Anfängen bis zur Perserzeit: Katalog, I: Von Tell Abu Farağ bis ʿAtlit* (Orbis Biblicus et Orientalis. Series Archaeologica, Vol. 13). Universitätsverlag; Vandenhoeck & Ruprecht.

Keel, O. (2013). *Corpus der Stempelsiegel-Amulette aus Palästina/Israel. Von den Anfängen bis zur Perserzeit: Katalog, IV: Von Tel Gamma bis Chirbet Husche* (Orbis Biblicus et Orientalis. Series Archaeologica, Vol. 33). Universitätsverlag; Vandenhoeck & Ruprecht.

Klemm, R., & Klemm, D. (2013). *Gold and Gold Mining in Ancient Egypt and Nubia. Geoarchaeology of the Ancient Gold Mining Sites in the Egyptian and Sudanese Eastern Deserts*. Springer.

Kolska Horwitz, L., & Tchernov, E. (1990). Cultural and environmental implications of hippopotamus bone remains in archaeological contexts in the Levant. *Bulletin of the American Schools of Oriental Research, 280*, 67–76.

Krzyszkowska, O. H., & Morkot, R. (2000). Ivory and related materials. In P. T. Nicholson & I. Shaw (Eds.), *Ancient Egyptian materials and technology* (pp. 320–331). Cambridge University Press.

Maniatis, Y., Panagiotaki, M., & Kaczmarczyk, A. (2008). Faience production in the East Mediterranean (συνδημοσίευση με τους M.S. Tite, Y. Maniatis and A. Kaczmarczyk). In M. S. Tite & A. J. Shortland (Eds.), *Production technology of Faience and related early vitreous materials* (pp. 111–125). Oxford University School of Archaeology.

Mansour, A. M. A. (2014). *Turquoise in the ancient Egypt concept and role* (BAR International Series). Oxford Archaeopress.

Martin, G. T. (1983). Appendix IV. A royal scarab from Hala Sultan Tekke (in (Niklasson 1983).

Miller, R. (1986). Elephants, ivory, and charcoal: An ecological perspective. *Bulletin of the American Schools of Oriental Research, 264*, 29–43.

Moorey, P. R. S. (1994). *Ancient Mesopotamian materials and industries: The archaeological evidence*. Clarendon.

Paule, A. (2018). Near Eastern materials, near Eastern techniques, near Eastern inspiration: Colourful jewellery from prehistoric, protohistoric and archaic Cyprus. In S. Di Paolo (Ed.), *Composite artefacts in the ancient near east. Exhibiting an imaginative materiality, showing a genealogical nature* (Ancient Near Eastern Archaeology 3) (pp. 85–96). Archaeopress Publishing Ltd.

Pulak, C. (2008). The Uluburun Shipwreck and Late Bronze Age trade. In J. Aruz, K. Benzel, & J. M. Evans (Eds.), *Beyond Babylon: Art, trade, and diplomacy in the second millennium B.C* (pp. 289–310). Metropolitan Museum of Art/Yale University Press.

Reese, D. S. (2008). Organic imports from Late Bronze Age Cyprus (with special reference to Hala Sultan Tekke). *Opuscula Atheniensia, 31–32*(2006–2007), 191–209.

Reese, D. S. (2018). Faunal evidence: Catalogues, worked bones, ivory, horn, shells. In P. M. Fischer & T. Bürge (Eds.), *Two Late Cypriot City Quarters at Hala Sultan Tekke: The Söderberg Expedition 2010–2017* (Studies in Mediterranean Archaeology, Vol. 147) (pp. 493–563). Åström.

Riis, P. J. (1970). *Sūkās I: The North-East Sanctuary and the first settling of Greeks in Syria and Palestine*. Publications of the Carlsberg expedition to Phoenicia 1; Historisk-filosoiske skriter 5/1. E. Munksgaard.